Volume

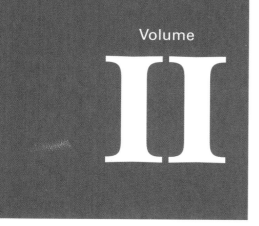

II

SEVENTH EDITION

The Humanistic Tradition

The Early Modern World to the Present

Volume

II

SEVENTH EDITION

The Humanistic Tradition

The Early Modern World to the Present

Gloria K. Fiero

McGraw Hill Education

Boston   Burr Ridge, IL   Dubuque, IA   New York   San Francisco   St. Louis
Bangkok   Bogotá   Caracas   Kuala Lumpur   Lisbon   London   Madrid   Mexico City
Milan   Montreal   New Delhi   Santiago   Seoul   Singapore   Sydney   Taipei   Toronto

THE HUMANISTIC TRADITION, VOLUME II
THE EARLY MODERN WORLD TO THE PRESENT
SEVENTH EDITION

Published by McGraw-Hill Education, 2 Penn Plaza, New York, NY 10121. Copyright 2015 by McGraw-Hill Education. All rights reserved. Printed in the United States of America. Previous edition © 2011, 2006, 2002, 1998, 1995, 1992. No part of this publication may be reproduced or distributed in any form or by any means, or stored in a database or retrieval system, without the prior consent of McGraw-Hill Education, including, but not limited to, in any network or other electronic storage or transmission, or broadcast for distance learning.

Some ancillaries, including electronic and print components, may not be available to customers outside the United States.

This book is printed on acid-free paper.

1 2 3 4 5 6 7 8 9 0 DOW/DOW 1 0 9 8 7 6 5

ISBN 978-1-259-35168-6
MHID 1-259-35168-8

Senior Vice President, Products & Markets: *Kurt L. Strand*
Vice President, General Manager, Products & Markets: *Michael Ryan*
Vice President, Content Design & Delivery: *Kimberly Meriwether David*
Managing Director: *William Glass*
Brand Manager: *Sarah Remington*
Director, Product Development: *Meghan Campbell*
Marketing Manager: *Kelly Odom*
Director of Development: *Dawn Groundwater*
Digital Product Developer: *Betty Chen*
Director, Content Design & Delivery: *Terri Schiesl*
Program Manager: *Debra Hash*
Content Program Manager: *Sheila Frank*
Buyer: *Susan K. Culbertson*
Printer: *R. R. Donnelley*

Permissions Acknowledgments appear on page 526, and on this page by reference.

Library of Congress Cataloging-in-Publication Data

Fiero, Gloria K.
 The humanistic tradition / Gloria K. Fiero. – Seventh edition.
   volumes cm
 Includes bibliographical references and index.

 Contents: BOOK 1. The First Civilizations and the Classical Legacy – BOOK 2. Medieval Europe and the World Beyond – BOOK 3. The European Renaissance, the Reformation, and Global Encounter – BOOK 4. Faith, Reason, and Power in the Early Modern World – BOOK 5. Romanticism, Realism, and the Nineteenth-Century World – BOOK 6. Modernism, Postmodernism, and the Global Perspective – VOLUME I. Prehistory to the Early Modern World – VOLUME II. The Early Modern World to the Present.

 ISBN 978-1-259-36066-4 (volume 1 : acid-free paper) – ISBN 1-259-36066-0 (volume 1 : acid-free paper) – ISBN 978-1-259-35168-6 (volume 2 : acid-free paper)) – ISBN 1-259-35168-8 (volume 2 : acid-free paper) – ISBN 978-0-07-337666-0 (looseleaf : book 1 : acid-free paper) – ISBN 0-07-337666-3 (looseleaf : book 1 : acid-free paper) – ISBN 978-1-259-35209-6 (looseleaf : book 2 : acid-free paper) – ISBN 1-259-35209-9 (looseleaf : book 2 : acid-free paper) – ISBN 978-1-259-35210-2 (looseleaf : book 3 : acid-free paper) – ISBN 1-259-35210-2 (looseleaf : book 3 : acid-free paper) – ISBN 978-1-259-35539-4 (looseleaf : book 4 : acid-free paper) – ISBN 1-259-35539-X (looseleaf : book 4 : acid-free paper) – ISBN 978-1-259-35540-0 (looseleaf : book 5 : acid-free paper) – ISBN 1-259-35540-3 (looseleaf : book 5 : acid-free paper) – ISBN 978-1-259-35211-9 (looseleaf : book 6 : acid-free paper)

 1. Civilization, Western–History–Textbooks. 2. Humanism–History–Textbooks. I. Title.
 CB245.F47 2015
 909'.09821–dc23

                              2014037553

The Internet addresses listed in the text were accurate at the time of publication. The inclusion of a website does not indicate an endorsement by the author or McGraw-Hill Education, and McGraw-Hill Education does not guarantee the accuracy of the information presented at these sites

www.mhhe.com

This book was designed and produced by Laurence King Publishing Ltd., London
www.laurenceking.com

Commissioning Editor: *Kara Hattersley-Smith*
Production: *Simon Walsh*
Designer: *Ian Hunt*
Picture Researcher: *Louise Thomas*
Text Permissions: *Rachel Thorne*
Copy-editor: *Rosanna Lewis*

Front cover (clockwise from left)
Anne-Louis Girodet-Trioson, *Jean-Baptiste Belley, Deputy from Santo Domingo* (detail), 1797. Oil on canvas, 62⅓ × 43⅔ in.

Toshusai Sharaku, *Bust Portrait of the Actor Segawa Tomisaburo as Yadorigi, the Wife of Ogishi Kurando* (detail), 1794–1795. Woodblock print, 14½ × 9¼ in.

Chuck Close, *Self-Portrait* (detail), 1991. Oil on canvas, 100 × 84 in.

Judith Leyster, *Self-Portrait* (detail), ca. 1630. Oil on canvas, 29⅜ × 25⅞ in.

Frontispiece and page xiv
Jean-Honoré Fragonard, *The Swing*, 1768–1769. Oil on canvas, 32 × 25½ in.

page 33
Pieter de Hooch, *Portrait of a Family Making Music* (detail), 1663. Oil on canvas, 38⅞ × 45¹⁵⁄₁₆ in.

page 207
Thomas Phillips, *Lord Byron Sixth Baron in Albanian Costume* (detail), 1813. Oil on canvas, 50 × 40 in.

page 351
Pablo Picasso, *Seated Woman* (detail), Paris, 1927. Oil on wood, 4 ft. 3⅛ in. × 3 ft. 2¼ in.

Series Contents

Volume II Contents

BOOK 6
Modernism, Postmodernism, and the Global Perspective

The Humanistic Tradition—a personalized learning

Each generation leaves a creative legacy, the sum of its ideas and achievements. This legacy represents the response to our effort to ensure our individual and collective survival, our need to establish ways of living in harmony with others, and our desire to understand our place in the universe. Meeting the challenges of *survival, communality,* and *self-knowledge,* we have created and transmitted the tools of science and technology, social and political institutions, religious and philosophic systems, and various forms of personal expression—the totality of which we call **culture**. Handed down from generation to generation, this legacy constitutes the humanistic tradition, the study of which is called *humanities.*

Understanding that a global humanities course is taught in varying ways, Gloria Fiero redefines the discipline for greater flexibility via a variety of innovative digital tools. Enhanced by McGraw-Hill Education's LearnSmart and SmartBook, Fiero delivers a learning experience tailored to the needs of each institution, instructor, and student. With the ability to incorporate new extended readings, streaming music, and artwork, *The Humanistic Tradition* renews the understanding of the relationship between world cultures and humankind's creative legacy.

Personalized Learning Experience

In **Connect Humanities**, you can access all of the art and music from *The Humanistic Tradition* on your computer or mobile device. Music logos (right) that appear in the margins of the text refer to listening selections available for streaming.

As part of McGraw-Hill Education's Connect Humanities, LearnSmart is an adaptive learning program designed to personalize the learning experience. LearnSmart helps students learn faster, study smarter, and retain more knowledge for greater success. Distinguishing what students know from what they don't, and touching on concepts they are most likely to forget, LearnSmart continuously adapts to each students' needs by building a personalized learning path. LearnSmart is proven to strengthen memory recall, keep students in class, and boost grades. By helping students master core concepts ahead of time, LearnSmart enables instructors to spend more meaningful time in the classroom.

SMARTBOOK™

Enhanced by LearnSmart, SmartBook is the first and only adaptive reading experience currently available.

- **Making It Effective** SmartBook creates a personalized reading experience by highlighting the most impactful concepts a student needs to learn at that moment in time. This ensures that every minute spent with SmartBook is returned to the student as the most valuable minute possible.
- **Make It Informed** Real-time reports quickly identify the concepts that require more attention from individual students—or the entire class.

Personalized Teaching Experience

Personalize and tailor your teaching experience to the needs of your humanities course with Create, Insight, and instructor resources.

Create What You've Only Imagined

No two humanities courses are the same. That is why Gloria Fiero has personally hand-picked additional readings that can be added easily to a customized edition of *The Humanistic Tradition*. Marginal icons (right) that appear throughout this new edition indicate additional readings, a list of which is found at the end of the Table of Contents.

To customize your book using McGraw-Hill Create™, follow these steps:
1. Go to http://create.mheducation.com and sign in or register for an instructor account.
2. Click Collections (top, right) and select the "Traditions: Humanities Readings Through the Ages" Collection to preview and select readings. You can also make use of McGraw-Hill's comprehensive, cross-disciplinary content as well as other third-party resources.
3. Choose the readings that are most relevant to your students, your curriculum, and your own areas of interest.
4. Arrange the content in a way that makes the most sense for your course.
5. Personalize your book with your course information and choose the best format for your students—color, black-and-white, or ebook. When you are done, you will receive a free PDF review copy in just minutes.

Or contact your McGraw-Hill Education representative, who can help you build your unique version of *The Humanisitic Tradition*.

Powerful Reporting on the Go

The first and only analytics tool of its kind, Connect Insight is a series of visual data displays—each framed by an intuitive question—that provide at-a-glance information regarding how your class is doing.
- **Intuitive** You receive an instant, at-a-glance view of student performance matched with student activity.
- **Dynamic** Connect Insight puts real-time analytics in your hands so you can take action early and keep struggling students from falling behind.
- **Mobile** Connect Insight travels from office to classroom, available on demand wherever and whenever it's needed.

Instructor Resources

Connect Image Bank is an instructor database of images from select McGraw-Hill Education art and humanities titles, including *The Humanistic Tradition*. It includes all images for which McGraw-Hill has secured electronic permissions. With Connect Image Bank, instructors can access a text's images by browsing its chapters, style/period, medium, and culture, or by searching with key terms. Images can be easily downloaded for use in presentations and in PowerPoints. The download includes a text file with image captions and information. You can access Connect Image Bank on the library tab in Connect Humanities (http://connect.mheducation.com).

Various instructor resources are available for *The Humanistic Tradition*. These include an instructor's manual with discussion suggestions and study questions, music listening guides, lecture PowerPoints, and a test bank. Contact your McGraw-Hill sales representative for access to these materials.

Letter from the Author

The Humanistic Tradition originated more than two decades ago. As a long-time humanities instructor, I recognized that the Western-only perspective was no longer adequate to understanding the cultural foundations of our global world. However, none of the existing humanities textbooks served my needs. The challenge was daunting—covering the history of Western literature, philosophy, art, music, and dance was already an ambitious undertaking for a humanities survey; how could I broaden the scope to include Asia, Africa, and the Americas without over-loading the course?

I found the solution in my classroom: Instead of assuming a strictly historical approach to the past, (as I did in my history classes), I would organize my humanities lectures topically, focusing on universal themes, major styles, and significant movements—gods and rulers, classicism, imperialism, the Romantic hero, racial and sexual equality, globalism—as they reflected or shaped the culture of a given time or place. What evolved was *The Humanistic Tradition*, a thematic, yet global and chronological approach to humanities, one that provokes thought and discussion without burying students under mountains of encyclopedic information.

Now in its seventh edition, *The Humanistic Tradition* continues to celebrate the creative mind by focusing on how the arts and ideas relate to each other, what they tell us about our own human nature and that of others on our planet. Its mission remains relevant to the present, and essential (I would hope) to enriching the future of each student who reads its pages.

The Seventh Edition of *The Humanistic Tradition*

To the seventh edition of *The Humanistic Tradition* I have added a new feature: **Looking Into** is a diagrammatic analysis of key works, such as Neolithic stone circles (including the latest archeological discoveries in Southeast Turkey), the Parthenon, the sonnets of Petrarch and Donne, *Shiva: Lord of the Dance*, Jan van Eyck's *Arnolfini Double Portrait*, and Judy Chicago's *Dinner Party*.

The new edition expands two popular features that promote critical thinking: **Exploring Issues**, which focuses on controversial ideas and current debates (such as the battle over the ownership of antiquities, and creationism versus evolution); and **Making Connections**, which brings attention to contrasts and continuities between past and present. To **Exploring Issues**, I have added the debate over the origins of India's Vedic culture (chapter 3). To **Making Connections** I offer a novel illustration of the contemporary affection for Chinese landscape painting (chapter 14).

The chapter-by-chapter integration of literary, visual, and aural primary sources remains a hallmark of *The Humanistic Tradition*. In an effort to provide the most engaging and accessible literary works, some selected readings in this edition appear in alternate translations. **Marginal logos** have been added to direct students to additional literary resources that are discussed but not included in the text itself.

Additions to the art program include the Nebra Sky Disk, Hellenistic mosaics, Delacroix's *Women of Algiers*, Oceania's art of tattoo, Japan's Amida Buddha, Charles Willson Peale's *Portrait of Yarrow Mamout* (the earliest known portrait of a Muslim in America), Ai Wei Wei's *Forever Bicycle*, Ernesto Neto's *Anthropodino*, and Zaha Hadid's Heydar Aliyev Center. Chapters 37 and 38, which treat the Information Age and Globalism, have been updated to present a cogent overview of contemporary issues, including terrorism, ecological concerns, ethnic conflict, and the digital arts.

The Humanistic Tradition pioneered a flexible six-book format in recognition of the varying chronological range of humanities courses. Each slim volume was also convenient for students to bring to classes, the library, and other study areas. The seventh edition continues to be available in this six-book format, as well as in a two-volume set for the most common two-term course configuration.

In preparing the seventh edition, I have depended on the excellent editorial and production team led by Donald Dinwiddie at Laurence King Publishing. Special thanks also go to Kara Hattersley-Smith at LKP and Sarah Remington at McGraw-Hill Higher Education.

Gloria K. Fiero

Studying humanities engages us in a dialogue with primary sources: works original to the age in which they were produced. Whether literary, visual, or aural, a primary source is a text; the time, place, and circumstances in which it was created constitute the context; and its various underlying meanings provide the subtext. Studying humanities from the perspective of text, context, and subtext helps us understand our cultural legacy and our place in the larger world.

Text

The *text* of a primary source refers to its medium (that is, what it is made of), its form (its outward shape), and its content (the subject it describes).

Literature: Literary form varies according to the manner in which words are arranged. So, *poetry*, which shares rhythmic organization with music and dance, is distinguished from *prose*, which normally lacks regular rhythmic patterns. Poetry, by its freedom from conventional grammar, provides unique opportunities for the expression of intense emotions. Prose usually functions to convey information, to narrate, and to describe.

Philosophy (the search for truth through reasoned analysis) and *history* (the record of the past) make use of prose to analyze and communicate ideas and information.

In literature, as in most forms of expression, content and form are usually interrelated. The subject matter or form of a literary work determines its *genre*. For instance, a long narrative poem recounting the adventures of a hero constitutes an *epic*, while a formal, dignified speech in praise of a person or thing constitutes a *eulogy*.

The Visual Arts: The visual arts employ a wide variety of media, ranging from the traditional colored pigments used in painting, to wood, clay, marble, and (more recently) plastic and neon used in sculpture, to a wide variety of digital media, including photography and film. The form or outward shape of a work of art depends on the manner in which the artist manipulates the elements of color, line, texture, and space. Unlike words, these formal elements lack denotative meaning.

The visual arts are dominantly spatial, that is, they operate and are apprehended in space. Artists manipulate form to describe or interpret the visible world (as in the genres of portraiture and landscape), or to create worlds of fantasy and imagination. They may also fabricate texts that are nonrepresentational, that is, without identifiable subject matter.

Music and Dance: The medium of music is sound. Like literature, music is durational: it unfolds over the period of time in which it occurs. The major elements of music are melody, rhythm, harmony, and tone color—formal elements that also characterize the oral life of literature. However, while literary and visual texts are usually descriptive, music is almost always nonrepresentational: it rarely has meaning beyond sound itself. For that reason, music is the most difficult of the arts to describe in words.

Dance, the artform that makes the human body itself the medium of expression, resembles music in that it is temporal and performance-oriented. Like music, dance exploits rhythm as a formal tool, and like painting and sculpture, it unfolds in space as well as in time.

Studying the text, we discover the ways in which the artist manipulates medium and form to achieve a characteristic manner of execution or expression that we call *style*. Comparing the styles of various texts from a single era, we discover that they usually share certain defining features and characteristics. Similarities between, for instance, ancient Greek temples and Greek tragedies, or between Chinese lyric poems and landscape paintings, reveal the unifying moral and aesthetic values of their respective cultures.

Context

The *context* describes the historical and cultural environment of a text. Understanding the relationship between text and context is one of the principal concerns of any inquiry into the humanistic tradition. To determine the context, we ask: In what time and place did our primary source originate? How did it function within the society in which it was created? Was it primarily decorative, didactic, magical, or propagandistic? Did it serve the religious or political needs of the community? Sometimes our answers to these questions are mere guesses. For instance, the paintings on the walls of Paleolithic caves were probably not "artworks" in the modern sense of the term, but, rather, magical signs associated with religious rituals performed in the interest of communal survival.

Determining the function of the text often serves to clarify the nature of its form, and vice-versa. For instance, in that the Hebrew Bible, the *Song of Roland*, and many other early literary works were spoken or sung, rather than read, such literature tends to feature repetition and rhyme, devices that facilitate memorization and oral delivery.

Subtext

The *subtext* of a primary source refers to its secondary or implied meanings. The subtext discloses conceptual messages embedded in or implied by the text. The epic poems of the ancient Greeks, for instance, which glorify prowess and physical courage, suggest an exclusively male perception of virtue. The state portraits of the seventeenth-century French king Louis XIV bear the subtext of unassailable and absolute power. In our own time, Andy Warhol's serial adaptations of Coca-Cola bottles offer wry commentary on the commercial mentality of American society. Examining the implicit message of the text helps us determine the values of the age in which it was produced, and offers insights into our own.

Protest and Reform: The Waning of the Old Order

ca. 1400–1600

"Now what else is the whole life of mortals but a sort of comedy, in which the various actors, disguised by various costumes and masks, walk on and play each one his part, until the manager waves them off the stage?"
Erasmus

Figure 19.1 ALBRECHT DÜRER, *The Four Horsemen of the Apocalypse*, ca. 1496. Woodcut, 15½ × 11 in. This illustration from the Revelation of Saint John, the last book of the New Testament, might be considered a grim prophecy of the sixteenth century, in which five million people would die in religious wars.

By the sixteenth century, the old medieval order was crumbling. Classical humanism and the influence of Italian Renaissance artist–scientists were spreading throughout Northern Europe (Map **19.1**). European exploration and expansion were promoting a broader world-view and new markets for trade. The rise of a global economy with vast opportunities for material wealth was inevitable. Europe's population grew from 69 million in 1500 to 188 million in 1600. As European nation-states tried to strengthen their international influence, political rivalry intensified. The "superpowers"—Spain, under the Hapsburg ruler Philip II (1527–1598), and England, under Elizabeth I (1533–1603)—contended for advantage in Atlantic shipping and trade. In order to resist the encroachment of Europe's stronger nation-states, the weaker ones formed balance-of-power alliances that often provoked war. The new order took Europe on an irreversibly modern course.

While political and commercial factors worked to transform the West, the event that most effectively destroyed the old medieval order was the Protestant Reformation. In the wake of Protestantism, the unity of European Christendom would disappear forever. Beginning in the fifteenth century, the Northern Renaissance, endorsed by middle-class patrons and Christian humanists, assumed a religious direction that set it apart from Italy's Classical revival. Its literary giants, from Erasmus to Shakespeare, and its visual artists, Flemish and German, shared little of the idealism of their Italian Renaissance counterparts. Their concern for the reality of human folly and for the fate of the Christian soul launched a message of protest and a plea for Church reform expedited by way of the newly perfected printing press.

The Temper of Reform

The Impact of Technology

In the transition from medieval to early modern times, technology played a crucial role. Gunpowder, the light cannon, and other military devices made warfare more impersonal and ultimately more deadly. At the same time, Western advances in navigation, shipbuilding, and maritime instrumentation propelled Europe into a dominant position in the world.

Just as the musket and the cannon transformed the history of European warfare, so the technology of mechanical printing revolutionized learning and communication. Block printing originated in China in the ninth century and movable type in the eleventh, but print technology did not reach Western Europe until the fifteenth century. By 1450, in the city of Mainz, the German goldsmith Johannes Gutenberg (ca. 1400–ca. 1468) perfected a printing press that made it possible to fabricate books more cheaply, more rapidly, and in greater numbers than ever before (Figure **19.2**). As information became a commodity for mass production, vast areas of knowledge—heretofore the exclusive domain of the monastery, the Church, and the university—became available to the public. The printing press facilitated the rise of popular education and encouraged individuals to form their own opinions by reading for themselves. It accelerated the growing interest in vernacular literature, which in turn enhanced national and individual self-consciousness. Print technology proved to

Figure 19.2 An early sixteenth-century woodcut of a printer at work.

Science and Technology

1320	paper adopted for use in Europe (having long been in use in China)
1450	the Dutch devise the first firearm small enough to be carried by a single person
1451	Nicolas of Cusa (German) uses concave lenses to amend nearsightedness
1454	Johannes Gutenberg (German) prints the Bible with movable metal type

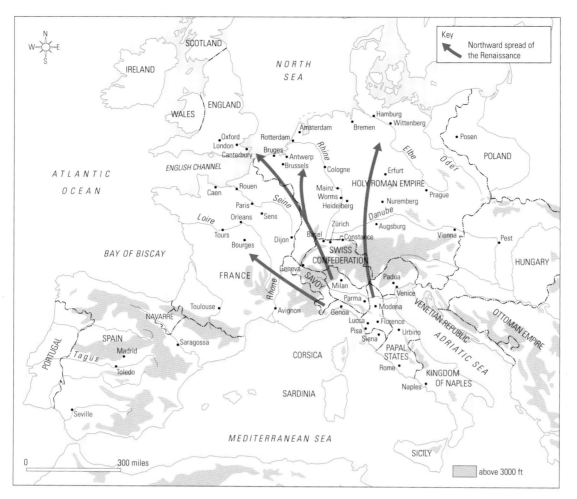

Map 19.1
Renaissance Europe,
ca. 1500.

be the single most important factor in the success of the Protestant Reformation, as it brought the complaints of Church reformers to the attention of all literate folk.

Christian Humanism and the Northern Renaissance

The new print technology broadcast an old message of religious protest and reform. For two centuries, critics had attacked the wealth, worldliness, and unchecked corruption of the Church of Rome. During the early fifteenth century, the rekindled sparks of lay piety and anticlericalism spread throughout the Netherlands, where religious leaders launched the movement known as the *devotio moderna* ("modern devotion"). Lay Brothers and Sisters of the Common Life, as they were called, organized houses in which they studied and taught Scripture. Living in the manner of Christian monks and nuns, but taking no monastic vows, these lay Christians cultivated a devotional lifestyle that fulfilled the ideals of the apostles and the church fathers. They followed the mandate of Thomas à Kempis (1380–1471), himself a Brother of the Common Life and author of the *Imitatio Christi* (*Imitation of Christ*), to put the message of Jesus into daily practice. After the Bible, the *Imitatio Christi* was the most frequently published book in the Christian West well into modern times.

The *devotio moderna* spread quickly throughout Northern Europe, harnessing the dominant strains of anticlericalism, lay piety, and mysticism, even as it coincided with the revival of Classical studies in the newly established universities of Germany. Although Northern humanists, like their Italian Renaissance counterparts, encouraged learning in Greek and Latin, they were more concerned with the study and translation of Early Christian manuscripts than with the Classical and largely secular texts that preoccupied the Italian humanists. This critical reappraisal of religious texts is known as Christian humanism. Christian humanists studied the Bible and the writings of the church fathers with the same intellectual fervor that the Italian humanists had brought to their examination of Plato and Cicero. The efforts of these Northern scholars gave rise to a rebirth (or renaissance) that focused on the late Classical world and, specifically, on the revival of church life and doctrine as gleaned from Early Christian literature. The Northern Renaissance put Christian humanism at the service of evangelical Christianity.

The leading Christian humanist of the sixteenth century—often called "the Prince of Humanists"—was Desiderius Erasmus of Rotterdam (1466–1536; Figure **19.3**). Schooled among the Brothers of the Common Life and learned in Latin, Greek, and Hebrew, Erasmus was a superb scholar and a prolific writer (see Reading 19.2). The first humanist to make extensive use of the printing press, he once dared a famous publisher to print his

Figure 19.3 ALBRECHT DÜRER, *Erasmus of Rotterdam*, 1526. Engraving, 9¾ × 7½ in. The Latin inscription at the top of the engraving reports that Dürer executed the portrait from life. The Greek inscription below reads, "The better image [is found] in his writings." The artist wrote to his friend that he felt the portrait was not a striking likeness.

words as fast as he could write them. Erasmus was a fervent Neoclassicist—he held that almost everything worth knowing was set forth in Greek and Latin. He was also a devout Christian. Advocating a return to the basic teachings of Christ, he criticized the Church and all Christians whose faith had been jaded by slavish adherence to dogma and ritual. Using four different Greek manuscripts of the Gospels, he produced a critical edition of the New Testament that corrected Jerome's mistranslations of key passages. Erasmus' New Testament became the source of most sixteenth-century German and English vernacular translations of this central text of Christian humanism.

The Protestant Reformation

During the sixteenth century, papal extravagance and immorality reached new heights, and Church reform became an urgent public issue. In the territories of Germany, loosely united under the leadership of the Holy Roman emperor Charles V (1500–1558), the voices of protest were more strident than anywhere else in Europe. Across Germany, the sale of indulgences (see chapter 15) for the benefit of the Church of Rome—specifically for the rebuilding of Saint Peter's Cathedral—provoked harsh criticism, especially by those who saw the luxuries of the papacy as a betrayal of apostolic ideals. As with

most movements of religious reform, it fell to one individual to galvanize popular sentiment. In 1505, Martin Luther (1483–1546), the son of a rural coal miner, abandoned his legal studies to become an Augustinian monk (Figure **19.4**). Thereafter, as a doctor of theology at the University of Wittenberg, he spoke out against the Church. His inflammatory sermons and essays offered radical remedies to what he called "the misery and wretchedness of Christendom."

Luther was convinced of the inherent sinfulness of humankind, but he took issue with the traditional medieval view—as promulgated, for instance, in *Everyman*—that salvation was earned through the performance of good works and grace mediated by the Church and its priesthood. Inspired by the words of Saint Paul, "the just shall live by faith" (Romans 1:17), Luther argued that salvation could be attained only by faith in the validity of Christ's sacrifice: human beings were saved by the unearned gift of God's grace, not by their good works on earth. Purchasing indulgences, venerating relics, making pilgrimages, and seeking the intercession of the saints were useless, because only the grace of God could save the Christian soul. Justified by faith alone, Christians should assume full responsibility for their own actions and intentions.

In 1517, in pointed criticism of Church abuses, Luther posted on the door of the collegiate church at Wittenberg a list of ninety-five subjects he intended for dispute with the leaders of the Church of Rome. The *Ninety-Five Theses*, which took the confrontational tone of the sample below, were put to press and circulated throughout Europe:

Figure 19.4 LUCAS CRANACH THE ELDER, *Portrait of Martin Luther*, 1533. Panel, 8 × 5¾ in.

27   They are wrong who say that the soul flies out of Purgatory as soon as the money thrown into the chest rattles.

32   Those who believe that, through letters of pardon [indulgences], they are made sure of their own salvation will be eternally damned along with their teachers.

37   Every true Christian, whether living or dead, has a share in all the benefits of Christ and of the Church, given by God, even without letters of pardon.

43   Christians should be taught that he who gives to a poor man, or lends to a needy man, does better than if he bought pardons.

44   Because by works of charity, charity increases, and the man becomes better; while by means of pardons, he does not become better, but only freer from punishment.

45   Christians should be taught that he who sees any one in need, and, passing him by, gives money for pardons, is not purchasing for himself the indulgences of the Pope but the anger of God.

49   Christians should be taught that the Pope's pardons are useful if they do not put their trust in them, but most hurtful if through them they lose the fear of God.

50   Christians should be taught that if the Pope were acquainted with the exactions of the Preachers of pardons, he would prefer that the Basilica of Saint Peter should be burnt to ashes rather than that it should be built up with the skin, flesh, and bones of his sheep.

54   Wrong is done to the Word of God when, in the same sermon, an equal or longer time is spent on pardons than on it.

62   The true treasure of the Church is the Holy Gospel of the glory and grace of God.

66   The treasures of indulgences are nets, wherewith they now fish for the riches of men.

67   Those indulgences which the preachers loudly proclaim to be the greatest graces, are seen to be truly such as regards the promotion of gain.

68   Yet they are in reality most insignificant when compared to the grace of God and the piety of the cross.

86   . . . why does not the Pope, whose riches are at this day more ample than those of the wealthiest of the wealthy, build the single Basilica of Saint Peter with his own money rather than with that of poor believers? . . .

Luther did not set out to destroy Catholicism, but rather to reform it. Gradually he extended his criticism of Church abuses to criticism of Church doctrine. For instance, because he found justification in Scripture for only two Roman Catholic sacraments—baptism and Holy Communion—he rejected the other five. He attacked monasticism and clerical celibacy. (Luther himself married, and fathered six children.) Luther's boldest challenge to the old medieval order, however, was his unwillingness to accept the pope as the ultimate source of religious authority. Denying that the pope was the spiritual heir to Saint Peter, he claimed that the head of the Church, like any other human being, was subject to error and correction. Christians, argued Luther, were collectively a priesthood of believers; they were "consecrated as priests by baptism." The ultimate source of authority in matters of faith and doctrine was Scripture, as interpreted by the individual Christian. To encourage the reading of the Bible among his followers, Luther translated the Old and New Testaments into German.

Luther's assertions were revolutionary because they defied both church dogma and the authority of the Church of Rome. In 1520, Pope Leo X issued an edict excommunicating the outspoken reformer. Luther promptly burned the edict in the presence of his students at the University of Wittenberg. The following year, he was summoned to the city of Worms in order to appear before the Diet—the German parliamentary council. Charged with heresy, Luther stubbornly refused to back down, concluding, "I cannot and will not recant anything, for to act against our conscience is neither safe for us, nor open to us. On this I take my stand. I can do no other. God help me. Amen." Luther's confrontational temperament and down-to-earth style are captured in this excerpt from his *Address to the German Nobility*, a call for religious reform written shortly before the Diet of Worms and circulated widely in a printed edition.

READING 19.1 From Luther's *Address to the German Nobility* (1520)

It has been devised that the Pope, bishops, priests, and   1
monks are called the *spiritual estate*; princes, lords,
artificers, and peasants are the *temporal estate*. This is
an artful lie and hypocritical device, but let no one be
made afraid by it, and that for this reason: that all
Christians are truly of the spiritual estate, and there is
no difference among them, save of office alone. As Saint
Paul says (1 Cor.:12), we are all one body, though each
member does its own work, to serve the others. This is
because we have one baptism, one Gospel, one faith,   10
and are all Christians alike; for baptism, Gospel, and
faith, these alone make spiritual and Christian people.

As for the unction by a pope or a bishop, tonsure,
ordination, consecration, and clothes differing from those
of laymen—all this may make a hypocrite or an anointed
puppet, but never a Christian or a spiritual man. Thus we
are all consecrated as priests by baptism. . . .

And to put the matter even more plainly, if a little
company of pious Christian laymen were taken prisoners
and carried away to a desert, and had not among them a   20
priest consecrated by a bishop, and were there to agree
to elect one of them, born in wedlock or not, and were to
order him to baptize, to celebrate the Mass, to absolve,
and to preach, this man would as truly be a priest, as if
all the bishops and all the popes had consecrated him.
That is why in cases of necessity every man can baptize
and absolve, which would not be possible if we were not
all priests. . . .

[Members of the Church of Rome] alone pretend to be considered masters of the Scriptures; although they learn nothing of them all their life. They assume authority, and juggle before us with impudent words, saying that the Pope cannot err in matters of faith, whether he be evil or good, albeit they cannot prove it by a single letter. That is why the canon law contains so many heretical and unchristian, nay unnatural, laws. . . .

And though they say that this authority was given to Saint Peter when the keys were given to him, it is plain enough that the keys were not given to Saint Peter alone, but to the whole community. Besides, the keys were not ordained for doctrine or authority, but for sin, to bind or loose; and what they claim besides this from the keys is mere invention. . . .

Only consider the matter. They must needs acknowledge that there are pious Christians among us that have the true faith, spirit, understanding, word, and mind of Christ: why then should we reject their word and understanding, and follow a pope who has neither understanding nor spirit? Surely this were to deny our whole faith and the Christian Church. . . .

Therefore when need requires, and the Pope is a cause of offence to Christendom, in these cases whoever can best do so, as a faithful member of the whole body, must do what he can to procure a true free council. This no one can do so well as the temporal authorities, especially since they are fellow-Christians, fellow-priests, sharing one spirit and one power in all things . . . Would it not be most unnatural, if a fire were to break out in a city, and every one were to keep still and let it burn on and on, whatever might be burnt, simply because they had not the mayor's authority, or because the fire perchance broke out at the mayor's house? Is not every citizen bound in this case to rouse and call in the rest? How much more should this be done in the spiritual city of Christ, if a fire of offence breaks out, either at the Pope's government or wherever it may! The like happens if an enemy attacks a town. The first to rouse up the rest earns glory and thanks. Why then should not he earn glory that decries the coming of our enemies from hell and rouses and summons all Christians?

But as for their boasts of their authority, that no one must oppose it, this is idle talk. No one in Christendom has any authority to do harm, or to forbid others to prevent harm being done. There is no authority in the Church but for reformation. Therefore if the Pope wished to use his power to prevent the calling of a free council, so as to prevent the reformation of the Church, we must not respect him or his power; and if he should begin to excommunicate and fulminate, we must despise this as the doings of a madman, and, trusting in God, excommunicate and repel him as best we may.

Q Which of Luther's assertions would the Church of Rome have found heretical? Why?

Q Which aspects of this selection might be called anti-authoritarian? Which might be called democratic?

The Spread of Protestantism

30 Luther's criticism constituted an open revolt against the institution that for centuries had governed the lives of Western Christians. With the aid of the printing press, his "protestant" sermons and letters circulated throughout Europe. His defense of Christian conscience worked to justify protest against all forms of dominion. In 1524, under the banner of Christian liberty, German common- ers instigated a series of violent uprisings against the oppressive landholding aristocracy. The result was full- scale war, the so-called Peasant Revolts that resulted in the 40 bloody defeat of thousands of peasants. Although Luther condemned the violence and brutality of the Peasant Revolts, social unrest and ideological warfare had only just begun. His denunciation of the lower-class rebels brought many of the German princes to his side; and some used their new religious allegiance as an excuse to seize and usurp Church properties and revenues within their own domains. As the floodgates of dissent opened wide, civil wars broke out between German princes who were faithful to Rome and those who called themselves 50 Lutheran. The wars lasted for some twenty-five years, until, under the terms of the Peace of Augsburg in 1555, it was agreed that each German prince should have the right to choose the religion to be practiced within his own domain. Nevertheless, religious wars resumed in the late sixteenth century and devastated German lands for almost a century.

Calvin

60 All of Europe was affected by Luther's break with the Church. The Lutheran insistence that enlightened Christians could arrive at truth by way of Scripture led reformers everywhere to interpret the Bible for them- selves. The result was the birth of many new Protestant sects, each based on its own interpretation of Scripture. In the independent city of Geneva, Switzerland, the French lawyer and theologian John Calvin (1509–1564) set up a government in which elected officials, using the Bible as the supreme law, ruled the community.

70 Calvin held that Christians were predestined from birth for either salvation or damnation, a circumstance that made good works irrelevant. The "Doctrine of Predestination" encouraged Calvinists to glorify God by living an upright life, one that required faith, obedience, and abstention from dancing, gambling, swearing, drunkenness, and all forms of public display. Although one's status was known only by God, Protestant Christians manifested that they were among the "elect" by their display of moral rectitude. Further, since Calvin taught that wealth was a sign of God's favor, Calvinists extolled the "work ethic" as consistent with 80 the divine will. Calvin's treatise *Institutes of the Christian Religion* (1536) was hugely influential in transforming Luther's teachings into a rational legal system, while his model city, Geneva, became a missionary center for Calvinist followers in Germany, England, the Netherlands, Scotland, and elsewhere.

Humanism and Religious Fanaticism: The Persecution of Witches

The age of Christian humanism witnessed the rise of religious fanaticism, the most dramatic evidence of which is the witch hunts that infested Renaissance Europe and Reformation Germany. While belief in witches dates back to humankind's earliest societies, the practice of persecuting witches did not begin until the late fourteenth century. Based in the medieval practice of finding evidence of the supernatural in natural phenomena, and fueled by the popular Christian belief that the Devil is actively engaged in human affairs, the first mass persecutions occurred at the end of the fifteenth century, reaching a peak approximately one hundred years later. Among Northern European artists, witches and witchcraft became favorite subjects (Figure **19.5**).

In 1484, two German theologians published the *Malleus Maleficarum* (*The Witches' Hammer*), an encyclopedia that described the nature of witches, their collusion with the Devil, and the ways in which they might be recognized and punished. Its authors reiterated the traditional claim that women—by nature more feeble than men—were dangerously susceptible to the Devil's temptation. As a result, they became the primary victims of the mass hysteria that prevailed during the so-called age of humanism. Women—particularly those who were single, old, or eccentric—constituted four-fifths of the roughly 70,000 witches put to death between the years 1400 and 1700. Females who served as midwives might be accused of causing infant deaths or deformities; others were condemned as witches at the onset of local drought or disease. One recent study suggests that witches were blamed for the sharp drops in temperature that devastated sixteenth-century crops and left many Europeans starving.

The persecution of witches may be seen as an instrument of post-Reformation religious oppression, or as the intensification of antifemale sentiment in an age when women had become more visible politically and commercially. Nevertheless, the witchcraft hysteria of the early modern era dramatizes the troubling gap between humanism and religious fanaticism.

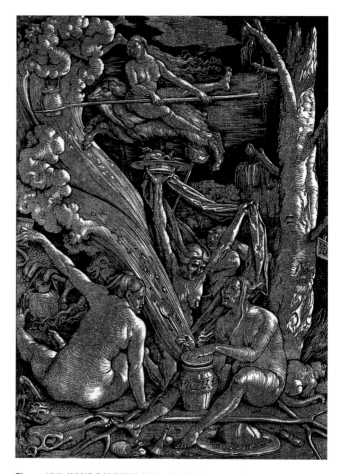

Figure 19.5 HANS BALDUNG ("Grien"), *Witches*, 1510. *Chiaroscuro* woodcut, 15⅞ × 10¼ in. Three witches, sitting under the branches of a dead tree, perform a black Mass. One lifts the chalice, while another mocks the Host by elevating the body of a dead toad. An airborne witch rides backward on a goat, a symbol of the Devil.

The Anabaptists

In nearby Zürich, a radical wing of the Protestant movement emerged: the Anabaptists (given this name by those who opposed their practice of "rebaptizing" adult Christians) rejected all seven of the sacraments (including infant baptism) as sources of God's grace. Placing total emphasis on Christian conscience and the voluntary acceptance of Christ, the Anabaptists called for the abolition of the Mass and the complete separation of Church and state: holding individual responsibility and personal liberty as fundamental ideals, they were among the first Westerners to offer religious sanction for political disobedience. Many Anabaptist reformers met death at the hands of local governments—the men were burned at the stake and the women were usually drowned. English offshoots of the Anabaptists—the Baptists and the Quakers—would come to follow Anabaptist precepts, including the rejection of religious ritual (and imagery) and a fundamentalist approach to Scripture.

The Anglican Church

In England, the Tudor monarch Henry VIII (1491–1547) broke with the Roman Catholic Church and established a church under his own leadership. Political expediency colored the king's motives: Henry was determined to leave England with a male heir, but when eighteen years of marriage to Catherine of Aragon produced only one heir (a daughter), he attempted to annul the marriage and take a new wife. The pope refused, prompting the king—formerly a staunch supporter of the Catholic Church—to break with Rome. In 1526, Henry declared himself head of the Church in England. In 1536, with the support of Parliament, he closed all Christian monasteries and sold Church lands, accumulating vast revenues for the royal treasury. His actions led to years of dispute and hostility between Roman Catholics and Anglicans (members of the new English Church). By the mid-sixteenth century, the consequences of Luther's protests were evident: the religious unity of Western Christendom was shattered forever. Social and political upheaval had become the order of the day.

Music and the Reformation

Since the Reformation clearly dominated the religious and social history of the sixteenth century, it also touched, directly or indirectly, all forms of artistic endeavor, including music. Luther himself was a student of music, an active performer, and an admirer of Josquin des Prez (see chapter 17). Emphasizing music as a source of religious instruction, he encouraged the writing of hymnals and reorganized the German Mass to include both congregational and professional singing. Luther held that all religious texts should be sung in German, so that the faithful might understand their message. The text, according to Luther, should be both comprehensible and appealing.

Luther's favorite musical form was the **chorale**, a congregational hymn that served to enhance the spirit of Protestant worship. Chorales, written in German, drew on Latin hymns and German folk tunes. They were characterized by monophonic clarity and simplicity, features that encouraged performance by untrained congregations. The most famous Lutheran chorale (the melody of which may not have originated with Luther) is "Ein' feste Burg ist unser Gott" ("A Mighty Fortress is our God")—a hymn that has been called "the anthem of the Reformation." Luther's chorales had a major influence on religious music for centuries. And although in the hands of later composers the chorale became a complex polyphonic vehicle for voices and instruments, at its inception it was performed with all voices singing the same words at the same time. It was thus an ideal medium for the communal expression of Protestant piety.

Other Protestant sects, such as the Anabaptists and the Calvinists, regarded music as a potentially dangerous distraction for the faithful. In many sixteenth-century churches, the organ was dismantled and sung portions of the service edited or deleted. Calvin, however, who encouraged devotional recitation of psalms in the home, revised church services to include the congregational singing of psalms in the vernacular.

This Lutheran chorale inspired Johann Sebastian Bach's Cantata No. 80, an excerpt from which is included among the Listening Selections for Chapter 22.

Northern Renaissance Art

Jan van Eyck

Prior to the Reformation, in the cities of Northern Europe, a growing middle class joined princely rulers and the Church to encourage the arts. In addition to traditional religious subjects, middle-class patrons commissioned portraits that—like those painted by Italian Renaissance artists (see chapter 17)—recorded their physical appearance and brought attention to their earthly achievements. Fifteenth-century Northern artists, unlike their Italian counterparts, were relatively unfamiliar with Greco-Roman culture; many of them moved in the direction of detailed Realism, already evident in the manuscript illuminations of the Limbourg brothers (see Figure 15.1).

The pioneer of Northern realism was the Flemish artist Jan van Eyck (ca. 1380–1441). Van Eyck, whom we met in chapter 17, was reputed to have perfected the art of oil painting (see Figure 17.11). His application of thin glazes of colored pigments bound with linseed oil achieved the impression of dense, atmospheric space, and simulated the naturalistic effects of light reflecting off the surfaces of objects. Such effects were almost impossible to achieve in fresco or tempera. While van Eyck lacked any knowledge of the system of linear perspective popularized in Florence, he achieved an extraordinary level of realism both in the miniatures he executed for religious manuscripts and in his panel paintings.

Van Eyck's full-length double portrait of 1434 is the first painting in Western art to have portrayed a secular couple in a domestic interior (see LOOKING INTO, Figure **19.6**). The painting has long been the subject of debate among scholars who have questioned its original purpose, as well as the identity of the sitters. It was long thought to represent the marriage of Giovanni di Nicolao Arnolfini (an Italian cloth merchant who represented the Medici bank in Bruges) to Jeanne Cenami, but it has recently been discovered that Jeanne died in 1433, a year before the date of the painting. Since so many elements in the painting suggest a betrothal or wedding vow, however, it is speculated that Giovanni, who knew van Eyck in Bruges for many years, might have remarried in 1434 and commissioned the artist to record the union.

In the painting, the richly dressed Arnolfini raises his right hand as if to greet or vow, while the couple joins hands, a gesture traditionally associated with engagement or marriage. Behind the couple, an inscription on the back wall of the chamber reads "*Johannes de Eyck fuit hic*" ("Jan van Eyck was here"); this testimonial is reiterated by the presence of two figures, probably the artist himself and a second observer, whose painted reflections are seen in the convex mirror below the inscription. Van Eyck's consummate mastery of minute, realistic details—from the ruffles on the young woman's headcovering to the whiskers of the monkey-faced dog—demonstrate the artist's determination to capture the immediacy of the physical world. This attention to detail and deliberate

Van Eyck's *Arnolfini Double Portrait*

Figure 19.6 JAN VAN EYCK, *Arnolfini Double Portrait*, 1434. Tempera and oil on panel, 32¼ × 23½ in.

The *Arnolfini Double Portrait* is typical of the Northern sensibility in the way in which the physical details "speak" to the function of the painting as a visual document related to marriage: the burning candle (traditionally carried to the marriage ceremony by the bride) suggests the all-seeing presence of Christ; the ripening fruit lying on and near the window sill both symbolizes fecundity and alludes to the union of the First Couple in the Garden of Eden; the carved image on the chairback near the bed represents Saint Margaret, the patron saint of childbirth.

The objects in this domestic interior suggest a world of material comfort and pleasure: the brass chandelier, convex mirror, and oriental carpet were luxuries in fifteenth-century Flanders, while the ermine and sable-trimmed outer garments and the very abundance of rich fabrics worn by both the merchant and his partner would have been recognized as signs of great wealth and prosperity. At the same time, however, many of these details make symbolic reference to a less tangible, spiritual reality. In this effort to reconcile the visible world with the invisible legacy of faith, van Eyck anticipated the unique character of Northern Renaissance art.

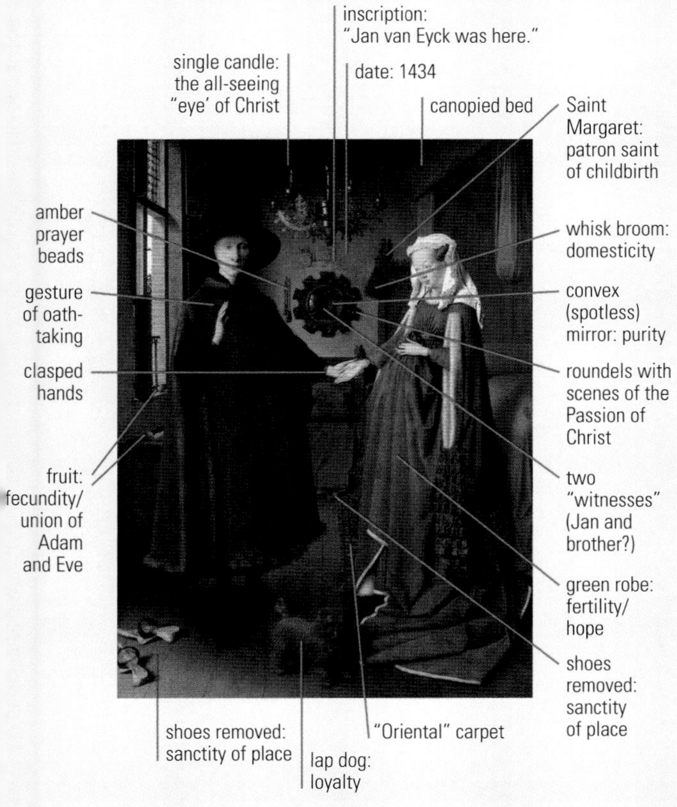

inscription: "Jan van Eyck was here."

single candle: the all-seeing "eye' of Christ

date: 1434

canopied bed

Saint Margaret: patron saint of childbirth

amber prayer beads

gesture of oath-taking

clasped hands

fruit: fecundity/ union of Adam and Eve

whisk broom: domesticity

convex (spotless) mirror: purity

roundels with scenes of the Passion of Christ

two "witnesses" (Jan and brother?)

green robe: fertility/ hope

shoes removed: sanctity of place

shoes removed: sanctity of place

lap dog: loyalty

"Oriental" carpet

Bosch

The generation of Flemish artists that followed Jan van Eyck produced one of the most enigmatic figures of the Northern Renaissance: Hieronymus Bosch (1460–1516). Little is known about Bosch's life, and the exact meaning of some of his works is much disputed. His career spanned the decades of the High Renaissance in Italy, but comparison of his paintings with those of Raphael or Michelangelo underscores the enormous difference between Italian Renaissance art and that of the European North: whereas Raphael and Michelangelo elevated the natural nobility of the individual, Bosch detailed the fallibility of humankind, its moral struggle, and its apocalyptic destiny.

Bosch's most famous work, the triptych known as *The Garden of Earthly Delights* (Figure **19.7**), was executed around 1510, the very time that Raphael was painting *The School of Athens*. A work of astonishing complexity, the imagery of Bosch's painting has baffled and intrigued viewers for centuries. For, while it seems to describe the traditional Christian theme of the Creation, Fall, and Punishment of humankind, it does so by means of an assortment of wildly unconventional images. When the wings of the altarpiece are closed, one sees an image of God hovering above a huge transparent globe: the planet earth in the process of creation. An accompanying inscription reads: "He spoke, and it came to be; he commanded and it was created" (Psalm 33.9). When the triptych is opened, the left wing shows the Creation of Eve, but the event takes place in an Eden populated with fabulous and predatory creations (such as the cat at lower left). In the central panel, amidst a cosmic landscape, hordes of youthful nudes cavort in a variety of erotic and playful pastimes. They frolic with oversized flora and fruit, real and imagined animals, gigantic birds, and strangely shaped vessels. In the right wing, Bosch pictures Hell as a dark and sulfurous inferno where the damned are tormented by an assortment of sinister creatures and infernal machines that inflict punishment on sinners appropriate to their sins (as in Dante's *Inferno*; see chapter 12). The hoarder (at the lower right), for instance, pays for his greed by excreting gold coins into a pothole, while the nude nearby, punished for the sin of lust, is fondled by demons.

The Garden of Earthly Delights has been described by some as an exposition on the decadent behavior of the descendants of Adam and Eve, but its distance from conventional religious iconography has made it the subject of endless scholarly interpretation. Bosch, a Roman Catholic, seems to have borrowed imagery from a variety of medieval and contemporary sources, including the Bible, popular proverbs, marginal grotesques in illuminated manuscripts, and pilgrimage badges, as well as the popular pseudo-sciences of his time: astrology, the study of the influence of heavenly bodies on human affairs (the precursor of astronomy); and alchemy, the art of transmuting base metals into gold (the precursor of chemistry). The egg-shaped vessels, beakers, and transparent tubes that appear in all parts of the

Figure 19.7 HIERONYMUS BOSCH, *The Creation of Eve: The Garden of Earthly Delights: Hell* (triptych), ca. 1510–1515. Oil on wood, 7 ft. 2⅜ in. × 12 ft. 8¾ in. Bosch probably painted this moralizing work for lay patrons. Many of its individual images would have been recognized as references to the Seven Deadly Sins, for instance: the bagpipe (a symbol of Lust) that sits on a disk crowning the Tree-Man (upper center) and the man who is forced to disgorge his food (symbolic of Gluttony) depicted beneath the enthroned frog (lower right).

triptych were commonly used in alchemical transmutation. The latter process may have been familiar to Bosch as symbolic of creation and destruction, and, more specifically, as a metaphor for the biblical Creation and Fall.

Regardless of how one interprets Bosch's *Garden*, it is clear that the artist transformed standard Christian iconography to suit his imagination. Probably commissioned by a

private patron, Bosch may have felt free to bring fantasy and invention to traditional subject matter. The result is a moralizing commentary on the varieties of human folly afflicting sinful creatures hopeful of Christian salvation.

More conventional in its imagery, Bosch's *Death and the Miser* (Figure **19.8**) belongs to the tradition of the *memento mori* (discussed in chapter 12), which warns the beholder of the inevitability of death. The painting also shows the influence of popular fifteenth-century handbooks on the art of dying (the *ars moriendi*), designed to remind Christians that they must choose between sinful pleasures and the way of Christ. As Death looms on the threshold, the miser, unable to resist worldly temptations even in his last minutes of life, reaches for the bag of gold offered to him by

Figure 19.8 HIERONYMUS BOSCH,
Death and the Miser, ca. 1485–1490. Oil on oak, 3 ft. ⅝ in. × 12⅛ in.

a demon. In the foreground, Bosch depicts the miser storing gold in his money chest while clutching his rosary. Symbols of worldly power—a helmet, sword, and shield—allude to earthly follies. The depiction of such still-life objects to symbolize vanity, transience, or decay would become a genre in itself among seventeenth-century Flemish artists.

Printmaking

The Protestant Reformation cast a long shadow upon the religious art of the North. Protestants rejected the traditional imagery of medieval piety, along with church relics and sacred images, which they associated with superstition and idolatry. Protestant iconoclasts stripped the stained glass from cathedral windows, shattered religious sculpture, whitewashed church frescoes, and destroyed altarpieces. At the same time, however, the voices of reform encouraged the proliferation of private devotional art, particularly that which illustrated biblical themes. In the production of portable devotional images, the technology of printmaking played a major role. Just as movable type had facilitated the dissemination of the printed word, so the technology of the print made devotional subjects available more cheaply and in greater numbers than ever before.

The two new printmaking processes of the fifteenth century were **woodcut**, the technique of cutting away all parts of a design on a wood surface except those that will be inked and transferred to paper (Figure **19.9**), and **engraving** (Figure **19.10**), the process by which lines are incised on a metal (usually copper) plate that is inked and run through a printing press. Books with printed illustrations

became cheap alternatives to the hand-illuminated manuscripts that were prohibitively expensive to all but wealthy patrons.

Dürer

The unassailed leader in Northern Renaissance printmaking, and one of the finest graphic artists of all time, was Albrecht Dürer of Nuremberg (1471–1528). Dürer earned international fame for his woodcuts and metal engravings. His mastery of the laws of linear perspective and human anatomy and his investigations into Classical principles of proportions (enhanced by two trips to Italy) equaled those of the best Italian Renaissance artist–scientists. In the genre of portraiture, Dürer was the match of Raphael, but, unlike Raphael, he recorded the features of his sitters with little idealization. His portrait engraving of Erasmus (see Figure 19.3) captures the concentrated intelligence of the Prince of Humanists.

Dürer brought to the art of his day a desire to convey the spiritual message of Scripture. His series of woodcuts illustrating the last book of the New Testament, the Revelation According to Saint John (also called the "Apocalypse"), reveals the extent to which he achieved his purpose. *The Four Horsemen of the Apocalypse*—one of fifteen woodcuts in the series—brings to life the terrifying events described in Revelation 6.1–8 (see Figure 19.1). Amidst billowing clouds, Death (in the foreground), Famine (carrying a pair of scales), War (brandishing a sword), and Pestilence (drawing his bow) sweep down upon humankind; their victims fall beneath

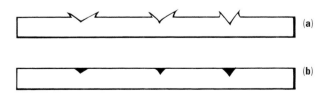

Figure 19.10 Engraving. An intaglio method of printing. The cutting tool, a *burin* or *graver*, is used to cut lines in the surface of metal plates. (**a**) A cross section of an engraved plate showing burrs (ridges) produced by scratching a burin into the surface of a metal plate; (**b**) the burrs are removed and ink is wiped over the surface and forced into the scratches. The plate is then wiped clean, leaving ink deposits in the scratches; the ink is forced from the plate onto paper under pressure in a special press.

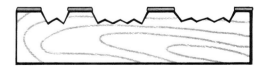

Figure 19.9 Woodcut. A relief printing process created by lines cut into the plank surface of wood. The raised portions of the block are inked and transferred by pressure to the paper by hand or with a printing press.

Figure 19.11 ALBRECHT DÜRER, *Knight, Death, and the Devil*, 1513. Engraving, 9⅝ × 7½ in. Dürer's engraving is remarkable for its wealth of microscopic detail. Objects in the real world—the horse, the dog, and the lizard—are depicted as precisely as those imagined: the devil and the horned demon.

the horses' hooves, or, as with the bishop in the lower left, are devoured by infernal monsters.

Dürer was a humanist in his own right and a great admirer of both the moderate Erasmus and the zealous Luther. In one of his most memorable engravings, *Knight, Death, and the Devil*, he depicted the Christian soul in the allegorical guise of a medieval knight (Figure **19.11**), a figure made famous in a treatise by Erasmus entitled *Handbook for the Militant Christian* (1504). The knight, the medieval symbol of fortitude and courage, advances against a dark and brooding landscape. Accompanied by his loyal dog, he marches forward, ignoring his fearsome companions: Death, who rides a pale horse and carries an hourglass, and the devil, a shaggy, cross-eyed, horned demon. Here is the visual counterpart of Erasmus' message that the Christian must hold to the path of virtue, and in spite of "all those spooks and phantoms" that come upon him, he must "look not behind." The knight's dignified bearing (probably inspired by heroic equestrian statues Dürer had seen in Italy) contrasts sharply with the bestial and cankerous features of his forbidding escorts. In the tradition of Jan van Eyck, but with a precision facilitated by the new medium of metal engraving, Dürer records every leaf and pebble, hair and wrinkle; and yet the final effect is not a mere piling up of minutiae but, like nature itself, an astonishing amalgam of organically related elements.

In addition to his numerous woodcuts and engravings, Dürer produced hundreds of paintings: portraits and large-scale religious subjects. His interest in the natural world inspired the first landscapes in Western art (Figure **19.12**). These detailed panoramic views of the countryside, executed in watercolor during his frequent travels to Italy and elsewhere, were independent works, not mere studies for larger, more formal subjects. To such landscapes, as well as to his meticulously detailed renderings of plants, animals, and birds, Dürer brought the eye of a scientific naturalist and a spirit of curiosity not unlike that of his Italian contemporary Leonardo da Vinci.

Grünewald

Dürer's German contemporary Matthias Gothardt Neithardt, better known as "Grünewald" (1460–1528), did not share Dürer's Classically inspired aesthetic ideals, nor his quest for realistic representation. The few paintings and drawings left by Grünewald (as compared with the hundreds of works left by Dürer) do not tell us whether the artist was Catholic or Protestant. In their spiritual intensity and emotional subjectivity, however, they are among the most striking devotional works of the Northern Renaissance.

Grünewald's landmark work, the Isenheim Altarpiece, was designed to provide solace to the victims of disease and especially plague at the Hospital of Saint Anthony in

Figure 19.12 ALBRECHT DÜRER, *Wire Drawing Mill*, undated. Watercolor, 11¼ × 16¾ in.

Figure 19.13 MATTHIAS GRÜNEWALD, Isenheim Altarpiece, ca. 1510–1515. Oil on panel, central panel 8 ft. × 10 ft. 1 in. The opened wings of the altarpiece show Saint Sebastian (left) and Saint Anthony (right), both protectors against disease and plague. Those afflicted with disease (including leprosy, syphilis, and poisoning caused by ergot, a cereal fungus), were able to contemplate the altarpiece daily in the hospital chapel.

Isenheim, near Colmar, France (Figure **19.13**). Like the *Imitatio Christi*, which taught Christians to seek identification with Jesus, this multipaneled altarpiece reminded its beholders of their kinship with the suffering Jesus, depicted in the central panel. Following the tradition of the devotional German *Pietà* (see Figure 15.11), Grünewald made use of expressive exaggeration and painfully precise detail: the agonized body of Jesus is lengthened to emphasize its weight as it hangs from the bowed cross, the flesh putrefies with clotted blood and angry thorns, the fingers convulse and curl, while the feet—broken and bruised—contort in a spasm of pain. Grünewald reinforces the mood of lamentation by placing the scene in a darkened landscape. He exaggerates the gestures of the attending figures, including that of John the Baptist, whose oversized finger points to the prophetic Latin inscription that explains his mystical presence: "He must increase and I must decrease" (John 3:30).

Cranach and Holbein

The German cities of the sixteenth century produced some of the finest draftsmen in the history of Western art. Dürer's contemporary Lucas Cranach the Elder (1472–1553) was a highly acclaimed court painter at Wittenberg

and, like Dürer, a convert to the Protestant reform. In 1522, he produced the woodcuts for the first German edition of the New Testament. Although he also worked for Catholic patrons, he painted and engraved numerous portraits of Protestant leaders, the most notable of whom was his friend Martin Luther, whose likeness he recreated several times. In the portrait illustrated in Figure 19.4, Cranach exercised his skill as a master draftsman, capturing both the authoritative silhouette and the confident demeanor of the famous reformer.

Hans Holbein the Younger (1497–1543), celebrated as the greatest of the German portraitists, was born in Augsburg, but spent much of his life in Switzerland, France, and England. With a letter of introduction from his friend Erasmus, Holbein traveled to England to paint the family of Sir Thomas More (see Figure 19.16)—Western Europe's first domestic group portrait (it survives only in drawings and copies). On a later trip to England, Holbein became the favorite of Henry VIII, whose likeness he captured along with portraits of the king's current and prospective wives. In common with Dürer and Cranach, Holbein was a master of line. All three artists manifested the integration of brilliant draftsmanship and precise, realistic detail that characterizes the art of the Northern Renaissance. Holbein, however, was unique in his minimal use of line to evoke a penetrating sense of the sitter's personality. So life-like are some of Holbein's portraits that modern scholars have suggested that he made use of technical aids, such as the *camera lucida*, in their preparation (see chapter 17, Exploring Issues).

Bruegel

The career of the last great sixteenth-century Flemish painter, Pieter Bruegel the Elder (1525–1569), followed the careers of most other Northern Renaissance masters by a generation. Like Dürer, Bruegel had traveled to Italy and absorbed its Classical culture; his style, however, would remain relatively independent of Italian influence. Closer in temperament to Bosch, he was deeply concerned with human folly, especially as it was manifested in the everyday life of his Flemish neighbors. Among his early works were crowded panoramas depicting themes of human pride and religious strife. Bruegel's *Triumph of Death* may be read as an indictment of the brutal wars that plagued sixteenth-century Europe (Figure **19.14**). In a cosmic landscape that resembles the setting of a Last Judgment or a Boschlike underworld, Bruegel depicts throngs of skeletons relentlessly slaughtering all ranks of men and women. The armies of the dead are without mercy. In the left foreground, a cardinal collapses in the arms of a skeleton; in the left corner, an emperor relinquishes his hoards of gold; on the right, death interrupts the pleasure of gamblers and lovers. Some of the living are crushed beneath the wheels of a death cart, others are hanged from scaffolds or subjected to torture. Bruegel's apocalyptic vision transforms the late medieval Dance of Death into a universal holocaust.

Many of Bruegel's best-known works were inspired by biblical parables or local proverbs, popular expressions of universal truths concerning human behavior. In his drawings, engravings, and paintings, he rendered these as visual narratives set in the Flemish countryside. His treatment of the details of rustic life, which earned him the title "Peasant Bruegel," and his landscapes illustrating the labors appropriate to each season were the culmination of a tradition begun in the innovative miniatures of the Limbourg brothers (see Figure 15.1). However, Bruegel's **genre paintings**

Figure 19.14 PIETER BRUEGEL THE ELDER, *Triumph of Death*, ca. 1562–1564. Oil on panel, 3 ft. 10 in. × 5 ft. 3¾ in.

Figure 19.15 PIETER BRUEGEL THE ELDER, *The Wedding Dance*, 1566. Oil on panel, 3 ft. 11 in. × 5 ft. 2 in.

(representations of the everyday life of ordinary folk) were not small-scale illustrations, but monumental (and sometimes allegorical) transcriptions of rural activities. *The Wedding Dance* (Figure **19.15**) depicts peasant revelry in a country setting whose earthiness is reinforced by rich tones of russet, tan, and muddy green. At the very top of the panel, an improvised wedding table appears among the trees. The red-haired bride, clothed in black (center left), has joined the villagers, who cavort to the music of the bagpipes (right foreground). Although Bruegel's figures are clumsy and often ill-proportioned, they share an ennobling vitality. In his art, as in that of other Northern Renaissance painters, we discover an unvarnished perception of human beings in mundane and unheroic circumstances—a sharp contrast to the idealized conception of humankind found in the art of Renaissance Italy.

Sixteenth-Century Literature

Erasmus: *The Praise of Folly*

European literature of the sixteenth century was marked by heightened individualism and a progressive inclination to clear away the last remnants of medieval orthodoxy. It was,

in many ways, a literature of protest and reform, and one whose dominant themes reflect the tension between medieval and modern ideas. European writers were especially concerned with the discrepancies between the noble ideals of Classical humanism and the ignoble reality of human behavior. Religious rivalry and the horrors of war, witch hunts, and religious persecution all seemed to contradict the optimistic view that the Renaissance had inaugurated a more enlightened phase of human self-consciousness.

Science and Technology

1540	the Swiss physician Paracelsus (Philippus von Hohenheim) pioneers the use of chemistry for medical purposes
1543	Copernicus (Polish) publishes *On the Revolution of the Heavenly Spheres*, announcing his heliocentric theory
1553	Michael Servetus (Spanish) describes the pulmonary circulation of the blood

Satire, a literary genre that conveys the contradictions between real and ideal situations, was especially popular during the sixteenth century. By means of satiric irony, Northern Renaissance writers held up prevailing abuses to ridicule, thus implying the need for reform.

The learned treatises and letters of Erasmus won him the respect of scholars throughout Europe; but his single most popular work was *The Praise of Folly*, a satiric oration attacking a wide variety of human foibles, including greed, intellectual pomposity, and pride. *The Praise of Folly* went through more than two dozen editions in Erasmus' lifetime, and influenced other humanists, including his lifelong friend and colleague Thomas More, to whom it was dedicated (in Latin, *moria* means "folly").

A short excerpt from *The Praise of Folly* offers some idea of Erasmus' keen wit as applied to a typical Northern Renaissance theme: the vast gulf between human fallibility and human perfectibility. The reading opens with the image of the world as a stage, a favorite metaphor of sixteenth-century painters and poets—not the least of whom was William Shakespeare. Dame Folly, the allegorical figure who is the speaker in the piece, compares life to a comedy in which the players assume various roles: in the course of the drama (she observes), one may come to play the parts of both servant and king. She then describes each of a number of roles (or disciplines), such as medicine, law, and so on, in terms of its affinity with folly. Erasmus' most searing words were reserved for theologians and church dignitaries, but his insights expose more generally (and timelessly) the frailties of all human beings.

READING 19.2 From Erasmus'
The Praise of Folly (1511)

Now what else is the whole life of mortals but a sort of comedy, in which the various actors, disguised by various costumes and masks, walk on and play each one his part, until the manager waves them off the stage? Moreover, this manager frequently bids the same actor go back in a different costume, so that he who has but lately played the king in scarlet now acts the flunkey in patched clothes. Thus all things are presented by shadows; yet this play is put on in no other way. . . .

[The disciplines] that approach nearest to common sense, that is, to folly, are held in highest esteem. Theologians are starved, naturalists find cold comfort, astrologers are mocked, and logicians are slighted. . . . Within the profession of medicine, furthermore, so far as any member is eminently unlearned, impudent, or careless, he is valued the more, even in the chambers of belted earls. For medicine, especially as now practiced by many, is but a subdivision of the art of flattery, no less truly than is rhetoric. Lawyers have the next place after doctors, and I do not know but that they should have first place; with great unanimity the philosophers—not that I would say such a thing myself—are wont to ridicule the law as an ass. Yet great matters and little matters alike are settled by the arbitrament of these

asses. They gather goodly freeholds with broad acres, while the theologian, after poring over chestfuls of the great corpus of divinity, gnaws on bitter beans, at the same time manfully waging war against lice and fleas. As those arts are more successful which have the greatest affinity with folly, so those people are by far the happiest who enjoy the privilege of avoiding all contact with the learned disciplines, and who follow nature as their only guide, since she is in no respect wanting, except as a mortal wishes to transgress the limits set for his status. Nature hates counterfeits; and that which is innocent of art gets along far the more prosperously.

What need we say about practitioners in the arts? Self-love is the hallmark of them all. You will find that they would sooner give up their paternal acres than any piece of their poor talents. Take particularly actors, singers, orators, and poets; the more unskilled one of them is, the more insolent he will be in his self-satisfaction, the more he will blow himself up. . . . Thus the worst art pleases the most people, for the simple reason that the larger part of mankind, as I said before, is subject to folly. If, therefore, the less skilled man is more pleasing both in his own eyes and in the wondering gaze of the many, what reason is there that he should prefer sound discipline and true skill? In the first place, these will cost him a great outlay; in the second place, they will make him more affected and meticulous; and finally, they will please far fewer of his audience. . . .

And now I see that it is not only in individual men that nature has implanted self-love. She implants a kind of it as a common possession in the various races, and even cities. By this token the English claim, besides a few other things, good looks, music, and the best eating as their special properties. The Scots flatter themselves on the score of high birth and royal blood, not to mention their dialectical skill. Frenchmen have taken all politeness for their province; though the Parisians, brushing all others aside, also award themselves the prize for knowledge of theology. The Italians usurp *belles lettres* and eloquence; and they all flatter themselves upon the fact that they alone, of all mortal men, are not barbarians. In this particular point of happiness the Romans stand highest, still dreaming pleasantly of ancient Rome. The Venetians are blessed with a belief in their own nobility. The Greeks, as well as being the founders of the learned disciplines, vaunt themselves upon their titles to the famous heroes of old. The Turks, and that whole rabble of the truly barbarous, claim praise for their religion, laughing at Christians as superstitious. . . .

[Next come] the scientists, reverenced for their beards and the fur on their gowns, who teach that they alone are wise while the rest of mortal men flit about as shadows. How pleasantly they dote, indeed, while they construct their numberless worlds, and measure the sun, moon, stars, and spheres as with thumb and line. They assign causes for lightning, winds, eclipses, and other inexplicable things, never hesitating a whit, as if they were privy to the secrets of nature, artificer of things, or as if they visited us fresh from the council of the gods. Yet all the while nature is laughing grandly at them and their conjectures. For to prove that they have good intelligence of nothing, this is a sufficient argument: they can never explain why they disagree with each other on every subject. Thus knowing nothing in general, they profess to know all things in particular; though they are ignorant even of themselves, and on occasion do not see the ditch or the stone lying across their path, because many of them are blear-eyed or absent-minded; yet they proclaim that they perceive ideas, universals, forms without matter. . . . Perhaps it were better to pass over the theologians in silence, [for] they may attack me with six hundred arguments, in squadrons, and drive me to make a recantation; which if I refuse, they will straightway proclaim me an heretic. By this thunderbolt they are wont to terrify any toward whom they are ill-disposed.

They are happy in their self-love, and as if they already inhabited the third heaven they look down from a height on all other mortal men as on creatures that crawl on the ground, and they come near to pitying them. They are protected by a wall of scholastic definitions, arguments, corollaries, implicit and explicit propositions; . . . they explain as pleases them the most arcane matters, such as by what method the world was founded and set in order, through what conduits original sin has been passed down along the generations, by what means, in what measure, and how long the perfect Christ was in the Virgin's womb, and how accidents subsist in the Eucharist without their subject.

But those are hackneyed. Here are questions worthy of the great and (as some call them) illuminated theologians, questions to make them prick up their ears—if ever they chance upon them. Whether divine generation took place at a particular time? Whether there are several sonships in Christ? Whether this is a possible proposition: God the Father hates the Son? Whether God could have taken upon Himself the likeness of a woman? Or of a devil? Of an ass? Of a gourd? Of a piece of flint? Then how would that gourd have preached, performed miracles, or been crucified? . . . .

Coming nearest to these in felicity are the men who generally call themselves "the religious" and "monks"— utterly false names both, since most of them keep as far away as they can from religion and no people are more in evidence in every sort of place. . . . For one thing, they reckon it the highest degree of piety to have no contact with literature, and hence they see to it that they do not know how to read. For another, when with asinine voices they bray out in church those psalms they have learned, by rote rather than by heart, they are convinced that they are anointing God's ears with the blandest of oil. Some of them make a good profit from their dirtiness and mendicancy, collecting their food from door to door with importunate bellowing; nay, there is not an inn, public

conveyance, or ship where they do not intrude, to the great disadvantage of the other common beggars. Yet according to their account, by their very dirtiness, ignorance, these delightful fellows are representing to us the lives of the apostles.

Q What disciplines does Dame Folly single out as having "the greatest affinity with folly"?

Q How does Erasmus attack the religious community of his day?

More's *Utopia*

In England, Erasmus' friend the scholar and statesman Sir Thomas More (1478–1535) served as chancellor to King Henry VIII at the time of Henry's break with the Catholic Church (Figure **19.16**). Like Erasmus, More was a Christian humanist and a man of conscience. He denounced the evils of acquisitive capitalism and religious fanaticism and championed religious tolerance and Christian charity. Unwilling to compromise his conviction as a Roman Catholic, he opposed the actions of the king and was executed for treason in 1535.

Figure 19.16 HANS HOLBEIN THE YOUNGER, *Sir Thomas More*, ca. 1530. Oil on panel, 29½ × 23¼ in. In his attention to minute detail and textural contrast— fur collar, velvet sleeves, gold chain, and Tudor rose pendant—Holbein refined the tradition of realistic portraiture initiated by Jan van Eyck (compare van Eyck's self-portrait, Figure 17.11).

In 1516, More completed his classic political satire on European statecraft and society, a work entitled *Utopia* (the Greek word meaning both "no place" and "a good place"). More's *Utopia*, the first literary description of an ideal state since Plato's *Republic*, was inspired, in part, by accounts of wondrous lands reported by sailors returning from the "New World" across the Atlantic (see chapter 18). More's imaginary island ("discovered" by a fictional explorer–narrator) is a socialistic state in which goods and property are shared, war and personal vanity are held in contempt, learning is available to all citizens (except slaves), and freedom of religion is absolute. Work, while essential to moral and communal well-being, is limited to six hours a day. In this ideal commonwealth, natural reason, benevolence, and scorn for material wealth ensure social harmony.

More's society differs from Plato's in that More gives to each individual, rather than to society's guardians, full responsibility for the establishment of social justice. Writing both a social critique and a satire, More draws the implicit contrast between his own corrupt Christian society and that of his ideal community. Although his Utopians are not Christians, they are guided by Christian principles of morality and charity. They have little use, for instance, for precious metals, jewels, and the "trifles" that drive men to war.

READING 19.3 From More's *Utopia* (1516)

[As] to their manner of living in society, the oldest man   1
of every family . . . is its governor. Wives serve their
husbands, and children their parents, and always the
younger serves the elder. Every city is divided into
four equal parts, and in the middle of each there is a
marketplace: what is brought thither, and manufactured
by the several families, is carried from thence to houses
appointed for that purpose, in which all things of a sort
are laid by themselves; and there every father goes and
takes whatsoever he or his family stand in need of,   10
without either paying for it or leaving anything in
exchange. There is no reason for giving a denial to any
person, since there is such plenty of everything among
them; and there is no danger of a man's asking for more
than he needs; they have no inducements to do this,
since they are sure that they shall always be supplied.
It is the fear of want that makes any of the whole race of
animals either greedy or ravenous; but besides fear, there
is in man a pride that makes him fancy it a particular
glory to excel others in pomp and excess. But by the   20
laws of the Utopians, there is no room for this. . . .

[Since the Utopians] have no use for money among
themselves, but keep it as a provision against events
which seldom happen, and between which there are
generally long intervening intervals, they value it no
farther than it deserves, that is, in proportion to its use.
So that it is plain they must prefer iron either to gold or
silver; for men can no more live without iron than
without fire or water, but nature has marked out no use
for the other metals so essential and not easily to be   30

dispensed with. The folly of men has enhanced the value
of gold and silver, because of their scarcity. Whereas,
on the contrary, it is their opinion that nature, as an
indulgent parent, has freely given us all the best things
in great abundance, such as water and earth, but has
laid up and hid from us the things that are vain and
useless. . . .

. . . They eat and drink out of vessels of earth, or glass,
which make an agreeable appearance though formed of
brittle materials: while they make their chamber-pots   40
and close-stools[1] of gold and silver, and that not only
in their public halls, but in their private houses: of the
same metals they likewise make chains and fetters for
their slaves; to some [slaves], as a badge of infamy, they
hang an ear-ring of gold, and [they] make others wear a
chain or coronet of the same metal; and thus they take
care, by all possible means, to render gold and silver of
no esteem. And from hence it is that while other nations
part with their gold and silver as unwillingly as if one
tore out their bowels, those of Utopia would look on   50
their giving in all they possess of those [metals] but
as the parting with a trifle, or as we would esteem the
loss of a penny. They find pearls on their coast, and
diamonds and carbuncles on their rocks; they do not
look after them, but, if they find them by chance, they
polish them, and with them they adorn their children,
who are delighted with them, and glory in them during
their childhood; but when they grow to years, and see
that none but children use such baubles, they of their
own accord, without being bid by their parents, lay   60
them aside; and would be as much ashamed to use them
afterward as children among us, when they come to
years, are of their puppets and other toys. . . .

They detest war as a very brutal thing; and which, to the
reproach of human nature, is more practiced by men than
by any sort of beasts. They, in opposition to the sentiments
of almost all other nations, think that there is nothing more
inglorious than that glory that is gained by war. And
therefore though they accustom themselves daily to
military exercises and the discipline of war—in which   70
not only their men but their women likewise are trained up,
that in cases of necessity they may not be quite useless—
yet they do not rashly engage in war, unless it be either to
defend themselves, or their friends, from any unjust
aggressors; or out of good-nature or in compassion
assist an oppressed nation in shaking off the yoke of
tyranny. They indeed help their friends, not only in
defensive, but also in offensive wars; but they never do
that unless they had been consulted before the breach
was made, and being satisfied with the grounds on which   80
they went, they had found that all demands of reparation
were rejected, so that a war was unavoidable. . . .

If they agree to a truce, they observe it so religiously that
no provocations will make them break it. They never lay
their enemies' country waste nor burn their corn, and even

---

[1] A covered chamber pot set in a stool.

in their marches they take all possible care that neither horse nor foot may tread it down, for they do not know but that they may have for it themselves. They hurt no man whom they find disarmed, unless he is a spy. When a town is surrendered to them, they take it into their protection; and when they carry a place by storm, they never plunder it, but put those only to the sword that opposed the rendering of it up, and make the rest of the garrison slaves, but for the other inhabitants, they do them no hurt; and if any of them had advised a surrender, they give them good rewards out of the estates of those that they condemn, and distribute the rest among their auxiliary troops, but they themselves take no share of the spoil.

Q What sort of social organization does More set forth in his Utopia?

Q How would you describe More's views on precious metals and on war?

Cervantes: *Don Quixote*

While Erasmus and More wrote primarily in Latin—*Utopia* was not translated into English until 1551—other European writers preferred the vernacular. The language of everyday speech was favored for such literary genres as the medieval romance (see chapter 11) and the more realistic and satiric **picaresque novel**, which emerged as a popular form of literary entertainment in sixteenth-century Spain. Narrated by the hero, the picaresque novel recounted the comic misadventures of a *picaro* ("rogue"). Its structure—a series of episodes converging on a single theme—anticipated the emergence of the novel in Western literature.

As a genre, the novel, a large-scale prose narrative, had its origins in eleventh-century Japan, with Murasaki Shikibu's *Tale of Genji*. However, in the West, the first such work in this genre was *Don Quixote*, written in two volumes (over a decade apart) by Miguel de Cervantes (1547–1616). *Don Quixote* resembles the picaresque novel in its episodic structure and in its satiric treatment of Spanish society, but the psychological complexity of its hero and the profundity of its underlying theme—the conflict between reality and the ideal—set it apart from the picaresque.

The fifty-year-old Alonso Quixado, who assumes the title of a nobleman, Don Quixote de la Mancha, sets out to roam the world as a knight errant, defending the ideals glorified in medieval books of chivalry. (Cervantes himself had fought in the last of the crusades against the Muslim Turks.) Seeking to bring honor to himself and his imaginary ladylove, he pursues a long series of adventures in which he repeatedly misperceives the ordinary for the sublime: he attacks a flock of sheep as a hostile army, advances on a group of windmills that he mistakes for giants. (The expression "tilting at windmills" has come to represent the futility of self-deluding action.) The hero's eternal optimism is measured against the practical realism of his potbellied sidekick, Sancho Panza, who tries to expose the Don's illusions of grandeur. In the end, the Don laments in self-reflection that the world "is nothing but schemes and plots."

Cervantes' masterpiece, *Don Quixote* attacks outworn medieval values, especially as they reflect sixteenth-century Spanish society. In Spain, on the eve of the early modern era, New World wealth was transforming the relationship between peasants and aristocrats; the tribunal of Catholic orthodoxy known as the Inquisition worked to expel the large populations of Jews and Muslims that had powerfully influenced earlier Iberian culture. While the novel emerged from this context of transformation and (often misguided) reform, it left a timeless, universal message, captured in the English word "quixotic," which means "foolishly idealistic" or "impractical."

READING 19.4 From Cervantes' *Don Quixote* (1605–1615)

The great success won by our brave Don Quijote[1] in his dreadful, unimaginable encounter with two windmills, plus other honorable events well worth remembering

Just then, they came upon thirty or forty windmills, which (as it happens) stand in the fields of Montiel, and as soon as Don Quijote saw them he said to his squire:

"Destiny guides our fortunes more favorably than we could have expected. Look there, Sancho Panza, my friend, and see those thirty or so wild giants, with whom I intend to do battle and to kill each and all of them, so with their stolen booty we can begin to enrich ourselves. This is noble, righteous warfare, for it is wonderfully useful to God to have such an evil race wiped from the face of the earth." 10

"What giants?" asked Sancho Panza.

"The ones you can see over there," answered his master, "with the huge arms, some of which are very nearly two leagues long."

"Now look, your grace," said Sancho, "what you see over there aren't giants, but windmills, and what seem to be arms are just their sails, that go around in the wind and turn the millstone."

"Obviously," replied Don Quijote, "you don't know much about adventures. Those are giants—and if you're frightened, take yourself away from here and say your prayers, while I go charging into savage and unequal combat with them." 20

Saying which, he spurred his horse, Rocinante, paying no attention to the shouts of Sancho Panza, his squire, warning him that without any question it was windmills and not giants he was going to attack. So utterly convinced was he they were giants, indeed, that he neither heard Sancho's cries nor noticed, close as he was, what they really were, but charged on, crying: 30

"Flee not, oh cowards and dastardly creatures, for he who attacks you is a knight alone and unaccompanied."

Just then the wind blew up a bit, and the great sails began to stir, which Don Quijote saw and cried out:

1

[1] A variant spelling of Quixote is Quijote, as in this excerpt.

"Even should you shake more arms than the giant Briareus himself, you'll still have to deal with me."

As he said this, he entrusted himself with all his heart to his lady Dulcinea, imploring her to help and sustain him at such a critical moment, and then, with his shield held high and his spear braced in its socket, and Rocinante at a full gallop, he charged directly at the first windmill he came to, just as a sudden swift gust of wind sent its sail swinging hard around, smashing the spear to bits and sweeping up the knight and his horse, tumbling them all battered and bruised to the ground. Sancho Panza came rushing to his aid, as fast as his donkey could run, but when he got to his master found him unable to move, such a blow had he been given by the falling horse.

"God help me!" said Sancho. "Didn't I tell your grace to be careful what you did, that these were just windmills, and anyone who could ignore that had to have windmills in his head?"

"Silence, Sancho, my friend," answered Don Quijote. "Even more than other things, war is subject to perpetual change. What's more, I think the truth is that the same Frestón the magician, who stole away my room and my books, transformed these giants into windmills, in order to deprive me of the glory of vanquishing them, so bitter is his hatred of me. But in the end, his evil tricks will have little power against my good sword."

"God's will be done," answered Sancho Panza.

Then, helping his master to his feet, he got him back up on Rocinante, whose shoulder was half dislocated. After which, discussing the adventure they'd just experienced, they followed the road toward Lápice Pass, for there, said Don Quijote, they couldn't fail to find adventures of all kinds, it being a well-traveled highway. But having lost his lance, he went along very sorrowfully, as he admitted to his squire, saying:

"I remember having read that a certain Spanish knight named Diego Pérez de Vargas, having lost his sword while fighting in a lost cause, pulled a thick bough, or a stem, off an oak tree, and did such things with it, that day, clubbing down so many Moors that ever afterwards they nicknamed him Machuca [Clubber], and indeed from that day on he and all his descendants bore the name Vargas y Machuca. I tell you this because, the first oak tree I come to, I plan to pull off a branch like that, one every bit as good as the huge stick I can see in my mind, and I propose to perform such deeds with it that you'll be thinking yourself blessed, having the opportunity to witness them, and being a living witness to events that might otherwise be unbelievable."

"It's in God's hands," said Sancho. "I believe everything is exactly the way your grace says it is. But maybe you could sit a little straighter, because you seem to be leaning to one side, which must be because of the great fall you took."

"True," answered Don Quijote, "and if I don't say anything about the pain it's because knights errant are never supposed to complain about a wound, even if their guts are leaking through it."

"If that's how it's supposed to be," replied Sancho, "I've got nothing to say. But Lord knows I'd rather your grace told me, any time something hurts you. Me, I've got to groan, even if it's the smallest little pain, unless that rule about knights errant not complaining includes squires, too."

Don Quijote couldn't help laughing at his squire's simplicity, and cheerfully assured him he could certainly complain any time he felt like it, voluntarily or involuntarily, since in all his reading about knighthood and chivalry he'd never once come across anything to the contrary. Sancho said he thought it was dinner-time. His master replied that, for the moment, he himself had no need of food, but Sancho should eat whenever he wanted to. Granted this permission, Sancho made himself as comfortable as he could while jogging along on his donkey and, taking out of his saddlebags what he had put in them, began eating as he rode, falling back a good bit behind his master, and from time to time tilting up his wineskin with a pleasure so intense that the fanciest barman in Málaga might have envied him. And as he rode along like this, gulping quietly away, none of the promises his master had made were on his mind, nor did he feel in the least troubled or afflicted—in fact, he was thoroughly relaxed about this adventure-hunting business, no matter how dangerous it was supposed to be.

In the end, they spent that night sleeping in a wood, and Don Quijote pulled a dry branch from one of the trees, to serve him, more or less, as a lance, fitting onto it the spearhead he'd taken off the broken one. Nor did Don Quijote sleep, that whole night long, meditating on his lady Dulcinea—in order to fulfill what he'd read in his books, namely, that knights always spent long nights out in the woods and other uninhabited places, not sleeping, but happily mulling over memories of their ladies. Which wasn't the case for Sancho Panza: with his stomach full, and not just with chicory water, his dreams swept him away, nor would he have bothered waking up, for all the sunlight shining full on his face, or the birds singing—brightly, loudly greeting the coming of the new day—if his master hadn't called to him. He got up and, patting his wineskin, found it a lot flatter than it had been the night before, which grieved his heart, since it didn't look as if they'd be making up the shortage any time soon. Don Quijote had no interest in breakfast, since, as we have said, he had been sustaining himself with delightful memories. They returned to the road leading to Lápice Pass, which they could see by about three that afternoon.

"Here," said Don Quijote as soon as he saw it, "here, brother Sancho Panza, we can get our hands up to the elbows in adventures. But let me warn you: even if you see me experiencing the greatest dangers in the world, never draw your sword to defend me, unless of course you see that those who insult me are mere rabble, people of low birth, in which case you may be permitted to help me. But if they're knights, the laws of knighthood make it absolutely illegal, without exception, for you to help me, unless you yourself have been ordained a knight."

"Don't worry, your grace," answered Sancho Panza. "You'll find me completely obedient about this, especially since I'm a very peaceful man—I don't like getting myself into quarrels and fights. On the other hand, when it comes to someone laying a hand on me, I won't pay much attention to those laws, because whether they're divine or human they permit any man to defend himself when anyone hurts him." **160**

"To be sure," answered Don Quijote. "But when it comes to helping me against other knights, you must restrain your natural vigor."

"And that's what I'll do," replied Sancho. "I'll observe this rule just as carefully as I keep the Sabbath."

Q **What rules of chivalry forbid Sancho's assisting his master in battle, and with what exception?**

Rabelais and Montaigne

Another master of vernacular prose, the French humanist François Rabelais (1495–1553), mocked the obsolete values of European society. Rabelais drew upon his experiences as a monk, a student of law, a physician, and a specialist in human affairs to produce *Gargantua and Pantagruel*, an irreverent satire filled with biting allusions to contemporary institutions and customs. The world of the two imaginary giants, Gargantua and Pantagruel, is one of fraud and folly drawn to fantastic dimensions. It is blighted by the absurdities of war, the evils of law and medicine, and the failure of Scholastic education. To remedy the last, Rabelais advocates education based on experience and action, rather than rote memorization. In the imaginary abbey of Thélème, the modern version of a medieval monastery, he pictures a coeducational commune in which well-bred men and women are encouraged to live as they please. *Gargantua and Pantagruel* proclaims Rabelais' faith in the ability of educated individuals to follow their best instincts for establishing a society free from religious prejudice, petty abuse, and selfish desire.

The French humanist Michel de Montaigne (1533–1592) was neither a satirist nor a reformer, but an educated aristocrat who believed in the paramount importance of cultivating good judgment. Trained in Latin, Montaigne was one of the leading proponents of Classical learning in

Renaissance France. He earned universal acclaim as the "father" of the personal **essay**, a short piece of expository prose that examines a single subject or idea. The essay—the word comes from the French *essayer* ("to try")—is a vehicle for probing or "trying out" ideas.

Montaigne regarded his ninety-four vernacular French essays as studies in autobiographical reflection—in them, he confessed, he portrayed himself. Addressing such subjects as virtue, friendship, old age, education, and idleness, he examined certain fundamentally humanistic ideas: that contradiction is a characteristically human trait, that self-examination is the essence of true education, that education should enable us to live more harmoniously, and that skepticism and open-mindedness are sound alternatives to dogmatic opinion. Like Rabelais, Montaigne defended a kind of teaching that posed questions rather than provided answers. In his essay on the education of children, he criticized teachers who might pour information into students' ears "as though they were pouring water into a funnel" and then demand that students repeat that information instead of exercising original thought.

Reflecting on the European response to overseas expansion (see chapter 18), Montaigne examined the ways in which behavior and belief vary from culture to culture. In his essay *On Cannibals*, a portion of which appears below, he weighted the reports of "New World" barbarism and savagery against the morals and manners of "cultured" Europeans. War, which he calls the "human disease," he finds less vile among "barbarians" than among Europeans, whose warfare is motivated by colonial expansion. Balancing his own views with those of Classical Latin writers, whom he quotes freely throughout his essays, Montaigne questions the superiority of any one culture over another. Montaigne's essays, an expression of reasoned inquiry into human values, constitute the literary high-water mark of the French Renaissance.

Science and Technology

1556	Georg Agricola (German) publishes *On the Principles of Mining*
1571	Ambroise Paré (French) publishes five treatises on surgery
1587	Conrad Gesner (Swiss) completes his *Historiae Animalum*, the first zoological encyclopedia
1596	Sir John Harington (English) invents the "water closet," providing indoor toilet facilities

READING 19.5 From Montaigne's *On Cannibals* (1580)

I had with me for a long time a man who had lived for **1**
ten or twelve years in that other world which has been
discovered in our century, in the place where Villegaignon
landed, and which he called Antarctic France.[1] This
discovery of a boundless country seems worthy of
consideration. I don't know if I can guarantee that some
other such discovery will not be made in the future, so
many personages greater than ourselves having been
mistaken about this one. I am afraid we have eyes bigger
than our stomachs, and more curiosity than capacity. **10**
We embrace everything, but we clasp only wind. . . .

This man I had was a simple, crude fellow—a character

---

[1] *La France antarctique* was the French term for South America. In 1555, Nicolas Durand de Villegaignon founded a colony on an island in the Bay of Rio de Janeiro, Brazil. The colony collapsed some years later, and many of those who had lived there returned to France.

fit to bear true witness; for clever people observe more things and more curiously, but they interpret them; and to lend weight and conviction to their interpretation, they cannot help altering history a little. They never show you things as they are, but bend and disguise them according to the way they have seen them; and to give credence to their judgment and attract you to it, they are prone to add something to their matter, to stretch it out and amplify it. We need a man either very honest, or so simple that he has not the stuff to build up false inventions and give them plausibility; and wedded to no theory. Such was my man; and besides this, he at various times brought sailors and merchants, whom he had known on that trip, to see me. So I content myself with his information, without inquiring what the cosmographers say about it.

We ought to have topographers who would give us an exact account of the places where they have been. But because they have over us the advantage of having seen Palestine, they want to enjoy the privilege of telling us news about all the rest of the world. I would like everyone to write what he knows, and as much as he knows, not only in this, but in all other subjects; for a man may have some special knowledge and experience of the nature of a river or a fountain, who in other matters knows only what everybody knows. However, to circulate this little scrap of knowledge, he will undertake to write the whole of physics. From this vice spring many great abuses.

Now to return to my subject, I think there is nothing barbarous and savage in that nation, from what I have been told, except that each man calls barbarism whatever is not his own practice; for indeed it seems we have no other test of truth and reason than the example and pattern of the opinions and customs of the country we live in. *There* is always the perfect religion, perfect government, the perfect and accomplished manners in all things. Those people are wild, just as we call wild the fruits that Nature has produced by herself and in her normal course; whereas really it is those that we have changed artificially and led astray from the common order, that we should rather call wild. The former retain alive and vigorous their genuine, their most useful and natural, virtues and properties, which we have debased in the latter in adapting them to gratify our corrupted taste. And yet for all that, the savor and delicacy of some uncultivated fruits of those countries is quite as excellent, even to our taste, as that of our own. It is not reasonable that art should win the place of honor over our great and powerful mother Nature. We have so overloaded the beauty and richness of her works by our inventions that we have quite smothered her. Yet wherever her purity shines forth, she wonderfully puts to shame our vain and frivolous attempts.

> *Ivy comes readier without our care;*
> *In lonely caves the arbutus grows more fair;*
> *No art with artless bird song can compare.*
> Propertius

All our efforts cannot even succeed in reproducing the nest of the tiniest little bird, its contexture, its beauty

and convenience; or even the web of the puny spider. All things, say Plato, are produced by nature, by fortune, or by art; the greatest and most beautiful by one or the other of the first two, the least and most imperfect by the last.

These nations, then, seem to me barbarous in this sense, that they have been fashioned very little by the human mind, and are still very close to their original naturalness. The laws of nature still rule them, very little corrupted by ours, and they are in such a state of purity that I am sometimes vexed that they were unknown earlier, in the days when there were men able to judge them better than we.

. . . .

They have their wars with the nations beyond the mountains, further inland, to which they go quite naked, with no other arms than bows or wooden swords ending in a sharp point, in the manner of the tongues of our boar spears. It is astonishing what firmness they show in their combats, which never end but in slaughter and bloodshed; for as to routs and terror, they know nothing of either.

Each man brings back as his trophy the head of the enemy he has killed, and sets it up at the entrance to his dwelling. After they have treated their prisoners well for a long time with all the hospitality they can think of, each man who has a prisoner calls a great assembly of his acquaintances. He ties a rope to one of the prisoner's arms, by the end of which he holds him, a few steps away, for fear of being hurt, and gives his dearest friend the other arm to hold in the same way; and these two, in the presence of the whole assembly, kill him with their swords. This done, they roast him and eat him in common and send some pieces to the absent friends. This is not, as people think, for nourishment, as of old the Scythians used to do; it is to betoken an extreme revenge.[2] And the proof of this came when they saw the Portuguese, who had joined forces with their adversaries, inflict a different kind of death on them when they took them prisoner, which was to bury them up to the waist, shoot the rest of their body full of arrows, and afterward hang them. They thought that these people from the other world, being men who had sown the knowledge of many vices among their neighbors and were much greater masters than themselves in every sort of wickedness, did not adopt this sort of vengeance without some reason, and that it must be more painful than their own; so they began to give up their old method and to follow this one.

I am not sorry that we notice the barbarous horror of such acts, but I am heartily sorry that, judging their faults rightly, we should be so blind as to our own. I think there is more barbarity in eating a man alive than in eating him dead; and in tearing by tortures and the rack a body still full of feeling, in roasting a man bit by bit, in having him bitten and mangled by dogs and swine (as we have not only read but seen within fresh memory, not among ancient enemies, but among neighbors and fellow citizens, and

---

[2] Montaigne overlooks the fact that ritual cannibalism might also involve the will to consume the power of the opponent, especially if he were a formidable opponent.

what is worse, on the pretext of piety and religion), than in roasting and eating him after he is dead.

. . . .

So we may well call these people barbarians, in respect of the rules of reason, but not in respect of ourselves, who surpass them in every kind of barbarity.

Their warfare is wholly noble and generous, and as excusable and beautiful as this human disease can be; its only basis among them is their rivalry in valor. They are not fighting for the conquest of new lands, for they still enjoy that natural abundance that provides them without toil and trouble with all necessary things in such profusion that they have no wish to enlarge their boundaries. They are still in that happy state of desiring only as much as their natural needs demand; any thing beyond that is superfluous to them.

130

— **Q** "Each man calls barbarism whatever is not his own practice," writes Montaigne. What illustrations does he offer? Does this claim hold true in our own day and age?

Shakespeare

No assessment of the early modern era would be complete without some consideration of the literary giant of the age: William Shakespeare (1564–1616; Figure **19.17**).

A poet of unparalleled genius, Shakespeare emerged during the golden age of England under the rule of Elizabeth I (1533–1603). He produced thirty-seven plays—comedies, tragedies, romances, and histories—as well as 154 sonnets and other poems. These works, generally considered to be the greatest examples of English literature, have exercised an enormous influence on the evolution of the English language and the development of the Western literary tradition.*

Little is known about Shakespeare's early life and formal education. He grew up in Stratford-upon-Avon in the English Midlands, married Anne Hathaway (eight years his senior), with whom he had three children, and moved to London sometime before 1585. In London, a city of some 80,000 inhabitants, he formed an acting company, the Lord Chamberlain's Company (also called "the King's Men"), in which he was shareholder, actor, and playwright. Like fifteenth-century Florence, sixteenth-century London (and especially the queen's court) supported a galaxy of artists, musicians, and writers who enjoyed a mutually stimulating interchange of ideas. Shakespeare's theater company performed at the court of Elizabeth I and that of her successor James I (1566–1625). But its main activities took place in the Globe, one of a handful of playhouses built

---

* The complete works of Shakespeare are available at the following website: http://shakespeare.mit.edu/works.html

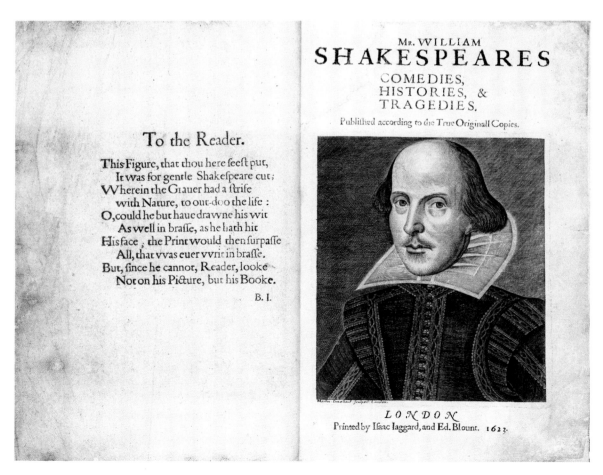

Figure 19.17 DROESHOUT, First Folio edition portrait of William Shakespeare, 1623. 13 × 18 in. (approx.).

just outside London's city limits—along with brothels and taverns, theaters were generally relegated to the suburbs.

Shakespeare's Sonnets

While Shakespeare is best known for his plays, he also wrote some of the most beautiful sonnets ever produced in the English language. Indebted to Petrarch (see LOOKING INTO in chapter 16), Shakespeare nevertheless devised most of his own sonnets in a form that would come to be called "the English sonnet": **quatrains** (four-line stanzas) with alternate rhymes, followed by a concluding **couplet**. Shakespeare's sonnets employ—and occasionally mock—such traditional Petrarchan themes as the blind devotion of the unfortunate lover, the value of friendship, and love's enslaving power. Some, like Sonnet 18, reflect the typically Renaissance (and Classical) concern for immortality achieved through art and love. In Sonnet 18, Shakespeare contrives an extended metaphor: like the summer day, his beloved will fade and die. But, exclaims the poet, she will remain eternal in and through the sonnet; for, so long as the poem survives, so will the object of its inspiration remain alive. Stripped of sentiment, Sonnet 116 defends the unchanging nature of love, its constancy and its ability to withstand adversity and the test of time. The poem exalts the "marriage of true minds" that most Renaissance humanists perceived as only possible among men. Sonnet 130, on the other hand, pokes fun at the literary conventions of the Petrarchan love sonnet. Satirizing the fair-haired, rosy-lipped heroine as object of desire, Shakespeare celebrates the real—though somewhat ordinary—features of his beloved.

— READING 19.6 From Shakespeare's Sonnets (1609)

Sonnet 18

Shall I compare thee to a summer's day?	1
Thou art more lovely and more temperate.	
Rough winds do shake the darling buds of May,	
And summer's lease[1] hath all too short a date.	
Sometime too hot the eye[2] of heaven shines,	5
And often is his gold complexion dimm'd;	
And every fair from fair sometime declines,[3]	
By chance or nature's changing course untrimm'd;[4]	
But thy eternal summer shall not fade	
Nor lose possession of that fair thou ow'st,	10
Nor shall Death brag thou wand'rest in his shade,	
When in eternal lines to time thou grow'st.[5]	
So long as men can breathe or eyes can see,	
So long lives this[6] and this gives life to thee.	

[1] Allotted time.
[2] The sun.
[3] Beautiful thing from beauty.
[4] Stripped of beauty.
[5] Your fame will grow as time elapses.
[6] The sonnet itself.

Sonnet 116

Let me not to the marriage of true minds	1
Admit impediments. Love is not love	
Which alters when it alteration finds,	
Nor bends with the remover to remove.[7]	
O, no, it is an ever-fixed mark,[8]	5
That looks on tempests and is never shaken;	
It is the star to every wand'ring bark,	
Whose worth's unknown, although his height be taken.[9]	
Love's not Time's fool, though rose lips and cheeks	
Within his bending sickle's compass come;	10
Love alters not with his brief hours and weeks,	
But bears it out even to the edge of doom.[10]	
If this be error, and upon me proved,	
I never writ, nor no man ever loved.	

Sonnet 130

My mistress' eyes are nothing like the sun;	1
Coral is far more red than her lips' red:	
If snow be white, why then her breasts are dun;	
If hairs be wires, black wires grow on her head.	
I have seen roses damasked, red and white,	5
But no such roses see I in her cheeks;	
And in some perfumes is there more delight	
Than in the breath that from my mistress reeks.	
I love to hear her speak, yet well I know	
That music hath a far more pleasing sound:	10
I grant I never saw a goddess go,—	
My mistress, when she walks, treads on the ground:	
And yet, by heaven, I think my love as rare	
As any she belied with false compare.	

Q **What does each of these sonnets convey about the nature of love?**

The Elizabethan Stage

In the centuries following the fall of Rome, the Church condemned all forms of pagan display, including the performance of comedies and tragedies. Tragedy, in the sense that it was defined by Aristotle ("the imitation of an action" involving "some great error" made by an extraordinary man), was philosophically incompatible with the medieval world-view, which held that all events were predetermined by God. If redemption was the goal of Christian life, there was no place for literary tragedy in the Christian cosmos. (Hence Dante's famous journey, though far from humorous, was called a "comedy" in acknowledgment of its "happy" ending in Paradise.) Elizabethan poets revived secular drama, adapting Classical and medieval texts to the writing of contemporary plays. While the context and the characters of such plays might be Christian, the plot and the dramatic action were secular in focus and in spirit.

[7] Changes as the beloved changes.
[8] Sea mark, an aid to navigation.
[9] Whose value is beyond estimation.
[10] Endures to the very Day of Judgment.

The rebirth of secular drama, Renaissance England's most original contribution to the humanistic tradition, unfolded during an era of high confidence. In 1588, the English navy defeated a Spanish fleet of 130 ships known as the "Invincible Armada." The victory gave clear advantage to England as the dominant commercial power in the Atlantic. The routing of the Spanish Armada was a victory as well for the partisans of Protestantism over Catholicism. It encouraged a sense of national pride that found its counterpart in a revival of interest in English history and its theatrical recreation. It also contributed to a renewed spirit of confidence in the ambitious policies of the "Protestant Queen," Elizabeth I (Figure **19.18**). In its wake followed a period of high prosperity, commercial expansion, and cultural vitality, all of which converged in London.

Elizabethan London played host to groups of traveling actors (or "strolling players") who performed in public spaces or for generous patrons. In the late sixteenth century, a number of playhouses were built along the River Thames across from the City of London. Begun in 1599,

the Globe, which held between 2000 and 3000 spectators, offered all levels of society access to professional theater (Figure **19.19**). The open-air structure consisted of three tiers of galleries and standing room for commoners (known as "groundlings") at the cost of only a penny—one-sixth of the price of a seat in the covered gallery. The projecting, rectangular stage, some 40 feet wide, included balconies (for musicians and special scenes, as in *Romeo and Juliet*), exits to dressing areas, and a trapdoor (used for rising spirits and for burial scenes, as in *Hamlet*). Stage props were basic, but costumes were favored, and essential for the male actors who played the female roles, since women were not permitted on the public stage. Performances were held in the afternoon and advertised by flying a flag above the theater roof. A globe, the signature logo, embellished the theater, along with a sign that read "*Totus mundus agit histrionem*" (loosely, "All the World's a Stage"). The bustling crowd that attended the theater—some of whom stood through two or more hours of performance—often ate and drank as they enjoyed the

Figure 19.18 GEORGE GOWER, *"Armada" Portrait of Elizabeth I*, ca. 1588. Oil on panel, 3 ft. 6 in. × 4 ft. 5 in. Bedecked with jewels, the queen rests her hand on the globe, an allusion to its circumnavigation by her vice-admiral, Sir Francis Drake. In the background at the right, the Spanish Armada sinks into the Atlantic amidst the "Protestant winds" of a fierce storm.

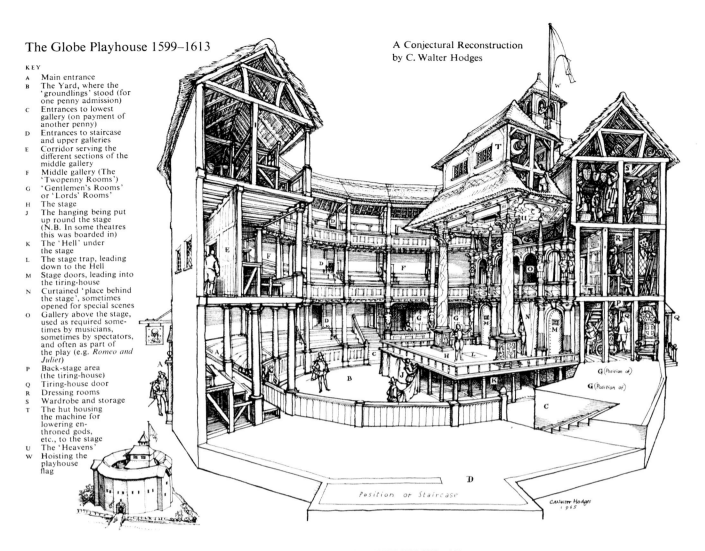

The Globe Playhouse 1599–1613

A Conjectural Reconstruction
by C. Walter Hodges

KEY

A   Main entrance
B   The Yard, where the 'groundlings' stood (for one penny admission)
C   Entrances to lowest gallery (on payment of another penny)
D   Entrances to staircase and upper galleries
E   Corridor serving the different sections of the middle gallery
F   Middle gallery (The 'Twopenny Rooms')
G   'Gentlemen's Rooms' or 'Lords' Rooms'
H   The stage
J   The hanging being put up round the stage (N.B. In some theatres this was boarded in)
K   The 'Hell' under the stage
L   The stage trap, leading down to the Hell
M   Stage doors, leading into the tiring-house
N   Curtained 'place behind the stage', sometimes opened for special scenes
O   Gallery above the stage, used as required sometimes by musicians, sometimes by spectators, and often as part of the play (e.g. *Romeo and Juliet*)
P   Back-stage area (the tiring-house)
Q   Tiring-house door
R   Dressing rooms
S   Wardrobe and storage
T   The hut housing the machine for lowering enthroned gods, etc., to the stage
U   The 'Heavens'
W   Hoisting the playhouse flag

Figure 19.19 Globe Playhouse, London, 1599–1613. Architectural reconstruction by **C. WALTER HODGES**, 1965.

most cosmopolitan entertainment of their time. A reconstruction of the Globe playhouse, located on the south bank of the Thames, opened in 1997.

Shakespeare's Plays

In Shakespeare's time, theater ranked below poetry as a literary genre. As popular entertainment, however, Shakespeare's plays earned high acclaim in London's thriving theatrical community. Thanks to the availability of printed editions, the Bard of Stratford was familiar with the tragedies of Seneca and the comedies of Plautus and Terence. He knew the popular medieval morality plays that addressed the contest between good and evil, as well as the popular improvisational form of Italian comic theater known as the *commedia dell'arte*, which made use of stock or stereotypical characters. All these resources came to shape the texture of his own plays. For his plots, Shakespeare drew largely on Classical history, medieval chronicles, and contemporary romances.

Like Machiavelli, Shakespeare was an avid reader of ancient and medieval history, as well as a keen observer of his own complex age; but the stories his sources provided became mere springboards for the exploration of human nature. His history plays, such as *Henry V* and *Richard III*, celebrate England's medieval past and its rise to power under the Tudors. The concerns of these plays, however, are not exclusively historical; rather, they explore the ways in which individuals behave under pressure: the weight of kingly responsibilities on mere humans and the difficulties of reconciling royal obligations and human aspirations.

Shakespeare's comedies, which constitute about one-half of his plays, deal with such popular themes as the battle of the sexes, rivalry among lovers, and mistaken identities. But here too, in such plays as *Much Ado About Nothing*, *All's Well That Ends Well*, and *The Taming of the Shrew*, it is Shakespeare's characters—their motivations exposed, their weaknesses and strengths laid bare—that command our attention.

It is in the tragedies, and especially the tragedies of his mature career—*Hamlet*, *Macbeth*, *Othello*, and *King Lear*—that Shakespeare achieved the concentration of thought and language that has made him the greatest English playwright of all time. Human flaws and failings—jealousy, greed, ambition, insecurity, and self-deception—give substance to most of Shakespeare's plays, but in these last tragedies they become definitive: they drive the action of the play. They are, in short, immediate evidence of the playwright's efforts to probe the psychological forces that motivate human action.

No discussion of Shakespeare's plays can substitute for the experience of live performance. Yet, in focusing on two of the late tragedies, *Hamlet* and *Othello*, it is possible to isolate Shakespeare's principal contributions to the humanistic tradition. These lie in the areas of character development and in the brilliance of the language with which characters are brought to life. Despite occasional passages in prose and rhymed verse, Shakespeare's plays were written in **blank verse**. This verse form was popular among Renaissance writers because, like Classical poetry, it was unrhymed, and it closely approximated the rhythms of vernacular speech. In Shakespeare's hands, the English language took on a breadth of expression and a majesty of eloquence that has rarely been matched to this day.

Shakespeare's *Hamlet*

Hamlet, the world's most quoted play, belongs to the popular Renaissance genre of revenge tragedy; the story itself came to Shakespeare from the history of medieval Denmark. Hamlet, the young heir to the Danish throne, learns that his uncle has murdered his father, the king of Denmark, and married his mother in order to assume the throne; the burden of avenging his father falls squarely on his shoulders. The arc of the play follows Hamlet's inability to take action—his melancholic lack of resolve that, in due course, results in the deaths of his mother (Gertrude), his betrothed (Ophelia), her father (Polonius), the king (Claudius), and, finally, Hamlet himself.

Shakespeare's protagonist differs from the heroes of ancient and medieval times: Hamlet lacks the sense of obligation to country and community, the religious loyalties, and the clearly defined spiritual values that impassioned Gilgamesh, Achilles, and Roland. He represents a new, multidimensional, and essentially modern hero, afflicted (even tormented) by self-questioning and brooding skepticism. Although sunk in melancholy, Hamlet shares Pico della Mirandola's view (see Reading 16.3) that human nature is freely formed by human beings themselves: He marvels, "What a piece of work is a man! How noble in reason! How infinite in faculty! In form and moving how express and admirable! In action how like an angel! In apprehension how like a god! The beauty of the world! The paragon of animals." Nevertheless, he qualifies this optimistic view of humankind with personal despair, concluding on a note of utter skepticism: "And yet, to me, what is this quintessence of dust?" (Act II, ii, ll. 303–309). It is by way of the oral examination of his innermost thoughts—a literary device known as the *soliloquy*—that Hamlet most fully reveals himself. He questions the motives for meaningful action and the impulses that prevent him from action; at the same time, he contemplates the futility of all human action. In the following excerpt

from the third act of this great play, two aspects of Hamlet's character come into focus: his deeply conflicted and self-reflective personality, and his peevish and dissembling behavior toward Ophelia.

READING 19.7 From Shakespeare's *Hamlet* (1602)

Hamlet, Act III, Scene 1
[The King, Queen, Polonius, Rosencrantz, and Guildenstern seek to determine the nature of Hamlet's recent changes in behavior by arranging his "accidental" meeting with Ophelia.]

King:	Sweet Gertrude, leave us too,	1

For we have closely sent for Hamlet hither,
That he, as 'twere by accident, may here
Affront Ophelia.
Her father and myself, lawful espials,
Will so bestow ourselves that seeing, unseen,
We may of their encounter frankly judge,
And gather by him, as he is behaved,
If 't be th' affliction of his love or no
That thus he suffers for.   10
Queen: I shall obey you.
And for your part, Ophelia, I do wish
That your good beauties be the happy cause
Of Hamlet's wildness. So shall I hope your virtues
Will bring him to his wonted way again,
To both your honors.
Ophelia: Madam, I wish it may.
                                                    [*Exit Queen.*]
Polonius: Ophelia, walk you here.—Gracious, so please you,
We will bestow ourselves. [*To Ophelia.*] Read on this
    book,   [*giving her a book*] 20
That show of such an exercise may color
Your loneliness. We are oft to blame in this—
'Tis too much proved—that with devotion's visage
And pious action we do sugar o'er
The devil himself.
King [*aside*]: O, 'tis too true!
How smart a lash that speech doth give my conscience!
The harlot's cheek, beautied with plastering art,
Is not more ugly to the thing that helps it
Than is my deed to my most painted word.   30
O heavy burden!
Polonius: I hear him coming. Let's withdraw, my lord.
                    [*The King and Polonius withdraw.*]
                    Enter Hamlet. [*Ophelia pretends to read a book.*]
Hamlet: To be, or not to be, that is the question:
Whether 'tis nobler in the mind to suffer

III.1. Location: The castle.
2 closely privately **4 Affront** confront, meet **5 espials** spies
15 wonted accustomed **18 Gracious** Your Grace (i.e., the king)
19 bestow conceal **21 exercise** religious exercise (the book she reads is one of devotion) **color** give a plausible appearance to **22 loneliness** being alone **23 too much proved** too often shown to be true, too often practiced **29 to** compared to **the thing** i.e., the cosmetic **32 s.d. withdraw** the King and Polonius may retire behind an arras. The stage directions specify that they "enter" again near the end of the scene.

The slings and arrows of outrageous fortune,
Or to take arms against a sea of troubles
And by opposing end them. To die, to sleep—
No more—and by a sleep to say we end
The heartache and the thousand natural shocks
That flesh is heir to. 'Tis a consummation   40
Devoutly to be wished. To die, to sleep;
To sleep, perchance to dream. Ay, there's the rub,
For in that sleep of death what dreams may come,
When we have shuffled off this mortal coil,
Must give us pause. There's the respect
That makes calamity of so long life.
For who would bear the whips and scorns of time,
Th' oppressor's wrong, the proud man's contumely,
The pangs of disprized love, the law's delay,
The insolence of office, and the spurns   50
That patient merit of th' unworthy takes,
When he himself might his quietus make
With a bare bodkin? Who would fardels bear,
To grunt and sweat under a weary life,
But that the dread of something after death,
The undiscovered country from whose bourn
No traveler returns, puzzles the will,
And makes us rather bear those ills we have
Than fly to others that we know not of?
Thus conscience does make cowards of us all;   60
And thus the native hue of resolution
Is sicklied o'er with the pale cast of thought,
And enterprises of great pitch and moment
With this regard their currents turn awry
And lose the name of action.—Soft you now,
The fair Ophelia. Nymph, in thy orisons
Be all my sins remembered.
Ophelia: Good my lord,
    How does your honor for this many a day?
Hamlet: I humbly thank you; well, well, well.   70
Ophelia: My lord, I have remembrances of yours,
    That I have longèd long to redeliver.
    I pray you, now receive them.   [*She offers tokens.*]
Hamlet: No, not I, I never gave you aught.
Ophelia: My honored lord, you know right well you did,
    And with them words of so sweet breath composed
    As made the things more rich. Their perfume lost,
    Take these again, for to the noble mind
    Rich gifts wax poor when givers prove unkind.
    There, my lord.   [*She gives tokens.*] 80
Hamlet: Ha, ha! Are you honest?

Ophelia: My lord?
Hamlet: Are you fair?
Ophelia: What means your lordship?
Hamlet: That if you be honest and fair, your honesty
    should admit no discourse to your beauty.
Ophelia: Could beauty, my lord, have better commerce
    than with honesty?
Hamlet: Ay, truly, for the power of beauty will sooner
    transform honesty from what it is to a bawd than the   90
    force of honesty can translate beauty into his likeness.
    This was sometime a paradox, but now the time gives
    if proof. I did love you once.
Ophelia: Indeed, my lord, you made me believe so.
Hamlet: You should not have believed me, for virtue
    cannot so inoculate our old stock but we shall relish of
    it. I loved you not.
Ophelia: I was the more deceived.
Hamlet: Get thee to a nunnery. Why wouldst thou be a
    breeder of sinners? I am myself indifferent honest, but   100
    yet I could accuse me of such things that it were better
    my mother had not borne me: I am very proud,
    revengeful, ambitious, with more offenses at my beck
    than I have thoughts to put them in, imagination to
    give them shape, or time to act them in. What should
    such fellows as I do crawling between earth and
    heaven? We are arrant knaves all; believe none of us.
    Go thy ways to a nunnery. Where's your father?
Ophelia: At home, my lord.
Hamlet: Let the doors be shut upon him, that he may   110
    play the fool nowhere but in 's own house. Farewell.
Ophelia: O, help him, you sweet heavens!
Hamlet: If thou dost marry, I'll give thee this plague for
    thy dowry: be thou as chaste as ice, as pure as snow,
    thou shalt not escape calumny. Get thee to a nunnery,
    farewell. Or, if thou wilt needs marry, marry a fool, for
    wise men know well enough what monsters you
    make of them. To a nunnery, go, and quickly too.
    Farewell.
Ophelia: Heavenly powers, restore him!   120
Hamlet: I have heard of your paintings too, well
    enough. God hath given you one face, and you make
    yourselves another. You jig, you amble, and you
    lisp, you nickname God's creatures, and make your
    wantonness your ignorance. Go to, I'll no more on 't;

---

35 slings missiles **42 rub** literally, an obstacle in the game of bowls **44 shuffled** sloughed, cast **coil** turmoil **45 respect** consideration **46 of . . . life** so long-lived, something we willingly endure for so long (also suggesting that long life is itself a calamity) **48 contumely** insolent abuse **49 disprized** unvalued **50 office** officialdom **spurns** insults **51 of . . . takes** receives from unworthy persons **52 quietus** acquittance; here, death **53 a bare bodkin** a mere dagger, unsheathed **fardels** burdens **56 bourn** frontier, boundar **61 native hue** natural color, complexion **62 cast** tinge, shade of color **63 pitch** height (as of a falcon's flight) **moment** importance **64 regard** respect, consideration **currents** courses **65 Soft you** i.e., wait a minute, gently

66 orisons prayers **81 honest** (1) truthful (2) chaste **83 fair** (1) beautiful (2) just, honorable **85 your honesty** your chastity **86 discourse to** familiar dealings with **87–88 commerce** dealings, intercourse **91 his** its **92 sometime** formerly **a paradox** a view opposite to commonly held opinion **the time** the present age **96 inoculate** graft, be engrafted to **96–97 but . . . it** that we do not still have about us a taste of the old stock, i.e., retain our sinfulness **99 nunnery** convent (with possibly an awareness that the word was also used derisively to denote a brothel) **100 indifferent honest** reasonably virtuous **103 beck** command **117 monsters** an illusion to the horns of a cuckold **you** i.e., you women **123 jig** dance **amble** move coyly **124 you nickname . . . creatures** i.e., you give trendy names to things in place of their God-given names **124–125 make . . . ignorance** i.e., excuse your affectation on the grounds of pretended ignorance **125 on 't** of it it hath made me mad. I say we will have no more marriage. Those that are married already—all but one—shall live. The rest shall keep as they are. To a nunnery, go. *Exit.*

Ophelia: O, what a noble mind is here o'erthrown!   130
The courtier's, soldier's, scholar's, eye, tongue, sword,
Th' expectancy and rose of the fair state,
The glass of fashion and the mold of form,
Th' observed of all observers, quite, quite down!
And I, of ladies most deject and wretched,
That sucked the honey of his music vows,
Now see that noble and most sovereign reason
Like sweet bells jangled out of tune and harsh,
That unmatched form and feature of blown youth   140
Blasted with ecstasy. O, woe is me,
T' have seen what I have seen, see what I see!

Q **What profound question does Hamlet address in his soliloquy?**

Q **What conclusion does Ophelia reach at the end of her conversation with Hamlet?**

Shakespeare's *Othello*

The Tragedy of Othello, the Moor of Venice was based on a story from a collection of tales published in Italy in the sixteenth century. The life of the handsome and distinguished Othello, an African soldier whose leadership in the Venetian wars against the Turks has brought him heroic esteem, takes a tragic turn when his ensign Iago beguiles him into thinking that his beautiful wife Desdemona has betrayed him with another man. Enraged with jealousy, Othello destroys the person he loves most in the world, his wife; and, in the unbearable grief of his error, he takes his own life as well. While Othello's jealousy is the flaw that brings about his doom, it is Iago whose unmitigated evil drives the action of the plot. Conniving Iago is the Machiavellian villain, "a demi-devil," as he is called in the play. In contrast, Desdemona is the paragon of virtue and beauty. Such characters hark back to the allegorical figures in medieval morality plays, but Shakespeare transforms these figures into complex personalities, allowing them full freedom to falter and fail through their own actions.

That Shakespeare made a black man the hero of one of his tragedies is significant, since his treatment of the character seems to have challenged Elizabethan stereotypes. Medieval and Renaissance literature described anyone who was black as vengeful, hot-blooded, and evil, black being the color traditionally associated with the Devil. But in Shakespeare's play, the Moor (the Elizabethan name for any African) is unwitting, ingenuous, and pure, while Iago, the white man who confounds him, is the personification of evil. Perhaps more significant than this irony is Shakespeare's implication that underlying the most untainted acts of heroism and the purest emotions of love is the dark possibility of misguided action that leads to self-defeat. Shakespeare's plays generally preach no explicit moral; rather, they suggest that, in a universe in which order and disorder coexist, human choices play a vital and potentially destructive part. The nihilism that darkens *Othello*, *Macbeth*, and *Hamlet* was unthinkable before the modern era.

READING 19.8 From Shakespeare's *Othello* (1604)

***Othello*, Act IV, Scene III**
Enter Othello, Lodovico, Desdemona, Emilia, and Attendants.

Lodovico: I do beseech you, sir, trouble yourself no further.   1
Othello: O, pardon me; 'twill do me good to walk.
Lodovico: Madam, good night. I humbly thank your ladyship.
Desdemona: Your honor is most welcome.
Othello: Will you walk, sir?
O, Desdemona!
Desdemona: My lord?
Othello: Get you to bed on th' instant; I will be return'd
forthwith. Dismiss your attendant there. Look 't be done.
Desdemona: I will, my lord.
                    Exit [*Othello, with Lodovico and Attendants*].
Emilia: How goes it now? He looks gentler than he did.   10
Desdemona: He says he will return incontinent,
And hath commanded me to go to bed,
And bade me to dismiss you.
Emilia: Dismiss me?
Desdemona: It was his bidding; therefore, good Emilia,
Give me my nightly wearing, and adieu.
We must not now displease him.
Emilia: I would you had never seen him!
Desdemona: So would not I. My love doth so approve him,
That even his stubbornness, his checks, his frowns—
Prithee unpin me—have grace and favor in them.   20
                    [*Emilia prepares Desdemona for bed.*]
Emilia: I have laid those sheets you bade me on the bed.
Desdemona: All's one. Good faith, how foolish are our minds!
If I do die before thee, prithee shroud me
In one of those same sheets.
Emilia: Come, come, you talk.
Desdemona: My mother had a maid call'd Barbary.
She was in love, and he she lov'd prov'd mad
And did forsake her. She had a song of "Willow,"
An old thing 'twas, but it express'd her fortune,
And she died singing it. That song tonight

---

133 expectancy hope **rose** ornament **134 The glass . . . form** the mirror of true self-fashioning and the pattern of courtly behavior **135 Th' observed . . . observers** i.e., the center of attention and honor in the court **137 music** musical, sweetly uttered **140 blown** blooming **141 Blasted** withered **ecstasy** madness

IV. iii Location: The citadel.
11 incontinent immediately **19 stubbornness** roughness **checks** rebukes **26 mad** wild, i.e., faithless

Will not go from my mind; I have much to do   30
   But to go hang my head all at one side
   And sing it like poor Barbary. Prithee, dispatch.
Emilia: Shall I go fetch your nightgown?
Desdemona: No, unpin me here.
   This Lodovico is a proper man.
Emilia: A very handsome man.
Desdemona: He speaks well.
Emilia: I know a lady in Venice would have walk'd barefoot
   to Palestine for a touch of his nether lip.
Desdemona [*Singing*]:
   "The poor soul sat sighing by a sycamore tree,
      Sing all a green willow;   40
   Her hand on her bosom, her head on her knee,
      Sing willow, willow, willow.
   The fresh streams ran by her, and murmur'd her moans;
      Sing willow, willow, willow;
   Her salt tears fell from her, and soft'ned the stones"—
   Lay by these.
[*Singing*]: "Sing willow, willow, willow"—
   Prithee, hie thee; he'll come anon.
[*Singing*] "Sing all a green willow must be my garland.
   Let nobody blame him; his scorn I approve"—   50
   Nay, that's not next.—Hark! Who is 't that knocks?
Emilia: It's the wind.
Desdemona [*Singing*]
   "I call'd my love false love; but what said he then?
      Sing willow, willow, willow;
   If I court moe women, you'll couch with moe men"—
   So, get thee gone; good night. Mine eyes do itch;
   Doth that bode weeping?
Emilia: '   Tis neither here nor there.
Desdemona: I have heard it said so. O, these men, these
      men!
   Dost thou in conscience think—tell me, Emilia—
   That there be women do abuse their husbands   60
   In such gross kind?
Emilia: There be some such, no question.
Desdemona: Wouldst thou do such a deed for all the world?
Emilia: Why, would not you?
Desdemona: No, by this heavenly light!
Emilia: Nor I neither by this heavenly light; I might do
   't as well i' th' dark.
Desdemona: Wouldst thou do such a deed for all the
   world?
Emilia: The world's a huge thing. It is a great price
   For a small vice.
Desdemona: Good troth, I think thou wouldst not.
Emilia: By my troth, I think I should; and undo 't when I
   had done. Marry, I would not do such a thing for a joint-   70
   ring, nor for measures of lawn, nor for gowns, petticoats,
   nor caps, nor any petty exhibition; but, for all the whole
   world—'ud's pity, who would not make her husband a
   cuckold to make him a monarch? I should venture
   purgatory for 't.

Desdemona: Beshrew me if I would do such a wrong for the
   whole world.
Emilia: Why, the wrong is but a wrong i' th' world; and
   having the world for your labor, 'tis a wrong in your own
   world, and you might quickly make it right.   80
Desdemona: I do not think there is any such woman.
Emilia: Yes, a dozen; and as many to th' vantage as
   would store the world they play'd for.
   But I do think it is their husbands' faults
   If wives do fall. Say that they slack their duties,
   And pour our treasures into foreign laps,
   Or else break out in peevish jealousies,
   Throwing restraint upon us? Or say they strike us,
   Or scant our former having in despite?
   Why, we have galls, and though we have some grace,
   Yet have we some revenge. Let husbands know   90
   Their wives have sense like them. They see, and smell,
   And have their palates both for sweet and sour,
   As husbands have. What is it that they do
   When they change us for others? Is it sport?
   I think it is. And doth affection breed it?
   I think it doth. Is 't frailty that thus errs?
   It is so too. And have not we affections,
   Desires for sport, and frailty, as men have?
   Then let them use us well; else let them know,
   The ills we do, their ills instruct us so.   100
Desdemona: Good night, good night. God me such uses
   send,
   Not to pick bad from bad, but by bad mend!   *Exeunt.*

Q **How do Emilia's views on women as wives
   compare with those of Desdemona?**

Chronology

1450	Gutenberg perfects the printing press
1517	Luther posts the *Ninety-Five Theses*
1524	German Peasant Revolts
1526	Henry VIII establishes the Anglican Church
1588	England defeats the Spanish Armada

30–31 I . . . hang I can scarcely keep myself from hanging **48 hie thee**
hurry **70–71 joint-ring** a ring made in separate halves **71 lawn** fine
linen **72 exhibition** gift **73 'ud's** i.e., God's

82 to th' vantage in addition, to boot **store** populate **85 pour . . .
laps** i.e., are unfaithful, give what is rightfully ours (semen) to other
women **88 scant . . . despite** reduce our allowance to spite us **89
have galls** i.e., are capable of resenting injury and insult **91 sense**
physical sense **101 uses** habit, practice **102 Not . . . mend** i.e., not to
learn bad conduct from others' badness (as Emilia has suggested women
learn from men), but to mend my ways by perceiving what badness is,
making spiritual benefit out of evil and adversity

The Temper of Reform

- The printing press facilitated the rise of popular education and encouraged individuals to form their own opinions by reading for themselves. The new print technology would be essential to the success of the Protestant Reformation.
- The Netherlandish religious movement known as the *devotio moderna* harnessed the dominant strains of anticlericalism, lay piety, and mysticism, even as it coincided with the revival of Classical studies in Northern Europe.
- Erasmus, the leading Christian humanist, led the critical study of the Bible and writings of the church fathers. Northern humanists brought to their efforts the same intellectual fervor that the Italian humanists had applied to their examination of Plato and Cicero.

The Protestant Reformation

- Across Germany, the sale of indulgences to benefit the Church of Rome provoked harsh criticism, especially by those who saw the luxuries of the papacy as a betrayal of apostolic ideals.
- Martin Luther was the voice of the Protestant Reformation. In his sermons and essays he criticized the worldliness of the Church and bemoaned "the misery and wretchedness of Christendom."
- Luther's greatest attempt at reforming the Catholic Church came in the form of his *Ninety-Five Theses* (1517), which listed his grievances against the Church and called for reform based on scriptural precedent.
- Luther's teachings, with the aid of the printing press, circulated throughout Europe, giving rise to other Protestant sects, including Calvinism and Anabaptism, and, in England, the Anglican Church.
- The Lutheran chorale became the vehicle of Protestant piety.

Northern Renaissance Art

- Even before the North felt the impact of the Italian Renaissance, Netherlandish artists initiated a painting style rich in realistic detail. Jan van Eyck's pioneering use of thin oil glazes captured the naturalistic effects of light on objects that, while tangible, also functioned as symbols.
- The paintings of Hieronymus Bosch infused traditional religious subjects with a unique combination of moralizing motifs drawn from illuminated manuscripts, pilgrimage badges, and the popular pseudo-sciences: astrology and alchemy.
- The Protestant Reformation, which rejected relics and sacred images as reflections of superstition and idolatry, favored devotional, and especially biblical, subjects. The two new graphic techniques, woodcutting and engraving, facilitated the mass production of devotional images that functioned as book illustrations and individual prints.
- A growing middle class provided patronage for portraiture, landscapes, and scenes of everyday life, subjects that were pursued by Albrecht Dürer, Lucas Cranach, Hans Holbein, and Pieter Bruegel. Nevertheless, deeply felt religious sentiment persisted in many Northern artworks, such as Matthias Grünewald's rivetingly expressive Isenheim Altarpiece.

Sixteenth-Century Literature

- Northern Renaissance writers took a generally skeptical and pessimistic view of human nature. Erasmus, More, and Rabelais lampooned individual and societal failings and described the ruling influence of folly in all aspects of human conduct.
- In France, Montaigne devised the essay as an intimate form of rational reflection, while in Spain, Cervantes' novel, *Don Quixote*, wittily attacked feudal values and outmoded ideals.
- Northern Renaissance literature was, in many ways, a literature of protest and reform, and one whose dominant themes reflect the tension between medieval and modern ideas.

Shakespeare

- Shakespeare emerged during the golden age of England, which flourished under the rule of Elizabeth I. He produced thirty-seven plays—comedies, tragedies, romances, and histories—as well as 154 sonnets and other poems. His work, along with that of other Northern artists and writers, brought the West to the threshold of modernity.
- The most powerful form of literary expression to evolve in the late sixteenth century was secular drama. In the hands of William Shakespeare, Elizabethan drama became the ideal vehicle for exposing the psychological forces that motivate human behavior.

Glossary

blank verse unrhymed lines of iambic pentameter, that is, lines consisting of ten syllables each with accents on every second syllable

chorale a congregational hymn, first sung in the Lutheran church

couplet two successive lines of verse with similar end-rhymes

engraving the process by which lines are incised on a metal plate, then inked and printed; see Figure 19.10

essay a short piece of expository prose that examines a single subject

genre painting art depicting scenes from everyday life; not to be confused with "genre," a term used to designate a particular category in literature or art, such as the essay (in literature) and portraiture (in painting)

picaresque novel a prose genre that narrates the comic misadventures of a roguish hero

quatrain a four-line stanza

woodcut a relief printing process by which all parts of a design are cut away except those that will be inked and printed; see Figure 19.9

Book 4

Faith, Reason, and Power in the Early Modern World

Summary of the Renaissance and the Reformation

The following paragraphs provide an overview of the Renaissance and Reformation, the two movements that ushered in the modern era in the West. This summary of fifteenth- and sixteenth-century culture (dealt with in detail in Book 3) offers some background to the materials contained in Books 4, 5, and 6, which deal with the modern era in a global context.

Classical Humanism

The effort to recover, edit, and study ancient Greek and Latin manuscripts, a movement known as Classical humanism, first occurred in fourteenth-century Italy, where it marked the beginnings of the Renaissance. This revival of Greco-Roman culture was to spread throughout Western Europe over the following 300 years. Petrarch, the father of humanism, provided the model for Renaissance scholarship and education. He promoted the study of the classic Greek and Latin writers, especially Cicero, encouraged textual criticism, and wrote introspective and passionate sonnets that were revered and imitated for centuries to come.

The city of Florence was the unrivaled center of Classical humanism in the first 150 years of the Renaissance. A thriving commercial and financial center dominated by a well-to-do middle class, Florence found political and cultural leadership in such wealthy and sophisticated families as the Medici. Classical humanism helped to cultivate a sense of civic pride, a new respect for oral and written eloquence, and a set of personal values that sustained the ambitions of the rising merchant class.

Fifteenth-century humanists carried on Petrarch's quest to recover the Classical past. Ficino translated the entire body of Plato's writings, while Pico's investigations in Hebrew and Arabic led him to believe that the world's great minds shared a single, universal truth. Pico's *Oration on the Dignity of Man* proclaimed the centrality of humankind and defended the unlimited freedom of the individual within the universal scheme.

Renaissance humanists cultivated the idea of the good life. Following Alberti's maxim, "A man can do anything he wants," they applied the moral precepts of the Classical past to such contemporary pursuits as diplomacy, politics, and the arts. While Petrarch and his peers were concerned primarily with the recovery of Classical manuscripts and the production of critical editions, Alberti, Castiglione, and Machiavelli infused scholarship with action. Allying their scrutiny of the past with an empirical study of the present, they fostered a heroic ideal of the individual that surpassed all Classical models. For Alberti, wealth and authority proceeded from the exercise of *virtù*; for Castiglione, the superior breed of human being was *l'uomo universale*,

the well-rounded person; for Machiavelli, only a ruthless master of power politics could ensure the survival of the state. Alberti, Castiglione, and Machiavelli were representative of the larger group of Renaissance humanists who envisioned self-knowledge and individualism as crucial to success in the secular world. Their views shaped the modern character of the humanistic tradition in the European West.

Renaissance Artists

The artists of the Renaissance brought a scientific curiosity to the study of the natural world and untiringly investigated its operations. Such Early Renaissance artists as Donatello, Pollaiuolo, Masaccio, and Brunelleschi studied the mechanics of the human body, the effects of light on material substances, and the physical appearance of objects in three-dimensional space. At the same time, Renaissance artists were masters of invention: they perfected the technique of oil painting, formulated the laws of perspective, and applied the principles of Classical art to the representation of Christian and contemporary subjects. Patronized by a wealthy middle class, they revived such this-worldly genres as portraiture and gave new attention to the nude body as an object of natural beauty.

The art of the High Renaissance marks the culmination of a hundred-year effort to wed the techniques of naturalistic representation to Classical ideals of proportion and order. Leonardo da Vinci, the quintessential artist–scientist, tried to reconcile empirical experience with abstract principles of design. The compositions of Raphael, with their monumental scale and unity of design, became standards by which Western paintings would be judged for centuries. The multitalented Michelangelo brought a heroic idealism to the treatment of traditional Christian and Classical themes. In Venice, Titian's painterly handling of the reclining female nude represented a new and more sensuous naturalism. The centrally planned buildings of Bramante and Palladio realized the architectural ideals of harmony, balance, and clarity pursued in the Early Renaissance by Brunelleschi and Alberti.

The Renaissance produced an equally splendid flowering in music, especially among Franco-Flemish composers. Secular compositions began to outnumber religious ones. The techniques of imitation and word painting infused both religious and secular music with homogeneity and increased expressiveness. Printed sheet music helped to popularize the madrigal and other secular, vernacular song forms. Instrumental music and dance now emerged as independent genres. Like their Classical predecessors, Renaissance artists placed human concerns and feelings at the center of their creative efforts. A spirit of optimism, combined with intellectual curiosity and increasing worldliness, fueled the early modern era in the West.

Shattering the Old Order: Protest and Reform

The sixteenth century was a time of rapid change marked by growing secularism, advancing technology, and European overseas expansion. It was also an age of profound religious and social upheaval. Northern humanists led by Erasmus of Rotterdam studied early Christian literature and urged a return to the teachings of Jesus and the early church fathers. Demands for Church reform went hand in hand with the revival of early Christian writings to culminate in the Protestant Reformation.

Aided by Gutenberg's printing press, Martin Luther challenged the authority of the Church of Rome. He held that Scripture was the sole basis for religious interpretation and emphasized the idea of salvation through faith in God's grace rather than through good works. As Lutheranism and other Protestant sects proliferated throughout Europe, the unity of medieval Christendom was shattered.

The music and the art of the Northern Renaissance reflect the mood of religious reform. In music, the Lutheran chorale became the vehicle of Protestant piety. In art, the increasing demand for illustrated devotional literature and private devotional art stimulated the production of woodcuts and metal engravings. The works of Dürer and Grünewald exhibit the Northern Renaissance passion for realistic detail and graphic expression, while the fantastic imagery of Hieronymus Bosch suggests a pessimistic and typically Northern concern with sin and death. Bosch's preoccupation with the palpable forces of evil found its counterpart in the witch hunts of the sixteenth century. In painting, too, such secular subjects as portraiture, landscapes, and scenes of everyday life mirrored the tastes of a growing middle-class audience for an unidealized record of the visual world.

Northern Renaissance writers took a generally skeptical and pessimistic view of human nature. Erasmus, More, and Rabelais lampooned individual and societal failings and described the ruling influence of folly in all aspects of human conduct. In France, Montaigne devised the essay as an intimate form of rational reflection. In Spain, Cervantes' novel, *Don Quixote*, wittily attacked outmoded feudal values and ideals. The most powerful form of literary expression to evolve in the late sixteenth century, however, was secular drama. In the hands of William Shakespeare, the play became the ideal vehicle for reconciling personality and circumstance. Shakespeare's tragedies (as opposed, for instance, to Montaigne's essays) reveal the human condition through overt action, rather than through private reflection.

By the end of the sixteenth century, national loyalties, religious fanaticism, and commercial rivalries for control of trade with Africa, Asia, and the Americas had splintered the European community. These conditions rendered ever more complex the society of the West. And yet, on the threshold of modernity, the challenges to the human condition—economic survival, communality, self-knowledge, and the inevitability of death—were no less pressing than they had been 2000 years earlier. If the technology of the sixteenth century offered greater control over nature than ever before, it also provided more devastating weapons of war and mass destruction. In the centuries to come, the humanistic tradition would be shaped and reshaped by changing historical circumstances that would put the West in a position of increasing world dominance.

BOOK 4

Faith, Reason, and Power in the Early Modern World

The Catholic Reformation and the Baroque Style

ca. 1550–1750

"So sweet are the colloquies of love which pass between the soul and God . . ."
Saint Teresa of Avila

Figure 20.1 CARAVAGGIO, *The Crucifixion of Saint Peter*, 1601. Oil on canvas, 7 ft. 6 in. × 5 ft. 9 in. While Caravaggio gives the saint a powerful body, he renders the face with an expression of vulnerability. Note how the highlighted areas of the composition seem to form the spokes of a wheel.

The early modern era, often called the Age of the Baroque, was a time of deep contradictions. In the West, fervent, even mystical, religious sentiment vied with dramatic advances in science and scientific methods of investigation. Newly developed theories of constitutional government contended with firmly entrenched claims to monarchy. The rising wealth of a small segment of the population came to contrast with widespread poverty and old aristocratic privilege. Overseas exploration and travel produced a broader and more accurate geographic perception of the planet. All these phenomena provided the context for the emergence of the style known as "the Baroque." Characterized by theatrical expressiveness and spatial grandeur, the Baroque became the hallmark of an age of vigorous expansion, fueled by the human ambition to master nature on a colossal scale. In Italy, it mirrored the religious fervor of the Catholic Reformation. In France and elsewhere under authoritarian regimes, it worked to glorify royal wealth and majesty. In Northern Europe, it conveyed the reflective spirit of Protestant devotionalism. Throughout the West, it embraced the new, dynamic view of the universe as set forth by proponents of the Scientific Revolution. Each of these aspects of the Baroque will be examined in the following chapters, beginning with its earliest phase during the advent of the Catholic Reformation.

The Catholic Reformation

The Protestant Reformation created a religious upheaval unlike any other in the history of Western Christendom. Luther's criticism of the Roman Catholic Church had encouraged religious devotion free of papal authority and had prepared the way for the rise of other Protestant sects (see chapter 19). The rival religious beliefs that fragmented Western Europe quickly accelerated into armed combat. The Thirty Years' War (1618–1648), which ended with the establishment of Protestantism throughout most of Northern Europe, caused the death of some five million Christians. During the sixteenth century, as Protestant sects began to lure increasing numbers of Christians away from Roman Catholicism, the Church launched an evangelical campaign to win back to Catholicism those who had strayed to Protestantism, a movement known as the Counter-Reformation. Even earlier, however, the Church had begun an internal program of papal and monastic reform, known as the Catholic Reformation. These two interdependent movements ultimately produced a renewed Catholicism that emphasized a return to the original ideals of the Church, ensuring its survival in the modern world.

Loyola and the Jesuits

The impetus for renewal came largely from fervent Spanish Catholics, the most notable of whom was Ignatius Loyola (1491–1556). A soldier in the army of King Charles I of Spain (the Holy Roman emperor Charles V; 1500–1558), Loyola brought to Catholicism the same iron will he had exercised on the battlefield. After his right leg was fractured by a French cannonball at the siege of Pamplona, Loyola became a religious teacher and a hermit, traveling lame and barefoot to Jerusalem in an effort to convert Muslims to Christianity. In the 1530s he founded the Society of Jesus, the most important of the many new monastic orders associated with the Catholic Reformation.

The Society of Jesus, or Jesuits, followed Loyola in calling for a militant return to fundamental Catholic dogma and the strict enforcement of traditional Church teachings. In addition to the monastic vows of celibacy, poverty, and obedience, the Jesuits took an oath of allegiance to the pope, whom they served as soldiers of Christ.

Under Loyola's leadership, the Jesuit order became the most influential missionary society of early modern times. Rigorously trained, its members acted as preachers, confessors, and teachers—leaders in educational reform and moral discipline. Throughout Europe, members of the newly formed order worked as missionaries to win back those who had strayed from "Mother Church." The Jesuits were fairly successful in stamping out Protestantism in much of France, southern Germany, and other parts of Europe. But their reach extended further: as pioneers in learning the languages and customs of India, China, and Japan, the Jesuits were the prime intermediaries between Europe and Asia from the sixteenth through the nineteenth centuries. In the Americas, which became prime targets for Jesuit activity, missionaries mastered Native American tribal languages and proceeded to convert thousands to Roman Catholicism. Their success in Mexico and Central and South America stamped these parts of the world with a distinctive cultural character.

The Jesuit order was a fascinating amalgam of two elements: mysticism and militant religious zeal. The first emphasized the personal and intuitive experience of God, while the second involved an attitude of unquestioned submission to the Church as the absolute source of truth. These two aspects of Jesuit training—mysticism and militancy—are reflected in Loyola's influential handbook, the *Spiritual Exercises*. In his introductory observations, Loyola explains that the spiritual exercises should do for the soul what physical exercise does for the body. As aids to the development of perfect spiritual discipline, these devotional exercises—each of which should occupy a full hour—engage the body in perfecting the soul. In the Fifth Exercise, a meditation on Hell, each of the five senses is summoned to heighten the mystical experience:

FIRST POINT: This will be to *see* in imagination the vast fires, and the souls enclosed, as it were, in bodies of fire.

SECOND POINT: To *hear* the wailing, the howling, cries, and blasphemies against Christ our Lord and against His saints.

THIRD POINT: With the sense of *smell* to perceive the smoke, the sulfur, the filth, and corruption.

FOURTH POINT: To *taste* the bitterness of tears, sadness, and remorse of conscience.

FIFTH POINT: With the sense of *touch* to feel the flames which envelop and burn the souls.

Loyola also insists on an unswerving commitment to traditional Church teachings. Among his "rules for thinking with the Church" is the admonition that Christians put aside all judgments of their own and remain obedient to the "holy Mother, the hierarchical Church."

READING 20.1 From Loyola's *Spiritual Exercises* (1548)

The following rules should be observed to foster the true attitude of mind we ought to have in the church militant.

1 We must put aside all judgment of our own, and keep the mind ever ready and prompt to obey in all things the true Spouse of Christ our Lord, our holy Mother, the hierarchical Church.

2 We should praise sacramental confession, the yearly reception of the Most Blessed Sacrament, and praise more highly monthly reception, and still more weekly Communion, provided requisite and proper dispositions are present.

3 We ought to praise the frequent hearing of Mass, the singing of hymns, psalmody, and long prayers whether in the church or outside; likewise, the hours arranged at fixed times for the whole Divine Office, for every kind of prayer, and for the canonical hours.[1]

4 We must praise highly religious life, virginity, and continency; and matrimony ought not be praised as much as any of these.

5 We should praise vows of religion, obedience, poverty, chastity, and vows to perform other works . . . conducive to perfection. . . .

6 We should show our esteem for the relics of the saints by venerating them and praying to the saints. We should praise visits to the Station Churches,[2] pilgrimages, indulgences, jubilees,[3] crusade indults,[4] and the lighting of candles in churches.

7 We must praise the regulations of the Church with regard to fast and abstinence. . . . We should praise works of penance,

[1] The eight times of the day appointed for special devotions; see chapters 11 and 15.

[2] Churches with images representing the stages of Christ's Passion.

[3] A time of special solemnity, ordinarily every twenty-five years, proclaimed by the pope; also, special indulgences granted during that time. The jubilee principle is based on a biblical injunction to free slaves, return land to its original owners, and leave fields untilled once every fifty years (Leviticus 25).

[4] Church indulgences granted to Christian Crusaders.

not only those that are interior but also those that are exterior.

8 We ought to praise not only the building and adornment of churches, but also images and veneration of them according to the subject they represent.

9 Finally, we must praise all the commandments of the Church, and be on the alert to find reasons to defend them, and by no means in order to criticize them. . . .

13 If we wish to proceed securely in all things, we must hold fast to the following principle: What seems to me white, I will believe black if the hierarchical Church so defines. For I must be convinced that in Christ our Lord, the bridegroom, and in His spouse the Church, only one Spirit holds sway, which governs and rules for the salvation of souls. For it is by the same Spirit and Lord who gave the Ten Commandments that our holy Mother Church is ruled and governed.

Q What is meant by "the true attitude of mind?" What by "the church militant?"

The Council of Trent

Loyola's affirmation of Roman Catholic doctrine anticipated the actions of the Council of Trent, the general church council that met between 1545 and 1563 to make doctrinal, ecclesiastical, and spiritual reforms. The Council of Trent reconfirmed all seven of the sacraments. It reasserted the basic tenets of Catholicism, including all theological matters that had been challenged by the Protestants. It set clear guidelines for the elimination of abuses among members of the clergy, emphasized preaching to the uneducated laity, and encouraged the regeneration of intellectual life within Catholic monasteries. Church leaders revived the activities of the Inquisition—the special court authorized to try and convict heretics (see chapter 12) and established the *Index Expurgatorius*, a list of books judged heretical and therefore forbidden to Catholic readers. Finally, the council approved a number of new religious orders, including the Jesuits, the Capuchins (an offshoot of the Franciscans notable as preachers and ministers to the poor), and the Ursulines (an order of females devoted to educating girls).

Over the course of more than ten years, Church reformers supported a broadly based Catholicism that emphasized the return to a personal relationship with Christ. At the same time, they encouraged an intuitive, even mystical, embrace of Mother Church. Although the Church of Rome would never reassume the universal authority it had enjoyed during the Middle Ages, both its internal reforms and its efforts to rekindle the faith restored its dignity in the minds and hearts of its followers.

Catholicism's Global Reach

The evangelical activities of the Jesuits and other religious orders were widespread, but not uniformly successful. In China, where European traders were regarded as "ocean devils," the Catholic missionaries developed a cordial relationship with the intellectual classes and succeeded in converting a number of Chinese scholars. By the eighteenth century, however, disputes between the Jesuits and the Dominicans over the veneration of Confucius (aggravated by papal condemnation of Confucian rites in 1744) weakened Catholic influence.

In Japan, the first Jesuit missionaries, admirers of Tokugawa culture (see chapter 21), diligently mastered the Japanese language and culture. While the Jesuits introduced the Japanese to European styles of painting and music, the Portuguese (and thereafter, Dutch and English) merchants brought commercial interests to Japan (see chapter 18), thus clouding the evangelical aims of the Jesuits with European material ambitions. The Jesuit efforts at conversion were also frustrated by rival Franciscan missionaries. Over time, the Jesuits fell into disfavor with Japanese Buddhists, who came to view all Christians as potentially subversive to the traditional social order. By 1606, following decades of disruption caused by European efforts to win trading privileges in Japan, the Japanese outlawed Christianity. In 1624, following a wave of brutal persecutions of both European Christians and Japanese converts to Catholicism, the country expelled almost all Western foreigners from Japanese soil.

Christian evangelism in the Americas proved to be far more successful. In sixteenth-century Mexico, where Spanish political authority went largely unchallenged, Catholicism went hand in hand with colonization. The arrival of the Jesuits in 1571 followed that of the Augustinians, the Dominicans, and the Franciscans in a vast program of Christianization. Just as the convergence of Europeans and Native Americans came to produce a unique new "Latin American" population, so the blend of European Catholic and native religious traditions produced a creolized Mexican culture. A formidable example of this phenomenon, and one that testifies to the powerful religious impact of Catholicism, is the Miracle of the Virgin of Guadalupe. In 1531, ten years after the conquest of Mexico by Hernán Cortés, on the site of a former shrine to the Aztec mother-goddess, the Virgin Mary appeared before a simple Mexican peasant named Juan Diego. Speaking in the native Aztec tongue, she asked that a church honoring her be built on that site. When the local bishop asked for a sign to prove the truth of Juan's story, the Virgin instructed the peasant to gather roses (blooming miraculously in winter) and deliver them to the bishop. As the roses were unloaded from Juan's cloak, the image of the Virgin was found imprinted on the fabric.

The legend of this miraculous apparition, commemorated in hundreds of carved and painted images (Figure **20.2**), became the basis for the most important religious cult in Mexican history: the cult of the Virgin of Guadalupe. The colonial cult of Guadalupe worships the Virgin in the traditional medieval guise of mother, intercessor, and protector, but it also exalts her as the symbol of Mexican national consciousness. At her shrine—the goal of thousands of pilgrims each year—and at hundreds of chapels throughout Mexico, the faithful pay homage to the Madonna, who is shown standing on a crescent moon, surrounded by a corona of sunrays and angels bearing the colors of the Mexican flag. The votive figure of the Virgin of Guadalupe was enthusiastically promoted by the Jesuits from the late sixteenth century, and her widespread popularity as protectress of Mexico has persisted even into modern times: in 1910, she was made an honorary general of the Mexican Revolution.

Literature and the Catholic Reformation

The ideals of the Catholic Reformation infused the arts of the sixteenth and seventeenth centuries. In literature, there appeared a new emphasis on heightened spirituality and on personal visionary experience. Like the Reformation itself, a number of its greatest mystics came from Spain. Juan de Yepes Alvarez, better known as Saint John of the Cross (1542–1591), left some of the finest religious poetry in the corpus of Spanish literature. His *Dark Night of the Soul* (1585) describes the journey of the soul from its bodily prison to spiritual union with God. A Carmelite priest and friar, Saint John worked to eliminate moral laxity and restore absolute poverty in the monasteries. His efforts at establishing new Carmelite houses in Spain were shared by the Carmelite nun Teresa of Avila.

Figure 20.2 *The Virgin of Guadalupe*, 1746. Oil on wood, 5 × 4 ft. (approx.). The cloak of Juan Diego bears the imprint of the Virgin surrounded by a gold mandorla and the roses that miraculously fell before the bishop. The basilica of Our Lady of Guadalupe in Mexico City remains the second most frequently visited religious shrine in the world.

Teresa of Avila

The early life of Teresa of Avila (1515–1582) was spent founding religious houses and defending the Carmelite practice of going without shoes (as an expression of humility). Traveling all over Spain, she became notorious as "the roving nun." It was not until she was almost forty years old that her life as a visionary began. Teresa's visions describe her firsthand experience of frequent visitations by Jesus Christ over a two-year period. Like the twelfth-century mystic Hildegard of Bingen (see chapter 12), Teresa embraced the intuitive knowledge of God. But unlike Hildegard, whose writings engage natural and supernatural details, Teresa's experience is physical (and explicitly sensory). Her love is the longing for oneness with God. In the *Visions*, physical suffering evokes psychic bliss; and her union with the divine, as illustrated in the following excerpt, is couched in the language of erotic desire and fulfillment. As the Lord's flaming arrow is withdrawn from her body, Teresa is left "completely afire."

READING 20.2 From Saint Teresa's *Visions* (1611)

It pleased the Lord that I should sometimes see the following   1
vision. I would see beside me, on my left hand, an angel in
bodily form—a type of vision which I am not in the habit of
seeing, except very rarely. Though I often see representations
of angels, my visions of them are of the type which I first
mentioned. It pleased the Lord that I should see this angel
in the following way. He was not tall, but short, and very
beautiful, his face so aflame that he appeared to be one of the
highest types of angel who seem to be all afire. They must be
those who are called cherubim: they do not tell me their names   10
but I am well aware that there is a great difference between
certain angels and others, and between these and others still,
of a kind that I could not possibly explain. In his hands I saw a
long golden spear and at the end of the iron tip I seemed to
see a point of fire. With this he seemed to pierce my heart
several times so that it penetrated to my entrails. When he
drew it out, I thought he was drawing them out with it and he
left me completely afire with a great love for God. The pain
was so sharp that it made me utter several moans; and so
excessive was the sweetness caused me by this intense pain   20
that one can never wish to lose it, nor will one's soul be
content with anything less than God. It is not bodily pain, but
spiritual, though the body has a share in it—indeed, a great
share. So sweet are the colloquies of love which pass between
the soul and God that if anyone thinks I am lying I beseech
God, in His goodness, to give him the same experience. . . .

Q Which strikes you as more effective: the written or the visual version of Saint Teresa's vision? Why so?

Crashaw

The language of religious ecstasy also infused the poetry of the English Catholic Richard Crashaw (1613–1649). Born into a Protestant family, Crashaw converted to Catholicism early in life. His religious poems, written in Latin and English, reflect the dual influence of Loyola's meditations and Teresa's visions. At least two of his most lyrical pieces are dedicated to Saint Teresa: *A Hymn to the Name and Honor of the Admirable Saint Teresa* and *The Flaming Heart, upon the Book and Picture of the Seraphical Saint Teresa, as She Is Usually Expressed with a Seraphim beside Her.* The latter poem suggests that Crashaw was familiar with Bernini's sculpted version of Teresa's vision before it was publicly unveiled in Rome (Figure **20.3**). Representative of this visionary sensibility, the last sixteen lines of *The Flaming Heart*, reproduced in Reading 20.3, are rhapsodic in their intense expression of personal emotion. Erasing boundaries between erotic and spiritual love, Crashaw pleads that Teresa ravish his soul, even as she has been ravished by God.

READING 20.3 From Crashaw's *The Flaming Heart* (1652)

O thou undaunted daughter of desires!   1
By all thou dower of lights and fires;
By all the eagle in thee, all the dove;
By all thy lives and deaths of love;
By thy large draughts of intellectual day,   5
And by thy thirsts of love more large than they;
By all thy brim-filled bowls of fierce desire,
By thy last morning's draught of liquid fire;
By the full kingdom of that final kiss
That seized thy parting soul, and sealed thee His;   10
By all the heavens thou hast in Him,
Fair sister of the seraphim,
By all of Him we have in thee;
Leave nothing of myself in me!
Let me so read thy life that I   15
Unto all life of mine may die.

Q What is the nature of the love that Crashaw describes?

Q Which images in this poem contribute to its erotic undertone?

The Visual Arts and the Catholic Reformation

Mannerist Painting in Italy

The religious zeal of the Catholic reformers inspired a tremendous surge of artistic activity, especially in Italy and Spain. In Venice and Rome, the centers of Italian cultural life, the clarity and order of High Renaissance art gave way to the visual eccentricities of *Mannerism* (from the Italian *maniera*, meaning "style"). Coined in the twentieth century, the term "Mannerism" describes a style characterized by virtuosity in execution, artificiality, and affectation. Flourishing between ca. 1520 and 1610, Mannerism became a vehicle for the spiritual upheavals of its time. Mannerist artists brought a new level of inventive fantasy and psychological intensity (bordering on disquiet) to

Figure 20.3 GIANLORENZO BERNINI, *The Ecstasy of Saint Teresa*, 1645–1652. Marble, height of group 11 ft. 6 in. (See also Figure 20.13)

Figure 20.4 MICHELANGELO BUONARROTI, *The Last Judgment* (after restoration), 1536–1540. Fresco, 48 × 44 ft. Below the athletic figure of Christ sits Saint Bartholomew, who suffered martyrdom by being flayed alive. He holds a knife and his own flayed skin, on which some scholars see a self-portrait of Michelangelo.

otherwise traditional subject matter. Their works mirrored the self-conscious spirituality and deep insecurity generated by Europe's religious wars and political rivalries.

The Mannerist style is already evident in *The Last Judgment* painted by the sixty-year-old Michelangelo on the east wall of the Sistine Chapel (Figure **20.4**). Between 1536 and 1540, only a few years after the armies of the Holy Roman Empire had sacked the city of Rome, Michelangelo returned to the chapel whose ceiling he had painted some twenty years earlier with the optimistic vision of salvation.

Now, in a mood of brooding pessimism, he filled the altar wall with agonized, writhing figures that press dramatically against one another. Surrounding the wrathful Christ are the Christian saints and martyrs, who carry the instruments of their torture, and throngs of the resurrected—originally depicted nude but in 1564, in the wake of Catholic reform, draped to hide their genitals. Michelangelo has replaced the Classically proportioned figures, calm balance, and spatial clarity of High Renaissance painting with a more troubled and turbulent vision of salvation.

The traits of the Mannerist style can be seen best in the *Madonna of the Long Neck* (Figure **20.5**) by Parmigianino (1503–1540). In this work, the traditional subject of Madonna and Child is given a new mood of theatricality (compare Raphael's *Alba Madonna*; see chapter 17). Perched precariously above a courtyard adorned with a column that supports no superstructure, the unnaturally elongated Mother of God— her spidery fingers affectedly touching her chest—gazes at the oversized Christ Child, who seems to slip lifelessly off her lap. Onlookers crowd into the space from the left, while a small figure (perhaps a prophet) at the bottom right corner of the canvas draws our eye into distant space. Cool coloring and an overall smokiness make the painting seem even more contrived and artificial, yet it is, by its very contrivance, unforgettable.

Figure 20.5 PARMIGIANINO,
Madonna of the Long Neck, 1534–1540.
Oil on panel, 7 ft. 1 in. × 4 ft. 4 in.

MAKING CONNECTIONS

The degree to which the Mannerists rejected the guiding principles of High Renaissance painting is nowhere better illustrated than in a comparison between *The Last Supper* (Figure **20.6**) by the Venetian artist Jacopo Tintoretto (1518–1594) and the fresco of the same subject by Leonardo da Vinci (see chapter 17) executed approximately a century earlier (Figure **20.7**). In his rendering of the sacred event, Tintoretto renounces the symmetry and geometric clarity of Leonardo's composition. The receding lines of the table and the floor in Tintoretto's painting place the viewer above the scene and draw the eye toward a vanishing point that lies in a distant and uncertain space beyond the canvas. The even texture

of Leonardo's fresco gives way in Tintoretto's canvas to vaporous contrasts of dark and light, produced by a smoking oil lamp. Clouds of angels flutter spectrally at the ceiling, and phosphorescent halos seem to electrify the agitated figures of the apostles. While Leonardo focuses on the human element of the Last Supper—the moment when Jesus acknowledges his impending betrayal—Tintoretto illustrates the miraculous moment when Jesus initiates the sacrament by which the bread and wine become his flesh and blood. Yet, in a move toward greater naturalism, he sets the miracle amidst the ordinary activities of household servants, who occupy the entire right-hand portion of the picture.

Figure 20.6 JACOPO TINTORETTO, *The Last Supper*, 1592–1594. Oil on canvas, 12 ft. × 18 ft. 8 in. Pictured against a concentrated burst of light at the upper end of the table, the Savior is pictured distributing the bread and wine to his disciples.

Figure 20.7 LEONARDO DA VINCI, *Last Supper*, ca. 1485–1498. Oil and tempera on plaster, 15 ft. 1⅛ in. × 28 ft. 10½ in.

Figure 20.8 EL GRECO, *The Agony in the Garden*, ca. 1585–1586. Oil on canvas, 6 ft. 1 in. × 9 ft. 1 in.

Mannerist Painting in Spain

The Mannerist passion for pictorial intensity was most vividly realized in the paintings of Domenikos Theotokopoulos, generally known (because of his Greek origins) as El Greco (1541–1614). Born in Crete, his early career was spent in Venice and Rome, but in the 1570s, he settled in Spain, where he remained—serving the Church and the Spanish king Philip II—until his death. El Greco preferred the expressive grace of Tintoretto to the more muscular vitality of Michelangelo. With the inward eye of a mystic, he produced visionary canvases marked by bold distortions of form, dissonant colors, and a daring handling of space. His elongated and flamelike figures, often highlighted by ghostly whites and yellow-grays, seem to radiate halos of light—auras that symbolize the luminous power of divine revelation. *The Agony in the Garden*, the scene of Jesus' final submission to the divine will, takes place in a moonlit landscape in which clouds, rocks, and fabrics billow and swell with mysterious energy (Figure **20.8**). Below the

tempestuous sky, Judas (the small figure on the lower right) leads the arresting officers to the Garden of Gethsemane. The sleeping apostles, tucked away in a cocoonlike shelter, violate rational space: they are too small in relation to the oversized image of Jesus and the angel who hovers above. El Greco's ambiguous spatial fields, which often include multiple vanishing points, his acrid greens and acid yellows, and his "painterly" techniques—his brushstrokes remain engagingly visible on the surface of the canvas—all contribute to the creation of a highly personal style that captured the mystical fervor of the new Catholicism.

The Baroque Style

The Baroque style, which flourished between roughly 1600 and 1750, brought heightened naturalism and a new level of emotionalism to Western art. Derived from the Portuguese word *barocco*, which describes the irregularly shaped pearls often featured in ornamental European decoration, the term *Baroque* is associated with such features as ornateness, spatial grandeur, and theatrical flamboyance. In painting, the Baroque is characterized by asymmetric compositions, strong contrasts of light and dark, vigorous brushwork, and bold, illusionistic effects. Baroque sculptors engaged light and space to convey physical energy and dramatic movement. A synthesis of the arts—painting, sculpture, and architecture—promoted the ambitions of rulers and the religious beliefs of Catholics and Protestants.

Baroque Painting in Italy

The Baroque style originated in Italy and came to dominate artistic production throughout Europe and in those parts of the Americas colonized by Spain. Baroque artists worked to increase the dramatic expressiveness of religious subject matter in order to give viewers the sense that they were participating in the action of the scene. They copied nature faithfully and without idealization. Such was the ambition of the north Italian artist Michelangelo Merisi, better known as Caravaggio (1571–1610). The leading Italian painter of the seventeenth century, Caravaggio flouted Renaissance artistic conventions, even as he flouted the law—he was arrested for violent acts that ranged from throwing a plate of artichokes in the face of a tavernkeeper to armed assault and murder. Having killed a tennis opponent in 1606, he was forced to flee Rome. In his paintings, Caravaggio renounced the grand style of the High Renaissance, which called for dignity, decorum, and the idealization of figures and setting. He recreated the Christian narrative as though its major events were occurring in the local taverns and streets of sixteenth-century Italy. Caravaggio dramatized these events with strong contrasts of light and dark that give his figures a sculptural presence. A golden light bathes Christ and his disciples in *The Supper at Emmaus* (Figure **20.9**); Caravaggio "spotlights" Jesus at the moment when, raising his hand to bless the bread, he is recognized as the Christ (Luke 24:30–31). Caravaggio commands our attention by means of explicit theatrical gestures and by the use of a perspective device known as **foreshortening**: Christ's right arm, painted at a right angle to the picture plane, seems to project sharply outward, as if to bless the viewer as well as the bread. At the moment of recognition, the disciple at the right flings his arms outward along a diagonal axis that draws the viewer into the composition, while the figure at the left grips the arm of his chair as though to rise in astonishment. Unlike the visionary El Greco, Caravaggio brings sacred subjects down to earth with an almost cameralike naturalism.

Figure 20.9 CARAVAGGIO, *The Supper at Emmaus*, ca. 1600. Oil on canvas, 4 ft. 7 in. × 6 ft. 5½ in. As Jesus raises his hand to bless the bread and wine, his two disciples recognize him as the Christ. Caravaggio dispenses with the traditional halo, but enshrouds Jesus with a dark shadow. Bread, fowl, and fruit are recreated in vivid realistic detail.

Figure 20.10 ARTEMISIA GENTILESCHI, *Judith Slaying Holofernes*, ca. 1614–1620. Oil on canvas, 6 ft. 6⅓ in. × 5 ft. 4 in.

Where El Greco's saints and martyrs are ethereal, Caravaggio's are solid, substantive, and often ordinary. Their strong physical presence and frank homeliness transform biblical miracles into human narratives—a bold repudiation of the Italian Renaissance conventions of beauty.

Caravaggio composed traditional religious subjects with unprecedented theatrical power and daring. In *The Crucifixion of Saint Peter* (see Figure **20.1**), he arranged the figures in a tense, off-centered pinwheel that captures the eccentricity of Saint Peter's torment (he was crucified upside down). By placing these large, vigorously modeled figures up against the picture plane, he reduced the psychological distance between the viewer and the subject. Staged against a darkened background, the action seems to take place within the viewer's space—a space whose cruel light reveals such banal details as the executioner's dirty feet. True to the ideals of the Catholic Reformation, Caravaggio's paintings appealed to the senses rather than to the intellect. They also introduced into European art a new and vigorously lifelike realization of the natural world—one that daringly mingled the sacred and the profane.

Caravaggio's powerful style had considerable impact throughout Europe; however, his most talented follower was also Italian. Born in Rome, Artemisia Gentileschi (1593–1653) was the daughter of a highly esteemed painter, himself a follower of Caravaggio. Artemisia was trained by her father, but soon outstripped him in technical proficiency and imagination. Since women were not permitted to draw from nude male models, they rarely painted large-scale canvases with biblical, historical, or mythological themes that usually required nude figures; instead, their efforts were confined to the genres of portrait painting and still life (see chapter 23). Gentileschi's paintings, however, challenged tradition. Her powerful rendering of Judith slaying Holofernes (Figure **20.10**), which compares in size and impact with Caravaggio's *Crucifixion of Saint Peter* (see Figure 20.1), illustrates the decapitation of an Assyrian general and enemy of Israel at the hands of a clever Hebrew widow. A story found in the Apocrypha (the noncanonical books of the Bible), the slaying of the tyrannical Holofernes was a favorite Renaissance allegory for liberty and religious defiance. Gentileschi brought to this subject the dramatic techniques of Caravaggio: realistically conceived figures, stark contrasts of light and dark, and a composition that brings the viewer painfully close to the event. She invested her subject with fierce intensity—the foreshortened body of the victim and the pinwheel arrangement of human limbs force the eye to focus on the gruesome action of the sword blade as it severs head from neck in a shower of blood.

Apocrypha, Book of Judith, 12:16–20; 13:1–10

Holofernes' heart was ravished with [Judith] and his passion was aroused, for he had been waiting for an opportunity to seduce her from the day he first saw her. [17]So Holofernes said to her, "Have a drink and be merry with us!" [18]Judith said, "I will gladly drink, my lord, because today is the greatest day in my whole life." [19]Then she took what her maid had prepared and ate and drank before him. [20]Holofernes was greatly pleased with her, and drank a great quantity of wine, much more than he had ever drunk in any one day since he was born.

[1]When evening came, his slaves quickly withdrew. . . . They went to bed, for they all were weary because the banquet had lasted so long. [2]But Judith was left alone in the tent, with Holofernes stretched out on his bed, for he was dead drunk. . . .

[4]Then Judith, standing beside his bed, said in her heart, "O Lord God of all might, look in this hour on the work of my hands for the exaltation of Jerusalem. [5]Now indeed is the time to help your heritage and to carry out my design to destroy the enemies who have risen up against us."

[6]She went up to the bedpost near Holofernes' head, and took down his sword that hung there. [7]She came close to his bed, took hold of the hair of his head, and said, "Give me strength today, O Lord God of Israel!" [8]Then she struck his neck twice with all her might, and cut off his head. [9]Next she rolled his body off the bed and pulled down the canopy from the posts. Soon afterward she went out and gave Holofernes' head to her maid, [10]who placed it in her food bag.

Gentileschi's favorite subjects were biblical heroines—she painted the Judith story some seven times. The violence she brought to these depictions may be said to reflect a personal sense of victimization: at the age of eighteen, she was raped by her drawing teacher and (during the sensational trial of her assailant) subjected to torture as a test of the truth of her testimony.

Baroque Sculpture in Italy

Gianlorenzo Bernini (1598–1680), Caravaggio's contemporary, brought the theatrical spirit of Baroque painting to Italian architecture and sculpture. A man of remarkable technical virtuosity, Bernini was the chief architect of seventeenth-century Rome, as well as one of its leading sculptors. Under Bernini's direction, Rome became the "city of fountains," a phenomenon facilitated by the early seventeenth-century revival of the old Roman aqueducts. Richly adorned with dolphins, mermaids, and tritons, the fountain—its waters dancing and sparkling in the shifting wind and light—was the favorite ornamental device of the Baroque era (Figure **20.11**).

Just as Caravaggio reshaped the tradition of Renaissance painting by way of pictorial illusionism, so Bernini challenged Renaissance sculptural tradition by investing it with a virtuosic naturalism and dramatic movement. He was determined, as he himself confessed, to "render the

Figure 20.11 GIANLORENZO BERNINI, *Fountain of the Four Rivers*, 1648–1651. Travertine and marble. Piazza Navona, Rome.

Figure 20.12 GIANLORENZO BERNINI,
David, 1623. Marble, 5 ft. 7 in.

marble flexible." His life-sized marble sculpture of David (Figure **20.12**) portrays this favorite biblical personality in a manner that recreates the very action of his assault on Goliath. In contrast with the languid and effeminate David of Donatello (see Figure 17.2) or the Classically posed hero of Michelangelo (see Figure 17.32), Bernini's David appears in mid-action, stretching the slingshot behind him as he prepares to launch the rock at his adversary: his torso twists vigorously at the waist, his face contorts with fierce determination, and his muscles strain with tense energy. The viewer, occupying the space "implied" by David's explosive action, is drawn unwittingly into the visual narrative.

Bernini's most important contribution to Baroque religious sculpture was his multimedia masterpiece *The Ecstasy of Saint Teresa* (see Figure 20.3), executed between 1645 and 1652 for the Cornaro Chapel of Santa Maria della Vittoria in Rome (Figure **20.13**). Bringing to life Saint Teresa's autobiographical description of divine seduction (see Reading 20.2), Bernini depicts the swooning saint with head sunk back and eyes half closed. A smiling angel, resembling a teenage cupid, gently lifts her bodice to withdraw the flaming arrow of divine love. Bold illusionism heightens the theatrical effect: the angel's marble draperies flutter and billow with tense energy, while Teresa's slack and heavy gown accents her ecstatic surrender. Teresa reclines on a marble cloud, which floats in heavenly space; the uncertain juxtaposition of the saint and the cloud below her suggests the experience of levitation described in her vision. Sweetness and eroticism dominate this extraordinary image.

But Bernini's conception goes beyond the medium of sculpture to achieve an unparalleled degree of theatrical illusionism. He situates Teresa beneath a colonnaded marble canopy from which gilded wooden rays appear to cast heaven's supernatural light. Real light entering through the glazed yellow panes of a concealed window above the chapel bathes the saint in a golden glow—an effect comparable to the spotlighting in a Caravaggio painting. From the ceiling of the chapel a host of angels both painted and sculpted in **stucco** (a light, pliable plaster) miraculously descends from the heavens. Agate and dark green marble walls provide a somber setting for the gleaming white and gold central image. On either side of the chapel, the members of the Cornaro family (executed in marble) behold Teresa's ecstasy from behind prayer desks that resemble theater boxes. These life-sized figures extend the supernatural space of the chapel and reinforce the viewer's role as witness to an actual event. It is no coincidence that Bernini's illusionistic tour de force appeared contemporaneously with the birth of opera in Italy, for both share the Baroque affection for dramatic expression on a monumental scale.

Figure 20.13 GIANLORENZO BERNINI, Cornaro Chapel, Santa Maria della Vittoria, Rome, 1642–1652. Bernini's *Ecstacy of Saint Teresa* (see Figure 20.3) appears beneath the marble canopy at the center of the chapel.

Baroque Architecture in Italy

The city of Rome carries the stamp of Bernini's flamboyant style. Commissioned to complete the *piazza* (the broad public space) in front of Saint Peter's Basilica, Bernini designed a trapezoidal space that opens out to a larger oval—the two shapes form, perhaps symbolically, a keyhole. Bernini's courtyard is bounded by a spectacular colonnade that incorporates 284 Doric columns (each 39 feet high) as well as ninety-six statues of saints (each 15 feet tall). In a manner consistent with the ecumenical breadth of Jesuit evangelism, the gigantic pincerlike arms of the colonnade reach out to embrace an area that can accommodate more than 250,000 people (Figure **20.14**)—a vast proscenium on which devotional activities of the Church of Rome are staged to this day. The Saint Peter's of Bernini's time was the locus of papal authority; then, as now, popes used the central balcony of the basilica to impart the traditional blessing, "Urbi et Orbi" ("To the city and to the world").

Figure 20.14 GIANLORENZO BERNINI, aerial view of colonnade and *piazza* of Saint Peter's, Rome, begun 1656. Travertine, longitudinal axis 800 ft. (approx.). Copper engraving by Giovanni Piranesi, 1750. The enormous *piazza* in front of the east façade of Saint Peter's can accommodate more than 250,000 people.

Figure 20.15 GIANLORENZO BERNINI, *Baldacchino* (canopy) ca. 1624–1633. Bronze with gilding, height 93 ft. 6 in. The four pillars of the *baldacchino* represent the columns of the Temple of Solomon, entwined by the Eucharist vines (symbolizing the New Testament). Decorative and symbolic details—vines, tassels, banners, and angelic figures—are all cast in bronze.

The proportions of Bernini's colonnade are symbolic of the Baroque preference for the grandiose, a preference equally apparent in the artist's spectacular setting for the Throne of Saint Peter and in the immense bronze canopy (*baldacchino*) he raised over the high altar of the basilica (Figure **20.15**).

As with Saint Peter's, Italian Baroque churches were designed to reflect the mystical and evangelical ideals of the Catholic Reformation. Il Gesù (the Church of Jesus) in Rome was the mother church of the Jesuit order and the model for hundreds of Counter-Reformation churches built throughout Europe and Latin America. Designed by Giacomo da Vignola (1507–1573), Il Gesù bears the typical features of the Baroque church interior: a broad Latin cross nave with domed crossing and deeply recessed chapels (Figure **20.16**). Lacking side aisles, the 60-foot-wide nave allowed a large congregation to assemble close enough to the high altar and the pulpit to see

Figure 20.16 GIACOMO DA VIGNOLA, interior of Il Gesù, Rome, 1568–1573. Length 240 ft. (approx.)

MAKING CONNECTIONS

The façade of Il Gesù, completed by Giacomo della Porta (Figure **20.17**) looks back to Alberti's two-story façade of Santa Maria Novella (Figure **20.18**). A comparison of the two provides insight into the differences between Renaissance and Baroque architectural styles. In contrast with the elegant linearity of the Florentine model, della Porta's façade is deeply carved, almost sculptural in its presence. Like a Caravaggio painting, it exploits dramatic contrasts of light and dark, of shallow and deep space. Pairs of pilasters and engaged Corinthian columns project from the surface, giving it weight and definition. Theatrical effect is heightened by niches bearing life-sized sculptures, by contrasting pediments (round and triangular), and by an ornate **cartouche** (oval tablet) over the central doorway and in the gable. While Alberti's façade was conceived in two dimensions, Il Gesù's was conceived in three. It inspired decades of imitation and architectural embellishment.

Figure 20.17 GIACOMO DA VIGNOLA and **GIACOMO DELLA PORTA**, façade of Il Gesù, Rome, ca. 1575–1584. Height 105 ft., width 115 ft.

Figure 20.18 LEON BATTISTA ALBERTI, façade of Santa Maria Novella, Florence, completed 1470. Width 117 ft. (approx.).

Figure 20.19 FRANCESCO BORROMINI, façade of San Carlo alle Quattro Fontane, Rome, 1667. Length 52 ft., width 34 ft., width of façade 38 ft.

the ceremony and hear the sermon. The wide nave also provided ample space for elaborate religious processions. Il Gesù's interior, with its magnificent altarpiece dedicated to Ignatius Loyola, exemplifies the Baroque inclination to synthesize various media, such as painted stucco, bronze, and precious stones, in the interest of achieving sumptuous and ornate effects.

The most daring of the Italian Baroque architects was Francesco Borromini (1599–1667). Borromini designed the small monastic church of San Carlo alle Quattro Fontane (Saint Charles at the Four Fountains; Figure **20.19**) to fit a narrow site at the intersection of two Roman streets. Rejecting the sobriety of Classical design, he combined convex and concave units to produce a sense of fluid, undulating movement. The façade consists of an assortment of deeply cut decorative elements: monumental Corinthian columns, a scrolled gable over the doorway, and life-sized angels that support a cartouche at the roofline. Borromini's aversion to the circle and the square—the "perfect" shapes of Renaissance architecture—extends to the interior of San Carlo, which is oval in plan. The dome, also oval, is lit by hidden windows that allow light to flood the church's interior. Carved with geometric motifs that diminish in size toward the apex, the shallow cupola appears to recede deep into space (Figure **20.20**). Such inventive illusionism, accented by dynamic spatial contrasts, characterized Roman Baroque church architecture at its best.

Baroque illusionism went further still, as artists turned houses of God into theaters for sacred drama. Such is the case with the church of Sant'Ignazio in Rome. Its barrel-vaulted ceiling bears a breathtaking *trompe l'oeil* vision of Saint Ignatius' apotheosis—his elevation to divine status (Figure **20.21**). A master of the techniques of linear perspective and dramatic foreshortening, the Jesuit architect and sculptor Andrea Pozzo (1642–1709) made the ceiling above the clerestory appear to open up, so that the viewer gazes "through" the roof into the heavens that receive the levitating body of the saint. Pozzo's cosmic rendering—one of the first of many illusionistic ceilings found in seventeenth- and eighteenth-century European churches and palaces—may be taken to reflect a new perception of the physical world inspired, in part, by European geographic exploration and discovery. Indeed, Pozzo underlines the global ambitions of Roman Catholic evangelism by adding at the four corners of the ceiling the allegorical figures of Asia, Africa, Europe, and America. The vast, illusionistic spatial fields of Italian Baroque frescoes also may be seen as a response to the new astronomy of the Scientific Revolution, which advanced

Figure 20.20 FRANCESCO BORROMINI, interior of dome, San Carlo alle Quattro Fontane, ca. 1638. Width 52 ft. (approx.). A dove, symbolizing the Holy Spirit, appears in the triangle at the apex of the dome, which is lit by partially hidden windows at its base.

a view of the universe as spatially infinite and dynamic rather than finite and static (see chapter 23). Whatever its inspiration, the spatial illusionism of Baroque painting and architecture gave apocalyptic grandeur to Catholic Reformation ideals.

Baroque Music

In an effort to rid sacred music of secular influence, the Council of Trent condemned the practice—common since the Late Middle Ages—of borrowing popular melodies for religious texts. It also banned complex polyphony that tended to obscure the sacred text: the function of music was to serve the text. The most notable representative of the Roman school of musical composition, Giovanni da Palestrina (1525–1594) took these recommendations as strict guidelines: his more than 100 polyphonic Masses and 450 motets feature clarity of text, skillful counterpoint, and regular rhythms. The *a cappella* lines of Palestrina's Pope Marcellus Mass flow with the smooth grace of a Mannerist painting. Often called "the music of mystic serenity," Palestrina's compositions embody the conservative and contemplative side of the Catholic Reformation.

In the religious compositions of Palestrina's Spanish contemporary Tomás Luis de Victoria (1548–1611), there is a brooding but fervent mystical intensity. Like El Greco, his colleague at the court of Philip II, Victoria brought passion and drama to religious themes. Recognizing that the Council of Trent had forbidden Palestrina to compose secular music, Victoria wrote not one note of secular song.

Figure 20.21 ANDREA POZZO,
Apotheosis of Saint Ignatius, 1691. Fresco.

The Genius of Gabrieli

At the turn of the sixteenth century, the opulent city of Venice was the center of European religious musical activity. Giovanni Gabrieli (1555–1612), principal organist at Saint Mark's Cathedral and one of the most influential composers of his time, ushered in a dramatic new style of **polychoral** and instrumental religious music. Abandoning the *a cappella* style favored in Rome, he composed works that brought together two or more choruses, solo instruments, and instrumental ensembles. The last often included trombones and **cornets** (an early type of trumpet) commonly used in Venetian ritual street processions (see Figure 17.37).

At Saint Mark's, where two organs were positioned on either side of the **chancel** (the space for clergy and choir surrounding the altar), Gabrieli stationed—on balconies high above the nave—instrumental groups and up to four separate voice choirs. The alternating bodies of sound, gloriously enhanced by the basilica's acoustics, produced a wide range of musical **dynamics** (degrees of loudness and softness), and rich, dramatic effects not unlike those achieved by the contrasts of light and shadow found in Baroque painting. Echo effects created by alternating voices and the use of unseen (offstage) voices achieved a degree of musical illusionism comparable to the pictorial illusionism of Baroque art. The motet "In Ecclesiis" illustrates the style of opposing or contrasting sonorities, known as *concertato*, that would become basic to the music of the Baroque era.

Gabrieli was among the first composers to specify an instrument for each part of a musical composition, a talent that earned him the title "the father of orchestration." He was also one of the first composers to write into his scores the words *piano* (soft) and *forte* (loud) to govern the dynamics of the piece. Gabrieli is also credited with advancing a system of major/minor tonality that came to dominate Western music. Based on the melodic and harmonic vocabulary of the major–minor key system, **tonality** refers to the arrangement of a musical composition around a central note, called the "tonic" or "home tone" (usually designated as the "key" of a given composition). A keynote or tonic can be built on any of the twelve tones of the **chromatic scale** (the seven white and five black keys of the piano keyboard). In Baroque music—as in most music written to this day—all the tones in the composition relate to the home tone. Tonality provided Baroque composers with a way of achieving dramatic focus in a piece of music—much in the way that light allowed Baroque painters to achieve dramatic focus in their compositions.

Monteverdi and the Birth of Opera

The first master of Baroque music-drama and the greatest Italian composer of the early seventeenth century was Claudio Monteverdi (1567–1643). Monteverdi served the court of Mantua until he became chapel master of Saint Mark's in Venice in 1621, a post he held for the rest of his life. During his long career, he wrote various kinds of religious music, as well as ballets, madrigals, and operas. Like Gabrieli, Monteverdi discarded the intimate dimensions of Renaissance chamber music and cultivated an expansive, dramatic style, marked by vivid contrasts of texture and color. His compositions reflect a typically Baroque effort to imbue music with a vocal expressiveness that reflected the emotional charge of poetry. "The [written] text," declared Monteverdi, "should be the master of the music, not the servant." Monteverdi linked "affections" or specific emotional states with appropriate sounds: anger, for instance, with the high voice register, moderation with the middle voice register, and humility with the low voice register. While the union of music and speech characterized almost all his religious music and smaller secular pieces, it was essential to the effectiveness of his operas.

Opera—a form of theater that combines music, drama, dance, and the visual arts—was the quintessential musical genre of the Baroque era. Born in Italy, it emerged out of Renaissance efforts to revive the music-drama of ancient Greek theater. While humanist composers had no idea what Greek music sounded like, they sought to imitate the ancient unity of music and poetry. The earliest performances of Western opera resembled the Renaissance masque, a form of musical entertainment that included dance and poetry, along with rich costumes and scenery. Baroque operas were more musically complex, however, and more dramatically cohesive than most Renaissance masques. The first opera house was built in Venice in 1637, and by 1700 Italy was home to seventeen more such houses, a measure of the vast popularity of the new genre. By the end of the seventeenth century, Italian courts and public theaters boasted all the essential features of the modern theater: the picture-frame stage, the horseshoe-shaped auditorium, and tiers of galleries or boxes (Figure **20.22**). Resplendent with life-sized sculptures and illusionistic frescoes, some of these opera houses are aesthetically indistinguishable from Italian Baroque church interiors (see Figures 20.13 and 20.16).

Orfeo, composed in 1607 for the duke of Mantua, was Monteverdi's first opera and one of the first full-length operas in music history. The **libretto** (literally, "little book") or text of the opera was written by Alessandro Striggio and based on a Classical theme—the descent of Orpheus, the Greek poet-musician, to Hades. Monteverdi's opera required an orchestra of more than three dozen instruments, including keyboard instruments, ten viols, three trombones, and four trumpets. The instrumentalists opened the performance with the **overture**, an orchestral introduction. They also accompanied the vocal line, which consisted of **arias** (elaborate solo songs or duets) alternating with **recitatives** (passages spoken or recited to sparse chordal accompaniment). The aria tended to develop a character's feelings or state of mind, while the recitative

See Music Listening Selections at end of chapter.

See Music Listening Selections at end of chapter.

Figure 20.22 PIETRO DOMENICO OLIVIER, *The Teatro Regio*, Turin, painting of the opening night, December 26, 1740. Oil on canvas, 4 ft. 2½ in. × 3 ft. 8⅛ in. Five tiers of boxes are fitted into the sides of the proscenium, one even perched over the semicircular pediment. Note the orchestra, without a conductor; the girls distributing refreshments; and the armed guard protecting against disorder.

served to narrate the action of the story or to heighten its dramatic effect.

Monteverdi believed that opera should convey the full range of human passions. To that end, he exploited the technique of word painting (the manipulation of music to convey the content of the text) popularized by the High Renaissance composer Josquin des Prez (see chapter 17). He engaged this device to reflect the emotional states of his characters, and to convey poetic images: a high tone for words like *stele* (stars) and *sole* (sun), a low tone for *morte* (death). He employed abrupt changes of key to emphasize shifts in mood and action. And he introduced such novel and expressive instrumental effects as **pizzicato**, the technique of plucking rather than bowing a stringed instrument. Integrating music, drama, and visual display, Italian opera became the ideal expression of the Baroque sensibility and the object of imitation throughout Western Europe.

LOOKING BACK

The Catholic Reformation

- In the wake of the Protestant Reformation, the Roman Catholic Church launched a reform movement known as the Catholic Reformation.
- Under the leadership of Ignatius Loyola, the Jesuit order became the most influential missionary society of early modern times. Members of the newly formed order worked as missionaries to win back those who had strayed from the "Mother Church."
- Between 1545 and 1563 the Council of Trent undertook papal and monastic reforms that eliminated corruption and restored Catholicism to many parts of Europe.

Catholicism's Global Reach

- Addressing the passions rather than the intellect, the arts broadcast the visionary message of Catholic reform to a vast audience that extended from Europe to Asia and the Americas.
- In China, where European traders were regarded as "ocean devils," Catholic missionaries developed a cordial relationship with the intellectual classes and succeeded in converting a number of Chinese scholars.
- Not all conversion attempts were successful. In 1624, Japan expelled almost all Western foreigners, after a wave of brutal persecutions of both European Christians and Japanese converts to Catholicism.
- Christian evangelism in the Americas proved to be far more successful.

In sixteenth-century Latin America, where Spanish political authority was largely unchallenged, Catholicism went hand in hand with colonization.

Literature and the Catholic Reformation

- The arts of the seventeenth century reflected the religious intensity of the Catholic Reformation. In literature, there appeared a new emphasis on heightened spirituality and on personal visionary experience acquired by way of the senses.
- The writings of Saint John of the Cross and Saint Teresa of Avila set the tone for a new, more mystical Catholicism.
- The English Catholic Richard Crashaw wrote rhapsodic lyrics that fused sensual and spiritual yearning.

The Visual Arts and the Catholic Reformation

- The Mannerist paintings of Parmigianino, Tintoretto, and El Greco mirrored the climate of insecurity in religiously divided and politically turbulent Europe.
- Mannerism anticipated the Baroque style by its use of figural distortions, irrational space, and bizarre colors, as well as its general disregard for the "rules" of Renaissance painting.

The Baroque Style

- The Baroque style brought new levels of naturalism and emotionalism to Western art. It featured dynamic contrasts of light and dark, an expanded sense of space, and the theatrical staging of the subject matter.

- Caravaggio and Gentileschi explored a variety of illusionistic techniques to draw the spectator into the space and action of the pictorial representation.
- Bernini challenged sculptural tradition by combining illusionism, naturalism, and implied movement. He brought a flamboyant style to the city of Rome, both in his fountain sculptures and in his designs for Italian Baroque churches.
- Italy's Catholic churches became ornate settings for the performance of ritual. Bernini's *The Ecstasy of Saint Teresa* and Pozzo's ceiling for the church of Sant'Ignazio achieved new heights of illusionistic theatricality.

Baroque Music

- Rome and Venice were fountainheads for Italian Baroque music. Palestrina's polyphonic Masses and motets emphasized both clarity of text and calm sublimity.
- Gabrieli's richly orchestrated polychoral compositions initiated the *concertato* style that would become a major feature of Baroque music.
- The most important development in seventeenth-century European music was the birth of opera as a genre. Borrowing themes from Classical mythology and history, Monteverdi integrated text and music to create the new art of music-drama.
- In its synthesis of all forms of performance—music, literature, and the visual arts—Italian opera became the supreme expression of the theatrical exuberance and vitality of the Baroque style.

Music Listening Selections

- Gabrieli, motet, "In Ecclesiis," excerpt, 1615.
- Monteverdi, *Orfeo*, aria: "In questo prato adorno," 1607.

Glossary

aria an elaborate solo song or duet, usually with instrumental accompaniment, performed as part of an opera or other dramatic musical composition

cartouche an oval tablet or medallion, usually containing an inscription or heraldic device

chancel the space for clergy and choir surrounding the altar in a church

chromatic scale a series of twelve tones represented by the seven white and five black keys of the piano keyboard; see also Glossary, chapter 5, "scale"

concertato (Italian, *concerto* = "opposing" or "competing") an early Baroque style in which voices or instruments of different rather than similar natures are used in an opposing or contrasting manner

cornet (French, *cornett*; German, *Kornett*; Spanish, *cururucho*) an early type of trumpet

dynamics the degree of loudness or softness in music

foreshortening a perspective device by which figures or objects appear to recede or project into space

libretto (Italian, "little book") the words of an opera or other textual musical composition

overture an instrumental introduction to a longer musical piece, such as an opera

piazza (Italian) a broad, open public space

pizzicato (Italian) the technique of plucking (with the fingers) rather than bowing a stringed instrument

polychoral music written for two or more choruses, performed both in turn and together

recitative a textual passage recited to sparse chordal accompaniment; a rhythmically free vocal style popular in seventeenth-century opera

stucco a light, pliable plaster made of gypsum, sand, water, and ground marble

tonality the use of a central note, called the tonic, around which all other tonal material of a composition is organized, and to which the music returns for a sense of rest and finality

Chapter

21

Absolute Power and the Aristocratic Style

ca. 1550–1750

"Virtue would not go nearly so far if vanity did not keep her company."
La Rochefoucauld

Figure 21.1 JULES HARDOUIN-MANSART, Salon de la Guerre (Drawing Room of War), Versailles. Length and width 33 ft. 8 in.; height 37 ft. 9 in. The stucco relief by Antoine Coysevox shows a larger-than-life equestrian image of Louis XIV. It is framed by panels of colored marble, mirrors, bronze and gilded sculptures, and ceiling frescoes painted by Le Brun.

The European state system had its beginnings in the early modern era. The first half of the seventeenth century witnessed the Thirty Years' War (1618–1648), a devastating religious conflict involving most of the European powers. In 1648, by the terms of the Treaty of Westphalia, the principle of national sovereignty was firmly established. By that principle, each European state would exercise independent and supreme authority over its own territories and inhabitants. In France a long tradition of absolutism prevailed. Absolutism made the claim that rulers obtained their power directly from God. During the seventeenth and well into the eighteenth century, divine-right kings exercised unlimited power within the individual nation-states of Europe. But the term "absolutism" is equally appropriate to describe the type of authority exercised in many of the states that prospered outside Europe. The rulers of the three great Muslim empires that flourished between ca. 1550 and 1750—Ottoman, Safavid, and Mogul—held power as divine-right monarchs, exercising unlimited control over vast territories. So too did the Ming and Qing emperors of China, and the Tokugawa rulers in Japan.

Absolute rulers maintained their authority by controlling a centralized bureaucracy and a standing army. They pursued economic policies designed to maximize the wealth of the state. In Western Europe, the mightiest of such potentates was the French king Louis XIV (1638–1715). During the nearly three-quarters of a century that he occupied the throne, he dictated the political, economic, and cultural policies of the country. Under his guidance, France assumed a position of political and military leadership in the West. By his hand, the grandeur of the Baroque style was invested with Classical features. The so-called Classical Baroque style would become the hallmark of French absolutism. It also impressed its stamp on the rest of Europe, and, somewhat later, on an emergent American culture. While absolutist states beyond the West did not share the Classical aspects of the Baroque style, their rulers manifested a typically Baroque taste for ornate theatricality and opulent grandeur. No less than in Louis' France, the aristocratic style that characterized the arts of absolutist regimes outside Europe was an expression of the majesty of the ruler and the wealth and power of the state.

The Aristocratic Style in Europe

Louis XIV and French Absolutism

Like the pharaohs of ancient Egypt and in the tradition of his medieval ancestors, Louis XIV governed France as the direct representative of God on earth. Neither the Church, nor the nobility, nor the will of his subjects limited his power. During his seventy-two years on the throne, the Estates General, France's representative assembly, was never once called into session. As absolute monarch, Louis brought France to a position of political and military preeminence among the European nation-states. He challenged the power of the feudal nobility and placed the Church under the authority of the state, thus centralizing all authority in his own hands. By exempting the nobility and upper middle class from taxation and offering them important positions at court, he turned potential opponents into supporters. Even if Louis never uttered the famous words attributed to him, "I am the state," he surely operated according to that precept. To distinguish his unrivaled authority, he took as his official insignia the image of the Classical sun god Apollo and referred to himself as *le roi soleil* ("the Sun King").

As ruler of France, Louis was one of the world's most influential figures. Under his leadership, the center of artistic patronage and productivity shifted from Italy to France. French culture in all its forms—from art and architecture to fashions and fine cuisine—came to dominate European tastes, a condition that prevailed until well into the early twentieth century. Although Louis was not an intellectual, he was shrewd and ambitious. He chose first-rate advisors to execute his policies and financed those

policies with money from taxes that fell primarily upon the backs of French peasants. Vast amounts of money were spent to make France the undisputed military leader of Western Europe. But Louis, who instinctively recognized the propaganda value of the arts, also used the French treasury to glorify himself and his office. His extravagances left France in a woeful financial condition, one that contributed to the outbreak of the revolution at the end of the eighteenth century. Incapable of foreseeing these circumstances, Louis cultivated the arts as an adjunct to majesty (see LOOKING INTO, Figure 21.2).

Versailles: Symbol of Royal Absolutism

Architecture played a vital role in the vocabulary of absolute power. The French royal family traditionally resided in Paris, at the palace known as the Louvre. But Louis, who detested Paris, moved his capital to a spot from which he might more directly control the nobility and keep them dependent upon him for honors and financial favors. Early in his career he commissioned a massive renovation of his father's hunting lodge at the village of Versailles, some

Science and Technology

1657	the first fountain pens are manufactured in Paris
1688	the French army introduces bayonets attached to muskets
1698	champagne is invented in France

Rigaud's *Portrait of Louis XIV*

This portrait of Louis XIV is the classic example of Baroque aristocratic portraiture (Figure **21.2**). Painted by Hyacinthe Rigaud (1659–1743) in 1701, the sixty-three-year-old monarch appears in his coronation garments, wearing the sword of state, and leaning on one of two royal scepters. The royal crown is seen on a cushion at the king's right. Louis wears ermine-lined coronation robes, silk stockings, a lace cravat, a well-manicured wig, and high-heeled shoes, which he himself designed to compensate for his short stature. All but the first of these were fashionable hallmarks of upper-class wealth in seventeenth and eighteenth-century France. Louis' mannered pose, which harks back to Classical models, reflects self-conscious pride in status. Symbolic devices enhance the themes of authority and regality: satin curtains frame the king theatrically, and a lone column compositionally and metaphorically underscores his fortitude. Such devices would become customary in European and American portraits of the eighteenth century (see Figures 22.2 and 26.23).

Figure 21.2 HYACINTHE RIGAUD, *Portrait of Louis XIV*, 1701. Oil on canvas, 9 ft. 1 in. × 6 ft. 4 in.

crown, and sword of state symbolizing royal authority

lone column signifying fortitude

two royal scepters: staff with *fleur-de-lis* ("lilyflower") and *main de justice* ("hand of justice"), emblems of authority

fleur-de-lis, heraldic symbol of the French monarchy

brocaded curtains theatrically framing the king and the royal throne

ermine-lined coronation robe

high-heeled shoes designed by Louis XIV to enhance his height

silk stockings, lace cravat, and wig: hallmarks of upperclass wealth

12 miles from Paris. It took 36,000 workers and nearly twenty years to build Versailles, but, in 1682, the French court finally established itself in the apartments of this magnificent unfortified *château* (castle). More than a royal residence, Versailles was—in its size and splendor—the symbol of Louis' supremacy over the landed aristocracy, the provincial governments, the urban councils, and the Estates General.

The wooded site that constituted the village of Versailles, almost half the size of Paris, was connected to the old capital by a grand boulevard that (following the path of the sun) ran from the king's bedroom—where most state business was transacted—to the Avenue de Paris. Even a cursory examination of the plan of Versailles, laid out by the French architect Louis Le Vau (1612–1670), reveals esteem for the rules of symmetry, clarity, and geometric regularity (Figure **21.3**). These principles, in combination with a taste for spatial grandeur, dramatic contrast, and theatrical display, were the distinguishing features of the Classical Baroque style.

Shaped like a winged horseshoe, the almost 2000-foot-long palace—best viewed in its entirety from the air—was the focus of an immense complex of parks, lakes, and forest (Figure **21.4**). Its central building was designed by Le Vau, while the two additional wings were added by Jules Hardouin-Mansart (1646–1708). Three levels of vertically

aligned windows march across the palace façade like soldiers in a formal procession (Figure **21.5**). Porches bearing free-standing Corinthian columns accent the second level, and ornamental statues at the roofline help to relieve the monotonous horizontality of the roofline. In its total effect, the palace is dignified and commanding, a synthesis of Classical and Palladian elements. Its calm nobility provides a striking contrast to the robust theatricality of most Italian Baroque structures (see Figures 20.17 and 20.19).

The grandeur and majesty of Versailles made it the model for hundreds of palace-estates and city planning projects in both Europe and America for the following two centuries. Le Vau's façade also became the prototype for the remodeled royal palace in Paris, the Louvre. Designed by Claude Perrault (1613–1688), the east façade of the Louvre echoes the basic Classical Baroque features of Louis' residence at Versailles: strong rectilinear organization, paired Corinthian columns, and a gabled entrance that provides dramatic focus (Figure **21.6**).

The palace at Versailles housed Louis' family, his royal mistresses (one of whom bore him nine children), and hundreds of members of the French nobility whose presence was politically useful to Louis. Life at the court of the Sun King was both formal and public—a small army of servants, courtiers, ministers, and pet animals constantly surrounded Louis. All behavior was dictated by

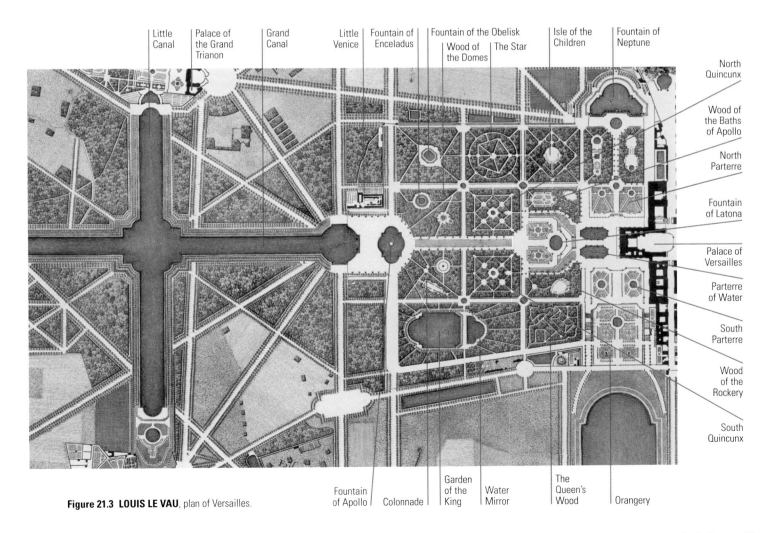

Figure 21.3 LOUIS LE VAU, plan of Versailles.

Figure 21.4 **ISIDORE-LAURENT DEROY**, the park and palace of Versailles, France, nineteenth century. Lithograph, 8 1/16 × 11 3/4 in.

Figure 21.5 **LOUIS LE VAU** and **JULES HARDOUIN-MANSART**, Parterre du Midi, Palace of Versailles, 1669–1685.

Figure 21.6 CLAUDE PERRAULT, LOUIS LE VAU, and **CHARLES LE BRUN**, east façade of the Louvre, Paris, 1667–1670. Louis XIV had originally commissioned Bernini to design the new Louvre. However, upon finding Bernini's design too ornate, he transferred the commission to his own architects, thus establishing the Classical Baroque as a major feature of the aristocratic style.

protocol. Rank at court determined where one sat at the dinner table and whether one or both panels of Versailles' "French doors" were to be opened upon entering.

Flanking the palace were barracks for honor guards, lodgings for more than 1500 servants, kennels, greenhouses, and an orangery with over 2000 orange trees. More than 7 square miles of gardens were designed by André Le Nôtre with the same compelling sense of order that Le Vau brought to the architecture. The great park featured an array of hedges clipped into geometric shapes (see Figure 21.5), sparkling fountains (that favorite of all Baroque mechanical devices), artificial lakes (Figure **21.7**), grottoes, a zoo, theaters, and outdoor "rooms" for private gatherings and clandestine meetings. When in bloom, the gardens—some planted with over four million tulip bulbs, which Louis imported annually from Holland—were a

Figure 21.7 Ornamental Lake and Fountain of Latona, Versailles. A bronze sculpture of the Roman river god adorns the lake.

spectacular sight. They embellished the long walkways that radiate from the central building. On the garden side of the palace, artificial pools reflected sculptures whose subject matter glorified the majesty of the king (see Figure 21.7). Itself a kind of outdoor theater, the royal palace provided the ideal backdrop for the ballets, operas, and plays that were regular features of court life (Figure **21.8**).

If the exterior of Versailles symbolized royal grandeur, the interior publicized princely self-indulgence (Figure **21.9**). Although now shorn of many of their original furnishings, Versailles' sumptuous *salons* (drawing rooms) still testify to Louis' success at cultivating French trades in such luxury items as crafted silver, clocks, lace, brocades, porcelain, and fine glass. During the seventeenth century, the silk industry reached its peak, French carpets competed with those of Turkey and Persia, the art of **marquetry** (inlaid wood) rivaled that of Italy, and the tapestries

produced at the Gobelins factory in Paris outclassed those woven in Flanders. Versailles' *salons* were adorned with illusionistic frescoes, gilded stucco moldings, crystal chandeliers, and huge, ornate mirrors. The rooms housed some of the most lavish *objets d'art* (art objects) in Western history, all of which, it is sobering to recall, were enjoyed at a time when the peasant majority of the French population lived in one-room, thatch-roofed houses filled with coarse wooden furniture. Equally sobering is the fact that, despite its splendor, the palace lacked any kind of indoor plumbing. Servants carried out the slops, but the unpleasant odor of human waste was difficult to mask, even with the finest French perfumes.

Each of Versailles' rooms illustrates a specific theme: the Salon de Venus was decorated by Charles Le Brun (1619–1690) with ceiling paintings portraying the influence of love on various kings in history. In the Salon de la

Figure 21.8 JEAN LE PAUTRE, A performance of Lully's *Alceste*, Marble Court, Versailles, 1674. Engraving, 12 × 16⅕ in.

Figure 21.9 Apartment of the Queen/Salon of the Nobles, Versailles. Length 31 ft., width 32 ft., height 24 ft. 8 in.

Guerre (Drawing Room of War) an idealized, equestrian Louis, carved in low-relief marble, is shown receiving the victor's crown (see Figure 21.1)—although, in fact, Louis himself rarely took part in combat. The most splendid interior space, however, is the 240-foot-long Galerie des Glaces (Hall of Mirrors; Figure **21.10**), which once connected the royal apartments with the chapel. Embellished with glorious frescoes, marble pilasters, and gilded bronze capitals, and furnished with ornate candelabra and bejeweled trees (the latter have since disappeared), the hall features a wall of seventeen mirrored arcades that face an equal number of high-arched windows opening onto the garden. Framing this opulent royal passageway, mirrors and windows set up a brilliant counterpoint of image and reflection. Mirrors were to Versailles what fountains were to Rome: vehicles for the theatrical display of changing light in unbounded space.

Louis as Patron of the Arts

At the center of his court, Louis was the arbiter of fashion and manners. Within his dining *salons*, linen napkins came into use, forks replaced fingers for eating, and elaborate dishes were served to suit the royal palate. Graced with an eye for beauty and a passion for aggrandizement, Louis increased the number of paintings in the French royal collection from the 200 he inherited upon his accession to the throne to the 2000 he left at his death. These

paintings formed the basis of the permanent collection at the Louvre, now a world-renowned art museum.

On a grander scale, Louis dictated the standards for all forms of artistic production. Following in the tradition of his father, Louis XIII (1601–1643), who had instituted the French Royal Academy of Language and Literature in 1635, he created and subsidized government-sponsored institutions in the arts, appointing his personal favorites to oversee each. In 1648, at the age of ten, Louis founded the Academy of Painting and Sculpture; in 1661 he established the Academy of Dance; in 1666, the Academy of Sciences; in 1669, the Academy of Music; and in 1671, the Academy of Architecture. The creation of the academies was a symptom of royal efforts to fix standards, but Louis also had something more personal in mind: he is said to have told a group of academicians, "Gentlemen, I entrust to you the most precious thing on earth—my fame." His trust was well placed, for the academies, which brought glory to the king, also set standards that would govern the arts for at least two centuries. These standards were inspired by the legacy of ancient Greece and Rome. Thus *Neoclassicism*—the revival of Classical style and subject matter—became the accepted style of academic art.

A typical example of the Neoclassical style in sculpture is seen in the work of the French academician François Girardon (1628–1715). Girardon drew on Hellenistic models for the ideally proportioned statues that he arranged

Figure 21.10 JULES HARDOUIN-MANSART and **CHARLES LE BRUN**, Galerie des Glaces (Hall of Mirrors), Versailles, ca. 1680. Length 240 ft. The opulence of Louis' court is exemplified in this hall, which functioned as a reception space for official state occasions. Thirty scenes of Louis' achievements were painted by Le Brun's studio on canvas and then attached to the ceiling. A $16 million, three-year renovation of the hall was completed in 2007.

in graceful tableaux for the gardens of Versailles. In one such tableau, Girardon's Neoclassical nymphs are seen entertaining the sun god Apollo—an obvious reference to Louis as *le roi soleil* (Figure **21.11**).

Academic Art: Poussin and Lorrain

Girardon's compositions owed much to the paintings of the leading exponent of French academic art, Nicolas Poussin (1594–1665). Poussin spent most of his life in Rome, absorbing the heritage of the Classical and Renaissance past. He revered the High Renaissance master Raphael as the leading proponent of the Classical style; and, like most Neoclassicists, he shared Raphael's esteem for lofty subjects drawn from Greco-Roman mythology and Christian legend. In an influential treatise on painting, Poussin formalized the rules that would govern academic art for centuries. Enshrined in the works of Raphael and expounded in the aesthetic theories of seventeenth-century Italian painters, these rules would come to characterize the Grand

Manner in Western art: artists should choose only serious and elevated subjects (such as battles, heroic actions, and miraculous events) drawn from Classical or Christian history, and reject crude, bizarre, and ordinary subject matter. As to the manner of representation, artists should make the physical action suit the mood of the narrative, avoiding, at all cost, the gross aspects of ordinary existence and any type of exaggeration. They should present their subjects clearly and evenly in harmonious compositions that were free of irrelevant and sordid details. Restraint, moderation, and decorum—that is, propriety and good taste—should govern all aspects of pictorial representation.

Poussin's paintings were faithful to the dictates of the academic style. His *Arcadian Shepherds*, completed in 1639, transports us to the idyllic region in ancient Greece known as Arcadia, a place where men and women were said to live in perfect harmony with nature (Figure **21.12**). Here, three shepherds have come upon an ancient tomb, a symbol of death; on the right, the stately muse of history meditates

Figure 21.11 FRANÇOIS GIRARDON, *Apollo Attended by the Nymphs*, ca. 1666–1672. Marble, life-sized. Louis XIV entrusted this sculptor with important commissions for the gardens of Versailles. Modeling the central figure on the famous Hellenistic *Apollo Belvedere* (see Figures 5.32 and 26.16), Girardon contributed to the propaganda that linked the Greek sun god with the French king.

Figure 21.12 NICOLAS POUSSIN, *Arcadian Shepherds*, 1638–1639. Oil on canvas, 33½ × 47⅝ in. Poussin's Classical compositions were an inspiration to the late nineteenth-century artist Paul Cézanne, who had a copy of this painting in his study.

Figure 21.13 CLAUDE LORRAIN (CLAUDE GELLÉE), *The Marriage of Isaac and Rebekah (The Mill)*, 1642. Oil on canvas, 4 ft. 11 in. × 6 ft. 5 in. The protagonists in the biblical story are barely visible in this idealized landscape. Featuring shepherds and their flocks, such scenes were often called "elevated pastorals."

upon the tomb's inscription, "*Et in Arcadia Ego*" ("I [Death] also dwell in Arcadia")—that is, death reigns even in this most perfect of places. Poussin's moral allegory, at once a pastoral elegy and a *memento mori*, instructs us that death is universal. Cool, bright colors and even lighting enhance the elegiac mood, while sharp contours and the sure use of line provide absolute clarity of design. But the real power of the painting lies in its rigorous composition. Poussin arrived at this composition by arranging and rearranging miniature wax models of his figures within a small rectangular box. He then posed these figures—statuesque, heroically proportioned, and idealized—so that their gestures served to narrate the story. All the elements in the painting, from the muse's feet (which parallel the horizontal picture plane) to the trees in the landscape and at the right edge of the tomb (which parallel the vertical picture plane) contribute to the geometry of the composition.

Despite the grand theatricality of Poussin's paintings, order dominates spontaneity. Both in form and in content, they are intellectual; they appeal to the mind rather than to the senses. In contrast to such Italian Baroque painters as Caravaggio, whose works he detested, Poussin advanced the aesthetics of Neoclassicism.

Poussin and his contemporary Claude Gellée (1600–1682), known as Claude Lorrain, were responsible for popularizing the genre known as the "ideal landscape," a landscape painted in the high-minded, idealized style usually found in traditional moral subjects. For such paintings, academic artists made careful renderings of the countryside around Rome. They then returned to the studio to assemble and combine the contents of their sketches according to the Classical ideals of balance and clarity. Lorrain's landscapes, characterized by haunting qualities of light, were tranquil settings for lofty mythological or biblical subjects (Figure **21.13**). Unlike the Dutch landscape painters, who rendered nature with forthright Realism (see Figure 23.11), academic artists imposed a preconceived, rationalized order upon the natural world.

Velázquez and Rubens

The aristocratic Baroque style was initiated in France, but it came to flourish in many other European courts. In seventeenth-century Spain, Diego Velázquez (1599–1660), court painter to King Philip IV (1605–1665), was that country's most prestigious artist. Velázquez excelled at modeling forms so that they convey the powerful presence of real objects in atmospheric space. For the Spanish court, Velázquez painted a variety of Classical and Christian subjects, but his greatest enterprise was the life-size group portrait known as *Las Meninas* (*The Maids of Honor*, Figure **21.14**).

In this painting, Velázquez depicted himself at his easel, alongside the members of the royal court: the *infanta* (the five-year-old daughter of the king), her maids of honor, her dwarf, a nun and priest, a mastiff hound, and the royal escorts. In the background is a mirror that reflects the images of the king and queen of Spain—presumably the subjects of the large canvas Velázquez is painting in the left foreground. Superficially, this is a group portrait of the kind commissioned by wealthy patrons since the

Figure 21.14 DIEGO VELÁZQUEZ, *Las Meninas* (*The Maids of Honor*), 1656. Oil on canvas, 10 ft. 5 in. × 9 ft. This unusual aristocratic group portrait depicts the royal family of Spain: King Philip IV and Queen Mariana are shown reflected in the mirror at the back of the room, while their daughter the Infanta Margarita stands at the center, surrounded by two maids of honor, a dwarf, and other court figures.

Renaissance. The addition of a mirror that reflects the presence of two figures outside the painting is, indeed, reminiscent of Jan van Eyck's Arnolfini double portrait (see Figure 19.6). However, Velázquez's composition is far more complex, for, although the painting is a record of the royal household (its original title was *Family of Philip IV*), it departs from traditional group portraits by minimizing its purported subject: the king and queen. Almost all the subjects in the painting, including the painter himself, are shown gazing at the royal couple, who must be standing outside the picture space in the very spot occupied by the viewer. Velázquez has expanded the spatial field, inviting the beholder into the picture space as if he or she were, in fact, the subject of the painting. His witty invention or "conceit" provokes a visual dialogue between artist and patron, and between the perceived and the perceiver.

A contemporary of Velázquez, the internationally renowned Flemish painter Peter Paul Rubens (1577–1640) established his reputation in the courts of Europe. Fluent in six languages, he traveled widely as a diplomat and art dealer for royal patrons in Italy, England, and France. He also led a large studio workshop that trained scores of assistants to help fulfill his many commissions—a total lifetime production of some 1800 paintings. For the Luxembourg Palace of Paris, Rubens and his studio executed twenty-one monumental canvases that glorified Marie de' Medici, Louis XIV's grandmother, and her late husband, King Henry IV of France. Like Poussin, Rubens studied in Italy and was familiar with both Classical and High Renaissance art. Rubens deeply admired the flamboyant colorists Titian and Tintoretto, and he developed a style that, in contrast with Poussin's, was painterly in its brushwork and dynamic in composition.

One of Rubens' most memorable canvases, the *Rape of the Daughters of Leucippus* (Figure **21.15**), depicts the abduction of two mortal women by the mythic heroes Castor and Pollux. Rubens' conception of the Classical story explodes with vigor: pressing against the picture plane are the fleshy bodies of the nude maidens, their limbs arranged in the pattern of a slowly revolving pinwheel. The masterful brushstrokes exploit sensuous contrasts of luminous pink flesh, burnished armor, gleaming satins, and dense horsehide. Probably commissioned to commemorate the double marriage of Louis XIII of France to a Spanish princess and Philip IV of Spain to a French princess (and, thus, to celebrate the diplomatic alliance of France and

Figure 21.15 PETER PAUL RUBENS, *Rape of the Daughters of Leucippus*, ca. 1618. Oil on canvas, 7 ft. 3 in. × 6 ft. 10 in. The twin sons of Zeus and Leda, Castor and Pollux (called the "Dioscuri," or "Sons of Zeus"), were popular heroes revered as brave horsemen by both the Greeks and the Romans. Their abduction of two women betrothed to their cousins provoked a battle in which Castor was killed. When his brother asked Zeus to let him die as well, Zeus granted them immortality.

Spain), the painting carries a subtext of (male) power over (female) privilege—and, by extension, of political absolutism. Images of subjugation by force, whether in the form of lion hunts (as in ancient Assyrian reliefs; see chapter 1) or in paintings and sculptures depicting mythological stories of rape, were metaphors for the sovereign authority of the ruler over his subjects, hence a veiled expression of political absolutism.

The Aristocratic Portrait

The Baroque was the great age of aristocratic portraiture. Commissioned by the hundreds by Louis XIV and the members of his court, aristocratic portraits differ dramatically from those by Dürer and Holbein (see chapter 19). Whereas these Renaissance artists investigated the personalities of their sitters, bringing to their likenesses a combination of psychological intimacy and forthrightness, most Baroque artists, such as Hyacinthe Rigaud (see Figure 21.2) were concerned primarily with outward appearance.

In England, the most accomplished advocate of the aristocratic portrait was the Flemish master Anthony van Dyck (1599–1641). Born in Antwerp, van Dyck had been an assistant to Rubens and may have worked with him on the *Rape of the Daughters of Leucippus.* Unwilling to compete with Rubens, he moved to Genoa and then to London, where he became court painter to King Charles I of England (1600–1649). Van Dyck's many commissioned portraits of European nobility are striking for their polished elegance and poise, features that are especially evident in his equestrian portrait of Charles I (see Figure 22.2). Here, van Dyck shows the king, who was actually short and undistinguished-looking, as handsome and regal. The combination of fluid composition and naturalistic detail, and the shimmering vitality of the brushwork, make this one of the most memorable examples of aristocratic Baroque portraiture.

Music and Dance at the Court of Louis XIV

The court at Versailles was the setting for an extraordinary outpouring of music, theater, and dance. To provide musical entertainments for state dinners, balls, and operatic performances, Louis established a permanent orchestra, the first in European history. Its director, the Italian-born (but French-educated) Jean-Baptiste Lully (1632–1687), also ran the French Academy of Music. Often called the "father of French opera," Lully oversaw all phases of musical performance, from writing scores and conducting the orchestra to training the chorus and staging operatic productions. Many of Lully's operas were based on themes from Classical mythology. Their semidivine heroes, prototypes of the king himself, flattered Louis' image as ruler.

Lully's operas shared the pomp and splendor of Le Brun's frescoes, the strict clarity of Poussin's paintings, and the formal correctness of Classical drama. Although Lully's compositions were generally lacking in spontaneity and warmth of feeling, they were faithful to the Neoclassical unity of words and music. Lully modified the music of

the recitative to follow precisely and with great clarity the inflections of the spoken word. He also introduced to opera the "French overture," an instrumental form that featured contrasts between a slow first part in homophonic texture and a fast, contrapuntal second part. Under Lully's leadership, French opera also developed its most characteristic feature: the inclusion of formal dance.

At the court of Louis XIV, dancing and fencing were the touchstones of aristocratic grace. All members of the upper class were expected to perform the basic court dances, including the very popular *minuet,* and the courtier who could not dance was judged rude and inept. Like his father, who had commissioned and participated in extravagantly expensive ballets, Louis XIV was a superb dancer. Dressed as the sun, he danced the lead in the performance of the *Ballet de la Nuit* in 1653 (Figure **21.16**). Of lasting significance was Louis' contribution to the birth of professional dance and the transformation of court dance into an independent artform. During the late seventeenth century, French ballet masters of the Royal Academy of Dance established rules for the five basic positions that have become the basis of classical dance. Fundamental ballet postures involving graceful movement were borrowed from the sport

Figure 21.16 King Louis XIV as the sun in the 1653 *Ballet de la Nuit.* Pen, wash, and gouache on paper, 10¼ × 6½ in.

of fencing. Clarity, balance, and proportion, along with studied technique—elements characteristic of Classicism in general—became the ideals of the classical ballet.

By 1685, female dancers were permitted to join the previously all-male French dance ensembles in staged performances. And in 1700, Raoul Auget Feuillet published a system of abstract symbols for recording specific dance steps and movements, thus facilitating the art of **choreography**. Ballet, itself a metaphor for the strict etiquette and ceremonial grace of court life, enriched all aspects of the French theater. However, since classical ballet demanded a rigorous attention to proper form, it soon became too specialized for any but professionals to perform, and so there developed the gap between performer and audience that exists to this day in the art of dance.

Seventeenth-Century French Literature

In literature, as with most forms of artistic expression in seventeenth-century France, Neoclassical precepts of form and content held sway. French writers addressed questions of human dignity and morality in a language that was clear, polished, and precise. Their prose is marked by refinement, good taste, and the concentrated presentation of ideas.

One literary genre that typified the Neoclassical spirit was the **maxim**. A maxim is a short, concise, and often witty saying, usually drawn from experience and offering some practical advice. Witty sayings that distilled wisdom into a few words were popular in many cultures, including those of the Hebrews, the Greeks, and the Africans. But in seventeenth-century France, the cautionary or moralizing aphorism was exalted as the ideal means of teaching good sense and decorum. Terse and lean, the maxim exalted precision of language and thought. France's greatest maxim writer was François de La Rochefoucauld (1613–1680), a nobleman who had participated in a revolt against Louis XIV early in his reign. Withdrawing from court society, La Rochefoucauld wrote with a cynicism that reflected his conviction that self-interest, hypocrisy, and greed motivated the behavior of most human beings—including and especially the aristocrats of his day. As the following maxims illustrate, however, La Rochefoucauld's insights into human behavior apply equally well to individuals of all social classes and to any age.

READING 21.1 From La Rochefoucauld's *Maxims* (1664)

Truth does less good in the world than its appearances do harm.

Love of justice in most men is only a fear of encountering injustice.

We often do good that we may do harm with impunity.

As it is the mark of great minds to convey much in few words, so small minds are skilled at talking at length and saying little.

Virtue would not go nearly so far if vanity did not keep her company.

We confess to small faults to create the impression that we have no great ones.

To be rational is not to use reason by chance, but to recognize it, distinguish it, appreciate it.

We all have strength enough to endure the misfortunes of others.

We are never so happy or so unhappy as we imagine we are.

Our minds are lazier than our bodies.

Quarrels would not last long were the wrong all on one side.

Q What is the effect of brevity in these maxims?

Q Which of these maxims might apply to the characters in Reading 21.2 (Molière)?

Like La Rochefoucauld's maxims, but on a larger scale, French drama reflected Neoclassical restraint, cool objectivity, and common sense. The leading French tragedian of the seventeenth century, Jean Racine (1639–1699), wrote plays that treated high-minded themes in an elevated language. Racine added to Aristotle's unities of action and time (see chapter 4) a strict unity of place, thus manifesting his abiding commitment to verisimilitude. In the play *Phèdre* (1677), itself based on Greek models, Racine explored the conflict between human passions (Phaedra's "unnatural" infatuation with her stepson) and human reason (Phaedra's sense of duty as the wife of Theseus, king of Athens). As do all Racine's tragedies, *Phèdre* illustrates the disastrous consequences of emotional indulgence—a weakness especially peculiar to Racine's female characters. Indeed, while Racine created some of the most dramatic female roles in Neoclassical theater, he usually pictured women as weak, irrational, and cruel.

Molière's Human Comedy

Jean-Baptiste Poquelin (1622–1673), whose stage name was Molière, was France's leading comic dramatist. The son of a wealthy upholsterer, he abandoned a career in law in favor of acting and writing plays. He learned much from the *commedia dell'arte*, a form of improvised Italian street theater that depended on buffoonery, slapstick humor, and pantomime. Molière's plays involve simple story lines that bring to life the comic foibles of such stock characters as the miser, the hypochondriac, the hypocrite, the misanthrope, and the would-be gentleman. The last of these is the subject of one of Molière's last plays, *Le Bourgeois Gentilhomme* (*The Tradesman Turned Gentleman*). The plot involves a wealthy tradesman (Monsieur Jourdain) who, aspiring to nobility, hires a variety of tutors to school him in the trappings of upper-class respectability. The play's fabric of deceit and self-deception is complicated by Jourdain's refusal to accept his daughter's choice of partner, the handsome but poor Cléonte. Only after Cléonte appears disguised as the son of the Grand Turk does the unwitting merchant bless the betrothal.

Essentially a farce or comedy of manners, Molière's play (like La Rochefoucauld's maxims) holds up to ridicule the fundamental flaws of human behavior, which might be corrected by applying the Classical norms of reason and moderation. By contrasting incidents of hypocrisy, pomposity, and greed with the solid good sense demonstrated, for instance, by Mr. Jourdain's wife, Molière probes the excesses of passion and vanity that enfeeble human dignity. *Le Bourgeois Gentilhomme* was designed as a **comédie-ballet**, a dramatic performance that incorporated interludes of song and dance (in a manner similar to modern musical comedy). Lully provided the music, choreographed the ballet, and directed the entire production, which, like many other of Molière's plays, was well received by the king and his court, a court that lavishly and regularly received the ambassadors of "exotic" countries, such as Turkey.

But even beyond Versailles, Molière's hilarious comedy had wide appeal. French aristocrats, convinced that they were above imitation, embraced the play. So did upper-middle-class patrons who, while claiming an increasingly prominent place in the social order, refused to see themselves as merchants longing to be aristocrats. Women found themselves endowed in Molière's play with confidence and guile, while servants discovered themselves invested with admirable common sense. The comedy, for all its farce, reflected the emerging class structure of early modern European society, with its firmly drawn lines between sexes and classes, its ambitions and high expectations. Yet, for all its value as a mirror of a particular time and place, *Le Bourgeois Gentilhomme* is universal and timeless. The following scenes offer a representative sampling of Molière's rollicking exposition of human nature.

READING 21.2 From Molière's *Le Bourgeois Gentilhomme* (1670)

The scene is at Paris

ACT I
Overture, played by a full orchestra; in the middle of the stage the Music-Master's Scholar, seated at a table, is composing the air for a serenade which Mr. Jourdain has ordered.

Scene I
Music-Master, Dancing-Master, Three Singers, Two Violinists, Four Dancers

Music-Master (*To the singers*): Here, step inside, and wait   1
until he comes.
Dancing-Master (*To the dancers*): And you too, this way.
Music-Master (*To his scholar*): Is it finished?
Scholar: Yes.
Music-Master: Let's see . . . That's good.
Dancing-Master: Is it something new?
Music-Master: Yes, 'tis the air for a serenade which I have
had him compose, while waiting for our gentleman to wake up.
Dancing-Master: May I see it?   10
Music-Master: You shall hear it, with the words, when he

comes. He won't be long.
Dancing-Master: You and I have no lack of occupation now.
Music-Master: That's true. We have found a man here who is just what we both needed. He's a nice little source of income for us, this Mr. Jourdain, with his visions of nobility and gallantry that he has got into his noddle. And 'twould be a fine thing for your dancing and my music if everybody were like him.
Dancing-Master: No, no, not quite; I could wish, for his   20
sake, that he had some true understanding of the good things we bring him.
Music-Master: 'Tis true he understands them ill, but he pays for them well; and that is what the arts need most nowadays.
Dancing-Master: For my part, I'll own, I must be fed somewhat on fame. I am sensitive to applause, and I feel that in all the fine arts 'tis a grievous torture to show one's talents before fools, and to endure the barbarous judgments of a dunce upon our compositions. There's great pleasure, I tell you,   30
in working for people who are capable of feeling the refinements of art, who know how to give a flattering reception to the beauties of your work, and recompense your toil by titillating praise. Yes, the most agreeable reward possible for what we do, is to see it understood, to see it caressed by applause that honors us. Nothing else, methinks, can pay us so well for all our labors; and enlightened praise gives exquisite delight.
Music-Master: I grant you that, and I relish it as you do. There is surely nothing more gratifying than such praise as you   40
speak of; but man cannot live on applause. Mere praise won't buy you an estate; it takes something more solid. And the best way to praise, is to praise with open hands. Our fellow, to be sure, is a man of little wit, who discourses at random about anything and everything, and never applauds but at the wrong time. But his money sets right the errors of his mind; there is judgment in his purse; his praises pass current; and this ignorant shopkeeper is worth more to us, as you very well see, than the enlightened lord who introduced us to his house.
Dancing-Master: There is some truth in what you say; but   50
methinks you set too much store by money; and self-interest is something so base that no gentleman should ever show a leaning towards it.
Music-Master: Yet I haven't seen you refuse the money our fellow offers you.
Dancing-Master: Certainly not; but neither do I find therein all my happiness; and I could still wish that with his wealth he had good taste to boot.
Music-Master: I could wish so too; and 'tis to that end that we are both working, as best we may. But in case, he gives   60
us the means to make ourselves known in the world; he shall pay for others, and others shall praise for him.
Dancing-Master: Here he comes.

[Act I, Scene II: Mr. Jourdain converses with his music- and dancing-masters, who dispute as to which is the more important art: music or dance. A dialogue in music, written by the music-master, follows, then a ballet choreographed by the dancing-master.]

Act II, Scene I: Mr. Jourdain dances the minuet for the dancing-master, and then learns how to make a "proper" bow.]

ACT II, Scene II

Mr. Jourdain, Music-Master, Dancing-Master, Lackey

Lackey: Sir, here is your fencing-master.   1

Mr. Jourdain: Tell him to come in and give me my lesson here. (*To the music-master and dancing-master*) I want you to see me perform.

Scene III

Mr. Jourdain, Fencing-Master, Music-Master, Dancing-Master, a Lackey with two foils

Fencing-Master (*Taking the two foils from the lackey and giving one of them to Mr. Jourdain*): Now, sir, your salute. The body erect. The weight slightly on the left thigh. The legs not so far apart. The feet in line. The wrist in line with the thigh. The point of your sword in line with your shoulder. The arm not quite so far extended. The left hand on a level   10 with the eye. The left shoulder farther back. Head up. A bold look. Advance. The body steady. Engage my sword in quart[1] and finish the thrust. One, two. Recover. Again, your feet firm. One, two. Retreat. When you thrust, sir, your sword must move first, and your body be held well back, and sideways. One, two. Now, engage my sword in tierce,[2] and finish the thrust. Advance. Your body steady. Advance. Now, from that position. One, two. Recover. Again. One, two. Retreat. On guard, sir, on guard (*the fencing-master gives him several thrusts*), on guard.   20

Mr. Jourdain: Well?

Music-Master: You do wonders.

Fencing-Master: I've told you already: the whole secret of arms consists in two things only: hitting and not being hit. And as I proved to you the other day by demonstrative logic, it is impossible that you should be hit if you know how to turn aside your adversary's sword from the line of your body; and that depends merely on a slight movement of the wrist, inwards or outwards.

Mr. Jourdain: So, then, without any courage, one may be   30 sure of killing his man and not being killed?

Fencing-Master: Certainly. Didn't you see the demonstration of it?

Mr. Jourdain: Yes.

Fencing-Master: And by this you may see how highly our profession should be esteemed in the State; and how far the science of arms excels all other sciences that are of no use, like dancing, music . . .

Scene VI

The Philosopher, Mr. Jourdain, Lackey

The Philosopher (*Straightening his collar*): Now for our lesson.   40

Mr. Jourdain: Oh! sir, I am sorry for the blows you got.

The Philosopher: That's nothing. A philosopher knows how to take things aright; and I shall compose a satire against them in Juvenal's manner,[3] which will cut them up properly. But let that pass. What do you want to learn?

Mr. Jourdain: Everything I can; for I have the greatest desire conceivable to be learned; it throws me in a rage to think that my father and mother did not make me study all the sciences when I was young.

The Philosopher: That is a reasonable sentiment; *nam,*   50 *sine doctrina, vita est quasi mortis imago.* You understand that, for of course you know Latin.

Mr. Jourdain: Yes; but play that I don't know it; and explain what it means.

The Philosopher: It means that, *without learning, life is almost an image of death*.

Mr. Jourdain: That same Latin's in the right.

The Philosopher: Have you not some foundations, some rudiments of knowledge?

Mr. Jourdain: Oh! yes, I can read and write.   60

The Philosopher: Where will you please to have us begin? Shall I teach you logic?

Mr. Jourdain: What may that same logic be?

The Philosopher: 'Tis the science that teaches the three operations of the mind.

Mr. Jourdain: And who are they, these three operations of the mind?

The Philosopher: The first, the second, and the third. The first is to conceive aright, by means of the universals; the second, to judge aright, by means of the categories; and the third, to   70 draw deductions aright, by means of the figures: *Barbara, Celarent, Darii, Ferio, Baralipton.*[4]

Mr. Jourdain: There's a pack of crabbed words. This logic doesn't suit me at all. Let's learn something else that's prettier.

The Philosopher: Will you learn ethics?

Mr. Jourdain: Ethics?

The Philosopher: Yes.

Mr. Jourdain: What is your ethics about?

The Philosopher: It treats of happiness, teaches men to moderate their passions, and . . .   80

Mr. Jourdain: No; no more of that. I am choleric as the whole pack of devils, ethics or no ethics; no, sir, I'll be angry to my heart's content, whenever I have a mind to it.

The Philosopher: Is it physics you want to learn?

Mr. Jourdain: And what has this physics to say for itself?

The Philosopher: Physics is the science which explains the principles of natural phenomena, and the properties of bodies; which treats of the nature of the elements, metals, minerals, stones, plants, and animals, and teaches us the causes of all such things as meteors, the rainbow, St. Elmo's fire,[5] comets,   90 lightning, thunder, thunderbolts, rain, snow, hail, winds, and whirlwinds.

Mr. Jourdain: There's too much jingle-jangle in that, too much hurly-burly.

The Philosopher: Then what to do you want me to teach you?

Mr. Jourdain: Teach me spelling.

The Philosopher: With all my heart.

Mr. Jourdain: And afterward, you shall teach me the almanac, so as to know when there's a moon, and when

---

[1] A defensive posture in the art of fencing.
[2] Another fencing posture.
[3] A Roman satirist of the early second century (see chapter 6).

[4] Part of a series of Latin names used by medieval logicians to help remember the valid forms of syllogisms.
[5] Electrical discharges seen by sailors before and after storms at sea and named after the patron saint of sailors.

there isn't.

The Philosopher: Very well. To follow up your line of thought logically, and treat this matter in true philosophic fashion, we must begin, according to the proper order of things, by an exact knowledge of the nature of the letters, and the different method of pronouncing each one. And on that head I must tell you that the letters are divided into vowels, so called—*vowels*—because they express the sounds of the voice alone; and consonants, so called—*con-sonants*—because they sound with the vowels, and only mark the different articulations of the voice. There are five vowels, or voices: A, E, I, O, U.

Mr. Jourdain: I understand all that.

The Philosopher: The vowel A is formed by opening the mouth wide: A.

Mr. Jourdain: A, A. Yes.

The Philosopher: The vowel E is formed by lifting the lower jaw nearer to the upper: A, E.

Mr. Jourdain: A, E; A, E. On my word, 'tis so. Ah! how fine!

The Philosopher: And the vowel I, by bringing the jaws still nearer together, and stretching the corners of the mouth toward the ears: A, E, I.

Mr. Jourdain: A, E, I, I, I, I. That is true. Science forever!

The Philosopher: The vowel O is formed by opening the jaws, and drawing in the lips at the corners: O.

Mr. Jourdain: O, O. Nothing could be more correct: A, E, I, O, I, O. 'Tis admirable! I, O; I, O.

The Philosopher: The opening of the mouth looks exactly like a little circle, representing an O.

Mr. Jourdain: O, O, O. You are right. O. Ah! What a fine thing it is to know something!

The Philosopher: The vowel U is formed by bringing the teeth together without letting them quite touch, and thrusting out the lips, at the same time bringing them together without quite shutting them: U.

Mr. Jourdain: U, U. Nothing could be truer: U.

The Philosopher: Your lips are extended as if you were pouting; therefore if you wish to make a face at anyone, and mock at him, you have only to say U.

Mr. Jourdain: U, U. 'Tis true. Ah! would I had studied sooner, to know all that!

The Philosopher: To-morrow, we will consider the other letters, namely the consonants.

Mr. Jourdain: Are there just as curious things about them as about these?

The Philosopher: Certainly. The consonant D, for instance, is pronounced by clapping the tip of the tongue just above the upper teeth: D.

Mr. Jourdain: D, D. Yes! Oh! what fine things! what fine things!

The Philosopher: The F, by resting the upper teeth on the lower lip: F.

Mr. Jourdain: F, F. 'Tis the very truth. Oh! father and mother of me, what a grudge I owe you!

The Philosopher: And the R by lifting the tip of the tongue to the roof of the mouth; so that being grazed by the air, which comes out sharply, it yields to it, yet keeps returning to the same point, and so makes a sort of trilling: R, Ra.

Mr. Jourdain: R, R, Ra, R, R, R, R, R, Ra. That is fine. Oh! what

a learned man you are, and how much time I've lost! R, R, R, Ra.

The Philosopher: I will explain all these curious things to you thoroughly.

Mr. Jourdain: Do, I beg you. But now, I must tell you a great secret. I am in love with a person of very high rank, and I wish you would help me to write her something in a little love note which I'll drop at her feet.

The Philosopher: Excellent!

Mr. Jourdain: 'Twill be very gallant, will it not?

The Philosopher: Surely. Do you want to write to her in verse?

Mr. Jourdain: No, no; none of your verse.

The Philosopher: You want mere prose?

Mr. Jourdain: No, I will have neither prose nor verse.

The Philosopher: It must needs be one or the other.

Mr. Jourdain: Why?

The Philosopher: For this reason, that there is nothing but prose or verse to express oneself by.

Mr. Jourdain: There is nothing but prose or verse?

The Philosopher: No, sir. All that is not prose is verse, and all that is not verse is prose.

Mr. Jourdain: But when we talk, what is that, say?

The Philosopher: Prose.

Mr. Jourdain: What! When I say: "Nicole, bring me my slippers and give me my nightcap," that's prose?

The Philosopher: Yes, sir.

Mr. Jourdain: Oh my word, I've been speaking prose these forty years, and never knew it; I am infinitely obliged to you for having informed me of this. Now I want to write to her in a note: *Fair Marquise,*[6] *your fair eyes make me die of love*; but I want it to be put in gallant fashion, and neatly turned.

The Philosopher: Say that the fires of her eyes reduce your heart to ashes; that night and day you suffer for her all the tortures of a. . .

Mr. Jourdain: No, no, no, I want none of all that. I will have nothing but what I told you: *Fair Marquise, your fair eyes make me die of love*.

The Philosopher: You must enlarge upon the matter a little.

Mr. Jourdain: No, I tell you. I'll have none but those very words in the note, but put in a fashionable way, arranged as they should be. Pray tell me over the different ways they can be put, so that I may see.

The Philosopher: You can first of all put them as you said:
Fair Marquise, your fair eyes make me die of love.
Or else: Of love to die me make, fair Marquise, your fair eyes.
Or else: Your fair eyes of love me make, fair Marquise, to die.
Or else: To die your fair eyes, fair Marquise, of love me make.
Or else: Me make your fair eyes die, fair Marquise, of love.

Mr. Jourdain: But which of all these ways is the best?

The Philosopher: The way you said it: *Fair Marquise, your fair eyes make me die of love*.

Mr. Jourdain: And yet I never studied, and I did it at the first try. I thank you with all my heart, and beg you to come again to-morrow early.

The Philosopher: I shall not fail to.

---

[6] The wife of a nobleman ranking below a duke and above an earl or count.

Scene IX

Mr. Jourdain, Master-Tailor, Journeyman-Tailor; Dancers, in the costume of journeymen-tailors

Master-Tailor (*To his journeymen*): Put on the gentleman's suit, in the style you use for persons of quality.

First Ballet

*Enter four journeymen-tailors, two of whom pull off
Mr. Jourdain's breeches that he has on for his exercise,
and the other two his jacket; then they put on his new suit; and
Mr. Jourdain walks about among them, showing off his suit, to see
if it is all right. All this to the accompaniment of full orchestra.*

  Journeyman-Tailor: Noble Sir, please give the tailor's men something to drink.
  Mr. Jourdain: What did you call me?
  Journeyman-Tailor: Noble Sir.   220
  Mr. Jourdain: Noble Sir! That is what it is to dress as a person of quality! You may go clothed as a tradesman all your days, and nobody will call you Noble Sir. (*Giving him money*) There, that's for Noble Sir.
  Journeyman-Tailor: My Lord, we are greatly obliged to you.
  Mr. Jourdain: My Lord! Oh! oh! My Lord! Wait, friend; My Lord deserves something, 'tis no mean word, My Lord! There, there's what His Lordship gives you.
  Journeyman-Tailor: My Lord, we will all go and drink Your Grace's health.   230
  Mr. Jourdain: Your Grace! Oh! oh! oh! wait; don't go. Your Grace, to me! (*Aside*) Faith, if he goes as far as Your Highness he'll empty my purse. (*Aloud*) There, there's for Your Grace.
  Journeyman-Tailor: My Lord, we thank you most humbly for your generosity.
  Mr. Jourdain: He did well to stop. I was just going to give it all to him. . . .

> **Q** How does Molière poke fun at aristocratic values?

> **Q** Describe the personality of Mr. Jourdain; is he a sympathetic character?

Absolute Power and the Aristocratic Style Beyond Europe

Imperial Islam

Between 1550 and 1700, three major Islamic empires flourished (Map **21.1**): the Ottoman Empire, which stretched from Eastern Europe through Anatolia and Syria, across North Africa and into Arabia; the Safavid Empire in Persia (modern-day Iran); and the Mogul Empire, which succeeded in unifying all of India. All three established absolute monarchies that depended on the support of an efficient bureaucracy and a powerful army. As with the kings of France, the rulers of these Muslim empires governed a rigidly stratified society, consisting of a wealthy elite and a large, and often impoverished, agrarian population. And as in early modern Europe, the empires of the Middle East confronted serious religious rifts. The establishment of Islamic authority over non-Muslims, and the militant animosity between Shi'ite and Sunni factions, ignited bitter conflicts not unlike those between Catholics and Protestants in Western Europe.

In the early modern era, both East and West shared a widening global perception that the "Old World" would never again live in isolation. Fueled by curiosity and commercial ambition, cross-cultural contact between Europe and Asia flourished. In the 1700s, ambassadors of the *shah* (king) of Persia and of other Asian potentates were splendidly received at Versailles, while, at the same time, Christian missionaries and official representatives of the European monarchs found their way to Hindu, Buddhist, and Muslim lands. France had long maintained diplomatic ties with the Ottoman Turks; in fact, the French king Francis I (1494–1547) had tried to tip the balance of power against the growing power of the Holy Roman Empire by forging an "unholy" alliance with the great Muslim leader, the **sultan** Suleiman (1494–1566).

The Ottoman Empire

The Ottoman Turks were the successors of the Seljuk Turks, who had converted to Islam in the eleventh century (see chapter 10). Having conquered Constantinople in 1453, they went on to establish an empire that, under the leadership of Suleiman, became the most powerful in the world. With a standing army of 70,000 and a navy of some 300 ships, Suleiman governed territories that stretched from Eastern Europe to the Persian Gulf (see Map 21.1). In 1555, a Western diplomat traveling in Istanbul wrote letters to the Hapsburg king, warning him of the vast superiority of Suleiman's army. The Turkish infantry consisted of *janissaries*, an elite slave force (originally recruited from lands conquered by the Ottomans), who eventually came to receive a regular cash salary for their services to the empire. Suleiman's court, more lavish than that of Louis XIV, supported an army of servants who dressed, bathed, and entertained the ruler, and served his meals on platters of gold and silver. Suleiman's position as caliph gave him religious authority over all Muslims; and while the Ottoman Sunnis militantly opposed the Shi'ites of Persia, Suleiman's regime granted religious toleration to Muslims and non-Muslims alike.

Suleiman's empire was a model of Muslim absolutism. In the sultan's hands lay unlimited political and religious authority. Known as the "Lawgiver," Suleiman oversaw the establishment of a legal code that, while respecting the *sharia* (Muslim sacred law), fixed specific penalties for routine crimes. He also introduced the concept of a balanced financial budget. State revenues some eighty times those of France permitted Suleiman to undertake an extensive program of architectural and urban improvement in the great cities of his empire: Mecca, Constantinople, and Jerusalem. A goldsmith and a poet of some esteem, he initiated a golden age of literature and art. Pomp and luxury characterized Suleiman's court, and the arts that flourished under his patronage shared with those of

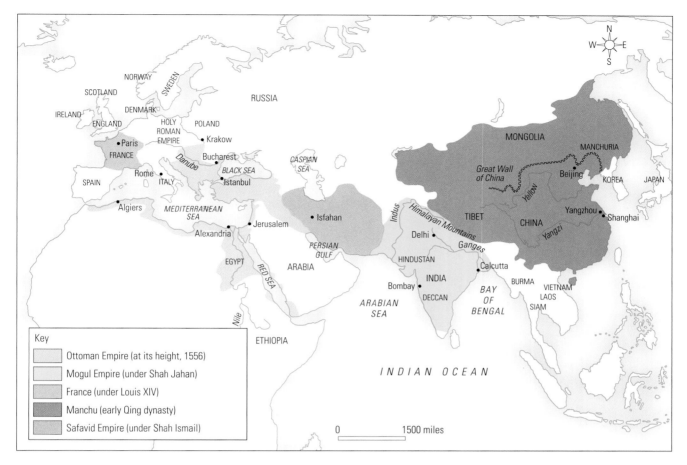

Map 21.1 Empires in the Late Sixteenth and Early Seventeenth Centuries. Note the strategically located capitals: Paris (French), Istanbul (Ottoman), Isfahan (Safavid), Delhi (Mogul), and Beijing (Manchu/Qing).

Figure 21.17 Ceremonial canteen, Ottoman Empire, second half of the sixteenth century. Gold decorated with jade plaques and gems, 11 × 9½ × 5 in.

seventeenth-century France a taste for the ornate and a high degree of technical skill (Figure **21.17**). Suleiman, whom Europeans called "the Magnificent," personally oversaw the activities of official court poets, painters, architects, and musicians. He established a model for imperial patronage that ensured the triumph of the aristocratic style not just in Turkish lands but in all parts of his multi-ethnic empire.

The Safavid Empire

The Ottoman Empire began to decline after Suleiman's death. In Persia, where Shi'ite leaders launched a *jihad* against the reigning Sunnis, the Safavid dynasty rose to power. (By the late seventeenth century, Persia's population was solidly Shi'ite, and that of modern-day Iran remains so.) Under the leadership of Shah Abbas (1557–1628), the multi-ethnic population of Persia was united. A political pragmatist and a brilliant strategist, Shah Abbas held absolute power over a prosperous empire. Establishing his capital at Isfahan, he commissioned the construction of new mosques, palaces, roads, and bridges. The government held monopolies in luxury goods, including silk production, and stimulated trade.

By the year 1600, Persian silk rivaled that of China in European markets. Carpet weaving became a national industry that employed more than 25,000 people in the city of Isfahan alone. Persian tapestries, intricately woven in silk and wool (Figure **21.18**), and finely ornamented ceramics were avidly sought across the world, and Persian manuscripts embellished with brightly printed illustrations came to be imitated throughout Asia.

Figure 21.18 Kirman shrub rug, Persia, seventeenth century. Silk and wool, 10 ft. 1 in. × 4 ft. 7 in. Court carpets were among the most magnificent products of sixteenth- and seventeenth-century Persia. This one features flowering trees and bushes that evoke the Qur'anic Garden of Paradise.

In the field of architecture, the outstanding monument to Safavid wealth and power was the Imperial Mosque, commissioned by Shah Abbas for the city of Isfahan (Figure **21.19**). Completed in 1637, this magnificent structure, flanked by minarets, encloses a square main hall covered by a splendid dome that rises to 177 feet. The surfaces of the mosque, both inside and out, are covered with colored glazed tiles (compare to the Ishtar Gate of ancient Babylon; see Figure 1.12) ornamented with calligraphic inscriptions and delicate blue and yellow floral motifs. French aristocrats in the service of Louis XIV brought back to France enthusiastic reports of the Imperial Mosque—a fact that has led scholars to detect the influence of Persian art on some of Louis' more lavish enterprises at Versailles.

The Mogul Empire

Muslims had ruled parts of India for almost a thousand years, but it was not until the sixteenth century that the Muslim dynasty known as the Moguls (the name derives from "Mongol") succeeded in uniting all of India (see Map 21.1). The earliest effort to establish a Muslim empire in India was led by Zahir al-Din Muhammad, known as Babur ("The Tiger"; 1483–1530), who captured Delhi in 1526, and recorded his mostly negative views of Hindu India in the *Babur-nama* (*Memoirs of Babur*). Distant cousins of the Safavid princes, the Moguls ruled India as absolute monarchs from 1526 to 1707. They imported Persian culture and language into India in much the same way that Louis XIV brought Italian culture into France. The creators of a culture that blended Muslim, Hindu, Turkish, Persian, Arabic, and African traditions, the Moguls encouraged the development of an aristocratic style, which—like that of the Sun King—served as an adjunct to majesty.

The architect of the Mogul Empire, Babur's grandson Akbar (1542–1605), came to the throne at the age of thirteen. Establishing an integrated state in north India, he laid the foundations for a luxurious court style that his son and grandson would perpetuate. India's most dynamic

Science and Technology

1717	inoculation against smallpox is introduced in Europe (from Ottoman Turkey)
1736	expansion of the Indian shipbuilding industry in Bombay
1780	a European version of Chinese silk-reeling machines is introduced in Bengal
1781	Turkish methods for producing high-quality cloth are copied in England
1790	India uses military rockets based on Ottoman technology in warfare

Figure 21.19 Imperial Mosque, Isfahan, Iran, 1637. Surface decorated with colored glazed tiles, height of dome 177 ft. The Imperial Mosque, which dates from the eighth century, was enlarged and renovated by numerous Muslim rulers. The Safavids were instrumental in making Shia Islam the official religion in Persia.

ruler since Emperor Asoka of the third century B.C.E., Akbar dominated a court consisting of thousands of ministers, servants, wives, and concubines. He exercised political control over feudal noblemen and royal officials who, unlike their French counterparts, received paid salaries. Amidst the primarily Hindu population, the Muslim ruler pursued a policy of religious toleration. So as not to offend India's Hindus, he became a vegetarian and gave up hunting, his favorite sport. Akbar's religious pluralism reflected his personal quest for a synthesis of faiths. Dedicated to "divine monotheism," he brought learned representatives of Christianity, Judaism, Hinduism, and other religions to his court to debate with Muslim theologians. He also made every effort to rid India of its outmoded traditions, such as the immolation of wives on their husbands' funeral pyres.

Despite Akbar's reforms, however, the lower classes and especially the peasants were taxed heavily (as was also the case in France under Louis XIV) to finance the luxuries of the upper-class elite.

In the seventeenth century, the Moguls governed the wealthiest state in the world, a state whose revenues were ten times greater than those of France. Akbar commissioned magnificent works of music, poetry, painting, and architecture—the tangible expressions of princely affluence and taste. As in Louis' court, most of these exquisite objects were designed for secular, not liturgical, use. A state studio of more than one hundred artists working under Persian masters created a library of over 24,000 illuminated manuscripts, the contents of which ranged from love poetry to Hindu epics and religious tales. One notable

Mogul innovation was the practice of recording and illustrating firsthand accounts of specific historical events. A miniature celebrating the birth of Akbar's son Nurud-din Salim Jahangir shows courtiers rejoicing: dancers sway to the rhythms of a lively musical ensemble while bread and alms are distributed outside the palace gate (Figure **21.20**). Such miniatures reveal the brilliant union of delicate line, rich color, and strong surface patterns—features that also dominate Asian carpet designs. The absence of perspective—a Western technique—gives the scene a flat, decorative quality.

The Arts of the Mogul Court

Under the rule of Akbar's son Jahangir (ruled 1605–1627), aristocratic court portraiture came into fashion in India. The new genre reflects the influence of European painting, which had been eagerly embraced by the Moguls, and suggests the gradual relaxation of the Muslim rule against the representation of the human figure. Relatively small in comparison with the aristocratic portraits executed by Rigaud or van Dyck (see Figures 21.2 and 22.2), the painted likeness of Jahangir (the name means "world seizer") featured in a small picture album glorifies the monarch in

Figure 21.20 *Rejoicing at the Birth of Prince Salim in 1569.* Color on paper, 9½ × 5 in. Manuscript illustration from the *Akbar-Nama*.

an international context (Figure **21.21**). The artist Bichitr (fl. 1625), whose self-portrait appears in the lower left corner, shows the *shah* enthroned atop an elaborate hourglass throne, a reference to the brevity of life and to Jahangir's declining health. Jahangir welcomes a Sufi (a Muslim mystic), who stands in the company of a Turkish dignitary and a European, King James I of England. While the latter invites the viewer into the scene, the turbaned Turk makes a gesture of submission to Jahangir. Yet Jahangir looks directly at the Sufi, who presents him with a book, perhaps a copy of the Qur'an. Four Western-style angels frame the scene: the upper two seem to lament the impermanence of worldly power, while the bottom two inscribe the base of the hourglass with the prayer, "O Shah, may the span of your life be a thousand years." Just as Louis XIV assumed the guise of the Sun King, so Jahangir—as notorious for his overconsumption of wine and opium as Louis was for fine food and sex—is apotheosized by a huge halo consisting of the sun and the moon. The miniature, an allegorical statement of the superiority of spiritual over secular power, is also an amalgam of Western and Eastern styles and motifs. Western-style illusionistic portraits are

Figure 21.21 *Jahangir Preferring a Sufi Shaikh to Kings,* from the *Leningrad Album of Bichitr,* seventeenth century. Color and gold on paper, 10 × 7⅛ in. The inscriptions above the halo proclaim Jahangir "Light of the Faith." King James I looks out at us to acknowledge our participation in the scene.

Figure 21.22 Anonymous Delhi artist, *The Red Fort*, ca. 1820. Opaque watercolor on paper, 8 × 10 in. (approx). The building dates from the Shah Jahan period, after 1638.

framed by an Eastern carpetlike background, the upper two angels are reminiscent of cherubs in Italian Renaissance paintings, and the halo is clearly inspired by Hindu and Buddhist art. This little hybrid masterpiece anticipates a global perspective that will overtake the world in the centuries to come.

Well before the seventeenth century, Mogul rulers had initiated the tradition of building huge ceremonial and administrative complexes, veritable cities in themselves. Such complexes symbolized Muslim wealth and authority in India, but, as in France, they were also political manifestations of the cult of royalty. Akbar had personally

Figure 21.23 Foliated arcades and perforated monolithic screens in the Red Fort (Shahjahanabad), Delhi, Shah Jahan period, after 1638.

Figure 21.24 Taj Mahal, Agra, India, 1623–1643.

overseen the construction of a palace complex near Agra, which, comparable with Versailles, featured an elaborate residence surrounded by courtyards and mosques, as well as by formal gardens and fountains watered by means of artificial conduits. The garden, a this-worldly counterpart of the Qur'anic Garden of Paradise (see chapter 10) and a welcome refuge from India's intense heat, was a characteristic feature of the Mogul palace complex.

Inspired by the elaborate ceremonial centers built by his father and his grandfather, Shah Jahan (1627–1666) commissioned the most sumptuous of all Mogul palaces, the Shahjahanabad (present-day Old Delhi). The red sandstone walls of the Shahjahanabad (nicknamed the "Red Fort") enclosed a palatial residence of white marble, flanked by magnificent gardens, public and private audience halls, courtyards, pavilions, baths, and the largest mosque in India (Figure **21.22**). The Red Fort's 3:4 rectangular plan was bisected by an axis that led through successive courts to the public audience hall, a pattern that anticipated the rigid symmetry of Versailles (compare Figure 21.3).

The hot Indian climate inclined Mogul architects to open up interior space by means of foliated arcades (see chapter 10) and latticed screens through which breezes might blow uninterrupted (Figure **21.23**). These graceful architectural features distinguish the *shah*'s palace at the Red Fort. The most ornate of all Mogul interiors, Shah Jahan's audience hall consists of white marble arcades and ceilings decorated with geometric and floral patterns popular in Mogul embroidery, a craft traditionally dominated by women. The rich designs consist of inlaid precious and semiprecious stones (***pietra dura***), a type of mosaic that the Moguls had borrowed from Italy. At the center of the hall, the *shah* sat on the prized Peacock Throne, fashioned in solid gold and studded with emeralds, rubies, diamonds, and pearls. Above the throne (which served imperial India until it was plundered by Persian warriors in 1732) was a canopy on which stood two gold peacocks, and above the canopy, around the ceiling of the hall, were inscribed the words, "If there is a paradise on the face of the earth, It is this, oh! it is this, oh! it is this."

Surpassing the splendor of the palace at Delhi (which was badly damaged by the British army during the nineteenth century) is Shah Jahan's most magnificent gift to world architecture: the Taj Mahal (Figure **21.24**). Shah Jahan built the Taj Mahal as a mausoleum to honor the memory of his favorite wife, Mumtaz Mahal (the name means "light of the world"). When Mumtaz died giving birth to their fourteenth child, her husband, legend has it, was inconsolable. He directed his architects to construct alongside the Jumna River a glorious tomb, a twin to one he planned for himself on the adjoining riverbank. Fabricated in cream-colored marble, the Taj rises majestically above a tree-lined pool that mirrors its elegant silhouette so that the mausoleum seems to be floating in air. Although the individual elements of the structure—slender minarets, bulbous domes, and octagonal base—recall Byzantine and Persian prototypes (see Figure 21.19), its total effect is unique: shadowy voids and bright solids play against one another on the surface of the exterior, while delicate patterns of light and dark animate the latticed marble screens and exquisitely carved walls of the interior. The garden complex, divided into quadrants by waterways and broad footpaths, is an earthly recreation of the Muslim Garden of Paradise. The Taj Mahal is the product of some 20,000 West Asian builders and craftsmen working under the direction of a Persian architect. It is a brilliant fusion of the best aspects of Byzantine, Muslim, and Hindu traditions and, hence, an emblem of Islamic cohesion. But it is also an extravagant expression of conjugal devotion and, to generations of Western visitors, an eloquent tribute to romantic love.

The Decline of the Islamic Empires

As these pages suggest, during the sixteenth and seventeenth centuries the aristocratic courts of Islam ruled vast parts of Asia, including India and the Near East (see Map 21.1). By the mid-eighteenth century, however, the great empires of the Ottomans, the Safavids, and the Moguls were either destroyed or in fatal decline. India came under the rule of Great Britain, and parts of the Ottoman Empire were lost to the control of other European powers. While the Islamic empires had depended on the West for modern weapons, they could not compete with the West's rapidly advancing commercialism and military technology. Conservative Muslim elements vigorously resisted all aspects of Western culture, including Western science and Christian learning. Threatened by the culture of the Christian West, some Muslim clerics even opposed the printing of books. Movements of Muslim revivalism would grow more militant in the following centuries, as Islam—once the imperial leader of the Asian world—struggled against European colonialism and the inevitable forces of Modernism.

Absolute Power and the Aristocratic Style in China

The Ming Dynasty

From the earliest days of Chinese history, Chinese emperors—the "Sons of Heaven"—ruled on earth by divine authority, or, as the Chinese called it, "the Mandate of Heaven" (see chapter 3). In theory, all China's emperors were absolute rulers. Nevertheless, over the centuries, their power was frequently contested by feudal lords, military generals, and government officials. In 1368, native Chinese rebels drove out the last of the Mongol rulers and

established the Ming dynasty, which ruled China until 1644. The Ming dynasty governed the largest and most sophisticated empire on earth, an empire of some 120 million people. In the highly centralized Chinese state, Ming emperors oversaw a bureaucracy that included offices of finance, law, military affairs, and public works. They rebuilt the Great Wall (see chapter 7) and revived the ancient Chinese tradition of the examination system, which had been suspended by the Mongols. By the seventeenth century, however, the Ming had become autocrats who, like the foreigners they had displaced, took all power into their own hands. They transformed the civil service into a nonhereditary bureaucracy that did not dare to threaten the emperor's authority. The rigid court protocol that developed around the imperial rulers of the late Ming dynasty symbolized this shift toward autocracy. Officials, for instance, knelt in the presence of the emperor, who, as the Son of Heaven, sat on an elevated throne in the center of the imperial precinct.

The Qing Dynasty

Beset by court corruption and popular revolts, the Ming fell prey to the invading hordes of East Asians (descendants of Mongols, Turks, and other tribes) known as the Manchu. Under the rule of the Manchu, who established the Qing dynasty (1644–1912), the conditions of imperial autocracy intensified. As a symbol of submission, every Chinese male was required to adopt the Manchu hairstyle, by which one shaved the front of the head and wore a plaited pigtail at the back. Qing rulers retained the administrative traditions of their predecessors, but government posts were often sold rather than earned by merit. When the Qing dynasty reached its zenith—during the very last years that Louis XIV ruled France—it governed the largest, the most populous, and one of the most unified states in the world (see Map 21.1). Despite internal peace, uprisings were common. They reflected the discontent of peasant masses beset by high taxes and rents and periodic famines. Like the lower classes of France and India, Chinese villagers and urban workers supported the luxuries of royal princes, government officials, and large landholders, who (as in France and India) were themselves exempt from taxation. The early Manchu rulers imitated their predecessors as royal sponsors of art and architecture. Like Louis XIV and Shah Jahan, the Chinese emperor and his huge retinue resided in an impressive ceremonial complex (Figure **21.25**). This metropolis, the symbol of entrenched absolutism and the majesty of the ruler, was known as the Forbidden City—so called because of its inaccessibility to ordinary Chinese citizens until 1925.

The Forbidden City

Comparable in size and conception to Versailles in the West and to the Mogul palaces of India, the Forbidden City—a walled complex of palaces, tombs, and gardens located in Beijing—was the most elaborate imperial monument of the Ming and Qing eras. Construction of the imperial palace began under fifteenth-century Ming emperors and was continued by the Manchus. For almost 500 years, this vast ceremonial complex—which, like Versailles, is

Figure 21.25 XU YANG, *Bird's-Eye View of the Capital*, 1770. Hanging scroll, ink and color on paper, 8 ft. 4¼ in. × 7 ft. 8 in. Commissioned in 1406, the Forbidden City was first occupied by the Ming court in 1421. It is said to have contained 9999 separate rooms; nine, an auspicious number, symbolizes the union of the five elements and the four cosmological directions.

now a park and museum—was the administrative center of China and the home of no fewer than twenty-four Ming and Qing emperors, their families, and the members of their courts. By the eighteenth century, some 9000 people, including guards, concubines, and domestic servants, resided within the complex.

Inside the 10-foot-high walls of the Forbidden City are royal meeting halls, grand avenues, broad courtyards, government offices, mansions for princes and dignitaries, artificial lakes, lush gardens, spacious temples, theaters, a library, and a printing house (Figure **21.26**). Entering from the south, one passes under the majestic five-towered entranceway through a succession of courtyards and gates reminiscent of the intriguing nests of boxes at which Chinese artisans excel. At the heart of the rectangular complex, one proceeds up a three-tiered stone terrace

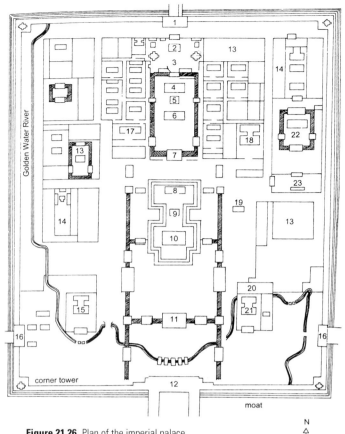

Figure 21.26 Plan of the imperial palace, Forbidden City, Beijing, China.

1 Gate of Divine Pride
2 Pavilion of Imperial Peace
3 Imperial Garden
4 Palace of Earthly Tranquility
5 Hall of Union
6 Palace of Heavenly Purity
7 Gate of Heavenly Purity
8 Hall of the Preservation of Harmony
9 Hall of Perfect Harmony
10 Hall of Supreme Harmony
11 Gate of Supreme Harmony
12 Meridian Gate
13 Kitchens
14 Gardens
15 Former Imperial Printing House
16 Flower Gate
17 Palace of the Culture of the Mind
18 Hall of the Worship of the Ancestors
19 Pavilion of Arrows
20 Imperial Library
21 Palace of Culture
22 Palace of Peace and Longevity
23 Nine Dragon Screen

(Figure **21.27**) into the Hall of Supreme Harmony (approximately 200 by 100 feet), where the Sons of Heaven sat enthroned, and beyond, to the imperial living quarters at the rear of the complex. Fragrant gardens, watered by fountains and artificial pools, once graced the private quarters of the royal officials.

During the seventeenth century, courtyard gardening itself developed into a fine art. Often flanked by a covered walkway from which it could be viewed, the Chinese garden was an arrangement of seemingly random (but actually carefully placed) rocks, plants, and trees—a miniature version of the natural world. Like the Chinese landscape scroll, the garden was an object of gentle contemplation, designed to be enjoyed progressively. Such gardens, with their winding, narrow paths, delicate ferns, and sheltering bamboos, have become a hallmark of East Asian culture.

The Forbidden City was the nucleus of imperial power and the symbol of Chinese absolutism. Laid out with a gridiron regularity that rivaled Mogul and French palatial complexes, the arrangement of buildings, courtyards, gates, and terraces was uniquely Chinese. It adhered to the ancient Chinese practice of *feng shui*, the arrangement of the physical environment in accordance with specific cosmological principles (see chapter 7). Lined up along the cosmic north–south axis, buildings are symmetrical, with square foundations symbolizing Earth, and yellow-tiled roofs symbolizing Heaven. (As the Son of Heaven, the emperor was expected to keep the two in balance.) Palace doors face the "good" southerly direction, while rear walls,

Figure 21.27 Three-tiered stone terrace and Hall of Supreme Harmony, Forbidden City, Ming dynasty. Hall approx. 200 × 100 ft. Number 10 in Figure 21.26, the largest throne hall in the complex, is positioned centrally on the 2-mile-long ceremonial axis.

facing north, are closed to the cold winds and the attacks of northern barbarians. The Forbidden City, however, also reflects the ceremonial dimension of royal absolutism. The sizes and functions of the buildings were determined by a strict protocol based on rank, age, and gender. During the Ming Era, for instance, imperial legislation prescribed nine rooms for the emperor, seven for a prince, five for a court official, and three for an ordinary citizen.

Most of the buildings of the Forbidden City are no more than a single story high, their walls serving only as screens that divide interior space. What the Chinese sacrificed in monumentality, however, they recovered in ornamental splendor and in the creation of an architecture that achieved harmony with (rather than dominance over) nature. Chinese architects preserved such traditional features as the rectangular hall with fully exposed wooden rafters and the pitched roof with projecting eaves and glazed yellow tiles—the latter symbolic of the mantle of heaven. Bronze lions and gilded dragons (symbols of royal power) guard the great halls and entrances. In the Forbidden City, Chinese court culture promoted a lavish aristocratic style that enhanced the majesty of the ruler.

The Arts of the Ming and Qing Courts

The Ming and Qing emperors were great patrons of the arts. They encouraged the traditional schools of landscape painting and oversaw the production of such luxury items as inlaid bronze vessels, carved ivory and jade, lacquerware, embroidered silk, and painted ceramics. Chinese porcelains had been much sought after since the seventh century; by the seventeenth century they were world famous, so much so that in the West the word "Ming" became synonymous with porcelain. (More generally, the word "china" has come to signify fine ceramics and tableware.)

Qing artists used bright colors more freely than in earlier times. Vessels with solid color glazes of ox-blood red and peach-blossom pink (Figure **21.28**) alternated with colorful landscapes filled with songbirds, flowering trees, human figures, and mythical animals. The central medallion of one Qing plate, ornamented with a rich five-color palette, shows a garden with three women, one of whom plays a *pipa* (see chapter 14). The surrounding eight scenes depict episodes from *The Journey to the West*, a picaresque adventure tale and popular Ming literary classic (Figure **21.29**). As these charming images suggest, neither the porcelains nor the paintings of Qing China manifest

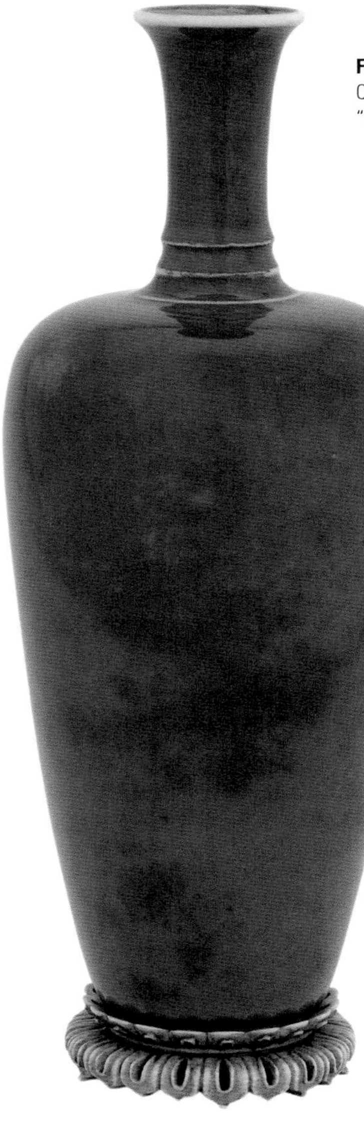

Figure 21.28 Flower vase, Qing dynasty. Chinese pottery, "peach-bloom" glaze, height 7¾ in.

Figure 21.29 *Famille verte*, Qing dynasty, early eighteenth century. Porcelain dish, diameter 13¾ in. Scenes from *The Journey to the West* depict the escapades of the Monkey King, wearing yellow trousers, who accompanied a seventh-century Chinese priest, shown in a yellow robe, on his journey to bring Buddhist texts from India to China.

Figure 21.30 Incense burner in the shape of a *li* (tripod), Ming dynasty, fifteenth or possibly early sixteenth century. *Cloisonné* enamel, diameter 7½ in.

an affection for the heroic and moralizing themes that dominated Baroque art in the West. This difference notwithstanding, imperial taste dictated the style of aristocratic art in China every bit as much as the royal academies of France influenced seventeenth-century French style. By 1680, there were over thirty official palace workshops serving the imperial court. Out of these workshops poured precious works of art: gem-encrusted jewelry, carved wood and lacquerware, painted enamel, *cloisonné* vessels (Figure **21.30**), intricate jade carvings, and heavily embroidered silk and gold textiles (Figure **21.31**). Many of these objects found their way into Europe, where they inspired **chinoiserie**, a style reflecting the influence of Chinese art and a taste for Chinese items that, in the 1700s, developed into something of a mania.

From China, by way of the Dutch, tea ("the Chinese drink") came into use in England, often smuggled into the country to avoid the high import tax. The fashionable tea service became the object of imitation in the West, most notably the blue and white wares of Delft, Holland. Cultural exchange between East and West, however, was mutual: delegations of Jesuits, who arrived in China in 1601, introduced the rules of linear perspective to Chinese art, even as they transmitted to Europe (often by means of prints and engravings) a knowledge of Chinese techniques and goods. And French prints in turn prompted early Manchu rulers to build a Chinese version of Versailles, complete with fountains, at the imperial summer palace northwest of Beijing.

Figure 21.31 Manchu-style man's *jifu* (semiformal court robe), Qing dynasty, second quarter of the eighteenth century. Silk and gold leaf over lacquered paper strips, 4 ft. 4¾ in. × 6 ft. 2⅓ in. The dragon, an age-old symbol of the emperor's supreme power, is the dominant motif on this robe. In the Hall of Supreme Harmony, the emperor sat on the Dragon Throne. Some additional 13,000 dragon images adorn the walls, ceilings, and other parts of the building.

Chinese Literature and the Theater Arts

Ming and Qing rulers worked hard to preserve China's rich literary heritage. Under Ming patronage, a group of 2000 scholars began the enormous task of collecting and copying the most famous of China's literary and historical works. The Manchu contemporary of Louis XIV, Emperor Kangxi (1654–1722), hired 15,000 calligraphers and 360 editors to compile a vast assortment of dictionaries and encyclopedias, and a thirty-six-volume anthology of the Chinese classics (Figure **21.32**). An increasing number of literate middle-class men and women in China's growing cities demanded printed books for everyday use. These included almanacs, guides to letter-writing, short stories, collections of proverbs and maxims, chronicles, ballads, and romances.

Novels, long works of fiction in the colloquial style, had emerged as early as the twelfth century in China and even earlier in Japan (see chapter 14), but in the Ming and Qing eras, this literary genre became ever more popular. The typical Chinese novel recounted historical events and often made fun of religious and secular authorities. In the early eighteenth century, Cao Xueqin produced China's greatest novel, *The Dream of the Red Chamber* (also known as *The Story of the Stone*). This 4000-page work, which was to become the most popular example of Chinese fiction, is a love story involving two aristocratic Beijing families. Filled with realistic detail as well as fantastic dream sequences, the novel provides a fascinating picture of upper-class Qing society.

Plots drawn from popular novels such as *The Dream of the Red Chamber* provided the themes for staged performances, which always included mime, dance, and vocal and instrumental music. This type of theatrical performance—which Westerners might call "opera"—was the only form of drama that existed in China prior to the twentieth century (when, imitating Western drama, Chinese writers began to produce exclusively spoken plays). In the Chinese theater, performers were always male, and male actors played the parts of such stock characters as the coquette or the virtuous maid. Since troupes of players moved from city to city, costumes and stage scenery were minimal. Chinese theater made use of conventional props to indicate setting or circumstance: a chair might represent a mountain, a whip might signify that the actor was on horseback, and a black cloth might be used to indicate that a character was invisible. Colors symbolized conventional character types: red represented loyalty and dignity, white symbolized villainy or treachery, and so on. During the Ming Era, when sumptuous costumes and masklike make-up became popular, such earlier stage symbols and conventions were still used. Indeed, to this day, Chinese theater retains many traditional, highly stylized features.

Despite the differences in their origins, Chinese and European opera developed during the same era—the seventeenth century. By the late eighteenth century the first permanent Chinese opera company emerged in the capital city of Beijing. Chinese opera shunned the

See Music Listening Selection 14, CD One, an excerpt from a Chinese opera described in chapter 14.

Figure 21.32 Anonymous, portrait of Emperor Kangxi reading. Ink and color on silk, 11½ × 17 in. Kangxi, a Confucian scholar who ruled China for sixty-one years, is shown seated against a background of string-bound books that made up part of his library. He is said to have introduced Western technology and Western musical instruments into China.

dramatic contrasts in texture and timbre that characterize Western opera (and Western music in general). While early European operas borrowed themes from Greco-Roman mythology and biblical history—themes that might glorify a royal patron or flatter upper-class tastes—Chinese operas mainly drew on a traditional repertory of love stories, social events, and the adventures of folk heroes. Such operas often featured stock characters resembling those of Molière's plays, and, like Molière's plays, they achieved wide and lasting popularity.

Absolute Power and the Aristocratic Style in Japan

By the seventeenth century, feudal Japan had taken the direction of a unified and centralized state led by members of the Tokugawa dynasty (1600–1868). In contrast to China, whose aristocracy consisted of a scholarly elite recruited through civil service examinations, Japan's aristocracy consisted of a warrior elite (the *samurai*) recruited in battle (see chapter 14). The Tokugawa **shogun** (general-in-chief) demanded that his feudal lords attend his court in Edo (modern-day Tokyo). Here he enforced court etiquette as faithfully as he solidified political and economic control. Unique to Japan was its self-enforced isolation from the West (see chapter 20). In the 1630s, Tokugawa

Figure 21.33 OGATA KORIN, *Irises at Yatsuhashi*, from the *Tale of Ise* (*Ise Monogatari*), Edo period. One of a pair of six-paneled screens, ink and color on gilded paper, with black lacquered frames, each screen 4 ft. 11 in. × 11 ft. 3 in. Ogata executed a number of these screens based on a nostalgic love poem; the first syllables of each line form the Japanese word for "iris."

rulers initiated a policy of national seclusion. Determined to maintain internal stability and peace, they expelled foreigners and forbade citizens to travel abroad, thus sealing off Japan from the outside world.

While a large segment of Japan's peasantry led barely subsistent lives, the pleasure-loving court at Edo (a city of one million people by the year 1700) and the rising commercial classes of the towns enjoyed one of the most creative periods in Japanese history. In the Tokugawa court, the traditional Japanese decorative style reached new heights. Luxury items included multipaneled screens (used to divide interior space), hand-painted scrolls, ceramics (including the decorative porcelain known as "Imari ware"), and lacquer boxes used for the tea ceremony. Japan's aristocratic style is best represented in its brightly painted multifold screens, adorned with stylized flowers, birds, or landscape motifs. In the large six-paneled screen by Ogata Korin (ca. 1658–1716) pictured in Figure **21.33**, bold, decorative shapes and the subtle balance of figure and ground (positive and negative space) achieve an astonishing purity of design. Such screens unite simplicity and luxury (the ground of the screen is gold leaf) with an elegance that distinguishes the Japanese court style at its very best.

The Floating World

Parallel with the flowering of the aristocratic style in Tokugawa Japan was the rise of popular culture and popular artforms. The new merchant class that occupied Japan's growing commercial cities demanded a variety of lively (and bawdy) entertainments. In the so-called floating world (*ukiyo*)—"floating" because Japan's middle class was not bound by aristocratic propriety—theaters and brothels provided leisure-time pleasures. *Ukiyo* was described by one of Japan's first professional writers, Asai Ryoi (1612–1691), in his *Tales of the Floating World* (ca. 1665):

Living only for the moment, turning our full attention to the pleasures of the moon, the snow, the cherry blossoms and the maples, singing songs, drinking wine, and diverting ourselves in just floating, floating, caring not a whit for the poverty staring us in the face, refusing to be disheartened, like a gourd floating along with the current: this is what we call *ukiyo*.

From the floating world of the Edo district came a new type of staged performance known as **kabuki**. The *kabuki* stage provided an alternative to Japan's oldest form of theater, Nō drama (see chapter 14), whose traditional literary subjects, stylized movements, and use of masks had much in common with ancient Greek theater. In its late fifteenth-century origins, *kabuki* (literally, "song-dance-art") was a female performance genre. But in 1629, some twenty years after its first appearance, the Japanese government issued an edict that forbade women to appear on stage. Thereafter, male actors wearing elaborate costumes, wigs, and make-up assumed all *kabuki* roles. *Kabuki* plays featured dance, song, and mime. Their plots, drawn from history, myth, puppet plays, and daily life, often involved tales of romance marked by violent passions and "love suicides." Action took place on a revolving stage that featured a long ramp leading from the audience to the rear of the stage (Figure **21.34**). Elegant backdrops and scenic effects embellished the action. Three to five plays might be performed in a single day, interrupted by intervals that allowed the audience to visit local teahouses and restaurants.

Woodcut prints celebrating celebrity actors and famous courtesans (some depicted in sexually explicit acts) became one of Japan's most popular genres (Figure **21.35**). Mass-produced and therefore inexpensive, *ukiyo-e* ("pictures of the floating world") were purchased by Edo patrons as souvenirs, much as people today collect posters of famous

Figure 21.34 MASANOBU (?), *Kabuki* stage, ca. 1740. Colored woodblock print, 11½ × 17 in.

personalities. Executed in black and white, and (by 1750) colored either by hand or with inked blocks, woodcut prints exemplify Japanese virtuosity in calligraphic design. They share with Ogata's screens the typically Japanese mastery of simplicity, elegance, and control.

The Way of Tea and Zen

A classic expression of Japanese culture is the ritual tea ceremony—a unique synthesis of art, theater, and everyday ritual. Introduced into Japan from China during the ninth century, strongly caffeinated tea served as an aid to Buddhist meditation. By the sixteenth century, the Way of Tea (as the practice of tea-drinking is called) was closely associated with Zen Buddhism, a strand of Buddhism that seeks spiritual enlightenment through intuitive illumination (see chapter 8). With the cultivation of better types of tea plant, tea-drinking became widely practiced in Japanese society, gradually establishing itself among *samurai* warriors and wealthy merchants. The four-hour tea ceremony is choreographed according to a strict set of rules and formal etiquette. An intimate ritual, incorporating the arts of ceramics, textiles, and flower-arranging, it remains a paradigm of the cultivated life.

Typical of Zen monastic practice, tea and the etiquette of tea-drinking coincided with a revival of Zen painting among eighteenth-century artist–monks. Zen calligraphers did not consider their paintings as works of art, but rather as acts of meditation involving intense concentration and focus. Absence of detail invited the beholder to complete the painting, and thus partake of the meditative process. One of the greatest Zen masters was Hakuin Ekaku (1685–1768), whose magnificent ink scrolls are noted for their vigorous yet subtle brushwork. In *Two Blind Men Crossing a Log Bridge* (Figure **21.36**), Hakuin illustrates his vision of the precarious nature of the human journey to spiritual enlightenment: two monks, one with his sandals hanging on his staff, make their way unsteadily across the narrow bridge. The figures, like the Japanese characters that record the accompanying poem (in the upper left corner), come to life by way of confident, calligraphic brushstrokes. Hakuin's poem reads:

> Both inner life and the floating world outside us
> Are like the blind man's round log bridge—
> An enlightened mind is the best guide.

Figure 21.35 TOSHUSAI SHARAKU, *Bust Portrait of the Actor Segawa Tomisaburo as Yadorigi, the Wife of Ogishi Kurando*, 1794–1795. Woodblock print, 14½ × 9¼ in.

Chronology

1520–1566	Suleiman rules Ottoman Empire
1556–1605	Akbar rules Mogul Empire
1588–1629	Shah Abbas rules Safavid Empire (Persia)
1600–1868	Tokugawa Shogunate in Japan
1605–1627	Jahangir rules Mogul Empire
1627–1666	Shah Jahan rules Mogul Empire
1643–1715	Louis XIV rules France
1661–1722	Kangxi (Qing dynasty) rules China

Figure 21.36 HAKUIN EKAKU, *Two Blind Men Crossing a Log Bridge*, Edo period. Hanging scroll, ink on paper, 11⅟₁₆ × 33 in.

In their improvisational spirit, the ink scrolls of the Zen master differ from the deliberately stylized Edo screens. Yet both share the Japanese preference for refinement and utmost simplicity.

Controlled simplicity is a major feature of Tokugawa lyric verse forms, the most notable of which is the *haiku*. The *haiku*—a seventeen-syllable poem arranged in three lines of 5/7/5 syllables—depends for its effectiveness on the absence of detail and the pairing of contrasting images. The unexpected contrast does not describe a condition or event, but rather evokes a mood or emotion. Much like the art of the Zen calligrapher, the *haiku* creates a provocative void between what is stated and what is left unsaid. In this void there lies an implied "truth," one that aims to close the gap between the world of things and the world of feelings. Witness the following five compositions by Japan's most famous *haiku* poet and Zen monk, Matsuo Bashō (1644–1694):

The beginning of all art
  a song when planting a rice field
    in the country's inmost part.

◆

The first day of the year:
  thoughts come—and there is loneliness;
    the autumn dusk is here.

◆

Oh, these spring days!
  A nameless little mountain,
    wrapped in morning haze!

◆

I'd like enough drinks
  to put me to sleep—on stones
    covered with pinks.

◆

Leaning upon staves
  and white-haired—a whole family
    visiting the graves.

LOOKING BACK

The Aristocratic Style in Europe

- As absolute monarch, Louis XIV brought France to a position of political and military preeminence among the European nation-states. He challenged the power of the nobility and the Church, centralizing authority in his own hands.
- Under Louis' leadership, the center of artistic patronage and productivity shifted from Italy to France. French culture in all its forms—from art and architecture to fashions and fine cuisine—came to dominate European taste.

- Louis recognized the propaganda value of the arts. Using the French treasury, he made the arts an adjunct to royalty. His extravagance left France in a woeful financial condition.
- At Versailles, Louis' newly constructed palace emerged as an amalgam of Greco-Roman subject matter, Classical principles of design, and Baroque theatricality. Luxury, grandeur, and technical refinement became the vehicles of French royal authority and the hallmarks of aristocratic elitism.

- Louis was the arbiter of fashion and manners. He dictated the standards for all forms of artistic production, and created government-sponsored academies in the arts, appointing his personal favorites to each.
- In Spain, Diego Velázquez, court painter to King Philip IV, became the country's most prestigious artist, thanks to his aristocratic portraits that conveyed the powerful presence of real objects in atmospheric space.

- The Flemish painter Peter Paul Rubens established his reputation in the courts of Europe. As court painter to King Charles I of England, Anthony van Dyck produced elegant, idealized portraits of his aristocratic patrons.

Music and Dance at the Court of Louis XIV

- The court at Versailles was the setting for music, theater, and dance. To provide musical entertainment for state dinners, balls, and operatic performances, Louis established a permanent orchestra. Its director, the Italian-born Jean-Baptiste Lully, headed the French Academy of Music.
- Lully introduced to opera the "French overture." Under his leadership, French opera also developed its most characteristic feature: the inclusion of formal dance.
- Of lasting significance was Louis' contribution to the birth of professional dance and the transformation of court dance into an independent artform.

Seventeenth-Century French Literature

- François de La Rochefoucauld wrote maxims that reflect the self-interest, hypocrisy, and greed of human beings— including and especially the aristocrats of his day.
- French drama reflected the Neoclassical effort to restrain passionate feeling by means of cool objectivity and common

sense. The French tragedian Jean Racine added unity of place to Aristotle's unities of action and time.
- France's leading comic playwright, Molière, brought to life the comic foibles of such stock characters as the miser, the hypochondriac, the hypocrite, the misanthrope, and the would-be gentleman. He learned much from the Italian *commedia dell'arte*, which incorporated buffoonery, slapstick humor, and pantomime.

Absolute Power and the Aristocratic Style beyond Europe

- In Southwest Asia, the Ottoman sultan Suleiman established a pattern of princely patronage that was imitated by Muslim rulers for at least two centuries.
- The Persian Shah Abbas and the Mogul rulers of India were great patrons of the arts and they commissioned some of the most magnificent monuments in architectural history.
- Like Versailles in France, the Imperial Mosque in Isfahan, the Red Fort in Old Delhi, and the Taj Mahal in Agra all epitomize the wealth, absolute authority, and artistic vision of a privileged minority.

Absolute Power and the Aristocratic Style in China

- The imperial complex at the Forbidden City in Beijing stands as a symbol of the absolutism of China's Ming and Qing emperors.

- Imperial patronage of the arts supported the production of porcelain, *cloisonné*, brocade, and woven textiles, many of which found their way to Europe.
- Under the emperor Kangxi, China's literary and historical writings were compiled and anthologized. Chinese fiction, in the form of the novel, and Chinese opera appealed to a growing number of the public.

Absolute Power and the Aristocratic Style in Japan

- The Tokugawa dynasty created a unified central state over which the *shogun* assumed political and economic control. After 1630, the Japanese expelled foreigners and sealed themselves off from the world.
- In Japanese multipaneled screens, painted scrolls, lacquerware, and ceramics the decorative tradition in the arts reached new heights of sophistication and refinement.
- Woodcut prints popularized the pleasures of Edo's "floating world" and celebrated the actors of Japan's popular *kabuki* plays.
- Tea and the etiquette of tea-drinking, associated with Zen Buddhist culture, came to define the Japanese way of life.
- The verse form known as *haiku* reflects the controlled simplicity of Zen expression.

Glossary

chinoiserie European imitation of Chinese art, architecture, and decorative motifs; also any objects that reflect such imitation

choreography the art of composing, arranging, and/or notating dance movements

comédie-ballet (French) a dramatic performance that features interludes of song and dance

haiku a light verse form consisting of seventeen syllables (three lines of five, seven, and five)

kabuki (Japanese, "song-dance art") a popular form of Japanese drama

marquetry a decorative technique in which patterns are created on a wooden surface by means of inlaid wood, shell, or ivory

maxim a short, concise, and often witty saying

objet d'art (French) art object

pietra dura (Italian, "hard stone") an ornamental technique involving inlaid precious and semiprecious stones

salon (French, "drawing room") an elegant apartment or drawing room

shah (Persian) king

sharia the body of Muslim law based on the Qur'an and the *Hadith*

shogun (Japanese, "general-in-chief") military ruler who exercised absolute rule under the leadership of the emperor

sultan a Muslim ruler

The Baroque in the Protestant North

ca. 1550–1750

"No man is an island entire of itself; every man is a piece of the continent, a part of the main."
John Donne

Figure 22.1
REMBRANDT VAN RIJN,
The Return of the Prodigal Son,
ca. 1662–1668. Oil on canvas,
8 ft. 8 in. × 6 ft. 8 in.

In Northern Europe, where Protestant loyalties remained strong, there emerged a phase of the Baroque that differed perceptibly from other expressions of that style. The largely middle-class populations of England and the Netherlands had little use for the aristocratic Baroque style that glorified absolutist France. The Protestant North also resisted the kinds of florid religious display that characterized the Baroque style of the Catholic Reformation in Italy, Spain, and parts of the Americas.

In contrast with the ornate church interiors of Italy, Northern houses of worship were stripped of ornamentation. In England, the Netherlands, and northern Germany, where Protestants were committed to private devotion rather than public ritual, the Bible exercised an especially significant influence. The Northern Baroque style emphasized personal piety and private devotion. It reflected the spirit of Pietism, a seventeenth-century German religious movement, and the ideals of the Puritans, English Protestants who advocated a "purity" of worship, doctrine, and morality. To both of these movements, as to the arts of the European North, the Bible was prized as the means of cultivating the "inner light."

The Rise of the English Commonwealth

In England, Queen Elizabeth I (1533–1603) was succeeded by the first Stuart monarch, James I (1566–1625). A Scot, and a committed proponent of absolute monarchy, James claimed, "There are no privileges and immunities which can stand against a divinely appointed King." His son, Charles I (1600–1649; Figure **22.2**), shared his father's view that kings held a God-given right to rule. Charles alienated Parliament by governing for more than a decade without its approval. He antagonized the growing number of Puritans, who demanded Church reform and greater strictness in religious observance. Allying with antiroyalist factions, mostly of the emergent middle class, the Puritans constituted a powerful political group. With their support, leaders in Parliament raised an army to oppose King Charles, ultimately defeating the royalist forces in a civil war that lasted from 1642 to 1648 and executing the king in 1649 on charges of treason. The government that followed this civil war, led by the Puritan general Oliver Cromwell (1599–1658), was known as the "Commonwealth."

Bearing the hallmarks of a republic, the new government issued a written constitution that proposed the formation of a national legislature elected by universal manhood suffrage. The Commonwealth, however, was unable to survive. A sorely reduced Parliament abolished many offices of state, and a newly formed one, which proved inept, was dissolved by Cromwell. The "Protector of the Realm" took on the role of a dictator, alienating many segments of English society. When Cromwell died, the monarchy was restored with Charles I's son, Prince Charles (1635–1685), returning from exile to become king. Charles II's successor, James II (1633–1701), came to power in 1685; but when he converted to Catholicism two years later, and attempted to fill a new Parliament with his Catholic supporters, the opposition rebelled.

In 1688, the English expelled the king and offered the crown to William of Orange, ruler of the Netherlands, and his wife, Mary, the Protestant daughter of James II. Following the "Glorious Revolution" of 1688, Parliament enacted a Bill of Rights prohibiting the king from suspending parliamentary laws or interfering with the ordinary course of justice. The Bill of Rights was followed by the Toleration Act of 1689, which guaranteed freedom of worship to non-Anglican sects. By 1689, Parliament's authority to limit the power of the English monarch was firmly established. The "bloodless revolution" reestablished constitutional monarchy and won a victory for popular sovereignty.

The King James Bible

These dramatic political developments, so closely tied to religious issues, occurred in the years following one of the most influential cultural events of the seventeenth century: the new English translation of the Bible. A committee of about fifty scholars recruited by James I of England had begun the work of translation in 1604. Drawing on a number of earlier English translations of Scripture, they produced an English-language edition of the Old and New Testaments that would shape the English language and all subsequent English literature. The "authorized" edition of Scripture, which was published in 1611, came about in part as a response to the problems that Puritan factions of the Anglican Church detected in earlier translations of the Bible. While this version was not actually authorized by any ministerial body, it quickly became the official Bible of the Church of England (and of most English-speaking Protestant sects). As the product of the decades that also witnessed the last works of William Shakespeare, it reflects the moment when the English language reached its peak in eloquence.

The new translation of Scripture preserved the spiritual fervor of the Old Testament Hebrew and the narrative vigor of the New Testament Greek. Some appreciation of these qualities may be gleaned from comparing the two following translations. The first, a sixteenth-century translation based on Saint Jerome's Latin Vulgate edition and published in the city of Douay in France in 1609, lacks the concise language, the poetic imagery, and the lyrical rhythms of the King James version (the second example), which, although deeply indebted to a number of sixteenth-century English translations, drew directly on manuscripts written in the original Hebrew.

Figure 22.2 ANTHONY VAN DYCK, *Charles I on Horseback*, ca. 1638. Oil on canvas, 12 ft. × 9 ft. 7in.

From the Douay Bible (1609)

Our Lord ruleth me, and nothing shall be wanting to me; in place of pasture there he hath placed me.

Upon the water of refection he hath brought me up; he hath converted my soul.

He hath conducted me upon the paths of justice, for his name.

For although I shall walk in the midst of the shadow of death, I will not fear evils; because thou art with me.

Thy rod and thy staff, they have comforted me.

Thou hast prepared in my sight a table against them that trouble me.

Thou hast fatted my head with oil, and my chalice inebriating, how goodly is it!

And thy mercy shall follow me all the days of my life.

And that I may dwell in the house of our Lord in longitude of days.

From the King James Bible (1611)

The Lord is my shepherd; I shall not want.

He maketh me to lie down in green pastures: he leadeth me beside the still waters.

He restoreth my soul: he leadeth me in the paths of righteousness for his name's sake.

Yea, though I walk through the valley of the shadow of death, I will fear no evil: for thou art with me; thy rod and thy staff they comfort me.

Thou preparest a table before me in the presence of mine enemies: thou anointest my head with oil; my cup runneth over.

Surely goodness and mercy shall follow me all the days of my life: and I will dwell in the house of the Lord for ever.

Q **What aspects of the King James version of the Twenty-Third Psalm make this translation memorable?**

English Literature of the Seventeenth Century

John Donne

One of the most eloquent voices of religious devotionalism in the Protestant North was that of the poet John Donne (1571–1631). Born and raised as a Roman Catholic, Donne studied at Oxford and Cambridge, but he renounced Catholicism when he was in his twenties. He traveled widely, entered Parliament in 1601, and converted to Anglicanism fourteen years later, soon becoming a priest of the Church of England.

A formidable preacher as well as a man of great intellectual prowess, Donne wrote eloquent sermons that challenged the parishioners at Saint Paul's Cathedral in London (Figure **22.3**), where he acted as dean. At Saint

Figure 22.3 CHRISTOPHER WREN, west façade of Saint Paul's Cathedral, London, 1675–1710. Width approx. 90 ft.

Paul's, Donne developed the sermon as a vehicle for philosophic meditation. In Meditation 17 (an excerpt from which follows), Donne pictures humankind—in typically Baroque terms—as part of a vast, cosmic plan. His image of human beings as "chapters" in the larger "book" of God's design is an example of Donne's affection for unusual, extended metaphors. The tolling bell that figures so powerfully in the last lines makes reference to an age-old tradition (perpetuated at Saint Paul's) of ringing the church bells to announce the death of a parishioner.

READING 22.2 From Donne's Meditation 17 (1623)

All mankind is of one author, and is one volume; when one man 1
dies, one chapter is not torn out of the book, but translated into
a better language; and every chapter must be so translated. God
employs several translators; some pieces are translated by age,
some by sickness, some by war, some by justice; but God's 5
hand is in every translation, and his hand shall bind up all
our scattered leaves again for that library where every book
shall lie open to one another. As therefore the bell that rings
to a sermon calls not upon the preacher only but upon the
congregation to come, so this bell calls us all. . . . No man is an 10
island entire of itself; every man is a piece of the continent, a
part of the main. If a clod be washed away by the sea, Europe is
the less, as well as if a promontory were, as well as if a manor
of thy friend's or of thine own were. Any man's death diminishes
me, because I am involved in mankind, and therefore never send 15
to know for whom the bell tolls; it tolls for thee.

Q **What three metaphors are invoked in Meditation 17?**

Donne's poetry was as unconventional as his prose: both abound in "conceits," that is, elaborate metaphors that compare two apparently dissimilar objects or emotions, often with the intention of shocking or surprising. In that the conceits of Donne (and other seventeenth-century writers) borrowed words and images from the new science (see chapter 23), critics called these devices and the poetry they embellished "metaphysical." Metaphysical poetry reflects the Baroque affection for dramatic contrast, for frequent and unexpected shifts of viewpoint, and for the dramatic synthesis of discordant images. These features are apparent in some of Donne's finest works, including the group of religious poems known as the Holy Sonnets (see LOOKING INTO).

In Sonnet 10, Donne addresses Death as an imaginary person, regarded by some as "mighty and dreadful." Donne mocks Death as being nothing more than a slave who keeps bad company ("poison, war, and sickness"). He teases his adversary for being less potent than pleasurable sleep. And in the final lines of the sonnet, he arrives at the brilliant paradox that Death itself shall die—in the eternal life afforded by Christianity.

READING 22.3 From Donne's *Holy Sonnets* (1610)

Holy Sonnet 10

Death be not proud, though some have called thee 1
Mighty and dreadful, for thou art not so;
For those whom thou think'st thou dost overthrow
Die not, poor Death, nor yet canst thou kill me.
From rest and sleep, which but thy pictures be, 5
Much pleasure, then from thee much more must flow,
And soonest our best men with thee do go,
Rest of their bones and souls' delivery.
Thou art slave to fate, chance, kings, and desperate men,
And dost with poison, war, and sickness dwell, 10
And poppy[1], or charms[2] can make us sleep as well,
And better than thy stroke; why swell'st[3] thou then?
One short sleep past, we wake eternally,
And Death shall be no more; Death, thou shalt die.

Q **Why might this sonnet be called "metaphysical?"**

The Genius of John Milton

John Milton (1608–1674) was a devout Puritan and a defender of the Cromwellian Commonwealth that collapsed in 1658. His career as a humanist and poet began at the University of Cambridge and continued throughout his eleven-year tenure as secretary to the English Council of State. Although shy and retiring, Milton became a political activist and a persistent defender of religious, political, and intellectual freedom. He challenged English society with expository prose essays on a number of controversial subjects. In one pamphlet, he defended divorce between couples who were spiritually and temperamentally incompatible—a subject possibly inspired by his first wife's unexpected decision to abandon him briefly just after their marriage. In other prose works, Milton opposed Parliament's effort to control free speech and freedom of the press. "Who kills a man kills a reasonable creature," wrote Milton, "but he who destroys a good book, kills reason itself."

Milton's verse compositions include lyric poems and elegies, but the greatest of his contributions are his two epic poems: *Paradise Lost* and *Paradise Regained*. Milton wrote both of these monumental poems during the last decades of his life, when he was totally blind—a condition he erroneously attributed to long nights of reading. Legend has it that he dictated the poems to his two young daughters. In *Paradise Lost* Milton created a cosmic (and earth-centered) vision of Heaven, Hell, and Paradise comparable to that drawn by Dante (see chapter 12) but more philosophic in its concern with the human experience of knowledge, sin, and free will. Considered the greatest of modern epics, *Paradise Lost* is impressive in its vast intellectual sweep, its wide-ranging allusions to history and literature, and its effort to embrace matters of time, space, and causality.

[1] Opium.
[2] Sleeping potion.
[3] Puff with pride.

John Donne's *Holy Sonnet 14* (1610)

In this poem, Donne uses the sonnet form (a fourteen-line lyric poem with a fixed scheme of rhyming) to compare himself to a fortress that has been seized by the enemies of the Lord. He describes Reason as the ruler who has failed to defend the fortress, that is, Donne himself. He pleads with God to "ravish" and "imprison" him so as to set him free from sin. Donne's

unexpected juxtapositions and richly worked figures of speech (such as paradox and alliteration) are typical of English metaphysical poetry. However, his rejection of conventional poetic language in favor of a conversational tone marked by fierce energy and sensual fervor represents a revolutionary (and modern) development in European literature.

(a)*	Batter my heart, three-personed God; for You	he asks to be assaulted as with the battering rams used against fortified medieval towns / three-personed God = the Trinity
(b)	As yet but knock, breathe, shine, and seek to mend;	he has felt only the milder "forces" of the Father, the Holy Ghost, and Jesus
(b)	That I may rise, and stand, o'erthrow me, and bend	**paradox**: if overthrown, he may rise
(a)	Your force, to break, blow, burn, and make me new.	**paradox**: by being overtaken he will be renewed, reborn; **alliteration**: break, blow, burn
(a)	I, like a usurped town to another due,	**simile**: he compares himself again to a beseiged town
(b)	Labour to admit You, but oh! to no end;	he longs to welcome and embrace God
(b)	Reason, Your viceroy in me, me should defend,	human reason, God's agent, should defend him from sin
(a)	But is captived and proves weak or untrue.	but reason is too weak and false
(c)	Yet dearly I love You, and would be loved fain	he loves God and would willingly be loved by God
(d)	But am betrothed unto Your enemy.	but he is wedded to Satan
(c)	Divorce me, untie, or break that knot again,	he begs God to divorce him from sin; note the "turn" from stating problem (first eight lines) to pleading for solution;
(d)	Take me to You, imprison me, for I	and take him captive
(e)	Except You enthrall me, never shall be free;	**paradox**: only if he is captured will he be free;
(e)	Nor ever chaste, except You ravish me.	only if he is taken by force (enraptured; raped) will he be pure (virginal)

Q Is faith, in this sonnet, a matter of knowledge or belief?

*(a), (b), (c), (d), (e) letters are used to indicate the rhyming scheme.

Milton was already fifty years old when he resolved to compose a modern epic that rivaled the majesty of the classic works of Homer and Virgil. At the outset, he considered various themes, one of which was the story of King Arthur. But he settled instead on a Christian subject that allowed him to examine an issue particularly dear to his Protestant sensibilities: the meaning of evil in a universe created by a benevolent God. The twelve books of *Paradise Lost* retell the story of the fall of Adam and Eve, beginning with the activities of the rebellious archangel Satan and culminating in the expulsion of the First Parents from Paradise. The poem concludes with the angel Michael's explanation to Adam of how fallen Man, through Christ, will recover immortality. This august theme, rooted in biblical history, permitted Milton to explore questions of human knowledge, freedom, and morality and, ultimately, to "justify the ways of God to Men."

Central in this cosmic drama is the figure of Satan, who is painted larger than life as God's adversary. Milton vividly recounts the demon's passage from Hell to Earth and the fall of the rebel angels—a lengthy account that was probably inspired by the English Civil War. The titanic Satan is a metaphor for the Puritan conception of evil in the world. Less vividly drawn, Adam is an expression of Protestant pessimism—a figure who, for all his majesty, is incapable of holding on to Paradise. *Paradise Lost* may be considered a Christian parable of the human condition. In its cosmic scope and verbal exuberance, it is also a mirror of the Baroque imagination.

The language of *Paradise Lost* is intentionally lofty; it is designed to convey epic breadth and to narrate (as Milton promised) "things unattempted yet in prose or rhyme." Like Shakespeare, Milton chose to write in blank verse: unrhymed lines of ten syllables each with accents on every second syllable. This device allowed Milton to carry the thread of a single thought past the end of the line, thereby grouping ideas in rich verse paragraphs. The following excerpts convey some sense of the power and majesty of Milton's verse. In the first twenty-six lines of Book I, Milton announces the subject of the poem: the loss of humankind's spiritual innocence. The second excerpt, also from Book I, relates the manner in which Satan tears himself from Hell's burning lake and proudly assumes his place as ruler of the fallen legions. In the third excerpt (from Book IX), Adam resolves to stand with his beloved partner, Eve, by eating the Forbidden Fruit. Milton's description of Eve and her "fatal trespass" (l. 71) perpetuated the misogynistic trope of flawed womankind well into the late nineteenth century. Finally, in the passage from Book XII, Adam hears the angel Michael's prophetic description of humankind's destiny as he prepares to leave Paradise.

READING 22.4 From Milton's *Paradise Lost* (1667)

Book I

Of Man's first disobedience, and the fruit   **1**
Of that forbidden tree whose mortal taste
Brought death into the World, and all our woe,
With loss of Eden, till one greater Man[1]
Restore us, and regain the blissful seat,
Sing, Heavenly Muse, that on the secret top
Of Oreb, or of Sinai,[2] didst inspire

---

[1] Christ.

[2] As was the case with epic poets of old, Milton here invokes a divine source of inspiration. Milton's muse, however, is an abstraction of Judeo-Christian wisdom, identified with the muse that inspired Moses at Mount Horeb (Deut. 4.10) or on Mount Sinai (Exod. 19.20).

[3] A spring near Mount Zion in Jerusalem where, in the Hebrew Bible, God spoke to his people.

That shepherd who first taught the chosen seed
In the beginning how the heavens and earth
Rose out of Chaos: or, if Sion hill   **10**
Delight thee more, and Siloa's brook[3] that flowed
Fast by the oracle of God, I thence
Invoke thy aid to my adventurous song,
That with no middle flight intends to soar
Above th' Aonian mount,[4] while it pursues
Things unattempted yet in prose or rhyme.
And chiefly thou, O Spirit, that dost prefer
Before all temples th' upright heart and pure,
Instruct me, for thou know'st; thou from the first
Wast present, and, with mighty wings outspread,   **20**
Dove-like sat'st brooding on the vast Abyss,
And mad'st it pregnant: what in me is dark
Illumine, what is low raise and support;
That, to the height of this great argument,
I may assert Eternal Providence,
And justify the ways of God to men.

. . . .

Forthwith upright he rears from off the pool
His mighty stature; on each hand the flames
Driven backward slope their pointing spires, and rolled
In billows, leave i' th' midst a horrid vale.   **30**
Then with expanded wings he steers his flight
Aloft, incumbent on the dusky air,
That felt unusual weight; till on dry land
He lights—if it were land that ever burned
With solid, as the lake with liquid fire,
And such appeared in hue as when the force
Of subterranean wind transports a hill
Torn from Pelorus,[5] or the shattered side
Of thundering Etna, whose combustible
And fuelled entrails, thence conceiving fire,   **40**
Sublimed with mineral fury, aid the winds,
And leave a singed bottom all involved
With stench and smoke. Such resting found the sole
Of unblest feet. Him followed his next mate;
Both glorying to have escaped the Stygian[6] flood
As gods, and by their own recovered strength,
Not by the sufferance of supernal Power.
   "Is this the region, this the soil, the clime,"
Said then the lost Archangel, "this the seat
That we must change for Heaven?—this mournful gloom   **50**
For that celestial light? Be it so, since he
Who now is sovereign can dispose and bid
What shall be right: farthest from him is best
Whom reason hath equalled, force hath made supreme
Above his equals. Farewell, happy fields,
Where joy for ever dwells! Hail, horrors! Hail,
Infernal world! And thou, profoundest Hell
Receive thy new possessor—one who brings

---

[4] In Greece, the muses were thought to live on Mount Helicon, also known as the "Aonian mountain."

[5] A promontory near the volcanic Mount Etna in Sicily.

[6] Referring to the River Styx, in Greek mythology the principal river of the underworld.

A mind not to be changed by place or time.
The mind is its own place, and in itself   60
Can make a Heaven of Hell, a Hell of Heaven.
What matter where, if I be still the same,
And what I should be, all but less than he
Whom thunder hath made greater? Here at least
We shall be free; th' Almighty hath not built
Here for his envy, will not drive us hence:
Here we may reign secure; and, in my choice,
To reign is worth ambition, though in Hell:
Better to reign in Hell, than serve in Heaven."

                .   .   .   .

Book IX

On the other side Adam, soon as he heard   70
The fatal trespass done by Eve, amazed,[7]
Astonied[8] stood and blank, while horror chill
Ran through his veins, and all his joints relaxed;
From his slack hand the garland wreathed for Eve
Down dropped, and all the faded roses shed:
Speechless he stood and pale, till thus at length
First to himself he inward silence broke.

    "O fairest of Creation, last and best
Of all God's works, Creature in whom excelled
Whatever can to sight or thought be formed,   80
Holy, divine, good, amiable, or sweet!
How art thou lost! How on a sudden lost,
Defaced, deflowered, and now to death devote![9]
Rather, how hast thou yielded to transgress
The strict forbiddance, how to violate
The sacred fruit forbidden! Some cursed fraud
Of enemy hath beguiled thee, yet unknown,
And me with thee hath ruined; for with thee
Certain my resolution is to die:
How can I live without thee! How forgo   90
Thy sweet converse, and love so dearly joined,
To live again in these wild woods forlorn!
Should God create another Eve, and I
Another rib afford, yet loss of thee
Would never from my heart: no, no! I feel
The link of Nature draw me: flesh of flesh,
Bone of my bone thou art, and from thy state
Mine never shall be parted, bliss or woe."

                .   .   .   .

Book XII

*["Greatly instructed," Adam prepares to depart from Paradise;
the angel Michael reminds him of humankind's limitations.]*

"This having learnt, thou hast attained the sum
Of wisdom; hope no higher, though all the stars   100
Thou knew by name, and all the ethereal powers,
All secrets of the deep, all nature's works,
Or works of God in heaven, air, earth, or sea,
And all the riches of this world enjoyed,

And all the rule, one empire; only add
Deeds to thy knowledge answerable, add faith,
Add virtue, patience, temperance, add love,
By name to come called charity, the soul
Of all the rest: then wilt thou not be loath
To leave this Paradise, but shalt possess   110
A paradise within thee, happier far.
Let us descend now therefore from this top
Of speculation; for the hour precise
Exacts our parting hence; and see the guards,
By me encamped on yonder hill, expect
Their motion,[10] at whose front a flaming sword,
In signal of remove,[11] waves fiercely round;
We may no longer stay: go, waken Eve;
Her also I with gentle dreams have calmed
Portending good, and all her spirits composed   120
To meek submission: thou at season fit
Let her with thee partake what thou hast heard,
Chiefly what may concern her faith to know,
The great deliverance by her seed to come
(For by the Woman's Seed) on all mankind.
That ye may live, which will be many days,
Both in one faith unanimous though sad,
With cause for evils past, yet much more cheered
With meditation on the happy end."

Q **Describe the appearance and the personality of
Satan (Book I).**

Q **Why does Adam decide to stay with the fallen Eve
(Book IX)?**

Q **What message does the angel give to Adam
(Book XII)?**

The London of Christopher Wren

London at the time of Donne and Milton was a city of vast extremes. England's commercial activities in India and the Americas made its capital a center for stock exchanges, insurance firms, and joint-stock companies. Yet living amongst the wealthy Londoners, a great number of people remained poor. One-fourth of London's 250,000 inhabitants could neither read nor write; meanwhile, English intellectuals advanced scientific learning. For some time Londoners enjoyed some of the finest libraries and theaters in Western Europe, but, under the Puritan-dominated Parliament of the 1640s, stage plays were suppressed, and many old theaters, including Shakespeare's Globe, were torn down. The restoration of the monarchy in 1660 brought with it a revived interest in drama and in the construction of indoor theaters (as opposed to the open-air theaters of Shakespeare's time).

In 1666, a devastating fire tore through London and destroyed three-quarters of the city, including 13,000

---

[7] Confused, terror-stricken.
[8] Stunned.
[9] Devoted, doomed.

[10] Await their marching orders.
[11] Departure.

homes, eighty-seven parish churches, and the cathedral church of Saint Paul's, where John Donne had served as dean some decades earlier. Following the fire, there was an upsurge of large-scale building activity and a general effort to modernize London. The architect Christopher Wren (1632–1723) played a leading role in this effort. A child prodigy in mathematics, then an experimental scientist and professor of astronomy at London and Oxford, Wren was one of the founding fathers of the Royal Society of London for Improving Natural Knowledge. Following the Great Fire, Wren prepared designs for the reconstruction of London. Although his plans for new city streets (based on the Roman grid) were rejected, he was commissioned to rebuild more than fifty churches,

including Saint Paul's—the first church in Christendom to be completed during the lifetime of its architect.

Wren's early designs for Saint Paul's featured the Greek cross plan that Michelangelo had proposed for Saint Peter's in Rome (see chapter 17). However, the clergy of Saint Paul's preferred a Latin cross structure. The final design was a compromise that combined Classical, Gothic, Renaissance, and Baroque architectural features. Saint Paul's handsome two-story façade, with its ornate twin clock towers and its strong surface contrasts of light and dark (see Figure 22.3), looks back to Borromini (see Figure 20.19), but its massive scale and overall design—a large dome set upon a Latin cross basilica—are reminiscent of Saint Peter's (see Figure 20.14). As at Saint Peter's, Wren's dome, which physically resembles that of Bramante's Tempietto (see Figure 17.28), is equal in its diameter (102 feet) to the combined width of the nave and side aisles. The dimensions of the cathedral are colossal: 366 feet from ground level to the top of the lantern cross (Saint Peter's reaches 452 feet).

Wren envisioned a dome that was both impressive from the outside and easily visible from the inside. He came up with an inventive and complex device: two domes, one exterior (made of timber covered with lead) and the other interior (made of light brick), are supported by a third, cone-shaped dome, which is hidden between the other two (Figure 22.4). The monumental silhouette of Wren's dome, which became the model for the United States capitol, remains an impressive presence on the London skyline. From within the church, there is the equally impressive illusionism of the *trompe l'oeil* heavens

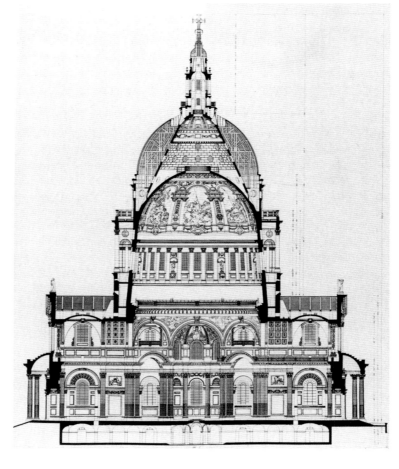

Figure 22.4 Cross section of Saint Paul's showing Wren's three domes.

painted on the inner surface of the central cupola. Like Milton's *Paradise Lost*, Wren's Saint Paul's is a majestic synthesis of Classical and Christian traditions, while its huge size, dramatic exterior, and light-filled interior are Baroque in conception and effect.

Protestant Devotionalism in the Netherlands

Since 1560, when Spain had invaded the Dutch Lowlands, the seventeen provinces of the Netherlands had been engaged in a bitter struggle against the Catholic forces of the Spanish king Philip II. In 1579, after years of bloodshed, the Dutch forced Philip's armies to withdraw. Two years later, the seven provinces of the north Netherlands declared their independence. By the end of the century the predominantly Calvinist Dutch Republic (later called "Holland") was a self-governing state and one of the most commercially active territories in Western Europe. Dutch shipbuilders produced some of the finest trading vessels on the high seas, while skilled Dutch seamen brought those vessels to all parts of the world. In Amsterdam, as in hundreds of other Dutch towns, merchants and craftspeople shared the responsibilities of local government, profiting handsomely from the smooth-running, primarily maritime, economy.

The autonomous towns of the north Netherlands, many of which supported fine universities, fostered freedom of thought and a high rate of literacy. Hardworking, thrifty, and independent-minded, the seventeenth-century Dutch enjoyed a degree of independence and material prosperity unmatched elsewhere in the world. Their proletarian tastes, along with a profound appreciation for the physical comforts of home and hearth, inspired their preference for such secular subjects as portraits, still lifes, landscapes, and scenes of domestic life (see chapter 23). Since Calvinism strongly discouraged the use of religious icons, sculpture was uncommon in the Protestant North. But paintings, especially those with scriptural subjects, were favored sources of seventeenth-century moral knowledge and instruction. The Old Testament was particularly popular among the Dutch, who viewed themselves as God's "chosen" people, elected to triumph over the forces of Catholic Spain.

Rembrandt

In this milieu emerged one of the world's great painters, Rembrandt van Rijn (1606–1669). Born in the city of Leiden, Rembrandt moved to Amsterdam, the new business capital of the Netherlands, in 1631, where he rose to fame as a portraitist (see chapter 23). In his religious works, he often chose subjects that were uncommon in Catholic art, focusing on the human, and even intimately personal, aspects of Old and New Testament stories. Rembrandt's Anabaptist upbringing, characterized by a fundamentalist approach to Scripture and a solemn attention to the role of individual conscience, surely contributed to this unique approach. The people who roamed the streets of Amsterdam, and the Spanish and Jewish refugees he regularly sketched in the city's ghettos, provided Rembrandt with a cast of characters who populated his religious paintings. His sympathetic and largely unidealized treatment of sacred subject matter captured the spirit of Protestant devotionalism.

A case in point is Rembrandt's moving painting *The Return of the Prodigal Son* (see Figure 22.1). Here, the artist has brought to life the moment when the wayward son of the parable (Luke 15:11–32), having returned home in rags, kneels humbly before his father to beg forgiveness. For theatrical effect, Rembrandt has pulled the figures out of the shadowy depths of the background. The father and son, bathed in golden light, form an off-center triangle balanced by the sharply lit vertical of the figure on the right. Rich areas of bright **impasto** (thick layers of pigment) contrast with dark, brooding passages, created by way of thinly brushed layers of oil paint. Rembrandt learned much about theatrical staging from the Italian Baroque master Caravaggio (see chapter 20), but in this simple and restrained composition, he reaches below surface appearance to explore the psychological subtlety of the drama.

Rembrandt's technical virtuosity as a draftsman made him more famous in his own time as a printmaker than as a painter. His medium of choice was **etching** (Figure **22.5**). Like the woodcuts and engravings of his Northern European predecessors Dürer and Holbein (see chapter 19), Rembrandt's etchings met the demands of middle-class patrons who sought private devotional images that—by comparison with paintings—were inexpensive. A consummate and prolific printmaker, Rembrandt used the **burin** (a steel cutting tool) to develop dramatic contrasts of rich darks and brilliant lights. These talents are evident in one of his most famous prints, *Christ Preaching*

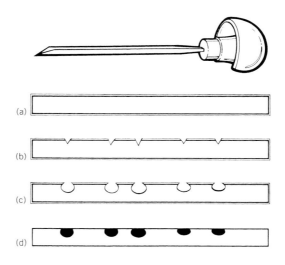

Figure 22.5 Etching is an intaglio printing process. A metal plate is coated with resin (a) then images are scratched through the coating with a burin or graver (b). Acid is applied, which "eats" or etches the metal exposed by the scratches (c). The resin is then removed and ink is rubbed into the etched lines on the metal plate (d). After the plate is wiped clean, it is pressed onto the paper and the ink-filled lines are deposited on the paper surface. Other intaglio processes include engraving and aquatint.

Figure 22.6 REMBRANDT VAN RIJN, *Christ Preaching* ("The Hundred-Guilder Print"), ca. 1648–1650. Etching, 11 × 15½ in. A group of Pharisees stands at the right hand of the preaching Jesus. One turns away from the preacher, a second is lost in thought, while a third, bathed in the light that surrounds the Christ, listens in rapt attention.

(Figure **22.6**)—also known as "The Hundred-Guilder Print," because it sold at a seventeenth-century auction for the then unimaginably high price of 100 Dutch guilders. Illustrating the Gospel of Matthew, it depicts Jesus addressing the members of the Jewish community: the sick and the lame (foreground), "the little children" (middle left), the ill and infirm (right), and an assembly of Pharisees (far left). With an extraordinary economy of line—no more than a few deft strokes of the pen—the artist has captured the lot of the poor, the downtrodden, and the aged. So colloquial is Rembrandt's handling of the biblical story that it seems an event that might have taken place in Rembrandt's own time and place.

The Music of the Protestant North

Handel and the English Oratorio

If the Protestant North produced memorable art, it also generated great music. The careers of two extraordinary German composers, George Frideric Handel (1685–1756) and Johann Sebastian Bach (1685–1750), represent the flowering of the Baroque style in Northern European music.

Born in the Lutheran trading city of Halle, Germany, Handel was determined to pursue his childhood musical talent. When his father, who intended for him a career in law, refused to provide him with a musical instrument, he smuggled a small clavichord into the attic. After proving himself at the keyboard and as a successful violinist and composer in the courts of Hamburg, Rome, Paris, Naples, and Venice, he emigrated to London in 1710, becoming a British citizen in 1726. Like many of his contemporaries, Handel began his career as a student of Italian opera. He composed forty-six operas in Italian and four in his native German. He also produced a prodigious number of instrumental works. But it was for his development of the **oratorio** that he earned fame among the English, who called him "England's greatest composer."

An oratorio is the musical setting of a long sacred or epic text; it is performed in concert by a narrator, soloists, chorus, and orchestra (Figure **22.7**). Like operas, oratorios are large in scale and dramatic in intent, but, unlike opera, they are produced without scenery, costumes, or dramatic action. Soloists and chorus assume the roles of the main characters in the narrative. The word "oratorio" refers to a church chapel, and most oratorios are religious in content;

Figure 22.7 Performance of an oratorio, 1750; Handel (far right) is conducting. Copper engraving, diameter 7⅞ in.

however, they were never intended for church services. Rather, they were performed in public concert halls. With the oratorio came the shift from music written and performed for church or court to music composed for concert halls (or opera houses) and enjoyed by the general public. Appropriately, in the late seventeenth century, public concerts (and entrance fees) made their first appearance in the social history of music.

In his lifetime, Handel composed more than thirty oratorios. Like the works of Rembrandt and Milton (whose verses he borrowed for the oratorio *Samson*), Handel's music brought Scripture to life. The most famous of Handel's oratorios is *Messiah*, which was written in the English of the King James Bible. Composed, remarkably enough, in just twenty-four days, it was performed for the first time in Dublin in 1742. It received instant acclaim. One of the most moving pieces of choral music ever written, *Messiah* celebrates the birth, death, and resurrection of Jesus. Unlike most of Handel's oratorios, it is not a biblical dramatization but rather a collection of verses from the Old and New Testaments. The first part of the piece recounts Old Testament prophecies of a Savior, the second relates the suffering and death of Jesus, and the

third rejoices in the redemption of humankind through Christ's resurrection.

Messiah is typical of the Baroque sensibility: indeed, the epic proportions of its score and libretto call to mind Milton's *Paradise Lost. Messiah* is also Baroque in its style, which features vigorous contrasts of tempo and dynamics and dramatic interaction between participating ensembles—solo voices, chorus, and instruments. A master of theatrical effects, Handel made use of word painting and other affective devices throughout the piece. For example, the music for the last words of the sentence "All we, like sheep, have gone astray" consists of deliberately divergent melodic lines.

The best-loved choral work in the English language, *Messiah* has outlasted its age. In many Christian communities, it has become traditional to perform the piece during both the Christmas and Easter seasons. The jubilant "Hallelujah Chorus" (which ends the second of the three parts of the oratorio) still brings audiences to their feet, as it did King George II of England, who introduced this

🎼 See Music Listening Selections at end of chapter.

Figure 22.8 ELIAS GOTTLOB HAUSSMANN, *Johann Sebastian Bach*, 1746. Oil on canvas, 30⅔ × 24 in.

tradition by rising from his seat when he first heard it performed in London in 1743.

Handel's *Messiah* features polyphonic textures at the start of many of the choruses, such as "For unto us a Child is born." Nevertheless, like Handel's other oratorios, *Messiah* is essentially **homophonic**; that is, its musical organization depends on the use of a dominant melody supported by chordal accompaniment. Homophony is the musical opposite of polyphony, the many-voiced texture that characterized most music prior to the seventeenth century. The chords in a homophonic composition serve to support—or, in the visual sense, to "spotlight"—a primary melody. In the seventeenth century, there evolved a form of musical shorthand that allowed musicians to fill in the harmony for the principal melody of a homophonic piece. The **figured bass**, as this shorthand was called, consisted of a line of music with numbers written below it to indicate the harmony accompanying the primary melody. The use of the figured bass (also called the "continuo," since it played throughout the piece) was one of the main features of Baroque music.

Bach and Religious Music

Johann Sebastian Bach (Figure **22.8**) was born in the small town of Eisenach, very near the castle in which Martin Luther—hiding from the wrath of the Roman papacy—had first translated the Bible into German. Unlike the cosmopolitan Handel, Bach never strayed more than a couple of hundred miles from his birthplace; the last twenty-seven years of his career were spent in nearby Leipzig. Nor did

he depart from his Protestant roots: Luther's teachings and Lutheran hymn tunes were Bach's major sources of religious inspiration, and the organ—the principal instrument of Protestant church music—was one of his favorite instruments. The Germans were the masters of the organ, and Bach was acknowledged to be the finest of organ virtuosi. He even served as a consultant for the construction of Baroque organs, whose ornately embellished casings made them the glory of many Protestant churches (Figure **22.9**). As organ master and choir director of the Lutheran church of Saint Thomas in Leipzig, Bach assumed the responsibility of composing music for each of the Sunday services and for holy days. A pious Lutheran, who, in the course of two marriages, fathered twenty children (five of whom became notable musicians), Bach humbly dedicated his compositions "to the glory of God."

Bach's religious vocal music included such forms as the oratorio, the Mass, and the **cantata**. The cantata is a multimovement work with a verse text sung by chorus and soloists and accompanied by a musical instrument or instruments. Like the oratorio, the cantata may be sacred or secular in subject matter and lyric or dramatic in style. Bach's 209 surviving cantatas are musical commentaries on the daily scriptural lessons of the Lutheran church service. At the beginning of the score for each cantata, Bach inscribed the initials "S.D.G.," standing for "Soli Deo Gloria" ("to the glory of God alone"). Unparalleled in their florid counterpoint, Bach's cantatas were inspired by the simple melodies of Lutheran chorales, with their regular rhythms and rugged melodies. Cantata No. 80 is based on Luther's "A Mighty Fortress is Our God," the most important hymn of the Lutheran Church (see chapter 19). Its melody unifies the eight movements of the cantata, which concludes with a four-part setting of the chorale melody, sung in the style of the congregational hymn. Bach drew on Protestant chorales not only for his cantatas but also as the basis for many of his instrumental compositions (see chapter 23), including the 170 organ **preludes** that he composed to precede and set the mood for congregational singing.

At the apex of Bach's achievement in vocal music is the *Passion According to Saint Matthew*, an oratorio written in 1727 for the Good Friday service at the church of Saint Thomas in Leipzig. This majestic work consists of the sung texts of chapters 26 and 27 of Matthew's Gospel, which describe Christ's Passion: the events between the Last Supper and the Resurrection. It is written for a double chorus, with soloists who take the parts of Jesus, the disciples, the Pharisees, and other characters in the Gospel account. A solo tenor sings the part of the Evangelist, who narrates the story. A double orchestra and two organs accompany the voices. Alternating with the Gospel verses, passages of commentary (a text written by a local German poet) moralize the narrative and develop the states of minds of the individual "characters."

The three-and-a-half-hour piece consists of two parts, the first originally to be sung before the Vespers sermon

See Music Listening Selections at end of chapter.

and the second after it. In Bach's time, the church congregation participated in the performance of the choral portions, thus adding to the sheer volume of sound produced by choirs and orchestras. Performed today in the church or in the concert hall, Bach's oratorio still conveys the devotional spirit of the Protestant North. In its imaginative use of Scripture, as well as in its compositional complexity, the *Passion According to Saint Matthew* compares with Rembrandt's religious paintings, Handel's *Messiah*, and Milton's *Paradise Lost.*

Figure 22.9 GOTTFRIED SILBERMANN, organ in Freiburg Cathedral (Saxony), Germany, 1710–1714.

LOOKING BACK

The Rise of the English Commonwealth

- Charles I, like his French counterparts, believed kings held a God-given right to rule. He alienated Parliament and antagonized the growing number of English Puritans until Parliament raised an army and initiated a civil war in 1642.
- After the execution of the king, the English Commonwealth, led by the Puritan general Oliver Cromwell, bore the hallmarks of a republic.

- Although the monarchy was reestablished after Cromwell's death, a rebellious Protestant opposition brought about the Glorious Revolution of 1688. Parliament's authority to limit the power of the English monarch was firmly established in 1689 after the passage of the Bill of Rights and the Toleration Act.

The King James Bible

- Drawing on a number of earlier English translations of Scripture made during

the sixteenth century, and manuscripts in the original Hebrew, a committee of about fifty scholars produced in 1611 an English-language edition of the Old and New Testaments known as the King James Bible.
- The King James Bible had a shaping influence on the English language and on all subsequent English literature.

English Literature of the Seventeenth Century

- Born and raised a Roman Catholic, John Donne converted to Anglicanism, becoming a priest of the Church of England. His sermons, developed as philosophical meditations, and his metaphysical sonnets featured ingenious conceits, extended metaphors, and paradoxical perspectives.
- John Milton, Puritan, humanist, and defender of Cromwell's Commonwealth, was the most notable English-language poet of the seventeenth century. His verse compositions include lyric poems and elegies; his two epic poems, *Paradise Lost* and *Paradise Regained*, are considered his greatest contributions to the humanistic tradition.
- *Paradise Lost* is impressive in its vast intellectual sweep, its wide-ranging allusions to history and literature, and its (typically Baroque) effort to address matters of time, space, and causality.

The London of Christopher Wren

- Following the devastating fire that destroyed three-quarters of London, Christopher Wren, an architect, scientist, and professor, and one of the founding fathers of the Royal Society of London, was commissioned to prepare designs for the city's reconstruction.
- Wren's design for Saint Paul's Cathedral was an ingenious combination of Classical, Gothic, Renaissance, and Baroque architectural features. Its huge size, dramatic exterior, and light-filled interior had a lasting impact on the field of architecture.

Protestant Devotionalism in the Netherlands

- The religious paintings of the Dutch master Rembrandt van Rijn represent a visual parallel to the deeply devotional works of Milton and Donne.
- Rembrandt illustrated the contents of Holy Scripture in paintings, drawings, and etchings that were at once realistic, theatrical, and psychologically profound. His bold compositions and inventive use of light recreated sacred events as though they were occurring in his own time and place.

The Music of the Protestant North

- The German composer George Frideric Handel dramatized scriptural narrative by means of the oratorio, a new musical form that typified the Baroque taste for rich color and dramatic effect. Handel's *Messiah*, an early landmark in homophonic composition, remains one of the most stirring examples of choral music.
- Handel's Lutheran contemporary Johann Sebastian Bach dedicated much of his life to composing music that honored God. His cantatas and preludes employ melodies borrowed largely from Lutheran hymns. His *Passion According to Saint Matthew* brought religious choral music to new heights of dramatic grandeur.

Music Listening Selections

- Handel, *Messiah*, "Hallelujah Chorus," 1742.
- Bach, Cantata No. 80, "Eine feste Burg ist unser Gott" ("A Mighty Fortress is Our God"), Chorale, 1724.

Glossary

alliteration a literary device involving the repetition of initial sounds in successive or closely associated words or syllables

burin a steel tool used for engraving and incising

cantata (Italian, *cantare* = "to sing") a multimovement composition for voices and instrumental accompaniment; smaller in scale than the oratorio

etching a kind of engraving in which a metal plate is covered with resin, then incised with a burin; acid is applied to "eat" away the exposed lines, which are inked before the plate is wiped clean and printed; see Figure 22.5

figured bass in Baroque music, the line of music with numbers written below (or above) it to indicate the required harmony, usually improvised in the form of keyboard chords accompanying the melody; also called "continuo"

homophony a musical texture consisting of a dominant melody supported by chordal accompaniment that is far less important than the melody; compare polyphony (see Glossary, chapter 13)

impasto the thick application of pigment to the surface of a painting

oratorio (Latin, *oratorium* = "church chapel") a musical setting of a long text, either religious or secular, for soloists, chorus, narrator, and orchestra; usually performed without scenery, costumes, or dramatic action

paradox a seemingly contradictory statement that may nevertheless be true

prelude a piece of instrumental music that introduces either a church service or another piece of music

simile a figure of speech in which two unlike things are compared

The Scientific Revolution and the New Learning
ca. 1550–1750

"Read not to contradict and confute; nor to believe and take for granted; nor to find talk and discourse, but to weigh and consider."
Francis Bacon

Figure 23.1 JAN STEEN, *The Drawing Lesson*, 1665. Oil on canvas, 19⅜ × 16¼ in. Often humorous and anecdotal, Steen's paintings are usually brilliant in composition. Here, he uses the canvas leaning on the trunk and the lute on the floor to lead our eyes into the scene.

While the early modern era was a time of heightened spirituality, it was also an age of scientific discovery. Between 1550 and 1750, European scientists challenged the model of the universe that had prevailed from the time of Aristotle to the sixteenth century. Advancing the sciences of physics, astronomy, and geology, they demystified nature, taking it out of the hands of priests and poets, and putting it into the laboratory. The Scientific Revolution would have a three-part focus: 1) the exercise of direct observation and experimentation; 2) the reliance on mathematical verification; and 3) the invention of new instruments by which to measure natural phenomena, test hypotheses, and predict the operations of nature.

The scientists of the early modern era differed from their predecessors in separating *scientia* (the Latin word for "knowledge") from religious truths. While their forerunners perceived the universe as the creation of an absolute and eternal God, they described it as a mechanism that operated according to the laws of nature. In consort with the new learning, a program of inquiry focused on inductive and deductive reasoning, they laid the groundwork for clear and objective thinking, and, ultimately, for the birth of modern philosophy and modern science.

The alliance of scientific inquiry and critical thinking ushered in a phase of the Baroque marked by an empirical attention to the real world; in art, an emphasis on light and space, and an increased demand for subjects that gave evidence of everyday experience: landscape, portraiture, still life, and the domestic interior. Developments in Baroque instrumental music, unique to this era, met the demands for secular entertainment made by a growing middle class.

The Scientific Revolution

The Background

The Scientific Revolution was not entirely sudden, nor were its foundations exclusively European. It owed much to a long history of empirical and theoretical inquiry that began in ancient Egypt and was furthered in China, in Hellenistic cities, and across the Muslim world. That history ranged from the invention of the magnetic compass to the formulation of Euclidian geometry, the birth of algebra, and the science of optics. Beginning with the Renaissance, however, as artist–scientists probed the workings of the visible world, the ambition to control nature by way of practical knowledge gained greater impetus in the West. In the pioneering efforts of Leonardo da Vinci, the empirical thrust of the Scientific Revolution was already initiated. Inspired by Leonardo's drawings of the human body, particularly those that investigated the internal organs, the Flemish physician Andreas Vesalius (1514–1564) published the first accurate analysis of human anatomy. Vesalius' treatise *On the Workings of the Human Body* (1543) became the virtual bible for seventeenth-century medical science.

A near contemporary of Vesalius, the Swiss alchemist Philippus von Hohenheim, known as Paracelsus (1493–1541), anticipated modern chemistry by compounding medical remedies from minerals rather than from botanical substances. At the same time, the Polish physician and astronomer Nicolas Copernicus (1473–1543) published his landmark treatise *On the Revolution of the Heavenly Spheres* (1543). Basing his work solely on mathematical calculations, Copernicus formulated a theory according to which the earth and all the planets circle around the sun. The **heliocentric** (sun-centered) model of the cosmos (Figure **23.2A**) stood in contradiction to the **geocentric** (earth-centered) model advanced by the renowned second-century Hellenistic astronomer Claudius Ptolemy. While other Hellenistic astronomers had argued in favor of a sun-centered universe, Ptolemy's detailed studies popularized the ancient Greek conception of the heavens as a series of concentric crystalline spheres (occupied

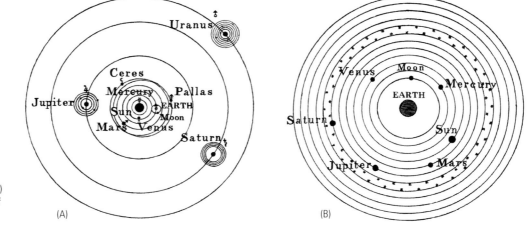

Figure 23.2 Heliocentric (A) and geocentric (B) models of the universe.

(A)

(B)

individually by the Moon, Mercury, Venus, the Sun, Mars, Jupiter, and Saturn), with Earth (and thus humankind) at the center (Figure **23.2B**)—a cosmos enshrined in Dante's *Divine Comedy* (see chapter 12). Planetary motion was circular, directed, according to Aristotle, by a first Cause or Unmoved Mover (in the later, Christian view, God). In the hundred years that followed the publication of Copernicus' treatise, these theories came under close scrutiny.

Kepler

The German mathematician Johannes Kepler (1571–1630) was among the first to make detailed records of planetary movements that substantiated the heliocentric theory. Challenging the conventional assumption that the planetary orbits were perfectly circular, Kepler also showed that the five known planets moved around the sun in elliptical paths. He argued that the magnetic force emitted by the sun determined their movements and their distances from the sun. Kepler's new physics advanced the idea of a universe in motion, contradicting the Aristotelian notion of a fixed and unchanging cosmos. It also generated strong opposition in religious circles. Not only did the theory of heliocentricity deprive God's ultimate creations—man and woman—of their paramount place in the universe, but also it conflicted with the Holy Bible—where, for example, the Hebrew hero Joshua is described as making the sun stand still (Joshua 10:12–13), a miraculous event that could have occurred only if the sun normally moved around the earth. The earth, according to Genesis (1:9–13), preceded the sun in the Divine Creation. Ultimately, then, the model of the universe defended by Kepler deprived human beings of their central place in the universe; it made humanity seem incidental to God's plan. Although Catholics and Protestants were at odds on many theological matters, in defending the inviolable truth of Scripture against the claims of the new science, they were united.

Galileo

Kepler's Italian contemporary Galileo Galilei (1564–1642) further advanced Kepler's research—and imperiled his own life by doing so. Galileo's inquiries into motion and gravity resulted in the formulation of the Law of Falling Bodies, which proclaims that the earth's gravity attracts all objects—regardless of shape, size, or density—at the same rate of acceleration. (Legend has it that he tested his theory by dropping different-sized weights from the top of the Leaning Tower of Pisa.)

In 1608, a Dutch lensmaker invented an instrument that magnified objects seen at a great distance. Intrigued by the device, Galileo went on to perfect it. His telescope literally revealed new worlds. Through its lens, one could see the craters of the moon, the rings of Saturn, and the moons of Jupiter, which, as Galileo observed, operated exactly like earth's moon. The telescope turned the heliocentric theory into fact.

Galileo's discoveries immediately aroused opposition from Catholics and Protestants committed to maintaining orthodox Christian beliefs, especially those set forth in Scripture. The first institutional attack on "the new science"

had occurred in 1600, when the Catholic Inquisition tried, condemned, and publicly executed the Italian astronomer Giordano Bruno, who had asserted that the universe was infinite and without center. Bruno had also suggested that other solar systems might exist in space. Sixteen years after Bruno was burned at the stake, the Church of Rome issued an edict that condemned Copernican astronomy as "false and contrary to Holy Scripture." The writings of Copernicus were put on the Catholic Index of Forbidden Books. Galileo added to the controversy by making his own findings public, and available to a wider audience because he wrote in Italian rather than in Latin, the traditional language of Western authority.

More inflammatory still was the publication of Galileo's *Dialogue Concerning the Two Principal Systems of the World* (1632), a fictional conversation between a Copernican and the defenders of the old order, one of whom resembled the pope. Written in the vernacular, this entertaining classic of science advanced, by way of biting sarcasm, the need for an open-minded examination of the cherished opinions of Aristotle and Ptolemy. Earlier in his career, when it had become evident that his gravitational theories contradicted Aristotle, Galileo had been forced to give up his position as mathematics professor at the University of Pisa. Now, ill with kidney stones and arthritis, he was dragged to Rome and brought before the Inquisition. After a long and unpleasant trial, Church officials, threatening torture, forced the aging astronomer to "admit his errors."

Legend has it that after publicly denying that the earth moved around the sun, he muttered under his breath, "Eppur si muove" ("But it *does* move!"). Although condemned to indefinite imprisonment, Galileo was permitted to reside—under "house arrest"—in a villa outside Florence. Imprisonment, however, did not daunt either his ingenuity or his sense of awe. On developing the compound microscope, he marveled, "I have observed many tiny animals . . . among which the flea is quite horrible, the gnat and the moth very beautiful; and with great satisfaction I have seen how flies and other little animals can walk attached to mirrors, upside down." His books banned by the Church, Galileo continued to receive personal visits from eminent figures, including the English poet John Milton.

The Instruments of the New Science

The Scientific Revolution produced new instruments for measurement and new procedures for experimentation and analysis. The slide rule, the magnet, the microscope, the mercury barometer, and the air pump (Figure **23.3**) were among the many products of the quest to calculate, investigate, and predict the workings of nature. Seventeenth-century scientists investigated the function of the human eye and explored the genesis and propagation of light, thus advancing the science of optics beyond the frontiers of Islamic and Renaissance scholarship. They accurately described the action of gases and the circulation of the blood. By 1660, with the aid of a more highly powered microscope, they identified protozoa and human blood cells. The mysterious process known to ancient

Figure 23.3 JOSEPH WRIGHT, *An Experiment on a Bird in the Air Pump*, 1768. Oil on canvas, 5 ft. 11⅝ in. × 7 ft. 11¾ in. Wright was the first Western artist to use scientific experimentation as dramatic subject matter. A vacuum is created by removing air from a glass bowl, which deprives the bird of oxygen. In a manner borrowed from Baroque religious art, Wright uses light to bring attention to the various expressions on the faces of the middle-class family.

and medieval societies as "generation" was described with some precision, when, between 1665 and 1680, scientists at the University of Leiden made key discoveries concerning human and animal reproduction. Based on William Harvey's hypothesis that all animals emerge from an egg, and Anton van Leeuwenhoek's microscopic studies of spermatozoa, science advanced an accurate theory of reproduction (see Science and Technology boxes).

Before the end of the century, the great minds of the age formulated the branches of higher mathematics known as analytic geometry, trigonometry, and infinitesimal calculus, by means of which modern scientists might analyze the phenomena of space and motion.

The New Learning

Bacon and the Empirical Method

One of the most characteristic features of the Scientific Revolution was its advancement of the empirical method. This method of inquiry depends on direct observation and scientific experimentation as the bases from which one arrives at general conclusions. The process that draws on the particulars of sensory evidence for the formulation of general principles (or axioms) is known as **inductive reasoning**.

The leading advocate of the empirical method was the English scientist and politician Francis Bacon (1561–1626).

Science and Technology

1608	Galileo improves the design of Dutch telescopes to obtain three-power magnification
1609	Hans Lippershey and Zacharias Janssen invent the compound microscope
1619	William Harvey accurately traces the circulation of the blood

In 1620, Bacon published his *Novum Organum* ("New Method"), an impassioned plea for objectivity and clear thinking and the strongest defense of the empirical method ever written. "Man, being the servant and interpreter of Nature," wrote Bacon, "can do and understand so much and so much only as he has observed in fact or in thought of the course of Nature: beyond this he neither knows anything nor can do anything."

Bacon argued that human beings might become "the masters and possessors of Nature" only through scientific study guided by precise methods. He promoted an objective system of experimentation, tabulation, and record keeping that became the touchstone of modern scientific inquiry.

Unlike earlier humanists, Bacon turned his back on Aristotle and Classical science. A prophet of the new learning, he sought to eliminate errors in reasoning derived from blind adherence to traditional sources of authority and religious belief. Advancing his own strategy for the acquisition of knowledge, Bacon warned against four "false notions" (or Idols, as he called them) that hinder clear and objective thinking.

READING 23.1 From Bacon's *Novum Organum* (1620)

39

There are four classes of Idols which beset men's minds. To these for distinction's sake I have assigned names,—calling the first class *Idols of the Tribe*; the second, *Idols of the Cave*; the third, *Idols of the Marketplace*; the fourth, *Idols of the Theatre*.

41

The Idols of the Tribe have their foundation in human nature itself, and in the tribe or race of men. For it is a false assertion that the sense of man is the measure of things. On the contrary, all perceptions as well of the sense as of the mind are according to the measure of the individual and not according to the measure of the universe. And the human understanding is like a false mirror, which, receiving rays irregularly, distorts and discolors the nature of things by mingling its own nature with it.

42

The Idols of the Cave are the idols of the individual man. For every one (besides the errors common to human nature in general) has a cave or den of his own, which refracts and discolors the light of nature; owing either to his own proper and peculiar nature; or to his education and conversation with others; or to the reading of books, and the authority of those whom he esteems and admires; or to the differences of impressions, accordingly as they take place in a mind preoccupied and predisposed or in a mind indifferent and settled; or the like. So that the spirit of man (according as it is meted out to different individuals) is in fact a thing variable and full of perturbation, and governed as it were by chance. Whence it was well observed by Heraclitus[1] that men look for sciences in their own lesser worlds, and not in the greater or common world.

43

There are also Idols formed by the intercourse and association of men with each other, which I call Idols of the Marketplace, on account of the commerce and consort of men there. For it is by discourse that men associate; and words are imposed according to the apprehension of the vulgar. And therefore the ill and unfit choice of words wonderfully obstructs the understanding. Nor do the definitions or explanations wherewith in some things learned men are wont to guard and defend themselves, by any means set the matter right. But words plainly force and overrule the understanding, and throw all into confusion, and lead men away into numberless empty controversies and idle fancies.

44

Lastly, there are Idols which have immigrated into men's minds from the various dogmas of philosophies, and also from wrong laws of demonstration. These I call Idols of the Theatre; because in my judgment all the received systems are but so many stage-plays, representing worlds of their own creation after an unreal and scenic fashion. Nor is it only of the systems now in vogue, or only of the ancient sects and philosophies, that I speak; for many more plays of the same kind may yet be composed and in like artificial manner set forth; seeing that errors the most widely different have nevertheless causes for the most part alike. Neither again do I mean this only of entire systems, but also of many principles and axioms in science, which by tradition, credulity, and negligence have come to be received.

Q How does the notion of an "idol" serve Bacon's purpose in writing this treatise?

Bacon observes that every culture and every age has "worshiped" the Idols. *Idols of the Tribe* are deceptive ideas that have their foundations in human nature (such as our natural inclination to accept and believe what we prefer to be true). He points to the fact that human understanding is self-reflective; it functions like a "false mirror," distorting universal truth. Privately held fallacies (*Idols of the Cave*), on the other hand, derive from individual education and background. One may assert, for instance, that one or another religion is the true faith, that certain racial or ethnic groups are superior to others, or that women

Science and Technology

1626	Francis Bacon uses snow in experiments to refrigerate chickens
1642	Blaise Pascal invents a mechanical calculator capable of addition and subtraction
1645	Otto von Guericke perfects the air pump
1650	Pascal invents the mercury barometer
1656	Christian Huygens develops the first accurate pendulum clock
1660	Anton van Leeuwenhoek discovers microscopic protozoa

---

[1] A Greek philosopher of ca. 500 B.C.E., who taught that all of nature was in a state of flux.

Science versus Religion

In an era dominated by fervent spirituality, Bacon demanded a separation of religion and science. "In every age," he observed, "Natural Philosophy has had a troublesome adversary . . . namely, superstition, and the blind and immoderate zeal of religion." In Bacon's time, the term "natural philosophy" (*philosophia naturalis*) described the objective study of nature and the physical universe. It is to this precursor of the natural sciences that Bacon refers in the *Novum Organum*:

> . . . the corruption of philosophy by a combination of superstition and theology is . . . widespread, and does the greatest harm both to whole philosophies and to their parts. Yet, some of the moderns have, with the greatest frivolity, indulged so far . . . as to try to found a natural philosophy on the first chapter of Genesis and the Book of Job and other sacred writings. . . . It is all the more important to

guard against and check this foolishness, for an unhealthy mixture of the divine and the human leads not only to fanciful philosophy but also to heretical religion. The healthy course therefore is to keep a sober mind and give to faith only that which is faith's.

The question of setting religious faith apart from science troubled early modern intellectuals, even as it does many thinkers in our own time. Some might argue that science and religion remain "locked in a death struggle." Moderates, however, would defend the idea that reason can function alongside faith to reduce suffering, end disease, and—by giving human beings greater power over nature—improve the conditions of everyday life. Nevertheless, where religion and science seem irreconcilable, such as in the case of current stem-cell research that might give humans the power to "compete with God's creation," the issue remains widely debated.

---

should be judged by a different set of standards from those applied to men.

The errors resulting from human association and communication, the *Idols of the Marketplace*, arise, according to Bacon, from an "ill or unfit choice of words," for example, the use of the noun "mankind" to designate all human beings. Finally, *Idols of the Theatre* are false dogmas perpetuated by social and political philosophies and institutions. Bacon probably would have regarded "divine-right monarchy" (see chapter 21) and "separate but equal education" as examples of these. To purge the mind of prejudice and false thinking, one must, argued Bacon, destroy the Idols.

Bacon's clarion call for objectivity and experimentation inspired the establishment in 1645 of what would become the Royal Society of London for Improving Natural Knowledge. The first of many such European and American societies for scientific advancement, the Royal Society has, over the centuries, attracted thousands of members. Their achievements have confirmed one nineteenth-century historian's assessment of Bacon as "the man that moved the minds that moved the world."

While Bacon wrote his scientific treatises in Latin, he used English for essays on law, rhetoric, and intellectual life. In *The Advancement of Learning* (1605), a sketch of his key ideas concerning methods for acquiring and classifying knowledge, and in the essay *Of Studies*, Bacon demonstrated the masterful use of prose as a tool for theorizing. Written in the poetic prose of the early seventeenth century, *Of Studies* describes the ways in which books serve the individual and society at large. In the excerpt that follows, Bacon defends reading as a source of pleasure, but, equally important, as a source of practical knowledge and power.

READING 23.2 From Bacon's
Of Studies from *Essays* (1625)

Studies serve for delight, for ornament, and for ability.   **1**
Their chief use for delight is in privateness and retiring; for
ornament, is in discourse; and for ability, is in the judgment
and disposition of business. For expert men can execute,
and perhaps judge of particulars, one by one; but the general
counsels and the plots and marshalling of affairs come best
from those that are learned. To spend too much time in studies
is sloth; to use them too much for ornament is affectation; to
make judgment wholly by their rules is the humor of a scholar.
They perfect nature, and are perfected by experience: for   **10**
natural abilities are like natural plants, that need pruning by
study; . . . Read not to contradict and confute; nor to believe
and take for granted; nor to find talk and discourse, but to
weigh and consider. Some books are to be tasted, others to
be swallowed, and some few to be chewed and digested; that
is, some books are to be read only in parts; others to be read,
but not curiously; and some few to be read wholly, and with
diligence and attention. . . . Reading maketh a full man;
conference a ready man; and writing an exact man. And
therefore, if a man write little, he had need have a great   **20**
memory; if he confer little, he had need have a present wit;
and if he read little, he had need have much cunning, to seem
to know that he does not. Histories make men wise; poets
witty; mathematics subtile; natural philosophy deep; moral
[philosophy] grave; logic and rhetoric able to contend. . . .

Q   In what ways do "studies," according to Bacon, "perfect nature?"

Q   What, in his view, are the benefits of reading, verbal discourse, and writing?

Descartes and the Birth of Modern Philosophy

Born in France, René Descartes (1596–1650) is regarded as the founder of modern Western philosophy. His writings revived the ancient Greek quest to discover how one knows what one knows, and his methods made the discipline of philosophy wholly independent of theology.

Whereas Bacon gave priority to knowledge gained through the senses, Descartes, the supreme rationalist, valued abstract reasoning and mathematical speculation. Descartes did not deny the importance of the senses in the search for truth, but he observed that our senses might deceive us. As an alternative to inductive reasoning, he championed the procedure for investigation called **deductive reasoning**. The reverse of the inductive method, the deductive process begins with clearly established general premises and moves toward the establishment of particular truths. In the *Discourse on the Method of Rightly Conducting the Reason and Seeking for Truth in the Sciences*, the most important of all his philosophic works, Descartes set forth his rules for reasoning: never accept anything as true that you do not clearly know to be true; dissect a problem into as many parts as possible; reason from simple to complex knowledge; and finally, draw complete and exhaustive conclusions. Descartes began the *Discourse* by systematically calling everything into doubt. He then proceeded to identify the first thing that he could not doubt—his existence as a thinking individual. This one clear and distinct idea of himself as a "thinking thing," expressed in the proposition "Cogito, ergo sum" ("I think, therefore I am"), became Descartes' "first principle" and the premise for all his major arguments.

For Descartes, the clear and unbiased mind was the source of all natural understanding. "Except [for] our own thoughts," he insisted, "there is nothing absolutely in our power." Having established rational consciousness as the only sure point of departure for knowledge, Descartes proceeded to examine the world. He made a clear distinction between physical and psychical phenomena, that is, between matter and mind, and between body and soul. According to this dualistic model, the human body operates much like a computer, with the immaterial mind (the software) "informing" the physical components of the body (the hardware). **Cartesian dualism**, the view that holds the mind (a thinking entity) as distinct from the body, dominated European philosophic thought until the end of the nineteenth century and still has some strong adherents today.

Beyond the domain of philosophy, Descartes earned renown as the father of analytic geometry, the discipline that uses algebra to solve problems of space and motion (Figure **23.4**). His program for defining geometric shapes by way of numerical information, presented in an appendix to the *Discourse*, provided the foundations for the branch of higher mathematics known as calculus.

Figure 23.4 PIERRE LOUIS DUMESNIL THE YOUNGER, detail of *Queen Christina of Sweden and Her Court*, 1649. Oil on canvas, 38 × 49½ in. Like many other monarchs of the seventeenth century, Queen Christina of Sweden invited scholars and artists to her court. At the right, Descartes is seen explaining his work to his female benefactor; he points to papers that lie among books and measuring instruments.

READING 23.3 From Descartes' *Discourse on Method* (Part IV) (1637)

. . . I do not know that I ought to tell you of the first meditations there made by me, for they are so metaphysical and so unusual that they may perhaps not be acceptable to everyone. And yet at the same time, in order that one may judge whether the foundations which I have laid are sufficiently secure, I find myself constrained in some measure to refer to them. For a long time I had remarked that it is sometimes requisite in common life to follow opinions which one knows to be most uncertain, exactly as though they were indisputable, as has been said above. But because in this case I wished to give myself entirely to the search after Truth, I thought that it was necessary for me to take an apparently opposite course, and to reject as absolutely false everything as to which I could imagine the least ground of doubt, in order to see if afterwards there remained anything in my belief that was entirely certain. Thus, because our senses sometimes deceive us, I wished to suppose that nothing is just as they cause us to imagine it to be; and because there are men who deceive themselves in their reasoning and fall into paralogisms,[1] even concerning the simplest matters of geometry, and judging that I was as subject to error as was any other, I rejected as false all the reasons formerly accepted by me as demonstrations. And since all the same thoughts and conceptions which we have while awake may also come to us in sleep, without any of them being at that time true, I resolved to assume that everything that ever entered into my mind was no more true than the illusions of my dreams. But immediately afterwards I noticed that whilst I thus wished to think all things false, it was absolutely essential that the "I" who thought this should be somewhat, and remarking that this truth "*I think, therefore I am*" was so certain and so assured that all the most extravagant suppositions brought forward by the sceptics were incapable of shaking it, I came to the conclusion that I could receive it without scruple as the first principle of the Philosophy for which I was seeking.

And then, examining attentively that which I was, I saw that I could conceive that I had no body, and that there was no world nor place where I might be; but yet that I could not for all that conceive that I was not. On the contrary, I saw from the very fact that I thought of doubting the truth of other things, it very evidently and certainly followed that I was; on the other hand if I had only ceased from thinking, even if all the rest of what I had ever imagined had really existed, I should have no reason for thinking that I had existed. From that I knew that I was a substance the whole essence or nature of which is to think, and that for its existence there is no need of any place, nor does it depend on any material thing; so that this "me," that is to say, the soul by which I am what I am, is entirely distinct from body, and is even more easy to know than is the latter; and even if body were not, the soul would not cease to be what it is.

After this I considered generally what in a proposition is requisite in order to be true and certain; for since I had just discovered one which I knew to be such, I thought that I ought also to know in what this certainly consisted. And having

remarked that there was nothing at all in the statement "*I think, therefore I am*" which assures me of having thereby made a true assertion, excepting that I see very clearly that to think it is necessary to be, I came to the conclusion that I might assume, as a general rule, that the things which we conceive very clearly and distinctly are all true—remembering, however, that there is some difficulty in ascertaining which are those that we distinctly conceive.

Following upon this, and reflecting on the fact that I doubted, and that consequently my existence was not quite perfect (for I saw clearly that it was a greater perfection to know than to doubt), I resolved to inquire whence I had learnt to think of anything more perfect than I myself was; and I recognised very clearly that this conception must proceed from some nature which was really more perfect. As to the thoughts which I had of many other things outside of me, like the heavens, the earth, light, heat, and a thousand others, I had not so much difficulty in knowing whence they came, because, remarking nothing in them which seemed to render them superior to me, I could believe that, if they were true, they were dependencies upon my nature, in so far as it possessed some perfection; and if they were not true, that I held them from nought, that is to say, that they were in me because I had something lacking in my nature. But this could not apply to the idea of a Being more perfect than my own, for to hold it from nought would be manifestly impossible; and because it is no less contradictory to say of the more perfect that it is what results from and depends on the less perfect, than to say that there is something which proceeds from nothing, it was equally impossible that I should hold it from myself. In this way it could but follow that it had been placed in me by a Nature which was really more perfect than mine could be, and which even had within itself all the perfections of which I could form any idea—that is to say, to put it in a word, which was God. . . .

Q How does Descartes arrive at his distinction between mind and matter?

Q Why does he conclude that he is "a substance the whole essence or nature of which is to think?"

Religion and the New Learning

The new learning, a composite of scientific method and rational inquiry, presented its own challenge to traditional religion. From "self-evident" propositions, Descartes arrived at conclusions to which empirical confirmation was irrelevant. His rationalism—like Plato's—involved a process of the mind independent of the senses. Reasoning that the concept of perfection ("something more perfect than myself") had to proceed from "some Nature which in reality was more perfect," Descartes "proved" the existence of God as Absolute Substance. Since something cannot proceed from nothing, argued Descartes, the idea of God held by human beings must come from God. Moreover, the idea of Perfection (God) embraces the idea of existence, for, if something is perfect, it must exist.

Raised by Jesuits, Descartes defended the existence of a Supreme Creator, but he shared with many seventeenth-century intellectuals the view that God was neither

---

[1] Fallacious arguments.

Caretaker nor personal Redeemer. Instead, Descartes identified God with "the mathematical order of nature." The idea that God did not interfere with the laws of humanity and nature was central to **deism**, a "natural" religion based on human reason rather than revelation. Deists purged religion of superstition, myth, and ritual. They viewed God as a master mechanic who had created the universe, and had then stepped aside and allowed his World-Machine to run unattended.

Unlike Bacon, Descartes did not envision any conflict between science and religion. He optimistically concluded that "all our ideas or notions contain in them some truth; for otherwise it could not be that God, who is wholly perfect and veracious, should have placed them in us." Like other deists of his time, Descartes held that to follow reason was to follow God.

Spinoza and Pascal

In Amsterdam, a city whose reputation for freedom of thought had attracted Descartes—he lived there between 1628 and 1649—the Jewish philosopher Baruch Spinoza (1632–1677) addressed the question of the new science versus the old faith. Spinoza posited "a universe ruled only by the cause and effect of natural laws, without purpose or design." Stripping God of his traditional role as Creator (and consequently finding himself ousted from the local synagogue), he claimed "God exists only philosophically." God, he suggested, is neither behind, nor beyond, nor separate from nature but, rather, identical with it; and every physical thing, including human beings, is an expression of God in some variation of mind combined with matter. In this pantheistic spirit, Spinoza held that the greatest good was the union of the human mind with the whole of nature.

For the French physicist–mathematician Blaise Pascal (1623–1662), on the other hand, science and religion were irreconcilable. Having undergone a mystical experience that converted him to devout Roman Catholicism, he believed that the path to God was through the heart rather than through the head. Although reason might yield a true understanding of nature, it could in no way prove God's existence. We are capable, wrote Pascal, of "certain knowledge and of absolute ignorance." In his collected meditations on human nature, called simply *Pensées* ("Thoughts"), Pascal proposed a wager that challenged the indifference of skeptics: if God does *not* exist, skeptics lose nothing by believing in him, but if God *does* exist, they reap eternal life. The spiritual quest for purpose and value in a vast, impersonal universe moved the sharp-minded Pascal to confess: "The eternal silence of these infinite spaces frightens me."

Locke and the Culmination of the Empirical Tradition

The writings of the English philosopher and physician John Locke (1632–1704) championed the empirical tradition in seventeenth-century thought. Written seventy years after Bacon's *Novum Organum*, Locke's *Essay Concerning Human Understanding* (1690) confirmed his predecessor's thesis that everything one knows derives from sensory experience. According to Locke, the human mind at birth is a *tabula rasa* ("blank slate") upon which experience—consisting of sensation, followed by reflection—writes the script. There are no innate moral principles or ideas; human knowledge consists only of the progressive accumulation of the evidence of the senses.

The implications of Locke's principles of knowledge moved European and (later) American thought to assume an optimistic view of human destiny. For, if experience influences human knowledge and behavior, then, surely, improving the social environment will work to perfect the human condition. Locke's ideas became basic to eighteenth-century liberalism, as well as to all ideologies that held that human knowledge, if properly applied, would produce happiness for humankind (see chapter 24).

READING 23.4 From Locke's *Essay Concerning Human Understanding* (1690)

Idea is the Object of Thinking.—Every man being conscious   1
to himself that he thinks, and that which his mind is applied
about whilst thinking, being the ideas that are there, it is past
doubt that men have in their minds several ideas, such as are
those expressed by the words whiteness, hardness, sweetness,
thinking, motion, man, elephant, army, drunkenness, and others.
It is in the first place then to be inquired how he comes by
them. I know it is a received doctrine that men have native
ideas and original characters stamped upon their minds in their
very first being. This opinion I have at large examined already;   10
and I suppose what I have [already] said . . . will be much more
easily admitted when I have shown whence the understanding
may get all the ideas it has, and by what ways and degrees they
may come into the mind; for which I shall appeal to every one's
own observation and experience.

All Ideas come from Sensation or Reflection.—Let us then
suppose the mind to be, as we say, white paper, void of all
characters, without any ideas; how comes it to be furnished?
Whence comes it by that vast store which the busy and
boundless fancy of man has painted on it with an almost   20
endless variety? Whence has it all the materials of reason and
knowledge? To this I answer in one word, from experience; in
that all our knowledge is founded, and from that it ultimately
derives itself. Our observation employed either about external
sensible objects, or about the internal operations of our minds,
perceived and reflected on by ourselves, is that which supplies
our understandings with all the materials of thinking. These two
are the fountains of knowledge from whence all the ideas we
have or can naturally have do spring.

The Objects of Sensation, one Source of Ideas.—First, our   30
senses, conversant about particular sensible objects, do convey
into the mind several distinct perceptions of things, according to
those various ways wherein those objects do affect them: and
thus we come by those ideas we have, of yellow, white, heat,
cold, soft, hard, bitter, sweet, and all those which we call
sensible qualities; which when I say the senses convey into
the mind, I mean, they from external objects convey into the
mind what produces there those perceptions. This great source
of most of the ideas we have, depending wholly upon our

senses, and derived by them to the understanding, I call Sensation. [40]

The Operations of our Minds, the other Source of them.—Secondly, the other fountain, from which experience furnishes the understanding with ideas, is the perception of the operations of our own mind within us, as it is employed about the ideas it has got; which operations, when the soul comes to reflect on and consider, do furnish the understanding with another set of ideas, which could not be had from things without; and such are perception, thinking, doubting, believing, reasoning, knowing, willing, and all the different actings of our own minds; which [50] we being conscious of, and observing in ourselves, do from these receive into our understandings as distinct ideas, as we do from bodies affecting our senses. This source of ideas every man has wholly in himself; and though it be not sense, as having nothing to do with external objects, yet it is very like it, and might properly enough be called internal sense. But as I call the other Sensation, so I call this Reflection, the ideas it affords being such only as the mind gets by reflecting on its own operations within itself. By reflection then, in the following part of this discourse, I would be understood to mean that [60] notice which the mind takes of its own operations, and the manner of them; by reason whereof there come to be ideas of these operations in the understanding. These two, I say, viz.,external material things, as the objects of sensation; and the operations of our own minds within, as the objects of reflection; are to me the only originals from whence all our ideas take their beginnings. . . .

All our Ideas are of the one or the other of these.—The understanding seems to me not to have the least glimmering of [70] any ideas which it doth not receive from one of these two. External objects furnish the mind with the ideas of sensible qualities, which are all those different perceptions they produce in us; and the mind furnishes the understanding with ideas of its own operations.

These, when we have taken a full survey of them, and their several modes, combinations, and relations, we shall find to contain all our whole stock of ideas; and that we have nothing in our minds, which did not come in one of these two ways. Let any one examine his own thoughts, and thoroughly search [80] into his understanding; and then let him tell me, whether all the original ideas he has there, are any other than of the objects of his senses, or of the operations of his mind, considered as objects of his reflection: and how great a mass of knowledge soever he imagines to be lodged there, he will, upon taking a strict view, see that he has not any idea in his mind, but what one of these two have imprinted. . . .

Q How does Locke's regard for the senses differ from Descartes'? On what aspects of the mind's operations might they agree?

Newton's Scientific Synthesis

The work of the great English astronomer and mathematician Isaac Newton (1642–1727) represents the culminating synthesis of seventeenth-century physics and mathematics. A tireless student of the sciences (so intent on his studies that he often forgot to eat), Newton moved the new

Science and Technology

1666	Isaac Newton uses a prism to analyze light
1671	Gottfried Wilhelm Leibniz invents a calculating machine that multiplies and divides
1684	Leibniz publishes his first paper on differential calculus
1687	Newton publishes his *Principia Mathematica*

learning from its foundations in methodical speculation (Copernicus) and empirical confirmation (Galileo) to its apogee in codification.

With the publication in 1687 of *Philosophiae Naturalis Principia Mathematica* (*Mathematical Principles of Natural Philosophy*),* commonly known as the *Principia*, Newton provided an all-embracing theory of universal gravitation that described every physical movement in the universe—from the operation of the tides to the effect of a planet on its moons. In its 550 pages (written in a mere eighteen months), he proved that nature's laws applied equally to terrestrial and celestial matter, thus unifying the work of Galileo and Kepler. He described the workings of the physical world with a single proposition that explained the universal force of gravity: "Every particle of matter attracts every other particle with a force propositional to the product of the masses and inversely proportional to the square of the distances between them" (Book III, Number 7).

The *Principia*, the fundamentals of which would go unchallenged until the late nineteenth century, proved to be the greatest work of science ever written. It advanced the concept of an orderly universe, one that operated as systematically as a well-oiled machine. Equally important, however, it promoted the optimistic notion that the physical universe was discoverable and knowable by human beings. Thus, it was an empowering force in the evolution of self-awareness. Newton's shaping influence is best described by his admiring British contemporary, Alexander Pope (see chapter 24): "Nature and Nature's Laws lay hid in Night./ God said, *Let Newton be*! And All was Light."

The Impact of the Scientific Revolution on Art

Northern Baroque Painting

If the new science engendered a spirit of objective inquiry in philosophy, it also inspired new directions in the visual arts. In the cities of seventeenth-century Holland, where Dutch lensmakers had produced the first telescopes and microscopes, artists paid obsessive attention to the appearance of the natural world. In still lifes, portraits, landscape, and scenes of everyday life—all secular subjects—Dutch

---

* The term "natural philosophy" meant primarily physics, astronomy, and the science of matter.

Figure 23.5 JAN VERMEER, *The Geographer*, ca. 1668. Oil on canvas, 20⅞ × 18¼ in. Vermeer renders the geographer at the moment when he pauses thoughtfully from his work. The painting, enriched by closely observed details, captures the spirit of intellectual inquiry that typified the Age of Science.

masters practiced the "art of describing."** The almost photographic realism of *The Geographer* (Figure **23.5**), a painting by the Delft master Jan Vermeer (see below), is typical of the new "Baconian" attention to the evidence of

the senses: from the calipers (a device used to measure distances) held in the geographer's right hand and the crisp parchment maprolls that lie on the table and floor, to the brocaded chair that stands against the wall, the objects of the real world are described with loving detail. References to Holland's global outreach, facilitated by its trading companies, appear in the inclusion of the handsome globe, the sea chart (so detailed that one can read the name of the

---

** See Svetlana Alpers, *The Art of Describing: Dutch Art in the Seventeenth Century*. Chicago: University of Chicago Press, 1983.

manufacturer), and the richly patterned carpet, an import from the East, commonly used in domestic interiors as a table cover or wall-hanging. Vermeer bathes these tangible objects in atmospheric light that pours in from the window, unifying the space.

Similar attention to detail is apparent in *The Drawing Lesson* (see Figure **23.1**), a delightful genre painting by Jan Steen (1626–1679). The Dutch studio interior is filled with artist's paraphernalia—canvases, a sketchbook, an easel, pens, paper, and plaster-cast models—as well as by various mundane items: bottles, books, and jugs. Two students are shown receiving instruction from a drawing master. The young female gazes with bewildered wonder at the skills of her mentor. Steen's representation gives evidence of an important phenomenon in seventeenth-century Dutch art: the growing number of women as master painters. Often excluded from membership in the local guilds, they learned their trade by drawing from plaster-cast reproductions. Forbidden to work from nude male models employed in traditional studio training, they inclined to the painting of portraits and still-life subjects.

Rachel Ruysch (1664–1750), the mother of ten children, produced precisely executed flower pieces for an international circle of patrons. Her works, which reflect the influence of the newly available botanical prints and drawings, suggest the close relationship between late seventeenth-century science and art. Especially popular were "tulip books," which catalogued varieties of the

popular flower first imported into Holland in the late sixteenth century from the Turkish court of Suleiman (see chapter 21). The tulip became a prized commodity whose value inspired a speculative financial "bubble" known as Tulip-mania (Figure **23.6**).

One of the most talented of Holland's floral painters was Maria van Oosterwyck (1630–1693), who worked in Delft, Utrecht, and Amsterdam. Drawing on the tradition of exacting realism initiated by Jan van Eyck (see chapters 17 and 19), van Oosterwyck brought a naturalist's passion for detail to still-life paintings that were popular among royal patrons throughout Europe. Her *Still Life* of 1668 (see LOOKING INTO, Figure **23.7**) includes a radiant Dutch tulip (a particularly desirable "broken" strain consisting of variant colors), a worn book, a meticulously painted astrological globe, a rotting skull, various insects (including a moth and a microscopically precise fly), a mouse nibbling at some grain, and a wine carafe (front left) that reflects a minute image of the artist.

In addition to still-life subjects, genre paintings (scenes of everyday life and especially family life) were in high demand in the Netherlands in the seventeenth century, generating a virtual golden age of Dutch art. The domestic scenes of Pieter de Hooch (1629–1684) show Dutch art to be societal—they are concerned with conviviality and companionship. In one painting, de Hooch uses a spacious courtyard filled with cool, bright light as the setting for such ordinary pleasures as pipe-smoking and beer-drinking

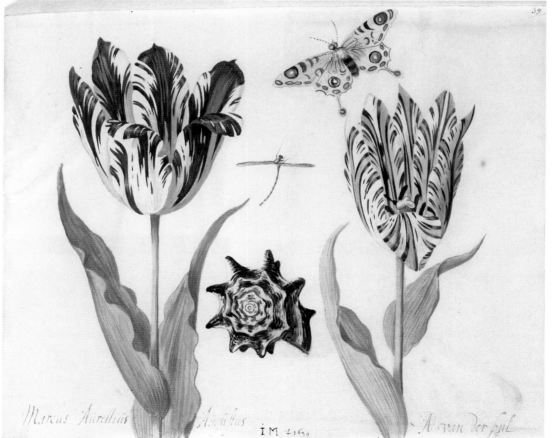

Figure 23.6 JACOB MARREL, *Two Tulips, a Butterfly and a Snail*, from *Book of Botanical Drawings*, 1637–1645. Pencil and watercolor on paper, 10⅔ × 13⅔ in. This 80-page book probably served as a catalogue used by those who wished to order tulip bulbs. Variegated or "flaming" multicolored tulips like those shown here were highly prized.

Van Oosterwyck's *Still Life*

Painted by one of Delft's most accomplished artists, this illusionistic still life, while brilliantly decorative, makes symbolic reference to the transience of temporal things. Red wine, exotic flowers, and musical instruments mark fleeting pleasures, while the symbols of corruption (the skull and the moth) remind us of the brevity of life. The books, entitled *Rekeningh* (*Reckoning*) and *Self-Stryt* (*Self-Struggle*), underline the need to take account of one's moral state. Ostensibly a celebration of earthly pleasures, the painting—a type known as **vanitas**—suggests the corruptibility of worldly goods, the futility of riches, and the inevitability of death.

Figure 23.7 MARIA VAN OOSTERWYCK, *Vanitas Still Life*, 1668. Oil on canvas, 29 × 35 in.

flowers, skull, and rotting corn: symbols of transience and death

moth symbolizing corruption and decay

astrological globe implying universality

hourglass symbolizing the passage of time and the inevitability of death

wine carafe signifying life's pleasures, with reflection of the artist in an interior

money bag and coins alluding to the futility of riches

recorder signifying music as a fleeting pleasure

fly symbolizing pestilence and misfortune

mouse symbolizing pestilence

butterfly: symbol of the immortal soul

books encouraging the need to take account of one's moral state

Figure 23.8 PIETER DE HOOCH, *A Dutch Courtyard*, 1658–1660. Oil on canvas, 26¾ × 23 in.

(Figure **23.8**). He captures a mood of domestic intimacy in his loving attention to humble fact: the crumbling brick wall, the gleaming tankard, the homely matron, and the pudgy child. The strict verticals and horizontals of the composition—established with Cartesian clarity and precision—create a sense of tranquility and order.

Amateur musical performances, one of the major domestic entertainments of the seventeenth century, are the subject of many Northern Baroque paintings, including de Hooch's *Portrait of a Family Making Music* (Figure **23.9**). The growing popularity of musical subjects reflects the emphasis on musical education and the rising number of private musical societies in the towns of the Dutch Republic. In the belief that listening to and making music were morally edifying (and thus more desirable than the all too popular pastime of drinking), many churches required musical recitals before and after services, and encouraged instrumental and choral expression among members of the congregation. Holland was a center for the manufacture of musical instruments; the Dutch household pictured by de Hooch would have owned the bass viol, recorder, cittern (a type of lute), and violin on which the family performed, their rhythm closely measured by the portly, no-nonsense matron of the house.

Music-making also figures in the delightful painting called *The Suitor's Visit* by Gerard ter Borch (1617–1681). The narrative is staged like a scene from a play: a well-dressed gentleman, who has just entered the parlor of a

Figure 23.9 PIETER DE HOOCH, *Portrait of a Family Making Music*, 1663. Oil on canvas, 38⅞ × 45¹⁵⁄₁₆ in.

well-to-do middle-class family, bows before a young woman whose coy apprehension suggests that she is the object of courtship (Figure **23.10**). The father and the family dog take note of the tense moment, while a younger woman, absorbed in playing the lute, ignores the interruption. Ter Borch was famous for his virtuosity in painting silk and satin fabrics that subtly gleam from within the shadowy depths of domestic interiors. Equally impressive, however, was his ability to invest an inconsequential social event with intimacy.

Vermeer and Dutch Painting

Seventeenth-century Dutch artists developed as a major subject the naturalistic landscape (the very word derives from the Dutch *landschap* meaning "landform"). In landscape painting as in genre subjects, they described nature with a close attention to detail and a sensitivity to atmosphere that rivaled the landscapes of their Northern European predecessors, Dürer and Bruegel (see chapter 19). Unlike their seventeenth-century French contemporaries Poussin and Claude Lorrain (see chapter 21), Dutch landscape painters depicted nature unidealized and free of moralizing narratives; they brought to life a sense of place and the vastness of nature itself.

Such is the case with the *View of Delft* (Figure **23.11**), the only landscape painted by the Dutch artist Jan Vermeer

Figure 23.10 GERARD TER BORCH, *The Suitor's Visit,* ca. 1658. Oil on canvas, 31½ × 29⅝ in.

Figure 23.11 JAN VERMEER, *View of Delft,* 1658. Oil on canvas, 3 ft. 2¾ in. × 3 ft. 10 in. This cityscape reflects the pride with which Dutch painters and patrons regarded their hometowns. Like other urban centers in the Lowlands, Delft was home to some of Europe's finest mapmakers.

Figure 23.12 A *camera obscura*; the image formed by the lens and reflected by the mirror on the ground glass is traced by the artist.

(1632–1675). An innkeeper and an art dealer, who produced fewer than forty canvases in his lifetime, Vermeer transformed everyday subjects by way of atmospheric space and evanescent light. His *View of Delft*, a topographical study of his native city, reveals a typically Dutch affection for the visible world. It also reflects the artist's delight in the physical effects of light on matter: the silvery surface of the water interrupted by boats and buildings, and the sunlight filtering down to illuminate some segments of the city, while others are clouded into shade. Vermeer lowers the horizon line to give increased attention to the sky—a reflection perhaps of his interest in the new astronomy. While the composition fixes a singular point of view and a precise place, the broad horizon seems to reach beyond the limits of the frame to suggest infinite space. Two groups of tiny figures (in the left foreground) invite us to share the view—as beholders and as minor players on the larger stage of nature.

It is likely that Vermeer and other Dutch masters shared an interest in the optical experiments of Galileo and Newton and in the optical devices (such as the *camera lucida*; see chapter 17) that facilitated an accurate and detailed depiction of the physical world. Scholars argue that Vermeer, the exemplar in an age of observation, executed his paintings with the aid of a *camera obscura* (Figure **23.12**), an apparatus that anticipated the modern pinhole camera (while lacking the means of capturing the image on film). The blurred contours and small beads of light that twinkle on the surface of his canvases suggest the use of an optical lens.

Vermeer's favorite subjects—women playing musical instruments, reading letters, or enjoying the company of suitors—are all depicted on small canvases in an intimate interior (possibly the artist's studio). Self-contained and self-possessed, and bathed in atmospheric light, they come to life in a strikingly personal manner. In Vermeer's *Woman Holding a Balance* (Figure **23.13**), a woman (perhaps pregnant) stands before a table contemplating a jeweler's balance. On the table, strands of pearls twinkle in the light that filters through the curtained window—a compositional strategy used in *The Geographer* (see Figure 23.5) and in many of Vermeer's domestic interiors. On the wall behind her is a painting of the Last Judgment. Is Vermeer's canvas a lofty allegory that alludes to the final weighing of souls, and the balance between worldly and otherworldly rewards? Or is it simply a delicately rendered record of a domestic activity? Either way, its exquisite intimacy and meditative tranquility are unique in Dutch art.

Figure 23.13 JAN VERMEER, *Woman Holding a Balance*, ca. 1664. Oil on canvas, 16¾ × 15 in.

Figure 23.14 FRANS HALS, *The Laughing Cavalier*, 1624. Oil on canvas, 33¾ × 27 in.

a courtly Dutch soldier, for instance, whose fleeting sideways glance flirts with the viewer (Figure **23.14**). A master of the brush, Hals brought his forms to life by means of quick, loose, staccato brushstrokes and impasto highlights. Immediacy, spontaneity, and impulsive movement—features typical of Baroque art—enliven Hals' portraits.

These qualities also appear in the work of Judith Leyster (1609–1660), a Netherlandish artist from the province of Utrecht, whose canvases until the twentieth century were attributed to her colleague Frans Hals. Leyster established a workshop in Haarlem and was one of only two females elected to the painters' guild of that city. Almost all her known paintings date from before her marriage at the age of twenty-six. Leyster's *Self-Portrait* achieves a sense of informality through the casual manner in which the artist turns away from her canvas as if to greet the viewer (Figure **23.15**). The laughing violinist that is the subject of the painting-within-the-painting provides an exuberant counterpoint to Leyster's robust visage. Leyster's portrait is a personal comment on the role of the artist as muse and artisan. It conveys the self-confidence of a middle-class woman who competed with the best of Holland's masters.

Dutch Portraiture

The vogue for portraiture in Northern Baroque art reflected the self-conscious materialism of a rising middle class. Like the portraits of wealthy Renaissance aristocrats (see chapter 17), the painted likenesses of seventeenth-century Dutch burghers fulfilled the ambition to immortalize one's worldly self. But in contrast to Italian portraits, the painted images of middle-class Dutch men and women are usually unidealized and often even unflattering. They capture a truth to nature reminiscent of late Roman portraiture (see chapter 6) but surpass even that in their self-scrutiny and probing, self-reflective character.

Two contemporaries, Frans Hals (1581–1666) and Rembrandt van Rijn (who was introduced in chapter 22), dominated the genre of portraiture in seventeenth-century Dutch painting. Hals was the leading painter of Haarlem and one of the great realists of the Western portrait tradition. His talent lay in capturing the personality and physical presence of his sitters: the jaunty self-confidence of

Figure 23.15 JUDITH LEYSTER, *Self-Portrait*, ca. 1630. Oil on canvas, 29⅜ × 25⅞ in. Shortly after her marriage, Leyster moved with her husband, Jan Molenaer, to Amsterdam, where she bore and reared at least five children. Although she may have helped her husband to execute his paintings, her own artistic output decreased dramatically.

Rembrandt's Portraits

Hals' and Leyster's portraits are astute records of surface appearance. By comparison, Rembrandt's portraits are studies of the inner life of his sitters, uncompromising explorations of flesh and blood. A keen observer of human character, Rembrandt became the leading portrait painter in the city of Amsterdam. The commissions he received at the beginning of his career exceeded his ability to fill them. But after a meteoric rise to fame, he saw his fortunes decline. Accumulated debts led to poverty, bankruptcy, and depression—the last compounded by the death of his beloved wife in 1642.

The history of Rembrandt's career is mirrored in his self-portraits, some forty of which survive. They are a kind of visual diary, a lifetime record of the artist's passionate enterprise in self-scrutiny. The *Self-Portrait* of 1661, with its slackened facial muscles and furrowed brow, engages the viewer with the image of a noble and yet utterly vulnerable personality (Figure **23.16**). Portraiture of this kind, which has no equivalent in any non-Western culture, may be considered among the outstanding examples of Northern Baroque art.

Among the most lucrative of Rembrandt's commissions was the group portrait, a genre that commemorated the achievements of wealthy Dutch families, guild members, and militia officers. Some of these paintings, which measure more than 12 by 14 feet, reflect the Baroque fondness for colossal proportion and theatrical setting. Even in his smaller group portraits, Rembrandt achieved a unity of dramatic effect typical of the Baroque style. The painting that established his reputation as a master portraitist, *The Anatomy Lesson of Dr. Nicolaes Tulp* (1632), is a case in point (Figure **23.17**). Here the artist has eliminated the posed look of the conventional group portrait by staging the scene as a dissection in progress. As in his religious compositions (compare Figure 22.1), he manipulates light for dramatic purposes: he spotlights the dissected corpse in the foreground and balances the darker area formed by the figure of the doctor with a triangle created by the brightly lit faces of the students (whose names

Figure 23.16 REMBRANDT VAN RIJN, *Self-Portrait as Saint Paul*, 1661. Oil on canvas, 35⅞ × 30⅜ in. As part of their training, Rembrandt's students copied the master's self-portraits. Recent scholarship has reduced the number of authentic Rembrandt self-portraits from sixty to around forty.

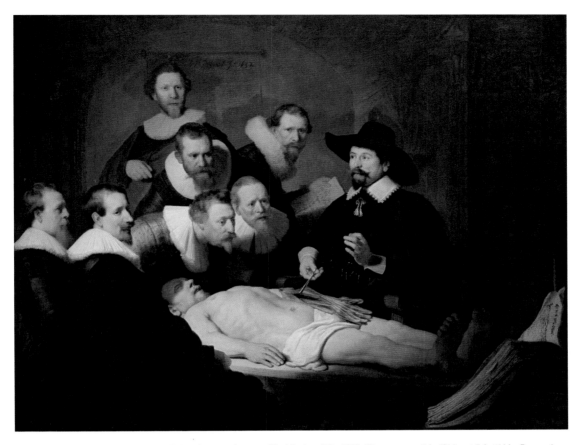

Figure 23.17 REMBRANDT VAN RIJN, *The Anatomy Lesson of Dr. Nicolaes Tulp*, 1632. Oil on canvas, 5 ft. 3⅜ in. × 7 ft. 1¼ in. Engaged in a public dissection witnessed by his students, the doctor is shown examining the muscles of the arm and hand of an executed prisoner. The large book in the lower right corner is doubtlessly a copy of Vesalius' monumental study *On the Workings of the Human Body*.

appear on the piece of paper held by the middle background figure). These faces bear the force of individual personalities and the spirit of inquisitiveness peculiar to the Age of Science.

Baroque Instrumental Music

Until the sixteenth century, almost all music was written for the voice rather than for musical instruments. Even during the Renaissance, instrumental music was, for the most part, the result of substituting an instrument for a voice in music written for singing or dancing. The seventeenth century marked the rise of music that lacked an extramusical text. Like a mathematical equation or a geometric formula, the instrumental music of the early modern era carried no explicit narrative content—it was neither a vehicle for religious expression nor a means of supporting a secular text. Such music was written without consideration for the content traditionally provided by a set of sung lyrics. The idea of music as an aesthetic exercise, composed for its own sake rather than to serve a religious or communal purpose, was a notable feature of seventeenth-century European culture.

Not surprisingly, the rise of instrumental music was accompanied by improvements in instruments and refinements in tuning. Indeed, instrumental music came to dominate musical composition at the very moment that Western musicians were perfecting such stringed instruments as the

violin, viola, and cello (see Figure 23.9) and such keyboard instruments as the organ and harpsichord (Figure **23.18**). By the early eighteenth century, musicians were adopting the system of tuning known as **equal temperament**, whereby the octave was divided into twelve half-steps of equal size. The collection of preludes and fugues known as the *Well-Tempered* [tuned] *Clavier* (1722–1742) shows how Bach made use of this uniform system of tuning to create sublime music—he wrote two pieces in every possible key. The new attention to improving instruments and systematizing keys mirrored the efforts of scientists and philosophers to bring precision and uniformity to the tools and methods of scientific inquiry.

In the seventeenth century, northern Italy was the world center for the manufacture of violins. The Amati, Guarneri, and Stradivari families of Cremona established the techniques of making high-quality violins that were sought in all the great courts of Europe. Transmitted from father to son, the construction techniques used to produce these instruments were kept so secret that modern violinmakers have never successfully imitated them. Elsewhere, around 1650, earlier instruments were standardized and refined. The ancient double-reed wind instrument known as the shawm, for instance, developed into the modern oboe. While amateur music-making was widespread, professional performance also took a great leap forward, as a new breed of virtuosi inspired the writing of treatises on performance techniques.

Three main types of composition—the sonata, the suite, and the concerto—dominated seventeenth-century instrumental music. All three reflect the Baroque taste for dramatic contrast in tempo and texture. The **sonata** (from the Italian word for "sounded," that is, music played and not sung) is a piece written for a few instruments—often no more than one or two. It usually consisted of three **movements** of contrasting tempo—fast/slow/fast—each based on a song or dance form of the time.

The **suite**, written for any combination of instruments, is a sequence or series of movements derived from various European court or folk dances—for example, the sarabande, the pavane, the minuet, and the gigue, or jig. Henry Purcell (1659–1695) in England, François Couperin (1668–1733) in France (see chapter 26), and Johann Sebastian Bach (1685–1750) in Germany all contributed to the development of the suite as a musical genre.

Finally, the **concerto** (from the same root as *concertato*, which describes opposing or contrasting bodies of sound; see chapter 20) is a composition consisting of two groups of instruments, one small and the other large, playing in "dialogue." The typical Baroque concerto, the **concerto grosso** ("large concerto"), had several movements, whose number and kind varied considerably.

Vivaldi

The leading Italian instrumental composer of the Baroque era was Antonio Vivaldi (1678–1741), a Roman Catholic priest and the son of a prominent violinist at Saint Mark's Cathedral in Venice. A composer of both sacred music and opera, he earned lasting fame as one of the most influential figures in the history of the concerto grosso. He wrote some 450 concertos, including concerti grossi and solo concertos, the latter mostly for violin. Vivaldi systematized the concerto grosso into a three-movement form (fast/slow/fast) and increased the distinction between solo and ensemble groups in each movement. He also perfected the form known as *ritornello* (literally, "return"), which makes use of a returning or recurring musical passage that (alternating with other musical episodes) brings dramatic unity to the composition.

Of Vivaldi's many compositions for solo violin and orchestra, the most glorious is *The Four Seasons*, a group of four violin concertos, each of which musically describes a single season. Vivaldi intended that this work be "programmatic," that is, carry meaning outside of the music itself. As if to ensure that the music duplicate the descriptive power of traditional vocal lines, he added poems at appropriate passages in the score for the instruction of the performers. At the section called "Spring," for instance, Vivaldi's verses describe "flowing streams" and "singing birds." While the music offers listeners the challenge of detecting such extramusical references, its brilliance lies not in its programmatic innovations but in its vibrant rhythms, its lyrical solos, and its exuberant "dialogues" between violin and orchestra.

See Music Listening Selections at end of chapter.

Figure 23.18 JOHANNES COUCHET (maker), Flemish harpsichord, double-banked, ca. 1650. Compass: four octaves and a fifth F to C (each keyboard). Case decorated with carving and gilt gesso work.

Bach and Instrumental Music

Johann Sebastian Bach, whom we met in chapter 22, served as a brilliant church musician for much of his life. However, he was also one of history's greatest composers of secular music, that is, music with no obvious religious function. Influenced by both Vivaldi's concertos and the Italian music style that inspired the expressive conjunction of solo and orchestral forms, Bach developed the musical potential of the concerto form more completely than any previous composer. He claimed that his study of Vivaldi had taught him to "think musically," and to endow the creative process with "order, coherence, and proportion." To the two dozen concertos he produced during his lifetime, Bach brought a high degree of rational control, expanding the *ritornello* sections and bringing solo episodes to new levels of complexity.

The six concertos known as the Brandenburg Concertos were composed over several years. In 1721, Bach sent them to Ludwig Christian, the margrave of Brandenburg, in the hope of securing a position at his court. Although there is no record that these concertos were ever performed during Bach's lifetime, they were intended for performance by the Brandenburg court orchestra.

The Brandenburg Concertos employ as soloists most of the principal instruments of the Baroque orchestra: violin, oboe, recorder, trumpet, and harpsichord. Bach applied himself to developing rich contrasts of tone and texture between the two "contending" groups of instruments—note especially the massive sound of the orchestra versus the lighter sounds of the small group (consisting of a violin and two recorders) in the first movement of the fourth concerto. Here, tightly drawn webs of counterpoint are spun between upper and lower instrumental parts, while musical lines, driven by an unflagging rhythm and energy, unfold majestically.

In the ten years before his death in 1750, Bach undertook one of the most monumental works of his career—a compelling example of Baroque musical composition that came to be called *The Art of Fugue*. A **fugue** (literally "flight") is a polyphonic composition in which a single musical theme (or subject) is restated in sequential phrases. As in the more familiar canon known as a "round"—for instance, "Three Blind Mice"—a melody in one voice part is imitated in a succession of other voices, so that the melody and repetitions overlap. The musical subject can be arranged to appear backward or inverted (or both), augmented (the length of the notes doubled, so that the melody moves twice as slowly), or diminished (note values halved, so that the melody moves twice as fast). In the hands of a great composer, this form of imitative counterpoint weaves a majestic tapestry of sound.

Such is the case with *The Art of Fugue*, which explores the contrapuntal possibilities of a single musical subject

See Music Listening Selections at end of chapter.

Chronology

1543   Copernicus publishes *De revolutionibus orbium*

1619   Kepler formulates three laws of planetary motion

1620   Bacon publishes *Novum Organum*

1633   Trial of Galileo

1637   Descartes publishes *Discourse on Method*

1645   Royal Society of London established

in eighteen separate compositions. Bach produced this *summa* of seventeenth-century musical science as a tool for instruction in the writing of fugues, which explores the contrapuntal possibilities of a single musical subject in eighteen separate compositions. In the last portion of the work he signed his name with a musical motif made up of the letters of his name—B flat, A, C, and B natural (referred to as H in German). Even the listener who cannot read music or understand the complexities of Bach's inventions is struck by their concentrated brilliance. No less than Newton's codification of the laws of nature, *The Art of Fugue* is a triumphant expression of the Age of Science.

LOOKING BACK

The Scientific Revolution

- Following Nicolas Copernicus, European scientists confirmed the reality of a heliocentric cosmos that operated according to fixed and understandable laws.
- Johannes Kepler's inquiries on planetary movements confirmed Copernicus' theories, and showed that the planets moved around the sun in elliptical paths.
- Galileo formulated the Law of Falling Bodies and used the telescope to confirm empirically the previously theoretical heliocentric universe.
- Between 1600 and 1700, new tools were invented for accurately measuring the physical world; the sciences of physics and astronomy, and the language of higher mathematics, were firmly established.

- The tenets of the new science contradicted scriptural teachings and met with opposition from both Catholics and Protestants.

The New Learning

- While scientists demystified nature, the new learning provided a methodology for more accurately describing and predicting its operations.
- The English scientist Francis Bacon, author of the *Novum Organum*, championed induction and the empirical method, which gave priority to knowledge gained through the senses.
- The English philosopher and physician John Locke defended the empirical tradition with the theory that all experience is imprinted on the human mind, a *tabula rasa* ("blank slate") at birth.

- Questioning the authority of the inductive method, René Descartes, the father of modern Western philosophy, gave priority to deductive reasoning and mathematical analysis in his *Discourse*.
- Descartes, along with many other intellectuals of new learning, embraced deism, which identified God as a master mechanic who did not interfere with the laws of nature.

Newton's Scientific Synthesis

- Bridging physics and mathematics, Isaac Newton moved the new learning from its theoretical and empirical phases to the stage of codification.
- Newton's *Principia* promoted the idea of a uniform and intelligible universe that operated as systematically as a well-oiled machine; his monumental work became the basis of modern physics.

The Impact of the Scientific Revolution on Art

- The Scientific Revolution and the new learning ushered in a phase of the Baroque style marked by an empirical attention to physical detail and a fascination with light and space.
- An increased demand for such secular subjects as still life, landscape, portraiture, and genre painting reflects the secular preoccupations and growing wealth of middle-class patrons, particularly in Northern Europe. Still-life subjects often incorporated a *vanitas* theme that drew attention to the brevity of life and its worldly pleasures.
- The definitive artworks of the seventeenth-century Northern Baroque include Vermeer's *View of Delft*, the portraits of Rembrandt, Hals, and Leyster, and the genre paintings of de Hooch and ter Borch, which explore the intimate pleasures of house and home.
- Rembrandt's psychologically penetrating self-portraits are the intimate equivalents of his masterful group portraits.

Baroque Instrumental Music

- During the seventeenth century, instrumental music came to dominate musical composition. String instruments, especially the violin, reached a new level of refinement.
- Keyboard instruments, and musical performance in general, benefited from the development of a uniform system of tuning; treatises on the art of instrumental performance became increasingly popular.
- The seventeenth century saw the rise of wholly instrumental music and of such instrumental forms as the sonata, the suite, and the concerto.
- Vivaldi was the most influential figure in the development of the Baroque concerto, especially the concerto grosso. Bach brought to perfection the art of the fugue in compositions whose complexity and brilliance remain unrivaled. These instrumental forms captured the exuberance of the Baroque spirit and the dynamic intellectualism of the age.

Music Listening Selections

- Vivaldi, *The Four Seasons*, "Spring," Concerto in E Major, Op. 8, No. 1, first movement, 1725.
- Bach, Brandenburg Concerto No. 4 in G Major, first movement, excerpt, 1721.
- Bach, *The Art of Fugue*, Canon in the 12th, harpsichord, 1749–1750.

Glossary

Cartesian of or relating to René Descartes or his philosophy

concerto (Italian, "opposing" or "competing") an instrumental composition consisting of one or more solo instruments and a larger group of instruments playing in "dialogue"

concerto grosso a "large concerto," the typical kind of Baroque concerto, consisting of several movements

deductive reasoning a method of inquiry that begins with clearly established general premises and moves toward the establishment of particular truths

deism a movement or system of thought advocating natural religion based on human reason rather than revelation; deists describe God as Creator, but deny that he interferes with the laws of the universe

dualism the view that holds the mind (a thinking entity) as distinct from the body

equal temperament a system of tuning that originated in the seventeenth century, whereby the octave is divided into twelve half-steps of equal size; since intervals have the same value in all keys, music may be played in any key, and a musician may change from one key to another with complete freedom

fugue ("flight") a polyphonic composition in which a theme (or subject) is imitated, restated, and developed by successively entering voice parts

geocentric earth-centered

heliocentric sun-centered

inductive reasoning a method of inquiry that begins with direct observation and experimentation and moves toward the establishment of general conclusions or axioms

movement a major section in a long instrumental composition

ritornello (Italian, "a little return") in Baroque music, an instrumental section that recurs throughout the movement

sonata an instrumental composition consisting of three movements of contrasting tempo, usually fast/slow/fast; see also Glossary, chapter 26

suite an instrumental composition consisting of a sequence or series of movements derived from court or folk dances

vanitas (Latin, "vanity") a type of still life consisting of objects that symbolize the brevity of life and the transience of earthly pleasures and achievements

Chapter 24

The Enlightenment: The Promise of Reason

ca. 1650–1800

"The time will . . . come when the sun will shine only on free men who know no other master but their reason."
Antoine Nicolas de Condorcet

Figure 24.1 JACQUES-LOUIS DAVID *Antoine-Laurent Lavoisier and His Wife (Marie-Anne Pierrette Paulze)*, 1788. Oil on canvas, 8 ft. 6¼ in. × 6 ft. 4⅝ in. The father of modern chemistry, Lavoisier wrote the first basic textbook on the subject; his wife translated English scientific documents, made sketches of laboratory instruments, and assisted him in his work.

In the year 1680, a comet blazed across the skies over Western Europe. The English astronomer Edmund Halley (1656–1742) observed the celestial body, calculated its orbit, and predicted its future appearances. Stripped of its former role as a portent of catastrophe or a harbinger of natural calamity, Halley's comet now became merely another natural phenomenon, the behavior of which invited scientific investigation. This new, objective attitude toward nature and the accompanying confidence in the liberating role of reason were hallmarks of the Enlightenment—the intellectual movement that occurred between 1687 (the date of Newton's *Principia*) and 1789 (the beginning of the French Revolution).

Also known as the Age of Reason, this era marks the divide between the medieval view of the world as governed by God and the principles of faith, and the modern, secular view of the world as dominated by humankind and the principles of reason. The light of reason, argued enlightened intellectuals, would dispel the mists of human ignorance, superstition, and prejudice. This spirit of buoyant optimism infused Enlightenment efforts to create a kind of happiness on earth that in former ages had been thought to exist only in heaven.

During the Age of Enlightenment, learning freed itself from the Church, and literacy became widespread. Among middle-class Europeans, 90 to 100 percent of men and almost 75 percent of women could read and write. This new, more literate middle class competed with a waning aristocracy for social and political prestige. The public interest in literature and the arts spurred the rise of the newspaper, the encyclopedia, the novel, and the symphony. While the major intellectual and cultural ideals of the Enlightenment did not directly touch the lives of millions of peasants and villagers, they influenced the course of modern history, not only in the West, but also, gradually, throughout the world.

Liberty and Political Theory

Natural Law

Eighteenth-century intellectuals were heirs to Newtonian science. As Newton had established the natural laws of the physical universe, so these rationalists sought to establish general laws of human behavior. As Newton had defined the operations of celestial bodies in the context of unchanging nature, so Enlightenment thinkers perceived human behavior in terms of *natural law*. Natural law, the unwritten and divinely sanctioned law of nature, held that there are certain principles of right and wrong that all human beings, by way of reason, can discover and apply in the course of creating a just society. "Natural rights" included life, liberty, property, and just treatment by the ruling order.

Enlightenment thinkers argued that a true understanding of the human condition was the first step toward progress, that is, toward the gradual betterment of human life. It is no wonder, then, that the eighteenth century saw the birth of the social sciences: anthropology, sociology, economics, and political science. Devoted to the study of humankind, these new disciplines were put at the service of an enlightened social order.

Hobbes and Locke

An enlightened social order required a redefinition of the role of government and the rights of citizens. In the early modern era, when European nation-states were on the rise, this subject dominated intellectual circles. Not since the Golden Age of Athens was so much attention given to the relationship between the ruler and the ruled.

During the sixteenth century, the pioneer political theorist Machiavelli had argued that the survival of the state was more important than the well-being of its citizens (see chapter 16). Later in that century, the French lawyer Jean Bodin (1530–1596) employed biblical precepts and long-standing tradition to defend theories of divine-right monarchy. In the seventeenth century, the Dutch statesman Hugo Grotius (1583–1645) proposed an all-embracing system of international law based on reason, which he identified with nature. Grotius' idea of a political contract based in natural law profoundly influenced the thinking of two of England's finest philosophers, Thomas Hobbes (1588–1679) and John Locke (whom we met in chapter 23).

Although a generation apart, Hobbes and Locke took up the urgent question of human rights versus the sovereignty of the ruler. Shaken by the conflict between royalist and antiroyalist factions that had fueled the English Civil War (see chapter 22), both thinkers rejected the principle of divine-right monarchy. Instead, they advanced the idea that government must be based in a **social contract**. For Hobbes, the social contract was a covenant among individuals who willingly surrendered a portion of their freedom to a governing authority or ruler, in whose hands should rest ultimate authority. Locke agreed that government must be formed by a contract that laid the basis for social order and individual happiness. But he believed that power must remain with the ruled.

The divergent positions of Hobbes and Locke proceeded from their contrasting perceptions of human nature. Whereas Locke described human beings as naturally equal, free, and capable (through reason) of defining the common good, Hobbes viewed human beings as selfish, greedy, and warlike. Without the state, he argued, human life was "solitary, poor, nasty, brutish, and short." Bound by an irrevocable and irreversible social contract, government under one individual or a ruling assembly was, according to Hobbes, society's only hope for peace and security. The collective safety of society lay in its willingness to submit to a higher authority, which Hobbes called the "Leviathan," after the mythological marine monster described in the Bible. Hobbes aired these views in a treatise of that name, which he published in 1651—only two years after England's antiroyalist forces had beheaded King Charles I.

— READING 24.1 From Hobbes' *Leviathan* (1651)

Part I   Chapter 13: Of the Natural Condition of Mankind as Concerning their Felicity and Misery

Nature has made men so equal in the faculties of the body and mind as that, though there be found one man sometimes manifestly stronger in body or of quicker mind than another, yet, when all is reckoned together, the difference between man and man is not so considerable as that one man can thereupon claim to himself any benefit to which another may not pretend as well as he. For as to the strength of body, the weakest has strength to kill the strongest, either by secret machination or by confederacy with others that are in the same danger with himself. . . .   **10**

From this equality of ability arises equality of hope in the attaining of our ends. And therefore if any two men desire the same thing, which nevertheless they cannot both enjoy, they become enemies; and in the way to their end, which is principally their own conservation, and sometimes their delectation[1] only, endeavor to destroy or subdue one another. And from hence it comes to pass that where an invader has no more to fear than another man's single power, if one plant, sow, build, or possess a convenient seat, others may probably be expected to come prepared with forces united to dispossess   **20** and deprive him, not only of the fruit of his labor, but also of his life or liberty. And the invader again is in the like danger of another. . . .

So that in the nature of man we find three principal causes of quarrel: first, competition; secondly, diffidence;[2] thirdly, glory.

The first makes men invade for gain, the second for safety, and the third for reputation. The first use violence to make themselves masters of other men's persons, wives, children, and cattle; the second, to defend them; the third, for trifles,   **30** as a word, a smile, a different opinion, and any other sign of undervalue, either direct in their persons or by reflection in their kindred, their friends, their nation, their profession, or their name.

Hereby it is manifest that, during the time men live without a common power to keep them all in awe, they are in that condition which is called war, and such a war as is of every man against every man. For war consists not in battle only, or the act

---

[1] Enjoyment; delight.
[2] Lack of confidence.

of fighting, but in a tract of time wherein the will to contend by battle is sufficiently known; and therefore the notion of time is   **40** to be considered in the nature of war as it is in the nature of weather. For as the nature of foul weather lies not in a shower or two of rain but in an inclination thereto of many days together, so the nature of war consists not in actual fighting but in the known disposition thereto, during all the time there is no assurance to the contrary. All other time is PEACE.

Whatsoever, therefore, is consequent to a time of war where every man is enemy to every man, the same is consequent to the time wherein men live without other security than what their own strength and their own invention shall furnish them withal.   **50** In such condition there is no place for industry, because the fruit thereof is uncertain; and consequently no culture of the earth; no navigation nor use of the commodities that may be imported by sea; no commodious building; no instruments of moving and removing such things as require much force; no knowledge of the face of the earth; no account of time; no arts; no letters; no society; and, which is worst of all, continual fear and danger of violent death; and the life of man solitary, poor, nasty, brutish, and short. . . .

Part II   Chapter 17: Of the Causes, Generation, and Definition of a Commonwealth

The final cause, end, or design of men, who naturally love   **60** liberty and dominion over others, in the introduction of that restraint upon themselves in which we see them live in commonwealths, is the foresight of their own preservation, and of a more contented life thereby—that is to say, of getting themselves out from that miserable condition of war which is necessarily consequent . . . to the natural passions of man when there is no visible power to keep them in awe and tie them by fear of punishment to the performance of their covenants and observations of [the] laws of nature. . . .

For the laws of nature—as *justice, equity, modesty, mercy,*   **70** and, in sum, *doing to others as we would be done to*—of themselves, without the terror of some power to cause them to be observed, are contrary to our natural passions, that carry us to partiality, pride, revenge, and the like. And covenants without the sword are but words, and of no strength to secure a man at all. Therefore, notwithstanding the laws of nature . . ., if there be no power erected, or not great enough for our security, every man will—and may lawfully—rely on his own strength and art for caution against all other men. . . .

The only way to erect such a common power as may be able   **80** to defend them from the invasion of foreigners and the injuries of one another, and thereby to secure them in such sort as that by their own industry and by the fruits of the earth they may nourish themselves and live contentedly, is to confer all their power and strength upon one man, or upon one assembly of men that may reduce all their wills, by plurality of voices, unto one will; which is as much as to say, to appoint one man or assembly of men to bear their person, and everyone to own and acknowledge to himself to be author of whatsoever he that so bears their person shall act or cause to be acted in those things   **90** which concern the common peace and safety, and therein to submit their wills every one to his will, and their judgments to his judgment. This is more than consent or concord; it is a real unity of them all in one and the same person, made by covenant of every man with every man, in which manner as if every man should say to every man, *I authorize and give up my right of governing myself to this man, or to this assembly of men, on this condition, that you give up your right to him and authorize all his actions in like manner.* This done, the multitude so united in one person is called a COMMONWEALTH, in Latin CIVITAS. This is the generation of that great LEVIATHAN (or rather, to speak more reverently, of that *mortal god*) to which we owe, under the *immortal God*, our peace and defense. For by this authority, given him by every particular man in the commonwealth, he has the use of so much power and strength conferred on him that, by terror thereof, he is enabled to form the wills of them all to peace at home and mutual aid against their enemies abroad. And in him consists the essence of the commonwealth, which, to define it, is *one person, of whose acts a great multitude, by mutual covenants one with another, have made themselves every one the author, to the end he may use the strength and means of them all as he shall think expedient for their peace and common defense.* And he that carries this person is called SOVEREIGN and said to have sovereign power: and everyone besides, his SUBJECT.

The attaining to this sovereign power is by two ways. One, by natural force. . . . The other is when men agree among themselves to submit to some man or assembly of men voluntarily, on confidence to be protected by him against all others. This latter may be called a political commonwealth, or commonwealth by *institution*, and the former a commonwealth by *acquisition.* . . .

Part II   Chapter 30: Of the Office of the Sovereign Representative

The office of the sovereign, be it a monarch or an assembly, consists in the end for which he was trusted with the sovereign power, namely, the procuration of the *safety of the people*; to which he is obliged by the law of nature, and to render an account thereof to God, the author of that law, and to none but him. But by safety here is not meant a bare preservation but also all other contentments of life which every man by lawful industry, without danger or hurt to the commonwealth, shall acquire to himself.

And this is intended should be done, not by care applied to individuals further than their protection from injuries when they shall complain, but by a general providence contained in public instruction, both of doctrine and example, and in the making and executing of good laws, to which individual persons may apply their own cases.

And because, if the essential rights of sovereignty . . . be taken away, the commonwealth is thereby dissolved and every man returns into the condition and calamity of a war with every other man, which is the greatest evil that can happen in this life, it is the office of the sovereign to maintain those rights entire, and consequently against his duty, first, to transfer to another or to lay from himself any of them. For he that deserts the means deserts the ends. . . .

— **Q** What is Hobbes' view of human nature?

— **Q** What is the function of a "Leviathan?"

Locke's Government of the People

John Locke (Figure **24.2**) rejected Hobbes' view of human-kind as self-serving and aggressive. If, he argued, human beings were born without any pre-existing qualities, their natural state must be one of perfect freedom. Whether people became brutish or otherwise depended solely upon their experiences and their environment. People have, by their very nature as human beings, reasoned Locke, the right to life, liberty, and estate (or "property"). Government must arbitrate between the exercise of one person's liberty and that of the next. The social contract thus preserves the natural rights of the governed. While individuals may willingly consent to give up some of their liberty in return for the ruler's protection, they may never relinquish their ultimate authority. If a ruler is tyranni-cal or oppressive, the people have not only the right but also the obligation to rebel and seek a new ruler. Locke's defense of political rebellion in the face of tyranny served as justification for the "Glorious Revolution" of 1688. It also inspired the revolutions that took place in America and France toward the end of the eighteenth century.

If for Hobbes the state was supreme, for Locke sover-eignty rested with the people, and government existed only to protect the natural rights of its citizens. In his first treatise, *On Government* (1689), Locke argued that indi-viduals might attain their maximum development only in a society free from the unnatural restrictions imposed by absolute rulers. In his second treatise, *Of Civil Government* (an excerpt from which follows), Locke expounded the

Figure 24.2 HERMAN VERELST, *Portrait of John Locke*, 1689. Oil on canvas, 35½ × 29¾ in.

idea that government must rest upon the consent of the governed. While Locke's views were basic to the development of modern liberal thought, Hobbes' views provided the justification for all forms of tyranny, including the enlightened despotism of such eighteenth-century rulers as Frederick of Prussia and Catherine II of Russia, who claimed that their authority was founded in the general consent of the people. Nevertheless, the notion of government as the product of a social contract between the ruler and the ruled has become one of the dominating ideas of modern Western—and more recently of Eastern European and Asian—political life.

READING 24.2 From Locke's *Of Civil Government* (1690)

Book II   Chapter II: Of the State of Nature

To understand political power right and derive it from its original, we must consider what state all men are naturally in, and that is a state of perfect freedom to order their actions and dispose of their possessions and persons as they think fit, within the bounds of the law of nature without asking leave or depending upon the will of any other man. 1

A state also of equality, wherein all the power and jurisdiction is reciprocal, no one having more than another; there being nothing more evident than that creatures of the same species and rank, promiscuously born to all the same 10 advantages of nature and the use of the same faculties, should also be equal one amongst another without subordination or subjection; unless the Lord and Master of them all should, by any manifest declaration of his will, set one above another and confer on him, by an evident and clear appointment, an undoubted right to dominion and sovereignty. . . .

Chapter V: Of Property

God, who hath given the world to men in common, hath also given them reason to make use of it to the best advantage of life and convenience. The earth and all that is therein is given to men for the support and comfort of their being. And though 20 all the fruits it naturally produces and beasts it feeds belong to mankind in common . . ., there must of necessity be a means to appropriate them some way or other before they can be of any use, or at all beneficial to any particular man. . . .

Though the earth and all inferior creatures be common to all men, yet every man has a property in his own person: this nobody has any right to but himself. The labor of his body, and the work of his hands we may say, are properly his. Whatsoever then he removes out of the state that nature has provided and left it in, he has mixed his labor with and joined 30 to it something that is his own, and thereby makes it his property. . . .

Chapter VIII: The Beginning of Political Societies

Men being, as has been said, by nature all free, equal, and independent, no one can be put out of this estate and subjected to the political power of another without his own consent. The only way whereby any one divests himself of his natural liberty and puts on the bonds of civil society is by agreeing with other men to join and unite into a community for their comfortable, safe, and peaceable living one amongst another, in a secure enjoyment of their properties, and a 40 greater security against any that are not of it. This any number of men may do, because it injures not the freedom of the rest; they are left as they were in the liberty of the state of nature. When any number of men have so consented to make one community or government, they are thereby presently incorporated and make one body politic, wherein the majority have a right to act and conclude the rest.

For when any number of men have, by the consent of every individual, made a community, they have thereby made that community one body, with a power to act as one body, which 50 is only by the will and determination of the majority: . . . And therefore we see that in assemblies empowered to act by positive laws, where no number is set by that positive law which empowers them, the act of the majority passes for the act of the whole and of course determines; as having, by the law of nature and reason, the power of the whole.

And thus every man, by consenting with others to make one body politic under one government, puts himself under an obligation to every one of that society to submit to the determination of the majority and to be concluded by it; or else 60 this original compact whereby he with others incorporate into one society, would signify nothing and be no compact if he be left free and under no other ties than he was in before in the state of nature. . . .

Chapter IX: Of the Ends of Political Society and Government

If man in the state of nature be so free as has been said; if he be absolute lord of his own person and possessions, equal to the greatest, and subject to nobody, why will he part with his freedom, why will he give up this empire and subject himself to the dominion and control of any other power? To which it is obvious to answer that though in the state of nature he has 70 such a right, yet the enjoyment of it is very uncertain and constantly exposed to the invasion of others; for all being kings as much as he, every man his equal and the greater part no strict observers of equity and justice, the enjoyment of the property he has in this state is very unsafe, very unsecure. This makes him willing to quit a condition, which, however free, is full of fears and continual dangers: and it is not without reason that he seeks out and is willing to join in society with others who are already united or have a mind to unite for the mutual preservation of their lives, liberties, and estates, which I call by the general 80 name property.

The great and chief end, therefore, of men's uniting into commonwealths, and putting themselves under government, is the preservation of their property. . . .

Chapter XVIII: Of Tyranny

As usurpation is the exercise of power, which another hath a right to, so tyranny is the exercise of power beyond right, which nobody can have a right to. And this is making use of the power any one has in his hands, not for the good of those who are under it, but for his own private, separate advantage—

when the governor, however entitled, makes not the law, but his will, the rule; and his commands and actions are not directed to the preservation of the properties of his people, but [to] the satisfaction of his own ambition, revenge, covetousness, or any other irregular passion. . . . 90

Wherever law ends, tyranny begins, if the law be transgressed to another's harm; and whosoever in authority exceeds the power given him by the law, and makes use of the force he has under his command, . . . ceases in that to be a [magistrate]; and, acting without authority, may be opposed as any other man who by force invades the right of another. . . . 100

"May the commands then of a prince be opposed? may he be resisted as often as any one shall find himself aggrieved, and but imagine he has not right done him? This will unhinge and overturn all politics, and, instead of government and order, leave nothing but anarchy and confusion."

To this I answer that force is to be opposed to nothing but to unjust and unlawful force; whoever makes any opposition in any other case, draws on himself a just condemnation both from God and man. . . .

⎣ **Q** **Why, according to Locke, are people willing to give up their freedom?**

⎣ **Q** **What, in Locke's view, is the function of law?**

The Influence of Locke on Montesquieu and Jefferson

Locke's political treatises were read widely. So too, his defense of religious toleration (issued even as Louis XIV forced all Calvinists to leave France), his plea for equality of education among men and women, and his arguments for the use of modern languages in place of Latin won the attention of many intellectuals. Published during the last decade of the seventeenth century, these writings became the wellspring of the Enlightenment in both Europe and America.

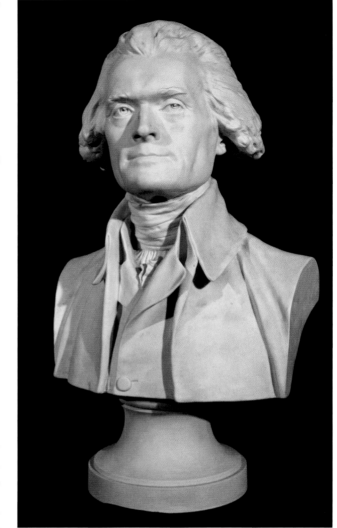

Figure 24.3 JEAN-ANTOINE HOUDON, *Thomas Jefferson*, 1789. Marble, height 21½ in.

EXPLORING ISSUES

The Right of Revolution

John Locke was among the many intellectuals—ancient and modern—who explored the relationship between individual rights and the well-being of the community. Like most seventeenth-century thinkers, Locke argued for the need for a social contract that protected both the citizen and the commonwealth. Following the Glorious Revolution of 1688, in his treatise *Of Civil Government* he tried to provide justification for popular revolt against a tyrannical ruler. Proclaiming that the function of government is the good of mankind, he asks:

. . . which is best for mankind, that the people should always be exposed to the boundless will of tyranny, or that rulers should

be sometimes liable to be opposed when they grow exorbitant in the abuse of their power, and employ it for the destruction and not the preservation of the properties of their people?

Locke's answer defended the use of force to unseat a ruler who, by his violation of the social contract, forfeited the right to rule. The question remains, however, whether, as Hobbes pointed out, the great masses of human beings (if indeed as selfish and competitive as Hobbes described them) should hold the privilege or the authority to unseat the sovereign forcefully. Might the community, as regulated by the decisions of the sovereign, ultimately be better served if the citizens' right to revolt were limited?

In France, the keen-minded aristocrat Charles Louis de Secondat Montesquieu (1689–1755) championed Locke's views on political freedom and expanded on his theories. Intrigued by the way in which nature appeared to govern social behavior, the Baron de Montesquieu investigated the effects of climate and custom on human conduct, thus pioneering the field of sociology. In an elegantly written thousand-page treatise, *The Spirit of the Laws* (1748), Montesquieu defended liberty as the free exercise of the will. He was among the first to condemn slavery as fundamentally "unnatural and evil."

Montesquieu, a proponent of constitutional monarchy, advanced the idea of a separation of powers among the executive, legislative, and judicial agencies of government, advising that each monitor the activities of the others in order to ensure a balanced system of government. He warned that when legislative and executive powers were united in the same person (or body of magistrates), or when judicial power was inseparable from legislative and executive powers, human liberty might be gravely threatened. Montesquieu's system of checks and balances was later enshrined in the Constitution of the United States of America (1787).

Across the Atlantic, many of Locke's ideas appeared in the preamble to the statement declaring the independence of the North American colonies from the rule of the British king George III. Written by the leading American apostle of the Enlightenment, Thomas Jefferson (1743–1826; Figure **24.3**), and adopted by the Continental Congress on July 4, 1776, the American Declaration of Independence echoes Locke's ideology of revolt as well as his view that governments derive their just powers from the consent of the governed. Following Locke and Montesquieu, Jefferson advocated the establishment of a social contract between ruler and ruled as the principal means of fulfilling natural law—the "unalienable right" to life, liberty, and the pursuit of happiness. While Jefferson did not include "property" among the unalienable rights, he was, as well, fully committed to the individual's right to own land and goods, including slaves.

READING 24.3 From Jefferson's Declaration of Independence (1776)

When, in the course of human events, it becomes necessary   1
for one people to dissolve the political bands which have
connected them with another, and to assume among the
powers of the earth, the separate and equal station to which
the laws of nature and of nature's God entitle them, a decent
respect to the opinions of mankind requires that they should
declare the causes which impel them to separation.

 We hold these truths to be self-evident: That all men are
created equal; that they are endowed by their Creator with
certain unalienable rights; that among these are life, liberty   10
and the pursuit of happiness; that to secure these rights
governments are instituted among men, deriving their just
powers from the consent of the governed; that whenever any
form of government becomes destructive of these ends, it is

the right of the people to alter or to abolish it, and to institute
new government, laying its foundation on such principles and
organizing its powers in such form, as to them shall seem most
likely to effect their safety and happiness. . . .

Q What is meant by "unalienable rights?"

Q How does Jefferson justify revolution?

The Declaration of Independence made clear the founding fathers' belief in equality among men. Equality between the sexes was, however, another matter: although both Locke and Jefferson acknowledged that women held the same natural rights as men, they did not consider women—or slaves, or children, for that matter—capable of exercising such rights. Recognizing this bias, Abigail Adams (d. 1818) wrote to her husband, John, who was serving as a delegate to the Second Continental Congress (1777), as follows:

> I . . . hear that you have declared an
> independency, and, by the way, in the new code
> of laws which I suppose it will be necessary for you
> to make, I desire you would remember the ladies
> and be more generous and favorable to them than
> were your ancestors. Do not put such unlimited
> power into the hands of husbands. Remember all
> men would be tyrants if they could. If particular
> care and attention are not paid to the ladies we
> are determined to foment a rebellion, and will
> not hold ourselves bound to obey any laws in
> which we have no voice or representation.

Despite the future First Lady's spirited admonitions, however, American women did not secure the legal right to vote or to hold political office until well into the twentieth century.

If the Declaration of Independence constituted a clear expression of Enlightenment theory in justifying revolution against tyrannical rule, the Constitution of the new United States of America represented the practical outcome of the revolution: the creation of a viable new nation with its government based ultimately on Enlightenment principles. The U.S. Constitution, framed in 1787 and ratified by popular vote in 1788–1789, articulated the mechanics of self-rule. First, it created a form of government new to the modern world: a system of representative government embodying the principle of "Republicanism," that is, government run by the elected representatives of the people. Second, following the precepts of Montesquieu, the framers of the Constitution divided the new government into three branches—legislative, executive, and judicial—each to be "checked and balanced" by the others to prevent the possible tyranny of any one branch. Third, the new republic was granted sufficient power to govern primarily through the authority granted the president to execute national laws and constitutional provisions. Withal, the U.S. Constitution would prove effective for more than two centuries, and would serve as the model for the constitutions of almost all new republics created throughout the world.

The Birth of Economic Theory

While Enlightenment thinkers were primarily concerned with matters of political equality, they also addressed questions related to the economy of the modern state. The Scottish philosopher Adam Smith (1723–1790) applied the idea of natural law to the domains of human labor, productivity, and the exchange of goods. His epoch-making synthesis of ethics and economics, *An Inquiry into the Nature and Causes of the Wealth of Nations*, set forth the "laws" of labor, production, and trade with an exhaustiveness reminiscent of Newton's *Principia Mathematica* (see chapter 23).

Smith contended that labor, a condition natural to humankind (as Locke had observed), was the foundation for prosperity. A nation's wealth is not its land nor its money, said Smith, but its labor force. In the "natural" economic order, individual self-interest guides the progress of economic life, and certain natural forces, such as the "law of supply and demand," motivate a market economy. Since government interference would infringe on the natural order, reasoned Smith, such interference is undesirable. He thus opposed all artificial restraints on economic progress and all forms of government regulation and control.

The modern concepts of free enterprise and ***laissez-faire*** (literally, "allow to act") economics spring from Smith's incisive formulations. In the following excerpt, Smith examines the origin of the division of labor among human beings and defends the natural and unimpeded operation of trade and competition among nations.

READING 24.4 From Smith's *An Inquiry into the Nature and Causes of the Wealth of Nations* (1776)

Book I   Chapter II: The Principle which Occasions the Division of Labor

[The] division of labor, from which so many advantages are derived, is not originally the effect of any human wisdom, which foresees and intends that general opulence to which it gives occasion. It is the necessary, though very slow and gradual, consequence of a certain propensity in human nature which has in view no such extensive utility; the propensity to truck, barter, and exchange one thing for another. 1

. . . . [This propensity] is common to all men, and to be found in no other race of animals, which seem to know neither this nor any other species of contracts. Two greyhounds, in running 10 down the same hare, have sometimes the appearance of acting in some sort of concert. Each turns her towards his companion, or endeavors to intercept her when his companion turns her towards himself. This, however, is not the effect of any contract, but of the accidental concurrence of their passions in the same object at that particular time. Nobody ever saw a dog make a fair and deliberate exchange of one bone for another with another dog. . . . In almost every other race of animals each individual, when it is grown up to maturity, is entirely independent, and in its natural state has occasion for the 20 assistance of no other living creature. But man has almost constant occasion for the help of his brethren, and it is in vain

for him to expect it from their benevolence only. He will be more likely to prevail if he can interest their self-love in his favor, and show them that it is for their own advantage to do for him what he requires of them. Whoever offers to another a bargain of any kind, proposes to do this. Give me that which I want, and you shall have this which you want, is the meaning of every such offer; and it is in this manner that we obtain from one another the far greater part of those good offices which we stand in 30 need of. It is not from the benevolence of the butcher, the brewer, or the baker, that we expect our dinner, but from their regard to their own interest. We address ourselves, not to their humanity, but to their self-love; and never talk to them of our own necessities, but of their advantages. . . .

As it is by treaty, by barter, and by purchase, that we obtain from one another the greater part of those mutual good offices which we stand in need of, so it is this same trucking disposition which originally gives occasion to the division of labor. In a tribe of hunters or shepherds a particular person 40 makes bows and arrows, for example, with more readiness and dexterity than any other. He frequently exchanges them for cattle or for venison with his companions; and he finds at last that he can in this manner get more cattle and venison, than if he himself went to the field to catch them. From a regard to his own interest, therefore, the making of bows and arrows grows to be his chief business. . . .

Book IV   Chapter III, Part II: Of the Unreasonableness of Restraints [on Trade]

Nations have been taught that their interest consisted in beggaring all their neighbors. Each nation has been made to look with an invidious eye upon the prosperity of all the 50 nations with which it trades, and to consider their gain as its own loss. Commerce, which ought naturally to be, among nations as among individuals, a bond of union and friendship, has become the most fertile source of discord and animosity. The capricious ambition of kings and ministers has not, during the present and the preceding century, been more fatal to the repose of Europe, than the impertinent jealousy of merchants and manufacturers. The violence and injustice of the rulers of mankind is an ancient evil, for which, I am afraid, the nature of human affairs can scarce admit of a remedy. But the 60 mean rapacity, the monopolizing spirit of merchants and manufacturers, who neither are, nor ought to be, the rulers of mankind, though it cannot perhaps be corrected, may very easily be prevented from disturbing the tranquility of anybody but themselves.

That it was the spirit of monopoly which originally both invented and propagated this doctrine, cannot be doubted; and they who first taught it were by no means such fools as they who believed it. In every country it always is and must be the interest of the great body of the people to buy whatever they 70 want of those who sell it cheapest. The proposition is so very manifest, that it seems ridiculous to take any pains to prove it; nor could it ever have been called in question had not the interested sophistry of merchants and manufacturers confounded the common sense of mankind. Their interest is, in this respect, directly opposed to that of the great body of the people. . . .

The wealth of a neighboring nation, though dangerous in war and politics, is certainly advantageous in trade. In a state of hostility it may enable our enemies to maintain fleets and armies superior to our own; but in a state of peace and commerce it must likewise enable them to exchange with us to a greater value and to afford a better market, either for the immediate produce of our own industry or for whatever is purchased with that produce. As a rich man is likely to be a better customer to the industrious people in his neighborhood, than a poor, so is likewise a rich nation. . . .

— **Q** **What natural forces dominate the economic life of the nation, according to Smith?**

— **Q** **Would you consider Smith a realist or an idealist?**

The *Philosophes*

When Louis XIV died, in 1715, the French nobility fled the palace of Versailles and settled in fashionable Paris townhouses. Socially ambitious noblewomen, many of whom championed a freer and more public role for their gender, organized gatherings in the *salons* of these houses (Figure **24.4**). Here, nobility and middle-class thinkers met to exchange views on morality, politics, science, and religion, and to voice opinions on everything ranging from diet to the latest fashions in theater and dress. Inevitably, as new ideas began to circulate in these meetings, Paris became the center of intellectual life. The well-educated

Figure 24.4 ANICET CHARLES GABRIEL LEMONNIER, *The Salon of Madame Geoffrin in 1755*, 1812. Oil on canvas, 51 × 77 in.

Bust of Voltaire

Rameau (composer)

Rousseau (philosopher)

Lekain (actor)

Diderot (encyclopedist)

Turgot (economist)

Montesquieu (philosopher)

Mme Geoffrin

Science and Technology

1702	the world's first daily newspaper is published in England
1704	the first alphabetical encyclopedia in English is printed
1714	a London engineer patents the first known typewriter
1765	Diderot's *Encyclopédie* is issued in seventeen volumes

individuals who graced the *salons* came to be known as *philosophes* (the French word for "philosophers"). Intellectuals rather than philosophers in the strictest sense of the term, the *philosophes* dominated the literary activity of the Enlightenment. Like the humanists of fifteenth-century Florence, their interests were mainly secular and social. Unlike their Renaissance counterparts, however, the *philosophes* scorned all forms of authority—they believed that they had surpassed the ancients, and they looked beyond the present state of knowledge to the establishment of a superior moral and social order.

Most *philosophes* held to the deist view of God as Creator and providential force behind nature and natural law, rather than as personal Redeemer. They believed in the immortality of the soul, not out of commitment to any religious doctrine, but because they regarded human beings as fundamentally different from other living creatures. They viewed the Bible as mythology rather than as revealed truth, and scorned church hierarchy and ritual. Their antipathy to irrationality, superstition, and religious dogma (as reflected, for instance, in the Catholic doctrine of Original Sin) alienated them from the Church and set them at odds with the established authorities—a position memorably expressed in Voltaire's acerbic pronouncement: "men will not be free until the last king is strangled with the entrails of the last priest." The quest for a nonauthoritarian, secular morality led the *philosophes* to challenge all existing forms of intolerance, inequality, and injustice. Their banner cry, "Ecrasez l'infame" ("Wipe out all evils"), sparked a commitment to social reforms that provoked the French Revolution (see chapter 25).

Diderot and the *Encyclopédie*

The reforming ideals of the Enlightenment were summed up in a monumental literary endeavor to which many of the *philosophes* contributed: the thirty-five-volume *Encyclopédie* (including eleven volumes of engraved plates) edited by Denis Diderot (1713–1784) and published between 1751 and 1772. Modeled on the two-volume Chambers' Encyclopedia printed in England in 1751, Diderot's *Encyclopédie*—also known as *The Analytical Dictionary of the Sciences, Arts, and Crafts*—was the largest compendium of contemporary social, philosophic, artistic, scientific, and technological knowledge ever produced in the West. A collection of "all the knowledge scattered over the face of

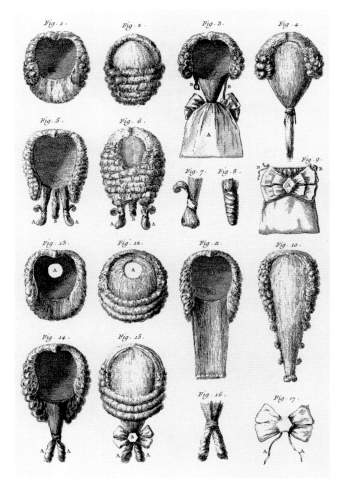

Figure 24.5 *Wigs*, a plate from the *Encyclopédie* illustrating the varieties of men's wig that were fashionable in Europe in the 1750s.

the earth," as Diderot explained, it manifested the zealous desire of the *philosophes* to dispel human ignorance and transform society. It was also, in part, a response to rising literacy and to the widespread public interest in the facts of everyday life. Not all members of society welcomed the enterprise, however: King Louis XV claimed that the *Encyclopédie* was doing "irreparable damage to morality and religion." Although the crown twice banned its printing, some volumes were published and distributed secretly.

Diderot's *Encyclopédie* was the most ambitious and influential literary undertaking of the eighteenth century. Almost 200 individuals contributed 72,000 entries on subjects ranging from political theory, cultural history, and art criticism to the technology of theater machinery, the making of silk stockings, and the varieties of wig (Figure **24.5**). Articles on Islam, India, and China indicate a more than idle curiosity about civilizations that remained to most Westerners remote and exotic. Diderot enlisted as contributors to the *Encyclopédie* the most progressive minds of the Enlightenment: François Marie Arouet (1694–1778), known as Voltaire, wrote on "matters of nature and art"; the French philosopher and educator Jean-Jacques Rousseau (1712–1778; see chapter 25) provided articles on music; François Quesnay wrote on political economy; Montesquieu (whose articles were published posthumously) examined the different types of government; Jean Le Rond d'Alembert (1717–1783) treated the subject of higher education; and Diderot himself prepared numerous entries on art and politics.

The *Encyclopédie* remains a monument to secular knowledge and to the Enlightenment faith in the promise of reason—a spirit summed up in Voltaire's proclamation, "Let the facts prevail." The following excerpts come from the entry on natural law written by the French lawyer Antoine-Gaspart Boucher d'Argis and from the long article on black Africans written by Le Romain (first name and dates unknown).

READING 24.5 From the *Encyclopédie* (1751–1772)

Law of Nature or Natural Law

In its broadest sense the term is taken to designate certain principles which nature alone inspires and which all animals as well as all men have in common. On this law are based the union of male and female, the begetting of children as well as their education, love of liberty, self-preservation, concern for self-defense. 1

It is improper to call the behavior of animals natural law, for, not being endowed with reason, they can know neither law nor justice.

More commonly we understand by natural law certain laws of justice and equity which only natural reason has established among men, or better, which God has engraved in our hearts. 10

The fundamental principles of law and all justice are: to live honestly, not to give offense to anyone, and to render unto each whatever is his. From these general principles derive a great many particular rules which nature alone, that is, reason and equity, suggest to mankind.

Since this natural law is based on such fundamental principles, it is perpetual and unchangeable: no agreement can debase it, no law can alter it or exempt anyone from the obligation it imposes. . . . 20

The principles of natural law, therefore, form part of the law of nations, particularly the primitive law of nations; they also form part of public and of private law: for the principles of natural law, which we have stated, are the purest source of the foundation of most of private and public law. . . .

The authority of natural laws stems from the fact that they owe their existence to God. Men submit to them because to observe them leads to the happiness of men and society. This is a truth demonstrated by reason. It is equally true that virtue 30 by itself is a principle of inner satisfaction whereas vice is a principle of unrest and trouble. It is equally certain that virtue produces great external advantage, while vice produces great ills. . . .

Negroes[1]

For the last few centuries the Europeans have carried on a trade in Negroes whom they obtain from Guinea and other coasts of Africa and whom they use to maintain the colonies established in various parts of America and in the West Indies. To justify this loathsome commerce, which is contrary to natural law, it is argued that ordinarily these slaves find the 40 salvation of their souls in the loss of their liberty, and that the Christian teaching they receive, together with their indispensable role in the cultivation of sugar cane, tobacco, indigo, etc., softens the apparent inhumanity of a commerce where men buy and sell their fellow men as they would animals used in the cultivation of the land.

Trade in Negroes is carried on by all the nations which have settlements in the West Indies, and especially by the French, the English, the Portuguese, the Dutch, the Swedes, and the Danes. The Spaniards, in spite of the fact that they possess the 50 greatest part of the Americas, have no direct way of acquiring slaves but have concluded treaties with other nations to furnish them with Negroes. . . .

As soon as the trade is completed no time must be lost in setting sail. Experience has shown that as long as these unfortunates are still within sight of their homeland, they are overcome by sorrow and gripped by despair. The former is the cause of many illnesses from which a large number perish during the crossing; the latter inclines them to suicide, which they effect either by refusing nourishment or by shutting off 60 their breathing. This they do in a way they know of turning and twisting their tongues which unfailingly suffocates them. Others again shatter their head against the sides of the ship or throw themselves into the sea if the occasion presents itself. . . .

Punishment of the Negroes, Policing, and Regulations Concerning these Matters:

If the Negro commits a slight offense the overseer may on his own responsibility punish him with a few strokes of the whip. If, however, it is a serious matter, the master has the culprit clapped in irons and then decides the number of strokes with which he will be punished. If all men were equally just, these 70 necessary punishments would be kept within limits, but it often happens that certain masters abuse the authority which they claim over their slaves and chastise these unfortunates too harshly. Yet the masters themselves may be responsible for the situation which led to the offense. To put an end to the cruelties of these barbarous men who would be capable of leaving their slaves without the basic necessities of life while driving them to forced labor, the officers of His Majesty, who are resident in the colonies, have the responsibility of enforcing the edict of the king, which is called the Black 80 Code. In the French islands of America this code regulates the governing and the administration of justice and of the police, as well as the discipline of the slaves and the slave-trade. . . .

Q What is the relationship between natural law and reason?

Q How is slavery assessed in this reading?

---

[1] A term originally used by the Spanish and Portuguese to identify black Africans.

Madame du Châtelet

Although women contributed moral and financial support to the *Encyclopédie*, none was invited to participate in its production. Moreover, not one of the thirty-one entries on women makes reference to the contributions of such exceptional eighteenth-century women as Gabrielle-Émilie Le Tonnelier de Breteuil, the Marquise du Châtelet (1706–1749). An impeccable scholar and a brilliant mathematician, Madame du Châtelet produced an annotated French translation of Newton's *Principia*—a monumental achievement that was near completion when she died, a few days after giving birth to her fourth child.

Proficient in Latin, Italian, and English, the marquise translated the works of Virgil, Horace, and Ovid into eloquent French; she wrote original poetry and conducted experiments in physics and chemistry. She was a reckless gambler, a feminist, a champion of the fashionably low-cut neckline (Figure **24.6**), and the mistress of Voltaire, who lived at her *château* until her death in 1749. As a woman, du Châtelet was deprived of education by the formal secondary schools that welcomed men. Nonetheless, she received independent instruction from some of Paris' most notable scholars, beginning lessons in advanced geometry and algebra at the age of twenty-six, and eventually becoming a respected authority in both of these fields, as well as in physics and calculus. Voltaire confessed that he could hardly live without the marquise, whose intellectual achievements, he insisted, qualified her as "a great man."

The Encyclopedic Cast of Mind

The *Encyclopédie* had an enormous impact on eighteenth-century culture. Although it was read and understood by few, it fostered an encyclopedic cast of mind. Its emphasis on the accumulation, codification, and systematic preservation of knowledge was, in part, a response to the Scientific Revolution and to that other Enlightenment "bible," Newton's *Principia*.

Eighteenth-century scientists made notable advances in the fields of chemistry, electricity, biology, and the medical sciences. They invented the mercury thermometer and the stethoscope and introduced the science of immunology to the West—some seven centuries after the Chinese had produced the first inoculations against smallpox. The French aristocrat Antoine Lavoisier (1743–1794) published the *Elementary Treatise of Chemistry* (1789), launching chemistry as an exact science. Assisted in the laboratory by his wife, Marie-Anne Pierrette Paulze, Lavoisier produced the first extensive list of chemical elements (see Figure 24.1). The Swede Carolus Linnaeus (1707–1778) produced a systematic method for classifying plants, and the French naturalist Georges Louis Leclerc, Comte de Buffon (1707–1788), made landmark advances in zoology.

Valuable efforts to accumulate and classify knowledge took place in the arts as well. The greatest literary critic of his time, Samuel Johnson (1709–1784) published the first dictionary of the English language. Occupying Johnson (and six assistants) for almost nine years, it consisted of

Figure 24.6 NICOLAS DE LARGILLIÈRE, *Gabrielle-Émilie Le Tonnelier de Breteuil, Marquise du Châtelet*, ca. 1740. Oil on canvas, 4 ft. 3½ in. × 3 ft. 4¼ in. Du Châtelet was the first woman whose writings were published by the French Royal Academy of Sciences. Managing a household, a husband, her children, and a series of lovers, she was forced to pursue her own work between midnight and 5 a.m. She died in childbirth at the age of 43.

definitions for some 40,000 words and more than 100,000 quotations from English literary works. The polymath Jean-Jacques Rousseau (see chapter 25) produced the first Western dictionary of music. In the social sciences, Voltaire's seven-volume general history (published in 1756), which included a monumental account of the age of Louis XIV, provided a model for a new universal and rationalist kind of history-writing. Voltaire was among the first to recognize Europe's debt to Arab science and Asian thought. He rejected faith-based explanations of the past and was generally critical of the role played by the Catholic Church in Western history. But it fell to the English historian Edward Gibbon (1737–1794) to provide the rationale that blamed Christianity for contributing to the collapse of Rome. *The Decline and Fall of the Roman Empire* (1776) was the product of Gibbon's unique interpretation of the sociological forces that shaped ancient cultures.

Eighteenth-century China lay beyond the immediate influence of the European Enlightenment; nevertheless, in the East an encyclopedic impulse similar to that prevailing in the West came to a climax at this time. Qing rulers followed their Ming predecessors in directing groups of scholars to assemble exhaustive collections of information, some filling as many as 36,000 manuscript volumes. These "encyclopedias" were actually anthologies of the writings of former Chinese artists and scholars, rather than comprehensive collections of contemporary knowledge. Nevertheless, as in France, some of China's rulers deemed the indiscriminate accumulation of information itself dangerous, and at least one eighteenth-century Qing emperor authorized the burning of thousands of books.

The Crusade for Progress

Leibniz and Beccaria

Among European intellectuals, the belief in the reforming powers of reason became the basis for a progressive view of human history. The German mathematician and philosopher Gottfried Wilhelm Leibniz (1646–1716) systematically defended the view that human beings live in perfect harmony with God and nature. Leibniz linked optimism to the logic of probability: his *principle of sufficient reason* held, simply, that there must be a reason or purpose for everything in nature. In response to the question, "Why does evil exist in a world created by a good God?," Leibniz answered that all events conformed to the divinely established harmony of the universe. Even evil, according to Leibniz, was necessary in a world that was "better than any other possible world"—a position that came to be known as "philosophic optimism."

For the *philosophes*, the key to social reform lay in a true understanding of human nature, which, they argued, might best be acquired by examining human history. They viewed, for instance, the transition from Paleolithic hunting and gathering to the rise of urban civilization as clear evidence of the steady march of social improvement. Faith in the reality of that march motivated the Enlightenment crusade for progress. The Italian lawyer

Science and Technology

1714	the mercury thermometer and the Fahrenheit scale are invented in Germany
1726	the first measurement of blood pressure is taken in England
1751	the first mental hospital opens in London
1774	Franz Mesmer (Austrian) uses hypnotism to aid in curing disease

and social reformer Cesare de Beccaria (1738–1794) enlisted in this crusade when he wrote his treatise *On Crimes and Punishments*. Here, for instance, he suggested that torturing criminals did not work to deter crime. Rather, argued Beccaria, society should seek methods by which to rehabilitate those who commit crimes. Although Beccaria's publication generated no immediate changes, it went through six editions in eighteen months and ultimately contributed to movements for prison reform in Europe and the United States. The questions Beccaria raised concerning the value of punishment are still being debated today.

Condorcet

The most passionate warrior in the Enlightenment crusade for progress was the French aristocrat Antoine Nicolas de Condorcet (1743–1794). Condorcet was a mathematician, a social theorist, and a political moderate amidst revolutionary extremists. His *Sketch for a Historical Picture of the Progress of the Human Mind*, written during the early days of the French Revolution, was the preface to a longer work he never completed—he committed suicide shortly after being imprisoned as an "enemy" of the revolution.

Condorcet believed that human nature could be perfected through the application of reason. All errors in politics and morals, he argued, were based on philosophic and scientific errors. "There is not a religious system nor a supernatural extravagance," he wrote, "that is not founded on ignorance of the laws of nature." Fiercely optimistic about the future of humankind, Condorcet was one of the first male champions of sexual equality. He called for the "complete annihilation of the prejudices that have brought about an inequality of rights between the sexes, an inequality fatal even to the party in whose favor it works." Such inequality, he protested, "has its origin solely in an abuse of strength, and all the later sophistical attempts that have been made to excuse it are vain."

In his *Sketch*, the visionary Condorcet traced the "progress" of humankind through ten stages, from ignorance and tyranny to the threshold of enlightenment and equality. The utopian tenth stage, subtitled "The Future Progress of the Human Mind" (an excerpt from which follows), sets forth ideas that were well ahead of their time, such as a guaranteed livelihood for the aged, a universal system of education, fewer work hours, and the refinement of technology for the accumulation of knowledge.

Map 24.1 The Intellectual Revolution of the Seventeenth and Eighteenth Centuries in Western Europe.

(How digital computers would have delighted this prophet of the Information Age!) The educational goals that Condorcet outlines toward the end of the excerpt still carry the force of sound judgment.

READING 24.6 From Condorcet's *Sketch for a Historical Picture of the Progress of the Human Mind* (1793)

If man can, with almost complete assurance, predict   1
phenomena when he knows their laws, and if, even when
he does not, he can still, with great expectation of success,
forecast the future on the basis of his experience of the
past, why, then, should it be regarded as a fantastic

undertaking to sketch, with some pretense to truth, the
future destiny of man on the basis of his history? The sole
foundation for belief in the natural sciences is this idea
that the general laws directing the phenomena of the universe,
known or unknown, are necessary and constant. Why should
this principle be any less true for the development of the   10
intellectual and moral faculties of man than for the other
operations of nature? Since beliefs founded on past experience
of like conditions provide the only rule of conduct for
the wisest of men, why should the philosopher be forbidden
to base his conjectures on these same foundations, so long
as he does not attribute to them a certainty superior to that
warranted by the number, the constancy, and the accuracy
of his observations? . . .

The time will therefore come when the sun will shine only

on free men who know no other master but their reason; when tyrants and slaves, priests and their stupid or hypocritical instruments will exist only in works of history and on the stage; and when we shall think of them only to pity their victims and their dupes; to maintain ourselves in a state of vigilance by thinking on their excesses; and to learn how to recognize and so to destroy, by force of reason, the first seeds of tyranny and superstition, should they ever dare to reappear among us.

In looking at the history of societies we shall have had occasion to observe that there is often a great difference between the rights that the law allows its citizens and the rights that they actually enjoy, and, again, between the equality established by political codes and that which in fact exists among individuals. . . .

These differences have three main causes: inequality in wealth, inequality in status between the man whose means of subsistence are hereditary and the man whose means are dependent on the length of his life, or, rather, on that part of his life in which he is capable of work; and, finally, inequality in education.

We therefore need to show that these three sorts of real inequality must constantly diminish without however disappearing altogether: for they are the result of natural and necessary causes which it would be foolish and dangerous to wish to eradicate. . . .

[As to education] we can teach the citizen everything that he needs to know in order to be able to manage his household, administer his affairs, and employ his labor and his faculties in freedom; to know his rights and to be able to exercise them; to be acquainted with his duties and fulfill them satisfactorily; to judge his own and other men's actions according to his own lights and to be a stranger to none of the high and delicate feelings which honor human nature; not to be in a state of blind dependence upon those to whom he must entrust his affairs or the exercise of his rights; to be in a proper condition to choose and supervise them; to be no longer the dupe of those popular errors which torment man with superstitious fears and chimerical hopes; to defend himself against prejudice by the strength of his reason alone; and, finally, to escape the deceits of charlatans who would lay snares for his fortune, his health, his freedom of thought, and his conscience under the pretext of granting him health, wealth, and salvation. . . .

The real advantages that should result from this progress, of which we can entertain a hope that is almost a certainty, can have no other term than that of the absolute perfection of the human race; since, as the various kinds of equality come to work in its favor by producing ampler sources of supply, more extensive education, more complete liberty, so equality will be more real and will embrace everything which is really of importance for the happiness of human beings. . . .

Q In what ways does this reading illustrate the optimism of Enlightenment thought?

Q What, according to Condorcet, are the three main causes of social discord?

Enlightenment and the Rights of Women

While Condorcet was among the first moderns to champion the equality of the sexes, his efforts pale before the impassioned defense of women launched by Mary Wollstonecraft (1759–1797; Figure **24.7**). This self-educated British intellectual applied Enlightenment principles of natural law,

Figure 24.7 JOHN OPIE, *Mary Wollstonecraft*, ca. 1797. Oil on canvas, 29½ × 24½ in. The author of the cornerstone treatise for women's liberation, Wollstonecraft was reviled by one of her male contemporaries as "a hyena in petticoats."

liberty, and equality to forge a radical rethinking of the roles and responsibilities of women in Western society. In *A Vindication of the Rights of Woman*, Wollstonecraft attacked the persistence of the female stereotype (docile, domestic, and childlike) as formulated by misguided, misogynistic, and tyrannical males, who, as she complained, "try to secure the good conduct of women by attempting to keep them in a state of childhood." Calling for a "revolution of female manners," she criticized the "disorderly kind of education" received by women, who, owing to their domestic roles, learn "rather by snatches."

Wollstonecraft emphasized the importance of reason in the cultivation of virtue, observing that "it is a farce to call any being virtuous whose virtues do not result from the exercise of its own reason." She criticized women for embracing their roles in "the great art of pleasing [men]." The minds of women, she insisted, were enfeebled by "false refinement," "sweet docility," and "slavish dependence."

Despite her high degree of critical acumen, however, Wollstonecraft seems to have been deeply conflicted by her own personal efforts to reconcile her sexual passions, her need for independence, and her free-spirited will. Her affair with an American speculator and timber merchant produced an illegitimate child and at least two attempts at suicide; and her marriage to the novelist William Godwin (subsequent to her becoming pregnant by him) proved no less turbulent. She died at the age of thirty-eight, following the birth of their daughter, the future Mary Shelley (see chapter 28). In contrast with her short and troubled life, Wollstonecraft's treatise has enjoyed sustained and significant influence; it stands at the threshold of the modern movement for female equality.

READING 24.7 From Wollstonecraft's *A Vindication of the Rights of Woman* (1792)

After considering the historic page, and viewing the living world with anxious solicitude, the most melancholy emotions of sorrowful indignation have depressed my spirits, and I have sighed when obliged to confess, that either nature has made a great difference between man and man, or that the civilization which has hitherto taken place in the world has been very partial. I have turned over various books written on the subject of education, and patiently observed the conduct of parents and the management of schools; but what has been the result?—a profound conviction that the neglected education of my fellow-creatures is the grand source of the misery I deplore; and that women, in particular, are rendered weak and wretched by a variety of concurring causes, originating from one hasty conclusion. The conduct and manners of women, in fact, evidently prove that their minds are not in a healthy state; for, like the flowers which are planted in too rich a soil, strength and usefulness are sacrificed to beauty; and the flaunting leaves, after having pleased a fastidious eye, fade, disregarded on the stalk, long before the season when they ought to have arrived at maturity.—One cause of this barren blooming I attribute to a false system of education, gathered from the books written on this subject by men who, considering females rather as women than human creatures, have been more anxious to make them [20] alluring mistresses than affectionate wives and rational mothers and the understanding of the sex has been so bubbled by this specious homage, that the civilized women of the present century, with a few exceptions, are only anxious to inspire love, when they ought to cherish a nobler ambition, and by their abilities and virtues exact respect.

In a treatise, therefore, on female rights and manners, the works which have been particularly written for their [30] improvement must not be overlooked; especially when it is asserted, in direct terms, that the minds of women are enfeebled by false refinement; that the books of instruction, written by men of genius, have had the same tendency as more frivolous productions; and that, in the true style of Mahometanism,[1] they are treated as a kind of subordinate beings, and not as a part of the human species, when improveable reason is allowed to be the dignified distinction which raises men above the brute creation, and puts a natural sceptre in a feeble hand. [40]

Yet, because I am a woman, I would not lead my readers to suppose that I mean violently to agitate the contested question respecting the equality or inferiority of the sex; but as the subject lies in my way, and I cannot pass it over without subjecting the main tendency of my reasoning to misconstruction, I shall stop a moment to deliver, in a few words, my opinion.—In the government of the physical world it is observable that the female in point of strength is, in general, inferior to the male. This is the law of nature; and it does not appear to be suspended or abrogated in [50] favour of woman. A degree of physical superiority cannot, therefore, be denied—and it is a noble prerogative! But not content with this natural preeminence, men endeavour to sink us still lower, merely to render us alluring objects for a moment; and women, intoxicated by the adoration which men, under the influence of their senses, pay to them, do not seek to obtain a durable interest in their hearts, or to become the friends of the fellow creatures who find amusement in their society. . . .

My own sex, I hope, will excuse me, if I treat them like [60] rational creatures, instead of flattering their *fascinating* graces, and viewing them as if they were in a state of perpetual childhood, unable to stand alone. I earnestly wish to point out in what true dignity and human happiness consists—I wish to persuade women to endeavour to acquire strength, both of mind and body, and to convince them that the soft phrases, susceptibility of heart, delicacy of sentiment, and refinement of taste, are almost synonymous with epithets of weakness, and that those beings who are only the objects of pity and that kind of [70] love, which has been termed its sister, will soon become objects of contempt.

Dismissing then those pretty feminine phrases, which the men condescendingly use to soften our slavish dependence, and despising that weak elegancy of mind, exquisite sensibility, and sweet docility of manners, supposed to be the sexual characteristics of the weaker vessel, I wish to shew that elegance is inferior to virtue, that the first object of

---

[1] A reference to the widespread Christian misconception that Islam denied that women had souls.

laudable ambition is to obtain a character as a human being, regardless of the distinction of sex; and that secondary views should be brought to this simple touchstone. . . . 80

The education of women has, of late, been more attended to than formerly; yet they are still reckoned a frivolous sex, and ridiculed or pitied by the writers who endeavour by satire or instruction to improve them. It is acknowledged that they spend many of the first years of their lives in acquiring a smattering of accomplishments; meanwhile strength of body and mind are sacrificed to libertine notions of beauty, to the desire of establishing themselves,—the only way women can rise in the world,—by marriage. And this desire making mere 90 animals of them, when they marry they act as such children may be expected to act:—they dress; they paint, and nickname God's creatures.—Surely these weak beings are only fit for a seraglio! Can they be expected to govern a family with judgment, or take care of the poor babes whom they bring into the world?

If then it can be fairly deduced from the present conduct of the sex, from the prevalent fondness for pleasure which takes place of ambition and those nobler passions that open and enlarge the soul; that the instruction which women have 100 hitherto received has only tended, with the constitution of civil society, to render them insignificant objects of desire—mere propagators of fools!—if it can be proved that in aiming to accomplish them, without cultivating their understandings, they are taken out of their sphere of duties, and made ridiculous and useless when the short-lived bloom of beauty is over, I presume that rational men will excuse me for endeavouring to persuade them to become more masculine and respectable. . . .

In the present state of society it appears necessary to go 110 back to first principles in search of the most simple truths, and to dispute with some prevailing prejudice every inch of ground. To clear my way, I must be allowed to ask some plain questions, and the answers will probably appear as unequivocal as the axioms on which reasoning is built; though, when entangled with various motives of action, they are formally contradicted, either by the words or conduct of men.

In what does man's pre-eminence over the brute creation consist? The answer is as clear as that a half is less than the whole; in Reason. 120

What acquirement exalts one being above another? Virtue; we spontaneously reply.

For what purpose were the passions implanted? That man by struggling with them might attain a degree of knowledge denied to the brutes; whispers Experience.

Consequently the perfection of our nature and capability of happiness, must be estimated by the degree of reason, virtue, and knowledge, that distinguish the individual, and direct the laws which bind society: and that from the exercise of reason, knowledge and virtue naturally flow, is equally undeniable, if 130 mankind be viewed collectively.

The rights and duties of man thus simplified, it seems almost impertinent to attempt to illustrate truths that appear so incontrovertible; yet such deeply rooted prejudices have clouded reason, and such spurious qualities have assumed the name of virtues, that it is necessary to pursue the course of reason as it has been perplexed and involved in error, by

various adventitious circumstances, comparing the simple axiom with casual deviations. Men, in general, seem to employ their reason to justify prejudices, which they have imbibed, 140 they can scarcely trace how, rather than to root them out. The mind must be strong that resolutely forms its own principles; for a kind of intellectual cowardice prevails which makes many men shrink from the task, or only do it by halves. . . .

Many are the causes that, in the present corrupt state of society, contribute to enslave women by cramping their understandings and sharpening their senses. One, perhaps, that silently does more mischief than all the rest, is their disregard of order.

To do every thing in an orderly manner, is a most important 150 precept, which women, who, generally speaking, receive only a disorderly kind of education, seldom attend to with that degree of exactness that men, who from their infancy are broken into method, observe. This negligent kind of guesswork, for what other epithet can be used to point out the random exertions of a sort of instinctive common sense, never brought to the test of reason? prevents their generalizing matters of fact—so they do to-day, what they did yesterday, merely because they did it yesterday.

This contempt of the understanding in early life has more baneful consequences that is commonly supposed; for the little 160 knowledge which women of strong minds attain, is, from various circumstances, of a more desultory kind than the knowledge of men, and it is acquired more by sheer observations on real life, than from comparing what has been individually observed with the results of experience generalized by speculation. Led by their dependent situation and domestic employments more into society, what they learn is rather by snatches; and as learning is with them, in general, only a secondary thing, they do not pursue any one branch with that persevering ardour necessary to give vigour to the faculties, and clearness to the judgment. In the present 170 state of society, a little learning is required to support the character of a gentleman; and boys are obliged to submit to a few years of discipline. But in the education of women, the cultivation of the understanding is always subordinate to the acquirement of some corporeal accomplishment; even while enervated by confinement and false notions of modesty, the body is prevented from attaining that grace and beauty which relaxed half-formed limbs never exhibit. Besides, in youth their faculties are not brought forward by emulation; and having no serious scientific study, if they have natural sagacity it is 180 turned too soon on life and manners. . . .

Strengthen the female mind by enlarging it, and there will be an end to blind obedience; but, as blind obedience is ever sought for by power, tyrants and sensualists are in the right when they endeavour to keep women in the dark, because the former only want slaves, and the latter a play-thing. The sensualist, indeed, has been the most dangerous of tyrants, and women have been duped by their lovers, as princes by their ministers, whilst dreaming that they reigned over them. . . .

It appears to me necessary to dwell on these obvious truths, 190 because females have been insulated, as it were; and, while they have been stripped of the virtues that should clothe humanity, they have been decked with artificial graces that enable them to exercise a short-lived tyranny. Love, in their bosoms, taking place of every nobler passion, their sole ambition is to be fair, to raise emotion instead of inspiring respect; and this ignoble desire, like the servility in absolute monarchies, destroys all strength of character. Liberty is the mother of virtue, and if women be, by their very constitution, slaves, and not allowed to breathe the sharp invigorating air of freedom, they must ever languish like exotics, and be reckoned beautiful flaws in nature. . . .

200

Make [women] free, and they will quickly become wise and virtuous, as men become more so; for the improvements must be mutual, or the injustice which one half of the human race are obliged to submit to, retorting on their oppressors, the virtue of men will be worm-eaten by the insects whom he keeps under his feet.

Let men take their choice, man and woman were made for each other, though not to become one being; and if they will not improve women, they will deprave them!

210

Q What does Wollstonecraft mean by "a false system of education"?

Q How does this system contribute to the plight of women?

Enlightenment Literature

The Journalistic Essay

As the writings of Condorcet and Wollstonecraft suggest, social criticism assumed an important place in Enlightenment thought. Such criticism now also manifested itself in a new literary genre: the journalistic essay. Designed to address the middle-class reading public, prose essays and editorials were the stuff of magazines and daily newspapers.

The first daily emerged in London during the eighteenth century, although a weekly had been published since 1642. At this time, London, with a population of some three-quarters of a million people, was the largest European city, and England claimed the highest rate of literacy in Western Europe. With the rise of newspapers and periodicals, the "poetic" prose of the seventeenth century—characterized by long sentences and magisterial phrases (see Bacon's *Of Studies*, Reading 23.2)—gave way to a more informal prose style, one that reflected the conversational chatter of the *salons* and cafés. Journalistic essays brought "philosophy out of the closets and libraries, schools and colleges, to dwell in clubs and assemblies, at tea-tables and in coffee houses," explained Joseph Addison (1672–1719), the leading British prose stylist of his day.

In collaboration with his lifelong friend Richard Steele (1672–1729), Addison published two London periodicals, the *Tatler* and the *Spectator*, which featured penetrating commentaries on current events and social behavior. The *Spectator* had a circulation of some 25,000 readers. Anticipating modern news magazines, eighteenth-century broadsheets and periodicals offered the literate public timely reports and diverse views on all aspects of popular culture. They provided entertainment even as they shaped popular opinion and cultivated an urban chauvinism. Samuel Johnson, a prolific contributor to the English periodicals of the day, expressed this civic pride by asserting:

"When a man is tired of London, he is tired of life: for there is in London all that life can afford."

The Modern Novel

The most important new form of eighteenth-century literary entertainment was the *novel*. The novel first appeared in world literature in China and Japan. The oldest of the early Japanese novels, *The Tale of Genji*, was written by an unknown eleventh-century author known as Lady Murasaki Shikibu (see chapter 14). In China, where the history of the novel reached back to the twelfth century, prose tales of travel, love, and adventure were popular sources for operas and plays (see chapter 21). Neither Japanese nor Chinese prose fiction had any direct influence on Western forerunners of the genre, such as Cervantes' *Don Quixote* (see chapter 19).

In both the West and in East Asia, the novel rose to prominence in part as a consequence of increasing urbanization and the emergence of a rising middle class seeking popular entertainment. Johnson distinguished the modern novel from its predecessors by asserting that such works "must arise from general converse and accurate observation of the living world." Not referred to as "novels" until the end of the century, the earliest fictional portrayals of contemporary life were presented as "histories." The popular *Robinson Crusoe* (1719) by Daniel Defoe (1660–1731) took the form of a counterfeit historical document, whose full title was *The Life and Strange Surprising Adventures of Robinson Crusoe of York, Mariner; Who lived Eight and Twenty Years, all alone in an un-inhabited Island on the Coast of America, near the Mouth of the Great River of Oronoque; Having been cast on shore by Shipwreck, where-in all the Men Perished but himself. With an Account how he was at last as strangely deliver'd by Pyrates. Written by Himself.* This "autobiography," inspired by stories of real-life castaways in an age of sea voyages, appealed to readers as truer to life than the fantasy-laden stories of Defoe's predecessors, Cervantes and Rabelais.

Often considered the first English novel, Samuel Richardson's best-selling *Pamela, Or, Virtue Rewarded* (1740) was first conceived as a conduct book—a moralizing genre designed to instruct and entertain. Purported to be based on letters written by the main character, it told the tale of a young domestic servant who makes her way to upper-class society. Its immense popularity provoked sequels as well as satiric ridicule. The adventures of Henry Fielding's hero Tom Jones (in the novel *The History of Tom Jones, a Foundling*, 1749), which turn on improbable coincidences and dramatic reversals of fortune, bring to life the escapades of criminals and prostitutes. In early modern novels, with their graphic accounts of the personalities of lower- and middle-class people, the reading public discovered passions and sentiments much like their own. No wonder such works appealed to the same individuals who enjoyed the spicy realism and journalistic prose of contemporary broadsheets.

Pope: Poet of the Enlightenment

If any single poet typified the spirit of the Enlightenment, it was surely Alexander Pope (1688–1744), the greatest

English poet of the eighteenth century. Pope, a semi-invalid from the age of twelve, was a great admirer of Newton and a champion of the scientific method. He was also a staunch Neoclassicist who devotedly revived the wit and polish of the golden age Roman poets Virgil and Horace. Largely self-taught (in his time, Roman Catholics were barred from attending English universities), Pope defended the value of education in Greek and Latin; his own love of the classics inspired him to produce new translations of Homer's *Iliad* and *Odyssey*. "A *little learning* is a dangerous thing," warned Pope in pleading for a broader and more thorough survey of the past.

Pope's poetry is as controlled and refined as a Poussin painting or a Bach fugue. His choice of the **heroic couplet** for most of his numerous satires, as well as for his translations of Homer, reflects his commitment to the fundamentals of balance and order. The concentrated brilliance and polish of each two-rhymed line bear out his claim that "True ease in writing comes from art, not chance,/ As those move easiest who have learned to dance."

Pope's most famous poem was his *Essay on Man*. Like Milton's *Paradise Lost*, but on a smaller scale, the *Essay* tries to assess humankind's place in the universal scheme. But whereas Milton explained evil in terms of human will, Pope—a Catholic turned deist—envisioned evil as part of God's design for a universe he describes as "A mighty maze! but not without a plan." Like Leibniz (whom he admired), Pope insisted that whatever occurs in nature has been "programmed" by God as part of God's benign and rational order. Pope lacked the reforming zeal of the *philosophes*, but he caught the optimism of the Enlightenment in a single line: "Whatever is, is right." In the *Essay on Man*, Pope warns that we must not presume to understand the whole of nature. Nor should we aspire to a higher place in the great "chain of being." Rather, he counsels, "Know then thyself, presume not God to scan;/ The proper study of Mankind is Man."

READING 24.8 From Pope's *Essay on Man* (1733–1734)

Epistle I

   IX What if the foot, ordain'd the dust to tread,   1
Or hand, to toil, aspir'd to be the head?
What if the head, the eye, or ear repin'd[1]
To serve mere engines to the ruling Mind?
Just as absurd for any part to claim
To be another, in his gen'ral frame:
Just as absurd, to mourn the tasks or pains.
The great directing Mind of All ordains.
   All are but parts of one stupendous whole,
Whose body Nature is, and God the soul;   10
That, chang'd thro' all, and yet in all the same;
Great in the earth, as in th' ethereal frame;
Warms in the sun, refreshes in the breeze,
Glows in the stars, and blossoms in the trees,

Lives thro' all life, extends thro' all extent,
Spreads undivided, operates unspent;
Breathes in our soul, informs our mortal part,
As full, as perfect, in a hair as heart:
As full, as perfect, in vile Man that mourns,
As the rapt Seraph[2] that adores and burns: 20
To him no high, no low, no great, no small;
He fills, he bounds, connects, and equals all.

   X Cease then, nor Order Imperfection name:
Our proper bliss depends on what we blame.
Know thy own point: This kind, this due degree
Of blindness, weakness, Heav'n bestows on thee.
Submit—In this, or any other sphere,
Secure to be as blest as thou canst bear:
Safe in the hand of one disposing Pow'r,
Or in the natal, or the mortal hour.   30
All Nature is but Art,[3] unknown to thee;
All Chance, Direction, which thou canst not see;
All Discord, Harmony not understood;
All partial Evil, universal Good:
And, spite of Pride, in erring Reason's spite,
One truth is clear, WHATEVER IS, IS RIGHT.

Epistle II

   I Know then thyself, presume not God to scan;[4]
The proper study of Mankind is Man.
Plac'd on this isthmus of a middle state,[5]
A Being darkly wise, and rudely great: 40
With too much knowledge for the Sceptic side,
With too much weakness for the Stoic's pride,
He hangs between; in doubt to act, or rest;
In doubt to deem himself a God, or Beast;
In doubt his Mind or Body to prefer,
Born but to die, and reas'ning but to err;
Alike in ignorance, his reason such.
Whether he thinks too little, or too much:
Chaos of Thought and Passion, all confus'd;
Still by himself abus'd, or disabus'd;   50
Created half to rise, and half to fall;[6]
Great lord of all things, yet a prey to all;
Sole judge of Truth, in endless Error hurl'd:[7]
The glory, jest, and riddle of the world!

Q **What aspects of this poem typify the spirit of the Enlightenment?**

Q **What does Pope see as Man's limitations?**

---

[1] Complained.

[2] A member of the highest order of angels.
[3] Compare Hobbes: "Nature is the art whereby God governs the world."
[4] Investigate.
[5] Between the angels (above) and the animal kingdom (below). Compare Pico della Mirandola's view of human beings as creatures who partake of both earthly and celestial qualities and can therefore ascend or descend the great "chain of being" (see chapter 16).
[6] See note 5.
[7] Cast back and forth.

Liberty and Political Theory

- In political thought, Thomas Hobbes and John Locke advanced the idea of government based on a social contract between ruler and ruled.
- While Hobbes envisioned this contract as a bond between individuals who surrendered some portion of their freedom to a sovereign authority, Locke saw government as an agent of the people—bound to exercise the will of the majority.
- Locke's writing provided the intellectual foundation for the Enlightenment faith in reason as the sure guide to social progress.
- Jefferson and Montesquieu applied Locke's views on natural law to political theory and practice, the basics of which are enshrined in America's Declaration of Independence.

The Birth of Economic Theory

- In *An Inquiry into the Nature and Causes of the Wealth of Nations*, Smith set forth the "laws" of labor, production, and trade leading to the modern concepts of free enterprise and *laissez-faire* economics.

The *Philosophes*

- In Paris, the hub of intellectual activity, the *philosophes* gathered in *salons* to exchange views on morality, politics, science, and religion.
- Seeking a nonauthoritarian, secular morality, the *philosophes* challenged existing forms of intolerance, inequality, and injustice.
- The prime symbol of the Enlightenment zeal for knowledge was the *Encyclopédie*, produced by Diderot with the assistance of the *philosophes*.
- A zeal for the ordering of socially useful information inspired the production of dictionaries, biographies, and histories.

The Crusade for Progress

- The Enlightenment crusade for progress stemmed from an optimistic faith in the progressive improvement of humankind.
- The idea that human beings, free from the bonds of ignorance and superstition and operating according to the principles of reason, might achieve the good life on earth inspired the philosophic optimism of Leibniz in Germany, the progressive theories of Beccaria in Italy, the visionary social reforms of Condorcet in France, and the defense of womankind by Wollstonecraft in England.

Enlightenment Literature

- The journalistic essay, a new literary genre, provided penetrating commentary on current events and social behavior, as popularized in the newspapers and periodicals of the day.
- The novel, which provided an expanding reading public with true-to-life characters drawn from everyday life, was the most important new form of literary entertainment.
- Alexander Pope's Neoclassical verses typified the spirit of the Age of Reason, and his *Essay on Man* advanced an optimistic view of human beings as the enlightened inhabitants of an orderly and harmonious universe.

Glossary

heroic couplet a pair of rhymed iambic pentameter lines that reach completion in structure and in sense at the end of the second line

laissez-faire (French, "allow to act") a general policy of noninterference in the economy, defended by such classical economists as Adam Smith

philosophes (French, "philosophers") the intellectuals of the European Enlightenment

social contract an agreement made between citizens leading to the establishment of the state

Chapter

25

The Limits of Reason

ca. 1700–1800

". . . many authors have hastened to conclude that man is naturally cruel and needs civil institutions to make him peaceable, whereas in truth nothing is more peaceable than man in his primitive state."
Rousseau

Figure 25.1 WILLIAM HOGARTH, *Gin Lane*, 1751. Engraving, 15⅓ × 12⅔ in. Above the doorway of the gin shop on the lower left are the words, "Drunk for a penny, dead drunk for two pence, clean straw for nothing." (The straw provided bedding for the poor.) Hogarth clearly intended this print as a satiric indictment of what he called the "idleness, poverty, misery, and ruin" consequent to the widespread addiction to gin in mid-eighteenth-century London.

Even that most enthusiastic champion of reason, Alexander Pope, acknowledged in his *Essay on Man* that human beings are "Born but to die, and reas'ning but to err"—that is, thinking creatures are finite and fallible. While generally committed to the belief in human perfectibility by way of reason, most Enlightenment thinkers realized that people are both imperfect and irrational. Reason is too frequently ignored or abandoned altogether. Perhaps the greatest obstacle to the promise of reason, however, lay in the hard reality of everyday urban life. In eighteenth-century Europe, where Enlightenment reformers exalted the ideals of human progress, there was clear evidence of ignorance, depravity, and despair, especially among those who felt the early effects of industrialization. Upon visiting the city of Paris, Jean-Jacques Rousseau lamented its "dirty stinking streets, filthy black houses," and alleys filled with beggars.

Indeed, outside the elegant drawing rooms of Paris and London, poverty, violence, and degradation prevailed.

Such conditions invited bitter attack, and none was more powerful than satire—the literary genre that engages humor to denounce human vice and folly. Satire became the intellectual weapon of the age, refined by the best thinkers of the time and devoured by the general public. Reform, however, would not be achieved exclusively by the pen. As the late eighteenth-century political revolutions in America and France proved, the musket would work to achieve what the pen had failed to secure. By the end of the eighteenth century, none of the age-old certainties were left unexamined: institutionalized religion, the autocratic rule of kings and despots, the agrarian way of life, the very social order—all fell under critical scrutiny and many came to crumble.

The Industrial Revolution

Early Industrialization

The Scientific Revolution of the seventeenth century encouraged the invention of new machinery and technology that contributed to the Industrial Revolution of the following two centuries. Industrialization involved a process that transformed agrarian and handicraft-dominated economies into those involving machine-manufactured goods. The textile industry was the first to be transformed. In England, the invention of the "flying shuttle" (a device that sped the weaving process), the "spinning jenny" (a multispooled spinning wheel), and the water-frame (a water-driven spinning machine) combined to revolutionize the production of textiles (see Science and Technology box).

Science and Technology

1733	John Kay invents the flying shuttle
1764	James Hargreaves invents the spinning jenny
1765	James Watt builds a model of a steam engine
1769	Richard Arkwright patents a hydraulic spinning machine
1779	the world's first iron bridge is erected at Coalbrookdale, England
1785	Edmund Cartwright's water-driven power loom revolutionizes England's weaving industry
1787	Friedrich Krupp establishes a steel plant at Essen, Germany
1792	Eli Whitney (American) manufactures the first effective cotton gin

The steam engine, invented by James Watt in 1765, was first employed to drain mine shafts, but soon came to serve England's flourishing textile industry. By the middle of the nineteenth century, it was used for everything from sawmills to railroads (see chapter 27). Industrialization was also advanced by the technology of cast iron, a medium processed by the Chinese as early as the fourth century, but not known in Europe until the early eighteenth century, when carbon-based fuel (coke) was used to produce iron strong enough to support structures.

With industrialization came the construction of factories and the mass production (and consumption) of goods. Industrialization would have significant social and economic effects, both positive and negative, throughout the West (see chapter 27), but it was primarily in England that the consequences of an expanding factory system were first visible. Allied with unregulated capitalism, the English factory system gave rise to dangerous working conditions and the exploitation of labor—mainly women and children. In many of London's factories, children tended the new machines for twelve- to fourteen-hour shifts, after which they were boarded in shabby barracks. And in the mines of Cornwall and County Durham, women and children were paid a pittance to labor like animals, pulling carts laden with coal. Some miners worked such long hours that they never saw the light of day.

The Transatlantic Slave Trade

In human terms, however, the most glaring evidence of the failure of the Enlightenment was the perpetuation of the slave trade, which, despite condemnation by many of the *philosophes*, flourished until the mid-nineteenth century. Begun by the Portuguese in the fifteenth century (see chapter 18), the transatlantic slave trade, by which millions of Africans were bought and shipped against their will to colonies in the "New World," reached its peak in the eighteenth century (Figure **25.2**). As England—lured by the lucrative sugar trade—became the leading player in the transatlantic traffic, some twelve million Africans—the exact number is much debated—were transported to work on sugar plantations in the West Indies and elsewhere in the Americas. British slave vessels were constructed in New England (notable for its outstanding timber), while nails, ropes, and anchors were provided by Liverpool.

The slave trade was big business; one eighteenth-century merchant described it as "the hinge on which all trade of this globe moves." In order to supply this market, Africans—including children—were frequently kidnapped by their unscrupulous countrymen, who profited hand-somely by selling their captives to white slave-traders. The fate of the African slave who survived the perilous "Middle Passage" between Africa and the Americas (it is estimated that roughly one-third perished in transit) was a life of unspeakable suffering.

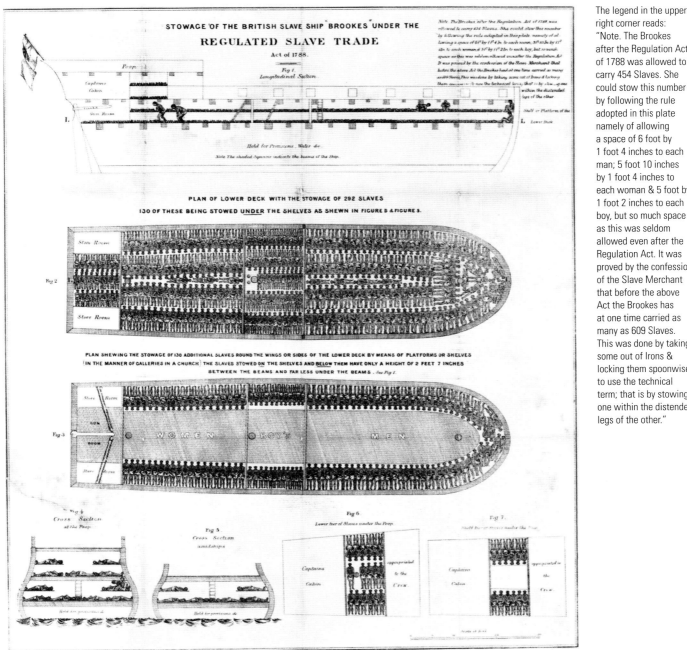

The legend in the upper right corner reads: "Note. The Brookes after the Regulation Act of 1788 was allowed to carry 454 Slaves. She could stow this number by following the rule adopted in this plate namely of allowing a space of 6 foot by 1 foot 4 inches to each man; 5 foot 10 inches by 1 foot 4 inches to each woman & 5 foot by 1 foot 2 inches to each boy, but so much space as this was seldom allowed even after the Regulation Act. It was proved by the confession of the Slave Merchant that before the above Act the Brookes has at one time carried as many as 609 Slaves. This was done by taking some out of Irons & locking them spoonwise, to use the technical term; that is by stowing one within the distended legs of the other."

Figure 25.2 Plan of the *Brookes*, a 320-ton British slave ship of the late eighteenth century.
Fig. 1 lengthwise cross section of the ship;
Fig. 2 lower deck with stowage of 292 slaves, 130 of these being stowed under platforms as seen in Figs. 4 and 5;
Fig. 3 lower deck with platforms stowing an additional 130 slaves;
Figs. 6 and 7 half-deck with and without platforms. The *Brookes* was one of eighteen vessels examined in 1788 by a committee making recommendations to Parliament for the regulation of slave ships.

Equiano and Slave Narratives

A firsthand account of this inhumane system is central to the many slave narratives that were written in the eighteenth century. A unique literary genre, slave narratives constitute a body of prose literature produced by Africans who suffered the cruelty of the transatlantic slave trade. The best-seller among these was an autobiography written by Olaudah Equiano (1745–1797). Equiano's *Travels* (1789) describes his birth in the West African kingdom of Benin, his kidnapping and enslavement at the age of eleven, and the horrific circumstances of his transatlantic journey. Both as a slave and after his release from slavery in 1766, Equiano traveled widely; during his stay in England (as one of only 30,000 black men and women in mid-eighteenth-century England), he mastered the English language and became an outspoken abolitionist (Figure **25.3**).

Recent scholarship has cast doubt on the accuracy of Equiano's story: baptismal records and naval rolls put his place of origin in South Carolina. If, however, Equiano fabricated his early life story to fuel the abolitionist cause, the accuracy of his descriptions of the Middle Passage is confirmed by the firsthand accounts of other slaves. Such literature ultimately served to convince readers of the immorality of this "peculiar institution." The following excerpt from Equiano's autobiographical narrative recounts with dramatic simplicity the traumatic experience of African men and women who were cruelly sold into bondage.

Figure 25.3 *Olaudah Equiano*, ca. 1780. Engraving, 6 × 4½ in.

READING 25.1 From Equiano's *Travels* (1789)

[Equiano describes his childhood, his kidnapping, and his tenure with African masters; he is sold a number of times (during a period of six to seven months) before he is taken to the sea coast.]

The first object which saluted my eyes when I arrived on the coast was the sea, and a slave ship which was then riding at anchor and waiting for its cargo. These filled me with astonishment, which was soon converted into terror when I was carried on board. I was immediately handled and tossed up to see if I were sound by some of the crew, and I was now persuaded that I had gotten into a world of bad spirits and that they were going to kill me. Their complexions too differing so much from ours, their long hair and the language they spoke (which was very different from any I had ever heard) united to confirm me in this belief. Indeed such were the horrors of my views and fears at the moment that, if ten thousand worlds had been my own, I would have freely parted with them all to have exchanged my condition with that of the meanest slave in my own country. When I looked round the ship too and saw a large furnace or copper boiling and a multitude of black people of every description chained together, every one of their countenances expressing dejection and sorrow, I no longer doubted of my fate; and quite overpowered with horror and anguish, I fell motionless on the deck and fainted. When I recovered a little I found some black people about me, who I believed were some of those who had brought me on board and had been receiving their pay; they talked to me in order to cheer me, but all in vain. I asked them if we were not to be eaten by those white men with horrible looks, red faces, and loose hair. They told me I was not, and one of the crew brought me a small portion of spirituous liquor in a wine glass, but being afraid of him I would not take it out of his hand. One of the blacks therefore took it from him and gave it to me, and I took a little down my palate, which instead of reviving me, as they thought it would, threw me into the greatest consternation at the strange feeling it produced, having never tasted any such liquor before. Soon after this the blacks who brought me on board went off, and left me abandoned to despair. 10 20 30

I now saw myself deprived of all chance of returning to my native country or even the least glimpse of hope of gaining the shore, which I now considered as friendly; and I even wished for my former slavery in preference to my present situation, which was filled with horrors of every kind, still heightened by my ignorance of what I was to undergo. I was not long suffered to indulge my grief; I was soon put down under the decks, and there I received such a salutation in my nostrils as I had never experienced in my life: so that with the loathsomeness of the stench and crying together, I became so sick and low that I was not able to eat, nor had I the least desire to taste anything. I now wished for the last friend, death, to relieve me; but soon, to my grief, two of the white men offered me eatables, and on my refusing to eat, one of them held me fast by the hands and laid me across I think the windlass,[1] and tied my feet while the other flogged me severely. I had never experienced anything of this kind 40 50

---
[1] The device that works the ship's anchor.

before, and although, not being used to the water, I naturally feared that element the first time I saw it, yet nevertheless could I have got over the nettings I would have jumped over the side, but I could not; and besides, the crew used to watch us very closely who were not chained down to the decks, lest we should leap into the water: and I have seen some of these poor African prisoners most severely cut for attempting to do so, and hourly whipped for not eating. This indeed was often the case with myself. In a little time after, amongst the poor chained men I found some of my own nation,[2] which in a small degree gave **60** ease to my mind. I inquired of these what was to be done with us; they gave me to understand we were to be carried to these white people's country to work for them. I then was a little revived, and thought if it were no worse than working, my situation was not so desperate: but still I feared I should be put to death, the white people looked and acted, as I thought, in so savage a manner; for I had never seen among my people such instances of brutal cruelty, and this not only shewn towards us blacks but also to some of the whites themselves. One white man in particular I saw, when we were permitted to be on deck, **70** flogged so unmercifully with a large rope near the foremast that he died in consequence of it; and they tossed him over the side as they would have done a brute. This made me fear these people the more, and I expected nothing less than to be treated in the same manner. I could not help expressing my fears and apprehensions to some of my countrymen: I asked them if these people had no country but lived in this hollow place (the ship): they told me they did not, but came from a distant one. "Then," said I, "how comes it in all our country we never heard of them?" They told me because they lived so very far off. I then asked where were **80** their women? had they any like themselves? I was told they had: "and why," said I, "do we not see them?" They answered, because they were left behind. . . . The stench of the hold while we were on the coast was so intolerably loathsome that it was dangerous to remain there for any time, and some of us had been permitted to stay on the deck for the fresh air; but now that the whole ship's cargo were confined together it became absolutely pestilential. The closeness of the place and the heat of the climate, added to the number in the ship, which was so crowded that each had scarcely room to turn himself, almost suffocated us. **90** This produced copious perspirations, so that the air soon became unfit for respiration from a variety of loathsome smells, and brought on a sickness among the slaves, of which many died, thus falling victims to the improvident avarice, as I may call it, of their purchasers. This wretched situation was again aggravated by the galling of the chains, now become insupportable, and the filth of the necessary tubs, into which the children often fell and were almost suffocated. The shrieks of the women and the groans of the dying rendered the whole a scene of horror almost inconceivable. Happily perhaps for myself I was soon reduced **100** so low here that it was thought necessary to keep me almost always on deck, and from my extreme youth I was not put in fetters. In this situation I expected every hour to share the fate of my companions, some of whom were almost daily brought upon deck at the point of death, which I began to hope would soon put an end to my miseries. Often did I think many of the inhabitants of

the deep much more happy than myself. I envied them the freedom they enjoyed, and as often wished I could change my condition for theirs. Every circumstance I met with served only to render my state more painful, and heighten my apprehensions **110** and my opinion of the cruelty of the whites. One day they had taken a number of fishes, and when they had killed and satisfied themselves with as many as they thought fit, to our astonishment who were on the deck, rather than give any of them to us to eat as we expected, they tossed the remaining fish into the sea again, although we begged and prayed for some as well as we could, but in vain; and some of my countrymen, being pressed by hunger, took an opportunity when they thought no one saw them of trying to get a little privately; but they were discovered, and the attempt procured them some very severe **120** floggings. One day, when we had a smooth sea and moderate wind, two of my wearied countrymen who were chained together (I was near them at the time), preferring death to such a life of misery, somehow made through the nettings and jumped into the sea: immediately another quite dejected fellow, who on account of his illness was suffered to be out of irons, also followed their example; and I believe many more would very soon have done the same if they had not been prevented by the ship's crew, who were instantly alarmed. Those of us that were the most active were in a moment put down under the deck, and **130** there was such a noise and confusion amongst the people of the ship as I never heard before, to stop her and get the boat out to go after the slaves. However two of the wretches were drowned, but they got the other and afterwards flogged him unmercifully for thus attempting to prefer death to slavery. In this manner we continued to undergo more hardships than I can now relate, hardships which are inseparable from this accursed trade. . . . At last we came in sight of the island of Barbados, at which the whites on board gave a great shout and made many signs of joy to us. We did not know what to think of this, but as the **140** vessel drew nearer we plainly saw the harbour and other ships of different kinds and sizes, and we soon anchored amongst them off Bridgetown. Many merchants and planters now came on board, though it was in the evening. They put us in separate parcels[3] and examined us attentively. They also made us jump[4] and pointed to the land, signifying we were to go there. We thought by this we should be eaten by these ugly men, as they appeared to us; and when soon after we were all put down under the deck again, there was much dread and trembling among us, and nothing but bitter cries to be heard all the night from these **150** apprehensions, insomuch that at last the white people got some old slaves from the land to pacify us. They told us we were not to be eaten but to work, and were soon to go on land where we should see many of our countrypeople. This report eased us much; and sure enough soon after we were landed there came to us Africans of all languages. We were conducted immediately to the merchant's yard, where we were all pent up together like so many sheep in a fold without regard to sex or age. . . . We were not many days in the merchant's custody before we were sold after their usual manner, **160** which is this: On a signal given (as the beat of a drum), the buyers rush at once into the yard where the slaves are confined, and

---

[2] Ethnic group.

[3] Groups.

[4] In order to determine whether they were healthy.

make choice of that parcel they like best. The noise and clamour with which this is attended and the eagerness visible in the countenances of the buyers serve not a little to increase the apprehensions of the terrified Africans, who may well be supposed to consider them as the ministers of that destruction to which they think themselves devoted. In this manner, without scruple, are relations and friends separated, most of them never to see each other again. I remember in the vessel in which I was   170
brought over, in the men's apartment there were several brothers who, in the sale, were sold in different lots; and it was very moving on this occasion to see and hear their cries at parting. O, ye nominal Christians! might not an African ask you, Learned you this from your God who says unto you, Do unto all men as you would men should do unto you? Is it not enough that we are torn from our country and friends to toil for your luxury and lust of gain? Must every tender feeling be likewise sacrificed to your avarice? Are the dearest friends and relations, now rendered more dear by their separation from their kindred,   180
still to be parted from each other and thus prevented from cheering the gloom of slavery with the small comfort of being together and mingling their sufferings and sorrows? Why are parents to lose their children, brothers their sisters, or husbands their wives? Surely this is a new refinement in cruelty which, while it has no advantage to atone for it, thus aggravates distress and adds fresh horrors even to the wretchedness of slavery. . . .

Q **Which of the circumstances and conditions described by Equiano strike you as most removed from the ideals of the *philosophes*?**

Phillis Wheatley

As Equiano suggests, the "gloom of slavery" itself left slaves little opportunity for self-expression. It is therefore notable that one particular slave would become America's first black woman poet. Phillis Wheatley (1754?–1784) was kidnapped from Senegal and sold at auction in Boston at the age of seven. She was educated along with the children of her master, John Wheatley, and learned to read and write English, as well as Greek and Latin. Producing her first poem at the age of thirteen, Wheatley had difficulty publishing her collection of poems in America, where the authenticity of her work was held in doubt. Following interrogation by a panel of eighteen illustrious Bostonians, it was concluded that "Phillis, a young Negro Girl, who was but a few Years since, brought an uncultivated Barbarian from Africa," had indeed written the verses in question.

In 1773, Wheatley's *Poems on Various Subjects; Religious and Moral* was published in England (which country was more receptive than America to black authors); it soon won acclaim in both Europe and America. An encouragement to the work of other black writers, it became a landmark in black literary achievement. John Wheatley emancipated Phillis in 1773, giving her the opportunity to travel and continue writing. The poem that follows, written in heroic couplets—the favorite meter of both Chaucer and Pope—is a terse and eloquent appeal to the Christian promise of equality before God, and the Enlightenment promise of reason.

READING 25.2 Wheatley's "On Being Brought from Africa to America" (1772)

'TWAS mercy brought me from my Pagan land,
Taught my benighted soul to understand
That there's a God, that there's a Saviour too:
Once I redemption neither sought nor knew.
Some view our sable[1] race with scornful eye,
"Their colour is a diabolic die."
Remember, *Christians*, Negros, black as Cain,
May be refin'd, and join th'angelic train.

Q **How does the tone of Wheatley's poem differ from that of Equiano's narrative?**

Enlightenment Bias

If slavery and industrialization in the West generated material conditions that were contrary to Enlightenment ideals, other factors served as serious obstacles to their realization. Ignorance, for example, the foundation for bias and (in many cases) unwitting prejudice, clouded the perception and judgment of some of the most educated *philosophes*. Diderot himself, who had no firsthand knowledge of the Muslim world, described Arabs (in his *Encyclopédie*) as "thievish and bellicose." Voltaire, who wrote a universal history that charted the customs of nations (including Russia and Africa), brought to his analysis an anti-Church, anti-Semitic, and antiblack bias.

Believing Africans to be intellectually inferior, America's leading Enlightenment thinker, Thomas Jefferson, defended the institution of slavery as a "necessary evil." His perception of African-American slaves was colored by prejudices that are shocking to modern sensibilities. In his *Notes on the State of Virginia*, Jefferson wrote:

"Comparing [blacks] by their faculties of memory, reason, and imagination, it appears to me that in memory they are equal to the whites; in reason much inferior . . . I advance it . . . as a suspicion only, that the blacks, whether originally a distinct race, or made distinct by time and circumstances, are inferior to the whites in the endowments both of body and mind . . . This unfortunate difference of color, and perhaps of faculty, is a powerful obstacle to the emancipation of these people."

In maintaining such opinions, which were shared by most of his fellow *philosophes*, Jefferson provided an implicit rationale for enslaving Africans. Clearly, such thinkers were all too capable of finding rationalizations for policies in which political or social advantage for the privileged few overrode the ideals of liberty and equality. Thus slavery persisted in the Western hemisphere (and elsewhere) for nearly a century beyond the Age of Enlightenment.

[1] Black or dark brown.

Satire: Weapon of the Enlightenment

The discrepancies between the sordid reality of eighteenth-century life and the progressive ideas of the Enlightenment provoked indignant protests, and none so potent as those couched in humor. The eighteenth century was history's greatest age of satire. This genre, which had served Juvenal in imperial Rome (see chapter 6) and Erasmus in the age of the Reformation (see chapter 19), now became the favorite weapon of social reformers, who drew attention to the vast contradictions between morals and manners, intentions and actions, and, more generally, between Enlightenment aspirations and contemporary degradation.

The Satires of Jonathan Swift

The premier British satirist of the eighteenth century was Jonathan Swift (1667–1745). Unlike the *philosophes*, this Dublin-born Anglican priest took a pessimistic view of human nature. He once confided (in a letter to the poet Alexander Pope) that he hated the human race, whose misuse of reason produced, in his view, an irredeemably corrupt society. Such negativity accompanied Swift's self-acclaimed "savage indignation." Yet Swift was not a man of despair, for no despairing personality could have produced such a profoundly moralizing body of literature. In 1726, he published his classic satire, *Gulliver's Travels*. At the simplest level, it is a story of travel and adventure that (somewhat like Equiano's true-to-life travels) describes the fortunes of a hero in imaginary lands peopled with midgets, giants, and other fabulous creatures. At a second, symbolic level, however, it is a social statement on the vagaries of human behavior. In one chapter, Gulliver visits the Lilliputians—"little people" whose moral pettiness and inhumanity seem to characterize humankind at its worst. In another, he meets noble horses whose rational behavior contrasts with the bestiality of their human-looking slaves, the Yahoos. An immediate popular sensation, *Gulliver's Travels* has become a landmark in fantasy literature and social satire.

Swift also wrote many pamphlets and letters protesting social and political ills. Among the most famous is an essay publicizing the wretched condition of the Irish peasants, who were exploited unmercifully by the British government. In his satirical treatise *A Modest Proposal*, Swift deals with the reality that many Irish peasants were too poor to feed their families; he proposes with deadpan frankness that Irish children should be bred and butchered for the English dining table, thus providing income for the poor and alleviating the misery of all. While *Gulliver's Travels* attacks conditions that are universal and timeless, *A Modest Proposal* mocks a specific crisis of Swift's own time.

READING 25.3 From Swift's *A Modest Proposal* (1729)

For Preventing the Children of Poor People in Ireland from Being a Burden to Their Parents or Country, and for Making Them Beneficial to the Public

It is a melancholy object to those who walk through this great town[1] or travel in the country, when they see the streets, the roads, and cabin-doors, crowded with beggars of the female sex, followed by three, four, or six children, all in rags, and importuning every passenger for an alms.[2] These mothers, instead of being able to work for their honest livelihood, are forced to employ all their time in strolling, to beg sustenance for their helpless infants, who, as they grow up, either turn thieves for want of work, or leave their dear native country to fight. . . in Spain, or sell themselves to the Barbadoes.[3] **10**

I think it is agreed by all parties that this prodigious number of children, in the arms, or on the backs, or at the heels of their mothers, and frequently of their fathers, is in the present deplorable state of the kingdom a very great additional grievance; and therefore whoever could find out a fair, cheap, and easy method of making these children sound, useful members of the commonwealth, would deserve so well of the public as to have his statue set up for a preserver of the nation.

But my intention is very far from being confined to provide only for the children of professed beggars; it is of a much greater extent, and shall take in the whole number of infants at a certain age, who are born of parents in effect as little able to support them as those who demand our charity in the streets. **20**

As to my own part, having turned my thoughts for many years upon this important subject, and maturely weighed the several schemes of other projectors,[4] I have always found them grossly mistaken in their computation. It is true, a child, just dropped from its dam,[5] may be supported by her milk for a solar year with little other nourishment, at most not above the value of two shillings, which the mother may certainly get, or the value in scraps, by her lawful occupation of begging; and it is exactly at one year old that I propose to provide for them in such a manner as instead of being a charge upon their parents or the parish, or wanting food and raiment[6] for the rest of their lives, they shall, on the contrary, contribute to the feeding and partly to the clothing of many thousands. **30**

There is likewise another great advantage in my scheme, that it will prevent those voluntary abortions, and that horrid practice of women murdering their bastard children, alas too frequent among us, sacrificing the poor innocent babes, **40**
I doubt, more to avoid the expense than the shame, which would move tears and pity in the most savage and inhuman breast.

The number of souls in this kingdom being usually reckoned one million and a half, of these I calculate there may be about two hundred thousand couple whose wives are breeders; from which number I subtract thirty thousand couple who are able to

---

[1] Dublin.
[2] Charity.
[3] As slaves in the West Indies.
[4] Speculators.
[5] Just born.
[6] Clothing.

maintain their own children, although I apprehend there cannot be so many under the present distresses of the kingdom; but this being granted, there will remain an hundred and seventy thousand breeders. I again subtract fifty thousand for those women who miscarry, or whose children die by accident or disease within the year. There only remain an hundred and twenty thousand children of poor parents annually born. The question therefore is, how this number shall be reared and provided for, which, as I have already said, under the present situation of affairs, is utterly impossible by all the methods hitherto proposed, for we can neither employ them in handicraft or agriculture; we neither build houses (I mean in the country) nor cultivate land; they can very seldom pick up a livelihood by stealing till they arrive at six years old, except where they are of towardly[7] parts, although I confess they learn the rudiments[8] much earlier. . . .

I am assured by our merchants that a boy or a girl before twelve years old is no saleable commodity, and even when they come to this age, they will not yield above three pounds, or three pounds and half-a-crown at most on the Exchange, which cannot turn to account either to the parents or kingdom, the charge of nutriment and rags having been at least four times that value. I shall now therefore humbly propose my own thoughts, which I hope will not be liable to the least objection.

I have been assured by a very knowing American of my acquaintance in London, that a young healthy child well nursed is at a year old a most delicious, nourishing, and wholesome food, whether stewed, roasted, baked, or boiled, and I make no doubt that it will serve in a fricassee or a ragout.

I do therefore humbly offer it to public consideration that of the hundred and twenty thousand children already computed, twenty thousand may be reserved for breed, whereof only one fourth part to be males, which is more than we allow to sheep, black cattle, or swine; and my reason is that these children are seldom the fruits of marriage, a circumstance not much regarded by our savages. Therefore one male will be sufficient to serve four females. That the remaining hundred thousand may at a year old be offered in sale to the persons of quality and fortune through the kingdom, always advising the mother to let them suck[9] plentifully in the last month, so as to render them plump and fat for a good table. A child will make two dishes at an entertainment for friends, and when the family dines alone, the fore or hind quarter will make a reasonable dish, and seasoned with a little pepper or salt will be very good boiled on the fourth day, especially in winter.

I have reckoned, upon a medium,[10] that a child just born will weigh 12 pounds, and in a solar year if tolerably nursed will increase to 28 pounds.

I grant this food will be somewhat dear, and therefore very proper for landlords, who, as they have already devoured most of the parents, seem to have the best title to the children.

Infants' flesh will be in season throughout the year, but more plentiful in March, and a little before and after, for we are told by a grave author,[11] an eminent French physician, that fish being

a prolific diet, there are more children born in Roman Catholic countries about nine months after Lent, than at any other season; therefore reckoning a year after Lent, the markets will be more glutted than usual, because the number of Popish infants is at least three to one in this kingdom, and therefore it will have one other collateral advantage, by lessening the number of Papists[12] among us.

I have already computed the charge of nursing a beggar's child (in which list I reckon all cottagers, labourers, and four-fifths of the farmers) to be about two shillings per annum, rags included, and I believe no gentleman would repine to give ten shillings for the carcass of a good fat child, which, as I have said, will make four dishes of excellent nutritive meat, when he has only some particular friend or his own family to dine with him. Thus the squire will learn to be a good landlord, and grow popular among his tenants, the mother will have eight shillings for net profit, and be fit for work till she produces another child.

Those who are more thrifty (as I must confess the times require) may flay the carcass; the skin of which, artificially dressed, will make admirable gloves for ladies, and summer boots for fine gentlemen.

As to our city of Dublin, shambles[13] may be appointed for this purpose in the most convenient parts of it, and butchers we may be assured will not be wanting, although I rather recommend buying the children alive, and dressing them hot from the knife, as we do roasting pigs.

A very worthy person, a true lover of his country, and whose virtues I highly esteem, was lately pleased, in discoursing on this matter, to offer a refinement upon my scheme. He said, that many gentlemen of this kingdom having of late destroyed their deer, he conceived that the want of venison might be well supplied by the bodies of young lads and maidens, not exceeding fourteen years of age, nor under twelve, so great a number of both sexes in every country being now ready to starve, for want of work and service, and these to be disposed of by their parents if alive, or otherwise by their nearest relations. But with due deference to so excellent a friend, and so deserving a patriot, I cannot be altogether in his sentiments; for as to the males, my American acquaintance assured me from frequent experience, that their flesh was generally tough and lean, like that of our schoolboys, by continual exercise, and their taste disagreeable, and to fatten them would not answer the charge. Then as to the females, it would, I think with humble submission, be a loss to the public, because they soon would become breeders themselves. And besides, it is not improbable that some scrupulous people might be apt to censure such a practice (although indeed very unjustly), as a little bordering upon cruelty, which, I confess, has always been with me the strongest objection against any project, however so will intended. . . .

I have too long digressed, and therefore shall return to my subject. I think the advantages by the proposal which I have made are obvious and many, as well as of the highest importance.

For first, as I have already observed, it would greatly lessen the number of Papists, with whom we are yearly over-run, being the principal breeders of the nation, as well as our most dangerous

---

[7] Handsome.
[8] Fundamentals; first principles.
[9] To nurse at the breast.
[10] On an average.
[11] François Rabelais (see chapter 19).

[12] Roman Catholics, especially those who ardently support the pope.
[13] Slaughterhouses.

enemies, and who stay at home on purpose to deliver the kingdom to the Pretender, hoping to take their advantage by the absence of so many good Protestants, who have chosen rather to leave their country, than stay at home, and pay tithes against their conscience, to an Episcopal curate. 160

Secondly, The poorer tenants will have something valuable of their own, which by law may be made liable to distress, and help to pay their landlord's rent, their corn and cattle being already seized, and money a thing unknown.

Thirdly, whereas the maintenance of an hundred thousand children, from two years old and upward, cannot be computed at less than ten shillings a piece per annum, the nation's stock will be thereby increased fifty thousand pounds per annum, besides the profit of a new dish, introduced to the tables of all gentlemen of fortune in the kingdom who have any refinement 170 in taste, and the money will circulate among ourselves, the good being entirely of our own growth and manufacture.

Fourthly, The constant breeders, beside the gain of eight shillings sterling per annum, by the sale of their children, will be rid of the charge of maintaining them after the first year.

Fifthly, This food would likewise bring great custom to taverns, where the vintners will certainly be so prudent as to procure the best receipts for dressing it to perfection, and consequently have their houses frequented by all the fine gentlemen who justly value themselves upon their knowledge 180 in good eating; and a skilful cook, who understands how to oblige his guests, will contrive to make it as expensive as they please.

Sixthly, This would be a great inducement to marriage, which all wise nations have either encouraged by rewards, or enforced by laws and penalties. It would increase the care and tenderness of mothers toward their children, when they were sure of a settlement for life, to the poor babes, provided in some sort by the public, to their annual profit instead of expense. We should see an honest emulation among the married women, 190 which of them could bring the fattest child to the market. Men would become as fond of their wives, during the time of their pregnancy, as they are now of their mares in foal, their cows in calf, their sows when they are ready to farrow, nor offer to beat or kick them (as is too frequent a practice) for fear of a miscarriage.

Many other advantages might be enumerated. For instance, the addition of some thousand carcasses in our exportation of barrelled beef, the propagation of swine's flesh, and improvement in the art of making good bacon, so much wanted among us by the great destruction of pigs, too frequent at our 200 table, which are no way comparable in taste, or magnificence, to a well-grown, fat yearling child, which roasted whole will make a considerable figure at a Lord Mayor's feast, or any other public entertainment. But this and many others I omit, being studious of brevity.

Supposing that one thousand families in this city would be constant customers for infants' flesh, beside others who might have it at merry-meetings, particularly at weddings and christenings, I compute that Dublin would take off annually about twenty thousand carcasses; and the rest of the kingdom 210 (where probably they will be sold somewhat cheaper) the remaining eighty thousand.

I can think of no one objection, that will possibly be raised against this proposal, unless it should be urged that the number of people will be thereby much lessened in the kingdom. This I freely own, and it was indeed one principal design in offering it to the world. I desire the reader to observe, that I calculate my remedy for this one individual kingdom of Ireland, and for no other that ever was, is, or I think, ever can be upon earth. Therefore let no man talk to me of other 220 expedients: Of taxing our absentees at five shillings a pound: Of using neither clothes, nor household furniture, except what is of our own growth and manufacture: Of utterly rejecting the materials and instruments that promote foreign luxury: Of curing the expensiveness of pride, vanity, idleness, and gaming[14] in our women: Of introducing a vein of parsimony, prudence and temperance: Of learning to love our Country, wherein we differ even from Laplanders, and the inhabitants of Topinamboo:[15] Of quitting our animosities and factions, nor act any longer like Jews, who were murdering one 230 another at the very moment their city was taken: Of being a little cautious not to sell our country and conscience for nothing: Of teaching landlords to have at least one degree of mercy toward their tenants. Lastly of putting a spirit of honesty, industry, and skill into our shopkeepers, who, if a resolution could now be taken to buy only our native goods, would immediately unite to cheat and exact upon us in the price, the measure, and the goodness, nor could ever yet be brought to make one fair proposal of just dealing, though often and earnestly invited to it. . . . 240

Q What aspects of Swift's proposal contribute to its effectiveness as a tool for political reform?

Voltaire and *Candide*

Swift's satires were an inspiration to that most scintillating of French *philosophes* and leading intellectual of French society, François-Marie Arouet (1694–1778), who used the pen name Voltaire (Figure **25.4** and see Figure 24.4). Born into a rising Parisian middle-class family and educated by Jesuits, Voltaire rose to fame as a poet, playwright, critic, and historian. His 2000 books and 20,000 letters and pamphlets earned him a central place among the members of the French *salons* (see Figure 24.4). In his writings, he championed freedom of thought and expression; he attacked bigotry as man-made evil, and injustice as institutional evil. In 1717, the royal condemnation of his biting verse-satires led to his imprisonment in the Bastille (the French state prison; see Figure 25.6). An enforced exile in 1726, which resulted in a three-year stay in England, instilled in him a high regard for constitutional government, the principles of toleration, and the concepts of equality found in the writings of John Locke—all of which he championed in his writings.

Voltaire's most famous historical work, *Le Siècle de Louis XIV* (*The Century of Louis XIV*), examined the social and cultural character of the age, rather than its military or economic features. Despite some narrowly personal opinions (see Enlightenment Bias), he extolled the traditions of non-Western cultures: having read the works of

---

[14] Gambling (the most popular pastime of the upper class).
[15] A district in Brazil supposedly inhabited by savages.

Figure 25.4 JEAN-ANTOINE HOUDON, *Voltaire in Old Age*, 1781. Marble, height 25⅛ in.

Confucius in Jesuit translations, he esteemed that ancient teacher as a philosopher–sage. Voltaire was the first modern intellectual to assess the role of Russia in world society. In his *Essay on Manners*, a universal history that examines the customs of nations around the world, Voltaire gave thoughtful attention to the history of the Russian state. His fascination with Russia as a curious blend of Asian and European traditions became the basis for a lifelong pursuit of things Russian, including a long correspondence with Catherine the Great, who ruled as empress of Russia from 1762 to 1796.

Like most of the *philosophes*, Voltaire condemned organized religion and all forms of religious fanaticism. He rejected the commonly held belief that the Bible was the inspired word of God. A declared deist, he once compared human beings to mice who, living in the recesses of an immense ship, know nothing of its captain or its destination. Any confidence Voltaire might have had in beneficent Providence was dashed by the terrible Lisbon earthquake and tidal wave of 1755, which took the lives of more than 20,000 Portuguese. For Voltaire, the reality of natural disaster and human cruelty was not easily reconciled with the belief that a good God had created the universe or that humans were by nature rational—views basic to Enlightenment optimism.

Voltaire's satirical masterpiece *Candide* (subtitled *Optimism*) addresses the age-old question of how evil can exist in a universe created and governed by the forces of good. A parody of the adventure romances and travel tales (Equiano and Swift both come to mind) in vogue in Voltaire's time, *Candide* relates the exploits of a naive and good-natured young man whose blissful life is daunted by a series of terrible (and hilarious) experiences. Initially, the youthful Candide (literally, "candid" or "frank") approaches life with the glib optimism taught to him by Dr. Pangloss (meaning "all tongue"), Voltaire's embodiment of Gottfried Wilhelm Leibniz (see chapter 24). But Candide soon discovers the folly of Leibniz's optimistic credo that "this is the best of [all] possible worlds." He experiences the horrors of war (the consequences of two equally self-righteous opposing armies), the evils of religious fanaticism (as manifested by the Spanish Inquisition), the disasters of nature (the Lisbon earthquake), and the dire effects of human greed (an affliction especially prevalent among the aristocracy and derived, according to Voltaire, from boredom). Experience becomes the antidote to the comfortable fatalism of Pope's "Whatever is, is right."

After a lifetime of sobering misadventures, Candide ends his days settled on a farm (in Turkey) in the company of his long-lost friends. (Not coincidentally, the aging Voltaire penned *Candide* while living on his farm retreat just outside Geneva.) "We must cultivate our garden," he concludes. This metaphor for achieving personal satisfaction in a hostile world relieves the otherwise devastating skepticism that underlies *Candide*. It is Voltaire's answer to blind optimism and to the foolish hope that human reason can combat evil.

Voltaire's genius, and the quality that separates his style from that of Swift, is his penetrating wit. Like the jouster's sword, Voltaire's satire is sharply pointed, precise in its aim, and devastating in its effect. With a sure hand, Voltaire manipulates the principal satirical devices: irony, understatement, and overstatement. Using irony—the contradiction between literal and intended meanings—he mocks serious matters and deflates lofty pretensions; he calls war, for instance, "heroic butchery" and refers to Paquetta's venereal disease as a "present" she received from "a very learned Franciscan." He exploits understatement when he notes, for example, that Pangloss "only lost one eye and one ear" (as the result of syphilis). And he uses overstatement for moral effect: the 350-pound baroness of Westphalia is "greatly respected"; thus corpulence—actually an indication of self-indulgence—becomes a specious sign of dignity and importance.

Voltaire's mock optimism, dispatched by Candide's persistent claim that this is "the best of all possible worlds" (even as he encounters repeated horrors), underscores the contradiction between the ideal and the real that lies at the heart of all satire. Although it was censored in many parts of Europe, *Candide* was so popular with the reading public that it went through forty editions in Voltaire's lifetime. A classic of Western satire, *Candide* has survived numerous adaptations, including a superb twentieth-century version as a comic operetta with lyrics by the American poet Richard Wilbur (b. 1921) and music by the American composer Leonard Bernstein (1918–1990).

Chapter 1

How Candide was Brought up in a Fine Castle, and How he was Expelled from Thence

There lived in Westphalia,[1] in the castle of my Lord the Baron **1**
of Thunder-ten-tronckh, a young man, on whom nature had
bestowed the most agreeable manners. His face was the index
to his mind. He had an upright heart, with an easy frankness;
which, I believe, was the reason he got the name of Candide.
He was suspected, by the old servants of the family, to be the
son of my Lord the Baron's sister, by a very honest gentleman
of the neighborhood, whom the young lady declined to marry,
because he could only produce seventy-one armorial
quarterings,[2] the rest of his genealogical tree having **10**
been destroyed through the injuries of time.

The Baron was one of the most powerful lords in
Westphalia; his castle had both a gate and windows; and his
great hall was even adorned with tapestry. The dogs of his
outer yard composed his hunting pack upon occasion, his
grooms were his huntsmen, and the vicar of the parish was
his chief almoner. He was called My Lord by everybody, and
everyone laughed when he told his stories.

My Lady the Baroness, who weighed about three hundred
and fifty pounds, attracted, by that means, very great **20**
attention, and did the honors of the house with a dignity that
rendered her still more respectable. Her daughter Cunegonde,
aged about seventeen years, was of a ruddy complexion, fresh,
plump, and well calculated to excite the passions. The Baron's
son appeared to be in every respect worthy of his father. The
preceptor, Pangloss,[3] was the oracle of the house, and little
Candide listened to his lectures with all the simplicity that was
suitable to his age and character.

Pangloss taught metaphysico-theologo-cosmoloonigology.[4]
He proved most admirably, that there could not be an effect **30**
without cause; that, in this best of possible worlds,[5] my Lord
the Baron's castle was the most magnificent of castles, and
my Lady the best of Baronesses that possibly could be.

"It is demonstrable," said he, "that things cannot be
otherwise than they are: for things having been made for some
end, they must necessarily be for the best end. Observe well,
that the nose has been made for carrying spectacles; therefore
we have spectacles. The legs are visibly designed for
stockings, and therefore we have stockings. Stones have been
formed to be hewn, and make castles; therefore my Lord has **40**
a very fine castle; the greatest baron of the province ought to
be the best accommodated. Swine were made to be eaten;

therefore we eat pork all the year round: consequently, those
who have merely asserted that all is good, have said a very
foolish thing; they should have said all is the best possible."

Candide listened attentively, and believed implicitly; for he
thought Miss Cunegonde extremely handsome, though he never
had the courage to tell her so. He concluded, that next to the
good fortune of being Baron of Thunder-ten-tronckh, the second
degree of happiness was that of being Miss Cunegonde, the **50**
third to see her every day, and the fourth to listen to the
teachings of Master Pangloss, the greatest philosopher
of the province, and consequently of the whole world.

One day Cunegonde having taken a walk in the environs of
the castle, in a little wood, which they called a park, espied
Doctor Pangloss giving a lesson in experimental philosophy to
her mother's chambermaid; a little brown wench, very
handsome, and very docile. As Miss Cunegonde had a strong
inclination for the sciences, she observed, without making any
noise, the reiterated experiments that were going on before **60**
her eyes; she saw very clearly the sufficient reason of the
Doctor, the effects and the causes; and she returned greatly
flurried, quite pensive, and full of desire to be learned;
imagining that she might be a sufficient reason for young
Candide, who also, might be the same to her.

On her return to the castle, she met Candide, and blushed;
Candide also blushed; she wished him good morrow with a
faltering voice, and Candide answered her, hardly knowing what
he said. The next day, after dinner, as they arose from table,
Cunegonde and Candide happened to get behind the screen. **70**
Cunegonde dropped her handkerchief, and Candide picked it up;
she, not thinking any harm, took hold of his hand; and the young
man, not thinking any harm neither, kissed the hand of the
young lady, with an eagerness, a sensibility, and grace, very
particular; their lips met, their eyes sparkled, their knees
trembled, their hands strayed.—The Baron of Thunder-ten-
tronckh happening to pass close by the screen, and observing
this cause and effect, thrust Candide out of the castle, with
lusty kicks [to the behind]. Cunegonde fell into a swoon and as
soon as she came to herself, was heartily cuffed on the ears **80**
by my Lady the Baroness. Thus all was thrown into confusion
in the finest and most agreeable castle possible.

Chapter 2

What Became of Candide Among the Bulgarians[6]

Candide being expelled the terrestrial paradise, rambled a long
while without knowing where, weeping, and lifting up his eyes
to heaven, and sometimes turning them towards the finest of
castles, which contained the handsomest of baronesses. He laid
himself down, without his supper, in the open fields, between
two furrows, while the snow fell in great flakes. Candide,
almost frozen to death, crawled next morning to the neighboring
village, which was called Waldber-ghoff-trarbk-dikdorff. **90**
Having no money, and almost dying with hunger and fatigue,

---

[1] A province in Germany.

[2] Genealogical degrees of noble ancestry; since each quartering
represents one generation, the family "tree" is over 2000 years old—
an obvious impossibility.

[3] The tutor's name is (literally) "all tongue."

[4] In the original French version, the word *nigaud* ("booby") was included
in the elaborate title of this pompous-sounding discipline.

[5] One of many allusions in *Candide* to the philosophic optimism
systematized by Leibniz and popularized by Pope (see chapter 24).

[6] Voltaire's name for the troops of Frederick the Great, king of Prussia,
who, like their king, were widely regarded as Sodomites; the
association between the name and the French *bougre* ("to bugger")
is patent.

he stopped in a dejected posture before the gate of an inn. Two men, dressed in blue,[7] observing him in such a situation, "Brother," says one of them to the other, "there is a young fellow well built, and of a proper height." They accosted Candide, and invited him very civilly to dinner.

"Gentlemen," replied Candide, with an agreeable modesty, "you do me much honor, but I have no money to pay my share."

"O sir," said one of the blues, "persons of your appearance and merit never pay anything; are you not five feet five inches high?"

"Yes, gentlemen, that is my height," returned he, making a bow.

"Come, sir, sit down at table; we will not only treat you, but we will never let such a man as you want money; men are made to assist one another."

"You are in the right," said Candide; "that is what Pangloss always told me, and I see plainly that everything is for the best."

They entreated him to take a few crowns, which he accepted, and would have given them his note; but they refused it, and sat down to table.

"Do not you tenderly love—"

"O yes," replied he, "I tenderly love Miss Cunegonde."

"No," said one of the gentlemen; "we ask you if you do tenderly love the King of the Bulgarians?"

"Not at all," said he, "for I never saw him."

"How! he is the most charming of kings, and you must drink his health."

"O, with all my heart, gentlemen," and drinks.

"That is enough," said they to him; "you are now the bulwark, the support, the defender, the hero of the Bulgarians; your fortune is made, and you are certain of glory." Instantly they put him in irons, and carried him to the regiment. They made him turn to the right, to the left, draw the ramrod, return the ramrod, present, fire, step double; and they gave him thirty blows with a cudgel. The next day, he performed his exercises not quite so badly, and received but twenty blows; the third day the blows were restricted to ten, and he was looked upon by his fellow-soldiers, as a kind of prodigy.

Candide, quite stupefied, could not well conceive how he had become a hero. One fine Spring day he took it into his head to walk out, going straight forward, imagining that the human, as well as the animal species, were entitled to make whatever use they pleased of their limbs. He had not traveled two leagues, when four other heroes, six feet high, came up to him, bound him, and put him into a dungeon. He is asked by a Court-martial, whether he chooses to be whipped six and thirty times through the whole regiment, or receive at once twelve bullets through the forehead? He in vain argued that the will is free, and that he chose neither the one nor the other; he was obliged to make a choice; he therefore resolved, in virtue of God's gift called freewill, to run the gauntlet six and thirty times. He underwent this discipline twice. The regiment being composed of two thousand men, he received four thousand lashes, which laid open all his muscles and nerves, from the nape of the neck to the back. As they were proceeding to a third course, Candide,

being quite spent, begged as a favor that they would be so kind as to shoot him; he obtained his request; they hoodwinked him, and made him kneel; the King of the Bulgarians passing by, inquired into the crime of the delinquent; and as this prince was a person of great penetration, he discovered from what he heard of Candide, that he was a young metaphysician, entirely ignorant of the things of this world; and he granted him his pardon, with a clemency which will be extolled in all histories, and throughout all ages. An experienced surgeon cured Candide in three weeks, with emollients prescribed by no less a master than Dioscorides.[8] His skin had already began to grow again, and he was able to walk, when the King of the Bulgarians gave battle to the King of the Abares.

[Candide escapes from the Bulgarians and travels to Holland, where he encounters the ailing Pangloss. Surviving a tempest and a shipwreck, they arrive in Portugal.]

Chapter 6

How a Fine *Auto-da-Fé*[9] was Celebrated to Prevent Earthquakes, and How Candide was Whipped

After the earthquake, which had destroyed three-fourths of Lisbon, the sages of the country could not find any means more effectual to prevent a total destruction, than to give the people a splendid *auto-da-fé*. It had been decided by the university of Coimbra, that the spectacle of some persons burnt to death by a slow fire, with great ceremony, was an infallible antidote for earthquakes.

In consequence of this resolution, they had seized a Biscayan, convicted of having married his godmother,[10] and two Portuguese, who, in eating a pullet, had stripped off the bacon.[11] After dinner, they came and secured Dr. Pangloss, and his disciple Candide; the one for having spoke too freely, and the other for having heard with an air of approbation. They were both conducted to separate apartments, extremely damp, and never incommoded with the sun.[12] Eight days after, they were both clothed with a gown[13] and had their heads adorned with paper crowns. Candide's crown and gown were painted with inverted flames, and with devils that had neither tails nor claws; but Pangloss' devils had claws and tails, and the flames were pointed upwards. Being thus dressed, they marched in procession, and heard a very pathetic speech followed by fine music on a squeaking organ. Candide was whipped on the back in cadence, while they were singing; the Biscayan, and the two men who would not eat lard, were burnt; and Pangloss, though it was contrary to custom, was hanged. The same day, the earth

---

[8] A famous Greek physician of the first century C.E. whose book on medicine was for centuries a standard text.

[9] The public ceremony (literally, "act of faith") by which those found guilty of heresy were punished.

[10] A swipe at papal efforts to condemn as incestuous marriages in which the parties might be bound by family relation.

[11] Unwittingly revealing that they were secretly Jews—Jewish dietary laws prohibit the eating of pork. Under the pressure of the Spanish and Portuguese Inquisitions, many Iberian Jews had converted to Christianity.

[12] Prison cells.

[13] Yellow penitential garments worn by the confessed heretic.

---

[7] The color of the uniforms worn by the soldiers of Frederick the Great.

shook anew,[14] with a most dreadful noise.

Candide, affrighted, interdicted, astonished, all bloody, all panting, said to himself: "If this is the best of possible worlds, what then are the rest? Supposing I had not been whipped now, I have been so, among the Bulgarians; but, Oh, my dear Pangloss; thou greatest of philosophers, that it should be my fate to see thee hanged without knowing for what! Oh! my dear Anabaptist! thou best of men, that it should be thy fate to be drowned in the harbor! Oh! Miss Cunegonde! the jewel of ladies, that it should be thy fate to have been outraged and slain!" **190**

He returned, with difficulty, supporting himself, after being lectured, whipped, absolved, and blessed, when an old woman accosted him, and said: "Child, take courage, and follow me."

Q What attitudes, beliefs, and institutions does Voltaire attack in *Candide*?

Q How does Voltaire's *Candide* "reply" to Pope's *Essay on Man*?

Satire in Chinese Literature

 While literary satire drew enthusiastic audiences in the West, the genre also came into vogue elsewhere in the world. Following the Manchu conquest of China in the mid-seventeenth century, Chinese writers produced bitter fictional tales that satirized a wide variety of contemporary practices, including Buddhist rituals, commercial banditry, and homosexual unions.

One of the cruelest satires of the eighteenth century consisted of a collection of stories attacking the absurdities of the examination system by which talented individuals were brought into China's civil service. *The Scholars*, as the novel is titled, written around 1750 by Wu Jingzi (1701–1754), reflects Wu's failure to pass the highly competitive exams, which often brought pseudo-scholars to positions of great wealth and political power. The satire emphasized the unpopular and anti-Confucian truth that the morally unscrupulous frequently gain great prizes in the world, while the virtuous often go unrewarded.

Chinese satire was also effective in attacking some of the more socially inhibiting practices of traditional Chinese culture, such as female footbinding. Beginning in the eleventh century, upper-class Chinese parents bound the feet of their young daughters (thus breaking the arch and stunting the feet to half the normal size) in order to exempt them from common labor, hence making them more physically attractive as marriage partners to wealthy men.

Toward the end of the great age of Chinese prose fiction, the philologist Li Ruzhen (1763–1830) attacked this practice in a satire entitled *Flowers in the Mirror*. An adventure tale similar to *Gulliver's Travels* and *Candide*, *Flowers* is a series of loosely woven stories that recount the experiences of a voyager to many strange lands, including the Country

of Two-Faced People, the Country of Long-Armed People, and the Country of Women. In the last of these fictional lands, the traditional roles of the sexes are reversed, and the ruling women of the country set upon the hero to prepare him as "royal concubine": they plait his hair, apply lipstick and powder to his face, pierce his ears, and, to his ultimate dismay, bind his feet in the traditional Chinese manner. Li Ruzhen's blunt social criticism and his bold assertion of equal rights for women fell on deaf ears, for despite the fact that Manchu rulers censured footbinding, the custom continued in many parts of China until the early twentieth century.

READING 25.5 From Li Ruzhen's *Flowers in the Mirror* (1828)

When Tang Ao heard that they had arrived at the Country of Women, he thought that the country was populated entirely by women, and was afraid to go ashore. But Old Tuo said, "Not at all! There are men as well as women, only they call men women, and women men. The men wear the skirts and take care of the home, while the women wear hats and trousers and manage affairs outside. If it were a country populated solely by women, I doubt that even Brother Lin here would dare to venture ashore, although he knows he always makes a good profit from sales here!" **1**

10

"If the men dress like women, do they use cosmetics and bind their feet?" asked Tang Ao.

"Of course they do!" cried Lin, and took from his pocket a list of the merchandise he was going to sell, which consisted of huge quantities of rouge, face powder, combs and other women's notions. "Luckily I wasn't born in this country," he said. "Catch me mincing around on bound feet!"

When Tang Ao asked why he had not put down the price of the merchandise, Lin said, "The people here, no matter rich or poor, from the 'King' down to the simplest peasant, are all mad about cosmetics. I'll charge them what I can. I shall have no difficulty selling the whole consignment to rich families in two or three days." **20**

Beaming at the prospect of making a good profit, Lin went on shore with his list.

Tang Ao and Old Tuo decided to go and see the city. The people walking on the streets were small of stature, and rather slim, and although dressed in men's clothes, were beardless and spoke with women's voices, and walked with willowy steps. **30**

"Look at them!" said Old Tuo. "They are perfectly normal-looking women. Isn't it a shame for them to dress like men?"

"Wait a minute," said Tang Ao. "Maybe when they see us, they think, 'Look at them, isn't it a shame that they dress like women'?"

"You're right. 'Whatever one is accustomed to always seems natural,' as the ancients say. But I wonder what the men are like?"

[Invited to sell his wares at the court of the "King," Lin visits the Palace.]

In a little time, Merchant Lin was ushered to a room upstairs

---

[14] A second earthquake occurred in Lisbon on December 21, 1755.

where victuals of many kinds awaited him. As he ate, however, he heard a great deal of noise downstairs. Several palace "maids" ran upstairs soon, and calling him "Your Highness," kowtowed to him and congratulated him. Before he knew what was happening, Merchant Lin was being stripped completely bare by the maids and led to a perfumed bath. Against the powerful arms of these maids, he could scarcely struggle. Soon he found himself being anointed, perfumed, powdered and rouged, and dressed in a skirt. His big feet were bound up in strips of cloth and socks, and his hair was combed into an elaborate braid over his head and decorated with pins. These male "maids" thrust bracelets on his arms and rings on his fingers, and put a phoenix headdress on his head. They tied a jade green sash around his waist and put an embroidered cape around his shoulders.

Then they led him to a bed, and asked him to sit down.

Merchant Lin thought that he must be drunk, or dreaming, and began to tremble. He asked the maids what was happening, and was told that he had been chosen by the "King" to be the Imperial Consort, and that a propitious day would be chosen for him to enter the "King's" chambers.

Before he could utter a word, another group of maids, all tall and strong and wearing beards, came in. One was holding a threaded needle. "We are ordered to pierce your ears," he said, as the other four "maids" grabbed Lin by the arms and legs. The white-bearded one seized Lin's right ear, and after rubbing the lobe a little, drove the needle through it.

"Ooh!" Merchant Lin screamed.

The maid seized the other ear, and likewise drove the needle through it. As Lin screamed with pain, powdered lead was smeared on his earlobes and a pair of "eight-precious" earrings was hung from the holes.

Having finished what they came to do, the maids retreated, and a black-bearded fellow came in with a bolt of white silk. Kneeling down before him, the fellow said, "I am ordered to bind Your Highness's feet."

Two other maids seized Lin's feet as the black-bearded one sat down on a low stool, and began to rip the silk into ribbons. Seizing Lin's right foot, he set it upon his knee, and sprinkled white alum powder between the toes and the grooves of the foot. He squeezed the toes tightly together, bent them down so that the whole foot was shaped like an arch, and took a length of white silk and bound it tightly around it twice. One of the others sewed the ribbon together in small stitches. Again the silk went around the foot, and again, it was sewn up.

Merchant Lin felt as though his feet were burning, and wave after wave of pain rose to his heart. When he could stand it no longer, he let out his voice and began to cry. The "maids" had hastily made a pair of soft-soled red shoes, and these they put on both his feet.

"Please, kind brothers, go and tell Her Majesty that I'm a married man," Lin begged. "How can I become her Consort? As for my feet, please liberate them. They have enjoyed the kind of freedom which scholars who are not interested in official careers enjoy! How can you bind them? Please tell your 'King' to let me go. I shall be grateful, and my wife will be very grateful."

But the maids said, "The King said that you are to enter his chambers as soon as your feet are bound. It is no time for talk of this kind."

When it was dark, a table was laid for him with mountains of meat and oceans of wine. But Merchant Lin only nibbled, and told the "maids" they could have the rest.

Still sitting on the bed, and with his feet aching terribly, he decided to lie down in his clothes for a rest.

At once a middle-aged "maid" came up to him and said, "Please, will you wash before you retire?"

No sooner was this said than a succession of maids came in with candles, basins of water and spittoon, dressing table, boxes of ointment, face powder, towels, silk handkerchiefs, and surrounded him. Lin had to submit to the motions of washing in front of them all. But after he had washed his face, a maid wanted to put some cream on it again.

Merchant Lin stoutly refused.

"But night time is the best time to treat the skin," the white-bearded maid said. "This powder has a lot of musk in it. It will make your skin fragrant, although I dare say it is fair enough already. If you use it regularly your skin will not only seem like white jade, but will give off a natural fragrance of its own. And the more fragrant it is, the fairer it will become, and the more lovely to behold, and the more lovable you will be. You'll see how good it is after you have used it regularly."

But Lin refused firmly, and the maids said, "If you are so stubborn, we will have to report this, and let Matron deal with you tomorrow."

Then they left him alone. But Lin's feet hurt so much that he could not sleep a wink. He tore at the ribbons with all his might, and after a great struggle succeeded in tearing them off. He stretched out his ten toes again, and luxuriating in their exquisite freedom, finally fell asleep.

The next morning, however, when the black-bearded maid discovered that he had torn off his foot-bandages, he immediately reported it to the "King," who ordered that Lin should be punished by receiving twenty strokes of the bamboo from the "Matron." Accordingly, a white-bearded "Matron" came in with a stick of bamboo about eight feet long, and when the others had stripped him and held him down, raised the stick and began to strike Lin's bottom and legs.

Before five strokes had been delivered, Lin's tender skin was bleeding, and the Matron did not have the heart to go on. "Look at her skin! Have you ever seen such white and tender and lovable skin? Why, I think indeed her looks are comparable to Pan An and Sung Yu!" the Matron thought to himself. "But what am I doing, comparing her bottom and not her face to them? Is that a compliment?"

The foot-binding maid came and asked Lin if he would behave from now on.

"Yes, I'll behave," Lin replied, and they stopped beating him. They wiped the blood from his wounds, and special ointment was sent by the "King" and ginseng soup was given him to drink.

Merchant Lin drank the soup, and fell on the bed for a rest. But the "King" had given orders that his feet must be bound again, and that he should be taught to walk on them. So with one maid supporting him on each side, Merchant Lin was marched up and down the room all day on his bound feet. When he lay down to sleep that night, he could not close his eyes for the excruciating pain.

But from now on, he was never left alone again. Maids took turns to sit with him. Merchant Lin knew that he was no longer in command of his destiny. . . . **160**

└ **Q** **What indignities are described in this satire?**

└ **Q** **What broader issues are suggested by the motif of role reversal?**

The Visual Satires of William Hogarth

The visual counterpart of literary satire is found in the paintings and prints of the English artist William Hogarth (1697–1764). A master draftsman, Hogarth produced a telling visual record of the ills of eighteenth-century British society. Popular novels and plays provided inspiration for what Hogarth called his "modern moral subjects." He illustrated the novels of Defoe and Swift, including *Gulliver's Travels*, and executed a series of paintings based on John Gay's *Beggar's Opera*—a mock-heroic comedy that equated low-class crime with high-class corruption. The theater prompted many of the devices Hogarth used for pictorial representation: boxlike staging, lighting from below, and a wealth of "props." "I have endeavored," he wrote, "to treat my subjects as a dramatic writer: my picture is my stage, and men and women my actors."

Hogarth made engraved versions of his paintings and sold them (just as the volumes of Diderot's *Encyclopédie* were vended) by subscription. So popular were Hogarth's prints that they were pirated and sold without his authorization (a practice that continued even after Parliament passed the first copyright law in 1735). Especially successful were two series of prints based on his paintings. The first ("The Harlot's Progress") illustrates the misfortunes of a young woman who becomes a London prostitute; the second ("The Rake's Progress") depicts the comic misadventures of an antihero and ne'er-do-well named Tom Rakewell.

Following these, Hogarth published a series of six engravings entitled "Marriage à la Mode," which describes the tragic consequences of a marriage of convenience between the son of a poverty-stricken nobleman and the daughter of a wealthy and ambitious merchant. The first print in the series, *The Marriage Transaction*, shows the two families negotiating the terms of the union (Figure **25.5**). The scene unfolds as if upon a stage: the corpulent Lord Squanderfield, victim of the gout (an ailment traditionally

Figure 25.5 WILLIAM HOGARTH, *The Marriage Transaction*, from the "Marriage à la Mode" series, 1742–1746. Engraving, 15 × 18 in.

linked with rich food and drink), sits pompously in his ruffled velvet waistcoat, pointing to his family tree, which springs from the loins of William the Conqueror. Across the table, the wealthy merchant and father of the bride carefully peruses the financial terms of the marriage settlement. On a settee in the corner of the room, the pawns of this socially expedient match turn away from each other in attitudes of mutual dislike. The earl's son, young Squanderfield, sporting a beauty patch, opens his snuffbox and vainly gazes at himself in a mirror, while his bride-to-be idly dangles her betrothal ring on a kerchief. She leans forward to hear the honeyed words of her future seducer, a lawyer named Lord Silvertongue. A combination of **caricature** (exaggeration of peculiarities or defects), comic irony, and symbolic detail, Hogarth's "stylish marriage" is drawn with a stylus every bit as sharp as Voltaire's pen.

Like Voltaire's Paris, Hogarth's London was not yet an industrial metropolis, but it was plagued by some of the worst urban conditions of the day. It lacked sewers, streetlights, and adequate law enforcement. A city of vast contrasts between rich and poor, it was crowded with thieves, drunks, and prostitutes, all of whom threatened the jealously guarded privileges of the rich. Hogarth represented mid-eighteenth-century London at its worst in the famous engraving *Gin Lane* (see Figure **25.1**). This devastating attack on the combined evils of urban poverty and alcoholism portrays poor, ragged, and drunk men and women in various stages of depravity. Some pawn their possessions to support their expensive addictions (upper left); others commit suicide (upper right corner); and one pours gin down the throat of a babe-in-arms (far right), following the common practice of using liquor and other drugs to quiet noisy infants. In the center of the print is the figure of a drunken mother—her leg covered with syphilitic sores—who carelessly allows her child to fall over the edge of the stair rail.

Hogarth's visual satirization of gin addiction was a heroic attack on the social conditions of his time and on drug abuse in general. But even Parliament's passage of the Gin Law in 1751, which more than doubled the gin tax, did little to reduce the widespread use of this popular alcoholic beverage in eighteenth-century England. While Hogarth's prints failed to reduce the ills and inequities of his society, they remain an enduring condemnation of human hypocrisy, cruelty, vanity, and greed.

Rousseau's Revolt Against Reason

Jean-Jacques Rousseau, introduced in chapter 24 as a contributor to Diderot's *Encyclopédie*, was one of the Enlightenment's most outspoken critics. A playwright, composer, and educator, Rousseau took issue with some of the basic precepts of Enlightenment thought, including the idea that the progress of the arts and sciences might improve human conduct. Human beings may be good by nature, argued Rousseau, but they are ultimately corrupted by society and its institutions. "God makes all things good," he wrote; "man meddles with them and they become evil." Rousseau condemned the artificiality of civilized life and,

although he did not advocate that humankind should return to a "state of nature," he exalted the "noble savage" as the model of the uncorrupted individual.

Rousseau's philosophy of the heart elevated the role of instinct over reason and encouraged a new appreciation of nature and the natural—principles that would underlie the Romantic movement of the early nineteenth century (see chapters 27 to 29). In the following excerpt from the *Discourse on the Origin of Inequality among Men* (1755), Rousseau gives an eloquent account of how, in his view, human beings came to lose their freedom and their innocence.

READING 25.6 From Rousseau's *Discourse on the Origin of Inequality among Men* (1755)

The first man who, having enclosed a piece of land, thought of saying "This is mine" and found people simple enough to believe him, was the true founder of civil society. How many crimes, wars, murders; how much misery and horror the human race would have been spared if someone had pulled up the stakes and filled in the ditch and cried out to his fellow men: "Beware of listening to this impostor. You are lost if you forget that the fruits of the earth belong to everyone and that the earth itself belongs to no one!" But it is highly probable that by this time things had reached a point beyond which they could [10] not go on as they were; for the idea of property, depending on many prior ideas which could only have arisen in successive stages, was not formed all at once in the human mind. It was necessary for men to make much progress, to acquire much industry and knowledge, to transmit and increase it from age to age, before arriving at this final stage of the state of nature. Let us therefore look farther back, and try to review from a single perspective the slow succession of events and discoveries in their most natural order.

Man's first feeling was that of his existence, his first [20] concern was that of his preservation. The products of the earth furnished all the necessary aids; instinct prompted him to make use of them. While hunger and other appetites made him experience in turn different modes of existence, there was one appetite which urged him to perpetuate his own species; and this blind impulse, devoid of any sentiment of the heart, produced only a purely animal act. The need satisfied, the two sexes recognized each other no longer, and even the child meant nothing to the mother, as soon as he could do without her.

Such was the condition of nascent[1] man; such was the life [30] of an animal limited at first to mere sensation; and scarcely profiting from the gifts bestowed on him by nature, let alone was he dreaming of wresting anything from her. But difficulties soon presented themselves and man had to learn to overcome them. The height of trees, which prevented him from reaching their fruits; the competition of animals seeking to nourish themselves on the same fruits; the ferocity of animals who threatened his life—all this obliged man to apply himself to bodily exercises; he had to make himself agile, fleet of foot,

---

[1] Early, developing.

and vigorous in combat. Natural weapons—branches of trees and stones—were soon found to be at hand. He learned to overcome the obstacles of nature, to fight when necessary against other animals, to struggle for his subsistence even against other men, or to indemnify[2] himself for what he was forced to yield to the stronger.

[Rousseau then describes how people devised a technology for hunting and fishing, invented fire, and developed superiority over other creatures.]

Instructed by experience that love of one's own wellbeing is the sole motive of human action, he found himself in a position to distinguish the rare occasions when common interest justified his relying on the aid of his fellows, and those even rarer occasions when competition should make him distrust them. In the first case, he united with them in a herd, or at most in a sort of free association that committed no one and which lasted only as long as the passing need which had brought it into being. In the second case, each sought to grasp his own advantage, either by sheer force, if he believed he had the strength, or by cunning and subtlety if he felt himself to be the weaker. . . .

. . . the habit of living together generated the sweetest sentiments known to man, conjugal love and paternal love. Each family became a little society, all the better united because mutual affection and liberty were its only bonds; at this stage also the first differences were established in the ways of life of the two sexes which had hitherto been identical. Women became more sedentary and accustomed themselves to looking after the hut and the children while men went out to seek their common subsistence. The two sexes began, in living a rather softer life, to lose something of their ferocity and their strength; but if each individual became separately less able to fight wild beasts, all, on the other hand, found it easier to group together to resist them jointly. . . .

To the extent that ideas and feelings succeeded one another, and the heart and mind were exercised, the human race became more sociable, relationships became more extensive and bonds tightened. People grew used to gathering together in front of their huts or around a large tree; singing and dancing, true progeny[3] of love and leisure, became the amusement, or rather the occupation, of idle men and women thus assembled. Each began to look at the others and to want to be looked at himself; and public esteem came to be prized. He who sang or danced the best; he who was the most handsome, the strongest, the most adroit[4] or the most eloquent became the most highly regarded, and this was the first step toward inequality and at the same time toward vice. From those first preferences there arose, on the one side, vanity and scorn, on the other, shame and envy, and the fermentation produced by these new leavens[5] finally produced compounds fatal to happiness and innocence.

As soon as men learned to value one another and the idea of consideration was formed in their minds, everyone claimed a right to it, and it was no longer possible for anyone to be refused consideration without affront. This gave rise to the first duties of civility, even among savages: and henceforth every intentional wrong became an outrage, because together with the hurt which might result from the injury, the offended party saw an insult to his person which was often more unbearable than the hurt itself. Thus, as everyone punished the contempt shown him by another in a manner proportionate to the esteem he accorded himself, revenge became terrible, and men grew bloodthirsty and cruel. This is precisely the stage reached by most of the savage peoples known to us; and it is for lack of having sufficiently distinguished between different ideas and seen how far those peoples already are from the first state of nature that so many authors have hastened to conclude that man is naturally cruel and needs civil institutions to make him peaceable, whereas in truth nothing is more peaceable than man in his primitive state. Placed by nature at an equal distance from the stupidity of brutes[6] and the fatal enlightenment of civilized man, limited equally by reason and instinct to defending himself against evils which threaten him, he is restrained by natural pity from doing harm to anyone, even after receiving harm himself: for according to the wise Locke: "Where there is no property, there is no injury."

But it must be noted that society's having come into existence and relations among individuals having been already established meant that men were required to have qualities different from those they possessed from their primitive constitution. . . .

As long as men were content with their rustic huts, as long as they confined themselves to sewing their garments of skin with thorns or fishbones, and adorning themselves with feathers or shells, to painting their bodies with various colors, to improving or decorating their bows and arrows; and to using sharp stones to make a few fishing canoes or crude musical instruments; in a word, so long as they applied themselves only to work that one person could accomplish alone and to arts that did not require the collaboration of several hands, they lived as free, healthy, good and happy men. . . .

. . . but from the instant one man needed the help of another, and it was found to be useful for one man to have provisions enough for two, equality disappeared, property was introduced, work became necessary, and vast forests were transformed into pleasant fields which had to be watered with the sweat of men, and where slavery and misery were soon seen to germinate and flourish with the crops. . . .

Q **What aspects of civilized life, according to Rousseau, weaken and corrupt society?**

Rousseau was haunted by contradictions within the social order and within his own mind (he suffered acute attacks of paranoia during the last fifteen years of his life). The opening words of his treatise *The Social Contract* (1762), "Man is born free, and everywhere he is in chains," reflect his apprehension concerning the inhibiting role of institutional authority. In order to safeguard individual liberty, said Rousseau, people should form a contract

---

[2] Compensate.
[3] Offspring.
[4] Skillful.
[5] Significant changes.

[6] Beasts.

among themselves. Unlike Hobbes, whose social contract involved transferring absolute authority from the citizens to a sovereign ruler, or Locke, whose social contract gave limited power to the ruler, Rousseau defined the state as "the general will" of its citizens. "The general will alone," he explained, "can direct the State according to the object for which it was instituted, that is, the common good." Rousseau insisted, moreover, that whoever refused to obey the general will should be constrained to do so by the whole society; that is, all humans should "be forced to be free." "As nature gives each man absolute power over all his members," wrote Rousseau, "the social compact gives the body politic absolute power over all its members also." Such views might have contributed to newly developed theories of democracy, but they were equally effective in justifying totalitarian constraints leveled in the name of the people.

Rousseau and Education

Rousseau's wish to preserve the natural also led him to propose revolutionary changes in education. If society is indeed hopelessly corrupt, then let children grow up in accord with nature, he argued. In *Emile* (1762), his treatise on education, Rousseau advanced the hypothesis—unheard of in his time—that the education of a child begins at birth. He divided childhood development into five stages over a twenty-five-year span and outlined the type of rearing desirable for each stage.

"Hands-on" experience was essential to education, according to Rousseau, especially in the period just prior to the development of reason and intellect, which he placed between the ages of twelve and fifteen. "Nature provides for the child's growth in her own fashion, and this should never be thwarted. Do not make him sit still when he wants to run about, nor run when he wants to be quiet."

Rousseau also made a clear distinction between the education of men and that of women. Arguing that a woman's place was in the home and beside the cradle, he proposed for her a domestic education that cultivated modesty, obedience, and other virtues agreeable to her mate. Describing Emile's ideal mate, Rousseau writes, "Her education is in no way exceptional. She has taste without study, talents without art, judgment without knowledge. Her mind is still vacant but has been trained to learn; it is a well-tilled land only waiting for the grain. What a pleasing ignorance! Happy is the man destined to instruct her." Thus Rousseau's views on female education were less "enlightened" (by the standards of Mary Wollstonecraft, for one) than those advanced by Castiglione some 200 years earlier in *The Book of the Courtier* (see chapter 16). Nevertheless, *Emile* became a landmark in educational theory. Rousseau's unique approach to education—particularly his emphasis on the cultivation of natural inquisitiveness over and above rote learning—influenced modern teaching methods such as those developed by the Italian educator Maria Montessori (1870–1952). Ironically, however, Rousseau saw fit to put all five of his own children in a foundling hospital rather than raise them himself.

Kant's Mind/World Revolution

The German philosopher Immanuel Kant (1724–1804) was a defender of Enlightenment values; but he was also a critic of its view of reason as the ultimate means of understanding reality. In his essay "An Answer to the Question, What is Enlightenment" (1784), he wrote, "Enlightenment is man's emergence from his self-imposed immaturity. Immaturity is the inability to use one's understanding without guidance from another." Rules, formulae, and traditional beliefs he regarded as "shackles" that inhibit us from thinking for ourselves. "*Sapare Aude!*" ("Dare to know!"), he proclaimed—that is, have the courage to think for yourself.

In the realm of philosophy, Kant fulfilled his own injunction, becoming one of the greatest philosophers of his time. His monumental *Critique of Pure Reason*, published in 1781, attacked previous philosophic theories that held reason as the sole means of discovering the nature of reality. In it, he argued that the manner in which one perceives the world depends on specific qualities in the perceiver's mind. The mind, according to Kant, is not a passive recipient of information (Locke's "blank slate"); rather, it participates in the process of knowing the world. Concepts such as time, space, and causality are innate conditions that organize experience. These intuitive forms, along with certain categories of thought (quantity, quality, relationship, and modality) exist in the mind from birth; they shape the data of the senses into a consistent picture of the world.

Kant claimed to have altered the relationship between mind and world as radically as Copernicus had changed the relationship between earth and sun. Shifting the focus of philosophic debate from the nature of objective reality to the question of cognition itself—the process by which the mind comprehends experience—he perceived the mind as not merely reflecting experience, but as organizing experience into a coherent pattern. The preeminence Kant gave to the role of the mind in constructing our idea of the world laid the basis for transcendental **idealism**, the doctrine that holds that reality consists of the mind and its forms of perception and understanding.

A giant in the field of modern ethics, Kant assessed the limits of reason with regard to morality. In contrast to Descartes and Locke, who held that knowledge was the key to intellectual advancement, Kant viewed knowledge as the vehicle of moral law. Recognizing that notions of good and evil differ widely in the world, Kant proposed a "supreme principle of morality," one that applied equally to all rational beings. In *Critique of Practical Reason* (1788) he advanced a universal moral law, known as the "categorical imperative": we must act as if we could will that the maxim of our actions become the law for all humankind. The basis of this moral law is the recognition of our duty to act in ways justified by reasons so universal that they are good for all people at all times. It is not enough that our acts have good effects; it is necessary that we *will* the good. Kant's notion of "good will" is not identical with the Christian concept of mercy. Nor is it the same as Jesus' commandment: "Do to others as you would wish them to do to you." In essence, ethical conduct is based not on love for humankind (which, after all, one may lack), but on the imperative to act rationally, a condition essential to human dignity.

The Revolutions of the Late Eighteenth Century

The American and French revolutions drew inspiration from the Enlightenment faith in the reforming power of reason. Both, however, demonstrated the limits of reason in the face of militant zeal.

The American Revolution

As early as 1776, North America's thirteen colonies had rebelled against the long-standing political control of the British government. In the Declaration of Independence (see chapter 24), Jefferson restated Locke's assertion that government must protect its citizens' rights to life, liberty, and property. The British government, however, in making unreasonable demands for revenue, threatened colonial liberty, igniting the passions of fervent populists who sought democratic reform. Following some seven years of armed conflict, several thousand battle deaths, and a war expense estimated at over $100 million, in 1783 the thirteen colonies achieved their independence. And, in 1789, they began to function under the Constitution of the United States of America. The British political theorist Thomas Paine (1737–1809) proclaimed that the revolution had done more to enlighten the world and diffuse a spirit of freedom among humankind than any event that had preceded it.

The French Revolution

The American Revolution did not go unnoticed in France. French intellectuals followed its every turn; the French government secretly aided the American cause and eventually joined in the war against Britain. However, the revolution that began on French soil in 1789 involved circumstances that were quite different from those in America. The French Revolution was, in the main, the product of two major problems: class inequality, and a serious financial crisis brought about by some 500 years of costly wars and royal extravagance (see chapter 21). In France, the lower classes sought to overturn long-standing social and political institutions and end upper-class privilege. With his nation on the verge of bankruptcy, King Louis XVI (1754–1793) sought new measures for raising revenue.

Throughout French history, taxes had fallen exclusively on the shoulders of the lower and middle classes, the so-called Third Estate. Almost four-fifths of the average peasant's income went to pay taxes, which supported the privileged upper classes. In a population of some twenty-five million people, the First Estate (the clergy) and the Second Estate (the nobility)—a total of only 200,000 citizens—controlled nearly half the land in France; yet they were exempt from paying taxes. Peasant grievances were not confined to matters of taxation: population growth and rising prices led to severe shortages of bread, the principal food of the lower classes.

When, in an effort to obtain public support for new taxes, Louis XVI called a meeting of the Estates General—its first in 175 years—the Third Estate withdrew. Declaring itself representative of the general will of the people, it formed a separate body claiming the right to approve or veto all taxation. This daring act set the revolution in motion. No sooner had the Third Estate proclaimed itself a national assembly than great masses of peasants and laborers began to riot throughout France.

On July 14, 1789, crowds stormed the Bastille and destroyed the visible symbol of the old French regime (Figure **25.6**). Less than one month later, on August 4, the

Figure 25.6 BRIFFAULT DE LA CHARPRAIS and **MME. ESCLAPART**, *The Siege of the Bastille, July 14, 1789*, 1791–1796. Engraving, 12 × 18¼ in.

National Assembly—as the new body established by the Third Estate called itself—issued decrees that abolished the last remnants of medieval feudalism, including manorial courts, feudal duties, and church tithes. It also made provisions for a limited monarchy and an elected legislative assembly. The decrees of the National Assembly became part of a constitution, prefaced by the Declaration of the Rights of Man and Citizen. Modeled on the American Declaration of Independence, the preface listed among its seventeen articles due process of law, religious freedom, and taxation based on the ability to pay. The body of the document promised a constitutional monarchy, a uniform code of law, and free public education.

Not all the "rights of man" applied equally to women. The right to vote, to sue for divorce, and to hold public office were all withheld from women. In 1791, Olympe de Gouges (1748–1793), a butcher's daughter and a vocal advocate of women's rights, drafted a Declaration of the Rights of Woman and the Female Citizen. If a woman has the right to mount the scaffold, claimed de Gouges, "she must equally have the right to mount the rostrum." The declaration demanded equal political rights and responsibilities for women, the sex de Gouges described as "superior in beauty and courage." Indeed, in October of 1789, some 6000 courageous women had marched on Versailles to protest the lack of bread in Paris (Figure **25.7**). For the first time in history, women constituted a collective revolutionary force, making demands for equal property rights, government employment for women, and equal educational opportunities—demands guaranteed by the Constitution of 1793 but lost less than two years later by the terms of a new constitution. Despite her tireless efforts, de Gouge's declaration was never passed into law.

While equality for women was not achieved in this era, in 1793, the Constitutional Convention voted to ban slavery

in all French colonies. The decision was inspired in part by the impassioned appeals of the former Senegalese slave Jean-Baptiste Belley (1746–1805; Figure **25.8**), one of three convention delegates from the French Caribbean island of Saint Domingue (present-day Haiti), where slaves under the leadership of Pierre-Dominique Toussaint-Louverture (1745–1803) had revolted two years earlier.

Enlightenment idealism, summed up in Rousseau's slogan "Liberty, Equality, Fraternity," had inflamed popular passions and inspired egalitarian reforms. Nevertheless, from the storming of the Bastille through the rural revolts and mass protests that followed, angry, unreasoning mobs controlled the course of the revolution. Divisions among the revolutionaries themselves soon led to a more radical phase of the revolution, called the Reign of Terror. This phase saw the failure of the existing government and sent Louis XVI and his queen, Marie Antoinette, to the guillotine. Between 1793 and 1794, over 40,000 people (including Olympe de Gouges) met their deaths at the guillotine. Others, members of the radical minority known as the Jacobins, met death by the hands of their ideological enemies. Jean-Paul Marat (1743–1793), a Jacobin hero and radical antiroyalist journalist, was assassinated in his bathtub, an event immortalized by his friend, the artist Jacques-Louis David (discussed in chapter 26). Shown in the wooden tub he bathed in to treat a skin condition, he holds the letter by which his assassin, the royalist extremist Charlotte Corday, gained entry to his chambers (Figure **25.9**). The painting, presented by David to the National Convention in October 1793, four months after Marat's death, became a highly celebrated image of patriotic martyrdom. Within eight months, however, David himself was imprisoned, as the Reign of Terror ended with the sweeping condemnation (and execution) of Jacobin extremists.

Figure 25.7 *March of the Women on Versailles, October 5, 1789,* late eighteenth century. Engraving, 6 × 10½ in.

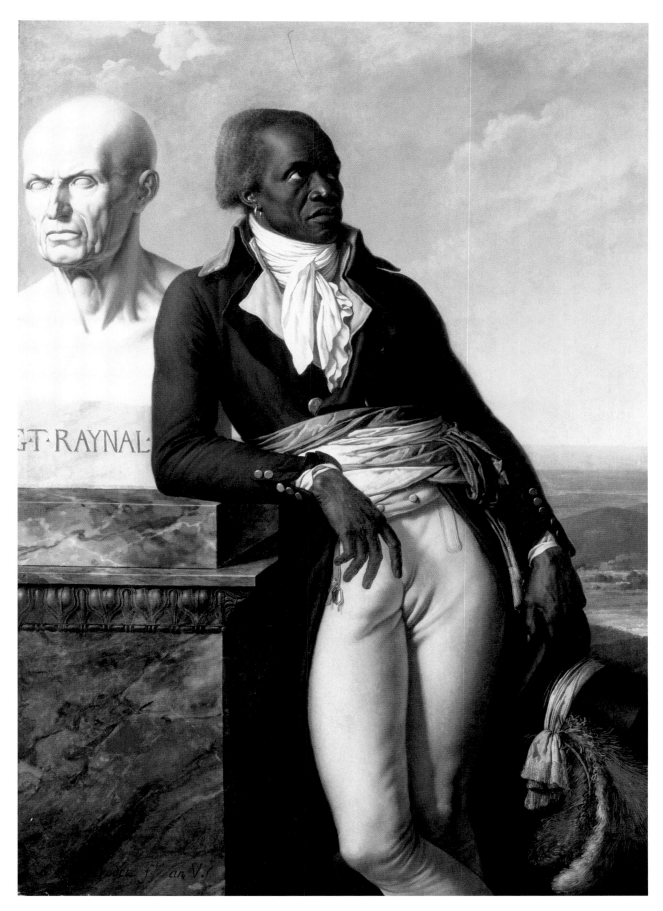

Figure 25.8 ANNE-LOUIS GIRODET-TRIOSON, *Jean-Baptiste Belley, Deputy from Santo Domingo*, 1797. Oil on canvas, 62⅓ × 43⅔ in. Belley, who publicly advocated liberty for all black people, is depicted by Girodet, a student of David, in the style of the aristocratic portrait (see chapter 21). Wearing the uniform of a member of the French National Convention, Belley stands before the bust of Guillaume-Thomas Raynal (1713–1796), an abolitionist and the author of a political history of the trade between Europe and the West Indies.

Finally, in 1794, a National Convention devised a system of government run by two legislative chambers and a five-man executive body of directors. One of these—Napoleon Bonaparte (1769–1821)—would turn France into a military dictatorship some five years later. If, indeed, the French Revolution defended the Enlightenment bastions of liberty and equality, its foundations of reason and rationality ultimately crumbled under the forces of extremism and violence. The radicals of this and many other world-historical revolutions to follow rewrote the words of the *philosophes* in blood.

Science and Technology

1752	Benjamin Franklin proves that lightning is a form of electricity
1783	the first parachute is used in France
1783	the French make the first manned hot-air balloon flight
1795	the Springfield flintlock musket is developed in the United States

Chronology

May 5, 1789	Meeting of the Estates General
July 14, 1789	Fall of the Bastille
August 26, 1789	Declaration of the Rights of Man and Citizen
October 1791	Legislative Assembly
September 1792	France declared a republic
January 1793	Louis XVI executed
1793–1794	Reign of Terror
1795–1799	Napoleon rules the Directory

Figure 25.9 JACQUES-LOUIS DAVID, *The Death of Marat*, 1793. Oil on canvas, 65 × 50½ in. When, during the phase of the French Revolution known as the Reign of Terror, David's antiroyalist friend was murdered in his bathtub, the artist paid tribute to him with this unforgettable painting. Having visited Marat the day before he died, David recreated the event in realistic detail; however, he idealized the scene by bathing Marat in ethereal gold light, as was common to images of Christian martyrdom.

The Industrial Revolution

- The invention of new mechanical devices worked to transform Europe's agrarian and handicraft-dominated economy into one dominated by the technology of mass production.
- The steam engine, the technology of cast iron, and the factory system had major effects on social and economic life, the most immediate of which involved the exploitation of labor.

The Transatlantic Slave Trade

- The failure of the Enlightenment promise of social justice and reform was nowhere better illustrated than in the inhumane activities of the transatlantic slave trade.
- Olaudah Equiano's autobiography, a key example of the popular slave narrative genre, protested the trade in African slaves that persisted throughout the eighteenth century.

Satire: Weapon of the Enlightenment

- In England, the keenest critic of Enlightenment idealism was Jonathan Swift, whose classic satires *Gulliver's Travels* and *A Modest Proposal* attack the moral pettiness and inhumanity of humankind.
- In France, the acerbic writings of Voltaire described human folly as a universal condition. Voltaire's *Candide* remains the classic statement of comic skepticism in Western literature.
- The European masters of satire found their East Asian counterpart in Li Ruzhen, an outspoken and witty critic of outmoded Chinese traditions.
- Voltaire's contemporary William Hogarth brought the bitter invective of the satirists to the visual arts. His engravings exposed the social ills and class discrepancies of British society, even as they mocked universal human vices.

Rousseau's Revolt Against Reason

- Questioning the value of reason for the advancement of the human condition, Jean-Jacques Rousseau argued that society itself corrupts humankind. He rejected the artificiality of the wig-and-silk-stocking culture in which he lived and championed "man in his primitive state."
- Rousseau's treatises on social history, government, and education explored ways in which individuals might retain their natural goodness and remain free and self-determining.

Kant's Mind/World Revolution

- In Germany, the philosopher Immanuel Kant examined the limits of the mind in the process of knowing.
- He argued that human beings have knowledge of the world through certain innate capabilities of mind.
- Kant appealed to "good will" as the basis for moral action.

The Revolutions of the Late Eighteenth Century

- While Enlightenment ideals fueled armed revolt in both America and France, the revolutions themselves blazed with antirational sentiment.
- French intellectuals followed the events of the American Revolution closely; the French government secretly aided the American cause and eventually joined in the war against Britain.
- In France, on July 14, 1789, crowds stormed the Bastille and destroyed the visible symbol of the old French regime. Less than one month later, the National Assembly was formed. In 1794, following a Reign of Terror, the French established a governing legislative system and executive directory.
- Those who fired the cannons of revolt found reason inadequate to the task of effecting social and political reform. Operating according to the dictates of their passions and their will, they gave dramatic evidence of the limits of reason in creating a heaven on earth.

Glossary

caricature the exaggeration of peculiarities or defects to produce comic or burlesque effects

idealism in philosophy, the theory that holds that reality consists of the mind and its ideas; transcendental (or critical) idealism is Kant's name for the doctrine that knowledge is a synthetic product of the logical self

Chapter 26

Eighteenth-Century Art, Music, and Society

ca. 1700–1820

"In the presence of this miracle of [ancient Greek] art, I forget the whole universe and my soul acquires a loftiness appropriate to its dignity."
Johann Joachim Winckelmann

Figure 26.1 FRANÇOIS BOUCHER, *Venus Consoling Love*, 1751. Oil on canvas, 3 ft. 6⅛ in. × 2 ft. 9⅜ in. Boucher is said to have established the erotic female nude as a popular Rococo genre.

The dynamics of class and culture shaped the arts of the eighteenth century. The Church and the royal courts remained the principal sources of artistic patronage, but a rising middle class presented opportunities for new audiences and contemporary subjects. While the arts of the era broadly reflect the intellectual ideals of the Enlightenment, they more closely mirror the tastes and values of different segments of society. No single style dominated the entire century, but three distinctive modes of expression emerged.

European aristocrats, who dominated artistic patronage between 1715 and 1750, found pleasure in an elegant and refined style known as the Rococo. Enlightenment reformers and members of the rising middle class favored genre paintings that described everyday life and the values of ordinary people. Genre painting became the visual equivalent of the popular novels, journalistic essays, and stage plays of the period. Toward the end of the century, the newly excavated ruins of ancient Greece and Rome inspired an archeological appreciation of antiquity and the rise of the Neoclassical style. Neoclassicism then conveyed the rationalism and political idealism of reformers and revolutionaries in France and the young American republic.

In music, the eighteenth century witnessed a move away from the playful and delicate Rococo style to the formal precision of the classical symphony and the string quartet. An increased demand for secular entertainment called forth new types of instrumental music and a musical language that featured clarity and order. Despite their stylistic diversity, the arts shared a spirit of optimism and vitality that ensured their endurance beyond the Age of Enlightenment.

The Rococo Style

The Rococo style was born in France among members of the leisured nobility who had outlived Louis XIV. At Versailles and in the elegant urban townhouses (or *hôtels*, as they were called) of Paris, where the wealthy gathered to enjoy the pleasures of dancing, dining, and conversing, the Rococo provided an atmosphere of elegant refinement. The word "Rococo" derives from *rocaille*, French for the fancy rock- or shellwork that was commonly used to ornament aristocratic gardens and grottoes. Rococo interiors display the organic vitality of seashells, plants, and flowers. Rococo artists preserved the ornate and luxuriant features of the Baroque style, but they favored elements of play and intimacy that were best realized in works of a small scale, such as porcelain figurines, furniture, and paintings suitable for domestic quarters.

The Salon de la Princesse in the Hôtel de Soubise in Paris typifies the Rococo style (Figure **26.2**): its interior is airy and fragile by comparison with a Louis XIV *salon* (see Figure 21.1). Brilliant white walls accented with pastel tones of rose, pale blue, and lime replace the ruby reds

Figure 26.2 GERMAIN BOFFRAND, Salon de la Princesse, Hôtel de Soubise, Paris, ca. 1740. Oval, max. 33 × 26 ft. The Hôtel de Soubise, a fourteenth-century manor house, was remodeled in the early eighteenth century. Its oval *salons*, ornamented with gilded carvings and mirrors, look out onto gardens.

and royal blues of the Baroque *salon*. The geometric regularity of the Baroque interior has given way to an organic medley of curves and countercurves, echoed in elegant mirrors and chandeliers. The walls, ornamented with gilded tendrils, playful cupids, and floral garlands, melt into sensuously painted ceiling vaults crowned with graceful moldings.

Rococo furnishings are generally more delicate than Baroque furnishings, and chairs are often fully upholstered—an innovation of the eighteenth century. Bureaus and tables may be fitted with panels of porcelain (Figure **26.3**)—a Chinese technique that Marie Antoinette, the consort of Louis XVI, introduced at Versailles. Aristocratic women—Marie Antoinette in France, Catherine the Great in Russia, and Maria Theresa in Austria—were enthusiastic patrons of the Rococo style. Indeed, the Rococo may be said to reflect the distinctive influence of eighteenth-century women of taste.

Beyond the *salon*, the garden was the favorite setting for the leisured elite. Unlike Versailles' geometrically ordered parks, Rococo gardens imitated the calculated naturalism of the Chinese garden. They featured undulating paths that gave false impressions of scale and distance. They might include artificial lakes, small colonnaded temples, ornamental pagodas, and other architectural "follies."

Figure 26.3 MARTIN CARLIN (master 1766–1785), Lady's desk, ca. 1775. Decorated with Sèvres porcelain plaques; tulipwood, walnut, and hardwood veneered on oak, 31⅞ × 25⅞ × 16 in. Known as a *bonheur-du-jour* ("delight-of-the-day"), this small writing desk was probably made for the Comtesse du Barry, Louise XV's mistress. Decorated at both front and back, it was meant to stand in the middle of the room.

Both outdoors and in, the fascination with imported Chinese objects and motifs—which began as a fashion in Europe around 1720—promoted the cult of *chinoiserie* (see chapter 21).

Although the Rococo style originated in France, it reached spectacular heights in the courts of secular princes elsewhere in Europe. In Austria and the German states, it became the favorite style for the ornamentation of rural pilgrimage churches. The walls of Bavaria's Benedictine abbey church of Ottobeuren, designed by the German architect Johann Michael Fischer (1692–1766), seem to disappear beneath a riot of stucco "frosting" as rich and sumptuous as that on any wedding cake (Figure **26.4**). By contrast with the more restrained elegance of French Rococo, this church interior erupts in a dazzling array of organic forms that sprout from the moldings and cornices like unruly flora. Shimmering light floods into the white-walled interior through the oval windows, and pastel-colored frescoes turn ceilings and walls into heavenly antechambers. Illusionism reigns: wooden columns and stucco cornices are painted to look like marble; angels and cherubs, tendrils and leaves, curtains and clouds—all made of wood and stucco that have been painted and gilded—come to life as props in a theater of miracles. At Ottobeuren, the somber majesty of the Roman Baroque church has given way to a sublime vision of paradise that is also a feast for the senses.

Rococo Painting: Watteau

The pursuit of pleasure—a major eighteenth-century theme—dominates the paintings of the Rococo masters. The first of these, the Flemish-born Antoine Watteau (1684–1721), began his career by painting theatrical scenes. In 1717, he submitted to the Royal Academy of Painting and Sculpture his *Departure from the Island of Cythera* (Figure **26.5**), a work that pays tribute to the fleeting joys of romantic love. The painting shows a group of fashionable men and women preparing to board a golden boat by which they will leave the island of Cythera, the legendary birthplace of Venus. They have made this outing—a *fête galante* (literally, "elegant entertainment")—in search of the goddess of love, whose rose-bedecked shrine appears at the far right. Amidst fluttering cupids, the pilgrims of love linger in pairs as they wistfully take leave of their florid hideaway. Watteau repeats the serpentine line formed by the figures in the delicate arabesques of the trees and rolling hills. He bathes this fictional moment of nostalgia in a misty, golden light.

Watteau's fragile forms and delicate colors, painted with feathery brushstrokes reminiscent of Rubens, evoke a mood of reverie and nostalgia. His doll-like men and women contrast sharply, however, with Rubens' physically powerful figures (see Figure 21.15) or, for that matter, with Poussin's idealized heroes (see Figure 21.12). Watteau's art conveys no moral or heroic message; rather, it explores the world of familiar but transitory pleasures. Not since the sixteenth-century artists Giorgione and Titian had any painter indulged so deeply in the pleasures of nature or the voluptuous world of the senses.

Figure 26.4 JOHANN MICHAEL FISCHER, interior, Benedictine abbey church, Ottobeuren, Bavaria, 1736–1766. Painted and gilded wood and stucco.

Figure 26.5 ANTOINE WATTEAU, *Departure from the Island of Cythera*, 1717. Oil on canvas, 4 ft. 3 in. × 6 ft. 4 in. Apprenticed to a stage designer in his early career, Watteau drew the subject of this painting from a popular play, *Les Trois Cousins*, written by Florent Dancourt, and performed in Paris in 1709. In the play, the central character invites her friends to visit the island birthplace of Venus, where a single man or woman might find a wife or husband.

Among Watteau's more intimate works are the drawings he executed in the new medium of **pastel**. Invented at the beginning of the eighteenth century, pastel crayons or chalks, which produced soft textures and light tones, were an ideal medium for the swift and spontaneous sketch and the portrait likeness.

Boucher

If Watteau's world was wistful and poetic, that of his contemporary François Boucher (1703–1770) was sensual and indulgent. Boucher, a specialist in designing mythological scenes, became head of the Gobelins tapestry factory in 1755 and director of the Royal Academy ten years later. He was First Painter to King Louis XV (1710–1774) and a good friend of the king's favorite mistress, Jeanne Antoinette Poisson, the Marquise de Pompadour (1721–1764). A woman of remarkable beauty and intellect—she owned two telescopes, a microscope, and a lathe that she installed in her apartments in order to carve cameos—Madame de Pompadour influenced state policy and dominated fashion and the arts at Versailles for almost twenty years.

With the idyllic *Venus Consoling Love*, Boucher flattered his patron by portraying her as the goddess of love (see Figure **26.1**). Surrounded by attentive doves and cupids, the nubile Venus relaxes on a bed of sumptuous rose and blue satin robes nestled in a bower of leafy trees and windswept grasses. Boucher delighted in sensuous contrasts of flesh, fabric, feathers, and flowers. His girlish women, with their unnaturally tiny feet, rosebud-pink nipples, and wistful glances, were coy symbols of erotic pleasure.

Boucher designed sets and costumes for the Royal Opera and motifs for tapestries and porcelains. From the Sèvres porcelain factory, located near Paris and founded by Madame de Pompadour, came magnificent porcelains ornamented with gilded wreaths, arabesque cartouches, and playful cupids floating on fleecy clouds (Figure **26.6**). Outside France, as well, in Germany and Austria, porcelain figurines of shepherds and shepherdesses advertised the eighteenth-century enthusiasm for the pastoral life.

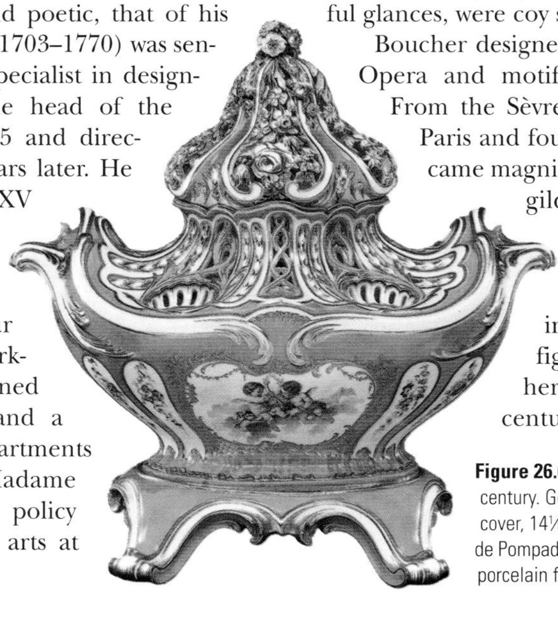

Figure 26.6 Sèvres porcelain potpourri vase, mid-eighteenth century. Gondola-shaped body, scrolled handles, four-lobed cover, 14⅛ × 14½ × 8 in. This vase, purchased by Madame de Pompadour, is one of the finest products of the Sèvres porcelain factory, which she sponsored and patronized.

Vigée-Lebrun

Fashion and fashionableness—public expressions of self-conscious materialism—were major themes of Rococo art. Marie-Louise-Elisabeth Vigée-Lebrun (1775–1842), one of only four women elected to the Royal Academy, produced refined portrait paintings for an almost exclusively female clientele. The favorite painter of Queen Marie Antoinette, she produced some 800 paintings in the course of her career. Most of these were glamorous likenesses that paid tribute to the French fashion industry: plumed headdresses and low-cut velvet gowns bedecked with lace and ribbons turned their subjects into conspicuous ornaments. (The size of women's billowing skirts required them to turn sideways in order to pass through an open door.)

Vigée-Lebrun's portrait of Marie Antoinette and her children (Figure **26.7**) is no exception. However, the elegant formality of the aristocratic portrait is humanized here by the presence of the queen's sweet-faced eldest daughter (at her right), the lively baby on her lap, and her son Louis-Joseph, who points to the empty cradle—drawing attention to the recent death of the queen's youngest child. In this painting, the artist casts Marie Antoinette in a manner reminiscent of the allegorical figure of Abundance; she is the embodiment of motherhood—a role designed, perhaps, to offset her public image of royal extravagance.

In response to the upper-class infatuation with pastoral and idyllic themes, Vigée-Lebrun also painted portraits of more modestly dressed women in muslin skirts and straw hats. Unlike Boucher, she did not cast her subjects as goddesses, but imparted to them a chic sweetness and artless simplicity. These talents earned her the equivalent of over $200,000 a year and allowed her an independence uncommon among eighteenth-century women.

Fragonard

Jean-Honoré Fragonard (1732–1806), the last of the great Rococo artists, was the undisputed master of translating the art of seduction into paint. Working shortly before the French Revolution, he captured the pastimes of a waning aristocracy, especially the pleasures of courtship and flirtation. In 1766, a wealthy aristocrat, the Baron of Saint Julien, commissioned Fragonard to paint a scene that showed his mistress seated on a swing being pushed by a friendly clergyman. *The Swing* depicts the frivolous encounter, which takes place in a garden bower filled with frothy trees, Classical statuary, and delicate light. The young woman, dressed in yards of satin and lace, kicks her tiny shoe into the air in the direction of a statue of Cupid, while her lover, hiding in the bushes below, peers delightedly beneath her billowing skirts (Figure **26.8**). Whether or not the young lady is aware of her lover's presence, her coy gesture and the irreverent *ménage à trois* (lover, mistress, and cleric) contribute to a theme of erotic intrigue common to popular comic operas and pornographic novels—the latter of which developed as a genre in eighteenth-century France. Although Fragonard immortalized the union of wealth, privilege, and pleasure enjoyed by the upper classes of the eighteenth century, he captured a spirit of sensuous abandon that has easily outlived the particulars of time, place, and social class.

Figure 26.7 MARIE-LOUISE-ELISABETH VIGÉE-LEBRUN, *Queen Marie Antoinette and Her Children*, 1787. Oil on canvas, 108¼ × 84⅝ in. The artist's travels in the Low Countries allowed her to study the works of Rubens and van Dyck, whose painterly style she greatly admired.

Figure 26.8 JEAN-HONORÉ FRAGONARD, *The Swing*, 1768–1769. Oil on canvas, 32 × 25½ in. Cupid, depicted as a watchful garden sculpture (on the left), reacts to the amorous flirtations below by coyly putting his finger to his lips. Fragonard's deft brushstrokes render the surrounding foliage in delicate tones of gold, green, and blue.

Rococo Sculpture

The finest examples of eighteenth-century sculpture are small in scale, intimate in mood, and almost entirely lacking in dramatic urgency and religious fervor. Intended for the boudoir or the drawing room, Rococo sculpture usually depicted elegant dancers, wooing couples, or other lighthearted subjects. The French sculptor Claude Michel, known as Clodion (1738–1814), who worked almost exclusively for private patrons, was among the favorite Rococo artists of the late eighteenth century. His *Intoxication of Wine* revived a Classical theme—a celebration honoring Dionysus, the Greek god of wine and fertility (Figure **26.9**). Flushed with wine and revelry, the **satyr** (a semibestial woodland creature symbolic of Dionysus) wildly embraces a **bacchante**, an attendant of Dionysus. Clodion made the piece in terracotta, a clay medium that requires rapid modeling, thus inviting the artist to capture a sense of spontaneity.

Figure 26.9 CLODION (Claude Michel), *The Intoxication of Wine*, ca. 1775. Terracotta, height 23¼ in.

Rococo painters sought similar effects through the use of loose and rapid brushstrokes and by sketching with pastels. The expressive impact of *The Intoxication of Wine* belies its tiny size—it is just under 2 feet high.

Rococo Music

By the middle of the eighteenth century, the Rococo (or *galant*) style began to challenge the popularity of Bach and Handel. Rococo composers abandoned the intricate counterpoint and dense textures of the Baroque in favor of light and graceful melodies organized into short, distinct phrases. As with Rococo art, Rococo music was delicate in effect, thin in texture, and natural in feeling. These qualities graced the works of the French composer François Couperin (1668–1733).

Couperin, a contemporary of Bach, wrote in both the Baroque and Rococo styles, as did many composers of the early eighteenth century. In 1716, Couperin published one of the most important musical treatises of the period,

Figure 26.10 JEAN-BAPTISTE GREUZE, *Village Betrothal*, 1761. Oil on canvas, 3 ft. × 3 ft. 10½ in.

The Art of Playing the Clavecin, which offers precise instructions for keyboard fingering and for the execution of musical ornaments known as *agréments*. The Rococo preference for intimate forms of expression cast in miniature is reflected in Couperin's suites for harpsichord (in French, *clavecin*). The individual sections of these suites bear playful titles based on women's names, parlor games, or human moods or attributes, such as Languor, Coquetry, and Jealousy. "Le Croc-en-jambe" (*donner un croc-en-jambe* means "to trip up" or "to play a dirty trick"), for example, is itself a tripping, lighthearted piece. Couperin's suites were written for solo instruments or for orchestral ensembles that accompanied such dances as the courante, the minuet, and the sarabande, all of which were performed in fashionable eighteenth-century *salons*. Embroidered with florid *agréments*, Couperin's music shares the lighthearted spirit and fragile elegance of the Rococo style in the visual arts.

Eighteenth-Century Genre Painting

Many of the *philosophes* found the works of Boucher, Clodion, and other Rococo artists intellectually trivial and morally degenerate. Diderot, for example, denounced

See Music Listening Selections at end of chapter.

Rococo boudoir imagery and demanded an art that made "virtue attractive and vice odious." He argued that art should seek "to move, to educate, to improve us, and to induce us to virtue." Artists favored by rationalist critics like Diderot avoided the indulgent themes and frivolous diversions of the Rococo. They focused instead on scenes of everyday life and behavior among the middle and lower classes. Genre painting, introduced earlier (in our treatment of Bruegel; see chapter 19), reflected the growing interest in middle-class tastes and values, as well as the popular fascination with the "modern moral subjects" that dominated the contemporary novel, the journal, and the theater.

Greuze

Jean-Baptiste Greuze (1725–1805), Diderot's favorite artist, exalted the natural virtues of ordinary people. His genre paintings brought to life moralizing subjects: *The Father Reading the Bible to His Children, The Well-Beloved Mother*, and *The Effects of Drunkenness*. In the manner of Hogarth (whose works he admired), Greuze chose engaging narratives that illustrated an unfolding story. With their obsessive attention to realistic detail and their intimate treatment of human vice and virtue, Greuze's canvases had much in common with the popular novels of the time.

Greuze's *Village Betrothal* (Figure **26.10**) of 1761 could easily have been an illustration of a scene from one of these novels or a play. It tells the story of an impending marriage among hardworking, simple-living rustics: the father, who has just given over the dowry to the humble groom, blesses the couple; the mother laments losing a daughter; while the other members of the household, including the hen and chicks (possibly a symbol of the couple's prospective progeny), look on approvingly. Greuze shunned the intellectualism of Poussin, the sensuality of Fragonard, and the satirical acrimony of Hogarth. His melodramatic representations appealed to common emotion and sentiment.

Understandably, they were among the most popular artworks of the eighteenth and nineteenth centuries.

Chardin

The art of Greuze's contemporary, Jean-Baptiste-Siméon Chardin (1699–1779), was less openly sentimental. He painted humble still lifes and genre scenes showing nurses, governesses, and kitchen maids at work (Figure **26.11**). Unlike Greuze, who illustrated his moral tales as literally as possible, Chardin avoided explicit moralizing and

Figure 26.11 JEAN-BAPTISTE-SIMÉON CHARDIN, *The Kitchen Maid*, 1738. Oil on canvas, 18⅛ × 14¾ in.

anecdotal themes. Yet Chardin's paintings bear a deep concern for commonplace humanity, and they convey an implicit message—that of the ennobling dignity of work and the virtues of domesticity. The forthright qualities of Chardin's subjects are echoed in his style: his figures are simple and monumental, and his compositions reveal an uncanny sense of balance reminiscent of the works of de Hooch and Vermeer. Each object seems to assume its proper and predestined place in the composition. Executed in mellow, creamy tones, Chardin's paintings evoke a mood of gentility and gravity.

Greuze and Chardin brought painting out of the drawing room and into the kitchen. Their canvases were in such high demand that they were sold widely in engraved copies. Ironically, while Chardin's subjects were humble and commonplace, his patrons were often bankers, foreign ambassadors, and royalty itself—Louis XV owned at least two of Chardin's paintings.

Not all eighteenth-century genre paintings contained the unstated moral meanings found in Chardin's works. Some, like the study of a man scraping chocolate by an

anonymous Spanish artist (Figure **26.12**), offer an unidealized record of common labor. Kneeling before a heated grinding stone (introduced into Spain from the Americas), a young man scrapes a large slab of chocolate, a luxury brought from the Americas to Europe in the sixteenth century. His efforts will produce patties of chocolate as seen in the foreground, as well as a grated chocolate paste (contained in the large bowl) that was the main ingredient for hot chocolate—a favorite drink among all social classes in Europe.

Figure 26.12 Anonymous, *A Man Scraping Chocolate*, Spain, ca. 1680–1780. Oil on canvas, 41 × 28 in. The *metate*, a type of grinding stone, was used by natives of Mexico and Guatemala to grind corn and chocolate. Like chocolate itself, it was brought to Europe by Spanish conquistadors.

Eighteenth-Century Neoclassicism

By mid-century, yet another style came to dominate the arts: Neoclassicism—the self-conscious revival of Greco-Roman culture—belonged to a tradition that stretched from the Early Renaissance through the age of Louis XIV. During the seventeenth century, Poussin and other artists of the European academies (see chapter 21) had resurrected the Classical ideals of clarity, simplicity, balance, and restraint, as configured in the Grand Manner of Raphael and other High Renaissance masters. During the eighteenth century, however, the long-standing respect for antiquity was infused by an important new development: the scientific study of Classical ruins.

In 1738, the king of Naples sponsored the first archeological excavations at Herculaneum, one of the two Roman cities in southern Italy buried under volcanic ash by the eruption of Mount Vesuvius in 79 C.E. The excavations at Pompeii would take place in 1748. These enterprises,

followed by European archeological expeditions to Greece and Asia Minor in 1750, inspired scholars to assemble vast collections of Greek and Roman artifacts (Figure **26.13**). Both the Louvre and the Vatican became museum repositories for the treasures of these expeditions, now available to artists, antiquarians, and the general public. For the first time in history, one was able to make clear distinctions between the artifacts of Greece and those of Rome. The result was a more archeologically correct Neoclassicism than any that had previously existed.

Winckelmann

Shortly after the first English expeditions to Athens, the German scholar Johann Joachim Winckelmann (1717–1768) began to study Greek and Roman antiquities. He published an eloquent assessment of these objects in a magnificently illustrated *History of Ancient Art* (1764). These and other of Winckelmann's texts offered a critical analysis of ancient art objects. Widely circulated, they

Figure 26.13 GIOVANNI PAOLO PANINI, *Gallery of Ancient Rome*, 1758. Oil on canvas, 7 ft. 7 in. × 9 ft. 1⅓ in. Art collecting paralleled the rise of the academies in the seventeenth century. In the eighteenth century, Classical antiquities and depictions of famous Classical monuments were found in picture galleries and private collections, alongside paintings by the old masters, copies after such works (note the *Laocoön* on the right), and portable examples of contemporary art.

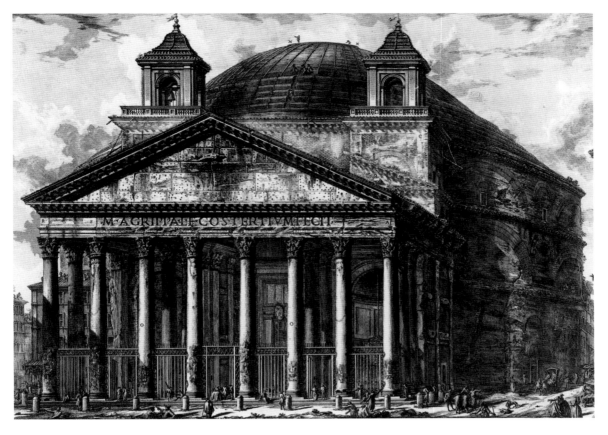

Figure 26.14 GIOVANNI BATTISTA PIRANESI, *The Pantheon*, from *Views of Rome*, ca. 1748–1778. Etching, 21⅝ × 30¼ in. The towers flanking the portico, which were added in the seventeenth century when the Pantheon functioned as a church, have since been removed.

established Winckelmann as the "father of modern art historical scholarship."

Although Winckelmann himself never visited Greece, he was infatuated with Hellenic and Hellenistic sculpture. He argued that artists of his time could become great only by imitating the ancient Greeks, in whose best works he discovered "a noble simplicity and a quiet grandeur." Of his favorite ancient statue, the *Apollo Belvedere* (see Figures 5.32 and 26.16, left), he proclaimed, "In the presence of this miracle of art, I forget the whole universe and my soul acquires a loftiness appropriate to its dignity." Winckelmann's reverence for antiquity typified the eighteenth-century attitude toward Classicism as a vehicle for the elevation of human consciousness. Here, finally, was the ideal mode of expression for the Enlightenment paradigm of reason, clarity, and order—a style that equated beauty with goodness, virtue, and truth. Winckelmann's publications became an inspiration for artists and aesthetes all over Europe. In Britain, the painter Sir Joshua Reynolds (1723–1792), founder of the Royal Academy of Arts in London, lectured on the Grand Manner; his *Discourses* were translated into French, German, and Italian. The lofty vision of a style that captured the nobility and dignity of the Greco-Roman past fired the imagination of intellectuals across Western Europe and America.

Piranesi

Since Renaissance times, Rome had been a favorite destination for educated tourists and artists. But during the eighteenth century, Rome and its monuments came under new scrutiny. Architects studied the monuments of antiquity, and artists made topographic sketches, often reproduced in copper engravings that were sold cheaply—in the manner of modern-day postcards. In 1740, the Venetian architect and engineer Giovanni Battista Piranesi (1720–1778) established himself in Rome as a printmaker. Piranesi's engravings of Rome were widely bought and appreciated (see Figure 20.14), while his studies of Roman monuments, with their precisely rendered technical details and inscriptions, exerted considerable influence on French and English architects of his time (Figure **26.14**). Piranesi's later works—nightmarish visions of dungeons inspired by the Roman sewer system—abandoned all Classical canons of objectivity and emotional restraint. Nevertheless, with European artists more eager than ever to rediscover antiquity through the careful study of its remains, the Neoclassical revival was underway.

Neoclassical Architecture

The Classical revival of the eighteenth century was unique in its accuracy of detail and its purity of design. Neoclassical architects made careful distinctions between Greek and Roman buildings and between the various Renaissance and post-Renaissance styles modeled on antiquity. They took inspiration from simple geometric shapes—spheres, cubes, and cylinders—to provide a new, more abstract and austere Classicism. They rejected the illusionistic theatricality of the Baroque style with its broken pediments, cartouches, and ornamental devices. They also turned their backs on the stucco foliage, cherubic angels, and "wedding-cake" fantasies of the Rococo. The ideal Neoclassical exterior was free of frivolous ornamentation, while its interior consisted of clean and rectilinear walls, soberly accented with engaged columns or pilasters, geometric motifs, and shallow niches that might house copies of antique statuary (see Figure 26.16).

The leading French Neoclassical architect, Jacques-Germain Soufflot (1713–1780), traveled to Italy and Greece to study ancient monuments. Commissioned by Louis XV to design the church of Sainte-Geneviève, honoring the patron saint of Paris (Figure **26.15**), Soufflot took inspiration from the Pantheon, which he had studied firsthand as a student at the French Academy in Rome. While the portico of the church is indebted to the Pantheon, its strict central plan, with four shallow domes covering each of the arms, followed an architectural tradition perfected by Bramante and Michelangelo at Saint Peter's in Rome. Saint-Geneviève's massive dome, supported entirely on pillars, rises over the crossing in a manner that looks back to Saint Paul's in London (see Figure 22.3).

Figure 26.15 JACQUES-GERMAIN SOUFFLOT, Sainte-Geneviève (renamed the "Panthéon" during the French Revolution), Paris, 1757–1792.

Figure 26.16 ROBERT ADAM, Marble Hall, Kedleston Hall, Derbyshire, England, 1763–1777. (Note copy of the *Apollo Belvedere* in niche at left.)

Clearly, Soufflot did not slavishly imitate any single landmark structure; rather, he selected specific features from some of history's greatest architectural monuments and combined them with clarity and reserve. During the French Revolution, when radicals rededicated many churches as "temples of reason," Sainte-Geneviève was renamed "the Panthéon". Inspired by the building that once honored the Roman gods, it would entomb the "gods" of the Enlightenment, including Voltaire and Rousseau.

Some of the purest examples of the Classical revival are found in late eighteenth-century English country houses. The interiors of these sprawling symbols of wealth and prestige reflect close attention to archeological drawings of Greek and Roman antiquities. Kedleston Hall in Derbyshire, England, designed by the Scottish architect Robert Adam (1728–1792), is a pristine synthesis of geometric shapes and Greco-Roman motifs (Figure **26.16**). In such estates as this, the Neoclassical spirit touched

Figure 26.17 ANTONIO CANOVA, *Pauline Borghese as Venus*, 1808. Marble, life-sized. Canova's idealized portrait of Napoleon's sister was intended for private viewing rather than for public display. While depicted here as a goddess, Pauline was notorious for her numerous illicit affairs and her self-indulgent habits—she was said to insist on being carried to the bath by her servants.

everything from sculpture (Figure **26.17**) and furniture to tea services and tableware. Among the most popular items of the day were the ceramics of the English potter Josiah Wedgwood (1730–1795). Wedgwood's wares were modeled on Greek and Roman vases and embellished with finely applied, molded white clay surface designs (Figure **26.18**).

The austerity and dignity of Neoclassicism made it the ideal style for public monuments and offices of state. In Paris, Berlin, and Washington, D.C., Neoclassical architects borrowed Greek and Roman temple designs for public and private buildings, especially for banks, where the modern-day gods of money and materialism replaced the ancient deities. In some instances (such as Soufflot's Panthéon), the spirit of revival produced daring architectural hybrids. In England, for instance, the Scottish architect James Gibbs (1682–1754) designed churches that combined a Classical portico with a Gothic spire (Figure **26.19**). This scheme, which united the Baroque love of dramatic contrast with the Neoclassical rule of perfect symmetry,

Figure 26.18 WEDGWOOD & SONS, copy of The Portland Vase (No. 7), ca. 1790. Blue-black jasperware, 10 × 7⅓ in. The Portland Vase is a Roman cameo glass vase that dates from the first century B.C.E. Excavated in the sixteenth century, it came into the hands of William Cavendish-Bentinck, the third duke of Portland, in the late eighteenth century, at which time it became an inspiration to makers of glass and porcelain wares. The identity of the reclining woman is much disputed; she has been identified as Ariadne, as Hecuba, and as Octavia, the wife of Mark Anthony.

Figure 26.19 JAMES GIBBS, Saint Martin-in-the-Fields, London, 1721–1726.

became extremely popular in America, primarily in the Congregational churches built across New England.

Neoclassicism in America

A tour of the city of Washington in the District of Columbia will convince any student of the impact of Neoclassicism on the architecture of the United States. The Neoclassical movement in America did not originate, however, in the capital city, whose major buildings date only from the nineteenth century, but rather among the founding fathers. One of the most passionate devotees of Greco-Roman art and life was the Virginia lawyer and statesman Thomas Jefferson (1743–1826), introduced in chapter 24. Farmer, linguist, educator, inventor, self-taught architect, musician, and politician, the man who served as third president of the United States was an eighteenth-century *uomo universale* (see Figure 24.3). Jefferson was a student of ancient and Renaissance treatises on architecture and an impassioned apostle of Neoclassicism. He understood that a nation's buildings not only create a national image, but also affect social conduct and human aspiration. In 1786, he designed the Virginia State Capitol, using as his model the ancient Roman Maison Carrée (see Figure 26.30).

Jefferson's tightly organized and geometrically correct plan for the campus of the University of Virginia reflects

MAKING CONNECTIONS

For the design of his country estate at Monticello (near Charlottesville, Virginia), and for the University of Virginia, America's first state university, Jefferson drew on that most admired of all Roman imperial monuments, the Pantheon (Figure **26.20**). In the Rotunda, which housed the original university library, he constructed the ancient Roman temple at two-thirds of its original size (Figure **26.21**). Considerably smaller than Soufflot's "Panthéon," the Rotunda is also purer

in form. It is faithful to the design of the Roman temple, and is unadorned, except for its Corinthian (rather than Doric) columns.

Figure 26.20 The Pantheon, Rome, ca. 118–125 C.E.

Figure 26.21 Thomas Jefferson, the Rotunda, University of Virginia, Charlottesville, Virginia, 1822–1826.

Figure 26.22 Great Seal of the United States.

the basic sympathy between Neoclassical design and the rationalist ideals of the Enlightenment. The "academical village," as Jefferson described it, was a community of the free-thinking elite—exclusively white, wealthy, and male—yet it provided both a physical and a spiritual model for nonsectarian education in the United States.

The young American nation drew on the heritage of the ancients (and especially the history of the Roman Republic) to symbolize its newly forged commitment to the ideals of liberty and equality. The leaders of the American Revolution regarded themselves as descendants of ancient Roman heroes. Like the humanists of Renaissance Italy, some even adopted Latin names. On the Great Seal of the United States, the Latin phrase "E pluribus unum" ("Out of many, one") and the bundle of arrows in the grasp of the American eagle (suggesting the Roman *fasces*: a bundle of rods surrounding an ax—the ancient symbol for power and authority) identified America as self-styled heir to republican Rome (Figure **26.22**).

Neoclassical Sculpture

Neoclassical sculptors heeded the Enlightenment call for an art that perpetuated the memory of illustrious men. Jean-Antoine Houdon (1741–1828), the leading portrait sculptor of Europe, immortalized in stone the features of his contemporaries. Reviving a tradition that had reached its high-water mark among the ancient Romans, Houdon's portrait busts met the popular demand for achieving a familiar likeness. Houdon had a special talent for catching characteristic gestures and expressions: the aging Voltaire, for example, addresses us with a grim and knowing smile (see Figure 25.4). While visiting America, Houdon carved portraits of Jefferson (see Figure 24.3), Franklin, and other "virtuous men" of the republic. His life-sized statue of George Washington renders the first president of the United States as country gentleman and eminent states-man (Figure **26.23**). Resting his hand on a columnar *fasces*, the poised but slightly potbellied Washington recalls (how-ever faintly) the monumental dignity of the Greek gods and the Roman emperors.

Figure 26.23 JEAN-ANTOINE HOUDON, *George Washington*, 1786–1796. Marble, life-size.

While Houdon invested Neoclassicism with a strong taste for Realism, most of his contemporaries preferred to idealize the human form. Such was the case with the Italian-born sculptor Antonio Canova (1757–1822). Considered the greatest sculptor of his generation, he received frequent commissions for portraits and multi-figured burial tombs. In 1802, Napoleon invited Canova to Paris, where the artist glorified the French ruler in a colossal free-standing nude image of Napoleon as Mars, the Roman god of war. Napoleon also commissioned Canova to portray his sister Pauline Borghese. Canova's life-sized marble portrait of Pauline is a sublime example of Neoclassical refinement and restraint (see Figure 26.17). Canova casts Pauline in the guise of a reclining Venus. Perfectly proportioned, she shares the flawless elegance of Classical statuary and Wedgwood reliefs. In contrast to the vigorously carved surfaces of Baroque sculpture (recall, for instance, Bernini's *Ecstasy of Saint Teresa*, Figure 20.3), Canova's figure is smooth and neutral—even stark. A comparison of Canova's *Pauline Borghese as Venus* with Clodion's *Intoxication of Wine* (see Figure 26.9) is also revealing: both depend on Classical themes and models, but whereas Clodion's piece is intimate, sensuous, and spontaneous, Canova's seems remote, controlled, and reserved. Its aesthetic distance is intensified by the ghostlike whiteness of the figure and its "blank" eyes—eighteenth-century sculptors were unaware that Classical artists painted parts of their statues to make them look more lifelike.

Neoclassical Painting and Politics: The Art of David

During the last decades of the eighteenth century, as the tides of revolution began to engulf the indulgent lifestyles of the French aristocracy, the Rococo style gave way to a sober new approach to picture-making. The pioneer of this style was the French artist Jacques-Louis David (1748–1825). David's early canvases were executed in the Rococo style of his teacher and distant cousin, Boucher. But after winning the coveted Prix de Rome, which took him to study in the foremost city of antiquity, David found his place among the Neoclassicists (see Figures 24.1 and 25.9). In 1784 he completed one of the most influential paintings of the late eighteenth century: *The Oath of the Horatii* (Figure **26.24**). The piece was commissioned by the French king some five years before the outbreak of the revolution; ironically, however, it would become a symbol of the very spirit that toppled the royal crown.

Figure 26.24 JACQUES-LOUIS DAVID, *The Oath of the Horatii*, 1784. Oil on canvas, 10 ft. 10 in. × 14 ft. One of the Horatii sisters, pictured at the right, had been engaged to marry a Curati warrior. Legend has it that when her brother returned triumphant and found her weeping over her lover's demise, he stabbed her to death.

Figure 26.25 JACQUES-LOUIS DAVID, *The Death of Socrates*, 1787. Oil on canvas, 4 ft. 3 in. × 6 ft. 5¼ in.

The Oath of the Horatii illustrates a dramatic event recorded in the first book of Livy's *History of Rome*: amidst a military contest for control of central Italy, the three sons of Horatius Proclus volunteer to meet the champions of the treacherous Curatii family in a win-or-die sword battle that will determine the future of Rome. Two of the Horatii brothers die in combat, but the third returns victorious, having killed all three of his opponents. In France, this historic legend, symbolic of the spirit of patriotism leading up to the French Revolution, became especially popular as the subject of a play by the French dramatist Pierre Corneille (1606–1684). David captured the spirit of the story in a single potent image: resolved to pursue their destiny as defenders of liberty, the Horatii lift their arms in a dramatic military salute. If David's subject matter was revolutionary, so was his style: geometric order, hard-edged contours, and somber colors—features that recalled the art of David's favorite artist, Poussin—replaced the sensuous curves, amorphous forms, and pastel tones of Rococo art. Bathed in golden light, the heroic figures stand along the strict horizontal line of the picture plane. The figure of the warrior on the far left forms a rigid triangle that is subtly repeated throughout the composition—in the arches of the colonnade, for instance, and in the group of grieving women. Austere, realistic, and Neoclassically precise—witness the archeologically correct helmets, sandals,

and swords—the *Oath* exalted sober simplicity and serious drama over and above the playful and luxuriant spirit of the Rococo.

David's painting was an immediate success: people lined up to see it while it hung in the artist's studio in Rome, and the city of Paris received it enthusiastically when it arrived there in 1785. The huge canvas (over 10 by 14 feet) came to be perceived as a clear denunciation of aristocratic pastimes. It proclaimed the importance of reason and the intellect above feeling and sentiment, and it defended the ideals of male heroism and self-sacrifice in the interest of one's country.

Three years after painting *The Oath of the Horatii*, David conceived the smaller but equally popular *Death of Socrates* (Figure **26.25**). The scene is a fifth-century B.C.E. Athenian prison. It is the moment before Socrates, the father of Greek philosophy, drinks the fatal hemlock. Surrounding Socrates are his students and friends, posed in various expressions of lament, while the apostle of reason himself—illuminated in the style of Caravaggio—rhetorically lifts his hand to heaven. Clarity and intellectual control dominate the composition: figures and objects are arranged as if plotted on a grid of lines horizontal and vertical to the picture plane. This ideal geometry, a metaphor for the ordering function of reason, complements the grave and noble message of the painting: reason

Ingres' *Apotheosis of Homer*

1 Virgil
2 Raphael
3 Sappho
4 Euripides
5 Demosthenes
6 Sophocles
7 Herodotus
8 Orpheus
9 Pindar
10 Hesiod
11 Plato
12 Socrates
13 Pericles
14 Michelangelo
15 Aristotle
16 Aristarchus
17 Alexander the Great
18 Dante
19 Iliad
20 Odyssey
21 Aesop
22 Shakespeare
23 La Fontaine
24 Tasso
25 Mozart
26 Poussin
27 Corneille
28 Racine
29 Molière
30 Glück
31 Apelles
32 Phidias

Figure 26.26 JEAN-AUGUSTE-DOMINIQUE INGRES, *The Apotheosis of Homer*, 1827. Oil on canvas, 12 ft. 8 in. × 16 ft. 10¾ in.

Surrounding Homer, the literary giant of antiquity, is an academic assembly that includes Plato, Dante, Raphael, Poussin, Racine, and other Western "luminaries" (thirty-two of whom are identified opposite). Ingres' iconic hero occupies the apex of the compositional pyramid. At his feet are the allegorical figures of his epics, the *Iliad* and the *Odyssey*, while behind him is a Neoclassical temple façade, not unlike that of "La Madeleine," which was then under construction in Paris (see Figure 26.29). Both in composition and in conception, the *Apotheosis* looks back to Raphael (see *The School of Athens*, Figure 17.27), but Ingres has brought self-conscious rigor to his application of the Neoclassical principles of clarity and symmetry.

guides human beings to live and, if need be, to die for their moral principles. In *The Death of Socrates*, as in *The Oath of the Horatii*, David put Neoclassicism at the service of a morality based on Greco-Roman Stoicism, self-sacrifice, and stern patriotism.

Ingres and Academic Neoclassicism

David's most talented pupil was Jean-Auguste-Dominique Ingres (1780–1867). The son of an artist–craftsman, Ingres rose to fame with his polished depictions of Classical history and mythology and with his accomplished portraits of middle- and upper-class patrons. He spent much of his career in Italy, where he came to prize (as he himself admitted) "Raphael, his century, the ancients, and above all the divine Greeks." Ingres shunned the weighty Realism of David in favor of the purity of line he admired in Greek vase-painting, in the published drawings of the newly unearthed Classical artifacts, and in late eighteenth-century engraved illustrations for the works of Homer and Hesiod.

Commissioned to paint a ceiling mural for the Louvre, Ingres produced a visual testament to Europe's esteem for its Classical heritage. The monumental *Apotheosis of Homer* shows the ancient Greek bard enthroned amidst forty-six notables of Classical and modern times; Homer is "deified" with a laurel crown bestowed by the winged figure of Victory (see LOOKING INTO, Figure **26.26**).

Late in his career, Ingres turned his nostalgia for the past to more exotic themes. Intrigued, for instance, by Turkish culture (publicized by Napoleon's campaigns in both Syria and North Africa), he painted languorous harem women, such as *La Grande Odalisque* (Figure **26.27**). A revisualization of both Titian's *Venus of Urbino* (see Figure 17.39) and Canova's *Pauline Borghese as Venus* (see Figure 26.17), Ingres' nude turns in a self-consciously seductive manner both away from and toward the beholder. The firm contours and polished brush-strokes are typically Neoclassical, but Ingres rejected Neoclassical canons of proportion by elongating the limbs in the tradition of the Italian Mannerists (see, for instance, Figure 20.5). The "incorrect" anatomy of the figure drew strong criticism from Ingres' contemporaries, who claimed that his subject had three too many vertebrae. Nevertheless (or perhaps because of its bold departures from both real and ideal norms), *La Grande Odalisque* remains one of the most arresting images of womanhood in Western art.

Kauffmann and Academic Neoclassicism

Well into the eighteenth century, the painting of large-scale historical, mythological, and religious subjects was dominated by male artists. Talented women, such as Maria van Oosterwyck (see Figure 23.7) and Judith Leyster (see Figure 23.15), confined themselves to still-life subjects and portrait painting, genres considered of lesser importance among academicians. Nevertheless, the Italian-trained Angelica Kauffmann (1741–1807),

Figure 26.27 JEAN-AUGUSTE-DOMINIQUE INGRES, *La Grande Odalisque*, 1814. Oil on canvas, 2 ft. 11¼ in. × 5 ft. 3¾ in. While criticized for depriving his female nudes of "bone and muscle," Ingres was celebrated for the exquisite perfection of his drawing, his subtle modeling, and his appreciation of antiquity. He was among the first artists to introduce exotic details of the East—the peacock fan, inlaid footstool, and embroidered turban—into his paintings.

Figure 26.28 ANGELICA KAUFFMANN, *Zeuxis Selecting Models for His Painting of Helen of Troy*, ca. 1765. Oil on canvas, 31 × 44 in. The only female painter of her time to produce historical narratives, Kauffmann was commissioned to decorate Saint Paul's in London and the walls of country houses designed by Robert Adam. Esteemed by artists and writers throughout Europe, she was a founding member of Britain's Royal Academy of Arts.

like Artemisia Gentileschi (see Figure 20.10), established a glowing reputation as a skilled painter of historical subjects. Kauffmann, the daughter of a Swiss artist who schooled her in music, history, and the visual arts, was one of the founding members of England's Royal Academy of Arts, to which she contributed many critically successful paintings based on Classical subjects. Commissioned to paint portrait likenesses of her contemporaries (including Winckelmann) during her sojourns in Rome, Florence, and London, she also became one of the most sought-after and highly paid portrait painters of her day.

Kauffmann's history subjects, many of which served as models for wall and ceiling designs in the Neoclassical interiors of Robert Adam (see Figure 26.16), reveal her familiarity with the figure types found in the wall-paintings of Pompeii and Herculaneum, her love of lyrical linear compositions, and her skillful, fluent brushwork. These features are especially apparent in the painting *Zeuxis Selecting Models for His Painting of Helen of Troy* (Figure **26.28**), in which the Greek artist is shown (as described by ancient historians) choosing the finest features of his various female models, so as to combine them in an idealized image of Helen of Troy. Kauffmann herself may have served as the model for the figure at the far right.

Neoclassicism under Napoleon

While Neoclassicism was the "official" style of the French Revolution, it soon became the vehicle of French imperialism. Under the leadership of Napoleon Bonaparte (1769–1821), the imagery of Classical Greece and republican Rome was abandoned for the more appropriate imagery of Augustan Rome. Like the Roman emperors, Napoleon used the arts to magnify his greatness. He appointed David to commemorate his military achievements, and he commissioned architects to redesign Paris in the spirit of ancient Rome. Paris became a city of straight, wide avenues and huge, impressive squares. Imaginary axes linked the Classically inspired monuments raised to honor the emperor, and older buildings were remodeled in the new Empire style.

Napoleon was also instrumental in reviving that best-known symbol of Roman imperialism: the triumphal arch. The Arc du Carrousel, which stands adjacent to

In 1806, Alexandre-Pierre Vignon (1763–1828) was commissioned to redesign the church of Saint Mary Magdalene (called "La Madeleine") as a Roman temple dedicated to the glory of the French army (Figure **26.29**). Originally dedicated to the saint, it was to become one of the monumental secular temples of Paris. Fifty-two Corinthian columns, each 66 feet tall, surround the temple, which rises on a 23-foot-high podium, like a gigantic version of the small Roman temple known as the Maison Carrée in Nîmes (Figure **26.30**). Vignon's gloomy interior—a nave crowned with three domes—falls short of reflecting the majesty of the exterior, despite his use of the Corinthian and Ionic orders in the decorative scheme.

Figure 26.29 ALEXANDRE-PIERRE VIGNON, Church of Saint Mary Magdalene ("La Madeleine"), Paris, 1807–1842. Length 350 ft., width 147 ft., height of podium 23 ft. Following the fall of Napoleon and the return of the monarchy, the Catholic king Louis XVIII rededicated the church to Mary Magdalene.

Figure 26.30 Maison Carrée, Nîmes, France, 16 B.C.E.

Figure 26.31 JEAN-FRANÇOIS THÉRÈSE CHALGRIN AND OTHERS, Arc de Triomphe, Paris, 1806–1836. Height 164 ft.

the Louvre, is faithful to its Roman model, the Arch of Constantine in Rome. And the grandest of Paris' triumphal arches, which occupies the crossing of twelve avenues at the end of the famous Avenue des Champs-Elysées (Figure **26.31**), closely resembles the Arch of Titus in the Roman Forum (see Figure 6.21). The 164-foot-high commemorative monument—which was dedicated to the French army—was larger than any arch built in ancient times. Napoleon would become one of the nineteenth century's most celebrated Romantic heroes (see chapter 28), but the monuments he commissioned for Paris were stamped unmistakably with the Classical spirit.

Eighteenth-Century Western Music

The eighteenth century was as rich in music as it was in the visual arts. Music filled the courts and concert halls, the latter as a response to a rising popular demand for public recitals. The eighteenth-century concert hall was small by modern standards. Its lights were rarely dimmed during performances and audiences were not expected to wait until the end of each piece to applaud. Often they showed their enthusiasm by applauding after a movement, insisting that it be repeated—a practice that is very much out of favor in our own time. Religious compositions were still in demand, but church music was overshadowed by the vast amounts of music composed for secular entertainment. Composers sought the patronage of wealthy aristocrats, at whose courts they often served. At the same time, they wrote music for amateur performance and for the concert hall. While opera remained the favorite vocal form, instrumental music began to free itself from religious and ceremonial functions.

During the eighteenth century, certain distinctive characteristics converged to set Western musical culture apart from that of the rest of the world. These included the idea that harmony is proper and essential to music, that a musical composition should be the original product of a single composer, and that a piece of music should be rehearsed and performed in much the same manner each time it is played. Such standards, which emphasize order and formality over spontaneity and improvisation, would come to characterize *classical* music—that is, "serious" or "art" music as distinct from the more ephemeral "popular" or "folk" music.

Classical Music

The term "classical" is also used more narrowly to describe a specific musical style that prevailed in the West between approximately 1760 and 1820. The music of this era shares the essential features of Neoclassical art: symmetry, order, and formal restraint. Unlike Neoclassical art and architecture, however, classical music had little to do with the heritage of Greece and Rome, for European composers had no surviving evidence of Greek and Roman music and, therefore, no antique musical models to imitate. Nevertheless, classical music would develop its own unique model for clarity of form and purity of design. Classical composers, most of whom came from Germany and Austria, wrote homophonic compositions with easy-to-grasp melodies, which are repeated or developed within a definitive formal structure. The liberation of melody from Baroque polyphony was anticipated by the light and graceful nature of French Rococo music (discussed earlier in this chapter).

While classical composers retained the fast/slow/fast contrasts of Baroque instrumental forms, they rid their

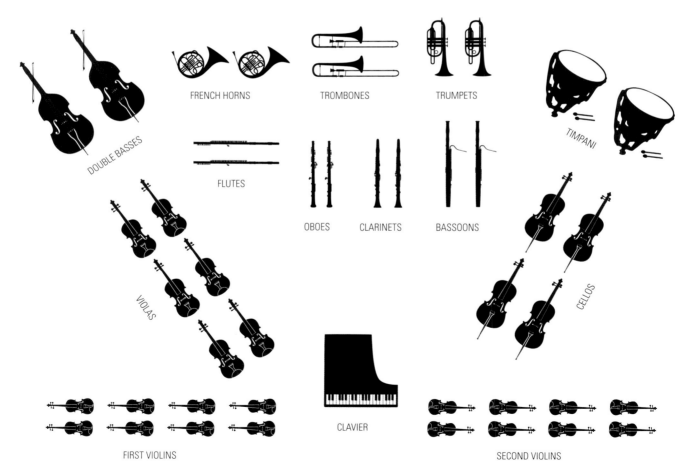

Figure 26.32 The classical symphony orchestra.

compositions of many Baroque features. They replaced, for instance, the abrupt changes from loud to soft with more gently graduated contrasts. They eliminated the unflagging rhythm and ornate embellishment of Baroque polyphony in favor of clear-cut musical phrases. While counterpoint continued to play an important role, the intricate webs of sound (as heard, for example, in Bach's fugues) gave way to a new harmonic clarity. In short, classical music developed formal attributes that reflect the Enlightenment quest for reasoned clarity and the Neoclassical commitment to balance and purity of design.

The Birth of the Symphony Orchestra

Eighteenth-century instrumental music served as secular entertainment in public theaters as well as in the *salons* of courtly residences. The most important instrumental grouping to emerge at this time was the orchestra. The eighteenth-century Bohemian composer Johann Stamitz (1717–1757), who settled in the south German town of Mannheim in the 1740s, organized what is thought to have been one of the earliest forms of the classical orchestra. It consisted of groups of related instruments, each with its own character or personality. The **strings**, made up of violins, violas, cellos, and double basses, formed the nucleus of the orchestra, since they were the most melodious and lyrical of the instrumental families. The **woodwinds**, consisting of flutes, oboes, clarinets, and bassoons, specialized in mellow harmony. The **brass** section, made up of trumpets and French horns (and, by the end of the century, trombones), added volume and resonance. Lastly, the **percussion** section, using kettledrums (also known as timpani), functioned as rhythm markers (Figure **26.32**).

Stamitz's orchestra was small by modern-day standards. It included some thirty-five pieces, many of which were still rudimentary: brass instruments lacked valves, and the clarinet was not perfected until roughly 1790. The piano, which was invented around 1720, remained until 1775 more closely related to the clavichord than to the modern grand piano. During the last quarter of the century, however, as the piano underwent technical refinement, it came to be the favorite solo instrument.

As musical instruments became more sophisticated, the orchestra, capable of an increasingly expressive and subtle range of sounds, grew in size and popularity. The eighteenth-century orchestra was led by a musician (often the composer himself) who played part of the composition on the clavier or other keyboard instrument located in the place now occupied by the conductor's podium. The string section was seated to the right and left, while the other

instruments were spread across the middle distance, in a pattern that persists to this day.

To facilitate the conductor's control over the music, the orchestra used a **score**, that is, a record of musical notation that indicates every sound to be played by each instrument. Each musical part appeared in groups of five-line staffs that enabled the conductor to "view" the composition as a whole. Separate parts were written out for each instrument as well. In the eighteenth century, both instrumentation and methods of scoring became standardized. Scores included a time signature, which indicated the number of beats per measure; a key signature, which noted the number of sharps or flats in the specified key; and abbreviations of the Italian words that indicated the dynamics of specific passages: *f* for *forte* ("loud") and *p* for *piano* ("soft"). Interpretive directions, such as *scherzando* ("sprightly") and *affettuoso* ("with feeling"), signified the intentions of the composer as to how a musical passage should be performed. All these notational devices served the principle of formality that governed eighteenth-century music and Western musical composition in general.

Classical Instrumental Compositions

Classical composers wrote music for a variety of instrumental groupings. The largest of these was the orchestral form known as the **symphony**. The Italian word *sinfonia* was used during the seventeenth century to describe various kinds of instrumental works; but by the mid-eighteenth century, the word came to mean an independent instrumental composition for full orchestra. In addition to the symphony, three other instrumental genres dominated the classical era: the **concerto**, a composition featuring one or more solo instruments and an orchestra; the **string quartet**, a piece for two violins, a viola, and a cello; and the **sonata**, a composition for an unaccompanied keyboard instrument or for another instrument with keyboard accompaniment.

Although the concerto and the sonata originated earlier (see chapter 23), they now took on a new formality. Indeed, all four instrumental forms—the symphony, the classical concerto, the string quartet, and the classical sonata—assumed the same formal structure: they were divided into three or four sections, or movements, each of which followed a specific tempo, or musical pace. The first movement was played *allegro* or in fast tempo; the second *andante* or *largo*, that is, in moderate or slow tempo; the third (usually omitted in concertos) in dance tempo (usually in three-quarter time); and the fourth again *allegro*.

For the organization of the first and last movements, classical composers used a special form known as **sonata form** (or **sonata allegro** form; Figure **26.33**). This calls for the division of the movement into three parts: the exposition, the development, and the recapitulation. In the exposition, the composer "exposes," or introduces, a theme in the "home" key, then contrasts it with a second theme in a different key. Musical effect is based on the tension of two opposing key centers. In the development, the composer moves to further contrasting keys, expanding and altering the themes stated in the exposition. Finally, in the recapitulation, the themes from the exposition are restated, both

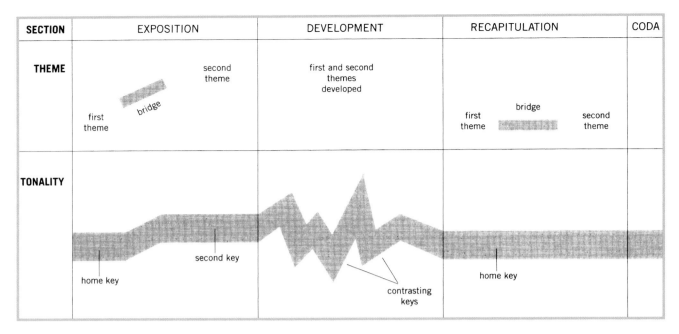

SECTION	EXPOSITION	DEVELOPMENT	RECAPITULATION	CODA
THEME	first theme bridge second theme	first and second themes developed	first theme bridge second theme	
TONALITY	home key second key	contrasting keys	home key	

Figure 26.33 Sonata form.

now in the home key, resolving the earlier tension. A **coda** ("tail") is often added as a definitive ending.

Also popular among classical composers was the form known as **theme and variations**, which might appear as an independent piece or as a musical idea within a symphony, string quartet, or sonata. As the name suggests, theme and variations features a basic musical idea that is repeated in a number of ways, that is, by changes in rhythm, harmony, melody, and so on. Already evident in Late Renaissance and Baroque music, this form was employed inventively in classical compositions that gave each variation of the theme its own identity.

Classical composers frequently deviated from sonata form, but they looked to it to provide the "rules" of musical design—the architectural guidelines, so to speak, for musical composition. Just as Neoclassical artists and writers favored clear definitions and an Aristotelian "beginning, middle, and end," so classical composers delighted in the threefold balance of the sonata form, the repetition of simple harmonies, and the crisp phrasing of bright, free-flowing melodies.

The Development of the Classical Style: Haydn

The classical style owes its development to the Austrian composer Franz Joseph Haydn (1732–1809). Of peasant birth, Haydn was recruited at the age of eight to sing in the choir of Saint Stephen's Cathedral in Vienna. As a young man, he taught music and struggled to make a living. In 1761, at the age of twenty-nine, he became musical director to the court of the powerful and wealthy Hungarian nobleman Prince Paul Anton Esterházy, who was also an accomplished musician. The magnificent Esterházy country estate (modeled on Versailles) had two theaters—one for opera and one for puppet plays—and two richly appointed concert halls. There, for almost thirty years, Haydn took charge of all aspects of musical entertainment:

he composed music, trained choristers, oversaw the repair of instruments, and rehearsed and conducted an orchestra of some twenty-five musicians. At the princely court, Haydn produced music for various instrumental groups. Tailoring his creative talents to suit special occasions and the taste of his wealthy patron, he wrote operas, oratorios, solo concertos, sonatas, overtures, and liturgical music. But his most original works were those whose forms he himself helped to develop: the classical symphony and the string quartet.

The "father of the symphony," as Haydn is often called, wrote 104 symphonies and 84 string quartets. The string quartet, a concentrated instrumental form, met the need for elite entertainment in a small room or chamber—hence the term "chamber music." Unlike the symphony, the string quartet requires close attention to the fine points of musical discourse between the instruments. Unfortunately, such works are today often performed in huge music halls, rather than in the intimate surroundings for which they were intended.

After the death of Prince Esterházy in 1790, Haydn was invited to perform in London, where he composed his last twelve symphonies. In the London symphonies, which he wrote for an orchestra of some sixty players, he explored an expanded harmonic range and a wealth of dramatic effects. For some of the symphonies he used folk melodies as themes, inventively repeating important fragments in different parts of the piece. Among the most memorable of the London compositions is the Symphony No. 94 in G Major. It is known as the *Surprise Symphony* because Haydn introduced an unexpected *fortissimo* ("very loud") instrumental crash on a weak beat in the second movement of the piece. Tradition has it that the blaring chord, occurring amidst a soft and folklike melody, was calculated to waken a drowsy audience—London concerts

See Music Listening Selections at end of chapter.

often lasted until well past midnight. It was also designed to entice them to anticipate the next jarring "surprise," which never occurs.

Haydn brought a lifetime of musical experience to his last works, and their witty phrasing and melodic effects made his symphonies enormously popular. His music was so popular, in fact, that eighteenth-century publishers often sold compositions falsely attributed to him. A celebrity in his old age, "Papa Haydn" (as he was affectionately called) was one of the first musicians to attain the status of cultural hero during his own lifetime.

The Genius of Mozart

The foremost musical genius of the eighteenth century—and, some would say, of all time—was Haydn's younger contemporary and colleague Wolfgang Amadeus Mozart (1756–1791). A child prodigy, Mozart wrote his first original composition at the age of six and his first symphony at the age of eight. His ability to sight-read, improvise, and transpose music, to identify the pitch of any sound, and to transcribe flawlessly whole compositions that he had heard only once, remains unequaled in the history of music. During his brief life, Mozart produced a total of some 650 works, including 41 symphonies, 60 sonatas, 27 piano concertos, 23 string quartets, and 20 operas. (These were catalogued and numbered in the late nineteenth century by Ludwig von Köchel, hence the "K." numbers used to identify them.)

Mozart, the son of a prominent composer, was born in Salzburg, Austria. With his father, Leopold, and his sister Nannerl, he toured Europe, performing hundreds of public and private concerts before he was thirteen (Figure **26.34**). He often performed his own pieces, particularly his piano concertos, which constitute some of his most important musical contributions. Unlike Haydn, Mozart did not invent any new forms. However, he brought to the instrumental genres of his time unparalleled melodic inventiveness. Mozart received frequent commissions for light musical entertainments performed by instrumental ensembles in the parks and gardens of Vienna. One such piece is the Serenade No. 13 in G Major, K. 525, also known as *Eine kleine Nachtmusik* (*A Little Night Music*), a work for small string orchestra. While lyrical and buoyant, it is structured (as is evident in the recorded excerpt) according to the formal divisions of sonata form: exposition, development, and recapitulation. Its adventurous shifts in melody and rhythm make it one of Mozart's most popular compositions.

Mozart brought an even broader range of musical invention to his symphonies, three of which (nos. 39, 40, and 41; K. 543, K. 550, and K. 551) were written during a six-week period in 1788. These pieces remain among the most eloquent examples of the classical symphonic form. They give substance to Mozart's claim that music "must never offend the ear, but must please the hearer, in other words, must never cease to be *music*."

After leaving the service of the archbishop of Salzburg in 1781, Mozart sought appointments in the aristocratic courts of Europe, but he never received adequate patronage and eventually had difficulty supporting himself and his family. Throughout his life, he was excessively concerned with money. When he died in Vienna at the age of thirty-six, he was, despite the public success of many of his works, deep in debt.*

During the last six years of his life, Mozart wrote four of his finest operas, receiving commissions for all but the first. These works are among the best loved in the Western operatic repertory: *Le nozze di Figaro* (*The Marriage of Figaro*, 1786), *Don Giovanni* (1787), *Così fan tutte* (*Thus Do All Women*, 1790), and *Die Zauberflöte* (*The Magic Flute*, 1791).

The *Marriage of Figaro* is an example of **opera buffa**, a type of comic opera that developed in Italy during the eighteenth century as a short, humorous entertainment. Formerly inserted between the acts of a serious play or opera, these **intermezzos** made use of stock comic types such as the clever servant, the miser, and the fool. Like the playwright Molière (see chapter 21), Mozart transformed the stereotyped characters of the Italian *opera buffa* into believable, sympathetic personalities—psychologically complex and often comical.

Sharing Molière's view that wealth and status are accidents of fortune and may have little to do with personal worth, Mozart used his characters to level a pointed attack at the decadence of the European aristocracy. The central intrigue of *Figaro*, for example, involves the maid Susanna and her fiancé, the valet Figaro, in a plot to outwit their master, Count Almaviva, who seeks to seduce Susanna. In an era dominated by aristocratic privilege, and one that still honored the feudal claim to "first-night rights" over a female servant, *The Marriage of Figaro* was unique: it championed the wit and ingenuity of the lower class (and especially the females of that class) over the self-serving arrogance of the nobility. And while such a theme might seem less than controversial today, it provoked heated debate in Mozart's time—Napoleon called the play by Pierre-Augustin Beaumarchais (1732–1799), on which the opera was based, "revolution already in action." Certainly Mozart was more interested in music than in political reform—he agreed to temper Beaumarchais' scolding satire by way of Lorenzo da Ponte's Italian libretto. But his scorn for the upper classes—perhaps stemming from his own personal difficulties with aristocratic patrons—is readily apparent in the piece.

Politics aside, the enduring beauty of *The Marriage of Figaro* lies in its lyrical elegance and its expressive ingenuity. In the aria "Dove sono," the wife of the philandering count laments the loss of her husband's affections; she nevertheless holds out hope for love's return. As this aria illustrates, Mozart had a special talent for shaping personalities by way

---

See Music Listening Selections at end of chapter.

* For a fascinating interpretation of Mozart's life, see the play *Amadeus* by Peter Shaffer (New York: Harper and Row, 1981) and the Academy Award-winning film version of the play produced in 1984.

See Music Listening Selections at end of chapter.

Figure 26.34 LOUIS CARMONTELLE, *The Mozarts in Concert: Leopold, Wolfgang (age seven), and Nannerl*, 1764. Engraving, 13 × 8 in. Between 1763 and 1766, Leopold Mozart gave up his career as a composer and a skilled violinist to tour Europe with his two musically gifted children, Maria Anna ("Nannerl"), age eleven, and Wolfgang, age seven. Leopold was both the teacher and the ambitious promoter of these prodigies, whose performances earned widespread acclaim.

of music. While the characters in the operas of Monteverdi and Lully were allegorical stick figures, Mozart's appeal to us as flesh-and-blood human beings. They convey a wide range of human expression, from grief and despair to hope and joy. Yet Mozart's vocal music is never sentimental; it retains the precision and clarity of the classical style and invests it with unparalleled melodic grace. Only by listening to Mozart's music can one appreciate why Haydn called him "the greatest composer known to me either in person or by name."

Beethoven: The Early Years

Generally considered the third of the great classical composers, Ludwig van Beethoven (1770–1827) spanned the era between the classical and Romantic styles in music.

Born in Bonn, in northern Germany, Beethoven spent the greater part of his life in Vienna, where he studied briefly with Haydn. His earliest works, mainly keyboard pieces composed between 1782 and 1792, reveal his debt to Mozart, as well as his facility with classical form and style.

Between 1793 and 1803, his first years in Vienna, Beethoven made his name as a virtuoso pianist, a composer of piano pieces, and a master of the string quartet. By 1799, however, he began to break with the more formal aspects of classical music. By the turn of the century, his compositions, which include the first two of his nine symphonies, would anticipate the tension and vigor, the emphasis on rhythm rather than melody, and the forceful instrumental language that would stretch classical form, and, ultimately, move in a new direction (see chapter 29).

LOOKING BACK

The Rococo Style

- The fashionable Rococo style reflected the taste of the European aristocracy. Notable for ornamental delicacy, intimacy, and playful elegance, this style dominated the *salons* of Paris and the courts and churches of Austria and Germany.
- In France, Watteau, Boucher, Vigée-Lebrun, Fragonard, and Clodion produced art that evoked a world of physical pleasure and sensuous delight.

Eighteenth-Century Genre Painting

- Encouraged by the *philosophes'* demand for an art of moral virtue, Greuze and Chardin produced genre paintings that dignified the life and work of ordinary individuals were among the most popular images of the eighteenth century, collected by middle- and upper-class patrons.

Eighteenth-Century Neoclassicism

- Archeological investigations in Greece and southern Italy encouraged new interest in Greco-Roman artifacts and produced a more accurate picture of Classical culture than had been available previously.
- In Europe Neoclassicism influenced all the arts, from Adam's English country houses and Soufflot's "Panthéon" to the portraits of Houdon and Canova, and the ceramics of Wedgwood.
- In America Neoclassicism was best expressed in the architectural achievements of Thomas Jefferson.
- Just as the French Revolution swept away the old regime, so Neoclassicism replaced the Rococo style. As Jacques-Louis David's stirring pictorial recreations of Greek and Roman history invoked a message of self-sacrifice and moral purpose, Neoclassicism came to symbolize the ideals of reason and liberty. These ideals are invoked in Ingres' monumental homage to Homer.
- During the reign of Napoleon, Neoclassicists drew on the arts of imperial Rome to glorify the French capital, Paris, and the emperor himself.

Eighteenth-Century Western Music

- The period between approximately 1760 and 1820 witnessed the birth of the orchestra and the development of the classical forms of Western instrumental music.
- Classical music was characterized by order, symmetry, and intellectual control—features similar to those admired by Neoclassical writers, painters, sculptors, and architects.
- Composers used sonata form to govern the composition of the symphony, the string quartet, the sonata, and the concerto.
- Franz Joseph Haydn shaped the character of the classical symphony and the string quartet; Mozart moved easily between light musical genres and classical instrumental forms, investing both with extraordinary melodic grace.
- In his operas as well as his symphonies, Mozart achieved a balance between lyrical invention and formal clarity that brought the classical style to its peak.

Music Listening Selections

- Couperin, "Le Croc-en-jambe" from Ordre No. 22, harpsichord, 1730.
- Haydn, Symphony No. 94 in G Major, *Surprise*, second movement, excerpt, 1791.
- Mozart, Serenade No. 13 in G Major, K. 525, *Eine kleine Nachtmusik*, first movement, excerpt, 1787.
- Mozart, *The Marriage of Figaro*, "Dove sono" aria, 1786.

Glossary

allegro (Italian, "cheerful") a fast tempo in music

andante (Italian, "going," i.e., a normal walking pace) a moderate tempo in music

bacchante a female attendant or devotee of Dionysus

brass a family of wind instruments that usually includes the French horn, trumpet, trombone, and tuba

coda (Italian, "tail") passage added to the closing section of a movement or musical composition in order to create the sense of a definite ending

concerto see Glossary, chapter 23; the classical concerto, which made use of **sonata form**, usually featured one or more solo instruments and orchestra

fête galante (French, "elegant entertainment") a festive diversion enjoyed by aristocrats, a favored subject in Rococo art

fortissimo (Italian, "very loud") a directive indicating that the music should be played very loudly; its opposite is *pianissimo* ("very soft")

intermezzo a short dramatic entertainment, with music, inserted between the acts of a play or opera

largo (Italian, "broad") a very slow tempo; the slowest of the conventional tempos in music

opera buffa a type of comic opera usually featuring stock characters

pastel a crayon made of dry powdered color and a gum binder, used for drawing

percussion a group of instruments that are sounded by being struck or shaken, used especially for rhythm

satyr a semibestial woodland creature symbolic of Dionysus

score the musical notation for all the instruments or voices in a particular composition; a composite from which the whole piece may be conducted or studied

sonata a composition for an unaccompanied keyboard instrument or for another instrument with keyboard accompaniment; see also Glossary, chapter 23

sonata form (or **sonata allegro form**) a structural form commonly used in the late eighteenth century for the first and fourth movements of symphonies and other instrumental compositions

string quartet a composition for four stringed instruments, each of which plays its own part

strings a family of instruments that usually includes the violin, viola, cello, and double bass (which are normally bowed); the harp, guitar, lute, and zither (which are normally plucked) can also be included, as can the viol, a bowed instrument common in the sixteenth and seventeenth centuries and a forerunner of the violin family

symphony an independent instrumental composition for orchestra

theme and variations a form employing a basic musical idea that is repeated with changes in rhythm, harmony, melody, dynamics, or tone color

woodwinds a family of wind instruments, usually consisting of the flute, oboe, clarinet, and bassoon

Book 5

Romanticism, Realism, and the Nineteenth-Century World

The Romantic View of Nature
ca. 1780–1880

"Beauty in art is truth bathed in an impression received from nature."
Corot

Figure 27.1 J. M. W. TURNER, *The Slave Ship (Slavers Throwing Overboard the Dead and Dying: Typhoon Coming On)*, 1840. Oil on canvas, 2 ft. 11¾ in. × 4 ft. ¼ in. Turner infused many of his paintings with a golden glow, achieved by working from a white (rather than a dark) ground and by the use of new yellow pigments commercially available after 1817. His detractors accused Turner of "yellow fever."

The nineteenth century is often called "the Romantic era." The term "Romanticism" describes a movement in the history of culture, an aesthetic style, and an attitude of mind. As a cultural *movement*, Romanticism reacted against the rationalism of the Enlightenment and the depersonalizing effects of Western industrialization. Spanning the late eighteenth century and continuing well into the twentieth, the Romantic movement revolted against academic convention, and authority, and opposed the limitations to freedom in personal, political, and artistic life.

As a *style*, Romanticism provided an alternative to the Enlightenment values of order, clarity, and rational restraint. In place of Neoclassical formality and the objective exercise of the intellect, Romanticism celebrated spontaneity and the subjective exercise of the imagination. In all the arts, the Romantics abandoned traditional formal constraints to explore new, imaginative avenues of expression.

As an *attitude of mind*, Romanticism may be seen as an assertion of intuitive individualism and the primacy of feeling. Romantics did not reject the value of reason as such, but they regarded emotions (and the role of the senses) as equally important to human experience—and as essential to creativity. They looked to nature as a source of divine inspiration and seized on the tumultuous events of their time: the exotic, the catastrophic, and the fantastic. They often indulged in acts of nonconformity that alienated them from conventional society.

The lives and works of the Romantics were marked by deep subjectivity—even self-indulgence. If their perceptions and passions were intense, their desire to devise a language adequate to that intensity of feeling often drove them to frustration, melancholy, despair, and early death: the poets Shelley, Keats, and Byron; the composers Chopin and Schubert; and the painters Gros and Géricault, all died before the age of forty.

The Progress of Industrialization

During the nineteenth century, the population of Europe doubled in size. At the same time, material culture changed more radically than it had in the previous thousand years. The application of science to practical invention, begun in the eighteenth century, had already sparked the beginnings of the Industrial Revolution—the mass production of material goods by machine. The first phase of industrialization occurred in mid eighteenth-century England, with the development of the steam engine and the machinery for spinning and weaving textiles (see chapter 25). Monopolized by the English for a half-century, the Industrial Revolution spread to the rest of Europe and to the United States by the 1830s. As increasing production of coal, iron, and steel encouraged the further expansion of industry and commerce, the West was transformed from an agrarian to an industrially based society. Goods that had been hand-produced in homes and workshops were increasingly manufactured in newly constructed factories, mills, and mines. Industrialization demanded enormous investments of capital and the efforts of a large labor force; it stimulated growth in Europe's urban centers. And ultimately, it provided the basis for the West's controlling influence over the rest of the world (see chapter 30).

Early Nineteenth-Century Thought

Romanticism found its formal philosophers largely among nineteenth-century German intellectuals. Gottlieb Fichte (1762–1814), Friedrich Schiller (1775–1854), and Arthur Schopenhauer (1788–1860) followed the philosophic idealism of Immanuel Kant, who exalted the role of the human mind in constructing an idea of the world (see chapter 25). According to the German idealists, the truths of empirical experience were not self-evident, as Locke had argued, and the truths of the mind were not clear and distinct, as Descartes had held. Much like Rousseau (see chapter 25) and the Romantic poets (discussed later in this chapter), the idealists prized the powers of human instinct and viewed nature in deeply subjective terms.

Schopenhauer defended the existence of a "life-will," a blind and striving impersonal force whose operations are without purpose or design, and whose activities give rise to disorder and delusion. In Schopenhauer's view, the only escape from malignant reality was selfless contemplation of the kind described in Hindu literature and the mystical treatises of Johannes Eckhart (see chapter 15). Welcoming the influence of Indian religious philosophy, Schopenhauer wrote: "Sanskrit literature will be no less influential for our time than Greek literature was in the fifteenth century for the Renaissance."

While Schopenhauer perceived existence as devoid of reason and burdened by constant suffering, others moved in the direction of mysticism. Some allied with notable visionaries, such as Friedrich von Hardenberg, better known as Novalis (1772–1801). Novalis shaped the German Romantic movement through poems and essays that expressed longing for the lost mythic past and a spiritually inspired future. "If God could become man," wrote Novalis, "then He can also become stone, plant, animal, and element and perhaps in this way there is redemption in Nature." The Romantic reawakening of religion embraced the doctrines of mysticism, confessional emotionalism, and pantheism, the last of which stressed the unity of God, man, and nature. According to the foremost German Protestant theologian and preacher, Friedrich E. D. Schleiermacher (1768–1834), the object of religion is "to love the spirit of the world" and "to become one with the infinite."

Hegel and the Hegelian Dialectic

The most influential philosopher of the nineteenth century was Georg Wilhelm Friedrich Hegel (1770–1831). A professor of philosophy at the University of Berlin, Hegel taught that the world consists of a single divine nature, which he termed "absolute mind" or "spirit." Spirit and matter obey an evolutionary process impelled by spirit seeking to know its own nature. He explained the operation of that process, or **dialectic**, as follows: every condition (or "thesis") confronts its opposite condition (or "antithesis"), which then generates a synthesis. The synthesis in turn produces its opposite, and so on, in a continuing evolution that moves toward the ultimate goal of spiritual freedom. For Hegel, all reality is a process that operates on the principle of the dialectic—thesis, antithesis, and synthesis—a principle that governs the realm of ideas, artistic creation, philosophic understanding . . . indeed, history itself. "Change in nature, no matter how infinitely varied it is," wrote Hegel, "shows only a cycle of constant repetition. In nature, nothing new happens under the sun."

Hegel's dense prose work *The Philosophy of History* (1807), a compilation of his own and his students' lecture notes, advances the idea that the essence of spirit is freedom, which finds its ultimate expression in the nation-state. According to Hegel, human beings possess free will (thesis), which, although freely exercised over property, is limited by duty to the universal will (antithesis). The ultimate synthesis is a stage that is reached as individual will comes into harmony with universal duty. This last stage, which represents real freedom, manifests itself in the concrete institutions of the state and its laws. Hegel's view of the state (and the European nation-state in particular) as the last stage in the development of spirit and the Hegelian dialectic in general had considerable influence on late nineteenth-century nationalism, as well as on the economic theories of Karl Marx (see chapter 30).

Darwin and the Theory of Evolution

Like Hegel, the British scientist Charles Darwin (1809–1882) perceived nature as constantly changing. A naturalist in the tradition of Aristotle, Darwin spent his early career amassing enormous amounts of biological and geological data, partly as the result of a five-year voyage to South America aboard the research vessel HMS *Beagle*. Darwin's study of fossils on the Galápagos Islands of the Pacific Ocean confirmed the view of his predecessors that complex forms of life evolved from a few extremely simple organic forms. The theory of evolution did not originate with Darwin—Goethe, for example, had already suggested that all forms of plant life had evolved from a single primeval plant, and the French biologist Jean-Baptiste de Lamarck (1744–1829) had shown that fossils give evidence of perpetual change in all species. Darwin, however,

substantiated the theory of evolution by explaining the process by which evolution occurs. Observing the tendency of certain organisms to increase rapidly over time while retaining traits favorable to their survival, he concluded that evolution operates by means of *natural selection.*

By natural selection, Darwin meant a process whereby nature "prunes away" unfavorable traits in a given species, permitting the survival of those creatures that are most suited to the struggle for life and to reproduction of that species. The elephant's trunk, the giraffe's neck, and the human brain were evidence, he argued, of adaptations made by each of these species to its environment and proof that any trait that remained advantageous to continuity would prevail. Failure to develop such traits meant the ultimate extinction of less developed species; only the "fittest" survived.

In 1859 Darwin published his classic work, *The Origin of Species by Means of Natural Selection, or the Preservation of the Favored Races in the Struggle for Life.* Less than a year later, a commentator observed: "No scientific work that has been published within this century has excited so much general curiosity." But curiosity was among the milder responses to this publication, for Darwin's theory of evolution, like Newton's law of gravity, challenged traditional ideas about nature and the world order. For centuries, most Westerners had held to the account of the Creation described in Scripture. Some, in fact, accepted the chronology advanced by the Irish Catholic bishop James Ussher (1581–1656), which placed earthly creation at 4004 B.C.E. Most scholars, however, perceived the likelihood of a far greater age for the earth and its species.

Darwin's thesis did not deny the idea of a divine creator—indeed, Darwin initially speculated that "it is just as noble a conception of the Deity to believe that He created a few original forms capable of self-development into other and needful forms, as to believe that He required a fresh act of creation to supply the voids caused by the action of His laws." But Darwin's theory implied that natural selection, not divine will, governed the evolutionary process. By suggesting that nature and its operations were impersonal, continuous, and self-governing, the theory of natural selection challenged the creationist view (supported by the Bible) that God had brought into being a fixed and unchanging number of species. Equally troubling was Darwin's argument (clarified in his later publication *The Descent of Man,* 1871) that the differences between humans and less complex orders of life were differences of degree,

Science and Technology

1799	paleontologist William Smith (British) theorizes that rock strata may be identified by fossils characteristic to each
1830	Charles Lyell (British) provides foundations for the modern study of geology in his *Principles of Geology*
1859	Darwin publishes *The Origin of Species*

Figure 27.2 Spoofing evolution, a cartoon of the day portrays an apelike Charles Darwin explaining his controversial theory of evolution to an ape with the help of a mirror. The work appeared in the *London Sketch Book* in May 1874, captioned by two suitable quotations from the plays of Shakespeare: "This is the ape of form" and "Four or five descents since."

not kind, and that all creatures were related to one another by their kinship to lower forms of life. The most likely ancestor for *Homo sapiens*, explained Darwin, was "a hairy, tailed quadruped, probably arboreal in its habits . . ." (Figure **27.2**).

Clearly, Darwin's conclusions (which nurtured his own reluctant agnosticism) toppled human beings from their elevated place in the hierarchy of living creatures. If the cosmology of Copernicus and Galileo had displaced earth from the center of the solar system, Darwin's theory robbed human beings of their preeminence on the planet. At a single blow, Darwin shattered the harmonious world-views of both Renaissance humanists and Enlightenment *philosophes*.

Yet, the theory of evolution by natural selection complemented a view of nature in keeping with Romanticism. As Thoreau (see Reading 27.6) mused, "Am I not partly leaves and vegetable mould myself?" And numerous passages from the writings of Wordsworth, Shelley, Emerson, and Whitman (the Romantics treated in this chapter) exhibit a similar pantheistic sentiment. At the same time, Darwin's ideas encouraged the late nineteenth-century movement of "scientism" (the proposition that the methods of the natural sciences should be applied in all areas of rational investigation). Darwin's writing also stimulated the rise of natural history museums, which, unlike the random collections of previous centuries, gave evidence of the common order of living things.

The consequences of Darwin's monumental theory were far-reaching, but his ideas were often oversimplified or misinterpreted. Among some thinkers, the theory of evolution provided the rationale for analyzing civilizations as living organisms with identifiable stages of growth, maturity, and decline. Then too, Darwin's use of the phrase "Favored Races" in the subtitle of his major work contributed to the theory of *social Darwinism*, which freely applied some of his ideas to political, economic, and cultural life.

The term "social Darwinism" did not come into use until 1879, but the idea that natural selection operated to determine the superiority of some individuals, groups, races, and nations over others was effective in justifying European policies of imperialism (see chapter 30). By their intelligence and wealth, argued the social Darwinists, Westerners (and white people in general) were clearly the "fittest," and therefore destined to dominate the less fit. Since Darwin meant by "fitness" the reproductive success of a species, not simply its survival, most applications of his work to contemporary social conditions represented a distortion of his ideas. Nevertheless, social Darwinism, expanded on by political theorists, would provide "scientific" justification for European colonialism. It also anticipated more threatening and extreme theories, such as **eugenics** (which focused on the elimination of society's "less fit" members) and the racist ideology of Adolf Hitler.

In the course of the twentieth century, modern biology, and particularly the science of molecular genetics (the study of the digital information preserved in DNA), has provided evidence to support Darwin's theory of natural selection. Nevertheless, today's scientists continue to probe the origins of life—where and how it first came into being. In the context of the nineteenth century, however, Darwin remains a leading figure. Like all Romantics, he was a keen and curious observer of nature, which he described as vast, energetic, and unceasingly dynamic. In *The Origin of Species*, he exults:

When we no longer look at an organic being as a savage looks at a ship, as something wholly beyond his comprehension; when we regard every production of nature as one which has had a long history; when we contemplate every complex structure and instinct as the summing up of many contrivances, each

Creationism versus Evolution

Darwin's *Origin of Species* generated much controversy in its own time and long thereafter. In the last 150 years, fossil research and molecular biology have provided overwhelming evidence to support the theory of evolution. Nevertheless, controversy continues. The debate centers on the question of origins, that is, whether human beings were divinely created or are the product of a series of biological "accidents" governed by natural selection. Creationists hold that the physical structure of the universe argues for the existence of a god whose "intelligent design" produced the world as we know it. While the defenders of Intelligent Design view Darwin's theory of natural selection as evidence for a random and undirected universe, Darwin himself, observing the "grandeur in this view of life, with its several powers, having been originally

breathed by the Creator . . . " speculated that natural selection and biological evolution might be part of a divine design.

Many religious faiths have no difficulty in accepting the idea that biological evolution governs the diversity of living things over billions of years, and thus find evolution and religious belief compatible. However, those who hold to the literal truth of Scripture find Darwin's theories in direct contradiction of their religious beliefs. The ongoing controversy, which flourishes mainly in the United States, centers on public education: whether creationism should be taught along with evolution in the classroom. The debate has provoked a number of related issues, including the definition and validity of "good science," and contemporary literal interpretations of the Book of Genesis.

---

useful to the possessor, in the same way as any great mechanical invention is the summing up of the labor, the experience, the reason, and even the blunders of numerous workmen; when we thus view each organic being, how far more interesting . . . does the study of natural history become!

And in the final paragraph of his opus, Darwin brings romantic fervor to his description of nature's laws:

It is interesting to contemplate a tangled bank, clothed with many plants of many kinds, with birds singing on the bushes, with various insects flitting about, and with worms crawling through the damp earth, and to reflect that these elaborately constructed forms, so different from each other, and dependent upon each other in so complex a manner, have all been produced by laws acting around us. These laws, taken in the largest sense, being Growth and Reproduction; Inheritance which is almost implied by reproduction; Variability from the indirect and direct action of the conditions of life, and from use and disuse; a Ratio of Increase so high as to lead to a Struggle for Life, and as a consequence to Natural Selection, entailing Divergence of Character and the Extinction of less-improved forms. Thus, from the war of nature, from famine and death, the most exalted object which we are capable of conceiving, namely, the production of the higher animals, directly follows. There is grandeur in this view of life, with its several powers, having been originally breathed by the Creator into a few forms or into one; and that, whilst this planet has gone cycling on according to the fixed law of gravity, from so simple a beginning endless forms most beautiful and most wonderful have been, and are being evolved.

Nature and the Natural in European Literature

One of the central features of nineteenth-century Romanticism was its love affair with nature. In nature, with its shifting moods and rhythms, the Romantics found solace, inspiration, and self-discovery. To Enlightenment thinkers, "nature" meant universal order, but to the Romantics, nature was the wellspring of divinity, the phenomenon that bound humankind to God. "Natural man" was one who was close to nature, unspoiled (as Rousseau had argued) by social institutions and imperatives.

The Romantics lamented the dismal effects of growing industrialization. In rural settings, they found a practical refuge from urban blight, smoke-belching factories, and poverty-ridden slums. The natural landscape, unspoiled and unpolluted, revealed the oneness of God and the universe. This **pantheistic** outlook, more typical of Eastern than Western religious philosophy, came to pervade the literature of European and American Romantics.

Wordsworth and the Poetry of Nature

In 1798, William Wordsworth (1780–1850) and his British contemporary Samuel Taylor Coleridge (1772–1834) produced the *Lyrical Ballads*, the literary work that marked the birth of the Romantic movement in England. When the book appeared in a second edition in 1800, Wordsworth added a preface that formally explained the aims of Romantic poetry. In this manifesto, Wordsworth described poetry as "the spontaneous overflow of powerful feelings," which takes its origin "from emotion recollected in tranquillity." The object of the poet is to choose incidents and situations from common life [and] to throw over them a certain colouring of the imagination . . . and above all, to make these incidents and situations interesting by tracing in them, truly though not ostentatiously, the primary laws of our nature.

The leading nature poet of the nineteenth century, Wordsworth was born in the English Lake District. He dated the beginning of his creative life from the time—at age fourteen—when he was struck by the image of tree boughs silhouetted against a bright evening sky. Thereafter, what he called "the infinite variety of natural appearances" became his principal source of inspiration and the primary subject of his poetry. Nature, he claimed, could restore to human beings their untainted, childhood sense of wonder. Moreover, through nature (as revealed to us by way of the senses), one might commune with the elemental and divine forces of the universe.

Wordsworth championed a poetic language that resembled "the real language of men in a state of vivid sensation." Although he did not always abide by his own precepts, his rejection of the artificial diction of Neoclassical verse in favor of this "real language" anticipated a new, more natural voice in poetry—one informed by childhood memories and deeply felt experiences. Wordsworth's verse reflects his preference for **lyric poetry**, which—like art song—describes deep personal feeling.

One of the most inspired poems in the *Lyrical Ballads* is "Lines Composed a Few Miles Above Tintern Abbey," the product of Wordsworth's visit to the ruins of a medieval monastery situated on the banks of the Wye River in

Figure 27.3 J. M. W. TURNER, *Interior of Tintern Abbey*, 1794. Watercolor, 12⅝ × 9⅞ in. At age nineteen, Turner explored the Wye Valley in search of picturesque subjects. This thirteenth-century abbey had fallen into ruin after the dissolution of the monasteries by Henry VIII in the 1530s.

southeast Wales (Figure **27.3**). The 159-line poem constitutes a paean to nature. Wordsworth begins by describing the sensations evoked by the British countryside; he then muses on the pleasures these memories provide as they are called up in recollection. The heart of the poem, however, is a joyous celebration of nature's moral value: nature allows the poet to "see into the life of things" (line 49), infusing him with "the still, sad music of humanity" (line 91), and ultimately bringing him into the sublime presence of the divine spirit. Nature, he exults, is the "anchor" of his purest thoughts, the "nurse" and "guardian" of his heart and soul (lines 109–110). In the final portion of the extract (lines 111–134), Wordsworth shares with his "dearest Friend," his sister Dorothy, the joys of his mystical communion with nature and humankind. "Tintern Abbey" set forth three of the key motifs of nineteenth-century Romanticism: the redemptive power of nature, the idea of nature's sympathy with humankind, and the view that one who is close to nature is close to God.

READING 27.1 From Wordsworth's
"Lines Composed a Few Miles
Above Tintern Abbey" (1798)

Five years have passed; five summers, with the length	1
Of five long winters! and again I hear	
These waters, rolling from their mountain-springs	
With a soft inland murmur. Once again	
Do I behold these steep and lofty cliffs,	5
That on a wild secluded scene impress	
Thoughts of more deep seclusion; and connect	
The landscape with the quiet of the sky.	
The day is come when I again repose	
Here, under this dark sycamore, and view	10
These plots of cottage-ground, these orchard tufts,	
Which at this season, with their unripe fruits,	
Are clad in one green hue, and lose themselves	
'Mid groves and copses. Once again I see	
These hedge-rows, hardly hedge-rows, little lines	15
Of sportive wood run wild: these pastoral farms,	
Green to the very door; and wreaths of smoke	
Sent up, in silence, from among the trees!	
With some uncertain notice, as might seem	
Of vagrant dwellers in the houseless woods,	20
Or of some Hermit's cave, where by his fire	
The hermit sits alone.	
These beauteous forms,	
Through a long absence, have not been to me	
As is a landscape to a blind man's eye;	
But oft, in lonely rooms, and 'mid the din	25
Of towns and cities, I have owed to them	
In hours of weariness, sensations sweet,	
Felt in the blood, and felt along the heart;	
And passing even into my purer mind,	
With tranquil restoration:—feelings too	30
Of unremembered pleasure: such, perhaps,	
As have no slight or trivial influence	

On that best portion of a good man's life,	
His little, nameless, unremembered acts	
Of kindness and of love. Nor less, I trust,	35
To them I may have owed another gift,	
Of aspect more sublime; that blessed mood,	
In which the burthen[1] of the mystery,	
In which the heavy and the weary weight	
Of all this unintelligible world,	40
Is lightened—that serene and blessed mood,	
In which the affections gently lead us on—	
Until, the breath of this corporeal frame	
And even the motion of our human blood	
Almost suspended, we are laid asleep	45
In body, and become a living soul;	
While with an eye made quiet by the power	
Of harmony, and the deep power of joy,	
We see into the life of things.	
If this	
Be but a vain belief, yet, oh! how oft—	50
In darkness and amid the many shapes	
Of joyless daylight; when the fretful stir	
Unprofitable, and the fever of the world,	
Have hung upon the beatings of my heart—	
How oft, in spirit, have I turned to thee,	55
O sylvan[2] Wye! thou wanderer through the woods,	
How often has my spirit turned to thee!	
And now, with gleams of half-extinguished thought,	
With many recognitions dim and faint,	
And somewhat of a sad perplexity,	60
The picture of the mind revives again;	
While here I stand, not only with the sense	
Of present pleasure, but with pleasing thoughts	
That in this moment there is life and food	
For future years. And so I dare to hope,	65
Though changed, no doubt, from what I was when first	
I came among these hills; when like a roe	
I bounded o'er the mountains, by the sides	
Of the deep rivers, and the lonely streams,	
Wherever nature led: more like a man	70
Flying from something that he dreads than one	
Who sought the thing he loved. For nature then	
(The coarser pleasures of my boyish days,	
And their glad animal movements all gone by)	
To me was all in all—I cannot paint	75
What then I was. The sounding cataract[3]	
Haunted me like a passion; the tall rock,	
The mountain, and the deep and gloomy wood,	
Their colours and their forms, were then to me	
An appetite; a feeling and a love,	80
That had no need of a remoter charm,	
By thought supplied, nor any interest	
Unborrowed from the eye. That time is past,	
And all its aching joys are now no more,	
And all its dizzy raptures. Not for this	85

---

[1] Burden.
[2] Wooded.
[3] A descent of water over a steep surface.

Faint I, nor mourn nor murmur; other gifts
Have followed; for such loss, I would believe,
Abundant recompense. For I have learned
To look on nature, not as in the hour
Of thoughtless youth; but hearing oftentimes   90
The still, sad music of humanity,
Nor harsh nor grating, though of ample power
To chasten and subdue. And I have felt
A presence that disturbs me with the joy
Of elevated thoughts; a sense sublime   95
Of something far more deeply interfused,
Whose dwelling is the light of setting suns,
And the round ocean and the living air,
And the blue sky, and in the mind of man:
A motion and a spirit, that impels   100
All thinking things, all objects of all thought,
And rolls through all things. Therefore am I still
A lover of the meadows and the woods,
And mountains; and of all that we behold
From this green earth; of all the mighty world   105
Of eye, and ear—both what they half create,
And what perceive; well pleased to recognize
In nature and the language of the sense,
The anchor of my purest thoughts, the nurse,
The guide, the guardian of my heart, and soul   110
Of all my moral being.
                              Nor perchance,
If I were not thus taught, should I the more
Suffer my genial spirits to decay:
For thou art with me here upon the banks
Of this fair river; thou my dearest Friend,[4]   115
My dear, dear Friend; and in thy voice I catch
The language of my former heart, and read
My former pleasures in the shooting lights
Of thy wild eyes. Oh! yet a little while
May I behold in thee what I was once,   120
My dear, dear Sister! and this prayer I make,
Knowing that Nature never did betray
The heart that loved her; 'tis her privilege,
Through all the years of this our life, to lead
From joy to joy: for she can so inform   125
The mind that is within us, so impress
With quietness and beauty, and so feed
With lofty thoughts, that neither evil tongues,
Rash judgments, nor the sneers of selfish men,
Nor greetings where no kindness is, nor all   130
The dreary intercourse of daily life,
Shall e'er prevail against us, or disturb
Our cheerful faith, that all which we behold
Is full of blessings. . . .

Q What does Wordsworth mean when he calls
nature "the anchor of my purest thoughts"?

Q Which lines in this selection best capture the
sublime aspects of nature?

---

[4] Wordsworth's sister Dorothy.

The Poetry of Shelley

Like Wordsworth, the English poet Percy Bysshe Shelley (1792–1822) embraced nature as the source of sublime truth, but his volcanic personality led him to engage the natural world with greater intensity and deeper melancholy than his older contemporary. A prolific writer and a passionate champion of human liberty, he provoked the reading public with a treatise entitled *The Necessity of Atheism* (1811), the circulation of which led to his expulsion from Oxford University. His pamphlet on the subject of the French Revolution, *A Declaration of Rights* (1812), endorsed a radical creed for political equality: "A Christian, a Deist, a Turk, and a Jew, have equal rights [in the benefits and burdens of government]."

Shelley was outspoken in his opposition to marriage, a union that he viewed as hostile to human happiness. He was as unconventional in his deeds as in his discourse: while married to one woman (Harriet Westbrook), with whom he had two children, he ran off with another (Mary Godwin). A harsh critic of Britain's rulers, he chose permanent exile in Italy in 1818 and died there four years later in a boating accident.

Shelley's *Defence of Poetry* (1821), a manifesto of the writer's function in society, hails poets as "the unacknowledged legislators of the world." Such creatures take their authority from nature, the fountainhead of inspiration. Shelley himself found in nature metaphors for the inconstant state of human desire. In "Ode to the West Wind" he appeals to the wind, a symbol of creativity, to drive his visions throughout the universe, as the wind drives leaves over the earth (stanza 1), clouds through the air (stanza 2), and waves on the seas (stanza 3). In the last stanza, he compares the poet to a lyre, whose "mighty harmonies," stirred by the wind of creativity, will awaken the world. Then, finally, he seeks his identity with the wind and nature itself: "Be thou, spirit fierce/My spirit! Be thou me, impetuous one!" By means of language that is itself musical, Shelley defends the notion of poetry as the music of the soul. Consider, for instance, his frequent use of the exclamatory "O" and the effective use of **assonance** and tonal color in lines 38 to 40: "while far below/The sea-blooms and the oozy woods which wear/The sapless foliage of the ocean, know."

READING 27.2 Shelley's
"Ode to the West Wind" (1819)

1

O wild West Wind, thou breath of Autumn's being   1
Thou, from whose unseen presence the leaves dead
Are driven, like ghosts from an enchanter fleeing,

Yellow, and black, and pale, and hectic red,
Pestilence-stricken multitudes: O thou,   5
Who chariotest to their dark wintry bed

The wingéd seeds, where they lie cold and low,
Each like a corpse within its grave, until
Thine azure sister of the spring shall blow

Her clarion o'er the dreaming earth, and fill   10
(Driving sweet buds like flocks to feed in air)
With living hues and odours plain and hill:

Wild Spirit, which art moving everywhere;
Destroyer and preserver; hear, oh, hear!

2

Thou on whose stream, 'mid the steep sky's commotion,   15
Loose clouds like earth's decaying leaves are shed,
Shook from the tangled boughs of Heaven and Ocean,

Angels of rain and lightning: there are spread
On the blue surface of thine aëry surge,
Like the bright hair uplifted from the head   20

Of some fierce Maenad,[1] even from the dim verge
Of the horizon to the zenith's height,
The locks of the approaching storm. Thou dirge

Of the dying year, to which this closing night
Will be the dome of a vast sepulchre,[2]   25
Vaulted with all thy congregated might

Of vapours, from whose solid atmosphere
Black rain, and fire, and hail will burst: O, hear!

3

Thou who didst waken from his summer dreams
The blue Mediterranean, where he lay,   30
Lulled by the coil of his crystalline streams,

Beside a pumice isle in Baiae's bay,[3]
And saw in sleep old palaces and towers
Quivering within the wave's intenser day,

All overgrown with azure moss and flowers   35
So sweet, the sense faints picturing them! Thou
For whose path the Atlantic's level powers

Cleave themselves into chasms, while far below
The sea-blooms and the oozy woods which wear
The sapless foliage of the ocean, know   40

Thy voice, and suddenly grow grey with fear,
And tremble and despoil themselves: O, hear!

4

If I were a dead leaf thou mightest bear;
If I were a swift cloud to fly with thee;
A wave to pant beneath thy power, and share   45

The impulse of thy strength, only less free
Than thou, O uncontrollable! If even
I were as in my boyhood, and could be

The comrade of thy wanderings over heaven,
As then, when to outstrip thy skiey speed   50
Scarce seemed a vision; I would ne'er have striven

As thus with thee in prayer in my sore need.
Oh! lift me as a wave, a leaf, a cloud!
I fall upon the thorns of life! I bleed!

A heavy weight of hours has chained and bowed   55
One too like thee: tameless, and swift, and proud.

5

Make me thy lyre, even as the forest is:
What if my leaves are falling like its own!
The tumult of thy mighty harmonies

Will take from both a deep, autumnal tone,   60
Sweet though in sadness. Be thou, spirit fierce,
My spirit! Be thou me, impetuous one!

Drive my dead thoughts over the universe
Like withered leaves to quicken a new birth!
And, by the incantation of this verse,   65

Scatter, as from an unextinguished hearth
Ashes and sparks, my words among mankind!
Be through my lips to unawakened earth

The trumpet of a prophecy! O, Wind,
If Winter comes, can Spring be far behind?   70

Q How would you describe the function of color in this poem?

Q What does this poem reveal about the personality of the poet?

The Poetry of Keats

The poetry of John Keats (1795–1821), the third of the great English nature poets, shares Shelley's elegiac sensibility. Keats lamented the fleeting nature of life's pleasures, even as he contemplated the brevity of life. He lost both his mother and his brother to tuberculosis, and he himself succumbed to that disease at the age of twenty-five. The threat of imminent death seems to have produced in Keats a heightened awareness of the virtues of beauty, human love, and friendship. He perceived these phenomena as fleeting forms of a higher reality made permanent only in art. For Keats, art is the great balm of the poet. Art is more than a response to the human experience of love and nature; it is the transmuted product of the imagination, a higher form of nature that triumphantly outreaches the mortal lifespan. These ideas are central to Keats' "Ode on a Grecian Urn." The poem was inspired by ancient Greek artifacts Keats had seen among those brought to London by Lord Elgin in 1816 and placed on display in the British Museum (see chapter 5).

In the "Ode," Keats contemplates a Greek vase (much like the one pictured in Figure **27.4**), whose delicately

---

[1] A female attendant of Dionysus; a bacchante (see chapter 26).
[2] Tomb.
[3] An ancient resort in southwest Italy.

Figure 27.4 SISYPHUS PAINTER, South Italian volute krater with women making music and centaur fight, late fifth century B.C.E. Red-figured pottery, height 29 in.

drawn figures are shown enjoying transitory pleasures. Frozen in time on the surface of such a vase, the fair youths will never grow old, the music of the pipes and lyres will never cease to sound, and the lovers will never cease to love. The "little town by river" and the other pastoral vignettes in the poem probably did not belong to any one existing Greek vase; yet Keats describes the imaginary urn (his metaphoric "Cold Pastoral") as a symbol of all great works of art, which, because of their unchanging beauty, remain eternally "true." The poem concludes with the joyous pronouncement: beauty and truth are one.

READING 27.3 Keats' "Ode on a Grecian Urn" (1818)

1

Thou still unravished bride of quietness,   1
 Thou foster-child of Silence and slow Time,
Sylvan historian, who canst thus express
 A flowery tale more sweetly than our rhyme:
What leaf-fringed[1] legend haunts about thy shape   5

Of deities or mortals, or of both,
 In Tempe[2] or the dales of Arcady?[3]
 What men or gods are these? What maidens loth?
What mad pursuit? What struggle to escape?
 What pipes and timbrels? What wild ecstasy?   10

2

Heard melodies are sweet, but those unheard
 Are sweeter; therefore, ye soft pipes, play on;
Not to the sensual ear, but, more endeared,
 Pipe to the spirit ditties of no tone:
Fair youth, beneath the trees, thou canst not leave   15
 Thy song, nor ever can those trees be bare;
 Bold Lover, never, never canst thou kiss,
Though winning near the goal—yet, do not grieve;
 She cannot fade, though thou hast not thy bliss,
 For ever wilt thou love, and she be fair!   20

3

Ah, happy, happy boughs! that cannot shed
 Your leaves, nor ever bid the Spring adieu;
And, happy melodist, unweariéd,
 For ever piping songs for ever new;
More happy love! more happy, happy love!   25
 For ever warm and still to be enjoyed,
 For ever panting, and for ever young;
All breathing human passion far above,
 That leaves a heart high-sorrowful and cloyed,
 A burning forehead, and a parching tongue.   30

4

Who are these coming to the sacrifice?
 To what green altar, O mysterious priest,
Lead'st thou that heifer lowing at the skies,
 And all her silken flanks with garlands drest?
What little town by river or sea shore,   35
 Or mountain-built with peaceful citadel,
 Is emptied of this folk, this pious morn?
And, little town, thy streets for evermore
 Will silent be; and not a soul to tell
 Why thou art desolate, can e'er return.   40

5

O Attic[4] shape! Fair attitude! with brede[5]
 Of marble men and maidens overwrought,
With forest branches and the trodden weed;
 Thou, silent form, dost tease us out of thought
As doth eternity: Cold Pastoral!   45
 When old age shall this generation waste,
 Thou shalt remain, in midst of other woe
Than ours, a friend to man, to whom thou say'st,
 "Beauty is truth, truth beauty,"—that is all

---

[1] A reference to the common Greek practice of bordering vases with stylized leaf forms (see Figure 27.4).

[2] A valley sacred to Apollo between Mounts Olympus and Ossa in Thessaly, Greece.

[3] Arcadia, the pastoral regions of ancient Greece (see Poussin's *Arcadian Shepherds*, Figure 21.12).

[4] Attica, a region in southeastern Greece dominated by Athens.

[5] Embroidered border.

Ye know on earth, and all ye need to know.   **50**

Q **How does this work of art—the painted urn—lead Keats to a perception of truth?**

Blake: Romantic Mystic

The British poet, painter, and engraver William Blake (1757–1827) shared the Romantic disdain for convention and authority. Blake, however, introduced a more mystical view of nature, God, and humankind. Deeply spiritual, he claimed "To see nature in a Grain of Sand,/ And Heaven in a Wild flower." This divine vision he brought to his poetry and his paintings; the former was often conceived along with visual images that he himself drew. Trained in the graphic arts, he prepared all aspects of his individual works, designing, illustrating, engraving, and hand-coloring each page. He also illustrated the literary works of others who, like himself, were horrified by the oppressive and inhumane treatment of rebellious slaves in the European colonies (see Figure 28.4).

Some of the best of Blake's artworks are illustrations for books of the Bible, and especially for such visionary landmarks as the Book of Revelation (Figure **27.5**). In these impassioned designs he drew more from the mind than from the eye. (Indeed, he credited conversations with angelic emissaries as a source of his imagery.)

Blake's early poems featured singular images with clear and vivid (and often) moral messages. "The Lamb," a short poem from his *Songs of Innocence* (1789), envisions that animal as a symbol of God's gentle goodness. In his

Figure 27.5 WILLIAM BLAKE, *The Great Red Dragon and the Woman Clothed with the Sun*, ca. 1805. Watercolor, 16¹⁄₁₆ × 13¼ in.

Songs of Experience (1794), childlike lyricism gives way to the disillusionment of maturity. The most famous poem in this collection, "The Tiger," asks whether goodness must be accompanied by evil, and whether God is responsible for both.

READING 27.4 Blake's "The Tiger"

Tiger! Tiger! Burning bright	**1**
In the forest of the night,	
What immortal hand or eye	
Could frame thy fearful symmetry?	
In what distant deeps or skies	**5**
Burnt the first of thine eyes?	
On what wings dare he aspire?	
What the hand dare seize the fire?	
And what shoulder, and what art,	
Could twist the sinews of thy heart?	**10**
And when thy heart began to beat,	
What dread hand? And what dread feet?	
What the hammer? What the chain?	
In what furnace was thy brain?	
What the anvil? What dread grasp	**15**
Dare its deadly terrors clasp?	
When the stars threw down their spears,	
And watered heaven with their tears,	
Did he smile his work to see?	
Did he who made the Lamb make thee?	**20**
Tiger! Tiger! Burning bright	
In the forests of the night,	
What immortal hand or eye,	
Dare frame thy fearful symmetry.	

Q **What kind of Creator does Blake envision? What preconceptions color Blake's view of nature?**

Blake's poetic imagination took much from the Bible and Milton's *Paradise Lost* (see chapter 22)—some scholars see in the fifth stanza of "The Tiger" an allusion to Milton's powerful Satan. Regardless of whether one perceives the Maker as satanic or divine or both, the poem seems to assert the typically Romantic view of the artist as sharing God's burden of creation and the creative process.

Nature and the Natural in Asian Literature

Although no literary movement in Chinese history has been designated "Romantic," there are clear examples of the Romantic sensibility in Chinese literature of the nineteenth century, especially in those works that exalt the emotional identification of the individual with nature. The Chinese writer Shen Fu (1763–1809) shares with Wordsworth, Shelley, and Keats the reflective view of nature and a heightened sensitivity to its transient moods. A bohemian spirit, Shen Fu failed the district civil examinations that guaranteed financial success for Chinese intellectuals. Often in debt and expelled from his family by an overbearing father, he found brief but profound joy in his marriage to a neighbor's daughter, Zhen Yuen. Shen Fu's autobiography, *Six Chapters from a Floating Life* (1809), is a confessional record of their life together, a life in which poverty is balanced by the pleasures of married love and an abiding affection for nature.

In the following excerpt from Shen's autobiography—a favorite with Chinese readers to this day—the writer describes the simple pleasures he and Zhen Yuen derived from growing flowers and designing "rockeries": natural arrangements of rocks and soil that resemble miniature gardens. The tender story of the destruction of the "Place of Falling Flowers," the couple's tiny version of the natural landscape, anticipates the central event of Shen's intimate life history: the death of his beloved wife. The story also functions as a reminder that all of nature is fragile and impermanent.

READING 27.5 From Shen Fu's *Six Chapters from a Floating Life* (1809)

As a young man I was excessively fond of flowers and loved to prune and shape potted plants and trees. When I met Chang Lan-p'o he began to teach me the art of training branches and supporting joints, and after I had mastered these skills, he showed me how to graft flowers. Later on, I also learned the placing of stones and designing of rockeries.

The orchid we considered the peerless flower, selecting it as much for its subtle and delicate fragrance as for its beauty and grace. Fine varieties of orchids were very difficult to find, especially those worthy of being recorded in the Botanical   10 Register. When Lan-p'o was dying he gave me a pot of spring orchids of the lotus type, with broad white centers, perfectly even "shoulders," and very slender stems. As the plant was a classic specimen of its type, I treasured its perfection like a piece of ancient jade. Yuen took care of it whenever my work as yamen secretary[1] called me away from home. She always watered it herself and the plant flourished, producing a luxuriant growth of leaves and flowers.

One morning, about two years later, it suddenly withered and died. When I dug up the roots to inspect them, I saw that   20 they were as white as jade, with many new shoots beginning to sprout. At first, I could not understand it. Was I just too unlucky, I wondered, to possess and enjoy such beauty? Sighing despondently, I dismissed the matter from my mind. But some time later I found out what had really happened. It seemed that a person who had asked for a cutting from the plant and had been refused, had then poured boiling water on it and killed it. After that, I vowed never to grow orchids again.

Azaleas were my second choice. Although the flowers had no fragrance they were very beautiful and lasted a long time.   30

[1] A government clerk.

The plants were easy to trim and to train, but Yuen loved the green of the branches and leaves so much that she would not let me cut them back, and this made it difficult for me to train them to correct shapes. Unfortunately, Yuen felt this way about all the potted plants that she enjoyed.

Every year, in the autumn, I became completely devoted to the chrysanthemum. I loved to arrange the cut flowers in vases but did not like the potted plants. Not that I did not think the potted flowers beautiful, but our house having no garden, it was impossible for me to grow the plants myself, and those for   40 sale at the market were overgrown and untrained; not at all what I would have chosen.

One day, as I was sweeping my ancestral graves in the hills, I found some very unusual stones with interesting streaks and lines running through them. I talked to Yuen about them when I went home.

"When Hsüan-chou stones are mixed with putty and arranged in white-stone dishes, the putty and stones blend well and the effect is very harmonious," I remarked. "These yellow stones from the hills are rugged and old-looking, but if   50 we mix them with putty the yellow and white won't blend. All the seams and gaps will show up and the arrangement will look spotty. I wonder what else we could use instead of putty?"

"Why not pick out some of the poor, uninteresting stones and pound them to powder," Yuen said. "If we mix the powdered stones with the putty while it is still damp, the color will probably match when it dries."

After doing as she suggested, we took a rectangular I-hsing pottery dish and piled the stones and putty into a miniature   60 mountain peak on the left side of it, with a rocky crag jutting out towards the right. On the surface of the mountain, we made criss-cross marks in the style of the rocks painted by Ni Tsan[2] of the Yuan dynasty. This gave an effect of perspective and the finished arrangement looked very realistic—a precipitous cliff rising sharply from the rocks at the river's edge. Making a hollow in one corner of the dish, we filled it with river mud and planted it with duckweed. Among the rocks we planted "clouds of the pine trees," bindweed. It was several days before the whole thing was finished.   70

Before the end of autumn the bindweed had spread all over the mountain and hung like wisteria from the rocky cliff. The flowers, when they bloomed, were a beautiful clear red. The duckweed, too, had sprouted luxuriantly from the mud and was now a mass of snowy white. Seeing the beauty of the contrasting red and white, we could easily imagine ourselves in Fairyland.

Setting the dish under the eaves, we started discussing what should be done next, developing many themes: "Here there should be a lake with a pavilion—" "This spot calls for a   80 thatched summerhouse—" "This is the perfect place for the six-character inscription 'Place of Falling Flowers and Flowing Water'"—"Here we could build our house—here go fishing—here enjoy the view"; becoming, by this time, so much a part of the tiny landscape, with its hills and ravines, that it seemed to us as if we were really going to move there to live.

One night, a couple of mis-begotten cats, fighting over food,

[2] A famous landscape painter (1301–1374) of the Yuan dynasty (1279–1368).

fell off the eaves and hit the dish, knocking it off its stand and smashing it to fragments in an instant. Neither of us could help crying.

"Isn't it possible," I sighed, "to have even a little thing like this without incurring the envy of the gods?"

— **Q** What aspects of this selection reflect East Asian attitudes toward nature and the natural?

— **Q** How does Shen Fu suggest the fragility of life?

Romantic Landscape Painting

Landscape painting originated as an independent genre not in the West, but in the East. While the ancient Romans had devised naturalistic settings for mythological subjects (see Figure 6.28), it was in tenth-century China that landscape painting first became a subject *in and of itself* (see Figure 14.15). By the thirteenth century, the Chinese landscape had overtaken figure painting in popularity. The genre soon spread to Japan and other parts of East Asia.

MAKING CONNECTIONS

Chinese landscape paintings generally achieve a sweeping unity of air, earth, and water that dwarfs the human figure. In one typically Chinese ink-on-paper album leaf, the artist Shen Zhou (1427–1509) pictures a solitary figure (possibly himself) atop a rugged cliff, overlooking a vast natural expanse (Figure **27.6**). To the painting, he has added these lines:

> White clouds encircle the waist of the hills like a belt;
> A stony ledge soars into the world, a narrow path into space.
> Alone, I lean on my thornwood staff and gaze calmly into the distance,
> About to play my flute in reply to the song of this mountain stream.*

The paintings of the nineteenth-century German artist Caspar David Friedrich (1774–1840), while not directly influenced by Chinese art, share some of its basic features. Friedrich's views of wintry graveyards and Gothic ruins usually show distant figures contemplating (with what the artist called "our spiritual eye") the mysteries of time and nature. In one of Friedrich's most notable paintings, two men stand at the brink of a steep cliff, overlooking an unseen valley (Figure **27.7**). A craggy, half-uprooted tree is silhouetted against the glowing, moonlit sky. Somber colors enhance a mood of poetic loneliness. While Shen Zhou's cosmic vista makes nature itself the subject matter, Friedrich's landscape—more closely focused and detailed—draws our attention to the figures. Nevertheless, both artists capture nature's power to free the individual from the confines of the material world. In spaces smaller than 2 feet square, they record the universal dialogue between humankind and nature.

*Translated by Daniel Bryant

Figure 27.6 SHEN ZHOU, *Poet on a Mountain Top*, from the "Landscape Album" series, ca. 1495–1500. Album leaf mounted as a handscroll; ink on paper or ink and light color on paper, 15¼ × 23¾ in.

Figure 27.7 CASPAR DAVID FRIEDRICH, *Two Men Looking at the Moon*, 1819–1820. Oil on panel, 13¾ × 17¼ in.

Typically vast and sweeping, Chinese landscapes achieve a cosmic unity of air, earth, and water that dwarfs the human figure (see Figure 27.6). Such landscapes are not literal imitations of reality, but expressions of a benign natural harmony. Executed in monochrome ink on silk, bamboo, or paper scrolls, they were intended as sources of personal pleasure and private retreat. Whether vertical or horizontal in format, they are "read" from a number of viewpoints, rather than from a single one. In all these features, Chinese landscapes differ from those of European artists.

In Europe, it was not until the Renaissance—among such painters as Leonardo da Vinci, Dürer, and Bruegel—that the natural landscape became a subject in its own right. Most Renaissance landscapes were visual records of a specific time and place (see Figure 19.12). During the seventeenth century, French academic painters cultivated the ideal landscape, a genre in which nature became the stage for mythological and biblical subjects (see Figure 21.13). The composition was conceived in the studio; key motifs, such as a foreground tree or a meandering road (often drawn from nature), were then incorporated into the design. Seventeenth-century Dutch masters, on the other hand, rejected the ideal landscape: Vermeer and Rembrandt rendered empirically precise views of

the physical world as perceived by the human eye (see Figure 23.12). During the following century, topographic landscapes—detailed descriptions of popular or remote locales—served the public as the picture postcards of their time. It was not until the nineteenth century, however, that the landscape became a primary vehicle for the expression of an artist's shifting moods and private emotions. The nineteenth-century "reinvention" of nature also coincided with a new interest in the age and evolution of the earth, a subject popularized by Darwin and his fellow geologists. Romantic painters would translate their native affection for the countryside into scenes that ranged from the picturesque to the sublime. Like Wordsworth and Shelley, these artists discovered in nature a source of inspiration and a mirror of their own sensibilities.

Constable and Turner

English artists took the lead in the genesis of the Romantic landscape. John Constable (1776–1837) owed much to the Dutch masters; yet his approach to nature was uncluttered by tradition. "When I sit down to make a sketch from nature," he wrote, "the first thing I try to do is

Figure 27.8 JOHN CONSTABLE, *The Haywain*, 1821. Oil on canvas, 4 ft. 3½ in. × 6 ft. 1 in. The artist originally titled this painting *Landscape: Noon.* On the specificity of time and place, he remarked: "No two days are alike, not even two hours; neither were there ever any two leaves alike since the creation of the world."

Figure 27.9 JOHN CONSTABLE, *Wivenhoe Park, Essex*, 1816. Oil on canvas, 1 ft. 10⅛ in. ✕ 3 ft. 3⅜ in. While Constable often made his sketches outdoors, where he was able to capture the effects of light in the landscape setting, he finished his paintings in his studio.

to forget that I have ever seen a picture." Constable's freshly perceived landscapes celebrate the physical beauty of the rivers, trees, and cottages of his native Suffolk countryside even as they describe the mundane labors of its inhabitants (Figure **27.8**). Like Wordsworth, who favored "incidents and situations from common life," Constable chose to paint ordinary subjects—"water escaping from mill-dams, willows, old rotten planks, slimy posts, and brickwork"— as he described them. And like Wordsworth, he drew on his childhood experiences as sources of inspiration. "Painting," Constable explained, "is with me but another word for feeling and I associate 'my careless boyhood' with all that lies on the banks of the Stour [River]; those scenes made me a painter, and I am grateful."

Constable brought to his landscapes a sensitive blend of empirical detail and painterly freedom. Fascinated by nineteenth-century treatises on the scientific classifications of clouds, he made numerous oil studies of cloud formations, noting on the reverse of each sketch the time of the year, hour of the day, and direction of the wind. "The sky," he wrote, "is the source of light in nature, and governs everything." He confessed to an "over-anxiety" about his skies and feared that he might destroy "that easy appearance which nature always has in all her movements." In order to capture the "easy appearance" of nature and the fugitive effects of light and atmosphere, he often stippled parts of the landscape with white dots (compare Vermeer; see chapter 23)—a device critics called "Constable's snow." His finished landscapes thus record not so much the "look" of nature as its fleeting moods.

In *Wivenhoe Park, Essex*, Constable depicts cattle grazing on English lawns that typically resemble well-manicured gardens (Figure **27.9**). From the distant horizon, the residence of the owners overlooks a verdant estate. Brilliant sunshine floods through the trees and across the fields onto a lake that is shared by swans and fishermen. But the real subject of the painting is the sky, which, with its wind-blown clouds, preserves the spontaneity of Constable's oil sketches.

If Constable's landscapes describe the gentle spirit of the English countryside, those of his English contemporary Joseph Mallord William Turner (1775–1851) invest nature with theatrical fervor. Trained in architectural draftsmanship, Turner began his career by making elegant drawings of Gothic ruins and popular tourist sites in England and Wales. These he sold to engravers, who mass-produced and marketed them. One of his early drawings, an intricate pencil sketch of the ruined monastery of Tintern Abbey, captures with some nostalgia the transient beauty of the medieval past (see Figure 27.3). Between 1814 and 1830, Turner traveled extensively throughout England and the Continent, making landscape studies of the mountains and lakes of Switzerland, the breathtaking reaches of the Alps, and the picturesque cities of Italy. His European tours inspired hundreds of rapid pencil sketches and luminous, eloquent studies executed in the spontaneous (and portable) medium of watercolor. His large-scale paintings of Venice, glorious explorations of the play of light on water, were among the most sought-after of his travel canvases.

In his mature style, the lyricism of Turner's early works gave way to impassioned studies of nature's more turbulent moods. Natural disasters—great storms and Alpine avalanches—and human catastrophes, such as shipwrecks and fires, became metaphors for human vulnerability before the forces of nature. Such expressions of the "sublime"—the terror human beings experience in the face of nature's overpowering forces—occupied the Romantic imagination. The sea, a symbol of nature's indomitable power, prevails as a Romantic theme in Coleridge's *Rime of the Ancient Mariner* (1798), Herman Melville's monumental novel *Moby-Dick* (1851), and Théodore Géricault's *The Raft of the "Medusa"* (see Figure 29.5), which Turner had seen in London.

In Turner's *Slave Ship* of 1840 (Figure **27.1**), the glowing sunset, turbulent seas, impending storm, and fantastic fish (that appear to devour the remains of the shackled body in the right foreground) do not immediately reveal the horror of the subject described in the original title: *Slavers Throwing Overboard the Dead and Dying: Typhoon Coming On.* While Britain had finally abolished slavery throughout its colonies in 1838, popular literature on the history of the slave trade published in 1839 recounted in some detail the notorious activity that inspired Turner's painting: the transatlantic traders' practice of throwing overboard the malnourished and disease-ridden bodies of African slaves, and then collecting insurance money on "goods lost" at sea. On the threshold of rising British commercialism (see chapter 30), Turner seems to suggest that the human capacity for evil rivals nature's cruelest powers.

Two years later, in *Snowstorm* (Figure **27.10**), Turner mounted his own Romantic engagement with nature: the 67-year-old artist claimed that, at his request, sailors lashed him to the mast of a ship caught for hours in a storm at sea so that he might "show what such a scene was like." He subtitled the painting "Steamboat off a Harbour's Mouth making Signals in Shallow Water . . . the Author was in this Storm on the Night the Ariel left Harwich." Since no ship by that name is listed in the records of the port of Harwich, Turner's imagination may have exceeded his experience. Nevertheless, as with many of Turner's late works, *Snowstorm* is an exercise in sensation and intuition. A swirling vortex of wind and waves, it is the imaginative transformation of an intense physical experience, which, recollected thereafter, evokes—as Wordsworth declared—"a sense sublime/ Of something far more deeply inter-fused,/ Whose dwelling is the light of setting suns,/ And the round ocean and the living air,/ And the blue sky, and in the mind of man." Turner's "landscapes of the sublime" come closer to capturing the spirit of Wordsworth's nature mysticism than do Constable's gentler views of the physical landscape. Their expanding and contracting forms and startling bursts of color, comparable to the impassioned

Figure 27.10 J. M. W. TURNER, *Snowstorm: Steamboat off a Harbour's Mouth*, 1842. Oil on canvas, 3 × 4 ft. Turner's claim that he was lashed to the mast may have been inspired by a similar event in the Greek epic the *Odyssey*. The English writer John Ruskin described *Snowstorm* as "one of the very grandest statements of sea motion, mist, and light that has ever been put on canvas."

Figure 27.11 JEAN-BAPTISTE-CAMILLE COROT, *Ville d'Avray*, 1870. Oil on canvas, 21⅝ × 31½ in. Even in his own time, forgeries of Corot's late paintings were produced in great numbers. Some of these were the result of Corot's practice of allowing his students to copy his works. One French collection is said to contain almost 2500 Corot forgeries.

rhythms and brilliant dynamics of much Romantic music, were daringly innovative at the time. Critics disparagingly called Turner's transparent veils of color—resembling his beloved watercolors—"tinted steam" and "soapsuds." In hundreds of canvases that he never dared to exhibit, Turner all but abandoned recognizable subject matter; these experiments in light and color anticipated those of the French Impressionists by more than three decades.

Landscape Painting in France

On the Continent, the artists of the Barbizon School—named after the picturesque village on the edge of the forest of Fontainebleau near Paris—were among the first to take their easels out of doors. Working directly from nature (although usually finishing the canvas in the studio), they painted modest landscapes and scenes of rural life. These unsentimental views of the local countryside were highly successful in capturing nature's moods.

The greatest French landscape painter of the mid-nineteenth century, Jean-Baptiste-Camille Corot (1796–1875), shared the Barbizon preference for working outdoors, but he brought to his compositions a breath-taking sense of harmony and order. Corot's early landscapes, executed for the most part in Italy, are as formally composed as the paintings of Poussin and David; they are, however, more personal and more serene. Corot's luminescent late paintings are intimate and contempla-tive (Figure **27.11**). He called them *souvenirs*, that is,

"remembrances," to indicate that they were recollections of previous visual experiences, rather than on-the-spot accounts. Like many artists, Corot kept notebooks in which he jotted his everyday thoughts. One passage per-fectly captures the Romantic point of view:

> Be guided by feeling alone. We are only simple mortals, subject to error, so listen to the advice of others, but follow only what you understand and can unite in your own feeling . . . Beauty in art is truth bathed in an impression received from nature.

Corot's poetic landscapes, filled with feathery trees and misty rivers, and bathed in nuances of silver light, became so popular in France and elsewhere that he was able to sell as many canvases as he could paint.

American Romanticism

Transcendentalism

Across the Atlantic, along the east-ern shores of the rapidly indus-trializing American continent, Romanticism took hold both as an attitude of mind and as a style. Romanticism infused all aspects of nineteenth-century American culture: it distinguished the frontier tales of James Fenimore Cooper (1789–1851), the mysteries of

Edgar Allan Poe (1809–1849), and the novels of Nathaniel Hawthorne (1804–1864) and Herman Melville (1819–1891). But it found its purest expression in the cultural movement known as *transcendentalism*. The group of New England Unitarian ministers who formed the first Transcendental Club took its name from a treatise by the German philosopher Friedrich Schiller. Schiller's *System of Transcendental Idealism* (1800) defended the oneness of Spirit and Nature and encouraged the realization of the higher spiritual self through sympathy with nature. The American transcendentalists—descendants of the English Puritans—held that knowledge gained by way of intuition transcended knowledge based on reason and logic. Reacting against the material excesses of advancing industrialization, they found sympathetic ideals in such mystical philosophies as Neoplatonism, and in the religions of East Asia, introduced into the Boston area in the early nineteenth century. From Hinduism and Buddhism, they adopted a holistic philosophy based in pantheism and in the ideal of a "universal brotherhood" shared by humanity, nature, and God.

The prime exemplar of the transcendentalists was Ralph Waldo Emerson (1803–1882), whose essays powerfully influenced nineteenth-century American thought. The son and grandson of clergymen, Emerson was ordained as a Unitarian minister when he was in his twenties. Like Wordsworth, he courted nature to "see into the life of things" and to taste its cleansing power. In the essay entitled "Nature" (1836), Emerson sets forth a pantheistic credo:

> In the woods is perpetual youth. Within these
> plantations of God, a decorum and sanctity reign,
> a perennial festival is dressed, and the guest sees not
> how he should tire of them in a thousand years. In

LOOKING INTO

Emerson's "Brahma" (1856)

Ralph Waldo Emerson's admiration for Asian philosophy, and Hinduism in particular, derived from his familiarity with the sacred Hindu texts, the *Upanishads* and the *Bhagavad-Gita*, in which Brahman is identified as the Universal Spirit. The three expressions of Brahmanic power—creation, preservation, and destruction—are represented by the gods Brahma, Vishnu, and Shiva (see chapter 14). In his poem "Brahma," the World Creator, Emerson reminds the reader that a single identity underlies the illusion of all apparent differences in nature. The universal forces, even life and death, are One, the knowledge of which surpasses the prospect of heaven.

If the red slayer think he slays,	/the Hindu warrior is mistaken to think he kills
Or if the slain think he is slain,	/the victim is mistaken to think he is dead
They know not well the subtle ways	/neither understand that Death and Life are the same
I keep, and pass, and turn again.	/in that I (Brahma) create, destroy, and recreate
Far or forgot to me is near;	/far and near are one in Brahma
Shadow and sunlight are the same;	/dark and light are one in Brahma
The vanished gods to me appear;	/all ancient divinities are present to Brahma
and one to me are shame and fame.	/all states of being coexist in Brahma
They reckon ill who leave me out;	/any who fail to recognize the Creator misunderstands
When me they fly, I am the wings;	/the Particular and the Individual are one and the same
I am the doubter and the doubt,	/Brahma is both subject and object
I am the hymn the Brahmin sings.	/the prayers of the Hindu priest are identical with Brahma
The strong gods pine for my abode;	/powerful deities envy Brahma's lofty status (passiveness trumps physical might)
And pine in vain the sacred Seven;	/Brahma is envied by the Saptarishi (seven Hindu sages descended from the constellation Ursa Major) who brought the Vedas and other sacred texts to humankind
But thou, meek lover of the good!	/thou=reader
Find me, and turn thy back on heaven.	/must seek oneness with Brahma, not salvation/heaven

Q What aspects of Hindu religion does Emerson's poem reflect?

Q How do they compare with typical Western religious beliefs?

the woods, we return to reason and faith. There I feel that nothing can befall me in life—no disgrace, no calamity (leaving my eyes), which nature cannot repair. Standing on the bare ground—my head bathed by the blithe air and uplifted into infinite space—all mean egotism vanishes. I become a transparent eyeball; I am nothing; I see all; the currents of the Universal Being circulate through me; I am part or parcel of God.

Although best known for his essays, especially those on the virtues of self-reliance and nonconformity, Emerson was a poet of considerable talent. He shared with Coleridge and Wordsworth (both of whom he had met in England) a mystic reverence for nature; but he also brought to his poetry a unique appreciation of Asian philosophy, which he had acquired by reading some of the central works of Hindu literature, including the *Bhagavad-Gita* (see chapter 3). In Emerson's short poem "Brahma" (see LOOKING INTO), the pantheistic philosophy of the transcendentalists is given lyric expression.

Emerson's friend Henry David Thoreau (1817–1862) set into practice many of the antimaterialist ideals of the transcendentalists. In his youth, Thoreau earned a bachelor's degree at Harvard University and made his way in the world by tutoring, surveying, and making pencils. An avid opponent of slavery, he was jailed briefly for refusing to pay a poll tax to a pro-slavery government. In an influential essay on civil disobedience, Thoreau defended the philosophy of passive resistance and moral idealism that he himself practiced—a philosophy embraced by the twentieth-century leaders Mohandas Karamchand Gandhi and Martin Luther King.

In 1845 Thoreau abandoned urban society to live in the Massachusetts woods near Walden Pond—an experiment that lasted twenty-six months. He described his love of the natural world, his nonconformist attitude toward society, and his deep commitment to monkish simplicity in his "handbook for living," called *Walden, or Life in the Woods*. In this intimate yet forthright diary, Thoreau glorifies nature as innocent and beneficent—a source of joy and practical instruction.

── READING 27.6 From Thoreau's *Walden* (1854)

Near the end of March, 1845, I borrowed an axe and went 1
down to the woods by Walden Pond, nearest to where
I intended to build my house, and began to cut down some tall,
arrowy white pines, still in their youth, for timber. . . . It was a
pleasant hillside where I worked, covered with pine woods,
through which I looked out on the pond, and a small open field
in the woods where pines and hickories were springing up. The
ice in the pond was not yet dissolved, though there were some
open spaces, and it was all dark-colored and saturated with
water. There were some slight flurries of snow during the days 10
that I worked there; but for the most part when I came out on
to the railroad, on my way home, its yellow sand-heap
stretched away gleaming in the hazy atmosphere, and the rails
shone in the spring sun, and I heard the lark and pewee and
other birds already come to commence another year with us.

They were pleasant spring days, in which the winter of man's discontent was thawing as well as the earth, and the life that had lain torpid began to stretch itself. One day, when my axe had come off and I had cut a green hickory for a wedge, driving it with a stone, and had placed the whole to soak in a pond- 20
hole in order to swell the wood, I saw a striped snake run into the water, and he lay on the bottom, apparently without inconvenience, as long as I stayed there, or more than a quarter of an hour; perhaps because he had not yet fairly come out of the torpid state. It appeared to me that for a like reason men remain in their present low and primitive condition; but if they should feel the influence of the spring of springs arousing them, they would of necessity rise to a higher and more ethereal life. I had previously seen the snakes on frosty mornings in my path with portions of their bodies still numb 30
and inflexible, waiting for the sun to thaw them. On the 1st of April it rained and melted the ice, and in the early part of the day, which was very foggy, I heard a stray goose groping about over the pond and cackling as if lost, or like the spirit of the fog. . . .

I went to the woods because I wished to live deliberately, to front only the essential facts of life, and see if I could not learn what it had to teach, and not, when I came to die, discover that I had not lived. I did not wish to live what was not life, living is so dear; nor did I wish to practice resignation, unless it was 40
quite necessary. I wanted to live deep and suck out all the marrow of life, to live so sturdily and Spartan-like as to put to rout all that was not life, to cut a broad swath and shave close, to drive life into a corner, and reduce it to its lowest terms, and, if it proved to be mean, why then to get the whole and genuine meanness of it, and publish its meanness to the world; or if it were sublime, to know it by experience, and be able to give a true account of it in my next excursion. For most men, it appears to me, are in a strange uncertainty about it, whether it is of the devil or of God, and have *somewhat hastily* concluded 50
that it is the chief end of man here to "glorify God and enjoy him forever." . . .

Simplicity, simplicity, simplicity! I say, let your affairs be as two or three, and not a hundred or a thousand; instead of a million count half a dozen, and keep your accounts on your thumb-nail. . . . Instead of three meals a day, if it be necessary eat but one; instead of a hundred dishes, five; and reduce other things in proportion. . . .

The indescribable innocence and beneficence of Nature,— of sun and wind and rain, of summer and winter,—such health, 60
such cheer, they afford forever! and such sympathy have they ever with our race, that all Nature would be affected, and the sun's brightness fade, and the winds would sigh humanely, and the clouds rain tears, and the woods shed their leaves and put on mourning in midsummer, if any man should ever for a just cause grieve. Shall I not have intelligence with the earth? Am I not partly leaves and vegetable mould myself? . . .

─ **Q** Was Thoreau's retreat to Walden Pond an adventure in practical survival or an extended mystical experience?

└─ **Q** What might Thoreau mean by "the indescribable innocence and beneficence of nature"?

Walt Whitman's Romantic Individualism

Although technically not a transcendentalist, Walt Whitman (1818–1892; Figure **27.12**) gave voice to the transcendental world-view and to the Emersonian credo of self-reliance. He worked as a Brooklyn printer and newspaper editor, a teacher, and a nurse in the American Civil War. His essays and poems, which have become an influential part of the American canon, assert his affection for the American landscape and its human inhabitants.

Like Wordsworth, Whitman took everyday life as his subject; he too had little use for the artificiality of traditional poetic diction. What he referred to as his "barbaric yawp" found ideal expression in **free verse** (poetry based on irregular rhythmic patterns rather than on the conventional use of meter). His unmetrical rhythms and sonorous cadences are rich in alliteration, assonance, and repetition. He loved Italian opera, and his style often simulates the musical grandeur of that genre.

The prevailing themes in Whitman's poetry are nationalism and democracy. He embraced the ordinary individual and sympathized with marginal people, felons, and prostitutes. Claiming to be a poet of the body as well as the soul, he defended an honest recognition of the physical self. The American scene was the source of endless inspiration for the sprawling, cosmic images that dominate his autobiographical masterpiece, *Leaves of Grass* (1855).

Figure 27.12 THOMAS EAKINS, *Walt Whitman*, 1888. Oil on canvas, 30⅛ × 24¼ in.

The first edition of this collection of poems was met with strident criticism for its freewheeling verse forms and its candid celebration of all forms of sexuality—one reviewer attacked the book as "a mixture of Yankee transcendentalism and New York rowdyism." "Song of Myself," the longest of the lyric poems included in *Leaves of Grass*, proclaims the expansive individualism of America's Romantic movement. At the same time, it voices Whitman's impassioned plea for unity with nature and with all humankind.

READING 27.7 From Whitman's
"Song of Myself" (1855)

1

I celebrate myself, and sing myself,   1
And what I assume you shall assume,
For every atom belonging to me as good belongs to you.

I loaf and invite my soul,
I learn and loaf at my ease observing a spear of summer grass.   5

My tongue, every atom of my blood, form'd from this soil,
    this air,
Born of parents born here from parents the same, and their
    parents the same,
I, now thirty-seven years old in perfect health begin,
Hoping to cease not till death.
Creeds and schools in abeyance,   10
Retiring back a while sufficed at what they are, but never
    forgotten,
I harbor for good or bad, I permit to speak at every hazard,
Nature without check with original energy.

24

Walt Whitman, a kosmos, of Manhattan the son,   1
Turbulent, fleshy, sensual, eating, drinking and breeding,
No sentimentalist, no stander above men and women or apart
    from them,
No more modest than immodest.

Unscrew the locks from the doors!   5
Unscrew the doors themselves from their jambs!
Whoever degrades another degrades me,
And whatever is done or said returns at last to me.
Through me the afflatus surging and surging, through me the
    current and index.

I speak the pass-word primeval, I give the sign of democracy,   10
By God! I will accept nothing which all cannot have their
    counterpart of on the same terms.

Through me many long dumb voices,
Voices of the interminable generations of prisoners and slaves,
Voices of the diseas'd and despairing and of thieves and
    dwarfs,
Voices of cycles of preparation and accretion,   15
And of the threads that connect the stars, and of wombs and

of the father-stuff,
And of the rights of them the others are down upon,
Of the deform'd, trivial, flat, foolish, despised,
Fog in the air, beetles rolling balls of dung.

Through me forbidden voices,   20
Voices of sexes and lusts, voices veil'd and I remove the veil,
Voices indecent by me clarified and transfigur'd.

I do not press my fingers across my mouth,
I keep as delicate around the bowels as around the head and
    heart,
Copulation is no more rank to me than death is.   25
I believe in the flesh and the appetites,
Seeing, hearing, feeling, are miracles, and each part and tag of
    me is a miracle.

Divine am I inside and out, and I make holy whatever I touch
    or am touch'd from,
The scent of these arm-pits aroma finer than prayer,
This head more than churches, bibles, and all the creeds.   30

52

The spotted hawk swoops by and accuses me, he complains of
    my gab and my loitering.   1

I too am not a bit tamed, I too am untranslatable,
I sound my barbaric yawp over the roofs of the world.

The last scud of day holds back for me,
It flings my likeness after the rest and true as any on the
    shadow'd wilds,   5
It coaxes me to the vapor and the dusk.

I depart as air, I shake my white locks at the runaway sun,
I effuse my flesh in eddies, and drift it in lacy jags.
I bequeath myself to the dirt to grow from the grass I love,
If you want me again look for me under your boot-soles.   10

You will hardly know who I am or what I mean,
But I shall be good health to you nevertheless,
And filter and fibre your blood.

Failing to fetch me at first keep encouraged,
Missing me one place search another,   15
I stop somewhere waiting for you.

Q **How does Whitman's poetry (and personality)**
compare with that of the European Romantics
(Readings 27.1 to 27.4)?

American Landscape Painting

Landscape painters in America mirrored the sentiments
of the transcendentalists by capturing what Thoreau
described as "the indescribable innocence and beneficence of nature." No less than the European Romantics,
American artists took clear delight in the beauty of nature
and its fleeting moods. But they also brought to their art
a nationalistic infatuation with one of their young nation's

unique features—its unspoiled and resplendent terrain.
Mountain ranges, broad lakes and rivers, and verdant
forests are precisely and lovingly documented. It is as if
these painters felt compelled to record with photographic
precision the majesty and moral power of the American
continent and, at the same time, capture the magnitude
of its untamed wilderness. Panorama and painstaking
detail are features found in the topographic landscapes of
the Hudson River School—a group of artists who worked
chiefly in the region of upstate New York during the 1830s
and 1840s.

One of the leading figures of the Hudson River School
was the British-born Thomas Cole (1801–1848), whose
Oxbow (Figure **27.13**) offers a view of the Connecticut River
near Northampton, Massachusetts. In this landscape, Cole
achieved a dramatic mood by framing the brightly lit hills
and curving river of the distant vista with the darker motifs
of a departing thunderstorm and a blighted tree.

Intrigued by America's drive to settle the West, the
German-born Albert Bierstadt (1830–1902) made panoramic depictions of that virginal territory. Bierstadt's landscape of the Rocky Mountains, which includes a Native
American encampment in the foreground, reflects his fascination with the templelike purity of America's vast, rugged spaces along the Western frontier (Figure **27.14**). The
isolated settlement, dwarfed and enshrined by snowcapped
mountains, a magnificent waterfall, and a looking-glass
lake—all bathed in golden light—is an American Garden
of Eden, inhabited by tribes of unspoiled "noble savages."
Bierstadt gave cosmic breadth to the ancient Roman genre
of the idyllic landscape, in which humankind and nature
flourish in perfect harmony. The huge dimensions of the
painting (some 6×10 feet) heralded the official establishment of landscape as a respectable genre, comparable to
historical and religious subjects that, in academic tradition,
commanded large canvases. Such "frontier landscapes"
also gave public evidence of American expansionism and
ascending nationalism.

Most nineteenth-century American artists visited
Europe and spent years studying abroad; however, for the
ordinary public, panoramic landscapes depicting remote
locales were substitutes for actual travel, and viewers were
known to carry binoculars to their showings, admission
to which usually required entrance fees. Such was in fact
the case with the paintings of Frederic Edwin Church
(1826–1900), a pupil of Thomas Cole. Church's celebrated
vista of Niagara Falls, displayed in a ticketed exhibition in
New York City, was visited by more than 100,000 spectators
(Figure **27.15**). His rendering of the Falls as seen from the
Canadian side includes almost no foreground, thus putting
viewers at the brink of the rushing water. The skyborne
rainbow, one of Church's favorite devices, would have
been recognized as a symbol of divine benevolence and
harmony. One critic called *Niagara* "the finest picture ever
painted on this side of the Atlantic."

Other Church landscapes, illustrating tropical storms,
erupting volcanoes, and gigantic icebergs, transported
American gallery patrons to the exotic places—Brazil,
Ecuador, Newfoundland—the artist himself had visited.

Figure 27.13 THOMAS COLE, *The Oxbow (View from Mount Holyoke, Northampton, Massachusetts, After a Thunderstorm)*, 1836. Oil on canvas, 4 ft. 3½ in. × 6 ft. 4 in. The loop made by the Connecticut River at Northampton was a well-known early nineteenth-century tourist spot. At the lower center of the canvas, Cole is pictured at his easel; his signature is found on his portfolio at the lower edge of the painting.

Figure 27.14 ALBERT BIERSTADT, *The Rocky Mountains, Lander's Peak*, 1863. Oil on canvas, 6 ft. 1 in. × 10 ft. ¾ in.

Figure 27.15 FREDERIC EDWIN CHURCH, *Niagara*, 1857. Oil on canvas, 42½ × 90½ in. Grand scale and fine detail characterize this typically nineteenth-century American painting. A contemporary newspaper critic exulted, "We know of no American landscape which unites as this does the merits of composition and treatment."

Such scenes, produced in the age of polar exploration and shipwrecks, conjured awe and a sense of the Romantic sublime. Called by his contemporaries "the Michelangelo of landscape art," Church became the most famous American painter of his time.

America and Native Americans

The Romantic fascination with unspoiled nature and "natural man" also inspired documentary studies of Native Americans, such as those executed by the artist–ethnologist George Catlin (1796–1872). During the 1830s, Catlin went to live among the Native Americans of the Great Plains. Moved by what he called the "silent and stoic dignity" of America's tribal peoples, he recorded their lives and customs in literature, as well as in hundreds of drawings and paintings (Figure **27.16**). Catlin's "Gallery of Indians," exhibited widely in mid-nineteenth-century Europe, drew more acclaim abroad than it did in his own country. Catlin popularized the image of Native Americans as people who deeply respected nature and the natural world (see chapter 18). He described exotic rituals designed to honor the Great Spirit (or Great Sun) and promote health and fertility. Observing that most tribes killed only as much game as was actually needed to feed themselves, Catlin brought attention to Native Americans as the first ecologists.

Harmony with nature and its living creatures was central to Native American culture, whose pantheistic idealism is eloquently conveyed in the proverbial teachings of the northwestern tribes: "The Earth does not belong to us; we belong to the earth . . . We did not weave the web of life; we are merely a strand in it. Whatever we do to the web,

we do to ourselves." Following ancestral tradition, Native Americans looked upon living things—plants, animals, and human beings—as sacred parts of an all-embracing, spiritually charged environment. Their arts, which for the most part served religious and communal purposes, reflect their need, at the same time, to protect the balance between these natural forces, and to take spiritual advantage of their transformative and healing powers. Woodcarving, pottery, basket-weaving, beadwork embroidery, sand painting, and other Native American crafts make significant use of natural imagery, but do so in ways that are profoundly different from the artistic enterprises of European and American Romantics: whereas Western artists perceived nature from "without," as a source of moral and aesthetic inspiration, Native American artists perceived nature from "within," as a power to be harnessed and respected. A polychrome water jar from the Zuni Pueblos of the American Southwest is treated as a living being whose spirit or breath may escape from the bowl by means of an opening in the path (the double line) painted around the vessel's shoulder (Figure **27.17**). In the body of the deer represented on the bowl, a "spirit" line links heart and mouth—a convention that derives from prehistoric pottery decoration.

Not the panoramic landscape, but the natural forces and living creatures immediate to that landscape, preoccupied native artists. As Catlin observed while living with the Plains Indians, natural forms embellished all ceremonial objects, one of the most important of which was the carved stone pipe. Pipes were often presented as gifts to seal tribal alliances. They were believed to be charged with supernatural power, and pipe-smoking—both public and private—was a sacred act. Among the Plains Indians, pipes were considered "activated" when the stem (symbolic of male power) was joined to the bowl (symbolic of the maternal earth). Often produced jointly by men and women, Plains pipes were carved out of catlinite, a red stone quarried in southwestern Minnesota (so named because Catlin was the first to bring east samples of this distinctive mineral). Legend identified the stone variously as the flesh of a mythical tribal people or the congealed blood of all dead Indians and dead buffalo. Catlinite pipes served in rituals for healing. They usually carry effigies of legendary birds, bears, or water creatures (Figure **27.18**).

Popularizing the culture of the Native American in literature, the American poet Henry Wadsworth Longfellow (1807–1882) offered a sentimental picture of American Indian life in his narrative poem *The Song of Hiawatha* (1885). This fictional tale is based on the life of a sixteenth-century Mohawk statesman. Unfortunately, neither Longfellow nor Catlin, nor the achievements of the Native Americans themselves, impeded the wholesale destruction of Native American cultures. Beginning in the 1830s, under pressure from the United States government, tribes were forced to cede their homelands and their hunting grounds to white settlers and to move into unoccupied lands in the American West. The perception of the Native American as the "devil savage" prevailed over the Romantic notion of the "noble savage" and came to justify America's effort to "civilize" its "savage" populations through policies (strongly criticized by Catlin and others) that forced most tribes to take up residence on "reservations" and, more often than not, to abandon their native languages, religions, and traditions. Persecution, humiliation, outright physical attack, and the continuing effects of disease further accelerated the decline and near extinction of America's indigenous peoples.

Figure 27.16 GEORGE CATLIN, *The White Cloud, Head Chief of the Iowas*, 1844–1845. Oil on canvas, 28 × 22⅞ in. Catlin considered the Native Americans of the northern plains, the frontier between the United States and Canada, the least corrupted by contact with other Americans. In paintings introduced to Europeans, he presented them as "nature's sovereign nobility."

Figure 27.17 Zuni water jar, nineteenth century. Height 9½ in.

Figure 27.18 Catlinite pipe (possibly a specialized medicine pipe or one for women's use) representing a fanged and crested water spirit, with fish effigy stem, 1850–1860. Sioux tribe, carved in Minnesota. Length 8⅝ in. After the Europeans introduced the horse to Native American culture, this animal joined the more traditional motifs used to ornament ritual pipes.

American Folk Art

American folk artists produced some of the most interesting artworks of the nineteenth century. Unlike professionally trained artists, such as Cole and Church, folk artists lacked technical schooling in the visual arts. Nevertheless, they were inspired to adorn their everyday surroundings with objects that often manifested extraordinary sensitivity to design and affection for natural detail.

One of the most distinctive of nineteenth-century folk art genres was the hand-stitched quilt, a utilitarian object produced almost exclusively by women. Unlike academic art objects, quilts were often communal projects. Several women embroidered or appliquéd designs onto individual fabric patches salvaged from leftover sewing materials. Then, at popular quilting "bees," they assembled the patches into bedcovers some 9 by 8 feet in size. Quilt motifs, frequently drawn from nature, were stylized and brightly colored (Figure **27.19**). Many became standardized patterns that were passed from mother to daughter and from household to household. Patchwork quilts might commemorate religious or family occasions (such as weddings) or public events, but they rarely

Figure 27.19 SARAH ANNE WHITTINGTON LANKFORD, probably Mary Evans, and possibly others, Baltimore Albion Quilt, ca. 1850. Appliqué, 8 ft. 3 in. × 7 ft. At the top of the quilt is pictured an American war memorial and a schematic rendering of the newly completed United States Capitol.

narrated a story. Rather, they conveyed meaning through abstract signs and symbols. A folk record of nature and the natural, quilt-making and related textile arts constitute a decorative yet intimate nineteenth-century American artform.

The Romantic sanctification of nature is even more vividly configured in *The Peaceable Kingdom* (Figure **27.20**), a painting by the American folk artist Edward Hicks (1780–1849). A Quaker minister in Bucks County, Pennsylvania, Hicks was also a popular sign-painter. His inspiration for more than one hundred versions of this utopian subject came from the Book of Isaiah: "The wolf also shall dwell with the lamb, and the leopard shall lie down with the kid . . . and a little child shall lead them" (11:6–9). Hicks set his charming, wide-eyed beasts and weightless, diminutive children in a verdant landscape. In the background, at the far left, Hicks' fellow Quaker William Penn displays the peace treaty signed with the Lenape tribe (an event that had also figured in academic American art). The decorative handling of the composition and its disregard for traditional perspective contributes to its visual immediacy; but it is in the gestures of the children, reaching out lovingly to the wild creatures in their midst, that Hicks establishes the link between natural innocence and peace.

Figure 27.20 EDWARD HICKS, *The Peaceable Kingdom*, ca. 1834. Oil on canvas, 30 × 35½ in. Hicks, a great admirer of his fellow Quaker William Penn, painted no less than sixty-one versions of this painting.

The Progress of Industrialization

- Nineteenth-century Europe experienced a population boom; increased production of coal, iron, and steel encouraged expansion of industry and commerce in the West. In this industrially based society, goods were increasingly made in factories rather than in homes.
- Advancing industrialization encouraged urbanization and spurred Western efforts to find markets and resources in other parts of the world.

Early Nineteenth-Century Thought

- German philosophers, influenced by Asian philosophy and Kantian idealism, viewed nature subjectively and in the direction of mysticism.
- Hegel proposed a dialectical model according to which all reality, all history, and all ideas progressed toward perfect spiritual freedom.
- Darwin argued that by means of natural selection, all living things, including human beings, evolved from a few simple forms: species either develop into higher forms of life or fail to survive.
- While the theory of natural selection displaced human beings from their elevated place in the hierarchy of living creatures, it advanced the idea of the unity of nature and humankind.

Nature and the Natural in European Literature

- Nature provided both a metaphor for the Romantic sensibility and a refuge from the evils of nineteenth-century industrialization and urbanization.
- William Wordsworth, the leading nature poet of the nineteenth century, embraced the redemptive power of nature. Exalting the natural landscape as the source of sublime inspiration and moral truth, Wordsworth and his English contemporaries initiated the Romantic movement.
- The Romantics stressed the free exercise of the imagination, the liberation of the senses, and the cultivation of a more natural language of poetic expression.
- Shelley compared the elemental forces of nature with the creative powers of the poet, while Keats rejoiced that nature's fleeting beauty might forever dwell in art. Blake's deeply spiritual poems reflect a visionary and moral perception of nature.

Nature and the Natural in Asian Literature

- The Romantic embrace of nature and natural imagery was not confined to the West: in Chinese literature, as reflected in Shen Fu's confessional prose, nature became a source of inspiration and personal solace.
- Chinese poets and painters described the natural landscape by way of a few carefully chosen words and images.

Romantic Landscape Painting

- It was among Western Romantics that the landscape became a major vehicle for the expression of the artist's moods and emotions.
- Constable's contemplative scenes of English country life and Turner's sublime vistas are the visual counterparts of the poems of Wordsworth.
- The elegiac landscapes of Friedrich in Germany and Corot in France reflect the efforts of Romantic artists to explore nature's shifting states as metaphors for human feeling.

American Romanticism

- American Romantics endowed the quest for natural simplicity with a robust spirit of individualism. The transcendentalists Emerson and Thoreau sought a union of self with nature; Walt Whitman proclaimed his untamed and "untranslatable" ego in sympathy with nature's energy.
- In the American landscapes of Cole, Bierstadt, and Church, nature becomes symbolic of an unspoiled and rapidly vanishing world; in the art of George Catlin, the native populations and traditions of America are lovingly documented.
- Among Native Americans, yet another (less Romantic but equally mystical) view of nature flourished, as evidenced in magnificent ceremonial objects.
- American folk art, as typified by the paintings of Edward Hicks, made use of natural imagery for decorative and symbolic purposes.

Glossary

assonance a literary device involving similarity in sound between vowels followed by different consonants

dialectic in Hegelian philosophy, the process by which every condition (or "thesis") confronts an opposite condition (or "antithesis") to resolve in synthesis

eugenics the science of improving human beings by means of genetic manipulation

free verse poetry that is based on irregular rhythmic patterns rather than on the conventional and regular use of meter

lyric poetry "lyric" means accompanied by the lyre, hence, verse that is meant to be sung rather than spoken; poetry marked by individual and personal emotion (see also chapter 5)

pantheism the belief that a divine spirit pervades all things in the universe

Chapter 28

The Romantic Hero

ca. 1780–1880

*"O hero, with whose bloodied story
Long, long the earth will still resound . . ."*
Pushkin

Figure 28.1 JACQUES-LOUIS DAVID, *Napoleon Crossing the Great Saint Bernard Pass*, 1800. Oil on canvas, 8 ft. 6 in. × 7 ft. 3 in. When the painting entitled *General Bonaparte's Passage over Mont St. Bernard* was first exhibited in London, it was described as follows: "He is here represented braving all the obstacles which Nature seemed to oppose to his passage; the winds, the cold, ice, snow, and thunder; nothing stops him; with one hand he is assisting his horse to mount these impractical rocks, with the other he is pointing out to his brave followers the dangers they have still to surmount, before they arrive where Glory calls them."

As the Romantics embraced nature, so they exalted the creative individual in the person of the hero. Heroes, whether mortal or divine, symbolize humanity at its best, most powerful, and godlike. Like the literary heroes of the past—Gilgamesh, Achilles, and Roland—the Romantic hero was a larger-than-life figure with extraordinary expectations, abilities, and goals. But whereas the literary hero defended the traditions and moral values of a society, the Romantic hero might challenge or seek to reform them.

The Romantics saw themselves as the visionaries of their time: as champions of a cult of the senses and of the heart. "*Exister, pour nous, c'est sentir*" ("For us, to exist is to feel"), proclaimed Rousseau, the late eighteenth-century prophet of Romanticism.

The spirit of the heroic self was anticipated in Rousseau's declaration: "I am made unlike anyone I have ever met; I will even venture to say that I am like no one in the whole world. I may be no better, but at least I am different." Working to fulfill their own personal vision, Romantic poets, painters, and composers freed themselves from dependence on the patronage of Church and state. At the same time, they defended the ideals of liberty and brotherhood associated with emerging nationalism. They opposed entrenched systems of slavery and institutional limitations to personal freedom. The nineteenth century did not produce more heroes than other centuries, but it celebrated the heroic personality as representative of the Romantic sensibility.

Nationalism and the Hero

Nationalism—the exaltation of the sovereign state—was one of the shaping forces of nineteenth-century culture. While the beginnings of the modern nation-state go back at least to the fourteenth century (see chapter 15), nationalism, an ideology (or belief system) grounded in a people's sense of cultural and political unity, did not gain widespread acceptance until roughly 1815. Modern nationalism flourished in the wake of the French Revolution and, thereafter, in resistance to the imperialistic expansion of Napoleonic France. One after another, European states, as well as some in Africa and in Latin America, rose up against foreign rulers. Love of nation and love of liberty became synonymous with the ideals of self-determination and political freedom. In its positive aspects, nationalism cultivated the revival and celebration of a common language, common customs, and a shared history, as expressed in poetry, music, and art. The collection of German fairy tales (1812–1815) by the brothers Jacob and Wilhelm Grimm serves as an example. But nationalism also manifested a malignant aspect: well into the twentieth century, nationalism and patriotic chauvinism motivated policies of imperialism and ignited warfare, not only between nations, but also among the ethnic populations of various regions. Indeed, as these chapters reveal, much of the art of the nineteenth century is a visceral response to brutal events associated with nascent nationalism.

Nineteenth-century intellectuals celebrated the heroic personality, especially in its dedication to the causes of liberty and equality. The British historian and essayist Thomas Carlyle (1795–1881) published a series of lectures, *On Heroes and Hero-Worship*, in which he glorified hero-gods, prophets, poets, priests, men of letters, and the quasi-legendary Napoleon Bonaparte. Walter Scott (1771–1832) and Alexandre Dumas (1802–1870) wrote historical novels that described the heroic adventures of swashbuckling soldiers and maidens in distress, while Victor Hugo (1802–1885) made sentimental heroes out of egalitarian patriots in the novel *Les Misérables*. Real-life heroes challenged literary heroes in courage and daring. The Zulu warrior Shaka (1787–1828) changed the destiny of the southern region of Africa by leading aggressive campaigns that united the local clans, thus forming the Zulu nation.

In America, heroic themes occupied the attention of the novelists Nathaniel Hawthorne (1804–1864) and Herman Melville (1819–1891). Each created brooding, melancholic fictional heroes whose moral strength was tested by the forces of evil. The two leading figures (Ishmael and Ahab) in Melville's great sea novel *Moby-Dick* are semi-autobiographical characterizations, inspired by Melville's adventures as the foremast hand on a whaling ship and as a sailor in the United States Navy. Then too, the Americas produced some notable real-life heroes and champions of political freedom, such as Simón Bolívar (1783–1830)—whose victories over the Spanish forces in South America won independence for Bolivia, Colombia, Ecuador, Peru, and Venezuela—and Frederick Douglass (1817–1895), the leading antislavery spokesman, whose autobiography details a heroic life of oppression and struggle.

Napoleon as a Romantic Hero

In 1799 the thirty-year-old Corsican army general Napoleon Bonaparte (1769–1821) seized control of the government of France. He ended civil strife, reorganized the educational system, and institutionalized the system of civil law known as the *Code Napoléon*. "The Revolution is ended," announced Napoleon as he proclaimed himself emperor in 1804. Over the following ten years, he pursued a policy of conquest that brought continental Western Europe to his feet. Throughout much of the West he abolished serfdom, expropriated Church possessions, curtailed feudal privileges, and introduced French laws, institutions, and influence. Spreading the revolutionary ideals of liberty, fraternity, and equality throughout his empire (Map **28.1**), he championed popular sovereignty and kindled sentiments of nationalism.

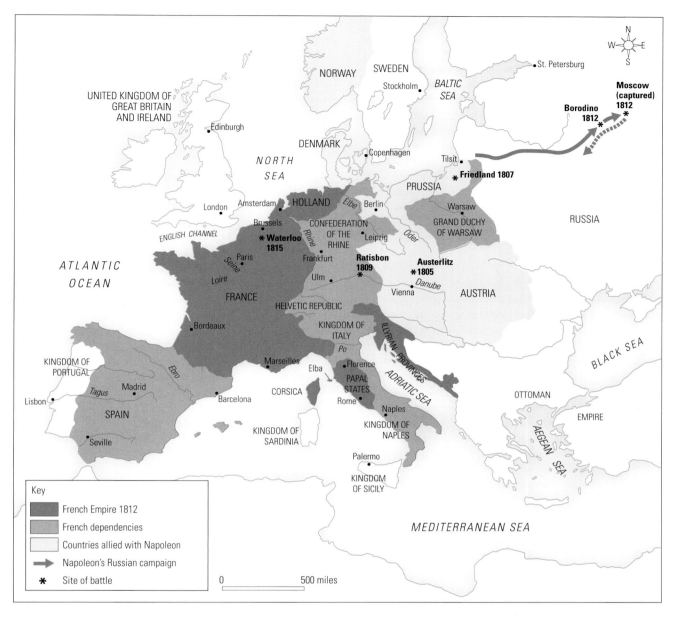

Map 28.1 The Empire of Napoleon at its Greatest Extent, 1812. In the lands he controlled directly and indirectly, Napoleon tried to initiate revolutionary reforms and institutions, an effort that generally met with resistance.

If Napoleon's ambitions were heroic, his military campaigns were stunning. Having conquered Italy, Egypt, Austria, Prussia, Portugal, and Spain, he pressed on to Russia where, in 1812, bitter weather and lack of food forced his armies to retreat. Only 100,000 of his army of 600,000 survived. In 1813, a coalition of European powers forced his defeat and exile to the island of Elba off the coast of Italy. A second and final defeat occurred after he escaped in 1814, raised a new army, and met the combined European forces led by the English duke of Wellington at the Battle of Waterloo (1815). The fallen hero spent the last years of his life in exile on the barren island of Saint Helena off the west coast of Africa.

Napoleon, the first of the modern European dictators, left a distinctly Neoclassical stamp upon the city of Paris (see chapter 26). However, he also became the nineteenth century's first Romantic hero, glorified in numerous European poems and paintings, and especially in the majestic portraits of Jacques-Louis David, his favorite artist. David's equestrian portrait of Napoleon (see Figure 28.1), which clearly draws on Roman imperial models, shows an idealized Napoleon—he actually crossed the Saint Bernard Pass on a mule—pursuing the destiny of such great military leaders as Hannibal and Charlemagne, whose names are carved on the foreground rocks. In this painting, one of five similar versions of the subject, David depicts Napoleon as a Romantic hero. Napoleon's diary, a record of personal reflection, a favorite genre of the nineteenth-century Romantics, corroborates that image. Entries made by Napoleon between 1800 and 1817 reveal many features that typify the Romantic personality: self-conscious individualism, a sense of personal power, unbridled egotism, and a high regard for the life of the imagination.

Milan, June 17, 1800: . . . What a thing is imagination! Here   1
are men who don't know me, who have never seen me, but
who only knew of me, and they are moved by my presence,
they would do anything for me! And this same incident arises
in all centuries and in all countries! Such is fanaticism!
Yes, imagination rules the world. The defect of our modern
institutions is that they do not speak to the imagination. By
that alone can man be governed; without it he is but a brute.

December 30, 1802: My power proceeds from my reputation,
and my reputation from the victories I have won. My power   10
would fall if I were not to support it with more glory and more
victories. Conquest has made me what I am; only conquest can
maintain me. . . .

Saint Helena, March 3, 1817: In spite of all the libels, I have
no fear whatever about my fame. Posterity will do me justice.
The truth will be known; and the good I have done will be
compared with the faults I have committed. I am not uneasy
as to the result. Had I succeeded, I would have died with the
reputation of the greatest man that ever existed. As it is,
although I have failed, I shall be considered as an extraordinary   20
man: my elevation was unparalleled, because unaccompanied
by crime. I have fought fifty pitched battles, almost all of which
I have won. I have framed and carried into effect a code of
laws that will bear my name to the most distant posterity.
I raised myself from nothing to be the most powerful monarch in
the world. Europe was at my feet. I have always been of [the]
opinion that the sovereignty lay in the people.

Q **What, according to Napoleon, is the role of
the imagination?**

Q **Why might Napoleon's self-image be considered
"romantic"?**

The Promethean Hero

The Promethean Myth in Literature

If Napoleon was nineteenth-century Europe's favorite
real-life hero, Prometheus was its favorite fictional hero.
Prometheus (the name means "forethought") was one
of the primordial deities of Greek mythology. According
to legend, Prometheus challenged Zeus by stealing from
his home on Mount Olympus the sacred fire (source of
divine wisdom and creative inspiration) and bestowing
this great gift upon humankind. As punishment, Zeus
chained him to a lonely rock, where an eagle fed daily on
his liver, which was miraculously restored each night. A
second, less dramatic aspect of the Prometheus story, more
popular among the Romans than the Greeks, credited
the hero with having fashioned human beings out of clay,
in the manner of the Babylonian hero-god Marduk (see
chapter 1).

Romantic poets embraced the figure of Prometheus as
the suffering champion of humanity—a symbol of freedom
and a deliverer whose noble ambitions had incurred the

wrath of the gods. Percy Bysshe Shelley, whom we met
in chapter 27, made Prometheus the savior-hero of his
four-act play *Prometheus Unbound* (1820). In this drama,
Prometheus frees the universe from the tyranny of the
gods. Two years earlier, in 1818, Shelley's second wife, Mary
Godwin Shelley (1797–1851), explored the Promethean
legend in her novel *Frankenstein; or, The Modern Prometheus*.
The daughter of William Godwin and the feminist writer
Mary Wollstonecraft (see chapter 24), Mary Shelley began
writing *Frankenstein* at the age of eighteen. Framed as a
series of letters, the novel relates the astonishing tale of
the scientist–philosopher Victor Frankenstein, who, having
discovered the secret of imparting life to inanimate matter,
produces a monster endowed with supernatural strength
(Figure **28.2**). A modern Prometheus, Frankenstein suffers the punishment for his ambitious designs when the
creature, excluded from the normal life of ordinary mortals, betrays his creator: "I was benevolent and good," he
protests, "misery made me a fiend." Like the fallen Lucifer,
Frankenstein's creation ultimately becomes a figure of
heroic evil.

Frankenstein belongs to a literary genre known as the
Gothic novel, a type of entertainment that features elements of horror and the supernatural cast in a medieval
("Gothic") setting. Such novels, the earliest of which was
Horace Walpole's *The Castle of Otranto* (1764), reflect the
rising tide of antirationalism and a revived interest in the
medieval past. Shelley's novel—actually a scientific horror
tale—has become a modern classic. The first literary work
to question the human impact of scientific research, it

Figure 28.2 The first illustration of the Frankenstein monster, frontispiece from
the Standards Novel edition of 1831. Engraving, 3½ × 2⅖ in.

has inspired numerous science-fiction "spinoffs," as well as cinematic and stage renderings. Ironically, however, it is not the scientist but the monster that has captured the modern imagination, even to the point of usurping the name of his creator.

READING 28.2 From Mary Shelley's *Frankenstein* (Chapters 4 and 5) (1818)

. . . One of the phenomena which had peculiarly attracted my attention was the structure of the human frame, and, indeed, any animal endued with life. Whence, I often asked myself, did the principle of life proceed? It was a bold question, and one which has ever been considered as a mystery: yet with how many things are we upon the brink of becoming acquainted, if cowardice or carelessness did not restrain our enquiries. I revolved these circumstances in my mind and determined thenceforth to apply myself more particularly to those branches of natural philosophy which relate to physiology. Unless I had   10
been animated by an almost supernatural enthusiasm, my application to this study would have been irksome and almost intolerable. To examine the causes of life, we must first have recourse to death. I became acquainted with the science of anatomy, but this was not sufficient; I must also observe the natural decay and corruption of the human body. In my education my father had taken the greatest precautions that my mind should be impressed with no supernatural horrors. I do not ever remember to have trembled at a tale of superstition or to have feared the apparition of a spirit. Darkness had no effect   20
upon my fancy, and a churchyard was to be merely the receptacle of bodies deprived of life, which, from being the seat of beauty and strength, had become food for the worm. Now I was led to examine the cause and progress of this decay and forced to spend days and nights in vaults and charnel-houses. My attention was fixed upon every object the most insupportable to the delicacy of the human feelings. I saw how the fine form of man was degraded and wasted; I beheld the corruption of death succeed to the blooming cheek of life; I saw how the worm inherited the wonders of the eye and brain.   30
I paused, examining and analysing all the minutiae of causation, as exemplified in the change from life to death, and death to life, until from the midst of this darkness a sudden light broke in upon me—a light so brilliant and wondrous, yet so simple, that while I became dizzy with the immensity of the prospect which it illustrated, I was surprised that among so many men of genius who had directed their enquiries towards the same science, that I alone should be reserved to discover so astonishing a secret.

Remember, I am not recording the vision of a madman. The sun does not more certainly shine in the heavens than that   40
which I now affirm is true. Some miracle might have produced it, yet the stages of the discovery were distinct and probable. After days and nights of incredible labour and fatigue, I succeeded in discovering the cause of generation and life; nay, more, I became myself capable of bestowing animation upon lifeless matter.

The astonishment which I had at first experienced on this discovery soon gave place to delight and rapture. After so much time spent in painful labour, to arrive at once at the summit of

my desires was the most gratifying consummation of my toils.   50
But this discovery was so great and overwhelming that all the steps by which I had been progressively led to it were obliterated, and I beheld only the result. What had been the study and desire of the wisest men since the creation of the world was now within my grasp. . . .

. . . Learn from me, if not by my precepts, at least by my example, how dangerous is the acquirement of knowledge and how much happier that man is who believes his native town to be the world, than he who aspires to become greater than his nature will allow.   60

When I found so astonishing a power placed within my hands, I hesitated a long time concerning the manner in which I should employ it. Although I possessed the capacity of bestowing animation, yet to prepare a frame for the reception of it, with all its intricacies of fibres, muscles, and veins, still remained a work of inconceivable difficulty and labour. I doubted at first whether I should attempt the creation of a being like myself, or one of simpler organization; but my imagination was too much exalted by my first success to permit me to doubt of my ability to give life to an animal as complex   70
and wonderful as man. The materials at present within my command hardly appeared adequate to so arduous an undertaking, but I doubted not that I should ultimately succeed. I prepared myself for a multitude of reverses; my operations might be incessantly baffled, and at last my work be imperfect; yet when I considered the improvement which every day takes place in science and mechanics, I was encouraged to hope my present attempts would at least lay the foundations of future success. Nor could I consider the magnitude and complexity of my plan as any argument of its impracticability. It was with   80
these feelings that I began the creation of a human being. As the minuteness of the parts formed a great hindrance to my speed, I resolved, contrary to my first intention, to make the being of a gigantic stature; that is to say, about eight feet in height, and proportionately large. After having formed this determination and having spent some months in successfully collecting and arranging my materials, I began.

No one can conceive the variety of feelings which bore me onwards, like a hurricane, in the first enthusiasm of success. Life and death appeared to be ideal bounds, which I should first   90
break through, and pour a torrent of light into our dark world. A new species would bless me as its creator and source; many happy and excellent natures would owe their being to me. No father could claim the gratitude of his child so completely as I should deserve theirs. Pursuing these reflections, I thought that if I could bestow animation upon lifeless matter, I might in process of time (although I now found it impossible) renew life where death had apparently devoted the body to corruption.

These thoughts supported my spirits, while I pursued my undertaking with unremitting ardour. My cheek had grown   100
pale with study, and my person had become emaciated with confinement. Sometimes, on the very brink of certainty, I failed; yet still I clung to the hope which the next day or the next hour might realize. One secret which I alone possessed was the hope to which I had dedicated myself; and the moon gazed on my midnight labours, while, with unrelaxed and breathless eagerness, I pursued nature to her hiding-places. Who shall conceive the horrors of my secret toil as I dabbled among the

unhallowed damps of the grave or tortured the living animal to animate the lifeless clay? My limbs now tremble, and my eyes swim with the remembrance; but then a resistless and almost frantic impulse urged me forward; I seemed to have lost all soul or sensation but for this one pursuit. It was indeed but a passing trance, that only made me feel with renewed acuteness so soon as, the unnatural stimulus ceasing to operate, I had returned to my old habits. I collected bones from charnel-houses and disturbed, with profane fingers, the tremendous secrets of the human frame. In a solitary chamber, or rather cell, at the top of the house, and separated from all the other apartments by a gallery and staircase, I kept my workshop of filthy creation: my eyeballs were starting from their sockets in attending to the details of my employment. The dissecting room and the slaughter-house furnished many of my materials; and often did my human nature turn with loathing from my occupation, whilst, still urged on by an eagerness which perpetually increased, I brought my work near to a conclusion. . . . 110

120

It was on a dreary night of November that I beheld the accomplishment of my toils. With an anxiety that almost amounted to agony, I collected the instruments of life around me, that I might infuse a spark of being into the lifeless thing that lay at my feet. It was already one in the morning; the rain pattered dismally against the panes, and my candle was nearly burnt out, when, by the glimmer of the half-extinguished light, I saw the dull yellow eye of the creation open; it breathed hard, and a convulsive motion agitated its limbs. 130

How can I describe my emotions at this catastrophe, or how delineate the wretch whom with such infinite pains and care I had endeavoured to form? His limbs were in proportion, and I had selected his features as beautiful. Beautiful! Great God! His yellow skin scarcely covered the work of muscles and arteries beneath; his hair was of a lustrous black, and flowing; his teeth of pearly whiteness; but these luxuriances only formed a more horrid contrast with his watery eyes, that seemed almost of the same colour as the dun-white sockets in which they were set, his shrivelled complexion and straight black lips. 140

The different accidents of life are not so changeable as the feelings of human nature. I had worked hard for nearly two years, for the sole purpose of infusing life into an inanimate body. For this I had deprived myself of rest and health. I had desired it with an ardour that far exceeded moderation; but now that I had finished, the beauty of the dream vanished, and breathless horror and disgust filled my heart. Unable to endure the aspect of the being I had created, I rushed out of the room and continued a long time traversing my bedchamber, unable to compose my mind to sleep. At length lassitude succeeded to the tumult I had before endured, and I threw myself on the bed in my clothes, endeavouring to seek a few moments of forgetfulness. But it was in vain; I slept, indeed, but I was disturbed by the wildest dreams. I thought I saw Elizabeth, in the bloom of health, walking in the streets of Ingolstadt. Delighted and surprized, I embraced her, but as I imprinted the first kiss on her lips, they became livid with the hue of death; her features appeared to change, and I thought that I held the corpse of my dead mother in my arms; a shroud enveloped her form, and I saw the grave-worms crawling in the folds of the flannel. I started from my sleep with horror; a cold dew 150

160

covered my forehead, my teeth chattered, and every limb became convulsed; when, by the dim and yellow light of the moon, as it forced its way through the window shutters, I beheld the wretch—the miserable monster whom I had created. He held up the curtain of the bed; and his eyes, if eyes they may be called, were fixed on me. His jaws opened, and he muttered some inarticulate sounds, while a grin wrinkled his cheeks. He might have spoken, but I did not hear; one hand was stretched out, seemingly to detain me, but I escaped and rushed downstairs. I took refuge in the courtyard belonging to the house which I inhabited, where I remained during the rest of the night, walking up and down in the greatest agitation, listening attentively, catching and fearing each sound as if it were to announce the approach of the daemoniacal corpse to which I had so miserably given life. . . . 170

180

— Q What are the dangers of "the acquirement of knowledge," according to Dr. Frankenstein?

— Q Why does he ultimately experience "breathless horror and disgust"?

Byron and the Promethean Myth

The Promethean myth found its most passionate champion in the life and works of the English poet George Gordon, Lord Byron (1788–1824). Byron was one of the most flamboyant personalities of the age (Figure **28.3**). Dedicated to pleasures of the senses, he was equally impassioned by the ideals of liberty and brotherhood. In his brief, mercurial life, he established the prototype of the Romantic hero, often called the Byronic hero.

As a young man, Byron traveled restlessly throughout Europe and the Mediterranean, devouring the landscape and the major sites. A physically attractive man (despite the handicap of a club foot) with dark, brooding eyes, he engaged in numerous love affairs, including one with his half-sister. In 1816, Byron abandoned an unsuccessful marriage and left England for good. He lived in Italy for a time with the Shelleys and a string of mistresses. By this time, he had earned such a reputation of dangerous nonconformity that an English woman, catching sight of the poet in Rome, warned her daughter: "Do not look at him! He is dangerous to look at." In 1824, Byron sailed to Greece to aid the Greeks in their war of independence against the Turks—one of the many episodes in the turbulent history of nineteenth-century nationalism. There, in his last heroic role, he died of a fever.

Throughout his life, Byron was given to periodic bouts of creativity and dissipation. A man of violent passions, he once described himself as "half-mad . . . between metaphysics, mountains, lakes, love indistinguishable, and the nightmare of my own delinquencies." Intent on sharing his innermost feelings, he became the hero of his two great poems, *Childe Harold's Pilgrimage* (1812–1818) and *Don Juan*, the latter written in installments between 1819 and 1824, and left unfinished at his death. The first poem narrates the wandering of Childe Harold, Byron's fictional self, whom he describes as "the most unfit/ Of men to herd with man; with whom he held/ Little in common."

The disillusioned hero finds solace, however, in nature, as Byron writes in Canto Three (13):

> He had the passion and the power to roam;
> The desert, forest, cavern, breaker's foam,
> Were unto him companionship; they spake
> A mutual language . . .

Begun in Venice, *Don Juan* drew on the legendary, fictional Spanish libertine who had also inspired Mozart's *Don Giovanni* (see chapter 26). Byron's don, however, is not the lustful womanizer of Mozart's opera; rather, he is a figure who stumbles into love in what might be called a romance of roguery, or—in Byron's words—"a satire on the abuses of society." Byron's disdain for the social conventions of his time and place are brilliantly mocked in a work that the author described as an "epic on modern life."

By comparison with the other heroes of his literary career, Prometheus, the god who "stole from Heaven the flame, for which he fell," preoccupied Byron as a symbol of triumphant individualism. For the poet, capturing the imagination in art or in life was comparable to stealing the sacred fire. In a number of his poems, he compares the fallen Napoleon to the mythic Prometheus—symbol of heroic ambition and ungovernable passions. But in the stirring ode called simply "Prometheus," Byron makes of the Promethean myth a parable for the Romantic imagination. He begins by recalling the traditional story of the hero whose "Godlike crime was to be kind." He goes on

Figure 28.3 THOMAS PHILLIPS, *Lord Byron Sixth Baron in Albanian Costume*, 1813. Oil on canvas, 50 × 40 in. Upon the death of his great-uncle in 1798, Byron became the sixth Baron Byron of Rochdale. Entitled to a seat in the House of Lords when he came of age in 1809, he attended only a few sessions. That same year, he bought this exotic costume (red-velvet jacket and Oriental headdress) while touring Greece and Albania. One of his lovers, Lady Caroline Lamb, characterized Byron as "mad, bad, and dangerous to know."

to identify Prometheus as a "symbol and a sign" to mortals who, although "part divine," are doomed to "funereal destiny." Like Prometheus, says Byron, we must strive to defy that destiny by pursuing the creative projects that will outlive us. Byron's voice sets defiance and hope against melancholy and despair.

READING 28.3 Byron's "Prometheus" (1816)

Titan! to whose immortal eyes	1
The sufferings of mortality,	
Seen in their sad reality,	
Were not as things that gods despise;	
What was thy pity's recompense?	5
A silent suffering, and intense;	
The rock, the vulture,[1] and the chain,	
All that the proud can feel of pain,	
The agony they do not show,	
The suffocating sense of woe,	10
Which speaks but in its loneliness,	
And then is jealous lest the sky	
Should have a listener, nor will sigh	
Until its voice is echoless.	

Titan! to thee the strife was given	15
Between the suffering and the will,	
Which torture where they cannot kill;	
And the inexorable Heaven,	
And the deaf tyranny of Fate,	
The ruling principle of Hate,	20
Which for its pleasure doth create	
The things it may annihilate,	
Refused thee even the boon to die:	
The wretched gift eternity	
Was thine—and thou hast borne it well.	25
All that the Thunderer[2] wrung from thee	
Was but the menace which flung back	
On him the torments of thy rack;	
The fate thou didst so well foresee,	
But would not to appease him tell;	30
And in thy Silence was his Sentence,	
And in his Soul a vain repentance,	
And evil dread so ill dissembled,	
That in his hand the lightnings trembled.	

Thy Godlike crime was to be kind,	35
To render with thy precepts less	
The sum of human wretchedness,	
And strengthen Man with his own mind;	
But baffled as thou wert from high,	
Still in thy patient energy,	40
In the endurance, and repulse	
Of thine impenetrable Spirit,	
Which Earth and Heaven could not convulse,	
A mighty lesson we inherit:	

Thou art symbol and a sign	45
To Mortals of their fate and force;	
Like thee, Man is in part divine,	
A troubled stream from a pure source;	
And Man in portions can foresee	
His own funereal destiny,	50
His wretchedness, and his resistance,	
And his sad unallied existence:	
To which his Spirit may oppose	
Itself—and equal to all woes,	
And a firm will, and a deep sense,	55
Which even in torture can descry	
Its own concenter'd recompense,[3]	
Triumphant where it dares defy,	
And making Death a Victory.	

Q How does Byron characterize Prometheus in this poem?

Q What aspects of the Byronic hero are configured in Prometheus?

Pushkin: The Byron of Russia

Napoleon's invasion of Russia in 1812 was one of the most dramatic events in nineteenth-century history. Sorely outnumbered by the Grand Army of Napoleon, Russian troops resorted to a "scorched earth" policy that produced severe shortages of food for French and Russians alike. As French forces advanced on Moscow, leaving a trail of bloody battles, the Russians burned their own capital city. Napoleon ultimately captured Moscow, but within a few months he and his badly diminished army retreated from Russia, never to return. Deeply moved by Napoleon's role in stirring Russian nationalism, Alexander Pushkin (1799–1837)—Russia's leading lyric poet and dramatist—eulogized the hero who, as he explains in the poem "Napoleon," had "launched the Russian nation/ Upon its lofty destinies."

Pushkin, whose maternal great-grandfather was a black African general, came from an old aristocratic family. Nevertheless, he claimed comradeship with Russia's humble commoners. He boasted: "I am a versewright and a bookman, . . . / No financier, no titled footman,/ A commoner: great on his own." Like Byron, Pushkin championed political freedom; he defended liberal causes, which resulted in his banishment to south Russia and ultimately to his dismissal from the foreign service. His agonizing death, at the age of thirty-seven, was the result of wounds suffered in a duel with his wife's alleged lover.

Pushkin's Romantic tragedies and long narrative poems reveal his great admiration for Shakespeare and Byron, and earned him a reputation as "the Byron of Russia." Some of Pushkin's works, such as *Boris Godunov* (1825) and *Eugene Onegin* (1833)—modeled in part on Byron's *Don Juan*—would inspire operas by the composers Modest Mussorgsky (1839–1881) and Peter Ilyich Tchaikovsky (see chapter 29) respectively. The lyric poem "Napoleon,"

---

[1] Byron replaces the mythological eagle with a vulture.
[2] Zeus, the supreme god of the Greeks.

[3] Catch a glimpse of the Spirit's own sufficient reward.

part of which follows, conveys Pushkin's gift for buoyant, energetic language and his profound respect for the figure whom he viewed as both oppressor and liberator.

READING 28.4 From Pushkin's "Napoleon" (1821)

A wondrous fate is now fulfilled,	1
Extinguished a majestic man.	
In somber prison night was stilled	
Napoleon's grim, tumultuous span.	
The outlawed potentate has vanished,	5
Bright Nike's mighty, pampered son;	
For him, from all Creation banished,	
Posterity has now begun.	
O hero, with whose bloodied story	
Long, long the earth will still resound,	10
Sleep in the shadow of your glory,	
The desert ocean all around . . .	
A tomb of rock, in splendor riding!	
The urn that holds your mortal clay,	
As tribal hatreds are subsiding,	15
Now sends aloft a deathless ray.	
How recently your eagles glowered	
Atop a disenfranchised world,	
And fallen sovereignties cowered	
Beneath the thunderbolts you hurled!	20
Your banners at a word would shower	
Destruction from their folds and dearth,	
Yoke after yoke of ruthless power	
You fitted on the tribes of earth.	
. . . .	
Vainglorious man! Where were you faring,	25
Who blinded that astounding mind?	
How came it in designs of daring	
The Russian's heart was not divined?	
At fiery sacrifice not guessing,	
You idly fancied, tempting fate,	30
We would seek peace and count it blessing;	
You came to fathom us too late . . .	
Fight on, embattled Russia mine,	
Recall the rights of ancient days!	
The sun of Austerlitz,[1] decline!	35
And Moscow, mighty city, blaze!	
Brief be the time of our dishonor,	
The auspices are turning now;	
Hail Moscow—Russia's blessings on her!	
War to extinction, thus our vow!	40
The diadem of iron[2] shaking	

In stiffened fingers' feeble clasp,	
He stares into a chasm, quaking,	
And is undone, undone at last.	
Behold all Europe's legions sprawling . . .	45
The wintry fields' encrimsoned glow	
Bore testimony to their falling	
Till blood-prints melted with the snow.	
. . . .	
Let us hold up to reprobation	
Such petty-minded men as chose	50
With unappeasable damnation	
To stir his laurel-dark repose!	
Hail him! He launched the Russian nation	
Upon its lofty destinies	
And augured ultimate salvation	55
For man's long-exiled liberties.	

Q In what ways does this poem reflect the sentiments of nationalism?

Q What, according to Pushkin, did Napoleon fail to recognize in Russia?

The Abolitionists: American Prometheans

Among the most fervent champions of liberty in nineteenth-century America were those who crusaded against the institution of slavery. Their efforts initiated a movement for black nationalism that would continue well into the twentieth century (see chapter 36). It is unlikely that the leaders of the abolitionist movement regarded themselves in the image of a Napoleon or the fictional Prometheus, but, as historical figures, the abolitionists were the heroes of their time. They fought against the enslavement of Africans (and their descendants), a practice that had prevailed in the Americas since the sixteenth century.* Although the abolitionists constituted only a small minority of America's population, their arguments were emotionally charged and their protests often dramatic and telling.

Antislavery novels—the most famous of which was *Uncle Tom's Cabin* (1852) by Harriet Beecher Stowe (1811–1896)—stirred up public sentiment against the brutality and injustice of the system. Originally serialized in an antislavery newspaper, Stowe's book sold more than one million copies within a year of its publication. But the most direct challenge to slavery came from the slaves themselves, and none more so than the slave rebels who—like Prometheus—mounted outright attacks against their owners and masters in their efforts to gain a prized privilege: freedom. While slave rebellions were rare in nineteenth-century America—between 1800 and 1860 only two reached the level of overt insurrection—the threat or rumor of rebellion was terrifying to slave-owners (Figure **28.4**).

One of the most notable insurrections of the century took place in Southampton County, Virginia, in 1831:

---

[1] The site of Napoleon's greatest victory, where, on December 2, 1805, he defeated the combined Austrian and Russian forces, acquiring control of European lands north of Rome and becoming king of Italy.

[2] The iron crown of Lombardy, dating back to the fifth century, which Napoleon had assumed some time after the Italian campaigns.

---

* The origins and history of the transatlantic slave trade are discussed in chapters 18 and 25.

Figure 28.4 WILLIAM BLAKE, *A Negro Hung Alive by the Ribs to a Gallows*, 1796. Colour engraving, 10½ × 8 in. Library of Congress #1835. Private Collection. John G. Stedman was a Dutch naval officer who volunteered for a military expedition to quell slave uprisings in the Dutch colony of Surinam in Guiana, and the east coast of South America. His drawings, produced to accompany his *Narrative of a Five-Years' Expedition against the Revolted Negroes of Surinam*, are eyewitness accounts of the varieties of torture inflicted by colonial masters on rebellious slaves. Blake's color engravings are based on Stedman's drawings.

Nat Turner (1800–1831), a slave preacher and mystic, believed that he was divinely appointed to lead the slaves to freedom. The Turner rebellion resulted in the deaths of at least fifty-seven white people (and many more black slaves, killed when the rebellion was suppressed) and the destruction of several plantations in the area. Following the defeat of the rebel slaves, the captive Turner explained his motives to a local attorney, who prepared a published version of his personal account in the so-called "Confessions of Nat Turner."

Frederick Douglass A longer, more detailed autobiography, the *Narrative of the Life of Frederick Douglass: An American Slave* (1845), came from the pen of the nineteenth century's leading African-American crusader for black freedom (Figure **28.5**). Born a slave on the east coast of Maryland, Douglass (1817–1895) taught himself how to read and write at an early age; he escaped bondage in Baltimore in 1838 and eventually found his way north to New England, where he joined the Massachusetts Antislavery Society. A powerful public speaker, who captivated his audiences

with accounts of his life, Douglass served as living proof of the potential of black slaves to achieve brilliantly as free persons. He wrote extensively and eloquently in support of abolition, describing the "dehumanizing character of slavery" (that is, its negative effects on both black and white people), and defending the idea that, by abandoning slavelike behavior, even slaves could determine their own lives. On occasion, he employed high irony—contradiction between literal and intended meanings—as is the case with his justification of theft as a moral act if perpetrated by a slave against his master. Although it is unlikely that Douglass had in mind any reference to the Promethean motif of heroic defiance, the parallel is not without significance. "A Slave's Right to Steal" comes from *My Bondage and My Freedom*, the revised and enlarged version of Douglass' autobiography.

READING 28.5 From Douglass' *My Bondage and My Freedom* (1855)

. . . There were four slaves of us in the kitchen, and four whites   1
in the great house—Thomas Auld, Mrs. Auld, Hadaway Auld
(brother of Thomas Auld), and little Amanda. The names of the
slaves in the kitchen, were Eliza, my sister; Priscilla, my aunt;
Henry, my cousin; and myself. There were eight persons in the
family. There was, each week, one half bushel of corn-meal
brought from the mill; and in the kitchen, corn-meal was
almost our exclusive food, for very little else was allowed us.
Out of this half bushel of corn-meal, the family in the great

Figure 28.5 *Portrait of Frederick Douglass*, 1847. Daguerreotype, 3¼ × 2¾ in.

house had a small loaf every morning; thus leaving us, in the kitchen, with not quite a half a peck of meal per week, apiece. This allowance was less than half the allowance of food on Lloyd's plantation. It was not enough to subsist upon; and we were, therefore, reduced to the wretched necessity of living at the expense of our neighbors. We were compelled either to beg, or to steal, and we did both. I frankly confess, that while I hated everything like stealing, *as such*, I nevertheless did not hesitate to take food, when I was hungry, wherever I could find it. Nor was this practice the mere result of an unreasoning instinct; it was, in my case, the result of a clear apprehension of the claims of morality. I weighed and considered the matter closely, before I ventured to satisfy my hunger by such means. Considering that my labor and person were the property of Master Thomas, and that I was by him deprived of the necessaries of life—necessaries obtained by my own labor— it was easy to deduce the right to supply myself with what was my own. It was simply appropriating what was my own to the use of my master, since the health and strength derived from such food were exerted in *his* service. To be sure, this was stealing, according to the law and gospel I heard from St. Michael's pulpit; but I had already begun to attach less importance to what dropped from that quarter, on that point, while, as yet, I retained my reverence for religion. It was not always convenient to steal from master, and the same reason why I might, innocently, steal from him, did not seem to justify me in stealing from others. In the case of my master, it was only a question of *removal*—the taking his meat out of the tub, and putting it into another; the ownership of the meat was not affected by the transaction. At first, he owned it in the *tub*, and last, he owned it in me. His meat house was not always open. There was a strict watch kept on that point, and the key was on a large bunch in Rowena's pocket. A great many times have we, poor creatures, been severely pinched with hunger, when meat and bread have been moulding under the lock, while the key was in the pocket of our mistress. This had been so when she *knew* we were nearly half starved; and yet, that mistress, with saintly air, would kneel with her husband, and pray each morning that a merciful God would bless them in basket and in store, and save them, at last, in his kingdom. But I proceed with the argument.

It was necessary that the right to steal from *others* should be established; and this could only rest upon a wider range of generalization than that which supposed the right to steal from my master.

It was sometime before I arrived at this clear right. The reader will get some idea of my train of reasoning, by a brief statement of the case. "I am," thought I, "not only the slave of Master Thomas, but I am the slave of society at large. Society at large has bound itself, in form and in fact, to assist Master Thomas in robbing me of my rightful liberty, and of the just reward of my labor; therefore, whatever rights I have against Master Thomas, I have, equally, against those confederated with him in robbing me of liberty. As society has marked me out as privileged plunder, on the principle of self-preservation I am justified in plundering in turn. Since each slave belongs to all; all must, therefore, belong to each."

I shall here make a profession of faith which may shock

some, offend others, and be dissented from by all. It is this: Within the bounds of his just earnings, I hold that the slave is fully justified in helping himself to the *gold and silver, and the best apparel of his master, or that of any other slaveholder; and that such taking is not stealing in any just sense of that word.*

The morality of *free* society can have no application to *slave* society. Slaveholders have made it almost impossible for the slave to commit any crime, known either to the laws of God or to the laws of man. If he steals, he takes his own; if he kills his master, he imitates only the heroes of the revolution. Slaveholders I hold to be individually and collectively responsible for all the evils which grow out of the horrid relation, and I believe they will be so held at the judgment, in the sight of a just God. Make a man a slave, and you rob him of moral responsibility. . . .

Q With what arguments does Douglass justify stealing?

Q Does moral responsibility alter according to the status of an individual?

Sojourner Truth While Frederick Douglass was among the first African-Americans to win international attention through his skills at public speaking, his female contemporary Sojourner Truth (ca. 1797–1883) brought wit and a woman's passion to the fight against slavery. Born to slave parents in Ulster County, New York, Isabella Baumfree was sold four times before the age of thirty, an inauspicious beginning for a woman who would become one of America's most vocal abolitionists, an evangelist, and a champion of women's rights.

After being emancipated in 1828, Baumfree traveled widely in the United States, changing her name to Sojourner Truth in 1843, as she committed her life to "sharing the truth" in matters of human dignity. Although she never learned to read or write, she was determined to have her voice heard across the nation and for future generations. To accomplish the latter, she dictated her story to a friend, Olive Gilbert. The narrative, which was published in 1850, recounts the major events of her life, including the tale of how Isabella engaged in a heroic legal battle to win back her five-year-old son, who was illegally sold into slavery in New York State. Sojourner Truth used her talents as an orator to voice her opposition to slavery, capital punishment, and the kidnapping and sale of black children (a common practice in some parts of the country). She also supported prison reform, helped to relocate former slaves, and defended the rights of women. Sharp-tongued and outspoken (and a lifelong pipe-smoker), Sojourner Truth won popular notoriety for the short, impromptu speech, "Ain't I a Woman?," delivered in 1851 to the Woman's Convention at Akron, Ohio. While scholars question the authenticity of various versions of the speech (which was published by abolitionists some twelve years later), no such debate clouds Sojourner's narrative, which, even in this short excerpt, captures the spirit of her straightforward rhetoric.

READING 28.6 From *The Narrative of Sojourner Truth* (1850)

Isabella's marriage

Subsequently, Isabella was married to a fellow-slave, named 1
Thomas, who had previously had two wives, one of whom, if
not both, had been torn from him and sold far away. And it is
more than probable, that he was not only allowed but
encouraged to take another at each successive sale. I say it is
probable, because the writer of this knows from personal
observation, that such is the custom among slaveholders at the
present day; and that in a twenty months' residence among
them, we never knew any one to open the lip against the
practice; and when we severely censured it, the slaveholder 10
had nothing to say; and the slave pleaded that, under existing
circumstances, he could do no better.

Such an abominable state of things is silently tolerated,
to say the least, by slaveholders—deny it who may. And what
is that religion that sanctions, even by its silence, all that is
embraced in the *"Peculiar Institution"*? If there can be any
thing more diametrically opposed to the religion of Jesus,
than the working of this soul-killing system—which is as truly
sanctioned by the religion of America as are her ministers
and churches—we wish to be shown where it can be found. 20

We have said, Isabella was married to Thomas—she was,
after the fashion of slavery, one of the slaves performing the
ceremony for them; as no true minister of Christ *can* perform,
as in the presence of God, what he knows to be a mere *farce*,
a *mock* marriage, unrecognized by any civil law, and liable to
be annulled at any moment, when the interest or caprice of the
master should dictate.

With what feelings must slaveholders expect us to listen to
their horror of amalgamation in prospect, while they are well
aware that we know how calmly and quietly they contemplate 30
the present state of licentiousness their own wicked laws have
created, not only as it regards the slave, but as it regards the
more privileged portion of the population of the South?

Slaveholders appear to me to take the same notice of the
vices of the slave, as one does of the vicious disposition of his
horse. They are often an inconvenience; further than that, they
care not to trouble themselves about the matter. . . .

Q **Why does Sojourner Truth claim that slavery is "sanctioned by the religion of America"?**

Slave Songs and Spirituals

The nineteenth century witnessed the flowering of a
unique type of folk song that expressed the heroic grief
and hopes of the American slave community. Slave songs,
sometimes termed "sorrow songs," formed the basis of what
later became known as "spirituals." These songs, the most
significant musical contribution of America's antebellum
population, were a distinctive cultural form that blended
the Methodist and Baptist evangelical church music of the
eighteenth century with musical traditions brought from
Africa to the Americas in the course of 200 years.

A communal vehicle that conveyed the fervent longing
for freedom, slave songs and spirituals based their content
on Bible stories, usually focused on deliverance—the passage of the "Hebrew children" out of Egyptian bondage,
for instance—and the promise of ultimate, triumphant
liberation. A typical spiritual, such as "Sometimes I Feel
Like a Motherless Child," tempers despair with enduring
faith. In form, spirituals embellished typically Protestant
melodies and antiphonal structures with the complex, percussive rhythms (such as polymeter and syncopation), overlapping call-and-response patterns, and improvisational
techniques of traditional African music (see chapter 18).

A powerful form of religious music, the spiritual came
to public attention only after 1871, when an instructor
of vocal music at Fisk University in Tennessee took the
school's student choir on a university fundraising tour. A
similar group was established by Hampton Institute (now
Hampton University in Virginia) in 1873. Beyond the commercial popularity of this song form, spirituals have come
to influence the development of numerous musical genres,
including jazz, gospel, and blues (see chapter 36).

Goethe's Faust: The Quintessential Romantic Hero

Of all literary heroes of the nineteenth century, perhaps
the most compelling is Goethe's Faust. The story of Faust
is based on a sixteenth-century German legend: a traveling physician and a practitioner of black magic, Johann
or Georg Faust, was reputed to have sold his soul to the
Devil in exchange for infinite knowledge. The story
became the subject of numerous dramas, the first of which
was *The Tragical History of Doctor Faustus* written by the
English playwright Christopher Marlowe (1564–1593).
Faust was the favorite Renaissance symbol of the lust for
knowledge and power balanced against the perils of eternal damnation—a theme that figured largely in literary
characterizations of Don Juan as well. In the hands of the
German poet Johann Wolfgang von Goethe (1749–1832),
Faust became the paradigm of Western man and the quintessential Romantic hero.

One of the literary landmarks of its time, *Faust* was the
product of Goethe's entire career: he conceived the piece
during the 1770s, published Part One in 1808, but did
not complete the play until 1832. Although ostensibly a
drama, *Faust* more closely resembles an epic poem. It is
written in a lyric German, with a richness of verse forms
that is typical of Romantic poetry. As a play, it deliberately
ignores the Classical unities of time and place—indeed,
its shifting "cinematic" qualities make it more adaptable
to modern film than to the traditional stage. Despite a
cosmic breadth, which compares with Milton's *Paradise
Lost* or Dante's *Divine Comedy*, Goethe's *Faust* focuses
more narrowly on the human condition. Goethe neither
seeks to justify God's ways to humanity nor to allegorize
the Christian ascent to salvation; rather, he uncovers the
tragic tension between heroic aspirations and human
limitations. A student of law, medicine, theology, theater,
biology, optics, and alchemy, Goethe seems to have modeled his hero on himself. Faust is a man of deep learning,

a Christian, and a scientist. Having mastered the traditional disciplines, he has turned to magic "to learn what it is that girds/ The world together in its inmost being." While the desire to know and achieve has driven his studies, he feels stale, bored, and deeply dissatisfied: "too old for mere amusement,/ Too young to be without desire." On the verge of suicide, he is enticed by Satan to abandon the world of the intellect for a fuller knowledge of life, a privilege that may cost him dearly.

The Prologue of *Faust* is set in Heaven, where (in a manner reminiscent of the Book of Job) a wager is made between Mephistopheles (Satan) and God. Mephistopheles bets God that he can divert Faust from "the path that is true and fit." God contends that, although "men make mistakes as long as they strive," Faust will never relinquish his soul to Satan. Mephistopheles then proceeds to make a second pact, this one with Faust himself, signed in blood: if he can satisfy Faust's deepest desires and ambitions to the hero's ultimate satisfaction, Mephistopheles will win Faust's soul. Mephistopheles lures the despairing scholar out of his study ("This God-damned dreary hole in the wall") and into the larger world of experience (Figure **28.6**). The newly liberated hero then engages in a passionate love affair with a young woman named Gretchen. Discovering

Figure 28.6 EUGÈNE DELACROIX, *Mephistopheles Appearing to Faust in his Study*, illustration for Goethe's *Faust*, 1828. Lithograph, 10¾ × 9 in. Dressed in a "suit of scarlet trimmed with gold," a "little cape of stiff brocade," and a stylish hat, Mephistopheles invites Faust to dress up like him and prepare to seek "pleasure and action." Goethe's drama inspired many contemporary visual illustrations, as well as musical settings by Berlioz and other composers (see chapter 29).

the joys of the sensual life, Faust proclaims the priority of the heart ("Feeling is all!") over the mind. Faust's romance, however, has tragic consequences, including the deaths of Gretchen's mother, her illegitimate child, her brother, and, ultimately, Gretchen herself. Nevertheless, at the close of Part One, Gretchen's pure and selfless love wins her salvation.

In the second part of the drama, the hero travels with Mephistopheles through a netherworld in which he meets an array of witches, sirens, and other fantastic creatures. He encounters the ravishing Helen of Troy, symbol of ideal beauty, who acquaints Faust with the entire history of humankind; but Faust remains unsated. His unquenched thirst for experience now leads him to pursue a life of action for the public good. He undertakes a vast land-reclamation project, which provides habitation for millions of people. In this Promethean effort to benefit humanity, the aged and near-blind Faust finally finds personal fulfillment. He dies, however, before fully realizing his dream, thus never declaring the satisfaction that will doom him to Hell. While Mephistopheles tries to apprehend Faust's soul as it leaves his body, God's angels, led by Gretchen (Goethe's symbol of the Eternal Female), intervene to shepherd Faust's spirit to Heaven.

The heroic Faust is a timeless symbol of the Western drive for consummate knowledge, experience, and the will to power over nature. Although it is possible to reproduce here only a small portion of Goethe's 12,000-line poem, the following excerpt conveys the powerful lyricism, the verbal subtlety, and the shifts between high seriousness and comedy that make Goethe's *Faust* a literary masterpiece.

READING 28.7 From Goethe's *Faust* (1808)

Prologue in Heaven

The Lord. The Heavenly Hosts. Mephistopheles following (the Three Archangels step forward).

Raphael: The chanting sun, as ever, rivals   1
The chanting of his brother spheres
And marches round his destined circuit—[1]
A march that thunders in our ears.
His aspect cheers the Hosts of Heaven
Though what his essence none can say;
These inconceivable creations
Keep the high state of their first day.

Gabriel: And swift, with inconceivable swiftness,
The earth's full splendor rolls around,   10
Celestial radiance alternating
With a dread night too deep to sound;
The sea against the rocks' deep bases
Comes foaming up in far-flung force,
And rock and sea go whirling onward
In the swift spheres' eternal course.

Michael: And storms in rivalry are raging

From sea to land, from land to sea,
In frenzy forge the world a girdle
From which no inmost part is free   20
The blight of lightning flaming yonder
Marks where the thunder-bolt will play;
And yet Thine envoys, Lord, revere
The gentle movement of Thy day.

Choir of Angels: Thine aspect cheers the Hosts of Heaven
Though what Thine essence none can say,
And all Thy loftiest creations
Keep the high state of their first day.
(Enter Mephistopheles) [2]

Mephistopheles: Since you, O Lord, once more approach and ask
If business down with us be light or heavy—   30
And in the past you've usually welcomed me—
That's why you see me also at your levee.
Excuse me, I can't manage lofty words—
Not though your whole court jeer and find me low;
My pathos certainly would make you laugh
Had you not left off laughing long ago.
Your suns and worlds mean nothing much to me;
How men torment themselves, that's all I see.
The little god of the world, one can't reshape, reshade him;
He is as strange to-day as that first day you made him.   40
His life would be not so bad, not quite,
Had you not granted him a gleam of Heaven's light;
He calls it Reason, uses it not the least
Except to be more beastly than any beast.
He seems to me—if your Honor does not mind—
Like a grasshopper—the long-legged kind—
That's always in flight and leaps as it flies along
And then in the grass strikes up its same old song.
I could only wish he confined himself to the grass!
He thrusts his nose into every filth, alas.   50

Lord: Mephistopheles, have you no other news?
Do you always come here to accuse?
Is nothing ever right in your eyes on earth?

Mephistopheles: No, Lord! I find things there as downright bad as ever.
I am sorry for men's days of dread and dearth;
Poor things, my wish to plague 'em isn't fervent.

Lord: Do you know Faust?

Mephistopheles: The Doctor?

Lord: Aye, my servant.[3]

Mephistopheles: Indeed! He serves you oddly enough,
I think.   60
The fool has no earthly habits in meat and drink.
The ferment in him drives him wide and far,
That he is mad he too has almost guessed;
He demands of heaven each fairest star
And of earth each highest joy and best,
And all that is new and all that is far
Can bring no calm to the deep-sea swell of his breast.

Lord: Now he may serve me only gropingly,

---

[1] The sun is treated here as one of the planets, all of which, according to Pythagoras, moved harmoniously in crystalline spheres.

[2] The name possibly derives from the Hebrew "Mephistoph," meaning "destroyer of the gods."

[3] Compare the exchange between God and Satan at the beginning of the Book of Job (see chapter 1).

Soon I shall lead him into the light.
The gardener knows when the sapling first turns green   70
That flowers and fruit will make the future bright.
    Mephistopheles: What do you wager? You will lose him yet,
Provided you give me permission
To steer him gently the course I set.
    Lord: So long as he walks the earth alive,
So long you may try what enters your head;
Men make mistakes as long as they strive.
    Mephistopheles: I thank you for that; as regards the dead,
The dead have never taken my fancy.
I favor cheeks that are full and rosy-red;   80
No corpse is welcome to my house;
I work as the cat does with the mouse.
    Lord: Very well; you have my full permission.
Divert this soul from its primal source
And carry it, if you can seize it,
Down with you upon your course—
And stand ashamed when you must needs admit:
A good man with his groping intuitions
Still knows the path that's true and fit.
    Mephistopheles: All right—but it won't last for long.   90
I'm not afraid my bet will turn out wrong.
And, if my aim prove true and strong,
Allow me to triumph wholeheartedly.
Dust shall he eat—and greedily—
Like my cousin the Snake renowned in tale and song.[4]
    Lord: That too you are free to give a trial;
I have never hated the likes of you.
Of all the spirits of denial
The joker is the last that I eschew.
Man finds relaxation too attractive—   100
Too fond too soon of unconditional rest;
Which is why I am pleased to give him a companion
Who lures and thrusts and must, as devil, be active.
But ye, true sons of Heaven,[5] it is your duty
To take your joy in the living wealth of beauty.
The changing Essence which ever works and lives
Wall you around with love, serene, secure!
And that which floats in flickering appearance
Fix ye it firm in thoughts that must endure.
    Choir of Angels: Thine aspect cheers the Hosts of
Heaven   110
Though what Thine essence none can say,
And all Thy loftiest creations
Keep the high state of their first day.
(Heaven closes)
    Mephistopheles *(Alone)*: I like to see the Old One now and then
And try to keep relations on the level
It's really decent of so great a person
To talk so humanely even to the Devil.

The First Part of the Tragedy Night

(In a high-vaulted narrow Gothic room Faust, restless, in a chair at his desk)

    Faust: Here stand I, ach, Philosophy
Behind me and Law and Medicine too
And, to my cost, Theology—[6]   120
All these I have sweated through and through
And now you see me a poor fool
As wise as when I entered school!
They call me Master, they call me Doctor,[7]
Ten years now I have dragged my college
Along by the nose through zig and zag
Through up and down and round and round
And this is all that I have found—
The impossibility of knowledge!
It is this that burns away my heart;   130
Of course I am cleverer than the quacks,
Than master and doctor, than clerk and priest,
I suffer no scruple or doubt in the least,
I have no qualms about devil or burning,
Which is just why all joy is torn from me,
I cannot presume to make use of my learning,
I cannot presume I could open my mind
To proselytize and improve mankind.

Besides, I have neither goods nor gold,
Neither reputation nor rank in the world;   140
No dog would choose to continue so!
Which is why I have given myself to Magic
To see if the Spirit may grant me to know
Through its force and its voice full many a secret,
May spare the sour sweat that I used to pour out
In talking of what I know nothing about,
May grant me to learn what it is that girds
The world together in its inmost being,
That the seeing its whole germination, the seeing
Its workings, may end my traffic in words.   150

O couldst thou, light of the full moon,
Look now thy last upon my pain,
Thou for whom I have sat belated
So many midnights here and waited
Till, over books and papers, thou
Didst shine, sad friend, upon my brow!
O could I but walk to and fro
On mountain heights in thy dear glow
Or float with spirits round mountain eyries
Or weave through fields thy glances glean   160
And freed from all miasmal theories
Bathe in thy dew and wash me clean![8]
Oh! Am I still stuck in this jail?
This God-damned dreary hole in the wall
Where even the lovely light of heaven
Breaks wanly through the painted panes!
Cooped up among these heaps of books

---

[4] In Genesis 3:14, God condemns the serpent to go on its belly and eat dust for the rest of its days.

[5] The archangels.

[6] Philosophy, law, medicine, and theology were the four programs of study in medieval universities.

[7] The two advanced degrees beyond the baccalaureate.

[8] Goethe's conception of nature as a source of sublime purification may be compared with similar ideas held by the nature poets and the transcendentalists discussed in chapter 27.

Gnawed by worms, coated with dust,
Round which to the top of the Gothic vault
A smoke-stained paper forms a crust. 170
Retorts and canisters lie pell-mell
And pyramids of instruments,
The junk of centuries, dense and mat—
Your world, man! World? They call it that!

And yet you ask why your poor heart
Cramped in your breast should feel such fear,
Why an unspecified misery
Should throw your life so out of gear?
Instead of the living natural world
For which God made all men his sons 180
You hold a reeking mouldering court
Among assorted skeletons.
Away! There is a world outside!
And this one book of mystic art
Which Nostradamus[9] wrote himself,
Is this not adequate guard and guide?
By this you can tell the course of the stars,
By this, once Nature gives the word,
The soul begins to stir and dawn,
A spirit by a spirit heard, 190
In vain your barren studies here
Construe the signs of sanctity.
You Spirits, you are hovering near;
If you can hear me, answer me!
(He opens the book and perceives the sign of the Macrocosm)[10]
Ha! What a river of wonder at this vision
Bursts upon all my senses in one flood!
And I feel young, the holy joy of life
Glows new, flows fresh, through nerve and blood!
Was it a god designed this hieroglyph to calm
The storm which but now raged inside me, 200
To pour upon my heart such balm,
And by some secret urge to guide me
Where all the powers of Nature stand unveiled around me?
Am I a God? It grows so light!
And through the clear-cut symbol on this page
My soul comes face to face with all creating Nature.
At last I understand the dictum of the sage:
"The spiritual world is always open,
Your mind is closed, your heart is dead;
Rise, young man, and plunge undaunted 210
Your earthly breast in the mourning red."
(He contemplates the sign)
Into one Whole how all things blend,
Function and live within each other!
Passing gold buckets to each other
How heavenly powers ascend, descend!
The odor of grace upon their wings,
They thrust from heaven through earthly things

And as all sing so the All sings!
What a fine show! Aye, but only a show!
Infinite Nature, where can I tap thy veins? 220

[Faust uses a magical sign to call forth the Earth Spirit; it appears but offers him no solace. He then converses with his assistant Wagner on the fruitlessness of a life of study. When Wagner leaves, Faust prepares to commit suicide; but he is interrupted by the sounds of church bells and choral music. Still brooding, he joins Wagner and the townspeople as they celebrate Easter Sunday. At the city gate, Faust encounters a black poodle, which he takes back with him to his studio. The dog is actually Mephistopheles, who soon makes his real self known to Faust.]

(The same room. Later)
    Faust: Who's knocking? Come in! Now who wants to annoy me?
    Mephistopheles *(outside door)*: It's I.
    Faust: Come in!
    Mephistopheles *(outside door)*: You must say "Come in" three times.
    Faust: Come in then!
    Mephistopheles *(entering)*: Thank you; you overjoy me.
We two, I hope, we shall be good friends;
To chase those megrims[11] of yours away 230
I am here like a fine young squire to-day,
In a suit of scarlet trimmed with gold
And a little cape of stiff brocade,
With a cock's feather in my hat
And at my side a long sharp blade,
And the most succinct advice I can give
Is that you dress up just like me,
So that uninhibited and free
You may find out what it means to live.
    Faust: The pain of earth's constricted life, I fancy, 240
Will pierce me still, whatever my attire;
I am too old for mere amusement,
Too young to be without desire.
How can the world dispel my doubt?
You must do without, you must do without!
That is the everlasting song
Which rings in every ear, which rings,
And which to us our whole life long
Every hour hoarsely sings.
I wake in the morning only to feel appalled, 250
My eyes with bitter tears could run
To see the day which in its course
Will not fulfil a wish for me, not one;
The day which whittles away with obstinate carping
All pleasures—even those of anticipation,
Which makes a thousand grimaces to obstruct
My heart when it is stirring in creation.
And again, when night comes down, in anguish
I must stretch out upon my bed
And again no rest is granted me, 260
For wild dreams fill my mind with dread.

---

[9] Michel de Notredame, or Nostradamus (1503–1566) was a French astrologer famous for his prophecies.
[10] Signs of the universe, such as the pentagram, were especially popular among those who practiced magic and the occult arts.

[11] Low or morbid spirits.

The God who dwells within my bosom
Can make my inmost soul react;
The God who sways my every power
Is powerless with external fact.
And so existence weighs upon my breast
And I long for death and life—life I detest.
    Mephistopheles: Yet death is never a wholly welcome guest.
    Faust: O happy is he whom death in the dazzle of victory
Crowns with the bloody laurel in the battling swirl!   270
Or he whom after the mad and breakneck dance
He comes upon in the arms of a girl!
O to have sunk away, delighted, deleted,
Before the Spirit of the Earth,[12] before his might!
    Mephistopheles: Yet I know someone who failed to drink
A brown juice on a certain night.[13]
    Faust: Your hobby is espionage—is it not?
    Mephistopheles: Oh I'm not omniscient—but I know a lot.
    Faust: Whereas that tumult in my soul
Was stilled by sweet familiar chimes   280
Which cozened[14] the child that yet was in me
With echoes of more happy times,
I now curse all things that encompass
The soul with lures and jugglery
And bind it in this dungeon of grief
With trickery and flattery.
Cursed in advance be the high opinion
That serves our spirit for a cloak!
Cursed be the dazzle of appearance
Which bows our senses to its yoke!   290
Cursed be the lying dreams of glory,
The illusion that our name survives!
Cursed be the flattering things we own,
Servants and ploughs, children and wives!
Cursed be Mammon[15] when with his treasures
He makes us play the adventurous man
Or when for our luxurious pleasures
He duly spreads the soft divan!
A curse on the balsam of the grape!
A curse on the love that rides for a fall!   300
A curse on hope! A curse on faith!
And a curse on patience most of all!
(The invisible Spirits sing again)
    Spirits: Woe! Woe!
You have destroyed it,
The beautiful world;
By your violent hand
'Tis downward hurled!
A half-god has dashed it asunder!
From under   310
We bear off the rubble to nowhere
And ponder
Sadly the beauty departed.
Magnipotent

---

[12]The Earth Spirit that Faust called forth earlier.
[13]Mephistopheles alludes to Faust's contemplation of suicide by poison earlier in the drama.
[14]Persuaded; cajoled.
[15]Riches or material wealth.

One among men,
Magnificent
Build it again,
Build it again in your breast!
Let a new course of life
Begin   320
With vision abounding
And new songs resounding
To welcome it in!
    Mephistopheles: These are the junior
Of my faction.
Hear how precociously they counsel
Pleasure and action.
Out and away
From your lonely day
Which dries your senses and your juices   330
Their melody seduces.
Stop playing with your grief which battens
Like a vulture on your life, your mind!
The worst of company would make you feel
That you are a man among mankind.
Not that it's really my proposition
To shove you among the common men;
Though I'm not one of the Upper Ten.
If you would like a coalition
With me for your career through life,   340
I am quite ready to fit in,
I'm yours before you can say knife.
I am your comrade;
If you so crave,
I am your servant, I am your slave.
    Faust: And what have I to undertake in return?
    Mephistopheles: Oh it's early days to discuss what that is.
    Faust: No, no, the devil is an egoist
And ready to do nothing gratis
Which is to benefit a stranger.   350
Tell me your terms and don't prevaricate!
A servant like you in the house is a danger.
    Mephistopheles: I will bind myself to your service in this world,
To be at your beck and never rest nor slack;
When we meet again on the other side,
In the same coin you shall pay me back.
    Faust: The other side gives me little trouble;
First batter this present world to rubble,
Then the other may rise—if that's the plan.
This earth is where my springs of joy have started.   360
And this sun shines on me when broken-hearted;
If I can first from them be parted,
Then let happen what will and can!
I wish to hear no more about it—
Whether there too men hate and love
Or whether in those spheres too, in the future,
There is a Below or an Above.
    Mephistopheles: With such an outlook you can risk it.
Sign on the line! In these next days you will get
Ravishing samples of my arts;   370
I am giving you what never man saw yet.
    Faust: Poor devil, can you give anything ever?
Was a human spirit in its high endeavor

Even once understood by one of your breed?
Have you got food which fails to feed?
Or red gold which, never at rest,
Like mercury runs away through the hand?
A game at which one never wins?
A girl who, even when on my breast,
Pledges herself to my neighbor with her eyes?   380
The divine and lovely delight of honor
Which falls like a falling star and dies?
Show me the fruits which, before they are plucked, decay
And the trees which day after day renew their green!

    Mephistopheles: Such a commission doesn't alarm me,
I have such treasures to purvey.
But, my good friend, the time draws on when we
Should be glad to feast at our ease on something good.

    Faust: If ever I stretch myself on a bed of ease,
Then I am finished! Is that understood?   390
If ever your flatteries can coax me
To be pleased with myself, if ever you cast
A spell of pleasure that can hoax me—
Then let that day be my last!
That's my wager!¹⁶

    Mephistopheles: Done!

    Faust: Let's shake!
If ever I say to the passing moment
"Linger for a while! Thou art so fair!"
Then you may cast me into fetters,   400
I will gladly perish then and there!
Then you may set the death-bell tolling,
Then from my service you are free,
The clock may stop, its hand may fall,
And that be the end of time for me!

[Faust agrees to sign the pact with a drop of his blood.]

Q **Compare the personalities of Faust and Mephistopheles.**

Q **Why might Faust be considered the quintessential Romantic hero?**

Romantic Love and Romantic Stereotypes

Romantic love, the sentimental and all-consuming passion for spiritual as well as sexual union with the opposite sex, was a favorite theme of nineteenth-century writers, painters, and composers. Many Romantics perceived friendship, religious love, and sexual love—both heterosexual and homosexual—as closely related expressions of an ecstatic harmony of souls. Passionate love, and especially unrequited or unfulfilled love, was the subject of numerous literary works. To name but three: Goethe's *Sorrows of Young Werther* (1774) told the story of a lovesick hero whose passion for a married woman leads him to commit suicide—the book was so popular that it made suicide something

¹⁶The wager between Faust and Mephistopheles recalls that between God and Mephistopheles in the Prologue.

of a nineteenth-century vogue; Hector Berlioz's *Symphonie fantastique* (1830–1831) described the composer's obsessive infatuation with a flamboyant actress (see chapter 29); and Richard Wagner's opera *Tristan and Isolde* (1859) dramatized the tragic fate of two legendary medieval lovers.

While Romantics generated an image of masculinity that emphasized self-invention, courage, and the quest for knowledge and power, they either glorified the female as chaste, passive, and submissive, or characterized her as dangerous and threatening. Romantic writers inherited the dual view of womankind that had prevailed since the Middle Ages: like Eve, woman was the *femme fatale*, the seducer and destroyer of mankind; like Mary, however, woman was also the source of salvation and the symbol of all that was pure and true. The Eve stereotype is readily apparent in such works as Prosper Mérimée's novella *Carmen*, on which the opera by Georges Bizet (1835–1875) was based. Set in Seville, Spain, Bizet's *Carmen* (1875) is a story of seduction, rejection, and fatal revenge. Carmen, a shameless flirt who works in a cigarette factory, lures the enamored Don José into deserting the army in order to follow her. Soon tiring of the soldier, she abandons him in favor of a celebrity toreador, only to meet her end at the hand of her former lover. Bizet's heroine became the late nineteenth-century symbol of faithless and dangerous Womankind.

At the other extreme, the Mary stereotype is present in countless nineteenth-century stories, including *Faust* itself, where Gretchen is cast as the Eternal Female, the source of procreation and personal salvation. The following lines by the German poet Heinrich Heine (1797–1856), which were set to music by his contemporary Robert Schumann (1810–1856), typify the female as angelic, ethereal, and chaste—an object that thrilled and inspired the imagination of many European Romantics.

READING 28.8 Heine's "You are Just Like a Flower" (1827)

You are just like a flower
So fair and chaste and dear;
Looking at you, sweet sadness
Invades my heart with fear.
I feel I should be folding
My hands upon your hair,
Praying that God may keep you
So dear and chaste and fair.

Q **What stereotype is established by the simile in this poem?**

Q **Why does the speaker experience "sweet sadness"?**

The Female Voice

The nineteenth century was the first great age of female writers. Examples include the English novelists George Eliot, a pseudonym for Mary Ann Evans (1819–1880);

Figure 28.7 LUIGI CALAMATA, *Portrait of George Sand*, 1837. Pencil on paper, 13 × 9¼ in. A prolific writer, Sand produced a 0body of work—some of which has still not been translated into English—that would fill at least 150 volumes, twenty-five of which, each a thousand pages long, would contain her correspondence with the leading artists and intellectuals of her day.

Emily Brontë (1818–1848), author of the hypnotic novel *Wuthering Heights*; her sister Charlotte Brontë (1816–1855), author of *Jane Eyre* (hailed as a masterpiece only after her death); and Mary Godwin Shelley, whose novel *Frankenstein* was discussed earlier. In France, Germaine Necker, known as Madame de Stael (1760–1817), was hailed by her contemporaries as the founder of the Romantic movement; she was a brilliant woman, if not a brilliant novelist, and her writings were widely read and admired in her own time. And in America, the Bostonian Louisa May Alcott (1832–1888) produced the classic novel *Little Women* (1868), a semiautobiographical work inspired by a childhood spent with her three sisters. Some of these writers struck a startling note of personal freedom in their lives. In their novels, however, they tended to perpetuate the Romantic stereotype of the chaste and clinging female. Even the most free-thinking of nineteenth-century women novelists might portray her heroine as a creature who submitted to the will and values of the superior male. In general, the dominant male-generated stereotype of the Romantic hero influenced female literary characterization well into the mid-nineteenth century.

The novels of Jane Austen (1775–1817) are something of an exception. In *Sense and Sensibility* (1811), which the author published at her own expense, Austen wittily attacks sentimental love and Romantic rapture. Here, as in her other novels, *Pride and Prejudice*, *Mansfield Park*, *Emma*, *Northanger Abbey*, and *Persuasion*, she turned her attention to the everyday concerns of England's provincial middle-class families. Her heroines, intelligent and generous in spirit, are concerned with reconciling economic security with proper social and moral behavior. Austen's keen eye for the details of family life, and for the comic contradictions between human actions and values, show her to be the first Realist in the English novel-writing tradition.

Among French writers of the Romantic era, the most original female voice was that of Amandine Aurore-Lucile Dupin, who used the pen name George Sand (1804–1876; Figure **28.7**). A woman who assumed the name of a man, Sand self-consciously examined the popular Romantic stereotypes, offering not one, but many different points of view concerning male–female dynamics. Defending the passions of Romantic love, one of Sand's heroines exclaims: "If I give myself up to love, I want it to wound me deeply, to electrify me, to break my heart or to exalt me . . . What I want is to suffer, to go crazy." Sand held that true and complete love involved the union of the heart, mind, and body. She avowed that "Love's ideal is most certainly everlasting fidelity," and most of her more than eighty novels feature themes of Romantic love and deep, undying friendship. But for some of her novels, she created heroines who freely exercised the right to love outside marriage. These heroines did not, however, physically consummate their love, even when that love was reciprocal.

Sand's heroines were very unlike Sand herself, whose numerous love affairs with leading Romantic figures—including the poet Alfred de Musset, the novelist Prosper Mérimée, and the composer Frédéric Chopin—impassioned her life and work. When Sand's affair with Musset came to an unhappy end, she cut off her hair and sent it to him encased in a skull. Sand defied society not only by adopting a life of bohemianism and free love, but also by her notorious habit of wearing men's clothes and smoking cigars. The female counterpart of the Byronic hero, Sand confessed: "My emotions have always been stronger than the arguments of reason, and the restrictions I tried to impose on myself were to no avail."

Sand may have been expressing her own ambiguities concerning matters of love and marriage in her third novel, *Lélia* (1833), the pages of which are filled with musings on the meaning of "true love." At one point in her spiritual odyssey, the disenchanted heroine openly ventures:

> As I continue to live, I cannot help realizing that youthful ideas about the exclusive passion of love and its eternal rights are false, even fatal. All theories ought to be allowed. I would give that of conjugal fidelity to exceptional souls. The majority have other needs, other strengths. To those others I would grant reciprocal freedom, tolerance, and renunciation of all jealous egotism. To others I would concede mystical ardors, fires brooded over in silence, a long and voluptuous reserve. Finally, to others I would admit the calm of angels, fraternal chastity, and an eternal virginity.—Are all souls alike? Do all men have the same abilities? Are not some born for the austerity of religious faith, others for voluptuousness, others for work and passionate struggle, and others, finally, for the vague reveries of the imagination? Nothing is more arbitrary than the understanding of *true love*. All loves are true, whether they be fiery or peaceful, sensual or ascetic, lasting or transient, whether they lead men to suicide or pleasure. The loves *of the mind* lead to actions just as noble as the loves *of the heart*. They have as much violence and power, if not as much duration.

Chronology

1804	Napoleon is crowned emperor
1812	Napoleon invades Russia
1814	Napoleon is exiled to Elba
1815	Battle of Waterloo
1829	Greece achieves independence from Turkey
1832	Goethe completes *Faust*

Sand's writings explore a variety of contradictory ideas concerning the fragile relationship between men and women; they also provide a wealth of information about nineteenth-century European life and culture. In addition to her novels and letters, Sand also left an autobiography and dozens of essays and articles championing socialism, women, and the working classes. She explained the power of Romantic creativity with these words: "The writer's trade is a violent, almost indestructible passion. Once it has entered a poor head, nothing can stop it . . . long live the artist's life! Our motto is freedom."

LOOKING BACK

Nationalism and the Hero

- For nineteenth-century Romantics, the hero was an expression of the expansive subjectivity of the individual. Characterized by superhuman ambition and talents, the hero, whether a historical figure or a fictional personality, experienced life with self-destructive intensity.
- Napoleon Bonaparte's remarkable career became a model for heroic action propelled by an unbounded imagination and ambition.
- To a great extent, Western literature of the early nineteenth century resembles a personal diary recording the moods and passions of the hero as a larger-than-life personality.

The Promethean Hero

- Prometheus, a Greek deity who selflessly imparted wisdom to humanity, influenced the Romantics as a symbol of heroic freedom. Mary Shelley, Byron, and other Romantics found in Prometheus an apt metaphor for the creative and daring human spirit. Byron in England and Pushkin in Russia took Napoleon as their source of inspiration.
- In America, Frederick Douglass, champion of the abolitionist movement, served as a prime example of Promethean defiance of authority and defense of human liberty.

Goethe's Faust: The Quintessential Romantic Hero

- Faust, the literary hero who symbolizes the quest to exceed the limits of knowledge and power, became the quintessential figure for Romantic

writers, painters, and composers (discussed in chapter 29).
- Goethe envisioned the legendary Faust as a symbol of the ever-striving human will to master all forms of experience, at the risk of imperiling his eternal soul.

Romantic Love and Romantic Stereotypes

- Romantic love was a popular theme among nineteenth-century writers, many of whom tended to stereotype females as either angels or *femmes fatales*.
- The nineteenth century, the first great age of female novelists, produced such outstanding writers as George Eliot, Mary Shelley, and Jane Austen.
- In the novels of George Sand, the Romantic heroine might be a self-directed creature whose passions incite her to contemplate (if not actually exercise) sexual freedom.

The Romantic Style in Art and Music

ca. 1780–1880

"Success is impossible for me if I cannot write as my heart dictates."
Verdi

Figure 29.1 EUGÈNE DELACROIX, *Women of Algiers*, 1834. Oil on canvas, 5 ft. 10⅞ in. × 7 ft. 6½ in. Delacroix's trip to North Africa in 1832 inspired more than one hundred paintings and drawings. His harem women in Moorish dress, flanked by a black attendant, reflect the Romantic taste for the exotic.

As with literature, so in the visual arts and music the Romantics favored subjects that gave free rein to the imagination. Nature and the natural landscape, the hero and heroism, and nationalist struggles for political independence—the very themes that intrigued Romantic writers—also inspired much of the art and music of the nineteenth century. Romantic artists abandoned the intellectual discipline of the Neoclassical style in favor of emotion and spontaneity. In place of the cool rationality and order of a Neoclassical composition, the Romantics introduced a studied irregularity and disorder.

Even the most superficial comparison of Neoclassical and Romantic paintings reveals essential differences in style: Neoclassical artists usually defined form by means of line (an artificial or "intellectual" boundary between the object and the space it occupied); Romantics preferred to model form by way of color. Neoclassicists generally used shades of a single color for each individual object, while Romantics might use touches of complementary colors to heighten the intensity of the painted object. And whereas Neoclassical painters smoothed out brushstrokes to leave an even and polished surface finish, Romantics often left their brushstrokes visible, as if to underline the immediacy of the creative act. They might deliberately blur details and exaggerate the sensuous aspects of texture and tone.

Rejecting the Neoclassical rules of propriety and decorum, they made room for temperament, accident, and individual genius. Romantic composers shared with the artists of their time the development of a more personal and unconstrained style. They tended to modify the "rules" of classical composition in order to increase expressive effect. They abandoned the clarity and precision of the classical composition, expanding and loosening form and introducing unexpected shifts of meter and tempo. Just as Romantic painters made free use of color to heighten the emotional impact of a subject, so composers gave **tone color**—the distinctive quality of musical sound made by a voice, a musical instrument, or a combination of instruments—a status equal to melody, harmony, and rhythm. During the nineteenth century, the symphony orchestra reached heroic proportions, while smaller, more intimate musical forms became vehicles for the expression of longing, nostalgia, and love. Program music, music-drama, and virtuoso instrumental forms added to the wide range of Romantic music.

Finally, the period saw the emergence of grand opera and the Romantic ballet, artforms that (as with the other arts of the nineteenth century) attracted the growing middle class. The exchange of ideas and themes among the artists of this era encouraged a new and lively synthesis of the arts.

Heroic Themes in Art

Gros and the Glorification of the Hero

Among the principal themes of Romantic art were those that glorified creative individualism, patriotism, and nationalism. Napoleon Bonaparte, the foremost living hero of the age and the symbol of French nationalism, was the favorite subject of many early nineteenth-century French painters. His imperial status was celebrated in the official portraits executed by his "first painter," Jacques-Louis David (see Figure 28.1); but the heroic dimension of his career was publicized by yet another member of his staff, Antoine-Jean Gros (1775–1835). Gros' representations of Napoleon's military campaigns became powerful vehicles of political propaganda.

Gros was a pupil of David, but, unlike David, he rejected the formal austerity of Neoclassicism. In his monumental canvas *Napoleon Visiting the Plague Victims at Jaffa* (Figure **29.2**), Gros converted a minor historical event—Napoleon's tour of his plague-ridden troops in Jaffa (in Palestine)—into an exotic allegorical drama that cast Napoleon in the guise of Christ as healer. He enhanced the theatricality of the scene by means of atmospheric contrasts of light and dark. Vivid details draw the eye from the foreground, filled with the bodies of the diseased and dying, into the background with its distant cityscape.

In its content, the painting manifested the Romantic taste for themes of personal heroism, suffering, and death. When it was first exhibited in Paris, an awed public adorned it with palm branches and wreaths. But the inspiration for Gros' success was also the source of his undoing: after Napoleon was sent into exile, Gros' career declined, and he committed suicide by throwing himself into the River Seine.

Popular Heroism in Goya and Géricault

Throughout most of Western history, the heroic image in art was bound up with Classical lore and Christian legend. But with Gros, we see one of the earliest efforts to glorify contemporary heroes and heroic events. The Spanish master Francisco Goya (1746–1828) helped to advance this phenomenon. He began his career as a Rococo-style tapestry designer and came into prominence as court painter to the Spanish king Charles IV. But following the invasion of Spain by Napoleon's armies in 1808, Goya's art took a new turn. Horrified by the guerrilla violence of the French occupation, he became a bitter social critic, producing some of the most memorable records of human warfare and savagery in the history of Western art.

The Third of May, 1808: The Execution of the Defenders of Madrid (Figure **29.3**) was Goya's nationalistic response to the events ensuing from an uprising of Spanish citizens against the French army of occupation. In a punitive measure, the French troops rounded up Spanish suspects in the streets of Madrid, and brutally executed them in the city outskirts. Goya recreated the episode with imaginative

Figure 29.2 **ANTOINE-JEAN GROS**, *Napoleon Visiting the Plague Victims at Jaffa*, 1804. Oil on canvas, 17 ft. 5 in. × 23 ft. 7 in.

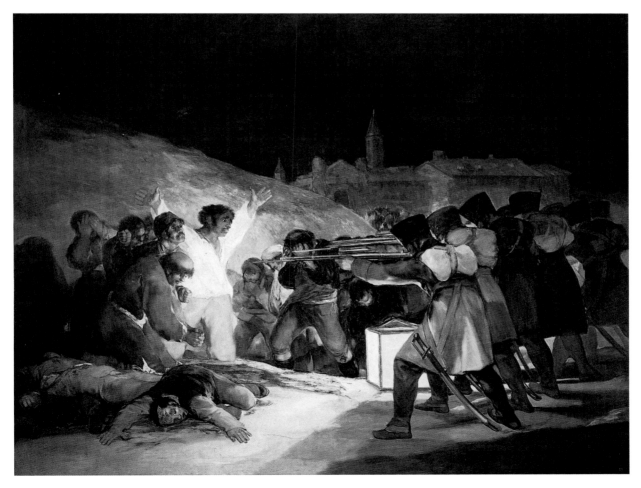

Figure 29.3 **FRANCISCO GOYA**, *The Third of May, 1808: The Execution of the Defenders of Madrid*, 1814. Oil on canvas, 8 ft. 8 in. × 10 ft. 4 in. Six years after the French were ousted, the Spanish government commissioned Goya to commemorate the massacre of May 8, 1808. Goya maintained that the work warned against future acts of brutality.

Figure 29.4 FRANCISCO GOYA, *Brave Deeds Against the Dead*, from the "Disasters of War" series, ca. 1814. Etching, 6 × 8¼ in. Goya himself wrote the biting captions for these etchings. Because some of the prints satirized the Church and other bastions of authority, they were not published until thirty-five years after the artist's death.

force, setting it against a dark sky and an ominous urban skyline. In the foreground, an off-center lantern emits a triangular beam of light that illuminates the Spanish rebels: some lie dead in pools of blood, while others cover their faces in fear and horror. Among the victims is a young man whose arms are flung upward in a final, Christlike gesture of terror and defiance. Goya deliberately spotlights this wide-eyed and bewildered figure as he confronts imminent death. On the right, in the shadows, the hulking executioners are lined up as anonymously as pieces of artillery. Emphatic contrasts of light and dark and the theatrical attention to graphic details heighten the intensity of a contemporary political event.

An indictment of butchery in the name of war, *The Third of May, 1808* is itself restrained compared to "The Disasters of War," a series of etchings and **aquatints** that Goya produced during the years of the French occupation of Spain. "The Disasters of War" have their source in historical fact as well as in Goya's imagination. *Brave Deeds Against the Dead* (Figure **29.4**) is a shocking record of the inhuman cruelty of Napoleon's troops, as well as a reminder that the heroes of modern warfare are often its innocent victims.

Goya's French contemporary Théodore Géricault (1791–1824) broadened the range of Romantic subjects. He found inspiration in the restless vitality of untamed horses and the ravaged faces of the clinically insane. Such subjects, uncommon in academic art, reflect the Romantic fascination with the life lying beyond the bounds of reason. The painting that brought Géricault instant fame was *The Raft of the "Medusa."* It immortalized a controversial event that made headlines in Géricault's own time: the wreck of a government frigate called the *Medusa* and the ghastly fate of its passengers (Figure **29.5**). When the ship hit a reef 50 miles off the coast of West Africa, the inexperienced captain, a political appointee, tried ignobly to save himself and his crew, who filled the few available lifeboats. Over a hundred passengers piled onto a makeshift raft, which was to be towed by the lifeboats. Cruelly, the crew set the raft adrift. With almost no food and supplies, chances of survival were scant; after almost two weeks, in which most died and several resorted to cannibalism, the raft was sighted and the fifteen survivors were rescued.

Géricault (a staunch opponent of the regime that appointed the captain of the *Medusa*) was so fired up by newspaper reports of the tragedy that he resolved to immortalize it in paint. He interviewed the few survivors, made drawings of the mutilated corpses in the Paris morgue, and even had a model of the raft constructed in his studio. The result was enormous, both in size (the canvas measures 16 feet 1 inch × 23 feet 6 inches) and in dramatic impact. In the decade immediately preceding the invention of photography, Géricault provided the public with a powerful visual record of a sensational contemporary event. He organized the composition on the basis of a double triangle: one triangle is formed by the two lines that stay the mast and is bisected by the mast itself; the other by the mass of agitated figures, culminating in the magnificently painted torso of a black man who signals the distant vessel that will make the rescue. Sharp diagonals, vivid contrasts of light and dark (reminiscent of Caravaggio), and muscular nudes (inspired by Michelangelo and Rubens) heighten the dramatic impact of the piece.

Géricault's *Raft* elevated ordinary men to the position of heroic combatants in the eternal struggle against the forces of nature. It celebrated their collective heroism in confronting deadly danger, a theme equally popular in Romantic literature, and, as with Turner's *Slave Ship* and Goya's *Third of May*, it publicly protested an aspect of contemporary political injustice. In essence, it brought together the reality of a man-made disaster and the more abstract theme of the Romantic *sublime*: the terror experienced by ordinary human beings in the face of nature's overpowering might.

Delacroix and Revolutionary Heroism

While Goya and Géricault democratized the image of the hero, Géricault's pupil and follower Eugène Delacroix (1798–1863) raised that image to Byronic proportions.

Figure 29.5 THÉODORE GÉRICAULT, *The Raft of the "Medusa,"* 1818. Oil on canvas, 16 ft. 1 in. × 23 ft. 6 in. Much like the panoramic landscapes of Frederic Church, Géricault's painting became an object of popular display and entertainment. Exhibited in London, it drew some 40,000 visitors between June and December 1820.

A melancholic and an intellectual, Delacroix shared Byron's hatred of tyranny, his sense of alienation, and his self-glorifying egotism—features readily discernible in the pages of his journal. Delacroix prized the imagination as "paramount" in the life of the artist. "Strange as it may seem," he observed, "the great majority of people are devoid of imagination. Not only do they lack the keen, penetrating imagination which would allow them to see objects in a vivid way—which would lead them, as it were, to the very root of things—but they are equally incapable of any clear understanding of works in which imagination predominates."

Delacroix loved dramatic narrative. He favored sensuous and violent subjects from contemporary life, popular literature, and ancient and medieval history. A six-month visit in 1832 to Morocco, neighbor of France's newly conquered colony of Algeria, provoked a lifelong interest in exotic subjects and a love of light and color. He depicted the harem women of Islamic Africa (see Figure **29.1**), recorded the poignant and shocking results of the Turkish massacres in Greece, brought to life Dante's *Inferno*, produced portrait likenesses of his contemporaries (see Figure 29.17), and made memorable illustrations for Goethe's

Faust (see Figure 28.6). Filled with fierce vitality and vivid detail, his narrative subjects make evident his declaration: "I have no love for reasonable painting." In his journal, Delacroix defended the artist's freedom to romanticize form and content: "The most sublime effects of every master," he wrote, "are often the result of *pictorial licence*, for example, the lack of finish in Rembrandt's work, the exaggeration in Rubens. Mediocre painters never have sufficient daring, they never get beyond themselves."

Delacroix's landmark work, *Liberty Leading the People*, transformed a contemporary event (the revolution of 1830) into a heroic allegory of the struggle for human freedom (see Figure 29.6). When King Charles X (1757–1836) dissolved the French legislature and took measures to repress voting rights and freedom of the press, liberal leaders, radicals, and journalists rose in rebellion. Delacroix envisioned this rebellion as a monumental allegory. Its central figure, a handsome, bare-breasted female—the personification of Liberty—leads a group of French rebels through the narrow streets of Paris and over barricades strewn with corpses. A bayonet in one hand and the tricolor flag of France in the other, she presses forward to challenge the forces of tyranny. She is champion of "the

Delacroix's painting *Liberty Leading the People* (Figure **29.6**) is often compared with David's *Oath of the Horatii* (Figure **29.7**) because both paintings are clear calls to heroic action. But in conception and in style, the two paintings are totally different. While David looked to the Roman past for his theme, Delacroix drew on the issues of his time, allegorizing real events in order to increase their dramatic impact. Whereas David's appeal was essentially elitist, Delacroix celebrated the collective heroism of ordinary people.

Delacroix was never a slave to the facts: for instance, the nudity of the fallen rebel in the left foreground (clearly related to the nudes of Géricault's *Raft*) has no basis in fact—it is uncommon to lose one's trousers in combat. The detail serves, however, to emphasize vulnerability and the imminence of death in battle. Stylistically, Delacroix's *Liberty* explodes with romantic passion. Surging rhythms link the smoke-filled background with the figures of the advancing rebels and the bodies of the fallen heroes heaped in the foreground. By comparison, David's Neoclassical *Oath* is cool and restrained, his composition gridlike, and his figures defined with linear clarity. Where Delacroix's canvas resonates with dense textures and loose, tactile brushstrokes, David's surfaces are slick and finished.

Figure 29.7 JACQUES-LOUIS DAVID, *The Oath of the Horatii*, 1785. Oil on canvas, 10 ft. 10 in. × 14 ft.

Figure 29.6 EUGÈNE DELACROIX, *Liberty Leading the People*, 1830. Oil on canvas, 8 ft. 6 in. × 10 ft. 7 in.

Figure 29.8 FRÉDÉRIC-AUGUSTE BARTHOLDI, Statue of Liberty (Liberty Enlightening the World), Liberty Island (Bedloe's Island), New York, 1871–1884. Framework constructed by A. G. Eiffel. Copper sheets mounted on steel frame, height 152 ft. While France gave America the statue, it did not provide the pedestal. To assist in raising funds for the latter, the poet Emma Lazarus was commissioned to write a poem. Her concern for the 2000 Russian-Jewish immigrants arriving monthly in New York inspired the famous lines that begin "Give me your tired, your poor,/ Your huddled masses yearning to breathe free."

people": the middle class, as represented by the gentleman in a frock coat; the lower class, as symbolized by the scruffy youth carrying pistols; and racial minorities, as conceived in the black saber-bearer at the left. She is, moreover, France itself, the banner-bearer of the spirit of nationalism that infused nineteenth-century European history.

Delacroix's *Liberty* instantly became a symbol of democratic aspirations. In 1884, France sent as a gift of friendship to the young American nation a monumental copper and cast-iron statue of an idealized female bearing a tablet and a flaming torch (Figure **29.8**). Designed by Frédéric-Auguste Bartholdi (1834–1904), the Statue of Liberty (Liberty Enlightening the World) is the "sister" of Delacroix's painted heroine; it has become a classic image of freedom for oppressed people everywhere.

Heroic Themes in Sculpture

In sculpture as in painting, heroic subjects served the cause of nationalism. *The Departure of the Volunteers of 1792* (Figure **29.9**) by François Rude (1784–1855) embodied the dynamic heroism of the Napoleonic Era. Installed at the foot of the Arc de Triomphe (see Figure 26.31), which stands at the end of the Champs-Elysées in Paris, the 42-foot-high stone sculpture commemorates the patriotism of a band of French volunteers—presumably the battalion of Marseilles, who marched to Paris in 1792 to defend the republic. Young and old, nude or clothed in ancient or medieval garb (a convention that augmented dramatic effect while universalizing the heroic theme), the spirited members of this small citizen army are led by the allegorical figure of Bellona, the Roman goddess of war. Like Delacroix's Liberty, Rude's Classical goddess urges the patriots onward. The vitality of the piece is enhanced by deep undercutting that achieves dramatic contrasts of light and dark. In this richly textured work, Rude captured the revolutionary spirit and emotional fervor of this battalion's marching song, "La Marseillaise," which the French later adopted as their national anthem.

Nineteenth-century nationalism stimulated an interest in the cultural heritage of ethnic groups beyond the European West. Just as Catlin found in the American West a wealth of fascinating visual resources, so Europeans turned to Africa and the East for exotic subjects (see Figure 29.1). Napoleon's invasion of Egypt (1798–1801) had started a virtual craze for things North African, and such interests were further stimulated by the French presence in Algeria beginning in the 1830s. In 1848, the French government abolished slavery in France and all its colonies.

Science and Technology

1836	Samuel Colt (American) produces a six-cylinder revolver
1841	the breech-loading rifle known as the "needlegun" is introduced
1847	an Italian chemist develops explosive nitroglycerin

Charles-Henri-Joseph Cordier (1827–1905), a member of Rude's studio and a favorite exhibitor in the academic Salon of Paris, requested a governmental assignment in Africa in order to make a record of its peoples. The result of Cordier's ethnological studies was a series of twelve busts of Africans and Asians, executed by means of innovative polychrome techniques that combined bronze or colored marble with porphyry, jasper, and onyx from Algerian quarries (Figure **29.10**). Cordier's portrait heads reveal a sensitivity to individual personality and a commitment to capturing the dignity of his models. Rather than perceiving his subject as an exotic "other," he regarded each as a racial type "at the point," as he explained, "of merging into one and the same people."

In America, the passage of the Thirteenth Amendment to the Constitution, in 1865, which outlawed the practice of slavery in the United States, was met with a similar outburst

Figure 29.11 **EDMONIA LEWIS**, *Forever Free*, 1867. Marble, height 40½ in.

Figure 29.10 **CHARLES-HENRI-JOSEPH CORDIER**, *African in Algerian Costume*, ca. 1856–1857. Bronze and onyx, 37¾ × 26 × 14 in. Rich details and sensuous materials characterize Cordier's portraits, which became famous as examples of a new visual anthropology focused on the physical appearance of what he called "the different indigenous types of the human race."

of heroic celebration. In the commemorative marble sculpture *Forever Free* (1867), a young slave who has broken his chains raises his arm in victory, while his female companion kneels in grateful prayer (Figure **29.11**). The artist who conceived this remarkable work of art, Edmonia Lewis (1845–ca. 1885), was the daughter of an African-American father and a Chippawa mother. Like most talented young American artists of this era, Lewis made her way to Europe for academic training. She remained in Rome to pursue her career and gained great recognition for her skillfully carved portrait busts and allegorical statues, some of which exalted heroic women in biblical and ancient history. Many of her works are now lost, and almost nothing is known of her life after 1885.

Figure 29.12 **CHARLES BARRY** and **A. W. N. PUGIN**, Houses of Parliament, London, 1840–1860. Length 940 ft. Following the fire of 1834, which destroyed the earlier structure (also known as the Palace of Westminster), a royal commission directed Barry to design a Neo-Gothic replacement. Pugin was largely responsible for the interior details. His designs seem to have coincided with his conversion to Roman Catholicism. He perceived purity of structure and the meaningful application of details as equivalent to the Catholic faith, but equally appropriate to the ideals of the largely Protestant nation.

Trends in Mid-Nineteenth-Century Architecture

Neomedievalism in the West

Architects of the early to mid-nineteenth century regarded the past as a source of inspiration and moral instruction. Classical Greek and republican Roman buildings embodied the political and aesthetic ideals of nation builders like Napoleon and Jefferson (see chapter 26); but the austere dignity of Neoclassicism did not appeal to all tastes. More typical of the Romantic imagination was a nostalgic affection for the medieval world, with its brooding castles and towering cathedrals. No less than Neoclassicism, *Neomedievalism*—the revival of medieval culture—served the cause of nationalism. It exalted the state by recapturing its unique historical and cultural past. On the eve of the unification of Germany (1848), and for decades thereafter, German craftsmen restored many of its most notable Gothic monuments, including its great cathedrals.

In England, where the Christian heritage of the Middle Ages was closely associated with national identity, writers embraced the medieval past: Alfred Lord Tennyson (1802–1892), poet laureate of Great Britain, for example, fused early British legend with the Christian mission in a cycle of Arthurian poems entitled *Idylls of the King*; while Sir Walter Scott immortalized medieval heroes and heroines in avidly read historical novels and Romantic poems.

The revival of the Gothic style was equally distinctive in architecture. The British Houses of Parliament, conceived by Charles Barry (1795–1860) and Augustus Welby Northmore Pugin (1812–1852) and begun in 1836,

Figure 29.13 **JAMES RENWICK** and **WILLIAM RODRIGUE**, Saint Patrick's Cathedral, Fifth Avenue and 50th Street, New York, 1853–1858.

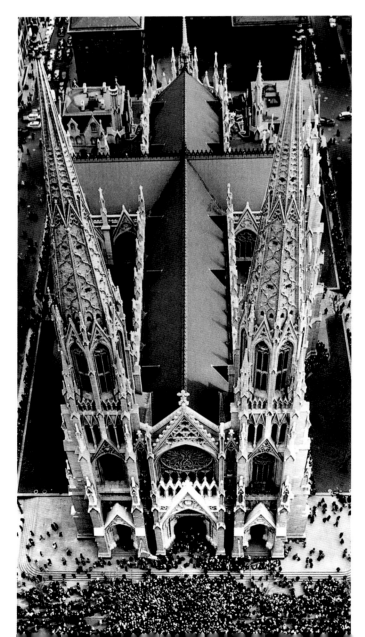

Figure 29.14 JOHN NASH, the Royal Pavilion, Brighton, from the northeast, 1815–1821.

are among the most aesthetically successful large-scale Neo-Gothic public buildings. The picturesque combination of spires and towers fronting on the River Thames in London was the product of Pugin's conviction that the Gothic style best expressed the dignity befitting the official architecture of a Christian nation (Figure **29.12**). Moreover, the Gothic style was symbolically appropriate for the building that epitomized the principles of parliamentary rule, pioneered in England with the signing of the Magna Carta in 1215. The Houses of Parliament might be said to reflect the importance of medieval historical tradition—both religious and political—in shaping England's self-image.

Neomedievalism gave rise to a movement for the archeological restoration of churches and castles throughout Europe: it also inspired some extraordinary new architectural activity in North America. Colleges and universities (such as Harvard and Yale), museums (such as the Smithsonian in Washington, D.C.), and numerous churches and cathedrals were modeled on medieval prototypes. One of the most elegant examples of the Gothic revival in the United States is Saint Patrick's Cathedral in New York City (Figure **29.13**), which (along with Grace Church in Manhattan and the Smithsonian) was designed by James Renwick (1818–1895) and William Rodrigue (1800–1867).

Exoticism in Western Architecture

Romantic architecture also drew inspiration from the "exotic" East, and especially those parts of the world in which the European powers were building colonial empires. The most intriguing Western pastiche of non-Western styles is the Royal Pavilion at Brighton, on the south coast of England. Designed by the English architect John Nash (1752–1835) between 1815 and 1821 as a seaside resort for the Prince Regent, it combines a fanciful assortment of Chinese, Indian, and Islamic motifs (Figure **29.14**). Nash raised bulbous domes and slender minarets over a hidden frame of cast iron, the structural medium that would soon come to dominate modern architecture (see chapter 30). The bizarre interior decor, which includes waterlily chandeliers and cast-iron palm trees with copper leaves, produced an eclectic style that Nash's critics called "Indian Gothic."

The Romantic Style in Music

"Music is the most romantic of all the arts—one might almost say, the only genuine romantic one—for its sole subject is the infinite." Thus wrote the German novelist and musician E. T. A. Hoffmann (1776–1822). Like many Romantic composers, Hoffmann believed that music held a privileged position in its capacity to express what he called "an inexpressible longing." For the Romantics, music—the most abstract and elusive of the arts—was capable of freeing the intellect and speaking directly to the heart.

The nineteenth century produced an enormous amount of music in all genres—a phenomenon that is reflected in the fact that audiences today listen to more nineteenth-century music than music of any previous time period. Its hallmark is personalized expression, a feature as apparent in large orchestral works as it is in small, intimate pieces.

During the Romantic era, the orchestra grew to grand proportions. Mid-nineteenth-century orchestras were often five times larger than those used by Haydn and Mozart. While the volume of sound expanded, the varieties of instrumental possibilities also grew larger, in part because of technical improvements made in the instruments themselves. Brass instruments (such as the trumpet and the tuba) gained new pitches and a wider range with the addition of valves; woodwind instruments (such as the flute and the clarinet) underwent structural changes that greatly facilitated fingering and tuning. Modifications to the violin lent the instrument greater power; and the early nineteenth-century piano, which acquired an iron frame, two or three pedals, and thicker strings, was capable of increased brilliance of tone and greater expressiveness—features that made it the most popular musical instrument of the century. Such mechanical improvements expanded the tonal potential of musical instruments and produced a virtual revolution in orchestral textures.

In terms of musical composition, the symphony and the concerto were the most important of the large orchestral forms. Equally significant, however, were song forms, especially songs that dealt with themes of love and death or nature and nature's moods. Composers found inspiration in heroic subjects, in contemporary events, and in the legends and histories of their native lands. Like the Romantic painters and writers, they embraced exotic themes. In both small musical forms and large operatic compositions, they made every effort to achieve an ideal union of poetry and music. The close association between the arts is seen in the many operas and symphonic pieces based on nineteenth-century plays, novels, and poems. The Faust legend and Goethe's *Faust* in particular inspired numerous musical settings. Bizet's *Carmen*, discussed in chapter 28, was based on a novella that was influenced in turn by Pushkin's narrative poem *The Gypsies* (1824); and Pushkin's verse poem *Eugene Onegin* (1832) inspired Peter Ilyich Tchaikovsky's opera of the same name. But it was Sir Walter Scott's historical novels that were the favorite source for at least a dozen operas by French, British, and Italian composers.

As in the eighteenth century, nineteenth-century composers were often also performers. They drew attention to their own technical abilities by writing **virtuoso** pieces (usually for piano or violin) that only highly accomplished musicians like themselves could perform with facility. No longer completely at the mercy of the patronage system, they indulged, often publicly, in bouts of euphoria, melancholy, and petty jealousy. The talented Genoese composer and violinist Niccolò Paganini (1782–1840), for instance, refused to publish his own pieces, which he performed with such astounding technical agility that rumor had it he had come by his virtuosity through a pact with the Devil.

The Genius of Beethoven

The leading composer of the early nineteenth century and one of the greatest musicians of all time was the German-born Ludwig van Beethoven (1770–1827). Beethoven's lifelong residency in Vienna brought him in contact with the music of Mozart and Haydn; he studied briefly with the latter. It also provided him with the fundamentals of the classical style. His indebtedness to classical composition, especially evident in his early works, makes him something of a bridge between the classical and Romantic eras.

Beethoven was a gifted pianist, organist, and violinist. While he composed works in almost every musical form and for many different kinds of instrument, his thirty-two piano sonatas reflect a lifelong love for the expressive potential of that instrument. His nine symphonies, which critics claim as his greatest achievement, generally adhere to the classical format, but they move beyond the bounds of classical structure. The Third Symphony, which he subtitled the *Eroica* ("Heroic"), is a case in point. It is longer and more complex than any previous orchestral work. While it follows the standard number and order of movements found in the classical symphony, it is almost twice as long as its typical twenty- to twenty-five-minute predecessors. The first movement, which one French critic called "the Grand Army of the soul," engages six (rather than the traditional two) themes dictated by the sonata form (see chapter 26). The movement begins with two commanding hammer strikes of the French horn—symbolic of the hero throughout the symphony. The second movement is a somber and solemn funeral march. For the third movement, instead of the traditional minuet, Beethoven introduces a vigorous **scherzo** ("joke"), which replaces the elegant courtly dance form with a melody that is fast and varied in tempo—a joke in that it is essentially undanceable! The last movement, a victory finale, brings the themes and variations of the first movement together with a long coda that again features the majestic horn section. It is worth noting that for the triumphant last movement of this stirring symphony, Beethoven included musical passages originally written for a ballet on the subject of Prometheus.

Beethoven had originally dedicated the Third Symphony to Napoleon, whom he admired both as a popular hero and a champion of liberty. But when Napoleon crowned himself emperor in 1804, Beethoven angrily scratched out the name "Buonaparte" and replaced it with a generalized dedication: "Heroic symphony, dedicated to the memory of a great man." "So, he is no more than a common mortal!" Beethoven is said to have exclaimed. "Now he will trample on all the rights of man and . . . become a tyrant." Ultimately, the symphony was dedicated and presented to a minor nobleman, Prince Joseph Franz Maximilian Lobkowicz.

Beethoven's genius lay in his use of compositional elements that gave his music unprecedented expressive power. He introduced into his compositions a new rhythmic vitality, strong and sudden contrasts of sound, and an expanded range of instrumental textures. By adding piccolo, bass clarinet, trombone, bass drum, and cymbals to the scoring and doubling the number of flutes, oboes, clarinets, and bassoons, he vastly broadened the expressive range and dramatic power of orchestral sound.

See Music Listening Selections at end of chapter.

In his use of musical **dynamics** (gradations of loudness and softness), Beethoven was more explicit and varied than his classical predecessors. Prior to 1812, he made use of only five terms to indicate the softness or loudness of piano performance; increasingly, however, he expanded the classical vocabulary with such words as *dolente* ("sorrowful") and *teneramente* ("tenderly") to indicate nuances. Like other Romantic artists—Delacroix, in particular, comes to mind—Beethoven blurred the divisions between the structural units of a composition, exploiting textural contrasts for expressive effect. He often broke with classical form, adding, for example, a fifth movement to his Sixth (or *Pastoral*) Symphony and embellishing the finale of his Ninth Symphony with a chorus and solo voices. Beethoven's daring use of dissonance, his sudden pauses and silences, and his brilliance of thematic and rhythmic invention reflect his preference for dramatic spontaneity over measured regularity. The powerful opening notes of the Fifth Symphony—a motif that Beethoven is said to have called "fate knocking at the door"—exemplify his affection for inventive repetition and surging rhythms that propel the music toward a powerful climax.

Difficult as it is to imagine, Beethoven wrote much of his greatest music when he was functionally deaf. From the age of twenty-nine, when he became aware of a progressive degeneration of his hearing, he labored against depression and despair. Temperamental and defiant, he scorned the patronage system that had weighed heavily upon both Mozart and Haydn, and often sold his musical compositions as an independent artist. He declared contempt for the nobility and ignored their demands. In 1802, he confided to his family: "I am bound to be misunderstood; for me there can be no relaxation with my fellow men, no refined conversations, no mutual exchange of ideas. I must live alone like one who has been banished." In retreat from society, the alienated composer turned to nature (Figure **29.15**).

In the woods outside Vienna, Beethoven roamed with his musical sketchbook under one arm, often singing to

Figure 29.15 *Beethoven Composing the "Pastoral" by a Brook,* from the Twenty-Second Almanac of the Zürich Musikgesellschaft for 1834: Biography of Ludwig van Beethoven. Colored lithograph, 6½ × 5⅖ in. In 1802, as his hearing became increasingly worse, Beethoven moved to the small village of Heiligenstadt, outside Vienna. His sense of isolation and his heroic struggle to overcome despair are reflected in his music.

himself in a loud voice. "Woods, trees and rock," he wrote in his diary, "give the response that man requires." His discovery that nature mirrored his deepest emotions inspired his programmatic Sixth Symphony (1808), which he subtitled "A recollection of country life." Each of the five movements of the *Pastoral* is labeled with a specific reference to nature: "Awakening of happy feelings on arriving in the country"; "By the brook"; "Joyous gatherings of country folk"; "Storm"; and "Shepherd's Song, happy and thankful feelings after the storm." In the tradition of Vivaldi's *Four Seasons* (see chapter 23), Beethoven occasionally imitated the sounds of nature. For example, at the end of the second movement, flute, oboe, and clarinet join to create bird calls; and a quavering *tremolo* (the rapid repetition of a tone to produce a trembling effect) on the lower strings suggests the sounds of a murmuring brook.

Some critics regard Beethoven's last symphony, the Ninth Symphony (1824), as his greatest work. It is the first example of a symphony that uses the human voice as a component of the instrumentation: In the last movement Beethoven took the unprecedented step of including four solo voices and a large chorus. The inspiration for the *Choral Symphony* was a poem by Friedrich Schiller (see chapter 27): *An die Freude* ("To Joy"), an ode that celebrates the joy of universal brotherhood. The final, choral movement of this long, ambitious symphony is a brilliant exposition of Beethoven's imaginative power and his defense of a humanistic ideal. At the premier performance of the symphony in Vienna, the aging composer shared the stage with the conductor, beating out the tempo for music he could hear only in his head.

Art Songs

The art songs of Beethoven's Austrian contemporary Franz Schubert (1797–1828) aptly reflect the nineteenth-century composer's ambition to unite poetry and music. Schubert is credited with originating the Romantic *lied* (German for "song," pl. *lieder*), an independent song for solo voice and piano. The *lied* is not a song in the traditional sense but, rather, a poem recreated in musical terms. Its lyric qualities, like those of simple folk songs, are generated by the poem itself. The *lieder* of Schubert, Robert Schumann (1810–1856), and Johannes Brahms (1833–1897), which set to music the poetry of Heine and Goethe, among others, are intimate evocations of personal feelings and moods. They recount tales of love and longing, describe nature and its moods (some forty songs are related to water or to fish), or lament the transience of human happiness.

Among Schubert's thousand or so works (which include nine symphonies, five operas, and numerous chamber pieces) are 600 *lieder*. Of these, his musical settings of Goethe's ballads rank as landmark expressions of the Romantic spirit of music. *Gretchen am Spinnrade* ("Gretchen at the Spinning Wheel"), written when the composer was only seventeen years old, is based on a poem by Goethe which occurs near the end of Part One of *Faust*. In the piece, Gretchen laments the absence of her lover, Faust, and anticipates the sorrows that their love will bring. Repeated three times are the poignant lines with which the song opens: "My peace is gone, my heart is sore:/ I shall find it never and never more." While the melody and tone color of the voice line convey the sadness expressed in the words of the poem, the propelling piano line captures the rhythms of the spinning wheel.

Another of Schubert's finest art songs is *Erlkönig* ("The Erlking"), which combines elements of the natural (a raging storm), the supernatural (the figure of death in the person of the legendary king of the elves), and the heroic (a father's desperate effort to save the life of his ailing son). Here, Schubert's music mingles the rhythms of the stormy ride on horseback, the struggle for survival, and the threatening lure of death. Schubert himself died of syphilis at the age of thirty-one.

The Programmatic Symphonies of Berlioz

The French composer Hector Berlioz (1803–1869) began his first symphony in 1830. An imaginative combination of the story of Faust and Berlioz's own life, the *Symphonie fantastique* tells the dramatic tale of Berlioz's "interminable and inextinguishable passion"—as he described it—for the captivating Irish actress Harriet Smithson. Berlioz wrote the symphony in the first flush of his passion, when he was only twenty-seven years old. Following an intense courtship, he married Harriet, only to discover that he and the woman he idolized were dreadfully mismatched—the marriage turned Smithson into an alcoholic and Berlioz into an adulterer.

The *Symphonie fantastique* belongs to the genre known as **program music**, that is, instrumental music endowed with a specific literary or pictorial content indicated by the composer. Berlioz was not the first to write music that was programmatic: in *The Four Seasons*, Vivaldi had linked music to poetic phrases, as had Beethoven in his *Pastoral Symphony*. But Berlioz was the first to build an entire symphony around a musical motif that tells a story. The popularity of program music during the nineteenth century testifies to the powerful influence of literature upon the other arts. Berlioz, whose second symphony, *Harold in Italy*, was inspired by Byron's *Childe Harold* (see chapter 28), was not alone in his attraction to literary subjects. The Hungarian composer Franz Liszt (1811–1886) wrote symphonic poems based on the myth of Prometheus and Shakespeare's *Hamlet*. He also composed the *Faust Symphony*, which he dedicated to Berlioz. The Russian composer Peter Ilyich Tchaikovsky (1840–1893) wrote many programmatic pieces, including the tone poem *Romeo and Juliet*. European political events inspired the composition of nationalistic program music, such as Beethoven's *Battle Symphony* of 1813 (also known as "Wellington's Victory") and Tchaikovsky's colorful *1812 Overture* (1880), which, commemorating Napoleon's retreat from Moscow, incorporated portions of the national anthems of both France and tzarist Russia.

In the *Symphonie fantastique*, Berlioz links a specific mood or event to a musical phrase, or **idée fixe** ("fixed idea").

See Music Listening Selections at end of chapter.

Figure 29.16 ANDREW GEIGER, *A Concert of Hector Berlioz in 1846*, 1846. Engraving, 9⅓ × 9⅓ in.

four, and combined instruments inventively so as to create unusual mixes of sound. In the third movement, for example, a solo English horn and an oboe create a mood of loneliness; thereafter, four timpani (kettledrums) produce the effect of "distant thunder." He also expanded tone color, stretching the register of clarinets to screeching highs, for instance, and playing the strings of the violin with the wood of the bow instead of with the hair. Berlioz's favorite medium was the full symphony orchestra, which he enlarged to include 150 musicians. Called "the apostle of bigness," Berlioz conceived an ideal orchestra that consisted of over 400 musicians, including 242 string instruments, 30 pianos, 30 harps, and a chorus of 360 voices. The monumental proportions of Berlioz's orchestras and choirs, and the volume of sound they produced, inspired spoofs in contemporary French and German journals. Cartoons showed the maestro, also spoofed for his extravagant hairstyles, beating time with an electric telegraph pole, recruiting orchestra members from the artillery of a garrison, and conducting a sea of instrumentalists (Figure **29.16**). But Berlioz, who was also a talented writer and a music critic for Parisian newspapers, thumbed his nose at the critics in lively essays that defended his own musical philosophy.

The Piano Music of Chopin

If the nineteenth century was the age of Romantic individualism, it was also the age of the virtuoso: composers wrote music that might be performed gracefully and accurately only by individuals with extraordinary technical skills. The quintessential example of this phenomenon is the Polish-born composer Frédéric Chopin (1810–1849). At the age of seven, Chopin gave his first piano concert in Warsaw. Slight in build even as an adult, Chopin had small hands that nevertheless could reach across the keys of the piano like "the jaws of a snake" (as one of his peers observed). After leaving Warsaw, Chopin became the acclaimed pianist of the Paris *salons* and a close friend of Delacroix (who painted the portrait in Figure **29.17**), Berlioz, and many of the leading novelists of his time, including George Sand (see chapter 28), with whom he had a stormy seven-year love affair.

In his brief lifetime—he died of tuberculosis at the age of thirty-nine—Chopin created an entirely personal musical idiom linked to the expressive potential of the modern piano. For that instrument, Chopin wrote over 200 pieces, most of which were short keyboard works, such as dances, *préludes*, **nocturnes** (slow, songlike pieces), **impromptus** (pieces that sound improvised), and *études* (instrumental studies designed to improve a player's technique).

This recurring motif becomes the means by which the composer binds together the individual parts of his dramatic narrative. Subtitled "Episode in the Life of an Artist," the *Symphonie fantastique* is an account of the young musician's opium-induced dream, in which, according to Berlioz's program notes, "the Beloved One takes the form of a melody in his mind, like a fixed idea which is ever returning and which he hears everywhere."

Unified by the *idée fixe*, the symphony consists of a sequence of five parts, each distinguished by a particular mood: the lover's "reveries and passions"; a ball at which the hero meets his beloved; a stormy scene in the country; a "March to the Scaffold" (marking the hero's dream of murdering his lover and his subsequent execution); and a final and feverishly orchestrated "Dream of a Witches' Sabbath" inspired by Goethe's *Faust*. (Berlioz's *Damnation of Faust*, a piece for soloists, chorus, and orchestra, likewise drew on Goethe's great drama.) The "plot" of the *Symphonie fantastique*, published along with the musical score, was (and usually still is) printed in program notes available to listeners. But the written narrative is *not* essential to the enjoyment of the music, for, as Berlioz himself explained, the music holds authority as absolute sound, above and beyond its programmatic associations. Indeed, after the first rehearsals of the *Symphonie*, Berlioz exclaimed that he had found the "March to the Scaffold" fifty times more frightening than he had expected.

The spiritual heir to Beethoven, Berlioz took liberties with traditional symphonic form. He composed the *Symphonie fantastique* in five movements instead of the usual

See Music Listening Selections at end of chapter.

His Etude in G-flat Major, **Opus** 10, No. 5, is a breathtaking piece that challenges the performer to play very rapidly on the black keys, which are less than half the width of the white ones.

Much like Delacroix, Chopin was given to violent mood swings. And, as with Delacroix's paintings, which although carefully contrived give the impression of spontaneity, much of Chopin's music seems improvised—the impetuous record of fleeting feeling, rather than the studied product of diligent construction. The most engaging of his compositions are marked by fresh turns of harmony and free tempos and rhythms. Chopin might embellish a melodic line with unusual and flamboyant devices, such as a rolling **arpeggio** (the sounding of the notes of a chord in rapid succession). His *préludes* provide bold contrasts of calm meditation and bravura, while his nocturnes—like the Romantic landscapes of Friedrich and Corot (see Figures 27.7 and 27.11)—are often dreamy and wistful. Of his dance forms, the polonaise and the mazurka preserve the robustness of the folk tunes of his native Poland, while the waltz mirrors the Romantic taste for a new type of dance, more sensuous and physically expressive than the courtly and formal minuet. Considered vulgar and lewd when it was introduced in the late eighteenth century, the waltz, with its freedom of movement, intoxicating rhythms, and close contact between partners became the most popular of all nineteenth-century dances.

Figure 29.17 EUGÈNE DELACROIX, *Frédéric Chopin*, 1838. Oil on canvas, 18 × 15 in. This unfinished portrait was originally part of a larger double portrait that showed George Sand listening to the virtuoso pianist at the keyboard.

See Music Listening Selections at end of chapter.

Figure 29.18 JEAN-LOUIS CHARLES GARNIER, the façade of the Opéra, Paris, 1860–1875. The 2200-seat theater is now used primarily for ballet. Both in its exterior design and in its lavish interior, it recalls the Palace of Versailles. The swampy foundation and underground lake that had to be pumped out during the building's construction were made famous in the French novel *The Phantom of the Opera* (1909) by Gaston Leroux.

Figure 29.19 JEAN-LOUIS CHARLES GARNIER, the Grand Staircase in the Opéra, Paris, 1860–1875. Engraving from Jean-Louis Charles Garnier, *Le Nouvel Opéra de Paris*, 1880, Vol. 2, plate 8. The Paris Opéra ruled that all works presented there must be in French, thus requiring foreign composers to translate their librettos. Also required was a second-act ballet, which became a standard device in French operas.

The Romantic Ballet

The theatrical artform known as "ballet" gained immense popularity in the Romantic era. While the great ballets of Tchaikovsky—*Swan Lake, The Nutcracker,* and *Sleeping Beauty*—brought fame to Russia toward the end of the 1800s, it was in early nineteenth-century Paris that Romantic ballet was born. By the year 1800, ballet had moved from the court to the theater, where it was enjoyed as a middle-class entertainment. Magnificent theaters, such as the Paris Opéra (Figure **29.18**), designed by Jean-Louis Charles Garnier (1825–1878), became showplaces for public entertainment.

The Neobaroque polychrome façade of the Paris opera house reflects Garnier's awareness that Greek architects had painted parts of their buildings; but the glory of the structure is its interior, which takes as its focus a sumptuous grand staircase (Figure **29.19**). Luxuriously appointed, and

Figure 29.20 JEAN-BAPTISTE CARPEAUX, *The Dance*, 1868. Stone, 13⁷⁄₁₀ × 9⁷⁄₁₀ × 4⁷⁄₁₀ ft. Created for the façade of the Opéra, Paris, now in Musée d'Orsay, Paris. Between 1854 and 1861, Carpeaux worked in Rome, where he studied the sculptures of the Renaissance masters. He broke with Classical and Renaissance traditions, however, in creating sculptures that incorporate spontaneous movement.

(choreographed by her father) was hailed as nothing less than virtuoso. Clothed in a diaphanous dress with a fitted bodice and a bell-shaped skirt (the prototype of the *tutu*), Taglioni performed perfect **arabesques**—a ballet position in which the dancer stands on one leg with the other extended behind her, and one or both arms held to create the longest line possible from one extremity to the other. She also astonished audiences by crossing the stage in three magnificent, floating leaps. While faithful to the exact steps of classical ballet, she brought to formal dance the new, more sensuous spirit of nineteenth-century Romanticism. Taglioni quickly became a celebrity: following her performances in London, dolls manufactured in the dress and style of the ballerina were in great demand. Legend has it that after her retirement from the stage in 1842, her fans cooked and ate a pair of her ballet shoes, covered with sauce.

Popular myths and fairy tales inspired many of the ballets of the Romantic era, including *La sylphide*, *Giselle*, and Tchaikovsky's more widely known *Swan Lake* and *Sleeping Beauty*. The central figure of each ballet is usually some version of the angelic female—a fictional creature drawn from fable, fairy tale, and fantasy. In *La sylphide*, a sylph (a mythical nature deity) enchants the hero and lures him away from his bride-to-be. Pursued by the hero,

Figure 29.21 RICHARD JAMES LANE, *Marie Taglioni in the Ballet Flore et Zephyre*, 1831. After a drawing by Alfred Edward Chalon. Hand-coloured engraving, 14¾ × 10½ in. Dancing *sur les points*, a talent that brought her fame as a prima ballerina, Taglioni is pictured here in her 1830 London debut as Flore. The ballet skirt of this era was shortened to display the dancer's legs, and reveal the virtuoso footwork that previously was reserved for male dancers.

illuminated by means of the latest technological invention, gaslight, the Paris Opéra became the model for public theaters throughout Europe. For the façade, Jean-Baptiste Carpeaux (1827–1875) created a 15-foot-high sculpture whose exuberant rhythms capture the spirit of dance as the physical expression of human joy (Figure **29.20**).

The ballets performed on the stage of the Paris Opéra were the culmination of a golden age in European dance. In Paris in 1830, the Italian-born **prima ballerina** (the first, or leading, female dancer in a ballet company) Maria Taglioni (1804–1884) perfected the art of dancing *sur les points* ("on the toes") in ballet shoes that were no more than flimsy slippers made from woven strips of silk ribbon and padded with cotton wool (Figure **29.21**). Taglioni's landmark performance in the ballet *La sylphide*

she nevertheless eludes his grasp and dies—the victim of a malevolent witch—before their love is consummated. The heroine of this and other Romantic ballets symbolized the elusive ideals of love and beauty that were a favorite subject of the Romantic poets. She conformed as well to the stereotype of the pure and virtuous female found in the pages of many Romantic novels. The traditional equation of beauty and innocence in the person of the idealized female is well illustrated in the comments of one French critic, who, describing "the aerial and virginal grace of Taglioni," exulted, "She flies like a spirit in the midst of transparent clouds of white muslin—she resembles a happy angel." Clearly, the nineteenth-century ballerina was the Romantic realization of the Eternal Female, a figure that fitted the stereotype of the angelic woman.

Romantic Opera

Verdi and Italian Grand Opera

Romantic opera, designed to appeal to a growing middle-class audience, came into existence after 1820. The culmination of Baroque theatricality, Romantic opera was grand both in size and in spirit. It was a flamboyant spectacle that united all aspects of theatrical production: music, dance, stage sets, and costumes. While Paris was the operatic capital of Europe in the first half of the nineteenth century, Italy ultimately took the lead in seducing the public with hundreds of wonderfully tuneful and melodramatic Romantic operas.

The art of singing, as it flourished in Italy in the first decades of the nineteenth century, established the **bel canto** tradition. Literally "beautiful singing" (or "beautiful song,") bel canto-style opera emphasizes the melodic line, and the vocalist's ability to execute such florid embellishments as rapid runs and trills. Two of the early nineteenth century's most famous bel canto operas are Gaetano Donizetti's Lucia di Lammermoor (1835), which is based on a novel by Sir Walter Scott, and Gioacchino Rossini's Il barbiere de Siviglia (The Barber of Seville, 1816). In these works, showpiece arias with long, winding melodic lines (usually sung in the upper register) demand stunning vocal agility.

The shift to operatic drama, marked by more intense and powerful singing, is evident in the music of the Italian composer Giuseppe Verdi (1813–1901). In his twenty-six operas, the long Italian operatic tradition that had begun with Monteverdi (see chapter 20) came to its peak. Reflecting on his gift for capturing high drama in music, Verdi exclaimed, "Success is impossible for me if I cannot write as my heart dictates." The heroines of Verdi's most beloved operas— Rigoletto (1851), La Traviata (1853), and Aïda (1870)—are also creatures of the heart, who all die for love.

Perhaps the most famous of Verdi's operas is Aïda, which was commissioned by the Turkish viceroy of Egypt to mark the opening of the Suez Canal. Aïda made a nationalistic plea for unity against foreign domination— one critic called the opera "agitator's music." Indeed, the aria "O patria mia" ("O my country") is an expression of Verdi's ardent love for the newly unified Italy. But Aïda is also the passionate love story of an Egyptian prince and an Ethiopian princess held as a captive slave. Verdi's stirring arias, vigorous choruses, and richly colored orchestral passages can be enjoyed by listening alone. But the dramatic force of this opera can be appreciated only by witnessing firsthand a theatrical performance—especially one that engages such traditional paraphernalia as horses, chariots, and, of course, elephants.

Wagner and the Birth of Music-Drama

In Germany, the master of opera and one of the most formidable composers of the century was Richard Wagner (1813–1883). The stepson of a gifted actor, he spent much of his childhood composing poems and plays and setting them to music. This union of music and literature culminated in the birth of what Wagner called **music-drama**—a continuous fabric of sound and story that replaced the traditional divisions of the opera into arias, duets, choruses, and instrumental passages. Wagner's conception of opera shattered long-standing Western theatrical traditions. He aimed, as he explained, "to force the listener, for the first time in the history of opera, to take an interest in a poetic idea by making him follow all its developments" as dramatized in music. While earlier composers generally told the story by way of the vocal line, Wagner made the orchestra an equal component in the drama. Heroic in size, Wagner's orchestra generally engulfs the listener in a maelstrom of uninterrupted melody. Characters and events emerge by way of the application of the *leitmotif*, a short musical phrase that—like the *idée fixe*—signifies a particular person, thing, or idea in the story.

Deeply nationalistic, Wagner based his music-dramas almost exclusively on heroic themes from Germany's medieval past. His librettos, which he himself wrote, brought to life the fabulous events and personalities of German folktales and legends. Among his recurring themes are two he shared with Goethe: the redeeming love of the Eternal Female and the Faustian lust for power. Magical devices— the ring, the sword, or the chalice—like the individual characters in the opera, might each assume its own musical phrase or *leitmotif.*

Of his nine principal operas, the most ambitious is a monumental fifteen-hour cycle of four music-dramas collectively titled Der Ring des Nibelungen (The Ring of the Nibelung). Based on Norse and Germanic mythology, The Ring involves the quest for a magical but cursed golden ring, whose power would provide its possessor with the potential to control the universe (Figure **29.22**). Out of a struggle between the gods of Valhalla and an assortment of giants, dragons, and dwarfs emerges the hero, Siegfried, whose valorous deeds secure the ring for his lover, Brünnhilde. In the end Siegfried loses both his love and his life, and Valhalla crumbles in flames, destroying the gods and eliciting the birth of a new order. Like Goethe, whose Faust was a lifetime effort and a tribute to his nation's past, Wagner toiled on the monumental Ring for more than twenty-five years, from 1848 to 1874.

While The Ring gives imaginative breadth to the hero myths of Germanic literary tradition, its music matches

Figure 29.22 Metropolitan Opera production of Wagner's *The Rhinegold* from *The Ring of the Nibelung*. In scene four, the giants Fasolt and Fafner refuse to relinquish their hostage Freia unless they are given enough gold to hide her body from view. Critics compare Wagner's story to J. R. R. Tolkien's fantasy trilogy *The Lord of the Rings* (1937–1949), which shares the mythical themes of loss and recovery and the epic quest for magical power.

its poetry in scope and drama. Wagner's orchestra for the cycle called for 115 pieces, including 64 string instruments. No fewer than twenty individual *leitmotifs* weave a complex web of dramatic musical density. "Every bar of dramatic music," proclaimed Wagner, "is justified only by the fact that it explains something in the action or in the character of the actor." In harmonic style, some Wagnerian passages anticipate the more radical experiments of twentieth-century music, such as dissonance and the dissolution of classical tonality (see chapter 32). Orchestral interludes that "describe" raging floods and rings of fire capture the Romantic sublime in musical form. The artist's mission, Wagner insisted, is to communicate "the necessary spontaneous emotional mood." In music-drama he not only fulfilled that mission, but also brought Romantic music to the threshold of modernity.

LOOKING BACK

Heroic Themes in Art

- Romantic artists generally elevated the heart over the mind and the emotions over the intellect. They favored subjects that gave free rein to the imagination, the mysteries of the spirit, and the cult of the ego.
- Increasingly independent of the official sources of patronage, Romantic artists saw themselves as the heroes of their age. They favored heroic themes and personalities, especially those illustrating the struggle for political independence.
- Gros, Géricault, Goya, and Delacroix stretched the bounds of traditional subject matter to include controversial contemporary events, exotic subjects,

and medieval legends. Their paintings gave substance to the spirit of nationalism that swept through nineteenth-century Europe.
- The Romantic turn to heroic themes was matched by new freedom in composition and technique. Neoclassical principles of pictorial balance, clarity, and restraint gave way to dynamic composition, bold color, and vigorous brushwork.

Trends in Mid-Nineteenth-Century Architecture

- The search for national identity is also evident in the Gothic revival in Western architecture. Neomedievalism challenged Neoclassicism in paying homage to Europe's historic past.

- Increasing familiarity with the cultures of Asia and Islam inspired exotic architecture, such as the Royal Pavilion of Brighton.

The Romantic Style in Music

- Romantic music found inspiration in heroic and nationalistic themes, as well as in nature's moods and the vagaries of human love. In their desire to express strong personal emotions, composers often abandoned classical models and stretched musical forms.
- The enlargement of the symphony orchestra in size and expressive range is apparent in the works of Beethoven, Berlioz, and Wagner. The creative giant of the age, Beethoven composed nine

symphonies and numerous instrumental works. Berlioz's *idée fixe* and Wagner's *leitmotif* tied sound to story, evidence of the Romantic search for an ideal union of poetry and music.
- Lyrical melody and tone color became as important to Romantic music as the free use of line and color was to Romantic painters.
- Schubert united poetry and music in the intimate form of the *lied*, while Chopin captured a vast range of moods and emotions in virtuoso piano pieces.

The Romantic Ballet

- Romantic ballet, which featured themes drawn from fantasy and legend, flowered in France and, later, in Russia.
- The ballets performed on the stage of the Paris Opéra were the culmination of a golden age in European dance. In Paris in 1830, Maria Taglioni perfected the art of dancing *sur les points*.
- Tchaikovsky heightened the importance of fantasy and story in his popular ballets *Swan Lake*, *The Nutcracker*, and *Sleeping Beauty*.

Romantic Opera

- Romantic opera, designed to appeal to a growing middle-class audience, came into existence after 1820. The culmination of Baroque theatricality, Romantic opera was grand both in size and in spirit. It was a flamboyant spectacle that united all aspects of theatrical production: music, dance, stage sets, and costumes.
- Grand opera was brought to its peak in Italy by Verdi and in Germany by Wagner, both of whom exploited nationalistic themes.

Music Listening Selections

- Beethoven, Symphony No. 3 in E-flat Major, *The Eroica*, first movement, excerpt, 1803–1804.
- Schubert, *Erlkönig*, 1815.
- Berlioz, *Symphonie fantastique*, Op. 14, "March to the Scaffold," fourth movement, excerpt, 1830.
- Chopin, Etude in G-flat Major, Op. 10, No. 5, 1833.

Glossary

aquatint a type of print produced by an engraving method similar to etching but involving finely granulated tonal areas rather than line alone

arabesque in ballet, a position in which the dancer stands on one leg with the other extended behind and one or both arms held to create the longest line possible from one extremity of the body to the other

arpeggio the sounding of the notes of a chord in rapid succession

bel canto (Italian, "beautiful singing" or "beautiful song") an operatic style characterized by lyricism and florid vocal embellishment

dynamics the gradations of loudness or softness with which music is performed

étude (French, "study") an instrumental piece designed to improve a player's performance technique

idée fixe (French, "fixed idea") a term used by Berlioz for a recurring theme in his symphonic works

impromptu (French, "improvised") a short keyboard composition that sounds as if it were improvised

leitmotif (German, "leading motif") a short musical theme that designates a person, object, place, or idea and that reappears throughout a musical composition

lied (German, "song," plural *lieder*) an independent song for solo voice and piano; also known as an "art song"

music-drama a unique synthesis of sound and story in which both are developed simultaneously and continuously; a term used to describe Wagner's later operas

nocturne a slow, songlike piece, usually written for piano; the melody is played by the right hand, and a steady, soft accompaniment is played by the left

opus (Latin, "work") a musical composition; followed by a number, it designates either the chronological place of a musical composition in the composer's total musical output or the order of its publication; often abbreviated "op."

prima ballerina the first, or leading, female dancer in a ballet company

program music instrumental music endowed with specific literary or pictorial content that is indicated by the composer

scherzo (Italian, "joke") in Beethoven's music and thereafter, a movement involving elements of vigor or surprise

tone color the distinctive quality of musical sound made by a voice, a musical instrument, or a combination of instruments; also called "timbre"

tremolo in music, the rapid repetition of a single pitch or two pitches alternately, producing a trembling effect

virtuoso one who exhibits great technical ability, especially in musical performance; also used to describe a musical composition demanding (or a performance demonstrating) great technical skill

"Show me an angel and I'll paint one."
Courbet

Figure 30.1 JEAN-FRANÇOIS MILLET, *Gleaners*, ca. 1857. Oil on canvas, approx. 2 ft. 9 in. × 3 ft. 8 in. Millet's portrayals of rural women at work—harvesting wheat, spinning, sewing, tending sheep, and feeding children—idealized the female as selfless and saintly. Nonetheless, his paintings brought attention to the fact that the French economy depended on the labor of the rural working class.

Nations have long drawn their strength and identity from their economic and military superiority over other nations. But during the late nineteenth century, nationalism and the quest for economic supremacy took on a more aggressive form. Fueled by advancing industrialization, Western nations not only competed among themselves for economic and political preeminence, but also sought control of markets throughout the world. The combined effects of nationalism, industrialization, and the consequent phenomena of imperialism and colonialism influenced the materialist direction of modern Western history and that of the world beyond the West as well.

It was in this climate that Realism emerged. As a cultural movement, Realism reflected popular demands for greater access to material wealth and well-being. In place of nostalgia and the sentimental embrace of the Romantic past, Realists manifested a renewed sense of social consciousness and a commitment to contemporary issues of class and gender. Unlike the Romantics, whose passionate subjectivity often alienated them from society, Realists regarded themselves as men and woman "of their time."

As a style, Realism called for an objective and unidealized assessment of everyday life. Artists, writers, and composers attacked the reigning stereotypes and pursued scientifically-based fidelity to nature. Lithography and photography encouraged the Realist sensibility. Advances in science and technology facilitated increased mobility and transformed urban life. The city, with its monumental skyscrapers and its bustling mix of people, became the site of new ideas and cultural norms that propelled the West toward Modernism.

The Global Dominion of the West

Advancing Industrialization

Industrialization provided the economic and military basis for the West's rise to dominion over the rest of the world. This process is well illustrated in the history of the railroad, the most important technological phenomenon of the early nineteenth century because it facilitated economic and political expansion. It was made possible by the combined technology of steam power, coal, and iron.

The first all-iron rails were forged in Britain in 1789, but it was not until 1804 that the British built their first steam railway locomotive, and several more decades before "iron horses" became a major mode of transportation. The drive to build national railways spread, encompassing Europe and the vast continent of North America. By 1850, some 23,000 miles of railway track crisscrossed Europe, linking the sources of raw materials—such as the coal mines of northern Germany's Ruhr valley—to factories and markets. The second half of the nineteenth century saw the unification of both Italy and Germany, the modernization of Russia, and the transformation of the United States into an economic powerhouse, fueled by abundant resources of iron ore and coal. Across the vast continent of North America, railroads facilitated rapid economic and political expansion. As Western nations colonized other parts of the globe, they took with them the railroad and other agents of industrialization.

Before the end of the nineteenth century, Western technology included the internal combustion engine, the telegraph, the telephone, the camera, and—perhaps most significant for the everyday life of human beings—electricity. Processed steel, aluminum, the steam turbine, and the pneumatic tire—all products of the 1880s—further altered the texture of life in the industrialized world. This technology, along with such lethal instruments of war as the fully automatic "machine gun," gave Europe clear advantages over other parts of the globe and facilitated Western imperialism in less industrially developed areas. In the enterprise of empire building, the industrialized nations of Britain, France, Belgium, Germany, Italy, and the United States took the lead.

Colonialism and the New Imperialism

The history of European expansion into Asia, Africa, and other parts of the globe dates back at least to the Renaissance. Between approximately 1500 and 1800, Europeans established trading outposts in Africa, China, and India. But not until after 1800, in the wake of the Industrial Revolution, did European imperialism transform the territories of foreign peoples into outright colonial possessions. Driven by the need for raw materials and markets for their manufactured goods, and aided

Science and Technology

1844	Samuel Morse (American) transmits the first telegraph message
1866	the first successful transatlantic telegraph cable is laid
1869	the first American transcontinental railroad is completed
1876	Alexander Graham Bell (Scottish) produces the first functional telephone in America

immeasurably by their advanced military technology, the industrial nations quickly colonized or controlled vast parts of Asia, Africa, and Latin America. So massive was this effort that, by the end of the nineteenth century, the West had established economic, political, and cultural dominion over much of the world.

European imperialists defended the economic exploitation of weaker countries with the view, inspired by social Darwinism, that in politics, as in nature, the strongest or "most fit" prevailed in the "struggle for survival." Since Caucasians had proved themselves the "most fit," they argued, it was the white population's "burden" to care for, protect, and rule over the "less fit," nonwhite peoples of the earth. Britain, the leader in European industrialization, spearheaded the thrust of colonization.

The self-appointed mission of Western rule in less technologically developed countries is best expressed in a poem by one of the most popular British writers of his time, Rudyard Kipling (1864–1936). Three verses of his poem "The White Man's Burden" sum up two of the key imperialist notions: racial superiority and the spirit of paternal and heroic deliverance.

READING 30.1 From Kipling's "The White Man's Burden" (1899)

Take up the White Man's burden—	1
Send forth the best ye breed—	
Go bind your sons to exile	
To serve your captive's need;	
To wait in heavy harness,	5
On fluttered folk and wide—	
Your new-caught, sullen peoples,	
Half-devil and half-child.	

. . . .

Take up the White Man's Burden—	
Ye dare not stoop to less—	10
Nor call too loud on Freedom	
To cloak your weariness;	
By all ye cry or whisper,	
By all ye leave to do,	
The silent, sullen peoples	15
Shall weigh your Gods and you.	

Take up the White Man's burden—	
Have done with childish days—	
The lightly proffered laurel,	
The easy, ungrudged praise.	20
Comes now, to search your manhood	
Through all the thankless years,	
Cold, edged with dear-bought wisdom,	
The judgment of your peers!	

Q To whom might the terms "half-devil" and "half-child" apply?

Q How is the "White Man" in this poem described?

Kipling dedicated "The White Man's Burden" to the United States to commemorate the American annexation of the Philippines in 1899, but the pattern for colonialism had been fixed by the British. In the race for overseas colonies, Britain led the way. The first major landmass to be subjugated was India, where commercial imperialism led to conquest, and, finally, to British rule in 1858. In less than a century, the nation had established control over so much territory across the globe that it could legitimately claim that "the sun never set" on the British Empire (Map 30.1).

The most dramatic example of the new imperialism was in Africa. In 1880, European nations controlled only 10 percent of the continent; but by 1900 all of Africa, save Ethiopia and Liberia, had been carved up by European powers, who introduced new models of political and economic authority, often with little regard for native populations. The partitioning of Africa began in 1830 with the French conquest of Algeria (in the north). In the decades thereafter, Belgium laid claim to the Congo, and the Dutch and the British fought each other for control of South Africa—both nations savagely wresting land from the Zulu and other African peoples.

A century-long series of brutal wars with the Asante Empire in West Africa left the British in control of the Gold Coast, while the conquest of the Sudan in 1898 saw 11,000 Muslims killed by British machine guns (the British themselves lost twenty-eight men). Profit-seeking European companies leased large tracts of African land from which native goods such as rubber, diamonds, and gold might be extracted; and increasingly Africans were forced to work on white-owned plantations and mines. The seeds of racism and mutual contempt were sown in this troubled era, an era that predictably spawned modern liberation movements, such as those calling for pan-Islamic opposition to colonialism (see chapter 36).

By the mid-nineteenth century, the United States (itself a colony of Britain until 1776) had joined the scramble for economic control. America forced Japan to open its doors to Western trade in 1853. This event, which marked the end of Japan's seclusion, ushered in the overthrow of the Tokugawa regime (see chapter 21) and marked the beginning of Japanese modernization under Meiji rule (1868–1912). In the Western hemisphere, the United States established its own overseas empire.

North Americans used the phrase "manifest destiny" to describe and justify a policy of unlimited expansion into the American West, Mexico, and elsewhere. The result was the United States' acquisition of more than half of Mexico, control of the Philippines and Cuba, and a dominant position in the economies of the politically unstable nations of Latin America. Although Westerners rationalized their militant expansionism by contending that they were "civilizing" the backward peoples of the globe, in fact their diplomatic policies contributed to undermining cultural traditions, to humiliating and often enfeebling the civilizations they dominated, and to creating conditions of economic dependency that would last well into the twentieth century (see chapter 36).

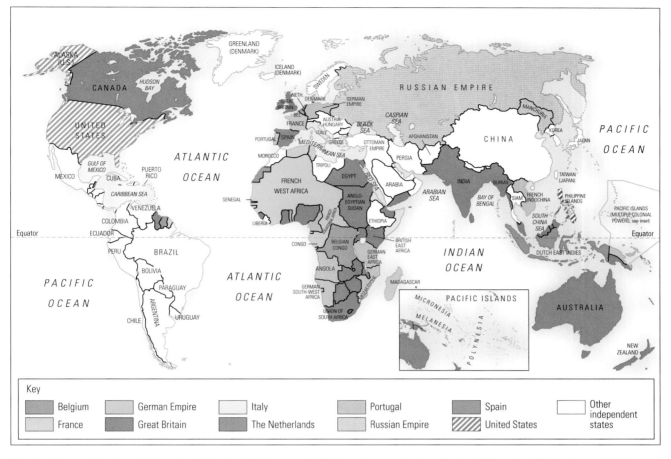

Key

Belgium	German Empire	Italy	Portugal	Spain	Other independent states
France	Great Britain	The Netherlands	Russian Empire	United States	

Map 30.1 European Colonies and Independent Nations in 1900. For many of the "independent states," such as Persia and China, the political and economic influence of the West presented an often destabilizing threat.

China and the West

The nineteenth century marked the end of China's long history as an independent civilization. The European powers, along with Russia and Japan, carved out trade concessions in China. And subsequent trade policies by China's imperial government, including efforts to restrict foreign trade, and the country's traditionally negative view of profit-taking, delayed any potential Chinese initiative toward industrialization.

More devastating still was the triangular trade pattern in opium and tea between India, China, and Britain. Established by Britain in the early nineteenth century, trade policy worked to stem the tide of British gold and silver that flowed to China to buy tea, a favorite British beverage. The Chinese had used narcotic opium for centuries, but as a result of the new arrangement large quantities of the drug—harvested in India—were exported directly to China. In exchange, the Chinese shipped tea to Britain. Opium addiction became an increasingly severe social problem in China. Following the opium-related death of the Chinese emperor's son, the Chinese made every effort to restrict the importation of the drug and stem the activities of opium smugglers (Figure **30.2**). British merchants refused to cooperate. The result was a series of wars

between Britain and China (the Opium Wars, 1839–1850) that brought China to its knees. In 1839, just before the first of these wars, the Chinese commissioner Lin Zexu (1785–1850) sent a detailed communication to the British queen pleading for Britain's assistance in ending opium smuggling and trade. Whether or not Queen Victoria ever read Lin's letter is unknown, but the document remains a literary tribute to the futile efforts of a great Asian civilization to achieve peace through diplomacy in the age of imperialism.

READING 30.2 From Lin Zexu's *Letter of Advice to Queen Victoria* (1839)

...The kings of your honorable country by a tradition handed   1
down from generation to generation have always been noted
for their politeness and submissiveness. We have read your
successive tributary memorials saying, "In general our
countrymen who go to trade in China have always received His
Majesty the Emperor's gracious treatment and equal justice,"
and so on. Privately we are delighted with the way in which the
honorable rulers of your country deeply understand the grand
principles and are grateful for the Celestial grace. For this
reason the Celestial Court in soothing those from afar has   10
redoubled its polite and kind treatment. The profit from trade

Zè vos dis qu'il faut, què vo ach'tè ce poisonne to d'suite, no vollons què vo empposonnièz vo vèritèblement, pou queno avions du thé bocoupe pou dègerer confortèblement nos **Beef-SteaKs!**..

Figure 30.2 Cartoon from a Paris newspaper, date unknown. The inscription reads: "I tell you that you have to buy this opium immediately so that you can poison yourself; and then you will buy a lot of tea to digest our beefsteaks in a comfortable manner."

has been enjoyed by them continuously for two hundred years. This is the source from which your country has become known for its wealth.

But after a long period of commercial intercourse, there appear among the crowd of barbarians both good persons and bad, unevenly. Consequently there are those who smuggle opium to seduce the Chinese people and so cause the spread of the poison to all provinces. Such persons who only care to profit themselves, and disregard their harm to others, are not 20 tolerated by the laws of heaven and are unanimously hated by human beings. His Majesty the Emperor, upon hearing of this, is in a towering rage. He has especially sent me, his commissioner, to come to Kwangtung, and together with the governor-general and governor jointly to investigate and settle this matter. . . .

We find that your country is [some 20,000 miles] from China. Yet there are barbarian ships that strive to come here for trade for the purpose of making a great profit. The wealth of China is used to profit the barbarians. That is to say, the great profit 30 made by barbarians is all taken from the rightful share of China. By what right do they then in return use the poisonous drug to injure the Chinese people? Even though the barbarians may not necessarily intend to do us harm, yet in coveting profit to an extreme, they have no regard for injuring others. Let us ask, where is your conscience? I have heard that the smoking of opium is very strictly forbidden by your country; that is because the harm caused by opium is clearly understood. Since it is not permitted to do harm to your own country, then

even less should you let it be passed on to the harm of other 40 countries—how much less to China! Of all that China exports to foreign countries, there is not a single thing which is not beneficial to people: they are of benefit when eaten, or of benefit when used, or of benefit when resold: all are beneficial. Is there a single article from China which has done any harm to foreign countries? Take tea and rhubarb, for example; the foreign countries cannot get along for a single day without them. If China cuts off these benefits with no sympathy for those who are to suffer, then what can the barbarians rely upon to keep themselves alive? Moreover the 50 [textiles] of foreign countries cannot be woven unless they obtain Chinese silk. If China, again, cuts off this beneficial export, what profit can the barbarians expect to make? As for other foodstuffs, beginning with candy, ginger, cinnamon, and so forth, and articles for use, beginning with silk, satin, chinaware, and so on, all the things that must be had by foreign countries are innumerable. On the other hand, articles coming from the outside to China can only be used as toys. We can take them or get along without them. Since they are not needed by China, what difficulty would there be if we closed 60 the frontier and stopped the trade? Nevertheless our Celestial Court lets tea, silk, and other goods be shipped without limit and circulated everywhere without begrudging it in the slightest. This is for no other reason but to share the benefit with the people of the whole world.

The goods from China carried away by your country not only supply your own consumption and use, but also can be divided up and sold to other countries, producing a triple profit. Even if you do not sell opium, you still have this threefold profit. How can you bear to go further, selling products injurious to others 70 in order to fulfil your insatiable desire?

Suppose there were people from another country who carried opium for sale to England and seduced your people into buying and smoking it; certainly your honorable ruler would deeply hate it and be bitterly aroused. We have heard heretofore that your honorable ruler is kind and benevolent. Naturally you would not wish to give unto others what you yourself do not want. We have also heard that the ships coming to Canton have all had regulations promulgated and given to them in which it is stated that it is not permitted to carry contraband 80 goods. This indicates that the administrative orders of your honorable rule have been originally strict and clear. Only because the trading ships are numerous, heretofore perhaps they have not been examined with care. Now after this communication has been dispatched and you have clearly understood the strictness of the prohibitory laws of the Celestial Court, certainly you will not let your subjects dare again to violate the law. . . .

Now we have set up regulations governing the Chinese people. He who sells opium shall receive the death penalty and 90 he who smokes it also the death penalty. Now consider this: if the barbarians do not bring opium, then how can the Chinese people resell it, and how can they smoke it? The fact is that the wicked barbarians beguile the Chinese people into a death trap. How then can we grant life only to these barbarians? He who takes the life of even one person still has to atone for it with his own life; yet is the harm done by opium limited to the taking of one life only? Therefore in the new regulations, in regard to those barbarians who bring opium to China, the penalty is fixed at decapitation or strangulation. This is what is called getting rid of a harmful thing on behalf of mankind. . . .

100

- Q What "balance of trade" is described in this letter?

- Q To what extent is Lin's letter an appeal to conscience?

To the European mind, the benefits of Western science, technology, and religion far outweighed the negative impact of colonialism. But the "gift" of progress was received in China with extreme caution and increasing isolationism. No dramatically new developments took place in the arts of China (nor, for that matter, in India) during the nineteenth century; in general, there was a marked decline in both productivity and originality. The full consequences of Western colonialism in Asia and elsewhere, however, would not become clear until the twentieth century.

Social and Economic Realities

In global terms, advancing industrialization polarized the nations of the world into the technologically advanced—the "haves"—and the technologically backward—the "have-nots." But industrialization had an equally profound impact within the industrialized nations themselves: it changed the nature and character of human work, altered relationships between human beings, and affected the natural environment.

Before 1800, the practice of accumulating capital for industrial production and commercial profit played only a limited role in European societies. But after this date, industrial production, enhanced by advances in machine technology, came to be controlled by a relatively small group of middle-class **entrepreneurs** (those who organize, manage, and assume the risks of a business) and by an even smaller number of **capitalists** (those who provide money to finance business).

Industrialization created wealth, but that wealth was concentrated in the hands of a small minority of the population. The vast majority of men and women lived hard lives supported by meager wages—the only thing they had to sell was their labor. Factory laborers, including women and children, worked under dirty and dangerous conditions for long hours—sometimes up to sixteen hours per day (Figure **30.3**). In the 1830s, almost half of London's funerals were for children under ten years old. Mass production brought more (and cheaper) goods to more people more rapidly, ultimately raising the standard of living for industrialized nations. But European industrialization and the unequal distribution of wealth contributed to a widening gap between capitalist entrepreneurs—the "haves" of society—and the working classes—the "have-nots." In 1846, the British statesman Benjamin Disraeli (1804–1881) described Britain under the rule of Queen Victoria (1819–1901) as two nations: the nation of the poor and the nation of the rich.

Beginning in 1848, the lower classes protested against these conditions with sporadic revolts. Economic unrest prevailed not only in the cities but also in rural areas. The

EXPLORING ISSUES

Islam and the West

The process of colonization had dramatic effects on the Islamic world. Muslims in the Middle East, India, Arabia, Malaya, and much of Africa regarded the European efforts at colonization as an assault on their cultures and their religious faith. Europeans, who tended to see premodern agrarian societies as backward, looked upon "Orientals" (a term that lumped together all Eastern people) as inherently inferior. Unlike Japan or China, which had never been colonized, and were therefore able to retain many of their economic and political traditions, Islamic states were often debilitated and humiliated by dependency on the West.

European colonization of the Islamic world began in the late eighteenth century. Napoleon had invaded the Near East in 1798, bringing with him a corpus of European literature and a printing press with Arabic type. Despite the failure of Napoleon's campaign in Egypt, the country made ambitious efforts to modernize. The failure of these efforts, however, which left Egypt bankrupt, led ultimately to British occupation.

A second instance of the Western presence in Islamic lands occurred in Persia (renamed Iran in 1935). Strategically located in the Middle East, Persia was forced into wars with Britain and Russia, whose rival interests in Middle Eastern territory threatened the autonomy of the Qajar dynasty (1794–1925). In the late nineteenth century, the Persian reformer Aqa Khan Kirmani (1853–1896) urged Muslims to adopt a program of Western-style modernization, to replace the *sharia* with a modern secular code of law, and to institute parliamentary representation. Iran's first modern college system would emerge in 1848. Others throughout the Islamic world, however, opposed the intrusion of the West and Western ways of life as a threat to Muslim traditions and religious ideals (see chapter 36). One of the most significant differences involved the political gulf between time-honored Islamic theocracy and Western representative democracy. Such issues have continued to trouble the world well into our own time.

Figure 30.3 **ADOLPH FRIEDRICH ERDMANN VON MENZEL**, *Iron Mill* (*Das Eisenwalzwerk—Moderne Zyklopen*), 1875. Oil on canvas, 5 ft. ¼ in. × 8 ft. 3⅝ in.

French population was two-thirds rural, largely poor, and often reduced to backbreaking labor (see Figure 30.10). Wealthy landowners in some parts of Europe treated their agricultural laborers as slaves. In America, until after the Civil War (1861–1865), most of those who worked the great Southern plantations were, in fact, African-American slaves. Between 1855 and 1861, there were almost 500 peasant uprisings across Europe (Figure **30.4**). Reform, however, was slow in coming. Outside England—in Germany, for instance—trade unions and social legislation to benefit the working classes did not appear until 1880 or later, while in Russia economic reform would require nothing less than a full-scale revolution (see chapter 34).

Nineteenth-Century Social Theory

Among nineteenth-century European intellectuals there developed a serious debate over how to address the social results of industrial capitalism. Matters of social reform were central to the development of ideologies that dictated specific policies of political and economic action. Traditional *conservatives* stressed the importance of maintaining order and perpetuating conventional power structures and religious authority. *Liberals*, on the other hand, whose ideas were rooted in Enlightenment theories of human progress and perfectibility (see chapter 24), supported gradual reform through enlightened legal systems, constitutional guarantees, and a generally equitable

distribution of material benefits. The British liberal Jeremy Bentham (1748–1832) advanced the doctrine of *utilitarianism*, which held that governments should work to secure "the greatest happiness for the greatest number of people"; while Bentham's student John Stuart Mill (1806–1873) expounded the ideology of social liberalism.

Mill emphasized freedom of thought over equality and personal happiness. He held that individuals must be free to direct their own lives, but, recognizing the disadvantages that might result from free competition, he argued that the state must protect its weaker members by acting to regulate the economy where private initiative failed to do so. Mill feared that the general will—the will of unenlightened, propertyless masses—might itself prove tyrannical and oppressive. In his classic statement of the liberal creed, *On Liberty* (1859), he concluded that "as soon as any part of a person's conduct affects prejudicially the interests of others, society has jurisdiction over it." For Mill, as for most nineteenth-century liberals, government was obliged to intervene to safeguard and protect the wider interests of society.

Such theories met with strenuous opposition from European *socialists*, for whom neither conservatism nor liberalism responded adequately to current social and economic inequities. Socialists attacked capitalism as unjust; they called for the common ownership and administration of the means of production and distribution in the interest of a public good. Society, according to the socialists, should operate entirely in the interest of the needs of the people, communally and cooperatively, rather than competitively.

The Limits of Authority

In *On Liberty*, Mill examined the nature of freedom, advocating individual rights over those of the state. He argued, however, that it was the legitimate duty of government to limit the exercise of any freedom that might harm other members of the community. Wrestling with key issues concerning limits to the authority of the state with regard to the individual, he asked: "What, then, is the rightful limit to the sovereignty of the individual over himself? Where does the authority of society begin? How much of human life should be assigned to individuality, and how much to society?"

Enlarging more generally on these questions, Mill's American contemporary Abraham Lincoln (1809–1865) observed: "The legitimate object of government is to do for a community of people whatever they need to have done, but can not do at all, or can not so well do for themselves in their separate and individual capacities." Is providing for the *needs* of the community—much like providing *protection* for its citizens—the function of the government? Suppose the political process of providing for these needs (like the obligation to protect the individual) comes at the cost of limiting the absolute freedom of others?

To one degree or another, most of the great political divisions emerging from nineteenth-century social thought proceeded from these questions. They are still debated today, mainly in the opposing political ideologies of *liberalism* and *conservatism*. Contemporary liberals would incline toward a relatively greater use of government authority in serving the needs of society. Conservatives would incline toward a relatively lesser exercise of such control.

The utopian socialist Pierre Joseph Proudhon (1809–1865) envisioned a society free of state control, while the more extreme *anarchists* favored the complete dissolution of the state and the elimination of the force of law.

The Radical Views of Marx and Engels

The German theorist Karl Marx (1818–1883) agreed with the socialists that bourgeois capitalism corrupted humanity, but his theory of social reform was even more radical, for it preached violent revolution that would both destroy the old order and usher in a new society. Marx began his career by studying law and philosophy at the University of Berlin. Moving to Paris, he became a lifelong friend of the social scientist and journalist Friedrich Engels (1820–1895). Marx and Engels shared a similar critical attitude in respect of the effects of European industrial capitalism. By 1848, they completed the *Communist Manifesto*, a short treatise published as the platform of a workers' association called the Communist League. The *Manifesto*, which remains the "guidebook" of Marxist socialism, demanded the "forcible overthrow of all existing social conditions" and the liberation of the **proletariat**, or working class. Marx offered an even more detailed criticism of the free enterprise system in *Das Kapital*, a work on which he toiled for thirty years.

The *Communist Manifesto* is a sweeping condemnation of the effects of capitalism on the individual and on society at large. It opens with a dramatic claim: "The history of all hitherto existing society is the history of class struggles." It further contends that capitalism concentrates wealth in the hands of the few, providing great luxuries for some, while creating an oppressed and impoverished proletariat. The psychological effects of such circumstances, it holds, are devastating: bourgeois capitalism alienates workers from their own productive efforts and robs individuals of their basic humanity. Finally, the *Manifesto* calls for revolution by which workers will seize the instruments of capitalistic production and abolish private ownership.

The social theories of Marx and Engels had enormous practical and theoretical influence. They not only supplied a justification for lower-class revolt, but also brought attention to the role of economics in the larger life of a society. Marx perceived human history in exclusively materialistic terms, arguing that the conditions under which one earned a living determined all other aspects of life: social, political, and cultural. A student of Hegel (see chapter 27), he viewed history as a struggle between "haves" (thesis) and "have-nots" (antithesis) that would resolve in the synthesis of a classless society. From Hegel, Marx also derived the utopian idea of the perfectibility of the state. The product of dialectical change, argued Marx, was a society free of class antagonism, and the ultimate dissolution of the state itself.

Although Marx and Engels failed to anticipate capitalism's potential to spread rather than to limit wealth, their manifesto gave sharp focus to prevailing class differences and to the actual condition of the European economy of their time. Despite the fact that they provided no explanation of *how* their classless society might function, their apocalyptic call to revolution would be heeded in the decades to come. Oddly enough, communist revolutions would occur in some of the least industrialized countries of the world, such as Russia and China, rather than in the most industrialized countries, as Marx and Engels expected. Elsewhere, communists would operate largely through *nonrevolutionary* vehicles, such as labor unions and political organizations, to initiate better working conditions, higher wages, and greater social equality. But the anticommunist revolutions and the collapse of the communist government

Figure 30.4 KÄTHE KOLLWITZ, *March of the Weavers*, from "The Weavers Cycle," 1897. Etching, 8⅜ × 11⅝ in. Kollwitz (1867–1945) was a German social realist, a pacifist, and a feminist. The series of prints known as "The Weavers" illustrates a play by Gerhart Hauptmann that dramatized the failed revolt of Silesian weavers in 1842. A sculptor as well as a printmaker, Kollwitz went on to create searing protest images of the two world wars.

in the Soviet Union in the late twentieth century reveal mounting frustration with the failure of most communist regimes to raise economic standards among the masses. Although the *Manifesto* did not accurately predict the economic destiny of the modern world, the treatise remains a classic expression of nineteenth-century social consciousness.

READING 30.3 From Marx's and Engels' *Communist Manifesto* (1848)

I Bourgeois and Proletarians[1]

The history of all hitherto existing society is the history of class struggles. 1

Freeman and slave, patrician and plebeian, lord and serf, guild-master[2] and journeyman, in a word, oppressor and oppressed, stood in constant opposition to one another, carried on an uninterrupted, now hidden, now open fight, a fight that each time ended either in a revolutionary reconstitution of society at large or in the common ruin of the contending classes.

In the earlier epochs of history we find almost everywhere a complicated arrangement of society into various orders, 10 a manifold gradation of social rank. In ancient Rome we have patricians, knights, plebeians, slaves; in the Middle Ages, feudal lords, vassals, guild-masters, journeymen, apprentices, serfs; in almost all of these classes, again, subordinate gradations.

The modern bourgeois society that has sprouted from the ruins of feudal society has not done away with class antagonisms. It has but established new classes, new conditions of oppression, new forms of struggle in place of the old ones. 20

Our epoch, the epoch of the bourgeoisie, possesses, however, this distinctive feature: it has simplified the class antagonisms. Society as a whole is splitting up more and more into two great hostile camps, into two great classes directly facing each other: Bourgeoisie and Proletariat.

---

[1] By bourgeoisie is meant the class of modern capitalists, owners of the means of social production and employers of wage labor. By proletariat, the class of modern wage-laborers who, having no means of production of their own, are reduced to selling their labor power in order to live.

[2] Guild-master, that is, a full member of a guild, a master within, not a head of a guild.

From the serfs of the Middle Ages sprang the chartered burghers of the earliest towns. From these burgesses the first elements of the bourgeoisie were developed.

The discovery of America, the rounding of the Cape, opened up fresh ground for the rising bourgeoisie. The East Indian and 30 Chinese markets, the colonization of America, trade with the colonies, the increase in the means of exchange and in commodities generally, gave to commerce, to navigation, to industry, an impulse never before known, and thereby, to the revolutionary element in the tottering feudal society, a rapid development.

The feudal system of industry, under which industrial production was monopolized by closed guilds, now no longer sufficed for the growing wants of the new markets. The manufacturing system took its place. The guild-masters were 40 pushed on one side by the manufacturing middle class; division of labor between the different corporate guilds vanished in the face of division of labor in each single workshop.

Meantime the markets kept ever growing, the demand ever rising. Even manufacture no longer sufficed. Thereupon, steam and machinery revolutionized industrial production. The place of manufacture was taken by the giant, Modern Industry, the place of the industrial middle class by industrial millionaires—the leaders of whole industrial armies, the modern bourgeois. Modern industry has established the world market, for which 50 the discovery of America paved the way. This market has given an immense development to commerce, to navigation, to communication by land. This development has, in its turn, reacted on the extension of industry; and in proportion as industry, commerce, navigation, railways extended, in the same proportion the bourgeoisie developed, increased its capital, and pushed into the background every class handed down from the Middle Ages.

We see, therefore, how the modern bourgeoisie is itself the product of a long course of development, of a series of 60 revolutions in the modes of production and of exchange.

Each step in the development of the bourgeoisie was accompanied by a corresponding political advance of that class. An oppressed class under the sway of the feudal nobility, an armed and self-governing association in the medieval commune,[3] here independent urban republic (as in Italy and Germany), there taxable "third estate" of the monarchy (as in France), afterward, in the period of manufacture proper, serving either the semi-feudal or the absolute monarchy as a counterpoise against the nobility, and, in fact, cornerstone of the great monarchies in general, the bourgeoisie has at last, since the establishment of Modern Industry and of the world market, conquered for itself, in the modern representative State, exclusive political sway. The executive of the modern State is but a committee for managing the common affairs of the whole bourgeoisie.

The bourgeoisie, historically, has played a most revolutionary part.

The bourgeoisie, wherever it has got the upper hand, has put an end to all feudal, patriarchal, idyllic relations. It has pitilessly torn asunder the motley feudal ties that bound man to his "natural superiors," and has left remaining no other nexus between man and man than naked self-interest, than callous "cash payment." It has drowned the most heavenly ecstasies of religious fervor, of chivalrous enthusiasm, of philistine sentimentalism, in the icy water of egotistical calculation. It has resolved personal worth into exchange value, and in place of the numberless indefeasible chartered freedoms has set up that single, unconscionable freedom— Free Trade. In one word, for exploitation, veiled by religious and political illusions, it has substituted naked, shameless, direct, brutal exploitation.

The bourgeoisie has stripped of its halo every occupation hitherto honored and looked up to with reverent awe. It has converted the physician, the lawyer, the priest, the poet, the man of science, into its paid wage-laborers.

The bourgeoisie has torn away from the family its sentimental veil, and has reduced the family relation to a mere money relation. . . .

The bourgeoisie, by the rapid improvement of all instruments of production, by the immensely facilitated means of communication, draws all, even the most barbarian, nations into civilization. The cheap prices of its commodities are the heavy artillery with which it batters down all Chinese walls, with which it forces the barbarians' intensely obstinate hatred of foreigners to capitulate. It compels all nations, on pain of extinction, to adopt the bourgeois mode of production; it compels them to introduce what it calls civilization into their midst, i.e., to become bourgeois themselves. In a word, it creates a world after its own image.

The bourgeoisie has subjected the country to the rule of the towns. It has created enormous cities, has greatly increased the urban population as compared with the rural, and has thus rescued a considerable part of the population from the idiocy of rural life. Just as it has made the country dependent on the towns, so it has made barbarian and semi-barbarian countries dependent on the civilized ones, nations of peasants on

[3] "Commune" was the name taken in France by the nascent towns even before they had conquered from their feudal lords and masters local self-government and political rights as the "Third Estate." Generally speaking, for the economic development of the bourgeoisie, England is here taken as the typical country; for its political development, France.

nations of bourgeois, the East on the West.

The bourgeoisie keeps doing away more and more with the scattered state of the population, of the means of production, and of property. It has agglomerated population, centralized means of production, and has concentrated property in a few hands. The necessary consequence of this was political centralization. Independent or but loosely connected provinces with separate interests, laws, governments and systems of taxation became lumped together into one nation, with one government, one code of laws, one national class interest, one frontier and one customs tariff.

The bourgeoisie during its rule of scarce one hundred years has created more massive and more colossal productive forces than have all preceding generations together. Subjection of nature's forces to man, machinery, application of chemistry to industry and agriculture, steam navigation, railways, electric telegraphs, clearing of whole continents for cultivation, canalization of rivers, whole populations conjured out of the ground—what earlier century had even a presentiment that such productive forces slumbered in the lap of social labor? . . .

But not only has the bourgeoisie forged the weapons that bring death to itself; it has also called into existence the men who are to wield those weapons—the modern working class, the proletarians.

In proportion as the bourgeoisie, i.e., capital, is developed, in the same proportion is the proletariat, the modern working class, developed—a class of laborers who live only as long as they find work, and who find work only as long as their labor increases capital. These laborers, who must sell themselves piecemeal, are a commodity like every other article of commerce, and are consequently exposed to all the vicissitudes of competition, to all the fluctuations of the market.

Owing to the extensive use of machinery and to division of labor, the work of the proletarians has lost all individual character and, consequently, all charm for the workman. He becomes an appendage of the machine, and it is only the most simple, most monotonous, and most easily acquired knack that is required of him. . . .

Modern industry has converted the little workshop of the patriarchal master into the great factory of the industrial capitalist. Masses of laborers, crowded into the factory, are organized like soldiers. As privates of the industrial army they are placed under the command of a perfect hierarchy of officers and sergeants. Not only are they slaves of the

Science and Technology

1839	Charles Goodyear (American) produces industrial-strength rubber
1846	Elias Howe (American) patents an interlocking-stitch sewing machine
1866	the first dynamo, capable of generating massive quantities of electricity, is produced
1876	Nikolaus Otto (German) produces a workable internal combustion engine

bourgeois class and of the bourgeois State; they are daily and hourly enslaved by the machine, by the overseer and, above all, by the individual bourgeois manufacturer himself. The more openly this despotism proclaims gain to be its end and aim, the more petty, the more hateful and the more embittering it is.

The less the skill and exertion of strength implied in manual labor, in other words, the more modern industry becomes developed, the more is the labor of men superseded by that of women. Differences of age and sex no longer have any 170 distinctive social validity for the working class. All are instruments of labor, more or less expensive to use, according to their age and sex.

No sooner is the exploitation of the laborer by the manufacturer so far at an end that he receives his wages in cash, than he is set upon by the other portions of the bourgeoisie, the landlord, and shopkeeper, the pawnkeeper, etc...

II Proletarians and Communists

... The Communist revolution is the most radical rupture with traditional property relations; no wonder that its development 180 involves the most radical rupture with traditional ideas.

But let us have done with the bourgeois objections to Communism.

We have seen above that the first step in the revolution by the working class is to raise the proletariat to the position of ruling class, to win the battle of democracy.

The proletariat will use its political supremacy to wrest, by degrees, all capital from the bourgeoisie, to centralize all instruments of production in the hands of the State, i.e., of the proletariat organized as the ruling class; and to increase the 190 total of productive forces as rapidly as possible. . . .

III Position of the Communists

... The Communists disdain to conceal their views and aims. They openly declare that their ends can be attained only by the forcible overthrow of all existing social conditions. Let the ruling classes tremble at a Communistic revolution. The proletarians have nothing to lose but their chains. They have a world to win.

WORKING MEN OF ALL COUNTRIES, UNITE!

Q Which of the *Manifesto's* arguments are the strongest? Which are the weakest?

Mill and Women's Rights

While Marx and Engels criticized a society that made middle-class women "mere instrument[s] of production," Mill described women of all classes as the unwilling subjects of more powerful males. In the treatise *The Subjection of Women,* Mill condemned the legal subordination of one sex to the other as objectively "wrong in itself, and . . . one of the chief hindrances to human improvement." Mill's optimism concerning the unbounded potential for social change—a hallmark of liberalism—may have been shortsighted, for women would not obtain voting rights in Britain until 1928.

In the United States, the first women's college—Mount Holyoke—was founded at South Hadley, Massachusetts,

in 1836; and in 1848, at Seneca Falls in upstate New York, American feminists, led by Elizabeth Cady Stanton (1815–1902) and Susan B. Anthony (1820–1906), issued the first of many declarations that demanded female equality in all areas of life.

The rights of women had been addressed in the literature of feminists from Christine de Pisan to Condorcet and Mary Wollstonecraft (see chapter 24), but nowhere was the plight of women more eloquently treated than in Mill's essay. Mill compared the subjection of women to that of other subject classes in the history of culture. But his most original contribution was his analysis of the male/female relationship and his explanation of how that relationship differed from that of master and slave.

READING 30.4 From Mill's *The Subjection of Women* (1869)

All causes, social and natural, combine to make it unlikely that 1 women should be collectively rebellious to the power of men. They are so far in a position different from all other subject classes that their masters require something more from them than actual service. Men do not want solely the obedience of women, they want their sentiments. All men, except the most brutish, desire to have, in the woman most nearly connected with them, not a forced slave but a willing one, not a slave merely, but a favorite. They have therefore put everything in practice to enslave their minds. The masters of all other 10 slaves rely, for maintaining obedience, on fear, either fear of themselves, or religious fears. The masters of women wanted more than simple obedience, and they turned the whole force of education to effect their purpose. All women are brought up from the very earliest years in the belief that their ideal of character is the very opposite to that of men; not self-will and government by self-control, but submission and yielding to the control of others. All the moralities tell them that it is the duty of women and all the current sentimentalities that it is their nature to live for others, to make complete abnegation of 20 themselves, and to have no life but in their affections. And by their affections are meant the only ones they are allowed to have—those to the men with whom they are connected, or to the children who constitute an additional and indefeasible tie between them and a man. When we put together three things—first, the natural attraction between opposite sexes; secondly, the wife's entire dependence on the husband, every privilege or pleasure she has being either his gift, or depending entirely on his will; and lastly, that the principal object of human pursuit, consideration, and all objects of social ambition 30 can in general be sought or obtained by her only through him, it would be a miracle if the object of being attractive to men had not become the polar star of feminine education and formation of character. And this great means of influence over the minds of women having been acquired, an instinct of selfishness made men avail themselves of it to the utmost as a means of holding women in subjection, by representing to them meekness, submissiveness, and resignation of all individual will into the hands of a man, as an essential part of sexual attractiveness. . . .

The preceding considerations are amply sufficient to show that custom, however universal it may be, affords in this case no presumption and ought not to create any prejudice in favor of the arrangements which place women in social and political subjection to men. But I may go further, and maintain that the course of history, and the tendencies of progressive human society afford not only no presumption in favor of this system of inequality of rights, but a strong one against it; and that, so far as the whole course of human improvement up to this time, the whole stream of modern tendencies warrants any inference on the subject, it is that this relic of the past is discordant with the future and must necessarily disappear.

For, what is the peculiar character of the modern world—the difference which chiefly distinguishes modern institutions, modern social ideas, modern life itself, from those of times long past? It is, that human beings are no longer born to their place in life and chained down by an inexorable bond to the place they are born to, but are free to employ their faculties and such favorable chances as offer, to achieve the lot which may appear to them most desirable. Human society of old was constituted on a very different principle. All were born to a fixed social position and were mostly kept in it by law or interdicted from any means by which they could emerge from it. As some men are born white and others black, so some were born slaves and others freemen and citizens; some were born patricians, others plebeians; some were born feudal nobles, others commoners. . . .

The old theory was that the least possible should be left to the choice of the individual agent; that all he had to do should, as far as practicable, be laid down for him by superior wisdom. Left to himself he was sure to go wrong. The modern conviction, the fruit of a thousand years of experience, is that things in which the individual is the person directly interested never go right but as they are left to his own discretion; and that any regulation of them by authority, except to protect the rights of others, is sure to be mischievous. . . .

Q How, in Mill's view, does the relationship between male and female differ from that of master and slave?

Q What does Mill consider to be the "peculiar character" of Modernism?

The New Historicism

While issues of class and gender preoccupied some of the finest minds of the nineteenth century, so too did matters surrounding the interpretation of the historical past. For many centuries, history was regarded as a branch of literature rather than a social science. The Romantic histories, such as those of Thomas Carlyle (see chapter 28), served to emphasize the role of great men in shaping the destinies of nations. At the same time, the spirit of high patriotism inspired nineteenth-century historians such as Thomas Babington Macaulay (1800–1859) in Britain and Fustel de Coulanges (1830–1889) in France to write nationalistic histories that brought attention to the greatness of their own people and culture.

Patriotism, however, also led historians to renew their efforts to retrieve the evidence of the past. Scholars compiled vast collections of primary source materials; and, enamored of the new, positivist zeal for objective measurement and recording, they applied scientific methods to the writing of history. The result was an effort to recreate history "as it actually was," a movement later called *historicism*. Led by the German historian Leopold von Ranke (1795–1886), historians produced historical works that depended on the objective interpretation of eyewitness reports and authentic documents. Von Ranke himself wrote sixty volumes on modern European history that rested on the critical study of sources that he had gleaned from numerous archives. This method of writing history came to dominate modern-day historiography.

The new historicism that scholars brought to the critical study of religious history stirred great controversy. Rejecting all forms of supernaturalism, some nineteenth-century scholars disputed the literal interpretation of the Bible, especially where its contents conflicted with scientific evidence (as in the case of the Virgin Birth). Since the facts of Jesus' life are so few, some also questioned the historicity of Jesus (that is, whether or not he had ever actually lived), while still others—such as the eminent French scholar Ernest Renan, author of the *Life of Jesus* (1863)—questioned his divinity. Renan and his followers offered a rationalist reconstruction of religious history that worked to separate personal belief and moral conduct from conventional religious history and dogma. As universal education spread throughout the literate world, Church and state moved further apart, and education became increasingly secularized.

Realism in Literature

The Novels of Dickens and Twain

Inequities of class and gender had existed throughout the course of history, but in an age that pitted the progressive effects of industrial capitalism against the realities of poverty and inequality, social criticism was inevitable. Many writers pointed to these conditions and described them with unembellished objectivity. This unblinking attention to contemporary life and experience was the basis for the style known as *literary realism*.

More than any other genre, the nineteenth-century novel—by its capacity to detail characters and conditions—fulfilled the Realist credo of depicting life with complete candor. In place of heroic and exotic subjects, the Realist novel portrayed men and women in actual, everyday, and often demoralizing situations. It examined the social consequences of middle-class materialism, the plight of the working class, and the subjugation of women, among other matters.

While Realism did not totally displace Romanticism as the dominant literary mode of the nineteenth century, it often appeared alongside the Romantic—indeed, Romantic and sentimental elements can be found in generally Realistic narratives. Such is the case in the novels

Figure 30.5 THOMAS ANNAN, *Close No. 193 High Street*, 1868–1877, print ca. 1877. Carbon print, 11 × 9¼ in. While Annan spent most of his life in Glasgow, Scotland, his photographs of disease-ridden slums are representative of similar circumstances in late nineteenth-century industrial centers. Annan's photographs were instrumental in the eventual demolition of Glasgow's slum areas.

of Charles Dickens (1812–1870) in England and Mark Twain, the pseudonym of Samuel Langhorne Clemens (1835–1910), in America. Twain's writings, including his greatest achievement, *The Adventures of Huckleberry Finn*, reveal a blend of humor and irony that is not generally characteristic of Dickens. But both writers employ a masterful use of dialect, sensitivity to pictorial detail, and a humanitarian sympathy in their descriptions of nineteenth-century life in specific locales—for Twain, the rural farmlands along the Mississippi River, and for Dickens, the streets of England's industrial cities.

The most popular English novelist of his time, Dickens came from a poor family who provided him with little formal education. His early experiences supplied some of the themes for his most famous novels: *Oliver Twist* (1838) vividly portrays the slums, orphanages, and boarding schools of London; *Nicholas Nickleby* (1839) is a bitter indictment of England's brutal rural schools; and *David Copperfield* (1850) condemns debtors' prisons and the conditions that produced them.

Dickens' novels are frequently theatrical, his characters may be drawn to the point of caricature, and his themes often suggest a sentimental faith in kindness and good cheer as the best antidotes to the bitterness of contemporary life. But, as the following excerpt illustrates, Dickens' evocation of realistic detail was acute, and his portrayal of physical ugliness was unflinching. In this passage from *The Old Curiosity Shop*, he painted an unforgettable picture of the horrifying urban conditions that gave rise to the despair of the laboring classes and inspired their cries for social reform (Figure **30.5**). His description of the English mill town of Birmingham, as first viewed by the novel's heroine, little Nell, and her grandfather, finds striking parallels in nineteenth-century visual representations of Europe's laboring poor; it also calls to mind the popular conceptions of Hell found in medieval art and literature (see chapter 12).

READING 30.5 From Dickens'
The Old Curiosity Shop (1841)

. . . A long suburb of red-brick houses—some with patches of garden-ground, where coal-dust and factory smoke darkened the shrinking leaves and coarse, rank flowers; and where the struggling vegetation sickened and sank under the hot breath of kiln and furnace, making them by its presence seem yet   1

more blighting and unwholesome than in the town itself— a long, flat, straggling suburb passed, they came by slow degrees upon a cheerless region, where not a blade of grass was seen to grow; where not a bud put forth its promise in the spring; where nothing green could live but on the surface of the stagnant pools, which here and there lay idly sweltering by the black roadside.   10

Advancing more and more into the shadow of this mournful place, its dark depressing influence stole upon their spirits, and filled them with a dismal gloom. On every side, as far as the eye could see into the heavy distance, tall chimneys, crowding on each other, and presenting that endless repetition of the same dull, ugly form, which is the horror of oppressive dreams, poured out their plague of smoke, obscured the light, and made foul the melancholy air. On mounds of ashes by the wayside,   20 sheltered only by a few rough boards, or rotten pent-house roofs, strange engines spun and writhed like tortured creatures; clanking their iron chains, shrieking in their rapid whirl from time to time as though in torment unendurable, and making the ground tremble with their agonies. Dismantled houses here and there appeared, tottering to the earth, propped up by fragments of others that had fallen down, unroofed, windowless, blackened, desolate, but yet inhabited. Men, women, children, wan in their looks and ragged in attire, tended the engines, fed their tributary fires, begged upon the road, or scowled half   30 naked from the doorless houses. Then came more of the wrathful monsters, whose like they almost seemed to be in their wildness and their untamed air, screeching and turning round and round again; and still, before, behind, and to the right and left, was the same interminable perspective of brick towers, never ceasing in their black vomit, blasting all things living or inanimate, shutting out the face of day, and closing in on all these horrors with a dense dark cloud.

But night-time in this dreadful spot!—night, when the smoke was changed to fire; when every chimney spirited up its flame; ₄₀ and places, that had been dark vaults all day, now shone red-hot, with figures moving to and fro within their blazing jaws, and calling to one another with hoarse cries—night, when the noise of every strange machine was aggravated by the darkness; when the people near them looked wilder and more savage; when bands of unemployed laborers paraded in the roads, or clustered by torch-light round their leaders, who told them in stern language of their wrongs, and urged them on to frightful cries and threats; when maddened men, armed with sword and firebrand, spurning the tears and prayers of women ₅₀ who would restrain them, rushed forth on errands of terror and destruction, to work no ruin half so surely as their own—night, when carts came rumbling by, filled with rude coffins (for contagious disease and death had been busy with the living crops); when orphans cried, and distracted women shrieked and followed in their wake—night, when some called for bread, and some for drink to drown their cares; and some with tears, and some with staggering feet, and some with bloodshot eyes, went brooding home—night, which, unlike the night that Heaven sends on earth, brought with it no peace, nor quiet, nor signs ₆₀ of blessed sleep—who shall tell the terrors of the night to that young wandering child!

Q **Which descriptive details are most effective in setting the tone of this novel?**

Mark Twain's literary classic *The Adventures of Huckleberry Finn* is the most widely taught book in American literature. Published as a sequel to the popular "boys' book" *The Adventures of Tom Sawyer* (1876), which, like Dickens' novels, appeared in serial format, the book recounts the exploits of the young narrator, Huck Finn, and the runaway slave, Jim, as the two make their way down the Mississippi River on a ramshackle raft. As humorist, journalist, and social critic, Twain offered his contemporaries a blend of entertainment and vivid insight into the dynamics of a unique time and place: the American South just prior to the Civil War. More generally, he conveys the innocence of youthful boyhood as it wrestles with the realities of greed, hypocrisy, and the moral issues arising from the troubled relations between black and white Americans in the mid-nineteenth century. These he captures in an exotic blend of dialects—the vernacular rhythms and idioms of local, untutored speech.

In the excerpt that follows, Huck, a poor, ignorant, but good-hearted Southern boy, experiences a crisis of conscience when he must choose between aiding and abetting a fugitive slave—a felony offense in the slave states of the South—and obeying the law by turning over his older companion and friend to the local authorities. Huck's moral dilemma, the theme of this excerpt, was central to

the whole system of chattel slavery. Historically, slaves were considered property (chattel), that is, goods that could be bought, sold, or stolen. Clearly, however, they were also human beings. In opting to help Jim escape, Huck is, in effect, an accomplice to a crime. Nevertheless, Huck chooses to aid Jim the *man*, even as he violates the law in harboring Jim the *slave*.

READING 30.6 From Twain's *The Adventures of Huckleberry Finn* (1884)

Chapter 16

We slept most all day, and started out at night, a little ways ₁ behind a monstrous long raft that was as long going by as a procession. She had four long sweeps[1] at each end, so we judged she carried as many as thirty men, likely. She had five big wigwams aboard, wide apart, and an open camp fire in the middle, and a tall flag-pole at each end. There was a power of style about her. It amounted to something being a raftsman on such a craft as that.

We went drifting down into a big bend, and the night clouded up and got hot. The river was very wide, and was walled with ₁₀ solid timber on both sides; you couldn't see a break in it hardly ever, or a light. We talked about Cairo,[2] and wondered whether we would know it when we got to it. I said likely we wouldn't, because I had heard say there warn't but about a dozen houses there, and if they didn't happen to have them lit up, how was we going to know we was passing a town? Jim said if the two big rivers joined together there, that would show. But I said maybe we might think we was passing the foot of an island and coming into the same old river again. That disturbed Jim—and me too. So the question was, what to do? I said, paddle ashore ₂₀ the first time a light showed, and tell them pap was behind, coming along with a trading-scow, and was a green hand at the business, and wanted to know how far it was to Cairo. Jim thought it was a good idea, so we took a smoke on it and waited.

There warn't nothing to do, now, but to look out sharp for the town, and not pass it without seeing it. He said he'd be mighty sure to see it, because he'd be a free man the minute he seen it, but if he missed it he'd be in the slave country again and no more show for freedom. Every little while he jumps up and says: ₃₀

"Dah she is!"

But it warn't. It was Jack-o-lanterns, or lightning-bugs;[3] so he set down again, and went to watching, same as before. Jim said it made him all over trembly and feverish to be so close to freedom. Well, I can tell you it made me all over trembly and feverish, too, to hear him, because I begun to get it through my head that he was most free—and who was to blame for it? Why, me. I couldn't get that out of my conscience, no how nor no way. It got to troubling me so I couldn't rest; I couldn't stay still in one place. It hadn't ever come home to me before, what ₄₀ this thing was that I was doing. But now it did; and it staid

---

[1] Long oars.
[2] A city in Illinois.
[3] Fireflies.

with me, and scorched me more and more. I tried to make out to myself that I warn't to blame, because I didn't run Jim off from his rightful owner; but it warn't no use, conscience up and says, every time, "But you knowed he was running for his freedom, and you could a paddled ashore and told somebody." That was so—I couldn't get around that, noway. That was where it pinched. Conscience says to me, "What had poor Miss Watson done to you, that you could see her nigger go off right under your eyes and never say one single word? What did that poor old woman do to you, that you could treat her so mean? Why, she tried to learn you your book, she tried to learn you your manners, she tried to be good to you every way she knowed how. That's what she done." 50

I got to feeling so mean and so miserable I most wished I was dead. I fidgeted up and down the raft, abusing myself to myself, and Jim was fidgeting up and down past me. We neither of us could keep still. Every time he danced around and says, "Dah's Cairo!" it went through me like a shot, and I thought if it was Cairo I reckoned I would die of miserableness. 60

Jim talked out loud all the time while I was talking to myself. He was saying how the first thing he would do when he got to a free State he would go to saving up money and never spend a single cent, and when he got enough he would buy his wife, which was owned on a farm close to where Miss Watson lived; and then they would both work to buy the two children, and if their master wouldn't sell them, they'd get an Ab'litionist to go and steal them.

It most froze me to hear such talk. He wouldn't ever dared to talk such talk in his life before. Just see what a difference it 70 made in him the minute he judged he was about free. It was according to the old saying, "give a nigger an inch and he'll take an ell."[4] Thinks I, this is what comes of my not thinking. Here was this nigger which I had as good as helped to run away, coming right out flat-footed and saying he would steal his children—children that belonged to a man I didn't even know; a man that hadn't ever done me no harm.

I was sorry to hear Jim say that, it was such a lowering of him. My conscience got to stirring me up hotter than ever, until at last I says to it, "Let up on me—it ain't too late, yet—I'll 80 paddle ashore at the first light, and tell." I felt easy, and happy, and light as a feather, right off. All my troubles was gone. I went to looking out sharp for a light, and sort of singing to myself. By-and-by one showed. Jim sings out:

"We's safe, Huck, we's safe! Jump up and crack yo' heels, dat's de good ole Cairo at las', I jis knows it!"

I says:

"I'll take the canoe and go see, Jim. It mightn't be, you know."

He jumped and got the canoe ready, and put his old coat in 90 the bottom for me to set on, and give me the paddle; and as I shoved off, he says:

"Pooty soon I'll be a-shout'n for joy, en I'll say, it's all on accounts o' Huck; I's a free man, en I couldn't ever ben free ef it hadn' ben for Huck; Huck done it. Jim won't ever forgit you, Huck; you's de bes' fren' Jim's ever had; en you's de *only* fren' ole Jim's got now."

I was paddling off, all in a sweat to tell on him; but when he

says this, it seemed to kind of take the tuck all out of me. I went along slow then, and I warn't right down certain whether 100 I was glad I started or whether I warn't. When I was fifty yards off, Jim says:

"Dah you goes, de ole true Huck; de on'y white genlman dat ever kep' his promise to old Jim."

Well, I just felt sick. But I says, I got to do it—I can't get *out* of it. Right then, along comes a skiff with two men in it, with guns, and they stopped and I stopped. One of them says:

"What's that, yonder?"

"A piece of a raft," I says.

"Do you belong on it?" 110

"Yes, sir."

"Any men on it?"

"Only one, sir."

"Well, there's five niggers run off to-night, up yonder above the head of the bend. Is you man white or black?"

I didn't answer up prompt. I tried to, but the words wouldn't come. I tried, for a second or two, to brace up and out with it, but I warn't man enough—hadn't the spunk of a rabbit. I see I was weakening; so I just give up trying, and up and says—

"He's white." 120

"I reckon we'll go and see for ourselves."

"I wish you would," says I, "because it's pap that's there, and maybe you'd help me tow the raft ashore where the light is. He's sick—and so is mam and Mary Ann."

"Oh, the devil! we're in a hurry, boy. But I s'pose we've got to. Come—buckle to your paddle, and let's get along."

I buckled to my paddle and they laid to their oars. When we had made a stroke or two, I says:

"Pap'll be mighty much obleeged to you, I can tell you. Everybody goes away when I want them to help me tow the 130 raft ashore, and I can't do it by myself."

"Well, that's infernal mean. Odd, too. Say, boy, what's the matter with your father?"

"It's the—a—the—well, it ain't anything, much."

They stopped pulling. It warn't but a mighty little ways to the raft, now. One says:

"Boy, that's a lie. What is the matter with your pap? Answer up square, now, and it'll be the better for you."

"I will, sir, I will, honest—but don't leave us, please. It's the—the—gentlemen, if you'll only pull ahead, and let me 140 heave you the head-line, you won't have to come a-near the raft—please do."

"Set her back, John, set her back!" says one. They backed water. "Keep away, boy—keep to looard.[5] Confound it, I just expect the wind has blowed it to us. Your pap's got the smallpox, and you know it precious well. Why didn't you come out and say so? Do you want to spread it all over?"

"Well," says I, a-blubbering, "I've told everybody before, and then they just went away and left us."

"Poor devil, there's something in that. We are right down 150 sorry for you, but we—well, hang it, we don't want the smallpox, you see. Look here, I'll tell you what to do. Don't you try to land by yourself, or you'll smash everything to pieces. You float along down about twenty miles and you'll come to a town on the left-hand side of the river. It will be long after sun-up,

---

[4] An English measure equal to 45 inches.

[5] Leeward; away from the wind.

then, and when you ask for help, you tell them your folks are all down with chills and fever. Don't be a fool again, and let people guess what is the matter. Now we're trying to do you a kindness; so you just put twenty miles between us, that's a good boy. It wouldn't do any good to land yonder where the light is—it's only a wood-yard. Say—I reckon your father's poor, and I'm bound to say he's in pretty hard luck. Here—I'll put a twenty dollar gold piece on this board, and you get it when it floats by. I feel mighty mean to leave you, but my kingdom! it won't do to fool with small-pox, don't you see?"

"Hold on, Parker," says the other man, "here's a twenty to put on the board for me. Good-bye, boy, you do as Mr. Parker told you, and you'll be all right."

"That's so, my boy—good-bye, good-bye. If you see any runaway niggers, you get help and nab them, and you can make some money by it."

"Good-bye, sir," says I, "I won't let no runaway niggers get by me if I can help it."

They went off, and I got aboard the raft, feeling bad and low, because I knowed very well I had done wrong, and I see it warn't no use for me to try to learn to do right; a body that don't get started right when he's little, ain't got no show[6]—when the pinch comes there ain't nothing to back him up and keep him to his work, and so he gets beat. Then I thought a minute, and says to myself, hold on,—s'pose you'd a done right and give Jim up; would you felt better than what you do now? No, says I, I'd feel bad—I'd feel just the same way I do now. Well, then, says I, what's the use you learning to do right, when it's troublesome to do right and ain't no trouble to do wrong, and the wages is just the same? I was stuck. I couldn't answer that. So I reckoned I wouldn't bother no more about it, but after this always do whichever come handiest at the time. . . .

Q How does Twain bring to life the personalities of Huck and Jim?

Q How does Huck resolve his moral dilemma?

Russian Realism: Dostoevsky and Tolstoy

More pessimistic than Dickens or Twain, and more profoundly analytic of the universal human condition, were the Russian novelists Fyodor Dostoevsky (1821–1881) and Leo Tolstoy (1828–1910). Both men were born and bred in wealth, but both turned against upper-class Russian society and sympathized with the plight of the lower classes.

Tolstoy ultimately renounced his wealth and property and went to live and work among the peasants. His historical novel *War and Peace* (1869), often hailed as the greatest example of Realistic Russian fiction, traces the progress of five families whose destinies unroll against the background of Napoleon's invasion of Russia in 1812. In this sprawling narrative, as in many of his other novels, Tolstoy exposes the privileged position of the nobility and the cruel exploitation of the great masses of Russian people. This task, along with sympathy for the cause of Russian nationalism in general, was shared by Tolstoy's friend and admirer Ilya Repin (1844–1930), whose portrait

[6] Has no chance.

Figure 30.6 ILYA REPIN, *Portrait of Leo Tolstoy*, 1887. Oil on canvas, 48⅘ × 34⅔ in. Repin was celebrated for his realistic depictions of contemporary Russian life and for the psychological insight he brought to his portraits of notable Russian writers and composers.

of Tolstoy brings the writer to life with skillful candor (Figure **30.6**). Russia's preeminent Realist painter, Repin rendered with detailed accuracy the miserable lives of ordinary Russians—peasants, laborers, and beggars—in genre paintings that might well serve as illustrations for the novels of Tolstoy and Dostoevsky.

Dostoevsky paid greater attention than Tolstoy to philosophical and psychological issues. His characters are often victims of a dual plight: poverty and conscience. Their energies are foiled by bitter efforts to resolve their own contradictory passions. Dostoevsky's personal life contributed to his bleak outlook: associated with a group of proletarian revolutionaries, he was arrested and deported to Siberia, where he spent five years at hard labor. The necessity of suffering is a central theme in his writing, as is the hope of salvation through suffering.

The novels *Crime and Punishment* (1866), *The Possessed* (1871), and *The Brothers Karamazov* (1880) feature protagonists whose irrational behavior and its psychological consequences form the central theme. In *Crime and Punishment*, Raskolnikov, a young, poor student, murders an old woman and her younger sister; his crime goes undetected. Thereafter, he struggles with guilt—the self-punishment for his criminal act. He also explores the problems arising from one's freedom to commit evil. In the following excerpt, the protagonist addresses the moral question of whether extraordinary individuals, by dint of their uniqueness, have the right to commit immoral acts. The conversation, which takes place between Raskolnikov and his friends, is spurred by an article on crime that Raskolnikov had published in a journal shortly after dropping out of university. This excerpt is typical of Dostoevsky's fondness for developing character through monologue and dialogue, rather than through descriptive detail. Dostoevsky's Realism (and his genius) lie in the way in which he forces the reader to understand the character as that character tries to understand himself.

READING 30.7 From Dostoevsky's *Crime and Punishment* (1866)

"... the 'extraordinary' man has the right ... I don't mean a   1
formal, official right, but he has the right in himself, to permit
his conscience to overstep ... certain obstacles, but only in
the event that his ideas (which may sometimes be salutary for
all mankind) require it for their fulfilment. You are pleased to
say that my article is not clear; I am ready to elucidate it for
you, as far as possible. Perhaps I am not mistaken in supposing
that is what you want. Well, then. In my opinion, if the
discoveries of Kepler and Newton, by some combination of
circumstances, could not have become known to the world
in any other way than by sacrificing the lives of one, or ten,   10
or more people, who might have hampered or in some way
been obstacles in the path of those discoveries, then Newton
would have had the right, or might even have been under an
obligation ... to *remove* those ten or a hundred people, so that
his discoveries might be revealed to all mankind. It does not
follow from this, of course, that Newton had the right to kill
any Tom, Dick, or Harry he fancied, or go out stealing from
market-stalls every day. I remember further that in my article
I developed the idea that all the ... well, for example, the
law-givers and regulators of human society, beginning with   20
the most ancient, and going on to Lycurgus, Solon, Mahomet,
Napoleon and so on, were without exception transgressors,[1]
by the very fact that in making a new law they *ipso facto* broke
an old one, handed down from their fathers and held sacred
by society; and, of course, they did not stop short of shedding
blood, provided only that the blood (however innocent and
however heroically shed in defence of the ancient law) was
shed to their advantage. It is remarkable that the greater
part of these benefactors and law-givers of humanity were

particularly blood-thirsty. In a word, I deduce that all of them,   30
not only the great ones, but also those who diverge ever so
slightly from the beaten track, those, that is, who are just
barely capable of saying something new, must, by their
nature, inevitably be criminals—in a greater or less degree,
naturally. Otherwise they would find it too hard to leave their
rut, and they cannot, of course, consent to remain in the rut,
again by the very fact of their nature; and in my opinion they
ought not to consent. In short, you see that up to this point
there is nothing specially new here. It has all been printed, and
read, a thousand times before. As for my division of people into   40
ordinary and extraordinary, that I agree was a little arbitrary, but
I do not insist on exact figures. Only I do believe in the main
principle of my idea. That consists in people being, by the law
of nature, divided *in general* into two categories: into a lower
(of ordinary people), that is, into material serving only for the
reproduction of its own kind, and into people properly speaking,
that is, those who have the gift or talent of saying *something
new* in their sphere. There are endless subdivisions, of course,
but the distinctive characteristics of the two categories are
fairly well marked: the first group, that is the material, are,   50
generally speaking, by nature staid and conservative, they live
in obedience and like it. In my opinion they ought to obey
because that is their destiny, and there is nothing at all
degrading to them in it. The second group are all law-breakers
and transgressors, or are inclined that way, in the measure of
their capacities. The aims of these people are, of course,
relative and very diverse; for the most part they require, in
widely different contexts, the destruction of what exists in the
name of better things. But if it is necessary for one of them, for
the fulfilment of his ideas, to march over corpses, or wade   60
through blood, then in my opinion he may in all conscience
authorize himself to wade through blood—in proportion,
however, to his idea and the degree of its importance—mark
that. It is in that sense only that I speak in my article of their
right to commit crime. (You will remember that we really began
with the question of legality.) There is, however, not much
cause for alarm: the masses hardly ever recognize this right of
theirs, and behead or hang them (more or less), and in this way,
quite properly, fulfil their conservative function, although in
following generations these same masses put their former   70
victims on a pedestal and worship them (more or less). The first
category are always the masters of the present, but the second
are the lords of the future. The first preserve the world and
increase and multiply; the second move the world and guide it
to its goal. Both have an absolutely equal right to exist. In short,
for me all men have completely equivalent rights, and—*vive
la guerre éternelle*—until we have built the New Jerusalem,
of course!"[2]

"You do believe in the New Jerusalem, then?"

"Yes, I do," answered Raskolnikov firmly; he said this with   80
his eyes fixed on one spot on the carpet, as they had been all
through his long tirade.

"A-and you believe in God? Forgive me for being so inquisitive."

---

[1] Raskolnikov's views are similar to those expressed by Napoleon III in his book *Life of Julius Caesar*. The newspaper *Golos* ("*Voice*") had recently summarized the English *Saturday Review's* analysis of Napoleon's ideas about the right of exceptional individuals (such as Lycurgus, Mahomet, and Napoleon I) to transgress laws and even to shed blood. The book appeared in Paris in March 1865; the Russian translation in April! [Lycurgus: the founder of the military regime of ancient Sparta; Solon: statesman and reformer in sixth-century B.C.E. Athens; Mahomet: Muhammad, the prophet of Allah and founder of the religion Islam.]

[2] New Jerusalem, symbolic of the ideal order, after the end of time, is a Heaven on Earth, a new paradise. See the description in Revelation 21 (the Apocalypse). The French phrase means "Long live perpetual war."

"Yes, I do," repeated Raskolnikov, raising his eyes to Porfiry.

"A-a-and do you believe in the raising of Lazarus?"

"Y-yes. Why are you asking all this?"

"You believe in it literally?"

"Yes."

"Ah . . . I was curious to know. Forgive me. But, returning to the previous subject—they are not always put to death. Some, on the contrary . . ."

"Triumph during their lifetime? Oh, yes, some achieve their ends while they still live, and then . . ."

"They begin to mete out capital punishment themselves?"

"If necessary, and, you know, it is most usually so. Your observation is very keen-witted."

"Thank you. But tell me: how do you distinguish these extraordinary people from the ordinary? Do signs and portents appear when they are born? I mean to say that we could do with rather greater accuracy here, with, so to speak, rather more outward signs: please excuse the natural anxiety of a practical and well-meaning man, but couldn't there be, for example, some special clothing, couldn't they carry some kind of brand or something? . . . Because, you will agree, if there should be some sort of mix-up, and somebody from one category imagined that he belonged to the other and began 'to remove all obstacles,' as you so happily put it, then really . . ."

"Oh, that very frequently happens! This observation of yours is even more penetrating than the last."

"Thank you."

"Not at all. But you must please realize that the mistake is possible only among the first group, that is, the 'ordinary' people (as I have called them, perhaps not altogether happily). In spite of their inborn inclination to obey, quite a number of them, by some freak of nature such as is not impossible even among cows, like to fancy that they are progressives, 'destroyers,' and propagators of the 'new world,' and all this quite sincerely. At the same time, they really take no heed of new people; they even despise them, as reactionary and incapable of elevated thinking. But, in my opinion, they cannot constitute a real danger, and you really have nothing to worry about, because they never go far. They might sometimes be scourged for their zealotry, to remind them of their place; there is no need even for anyone to carry out the punishment: they will do it themselves, because they are very well conducted: some of them do one another this service, and others do it for themselves with their own hands . . . And they impose on themselves various public penances besides—the result is beautifully edifying, and in short, you have nothing to worry about . . . This is a law of nature."

"Well, at least you have allayed my anxieties on that score a little; but here is another worry: please tell me, are there many of these people who have the right to destroy others, of these 'extraordinary' people? I am, of course, prepared to bow down before them, but all the same you will agree that it would be terrible if there were very many of them, eh?"

"Oh, don't let that trouble you either," went on Raskolnikov in the same tone. "Generally speaking, there are extremely few people, strangely few, born, who have a new idea, or are even capable of saying anything at all new. One thing only is clear, that the ordering of human births, all these categories and subdivisions, must be very carefully and exactly regulated

by some law of nature. This law is, of course, unknown at present, but I believe that it exists, and consequently that it may be known. The great mass of men, the common stuff of humanity, exist on the earth only in order that at last, by some endeavour, some process, that remains as yet mysterious, some happy conjunction of race and breeding, there should struggle into life a being, one in a thousand, capable, in however small a degree, of standing on his own feet. Perhaps one in ten thousand (I am speaking approximately, by way of illustration) is born with a slightly greater degree of independence, and one in a hundred thousand with even more. One genius may emerge among millions, and a really great genius, perhaps, as the crowning point of many thousands of millions of men. In short, I have not been able to look into the retort whence all this proceeds. But a definite law there must be, and is; it cannot be a matter of chance. . . ."

Q Into what two categories does Raskolnikov divide humankind?

Q How does he justify the transgressions of the "lords of the future"?

The Literary Heroines of Flaubert and Chopin

Nineteenth-century novelists shared a special interest in examining conflicts between social conventions and personal values, especially as they affected the everyday lives of women. Gustave Flaubert's *Madame Bovary* (1857), Tolstoy's *Anna Karenina* (1877), and Kate Chopin's *The Awakening* (1899) are representative of the writer's concern with the tragic consequences following from the defiance of established social and moral codes by passionate female figures. The heroines of these novels do not create the world in their own image; rather, the world—or more specifically, the social and economic environment—molds them and governs their destinies.

Flaubert (1821–1880), whom critics have called "the inventor of the modern novel," stripped his novels of sentimentality and of all preconceived notions of behavior. He aimed at a precise description of not only the stuff of the physical world but also the motivations of his characters. A meticulous observer, he sought *le mot juste* ("the exact word") to describe each concrete object and each psychological state—a practice that often prevented him from writing more than one or two pages of prose per week. One contemporary critic wittily claimed that Flaubert, the son of a surgeon, wielded his pen like a scalpel.

Flaubert's landmark novel, *Madame Bovary*, tells the story of a middle-class woman who desperately seeks to escape the boredom of her mundane existence. Educated in a convent and married to a dull small-town physician, Emma Bovary tries to live out the fantasies that fill the pages of her favorite romance novels, but her efforts to do so prove disastrous and lead to her ultimate destruction. With a minimum of interpretation, Flaubert reconstructs the particulars of Emma's provincial surroundings and her bleak marriage. Since the novel achieves its full effect through the gradual development of plot and character, no brief excerpt can possibly do it justice. Nevertheless, the following extract, which describes the deterioration of the adulterous affair between Emma Bovary and the young clerk Léon, illustrates Flaubert's ability to characterize places and persons by means of the fastidious selection and accumulation of descriptive details.

<hr/>

READING 30.8 From Flaubert's
Madame Bovary (1857)

In the end Léon had promised not to see Emma again; and he   1
reproached himself for not keeping his word, when he considered
the power this woman possessed to embroil him in dubious
situations, or inspire gossip, quite apart from the jokes that
circulated among his fellow clerks every morning, when they
gathered round the stove. Besides, he was about to be promoted
to head clerk; the time had come to be serious. So he gave up the
flute, and transports of emotion, and flights of imagination—for
every respectable middle-class man, in the ferment of his youth,
has seen himself, if only for one day, or one hour, as capable of   10
grand emotions and lofty enterprises! The most half-hearted
libertine has fantasized about Oriental queens; and every notary
carries within himself the vestigial traces of a poet.

He felt bored, now, when Emma, without warning, burst into
sobs in his arms; and, like a listener who can only endure a
certain dose of music and no more, his heart was growing torpid
with indifference towards this clamorous love, whose delicate
nuances he could no longer distinguish.

They knew one another too well to experience that
wonderment in mutual possession that increased its joy a   20
hundredfold. She was as sick of him as he was weary of her.
Emma was rediscovering, in adultery, all the banality of marriage.

But how to rid herself of him? And then, despite the humiliation
of craving such base pleasures, she had come, either out of habit
or depravity, to depend on them, and each day she pursued them
with a greater frenzy, exhausting every possibility of happiness
by the excess of her demands. She blamed Léon for her
disappointed hopes, as if he had betrayed her; and she even
longed for some disaster that would occasion their separation,
since she herself lacked the courage to bring this about.   30

But in spite of this she did continue to write him love letters,
faithful to the idea that a woman should always write to her
lover. But, as she wrote, she saw a different man, created from
her most passionate memories, her most beautiful passages of
fiction, and her most intense yearnings; and in the end he became
so real and tangible that her heart would throb in amazement, but
without her being able to conjure him up in precise detail, for, like
some god, his outline would be blurred by the very multiplicity of
his attributes. He inhabited that hazy blue region where silken
ladders sway from balconies, and the bright moonlight is heavy   40
with the scent of flowers. She could feel him close to her, he was
approaching, he would ravish her with a kiss and carry her off
with him. Then, afterwards, she would come back to earth utterly
spent and broken—for those vague amorous raptures left her
more exhausted than the most extreme debauchery.

Q **What insights into Emma's personality are offered in this brief excerpt? Into Léon's personality?**

Almost immediately after *Madame Bovary* appeared (in the form of six installments in the *Revue de Paris*), the novel was denounced as an offense against public and religious morals, and Flaubert, as well as the publisher and the printer of the *Revue*, was brought to trial before a criminal court. All three men were ultimately acquitted, but not before an eloquent lawyer had defended all the passages (including those in Reading 30.8) that had been condemned as wanton and immoral.

A similar situation befell the American writer Kate Chopin (1851–1904), whose novel *The Awakening* was banned in her native city of St. Louis shortly after its publication in 1899. The novel, a frank examination of female sexual passion and marital infidelity, violated the norms of the society in which Chopin had been reared. Unlike Flaubert, whose novels convey the staleness and inescapability of French provincial life, many of Chopin's stories deliberately ignore the specifics of time and place. Some are set in Louisiana, where Chopin lived for twelve years with her husband and six children. Chopin was successful in selling her Louisiana dialect stories, many of which explore matters of class, race, and gender within the world of Creole society, but her novels fell into obscurity soon after her death. *The Awakening*, whose heroine defies convention by committing adultery, did not receive positive critical attention until the 1950s.

While Chopin absorbed the Realist strategies and social concerns of Flaubert, she brought to her prose a sensitivity to the nuances of human (and especially female) behavior that challenged popular Romantic stereotypes (see chapter 28). Her work also reveals a remarkable talent for narrating a story with jewel-like precision. Her taut descriptive style reaches unparalleled heights in the short prose piece known as "The Story of an Hour." Here, the protagonist's brief taste of liberation takes on an ironic fatal turn.

<hr/>

READING 30.9 Kate Chopin's
"The Story of an Hour"
("The Dream of an Hour") (1894)

Knowing that Mrs. Mallard was afflicted with a heart trouble,   1
great care was taken to break to her as gently as possible the
news of her husband's death.

It was her sister Josephine who told her, in broken
sentences: veiled hints that revealed in half concealing. Her
husband's friend Richards was there, too, near her. It was he
who had been in the newspaper office when intelligence of the
railroad disaster was received, with Brently Mallard's name
leading the list of "killed." He had only taken time to assure
himself of its truth by a second telegram, and had hastened   10
to forestall any less careful, less tender friend in bearing the
sad message.

She did not hear the story as many women have heard the
same, with a paralysed inability to accept its significance. She
wept at once, with a sudden, wild abandonment, in her sister's
arms. When the storm of grief had spent itself she went away

to her room alone. She would have no one follow her.

There stood, facing the open window, a comfortable, roomy armchair. Into this she sank, pressed down by a physical exhaustion that haunted her body and seemed to reach into her soul.

She could see in the open square before her house the tops of trees that were all aquiver with the new spring life. The delicious breath of rain was in the air. In the street below a peddler was crying his wares. The notes of a distant song which some one was singing reached her faintly, and countless sparrows were twittering in the eaves.

There were patches of blue sky showing here and there through the clouds that had met and piled one above the other in the west facing her window.

She sat with her head thrown back upon the cushion of the chair, quite motionless, except when a sob came into her throat and shook her, as a child who has cried itself to sleep continues to sob in its dreams.

She was young, with a fair, calm face, whose lines bespoke repression and even a certain strength. But now there was a dull stare in her eyes, whose gaze was fixed away off yonder on one of those patches of blue sky. It was not a glance of reflection, but rather a suspension of intelligent thought.

There was something coming to her and she was waiting for it, fearfully. What was it? She did not know; it was too subtle and elusive to name. But she felt it, creeping out of the sky, reaching toward her through the sounds, the scents, the color that filled the air.

Now her bosom rose and fell tumultuously. She was beginning to recognize this thing that was approaching to possess her, and she was striving to beat it back with her will—as powerless as her white slender hands would have been.

When she abandoned herself a little whispered word escaped her slight parted lips. She said it over and over under her breath: "free, free, free!" The vacant stare and the look of terror that had followed it went from her eyes. They stayed keen and bright. Her pulses beat fast, and the coursing blood warmed and relaxed every inch of her body.

She did not stop to ask if it were not a monstrous joy that held her. A clear and exalted perception enabled her to dismiss the suggestion as trivial.

She knew that she would weep again when she saw the kind, tender hands folded in death: fixed and grey and dead. But she saw beyond that bitter moment a long procession of years to come that would belong to her absolutely. And she opened and spread her arms out to them in welcome.

There would be no one to live for her during those coming years; she would live for herself. There would be no powerful will bending hers in that blind persistence with which men and women believe they have a right to impose a private will upon a fellow-creature. A kind intention or a cruel intention made the act seem no less a crime as she looked upon it in that brief moment of illumination.

And yet she loved him—sometimes. Often she had not. What did it matter! What could love, the unsolved mystery, count for in the face of this possession of self-assertion which she suddenly recognized as the strongest impulse of her being!

"Free! Body and soul free!" she kept whispering.

Josephine was kneeling before the keyhole, imploring for admission. "Louise, open the door! I beg: open the door—you will make yourself ill. What are you doing, Louise? For heaven's sake open the door."

"Go away. I'm not making myself ill." No: she was drinking in a very elixir of life through that open window.

Her fancy was running riot along those days ahead of her. Spring days, and summer days, and all sorts of days that would be her own. She breathed a quick prayer that life might be long. It was only yesterday she had thought with a shudder that life might be long.

She arose at length and opened the door to her sister's importunities. There was a feverish triumph in her eyes, and she carried herself unwittingly like a goddess of Victory. She clasped her sister's wrist, and together they descended the stairs. Richards stood waiting for them at the bottom.

Some one was opening the front door with a latchkey. It was Brently Mallard who entered, a little travel-stained, composedly carrying his grip-sack and umbrella. He had been far from the scene of accident, and did not even know there had been one. He stood amazed at Josephine's piercing cry; at Richards' quick motion to screen him from the view of his wife.

But Richards was too late.

When the doctors came they said she had died of heart disease—of joy that kills.

Q. What does this story imply about the relationship between husband and wife?

Q. Would the story be equally effective if the roles of Louise and Brently Mallard were reversed?

Zola and the Naturalistic Novel

Kate Chopin's contemporary Emile Zola (1840–1902) initiated a variant form of literary Realism known as *naturalism*. Naturalist fiction was based on the premise that everyday life should be represented with scientific objectivity: faithfully and with detailed accuracy. Contrary to Romantic writers, naturalists refused to embellish or idealize experience. They went beyond the Realism of Flaubert and Dickens by conceiving their characters in accordance with psychological and sociological factors, and as products of the laws of heredity. This deterministic approach showed human beings as products of environmental or hereditary factors over which they had little or no control. Just as Marx held that economic life shaped all aspects of culture, so naturalists believed that material and social elements determined human conduct and behavior.

Zola (Figure **30.7**) treated the novel as a carefully researched study of commonplace, material existence. In his passion to describe his time and place with absolute fidelity, he studied labor problems, police records, and industrial history, amassing notebooks of information on a wide variety of subjects, including coal mining, the railroads, the stock market, and the science of surgery. He presented a slice of life that showed how social and material circumstances shaped the society of late nineteenth-century France. His twenty novels (known

Figure 30.7 EDOUARD MANET, *Zola*, exhibited 1868. Oil on canvas, 57 × 45 in. Manet's portrait has the quality of a snapshot. The writer is seen at his desk, which holds a copy of his short biography of the artist. Above the desk, he has posted a black-and-white reproduction of Manet's *Olympia*, a Japanese print of a sumo wrestler, and Goya's etching of a painting by Velázquez, favorite artists of both Manet and Zola.

as the "Rougon-Macquart" series) exploring the lives of French farmers, miners, statesmen, prostitutes, scholars, and artists constitutes a psycho-socio-biological history of his time. *The Grog Shop* (1877) offers a terrifying picture of the effects of alcoholism on industrial workers. *Nana* (1880) is a scathing portrayal of a beautiful but unscrupulous prostitute. The most scandalous of his novels, it inspired charges of pornography and "gutter-sweeping."

A later novel in the "Rougon-Macquart" series, *Germinal* (1885), exposes the bitter lives of coal miners in northern France. The excerpt that follows, which relates the hellish experience of the miner Maheu, reflects Zola's talent for detailed description that transforms his writing from mere social history to powerful fiction.

READING 30.10 From Zola's *Germinal* (1885)

The four cutters [miners] had stretched themselves out, head to   1
toe, over the whole surface of the sloping face. Separated by
hooked planks that caught the loosened coal, each of them
occupied about fifteen feet of the vein, which was so narrow—
scarcely twenty inches at this point—that they were squashed

in between the roof and the wall. They had to drag themselves
along on their knees and elbows, and were unable to turn
without bruising their shoulders. To get at the coal, they had to
lie sideways, their necks twisted and their raised arms wielding
the short-handled picks at an angle.   10

Zacharie was at the bottom. Levaque and Chaval above him,
and Maheu at the very top. Each one was hacking away at the
bed of shale with his pick, cutting two vertical grooves in the
vein, then driving an iron wedge into the top of the block and
freeing it. The coal was soft, and the block crumbled into pieces
and rolled down their stomachs and thighs. When these pieces,
caught by the planks, had heaped up beneath them, the cutters
disappeared, walled up in the narrow crevice.

Maheu was the one who suffered most. The temperature at
the top climbed as high as ninety-five degrees; the air did not   20
circulate, and the suffocating heat eventually became unbearable.
In order to see clearly, he had had to hang his lamp on a nail
right next to his head, and this additional heat beating down on
his skull made his blood sing in his ears. But the worst was the
dampness. Water was continually dripping down from the rock
only a few inches above his face, and there was a never-ending
stream of drops falling, with a maddening rhythm, always on the
same spot. It was no use twisting his neck or turning his head: the
drops kept beating against his face, splattering and spreading
without stop. At the end of a quarter of an hour he was soaked   30
through, coated with his own sweat, and steaming like a tub of
laundry. a That morning drop ceaselessly trickling into his eye
made him swear, but he wouldn't stop cutting, and his mighty
blows jolted him so violently between the two layers of rock that
he was like a plant-louse caught between two pages of a book—
in constant danger of being completely crushed.

Not a word was said. They were all hammering away, and
nothing could be heard except these irregular blows, muffled
and seemingly far away. The sounds were harsh in the echoless,
dead air, and it seemed as though the shadows had a strange   40
blackness, thickened by the flying coal dust and made heavier
by the gases that weighed down on their eyes. Behind metal
screens, the wicks of their lamps gave off only reddish points of
light, and it was hard to see anything. The stall opened out like a
large, flat, oblique chimney in which the soot of ten winters had
built up an unrelieved darkness. Phantom forms moved about,
dull beams of light giving glimpses of a rounded haunch, a brawny
arm, a distorted face blackened as if in preparation for a crime.
Occasionally, as blocks of coal came loose, they would catch
the light and shoot off crystal-like glitters from their suddenly   50
illuminated facets. Then it would be dark again, the picks would
beat out heavy dull blows, and there was nothing but the sound
of panting breaths, grunts of discomfort and fatigue in the stifling
air, and the dripping water from the underground streams.

Q Which of the senses does Zola engage in this description of coal mining?

Elements of naturalism are found in the novels of many late nineteenth-century writers in both Europe and America. Thomas Hardy (1840–1928) in England and Stephen Crane (1871–1900), Jack London (1876–1916) and Theodore Dreiser (1871–1945) in America are the most notable of the English-language literary naturalists.

Realist Drama: Ibsen

The Norwegian dramatist Henrik Ibsen (1828–1906) brought to the late nineteenth-century stage concerns similar to those in the novels of the Realists. A moralist and a critic of human behavior, he attacked the artificial social conventions that led people to pursue self-deluding and hypocritical lives. Ibsen was deeply concerned with contemporary issues and social problems. He shocked the public with prose dramas that addressed such controversial subjects as insanity, incest, and venereal disease. At the same time, he explored universal themes of conflict between the individual and society, between love and duty, and between husband and wife.

In 1879, Ibsen wrote the classic drama of female liberation, *A Doll's House*. Threatened with blackmail over a debt she had incurred years earlier, Nora Helmer looks to her priggish husband Torvald for protection. But Torvald is a victim of the small-mindedness and middle-class social restraints of his time and place. When he fails to rally to his wife's defense, Nora realizes the frailty of her dependent lifestyle. Awakened to the meaninglessness of her life as "a doll-wife" in "a doll's house," she comes to recognize that her first obligation is to herself and to her dignity as a human being.

Nora's revelation brings to life, in the forceful language of everyday speech, the psychological tension between male and female that Mill had analyzed only ten years earlier in his treatise on the subjection of women. Ibsen does not resolve the question of whether a woman's duties to husband and children come before her duty to herself; yet, as is suggested in the following exchange between Nora and Torvald (excerpted from the last scene of *A Doll's House*), Nora's self-discovery precipitates the end of her marriage. She shuts the door on the illusions of the past as emphatically as Ibsen shut out the world of Romantic idealism.

READING 30.11 From Ibsen's *A Doll's House* (1879)

Act III, Final Scene

[Late at night in the Helmers' living room. Instead of retiring, Nora suddenly appears in street clothes.]

Helmer: . . . What's all this? I thought you were going to 1
bed. You've changed your dress?

Nora: Yes, Torvald; I've changed my dress.

Helmer: But what for? At this hour?

Nora: I shan't sleep tonight.

Helmer: But, Nora dear—

Nora *[looking at her watch]*: It's not so very late—Sit down, Torvald; we have a lot to talk about.

[She sits at one side of the table.]

Helmer: Nora—what does this mean? Why that stern 10
expression?

Nora: Sit down. It'll take some time. I have a lot to say to you.

[Helmer sits at the other side of the table.]

Helmer: You frighten me, Nora. I don't understand you.

Nora: No, that's just it. You don't understand me; and I have never understood you either—until tonight. No, don't interrupt me. Just listen to what I have to say. This is to be a final settlement, Torvald.

Helmer: How do you mean? 20

Nora *[after a short silence]*: Doesn't anything special strike you as we sit here like this?

Helmer: I don't think so—why?

Nora: It doesn't occur to you, does it, that though we've been married for eight years, this is the first time that we two—man and wife—have sat down for a serious talk?

Helmer: What do you mean by serious?

Nora: During eight whole years, no—more than that—ever since the first day we met—we have never exchanged so much as one serious word about serious things. 30

Helmer: Why should I perpetually burden you with all my cares and problems? How could you possibly help me to solve them?

Nora: I'm not talking about cares and problems. I'm simply saying we've never once sat down seriously and tried to get to the bottom of anything.

Helmer: But, Nora, darling—why should you be concerned with serious thoughts?

Nora: That's the whole point! You've never understood me—A great injustice has been done me, Torvald; first by 40
Father, and then by you.

Helmer: What a thing to say! No two people on earth could ever have loved you more than we have!

Nora *[shaking her head]*: You never loved me. You just thought it was fun to be in love with me.

Helmer: This is fantastic!

Nora: Perhaps. But it's true all the same. While I was still at home I used to hear Father airing his opinions and they became my opinions; or if I didn't happen to agree, I kept it to myself— he would have been displeased otherwise. He used to call me 50
his doll-baby, and played with me as I played with my dolls. Then I came to live in your house—

Helmer: What an expression to use about our marriage!

Nora *[undisturbed]*: I mean—from Father's hands I passed into yours. You arranged everything according to your tastes, and I acquired the same tastes, or I pretended to—I'm not sure which—a little of both, perhaps. Looking back on it all, it seems to me I've lived here like a beggar, from hand to mouth. I've lived by performing tricks for you, Torvald. But that's the way you wanted it. You and Father have done me a great 60
wrong. You've prevented me from becoming a real person.

Helmer: Nora, how can you be so ungrateful and unreasonable! Haven't you been happy here?

Nora: No, never. I thought I was; but I wasn't really.

Helmer: Not—not happy!

Nora: No, only merry. You've always been so kind to me. But our home has never been anything but a play-room. I've been your doll-wife, just as at home I was Papa's doll-child. And the children, in turn, have been my dolls. I thought it fun when you played games with me, just as they thought it fun 70
when I played games with them. And that's been our marriage, Torvald.

Helmer: There may be a grain of truth in what you say, even though it is distorted and exaggerated. From now on things will be different. Play-time is over now; tomorrow lessons begin!

Nora: Whose lessons? Mine, or the children's?

Helmer: Both, if you wish it, Nora, dear.

Nora: Torvald, I'm afraid you're not the man to teach me to be a real wife to you. 80

Helmer: How can you say that?

Nora: And I'm certainly not fit to teach the children.

Helmer: Nora!

Nora: Didn't you just say, a moment ago, you didn't dare trust them to me?

Helmer: That was in the excitement of the moment! You mustn't take it so seriously!

Nora: But you were quite right, Torvald. That job is beyond me; there's another job I must do first: I must try and educate myself. You could never help me to do that; I must do it quite alone. So, you see—that's why I'm going to leave you. 90

Helmer: [jumping up]: What did you say—?

Nora: I shall never get to know myself—I shall never learn to face reality—unless I stand alone. So I can't stay with you any longer.

Helmer: Nora! Nora!

Nora: I am going at once. I'm sure Kristine will let me stay with her tonight—

Helmer: But, Nora—this is madness! I shan't allow you to do this. I shall forbid it! 100

Nora: You no longer have the power to forbid me anything. I'll only take a few things with me—those that belong to me. I shall never again accept anything from you.

Helmer: Have you lost your senses?

Nora: Tomorrow I'll go home—to what was my home, I mean. It might be easier for me there, to find something to do.

Helmer: You talk like an ignorant child, Nora—!

Nora: Yes. That's just why I must educate myself.

Helmer: To leave your home—to leave your husband, and your children! What do you suppose people would say to that? 110

Nora: It makes no difference. This is something I must do.

Helmer: It's inconceivable! Don't you realize you'd be betraying your most sacred duty?

Nora: What do you consider that to be?

Helmer: Your duty towards your husband and your children—I surely don't have to tell you that!

Nora: I've another duty just as sacred.

Helmer: Nonsense! What duty do you mean?

Nora: My duty towards myself.

Helmer: Remember—before all else you are a wife and mother. 120

Nora: I don't believe that any more. I believe that before all else I am a human being, just as you are—or at least that I should try and become one. I know that most people would agree with you, Torvald—and that's what they say in books. But I can no longer be satisfied with what most people say—or what they write in books. I must think things out for myself—get clear about them.

Helmer: Surely your position in your home is clear enough? Have you no sense of religion? Isn't that an infallible guide to you? 130

Nora: But don't you see, Torvald—I don't really know what religion is.

Helmer: Nora! How can you!

Nora: All I know about it is what Pastor Hansen told me when I was confirmed. He taught me what he thought religion was—said it was this and that. As soon as I get away by myself, I shall have to look into that matter too, try and decide whether what he taught me was right—or whether it's right for me, at least. 140

Helmer: A nice way for a young woman to talk! It's unheard of! If religion means nothing to you, I'll appeal to your conscience; you must have some sense of ethics, I suppose? Answer me! Or have you none?

Nora: It's hard for me to answer you, Torvald. I don't think I know—all these things bewilder me. But I do know that I think quite differently from you about them. I've discovered that the law, for instance, is quite different from what I had imagined; but I find it hard to believe it can be right. It seems it's criminal for a woman to try and spare her old, sick, father, or save her husband's life! I can't agree with that. 150

Helmer: You talk like a child. You have no understanding of the society we live in.

Nora: No, I haven't. But I'm going to try and learn. I want to find out which of us is right—society or I.

Helmer: You are ill, Nora; you have a touch of fever; you're quite beside yourself.

Nora: I've never felt so sure—so clear-headed—as I do tonight.

Helmer: "Sure and clear-headed" enough to leave your husband and your children? 160

Nora: Yes.

Helmer: Then there is only one explanation possible.

Nora: What?

Helmer: You don't love me any more.

Nora: No; that is just it.

Helmer: Nora!—What are you saying!

Nora: It makes me so unhappy, Torvald; for you've always been so kind to me. But I can't help it. I don't love you any more. 170

Helmer [mastering himself with difficulty]: You feel "sure and clear-headed" about this too?

Nora: Yes, utterly sure. That's why I can't stay here any longer. . . .

Q **What reasons does Nora give Helmer for leaving him?**

Q **What is Helmer's perception of Nora?**

Realism in the Visual Arts

The Birth of Photography

One of the most significant factors in the development of the materialist mentality was the birth of photography. While a painting or an engraving might bring to life the content of the artist's imagination, a photograph offered an authentic record of a moment vanished in time. Unlike the *camera obscura*, which captured an image only briefly (see chapter 23), the photograph fixed and preserved reality.

Photography—literally "writing with light"—had its beginnings in 1835, when William Henry Fox Talbot

Figure 30.8 JULIA MARGARET CAMERON,
Whisper of the Muse (G. F. Watts and Children), ca. 1865.
Photograph, 10¼ × 8½ in.

(1800–1877) fixed negative images on paper coated with light-sensitive chemicals, a process by which multiple prints might be produced from a single exposure. Slightly earlier, Talbot's French contemporary Louis J. M. Daguerre (1787–1851) had developed a similar process that fixed the image on a polished metal plate. Unlike Talbot's prints (produced from paper negatives), however, Daguerre's images could not be reproduced—each was a one-of-a-kind object. Nevertheless, in the next decades, his more widely publicized and technically improved product, known as a *daguerreotype*, came into vogue throughout Europe and America, where it fulfilled a growing demand for portraits. Gradual improvements in camera lenses and in the chemicals used to develop the visible image hastened the rise of photography as a popular way of recording the physical world with unprecedented accuracy.

Photography presented an obvious challenge to the authority of the artist, who, throughout history, had assumed the role of nature's imitator. But artists were slow to realize the long-range impact of photography—that is, the camera's potential to liberate artists from reproducing the physical "look" of nature. Critics proclaimed that photographs, as authentic facsimiles of the physical world, should serve artists as aids to achieving greater Realism in canvas painting; and many artists did indeed use photographs as factual resources for their compositions. Nevertheless, by mid-century, both Europeans and Americans were using the camera for a wide variety of other purposes: they made topographical studies of exotic geographic sites, recorded architectural monuments, and produced thousands of portraits. Photography provided ordinary people with portrait images that had previously been available only to those who could afford painted

Science and Technology

1835	William H. F. Talbot (English) invents the negative–positive photographic process
1837	Louis J. M. Daguerre (French) uses a copper plate coated with silver to produce the first daguerreotype
1860	production begins on the first Winchester repeating rifle (in America)
1866	explosive dynamite is first produced in Sweden
1888	George Eastman (American) perfects the "Kodak" box camera

likenesses. In the production of portraits, the daguerreotype proved most popular; by 1850, some 100,000 were sold each year in Paris. Such photographs were used as calling cards and to immortalize the faces of notable individuals (see Figure 28.5), as well as those of criminals, whose "mug shots" became a useful tool for the young science of criminology.

Some photographers, such as the British pioneer Julia Margaret Cameron (1815–1879), who began her career at the age of forty-eight, used the camera to recreate the style of Romantic painting. Imitating the effects of the artist's paintbrush, Cameron's moody lighting, shallow depth of field, and long exposure times produced soft-focus portraits that are Romantic in spirit and sentiment (Figure **30.8**). Others used the camera to document the factual reality of their time and place. The French photographer Gaspard-Félix Tournachon, known as Nadar (1820–1910), made vivid portrait studies of such celebrities as George Sand, Berlioz, and Sarah Bernhardt. Nadar was the first to experiment with aerial photography (see Figure 30.13). He also introduced the use of electric light for a series of extraordinary photographs that examined the sewers and catacombs beneath the city of Paris.

Inevitably, nineteenth-century photographs served as social documents: the black-and-white images of poverty-stricken families and ramshackle tenements (see Figure

30.5) produced by Thomas Annan (1829–1887), for instance, record with gritty Realism the notorious slums of nineteenth-century Glasgow, Scotland. Such photographs could easily illustrate the novels of Charles Dickens. In a similar vein, the eyewitness photographs of the American Civil War (1861–1865) produced by Mathew B. Brady (1823–1896) and his staff testify to the importance of the professional photographer as a chronicler of military combat. Brady's 3500 Civil War photographs include mundane scenes of barracks and munitions as well as unflinching views of human carnage (Figure **30.9**). By the end of the century, the Kodak "point and shoot" handheld camera gave vast numbers of ordinary people the freedom to take their own photographic images.

Courbet and French Realist Painting

In painting no less than in literature and photography, Realism came to challenge the Romantic style. The Realist preference for concrete, matter-of-fact depictions of everyday life provided a sober alternative to both the remote, exotic, and heroic imagery of the Romantics and the noble and elevated themes of the Neoclassicists. Obedient to the credo that artists must confront the experiences and appearances of their own time, Realist painters abandoned the nostalgic landscapes and heroic themes of Romantic art in favor of compositions depicting the consequences of industrialization (see Figure 30.3) and the lives of ordinary men and women.

The leading Realist of nineteenth-century French painting was Gustave Courbet (1819–1877). A farmer's son, he was a self-taught artist, an outspoken socialist, and a staunch defender of the Realist cause. "A painter," he protested, "should paint only what he can see." Indeed, most of Courbet's works—portraits, landscapes, and contemporary scenes—remain true to the tangible facts of his immediate vision. With the challenge "Show me an angel and I'll paint one," he taunted both the Romantics and the Neoclassicists. Not angels but ordinary individuals in their actual settings and circumstances interested Courbet.

In *The Stone-Breakers*, Courbet depicted two rural laborers performing the most menial of physical tasks (Figure **30.10**). The painting, which Courbet's friend Proudhon

Figure 30.9 MATHEW B. BRADY or staff, *Dead Confederate Soldier with Gun, Petersburg, Virginia*, 1865. Stereographic photograph using wet collodion and two glass plates, 5 × 5 in. (approx.). The four-year-long American Civil War produced the largest number of casualties of any war in American history. Brady hired staff photographers to assist him in photographing the military campaigns and battles, a project that produced some 3500 photographs but left him bankrupt.

Figure 30.10 GUSTAVE COURBET, *The Stone-Breakers*, 1849. Oil on canvas, 5 ft. 3 in. × 8 ft. 6 in.

called "the first socialist picture," outraged the critics because its subject matter is mundane and its figures are crude, ragged, and totally unidealized. Moreover, the figures were positioned with their backs turned toward the viewer, thus violating, by nineteenth-century standards, the rules of propriety and decorum enshrined in French academic art (see chapter 21). But despite such "violations," Courbet's painting appealed to the masses. In a country whose population was still two-thirds rural and largely poor, the stolid dignity of hard labor was a popular subject.

Courbet's contemporary Jean-François Millet (1814–1875) did not share his reformist zeal; he nevertheless devoted his career to painting the everyday lives of the rural proletariat. His depictions of hardworking farm laborers earned him the title "the peasant painter." In *Gleaners* (see Figure **30.1**), three peasant women pursue the menial task of gathering the bits of grain left over after the harvest. Delineated with ennobling simplicity, these stoop-laborers are as ordinary and anonymous as Courbet's stone-breakers, but, set against a broad and ennobling landscape, they appear dignified and graceful. While Courbet's scene has the "random" look of a snapshot, Millet's composition, in which the distant haystacks subtly echo the curved backs of the workers, appears more formal and contrived. Against Courbet's undiluted Realism, Millet's perception seems somewhat Romanticized.

A landmark even in its own time, *Gleaners* became a symbol of the dignity of hard work, a nostalgic reminder of a way of life quickly disappearing before encroaching industrialization. As such, it was copied and mass-produced in numerous engraved editions. Courbet, however, remained brutally loyal to nature and the mundane world; he knew that the carefree peasant was an idyllic stereotype that existed not in real life, but rather in the urban imagination. He would have agreed with his contemporary, the British novelist George Eliot (Mary Ann Evans), that "no one who is well acquainted with the English peasantry can pronounce them merry."

Courbet's most daring record of ordinary life was his monumental *Burial at Ornans* (see LOOKING INTO, Figure **30.11**). The huge canvas (over 10 × 21 feet) consists of fifty-two life-sized figures disposed informally around the edges of a freshly dug grave. Paintings of this size normally depicted historical or religious subjects. Here, however, inspired by the funeral of his great uncle, Courbet depicts the plain-looking (and even homely) townspeople of Ornans. When the painting was rejected by the Universal Exhibition of 1855, Courbet rented a space near the exhibition grounds, put up a tent, and displayed the *Burial* along with thirty-eight of his paintings. He called the space "The Pavilion of Realism." For this exhibition, the first one-man show in history, Courbet charged a small admission fee.

Daumier's Social Realism

The French artist Honoré Daumier (1808–1879) left the world a detailed record of the social life of his time. He had no formal academic education, but his earliest training was in **lithography**—a printmaking process created by drawing

Courbet's *Burial at Ornans*

Figure 30.11 GUSTAVE COURBET, *Burial at Ornans*, 1849–1850. Oil on canvas, 10 ft. 3 in. × 21 ft. 9 in. For the introduction to the catalogue that accompanied his one-man show, Courbet wrote a Realist Manifesto that stated his aim "to translate the customs, the ideas, and the appearance" of his epoch according to his own estimation. A leading critic claimed that Courbet had depicted "the modern bourgeois in all his ridiculousness, ugliness, and beauty."

In this ambitious painting, Courbet documented an actual event that took place in his hometown. He minimized the ritual aspects of death and disposal, and the display of pomp and ceremony traditional to Western representations of Christian burial. Here, the kneeling gravedigger and the attendant dog are as important to the picture as the priest and his retinue. And the mourners, while crowded together, play a more prominent role in the composition than the deceased. With the objectivity of a camera eye, Courbet banished from his painting all sentimentality and artifice.

limestone cliffs of Ornans

sacristan

crucifix and bearer

self-portrait of Courbet smoking a pipe

Courbet's father, wearing a tall, silk hat

Courbet's recently deceased grandfather

pallbearers (friends of Courbet)

coffin covered with white shroud bearing crossbones

altar boys

Courbet's three sisters

Mayor of Ornans, Claude-Hélène-Prosper Teste

Hippolyte Proudhon, a prominent local lawyer

local priest, the Abbé Benjamin Bonnet

two lay church officials

open grave

gravedigger, Antoine-Joseph Cassard

Figure 30.12 Lithography is a method of making prints from a flat surface; it is also called planography. An image is first drawn or painted with an oil-based lithographic crayon or pencil on a smooth limestone surface. The surface is wiped with water, which will not stick to the applied areas of greasy lithographic ink because oil and water do not mix. The greasy areas resist the water and are thus exposed. The surface is then rolled with printing ink, which adheres only to the parts drawn in the oil-based medium. Dampened paper is placed over the stone, and a special flatbed press rubs the back of the paper, transferring the work from the stone to the covering sheet.

Figure 30.13 **HONORÉ DAUMIER**, *Nadar Raising Photography to the Heights of Art*, 1862. Lithograph, 10¾ × 8¾ in. The balloonist, photographer, draftsman, and journalist Gaspard-Félix Tournachon, called Nadar, took his first photograph from a balloon. The aerial balloon, built in 1863, inspired some of the adventure novels of the science-fiction writer Jules Verne (see chapter 37). Nadar also pioneered the use of artificial lighting, by which he was able to photograph the catacombs of Paris.

on a stone plate (Figure **30.12**). Lithography, a product of nineteenth-century print technology, was a cheap and popular means of providing illustrations for newspapers, magazines, and books.

Daumier produced over 4000 lithographs, often turning out two or three per week for various Paris newspapers and journals. For his subject matter, he turned directly to the world around him: the streets of Paris, the theater, the law courts. The advancing (and often jarring) technology of modern life also attracted Daumier's interest: pioneer experiments in aerial photography (Figure **30.13**), the telegraph, the sewing machine, the repeating rifle, the railroad, and urban renewal projects that included widening the streets of Paris. But Daumier did not simply depict the facts of modern life; he frequently ridiculed them. Skeptical as to whether new technology and social progress could radically alter the human condition, he drew attention to characteristic human weaknesses, from the all too familiar complacency and greed of self-serving political figures to the pretensions of the *nouveaux riches*.

One of the popular institutions mocked by Daumier was the French *Salon* (Figure **30.14**). The *Salon de Paris* originated with the Royal Academy of Painting and Sculpture, founded in 1648 (see chapter 21). Exhibiting work at the *Salon* was a sign of royal favor and a sure path to success. Held annually during the eighteenth century at the palace of the Louvre, the juried exhibitions were public events that ran for weeks, attracting huge crowds, including newly minted art critics. Paintings were exhibited from floor to ceiling, taking up all the available space, and printed catalogues accompanied the exhibition. By the mid-nineteenth century, such annual government-sponsored juried exhibitions, held in large commercial halls, had become symbols of entrenched, academic taste. Daumier's lithographs satirized the *Salon* as a "grand occasion" attended by hordes of gaping urbanites.

The ancestors of modern-day political cartoons, Daumier's lithographs conveyed his bitter opposition to the monarchy, political corruption, and profiteering. Such criticism courted danger, especially since in mid-nineteenth-century France it was illegal to caricature individuals publicly without first obtaining their permission. Following the publication of his lithograph of 1831, which depicted the French king Louis Philippe as an obese Gargantua atop a commode/throne from which he defecated bags of gold, Daumier spent six months in jail.

Primarily a graphic artist, Daumier completed fewer than three hundred paintings. In *The Third-Class Carriage*, he

Science and Technology

1798	Aloys Senefelder (Bavarian) develops lithography
1822	William Church (American) patents an automatic typesetting machine
1844	wood-pulp production provides cheap paper for newspapers and periodicals

LE PUBLIC DU SALON

10

Maison Martinet, rVivienne 41 et 11 r.du Coq S^t. Honoré. Paris.   Imp.Ch.Trinocq Cour des Miracles, 9. Paris.

Un jour où l'on ne paye pas. __Vingt_cinq degrés de chaleur.

Figure 30.14 HONORÉ DAUMIER, *Free Admission Day—Twenty-Five Degree Heat*, from the series "Le Public du Salon," published in *Le Charivari* (May 17, 1852), p. 10. Lithograph, 11⅛ × 8⅝ in. The inscription reads "A day when one does not pay. Twenty-five degree [Celsius] heat."

captured on canvas the shabby monotony of nineteenth-century lower-class railway travel (Figure **30.15**). The part of the European train in which tickets were the least expensive was also, of course, the least comfortable: it lacked glass windows (hence was subject to more than average amounts of smoke, cinders, and clatter) and was equipped with hard wooden benches rather than cushioned seats. Three generations of poor folk—an elderly woman, a younger woman, and her children—occupy the foreground of Daumier's painting. Their lumpish bodies suggest weariness and futility, yet they convey a humble dignity reminiscent of Rembrandt's figures (see chapter 22). Dark and loosely sketched oil glazes underscore the mood of cheerless resignation. Daumier produced a forthright image of common humanity in a contemporary urban setting.

The Scandalous Realism of Manet

The French painter Edouard Manet (1832–1883) presented an unsettling challenge to the world of art. A native Parisian who chose painting over a career in law, Manet was

Figure 30.15 HONORÉ DAUMIER, *The Third-Class Carriage*, ca. 1862. Oil on canvas, 25¾ × 35½ in. A lower-class family, consisting of a grandmother, her daughter, and two children, are depicted with the candor and immediacy that typifies Daumier's on-the-spot visual records of Parisian life.

Figure 30.16 EDOUARD MANET, *Déjeuner sur l'herbe*, 1863. Oil on canvas, 7 ft. × 8 ft. 10 in. The still life in the lower left testifies to Manet's technical skills as a painter.

an admirer of the art of the old masters. He was equally enthralled by contemporary life, especially the middle-class pleasures of his fellow Parisians. In 1863, he shocked the public with a large, brilliantly painted canvas entitled *Déjeuner sur l'herbe* (*Luncheon on the Grass*; Figure **30.16**). This work shows a nude woman enjoying a picnic lunch

Figure 30.17 TITIAN (begun by Giorgione), *Pastoral Concert*, ca. 1505. Oil on canvas, 3 ft. 7¼ in. × 4 ft. 6¼ in.

with two fully clothed male companions, while a second, partially clothed woman bathes in a nearby stream.

From a historical perspective, Manet's subject matter—the female nude in a landscape—was familiar to artists, as well as to ordinary art patrons. Clearly, *Déjeuner* looks back to such Renaissance works as Titian's *Pastoral Concert* (Figure **30.17**). Its three central figures are drawn from a sixteenth-century engraving (Figure **30.18**) based on a Renaissance tapestry, itself derived from a lost painting by Raphael. The representation of the female nude was considered the ultimate subject in antiquity, and it remained so in academic art (see chapters 21 and 26). Her identity in Western art history was invariably that of a mythological or allegorical figure, such as Venus or Charity; however, Manet's nude appears as nothing more than an ordinary, naked woman. His figures are neither woodland nymphs nor Olympian gods; rather, they are the artist's favorite model (Victorine Meurent), and his future brother-in-law (the reclining male figure).

By taking a Classical subject and recasting it in modern terms, Manet violated academic tradition. And by picturing the female nude (brazenly staring out at the viewer) in a contemporary setting occupied by clothed men, he offended public morality. In "updating" traditional imagery with such off-hand, in-your-face immediacy, Manet was making a statement that—as with *Madame*

Figure 30.18 MARCANTONIO RAIMONDI, detail from *The Judgment of Paris*, ca. 1520. Engraving after Raphael tapestry.

Bovary—targeted the degeneracy of French society. Yet, like Flaubert, who combined authenticity of detail and an impersonal narrative style, the artist took a neutral stance that presented the subject with cool objectivity. It is no surprise that the jury of the Royal Academy rejected *Déjeuner*, refusing to hang it in the *Salon* exhibition of 1863.

Nevertheless, that same year it was displayed in an alternate venue: the *Salon des Refusés*, a landmark exhibition of rejected paintings, authorized by the French head of state in response to public agitation against the tyranny of the Academy.

No sooner was Manet's painting hung in public than visitors tried to poke holes in the canvas, and critics launched attacks on its coarse "improprieties." *Déjeuner* was pronounced scandalous. "The nude does not have a good figure," wrote one journalist, "and one cannot imagine anything uglier than the man stretched out beside her, who has not even thought of removing, out of doors, his horrible padded cap." While Manet's paintings met with repeated criticism, they were defended by his good friend Emile Zola, who penned a short biography of the artist in 1867 (see Figure 30.7). Zola praised Manet's works as "simple and direct translations of reality," observing with some acuity: "He treats figure paintings as the academic painter treats still lifes . . . He neither sings nor philosophizes. He paints, and that is all."

In a second painting of 1863, *Olympia*, Manet again "debased" a traditional subject: the reclining nude (Figure **30.19**). Lacking the subtle allure of a Titian Venus (see Figure 17.39) or an Ingres odalisque (see Figure 26.27), the short, stocky nude (Victorine Meurent again) looks boldly at the viewer. Her satin slippers, the black ribbon at her throat, and other provocative details (such as the black

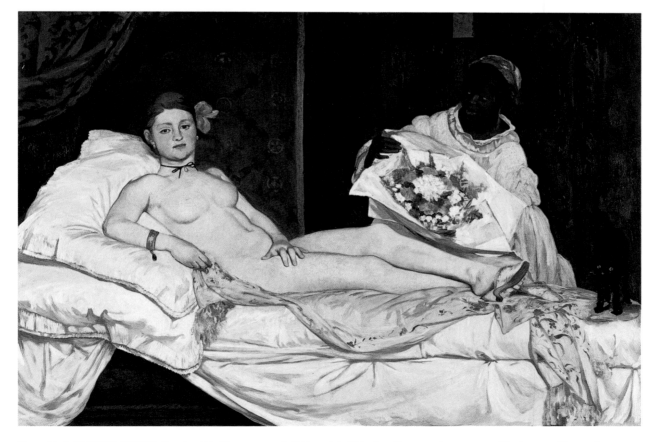

Figure 30.19 EDOUARD MANET, *Olympia*, 1863. Oil on canvas, 4 ft. 3¼ in. × 6 ft. 2¾ in. A maid presents the courtesan with a bouquet of flowers from an admirer, who, based on the startled response of the black cat, may have just entered the room. Commenting on the unmodulated flatness of the nude figure, Courbet compared Olympia to the Queen of Spades in a deck of playing cards.

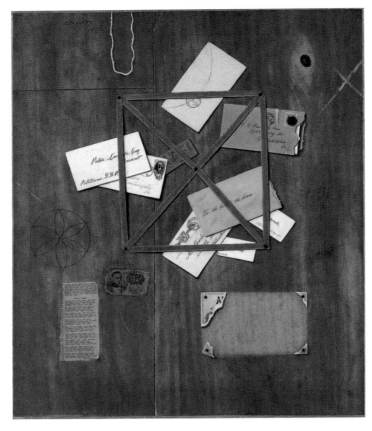

Figure 30.20 WILLIAM MICHAEL HARNETT, *The Artist's Letter Rack*, 1879. Oil on canvas, 30 × 25 in.

"alley cat," a symbol of sexuality) distinguish her as a courtesan—a high-class prostitute. Manet's urban contemporaries were not blind to this fact, but the critics were unsparingly brutal. One journalist called Olympia "a sort of female gorilla" and warned: "Truly, young girls and women about to become mothers would do well, if they are wise, to run away from this spectacle." Like Flaubert's *Madame Bovary* or Zola's *Nana*, Manet's *Olympia* desentimentalized the female image. By rendering the ideal in commonplace terms, he not only offended public taste, but also challenged the traditional view of art as the bearer of noble themes.

Manet also violated academic convention by employing new painting techniques. Imitating current photographic practice, he bathed his figures in bright light and, using a minimum of shading, flattened forms in a manner inspired by Japanese prints (see Figure 31.13). His practice of eliminating half-tones and laying on fresh, opaque colors (instead of building up form by means of thin, transparent glazes) anticipated Impressionism, a style he embraced later in his career.

Realism in American Painting

Although most American artists received their training in European art schools, their taste for Realism seems to have sprung from a native affection for the factual and the material aspects of their immediate surroundings. In the late nineteenth century, an era of gross materialism known as the Gilded Age, America produced

an extraordinary number of first-rate Realist painters. These individuals explored a wide variety of subjects, from still life and portraiture to landscape and genre painting. Like such literary giants as Mark Twain, American Realist painters fused keen observation with remarkable descriptive skills.

One of the most talented of the American Realists was William M. Harnett (1848–1892), a still-life painter and a master of *trompe l'oeil* ("fool the eye") illusionism. Working in the tradition of seventeenth-century Dutch masters, Harnett recorded mundane objects with such hair-fine precision that some of them—letters, newspaper clippings, and calling cards—seem to be pasted on the canvas (Figure **30.20**).

A master of early nineteenth-century portraiture and the founder of America's first museum (in Philadelphia), Charles Willson Peale (1741–1827) is renowned for his skillful likenesses of distinguished public figures, such as George Washington, Thomas Jefferson, and Andrew Jackson. But one of his most intriguing portraits is that of the African-American Yarrow Mamout (Figure **30.21**). A West African slave freed by his American owner after forty-five years of indenture, Mamout achieved prosperity and ultimately settled in his own home in Washington, D.C. Peale was seventy-seven years of age when he painted the eighty-three-year-old "Muhammad Yaro" (his African name). In his diary, the artist described his sitter as a cheerful man, notable for his "industry, frugality, and sobriety."

Figure 30.21 CHARLES WILLSON PEALE, *Portrait of Yarrow Mamout (Muhammad Yaro)*, 1819. Oil on canvas, 24 × 20 in. Mamout is pictured wearing the *kufic*, a brimless hat traditionally worn by natives of West Africa.

In 1889, Eakins accepted a commission offered by students at the University of Pennsylvania's School of Medicine to paint a portrait commemorating the retirement of one of their favorite professors. Eakins suggested a clinic scene that would include the surgeon's collaborators and class members. In drafting the composition, he surely had in mind Rembrandt's famous group portrait *The Anatomy Lesson of Dr. Nicolaes Tulp* (Figure **30.23**). Eakins' painting (Figure **30.22**) shares Rembrandt's dramatic staging, use of light to illuminate figures in darkened space, and dedication to realistic detail. Both paintings communicate a fresh and stubbornly precise record of the natural world.

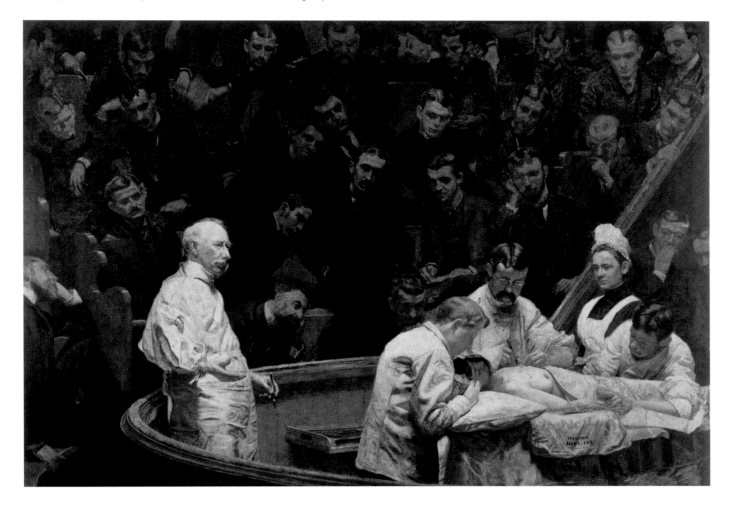

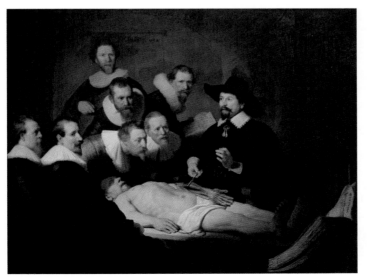

Figure 30.22 THOMAS EAKINS, *The Agnew Clinic*, 1889. Oil on canvas, 6 ft. 2½ in. × 10 ft. 10½ in. This wall-sized painting is the largest of Eakins' canvases. At the far right is the likeness of Eakins himself, painted by his wife, Susan.

Figure 30.23 REMBRANDT VAN RIJN, *The Anatomy Lesson of Dr. Nicolaes Tulp*, 1632. Oil on canvas, 5 ft. 3⅜ in. × 7 ft. 1¼ in.

Figure 30.24 HENRY OSSAWA TANNER, *The Banjo Lesson*, ca. 1893. Oil on canvas, 49 × 35½ in.

Walt Whitman (see Figure 27.12). Like most nineteenth-century American artists, Eakins received his training in European art schools, but he ultimately emerged as a painter of the American scene and as an influential art instructor in his own right. At the Pennsylvania Academy of Fine Arts, he was criticized for his insistence on working from nude models. After ten years of teaching at the Academy (1876–1886), he was forced to resign for removing the loincloth of a male model in a class that included female students.

Eakins was among the first artists to choose subjects from the world of sports, such as boxing and boating. A photographer of some note, he used the camera to collect visual data for his paintings. He was also among the first artists to use his own photographs as the basis for true-to-life pictorial compositions, and he encouraged his students to follow suit.

Eakins' fascination with scientific anatomy—he dissected cadavers at Jefferson Medical College in Philadelphia—led him to produce some unorthodox representations of medical training and practice. One of his most notable canvases, *The Agnew Clinic* (see Figure 30.22), is a dispassionate view of a hospital amphitheater in which the surgeon and professor P. Hayes Agnew lectures to students on the subject of the mastectomy that is being performed under his supervision.

Eakins' student Henry Ossawa Tanner (1859–1937)—like many other African-American artists—found Paris more receptive than America. A talented genre painter, landscape artist, and photographer, Tanner brought to his work a concern for simple, everyday events as practiced by working-class people. In *The Banjo Lesson*, he depicts an intimate domestic scene in which a young boy receives musical instruction from his grandfather (Figure **30.24**). A fine technician and a fluent colorist, Tanner showed his work regularly in Paris. In 1909, he was elected to the National Academy of Design, New York.

His portrait—the earliest known painting of a Muslim in American history—captures these qualities as well as Mamout's confident and resilient spirit.

In the generation following Peale, the Philadelphia artist Thomas Eakins (1844–1916) mastered the art of producing uncompromising likenesses such as that of the poet

American Realists were keenly aware of the new art of photography; some, like Tanner and Eakins, were themselves fine photographers. But they were also indebted to the world of journalism, which assumed increasing importance in transmitting literate culture. Winslow Homer (1836–1910) began his career as a newspaper illustrator and a reporter for the New York magazine *Harper's Weekly*. The first professional artist to serve

Figure 30.25 WINSLOW HOMER, *The War for the Union: A Bayonet Charge*, published in *Harper's Weekly*, July 12, 1862. Wood engraving, 13⅝ × 20⅝ in.

Figure 30.26 WINSLOW HOMER, *The Gulf Stream*, 1899. Oil on canvas, 2 ft. 4⅛ in. × 4 ft. 1⅛ in. Homer added the fully rigged sailing ship at the horizon on the left some time after the painting was exhibited.

as a war correspondent, he produced on-the-scene documentary paintings and drawings of the American Civil War, which *Harper's* converted to wood-engraved illustrations (Figure **30.25**). Although Homer often generalized the facts of the events he actually witnessed, he neither moralized nor allegorized his subjects (as did, for instance, Goya or Delacroix). His talent for graphic selectivity and dramatic concentration rivaled that of America's first war photographer, Mathew Brady (see Figure 30.9).

Apart from two trips to Europe, Homer spent most of his life in New England, where he painted subjects that were both ordinary and typically American. Scenes of hunting and fishing reveal his deep affection for nature, while his many genre paintings reflect a fascination with the activities of American women and children.

Homer was interested in the role of African-Americans in contemporary culture, but critical of visual representations that portrayed America's slaves as merry and content. One of his most provocative paintings, *The Gulf Stream*, shows a black man adrift in a rudderless boat surrounded by shark-filled waters that are whipped by the winds of an impending tornado (Figure **30.26**). While realistic in execution, the painting may be interpreted as a metaphor for the isolation and plight of black Americans in the decades following the Civil War. Homer shared with earlier nineteenth-century figures, including Turner, Melville, and Géricault, an almost obsessive interest in the individual's life-and-death struggle with the sea. However, compared (for instance) with Géricault's theatrical rendering of man against nature in *The Raft of the "Medusa"* (see Figure 29.5), which he probably saw in Paris, Homer's painting is a matter-of-fact study of human resignation in

the face of deadly peril. As with many publicly displayed nineteenth-century paintings, it provoked immediate critical response. Answering the critics, Eakins wryly replied: "The criticisms of *The Gulf Stream* by old women and others are noted. You may inform these people that the Negro did not starve to death, he was not eaten by the sharks, the water spout did not hit him, and he was rescued by a passing ship . . ."

American audiences loved their Realist painters, but, occasionally, critics voiced mixed feelings. The American novelist Henry James (1843–1916), whose novels probed the differences between European and American character, assessed what he called Homer's "perfect realism" with these words:

He is almost barbarously simple, and, to our eye, he is horribly ugly; but there is nevertheless something one likes about him. What is it? For ourselves, it is not his subjects. We frankly confess that we detest his subjects—his barren plank fences, his glaring, bald, blue skies, his big, dreary, vacant lots of meadows, his freckled, straight-haired Yankee urchins, his flat-breasted maidens, suggestive of a dish of rural doughnuts and pie, his calico sun-bonnets, his flannel shirts, his cowhide boots. He has chosen the least pictorial features of the least pictorial range of scenery and civilization; he has resolutely treated them as if they were pictorial, as if they were every inch as good as Capri or Tangiers; and, to reward his audacity, he has incontestably succeeded. It . . . is a proof that if you will only be doggedly literal, though you may often be unpleasing, you will at least have a stamp of your own.

Late Nineteenth-Century Architecture

In the nineteenth century, the history of architecture was revolutionized by the use of an exciting new structural medium: cast iron. Providing strength without bulk, cast iron allowed architects to span broader widths and raise structures to greater heights than achieved by traditional stone masonry. Although cast iron would change the history of architecture more dramatically than any advance in technology since the Roman invention of concrete, European architects were slow to realize its potential.

Science and Technology

1779	the first cast-iron bridge is built in England
1851	the first international industrial exposition opens in London
1856	Henry Bessemer (British) perfects the process for producing inexpensive steel
1857	E. G. Otis (American) installs the first safety elevator
1863	the first "subway" (the London Underground) begins operation

Figure 30.27 JOSEPH PAXTON, interior of Crystal Palace, 1851. Cast- and wrought-iron and glass, length 1851 ft. Assembled entirely on site from prefabricated components, the Crystal Palace housed some 14,000 exhibitions. The three-story structure, illuminated mainly by natural light, anticipated today's modern shopping malls.

In England, where John Nash had used cast iron in 1815 as the structural frame for the Brighton Pavilion (see Figure 29.14), engineers did not begin construction on the first cast-iron suspension bridge until 1836; and not until mid-century was iron used as skeletal support for mills, warehouses, and railroad stations.

The innovator in the use of iron for public buildings was, in fact, not an architect but a distinguished horticulturalist and greenhouse designer, Joseph Paxton (1801–1865). Paxton's Crystal Palace (Figure **30.27**), erected for the Great Exhibition in London in 1851, was the world's first prefabricated building and the forerunner of the "functional" steel and glass architecture of the twentieth century. Consisting entirely of cast- and wrought-iron girders and 18,000 panes of glass, and erected in only nine months, the 1851-foot-long structure—its length a symbolic reference to the year of the exhibition—resembled a gigantic greenhouse. Light entered through its transparent walls and air filtered in through louvered windows. Thousands flocked to see the Crystal Palace; yet most European architects found the glass and iron structure bizarre. Although heroic in both size and conception, it had almost no immediate impact on European architecture. Dismantled after the Great Exhibition and moved to a new site, however, it was hailed as a masterpiece of prefabrication and portability decades before it burned to the ground in 1936.

Like the Crystal Palace, the Eiffel Tower (Figure **30.28**) originated as a novelty, but it soon became emblematic of early Modernism. The viewing tower constructed by the engineer Gustave Eiffel (1832–1923) for the Paris World Exhibition of 1889 is, in essence, a tall (1063-foot-high) cast-iron skeleton equipped with elevators that offer visitors magnificent aerial views of Paris. Aesthetically, the tower linked the architectural traditions of the past with those of the future: its sweeping curves, delicate tracery, and dramatic verticality recall the glories of the Gothic cathedral, while its majestic ironwork anticipates the austere abstractions of International Style architecture (see chapter 32). Condemned as a visual monstrosity when it was first erected, the Eiffel Tower emerged as a positive symbol of the soaring confidence of the industrial age. This landmark of heroic materialism remained for four decades (until the advent of the American skyscraper) the tallest structure in the world.

In an age of advancing industrialization, ornamental structures such as the Crystal Palace and the Eiffel Tower gave way to functional ones. Inevitably, the skyscraper would become the prime architectural expression of modern corporate power and the urban scene. By 1850, there were seven American cities with more than 100,000 inhabitants, and before 1900 the populations of at least three of these—New York, Philadelphia, and Chicago—swelled as a result of the thousands of immigrants who came to live and work in the metropolitan community. The physical

Figure 30.28 GUSTAVE EIFFEL, Eiffel Tower, Paris, 1889. Wrought iron on a reinforced concrete base, original height 1063 ft.

Figure 30.29 LOUIS HENRY SULLIVAN and **DANKMAR ADLER**, Guaranty Building, Buffalo, New York, 1894–1895. Steel frame.

than cast iron, steel used as a frame could carry the entire weight of a structure, thus eliminating the need for solid weight-bearing masonry walls. Steel made possible a whole new concept of building design characterized by lighter materials, flat roofs, and large windows. In 1868, the six-story Equitable Life Insurance Building in New York City was the first office structure to install an electric elevator. By the 1880s, architects and engineers united the new steel frame with the elevator to raise structures more than ten stories. William Le Baron Jenney (1832–1907) built the first all-steel-frame skyscraper, the Home Insurance Building in Chicago, which, ironically, hides its metal skeleton beneath a traditional-looking brick and masonry façade. It fell to his successor Louis Henry Sullivan (1856–1924) to design multistory buildings, such as the Guaranty Building in Buffalo (Figure **30.29**), whose exteriors proudly reflect the structural simplicity of their steel frames. "Form should follow function," Sullivan insisted. Within decades, the American skyscraper became an icon of modern urban culture.

Nineteenth-century steel and cast-iron technology also contributed to the construction of bridges. In 1870, work began on the first steel-wire suspension bridge in the United States: the Brooklyn Bridge (Figure **30.30**). Designed by John Augustus Roebling (1806–1869), who had earlier engineered bridges in Pennsylvania, Ohio, and Texas, the Brooklyn Bridge (upon its completion in 1883) would be the largest suspension bridge in the world. Its main span, which crosses the East River between Manhattan and Brooklyn, measures some 1600 feet. This celebrated bridge reflects the marriage of modern steel technology and Neo-Gothic design, evident in the elegant granite and limestone arches.

Realism in Music

In Italian opera of the late nineteenth century, a movement called *verismo* (literally, "truth-ism," but more generally "Realism") paralleled the Realist style in literature and art. Realist composers rejected the heroic characters of Romantic grand opera and presented the problems and conflicts of people in familiar and everyday—if somewhat melodramatic—situations. The foremost "verist" was the Italian composer Giacomo Puccini (1858–1924).

Puccini's *La Bohème*, the tragic love story of young artists (called "bohemians" for their unconventional lifestyles) in the Latin Quarter of Paris, was based on a nineteenth-century novel called *Scenes of Bohemian Life*. The colorful orchestration and powerfully melodic arias of *La Bohème* evoke the joys and sorrows of true-to-life characters. While this poignant musical drama was received coldly at its premiere in 1897, *La Bohème* has become one of the best loved of nineteenth-century operas.

Another of Puccini's operas, *Madame Butterfly*, offered European audiences a timely, if moralizing, view of the Western presence in Asia and one that personalized the clash of radically different cultures. The story, which takes place in Nagasaki in the years following the reopening of Japanese ports to the West, begins with the wedding of a young United States navy lieutenant to a fifteen-year-old

character of the premodern city, whose buildings were no more than four stories high, changed enormously with the construction of skyscrapers.

Multistoried vertical buildings were made possible by the advancing technology of steel, a medium that was perfected in 1856. Lighter, stronger, and more resilient

Figure 30.30 JOHN AUGUSTUS ROEBLING and **WASHINGTON AUGUSTUS ROEBLING**, Brooklyn Bridge, New York, 1869–1883. Currier and Ives print, 1877, 25¾ × 37 in.

geisha (a Japanese girl trained as a social companion to men) known as "Butterfly." The American is soon forced to leave with his fleet, while for three years Butterfly, now the mother of his son, faithfully awaits his return. When, finally, he arrives (accompanied by his new American bride) only to claim the child, the grief-stricken Butterfly takes the only honorable path available to her: she commits suicide. This tragic tale, which had appeared as a novel, a play, and a magazine story, was based on a true incident. Set to some of Puccini's most lyrical music for voice and orchestra, *Madame Butterfly* reflects the composer's fascination with Japanese culture, a fascination most evident in his poetic characterization of the delicate Butterfly. While neither the story nor the music of the opera is authentically Japanese, its *verismo* lies in its frank (although poignant) account of the bitter consequences that often accompanied the meeting of East and West.

Chronology

1830	French conquest of Algeria
1839–1850	Opium Wars in China
1848	antigovernment revolutions in France and Central Europe
1868	beginning of Meiji rule in Japan
1860	unification of Italy
1861–1865	United States Civil War
1869	completion of the U.S. transcontinental railroad
1871	unification of Germany

The Global Dominion of the West

- During the second half of the nineteenth century, as Western industrialization accelerated, Realism came to rival Romanticism both as a style and as an attitude of mind.
- Western industrialization and the materialistic values with which it was allied precipitated imperialism and colonialism, both of which had a shaping influence on the non-Western world. The heavy hand of Western imperialism in some parts of Africa, Asia, and in the Middle East had a crippling effect on independent growth and productivity.

Nineteenth-Century Social Theory

- The ideologies of liberalism, conservatism, utilitarianism, and socialism offered varying solutions to nineteenth-century social and economic inequities. Marxist communism called for violent proletarian revolution that would end private ownership of the means of economic production.
- The leading proponent of liberalism, John Stuart Mill, defended the exercise of individual liberty as protected by the state.
- Mill's opposition to the subordination of women gave strong support to nineteenth-century movements for women's rights.

Realism in Literature

- In literature, Realism emerged as a style concerned with recording contemporary subject matter in true-to-life terms.
- Such novelists as Dickens in England, Dostoevsky and Tolstoy in Russia, Flaubert and Zola in France, and Twain and Chopin in America described contemporary social conditions sympathetically and with fidelity to detail.
- Flaubert and Chopin provided alternatives to Romantic idealism in their realistic characterizations of female figures.
- Zola's naturalistic novels pictured human beings as determined by hereditary and sociological factors, while Ibsen's fearless portrayal of class and gender opened a new chapter in modern drama.

Realism in the Visual Arts

- By the mid-nineteenth century the camera was used to document all aspects of contemporary life as well as to provide artists with detailed visual data.
- In painting, Courbet led the Realist movement with canvases depicting the activities of humble and commonplace men and women. Daumier employed the new technique of lithography to show his deep concern for political and social conditions in rapidly modernizing France.

- With the landmark paintings *Déjeuner sur l'herbe* and *Olympia*, Edouard Manet shocked public taste by modernizing Classical subjects and violating conventional painting techniques.
- American Realism is best represented by the *trompe l'oeil* paintings of William M. Harnett and the down-to-earth subjects of Thomas Eakins and Winslow Homer.

Late Nineteenth-Century Architecture

- Paxton's Crystal Palace, the world's first prefabricated cast-iron structure, offered a prophetic glimpse into the decades that would produce steel-framed skyscrapers.
- In an age of advancing industrialization, ornamental structures such as the Crystal Palace and the Eiffel Tower gave way to functional ones. Inevitably, the skyscraper would become the prime architectural expression of modern corporate power and the urban scene.

Realism in Music

- *Verismo* opera departed from Romantic tradition by seeking to capture the lives of men and women with a truth to nature comparable to that of Realist novels and paintings.
- In the opera *Madame Butterfly*, the Italian "verist" Giacomo Puccini presented a timely view of America's imperialistic presence in Asia.

Glossary

capitalist one who provides investment capital in economic ventures

entrepreneur one who organizes, manages, and assumes the risks of a business

lithography a printmaking process created by drawing on a stone plate; see Figure 30.12

proletariat a collective term describing industrial workers who lack their own means of production and hence sell their labor to live

verismo (Italian, "realism") a type of late nineteenth-century opera that presents a realistic picture of life, instead of a story based in myth, legend, or ancient history

The Move Toward Modernism

ca. 1875–1900

"Is not the nineteenth century . . . a century of decadence?"
Nietzsche

Figure 31.1 PIERRE-AUGUSTE RENOIR, *Le Moulin de la Galette*, 1876. Oil on canvas, 4 ft. 3½ in. × 5 ft. 9 in. Montmartre, the semirural working-class district of Paris, was not incorporated into the city limits until 1860. The Moulin ("mill") marked the spot of one of Montmartre's famous old windmills. Galettes, that is, buckwheat pancakes, were a specialty of the house. Dining, dancing, and enjoying the pleasures of urban life were among the favorite subjects of Renoir and the French Impressionists.

During the last quarter of the nineteenth century, France emerged as the center of Western artistic production. Paris became the melting pot for artists and intellectuals, composers and journalists. London and Paris hosted World's Fairs that brought the arts and cultures of Japan, Africa, and Oceania to the attention of astonished Westerners. In an era of relative world peace and urban prosperity, Western artists were preoccupied with the pleasures of life and the fleeting world of the senses. They initiated styles—Symbolism, Impressionism, and Postimpressionism—that neither idealized the world nor described it literally. Much of their art was driven by aesthetic principles that—similar to music—communicated no specific meaning, but, rather, evoked feeling by way of pure form and color. Their goals were described by Walter Pater in 1868 with the slogan *L'art pour l'art*, "art for art's sake."

Late nineteenth-century science and technology helped to drive this new approach in the arts. The last decades of the century saw the invention of synthetic oil paints available in portable tubes.

In 1873, the British physicist James Clerk Maxwell (1831–1879) published his *Treatise on Electricity and Magnetism*, which explained that light waves consisting of electromagnetic particles produced radiant energy. In 1879, after numerous failures, the American inventor Thomas Edison (1847–1931) moved beyond scientific theory to create the first efficient incandescent light bulb. Edison's light bulb provided a sharper perception of reality that—along with the camera—helped to shatter the world of romantic illusion. By the year 1880, the telephone transported the human voice over thousands of miles. In the late 1880s, Edison developed the technique of moving pictures. The invention of the internal combustion engine led to the production of automobiles in the 1890s, a decade that also witnessed the invention of the X-ray and the genesis of radiotelegraphy. Such technology accelerated the tempo of life and drew attention to the role of the senses in defining experience.

Late Nineteenth-Century Thought

Nietzsche's New Morality

The most provocative thinker of the late nineteenth century was the German philosopher and poet Friedrich Wilhelm Nietzsche (1844–1900). Nietzsche was a Classical philologist, a professor of Greek at the university of Basle, and the author of such notable works as *The Birth of Tragedy* (1872), *Thus Spoke Zarathustra* (1883–1892), and *On the Genealogy of Morals* (1887). In these, as in his shorter pieces, Nietzsche voiced the sentiments of the radical moralist. Deeply critical of his own time, he called for a revision of traditional values. He rejected organized religion, attacking Christianity and other institutionalized religions as contributors to the formation of a "slave morality." He was equally critical of democratic institutions, which he saw as the embodiment of rule by mass mediocrity. His goal for humanity was the emergence of a "superman" (*Übermensch*), whose singular vision and courage would, in his view, produce a "master" morality.

Nietzsche did not launch his ideas in the form of a well-reasoned philosophic system, but rather as aphorisms, maxims, and expostulations whose visceral force bear out his claim that he wrote "with his blood." Reflecting the spiritual cynicism of the late nineteenth century, he asked: "Is man merely a mistake of God's? Or God merely a mistake of man's?"

Nietzsche shared with Dostoevsky the view that European materialism had led inevitably to decadence and decline. In *The Antichrist*, published in 1888—shortly before Nietzsche became insane (possibly as a result of syphilis)—he wrote:

Mankind does not represent a development toward something better or stronger or higher in the sense accepted today. "Progress" is merely a modern idea, that is, a false ideal. The European of today is vastly inferior in value to the European of the Renaissance: further development is altogether not according to any necessity in the direction of elevation, enhancement, or strength.

The following readings demonstrate Nietzsche's incisive imagination and caustic wit. The first, taken from *The Gay Science* (1882) and entitled "The Madman," is a parable that harnesses Nietzsche's iconoclasm to his gift for prophecy. The others, excerpted from *Twilight of the Idols* (or *How One Philosophizes with a Hammer*, 1888), address the fragile relationship between art and morality and the "art for art's sake" spirit of the late nineteenth century.

READING 31.1 From the Works of Nietzsche

The Gay Science (1882)

The Madman. Have you not heard of that madman who lit a   1
lantern in the bright morning hours, ran to the market place,
and cried incessantly, "I seek God! I seek God!" As many of
those who do not believe in God were standing around just
then, he provoked much laughter. Why, did he get lost? said
one. Did he lose his way like a child? said another. Or is he
hiding? Is he afraid of us? Has he gone on a voyage? or
emigrated? Thus they yelled and laughed. The madman
jumped into their midst and pierced them with his glances.

   "Whither is God" he cried. "I shall tell you. *We have killed*   10 *him*—you and I. All of us are his murderers. But how have we done this? How were we able to drink up the sea? Who gave us the sponge to wipe away the entire horizon? What did we do when we unchained this earth from its sun? Whither is it moving now? Whither are we moving now? Away from all suns? Are we not plunging continually? Backward, sideward, forward, in all directions? Is there any up or down left? Are we not straying as through an infinite nothing? Do we not feel the breath of empty space? Has it not become colder? Is not night and more night coming on all the while? Must not lanterns be lit in the morning? Do we not hear anything yet of the noise of the gravediggers who are burying God? Do we not smell anything yet of God's decomposition? Gods too decompose. God is dead. God remains dead. And we have killed him. How shall we, the murderers of all murderers, comfort ourselves? What was holiest and most powerful of all that the world has yet owned has bled to death under our knives. Who will wipe this blood off us? What water is there for us to clean ourselves? What festivals of atonement, what sacred games shall we have to invent? Is not the greatness of this deed too great for us? Must not we ourselves become gods simply to seem worthy of it? There has never been a greater deed; and whoever will be born after us—for the sake of this deed he will be part of a higher history than all history hitherto."

Here the madman fell silent and looked again at his listeners; and they too were silent and stared at him in astonishment. At last he threw his lantern on the ground, and it broke and went out. "I come too early," he said then; "my time has not come yet. This tremendous event is still on its way, still wandering—it has not yet reached the ears of man. Lightning and thunder require time, the light of the stars requires time, deeds require time even after they are done, before they can be seen and heard. This deed is still more distant from them than the most distant stars—*and yet they have done it themselves.*"

It has been related further that on that same day the madman entered divers churches and there sang his *requiem aeternam deo.* Led out and called to account, he is said to have replied each time, "What are these churches now if they are not the tombs and sepulchers of God?"

Twilight of the Idols (1888)

L'art pour l'art. The fight against purpose in art is always a fight against the moralizing tendency in art, against its subordination to morality. *L'art pour l'art means,* "The devil take morality!" But even this hostility still betrays the overpowering force of the prejudice. When the purpose of moral preaching and of improving man has been excluded from art, it still does not follow by any means that art is altogether purposeless, aimless, senseless—in short, *l'art pour l'art,* a worm chewing its own tail. "Rather no purpose at all than a moral purpose!"—that is the talk of mere passion. A psychologist, on the other hand, asks: what does all art do? does it not praise? glorify? choose? prefer? With all this it strengthens or weakens certain valuations. Is this merely a "moreover"? an accident? something in which the artist's instinct had no share? Or is it not the very presupposition of the artist's ability? Does his basic instinct aim at art, or rather at the sense of art, at life? at a desirability of life? Art is the great stimulus to life: how could one understand

it as purposeless, as aimless, as *l'art pour l'art*?

One question remains: art also makes apparent much that is ugly, hard, and questionable in life; does it not thereby spoil life for us? And indeed there have been philosophers who attributed this sense to it: "liberation from the will" was what Schopenhauer taught as the over-all end of art; and with admiration he found the great utility of tragedy in its "evoking resignation." But this, as I have already suggested, is the pessimist's perspective and "evil eye." We must appeal to the artists themselves. What does the tragic artist communicate of himself? Is it not precisely the state *without* fear in the face of the fearful and questionable that he is showing? This state itself is a great desideratum;[1] whoever knows it, honors it with the greatest honors. He communicates it—*must* communicate it, provided he is an artist, a genius of communication. Courage and freedom of feeling before a powerful enemy, before a sublime calamity, before a problem that arouses dread—this triumphant state is what the tragic artist chooses, what he glorifies. Before tragedy, what is warlike in our soul celebrates its Saturnalia;[2] whoever is used to suffering, whoever seeks out suffering, the heroic man praises his own being through tragedy—to him alone the tragedian presents this drink of sweetest cruelty.

. . . .

One might say that in a certain sense the nineteenth century *also* strove for all that which Goethe as a person had striven for: universality in understanding and in welcoming, letting everything come close to oneself, an audacious realism, a reverence for everything factual. How is it that the over-all result is no Goethe, but chaos, a nihilistic sigh, an utter bewilderment, an instinct of weariness which in practice continually drives toward a recourse to the eighteenth century? (For example, as a romanticism of feeling, as altruism and hypersentimentality, as feminism in taste, as socialism in politics.) Is not the nineteenth century, especially at its close, merely an intensified, *brutalized* eighteenth century, that is, a century of *decadence*? So that Goethe would have been—not merely for Germany, but for all of Europe—a mere interlude, a beautiful "in vain"? But one misunderstands great human beings if one views them from the miserable perspective of some public use. That one cannot put them to any use, that in itself may belong to greatness. . . .

Q If art excludes moral purpose, what, according to Nietzsche, might be the purpose of art?

Bergson: Intellect and Intuition

While Nietzsche anticipated the darker side of Modernism, Henri Bergson (1859–1941) presented a more positive point of view. Bergson, the most important French philosopher of his time, offered a picture of the world that paralleled key developments in the arts and sciences and anticipated modern notions of time and space. Bergson

---

[1] Something desired as essential.
[2] An orgy, or unrestrained celebration.

viewed life as a vital impulse that evolved creatively, much like a work of art.

According to Bergson, two primary powers, intellect and intuition, governed the lives of human beings. While intellect perceives experience in individual and discrete terms, or as a series of separate and solid entities, intuition grasps experience as it really is: a perpetual stream of sensations. Intellect isolates and categorizes experience according to logic and geometry; intuition, on the other hand, fuses past and present into one organic whole. For Bergson, instinct (or intuition) is humankind's noblest faculty, and *duration*, or "perpetual becoming," is the very stuff of reality—the essence of life.

In 1889, Bergson published his treatise *Time and Freewill*, in which he described true experience as durational, a constant unfolding in time, and reality, which can only be apprehended intuitively, as a series of qualitative changes that merge into one another without precise definition.

Poetry in the Late Nineteenth Century: The Symbolists

Bergson's poetical view of nature had much in common with the aesthetics of the movement known as *Symbolism*, which flourished from roughly 1885 to 1910. The Symbolists held that the visible world does not constitute a true or universal reality. Realistic, objective representation, according to the Symbolists, failed to convey the pleasures of sensory experience and the intuitive world of dreams and myth. The artist's mission was to find a language that embraced the mystical, the erotic, and the ineffable world of the senses. For the Symbolists, reality was a swarm of sensations that could never be described but only *suggested* by poetic symbols—images that elicited moods and feelings beyond literal meanings.

In literature, the leading Symbolists were the French poets Charles Baudelaire (1821–1867), Paul Verlaine (1844–1896), Arthur Rimbaud (1854–1891), and Stéphane Mallarmé (1842–1898), and the Belgian playwright Maurice Maeterlinck (1862–1949). Rimbaud, who wrote most of his poetry while in his teens, envisioned the poet as seer. Freeing language from its descriptive function, his prose poems shattered the rational sequence of words and phrases, detaching them from their traditional associations and recombining them so as to create powerful sense impressions. In one of the prose poems from his *Illuminations*, for example, Rimbaud describes flowers as "Bits of yellow gold seeded in agate, pillars of mahogany supporting a dome of emeralds, bouquets of white satin and fine rods of ruby surround the water rose." The Symbolists tried to represent nature without effusive commentary, to "take eloquence and wring its neck," as Verlaine put it. In order to imitate the indefiniteness of experience itself, they might string words together without logical connections. Hence, in Symbolist poetry, images seem to flow into one another, and "meaning" often lies between the lines.

Mallarmé

For Stéphane Mallarmé, the "new art" of poetry was a religion, and the poet–artist was its oracle. Inclined to melancholy, he cultivated an intimate literary style based on the "music" of words. He held that art was "accessible only to the few" who nurtured "the inner life." Mallarmé's poems are tapestries of sensuous, dreamlike motifs that resist definition and analysis. To name a thing, Mallarmé insisted, was to destroy it, while to suggest experience was to create it.

Mallarmé's pastoral poem "L'après-midi d'un faune" ("The Afternoon of a Faun") is a reverie of an erotic encounter between two mythological woodland creatures, a faun (part man, part beast) and a nymph (a beautiful forest maiden). As the faun awakens, he tries to recapture the experiences of the previous afternoon. Whether his elusive memories belong to the world of dreams or to reality is uncertain; but, true to Bergson's theory of duration, experience becomes a stream of sensations in which past and present merge. As the following excerpt illustrates, Mallarmé's verbal rhythms are free and hypnotic, and his images, which follow one another with few logical transitions, are intimately linked to the world of the senses.

READING 31.2 From Mallarmé's "The Afternoon of a Faun" (1876)

I'd love to make them linger on, those nymphs. So fair,	1
their frail incarnate, that it flutters in the air	
drowsy with tousled slumbers.	
Did I love a dream?	
My doubt, hoard of old darkness, ends in a whole stream	5
of subtle branches which, remaining as the true	
forests, show that I've offered myself (quite alone, too)	
the roses' ideal failing as something glorious.	
Let me reflect . . .	
What if these women you discuss,	
faun, represent desires of your own fabulous	10
senses! Illusion flows out of the chilly blue	
eyes of the chaster one, like a fountain in tears:	
the other, though, all sighs, do you think she appears	
in contrast like a day's warm breeze across your fleece?	
Not at all: through the lazy languishing release	15
stifling with heat the cool dawn's struggles, not a sound	
of water but my flute's outpourings murmurs round	
the thicket steeped in music; and the one stir of air	
my dual pipes are swiftly shedding everywhere	
and then dispersing in a sonorous arid sleet,	20
is, over the horizon that no ripples pleat,	

the visible, serene and artificial sigh
of inspiration reascending to the sky.
O fringes of a placid mere in Sicily   25
thus plundered by my sun-rivalling vanity,
silent beneath the blooms of brilliant light, proclaim
—how I was cropping here the hollow reeds made tame
by talent, when, across the bluegreen gold of things
far off verdures devoting their vines to the springs—   30
came shimmering to rest a pallid animal glow;
and when the pipes were brought to birth, how at their slow
prelude this flight of swans—no! naiads—fled away
or dived.

             . . . .

How purple, freshly ripe, the pomegranates rise   35
and burst and murmur with the bees, my passion knows;
our blood, allured by what may seize its fancy, flows
for the swarm of desires eternally released.
Among the dead leaves, at times when the forest glows
with gold and ashen tints, there rises up a feast: 40
Etna![1] across your very slopes, then, Venus goes,
and on your laval ground she rests her artless toes
when sad slumbers are sounding and the flame has ceased.
I've seized the queen!
The punishment is certain . . .   45
No,
but the soul void of words and heavy body slowly
fall before noon's haughty calm. No more ado;
must sleep now, must forget the blasphemy and blame
spread on thirsty sands; and as I love to do   50
open my mouth to the wine's potent star!
Both of you, farewell; I'm going to see the shadow you become.

Q **How does this poem compare with those
of Wordsworth and Shelley (Readings 27.1
and 27.2)?**

Q **What aspects of Mallarmé's poem do you detect
in the music of Debussy and the paintings of
Monet?**

Music in the Late Nineteenth Century: Debussy

It is no surprise that Symbolist poetry, itself a kind of music, found its counterpart in music. Like the poetry of Mallarmé, the music of Claude Debussy (1862–1918) engages the listener through nuance and atmosphere. Debussy's compositions consist of broken fragments of melody, the outlines of which are blurred and indistinct. "I would like to see the creation . . . of a kind of music without themes and motives," wrote Debussy, "formed on a single continuous theme, which is uninterrupted and which never returns on itself."

Debussy owed much to Richard Wagner and the Romantic composers who had abandoned the formal clarity of classical composition (see chapter 29). He was also

---

[1] A volcanic mountain in Sicily.

Figure 31.2 Vaslav Nijinsky, *Afternoon of a Faun*, 1912. Photograph: L. Roosen. 9 × 5 in. (approx.). Dancing the part of the faun, Nijinsky moved across the stage in profile in imitation of the frieze on an ancient Greek vase. While he performed professionally for only ten years, his provocative choreography ushered in modern dance.

indebted to the exotic music of Bali in Indonesia, which he had heard performed at the World's Fair of 1889. Debussy experimented with nontraditional kinds of harmony, such as the five-tone scale found in East Asian music. He deviated from the traditional Western practice of returning harmonies to the tonic, or "home tone," introducing shifting harmonies with no clearly defined tonal center. His rich harmonic palette, characterized by unusually constructed chords, reflects a fascination with tone color that may have been inspired by the writings of the German physiologist Hermann von Helmholtz (1821–1894)—especially his treatise *On the Sensations of Tone as a Physiological Basis for the Theory of Music* (1863). But Debussy found his greatest inspiration in contemporary poetry and painting. A close friend of the Symbolist poets, he set a number of their texts to music. His first orchestral composition, *Prelude to "The Afternoon of a Faun"* (1894), was (in his words) a "very free illustration of Mallarmé's beautiful poem," which had been published eighteen years earlier. Debussy originally intended to write a dramatic piece based on the poem, but instead produced a ten-minute orchestral prelude that shares its dreamlike quality.

In 1912, Debussy's score became the basis for a twelve-minute ballet choreographed by Vaslav Nijinsky (1888–1950; Figure **31.2**). This brilliant Russian choreographer

---

See Music Listening Selections at end of chapter.

violated the formalities of classical dance by introducing sexually charged gestures and by dancing portions of the ballet barefoot. He outraged critics, who attacked the ballet for its "vile movements of erotic bestiality and gestures of extreme shamelessness."

Debussy had little use for the ponderous orchestras of the French and German Romantics. He scored the *Prelude* for a small orchestra whose predominantly wind and brass instruments might recreate Mallarmé's delicate mood of reverie. A sensuous melody for unaccompanied flute provides the composition's opening theme, which is then developed by flutes, oboes, and clarinets. Harp, triangle, muted horns, and lightly brushed cymbals contribute luminous tonal textures that—like the images of the poem itself—seem based in pure sensation. Transitions are subtle, and melodies seem to drift without resolution. Shifting harmonies with no clearly defined tonal center engulf the listener in a nebulous flood of sound that calls to mind the shimmering effects of light on water and the ebb and flow of ocean waves. Indeed, water—a favorite subject of Impressionist painters—is the subject of many of Debussy's orchestral sketches, such as *Gardens in the Rain* (1903), *Image: Reflections in the Water* (1905), and *The Sea* (1905).

Painting in the Late Nineteenth Century

Symbolism

In the visual arts, Symbolists gave emphasis to the simplification of line, arbitrary color, and expressive, flattened form. *The Chosen One* (Figure **31.3**), a painting by the Swiss artist Ferdinand Hodler (1853–1918), employs these features in depicting a young male child surrounded by a circle of angelic figures. The painting does not represent a specific event; rather, it suggests a mysterious and unnamed rite of passage. Symbolist emphasis on suggestion rather than depiction constituted a move in the direction of Modernist Abstraction and Expressionism (see chapters 32 and 33 respectively).

Science and Technology

1841	John G. Rand (American) invents the collapsible metal paint tube
1879	Edison produces the incandescent light bulb
1889	Edison invents equipment to take and show moving pictures
1898	Wilhelm C. Röntgen (German) discovers X-rays

Figure 31.3 FERDINAND HODLER, *The Chosen One*, 1893–1894. Tempera and oil on canvas, 7 ft. 3½ in. × 9 ft. 10½ in. Six angelic figures float above the ground on which a nude boy sits before a barren tree. While the images suggest renewal and rejuvenation, no clear narrative attaches to the scene.

Impressionism

The nineteenth-century art style that captured most fully the intuitive realm of experience, and thus closely paralleled the aesthetic ideals of Bergson, Mallarmé, and Debussy, was *Impressionism*. Luminosity, the interaction of light and form, subtlety of tone, and a preoccupation with sensation itself were the major features of Impressionist art.

Impressionist subject matter preserved the Romantic fascination with nature and the Realist preoccupation with daily life. But Impressionism departed from both the Romantic effort to idealize nature and the Realist will to record the natural world with unbiased objectivity. Often called an art of pure sensation, Impressionism was, in part, a response to nineteenth-century research into the physics of light, the chemistry of paint, and the laws of optics. *The Principles of Harmony and the Contrast of Colors* by the nineteenth-century French chemist Michel Chevreul (1786–1889), along with the treatises on the physical properties of color and musical tone by Hermann von Helmholtz mentioned above, offered new insights into the psychology of perception. These complemented the earliest appearance of synthetic pigments, which replaced traditional earth pigments. Of particular importance were chrome yellow, synthetic ultramarine, viridian, and emerald green, all of which gave the Impressionists a brighter range of color. Until the mid-nineteenth century, paint was stored in a pig's bladder, which was tapped and resealed as paint was needed. But the invention of the collapsible metal tube made it possible for artists to transport paint to outdoor sites and to store it for longer periods of time.

Monet: Pioneer Impressionist

In 1874, the French artist Claude Monet (1840–1926) exhibited a canvas that some critics consider to be the first modern painting. *Impression: Sunrise* (Figure **31.4**) is patently a seascape; but the painting says more about *how* one sees than about *what* one sees. It transcribes the fleeting effects of light and the changing atmosphere of water and air into a tissue of small dabs and streaks of color—the elements of pure perception. To increase luminosity, Monet coated the raw canvas with gesso, a chalky medium. Then, working in the open air and using the new synthetic paints, he applied brushstrokes of pure, occasionally unmixed, color. Monet ignored the brown underglazes artists traditionally used to build up form. Maintaining that there were no "lines" in nature, he avoided fixed contours. Instead of blending his colors to create a finished effect, he placed them side by side, building up a radiant impasto.

Figure 31.4 CLAUDE MONET, *Impression: Sunrise*, 1873. Oil on canvas, 19⅝ × 25½ in.

Figure 31.5 CLAUDE MONET, *Water-Lily Pond, Symphony in Green (Japanese Bridge)*, 1899. Oil on canvas, 3 ft. ⅗ in. × 2 ft. 11 in. The reflections of dense foliage in the surface of the waterlily pond eliminate distinctions between foreground and background and suggest a shifting play of light. Such paintings inspired the Symbolist Charles Morice to call Monet "master and king of the ephemeral."

In order to intensify visual effect, he juxtaposed complementary colors, putting touches of orange (red and yellow) next to blue and adding bright tints of rose, pink, and vermilion. He rejected the use of browns and blacks to create shadows; instead, he applied colors complementary to the hue of the object casting the shadow, thus approximating the prismatic effects of light on the human eye. Monet's canvases capture the external envelope: the instantaneous visual sensation of light itself.

Monet was by no means the first painter to deviate from academic techniques. Constable had applied color in rough dots and dabs, Delacroix had occasionally juxtaposed complementary colors to increase brilliance, and Manet had often omitted half-tones. But Monet went further by interpreting form as color itself—color so rapidly applied as to convey the immediacy of a sketch. Consequently, *Impression: Sunrise* struck the art world as a radically new approach. One critic dismissed the painting

as "only an impression," no better than "wallpaper in its embryonic state," thus unwittingly giving the name "Impressionism" to the movement that would dominate French art of the 1870s and 1880s.

Monet's early subjects include street scenes, picnics, café life, and boating parties at the fashionable tourist resorts that dotted the banks of the River Seine near Paris. However, as he began to find the intangible and shifting play of light more compelling than the pastimes of Parisian society, his paintings became more impersonal and abstract. Wishing to fix sensation, or, as he put it, to "seize the intangible," he painted the changing effects of light on such mundane objects as poplar trees and haystacks. Often working on a number of canvases at once, he might generate a series that showed his subject in morning light, under the noon sun, and at sunset. After visiting London in the 1890s, during which time he studied the works of Constable and Turner, his canvases became even more formless and radiant. At his private estate in Giverny, he lovingly painted dozens of views of the lily ponds, and the lavish gardens that he himself designed and cultivated (Figure **31.5**). These ravishing paintings brought him pleasure and fame at the end of his long career.

Monet may be considered an ultrarealist in his effort to reproduce with absolute fidelity the ever-changing effects of light. His freedom from preconceived ideas of nature prompted his contemporary Paul Cézanne to exclaim that he was "only an eye," but, he added admiringly, "what an eye!" Ironically, Monet's devotion to the physical truth of nature paved the way for modern abstraction—the concern with the intrinsic qualities of the subject, rather than with its literal appearance.

Renoir

Impressionism was never a single, uniform style. Nevertheless, it characterized the art of the group of Parisian artists who met regularly at the Café Guerbois and who showed their works together at no fewer than eight public exhibitions held between 1874 and 1886. To a greater or lesser extent, their paintings reflected Monet's manner of rendering nature in short strokes of brilliant color. Above all, they brought painterly spontaneity to a celebration of the leisure activities and diversions of urban life: dining, dancing, theater-going, boating, and socializing.

In this sense, the most typical Impressionist painter might be Pierre-Auguste Renoir (1841–1919). Le Moulin de la Galette, a popular outdoor café and dance-hall in Montmartre (the bohemian section of nineteenth-century Paris), provided the setting for one of Renoir's most seductive tributes to youth and informal pleasure (see Figure **31.1**). In the painting, elegantly dressed young men and women—artists, students, and working-class members of Parisian society—dance, drink, and flirt with one another in the flickering golden light of the late afternoon sun.

Pissarro

Renoir's colleague Camille Pissarro (1830–1903) was born in the West Indies but settled in Paris in 1855. The oldest and one of the most prolific of the Impressionists, he exhibited in all eight of the Impressionist group shows. Like Monet and Renoir, Pissarro loved outdoor subjects: peasants working in the fields, the magical effects of freshly fallen snow, and sunlit rural landscapes. Late in his career, however, as his eyesight began to fail, he gave up painting out-of-doors. Renting hotel rooms that looked out on the streets of Paris, he produced engaging cityscapes (Figure **31.6**)—sixteen of Paris' boulevards in 1897 alone.

Figure 31.6 CAMILLE PISSARRO, *Le Boulevard Montmartre: Rainy Weather, Afternoon*, 1897. Oil on canvas, 20⅝ × 26 in. During his long career, Pissarro painted hundreds of rural and urban landscapes. His techniques in capturing the effects of light influenced the work of his fellow Impressionists. Nevertheless, he sold very few paintings in his lifetime.

Figure 31.7 EDGAR DEGAS, *Two Dancers on a Stage*, ca. 1874. Oil on canvas, 24⅕ × 18 in. A comparison of this composition with that of the far left woodcut in Figure 31.10 reveals a similar treatment of negative space, a raked perspective, and the off-center arrangement of figures.

Strikingly similar to popular panoramic photographs of turn-of-the-century Paris, Pissarro's luminous scenes capture the rhythm of urban life; throngs of horse-drawn carriages and pedestrians are bathed in the misty atmosphere that envelops Paris after the rain. Asked by a young artist for advice on "how to paint," Pissarro responded that one should record visual perceptions with immediacy, avoid defining the outlines of things, observe reflections of color and light, and honor only one teacher: nature.

Degas

Edgar Degas (1834–1917) regularly exhibited with the Impressionists; but his style remained unique. Classically trained—he began copying Poussin at the Louvre when he was eighteen—he never sacrificed line and form to the beguiling qualities of color and light. He produced thousands of drawings and pastels, ranging from quick sketches to fully developed compositions. Whether depicting the urban world of cafés, racetracks, theaters, and shops, or the demimonde of laundresses and prostitutes, he concentrated his attention on the fleeting moment. He rejected the traditional "posed" model, seeking instead to capture momentary and even awkward gestures, such as stretching

and yawning. Degas was a consummate draftsman and a master designer. His innovative compositional techniques balance spontaneity and improvisation with artifice and calculation. In *Two Dancers on a Stage* (Figure **31.7**), for example, he presents two ballerinas as if seen from above and at an angle that leaves "empty" the lower left portion of the painting. In this feat of breathtaking asymmetry, part of the figure at the right seems to disappear off the edge of the canvas, while the body of a third figure at the left is cut off by the frame. The deliberately "random" view suggests the influence of photography, with its accidental "slice of life" potential, as well as the impact of Japanese woodcuts, which Degas enthusiastically collected after they entered Europe in the 1860s.

During the 1860s, Degas became interested in the subject of horse racing, which, like the theater, had become a fashionable leisure activity and social event (Figure **31.8**). His drawings and paintings of the races focused primarily on the anatomy and movement of the horses. In his studies of physical movement, he learned much from the British artist, photographer, and inventor Eadweard Muybridge (1830–1904), whose stop-action photographs of the 1870s and 1880s were revolutionary in their time (Figure **31.9**).

Figure 31.8 EDGAR DEGAS, *The False Start*, ca. 1870. Oil on canvas, 12⅝ × 15¾ in. The English sport of horse racing took hold in France in the 1830s when a track was built at Chantilly. In 1857, a fashionable racetrack was established at Longchamp in the Bois de Boulogne on the outskirts of Paris.

Figure 31.9 EADWEARD MUYBRIDGE, *Photo Sequence of Racehorse*, 1884–1885. Photograph, 7 × 10 in. (approx.).

Japanese Woodblock Prints and Western Art

Japanese woodblock prints entered Europe along with Asian trade goods (often as the wrappings for those goods) in the late nineteenth century. Although they were new to Europeans, they represented the end of a long tradition in Japanese art, one that began declining after Japan was forced to open its doors to the West in the 1860s. Produced in great numbers between 1660 and 1860, and sold as popular souvenirs, they recorded the pleasures of *ukiyo*, "the floating—or fleeting—world" of the courtesans, *kabuki* actors, and dancers (see Figure 31.12) who enlivened the streets of bustling, urban Edo (now Tokyo). Like the magnificent folding screens commissioned by wealthy patrons (see chapter 21), the prints feature flat, unmodulated colors, undulating lines, and compositions that are cropped or contain large areas of empty space. Their daring use of **negative space** and startling perspective was often the consequence of unusual vantage points, such as the bird's-eye view

Figure 31.10 KUNISADA, triptych showing the different processes of printmaking, ca. 1831. Japanese woodblock color print, each panel: 14½ × 10 in.
Left: the printer has just finished taking an impression by rubbing the *baren* (a round pad made of a coil of cord covered by a bamboo sheath) over the paper on the colored block; numerous brushes and bowls of color are visible. Kunisada has made the design more interesting by picturing women, although the craftsmen were almost always men (information from Julia Hutt, *Understanding Far Eastern Art*. New York: Dutton, 1987, 53).
Center: a woman (in the foreground) sizing paper sheets that are then hung up to dry; another is removing areas with no design from the block with a chisel.
Right: a woman with an original drawing pasted onto a block conversing with another who is sharpening blades on a whetstone.

seen in the prints of Kunisada (Figure **31.10**). Such prints were mass-produced, most often by men, despite Kunisada's rendering.

During the mid-nineteenth century, Japanese woodblock artists added landscapes to their repertory. The landscape prints, often produced as a series of views of local Japanese sites, resemble the topographical studies of European artists. But they operated out of entirely different stylistic imperatives: unlike the Romantics, the Japanese had little interest in the picturesque; rather, they gave attention to bold contrasts and decorative arrangements of abstract shapes and colors. The absence of *chiaroscuro* and aerial perspective reduced the illusion of spatial depth and atmospheric continuity between near and far objects. All these features are evident in one of the most famous mid-nineteenth-century Japanese landscape prints: *Mount Fuji Seen Below a Wave at Kanagawa* (Figure **31.11**), from the series "Thirty-Six Views of Mount Fuji" by Katsushika Hokusai (1760–1849).

When Japanese prints arrived in the West (see Figure 31.12), they had an immediate impact on fine and commercial art, including the art of the lithographic poster

(see Figure 31.13). Monet and Degas bought them (along with Chinese porcelain) in great numbers, and Vincent van Gogh, a great admirer of Hokusai, insisted that his own work was "founded on Japanese art."

Théodore Duret, a French art critic of the time and an enthusiast of Impressionist painting, was one of the first writers to observe the impact of Japanese prints on nineteenth-century artists. In a pamphlet called "The Impressionist Painters" (1878), Duret explained:

We had to wait until the arrival of Japanese albums before anyone dared to sit down on the bank of a river to juxtapose on canvas a boldly red roof, a white wall, a green poplar, a yellow road, and blue water. Before Japan it was impossible; the painter always lied. Nature with its frank colors was in plain sight, yet no one ever saw anything on canvas but attenuated colors, drowning in a general halftone.

As soon as people looked at Japanese pictures, where the most glaring, piercing colors were placed side by side, they finally understood that there were new methods for reproducing certain effects of nature.

Japonisme, the influence of Japan on European art of the late nineteenth century, proved to be multifaceted: the prints coincided with the Impressionist interest in casual urban subjects (especially those involving women) and inspired a new way of reconciling the illusion of the three-dimensional world with the flatness of the two-dimensional canvas. At the same time, the elegant naturalism and refined workmanship of Asian *cloisonné* enamels, ceramics, lacquerwares, ivories, silks, and other collectibles were widely imitated in the Arts and Crafts movements that flourished at the end of the century (see Figure 31.18).

Cassatt

One of the most notable artists to come under the influence of Japanese prints was the American painter Mary Cassatt (1844–1926). Cassatt spent most of her life in Paris, where she became a friend and colleague of Degas, Renoir, and other Impressionists, with whom she exhibited regularly. Like Degas, Cassatt painted mainly indoors, cultivating a style that combined forceful calligraphy, large areas of unmodulated color, and unusual perspectives—the major features of the Japanese woodcuts—with a taste for female subjects.

Figure 31.11 KATSUSHIKA HOKUSAI, *Mount Fuji Seen Below a Wave at Kanagawa*, from "Thirty-Six Views of Mount Fuji," Tokugawa period. Full-color woodblock print, 10⅕ × 14¾ in.

The pleasures and entertainments of *ukiyo*, "the floating world," were nowhere better represented than in Japanese woodblock prints of the seventeenth and eighteenth centuries. The hand-colored prints of *kabuki* performers are famous for their bright, flat colors, sinuous lines, and the sensitive integration of positive and negative space (Figure **31.12**). The popularity of such prints in the West coincided with the introduction of lithographic techniques used to record and publicize urban events (see Figures 30.13 and 30.14). Henri de Toulouse-Lautrec (discussed below) was not the first to produce commercial artworks for the world of entertainment. However, he was to become the father of the modern poster, generating some

thirty color lithographic posters during the last ten years of his life. Commissioned to design public advertisements for the popular Montmartre cabaret the Moulin Rouge ("Red Mill"), he immortalized its famous **can-can** dancer Louise Weber, known as La Goulue (the "glutton"), whose risqué, high-kicking physical displays attracted (and scandalized) audiences. A poster of the Parisian entertainer who replaced La Goulue, Jane Avril (Figure **31.13**), reveals the artist's brilliant combination of unmodulated primary colors, graceful, flowing lines, and the daring interplay of figure and ground—stylistic features that reflect the direct influence of Japanese woodblock prints.

Figure 31.12 TORII KIYONOBU, *Actor as a Monkey Showman*, ca. 1720. Woodblock print, 13¼ × 6¼ in.

Figure 31.13 HENRI DE TOULOUSE-LAUTREC, *Jane Avril*, 1899. Lithograph, printed in color, 22 × 14 in.

Figure 31.14 MARY CASSATT, *The Bath*, 1891–1892. Oil on canvas, 3 ft. 3½ in. × 2 ft. 2 in. Cassatt offers a bird's-eye view of all elements in the painting, with the exception of the pitcher in the lower right foreground and the chest of drawers in the background.

Cassatt brought a unique sensitivity to domestic themes that featured mothers and children enjoying everyday tasks and diversions (Figure **31.14**). These gentle and optimistic images appealed to American collectors and did much to increase the popularity of Impressionist art in the United States. Yet the so-called Madonna of American art preferred life in Paris to that in prefeminist America. "Women do not have to fight for recognition here if they do serious work," wrote Cassatt.

Toulouse-Lautrec

Cassatt's gentle visions of domestic life stand in strong contrast to the paintings of Henri de Toulouse-Lautrec (1864–1901). Toulouse-Lautrec, the descendant of an aristocratic French family, practiced many of the stylistic principles of Impressionism, but his choice of subject matter was often so bohemian that members of his own family condemned his work as unacceptable to "well-bred people." In paintings often executed on cardboard, he captured the seamy denizens of Parisian life—cabaret dancers, circus performers,

and prostitutes who, like Zola's Nana, lived on the margins of middle-class society. His intimate scenes of brothels, bars, and dance-halls (see LOOKING INTO, Figure **31.15**) chronicle the sensuous pleasures of nocturnal Montmartre.

Toulouse-Lautrec mocked traditional ideas of beauty and propriety in both subject matter and style. A pioneer in the technique of color lithography, he stylized figures—almost to the point of caricature—in bold and forceful silhouettes that became the celebrity images of popular urban posters (see Figure 31.13).

Art Nouveau

The posters of Toulouse-Lautrec bear the seductive stamp of *Art Nouveau* (French for "new art"), an ornamental style that became enormously popular in the late nineteenth century. *Art Nouveau* artists shared with members of the English Arts and Crafts movement a high regard for the fine artisanship of the preindustrial Middle Ages, an era that achieved an ideal synthesis of the functional and the

Toulouse-Lautrec's *At the Moulin Rouge*

At The Moulin Rouge shows the patrons and entertainers of Montmartre's famous music-hall, which opened in Paris in 1889. The painting, a glimpse of bohemian nightlife, stands in contrast to the genteel Impressionist depictions of daytime entertainments in Montmartre (see Figure 31.1). Inspired by Japanese prints (see Figure 31.10), the artist employed an unconventional perspective that forces the eye into the space above the diagonal axis of a railing that separated the promenade from the dance-hall. Here, one encounters a jaded-looking assembly of stylishly dressed and hatted men and women, including the celebrity dancer Jane Avril (see Figure 31.13) and the notable photographer Maurice Guibert, whose manipulated photographs anticipated experimental camera-work of the twentieth century. Flesh tones are distorted by electric lighting (which had recently come into use in Paris), and faces are altered by the stark white make-up (borrowed from Japanese theater) that was current in European fashion. Toulouse-Lautrec, who had been crippled by breaking both legs as a child, pictures himself in the background as a dwarfish caricature.

Figure 31.15 HENRI DE TOULOUSE-LAUTREC, *At The Moulin-Rouge*, 1893–1895. Oil on canvas, 4 ft. ⅜ in. × 4 ft. 7¼ in.

Toulouse-Lautrec

Toulouse-Lautrec's cousin
Dr. Tapié de Céleyran

La Macarona,
flamenco dancer

Edouard Dujardin,
poet and novelist

Jane Avril,
dancer

bentwood café chairs
designed by Michael
Thonet in 1830

La Goulue fixing
her hair before a
mirror

newly installed
electric lights

Paul Secau,
photographer

Maurice Guibert,
photographer
and vintner

the performer May
Milton, English
vaudeville dancer

decorative in daily life. The proponents of the new style also prized the decorative arts of Asia and Islam, which tended to favor bold, flat, organic patterns and semiabstract linear designs. Acknowledging the impact of the Japanese woodcut style, one French critic insisted that Japanese blood had mixed with the blood of *Art Nouveau* artists.

Art Nouveau originated in Belgium among architects working in the medium of cast iron, but it quickly achieved an international reach that affected painting, as well as the design of furniture, textiles, glass, ceramics, and jewelry. The Belgian founder of the style, Victor Horta (1861–1947), brought to his work the Arts and Crafts veneration for fine craftsmanship and the Symbolist glorification of the sensuous and fleeting forms in nature. A distinguished architect and a great admirer of Eiffel's 1063-foot-high tower (see Figure 30.28), Horta translated the serpentine lines and organic rhythms of flowers and plants into magnificent glass and cast-iron designs for public buildings and private residences (Figure **31.16**).

"Art in nature, nature in art" was the motto of *Art Nouveau*. The sinuous curves of blossoms, leaves, and tendrils, executed in iron, were immortalized in such notable

Figure 31.16 VICTOR HORTA, Tassel House, Brussels, 1892–1893.

monuments as the rapid transport system known as the Paris Métro. They also appear in wallpaper, posters, book illustrations, tableware, and jewelry. In *Art Nouveau*, as in late nineteenth-century literature and painting, women were a favorite subject: the female, often shown with long, luxuriant hair, might be pictured as seductress or enchantress. She might appear as a fairy or water nymph (Figure **31.17**), a poetic, sylphlike creature. In *Art Nouveau* pins, bracelets, and combs, she is the human counterpart of vines and flowers fashioned in delicately crafted metal armatures and semiprecious stones. Such images suggest that *Art Nouveau*, although modern in its effort to communicate meaning by way of shape, pattern, and decoration, was actually a waning expression of a century-long Romantic infatuation with nature.

In America, *Art Nouveau* briefly attracted the attention of such architects as Louis Sullivan (see chapter 30), who embellished some of his otherwise austere office buildings and department stores with floral cast-iron ornamentation. It also inspired the magnificent glass designs of Louis Comfort Tiffany (1848–1933). The son of Charles

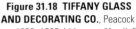

Figure 31.18 TIFFANY GLASS AND DECORATING CO., Peacock vase, 1892–1902. Iridescent "favrile" glass, blues and greens with feather and eye decorations, height 14⅛ in. A student of ancient and medieval glass practices, Tiffany patented in 1874 a way of mixing different colors of heated glass to produce the iridescent art glass he called "favrile" (a name derived from a Saxon word meaning "handmade").

Figure 31.17 EUGÈNE GRASSET, Comb, ca. 1900. 5¼ × 2¾ in.

L. Tiffany, founder of the famed New York jewelry house, Louis was a great admirer of Chinese *cloisonné* and ancient glass techniques. His innovative studio methods included assembly-line production, the use of templates, and the employment of female artisans who received the same wages as males—a policy that caused great controversy in Tiffany's time. Tiffany's inventive art glass, which featured floral arabesques and graceful geometric patterns, made him one of the masters of the international *Art Nouveau* style (Figure **31.18**).

Sculpture in the Late Nineteenth Century

Degas and Rodin

The two leading European sculptors of the late nineteenth century, Edgar Degas and Auguste Rodin (1840–1917), were masters at capturing the physical vitality of the human figure. Like the Impressionists, they were interested in lifelike movement and the sensory effects of light. To catch these fleeting qualities, they modeled their figures rapidly

Figure 31.19 EDGAR DEGAS, *Little Dancer Aged Fourteen*, ca. 1880–1881 (cast 1932). Bronze with net tutu and hair ribbon, 3 ft. 2½ in. × 14½ in. × 14¼ in. In Degas' time, young female dancers, called "little rats," usually came from working-class families, for whom they provided income.

Figure 31.20 AUGUSTE RODIN, *Dancing Figure*, 1905. Graphite with orange wash, 12⅞ × 9⅞ in.

in wet clay or wax. The bronze casts made from these originals preserve the spontaneity of the additive process. Indeed, many of Degas' bronze sculptures, cast posthumously, retain the imprints of his fingers and fingernails.

Degas often executed sculptures as exercises preliminary to his paintings. Throughout his life, but especially as his vision began to decline, he turned to making three-dimensional "sketches" of racehorses, bathers, and ballerinas—his favorite subjects. At his death, he left some 150 sculptures in his studio, some fully worked and others in various stages of completion. Only one of these sculptures, the *Little Dancer Aged Fourteen*, was exhibited as a finished artwork during Degas' lifetime. The reddish-brown wax original, made eerily lifelike by the artist's addition of a tutu, stockings, bodice, ballet shoes, a green satin ribbon, and hair from a horsehair wig (embedded strand by strand into the figure's head), was the subject of some controversy in the Parisian art world of 1881 (a world that would not see such mixed-media innovations for another half-century). The bronze cast of Degas' *Dancer* (Figure **31.19**), whose dark surfaces contrast sensuously with the fabric additions, retains the supple grace of the artist's finest drawings and paintings.

Like Degas, Rodin was keenly interested in movement and gesture. In hundreds of drawings, he recorded the dancelike rhythms of studio models whom he bid to move about freely rather than assume traditional, fixed poses (Figure **31.20**). But it was in the three-dimensional media that Rodin made his greatest contribution. One of his

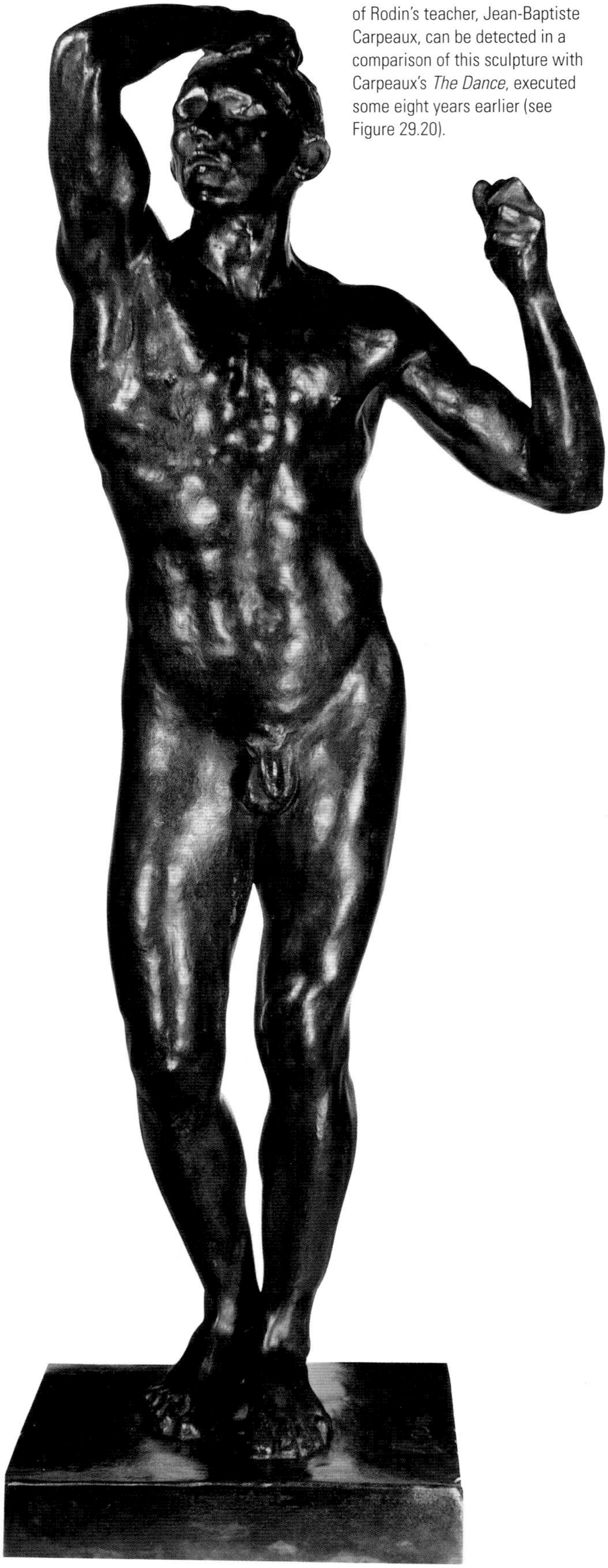

Figure 31.21 AUGUSTE RODIN, *The Age of Bronze*, 1876. Bronze, 25½ × 9⁹⁄₁₆ × 7½ in. The influence of Rodin's teacher, Jean-Baptiste Carpeaux, can be detected in a comparison of this sculpture with Carpeaux's *The Dance*, executed some eight years earlier (see Figure 29.20).

earliest sculptures, *The Age of Bronze* (Figure **31.21**), was so lifelike that critics accused him of forging the figure from plaster casts of a live model. In actuality, Rodin had captured a sense of organic movement by recreating the fleeting effects of light on form. He heightened the contrasts between polished and roughly textured surfaces, deliberately leaving parts of the piece unfinished. "Sculpture," declared Rodin, "is quite simply the art of depression and protuberance."

But Rodin moved beyond naturalistic representation. Anticipating Modernism, he used expressive distortion to convey a mood or mental disposition. He renounced formal idealization and gave his figures a nervous energy and emotional intensity that he found lacking in both Classical and Renaissance sculpture. "The sculpture of antiquity," he explained, "sought the logic of the human body; I seek its psychology." In this quest, Rodin was joined by his close friend the American dancer Isadora Duncan (1878–1927). Duncan introduced a language of physical expression

Figure 31.22 Isadora Duncan in *La Marseillaise*. Lantern slide, 5 × 4 in. Notorious for flouting the rules of academic dance as well as those of middle-class morality, the California-born Duncan achieved greater success in Europe than in the United States. She adopted the signature affectation of wearing scarves, one of which accidentally strangled her in a freak car mishap.

Figure 31.23 AUGUSTE RODIN, *The Gates of Hell*, 1880–1917. Bronze, 20 ft. 8 in. × 13 ft. 1 in. Below the Three Shades, in the center of the lintel (where Jesus is usually found in a traditional Christian Judgment scene), sits the Thinker, the human Creator, contemplating humankind doomed by its passions.

characterized by personalized gestures and improvised movements that were often fierce, earthy, and passionate (Figure **31.22**). Insisting that the rules of classical ballet produced ugly choreography, Duncan danced barefoot, often wearing Greek-style tunics in reference to ancient dance. "I have discovered the art that has been lost for two thousand years," she claimed.

Rodin's most ambitious project was a set of doors he was commissioned to design for the projected Museum of Decorative Arts in Paris. Loosely modeled on Ghiberti's *Gates of Paradise* (see Figure 17.19), *The Gates of Hell* (Figure **31.23**) consists of a swarm of figures inspired by the tortured souls of Dante's "Inferno" (see chapter 12). Rodin worked on the project for eight years, making hundreds of drawings and sculptures based on Dante's poem; but he never completed the doors, which were cast in bronze only years after his death. The figures that occupy *The Gates*, not all of which are identifiable, writhe and twist in postures of despair and yearning. Arrived at intuitively—like the images in a Mallarmé poem or a Monet landscape—they melt into one another without logical connection. Rodin admitted that he projected no fixed subject, "no scheme of illustrations or intended moral purpose." "I followed my own imagination," he explained, "my own sense of movement and composition." Collectively, his figures evoke a world of flux and chaos; their postures capture the restless discontent voiced by Nietzsche and by Gauguin (see below), and their random arrangement gives substance to Bergson's view of reality as a perpetual stream of sensations.

Throughout his career, Rodin remained compelled by the contents of *The Gates*. He cast in bronze many of its individual figures, and recreated others in marble. The two most famous of these are *The Kiss* (Figure **31.24**), based on the figures of the lovers Paola and Francesca (on the lower left door), and *The Thinker*. The latter—one of the best known of Rodin's works—originally represented Dante contemplating his imagined underworld from atop its portals.

Figure 31.24 AUGUSTE RODIN, *The Kiss*, 1886–1898. Marble, over life-size.

The Arts of Africa and Oceania

During the late nineteenth century, expanding Western commercialism and colonialism brought Europeans into closer contact with Africa and with Oceania (the islands of the South and Central Pacific). Nineteenth-century Africa and Oceania were essentially preindustrial and preliterate. Their social organization was usually highly stratified with clear distinctions between and among various classes: royalty, priests, and commoners held different ranks. Their economies were agricultural, and their gods and spirits were closely associated with nature and natural forces that were the object of communal and individual worship (see chapter 18). In some parts of Africa, kingdoms with long-standing traditions of royal authority were destroyed by colonial intrusion. But in other parts of Africa, ancient ways of life persisted. The royal traditions of Benin, Dahomey, Kongo, Yoruba, and other West African kingdoms (Map **31.1**) continued to flourish well into the modern era. During the nineteenth century, the oral traditions of African literature came to be recorded in written languages based on the Arabic and Western alphabets.

Africa and Oceania consisted of thousands of tightly knit communities in which reverence for the gods and the spirits of deceased ancestors was expressed by means of elaborate systems of worship. Reliquaries, masks, and other power objects were created by local artists to channel the spirits, celebrate rites of passage, and ensure the continuity and well-being of the community. As vessels for powerful spirits, they functioned to transmit supernatural energy. While sharing with some Western styles (such as Symbolism) a disregard for objective representation, the arts of these indigenous peoples stood far apart from nineteenth-century Western academic tradition. On the other hand, they had their roots in long-established cultural traditions—some extending back over thousands of years. Much of the art created in these regions during the nineteenth (and twentieth) century had its origins in conventional forms handed down from generation to generation. So, for example, masks produced in the nineteenth century by the Bambara people of Mali preserve the techniques and styles practiced almost without interruption since the founding of Mali's first empire in the thirteenth century (see Figure 18.8).

Africa

In Africa, even as the incursions of the French disrupted the Yoruba kingdoms of Nigeria (Map 31.1), royal authority asserted itself in the increased production of magnificent beaded objects, some of which served to identify and embellish the power and authority of the king. The beaded conical crown that belonged to King Glele (1858–1889) of Dahomey (the modern Republic of Benin) is surmounted by a bird that symbolizes potent supernatural powers and the all-surpassing majesty of the ruler (Figure **31.25**). Beadwork had been practiced in West Africa since the sixteenth century, when the Portuguese introduced Venetian glass beads to that continent. However, the golden age of beadwork occurred in the late nineteenth century, when uniformly sized European "seed beads" in a wide variety of colors first became available. It is noteworthy that in West Africa beading was an activity reserved exclusively for men.

A second example of high artistic productivity in nineteenth-century Africa comes from the genre of

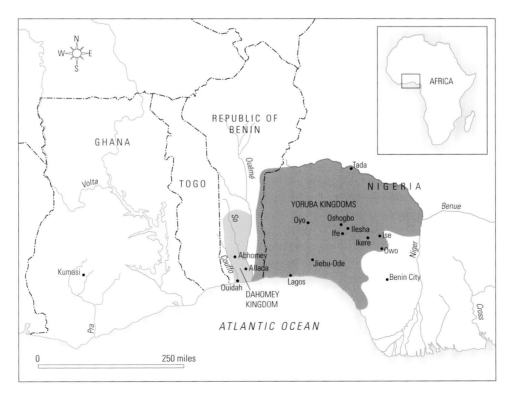

Map 31.1 The Kingdoms of Yoruba and Dahomey.

free-standing sculpture: the image of the war god Gu, commissioned by King Glele as a symbol of his own military might, was carved from wood and covered with hammered brass (said to have come from spent bullet shells). Brandishing two scimitars, the figure served to guard the gate of the city of Abhomey. Its fierce, scarified face with its jutting jaw, the wide flat feet, and taut, stylized physique reflect a powerful synthesis of naturalism and abstraction that typifies nineteenth-century African art, but, at the same time, adheres to a long tradition of West African sculpture (Figure **31.26**). The figure failed, however, in its protective mission: shortly after the death of King Glele in 1889, his kingdom fell to French colonial forces.

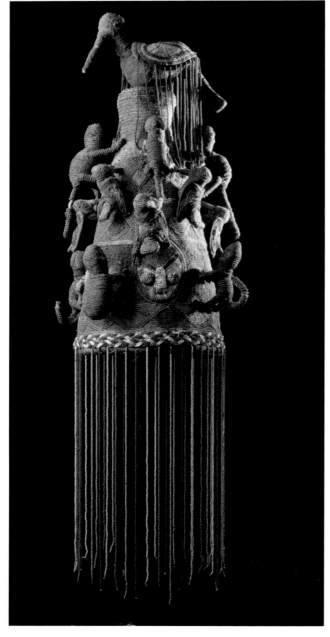

Figure 31.25 Yoruba headdress, African, nineteenth century. Beads and mixed media, height 37 in. (approx.). This crown of a Yoruba tribal prince is ornamented with figures of birds, chameleons, lizards, and human faces.

Figure 31.26 Attributed to **GANHU HUNTONDJI**, The war god Gu, nineteenth century. Brass and wood, height 41½ in.

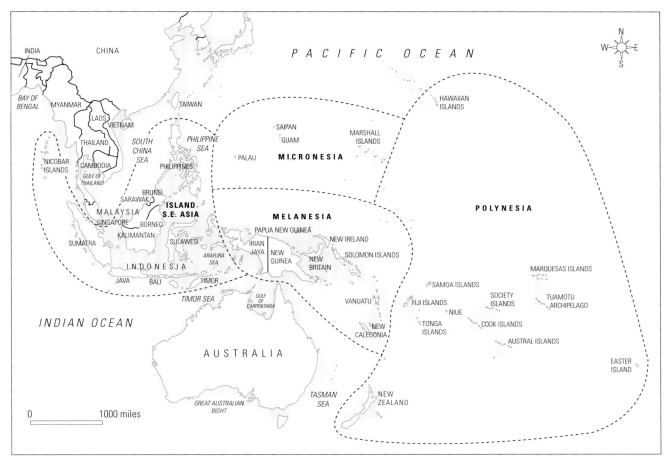

Map 31.2 The Islands of the South and Central Pacific.

Oceania

Although productivity from island to island in Oceania (Map **31.2**) varied dramatically, communities in this region generated some of their finest artwork during the nineteenth century. Among the Maori peoples of New Zealand, the art of woodcarving, usually involving the construction of elaborate wooden meeting houses, flourished during the 1800s. Teams of woodcarvers using European tools produced fierce totemic images embellished with elaborate patterns of spirals and scrolls (Figure **31.27**). Such designs resemble those used in the decorative body art known as "tattoo" (from the Polynesian *tatau*).

Especially popular among the Marquesas Islanders in the South Pacific, tattooing was considered a sacred art. Applied by specialists using a bone comb with sharp teeth, the tattoo, which might symbolize the specific rank and power of the wearer, served a protective function: a kind of visual armor. Its cultural significance, however, has inspired various interpretations. Expensive and painful, all-over body tattoos were usually worn by the wealthiest and most powerful individuals in the community (Figure **31.28**).

The serpentine patterns of Oceania tattoos and woodcarvings appear in the paintings of Paul Gauguin (see Figure 31.31) and in the many prints and sculptures that he produced during his stay in Tahiti. Tragically, as the cultures of Oceania came to be influenced by Western materialism and commercial exploitation, their brilliance and originality began to wane.

Primitivism

Europe had been involved in Africa and Oceania since the sixteenth century. By the nineteenth century, trade in goods, guns, and slaves had transformed African culture. In some areas, the availability of guns had led to violence and mayhem. Apart from imperialistic ambition, the Western penetration of the so-called Dark Continent was the product of intellectual curiosity, which had been stirred by Napoleon's Egyptian campaign (see chapter 29). Following the French invasion of Nigeria in 1830, and especially after medical science had recognized that quinine was effective against the dreaded malaria, Africa began to attract Western travelers and adventurers. Delacroix visited Morocco in 1831, bringing back to Europe seven sketchbooks of drawings and numerous watercolors. The British explorers David Livingstone (1813–1873) and Henry M. Stanley (1841–1904) spent years investigating Africa's vast terrain. Journalistic records of such expeditions drew attention to cultural traditions that differed sharply from those of the West. What often emerged was an oversimplified (and frequently distorted) understanding of the differences between and among a multitude of cultures, some of which were perceived as exotic, violent, and fundamentally inferior. Many Westerners characterized indigenous peoples as "primitive," implying simplicity and lack of sophistication. The French word *primitif* carried as well a positive charge, implying a closeness to nature exalted by those who decried the damaging effects of proto-modern industrialized society.

Figure 31.27 Fragment of a Maori doorpost (*poupou*) in the style of Te Arawa, from New Zealand. Wood, 18 in. (approx.).

Figure 31.28 Nuku Hiva islanders with various tattoos, 1813. Hand-colored copper plate engraving after original drawings by Wilhelm Gottlief von Tilenau, from Carl Bertuch, *Bilderbuch für Kinder*, vol. 8, Weimar (Landes-Industrie-Comptoir) 1813, no. 2. Nuku Hiva is the largest of the Marquesas Islands in French Polynesia.

Contributing to the European infatuation with non-Western culture was the *Exposition Universelle* (World's Fair) held in Paris in 1889, which brought to public view the arts of Asia, Africa, and Oceania. Reconstructions of villages from the Congo and Senegal, Japan and China, Polynesia and other South Sea islands introduced the non-Western world to astonished Europeans. Non-Western societies and their artistic achievements quickly became objects of research for the new disciplines of anthropology (the science of humankind and its culture) and ethnography (the branch of anthropology that studies preliterate peoples or groups). In 1890, the Scottish anthropologist Sir James Frazer (1854–1941) published *The Golden Bough*, a pioneer study of magic and religion as reflected in ancient and traditional folk customs. Collections of non-Western art filled the galleries of ethnographic museums, such as the American Museum of Natural History, which opened in New York in 1869, and the Musée d'Ethnographie du Trocadéro in Paris, founded in 1878. Tragically, however, it was often the case that even as these cultures were coming to be valued and their art collected and installed in Western museums, their brilliance and originality began to wane. The French painter Paul Gauguin, who recorded his impressions of Tahiti in his romanticized journal *Noa Noa* (*Fragrance*), lamented:

> The European invasion and monotheism have destroyed the vestiges of a civilization which had its own grandeur. . . . [The Tahitians] had been richly endowed with an instinctive feeling for the harmony necessary between human creations and the animal and plant life that formed the setting and decoration of their existence, but this has now been lost. In contact with us, with our school, they have truly become "savages" . . .

Gauguin objected to colonial efforts to impose French legal and economic policies on the Tahitians, and he also condemned the eradication of local religious beliefs by Catholic and Protestant missionaries. The appeal of "the primitive" among late nineteenth-century figures such as Gauguin reflected a more than casual interest in the world beyond the West. It provoked protests against what he called the "reign of terror" imposed by the West upon native non-Western populations. It also constituted a rebellion against Western values and societal taboos—a rebellion that would become full-blown in the primitivism of early modern art.

Postimpressionism

The art that followed the last of the Impressionist group shows in 1886 is generally designated as "Postimpressionist." Seeking a style that transcended the fleeting, momentary impression, the Postimpressionists gave increased emphasis to color and compositional form. They embraced an "art-for-art's sake" aestheticism that prized pictorial invention over pictorial illusion. Strongly individualistic, they were uninterested in satisfying the demands of public and private patrons; most of them made only sporadic efforts to sell what they produced. Like the Impressionists, the Postimpressionists looked to the natural world for inspiration. But unlike their predecessors, they brought an elemental emphasis to their compositions, following the inspired observation of the French Symbolist Maurice Denis (1870–1943) that a painting, before being a pictorial representation of reality, is "a flat surface covered with shapes, lines, and colors assembled in a particular order." This credo, as realized in Postimpressionist art, would drive most of the major modern art movements of the early twentieth century (see chapter 32).

Van Gogh

The Dutch artist Vincent van Gogh (1853–1890) was a passionate idealist whose life was marred by loneliness, poverty, depression, and a hereditary mental illness that ultimately drove him to suicide. During his career he produced over 700 paintings and thousands of drawings, of which he sold fewer than a half-dozen in his lifetime.

Van Gogh painted landscapes, still lifes, and portraits in a style that featured flat, bright colors, a throbbing, sinuous line, short, choppy brushstrokes, and bold compositions that betray his admiration for Japanese woodblock prints. His heavily pigmented surfaces were often manipulated with a palette knife or built up by applying paint directly from the tube. Deeply moved by music (especially the work of Wagner), he shared with the Romantics an attitude toward nature that was both inspired and ecstatic. His emotional response to an object, rather than its physical appearance, influenced his choice of colors, which he likened to orchestrated sound. As he explained to his brother Theo, "I use color more arbitrarily so as to express myself more forcefully."

Van Gogh's painting *The Starry Night* (Figure **31.29**), a view of the small French town of Saint-Rémy, is electrified

Figure 31.29 VINCENT VAN GOGH, *The Starry Night*, 1889. Oil on canvas, 2 ft. 5 in. × 3 ft. ¼ in. In 1889, Van Gogh began a year's stay at the mental hospital in Saint-Rémy near Arles, an area of southern France renowned for its intermittent fierce winds, known as "the mistral." Mistral winds and clear night skies filled with shooting stars may have provided inspiration for this painting.

Figure 31.30 VINCENT VAN GOGH, *Self-Portrait*, 1889. Oil on canvas, 25½ × 21¼ in.

by thickly painted strokes of white, yellow, orange, and blue. Cypresses writhe like flames, stars explode, the moon seems to burn like the sun, and the heavens heave and roll like ocean waves. Here, Van Gogh's expressive use of color invests nature with visionary frenzy.

In his letters to Theo (an art dealer by profession), Van Gogh pledged his undying faith in the power of artistic creativity. In 1888, just two years before he committed suicide, he wrote: "I can do without God both in my life and in my painting, but I cannot, ill as I am, do without something which is greater than I, which is my life—the power to create. And if, defrauded of the power to create physically, a man tries to create thoughts in place of children, he is still part of humanity." Assessing his own creativity, Van Gogh claimed that making portraits allowed him to cultivate what was "best and deepest." "Altogether," he explained, "it is the only thing in painting which moves me to the depths, and which more than anything else makes me feel the infinite." For Van Gogh, the challenge of portraiture lay in capturing the heart and soul of the model. His many portraits of friends and neighbors, and the twenty-four self-portraits he painted between 1886 and 1889, elevate Romantic subjectivity to new levels of confessional intensity. In the *Self-Portrait* of 1889 (Figure **31.30**), for instance, where the pale flesh tones of the head are set against an almost monochromatic blue field, the skull takes on a forbidding, even spectral presence—an effect enhanced by the lurid green facial shadows and the blue-green eyes, slanted (as he related to Theo) so as to make himself look Japanese. His brushstrokes, similar to those

that evoke the roiling heavens in *The Starry Night*, charge the surface with undulating rhythms that contrast sharply with the immobile figure. This visual strategy underscores the artist's monkish alienation. Indeed, Van Gogh confessed to his colleague Gauguin that he saw himself in this portrait as a simple Buddhist monk.

Gauguin

Van Gogh's friend and colleague Paul Gauguin (1848–1903) shared his sense of alienation from middle-class European society. Part-Peruvian, he spent his earliest childhood in South America; in his teens he joined the merchant marines before settling down in Paris. After ten years of marriage, he abandoned his wife, his five children, and his job as a Paris stockbroker to devote himself to painting. He traveled to Brittany in northwest France, to Martinique in the West Indies, to Tahiti in the South Seas, and to southern France, returning for good to the islands of the South Pacific in 1895.

Gauguin took artistic inspiration from the folk culture of Brittany, the native arts of the South Sea islands, and dozens of other nontraditional sources. What impressed him was the self-taught immediacy and authenticity of indigenous artforms, especially those that made use of powerful, totemic abstraction (see Figure 31.27). His own style, nurtured in the Symbolist precepts (discussed earlier in this chapter) and influenced by Japanese woodcuts and photographs of Japanese temple reliefs on view at the *Exposition Universelle* in 1889, featured flat, often distorted and brightly colored shapes that seem to float on the surface of the canvas.

In *The Day of the God* (Figure **31.31**), bright blues, yellows, and pinks form tapestrylike patterns reminiscent of Japanese prints and *Art Nouveau* posters. Gauguin's figures cast no shadows; his bold, unmodeled colors, like those of Van Gogh, are more decorative than illusionistic. Like the verbal images of the Symbolist poets, Gauguin's colored shapes carry an intuitive charge that lies beyond literal description. For example, the languid, organic shapes in the foreground pool of water and the fetal positions of the figures lying on the shore are suggestive of birth and regeneration. These and other figures in the painting seem spiritually related to the totemic guardian figure (pictured at top center of the canvas), who resembles the creator god and supreme deity of Maori culture.

Gauguin joined Van Gogh at Arles in southeastern France in the fall of 1888, and for a brief time the two artists lived and worked side by side. Volatile and temperamental, they often engaged in violent quarrels, during one of which part of Van Gogh's ear was cut off, either by Van Gogh himself, or (as some historians claim) by Gauguin. But despite their intense personal differences, the two artists were fraternal pioneers in the search for a provocative language of form and color. Gauguin's self-conscious effort to assume the role of "the civilized savage" was rooted in the notion of the *primitif*, the condition of unspoiled nature celebrated by Rousseau, Thoreau, and others. His flight to the South Seas represents the search for a lost Eden, and reflects the fascination with exotic non-Western cultures

Figure 31.31 PAUL GAUGUIN, *The Day of the God* (*Mahana no Atua*), 1894. Oil on canvas, 27⅜ × 35⅝ in. The blues in the background are of the same intensity as those in the foreground, thereby flattening space to create a tapestrylike surface. Gauguin denied that his paintings carried specific meanings. "My dream is intangible," he wrote a friend, "it comprises no allegory."

that swept through late nineteenth-century Europe. As such, Gauguin's bohemian nonconformity may have been the "last gasp" of Romanticism.

Seurat

Rejecting the formlessness of Impressionism, Georges Seurat (1859–1891) introduced strict methods of pictorial construction. Trained academically, he brought a degree of balance and order to his compositions that rivaled the works of Poussin and David. The figures in a Seurat painting seem plotted along an invisible grid of vertical and horizontal lines that run parallel to the picture plane. Every form assumes a preordained place. A similar fervor for order may have inspired Seurat's novel use of tiny dots of paint (in French, *points*). These he applied side by side (and sometimes one inside another) to build up dense clusters that intensified color and gave the impression of solid form—a style known as *pointillism*. He arrived at the technique of dividing color into component parts after studying the writings of Chevreul and other pioneers in color theory, such as the American physicist Ogden N. Rood (1831–1902), whose *Modern Chromatics, with Applications to Art and Industry* (translated into French in 1880) showed that optical mixtures of color were more intense than premixed colors. Leaving nothing to chance (Gauguin called him "the little green chemist"), Seurat applied each colored

dot so that its juxtaposition with the next would produce the desired degree of vibration to the eye of the beholder. Although Seurat shared the Impressionists' fascination with light and color, he shunned spontaneity, for while he made his sketches out-of-doors, he executed his paintings inside his studio, usually at night and under artificial light.

Seurat's monumental *Sunday Afternoon on the Island of La Grande Jatte* shows a holiday crowd of Parisians relaxing on a sunlit island in the River Seine (Figure **31.32**). Although typically Impressionistic in its subject matter—urban society at leisure—the painting (based on no fewer than twenty drawings and 200 oil studies) harbors little of the Impressionist's love for intimacy and fleeting sensation. Every figure is isolated from the next as if it were frozen in space and unaware of another's existence. Seurat claimed that he wished to invest his subjects with the gravity of the figures in a Greek frieze. Nevertheless, one critic railed: "Strip his figures of the colored fleas that cover them; underneath you will find nothing, no thought, no soul." Seurat's universe, with its atomized particles of color and its self-contained figures, may seem devoid of human feeling, but its exquisite regularity provides a comforting alternative to the chaos of experience. Indeed, the lasting appeal of *La Grande Jatte* lies in its effectiveness as a symbolic retreat from the tumult of everyday life and the accidents of nature.

Figure 31.32 GEORGES SEURAT, *Sunday Afternoon on the Island of La Grande Jatte*, 1884–1886. Oil on canvas, 6 ft. 9½ in. × 10 ft. ⅜ in. Nothing is left to chance in this highly formalized vision of the good life. Seurat died of diphtheria at the age of thirty-one, having completed barely a decade of mature work.

Figure 31.33 PAUL CÉZANNE, *The Basket of Apples*, ca. 1895. Oil on canvas, 25¾ × 32 in. The rear edge of the tabletop marks the horizon line at two different places; the top two lady-fingers are seen from above, while those below and the plate itself are seen straight on. Such deliberate deviations from optical realism characterize many of Cézanne's still lifes.

Figure 31.34 PAUL CÉZANNE, *Mont Sainte-Victoire*, 1902–1904. Oil on canvas, 27½ × 35¼ in. Between 1880 and his death in 1906, the so-called Master of Aix produced no fewer than twenty-five oil paintings and watercolors of his favorite mountain as seen from the countryside around his native city. In this rendering, dense patches of color come close to pure abstraction.

Cézanne

More so than Seurat, Paul Cézanne (1839–1906) served as a bridge between the art of the nineteenth century and that of the twentieth. Cézanne began his career as an Impressionist in Paris, but his traditional subjects—landscapes, portraits, and still lifes—show a greater concern for the formal aspects of a painting than for its subject matter. His effort to "redo nature after Poussin," that is, to find the enduring forms of nature that were basic to all great art, made Cézanne the first Modernist painter.

Cézanne's determination to invest his pictures with a strong sense of three-dimensionality (a feature often neglected by the Impressionists) led to a method of building up form by means of small, flat planes of color, larger than (but not entirely unlike) Seurat's colored dots. Abandoning the intuitive and loosely organized compositions of the Impressionists, Cézanne also sought to restore to painting the sturdy formality of academic composition. His desire to achieve pictorial unity inspired bold liberties of form and perspective: he might tilt and flatten surfaces; reduce (or abstract) familiar objects to basic geometric shapes—cylinders, cones, and spheres; or depict various objects in a single composition from different points of view. Cézanne's still lifes are not so much tempting likenesses of apples, peaches, or pears as they are architectural arrangements of colored forms (Figure **31.33**). Where narrative content often seems incidental, form itself takes on greater meaning.

Cézanne's mature style developed when he left Paris and returned to live in his native area of southern France. Here he tirelessly studied the local landscape: dozens of times he painted the rugged, stony peak of Mont Sainte-Victoire near his hometown of Aix-en-Provence. Among his last versions of the subject is a landscape in which trees and houses have become an abstract network of colored facets of paint (Figure **31.34**). By applying colors of the same intensity to different parts of the canvas—note the bright green and rich violet brushstrokes in both sky and landscape—Cézanne challenged traditional distinctions between foreground and background. In his canvases, all parts of the composition, like the flat shapes of a Japanese print, have become equal in value. Cézanne's methods, which transformed an ordinary mountain into a monumental icon, led the way to modern abstraction.

Late Nineteenth-Century Thought

- The provocative German thinker Friedrich Wilhelm Nietzsche, who detected in European materialism a deepening decadence, called for a revision of traditional values.
- While Nietzsche anticipated the darker side of Modernism, Henri Bergson presented a positive view of life as a vital impulse that evolved creatively and intuitively.

Poetry in the Late Nineteenth Century: The Symbolists

- Symbolist poets, such as Paul Verlaine and Arthur Rimbaud, devised a language of sensation that evoked rather than described feeling.
- In Stéphane Mallarmé's "L'après-midi d'un faune," sensuous images unfold as discontinuous literary fragments.

Music in the Late Nineteenth Century: Debussy

- Symbolist poetry found its counterpart in music. The compositions of Claude Debussy engage the listener through nuance and atmosphere.
- Inspired by Indonesian music, Wagnerian opera, and Symbolist poetry, Debussy created a mood of reverie in the shifting harmonies of his *Prelude to "The Afternoon of a Faun."*

Painting in the Late Nineteenth Century

- The Impressionists, led by Monet, were equally representative of the late nineteenth-century interest in sensation and sensory experience. These artists tried to record an instantaneous vision of their world, sacrificing the details of perceived objects in order to capture the effects of light and atmosphere.
- Renoir, Degas, and Pissarro produced informal, painterly canvases that offer a glimpse into the pleasures of nineteenth-century urban life.
- Two major influences on late nineteenth-century artists were stop-action photography and Japanese woodblock prints. The latter, originally popularized as souvenirs, entered Europe with Asian trade goods.
- In the domestic interiors of Cassatt and the cabarets of Toulouse-Lautrec, scenes of everyday life show the influence of Japanese prints.

Art Nouveau

- Originating in Belgium, *Art Nouveau* ("new art") was an ornamental style that became enormously popular in the late nineteenth century.
- The proponents of the style prized the arts of Asia and Islam, which featured bold, flat, organic patterns and semiabstract linear designs. In America, the style was advanced in the art glass of Louis Comfort Tiffany.

Sculpture in the Late Nineteenth Century

- The works of Degas and Rodin reflect a common concern for figural gesture and expressive movement.
- Rodin's efforts to translate inner states of feeling into physical form were mirrored by Isadora Duncan's innovations in modern dance.

The Arts of Africa and Oceania

- The late nineteenth century was a time of high artistic productivity in Africa and Oceania. Reliquaries, masks, and free-standing sculptures were among the power objects created to channel the spirits of ancestors, celebrate rites of passage, and ensure the well-being of the community.
- While sharing with some Western styles (such as Symbolism) a general disregard for objective representation, the visual arts of Africa and Oceania stood apart from nineteenth-century Western academic tradition.

Primitivism

- Colonialism and travel to Africa and Oceania worked to introduce the West to cultures that were perceived by some as exotic and violent, and by others as "primitive" and blissfully close to nature.
- The Paris *Exposition Universelle* of 1889 brought non-Western culture to public attention, encouraging the establishment of ethnographic collections and a broader interest in the world beyond the West.

Postimpressionism

- Renouncing their predecessors' infatuation with the fleeting effects of light, the Postimpressionists explored new pictorial strategies.
- Van Gogh and Gauguin used color not as an atmospheric envelope but rather as a tool for personal, symbolic, and visionary expression.
- Seurat and Cézanne reacted against the formlessness of Impressionism by inventing styles that featured architectural stability.

Music Listening Selection

- Debussy, *Prélude à "L'après-midi d'un faune,"* 1894.

Glossary

can-can (French, "scandal") a high-energy dance popular in Parisian music-halls of the late nineteenth century

negative space the background or ground area seen in relation to the shape of the (positive) figure

Book

6

Modernism, Postmodernism, and the Global Perspective

The Modernist Assault
ca. 1900–1950

*"What is real is not the external form,
but the essence of things."*
Constantin Brancusi

Figure 32.1 PABLO PICASSO, *Man with a Violin*, 1911. Oil on canvas, 3 ft. 3½ in. × 2 ft. 5⅞ in. Knit by a lively arrangement of flat shaded planes, monochromatic in color, figure and ground are almost indistinguishable in this Cubist canvas. Representational elements—the man and the violin—are evident in only bits and pieces abstracted from the whole.

Since the birth of civilization, no age has broken with tradition more radically or more self-consciously than the twentieth century. In its first decades, the spirit and the style of this new direction came to be called "Modernism." Modernism rejected former cultural values and conventions in favor of innovation, experimentation, and (at its most extreme) anarchy, the absolute dissolution of established norms.

The Modernist revolution in the creative arts responded to equally revolutionary changes in science and technology. The transformation in technology began at the end of the nineteenth century with the invention of the telephone (1876), wireless telegraphy (1891), and the internal combustion engine (1892), which made possible the first gasoline-powered automobiles. In France and the United States, the mass production of automobiles was underway by 1900. Among the swelling populations of modern cities, the pace of living became faster than ever before. By 1903, the airplane joined the string of enterprises that ushered in an era of rapid travel and communication—a "shrinking" of the planet that would produce the "global village" of the late twentieth century. Advances in scientific theory proved equally significant: atomic physics, which provided a new understanding of the physical universe, was as momentous for the twentieth century as metallurgy was for the fourth millennium B.C.E. But while the latter contributed to the birth of civilization, the former, which ushered in the nuclear age, threatened its survival.

The modern era—roughly the first half of the twentieth century—is considered thematically in the next three chapters. The first, chapter 32, deals with the Modernist assault on tradition in the arts. Chapter 33 examines the shaping influence of the great Austrian psychiatrist Sigmund Freud, whose writings had a shattering effect on every form of cultural expression. Chapter 34 considers the brutal impact of totalitarianism and the two world wars that put the potentially liberating tools of the new science and technology to horrifically destructive ends.

The New Physics

At the turn of the twentieth century, atomic physicists advanced a model of the universe that challenged the one Isaac Newton had provided two centuries earlier. Newton's universe operated according to smoothly functioning laws that generally corresponded with the world of sense perception. Modern physicists found, however, that at the physical extremes of nature—the microcosmic (the very small or very fast) realm of atomic particles and the macrocosmic world of heavy astronomical bodies—the laws of Newton's *Principia* did not apply. A more comprehensive model of the universe began to emerge after 1880 when two American physicists, Albert Michelson and Edward Morley, determined that the speed of light is a universal constant. In 1897, the English physicist Joseph J. Thompson (1846–1940) identified the electron, the elementary subatomic particle whose interaction between atoms is the main cause of chemical bonding. Three years later, the German physicist Max Planck (1858–1947) suggested that light waves sometimes behaved as *quanta*, that is, as separate and discontinuous bundles of energy.

Alongside this and other groundbreaking work in *quantum physics* (as the field came to be called), yet another German physicist, Albert Einstein (1879–1955), made public his *special theory of relativity* (1905), a radically new approach to the new concepts of time, space, motion, and light. While Newton had held that objects preserved properties such as mass and length whether at rest or in motion, Einstein theorized that as an object's speed approached the speed of light, its mass increased and its length contracted; no object could move faster than light, and light did not require any medium to carry it. In essence, Einstein's theory held that all measurable motion is relative to some other object, and that no universal coordinates, and no hypothetical ether, exist.

Building on Einstein's theories, Werner Heisenberg (1901–1976) theorized that since the very act of measuring subatomic phenomena altered them, the position and the velocity of a subatomic particle could not be measured simultaneously with absolute accuracy. Heisenberg's *principle of uncertainty* (1927)—the more precisely the position of a particle is determined, the less precisely its momentum can be known—replaced the absolute and rationalist model of the universe with one whose exact mechanisms at the subatomic level are indeterminate.

Science and Technology

1900	Max Planck (German) announces his quantum theory
1903	Henry Ford (American) introduces the Model A automobile
1905	Albert Einstein (German) announces his special theory of relativity
1910	Bertrand Russell and Alfred North Whitehead (British) publish their *Principia Mathematica*, a systematic effort to base mathematics in logic
1913	Niels Bohr (Danish) applies quantum theory to atomic structure
1916	Einstein announces his general theory of relativity

Quantum physics gave humankind greater insight into the workings of the universe, but it also made the operation of that universe more remote from the average person's understanding. The basic components of nature—subatomic particles—were inaccessible to both the human eye and the camera, hence beyond the realm of the senses. Nevertheless, the practical implications of the new physics were immense: radar technology, computers, and consumer electronics were only three of its numerous long-range consequences. Atomic fission, the splitting of atomic particles (begun only after 1920), and the atomic bomb itself (first tested in 1945) confirmed the validity of Einstein's famous formula, $E=mc^2$, which shows that mass and energy are different manifestations of the same thing; and therefore (in his words), "a very small amount of mass [matter] can be converted into a very large amount of energy." The new physics paved the way for the atomic age. It also radically altered the way in which human beings understood the physical world.

Early Twentieth-Century Poetry

Modern poets had little use for the self-indulgent sentiments of the nineteenth-century Romantics and the idealism of the Symbolists. They found in nature neither ecstasy nor redemption. If nature was indeed both random and relative, the job of these poets might be to find a new language for conveying its unique character, one that captured the disjunctive eccentricities of an indifferent cosmos. At the least, they would produce a style that was as conceptual and abstract as modern physics.

The Imagists

The leaders in the search for a more concentrated style of expression were a group of poets who called themselves *Imagists*. For the Imagist, the writer was like a sculptor, whose technique required that he carve away all extraneous matter in a process of **abstraction** that aimed to arrive at an intrinsic or essential form. Verbal compression, formal precision, and economy of expression were the goals of the Imagists. Renouncing traditional verse forms, fixed meter, and rhythm, their style of free verse became notorious for its abrupt and discontinuous juxtaposition of images. Essentially an English-language literary movement, Imagism attracted a number of talented American women, including Amy Lowell (1874–1925) and Hilda Doolittle (1886–1961), who signed her poems simply "H.D."

Imagism's most influential poet was the American expatriate Ezra Pound (1885–1972). By the age of twenty-three, Pound had abandoned his study of language and literature at American universities for a writing career that led him to Europe, where he wandered from England to France and Italy. A poet, critic, and translator, Pound was thoroughly familiar with the literature of his contemporaries, but he cast his net wide: he studied the prose and poetry of ancient Greece and Rome, China and Japan, medieval France and Renaissance Italy—often reading such works in their original language. As a student of East Asian calligraphy, he drew inspiration from the sparseness and subtlety of Chinese characters. He was particularly fascinated by the fact that the Chinese poetic line, which presented images without grammar or syntax, operated in the same intuitive manner that nature worked upon the human mind. It was this vitality that Pound wished to bring to poetry.

In Chinese and Japanese verse—especially in the Japanese poetic genre known as **haiku** (see chapter 21)—Pound found the key to his search for concentrated expression. Two of his most famous *haiku*-like poems are found in the collection called *Personae*. He claimed that it took him a year and a half to write the first of these poems, cutting down the verse from thirty lines to two.

READING 32.1 From Pound's *Personae* (1926)

"In a Station of the Metro"
The apparition of these faces in the crowd;
Petals on a wet, black bough.

"The Bath Tub"
As a bathtub lined with white porcelain,
When the hot water gives out or goes tepid,
So is the slow cooling of our chivalrous passion,
O my much praised but-not-altogether-satisfactory lady.

Q In what ways are these poems abstract?

Q What effects are created by the juxtaposition of the key images?

Pound imitated the *haiku*-style succession of images to evoke subtle, metaphoric relationships between things. He conceived what he called the "rhythmical arrangement of words" to produce an emotional "shape."

In the *Imagist Manifesto* (1913) and in various interviews, Pound outlined the cardinal points of the Imagist doctrine: poets should use "absolutely no word that does not contribute to the presentation"; and they should employ free verse rhythms "in sequence of the musical phrase." Ultimately, Pound summoned his contemporaries to cast aside traditional modes of Western verse-making and "make it new"—a dictum allegedly scrawled on the bathtub of an ancient Chinese emperor. "Day by day," wrote Pound, "make it new/cut underbrush/pile the logs/keep it growing." The injunction to "make it new" became the rallying cry of Modernism.

The Imagist search for an abstract language of expression stood at the beginning of the Modernist revolution in poetry. It also opened the door to a more concealed and elusive style of poetry, one that drew freely on the cornucopia of world literature and history. The poems that Pound wrote after 1920, particularly the *Cantos* (the unfinished opus on which Pound labored for fifty-five years), are filled with foreign language phrases, obscene jokes, and arcane literary and historical allusions juxtaposed without connective tissue. These poems contrast sharply with the terse precision and eloquent purity of Pound's early Imagist efforts.

T. S. Eliot

No English-speaking poet advanced the Modernist agenda more powerfully than the American-born writer T. S. (Thomas Stearns) Eliot (1888–1965). Meeting Pound in 1914, Eliot joined him in the effort to rid modern poetry of romantic sentiment. He held that poetry must seek the verbal formula or "objective correlative" (as he called it) that gives precise shape to feeling. Eliot's style soon became notable for its inventive rhythms, irregular cadences, and startling images, many of which draw on personal reminiscences and obscure literary resources.

Educated at Harvard University in philosophy and the classics, Eliot was studying at Oxford when World War I broke out. He remained in England after the war, becoming a British citizen in 1927 and converting to the Anglican faith in the same year. His intellectual grasp of modern philosophy, world religions, anthropology, and the classical literature of Asia and the West made him the most erudite literary figure of his time.

Begun in 1910, Eliot's poem "The Love Song of J. Alfred Prufrock" (reproduced here in full) captures the waning idealism that pervaded the years leading up to World War I. The "love song" is actually the dramatic monologue of a timid, middle-aged man who has little faith in himself or his capacity for effective action. Prufrock's cynicism anticipated the disillusion and the sense of impotence that marked the postwar generation (discussed in greater detail in chapter 34).

READING 32.2 Eliot's "The Love Song of
J. Alfred Prufrock" (1915)

*S'io credesse che mia risposta fosse
A persona che mai tornasse al mondo,
Questa fiamma staria senza piu scosse.
Ma perciocche giammai di questo fondo
Non torno vivo alcun s'i'odo il vero,
Senza tema d'infamia ti rispondo.*[1]

Let us go then, you and I,   1
When the evening is spread out against the sky
Like a patient etherised upon a table;
Let us go, through certain half-deserted streets,
The muttering retreats   5
Of restless nights in one-night cheap hotels
And sawdust restaurants with oyster-shells:
Streets that follow like a tedious argument
Of insidious intent
To lead you to an overwhelming question . . .   10
Oh, do not ask, "What is it?"
Let us go and make our visit.

In the room the women come and go
Talking of Michelangelo.

The yellow fog that rubs its back upon the window-panes,   15
The yellow smoke that rubs its muzzle on the window-panes
Licked its tongue into the corners of the evening,
Lingered upon the pools that stand in drains,
Let fall upon its back the soot that falls from chimneys,
Slipped by the terrace, made a sudden leap,   20
And seeing that it was a soft October night,
Curled once about the house, and fell asleep.

And indeed there will be time
For the yellow smoke that slides along the street,
Rubbing its back upon the window-panes;   25
There will be time, there will be time
To prepare a face to meet the faces that you meet;
There will be time to murder and create,
And time for all the works and days of hands[2]
That lift and drop a question on your plate;   30
Time for you and time for me,
And time yet for a hundred indecisions,
And for a hundred visions and revisions,
Before the taking of a toast and tea.

In the room the women come and go   35
Talking of Michelangelo.

And indeed there will be time
To wonder, "Do I dare?" and, "Do I dare?"
Time to turn back and descend the stair,
With a bald spot in the middle of my hair—   40
(They will say: "How his hair is growing thin!")
My morning coat, my collar mounting firmly to the chin,
My necktie rich and modest, but asserted by a simple pin—
(They will say: "But how his arms and legs are thin!")
Do I dare   45
Disturb the universe?
In a minute there is time
For decisions and revisions which a minute will reverse.

For I have known them all already, known them all—
Have known the evenings, mornings, afternoons,   50
I have measured out my life with coffee spoons;
I know the voices dying with a dying fall
Beneath the music from a farther room.
    So how should I presume?

And I have known the eyes already, known them all—   55
The eyes that fix you in a formulated phrase,
And when I am formulated, sprawling on a pin,
When I am pinned and wriggling on the wall,
Then how should I begin
To spit out all the butt-ends of my days and ways?   60
    And how should I presume?

---

[1] Lines from Dante's "Inferno," Canto 27, 61–66, spoken by Guido da Montefeltro, who was condemned to Hell for the sin of false counseling. In explaining his punishment to Dante, Guido is still apprehensive of the judgment of society.

[2] An ironic allusion to the poem "Works and Days" by the eighth-century B.C.E. poet Hesiod, which celebrates the virtues of hard labor on the land.

And I have known the arms already, known them all—
Arms that are braceleted and white and bare
(But in the lamplight, downed with light brown hair!)
Is it perfume from a dress   65
That makes me so digress?
Arms that lie along a table, or wrap about a shawl.
    And should I then presume?
    And how should I begin?

. . . .

    Shall I say, I have gone at dusk through narrow streets   70
And watched the smoke that rises from the pipes
Of lonely men in shirt-sleeves, leaning out of windows? . . .

    I should have been a pair of ragged claws
Scuttling across the floors of silent seas.

. . . .

    And the afternoon, the evening, sleeps so peacefully!   75
Smoothed by long fingers,
Asleep . . . tired . . . or it malingers,
Stretched on the floor, here beside you and me.
Should I, after tea and cakes and ices,
Have the strength to force the moment to its crisis?   80
But though I have wept and fasted, wept and prayed,
Though I have seen my head (grown slightly bald)
    brought in upon a platter,
I am no prophet—and here's no great matter;[3]
I have seen the moment of my greatness flicker,
And I have seen the eternal Footman hold my coat, and
    snicker,   85
And in short, I was afraid.

    And would it have been worth it, after all,
After the cups, the marmalade, the tea,
Among the porcelain, among some talk of you and me,
Would it have been worth while,   90
To have bitten off the matter with a smile,
To have squeezed the universe into a ball[4]
To roll it toward some overwhelming question,
To say: "I am Lazarus, come from the dead,[5]
Come back to tell you all, I shall tell you all"—   95
If one, settling a pillow by her head,
    Should say: "That is not what I meant at all,
    That is not it, at all."

    And would it have been worth it, after all,
Would it have been worth while,   100
After the sunsets and the dooryards and the sprinkled streets,
After the novels, after the teacups, after the skirts that
    trail along the floor—

And this, and so much more?—
It is impossible to say just what I mean!
But as if a magic lantern threw the nerves in patterns on
    a screen: 105
Would it have been worth while
If one, settling a pillow or throwing off a shawl,
And turning towards the window, should say:
    "That is not it at all,
    That is not what I meant, at all."   110

. . . .

    No! I am not Prince Hamlet, nor was meant to be;
Am an attendant lord, one that will do
To swell a progress, start a scene or two,
Advise the prince; no doubt, an easy tool,[6]
Deferential, glad to be of use,   115
Politic, cautious, and meticulous;
Full of high sentence, but a bit obtuse;
At times, indeed, almost ridiculous—
Almost, at times, the Fool.

    I grow old . . . I grow old . . .   120
I shall wear the bottoms of my trousers rolled.[7]

    Shall I part my hair behind? Do I dare to eat a peach?
I shall wear white flannel trousers, and walk upon the beach.
I have heard the mermaids singing, each to each.
I do not think that they will sing to me.   125
I have seen them riding seaward on the waves
Combing the white hair of the waves blown back
When the wind blows the water white and black.

We have lingered in the chambers of the sea
By sea-girls wreathed with seaweed red and brown   130
Till human voices wake us, and we drown.

Q How would you describe the personality of Eliot's
Prufrock?

Q What do each of the literary allusions add to our
understanding of the poem?

The tone of Eliot's poem is established by way of powerfully compressed (and gloomy) images: "one-night cheap
hotels," "sawdust restaurants," "soot that falls from chimneys," "narrow streets," and "lonely men in shirt-sleeves."
Eliot's literary vignettes, and allusions to biblical prophets and to the heroes of history and art (Hamlet and
Michelangelo), work as foils to Prufrock's bankrupt idealism, underlining his self-conscious retreat from action, and
his loss of faith in the conventional sources of wisdom. The
voices of inspiration, concludes Prufrock, are submerged
by all-too-human voices, including his own. Prufrock's
moral inertia made him an archetype of the condition of
spiritual loss associated with Modernism.

---

[3] A reference to John the Baptist, who was beheaded by Herod
(Matthew 14: 3–11). Prufrock perceives himself as victim but as
neither saint nor martyr.

[4] A reference to the line "Let us roll all our strength and all our
sweetness up into one ball," from the poem "To his Coy Mistress"
by the seventeenth-century English poet Andrew Marvell, in which
Marvell presses his lover to "seize the day."

[5] According to the Gospel of John (11: 1–44), Jesus raised Lazarus from
the grave.

[6] A reference to Polonius, the king's advisor in Shakespeare's *Hamlet*,
as well as to Guido da Montefeltro—both of them false counselors.

[7] In Eliot's time, rolled or cuffed trousers were considered fashionable.

Frost and Lyric Poetry

Robert Frost (1874–1963), the best known and one of the most popular of American poets, offered an alternative to the abstract style of the Modernists. While Frost rejected the romantic sentimentality of much nineteenth-century verse, he embraced the older tradition of Western lyric poetry. He wrote in metered verse and jokingly compared the Modernist use of free verse to playing tennis without a net. Frost avoided dense allusions and learned references. In plain speech he expressed deep affection for the natural landscape and an abiding sympathy with the frailties of the human condition. He described American rural life as uncertain and enigmatic—at times, notably dark. "My poems," explained Frost, "are all set to trip the reader head foremost into the boundless." Frost's "The Road Not Taken" is written in the rugged and direct language that became the hallmark of his mature style. The poem exalts a profound individualism as well as a sparseness of expression in line with the Modernist injunction to "make it new."

READING 32.3 Frost's "The Road Not Taken" (1916)

Two roads diverged in a yellow wood,	1
And sorry I could not travel both	
And be one traveler, long I stood	
And looked down one as far as I could	
To where it bent in the undergrowth;	5
Then took the other, as just as fair,	
And having perhaps the better claim,	
Because it was grassy and wanted wear,	
Though as for that the passing there	
Had worn them really about the same,	10
And both that morning equally lay	
In leaves no step had trodden black.	
Oh, I kept the first for another day!	
Yet knowing how way leads on to way,	
I doubted if I should ever come back.	15
I shall be telling this with a sigh	
Somewhere ages and ages hence:	
Two roads diverged in a wood, and I—	
I took the one less traveled by,	
And that has made all the difference.	20

Q Why might Frost's choice of roads have made "all the difference"?

Q How does the poem illustrate Frost's fondness for direct language?

Early Twentieth-Century Art

As with Modernist poetry, the art of the early twentieth century came to challenge all that preceded it. Liberated by the camera from the necessity of imitating nature, **avant-garde** artists questioned the value of art as

a faithful recreation of the visible world. They pioneered an authentic, "stripped down" style that, much like Imagist poetry, *evoked* rather than *described* experience. They pursued the intrinsic qualities and essential meanings of their subject matter to arrive at a concentrated emotional experience. The language of pure form did not, however, rob modern art of its humanistic dimension; rather, it provided artists with a means by which to move beyond traditional ways of representing the visual world. Abstraction—one of the central tenets of Modernism—promised to purify nature so as to come closer to its true reality.

Early Modern artists probed the tools and techniques of formal expression more fully than any artists since the Renaissance. Deliberately blurring the boundaries between painting and sculpture, they attached three-dimensional objects to two-dimensional surfaces, thereby violating traditional categories of style and format. Like the Imagists, they found inspiration in non-Western cultures in which art shared the power of ritual. Innovation, abstraction, and experimentation became the hallmarks of the Modernist revolt against convention and tradition.

Picasso

The giant of twentieth-century art was the Spanish-born Pablo Picasso (1881–1973). During his ninety-two-year life, Picasso worked in almost every major art style of the century, some of which he himself inaugurated. He produced thousands of paintings, drawings, sculptures, and prints—a body of work that in its size, inventiveness, and influence is nothing short of phenomenal. As a child, he showed an extraordinary gift for drawing, and by the time he was twenty his precise and lyrical line style rivaled that of Raphael and Ingres. In 1903, the young painter left his native Spain to settle in Paris. There, in the bustling capital of the Western art world, he came under the influence of Impressionist and Postimpressionist painting, taking as his subjects café life, beggars, prostitutes, and circus folk. Much like the Imagists, Picasso worked to refine form and color in the direction of concentrated expression, reducing the colors of his palette first to various shades of blue and then, after 1904, to tones of rose.

By 1906, Picasso began to abandon traditional Western modes of pictorial representation. In that year he started a large painting that would become his foremost assault on tradition: *Les Demoiselles d'Avignon* (see Figure 32.2). *Les Demoiselles* depicts five nude women—the prostitutes of a Barcelona bordello in the Carrer d'Avino (Avignon Street). The subject matter of the work looked back to the long, respectable Western tradition of representing the female nude or group of nudes in a landscape setting (see Figure 32.3). However, *Les Demoiselles* violated every shred of tradition.

The manner in which Picasso "made new" a traditional subject in Western art is worth examining: in the early sketches for the painting, originally called *The Philosophical Brothel*, Picasso included two male figures, one of whom resembled the artist himself. However, in 1906, Picasso came under the influence of a number of important exhibitions: a show of archaic Iberian sculptures at the Louvre,

Picasso's *Les Demoiselles d'Avignon* (Figure **32.2**) reflects the artist's keen attention to the art of his time, publically displayed in the salons and museums of Paris. In Cézanne's canvases, with their flattened planes and arbitrary colors (Figure **32.3**), Picasso recognized a rigorous new language of form that seemed to define nature's underlying structure. And in African and Oceanic sculpture he discovered the power of art as the palpable embodiment of potent supernatural forces. Of the tribal masks and sculptures (Figure **32.4**), Picasso later explained: "For me, [they] were not just sculptures; they were magical objects . . . intercessors against unknown, threatening spirits." The union of expressive abstraction and dynamic distortion clearly characterizes both the Etoumbi image and the treatment of the two figures on the right in *Les Demoiselles d'Avignon*.

Figure 32.2 PABLO PICASSO,
Les Demoiselles d'Avignon, 1907.
Oil on canvas, 8 ft. × 7 ft. 8 in.

Figure 32.3 PAUL CÉZANNE, *The Large Bathers*, 1906. Oil on canvas, 6 ft. 10⅞ in. × 8 ft. 2¾ in. Picasso came to call this artist "the father of us all."

Figure 32.4 Mask from Etoumbi region, Democratic Republic of Congo. Wood, height 14 in. Scholars continue to debate exactly which works of tribal art Picasso viewed on his visits to the Musée d'Ethnographie du Trocadéro in Paris and which he encountered as African imports sold by Paris art dealers. The latter were purchased by artists (including Picasso himself) and collectors, such as Picasso's expatriate American friends Gertrude Stein and her brother, who resided in Paris.

an exhibition of Gauguin's Polynesian paintings and sculptures at the Salon d'Automne, and, the following year, a huge retrospective of Cézanne's major works. Finally, in the summer of 1907, Picasso fell deeply under the spell of African and Oceanic art on display both in local galleries and at the Musée d'Ethnographie du Trocadéro in Paris.

Reworking *The Philosophical Brothel*, Picasso eliminated the male figures and transformed the five prostitutes into a group of fierce iconic females, forbidding rather than seductive. For what he would later call his "first exorcism picture," he painted out the faces of the figures, giving the two on the right the features of African masks. He seems to have taken apart and reassembled the figures as if to test the physics of disjunction and discontinuity. At least three of the nudes are rendered not from a single vantage point but from multiple viewpoints, as if one's eye could travel freely in time and space. The body of the crouching female on the far right is seen from the back, while her face, savagely striated like the scarified surfaces of African and Polynesian sculptures (see Figures 18.10, 31.27, and 32.4), is seen from the front. The noses of the two central females appear in profile, while their eyes are frontal—a convention Picasso may have borrowed from ancient Egyptian frescoes (see Figure 2.17). The relationship between the figures and the shallow area they occupy is equally disjunctive: background becomes indistinguishable from foreground, and pictorial space is shattered by brutally fractured planes—brick reds and vivid blues—that resemble shards of glass. Stripping his "demoiselles" of all sensuous appeal, Picasso banished the alluring female nude from the domain of Western art.

The Birth of Cubism

Les Demoiselles was the precursor of an audacious new style known as *Cubism*, a bold and distinctive formal language that came to challenge the principles of Renaissance painting as dramatically as Einstein's theory of relativity had challenged Newtonian physics. In the Cubist canvas, the recognizable world of the senses disappears beneath a scaffold of semitransparent planes and short, angular lines; ordinary objects are made to look as if they have exploded and been reassembled somewhat arbitrarily in

geometric bits and pieces that rest on the surface of the picture plane (see Figure **32.1**). A comparison of this early Cubist painting with *Les Demoiselles d'Avignon* (see Figure 32.2) shows how far toward abstraction Picasso had moved in less than four years.

With *Analytic Cubism*, as the style came to be called, a multiplicity of viewpoints replaced one-point perspective. The Cubist image, conceived as if one were moving around, above, and below the subject and even perceiving it from within, appropriates the fourth dimension—time itself. Abrupt shifts in direction and an ambiguous spatial field call up the uncertainties of the new physics. As Picasso and his French colleague Georges Braque (1882–1963) collaborated in a search for an ever more pared-down language of form, their compositions became increasingly abstract and colors became cool and controlled: Cubism came to offer a new formal language, one wholly unconcerned with narrative content. Years later, Picasso defended the viability of this new language: "The fact that for a long time Cubism has not been understood . . . means nothing. I do not read English, an English book is a blank book to me. This does not mean that the English language does not exist."

Around 1912, a second phase of Cubism, namely *Synthetic Cubism*, emerged, when Braque first included three pieces of wallpaper in a still-life composition. Picasso and Braque, who thought of themselves as space pioneers (much like the Wright brothers), pasted mundane objects such as wine-bottle labels, playing cards, and scraps of newspaper onto the surface of the canvas—a technique known as **collage** (from the French *coller*, "to paste"). The result was a kind of art that was neither a painting nor a sculpture, but both at the same time. The two artists filled their canvases with puns, hidden messages, and subtle

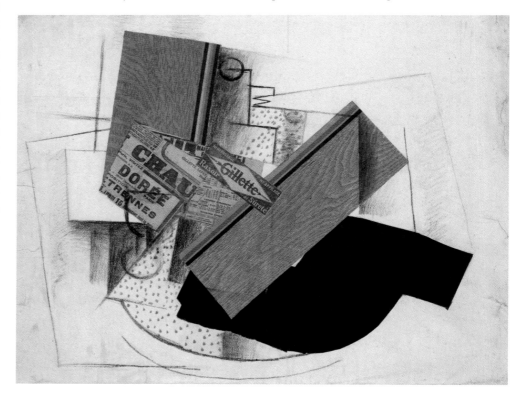

Figure 32.5 GEORGES BRAQUE, *Still Life on a Table*, ca. 1914. Collage on paper, 18⅞ × 24⅜ in. Trained as a decorator, Braque introduced stenciled letters, sand, and sawdust into his artworks. His use of newspaper clippings, wallpaper, wine-bottle labels, and wrappers gave his works greater density and challenged viewers to view everyday objects from different perspectives—conceptual and perceptual.

references to contemporary events; but the prevailing strategy in all these artworks was to test the notion of art as illusion.

In Braque's *Still Life on a Table* (Figure **32.5**), strips of imitation wood graining, a razor-blade wrapper, and newspaper clippings serve the double function of "presenting" and "representing." Words and images wrenched out of context here play off one another like some cryptographic billboard. Prophetic of twentieth-century art in general, Braque would proclaim: "The subject is not the object of the painting, but a new unity, the lyricism that results from method."

Assemblage

In these years, Picasso also created the first **assemblages**—artworks that were built up, or pieced together, from miscellaneous or commonplace materials. Like the collage, the three-dimensional assemblage depended on the inventive combination of found objects and materials. As such, it constituted a radical alternative to traditional techniques of carving in stone, metal casting, and modeling in clay or plaster. The art of assemblage clearly drew inspiration from African and Oceanic traditions of combining natural materials (such as cowrie shells, beads, and raffia) for masks and costumes; it also took heed of the expressive simplifications that typify power objects, reliquaries, and other tribal artforms. Picasso's *Guitar* of 1912–1913 achieves its powerful effect by means of fragmented planes, deliberate spatial inversions (note the projecting soundhole), and the wedding of sheet metal and wire (Figure **32.6**).

Within a decade, Western sculptors were employing the strategies of Synthetic Cubism in ways that reflected abstract models of time and space. The Russian-born cubist Alexander Archipenko (1887–1964), for instance, fashioned the female form so that an area of negative space actually constitutes the head (Figure **32.7**).

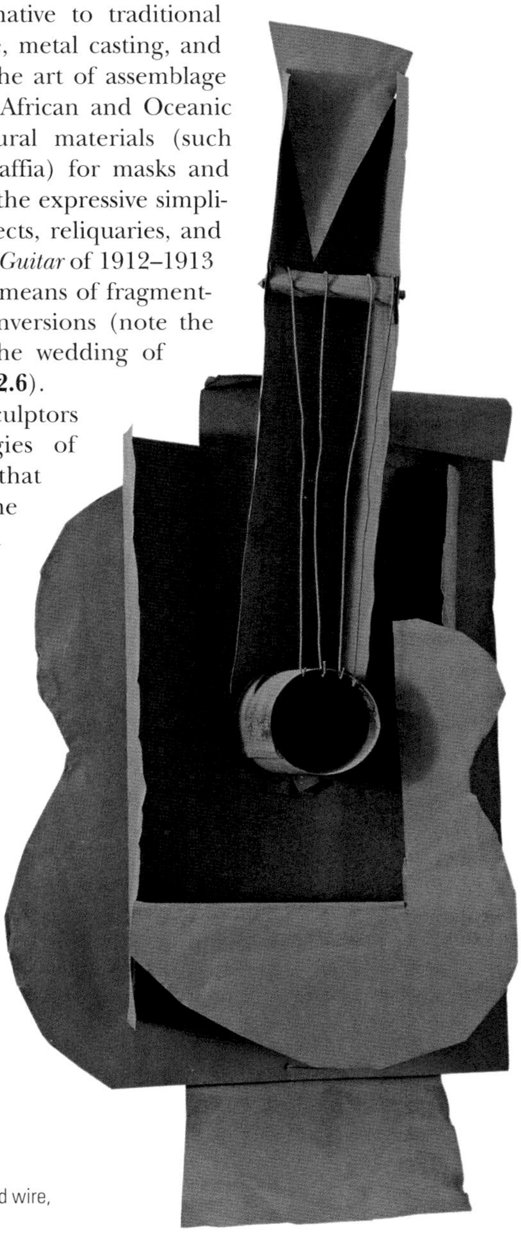

Figure 32.7 ALEXANDER ARCHIPENKO, *Woman Combing Her Hair*, 1915. Bronze, 13¾ × 3¼ × 3⅛ in. (including base).

Figure 32.6 PABLO PICASSO, *Guitar*, 1912–1913. Construction of sheet metal and wire, 30½ × 13¾ × 7⅝ in.

Science and Technology

1901	the first international radio broadcast is made by Guglielmo Marconi (Italian)
1903	Orville and Wilbur Wright (American) make the first successful airplane flight
1927	the first motion picture with synchronized sound (*The Jazz Singer*) is released
1927	Werner Heisenberg (German) announces his "uncertainty principle"

Futurism

Intrigued by the dynamism of modern technology, the avant-garde movement known as *Futurism* emerged in Italy. Originally a literary movement, it soon came to embrace all the arts, including architecture, poetry, music, and film. Its founder, the poet and iconoclast Filippo Tommaso Marinetti (1876–1944), issued a series of manifestoes attacking literary formalism, museum art, and academic culture. He called for a style that linked contemporary expression to industry, technology, and urban life. Marinetti, who held that "war was the only healthgiver of the world," demanded an art of "burning violence" that would free Italy from its "fetid gangrene of professors, archeologists, antiquarians, and rhetoricians." "We declare," he wrote in his *Futurist Manifesto* of 1909, "that there can be no modern painting except from the starting point of an absolutely modern sensation. . . . A roaring motorcar is more beautiful than the winged *Victory of Samothrace*" (the famous Hellenistic sculpture illustrated as Figure 5.33). "The gesture that we would reproduce on canvas shall no longer be a fixed moment in universal dynamism. It shall simply be the dynamic sensation itself."

The Futuristic alternative to static academicism was produced by Umberto Boccioni (1882–1916). His near life-sized bronze sculpture captures the sensation of motion as it pushes forward like an automated robot (Figure **32.8**). The striding figure, which consists of an aggressive series of dynamic, jagged lines, is clearly human in form, despite Boccioni's assertion (in his *Technical Manifesto of Futurist Sculpture*, 1912) that artists should "abolish . . . the traditionally exalted place of subject matter."

The Futurists were enthralled by the speed and dynamism of automobiles, trains, and airplanes, and by such new forms of technology as the machine gun and the electric Brunt Arc lamps that were installed in the streets of Rome during the first decade of the century. One Futurist whimsically claimed that by outshining moonlight, the electric light hailed the demise of Romantic art in the West. In literature, the Futurists shared with the Imagists a desire to "free the word" from traditional meter and syntax. And in music, Futurist composers introduced noise generators and the sounds of airplane propellers and industrial machinery.

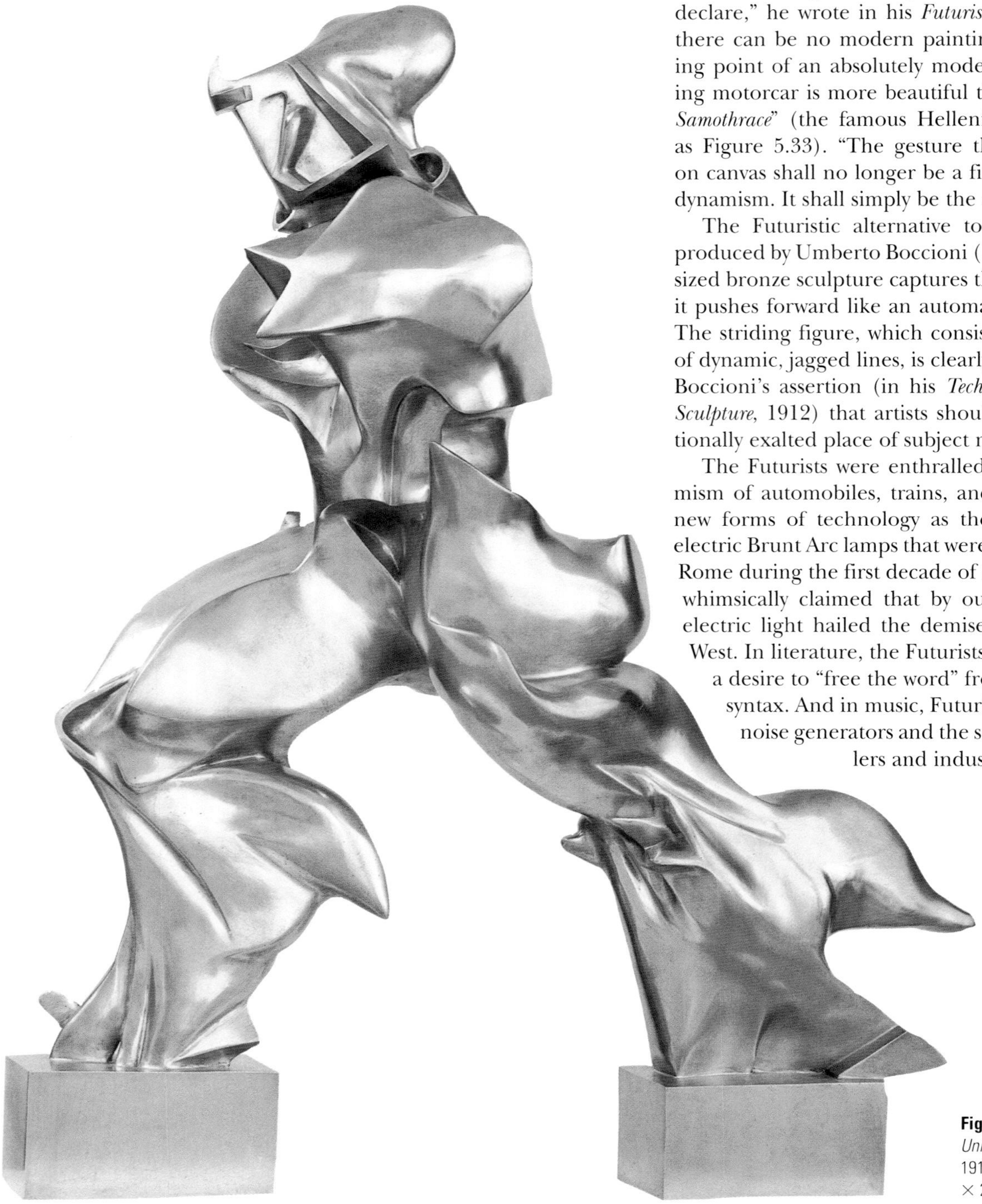

Figure 32.8 UMBERTO BOCCIONI, *Unique Forms of Continuity in Space*, 1913. Bronze (cast 1931), 3 ft. 7⅞ in. × 2 ft. 10⅞ in. × 1 ft. 3¾ in.

Figure 32.9 MARCEL DUCHAMP, *Nude Descending a Staircase, No. 2*, 1912. Oil on canvas, 4 ft. 10 in. × 2 ft. 11 in. Movement is suggested by the successive superimposition of figures, a technique that mimics the motion of a stroboscope, a device invented in 1832.

Futurists were also inspired by the time-lapse photography of Eadweard Muybridge (see Figure 31.9), the magical properties of X-rays (not in wide use until 1910), and pioneer efforts in the new industry of motion pictures, in which "multiple profiles" gave the appearance of movement in time and space. These modern phenomena shaped the early career of the French artist Marcel Duchamp (1887–1968). When Duchamp's *Nude Descending a Staircase, No. 2* (Figure **32.9**) was exhibited at the International Exhibition of Modern Art (known as the Armory Show) in New York City, one critic mockingly called it "an explosion in a shingle factory." Yet, from the time of its first showing in 1913, the painting (and much of the art in the Armory exhibition) had a formative influence on the rise of American Modernism. Futurism did not last beyond the end of World War I, but its impact was felt in both the United States and Russia, where Futurist efforts to capture the sense of form in motion would coincide with the first developments in the technology of cinematography.

The Birth of Motion Pictures

It is no coincidence that the art of motion pictures was born at a time when artists and scientists were obsessed with matters of space and time. Indeed, as an artform that captures rapidly changing experience, cinema is the quintessentially modern medium. The earliest public film presentations took place in Europe and the United States in the mid-1890s: in 1895, Thomas Edison (1847–1931) was the first American to project moving images onto a screen. In France the brothers Auguste and Louis Lumière (1862–1954; 1864–1948) perfected the process by which cellulose film ran smoothly in a commercial projector. They pioneered the first cinematic projection in an auditorium equipped with seats and piano accompaniment. These first experiments delighted audiences with moving pictures of everyday subjects.

It was not until 1902, however, that film was used to create a reality all its own: in that year the French filmmaker Georges Méliès (1861–1938) completed a fourteen-minute theatrical sequence called *A Trip to the Moon*, an engaging fantasy based on a novel by Jules Verne. One year later, the American director Edwin S. Porter (1869–1941) produced the twelve-minute silent film *The Great Train Robbery*, which treated the myth of American frontier life in its story of a sensational holdup, followed by the pursuit and capture of the bandits. These pioneer narrative films established the idiom for two of the most popular genres in cinematic history: the science-fiction film and the "western."

Between 1908 and 1912, Hollywood became the center of American cinema. D. W. Griffith (1875–1948), the leading director of his time, made major innovations in cinematic technique. He introduced the use of multiple cameras and camera angles, as well as such new techniques as close-ups, fade-outs, and flashbacks, which, when joined together in an edited sequence, greatly expanded the potential of film narrative. Griffith's three-hour silent film *The Birth of a Nation* (1915) was an epic account of the American Civil War and the Reconstruction Era that followed in the South. Unfortunately, despite the film's technical excellence, its negative portrayal of African-Americans contributed to stereotyping them as violent and ignorant savages.

Until the late 1920s, all movies were silent—filmmakers used captions to designate the spoken word wherever appropriate, and live musical accompaniment was often provided in the theater. Well before the era of the "talkies," cinematographers began to use the camera not simply as a disinterested observer, but as a medium for conveying the emotional states of the characters. In the absence of sound, they were forced to develop the affective structure of the film by essentially visual means. According to some film critics, the aesthetics of film as a medium were compromised when sound was added. Nevertheless, by 1925 it was apparent that film was destined to become one of the major artforms of the modern era.

Matisse and Fauvism

While Cubists and Futurists were principally concerned with matters of space and motion, other Modernists, led by the French artist Henri Matisse (1869–1954), made *color* the principal feature of their canvases. This group, branded as "Fauves" (from the French *fauve*, "wild beast") by a critic who saw their work at an exhibition in Paris in 1905, employed flat, bright colors in the arbitrary manner of Van Gogh and Gauguin. But whereas the latter had used color to evoke a mood or a symbolic image, the younger artists were concerned with color only as it served pictorial structure; their style featured bold spontaneity and the direct and instinctive application of pigment. Critics who called these artists "wild beasts" were in fact responding to the use of color in ways that seemed both crude and savage. They attacked the new style as "color madness" and "the sport of a child." For Matisse, however, color was the font of pure and sensuous pleasure. In his portrait

of Madame Matisse (which he subtitled *The Green Line*), broad, flat swaths of paint give definition to a visage that is bisected vertically by an acid-green stripe (Figure **32.10**).

Matisse brought daring to Cézanne's flat color patches, using them to simplify form that achieved the visual impact of the tribal artworks he collected. At the same time, he invested the canvas with a thrilling color radiance, that, like smell (as Matisse himself observed), subtly but intensely suffuses the senses. In contrast with Picasso, who held that art was a weapon with which to jar the senses, Matisse sought "an art of balance, of purity and serenity, devoid of troubling or depressing subject matter . . . something like a good armchair in which to rest from physical fatigue."

Matisse was among the first to articulate the Modernist scorn for representational art: "Exactitude is not truth," he insisted. In *Notes of a Painter*, published in 1908, he described colors and shapes as the equivalent of feelings

Figure 32.10 HENRI MATISSE, *Madame Matisse (The Green Line)*, 1905. Oil on canvas, 16 × 12¾ in.

Figure 32.11 HENRI MATISSE, *Dance 1*, 1909. Oil on canvas, 8 ft. 6½ in. × 12 ft. 9½ in. Matisse painted a second version of *The Dance* for the home of his patron, the Russian art collector Sergei Shchukin. It is now in Saint Petersburg's Hermitage Museum.

rather than the counterpart of forms in nature. Gradually, as he came to be influenced by Islamic miniatures and Russian icons, his style moved in the direction of linear simplicity and sensuousness of color. A quintessential example of his facility for color abstraction is *Dance I* (Figure **32.11**). In its lyrical arabesques and unmodeled fields of color, the painting calls to mind the figural grace of ancient Greek vase paintings. At the same time, it captures the exhilaration of the primordial round—the traditional dance of almost all Mediterranean cultures.

Brancusi and Abstraction

Although Cubists, Futurists, and Fauves pursued their individual directions, they all shared the credo of abstract art: the artist must evoke the essential and intrinsic qualities of the subject rather than describe its physical properties. In early modern sculpture, the guardian of this credo was Constantin Brancusi (1876–1957). Born in Romania and trained in Bucharest, Vienna, and Munich, Brancusi came to Paris in 1904. There, after a brief stay in Rodin's studio, he fell under the spell of ancient fertility figures and the sculpture of Africa and Polynesia. Inspired by these

objects, whose spiritual power lay in their visual immediacy and their truth to materials, Brancusi proceeded to create an art of radically simple, organic forms. While he began by closely observing the living object—whether human or animal—he progressively eliminated all naturalistic details until he arrived at a form that captured the essence of the subject. Like his good friend Ezra Pound, Brancusi achieved a concentrated expression in forms so elemental that they seem to speak a universal language.

A case in point is *Bird in Space* (Figure **32.12**), of which Brancusi made more than thirty versions in various sizes and materials. The sculpture is of no particular species of feathered creature, but it captures perfectly the concept of "birdness." It is, as Brancusi explained, "the essence of flight." "What is real," he insisted, "is not the external form, but the essence of things." The elegant form, curved like a feather, unites birdlike qualities of grace and poise with the dynamic sense of soaring levitation characteristic of mechanical flying machines, such as rockets and airplanes. Indeed, when Brancusi's bronze *Bird* first arrived in America, United States customs officials mistook it for a piece of industrial machinery.

Figure 32.13 **EDWARD WESTON**, *Two Shells*, 1927. Photograph. Print by Cole Weston, 9¼ × 7¼ in.

Abstraction and Photography

Photographers also enthusiastically embraced the Modernist aesthetic. The American photographer Edward Weston (1886–1953) was among the pioneers of photographic abstraction. His close-up photograph of two nautilus shells evokes the twin ideas of flower (a magnolia blossom, according to Weston himself) and female (Figure **32.13**). Weston took photography beyond the realm of the representational: he used the camera not simply to record the natural world, but to explore new avenues of visual experience.

Nonobjective Art

Between 1909 and 1914, three artists working independently of one another in different parts of Europe moved to purge art of all recognizable subject matter. The Russians Wassily Kandinsky (1866–1944) and Kasimir Malevich (1878–1935) and the Dutchman Piet Mondrian (1872–1944), pioneers of **Nonobjective Art**, had all come into contact with the principal art movements of the early twentieth century: Cubism, Futurism,

Figure 32.12 **CONSTANTIN BRANCUSI**, *Bird in Space*, 1928. Polished bronze, height 4 ft. 6 in.

and Fauvism. They acknowledged the Postimpressionist premise that a painting was, first and foremost, a flat surface covered with colors assembled in a particular order. But their quest for subjectless form had a unique goal: that of achieving an art whose purity would offer a spiritual remedy for the soullessness of modern life.

Kandinsky Kandinsky, whose career in art began only at the age of forty, was deeply influenced by the Fauves, the Symbolists (see chapter 31), and by Russian folk art. While he filled his early paintings with vibrant hues, he observed with some dismay that the subject matter in his canvases tended to "dissolve" into his colors. One evening, upon returning to his studio in Munich, Kandinsky experienced a "revelation" that led him to abandon pictorial subject matter. The incident is described in his *Reminiscences* of 1913:

> I saw an indescribably beautiful
> picture drenched with an inner
> glowing. At first I hesitated, then
> I rushed toward this mysterious
> picture, of which I saw nothing but
> forms and colors, and whose content
> was incomprehensible. Immediately
> I found the key to the puzzle: it was a
> picture I had painted, leaning against
> the wall, standing on its side. . . . Now
> I knew for certain that the [pictorial]
> object harmed my paintings.

From this point on, Kandinsky began to assemble colors, lines, and shapes without regard for recognizable objects (Figure **32.14**). He called his nonrepresentational paintings "improvisations" or "abstract compositions" and numbered them in series. In his treatise *Concerning the Spiritual in Art* (1910), he argued that form and color generate meaning without reference to the natural world. "Color can exercise enormous influence upon the body," he wrote; it functions to influence mood. Such insights anticipated modern research in chromotherapy, that is, the use of colors and colored light to affect body states. According to Kandinsky, painting was a spiritually liberating force akin to music—he himself was an amateur cellist and friend of many avant-garde composers. "Painting," he proclaimed, "is a thundering collision of different worlds, intended to create a new world."

Figure 32.14 WASSILY KANDINSKY, *Panel for Edwin Campbell No. 1*, 1914. Oil on canvas, 5 ft. 4 in. × 3 ft. ¼ in. Kandinsky was among the first of the Modernists to confess indebtedness to atomic theory. He urged young artists to study the new physics.

Figure 32.15 KASIMIR MALEVICH, *Suprematist Composition: White on White*, 1918. Oil on canvas, 31¼ × 31¼ in.

Malevich Kandinsky's Russian contemporary Kasimir Malevich arrived at nonrepresentational art not by way of Fauvism but through the influence of Analytic Cubism, which asserted the value of line over color. Seeking to "free art from the burden of the object" and to rediscover "pure

feeling in creative art," Malevich created an austere style limited to the strict geometry of the square, the circle, and the rectangle (Figure **32.15**). Malevich called these shapes "suprematist elements" and his style *Suprematism*. "To the suprematist," wrote Malevich, "the visual phenomena of the objective world are, in themselves, meaningless; the significant thing is feeling . . . quite apart from the environment in which it is called forth." By restricting his art to the arrangement of ideal geometric shapes on the two-dimensional picture plane, Malevich replaced the world of appearance with a language of form as abstract and exacting as that of modern physics.

Mondrian The early works of the third pioneer of Nonobjective Art, Piet Mondrian, reveal his affection for the landscape of his native Holland. By 1910, however, as he began to impose an abstract, geometric regularity on the natural environment, he slowly stripped away recognizable subject matter (Figure **32.16**). Eventually, he limited his visual vocabulary to "pure" forms: the square or rectangle laid out on a grid of horizontal and vertical lines, the three primary colors (red, yellow, and blue), and three values—white, gray, and black (Figure **32.17**). The paring-down process achieved a compositional balance of geometric elements, an "equivalence of opposites" similar to the dynamic equilibrium of an algebraic equation.

Although Mondrian would eventually emigrate to America, the movement he helped to create would

Figure 32.16 PIET MONDRIAN, *Tree*, 1912. Oil on canvas, 29¼ × 43⅞ in. In this early study of a tree, the transition from a realistic depiction to abstract design is evident. Mondrian finally stripped away all representational associations to arrive at his signature grid patterns. © 2014 Mondrian/Holtzman Trust c/o HCR International, USA.

continue to flourish. Taking its name from a magazine founded in 1917, it was called simply *De Stijl* ("the Style"). Its Dutch adherents advanced a radical utopian program devoted to the evolution of pure, abstract art: "a direct expression of the universal." Despite differences of opinion among its members—Mondrian resigned in 1925 in opposition to a colleague's use of diagonals—De Stijl was to have worldwide impact, especially on architecture and furniture design (Figure **32.18**).

The disappearance of the object in early twentieth-century art is often mistakenly associated with the dehumanization of modern life. However, one of the great ironies of the birth of Nonobjective Art is its indebtedness to the mystical and transcendental philosophies that were current in the early modern era. One of the most influential of these was *theosophy*, a blend of Eastern and Western religions that emphasizes communion with nature by purely spiritual means. Mondrian, a member of the Dutch Theosophical Society, regarded geometric clarity as an expression of spiritual progress. In his view, the law of equivalence reflected "the true content of reality." "Not only science," wrote Mondrian, "but art also, shows us that reality, at first incomprehensible, gradually reveals itself by the mutual relations that are inherent in things. Pure science and pure art, disinterested and free, can lead the advance in the recognition of the laws which are based on these relationships." The commitment to pure abstraction as the universal language of spirituality—a commitment central to the careers of Kandinsky, Malevich, and Mondrian—reflects the utopian humanism of Modernists who perceived their art as a wellspring of social harmony and order.

Russian Constructivism

While utopian Modernism swept across Europe, one of the most utilitarian of the movements for "pure art" flourished in pre-revolutionary Russia. *Constructivism*, which had its roots in both Futurism and the purist teachings of Malevich, advocated the application of geometric abstraction to all forms of social enterprise. Russian Constructivists, who called themselves "artist–engineers,"

Figure 32.18 GERRIT RIETVELD, *Red Blue Chair*, 1923. Painted wood, 34⅛ × 26 × 33 in; seat height 13 in.

Figure 32.19 LIUBOV POPOVA, set design for Fernand Crommelynk, *Le Cocu magnifique*, State Institute of Theatrical Art, Moscow, 1922. Gouache on paper, 19½ × 27 in.

worked to improve the everyday lives of the masses by applying the new abstraction to the industrial arts, theater, film, typography, textile design, and architecture. Liubov Popova (1889–1924), one of the many talented female advocates of this movement, designed stage sets and costumes for the Russian theater (Figure **32.19**), thus putting into practice the Constructivist motto "Art into production." Like other Modernists, the Constructivists worked to break down the barriers between fine and applied art, but unlike any other modern art movement, Constructivism received official state sanction. Following the Russian Revolution, however, the Soviet Union would bring about its demise, almost obliterating Russia's most innovative contribution to twentieth-century Modernism (see chapter 34).

Abstraction and Film

Inspired by theosophy and by the abstract works of Kandinsky, the German filmmaker Oskar Fischinger (1900–1967) produced Europe's first abstract animated films. In Fischinger's *Raumlichtkunst* (*Space-Light-Art*, 1926), nitrate film loops of abstract shapes and colors (created with melted wax, tinted liquids, and other ingenious mediums) were projected simultaneously onto three screens and accompanied by music, creating what the artist called "intoxication by light." Fischinger, who emigrated to the United States in 1936, contributed to the production of Walt Disney's *Fantasia* and *Pinocchio* (both 1940), two of America's classic animated films.

Early Twentieth-Century Architecture

The revolution in visual abstraction found monumental expression in architecture. Early modern architects made energetic use of two new materials—structural steel and **ferroconcrete**—in combination with **cantilever** construction. The cantilever, a horizontal beam supported at only one end and projecting well beyond the point of support, had first appeared in the timber buildings of China (see chapter 14); but the manufacture of the structural steel cantilever ushered in a style whose austere simplicity had no precedents. That style was inaugurated by Frank Lloyd Wright (1869–1959), the leading figure in the history of early modern architecture.

The Architecture of Wright

Frank Lloyd Wright, the first American architect of world significance, was the foremost student of the Chicago architect Louis Sullivan (see chapter 30). Wright's style combined the new technology of steel and glass with the aesthetic principles of Asian architecture. Wright visited Japan when he was in his thirties and was impressed by the grace and purity of Japanese art. He especially admired the respect for natural materials and the sensitivity to the relationship between setting and structure that characterized traditional Japanese architecture (see chapter 14). In his earliest domestic commissions, Wright embraced the East Asian principle of horizontality, by which the building might hug the earth. He imitated the low, steeply pitched roofs of Japanese pavilions and temples. From Japanese interiors, where walls often consist of movable screens, Wright borrowed the idea of

Figure 32.20 FRANK LLOYD WRIGHT, Robie House, Chicago, Illinois, 1909. Brick, glass, natural rock.

interconnecting interior and exterior space. He used the structural steel frame and the cantilever to create large areas of uninterrupted space. In every one of Wright's designs, the exterior of the structure reflects the major divisions of its interior space. Wright refined this formula in a series of innovative homes in the American Midwest, pioneering the so-called Prairie School of architecture that lasted from roughly 1900 until World War I.

The classic creation of Wright's early career was the Robie House in Chicago, completed in 1909 (Figure **32.20**). The three-story house marks the first use of welded steel beams in residential construction. Making the fireplace the center of the architectural plan, Wright crossed the long main axis of the house with counteraxes of low cantilevered roofs that push out into space over terraces and verandas. He subordinated decorative details to the overall design, allowing his materials—brick, glass, and natural rock—to assume major roles in establishing the unique character of the structure. As Wright insisted, "To use any material wrongly is to abuse the integrity of the whole design." The result was a style consisting of crisp, interlocking planes, contrasting textures, and interpenetrating solids and voids—a domestic architecture that was as abstract and dynamic as an Analytic Cubist painting.

Wright's use of the cantilever and his integration of landscape and house reached new imaginative heights in Fallingwater, the residence he designed in 1936 for the American businessman Edgar J. Kaufmann at Bear Run, Pennsylvania (Figure **32.21**). Embracing a natural waterfall, the structure of ferroconcrete and stone seems to grow organically out of the natural, wooded setting, yet dominates that setting through its pristine equilibrium.

Figure 32.21 FRANK LLOYD WRIGHT, Fallingwater, Kaufmann House, Bear Run, Pennsylvania, 1936–1939. Reinforced concrete, stone, masonry, steel-framed doors and windows, enclosed area 5800 sq. ft. Wright rejected the machinelike qualities of International Style architecture. At Fallingwater, he made use of the local stone, integrating the cascading waters of a stream into the design.

The Bauhaus and the International Style

Wright's synthesis of art and technology anticipated the establishment of the *Bauhaus*, Modernism's most influential school of architecture and applied art. Founded in 1919 by the German architect and visionary Walter Gropius (1883–1969), the Bauhaus pioneered an instructional program that united the technology of the Machine Age with the purest principles of functional design. Throughout its brief history (1919–1933), and despite its frequent relocation (from Weimar to Dessau, and finally Berlin), the Bauhaus advocated a close relationship between the function of an object and its formal design, whether in furniture, lighting fixtures, typography, photography, industrial products, or architecture.

Bauhaus instructors had little regard for traditional academic styles; they endorsed the new synthetic materials of modern technology, a stark simplicity of design, and the standardization of parts for affordable, mass-produced merchandise, as well as for large-scale housing. Some of Europe's leading artists, including Kandinsky and Mondrian, taught at the Bauhaus. Like Gropius, these artists envisioned a new industrial society liberated by the principle of abstraction. They shared with the Russian Constructivists the utopian belief in the power of the arts to transform society. When the Nazis closed down the school in 1933, many of its finest instructors, such as the photographer László Moholy-Nagy, architect and designer Marcel Breuer, and artist Josef Albers, emigrated to the United States, where they exercised tremendous influence on the development of American architecture and industrial art. (In 1929, a group of wealthy Americans had already established the first international collection of modern art: New York City's Museum of Modern Art.)

Under the direction of Gropius, the Bauhaus launched the *International Style* in architecture, which brought to the marriage of structural steel, ferroconcrete, and sheet glass a formal precision and geometric austerity resembling a Mondrian painting (see Figure 32.17). In the four-story glass building Gropius designed to serve as the Bauhaus craft shops in Dessau, unadorned curtain walls of glass (which meet uninterrupted at the corners of the structure) were freely suspended on structural steel cantilevers (Figure **32.22**). This fusion of functional space and minimal structure produced a purist style that paralleled the abstract trends in poetry, painting, and sculpture discussed earlier in this chapter.

Le Corbusier

The revolutionary Swiss architect and town planner Charles-Edouard Jeanneret (1887–1965), who called himself Le Corbusier (a pun on the word "raven"), was not directly affiliated with the Bauhaus, but he shared Gropius' fundamental concern for efficiency of design, standardization of building techniques, and the promotion of low-cost housing. In 1923, Le Corbusier wrote the treatise *Towards a New Architecture*, in which he proposed that modern architectural principles should imitate the efficiency of the

Figure 32.22 WALTER GROPIUS, workshop wing, Bauhaus Building, Dessau, Germany, 1925–1926. Steel and glass.

Figure 32.23 LE CORBUSIER, Villa Savoye, Poissy, France, 1928–1929. Ferroconcrete and glass. The house illustrates the five principles for domestic architecture laid out by Le Corbusier in 1923: 1) elevation above the ground, 2) the flat roof, 3) the open floor plan, 4) exterior curtain walls, and 5) horizontal bands of windows.

machine. "Machines," he predicted, "will lead to a new order both of work and of leisure." Just as form follows function in the design of airplanes, automobiles, and machinery in general, so it must in modern domestic architecture. Le Corbusier was fond of insisting that "the house is a machine for living [in]." With utopian fervor he urged,

> We must create the mass-production spirit.
> The spirit of constructing mass-production houses.
> The spirit of living in mass-production houses.
> The spirit of conceiving mass-production houses.

> If we eliminate from our hearts and minds all
> dead concepts in regard to the house, and look at
> the question from a critical and objective point of
> view, we shall arrive at the "House-Machine," the
> mass-production house, healthy (and morally so too)
> and beautiful in the same way that the working
> tools and instruments that accompany our existence
> are beautiful.

In the Villa Savoye, a residence located outside Paris at Poissy, Le Corbusier put these revolutionary concepts to work (Figure **32.23**). The residence, now considered a "classic" of the International Style, consists of simple and unadorned masses of ferroconcrete punctured by ribbon windows. It is raised above the ground on *pilotis*, pillars that free the ground area of the site. (More recently, architects have abused the pilotis principle to create parking space for automobiles.) The Villa Savoye features a number of favorite Le Corbusier devices, such as the roof garden, the open floor plan that allows one to close off or open up

space according to varying needs, and the free façade that consists of large areas of glass—so-called curtain walls.

Le Corbusier's genius for fitting form to function led, during the 1930s, to his creation of the first high-rise urban apartment buildings—structures that housed more than a thousand people and consolidated facilities for shopping, recreation, and child care under a single roof (Figure **32.24**). These "vertical cities," as stripped of decorative details as the sculptures of Brancusi, became hallmarks of urban Modernism.

Early Twentieth-Century Music

The music of the early twentieth century shared the Modernist assault on tradition, and most dramatically so in the areas of tonality and meter. Until the late nineteenth century, most music was tonal; that is, structured on a single key or tonal center. However, by the second decade of the twentieth century, musical compositions might be **polytonal** (having several tonal centers) or **atonal** (without a tonal center). Further, instead of following a single meter, a modern composition might be **polyrhythmic** (having two or more different meters at the same time), or (as with Imagist poems) it might obey no fixed or regular metrical pattern at all.

Modern composers tended to reject conventional modes of expression, including traditional harmony and instrumentation. Melody—like recognizable subject matter in painting—became of secondary importance to formal composition. Modernists invented no new forms comparable to the fugue or the sonata; rather, they

Figure 32.24 LE CORBUSIER, Unité d'Habitation apartment block, Marseilles, France, 1946–1952. The twelve-story building, made of rough-cast concrete supported by pilotis, featured the *brise-soleil* or sun-break that sheltered the interior from sunlight, an advantage in hot locations.

explored innovative effects based on dissonance, the free use of meter, and the inventive combination of musical instruments, some of which they borrowed from non-Western cultures. They employed unorthodox sources of sound, such as sirens, bullhorns, and doorbells. Some incorporated silence in their compositions, much as Cubist sculptors introduced negative space into mass. The results were as startling to the ear as Cubism was to the eye.

Schoenberg

The most radical figure in early twentieth-century music was the Austrian composer Arnold Schoenberg (1874–1951). Schoenberg was born in Vienna, the city of Mozart and Beethoven. He learned to play the violin at the age of eight and began composing music in his late teens. Schoenberg's first compositions were conceived in the Romantic tradition, but by 1909 he began to develop a new musical language punctuated by dissonant and unfamiliar chords. Instead of organizing tones around a home key (the tonal center) in the time-honored tradition of Western musical composition, he treated all twelve notes of the chromatic scale equally. Schoenberg's atonal works use abrupt changes in rhythm, tone color, and dynamics—features evidenced in his expressionistic song cycle *Pierrot Lunaire* (*Moonstruck Pierrot*; see also chapter 33) and in his *Five Pieces for Orchestra*, Opus 16, both written in 1912.

See Music Listening Selections at end of chapter.

In the former work, which one newspaper critic described as "incomprehensible as a Tibetan poem," the instruments produce a succession of individual, contrasting tones that, like the Nonobjective canvases of Schoenberg's good friend Kandinsky, resist familiar harmonies and soothing resolution.

During the 1920s, Schoenberg went on to formulate a unifying system for atonal composition based on **serial technique**. His type of *serialism*, called the "**twelve-tone system**," demanded that the composer use all twelve tones of the chromatic scale either melodically or in chords before any one of the other eleven notes might be repeated. The twelve-tone row might be inverted or played upside down or backwards—there are actually forty-eight possible musical combinations for each tone row. Serialism, like quantum theory or Mondrian's "equivalence of opposites," involved the strategic use of a sparse and elemental language of form. It engaged the composer in a rigidly formulaic (even mathematical) disposition of musical elements. In theory, the serial technique invited creative invention rather than mechanical application. Nevertheless, to the average listener, who could no longer leave the concert hall humming a melody, Schoenberg's atonal compositions seemed forbidding and obscure.

Stravinsky

In 1913—the same year Ezra Pound issued his *Imagist Manifesto* and Malevich and Kandinsky painted their first

Nonobjective canvases—a Paris audience witnessed the premiere of the ballet *Le Sacre du printemps* (*The Rite of Spring*). The piece was performed by the Ballets Russes, a company of expatriate Russian dancers led by Sergei Diaghilev (1872–1929), and the music was written by the Russian composer Igor Stravinsky (1882–1971; Figure **32.25**). Shortly after the music began, catcalls, hissing, and booing disrupted the performance, as members of the audience protested the "shocking" sounds that were coming from the orchestra. By the time the police arrived, Stravinsky had disappeared through a backstage window. What offended this otherwise sophisticated audience was Stravinsky's bold combination of throbbing rhythms and dissonant harmonies, which, along with the jarring effects of a new style in choreography, marked the birth of modern music.

Stravinsky was one of the most influential figures in the history of twentieth-century music. Like Schoenberg, he began to study music at a young age. His family pressed him to pursue a career in law, but Stravinsky was intent on becoming a composer. At the age of twenty-eight, he left Russia for Paris, where he joined the Ballets Russes. Allied with some of the greatest artists of the time, including Picasso, the writer Jean Cocteau, and the choreographer Vaslav Nijinsky, Stravinsky was instrumental in making the Ballets Russes a leading force in modern dance theater. His influence on American music was equally great, especially after 1939, when he moved permanently to the United States.

Russian folk tales and songs provided inspiration for many of Stravinsky's early compositions, including *The Rite of Spring*. Subtitled *Pictures from Pagan Russia*, this landmark piece was based on an ancient Slavonic ceremony that invoked the birth of spring with the ritual sacrifice of a young girl. The themes of death and resurrection associated with traditional pagan celebrations of seasonal change provided the structure of the suite, which was divided into two parts: "The Fertility of the Earth" and "The Sacrifice." Like Picasso and Gauguin, Stravinsky was captivated by primitivism; he shared the fascination with ancient rituals and tribal culture that had gripped late nineteenth-century Europe (see chapter 31). These subjects were popularized by Sir James Frazer in his widely acclaimed book *The Golden Bough* (1890), which had been reissued in twelve volumes between 1911 and 1915.

The Rite of Spring is a pastoral piece, but its music lacks the calm grace traditionally associated with that genre. Its harsh chordal combinations and jarring shifts of meter set it apart from earlier pastorals, such as Debussy's *Prelude to "The Afternoon of a Faun."* While Debussy's tonal shifts are as

See Music Listening Selections at end of chapter.

Figure 32.25 PABLO PICASSO, *Igor Stravinsky*, 1920. Drawing, 24½ × 19 in. Picasso, a master draftsman, was capable of switching from one style to another with great ease. Even as he executed drawings like this one, he was painting abstract canvases in the Synthetic Cubist style.

subtle and nuanced as a Monet seascape, Stravinsky's are as abrupt and disjunctive as Picasso's *Demoiselles*, so disjunctive, in fact, that critics questioned whether the composer was capable of writing conventional musical transitions. Although not atonal, portions of the composition are polytonal, while other passages are ambiguous in tonality, especially in the opening sections. If the shifting tonality and pounding rhythms of the piece were "savage," as critics claimed, so too were its orchestral effects: Stravinsky's unorthodox scoring calls for eighteen woodwind instruments, eighteen brass instruments, and a *quiro* (a Latin American gourd that is scraped with a wooden stick). *The Rite* had an impact on twentieth-century music comparable to that of *Les Demoiselles d'Avignon* on the visual arts. It shattered the syntax of traditional musical language with a force similar to that with which this painting had attacked traditional pictorial norms. It rewrote the rules of musical composition as they had been practiced for centuries. No greater assault on tradition could have been imagined at the time.

The Beginnings of Modern Dance

Nijinsky

Only a year after his daring performance in Debussy's *Afternoon of a Faun* (see chapter 31), Vaslav Nijinsky aroused even greater controversy with his choreography for *The Rite of Spring*. He took the raw, rhythmic complexity of Stravinsky's score as inspiration for a series of frenzied leaps and wild, wheeling rounds that shocked the audience—and even disturbed Stravinsky. "They paw the ground, they stamp, they stamp, they stamp, and they stamp," complained one French critic. Like *The Rite* itself, such choreography seemed to express what the critics called "the hidden primitive in man." Interestingly enough, some of Nijinsky's body movements—angular, disjunctive, and interrupted by frozen stillness (see Figure 31.2)—were reminiscent of Cubist paintings. Tragically, Nijinsky's career came to an end in 1917, when he became incurably insane. In his ten years as the West's first dance superstar, Nijinsky choreographed only four ballets; and not until 1987 was his most famous ballet, *The Rite of Spring*, revived for the American stage.

Graham

The innovative character of early modern dance owed much to the pioneer American choreographer Martha

Graham (1894–1991). Following Isadora Duncan (see chapter 31) and Nijinsky, Graham rejected the rules and conventions of classical ballet, preferring to explore the expressive power of natural movement. Drawing on the dance traditions of Asia, Africa, and Native America, she sought a direct correspondence between intangible emotions and physical gesture. Much of her choreography, such as that produced for Aaron Copland's ballet suite *Appalachian Spring* (1944), provided the visual narrative for a specific story (see chapter 34). Just as the Imagists arranged words to convey an emotional "shape" or sensation, so Graham found definitive gestures to express ineffable states of mind. Her dancers were trained to expose the process and techniques of dancing, rather than to conceal displays of physical effort, as was expected in classical dance.

Balanchine

In contrast with Graham, George Balanchine (1904–1983) developed a dance idiom that was storyless, abstract, and highly structured. Balanchine was a Russian choreographer who spent his early career in Paris with Diaghilev's Ballets Russes. He was deeply influenced by the musical innovations of his friend and compatriot Igor Stravinsky, with whom he often collaborated—Stravinsky wrote the scores for at least four of his ballets.

Balanchine prized musically driven dance and pure artistic form. Loyal to the 350-year-old idiom of classical ballet, he insisted on rigorous academic dance training and the use of traditional toe-shoes. However, he rejected the dance-drama vocabulary of the nineteenth century, preferring a Modernist energy and verve that drew enthusiastically on the irregular rhythmic structures of Stravinsky. He pioneered the twentieth-century practice of choreographing concertos, symphonies, and other classical forms never intended for dance. His choreography, according to one critic, "pushed dance into the space age." In 1934, Balanchine was persuaded to come to the United States, where he helped to found the School of American Ballet.

Dunham

The development of modern dance owes much to the genius of Katherine Dunham (1909–2006). The "Mother of Black Dance," Dunham was both a choreographer and a trained anthropologist. Her doctoral work at the University of Chicago investigated the vast resources of the black heritage, ranging from African-American slave dances to the dance histories of the Caribbean. Her choreography drew on the dance styles of the late nineteenth century, when all-black theatrical companies and minstrel shows toured the United States. Freely improvising on tap-dance styles and on popular American dances such as the high-stepping cakewalk, she would in her later career give serious attention to the dance idioms of native societies in Haiti and Trinidad (see Figure 36.10). In the 1930s, she formed her own company—the first, and for some thirty years, the only black dance company in America.

LOOKING BACK

The New Physics

- During the first decades of the twentieth century, quantum physicists provided a new model of the universe. Albert Einstein theorized that matter is a form of energy, and time and space are relative to the position of the observer. Werner Heisenberg concluded that the operations of the universe cannot be measured with absolute certainty.
- Revolutionary changes in science and technology provided the context for the Modernist assault on traditional modes of expression.

Early Twentieth-Century Poetry

- Modern poets moved away from Romanticism to adopt a conceptual and abstract literary style. The poems of the Imagists demonstrated a reduction

of form that overtook naturalism and realistic representation.
- Led by Ezra Pound, the Imagists used free verse in the concentrated style of the Japanese *haiku*. Pound called on other writers to "make it new" by eliminating all extraneous expression from their poems.
- T. S. Eliot's *Prufrock* conveys the spiritual condition of the modern urban antihero in erudite free verse. Robert Frost's straightforward, metered lyrics provided an alternative to the Modernist taste for dense literary allusions.

Early Twentieth-Century Art

- Picasso assaulted tradition with the landmark painting *Les Demoiselles d'Avignon,* which led the way to Cubism. Inspired by the works of Cézanne and by African art, Picasso, Braque, and

Brancusi pursued the concentrated reduction of form.
- In Italy Futurists linked artistic expression to the machine technology of speed, electric lighting, and the new phenomenon of moving pictures.
- Matisse led the Fauves in employing flat, bright colors for canvases that critics condemned as "color madness."
- With Kandinsky, Malevich, and Mondrian, painting freed itself entirely of recognizable objects. These artists shared a utopian faith in the reforming power of purist, Nonobjective Art.
- A more practical application of Nonobjective abstraction was undertaken by the Russian Constructivists, who applied purist design to functional products, including industrial arts, theater sets, textile design, typography, and architecture.

Early Twentieth-Century Architecture

- Frank Lloyd Wright invested the techniques of glass and steel technology and the functional principle of the cantilever with the aesthetics of Japanese art to create a modern style of domestic architecture.
- Gropius, founder of the Bauhaus in Germany, established a program of functional design that featured the use of new synthetic materials and the pursuit of geometric austerity in art and architecture. Bauhaus instructors provided the models for modern industrial design.
- Le Corbusier, pioneer of the vertical city, developed the International Style, which proclaimed the credo "form follows function." Insisting that "the house is a machine for living [in]," Le Corbusier introduced some of the classic elements of modern urban architecture, including the open floor plan, the flat roof, and the use of glass "curtain walls."

Early Twentieth-Century Music

- Arnold Schoenberg and Igor Stravinsky introduced atonality, polytonality, and polyrhythm as formal alternatives to the time-honored Western traditions of pleasing harmonies and uniform meter.
- Schoenberg, who started working in traditional forms, turned to atonality with a serial technique known as the "twelve-tone system," by which the composer makes use of all twelve tones on the chromatic scale before repeating any one of the other tones.
- As a powerful form of disjunctive expression, Stravinsky's *Rite of Spring* had an effect on musical composition equivalent to that of *Les Demoiselles d'Avignon* on painting.

The Beginnings of Modern Dance

- The Russian dancer Vaslav Nijinsky followed the call to "make it new" with wild and frenzied choreography that broke with the traditions of academic dance.
- America's Martha Graham, who studied the dance history of other cultures, emphasized expressive natural movement to reflect human emotions in her choreography.
- Working closely with Stravinsky, George Balanchine created non-narrative ballets that invested Modernist abstraction with rigorous academic dance training.
- The first black dance company was founded by Katherine Dunham, who was strongly influenced by popular American dance styles and by the dance traditions of Haiti and Trinidad.

Music Listening Selections

- Schoenberg, *Pierrot Lunaire*, Op. 21, Part 3, No. 15, "Heimweh," 1912.
- Stravinsky, *The Rite of Spring*, "Sacrificial Dance," 1913, excerpt.

Glossary

abstraction the process by which subject matter is pared down or simplified in order to capture its intrinsic or essential qualities; also, any work of art that reflects this process

assemblage an artwork composed of three-dimensional objects, either natural or manufactured; the sculptural counterpart of collage

atonality in music, the absence of a tonal center or definite key

avant-garde (French, "vanguard") those who create or produce styles and ideas ahead of their time; also, an unconventional movement or style

cantilever a projecting beam firmly anchored at one end and unsupported at the other

collage (French, *coller*, "to paste") a composition created by pasting materials such as newspaper, wallpaper, photographs, or cloth onto a flat surface or canvas

ferroconcrete a cement building material reinforced with embedded wire or iron rods; also called "reinforced concrete"

haiku a Japanese light verse form consisting of seventeen syllables (three lines of five, seven, and five)

Nonobjective Art art that lacks recognizable subject matter; also called "nonrepresentational art"

polyrhythm in music, the device of using two or more different rhythms at the same time; also known as "polymeter"

polytonality in music, the simultaneous use of multiple tonal centers or keys; for compositions using only two tonal centers, the word "bitonality" applies

serial technique in music, a technique that involves the use of a particular series of notes, rhythms, and other elements that are repeated over and over throughout the piece

twelve-tone system a kind of serial music that demands the use of all twelve notes of the chromatic scale (all twelve half-tones in an octave) in a particular order or series; no one note can be used again until all eleven others have appeared

33

The Freudian Revolution

ca. 1900–1950

"Only children, madmen, and savages truly understand the 'in-between' world of spiritual truth."
Paul Klee

Figure 33.1 JOAN MIRÓ, *The Harlequin's Carnival*, 1924. Oil on canvas, 26 × 36½ in. Years after painting this picture, Miró claimed that some of the images in his early Surrealist pieces were inspired by hallucinations brought on by hunger and by staring at the cracks in the plaster walls of his shabby Paris apartment.

No figure in modern Western history has had more influence on our perception of ourselves than Sigmund Freud. This brilliant physician rocked the modern West with writings that opened the subjects of human sexuality and behavior to public discourse and debate. He was the first to map the geography of the *psyche* (mind), making it the object of methodical, scientific research. Freud's theories suggested that the conscious self was only a small part of one's psychical life. He presented a radical model of the human mind that would resonate through the arts of the twentieth century, affecting literature and theater, music and the visual arts, including the new medium of film.

While Freud himself believed as firmly as any Enlightenment *philosophe* in the reforming power of reason, his model of the unconscious challenged the supremacy of reason itself. Copernicus had dislodged human beings from their central place in the cosmos; Darwin had deposed *Homo sapiens* from his privileged status as God's ultimate creation; now Freud, uncovering the mysterious realm of the unconscious, challenged the long-standing belief that reason was the fundamental monitor of human behavior.

Freud

Sigmund Freud (1856–1939) graduated in medicine from the University of Vienna in 1880. His early work with severely disturbed patients, followed by a period of intensive self-analysis, led him to develop a systematic procedure for treating emotional illnesses. The founder of *psychoanalysis*, a therapeutic method by which repressed desires are brought to the conscious level to reveal the sources of emotional disturbance, Freud pioneered its principal tools: dream analysis and "free association" (the spontaneous verbalization of thoughts). He favored these techniques over hypnosis, the procedure preferred by notable physicians with whom he had studied.

Freud theorized that instinctual drives, especially the *libido*, or sex drive, governed human behavior. Guilt from the repression of instinctual urges dominates the unconscious life of human beings and manifests itself in emotional illness. Most psychic disorders, he argued, were the result of sexual traumas stemming from the child's unconscious attachment to the parent of the opposite sex and jealousy of the parent of the same sex, a phenomenon Freud called the Oedipus complex (in reference to the ancient Greek legend in which Oedipus, king of Thebes, unwittingly kills his father and marries his mother). Freud shocked the world with his analysis of infant sexuality and, more generally, with his claim that the psychic lives of human beings were formed by the time they were five years old.

Of all his discoveries, Freud considered his research on dream analysis the most important. In 1900 he published *The Interpretation of Dreams*, in which he defended the significance of dreams in deciphering the unconscious life of the individual. In *Totem and Taboo* (1913), he examined the function of the unconscious in the evolution of the earliest forms of religion and morality. And in "The Sexual Life of Human Beings," a lecture presented to medical students at the University of Vienna in 1916, he examined the psychological roots of sadism, homosexuality, fetishism, and voyeurism—sexual subjects still considered taboo in some social circles. Freud's theories opened the door to the clinical appraisal of these previously guarded types of human behavior. By bringing attention to the central place of erotic desire in human life, his writings irrevocably altered popular attitudes toward human sexuality. His work also had a major impact on the treatment of the mentally ill. Until at least the eighteenth century, people generally regarded psychotic behavior as evidence of possession by demonic or evil spirits, and the mentally ill were often locked up like animals. Freud's studies argued that neuroses and psychoses were illnesses that required medical treatment.

The Tripartite Psyche

In describing the activities of the human mind, Freud proposed a theoretical model, the terms of which (although often oversimplified and misunderstood) have become basic to *psychology* (the study of mind and behavior) and fundamental to our everyday vocabulary. This model pictures the psyche as consisting of three parts: the *id*, the *ego*, and the *superego*. The id, according to Freud, is the seat of human instincts and the source of all physical desires, including nourishment and sexual satisfaction. Seeking fulfillment in accordance with the pleasure principle, the id (and in particular the libido) is the compelling force of the unconscious realm.

Freud described the second part of the psyche, the ego, as the administrator of the id: the ego is the "manager" that attempts to adapt the needs of the id to the real world. Whether by dreams or by **sublimation** (the positive modification and redirection of primal urges), the ego mediates between potentially destructive desires and social necessities. In Freud's view, civilization is the product of the ego's effort to modify the primal urges of the id. The third agent in the psychic life of the human being, the superego, is the moral monitor commonly called the "conscience." The superego monitors human behavior according to principles inculcated by parents, teachers, and other authority figures.

Civilization and Its Discontents

By challenging reason as the governor of human action, Freud questioned the very nature of human morality. He described benevolent action and altruistic conduct as mere masks for self-gratification, and religion as a form of mass delusion. Such views were central to the essay *Civilization and Its Discontents*, in which Freud explored at length the relationship between psychic activity and human society. Enumerating the various ways in which all human beings attempt to escape the "pain and unpleasure" of life, Freud argued that civilization itself was the collective product of sublimated instincts. The greatest impediment to civilization, he claimed, was human aggression, which he defined as "an original, self-subsisting instinctual disposition in man." The following excerpts offer some idea of Freud's incisive analysis of the psychic life of human beings.

READING 33.1 From Freud's *Civilization and Its Discontents* (1930)

We will . . . turn now to the more modest question of what [1]
human beings themselves reveal, through their behavior,
about the aim and purpose of their lives, what they demand
of life and wish to achieve in it. The answer can scarcely be
in doubt: they strive for happiness, they want to become happy
and remain so. This striving has two goals, one negative
and one positive: on the one hand it aims at an absence of pain
and unpleasurable experiences, on the other at strong feelings
of pleasure. "Happiness," in the strict sense of the word, relates
only to the latter. In conformity with this dichotomy in its aims, [10]
human activity develops in two directions, according to
whether it seeks to realize—mainly or even exclusively
—the one or the other of these aims.

As we see, it is simply the program of the pleasure
principle that determines the purpose of life. This principle
governs the functioning of our mental apparatus from the
start; there can be no doubt about its efficacy, and yet its
program is at odds with the whole world—with the
macrocosm as much as with the microcosm. It is quite
incapable of being realized; all the institutions of the universe [20]
are opposed to it; one is inclined to say that the intention that
man should be "happy" has no part in the plan of "creation."
What we call happiness, in the strictest sense of the word,
arises from the fairly sudden satisfaction of pent-up needs.
By its very nature it can be no more than an episodic
phenomenon. Any prolongation of a situation desired by the
pleasure principle produces only a feeling of lukewarm
comfort; we are so constituted that we can gain intense
pleasure only from the contrast, and only very little from
the condition itself. Hence, our prospects of happiness are [30]
already restricted by our constitution. Unhappiness is much
less difficult to experience. Suffering threatens us from
three sides: from our own body, which, being doomed to
decay and dissolution, cannot dispense with pain and anxiety
as warning signals; from the external world, which can unleash
overwhelming, implacable, destructive forces against us; and
finally from our relations with others. The suffering that arises

from this last source perhaps causes us more pain than any
other; we are inclined to regard it as a somewhat superfluous
extra, though it is probably no less ineluctable[1] than [40]
suffering that originates elsewhere.

Unrestricted satisfaction of all our needs presents itself
as the most enticing way to conduct one's life, but it means
putting enjoyment before caution, and that soon brings its
own punishment. The other methods, which aim chiefly at
the avoidance of unpleasurable experience, differ according
to which source of such experience is accorded most
attention. Some of them are extreme and others moderate;
some are one-sided, and some tackle the problem at several
points simultaneously. Deliberate isolation, keeping others at [50]
arm's length, affords the most obvious protection against any
suffering arising from interpersonal relations. One sees that
the happiness that can be attained in this way is the happiness
that comes from peace and quiet. Against the dreaded external
world one can defend oneself only by somehow turning away
from it, if one wants to solve the problem unaided. There is of
course another, better path: as a member of the human
community one can go on the attack against nature with the
help of applied science, and subject her to the human will.
One is then working with everyone for the happiness of all. [60]
The most interesting methods of preventing suffering are
those that seek to influence one's own constitution.
Ultimately, all suffering is merely feeling; it exists only in so
far as we feel it, and we feel it only because our constitution
is regulated in certain ways.

The crudest, but also the most effective method of
influencing our constitution is the chemical one—
intoxication. No one, I think, fully understands how it works,
but it is a fact that there are exogenous[2] substances
whose presence in the blood and tissues causes us direct [70]
feelings of pleasure, but also alters the determinants of our
sensibility in such a way that we are no longer susceptible
to unpleasurable sensations. Both effects not only occur
simultaneously; they also seem closely linked. However,
there must also be substances in the chemistry of our bodies
that act in a similar way, for we know of at least one morbid
condition—mania—in which a condition similar to intoxication
occurs, without the introduction of any intoxicant. Moreover,
in our normal mental life there are oscillations between fairly
easy releases of pleasure and others that are harder to [80]
come by, and these run parallel to a lesser or a greater
susceptibility to unpleasurable feelings. It is much to be
regretted that this toxic aspect of mental processes has
so far escaped scientific investigation. The effect of
intoxicants in the struggle for happiness and in keeping
misery at a distance is seen as so great a boon[3]
that not only individuals, but whole nations, have
accorded them a firm place in the economy of the libido.[4]
We owe to them not only a direct yield of pleasure, but a
fervently desired degree of independence from the external [90]

---

[1] inevitable.

[2] foreign.

[3] blessing.

[4] The instinctual desires of the id, most specifically, the sexual urge.

world. We know, after all, that by "drowning our sorrows" we can escape at any time from the pressure of reality and find refuge in a world of our own that affords us better conditions for our sensibility. It is well known that precisely this property of intoxicants makes them dangerous and harmful. In some circumstances they are responsible for the futile loss of large amounts of energy that might have been used to improve the lot of mankind. . . .

Another technique for avoiding suffering makes use of the displacements of the libido that are permitted by our psychical apparatus and lend its functioning so much flexibility. Here the task is to displace the aims of the drives in such a way that they cannot be frustrated by the external world. Sublimation of the drives plays a part in this. We achieve most if we can sufficiently heighten the pleasure derived from mental and intellectual work. Fate can then do little to harm us. This kind of satisfaction—the artist's joy in creating, in fashioning forth the products of his imagination, or the scientist's in solving problems and discovering truths—has a special quality that it will undoubtedly be possible, one day, to describe in metapsychological terms. At present we can only say, figuratively, that they seem to us "finer and higher," but their intensity is restrained when compared with that which results from the sating of crude, primary drives: they do not convulse our physical constitution. The weakness of this method, however, lies in the fact that it cannot be employed universally, as it is accessible only to the few. It presupposes special aptitudes and gifts that are not exactly common, not common enough to be effective. And even to the few it cannot afford complete protection against suffering; it does not supply them with an armor that is proof against the slings and arrows of fortune, and it habitually fails when one's own body becomes the source of the suffering. . . .

Another method, which operates more energetically and more thoroughly, sees reality as the sole enemy, the source of all suffering, something one cannot live with, and with which one must therefore sever all links if one wants to be happy, in any sense of the word. The hermit turns his back on the world and refuses to have anything to do with it. But one can do more than this: one can try to re-create the world, to build another in its place, one in which the most intolerable features are eliminated and replaced by others that accord with one's desires. As a rule anyone who takes this path to happiness, in a spirit of desperate rebellion, will achieve nothing. Reality is too strong for him. He will become a madman and will usually find nobody to help him realize his delusion. It is asserted, however, that in some way each of us behaves rather like a paranoic, employing wishful thinking to correct some unendurable aspect of the world and introducing this delusion into reality. Of special importance is the case in which substantial numbers of people, acting in concert, try to assure themselves of happiness and protection against suffering through a delusional reshaping of reality. The religions of mankind too must be described as examples of mass delusion. Of course, no one who still shares a delusion will ever recognize it as such. . . .

Religion interferes with this play of selection and adaptation by forcing on everyone indiscriminately its own path to the attainment of happiness and protection from suffering. Its technique consists in reducing the value of life and distorting the picture of the real world by means of delusion; and this presupposes the intimidation of the intelligence. At this price, by forcibly fixing human beings in a state of psychical infantilism and drawing them into a mass delusion, religion succeeds in saving many of them from individual neurosis. But it hardly does any more. . . .

In recent generations the human race has made extraordinary advances in the natural sciences and their technical application, and it has increased its control over nature in such a way that would previously have been unimaginable. The details of these advances are generally known and need not be enumerated. Human beings are proud of these achievements, and rightly so. Yet they believe they have observed that this newly won mastery over space and time, this subjugation of the forces of nature—the fulfilment of an age-old longing—has not increased the amount of pleasure they can expect from life or made them feel any happier. We ought to be content to infer from this observation that power over nature is not the sole condition of human happiness, just as it is not the sole aim of cultural endeavors, rather than to conclude that technical progress is of no value in the economy of our happiness. By way of objection it might be asked whether it is not a positive addition to my pleasure, an unequivocal increment[5] of my happiness, if I can hear, as often as I wish, the voice of the child who lives hundreds of miles away, or if a friend can inform me, shortly after reaching land, that he has survived his long and arduous voyage. Is it of no importance that medicine has succeeded in significantly reducing infant mortality and the risk of infection to women in childbirth, and in adding a good many years to the average life-span of civilized man? We can cite many such benefits that we owe to the much-despised era of scientific and technical advances. At this point, however, the voice of pessimistic criticism makes itself heard, reminding us that most of these satisfactions follow the pattern of the "cheap pleasure" recommended in a certain joke, a pleasure that one can enjoy by sticking a bare leg out from under the covers on a cold winter's night, then pulling it back in. If there were no railway to overcome distances, my child would never have left his home town, and I should not need the telephone in order to hear his voice. If there were no sea travel, my friend would not have embarked on his voyage, and I should not need the telegraph service in order to allay my anxiety about him. . . .

It is the existence of this tendency to aggression, which we detect in ourselves and rightly presume in others, that vitiates[6] our relations with our neighbor and obliges civilization to go to such lengths. Given this fundamental hostility of human beings to one another, civilized society is constantly threatened with disintegration. A common interest in work would not hold it together: passions that derive from the [instinctual] drives are stronger than reasonable interests. Civilization has to make every effort

---

[5] increase.

[6] impairs.

to limit man's aggressive drives and hold down their manifestations through the formation of psychical reactions. This leads to the use of methods that are meant to encourage people to identify themselves with others and enter into aim-inhibited erotic relationships, to the restriction of sexual life, and also to the ideal commandment to love one's neighbor **210** as oneself, which is actually justified by the fact that nothing else runs so much counter to basic human nature. For all the effort invested in it, this cultural endeavor has so far not achieved very much. It hopes to prevent the crudest excesses of brutal violence by assuming the right to use violence against criminals, but the law cannot deal with the subtler manifestations of human aggression. There comes a point at which each of us abandons, as illusions, the expectations he pinned to his fellow men when he was young and can **220** appreciate how difficult and painful his life is made by their ill will. . . .

Q What, according to Freud, are the three main sources of human suffering? By what means does one fend off suffering?

Q What role, according to Freud, does religion play in civilized society?

Freud's Followers

Freud's immediate followers recognized that they stood in the shadow of an intellectual giant. Although some theorists disagreed with his dogmatic assertion that all neuroses stemmed from the traumas of the id, most took his discoveries as the starting point for their own inquiries into human behavior. For instance, Freud's Viennese associate Alfred Adler (1870–1937), who pioneered the field of individual psychology, worked to explain the ego's efforts to adapt to its environment. Coining the term "inferiority complex," Adler concentrated on analyzing

problems relating to the ego's failure to achieve its operational goals in everyday life.

Another of Freud's colleagues, the Swiss physician Carl Gustav Jung (1875–1961), found Freud's view of the psyche too narrow and overly deterministic. Jung argued that the personal, unconscious life of the individual rested on a deeper and more universal layer of the human psyche, which he called the **collective unconscious**. According to Jung, the collective unconscious belongs to humankind at large, that is, to the human family. It manifests itself throughout history in the form of dreams, myths, and fairy tales. The **archetypes** (primal patterns) of that realm reflect the deep psychic needs of humankind as a species. They reveal themselves as familiar motifs and characters, such as "the child-god," "the hero," and "the wise old man." Jung's investigations into the cultural history of humankind disclosed similarities between the symbols and myths of different religions and bodies of folklore. These he took to support his theory that the archetypes were the innate, inherited contents of the human mind.

Some of Jung's most convincing observations concerning the life of the collective unconscious appear in his essay "Psychological Aspects of the Mother Archetype" (1938). Here, Jung discusses the manifestations of the female archetype in personal life, as mother, grandmother, stepmother, nurse, or governess; in religion, as the redemptive Mother of God, the Virgin, Holy Wisdom, and the various nature deities of ancient myth and religion; and in the universal symbols associated with fertility and fruitfulness, such as the cornucopia, the garden, the fountain, the cave, the rose, the lotus, the magic circle, and the uterus. The negative aspect of the female archetype, observed Jung, usually manifests itself as the witch in traditional fairy tales and legends.

Jung emphasized the role of the collective unconscious in reflecting the "psychic unity" of all cultures. He treated

EXPLORING ISSUES

Freud versus the Critics

As with most great thinkers, Freud made some questionable judgments, many of which came under attack before the end of the twentieth century. Revisionists questioned his theories on repression, arguing that they were scientifically untestable. Feminists took issue with his analysis of female sexuality (which holds that "penis envy" afflicts women), and his patriarchal perception of womankind as passive, weak, and dependent (see chapter 36). Proponents of biomedical psychiatry and behavioral psychology questioned the effectiveness of psychoanalysis itself. Still in progress is the debate as to whether mental illnesses are *biological* dysfunctions (best treated pharmacologically), *psychological* dysfunctions related

to infant or early childhood trauma (best treated by some form of psychotherapy), or both.

While Freud may be less valued today as an empirical scientist, he remains celebrated as a monumental visionary. His writings anticipated many of the recent developments in neuropsychiatry, the branch of medicine dealing with diseases of the mind and the nervous system. His theories continue to be tested. In the long run, however, Freud's most important contributions may be found to lie in modern intellectual history, specifically, in his thesis that the inner functions of the mind are valid and meaningful elements of the personality, and in his assertion that dreams and fantasies are as vital to human life as reason itself.

the personal psyche as part of the larger human family, and, unlike Freud, he insisted on the positive value of religion in satisfying humankind's deepest psychic desires. Currently, Jungian analysts focus on building an ongoing relationship between the individual and the unconscious domain.

The New Psychology and Literature

The impact of the new psychology was felt throughout Europe. Freud's theories, and particularly his pessimistic view of human nature, intensified the mood of uncertainty produced by the startling revelations of atomic physics and the outbreak of World War I. The Freudian revolution affected all aspects of artistic expression, not the least of which was literature. A great many figures in early twentieth-century fiction were profoundly influenced by Freud; three of the most famous of these are Marcel Proust, Franz Kafka, and James Joyce. In the works of these novelists, the most significant events are those that take place in the psychic life of dreams and memory. The narrative line of the story may be interrupted by unexpected leaps of thought, intrusive recollections, self-reflections, and sudden dead ends. Fantasy may alternate freely with rational thought. The lives of the heroes—or, more exactly, antiheroes—in these stories are often inconsequential, while their concerns, although commonplace or trivial, may be obsessive, bizarre, and charged with passion.

Proust's Quest for Lost Time

Born in Paris, Marcel Proust (1871–1922) spent his youth troubled by severe attacks of asthma and recurring insecurity over his sexual orientation. Devastated by the death of his mother in 1905, Proust withdrew completely from Parisian society. He retreated into the semidarkness of a cork-lined room, where, shielded from noise, light, and frivolous society, he pursued a life of introspection and literary endeavor. Between 1909 and 1922 Proust produced a sixteen-volume novel entitled *A la recherche du temps perdu* (literally, "In Search of Lost Time," but usually translated as *Remembrance of Things Past*). This lengthy masterpiece provides a reflection of the society of turn-of-the-century France, but its perception of reality is wholly internal. It is widely regarded as the first European novel to feature homosexuality in the lives of some of its characters. Its central theme, however, is the role of memory in retrieving past experience and in shaping the private life of the individual. Proust's mission was to rediscover a sense of the past by reviving sensory experiences buried deep within his psyche, that is, to bring the unconscious life to the conscious level. "For me," explained Proust, "the novel is . . . psychology in space and time."

In the first volume of *A la recherche du temps perdu*, entitled *Swann's Way*, Proust employs the Freudian technique of "free association" to recapture from the recesses of memory the intense moment of pleasure occasioned by the taste of a piece of cake soaked in tea. The following excerpt illustrates Proust's ability to free experience from the rigid order of mechanical time and to invade the richly textured storehouse of the psyche. It also illustrates the modern notion of the mental process as a "stream of thought," a concept that had appeared as early as 1884 in the writings of the American psychologist William James (1842–1910) and in the works of Henri Bergson (1859–1941), who described reality as a perpetual flux in which past and present are inseparable (see chapter 31).

READING 33.2 From Proust's *Swann's Way* (1913)

The past is hidden somewhere outside the realm, beyond the   1
reach of intellect, in some material object (in the sensation
which that material object will give us) which we do not
suspect. And as for that object, it depends on chance
whether we come upon it or not before we ourselves must die.

Many years had elapsed during which nothing of Combray,
save what was comprised in the theatre and the drama of my
going to bed there, had any existence for me, when one day
in winter, as I came home, my mother, seeing that I was cold,
offered me some tea, a thing I did not ordinarily take. I   10
declined at first, and then, for no particular reason, changed
my mind. She sent out for one of those short, plump little
cakes called "petites madeleines," which look as though they
had been moulded in the fluted scallop of a pilgrim's shell.
And soon, mechanically, weary after a dull day with the
prospect of a depressing morrow, I raised to my lips a spoonful
of the tea in which I had soaked a morsel of the cake. No
sooner had the warm liquid, and the crumbs with it, touched
my palate than a shudder ran through my whole body, and I
stopped, intent upon the extraordinary changes that were   20
taking place. An exquisite pleasure had invaded my senses,
but individual, detached, with no suggestion of its origin.
And at once the vicissitudes of life had become indifferent to
me, its disasters innocuous, its brevity illusory—this new
sensation having had on me the effect which love has of filling
me with a precious essence; or rather this essence was not in
me, it was myself. I had ceased now to feel mediocre,
accidental, mortal. Whence could it have come to me, this all-
powerful joy? I was conscious that it was connected with the
taste of tea and cake, but that it infinitely transcended those   30
savours, could not, indeed, be of the same nature as theirs.
Whence did it come? What did it signify? How could I seize
upon and define it?

I drink a second mouthful, in which I find nothing more
than in the first, a third, which gives me rather less than the
second. It is time to stop; the potion is losing its magic. It is
plain that the object of my quest, the truth, lies not in the cup
but in myself. The tea has called up in me, but does not itself
understand, and can only repeat indefinitely with a gradual
loss of strength, the same testimony; which I, too, cannot   40
interpret, though I hope at least to be able to call upon the tea
for it again and to find it there presently, intact and at my
disposal, for my final enlightenment. I put down my cup and
examine my own mind. It is for it to discover the truth. But
how? What an abyss of uncertainty whenever the mind feels
that some part of it has strayed beyond its own borders; when

it, the seeker, is at once the dark region through which it must go seeking, where all its equipment will avail it nothing. Seek? More than that: create. It is face to face with something which does not so far exist, to which it alone can give reality and substance, which it alone can bring into the light of day. 50

And I begin again to ask myself what it could have been, this unremembered state which brought with it no logical proof of its existence, but only the sense that it was a happy, that it was a real state in whose presence other states of consciousness melted and vanished. I decide to attempt to make it reappear. I retrace my thoughts to the moment at which I drank the first spoonful of tea. I find again the same state, illumined by no fresh light. I compel my mind to make one further effort, to follow and recapture once again the 60 fleeting sensation. And that nothing may interrupt it in its course I shut out every obstacle, every extraneous idea, I stop my ears and inhibit all attention to the sounds which come from the next room. And then, feeling that my mind is growing fatigued without having any success to report, I compel it for a change to enjoy that distraction which I have just denied it, to think of other things, to rest and refresh itself before the supreme attempt. And then for the second time I clear an empty space in front of it. I place in position before my mind's eye the still recent taste of that first mouthful, and I feel 70 something start within me, something that leaves its resting-place and attempts to rise, something that has been embedded like an anchor at a great depth; I do not know yet what it is, but I can feel it mounting slowly; I can measure the resistance, I can hear the echo of great spaces traversed.

Undoubtedly what is thus palpitating in the depths of my being must be the image, the visual memory which, being linked to that taste, has tried to follow it into my conscious mind. But its struggles are too far off, too much confused; scarcely can I perceive the colorless reflection in which are 80 blended the uncapturable whirling medley of radiant hues, and I cannot distinguish its form, cannot invite it, as the one possible interpreter, to translate to me the evidence of its contemporary, its inseparable paramour, the taste of cake soaked in tea; cannot ask it to inform me what special circumstance is in question, of what period in my past life.

Will it ultimately reach the clear surface of my consciousness, this memory, this old, dead moment which the magnetism of an identical moment has travelled so far to importune, to disturb, to raise up out of the very depths of my being? I cannot tell. 90 Now that I feel nothing, it has stopped, has perhaps gone down again into its darkness, from which who can say whether it will ever rise? Ten times over I must essay the task, must lean down over the abyss. And each time the natural laziness which deters us from every difficult enterprise, every work of importance, has urged me to leave the thing alone, to drink my tea and to think merely of the worries of to-day and of my hopes for tomorrow, which let themselves be pondered over without effort or distress of mind.

And suddenly the memory returns. The taste was that of 100 the little crumb of madeleine which on Sunday mornings at Combray (because on those mornings I did not go out before church-time), when I went to say good day to her in her bedroom, my aunt Léonie used to give me, dipping it first in her own cup of real or of lime-flower tea. The sight of the little madeleine had recalled nothing to my mind before I tasted it; perhaps because I had so often seen such things in the interval, without tasting them, on the trays in pastry-cooks' windows, that their image had dissociated itself from those Combray days to take its place among others more recent; 110 perhaps because of those memories, so long abandoned and put out of mind, nothing now survived, everything was scattered; the forms of things, including that of the little scallop-shell of pastry, so richly sensual under its severe, religious folds, were either obliterated or had been so long dormant as to have lost the power of expansion which would have allowed them to resume their place in my consciousness. But when from a long-distant past nothing subsists, after the people are dead, after the things are broken and scattered, still, alone, more fragile, but with more vitality, more 120 unsubstantial, more persistent, more faithful, the smell and taste of things remain poised a long time, like souls, ready to remind us, waiting and hoping for their moment, amid the ruins of all the rest; and bear unfaltering, in the tiny and almost impalpable drop of their essence, the vast structure of recollection. . . .

Q **What links does Proust draw between his unconscious and his conscious self?**

Q **What role does the madeleine play in these relationships?**

The Nightmare Reality of Kafka

For Proust, memory was a life-enriching phenomenon, but for the German-Jewish novelist Franz Kafka (1883–1924), the subconscious life gave conscious experience bizarre and threatening gravity. Written in German, Kafka's novels and short stories take on the reality of dreams in which characters are nameless, details are precise but grotesque, and events lack logical consistency. In the nightmarish world of his novels, the central characters become victims of unknown or imprecisely understood forces. They may be caught in absurd but commonplace circumstances involving guilt and frustration, or they may be threatened by menacing events that appear to have neither meaning nor purpose. In *The Trial* (1925), for instance, the protagonist is arrested, convicted, and executed, without ever knowing the nature of his crime. In "The Metamorphosis," one of the most disquieting short stories of the twentieth century, the central character, Gregor Samsa, wakes one morning to discover that he has turned into a large insect. The themes of insecurity and vulnerability that recur in Kafka's novels reflect the mood that prevailed during the early decades of the century. Kafka himself was afflicted with this insecurity: shortly before he died in 1924, he asked a close friend to burn all his manuscripts; the friend disregarded the request and saw to it that Kafka's works, even some that were unfinished, were published. Consequently, Kafka's style, which builds on deliberate ambiguity and fearful contradiction, has had a major influence on modern fiction. Although "The Metamorphosis" is too long to reproduce here in full, the excerpt that follows conveys some idea of Kafka's surreal narrative style.

READING 33.3 From Kafka's "The Metamorphosis" (1915)

When Gregor Samsa awoke from troubled dreams one morning, he found that he had been transformed in his bed into an enormous bug. He lay on his back, which was hard as armor, and, when he lifted his head a little, he saw his belly—rounded, brown, partitioned by archlike ridges—on top of which the blanket, ready to slip off altogether, was just barely perched. His numerous legs, pitifully thin in comparison to the rest of his girth, flickered helplessly before his eyes.

"What's happened to me?" he thought. It was no dream. His room, a real room meant for human habitation, though a little too small, lay peacefully within its four familiar walls. Above the table, on which an unpacked sampling of fabric swatches was strewn—Samsa was a traveling salesman—hung the picture that he had recently cut out of an illustrated magazine and had placed in a pretty gilt frame. It depicted a lady who, decked out in a fur hat and a fur boa, sat upright, raising toward the viewer a heavy fur muff in which her whole forearm was encased.

Gregor's gaze then turned toward the window, and the dismal weather—you could hear raindrops beating against the window gutter—made him quite melancholy. "What if I went back to sleep for another while and forgot all this foolishness?" he thought; but that was totally out of the question, because he was used to sleeping on his right side, and in his present state he couldn't get into that position. No matter how energetically he threw himself onto his right side, each time he rocked back into the supine position. He must have tried a hundred times, closing his eyes to avoid seeing his squirming legs, not stopping until he began to feel a slight, dull pain in his side that he had never felt before.

"My God," he thought, "what a strenuous profession I've chosen! Traveling day in and day out. The turmoil of business is much greater than in the home office, and on top of that I'm subjected to this torment of traveling, to the worries about train connections, the bad meals at irregular hours, an association with people that constantly changes, never lasts, never becomes cordial. The devil take it all!" He felt a slight itch up on his belly; slowly shoved himself on his back closer to the bedpost, so he could lift his head better; found the itchy place, which was all covered with little white spots that he was unable to diagnose; and wanted to feel the area with one leg, but drew it back immediately, because when he touched it he was invaded by chills. . . .

He glanced over toward his alarm clock, which was ticking on the chest. "Father in Heaven!" he thought. It was half past six, and the hands were moving ahead peacefully; in fact, it was later than half past, it was almost a quarter to seven. Could the alarm have failed to ring? From the bed he could see that it was correctly set for four; surely, it had also rung. Yes, but was it possible to sleep peacefully through that furniture-shaking ring? Well, he hadn't slept peacefully, but probably all the more soundly for that. Yet what should he do now? The next train left at seven; to catch it he would have to make a mad dash, his sample case wasn't packed yet, and he himself definitely didn't feel particularly fresh and lively. And even if he caught the train, he couldn't escape a bawling out from his boss, because the office messenger had waited at the five-o'clock train and had long since made a report about his negligence. . . .

While he was considering all this in the greatest haste, still unable to decide whether to get out of bed—the clock was just striking six forty-five—there was a cautious knock on the door at the head of his bed. "Gregor," a voice called—it was his mother—"it's six forty-five. Didn't you intend to make a trip?" That gentle voice! Gregor was frightened when he heard his own answering voice, which, to be sure, was unmistakably his accustomed one, but in which there now appeared, as if rising from below, an irrepressible, painful peeping sound, so that his words retained their clarity only at the very outset but became distorted as they faded away, so that you couldn't tell if you had heard them correctly. Gregor had meant to give a detailed answer and explain everything, but under the circumstances he merely said: "Yes, yes; thanks, Mother; I'm getting up now." Because the door was made of wood, the alteration in Gregor's voice was probably not noticeable, since his mother was pacified by that explanation and shuffled away. But as a result of that brief conversation the other members of the family had become aware that, contrary to expectation, Gregor was still at home; and his father was soon knocking at one of the side doors, softly, but with his fist. "Gregor, Gregor," he called, "what's going on?" And before very long he admonished him again, in a deeper voice: "Gregor! Gregor!" But at the other door his sister was quietly lamenting: "Gregor? Aren't you well? Do you need anything?" Gregor answered in both directions: "Be right there!" He made an effort, by enunciating most carefully and by inserting long pauses between the individual words, to free his voice of anything out of the ordinary. His father then returned to his breakfast, but his sister whispered: "Gregor, open up, I beg you." . . . .

[Unexpectedly, the chief clerk arrives to find out why Gregor is not at work. He demands to see him.]

Gregor shoved himself slowly to the door, using the chair; once there, he let it go and threw himself against the door, holding himself upright against it—the balls of his little feet contained some sticky substance—and rested there from his exertions for the space of a minute. But then he prepared to turn the key in the lock with his mouth. Unfortunately it seemed that he had no real teeth—what was he to grasp the key with?—but, instead, his jaws were actually pretty strong; with their help he did really get the key to move, paying no heed to the fact that he was doubtless doing himself some injury, because a brown fluid issued from his mouth, ran down over the key and dripped onto the floor. "Listen there," said the chief clerk in the adjoining room, "he's turning the key." That was a great encouragement for Gregor; but all of them should have called out to him, even his father and mother; "Go to it, Gregor!" they should have called, "keep at it, work on that lock!" And, imagining that they were all following his efforts in suspense, he bit recklessly into the key with all the strength he could muster. He danced around the lock, now here, now there, following the progress of the key as it turned; now he was keeping himself upright solely with his mouth, and, as the need arose, he either hung from the key or pushed it down again with the full weight of his body. The sharper sound of the lock, as it finally snapped back, woke Gregor up completely. With a sigh of relief he said to himself: "So then, I didn't need the locksmith," and he placed his head on the handle, in order to open the door all the way.

Since he had to open the door in this manner, he was still out of sight when it was already fairly wide open. First he had to turn his body slowly around one leaf of the double door, and very carefully at that, if he didn't want to fall squarely on his back right before entering the room. He was still occupied by that difficult maneuver and had no time to pay attention to anything else, when he heard the chief clerk utter a loud "Oh!" —it sounded like the wind howling—and now he saw him as well. He had been the closest to the door; now, pressing his hand against his open mouth, he stepped slowly backward as if driven away by some invisible force operating with uniform pressure. Gregor's mother—despite the presence of the chief clerk, she stood there with her hair still undone from the previous night and piled in a high, ruffled mass—first looked at his father with folded hands, then took two steps toward Gregor and collapsed in the midst of her petticoats, which billowed out all around her, her face completely lost to view and sunk on her chest. His father clenched his fist with a hostile expression, as if intending to push Gregor back into his room; then he looked around the parlor in uncertainty, shaded his eyes with his hands and wept so hard that it shook his powerful chest . . . .

Q How would you describe Gregor Samsa's personality?

Q What details in this story establish a sense of reality? Of unreality? Of fear?

Joyce and Stream-of-Consciousness Prose

One of the most influential writers of the early twentieth century, and also one of the most challenging, was the Irish expatriate James Joyce (1882–1941). Born in Dublin and educated in Jesuit schools, Joyce abandoned Ireland in 1905 to live abroad. In Paris, he studied medicine and music but made his livelihood there and elsewhere by teaching foreign languages and writing short stories. Joyce's prose reflects his genius as a linguist and his keen sensitivity to the musical potential of words. His treatment of plot and character is deeply indebted to Freud, whose earliest publications Joyce had consumed with interest. From Freud's works, he drew inspiration for the **interior monologue**, a literary device consisting of the private musings of a character in the form of a "stream of consciousness"—a succession of images and ideas connected by free association rather than by logical argument or narrative sequence. The stream-of-consciousness device recalls the technique of free association used by Freud in psychotherapy; it also recalls the discontinuous-verse style of the Imagist poets (see chapter 32). In a stream-of-consciousness novel, the action is developed through the mind of the principal character as he or she responds to the dual play of conscious and subconscious stimuli. The following passage from Joyce's 600-page novel *Ulysses* (1922) provides a brief example:

He crossed to the bright side, avoiding the loose cellarflap of number seventy-five. The sun was nearing the steeple of George's church. Be a warm day I fancy, Specially in these black clothes feel it more. Black conducts, reflects (refracts is it?), the heat. But I couldn't go in that light suit. Make a picnic of it. His Boland's breadvan delivering with trays our daily but she prefers yesterday's loaves turnovers crisp crowns hot. Makes you feel young. Somewhere in the east: early morning: set off at dawn, travel round in front of the sun, steal a day's march on him. Keep it up for ever never grow a day older technically. . . . Wander along all day. Meet a robber or two. Well, meet him. Getting on to sundown. The shadows of the mosques along the pillars: priest with a scroll rolled up. A shiver of the trees, signal, the evening wind. I pass on. Fading gold sky. A mother watches from her doorway. She calls her children home in their dark language. High wall: beyond strings twanged. Night sky moon, violet, colour of Molly's new garters. Strings. Listen. A girl playing one of these instruments what do you call them: dulcimers. I pass. . . .

Joyce modeled his sprawling novel on the Homeric epic the *Odyssey*. But Joyce's version differs profoundly from Homer's. Leopold Bloom, the main character of *Ulysses*, is as ordinary as Homer's Odysseus was heroic; his adventures seem trivial and insignificant by comparison with those of his Classical counterpart. Bloom's commonplace experiences, as he wanders from home to office, pub, and brothel, and then home again—a one-day "voyage" through the streets of Dublin— constitute the plot of the novel. The real "action," however, takes place in the minds of the principal characters: Bloom, his acquaintances, and his wife, Molly. Their collective ruminations produce an overwhelming sense of desolation and a startling awareness that the human psyche can never extricate itself from the timeless blur of experience.

Joyce's stream-of-consciousness technique and his dense accumulation of unfamiliar and oddly compounded words make this monumental novel difficult to grasp—yet it remains more accessible than his experimental, baffling prose work *Finnegans Wake* (1939). Initially, however, it was censorship that made *Ulysses* inaccessible to the public: since Joyce treated sexual matters as intimately as all other aspects of human experience, critics judged his language obscene. The novel was banned in the United States until 1933.

The combined influence of Freud and Joyce was visible in much of the first-ranking literature of the twentieth century. Writers such as Gertrude Stein (1874–1946) and the Nobel laureates Thomas Mann (1875–1955) and William Faulkner (1897–1962) extended the use of the stream-of-consciousness technique. In theater, the American playwright Eugene O'Neill (1888–1953) fused Greek myth with Freudian concepts of guilt and repression in the dramatic trilogy *Mourning Becomes Electra* (1931). He devised dramatic techniques that revealed the characters' buried emotions, such as two actors playing different aspects of a single individual, the use of masks, and the embellishment of dialogue with accompanying asides.

The new psychology extended its influence to performance style as well: Freud's emphasis on the interior life inspired the development of **method acting**, a style of modern theatrical performance that tried to harness "true emotion" and "affective memory" (from childhood experience) in the interpretation of dramatic roles. The pioneer in method acting was the Russian director and actor Konstantin Stanislavsky (1863–1938), whose innovative techniques as head of the Moscow Art Theater spread to the United States in the early 1930s. There, his method inspired some of America's finest screen and stage actors, such as James Dean (1931–1955) and Marlon Brando (1924–2004).

The New Freedom in Poetry

Modern poets avidly seized upon stream-of-consciousness techniques to emancipate poetry from syntactical and grammatical bonds—a mission that had been initiated by the Symbolists and refined by the Imagists. The French writer Guillaume Apollinaire (1880–1918), a close friend of Picasso and an admirer of Cubism, wrote poems that not only liberated words from their traditional placement in the sentence but also freed sentences from their traditional arrangement on the page. Inspired by the designs of ordinary handbills, billboards, and signs, Apollinaire created **concrete poems**, that is, poems produced in the shape of external objects, such as watches, neckties, and pigeons. He arranged the words in the poem "Il Pleut" ("It Rains"), for instance, as if they had fallen onto the page like raindrops from the heavens. Such word-pictures, which Apollinaire called "lyrical ideograms," inspired the poet to exult: "I too am a painter!"

The American poet E. E. Cummings (1894–1962) arrived in France in 1917 as a volunteer ambulance driver for the Red Cross. Like Apollinaire, Cummings wrote poems that violated the traditional rules of verse composition. To sharpen the focus of a poem, he subjected typography and syntax to acrobatic distortions that challenged the eye as well as the ear. Cummings poked fun at modern society by packing his verse with slang, jargon, and sexual innuendo. As the following poem suggests, his lyrics are often infused with large doses of playful humor.

┌─ **READING 33.4** Cummings'
│   [she being Brand] (1926)
│
│ she being Brand   1
│
│ -new;and you
│ know consequently a
│ little stiff i was
│ careful of her and(having   5
│ thoroughly oiled the universal
│ joint tested my gas felt of
│ her radiator made sure her springs were O.
│
│ K.)i went right to it flooded-the-carburetor cranked her

up, slipped the   10
clutch(and then somehow got into reverse she
kicked what
the hell)next
minute i was back in neutral tried and

again slo-wly;bare,ly nudg.   ing(my   15

lev-er Right-
oh and her gears being in
A 1 shape passed
from low through
second-in-to-high like   20
greasedlightning) just as we turned the corner of Divinity

avenue i touched the accelerator and give

her the juice,good

                              (it

was the first ride and believe i we was   25
happy to see how nice she acted right up to
the last minute coming back down by the Public
Gardens i slammed on

the
internalexpanding   30
&
externalcontracting
brakes Bothatonce and

brought allofher tremB
-ling   35
to a: dead.

stand-
;Still)

─ **Q** Who is the "she" in this poem?

─ **Q** What liberties does the poet take with form? With subject matter?

The New Psychology and the Visual Arts

It was in the visual arts that the new psychology made its most dramatic and longlasting impact. As artists brought to their work their hidden emotions, their repressed desires, and their dreams and fantasies, art became the vehicle of the subconscious. The irrational and antirational forces of the id were the subject and the inspiration for an assortment of styles. These include Expressionism, Metaphysical art, Dada, and Surrealism. Expressionism and Surrealism had particularly important effects on photography and film, as well as on the fields of commercial and applied arts. In every aspect of our daily life, from fashion designs to magazine and television advertisements, the evidence of the Freudian revolution is still visible.

Expressionism

The pioneer Expressionist painter of the twentieth century was the Norwegian Edvard Munch (1863–1944). Munch was a great admirer of Henrik Ibsen, whose plays (see chapter 30) examine the inner conflicts and repressed desires of their characters. Obsessed with the traumas of puberty and frustrated sexuality, Munch was also deeply troubled by personal associations with illness and death—tuberculosis had killed both his mother and his sister. Such subjects provided the imagery for his paintings and woodcuts; but it was in his style—a haunting synthesis of distorted forms and savage colors—that he captured the anguished intensity of the neurosis that led to his mental collapse in 1908.

The Scream (Figure **33.2**), a painting that has become a universal symbol of the modern condition, takes its mood of urgency and alarm from the combined effects of sinuous clouds, writhing blue-black waters, and a dramatically receding pier (a popular meeting spot near Munch's summer cottage). These visual rhythms suggest the resonating sound of the voiceless cry described by Munch in the notes to a preliminary drawing for the painting: "I walked with two friends. Then the sun sank. Suddenly the sky turned red as blood. . . . My friends walked on, and I was left alone, trembling with fear. I felt as if all nature were filled with one mighty unending shriek."

Munch's impassioned style foreshadowed *German Expressionism.* Like the Italian Futurists, young artists in Germany rebelled against the "old-established forces" of academic art. Influenced by Freud and by the arts of Africa and Oceania, two Modernist groups emerged: in Dresden, *Die Brücke* (The Bridge) was founded in 1905; the second, established in Munich in 1911, called itself *Der Blaue Reiter* (The Blue Rider). Although divided by strong personal differences, the artists of these two groups shared a style marked by pathos, violence, and emotional intensity. The German Expressionists inherited the brooding, romantic sensibility of Goethe, Nietzsche, and Wagner. They favored macabre and intimate subjects, which they rendered by means of distorted forms, harsh colors, and the bold and haunting use of black.

Led by Ernst Ludwig Kirchner (1880–1938), members of *Die Brücke,* including Erich Heckel (1883–1970), Karl Schmidt-Rottluff (1884–1976), and Emil Nolde (1867–1956), envisioned their movement as a "bridge" to Modernism. They embraced art as an outpouring of "inner necessity," emotion, and ecstasy. Seized by the prewar tension of urban Germany, they painted probing self-portraits, tempestuous landscapes, and ominous cityscapes. In *Street, Berlin* (Figure **33.3**), Kirchner's jagged lines and dissonant colors, accented by aggressive areas of black, evoke the image of urban life as crowded, impersonal, and threatening. His convulsive distortions of figural form reveal the influence of African sculpture, while the nervous intensity of his line style reflects his indebtedness to the German graphic tradition pioneered by Albrecht Dürer (see chapter 19). Like Dürer, Kirchner rendered many of his subjects (including portraits and cityscapes) in woodcut—the favorite medium of German Expressionism.

Figure 33.2 EDVARD MUNCH, *The Scream*, 1893. Oil, pastel, and casein on cardboard, 35¾ × 29 in. The ghostly foreground figure (Munch himself) may have been inspired by an Inca mummy viewed by the artist in the Paris Exhibition of 1899. The blood-red sky may owe something to a volcanic eruption that took place in Indonesia in August 1883, the effects of which reached Munch's hometown in Norway.

Chirico commented: "There are more enigmas in the shadow of a man who walks in the sun than in all the religions of past, present, and future." De Chirico anticipated a mode of representation known as *Magic Realism*, in which commonplace objects and events are exaggerated or juxtaposed in unexpected ways that evoke a mood of mystery or fantasy.

The Russian-born artist Marc Chagall (1887–1985) arrived in Paris in 1910. Like his countryman and fellow expatriate Igor Stravinsky, Chagall infused his first compositions with the folktales and customs of his native land. His nostalgic recollection of rural Russia called *I and the Village*

Figure 33.3 **ERNST LUDWIG KIRCHNER**, *Street, Berlin*, 1913. Oil on canvas, 3 ft. 11½ in. × 2 ft. 11⅞ in. Two stylishly dressed prostitutes press forward along a wildly tilted city street. Lurid pinks, acid blues, and charcoal blacks add to the claustrophobic atmosphere. Kirchner painted this and similar scenes after moving from Dresden to Berlin, during a time he described as being one of loneliness and depression.

Metaphysical Art and Fantasy

While the German Expressionists brought a new degree of subjective intensity to the depiction of the visible world, other artists explored the life that lay beyond the senses. One of these artists was Giorgio de Chirico (1888–1978). Born in Greece, de Chirico moved to Italy in 1909. Rejecting the tenets of Italian Futurism (see chapter 32), he pioneered a style that he called "metaphysical," that is, "beyond physical reality." In canvases executed between 1910 and 1920, he introduced the landscape of the psyche into the realm of art. His sharply delineated images, contradictory perspectives, unnatural colors, and illogically cast shadows produced disturbing, dreamlike effects similar to those in Kafka's prose.

In *The Nostalgia of the Infinite* (Figure **33.4**), two figures, dwarfed by eerie shadows, stand in the empty courtyard; five flags flutter mysteriously in an airless, acid-green sky. The vanishing point established by the orthogonal lines of the portico on the right contradicts the low placement of the distant horizon. Of his disquieting cityscapes, de

Figure 33.4 **GIORGIO DE CHIRICO**, *The Nostalgia of the Infinite*, 1914; dated on painting 1911. Oil on canvas, 4 ft. 5¼ in. × 2 ft. 1½ in.

behavior—with works that deliberately violated good taste, middle-class values, and artistic convention.

The Dadaists met regularly at the Café Voltaire in Zürich, where they orchestrated "noise concerts" and recited poetry created by way of **improvisation** and free association. The Romanian poet Tristan Tzara (1896–1963) produced poems from words cut out of newspapers and randomly scattered on a table, while the French sculptor and poet Jean Arp (1887–1966) constructed collages and relief sculptures from shapes dropped at random on a canvas and left "according to the laws of chance." Dada's attacks on rationalist tradition and on modern technocracy in general reflected the spirit of **nihilism** (the denial of traditional and religious and moral principles) that flowered in the ashes of the war. In his "Lecture on Dada" in 1922, Tzara declared: "The acts of life have no beginning or end. Everything happens in a completely idiotic way. Simplicity is called dada. . . . Like everything in life, dada is useless."

As with poetry and painting, Dada theater paid homage to Freud by liberating "everything obscure in the mind, buried deep, unrevealed," as one French playwright explained. Narrative realism and traditional characterization gave way to improvisation and the performance of random and bizarre incidents. One form of Dada theater, the *theater of cruelty*, known for its violent and scatological themes, anticipated the theater of the absurd plays written during the 1950s and 1960s (see chapter 35).

The spirit of the Dadaists was most vividly realized in the work of the French artist Marcel Duchamp

Figure 33.5 MARC CHAGALL, *I and the Village*, 1911. Oil on canvas, 6 ft. 3⅝ in. × 4 ft. 11⅝ in.

(Figure **33.5**) owes much to the lessons of Cubism and Fauvism. However, the disjunctive sizes and positions of the figures and the variety of arbitrary colors obey the whimsy of the unconscious. Chagall freely superimposed images upon one another or showed them floating in space, defying the laws of gravity. Autobiographical motifs, such as violin players and levitating lovers, became Chagall's hallmarks in the richly colored canvases, murals, and stained glass windows of his long and productive career.

The Dada Movement

While Expressionism and fantasy investigated the Freudian unconscious, neither attacked nationalist tradition as aggressively as the movement known as *Dada*. Founded in 1916 in Zürich, Switzerland, the Dada movement consisted of a loosely knit group of European painters and poets who, perceiving World War I as evidence of a world gone mad, dedicated themselves to spreading the gospel of irrationality. The nonsensical name of the movement, "dada" ("hobbyhorse"), which was chosen by inserting a penknife at random into the pages of a dictionary, symbolized their irreverent stance. If the world had gone mad, should not its creative endeavors be equally mad? Dada answered with art that was the product of chance, accident, or outrageous

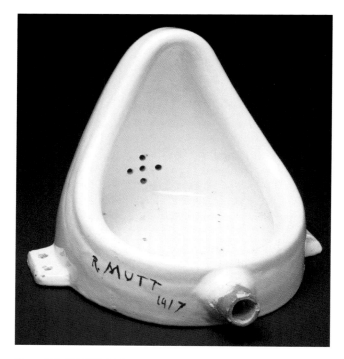

Figure 33.6 MARCEL DUCHAMP, *Fountain (Urinal)*, 1917. Ready-made, height 24 in. There are eight factory-made replicas of *Fountain*, "signed" by Duchamp in 1964. In 1993, an artist attacked the piece on display in Nîmes, France. Claiming the right to use it for its original purpose, he urinated in it.

Figure 33.7 MARCEL DUCHAMP, *L.H.O.O.Q.*, 1919. Rectified ready-made, pencil on a reproduction of the *Mona Lisa*, 7¾ × 4⅞ in.

Perhaps most importantly, however, *Fountain* introduced to modern art the revolutionary notion that a work of art was first and foremost about an artist's *idea*. *Fountain* was not art because Duchamp had "made" it, but because he had chosen to remove it from the context of everyday life and had given it a whole new identity (as art). Pursuing this logic, the artist might also alter (or "remake") existing art, as, for example, when Duchamp drew a mustache on a reproduction of Leonardo da Vinci's venerable *Mona Lisa*, adding a series of letters at the bottom that, when recited rapidly (in French), describe the sitter in lusty street slang (Figure **33.7**). This "corrected ready-made," as Duchamp called the piece, expressed the Dada disdain for Western high art. It established the modern artist as maverick—the self-appointed prophet and defiler of tradition.

Moving to New York City in 1918, Duchamp labored for ten years on his magnum opus, a large glass and wire assemblage filled with esoteric sexual symbolism. He called it *The Bride Stripped Bare by Her Bachelors, Even*. After 1920, Duchamp went "underground," spending as much time perfecting his chess game (his favorite pastime) as making art. Nevertheless, his small, pioneering body of work and his irreverent view that art "has absolutely no existence as . . . truth" have had a powerful influence on scores of poets, painters, and composers even into the twenty-first century.

Surrealism and Abstract Surrealists: Picasso, Miró, and Klee

One of Modernism's most distinctive movements, *Surrealism* (the term coined by Guillaume Apollinaire in 1917), was devoted to giving physical expression to the workings of the unconscious mind. The Surrealists paid explicit homage to Freud and his writings, especially those on free association and dream analysis. In the first "Surrealist Manifesto" (1924), the French critic and spiritual godfather of Surrealism, André Breton (1896–1966) proclaimed the artist's liberation from reason and from the demands of conventional society. Having visited Freud in Vienna in 1921, Breton described the Surrealist commitment to the irrational as follows:

> We are still living under the reign of logic. . . . But in this day and age logical methods are applicable only to solving problems of secondary interest. The absolute rationalism that is still in vogue allows us to consider only facts relating directly to our experience. . . . [Experience] is protected by the sentinels of common sense. Under the pretense of civilization and progress, we have managed to banish from the mind everything that may rightly or wrongly be termed superstition, or fancy; forbidden is any kind of search for truth which is not in conformance with accepted practices. It was, apparently, by pure chance, that a part of our mental world which we pretended not to be concerned with any longer—and, in my opinion, by far the most important part—has been brought back to light. For this we must give thanks to the discoveries of Sigmund Freud. . . . The imagination is perhaps on the point of reasserting itself, of reclaiming its rights.

(1887–1968). Early in his career, Duchamp had flirted with Cubism and Futurism, producing the influential *Nude Descending a Staircase, No. 2* (see Figure 32.9); but after 1912, he abandoned professional painting and turned to making—or remaking—art objects. In 1913 he mounted a bicycle wheel atop a barstool, thus producing the first "ready-made," as well as the first **mobile** (a sculpture with moving parts). Four years later, Duchamp would launch the landmark ready-made of the century: he placed a common factory-produced urinal on a pedestal, signed the piece with the fictitious name "R. Mutt," and submitted it for an exhibition held by the American Society of Independent Artists (Figure **33.6**). The piece, which he called *Fountain*, was rejected, but its long-term impact was enormous. By calling the "found object" a work of art, Duchamp mocked conventional techniques of making art. Moreover, by wrenching the object out of its functional context, he suggested that the image obeyed a logic of its own, a logic whose "rules" flouted traditional aesthetic norms. *Fountain* not only attacked the barrier between art and life, but also called for art that exalted the nonsensical, the accidental, and the absurd.

Figure 33.8 PABLO PICASSO, *Seated Woman*, Paris, 1927. Oil on wood, 4 ft. 3⅛ in. × 3 ft. 2¼ in.

dissection and savage distortion dominated his art. In 1927, Picasso painted the *Seated Woman* (Figure **33.8**), the image of a "split personality" that seemed to symbolize Freud's three-part psyche. The head of the female consists of a frontal view, as well as at least two profile views, each of which reveals a different aspect of her personality. The "split personality" motif continued to preoccupy Picasso throughout his long artistic career. In scores of paintings and sculptures, as well as in the stream-of-consciousness prose he wrote during the 1930s, Picasso pursued double meanings and visual puns, thus securing his reputation as the master of metamorphosis in twentieth-century art.

In the paintings of the Spanish artist Joan Miró (1893–1983), the Surrealist's search for subconscious experience kindled the artist's personal mythology. Miró's simple, childlike figures, his biomorphic creatures, and spiny, abstract organisms became the denizens of a fantastic universe. The creatures in *The Harlequin's Carnival*—amoeba, snakes, and insects—cavort in unbounded space (see Figure **33.1**). A ladder leads to an eyelash; a window opens onto a pyramid. "In my pictures," explained Miro, "there are tiny forms in vast, empty spaces. Empty space, empty horizons, empty plains, everything that is stripped has always impressed me."

Breton defined Surrealism as "psychic automatism, in its pure state," that is, creative effort guided by thought functions free of rational control and he also said that it should be "exempt from any aesthetic or moral concern." In addition he emphasized the omnipotence of the dream state in guiding the Surrealist enterprise.

Just as writers developed new literary techniques to achieve freedom from rational control, so visual artists devised new methods and processes to liberate the visual imagination. Some explored psychic automatism, allowing the hand to move spontaneously and at random, as if casually doodling or improvising. Others tried to recover a sense of childlike spontaneity by filling their paintings with free-spirited, biomorphic shapes. Fundamentally, however, the paradox of Surrealist art rested on the artist's *conscious* effort to capture *unconscious* experience.

Breton recognized Picasso as one of the pioneers of Surrealist art. As early as 1907, in *Les Demoiselles d'Avignon* (see Figure 32.2), Picasso had begun to radicalize the image of the human figure; by the mid-1920s, brutal

The Swiss-born painter Paul Klee (1879–1940) stood on the fringes of Surrealism. One of the most sophisticated artists of the century, Klee was a brilliant draftsman who created physically small artworks that resemble hieroglyphic puzzles. His abstractions, like the entries in his personal diaries, are characterized by gentle humor and exquisite finesse; they belong to the substratum of the mind—the subconscious repository of mysterious symbols. "Art does not represent the visible," Klee insisted, "rather, it renders visible [the invisible]."

Klee's *Fish Magic* (Figure **33.9**), painted during his tenure as a teacher at the Bauhaus, consists of a group of carefully arranged organic motifs that resemble sacred signs. Flowers, fish, and human figure, all executed with pictographic simplicity, share the ambient space of planets whose rhythms are measured by a mysteriously suspended clock. Klee was among the first artists to recognize the art of the untutored and the mentally ill. "Only children, madmen, and savages," he wrote, "truly understand the 'in-between' world of spiritual truth."

Figure 33.9 PAUL KLEE, *Fish Magic*, 1925. Oil on canvas, mounted on board, 2 ft. 6⅜ × 3 ft. 2½ in. This pictorial fairy tale may have been inspired by Klee's visit to an aquarium in Naples, Italy. Describing his style, Klee wrote: "My aim is to create much spirituality out of little."

Visionary Surrealists: Magritte and Dalí

While Picasso, Miró, and Klee favored abstract and biomorphic images, other Surrealists juxtaposed meticulously painted objects in ways that were often shocking or unexpected. The most notable of these visionary Surrealists were René Magritte and Salvador Dalí. Both were superb draftsmen whose *trompe l'oeil* skills elicited a disquieting dream reality.

Trained as a commercial illustrator, and profoundly influenced by de Chirico, the Belgian artist Magritte (1898–1967) combined realistically detailed objects in startling and irrational ways. In one of his paintings, a coffin takes the place of a reclining figure; in another, a bird cage is substituted for the head of the sitter; and in still another, human toes appear on a pair of leather shoes. In such discordant images, Magritte brought mystery to the objects of everyday experience. "I don't paint visions," Magritte wrote, "I describe objects—and the mutual relationships of objects—in such a way that none of our habitual concepts or feelings is necessarily linked with them."

The small piece entitled *The Betrayal of Images* (1928) depicts with crisp and faultless accuracy a briar pipe, beneath which appears the legend "This is not a pipe" (Figure **33.10**). The painting addresses the age-old distinction between the real world—the world of the *actual* pipe—and the painted image, whose reality is the virtual *illusion* of a pipe. "Who could smoke a pipe from one of my paintings?" quipped Magritte. At the same time, the

Figure 33.10 RENÉ MAGRITTE, *The Betrayal of Images*, ca. 1928–1929. Oil on canvas, 25⅜ × 37 in. "People who look for symbolic meanings fail to grasp the inherent poetry and mystery of the image," complained Magritte. "By asking, 'What does this mean,' they express a wish that everything be understandable."

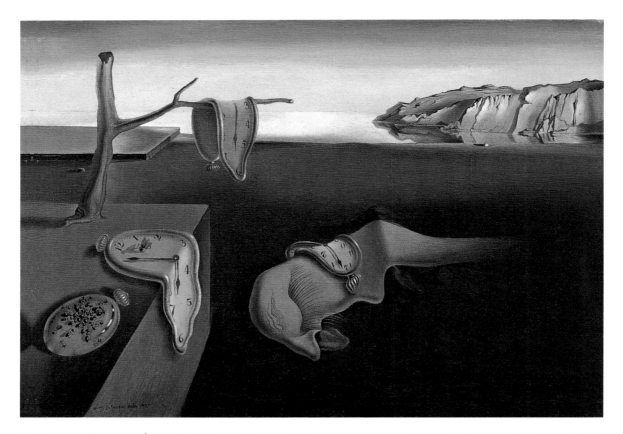

Figure 33.11 **SALVADOR DALÍ**, *The Persistence of Memory* (*Persistance de la Mémoire*), 1931. Oil on canvas, 9½ × 13 in. One of the most deceptive aspects of this painting is its size: while it appears to be a large canvas, it is actually not much larger than this page.

work anticipates Modernist efforts to question how words and images differ in conveying information. "The object," observed Magritte, "is not so possessed of its name that one cannot find for it another that suits it better."

The Spanish painter and impresario Salvador Dalí (1904–1989) was as much a showman as an artist.

Cultivating the bizarre as a lifestyle, Dali exhibited a perverse desire to shock his audiences. Drawing motifs from his own erotic dreams and fantasies, he executed both natural and unnatural images with meticulous precision, combining them in unusual settings or giving them grotesque attributes.

Dada and Surrealist Film

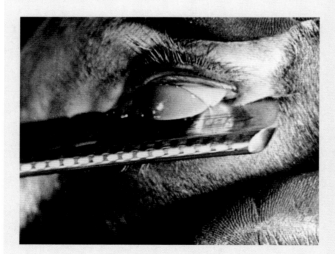

Figure 33.12 **LUIS BUÑUEL AND SALVADOR DALÍ**, *Un Chien Andalou*, 1928, film still.

The pranksters of Dada looked to film as a vehicle of the nonsensical. Duchamp and the American photographer Man Ray (1890–1976) matched wits in New York City to make one of the earliest Dada films, the entire action of which showed a courtesan, who called herself the baroness Elsa von Freytag-Loringhoven, shaving her pubic hair. In 1928, Salvador Dalí teamed up with the Spanish filmmaker Luis Buñuel (1900–1983) to create the pioneer Surrealist film, *Un Chien Andalou*. Violence and eroticism are the dominant motifs of this plotless twenty-one-minute silent film, whose more famous scenes include ants crawling out of a hole in a man's palm (an oblique reference to Christ's stigmata), a man bleeding from the mouth as he fondles a woman, a woman poking a stick at an amputated hand that lies on the street, an eyeball being sliced with a razor blade (Figure **33.12**), and two pianos filled with the mutilated carcasses of donkeys. Such special techniques as slow motion, close-up, and quick cuts from scene to scene create jolting, dreamlike effects. It is no surprise that Surrealist film had a formative influence on some of the twentieth century's most imaginative filmmakers, including Jean Cocteau, Jean Renoir, Ingmar Bergman, and Federico Fellini.

Dali's infamous *The Persistence of Memory* (Figure **33.11**) consists of a broad and barren landscape occupied by a leafless tree, three limp watches, and a watchcase crawling with ants. One of the timepieces plays host to a fly, while another rests upon a mass of brain matter resembling a profiled self-portrait—a motif that the artist frequently featured in his works. To seek an explicit message in this painting—even one addressing modern notions of time—would be to miss the point, for, as Dalí himself warned, his "hand-painted dream photographs" were merely designed to "stamp themselves indelibly upon the mind."

The Women of Surrealism

Perhaps more than any other movement in the history of early Modernism, Surrealism attracted a good many women artists. Arguably the most celebrated of these was Mexico's Frida Kahlo (1907–1954). Kahlo's paintings, of which more than one-third are self-portraits, reflect the determined effort (shared by many feminists) to present the female image as something other than the object of male desire. Her art bears testimony to what she called the "two great accidents" of her life: a bus crash that at the age of eighteen left her disabled, and her stormy marriage to

Figure 33.13 FRIDA KAHLO, *The Broken Column*, 1944. Oil on canvas, 15¾ × 12¼ in. Visiting Mexico, André Breton declared Kahlo to be a superb Surrealist; but Kahlo protested, "I never painted dreams. I painted my own reality."

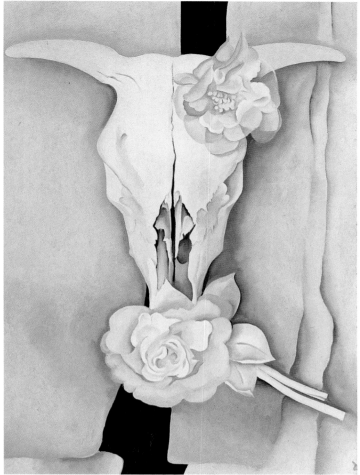

Figure 33.14 GEORGIA O'KEEFFE, *Cow's Skull: with Calico Roses*, 1931. Oil on canvas, 3 ft. 5/16 in. × 2 ft. ⅛ in. After an early career aided by the American photographer Alfred Stieglitz (whom she later married), O'Keeffe left New York City, settling in New Mexico in 1934. Her earliest abstract drawings were inspired by her reading of Wassily Kandinsky's *On the Spiritual in Art*.

the notorious Mexican mural painter Diego Rivera (see chapter 34). Like Rivera, Kahlo was a fervent Marxist and a nationalist who supported the revolutionary government that took control of Mexico in 1921. But the principal subject matter of Kahlo's art is Frida herself: "I am the subject I know best," she explained. Her paintings bring to life the experience of chronic pain, both physical (her accident required some thirty surgeries and ultimately the amputation of her right leg) and psychological (repeated miscarriages, for example, left her incapable of bearing a child).

Kahlo's canvases reveal her close identification with Mexican folk art, which traditionally features visceral and diabolical details. At the same time, her taste for realistically conceived but shockingly juxtaposed images reflects her debt to de Chirico and the Magic Realist style. In *The Broken Column* (Figure **33.13**), Kahlo pictures herself as sufferer and savior, an emblematic figure that recalls the devotional icons of Mexico's religious shrines.

A pioneer Modernist on the American scene, Georgia O'Keeffe (1887–1986) is often classified with America's regional painters. However, her treatment of haunting, biomorphic images abstracted from greatly enlarged flowers and bleached animal bones gives her early paintings a menacing presence (Figure **33.14**). In a fluid line style

Figure 33.15 **MERET OPPENHEIM**, *Object: Breakfast in Fur* (*Objet: Le Déjeuner en fourrure*), 1936. Fur-covered cup, saucer, and spoon; cup 4⅜ in. diameter; saucer 9⅜ in. diameter; spoon 8 in. long; overall height 2⅜ in.

that distills the essence of the subject, the so-called high priestess of early Modernism brought a visionary clarity to the most ordinary ingredients of the American landscape.

The unorthodox combination of commonplace objects—the hallmark of the visionary Surrealists—was a particularly effective strategy for Surrealist sculptors; and in this domain as well, women made notable contributions. The fur-lined cup and saucer (Figure **33.15**) conceived by the Swiss-German sculptor Meret Oppenheim (1913–1985) is shocking in its union of familiar but disparate elements. Conceived in the irreverent spirit of Duchamp's modified ready-mades, Oppenheim's *Object: Breakfast in Fur* provokes a sequence of discomfiting narrative associations.

Dada and Surrealist Photography

Photography was an ideal medium with which to explore the layers of the unconscious mind. Modernist photographers experimented with double exposure and unorthodox darkroom techniques to create unusual new effects similar to those of visionary Surrealist painters and sculptors. Liberating photography from traditional pictorialism, a group of Berlin Dadaists invented a new kind of collage called **photomontage**. The photomontage consisted of "found" photographic images cut from books, magazines, and newspapers, and pasted onto a flat surface. A champion of the technique, Raoul Hausmann (1886–1971), called photomontage "the 'alienation' of photography." By this, he implied that photomontage destroyed the role of photography as a medium for recreating physical reality. But the statement also suggests that by its dependence on fragmentation and dislocation, photomontage offered "a visually and conceptually new image of the chaos of an age of war and revolution."

The only female member of the group, Hannah Höch (1889–1979), was schooled in the visual arts and advertising. Her early training in Berlin, preparing advertising brochures directed at a female audience, opened her eyes to the way in which mass media targeted women. To her photomontages Höch brought her personal involvement with feminist issues and a wary recognition of the growing corruption and militarism of Weimar Germany (the period between 1919 and Hitler's seizure of power in 1933). Her *Cut with the Kitchen Knife through the Last Weimar Beer Belly Cultural Epoch of Germany* consists of select words and images clipped from newspapers and magazines: the wheels and cogs of military technology, the faces of German celebrities, and androgynous figures formed by pasting the head of one sex onto the body of the other (middle and lower right) that reference her own bisexuality (Figure **33.16**). The disjunctive series of "quick cuts" between individual images anticipated experiments in cinematic montage that were to transform the history of film (see chapter 34).

The New Psychology and Music

During the 1920s, composers moved beyond the exotic instrumental forays of Stravinsky's *Rite of Spring* to explore even more unorthodox experiments in sound. A group of six artists that included the French composer Eric Satie (1866–1925) incorporated into their music such "instruments" as doorbells, typewriters, and roulette wheels. Satie's style, which is typically sparse, rhythmic, and witty, has much in common with the poetry of Apollinaire and Cummings. His compositions, to which he gave such titles as *Flabby Preludes*, *Desiccated Embryos*, and *Three Pieces in the Form of a Pear*, were, however, less eccentric than was his lifestyle—he ate nothing but white foods and wore only gray suits.

Strauss and Bartók

The Freudian impact on music was most evident in the medium of musical drama, which, by the second decade of the century, incorporated themes of sexuality, eroticism, female hysteria, and the life of dreams. In the opera *Salome* (1905), a modern interpretation of the martyrdom of John the Baptist, the German composer Richard Strauss

Figure 33.16 HANNAH HÖCH, *Cut with the Kitchen Knife*, 1919. Collage of pasted papers, 3 ft. 8⅜ in. × 2 ft. 11½ in. In this allegorical critique of Weimar culture, Höch irreverently assembles photographic images of political leaders, sports stars, scientists, Dada artists, urban activists, and (at the lower right corner) a map showing the progress of women's enfranchisement.

(*Expectation*), Schoenberg took as his subject a woman's frenzied search for the lover who has deserted her. In *Pierrot Lunaire* (*Moonstruck Pierrot*) of 1912, a cycle of twenty-one songs for female voice and small instrumental ensemble, Schoenberg brought to life the dreamworld of a mad clown.

The texts of his atonal and harshly dissonant song cycles resemble stream-of-consciousness monologues. They are performed in **Sprechstimme** (or "speech-song"), a style in which words are spoken at different pitches. Neither exclusively song nor speech, *Sprechstimme* is a kind of operatic recitation in which pitches are approximated and the voice may glide in a wailing manner from note to note. Many of the critics found *Pierrot Lunaire* "depraved" and "ugly." But despite the controversy ignited by his disquieting music, Schoenberg attracted a large following. Even after he moved to the United States in 1933, young composers—including many associated with Hollywood films—flocked to study with him. And modern movie audiences were quick to accept the jolting dissonances of scores that worked to lend emotional expressiveness to the cinematic narrative.

Berg

Schoenberg's foremost student, Alban Berg (1885–1935), produced two of the most powerful operas of the twentieth century. Although less strictly atonal than Schoenberg's song cycles, Berg's operas *Wozzeck* (1921) and *Lulu* (1935) make use of serial techniques and the *Sprechstimme* style. Thematically, they feature the highly charged motifs of sexual frustration, murder, and suicide.

The unfinished *Lulu* is the story of a sexually dominated woman who both destroys and is destroyed by her lovers. It has been called "sordid," "psychotic," and "shocking." It explores such Freudian subjects as female hysteria and repressed sexuality, while at the same time it exploits the age-old image of woman as serpent. Both the music and the story of *Lulu* evoke a nightmarelike atmosphere, which, in modern multimedia productions, has been enhanced by the use of onstage digital projections.

(1864–1949) dramatized the obsessive erotic attachment of King Herod's beautiful niece to the Christian prophet. Revolutionary in sound (in some places the meter changes in every bar) and in its frank treatment of a biblical subject, *Salome* shocked critics so deeply that a performance slated for Vienna in 1905 was cancelled; in America, the opera was banned for almost thirty years after its New York performance in 1907.

Bluebeard's Castle (1918), a one-act opera by the leading Hungarian composer of the twentieth century, Béla Bartók (1881–1945), did not suffer so harsh a fate, despite the fact that the composer had boldly recast a popular fairy tale into a parable of repressed tension and jealousy between the sexes.

Schoenberg

The mood of anxiety and apprehension that characterized Expressionist and Surrealist art was, however, most powerfully realized in the compositions of Arnold Schoenberg, whose experiments in atonality were introduced in chapter 32. Schoenberg's song cycles, or **monodramas**, were dramatic pieces written for a single (usually deeply disturbed) character. In the monodrama *Erwartung*

🎵 See Music Listening Selections at end of chapter.

Freud

- Sigmund Freud's theories concerning the nature of the human psyche, the significance of dreams, and the dominating role of human sexuality had a revolutionary effect on modern society and on the arts.
- As the events of the two world wars would confirm Freud's pessimistic analysis of human nature, so the arts of the twentieth century acknowledged his view that human reason was not the "keeper of the castle"; the castle itself was perilously vulnerable to the dark forces of the human mind.

The New Psychology and Literature

- Proust, Kafka, and Joyce are representative of the modern novelist's preoccupation with the unconscious mind and with the role of memory and dreams in shaping reality.
- Stream-of-consciousness narrative and the interior monologue are among the Modernist literary techniques used to develop plot and character.
- American playwrights responded to the stream-of-consciousness technique, even as modern theater and film investigated a new performance style based on method acting.
- The poetry of E. E. Cummings reveals the influence of free association in liberating words from the bounds of syntax and conventional transcription.

The New Psychology and the Visual Arts

- In the visual arts, the impact of Freud's work generated styles that gave free play to fantasy and dreams: the Expressionism of Munch and Kirchner, the Metaphysical art of de Chirico, and the whimsical fantasies of Chagall.
- Marcel Duchamp, the most outrageous of the Dada artists, championed a nihilistic, antibourgeois, anti-art spirit that had far-reaching effects in the second half of the century.
- In 1924, André Breton launched Surrealism, an international movement to liberate the life of the mind from the bonds of reason. Strongly influenced by Freud, the Surrealists viewed the unconscious realm as a battleground of conflicting forces dominated by the instincts.
- Picasso, Miró, and Klee explored the terrain of the interior life in abstract paintings filled with both playful and ominous images, while Dalí and Magritte questioned illusion itself by way of realistically detailed yet irrationally juxtaposed objects.
- Kahlo, O'Keeffe, Oppenheim, and Höch were among the female Surrealists who manipulated the stuff of the real world so as to evoke jolting dreamlike effects and disquieting personal truths.
- Both photography and film responded enthusiastically to the disjunctive and absurd characteristics of the Surrealist style.

The New Psychology and Music

- In music, Eric Satie made use of mundane sounds with the same enthusiasm that E. E. Cummings brought to slang and Duchamp exercised for "found objects."
- Freud's impact was most powerfully realized in the Expressionistic monodramas of Schoenberg and the sexually charged operas of Strauss, Bartók, and Berg.

Music Listening Selection

- Schoenberg, *Pierrot Lunaire*, Op. 21, Part 3, No. 15, "Heimweh," 1912.

Glossary

archetype the primal patterns of the collective unconscious, which Carl Jung described as "mental forms whose presence cannot be explained by anything in the individual's own life and which seem to be aboriginal, innate, and inherited shapes of the human mind"

collective unconscious according to Jung, the universal realm of the unconscious life, which contains the archetypes

concrete poetry poetry produced in the shape of ordinary, external objects

improvisation the invention of the work of art as it is being performed

interior monologue a literary device by which the stream of consciousness of a character is presented; it records the internal, emotional experience of the character on one or more levels of consciousness

method acting a modern style of theatrical performance that tries to harness childhood emotions and memories in the service of interpreting a dramatic role

mobile a sculpture constructed so that its parts move by natural or mechanical means

monodrama in music, a dramatic piece written for only one character

nihilism a viewpoint that denies objective moral truths and traditional religious and moral principles

photomontage the combination of freely juxtaposed and usually heterogeneous photographic images (see also Glossary, chapter 34, "montage")

Sprechstimme (German, "speech-song") a style of operatic recitation in which words are spoken at different pitches

sublimation the positive modification and redirection of primal urges that Freud identified as the work of the ego

Chapter 34

Total War, Totalitarianism, and the Arts

ca. 1900–1950

"Where is God now?"
Elie Wiesel

Figure 34.1 LEE MILLER, *Buchenwald, Germany*, April 30, 1945. Photograph, 6 × 6 in. (approx.). Some six million Jews and others targeted as "undesirables," the victims of inhumane Nazi policies, were put to death in concentration camps such as those at Buchenwald and Dachau, Germany. Miller made this photograph only days after American troops liberated Buchenwald.

Two fundamentally related calamities afflicted the twentieth century: total war and totalitarian dictatorship. The consequences of both were so great that the world has still not recovered from them. Total war and totalitarianism, facilitated by sophisticated military technology and electronic forms of mass communication, caused the twentieth century to be the bloodiest in world history. Unlike the Black Death, the Lisbon earthquake, and other natural disasters, the wars and totalitarian regimes of the modern era were perpetrated on human beings *by* human beings. These human-made disasters not only challenged the belief that technology would improve the quality of human life, but also seemed to validate Freud's theory that mortals are driven by base instincts and the dark forces of self-destruction.

The two world wars of the twentieth century provide the context for the arts of this era. Many writers, painters, and composers responded directly with visceral antiwar statements. Others, acknowledging the requirements of totalitarian regimes (those of Hitler in Germany, Stalin in Russia, and Mao in China), produced works that responded to the revolutionary ideologies of the state. Photography and film—media that appealed directly to the masses—became important wartime vehicles, functioning both as propaganda and as documentary evidence of brutality and despair. The era inspired two of the twentieth century's leading artists to produce landmark Modernist works: T. S. Eliot's *The Waste Land* and Pablo Picasso's *Guernica*.

Total Wars

In the West, the end of the nineteenth century was a time of relative peace and optimistic faith in the progress of humankind. Throughout the world, however, sharp contrasts existed between rich and poor, and between technologically backward and technologically advanced nations. As the more powerful states jockeyed for political and economic primacy, and as Europe and the United States continued to build their industrial and military strength, few anticipated the possibility of widespread armed conflict. In 1914, however, that possibility became reality with the outbreak of the first of two world wars. World War I, the first *total* war in world history, ended forever the so-called age of innocence. And by the end of World War II in 1945, nothing would ever seem certain again.

The Great War of 1914, as World War I was called, and World War II, which followed in 1939, are called "total" not only because they involved more nations than had ever before been engaged in armed combat, but because they killed—along with military personnel—large numbers of civilians. Further, they were total in the sense that they were fought with a "no holds barred" attitude—all methods of destruction were used in the name of conquest.

The weapons of advanced technology made warfare more impersonal and more devastating than ever before. World War I combatants used machine guns, heavy artillery, hand grenades, poison gas, flame throwers, armored tanks, submarines, dirigibles (airships), and airplanes. From their open cockpits, pilots fired on enemy aircraft, while on land soldiers fought from lines of trenches dug deep into the ground. The rapid-firing, fully automatic machine gun alone caused almost 80 percent of the casualties. The cost of four years of war was approximately $350 billion, and the death toll was staggering. In all, seventy million armed men fought in World War I, and more than eight million of them died. In World War II, airplanes and aerial bombs (including, ultimately, the atomic bomb) played major roles; war costs were triple those of World War I, and casualties among the Allied forces alone rose to over eighteen million people.

The underlying cause of both wars was aggressive rivalry between European powers. During the nineteenth century, nationalism and industrialism had facilitated militant competition for colonies throughout the world (see chapter 30); the armed forces became the embodiment of a nation's sovereign spirit and the primary tool for imperialism. National leaders fiercely defended the notion that military might was the best safeguard of peace: "*Si vis pacem, para bellum*"—"if you want peace, prepare for war," they argued. Nations believed their safety lay in defensive alliances. They joined with their ideological or geographic neighbors in order to create a system of alliances that, by the early twentieth century, divided Europe into two potentially hostile camps, each equipped to mobilize their armies if threatened.

World War I

The circumstances that led to World War I involved the increasingly visible efforts of Austria-Hungary and Germany to dominate vast portions of Eastern Europe. Having risen to power during the nineteenth century, Germany rivaled all other European nations in industrial might. By the early twentieth century, German efforts to colonize markets for trade took the form of militant imperialism in Eastern Europe. In July 1914, Austria-Hungary, seeking to expand Austrian territory to the south, used the political assassination of Archduke Francis Ferdinand (heir to the throne of Austria-Hungary) as a pretext to declare war on Serbia. Almost immediately, two opposing alliances came into confrontation: the Central Powers of Austria-Hungary, Germany, and the Ottoman Empire versus the Allied forces of Serbia, Belgium, France, Great Britain, and Russia. Clearly, the policy of peace through military strength had not prevented war but actually encouraged it.

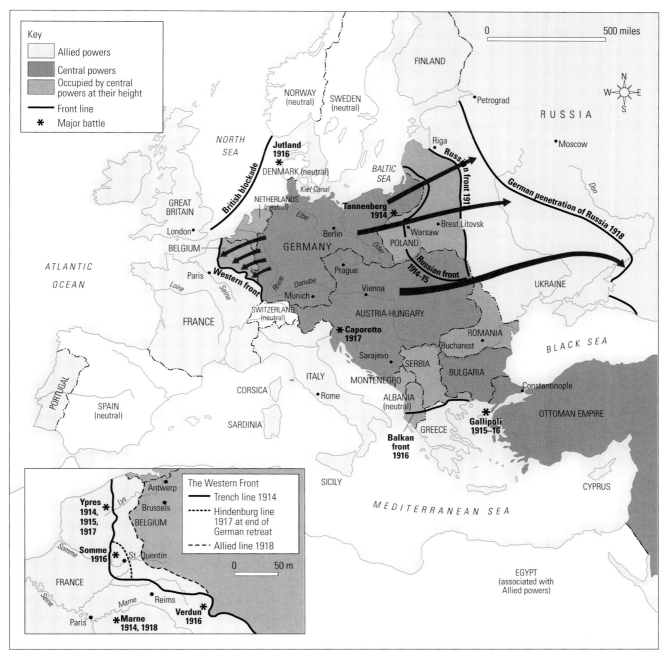

Map 34.1 World War I, 1914–1918.

At the beginning of the war, the Central Powers won early victories in Belgium and Poland, but the Allies stopped the German advance at the First Battle of the Marne in September 1914 (Map **34.1**). The opposing armies settled down to warfare along the western front—a solid line of two opposing trenches that stretched 500 miles from the English Channel to the Swiss border. At the same time, on the eastern front, Russian armies lost over a million men in combat against the combined German and Austrian forces. In the early years of the war, the United States remained neutral, but when German submarines began sinking unarmed passenger ships in 1917, the American president Woodrow Wilson opted to aid the Allies in order to "make the world safe for democracy." Fortified by American supplies and troops, the Allies

moved toward victory. In November 1918, the fighting ended with an armistice.

World War I Literature

World War I Poetry

Writers responded to the war with sentiments ranging from buoyant idealism and militant patriotism to frustration and despair. The most enduring literature of the era, however, expressed the bitter anguish of the war experience itself. The poetry of the young British officer Wilfred Owen (1893–1918) reflects the sense of cynicism and futility that was voiced toward the end of the war. Owen viewed war as a senseless waste of human resources and a barbaric form of human behavior. His poems, which question the meaning of wartime heroism, unmask "the old Lie" that it is "fitting and proper to die for one's country." The poet was killed in combat at the age of twenty-five, just one week before the armistice was signed.

READING 34.1 Owen's "Dulce Et Decorum Est"[1] (1918)

Bent double, like old beggars under sacks,   **1**
Knock-kneed, coughing like hags, we cursed through sludge,
Till on the haunting flares we turned our backs,
And towards our distant rest began to trudge.
Men marched asleep. Many had lost their boots,   **5**
But limped on, blood-shod. All went lame, all blind;
Drunk with fatigue; deaf even to the hoots
Of tired, outstripped Five-Nines[2] that drop behind.

Gas! GAS! Quick, boys!—An ecstasy of fumbling
Fitting the clumsy helmets just in time,   **10**
But someone still was yelling out and stumbling
And flound'ring like a man in fire or lime.—
Dim through the misty panes and thick green light,
As under a green sea, I saw him drowning.

In all my dreams before my helpless sight   **15**
He plunges at me, guttering, choking, drowning.

If in some smothering dreams, you too could pace
Behind the wagon that we flung him in,
And watch the white eyes writhing in his face,
His hanging face, like a devil's sick of sin,   **20**
If you could hear, at every jolt, the blood
Come gargling from the froth-corrupted lungs
Bitter as the cud
Of vile, incurable sores on innocent tongues,—
My friend, you would not tell with such high zest   **25**
To children ardent for some desperate glory,
The old Lie: *Dulce et decorum est*
Pro patria mori.

Q **Why does the poet try to reconcile the technology of modern war with traditional ideals of patriotism?**

Other poets viewed the war as symbolic of a dying Western civilization. The poet T. S. Eliot, whom we met in chapter 32, summed up this view in his classic poem *The Waste Land* (1922). This requiem for a dry and sterile culture is structured as a collection of individual poems, each narrated by a different speaker at a different time, but all evoking the themes of loss and hope for redemption. Incorporating quotations in Greek, Italian, German, and Sanskrit, the poem makes reference to Classical and Celtic mythology, the Bible, Saint Augustine, Dante, Chaucer, Shakespeare, Whitman, Wagner, the Hindu Upanishads, the sermons of the Buddha, James Frazer's *The Golden Bough* (see chapter 31), and other canonic works. The inclusion of such references, while indicative of Eliot's erudition, required that the poet himself append footnotes to the text. *The Waste Land* became the single most influential poem in early modern literature. Its incantatory rhythms and profound allusions established the idiom of modern poetry as compressed, complex, and serious.

READING 34.2 From Eliot's *The Waste Land* (1922)

V. What the Thunder Said

After the torchlight red on sweaty faces   **1**
After the frosty silence in the gardens
After the agony in stony places
The shouting and the crying
Prison and palace and reverberation   **5**
Of thunder of spring over distant mountains
He who was living is now dead
We who were living are now dying
With a little patience
    Here is no water but only rock   **10**
Rock and no water and the sandy road
The road winding above among the mountains
Which are mountains of rock without water
If there were water we should stop and drink
Amongst the rock one cannot stop or think   **15**
Sweat is dry and feet are in the sand
If there were only water amongst the rock
Dead mountain mouth of carious teeth that cannot spit
Here one can neither stand nor lie nor sit
There is not even silence in the mountains   **20**
But dry sterile thunder without rain
There is not even solitude in the mountains
But red sullen faces sneer and snarl
From doors of mudcracked houses
                              If there were water   **25**
    And no rock
    If there were rock
    And also water
    And water
    A spring   **30**
    A pool among the rock
    If there were the sound of water only
    Not the cicada
    And dry grass singing
    But sound of water over a rock   **35**
Where the hermit-thrush sings in the pine trees
Drip drop drip drop drop drop drop
But there is no water
                    · · · · · · · · · ·

Q **It has been said that Eliot favored "biblical rhythms." Do you detect any in this excerpt? What effects do they achieve?**

---

[1] "It is fitting and proper to die for one's country." A line from "Ode III" by the Roman poet Horace (see chapter 6).
[2] Gas shells.

Eliot's contemporary and one of the greatest lyricists of the century, William Butler Yeats (1865–1939), responded to the violence of World War I and to the prevailing mood of unrest in his native Ireland with the apocalyptic poem "The Second Coming." The title of the poem alludes both to the long-awaited Second Coming of Jesus and to the nameless force that, in Yeats' view, threatened to enthrall the world in darkness.

READING 34.3 Yeats' "The Second Coming" (1921)

Turning and turning in the widening gyre[1]	1
The falcon cannot hear the falconer;	
Things fall apart; the center cannot hold;	
Mere anarchy is loosed upon the world,	
The blood-dimmed tide is loosed, and everywhere	5
The ceremony of innocence is drowned;	
The best lack all conviction, while the worst	
Are full of passionate intensity.	
Surely some revelation is at hand;	
Surely the Second Coming is at hand.	10
The Second Coming! Hardly are those words out	
When a vast image out of Spiritus Mundi[2]	
Troubles my sight: somewhere in sands of the desert	
A shape with lion body and the head of a man,	
A gaze blank and pitiless as the sun,	15
Is moving its slow thighs, while all about it	
Reel shadows of the indignant desert birds.	
The darkness drops again; but now I know	
That twenty centuries of stony sleep	
Were vexed to nightmare by a rocking cradle,	20
And what rough beast, its hour come round at last,	
Slouches towards Bethlehem to be born?	

Q **Is the Second Coming Yeats describes one of deliverance or destruction?**

World War I Fiction

World War I also inspired some of the twentieth century's outstanding fiction—much of it written by men who had engaged in field combat. The American Ernest Hemingway (1899–1961) immortalized the Allied offensive in Italy in *A Farewell to Arms* (1929). The novel, whose title reflects the desperate hope that World War I would be "the war to end all wars," is a study in disillusionment and a testament to the futility of armed combat. Hemingway's prose is characterized by understatement and journalistic succinctness. His profound respect for physical and emotional courage, apparent in all his novels, was forged on the battlefields of the war, which he observed firsthand.

Armed conflict had a similar influence on the life and work of the novelist Erich Maria Remarque (1898–1970).

[1] A circular course traced by the upward sweep of a falcon. The image reflects Yeats' cyclical view of history.
[2] World Spirit, similar to the Jungian Great Memory of shared archetypal images.

Remarque, a German soldier who was wounded in combat several times, brought firsthand experience of World War I to his book *All Quiet on the Western Front*. Perhaps the finest war novel of the twentieth century, it portrays with horrifying clarity the brutal reality of trench warfare and poison gas, two of the most chilling features of the war. Remarque tells the story in first-person, present-tense narrative, a style that compels the reader to share the apprehension of the protagonist. Over one million copies of Remarque's novel were sold in Germany during the year of its publication alone, and similar success greeted it in translation and in its three movie versions. In 1939, however, the Nazi regime in Germany condemned Remarque's outspoken antimilitarism by publicly burning his books and depriving him of German citizenship. Shortly thereafter, Remarque moved to the United States, where he became an American citizen.

READING 34.4 From Remarque's *All Quiet on the Western Front* (1929)

An indigent looking wood receives us. We pass by the soup-kitchens. Under cover of the wood we climb out. The lorries turn back. They are to collect us again in the morning, before dawn. [1]

Mist and the smoke of guns lie breast-high over the fields. The moon is shining. Along the road troops file. Their helmets gleam softly in the moonlight. The heads and the rifles stand out above the white mist, nodding heads, rocking carriers of guns.

Farther on the mist ends. Here the heads become figures; coats, trousers, and boots appear out of the mist as from a milky pool. They become a column. The column marches on, straight ahead, the figures resolve themselves into a block, individuals are no longer recognizable, the dark wedge presses onward, fantastically topped by the heads and weapons floating off on the milky pool. A column—not men at all. [10]

Guns and munition wagons are moving along a crossroad. The backs of the horses shine in the moonlight, their movements are beautiful, they toss their heads, and their eyes gleam. The guns and the wagons float before the dim background of the moonlit landscape, the riders in their steel helmets resemble knights of a forgotten time; it is strangely beautiful and arresting. [20]

We push on to the pioneer dump. Some of us load our shoulders with pointed and twisted iron stakes; others thrust smooth iron rods through rolls of wire and go off with them. The burdens are awkward and heavy.

The ground becomes more broken. From ahead come warnings: "Look out, deep shell-holes on the left"—"Mind, trenches"— — — [30]

Our eyes peer out, our feet and our sticks feel in front of us before they take the weight of the body. Suddenly the line halts; I bump my face against the roll of wire carried by the man in front and curse.

There are some shell-smashed lorries in the road. Another order: "Cigarettes and pipes out." We are getting near the line.

In the meantime it has become pitch dark. We skirt a small wood and then have the front-line immediately before us.

An uncertain, red glow spreads along the skyline from one

end to the other. It is in perpetual movement, punctuated with the bursts of flame from the muzzles of the batteries. Balls of light rise up high above it, silver and red spheres which explode and rain down in showers of red, white, and green stars. French rockets go up, which unfold a silk parachute to the air and drift slowly down. They light up everything as bright as day, their light shines on us and we see our shadows sharply outlined on the ground. They hover for the space of a minute before they burn out. Immediately fresh ones shoot up to the sky, and again, green, red, and blue stars.

"Bombardment," says Kat.

The thunder of the guns swells to a single heavy roar and then breaks up again into separate explosions. The dry bursts of the machine-guns rattle. Above us the air teems with invisible swift movements, with howls, piping, and hisses. They are the smaller shells;—and amongst them, booming through the night like an organ, go the great coal-boxes and the heavies. They have a hoarse, distant bellow like a rutting stag and make their way high above the howl and whistle of the smaller shells. It reminds me of flocks of wild geese when I hear them. Last autumn the wild geese flew day after day across the path of the shells.

The searchlights begin to sweep the dark sky. They slide along it like gigantic tapering rulers. One of them pauses, and quivers a little. Immediately a second is beside him, a black insect is caught between them and tries to escape—the airman. He hesitates, is blinded and falls. . . .

We go back. It is time we returned to the lorries. The sky is become a bit brighter. Three o'clock in the morning. The breeze is fresh and cool, the pale hour makes our faces look grey.

We trudge onward in single file through the trenches and shell-holes and come again to the zone of mist. Katczinsky is restive, that's a bad sign.

"What's up, Kat?" says Kropp.

"I wish I were back home." Home—he means the huts.

"It won't last much longer, Kat."

He is nervous. "I don't know, I don't know— — —"

We come to the communication-trench and then to the open fields. The little wood reappears; we know every foot of ground here. There's the cemetery with the mounds and the black crosses.

That moment it breaks out behind us, swells, roars, and thunders. We duck down—a cloud of flame shoots up a hundred yards ahead of us.

The next minute under a second explosion part of the wood rises slowly in the air, three or four trees sail up and then crash to pieces. The shells begin to hiss like safety-valves—heavy fire— — —

"Take cover!" yells somebody—"Cover!"

The fields are flat, the wood is too distant and dangerous—the only cover is the graveyard and the mounds. We stumble across in the dark and as though spirited away every man lies glued behind a mound.

Not a moment too soon. The dark goes mad. It heaves and raves. Darkness blacker than the night rushes on us with giant strides, over us and away. The flames of the explosions light up the graveyard.

There is no escape anywhere. By the light of the shells I try to get a view of the fields. They are a surging sea, daggers of flame from the explosions leap up like fountains. It is impossible for anyone to break through it.

The wood vanishes, it is pounded, crushed, torn to pieces. We must stay here in the graveyard.

The earth bursts before us. It rains clods. I feel a smack. My sleeve is torn away by a splinter. I shut my fist. No pain. Still that does not reassure me: wounds don't hurt till afterwards. I feel the arm all over. It is grazed but sound. Now a crack on the skull, I begin to lose consciousness. Like lightning the thought comes to me: Don't faint, sink down in the black broth and immediately come up the top again. A splinter slashes into my helmet, but has travelled so far that it does not go through. I wipe the mud out of my eyes. A hole is torn up in front of me. Shells hardly ever land in the same hole twice, I'll get into it. With one bound I fling myself down and lie on the earth as flat as a fish; there it whistles again, quickly I crouch together, claw for cover, feel something on the left, shove in beside it, it gives way, I groan, the earth leaps, the blast thunders in my ears, I creep under the yielding thing, cover myself with it, draw it over me, it is wood, cloth, cover, cover, miserable cover against the whizzing splinters.

I open my eyes—my fingers grasp a sleeve, an arm. A wounded man? I yell to him—no answer—a dead man. My hand gropes farther, splinters of wood—now I remember again that we are lying in the graveyard.

But the shelling is stronger than everything. It wipes out the sensibilities, I merely crawl still deeper into the coffin, it should protect me, and especially as Death himself lies in it too.

Before me gapes the shell-hole. I grasp it with my eyes as with fists. With one leap I must be in it. There, I get a smack in the face, a hand clamps on to my shoulder—has the dead man waked up?—The hand shakes me, I turn my head, in the second of light I stare into the face of Katczinsky, he has his mouth wide open and is yelling. I hear nothing, he rattles me, comes nearer, in a momentary lull his voice reaches me: "Gas—Gaas—Gaaas—Pass it on."

I grab for my gas-mask. Some distance from me there lies someone. I think of nothing but this: That fellow there must know: Gaaas—Gaaas— — —

I call, I lean toward him, I swipe at him with the satchel, he doesn't see—once again, again—he merely ducks—it's a recruit—I look at Kat desperately, he has his mask ready—I pull out mine too, my helmet falls to one side, it slips over my face, I reach the man, his satchel is on the side nearest me, I seize the mask, pull it over his head, he understands, I let go and with a jump drop back into the shell-hole.

The dull thud of the gas-shells mingles with the crashes of the high explosives. A bell sounds between the explosions, gongs, and metal clappers warning everyone—Gas—Gas—Gaas.

Someone plumps down behind me, another. I wipe the goggles of my mask clear of the moist breath. It is Kat, Kropp, and someone else. All four of us lie there in heavy, watchful suspense and breathe as lightly as possible.

These first minutes with the mask decide between life and death: is it tightly woven? I remember the awful sights in the hospital: the gas patients who in day-long suffocation cough their burnt lungs up in clots.

Cautiously, the mouth applied to the valve, I breathe. The gas still creeps over the ground and sinks into all hollows. Like a big, soft jelly-fish it floats into our shell-hole and lolls there obscenely. I nudge Kat, it is better to crawl out and lie on top than to stay here where the gas collects most. But we don't get as far as that; a second bombardment begins. It is no longer as though the shells roared; it is the earth itself raging. 160

With a crash something black bears down on us. It lands close beside us; a coffin thrown up.

I see Kat move and crawl across. The coffin has hit the fourth man in our hole on his outstretched arm. He tries to tear off his gas-mask with the other hand. Kropp seizes him just in time, twists the hand sharply behind his back and holds it fast.

Kat and I proceed to free the wounded arm. The coffin lid is 170 loose and bursts open, we are easily able to pull it off, we toss the corpse out, it slides to the bottom of the shell-hole, then we try to loosen the under-part.

Fortunately the man swoons and Kropp is able to help us. We no longer have to be careful, but work away till the coffin gives with a sigh before the spade that we have dug in under it.

It has grown lighter. Kat takes a piece of the lid, places it under the shattered arm, and we wrap all our bandages round it. For the moment we can do no more.

Inside the gas-mask my head booms and roars—it is nigh 180 bursting. My lungs are tight, they breathe always the same hot, used-up air, the veins on my temples are swollen, I feel I am suffocating.

A grey light filters through to us. I climb out over the edge of the shell-hole. In the dirty twilight lies a leg torn clean off; the boot is quite whole, I take that all in at a glance. Now someone stands up a few yards distant. I polish the windows, in my excitement they are immediately dimmed again, I peer through them, the man there no longer wears his mask.

I wait some seconds—he has not collapsed—he looks 190 around and makes a few paces—rattling in my throat I tear my mask off too and fall down, the air streams into me like cold water, my eyes are bursting, the wave sweeps over me and extinguishes me. . . .

Q **What elements contribute to a sense of the macabre in this piece?**

Q **How does Remarque achieve cinematic momentum?**

World War I Art

Ernst

In Germany, World War I brought impassioned protests from many visual artists. One of the most outspoken was Max Ernst (1891–1976), whose career flowered in the Dada and Surrealist movements. Shortly after the war, Ernst began to create unsettling visual fantasies assembled from bits of photographs and prints that he cut from magazines, books, and newspapers. In the collage-painting *Two Ambiguous Figures* (Figure **34.2**), he combined the paraphernalia of modern warfare with the equipment of the scientist's laboratory.

Ernst's machinelike monsters are suspiciously reminiscent of the gas-masked soldiers that he encountered during his four-year stint in the German infantry. Sadly

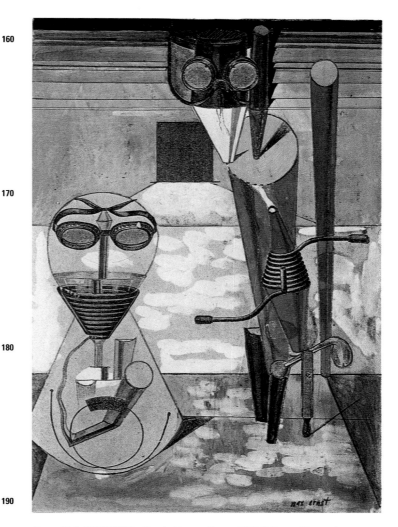

Figure 34.2 MAX ERNST, *Two Ambiguous Figures*, 1919. Collage with gouache and pencil, 9½ × 6½ in. Ernst produced this provocative image by painting over a page torn from a teaching-aids catalogue for scientific equipment used in chemistry and biology.

enough, Ernst's demons have become prophetic icons of modern warfare. Poison gas, used by the Iraqis in the 1980s war with Iran, received renewed international attention during the widely televised Gulf War of 1991, when images of both soldiers and civilians donning gas masks were a common, if appalling, sight.

Grosz

The art of George Grosz (1893–1959) was unique in its imaginative blend of social criticism and biting satire. Discharged from the army in 1916 after a brief experience at the front, Grosz mocked the German military and its corrupt and mindless bureaucracy in sketchy, brittle compositions filled with pungent caricatures. For example, the wartime pen-and-ink drawing *Fit for Active Service* (Figure **34.3**) shows a fat German army doctor pronouncing a skeletal cadaver "O.K."—fit to serve in combat. Here, Grosz makes pointed reference to the prevailing military practice of drafting old (and even ill) recruits. In a trenchant line style, he evokes a sense of the macabre similar to that captured by Remarque in *All Quiet on the Western Front.*

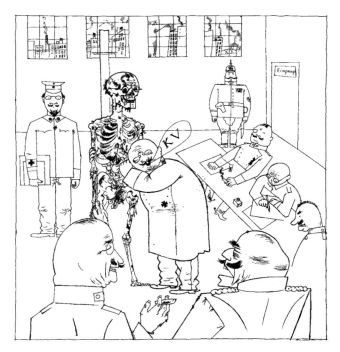

Figure 34.3 GEORGE GROSZ, *Fit for Active Service*, 1916–1917. Pen and brush and ink on paper, 20 × 14⅜ in. Grosz delighted in mocking the corrupt "fat cats" of Weimar society. At the top of this drawing, he shows factory chimneys spewing smoke that pollutes the already tainted political environment of his native Berlin.

Like Remarque (and hundreds of other European artists and writers), Grosz fled Nazi Germany in the 1930s for the United States, where he eventually became an American citizen.

Léger

The art of Fernand Léger (1881–1955) is usually classed with that of the Cubists, but it was the French artist's wartime experience that actually shaped his long and productive career. During his four years on the front, Léger witnessed the horrors of war, coming close to death in a mustard-gas

Experimental Film

Fernand Léger produced one of the earliest and most influential post-Cubist films in the history of motion pictures. Developed in collaboration with the American journalist Dudley Murphy, *Ballet mécanique* (*Mechanical Ballet*, 1923–1924) puts into motion a series of abstract shapes and mundane objects (such as bottles and kitchen utensils), which, interspersed with figurative elements, convey a playful but dehumanized sense of everyday experience. The rhythms and juxtapositions of the images suggest—without any narrative—the notion of modern life as mechanized, routine, standardized, and impersonal. The repeated image of a laundry woman, for instance, alternating with that of a rotating machine part, plays on the associative qualities of visual motifs in ways that would influence filmmakers for decades.

attack by German troops at Verdun. Nevertheless, the artist came to appreciate both the visual eloquence of modern machinery and the common humanity of the working-class soldiers with whom he shared the trenches. "Dazzled" (as he put it) by the breech of a 75-millimeter gun as it stood in the sunlight, Léger discovered similar kinds of beauty in ordinary human beings and in everyday objects—"the pots and pans on the white wall of your kitchen." "I invent images from machines," he claimed. The anonymity of urban life and the cold monumentality of the city—gray, hard, and sleek—became major themes for Léger in the postwar years. This "mechanical" aesthetic (which he called "painting in slang") is visible in *Three Women* (Figure **34.4**). Robust and robotic, the near-identical nudes (and their cat) share an austere and lively geometry.

The Russian Revolution

One of the last of the European powers to become industrialized, Russia entered World War I in 1914 under the leadership of Tzar Nicholas II (1868–1918). Russian involvement in the war, compounded by problems of government corruption and a weak and essentially agrarian economy, reduced the nation to desperate straits. Within a single year, the Russian army lost over one million men; a million more soldiers deserted. Food and fuel shortages threatened the entire civilian population. By 1917, a full-scale revolution was underway: strikes and riots broke out in the cities, while in the countryside peasants seized the lands of their aristocratic landlords. The revolution of 1917 forced the abdication of the tzar and ushered in a new regime, which, in turn, was seized by members of the Russian socialist party under the leadership of the Marxist revolutionary Vladimir Ilyich Lenin (1870–1924).

Between 1917 and 1921, by means of shrewd political manipulation as well as a reign of terror conducted by the Red Army and the secret police, Lenin installed the left-wing faction of the Marxist socialists—the Bolsheviks—as the party that would govern a nation of more than 150 million people. Tailoring Marxist ideas to the needs of revolutionary Russia, Lenin became the architect of Soviet communism.

Before and after his rise to power, Lenin formulated and published his political theories. He followed Marx in describing imperialism as an expression of the capitalist effort to monopolize raw materials and markets throughout the world. He agreed that a "dictatorship of the proletariat" was the first step in liberating the workers from bourgeois suppression. While condemning the state as "the organ of class domination," he projected the transition to a classless society in a series of phases, which he outlined in the influential pamphlet "The State and Revolution" (1917). According to Lenin, in the first phase of communist society (generally called socialism), private property would be converted into property held in common and the means of production and distribution would belong to the whole of society. Every member of society would perform a type of labor and each would be entitled to a "quantity of products" (drawn from public warehouses)

Figure 34.4 FERNAND LÉGER, *Three Women* (*Le Grand Déjeuner*), 1921. Oil on canvas, 6 ft. ½ in. × 8 ft. 3 in. Sturdy women share the objectlike quality of a breakfast still life. "I have made use of the machine as others have used the nude body or the still life," explained Léger.

that corresponded to his or her "quantity of work." (A favorite Lenin slogan ran: "He who does not work does not eat.") In the first phase of communism, the socialist state prevailed. As Lenin explained, "a form of state is still necessary, which, while maintaining public ownership of the means of production, would preserve the equality of labor and equality in the distribution of products."

In the second phase of communism, however, the state would disappear altogether:

> The state will be able to wither away completely when society has realized the rule: "From each according to his ability; to each according to his needs," *i.e.,* when people have become accustomed to observe the fundamental rules of social life, and their labor is so productive that they voluntarily work *according to their ability.* . . . There will then be no need for any exact calculation by society of the quantity of products to be distributed to each of its members; each will take freely according to his needs.

Lenin was aware that such a social order might be deemed "a pure Utopia"; yet, idealistically, he anticipated the victory of communist ideals throughout the world. The reality was otherwise. In early twentieth-century Russia, the Bolsheviks created a dictatorship *over* rather than *of* the proletariat.

In 1918, when the Constituent Assembly refused to approve Bolshevik power, Lenin dissolved the assembly. (In free elections Lenin's party received less than a quarter of one percent of the vote.) He then eliminated all other parties and consolidated the Communist Party in the hands of five men—an elite committee called the Politburo, which Lenin himself chaired. Russia was renamed the Union of Soviet Socialist Republics (U.S.S.R.) in 1922, and in 1924 the constitution established a sovereign Congress of Soviets. But this body was actually governed by the leadership of the Communist Party, which maintained absolute authority well after Lenin's death.*

The Communist Party established the first **totalitarian** regime of the twentieth century. Totalitarianism subordinated the life of the individual to the needs of the state. Through strict control of political, economic, and cultural life, and by means of coercive measures such as censorship and terrorism, Soviet communists persecuted those whose activities they deemed threatening to the state. Using educational propaganda and the state-run media, they worked tirelessly to indoctrinate Soviet citizens with the virtues of communism.

---

* The Communist Party ceased to rule upon the collapse of the Soviet Union in 1991.

Under the rule of Joseph Stalin (1879–1953), who took control of the communist bureaucracy in 1926, the Soviets launched vast programs of industrialization and agricultural collectivization (the transformation of private farms into government-run units) that demanded heroic sacrifice from the Soviet people. Peasants worked long hours on state-controlled farms, earning a bare subsistence wage. Stalin crushed all opposition: his secret police "purged" the state of dissidents, who were either imprisoned, exiled to *gulags* (labor camps), or executed. Between 1928 and 1938, the combination of severe famine and Stalin's inhuman policies (later known as "the great terror") took the lives of fifteen to twenty million Russians.

Communism enforced totalitarian control over all aspects of cultural expression. In 1934, the First All-Union Congress of Soviet Writers officially approved the style of *socialist realism* in the arts. It condemned all manifestations of "Modernism" (from Cubist painting to hot jazz) as "bourgeois decadence." The congress called upon Soviet artists to create "a true, historically concrete portrayal of reality in its revolutionary development." Artists—including Malevich and the pioneer Russian Constructivists—were

Figure 34.5 A. I. STRAKHOV, *Emancipated Women Build Socialism! 8th March, Day of the Liberation of Women*, 1920. Colored lithograph, 3 ft. 6½ in. × 2 ft. 2¾ in. Strong, simple forms, flat, bright colors, and short, easily memorized texts were the main characteristics of the Bolshevik political posters produced in the early decades of the twentieth century.

instructed to communicate simply and directly, to shun all forms of decadent (that is, modern) Western art, and to describe only the positive aspects of socialist society. In realistically conceived posters, the new Soviet man and woman were portrayed earnestly operating tractors or running factory machinery (Figure **34.5**). Thus the arts served to reinforce in the public mind the ideological benefits of communism. Socialist realism and the philosophy of art as mass propaganda lent support to almost every totalitarian regime of the twentieth century.

The Great Depression and the American Scene

World War I left Europe devastated, and massive economic problems burdened both the Central Powers and the Allied nations. In the three years following the war, world industrial production declined by more than a third, prices dropped sharply, and over thirty million people lost their jobs. The United States emerged from the war as the great creditor nation, but its economy was inextricably tied to world conditions. Following the inevitable crash of inflated stock prices in 1929, a growing paralysis swept through the American economy that developed into the Great Depression—a world crisis that lasted until the 1940s.

Literature

The Great Depression inspired literary descriptions of economic oppression and misery that were often as much social documents as fictional narratives. The most memorable of these is the American novel *The Grapes of Wrath*, written in 1939 by John Steinbeck (1902–1968). The story recounts the odyssey of a family of Oklahoma migrant farmers who make their way to California in search of a living. In straightforward and photographically detailed prose, Steinbeck describes courageous encounters with starvation, injustice, and sheer evil. Like the soldiers in Remarque's regiment, the members of the Joad family (and especially the matriarch, Ma Joad) display heroism in sheer survival.

The Grapes of Wrath is an example of *Social Realism*, a style that presents socially significant subject matter in an objective and lifelike manner. Not to be confused with socialist realism, which operated to glorify the socialist state, Social Realism was a vehicle of criticism and political protest. A writer, declared Steinbeck, is "the watchdog of society"; he must "set down his time as nearly as he can understand it."

The Visual Arts

During the Depression, Social Realism also dominated America's visual arts. In opposition to Modernism, which sacrificed subject matter to formal abstraction, Social Realism made use of recognizable imagery that communicated the concerns of the masses. The Missouri-born Thomas Hart Benton (1889–1975) devoted his career to

Science and Technology

1927	the first television transmission is viewed in America
1930	the British invent a workable jet engine
1938	the Germans split the atom to achieve nuclear fission
1939	British scientists produce pure penicillin
1945	the first experimental atomic bomb is exploded, at Alamogordo, New Mexico

depicting scenes that called into question the political and economic policies leading to the Great Depression. Benton aimed to commemorate "true" American values by immortalizing the lives of ordinary men and women, whom he pictured as rugged and energetic. In three sets of public **murals** completed between 1930 and 1933, he created an extraordinary pictorial history of the United States. He portrayed steelworking, mining, farming, and other working-class activities, as well as bootlegging, gospel singing, crap shooting, and a wide variety of essentially familiar pastimes.

Benton's *City Activities*, one of ten panels from *America Today*, a mural depicting American life during the Prohibition era, is a montage of "vignettes" from such popular urban entertainments as the circus, the movie theater, and the dance-hall (see LOOKING INTO, Figure **34.6**). A ticker-tape machine—the symbol of Wall Street commercialism and American greed—appears in the upper part of the mural; it is balanced in the lower foreground by another instrument of commercialism—bootlegging equipment. In Benton's hands the mural was not mere decoration. It was a major form of public art, one that revealed ordinary American life as vividly as Renaissance murals mirrored the elitist world of sixteenth-century Italy.

Mexico's Mural Renaissance

Benton drew inspiration from the work of two great Mexican muralists: José Clemente Orozco (1883–1949) and Diego Rivera (1886–1957). Their paintings, characterized by simple yet powerful forms and bold colors, capture the vitality and the futility of the Mexican Revolution—one of many militant efforts at reforming economic and social conditions in Central and South America during the first half of the twentieth century (Figure **34.7**).

The Mexican Revolution (1910–1920) was particularly significant as the first social revolution of the century to engage the active participation of great masses of peasants and urban workers. United under the banner of "Land Liberty," Mexico's farmers and laborers opposed the promotion of industry and the reallocation of farmland at their expense. Rivera championed their cause in murals that featured the sympathetic depiction of peasants, often inspired by the art of their Maya and Aztec forebears. By emphasizing the Amerindian aspect of Mexico's history, Rivera's art—like the revolution itself—helped to effect a change in Mexico's self-image.

Thomas Hart Benton's *City Activities*

City Activities is one of a series of panels depicting rural and urban America on the eve of the Great Depression. As Benton explained in an interview in 1968, *America Today* was intended as "a report on American life." He claimed he found his inspiration for the subject matter by traveling around the country "sketching and talking to people." Benton, who appears with paintbrush in hand in the lower right corner of the panel, admired the purity of the rural Midwest. By contrast, he regarded America's cities as "nothing but coffins for living and thinking." Nevertheless, in this lively collection of images, he captured the vital, energetic rhythm of the urban scene.

Figure 34.6 THOMAS HART BENTON, *City Activities with Dance Hall*, from the mural series *America Today*, 1930. Distemper and egg tempera on gessoed linen with oil glaze, 7 ft. 8 in. × 11 ft. 2½ in. Benton's *America Today* murals are set in the Prohibition Era: effective January 16, 1920, the Eighteenth Amendment to the United States Constitution prohibited the manufacture and sale of alcohol. Unpopular and unenforceable, the amendment was repealed in 1933.

beer, bootlegged during Prohibition

ticker-tape machine and Wall Street traders

trapeze artist and circus performers

cigarettes advertisement

Jazz Age dance-hall

soda "jerk" in drugstore ice-cream parlor

Elizabeth Pollock, wife of Benton's student

sign above books alluding to popular mystery novels of "S. S. Van Dine"

whiskey (illicit at the time), and shot glass

Benton with paintbrush and highball, toasting Director of New School for Social Research who commissioned the murals

homemade still for making "bathtub gin"

woman reading cinema handbill

Benton's wife and son with Caroline Pratt, progressive educator and founder of the first nursery school in America

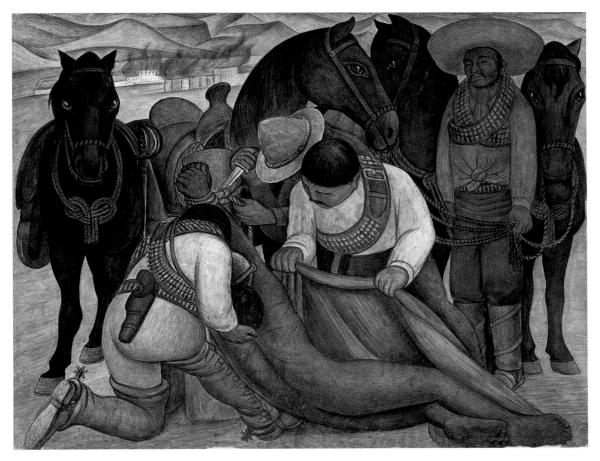

Figure 34.7 DIEGO RIVERA, *Liberation of the Peon*, 1931. Fresco, 6 ft. 2 in. × 7 ft. 11 in. Rivera helped to launch Mexico's mural renaissance. His large, simplified figures and bold colors look back to Maya relief sculptures and frescoes.

Photography

During the Great Depression, photography was pressed into political service. United States federal agencies sponsored a program to provide a permanent record of economic and social conditions in rural America. Migration and rural poverty—bread lines, beggars, and the shanty towns of America's impoverished classes— became the primary subjects of *documentary photography*. The New York photographer Dorothea Lange (1895– 1965) traveled across the country to record the conditions of destitute farmers who had fled the Midwestern dust bowl for the fields of California. *Migrant Mother* (Figure **34.8**), which Lange photographed at a farm camp in Nipomo, California, is the portrait of a gaunt thirty-two-year-old woman who had become the sole supporter of her six children. Forced to sell her last possessions for food, the anxious but unconquerable heroine in this photograph might have stepped out of the pages of Steinbeck's *Grapes of Wrath*. Lange's moving image reaches beyond a specific time and place to universalize the twin evils of poverty and oppression.

Figure 34.8 DOROTHEA LANGE, *Migrant Mother, Nipomo, California,* 1936. Gelatin-silver print, 5 × 4 in. (approx.). *Migrant Mother* has been hailed as the Depression era equivalent of the medieval Madonna: an image of protective anguish and despair.

Totalitarianism and World War II

The Rise of Hitler

In Germany, widespread discontent and turmoil followed the combined effects of the Great Depression and the humiliating peace terms dictated by the victorious Allies. Crippling debts forced German banks to close in 1931, and at the height of the Depression only one-third of all Germany's workers were fully employed. In the wake of these conditions, the young ideologue Adolf Hitler (1889–1945) rose to power. By 1933, Hitler was chancellor of Germany and the leader (in German, *Führer*) of the National Socialist German Workers' party (the *Nazi* party), which would lead Germany again into a world war.

A fanatic racist, Hitler shaped the Nazi platform. He blamed Germany's ills on the nation's internal "enemies," whom he identified as Jews, Marxists, bourgeois liberals, and "social deviates." Hitler promised to "purify" the German state of its "threatening" minorities and rebuild the country into a mighty empire. He manipulated public opinion by using all available means of propaganda—especially the radio, which brought his voice into every German home. In his autobiographical work *Mein Kampf* (*My Struggle*), published in 1925, Hitler set forth a misguided theory of "Aryan racial superiority" that would inspire some of the most malevolent episodes in the history of humankind, including genocide: the systematic extermination of millions of Jews, along with thousands of Roman Catholics, gypsies, homosexuals, and other minorities. Justifying his racist ideology, he wrote:

> What we must fight for is to safeguard the existence and reproduction of our race and our people, the sustenance of our children and the purity of our blood, the freedom and independence of the fatherland so that our people may mature for the fulfillment of the mission allotted to it by the creator of the universe.

Mein Kampf exalted the totalitarian state as "the guardian of a millennial future in the face of which the wishes and the selfishness of the individual must appear as nothing and submit." "The state is a means to an end," insisted Hitler. "Its end lies in the preservation and advancement of physically and psychically homogeneous creatures."

Less than twenty years after the close of World War I, the second, even more devastating, world war threatened. The conditions that contributed to the outbreak of World War II included the failure of the peace settlement that had ended World War I and the undiminished growth of nationalism and militarism. But the specific event that initiated a renewal of hostilities was Hitler's military advance into Poland in 1939.

The Holocaust

Hitler wielded unlimited and often ruthless authority. He destroyed democratic institutions in Germany, condemned avant-garde art, modern architecture, atonal music, and jazz as "degenerate," attacked Einstein's theories as "Jewish physics," and proceeded to eliminate—by means of the *Gestapo* (the Nazi secret police)—all opposition to his program of purification and mass conformity. In 1933, over 35,000 Germans died either by suicide or from "unexplained causes." Beginning in 1941, the Nazis dispatched thousands of military "action squads" to kill entire populations of Jews and other "undesirables." The ultimate or "final solution" was reached by the Nazi leadership in 1942, when concentration camps were constructed in Austria, Poland, and Germany to house Hitler's "impure" minorities. Prisoners, transported to the camps in cattle cars and branded with numbers burnt onto their arms, were exterminated (often in lethal gas chambers) if deemed unable to work in these forced-labor prisons. It is estimated that six million Jews and five million non-Jews were put to death in Nazi gas chambers—a hideous episode in European history known as the Holocaust.

World War II

Once again, two opposing alliances were formed: Germany, Italy, Bulgaria, and Hungary comprised the Axis powers (the term describing the imaginary line between Rome and Berlin), while France and Britain and, in 1941, the United States and the Soviet Union constituted the major Allied forces. Germany joined forces with totalitarian regimes in Italy (under Benito Mussolini) and in Spain (under General Francisco Franco), and the hostilities quickly spread into North Africa, the Balkans, and elsewhere. The fighting that took place during the three-year civil war in Spain (1936–1939) and in the German attack on the Netherlands in 1940 anticipated the merciless aspects of total war. In Spain, Nazi dive-bombers destroyed whole cities, while in the Netherlands, German tanks, parachute troops, and artillery overran the country in less than a week. The tempo of death was quickened as German air power attacked both military and civilian targets. France fell to Germany in 1940, and Britain became the target of systematic German bombing raids. At the same time, violating a Nazi–Soviet pact of 1939, Hitler invaded the Soviet Union, only to suffer massive defeat in the Battle of Stalingrad in 1942 (Map **34.2**).

The United States, although supportive of the Allies, again tried to hold fast to its policy of "benevolent neutrality." It was brought into the war nevertheless by Japan, which had risen rapidly to power in the late nineteenth century. Japan had defeated the Russians in the Russo–Japanese War of 1904. The small nation had successfully invaded Manchuria in 1931 and established a foothold in China and Southeast Asia. In December 1941, in opposition to United States efforts at restricting Japanese trade, the Japanese naval air service dropped bombs on the American air base at Pearl Harbor in Hawaii. The United States, declaring war on Japan, joined the twenty-five other nations that opposed the Axis powers and sent combat forces to fight in both Europe and the Pacific.

The war against Japan was essentially a naval war, but it involved land and air attacks as well. Its terrible climax was America's attack on two Japanese cities, Hiroshima and Nagasaki, in August 1945. The bombing, which

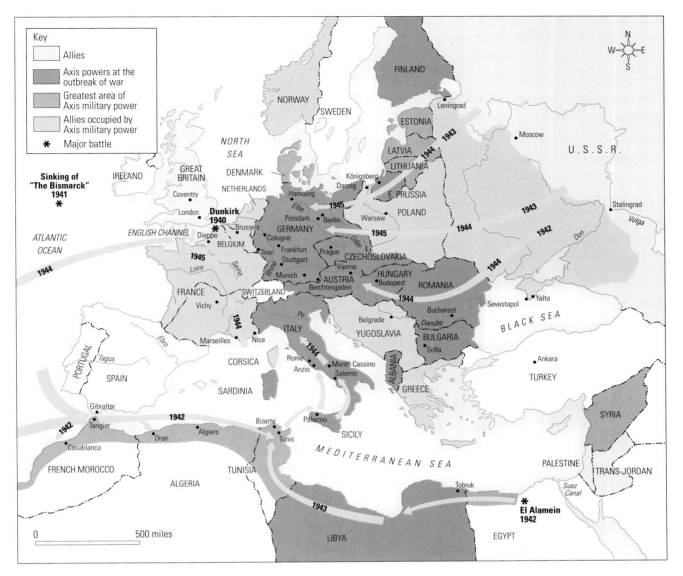

Map 34.2 World War II: The Defeat of the Axis Powers, 1942–1945.

annihilated over 120,000 people (mostly civilians) and forced the Japanese to surrender within a matter of days, ushered in the atomic age. Just months before, as German forces had given way to Allied assaults on all fronts, Hitler committed suicide. World War II came to a close with the surrender of both Germany and Japan in 1945.

The New Journalism

The bombing of Hiroshima ushered in the atomic age; it also inspired some of the earliest examples of the new journalism, a genre that adapts the techniques of fiction to non-fiction reportage of actual events. A notable example of the new journalism is the 31,000-word article that soon became the Pulitzer Prize-winning book *Hiroshima* (1946) by John Hersey (1914–1993). Hersey recounts the horrific consequences of the American bombing as told to the author by six survivors. Other firsthand accounts by Japanese survivors, such as Yamaoka Michiko's "Eight Hundred Meters from the Hypocenter," are almost too chilling to read.

World War II Poetry

Around the globe, World War II poetry carried to new extremes the sentiments of despair and futility. The American poet and critic Randall Jarrell (1914–1965), who served in the U. S. Army Air Corps from 1942 to 1946, condemned military combat as dehumanizing and degrading. In the short poem "The Death of the Ball Turret Gunner," a World War II airman, speaking from beyond the grave, recounts his fatal experience as an airforce gunner. Encased in the Plexiglas bubble dome of an airplane ball turret—like an infant in his mother's womb—he "wakes" to "black flak" and dies; the startling image of birth in death conflates dreaming and waking. Jarrell observed that modern combat, fueled by sophisticated technical instruments, neither fostered pride nor affirmed human nobility. Rather, such combat turned the soldier into a technician and an instrument of war. It robbed him of personal identity and reduced him to the level of an object—a thing to be washed out by a high-pressure steam hose. The note to the title of the poem was provided by the poet himself.

READING 34.5 Jarrell's "The Death of the Ball Turret Gunner"[1] (1945)

From my mother's sleep I fell into the State,
And I hunched in its belly till my wet fur froze.[2]
Six miles from earth, loosed from its dream of life,
I woke to black flak and the nightmare fighters.
When I died they washed me out of the turret with a hose.

Q How are the images of birth and death conflated by Jarrell?

In Japan, lamentation preceded rage. The *haiku*, the light verse form that had traditionally enshrined such images as cherry blossoms and spring rain, now became the instrument by which Japanese poets evoked the presence of death. Kato Shuson (1905–1993) introduced the three *haikus* reproduced below with the following words: "In the middle of the night there was a heavy air raid. Carrying my sick brother on my back I wandered in the flames with my wife in search of our children."

READING 34.6 Shuson's *haikus* (ca. 1945)

Hi no oku ni	In the depths of the flames
Botan kuzururu	I saw how a peony
Sama wo mitsu	Crumbles to pieces.

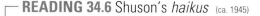

Kogarashi ya	Cold winter storm—
Shōdo no kinko	A safe-door in a burnt-out site
Fukinarasu	Creaking in the wind.

Fuyu kamome	The winter sea gulls—
Sei no ie nashi	In life without a house,
Shi no haka nashi	In death without a grave.

Q What effects are achieved by verbal compression?

World War II Fiction

As in the poetry of Jarrell, the novels of World War II were characterized by nihilism and resignation, their heroes robbed of reason and innocence. In *From Here to Eternity* (1951) by James Jones (1921–1977) and *The Naked and the Dead* (1948) by Norman Mailer (1923–2007), war makes men and machines interchangeable—the brutality of total war dehumanizes its heroes. Mailer's raw, naturalistic novels, which are peppered with the four-letter words that characterize so much modern fiction, portray a culture dominated by violence and sexuality. Stylistically, Mailer often deviated from the traditional "beginning, middle and end" narrative format, using instead such cinematic techniques as flashback.

This episodic technique also prevails in the novels of Joseph Heller (1923–1999), Kurt Vonnegut (1922–2007), and other **gallows humor** writers. "Gallows" (or "black") humor is a form of literary satire that mocks modern life by calling attention to situations that seem too ghastly or too absurd to be true. Such fiction describes the grotesque and the macabre in the passionless and nonchalant manner of a contemporary newspaper account. Like an elaborate hate joke, the gallows-humor novel provokes helpless laughter at what is hideous and awful. Modern war, according to these humorists, is the greatest of all hate jokes: dominated by bureaucratic capriciousness and mechanized destruction, it is an enterprise that has no victors, only victims.

Heller's *Catch-22* (1955), one of the most popular gallows-humor novels to emerge from World War II, marks the shift from the realistic description of modern warfare (characteristic of the novels of Remarque, Jones, and Mailer) to its savage satirization. Heller based the events of *Catch-22* on his own experiences as an air-force bombardier in World War II. The novel takes place on an air base off the coast of Italy, but its plot is less concerned with the events of the war than with the dehumanizing operations of the vast military bureaucracy that runs the war. Heller describes this bureaucracy as symbolic of "the humbug, hypocrisy, cruelty and sheer stupidity of our mass society." His rendering of the classic armed-forces condolence form-letter satirizes the impersonal character of modern war and provides a brief example of his biting style:

> Dear Mrs.,/Mr.,/Miss,/or Mr. and Mrs.— — —: Words cannot express the deep personal grief I experienced when your husband,/son,/father,/or brother was killed,/wounded,/or reported missing in action.

Catch-22 is a caustic blend of nihilism and forced cheerfulness. The characters in the novel—including a navigator who has no sense of direction and an aviator who bombs his own air base for commercial advantage—operate at the mercy of a depersonalizing system. As they try their best to preserve their identity and their sanity, they become the enemies of the very authorities that sent them to war.

Responses to Totalitarianism

While total war became a compelling theme in twentieth-century fiction, so too did totalitarianism, especially as it was described by those who had experienced it firsthand. Until Stalin's death in 1953, a reign of terror prevailed in the Soviet Union. As many found out, the slightest deviation from orthodox Marxist-Stalinist decorum resulted in imprisonment, slave labor, or execution. Between 1929 and 1953 some eighteen million people were sent to prison camps and another six million were exiled to remote parts of the Soviet Union. Aleksandr Solzhenitsyn (1918–2008) served in the Russian army during World War II, and although he had twice received recognition for bravery in combat, he was arrested in 1945 for veiled anti-Stalinist comments that he had made in a letter to a friend. He was sentenced to eight years of imprisonment, spending half

---

[1] "A ball turret was a Plexiglas sphere set into the belly of a B-17 or B-24 and inhabited by two .50 caliber machine-guns and one man, a short, small man. When this gunner traced with his machine-guns a fighter attacking his bomber from below, he revolved with the turret; hunched upside-down in his little sphere, he looked like the fetus in the womb. The fighters which attacked him were armed with cannon firing explosive shells. The hose was a steam hose."

[2] The airman's fur-lined flight jacket.

the term in a *gulag* in Siberia and the other half teaching mathematics in a Moscow prison. His Siberian experience provided the eyewitness material for his first novel, *One Day in the Life of Ivan Denisovich* (1962). It was followed in 1973–1976 by *The Gulag Archipelago*, a documentary description of Soviet prison life. These dispassionate accounts of the grim conditions of totalitarianism are searing indictments of inhumanity, and testaments to the heroism of the victims of Soviet political oppression.

In Germany, the voices of actual witnesses to the atrocities of the Holocaust were for the most part silenced by death, but drawings by camp inmates and documentary photographs taken just after the war (see Figure **34.1**) provide shocking visual evidence of modern barbarism. One of the most eloquent survivors of the Holocaust is the writer Elie Wiesel (b. 1928), recipient of the Nobel Peace Prize in 1986. At the age of fifteen, Wiesel, a Romanian Jew, was shipped with his entire family to the concentration camp at Auschwitz, Poland. There the family was split up, and Wiesel and his father were sent to the forced-labor camp at Buchenwald, Germany, where the boy saw his father and hundreds of others killed by the Nazis. Liberated in 1945, Wiesel transmuted the traumatic experiences of his childhood into prose. "Auschwitz," he wrote, "represents the negation and failure of human progress: it negates the human design and casts doubts on its validity." *Night*, Wiesel's autobiographical record of Nazi genocide, is a graphic account of Hitler's crimes against humanity. The brief excerpt that follows reveals the anguish Wiesel and other Jews experienced in confronting what appeared to be God's silence in the face of brutal injustice.

READING 34.7 From Wiesel's *Night* (1958)

One day, the power failed at the central electric plant in Buna. 1
The Gestapo, summoned to inspect the damage, concluded that it was sabotage. They found a trail. It led to the block of the Dutch *Oberkapo*.[1] And after a search, they found a significant quantity of weapons.

The *Oberkapo* was arrested on the spot. He was tortured for weeks on end, in vain. He gave no names. He was transferred to Auschwitz. And never heard from again.

But his little *pipel*[2] remained behind in solitary confinement. He too was tortured, but he too remained 10
silent. The SS[3] condemned him to death, him and two other inmates who had been found to possess arms.

One day, as we returned from work, we saw three gallows, three black ravens, erected on the Appelplatz.[4] Roll call.
The SS surrounding us, machine guns aimed at us: the usual ritual. Three prisoners in chains—and, among them, the little *pipel*, the sad-eyed angel.

The SS seemed more preoccupied, more worried than

---

[1] The foreman of the prisoners, selected from among
  them by the Nazis.
[2] The servant to the *Oberkapo*.
[3] A special police force that operated the camps.
[4] The assembly place of the camp.

---

usual. To hang a child in front of thousands of onlookers was not a small matter. The head of the camp read the verdict. 20
All eyes were on the child. He was pale, almost calm, but he was biting his lips as he stood in the shadow of the gallows.

This time, the *Lagerkapo*,[5] refused to act as executioner. Three SS took his place.

The three condemned prisoners together stepped onto the chairs. In unison, the nooses were placed around their necks.

"Long live liberty!" shouted the two men.

But the boy was silent.

"Where is merciful God, where is He?" someone behind me was asking. 30

At the signal, the three chairs were tipped over.

Total silence in the camp. On the horizon, the sun was setting.

"Caps off!" screamed the *Lagerälteste*.[6] His voice quivered.
As for the rest of us, we were weeping.

"Cover your heads!"

Then came the march past the victims. The two men were no longer alive. Their tongues were hanging out, swollen and bluish. But the third rope was still moving: the child, too light, was still breathing. . . .

And so he remained for more than half an hour, lingering 40
between life and death, writhing before our eyes.
And we were forced to look at him at close range. He was still alive when I passed him. His tongue was still red, his eyes not yet extinguished.

Behind me, I heard the same man asking:

"For God's sake, where is God?"

And from within me, I heard a voice answer:

"Where He is? This is where—hanging here from this gallows. . . ."

That night the soup tasted of corpses. . . .

Q What similarities and differences do you detect between the circumstances described here and those described by Remarque (Reading 34.4)?

Q How do the styles of Wiesel and Remarque compare?

The Visual Arts in the War Era

Photojournalism

The realities of World War II were recorded by an international array of photojournalists. One of the most gifted was Lee Miller (1907–1977), an American debutante who became the first female wartime photojournalist and an early witness to the horrors of the German concentration camps (see Figure 34.1). The American photographer Robert Capa (1897–1954) produced notable pictures of World War II paratroopers, and the French photographer Henri Cartier-Bresson (1908–2004) immortalized the plight of war-torn Europe in hundreds of aesthetically compelling Social Realist photographs.

The distinction between documentary photography and photojournalism is a slippery one. However, a contrast might be made between documentary photographers (for

---

[5] The prisoner who acted as foreman of the warehouse.
[6] The head of the camp.

instance, Dorothea Lange), who gather and create images as a form of storytelling (see Figure 34.8), and photojournalists (such as Miller, Capa, and Cartier-Bresson), whose photos represent an immediate and instinctive reaction to random visual information.

In the Soviet Union, photography came under the totalitarian knife, as Stalin's propagandists carefully excised from official photographs unseemly images of political brutality. The "remaking" of history via photomanipulation—a technique that would become popular among American filmmakers at the end of the century (see chapter 38)—had its ignoble beginnings in the war era.

Picasso's *Guernica*

On the afternoon of April 26, 1937, during the Spanish Civil War (1936–1939), which pitted republican forces against the Fascist dictatorship of General Francisco Franco, the German air force (in league with the Spanish Fascists) dropped incendiary bombs on Guernica, a small Basque market town in northeast Spain. During three and a half hours of bombing, the town was leveled and hundreds of people were killed. News of the event—the world's first aerial bombardment of a civilian target—reached Paris, where the horrified Pablo Picasso read illustrated newspaper accounts of the attack as the death toll mounted.

MAKING CONNECTIONS

Figure 34.9 PABLO PICASSO, *Guernica*, 1937. Oil on canvas, 11 ft. 5½ in. × 25 ft. 5¾ in.

Picasso regarded himself as heir to the historical giants of world art, and especially those who came from his own native Spain. Familiar with Goya's painting *The Third of May, 1808* (Figure **34.10**), which immortalizes the massacre of Madrid's citizens by the invading forces of France, he expropriated some of its most effective devices, such as the triangular beam of light that unifies the composition and the sharp contrasts of light and dark that create dramatic tension. In the image of the burning woman in *Guernica* (Figure **34.9**), Picasso makes reference to the unforgettable figure of Goya's protagonist, who, facing the French firing squad, flings his arms above his head in a gesture of rage and despair. Since the return of *Guernica* to Spain in 1981, it has become, like Goya's *Third of May*, a national monument.

Figure 34.10 FRANCISCO GOYA, *The Third of May, 1808: The Execution of the Defenders of Madrid*, 1814. Oil on canvas, 8 ft. 6 in. × 10 ft. 4 in.

Earlier in the year, the artist had been invited to contribute a painting for the Spanish Pavilion of the Paris World's Fair. The bombing of Guernica provided him with inspiration for the huge mural that would become the twentieth century's most famous antiwar painting (Figure **34.9**).

More powerful than any literary description, *Guernica* captures the grim brutality and suffering of the wartime era. For the painting, almost 12 feet high and as wide as the 26 feet of his studio wall, Picasso chose monochromatic tones—the ashen grays of incineration—which also call to mind the documentary media of mass communication: newspapers, photographs, and film. However, *Guernica* is far from documentary. Its flat, abstract figures and airless spatial field, distilled from the language of Cubism, provide a sharp contrast with the Social Realist style that dominated much of the art produced in Europe and America between the wars. While ignoring true-to-life details, the painting conflates the actual event of the bombing with an assortment of images drawn from Picasso's personal pictorial vocabulary, especially those of the Spanish bullfight, the ancient ritual of sacrificial death that intrigued the artist. The bull, at once hero and victim of the traditional combat, stands at the left of the shallow stage; the horse, whose body bears the gaping wound of a spear, rears its head in an agonized cry, its role in this massacre no less devastating than the one it often plays in the bullring, when attacked by the bull itself. Four women—one carrying a dead infant, a second holding a lamp, a third consumed in the flames of a burning building—issue voiceless screams configured to repeat that of the wounded horse. The dead warrior at the bottom of the composition—actually a broken statue—makes reference to war's corrupting effect on the artifacts of high culture, while mocking the militant idealism represented by traditional war monuments. By the unique conjunction of powerful images—a screaming woman, a dead baby, a severed arm, a victimized animal—Picasso created a universal icon for the inhuman atrocities of war, one that has made good his claim that art is "a weapon against the enemy."

Music in the War Era

Every totalitarian government in history has feared the power of music. In Nazi Germany, jazz was forbidden on the basis of its free and improvised style and its association with black musicians; in communist China, Beethoven's music was banned as the sound of the independent spirit. In Soviet Russia, Lenin's regime laid down the specific rule that composers write only music that "communicated" to the people. Atonality, associated with elitism and inscrutability, was to be avoided, along with other expressions of Western "decadence." "Music," observed Lenin, "is a means of unifying great masses of people."

Shostakovich

The career of the eminent Russian composer Dmitri Shostakovich (1906–1975) illustrates the challenges faced by Soviet composers in the time of Stalin. Enrolled at thirteen in the Leningrad Conservatory, Shostakovich was the product of rigorous classical training. His compositions, including fifteen symphonies, fifteen string quartets, and numerous scores for ballet, opera, plays, and motion pictures, incorporate songlike melodies and insistent rhythmic repetition. They are essentially tonal, but they make dramatic use of dissonance. One of his first operas, *Lady Macbeth of Mtsensk* (1934), was hailed by the Soviet press as a loyal expression of socialist ideology. However, within two years, *Pravda*, the official Soviet newspaper, condemned the piece as "*antinarodnaya*," that is, "antipeople." In 1941, the Seventh ("Leningrad") Symphony was hailed as a celebration of the Soviet triumph against the Nazi invasion of Leningrad. Nevertheless, in 1948, it received harsh criticism for its "bourgeois formalism." That same year, Shostakovich was denounced by the government and dismissed from his posts at the Moscow and Leningrad conservatories.

The fact that music rarely has meaning beyond sound itself worked, however, in the composer's favor: passages featuring militaristic rhythms might be taken as a sign of militant triumph, but they might also be heard as a reference to freedom from oppression. Only after 1979, when the memoirs of Shostakovich were smuggled out of the Soviet Union, did it become apparent that the composer intended the symphony as an attack on Stalin's inhumanity toward his own people.

Prokofiev

The career of the Russian composer Sergei Prokofiev (1891–1953) was equally turbulent. Permitted to leave Russia in 1918, he was persuaded to return in 1936. Defending Soviet principles, he proclaimed: "The composer . . . is in duty bound to serve man, the people. He must be a citizen first and foremost, so that his art may consciously extol human life and lead man to a radiant future." In 1948, the Soviets nevertheless denounced Prokofiev's music as "too modern"; and, along with Shostakovich, Prokofiev was relieved of his position at the Soviet music conservatories.

Prokofiev's compositions, most of which reveal his preference for classical form, are tonal and melodic, but they are boldly inventive in modulation and harmonic dissonance. In his scores for the ballets *Romeo and Juliet* (1935) and *Cinderella* (1944), and in his cantata for the Sergei Eisenstein film *Alexander Nevsky* (1938), Prokofiev demonstrated a talent for driving rhythms, sprightly marches, and unexpected, often whimsical shifts of tempo and melody. These features are found as well in his two delightful modern-day classics: the *Lieutenant Kije Suite* (1934) and the symphonic fairy tale *Peter and the Wolf* (1936).

Britten

Twentieth-century composers were frequently moved to commemorate the horrors of war. The most monumental example of such music is the *War Requiem* (1963) by the British composer Benjamin Britten (1913–1976) to accompany the consecration of England's new Coventry Cathedral, built alongside the ruins of the fourteenth-century cathedral that had been virtually destroyed by German bombs in World War II. Britten was a master at setting text to music. In the *War Requiem* he juxtaposed the

Figure 34.11 SERGEI M. EISENSTEIN, *Battleship Potemkin*, 1925. Film stills from Act IV, "The Odessa Steps Massacre." A woman, whose face will be slashed by a soldier, watches the careening baby carriage as it rolls down the steps. The Odessa Steps sequence, whose rapidly increasing tempo evokes apprehension and terror, is an ingenious piece of editing that has been imitated with great frequency by modern filmmakers.

Film in the War Era

Eisenstein

Film provided a permanent historical record of the turbulent military and political events of the early twentieth century. It also became an effective medium of political propaganda. In Russia, Lenin envisioned film as an invaluable means of spreading the ideals of communism. Following the Russian Revolution, he nationalized the fledgling motion-picture industry. In the hands of the Russian filmmaker Sergei Eisenstein (1898–1948), film operated both as a vehicle for political persuasion and as a fine art. He shaped the social and artistic potential of cinema by combining realistic narrative with symbolic imagery.

In *Battleship Potemkin* (1925), his silent-film masterpiece, Eisenstein told the story of a mutiny of 1905 led by the crew of a Russian naval vessel, and the subsequent massacre of their sympathizers—the citizens of Odessa. While this singular event did not actually occur, Eisenstein drew on similar episodes of brutality described in the Russian press. To recreate the effect of an on-the-spot documentary, he made use of **montage**, the cinematic technique that depends on a rapid succession of images. The so-called Odessa Steps sequence at the end of the film interposes 155 separate images in less than five minutes; the footage shows the advancing tzarist soldiers attacking their civilian victims, including a mother who is killed trying to save her infant in a baby carriage that slowly careens down a broad flight of stairs (Figure **34.11**). Alternating close-ups and long shots, shots from below and above, fixed shots and traveling shots, the Odessa Steps sequence gave the fictional massacre of Odessa's civilian victims unprecedented dramatic authenticity.

Two years later, in 1927, Eisenstein made the Russian Revolution itself the subject of the film *Ten Days That Shook the World*. Both in his silent movies and in those he made later with sound, Eisenstein developed techniques that drew the viewer into the space of the film. He deliberately cut off parts of faces to bring attention to the eyes, played one shot off the next to build a conflicting and often discontinuous sequence, and devised visual angles that, in true constructivist fashion, produced startling asymmetrical abstractions.

The masterpiece of Eisenstein's post-silent-film career was *Alexander Nevsky* (1938), a film that exalted the thirteenth-century Russian prince who defended the motherland against the onslaught of the Teutonic Knights. Here Eisenstein linked the musical score (composed by Sergei Prokofiev) to the pacing of the cinematic action: specifically, to the compositional flow of individual shots in the visual sequence—a technique known as "vertical montage." In place of the operatic crowd scenes of his earlier films, he framed the protagonist within landscapes and battle scenes that were as gloriously stylized as monumental paintings. *Alexander Nevsky* earned the approval of Joseph Stalin and the acclaim of the Russian people. It survives as a landmark in the history of inventive filmmaking.

Riefenstahl

While Eisenstein used film to glorify the collective and individual heroism of the Soviet people, German filmmakers working for Hitler turned motion pictures into outright vehicles of state propaganda. The filmmaker and former actress Leni Riefenstahl (1902–2003) received unlimited state subsidy to produce the most famous propaganda film of all time, *The Triumph of the Will* (1934). She engaged a crew of 135 people to film the huge rallies and ceremonies staged by Hitler and the Nazi party, including its first meeting in Nuremberg. *The Triumph of the Will* is a synthesis of documentary fact and sheer artifice. Its bold camera angles and stark compositions seem in themselves totalitarian—witness the absolute symmetry and exacting conformity of the masses of troops that frame the tiny figures of Hitler and his compatriots at the Nuremberg rally (Figure **34.12**).

Film in America

In America, film served to inform, to boost morale, and to propagandize for the Allied cause; but it also served as entertainment and escape. At the height of the Depression as well as during the war era, millions of Americans flocked to movie theaters each week. While such prize-winning movies as *All Quiet on the Western Front* (1930) and *From Here to Eternity* (1953) were painfully realistic, numerous other films romanticized and glamorized the war. An exception to the standard war-movie fare was *The Great Dictator* (1940), which was directed by the multitalented British-born actor and filmmaker Charlie Chaplin (1889–1977). In this hilarious satire of Fascist dictatorship, Adolf Hitler (known in the film as Adenoid Hynkel and played by Chaplin) rises to power as head of the "Double Cross Party," only to be arrested by his own troops, who mistake him for a Jewish barber.

Figure 34.12 LENI RIEFENSTAHL, *The Triumph of the Will*, 1934. Film still showing Heinrich Himmler, Hitler, and Viktor Lutze framed by columns of people as they approach the memorial monument in Nuremberg, Germany.

Roman Catholic Mass for the Dead (the Latin Requiem Mass) with lines from the poems of Wilfred Owen. The latter convey the composer's antiwar convictions. Britten's imaginative union of sacred ritual and secular song calls for orchestra, chorus, boys' chorus, and three soloists. Poignant in spirit and dramatic in effect, this oratorio may be seen as the musical analogue of Picasso's *Guernica*.

Penderecki

If it were possible to capture in music the agony of war, the Polish composer Krzysztof Penderecki (b. 1933) has come closest to doing so. His *Threnody in Memory of the Victims of Hiroshima* (1960) consists of violent torrents of dissonant, percussive sound, some of which is produced by beating on the bodies of the fifty-two stringed instruments for which the piece is scored. The ten-minute song of lamentation for the dead begins with a long, screaming tone produced by playing the highest pitches possible on the violins; it is followed by passages punctuated by **tone clusters** (groups of adjacent dissonant notes). The rapid shifts in density, timbre, rhythm, and dynamics are jarring and disquieting—effects consistent with the subject matter of the piece.

Threnody was said to be the "anguished cry" that proclaimed the birth of the musical avant-garde behind the Iron Curtain. Penderecki's angry blurring of tones also characterizes his *Dies Irae* (1967), subtitled *Oratorio Dedicated to the Memory of those Murdered at Auschwitz*. Like Britten's *War Requiem*, it draws on Christian liturgy—here the traditional hymn of Last Judgment (the "Day of Wrath")—to convey a mood of darkness and despair. The *Dies Irae*, first performed on the grounds of a former concentration camp, is punctuated by clanking chains and piercing sirens. Harsh and abrasive, it remains a symbol of the Holocaust's haunting impact.

Copland and the American Sound

One of America's finest twentieth-century composers, Aaron Copland (1900–1990) turned away from the horrors of war; however, just as the music of Shostakovich and Prokofiev was rooted in Russian soil, so that of Copland drew nourishment from native American idioms. The New York composer spiced his largely tonal compositions with the simple harmony of American folk songs, the clarity of Puritan hymns, and the lively and often syncopated rhythms of jazz and Mexican dance. In 1941, Copland advised American composers to find alternatives to the harsh and demanding serialism of their European colleagues: "The new musical audiences will have to have music they can comprehend," he insisted. "It must therefore be simple and direct . . . Above all, it must be fresh in feeling." Copland achieved these goals in all his compositions, especially in the ballet scores *Billy the Kid* (1938), *Rodeo* (1940), and *Appalachian Spring* (1944).

Appalachian Spring, commissioned by the Martha Graham Dance Company, was originally called "Ballet for Martha." The choreographer chose its title, which is based on the first line of a poem by the American writer Hart Crane

See Music Listening Selections at end of chapter.

(1899–1932). (The "spring" in the title refers not to a season but to a source of water.) Graham's ballet tells the story of a newly betrothed Pennsylvania frontier couple, who are welcomed to their new community by a revivalist preacher and his congregation. An orchestral suite for small chamber orchestra, it features five variations on the familiar Shaker song "'Tis the Gift to Be Simple." In directing an orchestral rehearsal for the piece in 1974, Copland urged: "Make it more American in spirit, in that the sentiment isn't shown on the face." Copland also composed for film, winning an Oscar in 1949 for his score for *The Heiress*. Like the murals of Thomas Hart Benton, Copland's music wedded American themes to a vigorous and readily accessible language of form.

The Communist Revolution in China

The history of totalitarianism is not confined to the West. In the course of the twentieth century, modern tyrants wiped out whole populations in parts of Cambodia, Vietnam, Iraq, Africa, and elsewhere. Of all the Asian countries, however, China experienced the most dramatic changes. In 1900, less than 10 percent of the Chinese population owned almost 80 percent of the land. Clamoring for reform, as well as for independence from foreign domination, nationalist forces moved to redistribute land among the enormous peasant population. By 1911, the National People's Party had overthrown the Manchu leaders (see chapter 21) and established a republican government. But the Nationalists failed to provide an efficient program for land redistribution. Consequently, after 1937, they lost much of their popular support. Following World War II, the communist forces under the leadership of Mao Zedong (1893–1976) rose to power. In 1949, they formed the People's Republic of China.

In China as in Russia, the Communist Party gained exclusive control of the government, with Mao serving as both chairman of the party and head of state. Mao called upon the great masses of citizens to work toward radical reform. "The theory of Marx, Engels, Lenin and Stalin is universally applicable," he wrote. However, he added, "We should regard it not as a dogma, but as a guide to action." A competent poet and scholar, Mao drew up the guidelines for the new society of China, a society that practiced cooperative endeavor and self-discipline. These guidelines were published in 1963 as the *Quotations from Chairman Mao*. Mao's "little red book" soon became the "bible" of the Chinese Revolution. On youth, Mao wrote: "The world is yours, as well as ours, but in the last analysis, it is yours. You young people, full of vigor and vitality, are in the bloom of life, like the sun at eight or nine in the morning. Our hope is placed in you." On women: "In order to build a great socialist society, it is of the utmost importance to arouse the broad masses of women to join in productive activity. Men and women must receive equal pay for equal work in production." And on the masses: "The masses have boundless creative power . . . the revolutionary war is a war of the masses; it can be waged only by mobilizing the masses and relying on them."

Mao's ambitious reforms earned the support of the landless masses, but his methods for achieving his goals struck at the foundations of traditional Chinese culture. He moved to replace the old order, and especially the Confucian veneration of the family, with new socialist values that demanded devotion to the local economic unit—and ultimately to the state. To carry out his series of five-year plans for economic development in industry and agriculture, he instituted iron-handed totalitarian practices, including indoctrination, exile, and repeated purges of the voices of opposition. Between 1949 and 1952, Mao authorized the execution of some two to five million people, including the wealthy landowners themselves.

Like the century's other totalitarian leaders, Mao directed writers to infuse their works with ideological content that celebrated the creative power of the masses. To some extent, however, the movement for a "people's literature" advanced reforms that had already been launched during the political revolution of 1911: at that time, traditional styles of writing, including the "book language" of the classics, gave way to the language of common, vernacular speech. The new naturalistic style was strongly influenced by Western literature and journalism. Chinese writers responded enthusiastically to modern European novels, short stories, and psychological dramas—poets even imitated such Western forms as the sonnet.

In the visual arts, the influence of late nineteenth-century Western printmakers such as Käthe Kollwitz (see chapter 30), helped to shape the powerful realism of many

Figure 34.13 LI HUA, *Roar!*, 1936. Woodcut, 8 × 6 in. Li Hua's woodcut is representative of the modern woodcut movement that flourished in China during the 1930s. The movement was a significant expression of China's avant-garde.

Chinese artists, including Li Hua (1907–1994). Li's stark and searing woodcut of a bound man (Figure 34.13)—a metaphor for modern China—reiterates the silent scream of Munch (see Figure 33.2) and Eisenstein (see Figure 34.11). During the Cultural Revolution (1966–1976), China's communist regime reinstated the official policy of socialist realism as it had been defined by the First All-Union Congress of Soviet Writers in 1934. The consequences of this policy would work to foment the liberation movements of the last decades of the century.

Chronology

1910–1920	Mexican Revolution
1911	Nationalist Revolution in China
1914–1918	World War I
1917	Russian Revolution
1926	Stalin becomes Soviet dictator
1929	Stock market crashes
1936–1939	Spanish Civil War
1939–1945	World War II
1949	People's Republic of China formed under Mao

LOOKING BACK

Total Wars

- The twentieth century was molded in the crucible of total war and totalitarianism.
- World Wars I and II were more devastating in nature and effect than any preceding wars in world history. They involved numerous nations, killed an unprecedented number of civilians, and employed the weapons of modern technology: machine guns, poison gas, tanks, and, finally, atomic bombs.

World War I Literature

- Writers responded to total war and totalitarianism with rage, disbelief, and compassion.
- Bitter indictments of World War I are found in the poetry of Owen, Eliot, and Yeats, who viewed war as an indication of the decay of Western civilization.
- The novelist Erich Remarque produced a firsthand account of trench warfare and the devastating nature of World War I.

World War I Art

- Visual artists also protested against the calamities of war. Max Ernst used collage-paintings to create bizarre dehumanized images, while George Grosz produced mocking depictions of the German military machine.
- Léger's Cubist paintings reflect his appreciation of modern weaponry and machinery. He produced one of the first abstract films, *Ballet mécanique*, which

pictured modern life as mechanized and impersonal.

The Russian Revolution

- World War I, a corrupt tsarist government, and a weak economy led to discontent in Russia. The Russian Revolution of 1917 marked the beginnings of Soviet communism and ushered in decades of totalitarian rule inspired by the Marxist ideology of Vladimir Lenin.
- Following Lenin, Joseph Stalin took control of Russia. Under his totalitarian regime dissidents were imprisoned, executed, or exiled, and all expressions of "Modernism" were condemned. In the arts, socialist realism promoted the ideological benefits of communism.

The Great Depression and the American Scene

- America's economy, like that of the rest of the world, suffered after World War I, and the country was swept into the Great Depression.
- Social Realism, often a vehicle of social criticism and protest, dominated the novels of John Steinbeck and the murals of Thomas Hart Benton. As with the mural paintings of revolutionary Mexico, Benton's murals depicting American occupations and pastimes became a major form of public art.
- Dorothea Lange and other photographers of the Great Depression left a documentary record of rural poverty and oppression.

Totalitarianism and World War II

- Under Adolf Hitler, the Nazi policy of militant racism brought about the brutal deaths of millions throughout Europe.
- In the poems of Randall Jarrell, the fiction works of Norman Mailer, and the gallows-humor novels of Joseph Heller, World War II literature emphasized the dehumanizing effects of war.
- The firsthand experiences of Solzhenitsyn in the Russian *gulags* and Wiesel in Nazi concentration camps are shocking records of totalitarian inhumanity.

The Visual Arts in the War Era

- Photography documented the horrifying visual history of World War II. The first female war photojournalist, Lee Miller, made moving images of Nazi concentration camps.
- Working in Paris, Picasso responded to news reports of the German aerial bombing of a Spanish market town; *Guernica* has become the quintessential antiwar painting of the twentieth century.

Film in the War Era

- The Russian filmmaker Sergei Eisenstein pioneered the technique of cinematic montage to brilliant effect in the classic film *Battleship Potemkin*.
- American films generally served as morale boosters and vehicles of Allied propaganda; the British actor Charlie Chaplin satirized Fascist dictatorship.

Music in the War Era

- Living under the critical eye of the communist regime, Dmitri Shostakovich and Sergei Prokofiev composed in distinctly different but memorable musical styles.
- In England, Benjamin Britten commemorated World War II in his *War Requiem*, while in Poland Krzysztof Penderecki immortalized in atonal compositions the harsh reality of twentieth-century genocide.
- Native idioms, such as folk songs and Mexican dance, were integrated into the readily accessible music of one of America's most notable composers, Aaron Copland.

The Communist Revolution in China

- After Nationalist forces in China failed to provide much-needed land reforms, the Communist Party, under the leadership of Mao Zedong, gained control, forming the People's Republic of China in 1949.
- Economic reform went hand in hand with the eradication of age-old traditions and the execution of dissidents and landowners. Mao's "little red book," which encouraged the empowerment of the masses, became the "bible" of the Chinese Revolution.

Music Listening Selection

- Copland, *Appalachian Spring*, excerpt, 1944.

Glossary

gallows humor (or "black humor") the use of morbid and absurd situations for comic and satirical purposes in modern fiction and drama

montage in art, music, or literature, a composite made by freely juxtaposing usually heterogeneous images; in cinema, the production of a rapid succession of images to present a stream of interconnected ideas (see also Glossary, chapter 33, "photomontage")

mural a painting applied to a large wall or ceiling

tone cluster a group of adjacent dissonant notes, such as the notes of a scale, that are sounded together

totalitarian a political regime that imposes the will of the state upon the life and conduct of the individual

Chapter 35

The Quest for Meaning

ca. 1940–1960

"Man is nothing else but what he makes of himself."
Jean-Paul Sartre

Figure 35.1 MARK ROTHKO, *Untitled*, 1960. Oil on canvas, 5 ft. 9 in. × 4 ft. 2⅛ in. Devoid of figural representation, Rothko's huge, luminous paintings invite sustained contemplation. The artist held that the spiritual intimacy between artwork and viewer would be achieved if the latter stood no more than 18 inches from the canvas.

The nightmare of World War II left the world's population in a state of shock and disillusionment. The Western democracies had held back the forces of totalitarian aggression, but the future seemed as threatening as ever. The treaty settlements that ended World War II left two large blocs of powerful nations ranged against each other in an effort to further their individual political, social, and ideological ends. The largest of these ideological power blocs, the nations led by the United States and its democratic/capitalistic ideology, stood opposed to the Soviet/communist bloc, which came to include most of the East European countries adjacent to Russia. Communism and capitalist democracy now confronted each other in hostile distrust. And both possessed nuclear capability with the potential to extinguish the human race.

The pessimism that accompanied the two world wars was compounded by a loss of faith in the bedrock beliefs of former centuries. The realities of trench warfare, the Holocaust, and Hiroshima made it difficult to maintain that human beings were rational by nature, that technology would work to advance human happiness, and that the universe was governed by a benevolent God. It is little wonder that the events of the first half of the twentieth century caused a loss of confidence in moral absolutes. The sense of estrangement from God and from reason produced a condition of anxious withdrawal that has been called "alienation." By mid-century, the quest for meaning had produced the philosophy of Existentialism, while the mood of alienation and anxiety pervaded the literature of dystopia, the personality of the fictional antihero, and a host of new directions in the arts. Avant-garde movements in painting, music, and dance launched America to a position of cultural leadership in the West.

The Cold War

The contest for world domination—the so-called cold war that followed World War II—determined the course of international relations during the second half of the twentieth century. In Europe, postwar Germany was politically divided, most visibly by the Berlin Wall, which separated Soviet-dominated East Germany from the West German Democratic Republic. As "power vacuums" occurred in the post-colonial regions of East Asia, the cold war grew hot. In the Korean peninsula, the two superpowers, the Soviet Union and the United States, wrestled diplomatically but unsuccessfully for dominion in what would ultimately become all-out war. The Korean War (1950–1953), fought virtually to a standoff with both sides suffering terrible losses (three million Koreans, mostly civilians, died), ended with the division of the country into a northern communist state (the Korean People's Democratic Republic) and a southern democratic state (the Republic of Korea). The destabilized circumstances of the lingering cold war contributed to the anxiety of the postwar era.

Existentialism

Existentialism, the most important philosophic movement of the twentieth century, examined the unique nature of individual experience within an indifferent universe. Focusing on matters of human freedom, choice, and responsibility, it had its roots in the late nineteenth century, most notably in the writings of the Danish philosopher Søren Kierkegaard (1813–1855). But it rose to prominence through the efforts of the French left-wing intellectual Jean-Paul Sartre.

The Philosophy of Sartre

Jean-Paul Sartre (1905–1980), the leading philosopher of the twentieth century, made significant contributions as a playwright, novelist, journalist, and literary critic. Sartre fought in World War II and was active in the French resistance to the German occupation of France. Committed to social reform, he supported the working-class ideals of Marxist communism, but never became a member of the French Communist Party.

Sartre's philosophy, as expounded in his classic work *Being and Nothingness* (1943), took as its premise the idea that existence precedes essence, that is, that one's material being exists prior to and independent of any intrinsic factors. Sartre's premise challenged the fundamentals of traditional philosophy: Plato had identified "essence" as Forms (or Ideas) that were eternal and unchanging. For Aristotle, reason—humankind's capacity for rational thought—was the "essence" that separated human beings from the lower animals. Philosophers from Descartes through Kant followed the ancients by defending the notion that primary internal principles of being preceded being itself—a view that was metaphysically compatible with Christian theology.

Sartre proposed, however, that there is no pre-existing blueprint for human beings, no fixed essence or nature. We are not imbued with any special divinity, nor are we (by nature) rational. We are neither imprisoned by unconscious forces (as Freud had held) nor determined by specific economic conditions (as Marx had maintained). Born into the world as body/matter, we proceed to make the choices by which we form our own natures. In Sartre's analysis, each individual is the sum of his or her actions; "We are what we choose to be," he insisted. Because we must choose at every turn between a variety of possibilities, we are "condemned to be free." Moreover, since every choice we make implies a choice for all humankind, we bear the overwhelming burden of total responsibility—a condition that Sartre called "anguish."

Sartre's viewpoint struck a balance between optimism and despair. While freedom and meaning depend on human action, all human actions, by necessity, are played out within a moral void—that is, within a universe lacking divine guidance and absolute values. To our profound despair, we seek meaning in a meaningless world. Yet, because human life is all there is, it must be cherished. According to Sartre, the human condition is one of anxiety experienced in the face of nothingness and the inevitability of death. Such anxiety is compounded because we alone are responsible for our actions. To disclaim responsibility for those actions by blaming external causes—"the Devil made me do it," "The ghetto turned me into a criminal," or "My parents were too lenient"—is to act in "bad faith." For Sartre, no forms of human engineering, technocratic or otherwise, can usurp the human potential for free action. A flight from freedom and responsibility is a form of self-deception and inauthenticity. "We are alone, with no excuses," he concluded.

In addition to his major philosophic work, Sartre wrote a number of significant novels, short stories, and plays. The most gripping of his plays, *No Exit* (1945), features three characters trapped in a "hell" they have created by their efforts to justify the acts of bad faith that have shaped their lives. The principal ideas set forth in these most famous of Sartre's writings are summarized in the lecture entitled "Existentialism," which Sartre presented in Paris in 1945. In the following excerpt, Sartre discusses Existentialism as an ethics of action and involvement, and explores the meaning of existential anguish.

READING 35.1 From Sartre's "Existentialism" (1945)

. . . Atheistic existentialism . . . states that if God does not   1
exist, there is at least one being in whom existence precedes
essence, a being who exists before he can be defined by any
concept, and that this being is man, or, as Heidegger[1] says,
human reality. What is meant here by saying that existence
precedes essence? It means that, first of all, man exists, turns
up, appears on the scene, and, only afterwards, defines
himself. If man, as the existentialist conceives him, is
indefinable, it is because at first he is nothing. Only afterward
will he be something, and he himself will have made what he   10
will be. Thus, there is no human nature, since there is no God
to conceive it. Not only is man what he conceives himself to
be, but he is also only what he wills himself to be after this
thrust toward existence.

   Man is nothing else but what he makes of himself. Such is
the first principle of existentialism. It is also what is called
subjectivity, the name we are labeled with when charges are
brought against us. But what do we mean by this, if not that

---

[1] A German philosopher (1889–1976) whose writings had a major influence on Sartre and other Existentialists.

man has a greater dignity than a stone or table? For we mean
that man first exists, that is, that man first of all is the being   20
who hurls himself toward a future and who is conscious of
imagining himself as being in the future. Man is at the start a
plan which is aware of itself, rather than a patch of moss, a
piece of garbage, or a cauliflower; nothing exists prior to this
plan; there is nothing in heaven; man will be what he will
have planned to be. Not what he will want to be. Because
by the word "will" we generally mean a conscious decision,
which is subsequent to what we have already made of
ourselves. I may want to belong to a political party, write a
book, get married; but all that is only a manifestation of an   30
earlier, more spontaneous choice that is called "will." But if
existence really does precede essence, man is responsible for
what he is. Thus, existentialism's first move is to make every
man aware of what he is and to make the full responsibility
of his existence rest on him. And when we say that a man
is responsible for himself, we do not only mean that he is
responsible for his own individuality, but that he is responsible
for all men.

   The word subjectivism has two meanings, and our
opponents play on the two. Subjectivism means, on the one   40
hand, that an individual chooses and makes himself; and, on
the other, that it is impossible for man to transcend human
subjectivity. The second of these is the essential meaning of
existentialism. When we say that man chooses his own self,
we mean that every one of us does likewise; but we also
mean by that that in making this choice he also chooses all
men. In fact, in creating the man that we want to be, there is
not a single one of our acts which does not at the same time
create an image of man as we think he ought to be. To choose
to be this or that is to affirm at the same time the value of   50
what we choose, because we can never choose evil. We
always choose the good, and nothing can be good for us
without being good for all.

   If, on the other hand, existence precedes essence, and if
we grant that we exist and fashion our image at one and the
same time, the image is valid for everybody and for our whole
age. Thus, our responsibility is much greater than we might
have supposed, because it involves all mankind. If I am a
workingman and choose to join a Christian trade-union rather
than be a communist, and if by being a member I want to   60
show that the best thing for man is resignation, that the
kingdom of man is not of this world, I am not only involving
my own case—I want to be resigned for everyone. As a result,
my action has involved all humanity. To take a more individual
matter, if I want to marry, to have children; even if this marriage
depends solely on my own circumstances or passion or wish,
I am involving all humanity in monogamy and not merely myself.
Therefore, I am responsible for myself and for everyone else.
I am creating a certain image of man of my own choosing.
In choosing myself, I choose man.   70

   This helps us understand what the actual content is of such
rather grandiloquent words as anguish, forlornness, despair.
As you will see, it's all quite simple.

   First, what is meant by anguish? The existentialists say at
once that man is anguish. What that means is this: the man
who involves himself and who realizes that he is not only the
person he chooses to be, but also a lawmaker who is, at the

Communism versus Capitalism

For roughly a half-century following World War II, the great powers of the world were divided into two opposing ideological camps, popularly known as "communism" and "capitalism." Each of these power blocs fervently defended its superiority, and the necessity of its success in the world struggle for dominance. "Communism"—in reality one of several forms of Marxist–Leninist socialism—describes a social and political system committed to the principle that the central state should own and operate the nation's means of production and distribution of goods, with the entire population sharing the resulting wealth equally (see chapters 30 and 34). "Capitalism" describes a system based on the principle that the world's economic capital should function according to free market forces, described by Adam Smith (see chapter 24), and that government should have little to do with regulation of the economic and financial world. Individual initiative and enterprise would then function to produce and distribute goods among the population.

These two seemingly incompatible and competing ideologies fueled the cold war of the postwar years. While the cold war has only occasionally turned hot in the past half-century—most recently in the Vietnam War (see chapter 36)—the competing ideologies of communism and capitalism, and the policies guided by these ideas, worked to destabilize international relations during most of the twentieth century.

---

same time, choosing all mankind as well as himself, cannot escape the feeling of his total and deep responsibility. Of course, there are many people who are not anxious; but we **80** claim that they are hiding their anxiety, that they are fleeing from it. Certainly, many people believe that when they do something, they themselves are the only ones involved, and when someone says to them, "What if everyone acted that way?" they shrug their shoulders and answer, "Everyone doesn't act that way." But really, one should always ask himself, "What would happen if everybody looked at things that way?" There is no escaping this disturbing thought except by a kind of double-dealing. A man who lies and makes excuses for himself by saying "not everybody does that," is someone **90** with an uneasy conscience, because the act of lying implies that a universal value is conferred upon the lie. . . .

The existentialist . . . thinks it very distressing that God does not exist, because all possibility of finding values in a heaven of ideas disappears along with Him; there can no longer be an *a priori* Good, since there is no infinite and perfect consciousness to think it. Nowhere is it written that the Good exists, that we must be honest, that we must not lie; because the fact is we are on a plane where there are only men. Dostoevsky said, "If God didn't exist, everything would be **100** possible." That is the very starting point of existentialism. Indeed, everything is permissible if God does not exist, and as a result man is forlorn, because neither within him nor without does he find anything to cling to. He can't start making excuses for himself.

If existence really does precede essence, there is no explaining things away by reference to a fixed and given human nature. In other words, there is no determinism, man is free, man is freedom. On the other hand, if God does not exist, we find no values or commands to turn to which legitimize **110** our conduct. So, in the bright realm of values, we have no excuse behind us, nor justification before us. We are alone, with no excuses.

That is the idea I shall try to convey when I say that man is condemned to be free. Condemned, because he did not create himself, yet, in other respects is free; because, once thrown into the world, he is responsible for everything he does. The existentialist does not believe in the power of passion. He will never agree that a sweeping passion is a ravaging torrent which fatally leads a man to certain acts and is therefore an **120** excuse. He thinks that man is responsible for his passion.

The existentialist does not think that man is going to help himself by finding in the world some omen by which to orient himself. Because he thinks that man will interpret the omen to suit himself. Therefore, he thinks that man, with no support and no aid, is condemned every moment to invent man. Ponge,[2] in a very fine article, has said, "Man is the future of man." That's exactly it. But if it is taken to mean that this future is recorded in heaven, that God sees it, then it is false, because it would really no longer be a future. If it is taken to **130** mean that whatever a man may be, there is a future to be forged, a virgin future before him, then this remark is sound. But then we are forlorn. . . .

Now, for the existentialist there is really no love other than one which manifests itself in a person's being in love. There is no genius other than one which is expressed in works of art; the genius of Proust is the sum of Proust's works; the genius of Racine is his series of tragedies. Outside of that, there is nothing. Why say that Racine could have written another tragedy, when he didn't write it? A man is involved in life, **140** leaves his impress on it, and outside of that there is nothing. To be sure, this may seem a harsh thought to someone whose life hasn't been a success. But, on the other hand, it prompts people to understand that reality alone is what counts, that dreams, expectations, and hopes warrant no more than to define a man as a disappointed dream, as miscarried hopes, as vain expectations. In other words, to define him negatively and

---

[2] Francis Ponge (1899–1987) was a French poet and critic.

not positively. However, when we say, "You are nothing else than your life," that does not imply that the artist will be judged solely on the basis of his works of art; a thousand other things will contribute toward summing him up. What we mean is that a man is nothing else than a series of undertakings, that he is the sum, the organization, the ensemble of the relationships which make up these undertakings. . . .

If it is impossible to find in every man some universal essence which would be human nature, yet there does exist a universal human condition. It's not by chance that today's thinkers speak more readily of man's condition than of his nature. By condition they mean, more or less definitely, the *a priori* limits which outline man's fundamental situation in the universe. Historical situations vary; a man may be born a slave in a pagan society or a feudal lord or a proletarian. What does not vary is the necessity for him to exist in the world, to be at work there, to be there in the midst of other people, and to be mortal there. . . .

But there is another meaning of humanism. Fundamentally it is this: man is constantly outside of himself; in projecting himself, in losing himself outside of himself, he makes for man's existing; and, on the other hand, it is by pursuing transcendent goals that he is able to exist; man, being this state of passing-beyond, and seizing upon things only as they bear upon this passing-beyond, is at the heart, at the center of this passing-beyond. There is no universe other than a human universe, the universe of human subjectivity. This connection between transcendency, as a constituent element of man— not in the sense that God is transcendent, but in the sense of passing beyond—and subjectivity, in the sense that man is not closed in on himself but is always present in a human universe, is what we call existentialist humanism. Humanism, because we remind man that there is no lawmaker other than himself, and that in his forlornness he will decide by himself; because we point out that man will fulfill himself as man, not in turning toward himself, but in seeking outside of himself a goal which is just this liberation, just this particular fulfillment.

From these few reflections it is evident that nothing is more unjust than the objections that have been raised against us. Existentialism is nothing else than an attempt to draw all the consequences of a coherent atheistic position. It isn't trying to plunge man into despair at all. But if one calls every attitude of unbelief despair, like the Christians, then the word is not being used in its original sense. Existentialism isn't so atheistic that it wears itself out showing that God doesn't exist. Rather, it declares that even if God did exist, that would change nothing. There you've got our point of view. Not that we believe that God exists, but we think that the problem of His existence is not the issue. In this sense existentialism is optimistic, a doctrine of action, and it is plain dishonesty for Christians to make no distinction between their own despair and ours and then to call us despairing.

Q In your own words, explain: "existence precedes essence" and "existential anguish."

Q Evaluate Sartre's claims: "You are nothing else than your life," and "Man is condemned to be free."

Christian Existentialism

While Sartre excluded the question of God's existence from his speculations, Christian Existentialists saw little contradiction between the belief in a Supreme Being and the ethics of human freedom and responsibility. They held that religious philosophy need not concern itself with the proof or disproof of God's existence; rather, it should focus on the moral life of the individual. Beyond what Kierkegaard had called the "leap of faith" from which all religious belief proceeded, there lay a continuing moral responsibility for one's own life. According to the philosophers Karl Jaspers (1883–1969) and Gabriel Marcel (1889–1973), God had challenged human beings to act as free and responsible creatures.

Among Christian theologians, a similar concern for the moral life of the individual moved religion out of the seminaries and into the streets. The Protestant theologian Reinhold Niebuhr (1892–1971) criticized doctrinaire theology and called for the revival of moral conduct in an immoral society. Convinced that human participation was essential to social redemption, Niebuhr urged Christians to cultivate humility and advance justice in modern society. Niebuhr's contemporary and fellow Lutheran Paul Tillich (1886–1965) boldly rejected the concept of a *personal* god. For Tillich, anxiety and alienation were conditions preliminary to the mystical apprehension of a "God above the God of theism."

Literature at Mid-Century

Utopias and Dystopias

In the postwar era, the breach between humanism and science seemed wider than ever. Increasingly, intellectuals questioned the social value of scientific knowledge as it applied to human progress. Optimists still envisioned modern technology as a liberating force for humankind. The American behavioral psychologist B. F. Skinner (1904–1990), for instance, anticipated a society in which the behavior of human beings might be scientifically engineered for the benefit of both the individual and the community. In the futuristic novel *Walden Two* (1948), Skinner created a fictional society in which the "technology of behavior" replaced traditional "prescientific" views of freedom and dignity. *Walden Two* is typical of a large body of *utopian literature* that exalted science as a positive force in shaping the future.

Pessimists, on the other hand, feared—and still fear— that modern technology might produce catastrophes ranging from a nuclear holocaust to the absolute loss of personal freedom. *Dystopian literature*, that is, works that picture societies in which conditions are dreadful and bleak, reflect this negative outlook. The most notable of these are *Brave New World* (1932) by the English writer Aldous Huxley (1894– 1963), *1984* (1949) by his compatriot George Orwell (the pen name of Eric Arthur Blair; 1903–1950), and *Fahrenheit 451* (1953) by the American Ray Bradbury (1920–2012). All three of the novels present fictional totalitarian societies in which modern technology and the techniques of human engineering operate to destroy human freedom— a theme that has been updated in the dystopian literature of the twenty-first century (see chapter 37).

Brave New World describes an imaginary society of the seventh century "A.F." ("after Henry Ford," the early twentieth-century American automobile manufacturer). In Huxley's futuristic society, babies are conceived in test tubes and, following the assembly-line methods invented by Ford for the manufacture of cars, individuals are behaviorally conditioned to perform socially beneficial tasks. From this "brave new world," the concept and practice of family life have been eradicated; human anxiety is quelled by means of *soma* (a mood-altering drug); and art, literature, and religion—all of which, according to the custodians of technology, threaten communal order and stability—have been ruthlessly purged.

The Literary Antihero

The postwar era witnessed the birth of a new kind of literary hero: one who, deprived of traditional values and religious beliefs, bears the burden of freedom and the total responsibility for his actions. The existential hero—or, more exactly, antihero—takes up the quest for meaning: alienated by nature and circumstance, he makes choices in a world lacking moral absolutes, a world in which no act might be called "good" unless it is chosen in conscious preference to its alternatives. Unlike the heroes of old, the modern antihero is neither noble nor sure of purpose. He might act decisively, but with full recognition of the absence of shared cultural values or personal reward. Trapped rather than liberated by freedom, he might have trouble getting along with others or simply making it through the day—"Hell," says one of Sartre's characters in *No Exit*, "is other people." Confronting meaninglessness and irrationality, the antihero might achieve nothing other than the awful recognition of life's absurdity.

Twentieth-century literature is filled with antiheroes—characters whose lives illustrate the absurdity of the human condition. Sartre's compatriot Albert Camus (1913–1960) defined the absurd as the "divorce between man and life, actor and setting." In Camus' short stories and novels, the antihero inevitably confronts the basic existential imperatives: "Recognize your dignity as a human being"; "Choose

Science and Technology

1944	a Canadian bacteriologist proves DNA is fundamental in determining heredity
1946	the first functional electronic digital computer is tested in America
1947	quantum electrodynamics (QED) studies "irregular" behavior of subatomic particles
1948	Bell Laboratories develop the transistor
1951	nuclear reactors are utilized successfully to produce electricity

and commit yourself to action." The central character of Camus' classic work *The Stranger* (1942) is the quintessential alienated man: he is estranged from traditional social values and unable to establish his sense of being except through continual rebellion. Camus' view of human nature was less cynical than Sartre's and more concerned with the value of benevolent reconciliation between individuals. At the same time, the situations described in his novels—and his own death in an automobile crash—seem inescapably arbitrary and absurd.

Although Existentialism was an essentially European phenomenon, the existential hero appears in the literature of twentieth-century writers throughout the world, most notably in the novels of Argentina's Jorge Luis Borges (see chapter 37) and Japan's Oē Kenzaburo (b. 1935). In postwar America, the existential perspective cut across regional lines, from the deep South of William Faulkner (1897–1962) and Walker Percy (1916–1990) to John Cheever's (1912–1982) New England and the New York of Bernard Malamud (1914–1986); and from the urban Midwest of Saul Bellow (1915–2005) to California's Beat Generation. The Beat Generation were a group of writers who prized bohemian creativity, anticonformity, and a spontaneous lifestyle. They are best represented by Jack Kerouac's *On the Road* (1951), a saga of youthful restlessness that Kerouac called his "true-story novel"; and by Allen Ginsberg's long, in-your-face poem *Howl* (1955). The latter, a ranting lament on America's loss of values, makes notorious reference to illicit drugs, to sexuality and homosexuality, and to the evils of American commercialism. It opens with these angry lines:

> I saw the best minds of my generation destroyed by
>   madness, starving hysterical naked,
> dragging themselves through the negro streets at
>   dawn looking for an angry fix;
> angel-headed hipsters burning for the ancient
>   heavenly connection
> to the starry dynamo in the machinery of night, ...

Postwar dramatists also treated the existential experience: in the Pulitzer prize-winning play *Death of a Salesman* (1949) by Arthur Miller (1915–2005), the antihero is a quintessentially American figure. Miller's protagonist, Willy Loman, is a salesman, a "little man" who has met failure at every turn, but he cannot recognize the inauthenticity of his false claims to material success nor escape the futility of his self-deception. An American classic, *Salesman* depends on traditional dramatic structure in bringing to life a complex but ultimately sympathetic existential figure. An entirely different type of theater, however, would come to dominate the postwar era.

Theater of the Absurd

The international movement known as *theater of the absurd* so vividly captured the anguish of modern society that late twentieth-century critics called it "the true theater of our time." Abandoning Classical theater from Sophocles and Shakespeare through Ibsen and Miller, Absurdist playwrights rejected traditional dramatic structure (in which action moves from conflict to resolution), along with traditional modes of character development. The Absurdist play, which drew stylistic inspiration from Dada performance art and Surrealist film (see chapter 33), lacks dramatic progression, direction, and resolution. Its characters undergo little or no change, dialogue contradicts actions, and events follow no logical order. Dramatic action, leavened with gallows humor, may consist of irrational and grotesque situations that remain unresolved at the end of the performance—as is often the case in real life.

The principal figures of Absurdist theater reflect the international character of the movement: they include Samuel Beckett (Irish), Eugène Ionesco (Romanian), Harold Pinter (British), Fernando Arrabal (Spanish), Jean Genet (French), and Edward Albee (American). Of these, Samuel Beckett (1906–1989), recipient of the Nobel Prize in 1969, earned the greatest distinction. Early in his career, Beckett came under the influence of James Joyce, parts of whose novel *Finnegans Wake* he recorded from dictation, as the aging Joyce was losing his eyesight. Beckett admired Joyce's experimental use of language. He also shared the views of the Austrian linguistic philosopher Ludwig Wittgenstein (see chapter 37), who held that human beings were imprisoned by language and consequently cut off from the possibility of true understanding.

The concept of language as the prisonhouse of the mind—a point of view that had far-reaching consequences in Postmodern philosophy—was fundamental to Beckett's dramatic style. It is particularly apparent in his most notable work, *Waiting for Godot*, written in 1948 and first staged in 1952. The main "action" of the play consists of a running dialogue—terse, repetitive, and often comical—between two tramps as they await the mysterious "Godot" (who, despite their anxious expectations, never arrives). Some find in Godot a symbol of salvation, revelation, or, most commonly, God—an interpretation that Beckett himself rejected. Nevertheless, the absent "deliverer" (perhaps by his very absence) gives a modicum of meaning to the lives of the central characters. Their longings and delusions, their paralysis and ignorance, are anticipated in the play's opening line, "Nothing to be done." The progress of the play, animated by an extraordinary blend of biblical references, broad slapstick, comic wordplay, Zenlike propositions, and crude jokes, gives life to Sartre's observation that "man first of all is the being who hurls himself toward a future" (see Reading 35.1). A parable of the existential condition, *Waiting for Godot* animates the divorce between expectation and event. At the same time (and as the brief excerpt from the end of Act Two illustrates), the play underscores the futility of communication between two frail creatures who cling (and wait) together.

READING 35.2 From Beckett's *Waiting for Godot* (1948)

Estragon: Where shall we go? 1
Vladimir: Not far.
Estragon: Oh yes, let's go far away from here.
Vladimir: We can't.

Estragon: Why not?
Vladimir: We have to come back to-morrow.
Estragon: What for?
Vladimir: To wait for Godot.
Estragon: Ah! *(Silence.)* He didn't come?
Vladimir: No. 10
Estragon: And now it's too late.
Vladimir: Yes, now it's night.
Estragon: And if we dropped him. *(Pause.)* If we dropped him?
Vladimir: He'd punish us. *(Silence. He looks at the tree.)* Everything's dead but the tree.
Estragon *(Looking at the tree)*: What is it?
Vladimir: It's the tree.
Estragon: Yes, but what kind?
Vladimir: I don't know. A willow. 20
(Estragon draws Vladimir towards the tree. They stand motionless before it. Silence.)
Estragon: Why don't we hang ourselves?
Vladimir: With what?
Estragon: You haven't got a bit of rope?
Vladimir: No.
Estragon: Then we can't.
(Silence.)
Vladimir: Let's go.
Estragon: Wait, there's my belt.
Vladimir: It's too short.
Estragon: You could hang on to my legs.
Vladimir: And who'd hang on to mine? 30
Estragon: True.
Vladimir: Show all the same. *(Estragon loosens the cord that holds up his trousers which, much too big for him, fall about his ankles. They look at the cord.)* It might do at a pinch. But is it strong enough?
Estragon: We'll soon see. Here.
(They each take an end of the cord and pull. It breaks. They almost fall.)
Vladimir: Not worth a curse.
(Silence.)
Estragon: You say we have to come back to-morrow?
Vladimir: Yes.
Estragon: Then we can bring a good bit of rope. 40
Vladimir: Yes.
(Silence.)
Estragon: Didi.
Vladimir: Yes.
Estragon: I can't go on like this.
Vladimir: That's what you think.
Estragon: If we parted? That might be better for us.
Vladimir: We'll hang ourselves tomorrow. *(Pause.)* Unless Godot comes.
Estragon: And if he comes?
Vladimir: We'll be saved. 50
(Vladimir takes off his hat (Lucky's), peers inside it, feels about inside it, shakes it, knocks on the crown, puts it on again.)
Estragon: Well? Shall we go?
Vladimir: Pull on your trousers.
Estragon: What?
Vladimir: Pull on your trousers.

Estragon: You want me to pull off my trousers?

Vladimir: Pull ON your trousers.

Estragon *(Realizing his trousers are down)*: True. *(He pulls up his trousers.)*

Vladimir: Well? Shall we go?

Estragon: Yes, let's go.   60

(They do not move.)

(Curtain.)

— **Q** What aspects of "the absurd" are communicated in this reading?

— **Q** Do the two protagonists differ in personality?

Poetry at Mid-Century: Dylan Thomas

Dylan Thomas (1914–1953) took a thoughtful attitude toward the modern condition, which he viewed as a mere stopping point between birth and death. Calling himself a Welshman first and a drunkard second, he became famous in America for his rhapsodic public readings and for the sheer musicality of his poetry. His poem "Do Not Go Gentle Into That Good Night," published just after the death of his father in 1951, makes a plea for life-affirming action even in the face of death. Thomas creates a rhythmic litany with the phrases "wise men," "good men," "wild men," "grave men"—resolving four of the six stanzas with the imperative: "rage against the dying of the light." The reference to those "who see with blinding sight" was probably inspired by the loss of vision that the poet's schoolteacher father suffered during his last years of life, but it also may be taken as an allusion to his father's agnosticism, that is, to his spiritual blindness—and, more generally, to the mood of alienation afflicting a generation of modern disbelievers. In 1954, Igor Stravinsky used this poem as the basis for *In Memoriam Dylan Thomas*, a piece written for tenor, string orchestra, and two trombones.

— **READING 35.3** Thomas' "Do Not Go Gentle Into That Good Night" (1951)

Do not go gentle into that good night,   1
Old age should burn and rave at close of day;
Rage, rage against the dying of the light.

Though wise men at their end know dark is right,
Because their words had forked no lightning they   5
Do not go gentle into that good night.

Good men, the last wave by, crying how bright
Their frail deeds might have danced in a green bay,
Rage, rage against the dying of the light.

Wild men who caught and sang the sun in flight,   10
And learn, too late, they grieved it on its way,
Do not go gentle into that good night.

Grave men, near death, who see with blinding sight
Blind eyes could blaze like meteors and be gay,

Rage, rage against the dying of the light.   15
And you, my father, there on the sad height,
Curse, bless, me now with your fierce tears, I pray.
Do not go gentle into that good night.
Rage, rage against the dying of the light.

— **Q** How does Thomas use the imagery of light and dark in this poem?

— **Q** Does religious faith play any part here?

Rabindranath Tagore

In contrast with Thomas, the poet Rabindranath Tagore (1861–1941) saw a world in spiritual deterioration. For Tagore, the crisis of modern society lay in a set of misplaced values that prized the rush of business and the acquisition of material comforts at the expense of beauty, creativity, and spiritual harmony. Born in Bengal, India (while the province was still under British control), Tagore was raised in a family of artists, musicians, and social reformers. After a brief stay in England, he returned to India, where he became a prolific writer, publishing some sixty volumes of poetry, plays, stories, and novels.

In India, Tagore pursued his ambition to foster a "spiritual unity of all races" by founding an international educational institute for the exchange of ideas between Western scholars and Indian students. Awarded the Nobel Prize in literature in 1913, Tagore left a body of writings that offers an Eastern, and specifically Hindu, approach to the modern quest for meaning. In his narrative poem "The Man Had No Useful Work," he deals with the existential responsibility for individual choice. This provocative allegory questions the value of the practical, goal-oriented pursuits that drive most modern societies. It also plays on the ironic possibility that works of art may be both meaningless and essential.

— **READING 35.4** Tagore's "The Man Had No Useful Work" (1921)

The man had no useful work, only vagaries of various kinds.   1
Therefore it surprised him to find himself in Paradise after a
   life spent perfecting trifles.
Now the guide had taken him by mistake to the wrong
Paradise—one meant only for good, busy souls.

In this Paradise, our man saunters along the road only to
   obstruct the rush of business.
He stands aside from the path and is warned that he tramples
   on sown seed. Pushed, he starts up: hustled, he moves on.   5
A very busy girl comes to fetch water from the well. Her feet
   run on the pavement like rapid fingers over harp-strings.
   Hastily she ties a negligent knot with her hair, and loose
   locks on her forehead pry into the dark of her eyes.
The man says to her, "Would you lend me your pitcher?"
"My pitcher?" she asks, "to draw water?"
"No, to paint patterns on."
"I have no time to waste," the girl retorts in contempt.   10

Now a busy soul has no chance against one who is supremely
    idle.
Every day she meets him at the well, and every day he repeats
    the same request, till at last she yields.
Our man paints the pitcher with curious colors in a mysterious
    maze of lines.
The girl takes it up, turns it round and asks, "What does it mean?
"It has no meaning," he answers.   15

The girl carries the pitcher home. She holds it up in different
    lights and tries to con its mystery.
At night she leaves her bed, lights a lamp, and gazes at it from
    all points of view.
This is the first time she has met with something without
    meaning.

On the next day the man is again near the well.
The girl asks, "What do you want?"   20
"To do more work for you!"
"What work?" she enquires.
"Allow me to weave colored strands into a ribbon to bind your
    hair."
"Is there any need?" she asks.
"None whatever," he allows.   25
The ribbon is made, and thenceforward she spends a great
    deal of time over her hair.

The even stretch of well-employed time in that Paradise
    begins to show irregular rents.
The elders are troubled; they meet in council.
The guide confesses his blunder, saying that he has brought
    the wrong man to the wrong place.
The wrong man is called. His turban, flaming with color,
    shows plainly how great that blunder has been.   30
The chief of the elders says, "You must go back to the earth."
The man heaves a sigh of relief: "I am ready."
The girl with the ribbon round her hair chimes in: "I also!"
For the first time the chief of the elders is faced with a
    situation which has no sense in it.

Q **What does each figure in Tagore's allegory
represent?**

Q **Is there a "moral" to this story?**

The Visual Arts at Mid-Century

 The major figure in postwar
European art was the Dublin-born
painter Francis Bacon (1909–
1992). Self-trained, Bacon infused
European Expressionism with an
eccentric approach to form that turned human and animal
figures into flayed carcasses and mangled skeletons. Like
a sorcerer, he transformed his favorite images from film,
magazine illustrations, and the history of art into grotesque
and deformed (but sensuously painted) icons.

Bacon had never seen the original portrait of Pope
Innocent X executed in 1650 by Diego Velázquez (see

Figure 35.2 FRANCIS BACON, *Head VI*, 1949. Oil on canvas, 36¾ × 30¼ in.
The painting has become an icon of existential despair. The pope's gaping mouth
was inspired by the screaming woman from the Odessa Steps sequence in
Eisenstein's *Battleship Potemkin* (see Figure 34.11), and by graphic illustrations
of diseases of the mouth in a book the artist had purchased in Paris.

chapter 21); however, he owned many reproductions of
the work and was haunted by the lonely presence of its
subject. Painting more than twenty-five versions of the
portrait, Bacon imprisoned the figure in a transparent
cage, immobilized by ambiguous lines of force (Figure
35.2). The venerable pope became a visceral expression
of anguish and alienation. His silent scream, a logo for
despiritualized Modernism, looks back to Munch (Figure
33.2), Eisenstein (Figure 34.11), and Picasso (Figure 34.9),
all of whom Bacon admired.

Abstract Expressionism

For hundreds of years, almost all important new styles in
painting had originated in Paris or other European cities.
After 1945, however, the United States, and New York City
in particular, took the lead with a radical new style called
Abstract Expressionism. Abstract Expressionism had its roots
in the Modernist assault on traditional, representational
art. It took inspiration from the reductionist abstractions
of Picasso and Matisse, the colorist experiments of Wassily
Kandinsky, the nonsensical performances of Dada, and the
"automatic" art of the Surrealists. The new style embraced
the role of chance with existential fervor; it also seemed
resonant of the quantum physicist's description of the universe as a series of continuously shifting random patterns.
Whether or not such theories directly influenced the visual

arts, they paralleled the experiments in random art that occurred at this time.

In America, Abstract Expressionism ushered in the so-called heroic age of American painting. The pioneers of the movement were a group of talented immigrants who had escaped Nazi oppression and the perils of war-torn Europe. These artists included Arshile Gorky (1905–1948), Hans Hofmann (1880–1966), and Willem de Kooning (1904–1997), all of whom moved to New York between 1920 and 1930. Working on large canvases and using oversized brushes, paint was applied in a loose, free, and instinctive manner that emphasized the physical gesture—the very *act* of painting.

Abstract Expressionist paintings are usually nonrepresentational, but where recognizable subject matter appears, as in de Kooning's series of fierce, totemic women—one of his favorite subjects—it is rendered with frenzied, subjective urgency (Figure **35.3**). De Kooning's wide-eyed females, with their huge breasts and toothy grins, were thought by some to reflect a negative view of women. Actually, however, they took their inspiration from Sumerian votive sculptures and Earth Mother images (see Figures 0.4 and 1.2). De Kooning joked that his women were the sisters of popular pin-ups and billboard goddesses, celebrated for their vacant "American smile."

By contrast, the huge black-and-white canvases of Franz Kline (1910–1962) consist entirely of imposing, abstract shapes. Although wholly nonrepresentational, they call to mind the powerful angularity of bridges, steel mills, and other monuments of postwar urban expansion (Figure **35.4**). Kline, who used housepainters' brushes on canvases that often measured over 10 feet square, achieved a sense of rugged immediacy (which he called "snap").

Figure 35.3 WILLEM DE KOONING, *Woman and Bicycle*, 1952–1953. Oil, enamel, and charcoal on linen, 6 ft. 4½ in. × 4 ft. 1 in. Despite what seem to be urgent and spontaneous brushstrokes, the painting required more than eighteen months of effort, during which the artist repeatedly laid on, scraped away, and restored color to the canvas.

Figure 35.4 FRANZ KLINE, *Mahoning*, 1956. Oil and paper collage on canvas, 6 ft. 8 in. × 8 ft. 4 in.

For centuries, Japan's Zen masters practiced calligraphy, an art that was revived in the eighteenth century (see chapter 21). Executed with large brushes dipped in black ink, Zen paintings were acts of meditation that required concentration and focus, and an intuitive balance of improvisation and control (Figure **35.5**). Usually confined to silk or paper scrolls no more than 4 or 5 feet in length, these calligraphic works convey the vigor of larger paintings like those of the Abstract Expressionists (see Figure 35.4). While the latter may not have been directly influenced by the Zen masters, they were probably aware of the radical Japanese postwar group known as

Figure 35.5 TOREI ENJI, *Calligraphic Talisman*, late eighteenth century. Sumi on paper, 4 ft. 2¾ in. × 10⅞ in.

the Gutai Bijutsu Kyokai (Concrete Art Association). The indirect heirs of the Zen masters, the Gutai sponsored "action events" that harnessed physical action to chance. Their performances featured the spontaneous and occasionally outrageous manipulation of paint, which might be flung or hurled at the canvas. Like America's Abstract Expressionists, the Gutai achieved an unmediated encounter between artist, gesture, and materials.

Pollock

The best known of the Abstract Expressionists is Wyoming-born Jackson Pollock (1912–1956). His early paintings reveal a coarse figural style and brutal brushwork similar to de Kooning's, but by 1945 Pollock had devised a technique that made action itself the subject of the painting. Instead of mounting the canvas on an easel, he strapped it to the floor of his studio and proceeded to drip, splash, pour, and spread oil, enamel, and commercial aluminum paints across its surface (Figure **35.6**). Layered filaments of paint—the

artist's seductive "handwriting"—mingled with sand, nails, matches, bottle shards, and occasional cigarette butts.

Pollock's daring new method, which came to be called *action painting*, allowed him (as he explained) "to walk around [the canvas], work from the four sides and literally be *in* the painting," a method inspired by the healing rituals of Navajo sand painting whose union of intuition, improvisation, and rigorous control he admired. "It seems to me," he observed, "that the modern painter cannot express his age, the airplane, the atom bomb, the radio, in

Figure 35.6 Jackson Pollock at work in his Long Island studio, 1950.

the old forms of the Renaissance or of any other past culture. Each age finds its own technique." Pollock's canvases are baffling studies in sensation, density, and rhythm, but they are apt metaphors for an age that defined physical reality in terms of process, uncertainty, and chance. Like

the currents in some cosmic whirlpool, the galactic paint threads of *Autumn Rhythm* (Figure **35.7**) seem to expand beyond the limits of the canvas, as if to mirror postwar theories of quantum forces in an expanding universe. Pollock viewed each of his works of art as having a life of its own, but he insisted that *he* controlled its direction: "There is no accident, just as there is no beginning and no end."

Color-Field Painting

One variety of Abstract Expressionism, known as *color-field painting*, involved the application of large, often transparent layers of paint to the surface of the canvas. The paintings of Mark Rothko (1903–1970) consist of translucent, soft-edged blocks of color that float mysteriously on the surfaces of yet other fields of color (see Figure **35.1**). These huge, iconic compositions derive their sensuous power from the subtle interaction of rich layers of paint, which seem to glow from within. Rothko experienced the existential alienation of the postwar era. He claimed to express in his work the basic human emotions: "tragedy, ecstasy, and doom." "The people who weep before my pictures are having the same religious experience I had when I painted them," he contended; "if you . . . are moved only by their color relationships, then you miss the point." Rothko took his own life in 1970.

While Rothko's abstract shapes are usually self-contained, those of Helen Frankenthaler (1928–2011) tend to swell and expand like exotic blooms (Figure **35.8**). Frankenthaler cultivated the practice of pouring thin washes of paint directly from coffee tins onto raw or **unprimed** (without gesso undercoat) canvas. Her lyrical

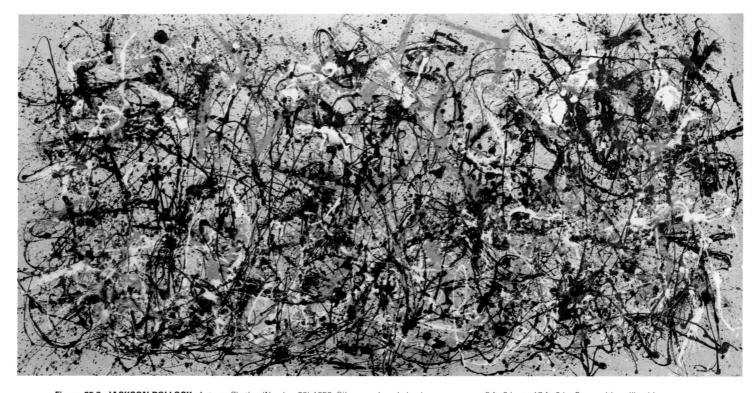

Figure 35.7 JACKSON POLLOCK, *Autumn Rhythm (Number 30)*, 1950. Oil, enamel, and aluminum on canvas, 8 ft. 9 in. × 17 ft. 3 in. Compositions like this one anticipated some of the photographs of outer space taken in the mid-1990s by the Hubble space telescope.

Figure 35.8 HELEN FRANKENTHALER, *Before the Caves*, 1958. Oil on canvas, 8 ft. 6⅛ in. × 8 ft. 8⅜ in.

compositions, often heroic in scale, capture the transparent freshness of watercolors.

In a culture increasingly dominated by mass mechanization, American Abstractionists asserted their preference for an art that was gestural, personal, and spontaneous. The *process* of making art was becoming as important as the *product*. At the same time, these artists seemed to turn their backs on bourgeois taste by creating artworks that were simply too large to hang in the average living room. As the movement developed, in fact, the size of the canvas grew as if to accommodate the heroic ambitions of the artists themselves. Ironically, however, these artworks, which scorned the depersonalizing effects of capitalist technology, came to be prized by the guardians of that very technology. Abstract Expressionist paintings, which now hang in corporate offices, hotels, banks, and sanctuaries (such as Houston's nondenominational Rothko Chapel), have become hallmarks of modern sophistication.

Hopper's America

The Abstract Expressionists represented a decisive break with the Realist tradition in American painting and with Social Realism in particular. Nevertheless, throughout the century, representational art continued to flourish. The paintings of the New York artist Edward Hopper (1882–1967), for instance, present a figurative view of an urban America that is bleak and empty of meaningful relationships. Hopper's fondness for American cinema and theater is reflected in oddly cropped, artificially lit compositions that often resemble film stills. Like the film still, Hopper's frozen moments seem to belong to a larger, existential narrative. In *Nighthawks* (Figure **35.9**), Hopper depicts a

Figure 35.9 EDWARD HOPPER, *Nighthawks*, 1942. Oil on canvas, 2 ft. 9⅛ in. × 5 ft. ⅛ in. Hopper was notorious for painting the joyless, mundane activities of everyday urban life. A native New Yorker, he reported that his inspiration for this melancholy scene was a restaurant on the wedge-shaped corner of Greenwich Avenue and West Eleventh and Twelfth streets.

Figure 35.10 ALBERTO GIACOMETTI, *City Square (La Place)*, 1948. Bronze, 8½ × 25⅜ × 17¼ in. The isolation of each individual (on what might be an urban street) is conveyed by the fact that no figure, if extended in its forward movement, would encounter another figure in the spatial field.

harshly lit all-night diner, whose occupants share the same small space but little intimacy. His characters, estranged and isolated from one another in the mundane interiors of "one-night cheap hotels" and "sawdust restaurants," call to mind Eliot's Prufrock (see Reading 32.2).

Sculpture at Mid-Century

Giacometti

The mood of existential anxiety also dominated international sculpture. What the art critic Herbert Read called a "geometry of fear" is evident in the figurative and non-figurative sculpture of the Swiss artist Alberto Giacometti (1901–1966). In 1930, Giacometti came under the influence of Surrealism, but in the postwar era he devised a new language with which to describe the human figure and the human condition. In both small and large clay works, thereafter cast in bronze, he transformed figurative subjects into haunting, spindly creatures that seem to symbolize existential solitude (Figure **35.10**). Giacometti's disengaged and ravaged figures were greatly admired by Sartre, who wrote the introduction to the catalogue for the artist's one-man exhibition in New York City in 1948. Giacometti's ties to Existentialist writers secured his commission to design the set for the original production of Beckett's *Waiting for Godot*.

Segal

In America, the haunting works of George Segal (1924–2000) captured the modern mood of alienation. Segal devised a unique method of constructing life-sized figures from plaster casts of live models—often friends and members of his own family. He installed these ghostly replicas in mundane settings staged with ordinary, uncast props:

Figure 35.11 GEORGE SEGAL, *Bus Riders*, 1962. Plaster, cotton gauze, steel, wood, and vinyl, 5 ft. 10 in. × 3 ft. 6⅜ in. × 7 ft. 6¾ in. Segal used actual plaster-bandage casts of the models in his early sculptures. Later, he began painting them with bright colors; and finally, they were cast in bronze with a white patina to resemble the original ghostly plaster.

barstools, streetlights, beds, bus seats (Figure **35.11**). These "assembled environments," as he called them, allowed Segal to comment on matters of alienation, social injustice, and the failure of communication in modern life. Stylistically, Segal's tableaux link the tradition of Realist sculpture to the Pop and performance-art movements of the later twentieth and twenty-first centuries (see chapter 37).

Smith

The nonfigurative sculpture of the postwar era shared the improvisatory vitality of Abstract Expressionist painting. American sculptors, exploiting such industrial materials as welded iron and steel, constructed iconic abstractions that were monumental in size and dynamic in spirit. Among the pioneers of *constructed sculpture* was the Midwestern artist David Smith (1906–1965). Smith learned to weld while at

Figure 35.12 DAVID SMITH, *Cubi XII*, 1963. Stainless steel, height 9 ft. 1⅝ in. Smith made cardboard maquettes of each *Cubi* from old liquor cartons before transposing them into stainless steel forms. He likened the marks on the burnished surfaces to brushstrokes.

college, during a summer job at an automobile plant, and he mastered a variety of other industrial processes while working in a wartime locomotive factory. His early pieces were large welded iron forms sprayed with multiple layers of automobile enamel. Between 1961 and 1965, he constructed the twenty-eight boxlike stainless steel forms (the "Cubi" series), whose surfaces he burnished and scraped with motorized tools so that they reflected the colors of their surroundings (Figure **35.12**).

Smith forged a new structural style based on industrial techniques. His heroic forms share the calligraphic energy of Franz Kline's gestural abstractions: they capture a sense of aggressive movement that animates the space around them. While the efforts of Giacometti and Segal may reflect existential despair, Smith's sculptures symbolize the optimistic spirit of postwar America. "The metal itself," he insisted, "possesses little art history. What associations it possesses are those of this century: power, structure, movement, progress, suspension, destruction, brutality."

Calder

The American sculptor Alexander Calder (1898–1976) was a contemporary of the Surrealists, whom he met in Paris in 1926. Influenced by the work of Duchamp and Miró, Calder created abstract wire constructions. These he motorized or hung from ceilings so that they floated freely in the air. Calder's wind-driven mobiles, which range from a few inches in size to enormous proportions, take advantage of the "chance" effects of air currents to create constantly changing relationships between volumes and voids, that is, between brightly colored, biomorphic aluminum shapes and the surrounding space (Figure **35.13**).

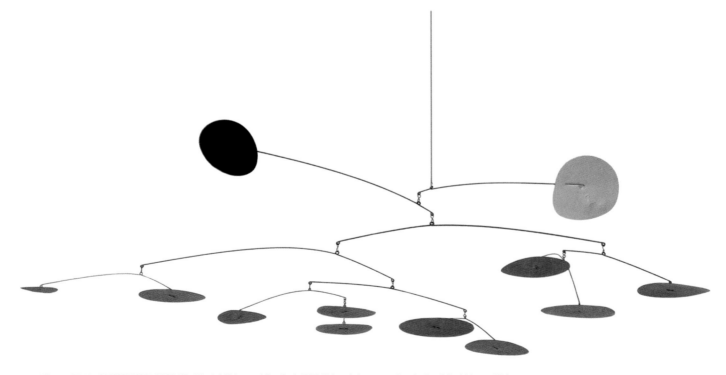

Figure 35.13 ALEXANDER CALDER, *Black, White, and Ten Red*, 1957. Painted sheet metal and wire, 2 ft. 11 in. × 12 ft.

Film at Mid-Century

In the postwar era, filmmakers took a number of new directions. In Italy, the *Neorealism* of Roberto Rossellini (1906–1977) probed the bitter consequences of Fascism. With the film *Open City* (1945), Rossellini replaced the cinema of entertainment with a brutal new genre that chronicled human tragedies as if they were natural disasters. Wedded to Realism in both style and substance, Rossellini employed nonprofessional actors and filmed entirely on location. Neorealist cinema self-consciously rejected the artifice of cinematic moralizing and Hollywood "staging," seeking instead to depict the harsh reality of commonplace existence.

A second direction in postwar film appeared in the form of *film noir*, a cinematic style (especially popular in Germany, France, and America) that dealt with the dark world of crime and intrigue. Unlike the gangster movies of the 1930s, film noir conveyed a mood of disillusion and resignation proceeding from moral ambiguity between good and evil. In the American film *Double Indemnity* (1944), the *femme fatale* (the dangerous, seductive woman) made one of her earliest cinematic appearances. And in the film noir classic *A Touch of Evil* (1958), the multitalented director and actor Orson Welles (1915–1985) used long takes (shots of twenty or more seconds), high and low camera positions, and off-center compositions to create sinister characters and ominous settings.

A third film genre, the *thriller*, dominated by the impresario Alfred Hitchcock (1899–1980), depended for its impact on suspense rather than graphic violence. Hitchcock's unique combination of story and style—quick shots that alternate between the character and the (often fearful) object of his gaze—were particularly successful in such films as *Rear Window* (1954) and *Psycho* (1960).

Postwar cinema took up the quest for meaning by way of films that challenged traditional moral values. The pioneer Japanese filmmaker Akira Kurosawa (1910–1998) explored the complexity of modern life by revisiting traditional *samurai* culture (see chapter 14). A highly skilled director, he used unusual camera angles, flashbacks, and a stringent economy of expression in the classics *Rashōmon* (1950) and *The Seven Samurai* (1954). These films convey Kurosawa's utopian view that positive social action can redeem the world's evils.

Bergman

Less optimistic concerning the fate of humankind was the Swedish cinematic giant Ingmar Bergman (1918–2007). In his almost four dozen films, Bergman probed the troubled lives of modern men and women. The loss of God, the acknowledgment of spiritual and emotional alienation, and the anxiety that accompanies self-understanding are his principal themes. Bergman's most notable films are *The Seventh Seal* (1956), *Wild Strawberries* (1957), and *Persona* (1966). His landmark work, *The Seventh Seal*, is an allegorical tale of despair in the face of impending death. Set in medieval Europe (and inspired by the Revelation of Saint John in the New Testament), it is the story of a knight who returns home from the Crusades, only to confront widespread plague and human suffering. Disillusioned, he ultimately challenges Death to a game of chess, the stakes of which are life itself. Bergman compared filmmaking to composing music: a non-narrative and largely intuitive enterprise. His apocalyptic visions, translated to film, proceeded from what he called "the administration of the unspeakable."

Architecture at Mid-Century

By the middle of the twentieth century, public architecture assumed a distinctly international character. The principles of International Style architecture, based on the use of structural steel, ferroconcrete, and glass, had gained popularity through the influence of Bauhaus-trained architects and Le Corbusier (see chapter 32). Standardization and machinelike efficiency became the hallmarks of high-rise urban apartment buildings, constructed in their thousands to provide low-rent housing in the decades after 1930. In the building of schools, factories, and offices, the simplicity and austerity of the International Style echoed the mood of depersonalization that prevailed in the arts. International Style skyscrapers became symbols of corporate wealth and modern technocracy. They reflected the materialism of the twentieth century as powerfully as the Gothic cathedral summed up the spirituality of the High Middle Ages.

Mies van der Rohe

Among the most daring of the International Style proponents was the Dutch architect (and the last director of the Bauhaus) Ludwig Mies van der Rohe (1886–1969). Mies' credo, "Less is more," inspired such austere structures as the Seagram Building in New York City, designed in partnership with Philip Johnson (1906–2005) in 1958 (Figure **35.14**). This sleek, unadorned slab of metallic bronze and amber glass was "the last word" in sophisticated machine engineering and a monument to the "form follows function" credo of the International Style. The proportions of the building are as impeccable as those of any Classical structure: the raised level at the bottom is balanced at the top by a four-story band of darker glass. For decades, the Seagram Building influenced glass-and-steel-box architecture; unfortunately, in many of its imitators, it was the cool, impersonal quality of the building and not its poetic simplicity that prevailed.

At mid-century, some of the world's leading architects reacted against the strict geometry and functional purism

Figure 35.14 LUDWIG MIES VAN DER ROHE, Seagram Building, New York, 1954–1958. Metallic bronze and amber glass.

of International Style architecture. Instead, they provided subjective, personal, and even romantic alternatives to the cool rationalism of the International Style. Using the medium of cast concrete, they created organically shaped structures that were as gestural as the sculptures of Smith and as lyrical as the paintings of Frankenthaler. The Trans World Airlines Terminal at New York's Kennedy Airport (Figure **35.15**), for example, designed by the Finnish architect Eero Saarinen (1910–1961), is a metaphor for flight: its cross-vaulted roof—a steel structure surfaced with concrete—flares upward like a gigantic bird. The interior of the terminal unfolds gradually and mysteriously to embrace fluid, uninterrupted space.

Wright at Mid-Century

One of the most original minds of the twentieth century, Frank Lloyd Wright had produced notable examples of domestic architecture as early as 1909 (see Figures 32.20 and 32.21). At mid-century, he designed one of the most unique buildings in America: the Guggenheim Museum in New York City. An architectural landmark that contrasts vividly with Manhattan's typically boxy vertical buildings, the museum is configured as a ribbon of white ferroconcrete that winds into a cylindrical shape, narrowing from top to bottom. Its interior, which resembles the inside of a huge snail shell, consists of a continuous spiral ramp fixed around a central well and 96-foot-high skylight (Figure **35.16**). A clear glass dome at the top allows natural light to bathe the interior, whose breathtaking enclosure competes seductively with most of the artwork exhibited therein. A ten-story limestone extension added in 1992 has reduced the dramatic contrast between the rotunda and its urban

Figure 35.15 EERO SAARINEN, Trans World Airlines Terminal, Kennedy Airport, New York, 1962.

Figure 35.16 FRANK LLOYD WRIGHT, The Solomon R. Guggenheim Museum interior, 1957–1959. Objecting to the problems associated with hanging paintings on walls that are not strictly vertical, Willem de Kooning and twenty other artists wrote a letter refusing to show their works in the museum. In 1992, traditionally configured rooms and an adjacent tower were added to Wright's original design.

Figure 35.17 FRANK LLOYD WRIGHT, The Solomon R. Guggenheim Museum, New York, 1957–1959.

Figure 35.18 RICHARD BUCKMINSTER FULLER, geodesic dome, U.S. Pavilion, Montreal International Exposition, 1967. The original dome, which served as the United States Pavilion at Expo '67, was 250 feet in diameter and 200 feet high. In 1976, a fire destroyed the acrylic surface but left the lattice frame of the dome, which has since been restored.

setting, but it does not destroy the eloquence of the original design (Figure **35.17**). The Guggenheim remains the definitive example of the modern architectural imagination.

Fuller

The architectural visionary and pioneer environmentalist Richard Buckminster Fuller (1895–1983) saw few of his futuristic ideas realized in tangible form. Fuller was ahead of his time in realizing that the earth's resources are finite and the planet (which he called "spaceship Earth") is a fragile entity. His campaigns for energy-efficient, affordable housing inspired one of the earliest prefabricated house designs: the Dymaxion (1927), a metal structure hung from a central mast with outer walls of continuous glass.

Fuller is best known for his **geodesic domes**, which depend on the tensile properties of lightweight triangular elements. This type of construction, which uses a minimum of structure to create maximum strength, could be mass-produced cheaply and flown anywhere by helicopter to provide instant shelter. Like the Dymaxion, the geodesic dome that he designed for the International Exposition of 1967 in Montreal (Figure **35.18**) had little impact on architectural construction until the end of the twentieth century (see Figure 37.22).

Music and Dance at Mid-Century

Cage

The most inventive figure in mid-twentieth-century music was the American composer John Cage (1912–1992). Cage styled himself as a student of architecture and gardening, and a devotee of Zen Buddhism. He studied with Arnold Schoenberg (see chapter 32), who described him as an inventor, rather than a composer. A leading spokesman for experimentation, Cage once defined music as a combination of sounds (specific pitches), noise (nonpitched sounds), and silence, with rhythm as the common denominator. "Everything we do is music," he insisted.

In 1938, Cage invented the prepared piano, a traditional Steinway piano modified by attaching to its strings pieces of rubber, bamboo slats, bolts, and other objects. When played, the prepared piano becomes something like a percussion instrument, the sounds of which resemble those of a Balinese orchestra; as Cage observed, "a percussive orchestra under the control of a single player." The *Sonata V* (1948), written for the prepared piano, belongs to a series of sixteen sonatas and four interludes that reflect the

♪ See Music Listening Selections at end of chapter.

composer's introduction to Indian music and philosophy. These early compositions are delicate in timbre and texture and elegant in percussive rhythms.

Cage's later works were radically experimental, especially in their effort to accommodate silence and nonpitched sound. In 1953, Cage composed *4′ 33″*, a piece in which a performer sits motionless before the piano for four minutes and thirty-three seconds. The "music" of *4′ 33″* consists of the fleeting, random sounds that occur during the designated time period—the breathing of the pianist, the shuffling of the audience's feet, or the distant hum of traffic outside the concert hall.

Much of Cage's music is **aleatory**, that is, based on chance or random procedures. To determine the placement of notes in a musical composition, Cage might apply the numbers dictated in a throw of the dice or incorporate the surface stains and imperfections on an otherwise blank piece of sheet music. He found inspiration for these techniques in Zen Buddhism, in the *I jing* (China's ancient oracular *Book of Changes*), and in the psychic automatism of the Surrealists. Accident and chance were basic to his *Imaginary Landscape No. 4* (1951), a composition that calls for twelve radios playing simultaneously with twenty-four performers (two at each radio) randomly turning the volume and selector controls. Such antimusical music celebrates the absurd and random nature of the modern experience. At the same time, it blurs the traditional relationship between composers and performers, and between artistic conception and execution. Nevertheless, despite Cage's chance methods, each of his compositions is fully scored: even the most unconventional passages follow his explicit directions. These "scored improvisations" acknowledge the existential credo that every creative act involves choice. The decision to operate at random (whether by a roll of the dice, a toss of coins, or some other method), even the decision *not* to act, represents a choice.

Cage's avant-garde methods, as publicized in his numerous essays and lectures, have had an enormous influence on younger artists well into the twenty-first century. His "chance" aesthetic inspired the international Neodada movement known as *Fluxus*. Fluxus artists, writers, filmmakers, and musicians experimented with minimal, performance-oriented works that left the viewer to complete the work of art.

Cunningham

In the mid-1940s, Cage met the American choreographer Merce Cunningham (1922–2009) and the young painter Robert Rauschenberg (1925–2008; see chapter 37). At Black Mountain College in Asheville, North Carolina, they collaborated in staging performances that employed improvisational techniques and inventive combinations of dance, mime, poetry, music, photographic projections, and film.

Cunningham's contribution to modern choreography stems from his radical disassociation of music and dance. Rejecting the narrative, storytelling dance style of his teacher Martha Graham (see chapter 32), he concentrated exclusively on movement and form. In a Cunningham piece, dance may proceed without music, or music may coexist with dance, but the tempo of the music may be wholly irrelevant to the movements of the dancers. Cunningham disclaimed traditional dance positions and ignored traditional staging (whereby dancers are assigned to specific spaces). The number of dancers and the length of time they would dance might be determined by the methods of chance employed by his life partner, John Cage, and his choreography called for clean, expansive body gestures that occupied large, spatial fields. Like a Pollock painting or a Cage composition, a Cunningham performance might unfold along a broad continuum, lacking a fixed center. All body movements (even the ordinary actions of running, jumping, and falling) are treated equally; and such movements may occur by way of improvisation or—as with the music of Cage—by chance. Nevertheless, as with Cage's compositions, even improvisation is planned (or choreographed) by the artist.

One of Cunningham's early works, entitled *Summerspace* (1958), shared the raw energy and spontaneity that typified the canvases of the Abstract Expressionists (Figure **35.19**). In this multimedia piece, Cunningham explored the tension between chance and choice and between freedom and control, that lies at the heart of existential expression.

Figure 35.19 MERCE CUNNINGHAM, *Summerspace,* 1958. Cage became director of Cunningham's dance company, founded in 1953. With Rauschenberg, who designed the sets and costumes for *Summerspace,* he and Cunningham produced some of the most innovative mixed-media performances of the predigital era.

The Cold War

- Alienation and anxiety were two of the principal conditions of the postwar mentality.
- Following World War II, a contest for world domination known as the "cold war" determined the course of international relations. Two seemingly incompatible ideologies, communism and capitalism, competed for prominence in the global arena.
- Capitalism found its roots in Adam Smith's free market philosophy, while communism gave a central state the power to distribute wealth equally.

Existentialism

- Existentialism, a humanistic philosophy formulated by Jean-Paul Sartre, emphasized the role of individual choice in a world that lacked moral absolutes.
- Both secular and Christian Existentialism charged human beings with full responsibility for their freely chosen actions.

Literature at Mid-Century

- Twentieth-century writers gave voice to the existential challenge and to the anguish produced by the individual's freedom to choose. Pessimists feared the destructive potential of modern technology and anticipated the demise of human freedom.
- Modern antiheroes, such as the burlesque tramps in Samuel Beckett's theater-of-the-absurd *Waiting for Godot*, contend with the despair of making choices in an essentially meaningless universe. Their survival seems to depend upon an authentic commitment to action.
- Asian writers such as Rabindranath Tagore pursued the quest for meaning in parts of the world where Modernism did as much to threaten as to reshape tradition.

The Visual Arts at Mid-Century

- In the visual arts, the center of gravity shifted from Paris to New York City. The movement known as Abstract Expressionism marked a heroic effort at self-actualization through the gestural and often brutal application of paint to canvas.
- The action paintings of Jackson Pollock and the color-field paintings of Helen Frankenthaler and Mark Rothko explore the dynamic balance between chance and choice.

Sculpture at Mid-Century

- Existential anxiety characterizes the sculptures of Alberto Giacometti and George Segal, whose figures evoke a mood of alienation, even as they occupy the crowded urban environment.
- David Smith's large-scale works introduced industrial techniques to abstract sculptures fabricated in iron and stainless steel.

Film at Mid-Century

- Italian director Roberto Rossellini's Neorealist style used nonprofessional actors and on-site filming to depict reality at its fullest.
- The film noir genre dealt with the dark, moral ambiguities of the criminal world. Alfred Hitchcock's thrillers focused on suspense rather than graphic violence.
- Masters of postwar films, Akira Kurosawa and Ingmar Bergman questioned traditional moral values, often using allegory to probe states of disillusion and despair.

Architecture at Mid-Century

- The International Style in architecture culminated in classic glass-box skyscrapers; despite some exceptions, these buildings reinforced the impersonal nature of the modern urban community.
- Buckminster Fuller's geodesic dome and a new wave of seductive ferroconcrete buildings, exemplified in Frank Lloyd Wright's Guggenheim Museum, challenged the austerity of the International Style.

Music and Dance at Mid-Century

- In the domains of music and dance, as in the visual arts, the postwar generation took the absence of absolutes as the starting point for free experimentation.
- John Cage, the foremost member of the musical avant-garde, integrated silence, noise, and chance into his compositions.
- Merce Cunningham redefined modern dance as movement stripped of both thematic and musical associations.

Music Listening Selection

- Cage, *Sonata V*, 1948, excerpt.

Glossary

aleatory (Latin, *alea*, "dice") any kind of music composed according to chance or random procedures

geodesic dome a spherical structure formed by lightweight elements held in tension

unprimed lacking the gesso undercoat that is normally applied to the surface of the canvas

Chapter

36

Liberation and Equality

ca. 1930–present

"This world is white no longer, and it will never be white again."
James Baldwin

Figure 36.1 KEHINDE WILEY, *World Stage Series*, 2011–2012. Oil and enamel on canvas, 96 × 72 in. Wiley photographs his subjects (usually attired in street clothes) before painting them. His studio assistants apply the ornamental tendrils that enmesh the figures in a brightly colored tapestry.

While the mood of despair pervaded much of the postwar era, a second, more positive spirit fueled movements to achieve liberation and equality in many parts of the world. Two major liberation movements marked the second half of the twentieth century. The first involved efforts on the part of colonial nations to secure political, economic, religious, and ethnic independence. It also aimed to reduce poverty and raise standards of living in the world's industrially underdeveloped nations, thus bringing them to the productive status of nations with more highly developed economies.

The second movement for liberation, fired by opposition to age-old social injustice and ingrained prejudice, involved the demand for racial, ethnic, and gender equality. Engaging worldwide participation, the movement embraced a lengthy struggle for civil rights in the African-American population of the United States, the demand for equality among feminists throughout the West, and a recognition of the inequalities suffered by those of untraditional sexual orientation.

The movements for liberation and equality—colonial, racial, and sexual—provided the context for some of the most significant literature, art, and music of the twentieth and twenty-first centuries. In the long run, all art must be judged without reference to the politics, race, or gender of the artist. Nevertheless, the works that are featured in this chapter are examined in the context of the ongoing quest for equality, a key theme in the history of the humanistic tradition.

Anticolonialism and Liberation

In the postwar era, the weakened European nations were unable to maintain the military and economic forces necessary to sustain their empires. At the same time, their colonial subjects increased their efforts to free themselves from Western rulers.

One of the earliest revolts against colonial rule took place in India. During World War I, the Indian National Congress came under the influence of the Hindu Mohandas Karamchand Gandhi (1869–1948). Gandhi, whose followers called him "Mahatma," or "great soul," led India's struggle for independence from Great Britain. Guided by the precepts of Hinduism, as well as by the Sermon on the Mount and the writings of Thoreau and Tolstoy, Gandhi initiated a policy of peaceful protest against colonial oppression. His program of nonviolent resistance, including fasting and peaceful demonstrations, influenced subsequent liberation movements throughout the world. Gandhi's involvement was crucial to India's emancipation from British control, which occurred in 1947, only one year before he was assassinated by a Hindu fanatic who opposed his conciliatory gestures toward India's Muslim minority.

Between 1944 and 1960, many nations, including Jordan, Burma, Palestine, Sri Lanka, Ghana, Malaya, Cyprus, and Nigeria, freed themselves from British rule. Syria, Lebanon, Cambodia, Laos, North and South Vietnam, Morocco, Tunisia, Cameroon, Mali, and other African states won independence from France. And still other territories claimed their freedom from the empires of the United States, Japan, the Netherlands, Belgium, and Italy.

In Central America, Southeast Asia, and elsewhere, however, internal conflicts provoked military intervention by First World powers, that is, the industrialized capitalist nations, including the United States, most of Western Europe, Japan, and Canada. Between 1964 and 1975, the United States succeeded France in an unsuccessful effort to defend South Vietnam from the incursion of communist-controlled North Vietnam. The Vietnam War—the longest war in American history—cost the lives of some 50,000 Americans and more than fifteen million Vietnamese. More recently, in Eastern Europe and parts of Russia, the demise of Soviet authority has unleashed age-old ethnic conflicts, producing fragmentation and bloodshed.

Liberation and Literature in the Islamic World

While India achieved its emancipation from British control, a related drive for liberation was underway among the members of the country's Muslim minority. The quest for an autonomous Muslim state on the Indian subcontinent resulted in the creation of an independent Pakistan in 1947. Other parts of the Islamic world, however, were not so successful. For instance, brutal massacres, riots, and revolution plagued Egypt for decades before it became an independent nation in 1971. Impeding the success of independent Muslim states was the fact that the West, even after granting them their independence, continued to influence key aspects of their economies, such as the production of oil.

Equally challenging was the process of modernization itself: specifically, the incompatibility between the agenda of modernization, focused on Western-style capitalism and democratic reform, and the fundamentals of Muslim tradition based on the Qur'an and a governing theocracy. In most parts of the Islamic world, the difficulties of introducing modern legal and constitutional innovations into centuries-old Islamic societies proved overwhelming. To this day, in fact, minority elements within the Islamic world remain in violent opposition to the culture of modernization and to Western intrusion in Muslim affairs.

If Western technology and imperialism have weighed heavily in the transition from ancient to modern times, Muslim culture has nonetheless flourished. In India, the poet and philosopher Muhammad Iqbal (1876–1938) envisioned Islam as the leading moral force in South Asia. While supporting the formation of an independent Muslim state in Pakistan, he emphasized the importance of achieving brotherhood among India's Muslim, Christian, and Hindu populations. Educated in law and philosophy at the University of Oxford, Iqbal anticipated a pan-Islamic community that transcended ethnic, racial, and national loyalties. He urged his followers to replace Islamic mysticism and passive contemplation with an activist spirit. In his poems, he gave voice to the despair felt by Muslims who viewed imperialism and Modernism as twin threats to spirituality and divine law.

READING 36.1 Islamic Poems

Iqbal's "Revolution" (1938)

Death to man's soul is Europe, death is Asia
To man's will: neither feels the vital current.
In man's hearts stirs a revolution's torrent;
Maybe our old world too is nearing death.

Iqbal's "Europe and Syria" (1936)

This land of Syria gave the West a Prophet
Of purity and pity and innocence;
And Syria from the West as recompense
Gets dice and drink and troops of prostitutes.

Q Based on the evidence of these two poems, how would you describe the Muslim response to Western values?

Liberation and Literature in Latin America

From the time of Christopher Columbus, the peoples of Latin America have served the political and economic interests of First World countries more powerful than their own. And even after the European nations departed from the shores of Argentina, Brazil, Mexico, Peru, and other Latin American states in the early nineteenth century, the intolerable conditions that had prevailed in the long era of colonialism persisted: the vast majority of Latin Americans, including great masses of peasants of Native American descent, lived in relative poverty, while small, wealthy, landowning elites held power. These elites maintained their position by virtue of their alliance with the financial and industrial interests of First World nations, including (especially since the 1890s) the United States.

Spanish-speaking and predominantly Catholic, the rapidly growing populations of the more than two dozen nations of Latin America have suffered repeated social upheaval in their attempts to cope with persistent problems of inequality, exploitation, and underdevelopment. The long and bitter history of the Mexican Revolution, commemorated in the murals of Diego Rivera (see Figure 34.7), provides a vivid example. From country to country, political and social reformers have struggled to revolutionize the socioeconomic order, to liberate Latin America from economic colonialism, and to bring about a more equitable distribution of wealth. Support for these essentially socialist movements has come from representatives of the deprived elements of society, including organized labor, and, often enough, from the Catholic Church, which has acted on behalf of the masses as an agent of social justice. The "liberation theology" preached by reformist elements in the clergy advanced a powerful new rendering of Christian dogma.

Latin America's artists rallied to support movements for liberation. During the 1960s, the outpouring of exceptionally fine Latin American prose and poetry constituted a literary boom, the influence of which is still being felt worldwide. Among the champions of reform was the Chilean Pablo Neruda (1904–1973), one of Latin America's most prolific Spanish-language poets. His poems, often embellished with violent, Surrealist images, endorse a radical, populist ideology. In "The United Fruit Co.," he describes the corruption of justice and freedom in the "Banana Republics" of Latin America. The poem, which is phrased as a mock Last Judgment, smolders with indignation at the United States' policies of commercial exploitation in the nations south of its borders.

READING 36.2 Neruda's "United Fruit Co." (1950)

When the trumpets had sounded and all	1
was in readiness on the face of the earth,	
Jehovah divided his universe:	
Anaconda, Ford Motors,	
Coca-Cola Inc., and similar entities:	5
the most succulent item of all,	
The United Fruit Company Incorporated	
reserved for itself: the heartland	
and coasts of my country,	
the delectable waist of America.	10
They rechristened their properties:	
the "Banana Republics"—	
and over the languishing dead,	
the uneasy repose of the heroes	
who harried that greatness,	15
their flags and their freedoms,	
they established an *opéra bouffe*:	
they ravished all enterprise,	
awarded the laurels like Caesars,	
unleashed all the covetous, and contrived	20
the tyrannical Reign of the Flies—	
Trujillo the fly, and Tacho the fly,	
the flies called Carias, Martinez,	

[1] The twentieth-century dictators of Latin America: Rafael Molina Trujillo brutally dominated the Dominican Republic from 1930 to 1961; "Tacho" was the nickname for Anastasio Somoza, who controlled Nicaragua from 1937 until his assassination in 1956; Tiburcio Carias, self-styled dictator of Honduras, was supported during the 1930s and 1940s by the United Fruit Company; Maximilian Martinez was the ruthless dictator of El Salvador during the 1930s and 1940s; Jorge Ubico seized power in Guatemala in 1931 and served as a puppet of the United States until 1944.

Ubico[1]—all of them flies, flies
dank with the blood of their marmalade   25
vassalage, flies buzzing drunkenly
on the populous middens:
the fly-circus fly and the scholarly
kind, case-hardened in tyranny.
Then in the bloody domain of the flies   30
The United Fruit Company Incorporated
sailed off with a booty of coffee and fruits
brimming its cargo boats, gliding
like trays with the spoils
of our drowning dominions.   35
And all the while, somewhere in the sugary
hells of our seaports,
smothered by gases, an Indian
fell in the morning:
a body spun off, an anonymous   40
chattel, some numeral tumbling,
a branch with its death running out of it
in the vat of the carrion, fruit laden and foul.

  Q **What sentiments dominate this poem?**

  Q **What is the function of Neruda's mock Last Judgment?**

The Quest for Racial Equality

The most turbulent liberation movement of the twentieth century addressed the issue of racial equality—an issue so dramatically reflected in the African-American experience that some observers have dubbed the century "The Race Era." Since the days of slavery, millions of black Americans had existed as an underprivileged minority population living within an advanced industrial state.

The Dutch took the first Africans to America in 1619, and during the late seventeenth and eighteenth centuries, thousands of slaves were imported to the American colonies, especially those in the South. For 250 years, until the end of the Civil War, slavery was a fact of American life. The Emancipation Proclamation issued by Abraham Lincoln in 1863 facilitated the liberation of the slaves, but it was not until 1865—with the Thirteenth Amendment to the United States Constitution—that all slaves were finally freed. This and other constitutional amendments guaranteed the rights of black people; nevertheless, the lives of African-Americans continued to be harsh and poor by comparison with those of their former white masters. Separation of the races by segregated housing, inferior schools, and exclusion from voting and equal employment were only a few of the inequities suffered by this minority in the post-emancipation United States. It was to these issues and to the more general problem of racism that many African-Americans addressed themselves after World War I.

The Harlem Renaissance

World War I provided African-Americans with new opportunities in education and employment. During and after

Figure 36.2 JACOB LAWRENCE, "Race riots were numerous. White workers were hostile toward the migrants who had been hired to break strikes." Panel 50 from *The Migration of the Negro*, 1940–1941; text and title revised by the artist, 1993. Tempera on gesso on composition board, 18 × 12 in.

the war, over five million African-Americans migrated from the South to the northern states. New York City became the center of economic opportunity, as well as the melting pot for black people from other parts of the world. But white frustration and fear of black competition for jobs led to race riots in over twenty-five cities during the "Bloody Summer" of 1919 (Figure **36.2**).

Between 1920 and 1940, the quest for racial equality and a search for self-identity among African-Americans inspired an upsurge of creative expression in the arts. Centered in Harlem—a part of Manhattan occupied largely by African-Americans—poets, painters, musicians, and dancers forged the movement that came to be called the Harlem Renaissance.

The Harlem Renaissance made the self-conscious "rebirth" of the African heritage the principal part of an intellectual and cultural quest for racial identity and equality. A leading figure of the movement was the writer, folklorist, and anthropologist Zora Neale Hurston (1891–1960). Hurston made use of African-American dialect to create some of the strongest female characters in early twentieth-century fiction. Her novel *Their Eyes Were Watching God* is widely regarded as a classic of black literature.

Hurston's contemporary Langston Hughes (1902–1967) was one of the most eloquent voices of the Harlem Renaissance. Hughes was born in Missouri and moved to New York in 1921, where he became the first African-American to support himself as a professional writer. A musician as well as a journalist and a novelist, Hughes was the rare poet whose powerful phrases ("a dream deferred," "a raisin in the sun," and "black like me") are enshrined in the canon of American literature and in the English language. His poems, which capture the musical qualities of the African oral tradition, fuse everyday speech with the rhythms of blues and jazz. Hughes, who regarded poets as "lyric historians," drew deeply on his own experience: his "Theme for English B" records his response to the education of black students in a dominantly white culture. In "Harlem," a meditation on the Bloody Summer of 1919, Hughes looks to the immediate past to presage the angry riots that have recurred regularly since the 1960s in America's black ghettos.

Like the writers of the Harlem Renaissance, the Chicago-born poet Gwendolyn Brooks (1917–2000) drew upon the idioms of jazz and street slang to produce a vivid picture of the black ghettos in her city. The first African-American to receive the Pulitzer Prize for poetry (1949), Brooks brought to attention the plight of black people—especially young black men and women—in American society. The two poems in Reading 36.4 are representative of the early part of her long and productive career.

READING 36.3 The Poems of Hughes

Theme for English B (1949)

The instructor said,   1

   Go home and write
   a page tonight.
   And let that page come out of you—
   Then, it will be true.   5

I wonder if it's that simple?

I am twenty-two, colored, born in Winston-Salem.
I went to school there, then Durham, then here
to this college on the hill above Harlem.
I am the only colored student in my class.   10
The steps from the hill lead down into Harlem,
through a park, then I cross St. Nicholas,
Eighth Avenue, Seventh, and I come to the Y,
the Harlem Branch Y, where I take the elevator
up to my room, sit down, and write this page: 15

It's not easy to know what is true for you or me
at twenty-two, my age. But I guess I'm what

I feel and see and hear, Harlem, I hear you:
hear you, hear me—we two—you, me, talk on this page.
(I hear New York, too.) Me—who?   20
Well, I like to eat, sleep, drink, and be in love.
I like to work, read, learn, and understand life.
I like a pipe for a Christmas present,
or records—Bessie, bop, or Bach.
I guess being colored doesn't make me not like   25
the same things other folks like who are other races.
So will my page be colored that I write?
Being me, it will not be white.
But it will be
a part of you, instructor.   30
You are white—
yet a part of me, as I am a part of you.
That's American.
Sometimes perhaps you don't want to be a part of me.
Nor do I often want to be a part of you.   35
But we are, that's true!
I guess you learn from me—
although you're older—and white—
and somewhat more free.

This is my page for English B.   40

Harlem (1951)

What happens to a dream deferred?   1

Does it dry up
like a raisin in the sun?
Or fester like a sore—
And then run?   5
Does it stink like rotten meat?
Or crust and sugar over—
like a syrupy sweet?
Maybe it just sags
like a heavy load.   10

Or does it explode?

Q To what extent do the circumstances described in these poems (written more than sixty years ago) still pertain?

READING 36.4 The Poems of Brooks

The Mother (1945)

Abortions will not let you forget.   1
You remember the children you got that you did not get,
The damp small pulps with a little or with no hair,
The singers and workers that never handled the air.
You will never neglect or beat   5
Them, or silence or buy with a sweet.
You will never wind up the sucking-thumb
Or scuttle off ghosts that come.
You will never leave them, controlling your luscious sigh,
Return for a snack of them, with gobbling mother-eye.   10

I have heard in the voices of the wind the voices of my
    dim killed children.
I have contracted. I have eased
My dim dears at the breasts they could never suck.
I have said, Sweets, if I sinned, if I seized
Your luck   15
And your lives from your unfinished reach,
If I stole your births and your names,
Your straight baby tears and your games,
Your stilted or lovely loves, your tumults, your marriages,
    aches, and your deaths,

If I poisoned the beginnings of your breaths,   20
Believe that even in my deliberateness I was not deliberate.
Though why should I whine,
Whine that the crime was other than mine?—
Since anyhow you are dead.
Or rather, or instead,   25
You were never made.

But that too, I am afraid,
Is faulty: oh, what shall I say, how is the truth to be said?
You were born, you had body, you died.
It is just that you never giggled or planned or cried.   30

Believe me, I loved you all.
Believe me, I knew you, though faintly, and I loved,
    I loved you
All.

We Real Cool (1959)

The Pool Players.
Seven at the Golden Shovel.

    We real cool. We
    Left school. We

    Lurk late. We
    Strike straight. We

    Sing sin. We
    Thin gin. We

    Jazz June. We
    Die soon.

Q In what ways are these poems descriptive?
Are they also didactic? How so?

Richard Wright and the Reality of Racism

Richard Wright (1908–1960) was born on a cotton plantation in Mississippi and came to New York City in 1937,
just after the heyday of the Harlem Renaissance. Wright
brought to his writings the anger of a man who had
known physical punishment and repeated injustice at the
hands of white people. In his novel *Native Son* (1940),
the nightmarish story of a poor, young black man who
kills his white employer's daughter, Wright examined the

ways in which the frustrated search for identity led some
African-Americans to despair, defiance, and even violent
crime. The novel won Wright immediate acclaim and was
adapted for the New York stage in 1941.

In the autobiographical sketch *The Ethics of Living Jim
Crow* (1938), Wright records with grim frankness the experience of growing up in a racially segregated community
in the American South. "Jim Crow," the stage name of a
popular nineteenth-century minstrel performer, Thomas
D. Rice, had come to describe anything pertaining to
African-Americans, including matters of racial segregation.

READING 36.5 From Wright's *The Ethics of Living Jim Crow* (1938)

My first lesson in how to live as a Negro came when I was   1
quite small. We were living in Arkansas. Our house stood
behind the railroad tracks. Its skimpy yard was paved with
black cinders. Nothing green ever grew in that yard. The only
touch of green we could see was far away, beyond the tracks,
over where the white folks lived. But cinders were good
enough for me and I never missed the green growing things.
And anyhow cinders were fine weapons. You could always
have a nice hot war with huge black cinders. All you had to do
was crouch behind the brick pillars of a house with your hands   10
full of gritty ammunition. And the first woolly black head you
saw pop out from behind another row of pillars was your
target. You tried your very best to knock it off. It was great
fun. I never fully realized the appalling disadvantages of a
cinder environment till one day the gang to which I belonged
found itself engaged in a war with the white boys who lived
beyond the tracks. As usual we laid down our cinder barrage,
thinking that this would wipe the white boys out. But they
replied with a steady bombardment of broken bottles. We
doubled our cinder barrage, but they hid behind trees, hedges,   20
and the sloping embankment of their lawns. Having no such
fortifications, we retreated to the brick pillars of our homes.
During the retreat a broken milk bottle caught me behind the
ear, opening a deep gash which bled profusely. The sight of
blood pouring over my face completely demoralized our ranks.
My fellow-combatants left me standing paralyzed in the center
of the yard, and scurried for their homes. A kind neighbor
saw me, and rushed me to a doctor, who took three stitches
in my neck.

I sat brooding on my front steps, nursing my wound and   30
waiting for my mother to come from work. I felt that a grave
injustice had been done me. It was all right to throw cinders.
The greatest harm a cinder could do was leave a bruise.
But broken bottles were dangerous; they left you cut, bleeding,
and helpless.

When night fell, my mother came from the white folks'
kitchen. I raced down the street to meet her. I could just feel
in my bones that she would understand. I knew she would tell
me exactly what to do next time. I grabbed her hand and
babbled out the whole story. She examined my wound, then   40
slapped me.

"How come yuh didn't hide?" she asked me. "How come yuh
awways fightin'?"

I was outraged, and bawled. Between sobs I told her that I didn't have any trees or hedges to hide behind. There wasn't a thing I could have used as a trench. And you couldn't throw very far when you were hiding behind the brick pillars of a house. She grabbed a barrel stave, dragged me home, stripped me naked, and beat me till I had a fever of one hundred and two. She would smack my rump with the stave, and, while the skin was still smarting impart to me gems of Jim Crow wisdom. I was never to throw cinders any more. I was never to fight any more wars. I was never, never, under any conditions, to fight white folks again. And they were absolutely right in clouting me with the broken milk bottle. Didn't I know she was working hard every day in the hot kitchens of the white folks to make money to take care of me? When was I ever going to learn to be a good boy? She couldn't be bothered with my fights. She finished by telling me that I ought to be thankful to God as long as I lived that they didn't kill me. 50 60

All that night I was delirious and could not sleep. Each time I closed my eyes I saw monstrous white faces suspended from the ceiling, leering at me.

From that time on, the charm of my cinder yard was gone. The green trees, the trimmed hedges, the cropped lawns grew very meaningful, became a symbol. Even today when I think of white folks, the hard, sharp outlines of white houses surrounded by trees, lawns, and hedges are present somewhere in the background of my mind. Through the years they grew into an overreaching symbol of fear. 70

It was a long time before I came in close contact with white folks again. We moved from Arkansas to Mississippi. Here we had the good fortune not to live behind the railroad tracks, or close to white neighborhoods. We lived in the very heart of the local Black Belt. There were black churches and black preachers; there were black schools and black teachers; black groceries and black clerks. In fact, everything was so solidly black that for a long time I did not even think of white folks, save in remote and vague terms. But this could not last forever. As one grows older one eats more. One's clothing costs more. When I finished grammar school I had to go to work. My mother could no longer feed and clothe me on her cooking job. 80

There is but one place where a black boy who knows no trade can get a job, and that's where the houses and faces are white, where the trees, lawns, and hedges are green. My first job was with an optical company in Jackson, Mississippi. The morning I applied I stood straight and neat before the boss, answering all his questions with sharp yessirs and nosirs. I was very careful to pronounce my *sirs* distinctly, in order that he might know that I was polite, that I knew where I was, and that I knew he was a *white* man. I wanted that job badly. 90

He looked me over as though he were examining a prize poodle. He questioned me closely about my schooling, being particularly insistent about how much mathematics I had had. He seemed very pleased when I told him I had had two years of algebra.

"Boy, how would you like to try to learn something around here?" he asked me. 100

"I'd like it fine, sir," I said, happy. I had visions of "working my way up." Even Negroes have those visions.

"All right," he said. "Come on."

I followed him to the small factory.

"Pease," he said to a white man of about thirty-five, "this is Richard. He's going to work for us."

Pease looked at me and nodded.

I was then taken to a white boy of about seventeen.

"Morrie, this is Richard, who's going to work for us."

"Whut yuh sayin' there, boy!" Morrie boomed at me. 110

"Fine!" I answered.

The boss instructed these two to help me, teach me, give me jobs to do, and let me learn what I could in my spare time.

My wages were five dollars a week.

I worked hard, trying to please. For the first month I got along O.K. Both Pease and Morrie seemed to like me. But one thing was missing. And I kept thinking about it. I was not learning anything and nobody was volunteering to help me. Thinking they had forgotten that I was to learn something about the mechanics of grinding lenses, I asked Morrie one day to tell me about the work. He grew red. 120

"Whut yuh tryin' t' do, nigger, get smart?" he asked.

"Naw; I ain' tryin' t' git smart," I said.

"Well, don't, if yuh know whut's good for yuh!"

I was puzzled. Maybe he just doesn't want to help me, I thought. I went to Pease.

"Say, are yuh crazy, you black bastard?" Pease asked me, his gray eyes growing hard.

I spoke out, reminding him that the boss had said I was to be given a chance to learn something. 130

"Nigger, you think you're white, don't you?"

"Naw, sir!"

"Well, you're acting mighty like it!"

"But, Mr. Pease, the boss said . . ."

Pease shook his fist in my face.

"This is a *white* man's work around here, and you better watch yourself!"

From then on they changed toward me. They said good-morning no more. When I was just a bit slow in performing some duty, I was called a lazy black son-of-a-bitch. 140

Once I thought of reporting all this to the boss. But the mere idea of what would happen to me if Pease and Morrie should learn that I had "snitched" stopped me. And after all the boss was a white man, too. What was the use?

The climax came at noon one summer day. Pease called me to his workbench. To get to him I had to go between two narrow benches and stand with my back against a wall.

"Yes, sir," I said.

"Richard, I want to ask you something," Pease began pleasantly, not looking up from his work. 150

"Yes, sir," I said again.

Morrie came over, blocking the narrow passage between the benches. He folded his arms, staring at me solemnly.

I looked from one to the other, sensing that something was coming.

"Yes, sir," I said for the third time.

Pease looked up and spoke very slowly.

"Richard, *Mr.* Morrie here tells me you called me *Pease.*"

I stiffened. A void seemed to open up in me. I knew this was the showdown. 160

He meant that I had failed to call him Mr. Pease. I looked at

Morrie. He was gripping a steel bar in his hands. I opened my mouth to speak, to protest, to assure Pease that I had never called him simply *Pease*, and that I had never had any intentions of doing so, when Morrie grabbed me by the collar, ramming my head against the wall.

"Now be careful, nigger!" snarled Morrie, baring his teeth. "*I* heard yuh call 'im *Pease*! 'N' if yuh say yuh didn't, yuh're callin' me a *lie*, see?" He waved the steel bar threateningly.

If I had said: No, sir, Mr. Pease, I never called you *Pease*   **170** I would have been automatically calling Morrie a liar. And if I said: Yes, sir, Mr. Pease, I called you *Pease*, I would have been pleading guilty to having uttered the worst insult that a Negro can utter to a southern white man. I stood hesitating, trying to frame a neutral reply.

"Richard, I asked you a question!" said Pease. Anger was creeping into his voice.

"I don't remember calling you *Pease*, Mr. Pease," I said cautiously. "And if I did, I sure didn't mean . . ."

"You black son-of-a-bitch! You called me *Pease*, then!" he   **180** spat, slapping me till I bent sideways over a bench. Morrie was on top of me, demanding:

"Didn't you call 'im *Pease*? If yuh say yuh didn't, I'll rip yo' gut string loose with this bar, yuh black granny dodger! Yuh can't call a white man a lie 'n' git erway with it, you black son-of-a-bitch!"

I wilted. I begged them not to bother me. I knew what they wanted. They wanted me to leave.

"I'll leave," I promised. "I'll leave right *now*."

They gave me a minute to get out of the factory. I was   **190** warned not to show up again, or tell the boss.

I went.

When I told the folks at home what had happened, they called me a fool. They told me that I must never again attempt to exceed my boundaries. When you are working for white folks, they said, you got to "stay in your place" if you want to keep working. . . .

Q **Which of the details in this selection bring to life the plight of young blacks in the American South?**

Q **Describe the character, Pease: is he a believable figure?**

The Civil Rights Movement

Well after World War II, racism remained an undeniable obstacle to equality. Ironically, while Americans had fought to oppose Nazi racism in Germany, black Americans endured a system of inferior education, restricted jobs, ghetto housing, and generally low living standards. High crime rates, illiteracy, and drug addiction were evidence of affluent America's awesome failure to assimilate a population that suffered in its midst. The fact that African-Americans had served in great numbers in World War II inspired a redoubled effort to end persistent discrimination and segregation in the United States. During the 1950s and 1960s, that effort came to flower in the civil rights movement.

Civil rights leaders of the 1950s demanded enforcement of all the provisions for equality promised in the

United States Constitution. Their demands led to a landmark Supreme Court decision in 1954 that banned school segregation; by implication, the ruling undermined the entire system of legalized segregation in the United States. Desegregation was met with fierce resistance, especially in the American South. In response, the so-called Negro Revolt began in 1955 and continued for more than a decade. It took the form of nonviolent, direct-action protests, including boycotts of segregated lunch counters, peaceful "sit-ins," and protest marches. Leading the revolt was Dr. Martin Luther King, Jr. (1929–1968), a Protestant pastor and civil rights activist who modeled his campaign of peaceful protest on the example of Gandhi. As president of the Southern Christian Leadership Conference, King served as an inspiration to all African-Americans.

The urgency of their cause is conveyed in a letter King wrote while confined to jail for marching without a permit in the city of Birmingham, Alabama. It addressed a group of local white clergy, who had publicly criticized King for breaking laws that prohibited black people from using public facilities and for promoting "untimely" demonstrations. After King's letter was published in *The Christian Century* (June 12, 1963), it became (in a shorter version edited by King himself) the key text in a nationwide debate over civil rights: it provided philosophic justification for the practice of civil disobedience as a means of opposing injustice. King's measured eloquence and reasoned restraint stand in ironic contrast to the savagery of the opposition, who had used guns, hoses, and attack dogs against the demonstrators, 2400 of whom were jailed along with King.

READING 36.6 From King's *Letter from Birmingham Jail* (1963)

My dear Fellow Clergymen,
While confined here in the Birmingham City Jail, I came   **1** across your recent statement calling our present activities "unwise and untimely." Seldom, if ever, do I pause to answer criticism of my work and ideas. But since I feel that you are men of genuine goodwill and your criticisms are sincerely set forth, I would like to answer your statement in what I hope will be patient and reasonable terms.

I think I should give the reason for my being in Birmingham, since you have been influenced by the argument of "outsiders coming in." Several months ago our local affiliate here in   **10** Birmingham invited us to be on call to engage in a nonviolent direct action program if such were deemed necessary. We readily consented and when the hour came we lived up to our promises. So I am here, along with several members of my staff, because we were invited here. Beyond this, I am in Birmingham because injustice is here.

Moreover, I am cognizant of the interrelatedness of all communities and states. I cannot sit idly by in Atlanta and not be concerned about what happens in Birmingham. Injustice anywhere is a threat to justice everywhere. We are caught in   **20** an inescapable network of mutuality tied in a single garment of destiny. Never again can we afford to live with the narrow, provincial "outsider agitator" idea. Anyone who lives inside the

United States can never be considered an outsider anywhere in this country.

You deplore the demonstrations that are presently taking place in Birmingham. But I am sorry that your statement did not express a similar concern for the conditions that brought the demonstrations into being. I would not hesitate to say that it is unfortunate that so-called demonstrations are taking place in Birmingham at this time, but I would say in more emphatic terms that it is even more unfortunate that the white power structure of this city left the Negro community with no other alternative.

In any nonviolent campaign there are four basic steps: 1) collection of the facts to determine whether injustices are alive; 2) negotiation; 3) self-purification; and 4) direct action.

You may well ask, "Why direct action? Why sit-ins, marches, etc.? Isn't negotiation a better path?" You are exactly right in your call for negotiation. Indeed, this is the purpose of direct action. Nonviolent direct action seeks to create such a crisis and establish such creative tension that a community that has constantly refused to negotiate is forced to confront the issue. So the purpose of the direct action is to create a situation so crisis-packed that it will inevitably open the door to negotiation.

My friends, I must say to you that we have not made a single gain in civil rights without determined legal and nonviolent pressure. History is the long and tragic story of the fact that privileged groups seldom give up their privileges voluntarily. Individuals may see the moral light and voluntarily give up their unjust posture; but as Reinhold Niebuhr[1] has reminded us, groups are more immoral than individuals.

We know through painful experience that freedom is never voluntarily given by the oppressor; it must be demanded by the oppressed. For years now I have heard the word "Wait!" It rings in the ear of every Negro with a piercing familiarity. This "wait" has almost always meant "never." We must come to see with the distinguished jurist of yesterday that "justice too long delayed is justice denied." We have waited for more than three hundred and forty years for our constitutional and God-given rights.

You express a great deal of anxiety over our willingness to break laws. This is certainly a legitimate concern. Since we so diligently urge people to obey the Supreme Court's decision of 1954 outlawing segregation in the public schools, it is rather strange and paradoxical to find us consciously breaking laws. One may well ask, "How can you advocate breaking some laws and obeying others?" The answer is found in the fact that there are two types of laws. There are *just* laws and there are *unjust* laws. One has not only a legal but a moral responsibility to obey just laws. Conversely, one has a moral responsibility to disobey unjust laws.

Now what is the difference between the two? A just law is a man-made code that squares with the moral law or the law of God. An unjust law is a code that is out of harmony with the moral law. Any law that degrades human personality is unjust. All segregation statutes are unjust because segregation distorts the soul and damages the personality. It gives the segregator a false sense of superiority and the segregated a false sense of inferiority.

Let us turn to a more concrete example of just and unjust laws. An unjust law is a code that a majority inflicts on a minority that is not binding on itself. This is *difference* made legal. On the other hand a just law is a code that a majority compels a minority to follow and that it is willing to follow itself. This is *sameness* made legal.

I hope you can see the distinction I am trying to point out. In no sense do I advocate evading or defying the law as the rabid segregationist would do. This would lead to anarchy. One who breaks an unjust law *openly, lovingly*, and with a willingness to accept the penalty by staying in jail to arouse the conscience of the community over its injustice, is in reality expressing the very highest respect for law.

Of course there is nothing new about this kind of civil disobedience. It was seen sublimely in the refusal of Shadrach, Meshach, and Abednego to obey the laws of Nebuchadnezzar[2] because a higher moral law was involved. It was practiced superbly by the early Christians.

We can never forget that everything Hitler did in Germany was "legal" and everything the Hungarian freedom fighters did in Hungary was "illegal." It was "illegal" to aid and comfort a Jew in Hitler's Germany.

In your statement you asserted that our actions, even though peaceful, must be condemned because they precipitate violence. But can this assertion be logically made? Isn't this like condemning the robbed man because his possession of money precipitated the evil act of robbery? We must come to see, as federal courts have consistently affirmed, that it is immoral to urge an individual to withdraw his efforts to gain his basic constitutional rights because the quest precipitates violence. Society must protect the robbed and punish the robber.

Over the last few years I have consistently preached that nonviolence demands that the means we use must be as pure as the ends we seek. So I have tried to make it clear that it is wrong to use immoral means to gain moral ends. But now I must affirm that it is just as wrong, or even more so, to use moral means to preserve immoral ends. T. S. Eliot has said that there is no greater treason than to do the right deed for the wrong reason.

I wish you had commended the Negro sit-inners and demonstrators of Birmingham for their sublime courage, their willingness to suffer, and their amazing discipline in the midst of the most inhuman provocation. One day the South will recognize its real heroes. They will include old, oppressed, battered Negro women, symbolized in a seventy-two-year-old woman of Montgomery, Alabama, who rose up with a sense of dignity and with her people decided not to ride the segregated buses, and responded to one who inquired about her tiredness with ungrammatical profundity: "My feets is tired, but my soul is rested." One day the South will know that when these disinherited children of God sat down at the lunch

---

[1] An American Protestant theologian (1892–1971) who urged ethical realism in Christian approaches to political debate (see chapter 35).

[2] The Chaldean king of the sixth century B.C.E., who, according to the Book of Daniel, demanded that these Hebrew youths worship the Babylonian gods. Nebuchadnezzar cast them into a fiery furnace, but they were delivered unhurt by an angel of God (see chapter 9, LOOKING INTO Figure 9.7).

counters they were in reality standing up for the best in the American dream and the most sacred values in our Judeo-Christian heritage, and thus carrying our whole nation back to great wells of democracy which were dug deep by the founding fathers in the formulation of the Constitution and the Declaration of Independence.

I hope this letter finds you strong in the faith. I also hope 140 that circumstances will soon make it possible for me to meet each of you, not as an integrationist or a civil rights leader, but as a fellow clergyman and a Christian brother. Let us hope that the dark clouds of racial prejudice will soon pass away and the deep fog of misunderstanding will be lifted from our fear-drenched communities and in some not too distant tomorrow the radiant stars of love and brotherhood will shine over our great nation with all of their scintillating beauty.

> *Yours for the cause of*
> *Peace and Brotherhood* 150
> Martin Luther King, Jr.

Q **What arguments does Dr. King make for nonviolence and negotiation?**

Q **Evaluate the claim (line 53) that "groups are more immoral than individuals."**

While Dr. King practiced the tactics of nonviolence to achieve the goals of racial integration and civil rights in America, another protest leader took a very different tack: Malcolm Little (1925–1965), who called himself "Malcolm X," experienced firsthand the inequities and degradation of life in white America. For a time he turned to crime and drugs as a means of survival. Arrested and imprisoned in 1946, he took the opportunity to study history and religion, and most especially the teachings of Islam. By the time he was released in 1952, he had joined the Nation of Islam and was prepared to launch his career as a Muslim minister.

Malcolm and other "Black Muslims" despaired over persistent racism in white America. They determined that black people should pursue a very different course from that of Dr. King and the Southern Christian Leadership Conference. African-Americans, argued Malcolm, should abandon aspirations for integration. Instead, they should separate from white Americans in every feasible way; they should create a black nation in which—through hard work and the pursuit of Muslim morality—they might live equally, in dignity, free of the daily affronts of white racism. These goals should be achieved by all available means, violent if necessary (armed self-defense was a first step). Only by fighting for black nationalism would African-Americans ever gain power and self-respect in racist America. Little wonder that Malcolm was feared and reviled by white Americans and deemed a dangerous radical by more moderate black people as well.

In 1963, Malcolm addressed a conference of black leaders in Detroit, Michigan. In this speech, which later came to be called "Message to the Grass Roots," Malcolm addressed a large audience representing a cross section of the African-American community. The power and immediacy of his style is best captured on the tape of the speech published by the African-American Broadcasting and Record Company. Nevertheless, the following brief excerpt provides a glimpse into the ferocious eloquence that Malcolm exhibited throughout his brief career—until his death by assassination in 1965.

READING 36.7 From Malcolm X's "Message to the Grass Roots" (1963)

. . . America has a very serious problem. Not only does 1 America have a very serious problem, but our people have a very serious problem. America's problem is us. We're her problem. The only reason she has a problem is she doesn't want us here. And every time you look at yourself, be you black, brown, red or yellow, a so-called Negro, you represent a person who poses such a serious problem for America because you're not wanted. Once you face this as a fact, then you can start plotting a course that will make you appear intelligent, instead of unintelligent. 10

What you and I need to do is learn to forget our differences. When we come together, we don't come together as Baptists or Methodists. You don't catch hell because you're a Baptist, and you don't catch hell because you're a Methodist. You don't catch hell because you're a Methodist or Baptist, you don't catch hell because you're a Democrat or a Republican, you don't catch hell because you're a Mason or an Elk, and you sure don't catch hell because you're an American; because if you were an American, you wouldn't catch hell. You catch hell because you're a black man. You catch hell, all of us catch 20 hell, for the same reason.

So we're all black people, so-called Negroes, second-class citizens, ex-slaves. You're nothing but an ex-slave. You don't like to be told that. But what else are you? You are ex-slaves. You didn't come here on the "Mayflower." You came here on a slave ship. In chains, like a horse, or a cow, or a chicken. And you were brought here by the people who came here on the "Mayflower," you were brought here by the so-called Pilgrims, or Founding Fathers. They were the ones who brought you here. 30

We have a common enemy. We have this in common: We have a common oppressor, a common exploiter, and a common discriminator. But once we all realize that we have a common enemy, then we unite—on the basis of what we have in common. And what we have foremost in common is that enemy—the white man. . . .

As long as the white man sent you to Korea, you bled. He sent you to Germany, you bled. He sent you to the South Pacific to fight the Japanese, you bled. You bleed for white people, but when it comes to seeing your own churches being 40 bombed and little black girls murdered, you haven't got any blood. You bleed when the white man says bleed; you bite when the white man says bite; and you bark when the white man says bark. I hate to say this about us, but it's true. How are you going to be nonviolent in Mississippi, as violent as you were in Korea? How can you justify being nonviolent in Mississippi and Alabama, when your churches are being bombed, and your little girls are being murdered, and at the same time you are going to get violent with Hitler, and Tojo, and somebody else you don't even know? **50**

If violence is wrong in America, violence is wrong abroad. If it is wrong to be violent defending black women and black children and black babies and black men, then it is wrong for America to draft us and make us violent abroad in defense of her. And if it is right for America to draft us, and teach us how to be violent in defense of her, then it is right for you and me to do whatever is necessary to defend our own people right here in this country. . . .

Q How does Malcolm justify black violence?

Q How do his perceptions differ from King's?

The Literature of the Black Revolution

The passage of the Civil Rights Act in America in 1964 provided an end to official segregation in public places; but continuing discrimination and the growing militancy of some civil rights groups provoked a more violent phase of the protests during the late 1960s and thereafter. Even before the assassination of Martin Luther King, Jr., in 1968, the black revolution had begun to assume a transnational fervor. American voices joined those of their black neighbors in the West Indies, South Africa, and elsewhere in the world. Fired by **apartheid**, the system of strict racial segregation that prevailed legally in South Africa until 1994, the poet Bloke Modisane (1923–1986) lamented:

> it gets awful lonely,
> lonely;
> like screaming,
> screaming lonely
> screaming down dream alley,
> screaming blues, like none can hear

In *Black Skin, White Masks* (1958)—the handbook for African revolution—the West Indian essayist and revolutionary Franz Fanon (1925–1961) defended violence as necessary and desirable in overcoming the tyranny of whites over blacks in the colonial world. "At the level of individuals," he wrote, "violence is a cleansing force." In the United States, where advertising media made clear the disparity between the material comforts of black and white Americans, the black revolution swelled on a tide of rising expectations. LeRoi Jones (1934–2014), who in 1966 adopted the African name Imamu Amiri Baraka, echoed the message of Malcolm X in poems and plays that advocated militant action and pan-Africanism. Rejecting white Western literary tradition, Baraka called for "poems that kill"; "Let there be no love poems written," he entreats, "until love can exist freely and cleanly."

Baldwin and Ellison Two luminaries of American black protest literature were James Baldwin (1924–1987) and Ralph Ellison (1914–1994). Baldwin, the eldest of nine children raised in Harlem in conditions of poverty, began writing when he was fourteen years old. Encouraged early in his career by Richard Wright, he became a formidable preacher of the gospel of equality. For Baldwin, writing was a subversive act. "You write," he insisted, "in order to change the world, knowing perfectly well that you probably can't, but also knowing that literature is indispensable to the world. In some way, your aspirations and concern for a single man in fact do begin to change the world. The world changes according to the way people see it, and if you alter, even by a millimeter, the way a person looks or people look at reality, then you can change it."

In his novels, short stories, and essays, Baldwin stressed the affinity African-Americans felt with other poverty-stricken populations. Yet, as he tried to define the unique differences between black and white people, he observed that the former were strangers in the modern world—a world whose traditions were claimed by those who were white. As he explained in the essay "Stranger in the Village" (1953):

> [European Whites] cannot be, from the point of view of power, strangers anywhere in the world; they have made the modern world, in effect, even if they do not know it. The most illiterate among them is related, in a way that I am not, to Dante, Shakespeare, Michelangelo, Aeschylus, da Vinci, Rembrandt, and Racine; the cathedral at Chartres says something to them which it cannot say to me. . . . Out of their hymns and dances come Beethoven and Bach. Go back a few centuries and they are in their full glory—but I am in Africa, watching the conquerors arrive.

But Baldwin uncovered a much overlooked truth about the character of the modern world: that black culture has influenced white culture, and especially American culture, in a profound and irreversible manner:

> The time has come to realize that the interracial drama acted out on the American continent has not only created a new black man, it has created a new white man, too. . . . One of the things that distinguishes Americans from other people is that no other people has ever been so deeply involved in the lives of black men, and vice versa. . . . It is precisely this black–white experience which may prove of indispensable value to us in the world we face today. This world is white no longer, and it will never be white again.

Baldwin's contemporary Ralph Ellison, a native of Oklahoma and an amateur jazz musician, came to Harlem during the 1930s to study sculpture and musical composition. He was influenced by both Hughes and Wright, and soon turned to writing short stories and newspaper reviews. In 1945, he began the novel *Invisible Man*, a fiction masterpiece that probes the black estrangement from white culture. The prologue to the novel, an excerpt of which follows, offers a glimpse into the spiritual odyssey of the "invisible" protagonist, an unnamed black man who lives rent-free in a Harlem basement flat illuminated by 1369 light bulbs he has connected (illegally) to the city's electrical grid (Figure **36.3**). It broaches, with surrealistic

Figure 36.3 JEFF WALL, *After Invisible Man by Ralph Ellison, "The Preface," Edition of 2*, 1999–2000. Cibachrome transparency, aluminum light box, fluorescent bulbs, 75¼ × 106¼ × 10¼ in. Wall made this large-scale backlit cibachrome photograph from a scene he himself staged with a hired actor and a fabricated set. He is inspired by subjects and images drawn from the history of art and literature.

intensity, some of Ellison's most important themes: the nightmarish quality of urban life and the alienation experienced by both black and white Americans in the modern United States.

READING 36.8 From Ellison's *Invisible Man* (1952)

I am an invisible man. No, I am not a spook like those who   1
haunted Edgar Allan Poe;[1] nor am I one of your Hollywood-
movie ectoplasms. I am a man of substance, of flesh and
bone, fiber and liquids—and I might even be said to possess a
mind. I am invisible, understand, simply because people refuse
to see me. Like the bodiless heads you see sometimes in circus
sideshows, it is as though I have been surrounded by mirrors of
hard, distorting glass. When they approach me they see only
my surroundings, themselves, or figments of their
imagination—indeed, everything and anything except me.   10
    Nor is my invisibility exactly a matter of a bio-chemical
accident to my epidermis. That invisibility to which I refer

---

[1] A leading American poet, literary critic, and short-story writer (1809–1849), noted for his tales of terror and his clever detective stories.

occurs because of a peculiar disposition of the eyes of those
with whom I come in contact. A matter of the construction of
their inner eyes, those eyes with which they look through their
physical eyes upon reality. I am not complaining, nor am
I protesting either. It is sometimes advantageous to be unseen,
although it is most often rather wearing on the nerves. Then
too, you're constantly being bumped against by those of
poor vision. Or again, you often doubt if you really exist. You   20
wonder whether you aren't simply a phantom in other people's
minds. Say, a figure in a nightmare which the sleeper tries
with all his strength to destroy. It's when you feel like this
that, out of resentment, you begin to bump people back. And,
let me confess, you feel that way most of the time. You ache
with the need to convince yourself that you do exist in the real
world, that you're a part of all the sound and anguish, and you
strike out with your fists, you curse and you swear to make
them recognize you. And, alas, it's seldom successful.
    One night I accidentally bumped into a man, and perhaps   30
because of the near darkness he saw me and called me an
insulting name. I sprang at him, seized his coat lapels and
demanded that he apologize. He was a tall blond man, and as
my face came close to his he looked insolently out of his blue
eyes and cursed me, his breath hot in my face as he struggled.
I pulled his chin down sharp upon the crown of my head,

butting him as I had seen the West Indians do, and I felt his flesh tear and the blood gush out, and I yelled, "Apologize! Apologize!" But he continued to curse and struggle, and I butted him again and again until he went down heavily, on his **40** knees, profusely bleeding. I kicked him repeatedly, in a frenzy because he still uttered insults though his lips were frothy with blood. Oh yes, I kicked him! And in my outrage I got out my knife and prepared to slit his throat, right there beneath the lamplight in the deserted street, holding him by the collar with one hand, and opening the knife with my teeth—when it occurred to me that the man had not seen me, actually; that he, as far as he knew, was in the midst of a walking nightmare! And I stopped the blade, slicing the air as I pushed him away, letting him fall back to the street. I stared at him hard as the **50** lights of a car stabbed through the darkness. He lay there, moaning on the asphalt; a man almost killed by a phantom. It unnerved me. I was both disgusted and ashamed. I was like a drunken man myself, wavering about on weakened legs. Then I was amused. Something in this man's thick head had sprung out and beaten him within an inch of his life. I began to laugh at this crazy discovery. Would he have awakened at the point of Death? Would Death himself have freed him for wakeful living? But I didn't linger. I ran away into the dark, laughing so hard I feared I might rupture myself. The **60** next day I saw his picture in the Daily News, beneath a caption stating that he had been "mugged." Poor fool, poor blind fool, I thought with sincere compassion, mugged by an invisible man! . . .

Q **What does Ellison's protagonist mean when he says he is "an invisible man"?**

Morrison and Walker In the literature of the black revolution, especially that of the last three decades of the twentieth century, many of the most powerful voices were female. Succeeding such notable Harlem Renaissance writers as Hurston and Dorothy West (1912–1998), two contemporary figures—Toni Morrison (b. 1931) and Alice Walker (b. 1944)—have risen to eminence.

Toni Morrison is celebrated as one of America's finest writers. Her novels, rich in epic themes, memorable characters, and vivid oral rhythms, examine the long-range consequences of slavery in America. Many of her characters, Afro-American women, suffer displacement and despair in their homes and communities. The Pulitzer Prize-winning *Beloved* (1988), inspired by the true story of an African-American slave, is a story of racism's power to destroy the natural impulses of human love. Morrison's novel *Jazz* (1992) mirrors the various rhythms of that unique musical genre by way of the verbal "improvisations" of its characters. In 1993, Morrison became the first black woman to be honored with the Nobel Prize in literature.

Alice Walker, whose highly acclaimed novel *The Color Purple* won the Pulitzer Prize in fiction in 1982, is celebrated for her candid characterizations of black women facing the perils of racism, domestic violence, and sexual abuse. Her short story "Elethia" probes the dual issues of identity and liberation as they come to shape the destiny of a young black female.

READING 36.9 Walker's "Elethia" (1981)

A certain perverse experience shaped Elethia's life, and made **1** it possible for it to be true that she carried with her at all times a small apothecary jar of ashes.

There was in the town where she was born a man whose ancestors had owned a large plantation on which everything under the sun was made or grown. There had been many slaves, and though slavery no longer existed, this grandson of former slaveowners held a quaint proprietary point of view where colored people were concerned. He adored them, of course. Not in the present—it went without saying—but at **10** that time, stopped, just on the outskirts of his memory: his grandfather's time.

This man, whom Elethia never saw, opened a locally famous restaurant on a busy street near the center of town. He called it "Old Uncle Albert's." In the window of the restaurant was a stuffed likeness of Uncle Albert himself, a small brown dummy of waxen skin and glittery black eyes. His lips were intensely smiling and his false teeth shone. He carried a covered tray in one hand, raised level with his shoulder, and over his other arm was draped a white napkin. **20**

Black people could not eat at Uncle Albert's, though they worked, of course, in the kitchen. But on Saturday afternoons a crowd of them would gather to look at "Uncle Albert" and discuss how near to the real person the dummy looked. Only the very old people remembered Albert Porter, and their eyesight was no better than their memory. Still there was a comfort somehow in knowing that Albert's likeness was here before them daily and that if he smiled as a dummy in a fashion he was not known to do as a man, well, perhaps both memory and eyesight were wrong. **30**

The old people appeared grateful to the rich man who owned the restaurant for giving them a taste of vicarious fame. They could pass by the gleaming window where Uncle Albert stood, seemingly in the act of sprinting forward with his tray, and know that though niggers were not allowed in the front door, ole Albert was already inside, and looking mighty pleased about it, too.

For Elethia the fascination was in Uncle Albert's fingernails. She wondered how his creator had got them on. She wondered also about the white hair that shone so brightly **40** under the lights. One summer she worked as a salad girl in the restaurant's kitchen, and it was she who discovered the truth about Uncle Albert. He was not a dummy; he was stuffed. Like a bird, like a moose's head, like a giant bass. He was stuffed.

One night after the restaurant was closed someone broke in and stole nothing but Uncle Albert. It was Elethia and her friends, boys who were in her class and who called her "Thia." Boys who bought Thunderbird and shared it with her. Boys who laughed at her jokes so much they hardly remembered **50** she was also cute. Her tight buddies. They carefully burned Uncle Albert to ashes in the incinerator of their high school, and each of them kept a bottle of his ashes. And for each of them what they knew and their reaction to what they knew was profound.

The experience undercut whatever solid foundation Elethia had assumed she had. She became secretive, wary, looking over her shoulder at the slightest noise. She haunted the museums of any city in which she found herself, looking, usually, at the remains of Indians, for they were plentiful everywhere she went. She discovered some of the Indian warriors and maidens in the museums were also real, stuffed people, painted and wigged and robed, like figures in the Rue Morgue. There were so many, in fact, that she could not possibly steal and burn them all. Besides, she did not know if these figures—with their valiant glass eyes—would wish to be burned.

About Uncle Albert she felt she knew.
What kind of man was Uncle Albert?

Well, the old folks said, he wasn't nobody's uncle and wouldn't sit still for nobody to call him that, either.

Why, said another old-timer, I recalls the time they hung a boy's privates on a post at the end of the street where all the black folks shopped, just to scare us all, you understand, and Albert Porter was the one took 'em down and buried 'em. Us never did find the rest of the boy though. It was just like always—they would throw you in the river with a big old green log tied to you, and down to the bottom you sunk.

He continued.

Albert was born in slavery and he remembered that his mama and daddy didn't know nothing about slavery'd done ended for near 'bout ten years, the boss man kept them so ignorant of the law, you understand. So he was a mad so-an'-so when he found out. They used to beat him *severe* trying to make him forget the past and grin and act like a nigger. (Whenever you saw somebody acting like a nigger, Albert said, you could be sure he seriously disremembered his past.) But he never would. Never would work in the big house as head servant, neither—always broke up stuff. The master at that time was always going around pinching him too. Looks like he hated Albert more than anything—but he never would let him get a job anywhere else. And Albert never would leave home. Too stubborn.

Stubborn, yes. My land, another one said. That's why it do seem strange to see that dummy that sposed to be old Albert with his mouth open. All them teeth. Hell, all Albert's teeth was knocked out before he was grown.

Elethia went away to college and her friends went into the army because they were poor and that was the way things were. They discovered Uncle Alberts all over the world. Elethia was especially disheartened to find Uncle Alberts in her textbooks, in the newspapers and on t.v.

Everywhere she looked there was an Uncle Albert (and many Aunt Albertas, it goes without saying).

But she had her jar of ashes, the old-timers' memories written down, and her friends who wrote that in the army they were learning skills that would get them through more than a plate glass window.

And she was careful that, no matter how compelling the hype, Uncle Alberts, in her own mind, were not permitted to exist.

Q **What are "Uncle Alberts"?**

Q **What social contradictions does Walker attack in this story?**

African-Americans and the Visual Arts

During the Harlem Renaissance, African-American painters and sculptors made public the social concerns of black poets and writers. In picturing their experience, they drew on African folk idioms and colloquial forms of native expression; but they also absorbed the radically new styles of European Modernism. Among these painters, there emerged a "blues aesthetic" that featured bold colors, angular forms, and rhythmic, stylized compositions.

Lawrence and Bearden One of the most notable artists of the twentieth century, Jacob Lawrence (1917–2000) migrated to Harlem with his family in 1930. Lawrence's powerful style features flat, unmodulated colors and angular, abstract forms that owe as much to African art as to Synthetic Cubism and Expressionism. At the same time, his lifelong commitment to social and racial issues made him heir to the nineteenth-century artist–critics Goya and Daumier, whom he admired. Painting in tempera on masonite panels, Lawrence won early acclaim for serial paintings that deal with black history and with the lives of black American heroes and heroines. Among the most famous of these is a series of sixty panels known as *The Migration of the Negro* (1940–1941). For *The Migration*—an expressionistic narrative of the great northward movement of African-Americans after World War I—Lawrence drew on textual sources rather than firsthand visual experience. The drama of each episode (see Figure 36.2) is conveyed by means of bold rhythms and vigorous, geometric shapes that preserve what Lawrence called "the magic of the picture plane."

Lawrence's contemporary Romare Bearden (1916–1988) was born in North Carolina, but grew up in Harlem. He knew the major figures of the Harlem Renaissance, including Lawrence, Langston Hughes, and the leading jazz musicians of New York. Bearden's favorite medium was collage (see chapter 32). The earliest of his works in this technique emerged against the backdrop of the civil rights movement and took as their theme the African-American struggle. Much like Hannah Höch (see Figure 33.16), Bearden cut bits and pieces of images from popular magazines; but his semiabstract compositions developed narrative themes drawn from everyday life. Their abrupt shifts in scale and strident colors call to mind the improvisational phrasing and syncopated rhythms of jazz. Music, in fact, provided the subject matter for some of Bearden's most notable works, such as *Train Whistle Blues* (1964), *Three Folk Musicians* (1967), *New Orleans Ragging Home* (1974), and *Empress of the Blues* (1974; see Figure 36.7).

Saar and Colescott Since the mid-twentieth century, African-American artists have taken ever more cynical approaches to themes of race discrimination and racial stereotyping. The California sculptor Betye Saar (b. 1926) abandoned the African-inspired fetishlike sculptures of her early career and turned to fabricating boxed constructions that attacked the icons of commercial white culture. In the mixed-media piece entitled *The Liberation of Aunt Jemima,*

Saar attacked the "mammy" stereotype by presenting a gun-toting version of the image developed by R. T. Davis in 1890 to sell ready-made pancake mix (Figure **36.4**). "My interest," explained Saar, "was to transform a negative, demeaning figure into a positive, empowered woman . . . A warrior ready to combat servitude and racism."

The satirist–artist Robert Colescott (1925–2009) created parodies of famous paintings in which whites are recast as cartoon-style, stereotyped black men and women. In doing so, Colescott called attention to their exclusion from Western art history. His bitter parody of Delacroix's *Liberty Leading the People* (1976) features a crew of brashly painted African-American rebels commanded by a black-faced Liberty (see Figure 29.6). Colescott's *Les Demoiselles d'Alabama* (Figure **36.5**), an obvious funk-art clone of Picasso's landmark painting (see Figure 32.2), slyly challenges contemporary definitions of Primitivism and Modernism. Colescott observes: "Picasso started with European art and abstracted through African art, producing 'Africanism' but keeping one foot in European art.

I began with Picasso's Africanism and moved toward European art, keeping one foot in Africanism. . . ."

Walker and Wiley The American artist Kara Walker (b. 1969) appreciates the fact that liberation and racial freedom are ongoing processes. Using her trademark silhouettes, she brings to contemporary art a subtle and complex examination of the tangled relationships between white and black Americans, especially as they played out between the male masters and female slaves of the nineteenth-century American South. In the piece *A Work on Progress* (Figure **36.6**), she pictures a stereotypical African-American housemaid sweeping out a sister figure whose chains are newly broken. The liberated female, observes Walker, may represent the end of slavery, but like the trash she sweeps from the house, she holds an undefined (and unwelcome) place in society.

The African-American artist Kehinde Wiley (b. 1977) began his career by appropriating famous Renaissance and Baroque portraits as models for hyperrealistic, theatrically posed images of young black men dressed in hip-hop street garb: hoodies and baggy sportswear. More recently, with the intent of "charting the presence of black and brown people throughout the world," he has made visits to Brazil, Israel, and various parts of Africa, including his father's homeland, Nigeria. In Israel, he photographed and painted portraits of black Ethiopian Jews whose current musical practices (hip-hop and reggae) resonate with segments of African-American populations.

Figure 36.4 BETYE SAAR, *The Liberation of Aunt Jemima*, 1972. Mixed media assemblage, 11¾ × 8 × 2¾ in., signed. Saar drew attention to unflattering stereotypes of African-Americans: Uncle Tom, Little Black Sambo, and Aunt Jemima. Her version of the trademark figure associated with a popular pancake mix is seen here as a domestic servant with a rifle, a pistol, and a broom. A second version shows her as a nanny, holding a squalling white baby.

African-Americans and Film

The first African-American to establish himself as a major Hollywood filmmaker, Shelton Jackson "Spike" Lee (b. 1957), has won international acclaim for films that explore race conflict in the inner city (*Do the Right Thing*, 1989), modern black history (*Malcolm X*, 1992), the black minstrel tradition (*Bamboozled*, 2000), drug-dealing (*25th Hour*, 2002), and the black infantrymen, the so-called buffalo soldiers of World War II (*Miracle at St. Anna*, 2008). Lee uses the camera inventively to underline social conflict, as in his radical close-ups of faces caught in bitter, heated disputes. He favors short, disconnected scenes, the "accidental" effects of the handheld camera, and editing techniques that often leave the narrative themes of his films unresolved but filled with implications. Lee opened the door for a new wave of black filmmakers that includes John Singleton (*Boyz in the Hood*, 1991) and Julie Dash (*Daughters of the Dust*, 1991).

The British-born director Steve McQueen (b. 1969) recently engaged the viewing public with the powerful film *12 Years a Slave* (2013), an adaptation of the autobiography of Solomon Northup (1853). The novel, searingly recreated in the film, tells the brutal story of a free black man, a citizen of New York, who was kidnapped in Washington, D.C., in 1841 and rescued twelve years later from a cotton plantation near the Red River in Louisiana.

Figure 36.5 ROBERT COLESCOTT,
Les Demoiselles d'Alabama (Vestidas),
1985. Acrylic on canvas, 8 ft. × 7 ft. 8 in.

In Wiley's exquisitely executed paintings, embellished with designs drawn from Arab, Israeli, and European decorative arts, he may pose his subjects in positions drawn from traditional Mali statuary (see Figure **36.1**). Aiming to dispel the negative and violent post-colonial stereotypes that dominate the media, he invests his subjects with masculinity, heroic power, and an attitude of self-conscious superiority borrowed from Western, white aristocratic portraiture (see Figures 21.2, 22.2, and 28.3).

Figure 36.6 KARA WALKER,
A Work on Progress, 1998. Cut paper and adhesive, 5 ft. 9 in. × 6 ft. 8 in. Installation view at the Walker Art Center, 2007. Walker made use of the popular folk-art tradition of cut-paper silhouettes, which were often used for late eighteenth-century portraits. She recently employed this technique to illustrate the poems of Toni Morrison.

Figure 36.7 ROMARE BEARDEN, *Empress of the Blues*, 1974. Acrylic and pencil on paper and printed paper on paperboard, 3 ft. 10 in. × 4 ft. 2 in. Bearden depicts Bessie Smith, the singer known as the "Empress of the Blues." The artist's working methods gave visual substance to the "call-and-response" patterns in African music and jazz: "You put down one color, and it calls for an answer," he explained.

African-Americans and Jazz

Possibly the most important contribution made by African-Americans to world culture occurred in the area of music, specifically in the birth and development of that unique form of modern music known as jazz. Jazz is a synthesis of diverse musical elements that came together in the first two decades of the twentieth century, but it was after World War I that jazz came to full fruition as an artform. Although some music historians insist that jazz is the product of place, not race, the primary role of African-Americans in the origins and evolution of jazz is indisputable.

Jazz is primarily a performer's rather than a composer's art. Dominated by Afro-Caribbean rhythmic styles, it incorporates a wide range of European and African-American concepts of harmony, melody, and tone color. In its evolution, jazz absorbed the musical idioms of the marching brass band, the minstrel stage, the blues, and the piano style known as *ragtime*. Ragtime is a form of piano composition and performance featuring highly syncopated rhythms and simple, appealing melodies. It apparently originated in the lower Mississippi valley, but it migrated north after the Civil War and became popular during the 1890s. Its most inspired proponent (if not its inventor) was the black composer and popular pianist Scott Joplin (1868–1917). Early jazz performers, like "Jelly Roll" Morton (Ferdinand Joseph LaMonthe, 1885–1941), who claimed to have invented jazz, used ragtime rhythms in developing the essential features of the new form.

Blues, a formative element in the evolution of jazz, had begun as a vocal rather than an instrumental genre.

Native to the southern United States, but possibly stemming from African song forms, it is an emotive type of individual expression for lamenting one's troubles, loneliness, and despair. A blues song may recall the wailing cries of plantation slaves; it may describe the anguish of separation and loss or the hope for deliverance from oppression. Such classics as W. C. Handy's "St. Louis Blues" (1914) begin with a line that states a simple plaint ("I hate to see the evening sun go down"); the plaint is repeated in a second line, and it is "answered" in a third ("It makes me think I'm on my last go-round")—a pattern derived perhaps from African call-and-response chants (see chapter 18). Technically, blues makes use of a special scale known as a "blues scale," which features (among other things) the flatted forms of E, G, and B within the standard C major scale.

Both ragtime and blues contributed substantially to the development of jazz as a unique musical idiom. But if jazz manifests any single defining quality, that quality would have to be improvisation—individual and collective. Most jazz performances are based on standard melodies—often familiar popular tunes; the individual performers (and sometimes a group of performers within an ensemble) then "improvise" on the base melody. They invent passages while in the process of performing them—a form of "composing as you go"—or they incorporate bits of other (often familiar) melodies into their solos. Most scholars agree that improvisation, either individual or collective, constitutes the single element that most distinguishes jazz from other musical idioms.

See Music Listening Selections at end of chapter.

Figure 36.8 King Oliver's Creole Jazz Band, 1923. Photograph, 7¼ × 9¾ in. Honore Dutrey, Warren "Baby" Dodds, Joe Oliver, Louis Armstrong, Lillian Hardin, Bill Johnson, and Johnny Dodds.

Finally, jazz employs a unique variation on standard rhythms that performers and aficionados term "**swing**." While it is virtually impossible to define the concept of "swing," it may best be described as the practice of playing just off the beat—slightly ahead or behind. "Swinging" normally involves achieving a certain rhythmic "groove"— a combination of rhythm and harmony that vitalizes the ensemble and propels the performance forward. (In the words of a 1940s popular song, "It don't mean a thing if it ain't got that swing!")

As a performance art, jazz depends on the interaction of the ensemble's members as they create an essentially new composition in the very act of performing it. Although syncopated rhythms, the blues motif, harmonic flexibility, and improvisation were not in themselves new, their combination—when vitalized by a "swinging" performance— produced an essentially new artform, one that would have a major impact on Western music for years to come.

Armstrong The beginnings of American jazz are found in New Orleans, Louisiana, a melting pot for the rich heritage of Spanish, French, African, Caribbean, Indian, and Black Creole musical traditions. Here, black and white musicians drew on the intricate rhythms of African tribal dance and the European harmonies of traditional marching bands. The street musicians who regularly marched behind funeral or wedding processions, many of whom were neither formally trained nor able to read music, might play trumpets, trombones, and clarinets; rhythm was provided by tubas as well as snare and bass drums. These musicians made up the "front line" of the parade; the crowd that danced behind them was called the "second line."* Parade bands

performed perhaps the earliest version of what became jazz. Similar bands also played the popular music of the time in nightclubs and dance-halls.

Louis Armstrong (1900–1971), a native of New Orleans, began playing the cornet at the age of twelve. By the 1920s he had emerged as the foremost jazz musician of the period. Armstrong's innovative solos provided the breakthrough by which solo improvisation became central to jazz performance. His ability to redirect the harmony and to invent reworkings of standard melodies in his solos—all performed with breathtaking virtuosity—elevated the jazz soloist to the foremost role in ensemble performance.

"Satchmo" ("Satchelmouth") Armstrong was also a jazz singer with formidable musical gifts. He often embellished jazz with **scat singing**—an improvised set of nonsense syllables. His compelling personality and unfailing good spirits brought joy to millions and turned jazz into an internationally respected musical form. "Hotter Than That" (1927), a composition by Lillian Hardin (Armstrong's wife), exemplifies the style termed "hot jazz" (Figure **36.8**) —a style that the French in particular elevated to the status of a craze.

The Jazz Age In the 1920s jazz spread north to the urban centers of Chicago, Kansas City, and New York. Armstrong moved to Chicago in 1922. In New York, extraordinary jazz and blues singers like Bessie Smith (1898–1937), known by her fans as the "Empress of the Blues" (see Figure 36.7), and Billie Holiday (1915–1959)—"Lady Day"—drew worldwide acclaim through the phenomena of radio and phonograph records. In the so-called Jazz Age, jazz had a major impact on other musical genres. The American composer George Gershwin (1898–1937) incorporated the rhythms of jazz into the mesmerizing *Rhapsody in Blue*

---

* Not to be confused with a variant usage of the term, which distinguishes the rhythm section of a band from the "front line" of reed and brass solo instrumentalists.

See Music Listening Selections at end of chapter.

(1924), a concert piece for piano and orchestra. Gershwin's *Porgy and Bess* (1935), a fully composed opera dealing with the life of poverty-stricken Charleston African-Americans, combined jazz, blues, and spiritual and folk idioms to produce a new style of American musical theater featuring an all-black cast.

Popular music of the 1930s and 1940s was closely tied to the vogue for big-band jazz and the danceable rhythms of swing, a big-band jazz style that fed the dance craze of the 1940s. The white swing bands of Tommy Dorsey, Glenn Miller, and Benny Goodman (who later integrated his band—the first bandleader to do so) played a mix of instrumental swing and popular ballads, while black swing bands like that of William "Count" Basie (1904–1984) leaned more toward blues and a dynamic big-band sound.

Postwar Jazz In the years following World War II, jazz took on some of the complex and sophisticated characteristics of "art music." The beguiling suite *Black, Brown, and Beige* (1948) composed by Edward Kennedy "Duke" Ellington (1899–1974) paved the way for concert-hall jazz, a form that has enjoyed a revival since the 1990s. Ellington was a prolific musician, unquestionably the foremost composer in the jazz idiom (and arguably in *any* idiom) that the United States has produced.

On a smaller scale, among groups of five to seven instruments, the jazz of the late 1940s and 1950s engaged the unique improvisational talents of individual performers. New forms included "bebop" (or "bop")—a jazz style characterized by frenzied tempos, complex chord progressions, and dense polyrhythms—and "cool" jazz, a more restrained and gentler style associated with the West Coast. "Koko," performed by the saxophonist Charlie Parker (1920–1955) and the trumpeter John "Dizzy" Gillespie (1917–1993), epitomizes the bebop style of the 1940s: the piece is an improvised version of the popular jazz standard "Cherokee" by the British composer Ray Noble (1903–1978).

See Music Listening Selections at end of chapter.

Since the jazz renaissance of the 1980s, the New Orleans composer, trumpet prodigy, and teacher Wynton Marsalis (b. 1961) has reconfirmed the role of jazz as America's classical music. Awarded the Pulitzer Prize in 1995 for his jazz oratorio on slavery, *Blood on the Field*, Marsalis has become the world's most articulate spokesperson for the jazz genre. Likening jazz to the open exchange of ideas, Marsalis holds: "Jazz is more than the best expression there is of American culture; it is the most democratic of arts." To this day, jazz remains a unique kind of chamber music that combines the best of classical and popular musicianship.

Hip-Hop Like the "blues aesthetic" in the poetry and painting of the Harlem Renaissance, a "jazz aesthetic" featuring spontaneity and improvisation infused the 1970s performance phenomenon known as *hip-hop*. A product of the inner-city American subculture, hip-hop brings together loud, percussive music (often electronically "mixed" by disc jockeys), the spoken word, and street-dance, generating a raw vitality that borders on the violent (see chapter 38).

The paintings of the short-lived Jean-Michel Basquiat (1960–1988) embrace the free improvisations and

Figure 36.9 JEAN-MICHEL BASQUIAT, *Horn Players*, 1983. Acrylic and mixed media on canvas, 8 ft. × 6 ft. 3 in. The death's head at the center of the piece is a favorite motif of the artist and appears in many of his works. It is seen by some to have anticipated Basquiat's death from an overdose of cocaine and heroin at the age of twenty-eight.

borrowed "riffs" of modern jazz, even as they are infused with the staccato rhythms and jarring lyrics of hip-hop. Basquiat's artworks conflate crude, childlike but familiar images, grim cartoon logos, street art, and scrawled graffiti (see chapter 38)—an urban folk-art style that vents the rage and joy of inner-city youths (like Basquiat himself). *Horn Players* (Figure **36.9**), executed with portable oil sticks on a blackboardlike surface, pays homage to the jazz giants Dizzy Gillespie (shown playing his saxophone at left) and Charlie Parker (holding his trumpet at right). The word "ornithology" is a witty reference to a bebop jazz standard of that name, and to Parker's nickname: "Bird."

African-Americans and Dance

The African-American impact on twentieth-century dance rivaled that on music. For centuries, dance served African-Americans as a primary language of religious expression and as a metaphor of physical freedom. By the late nineteenth century, as all-black theatrical companies and minstrel shows toured the United States, black entertainment styles began to reach white audiences. Popular black dances such as the high-kicking cakewalk became the international fad of the early 1900s, and dances such as the black bottom and lindy hop came to influence both social and theatrical performance.

With the pioneer African-American choreographer Katherine Dunham, introduced in chapter 32, black dance moved beyond the level of stage entertainment. After completing her doctorate in anthropology at the University of Chicago in 1939, Dunham traveled to Jamaica, Trinidad, Martinique, and Haiti to do research, some of which explored the relationship between dance and voodoo practice. An avid student of Caribbean dance, Dunham drew heavily on Afro-Caribbean and African culture in both choreography and the sets and costumes designed by her husband, John Pratt (Figure **36.10**). Dunham's troupe borrowed from Caribbean music the rhythms of the steel band, an instrumental ensemble consisting entirely of steel drums fashioned from oil containers. Originating in Trinidad, steel bands provided percussive accompaniment for calypso and other improvised dance forms. In her book *Dances of Haiti*, Dunham examines the sociological function of dance—for instance, how communal dance captures the spirit of folk celebrations and how African religious dance interacts with European secular dance.

Dunham's work inspired others. Born in Trinidad and raised in New York City, Pearl Primus (1919–1994) used her studies in choreography and anthropology (like Dunham, she earned a doctorate in this field) to become the world's foremost authority on African dance. Following a trip to Africa in the 1940s, she brought to modern dance the spirit and substance of native tribal rituals. She also choreographed theatrical versions of African-American spirituals and poems, including those of Langston Hughes.

Figure 36.10 Katherine Dunham in the 1945–1946 production of *Tropical Revue*. While working on her master's degree, the "dancing anthropologist" had to choose between dance and an academic career. While she went on to complete the doctorate, she ultimately chose dance, establishing in 1945 her own dance company, with which she toured the world.

In her book *African Dance*, Primus declared: "The dance is strong magic. . . . It turns the body to liquid steel. It makes it vibrate like a guitar. The body can fly without wings. It can sing without voice."

The achievements of Dunham and Primus gave African-American dance theater international stature. Since 1950, such outstanding choreographers as Alvin Ailey (1931–1989), Donald McKayle (b. 1930), and Arthur Mitchell (b. 1934) have graced the history of American dance. Ailey's *Revelations* (1960), a suite that drew on his Texas roots and his affection for African-American spirituals, song-sermons, and gospel music, is an enduring tribute to the cultural history of the American South.

The Quest for Gender Equality

Throughout history, misogyny (the dislike or hatred of women) and the perception of the female sex as inferior in intelligence and strength have enforced conditions of gender inequality. While women make up the majority of the population in many cultures, they have exercised little significant political or economic power. Like many ethnic minorities, women have long been relegated to the position of second-class citizens. In 1900, women were permitted to vote in only one country in the world: New Zealand. By mid-century, women in most First World countries had gained voting rights; nevertheless, their social and economic status has remained far below that of men. As recently as 1985, the World Conference on Women reported that while women represent 50 percent of the world's population and contribute nearly two-thirds of all working hours, they receive only one-tenth of the world's income and they own less than one percent of the world's property. Although female inequality has been a fact of history, it was not until the twentieth century that the quest for female liberation took the form of an international movement.

The Literature of Feminism: Woolf

The history of **feminism** (the principle advocating equal social, political, and economic rights for men and women) reaches back at least to the fourteenth century, when the French poet Christine de Pisan took up the pen in defense of women (see chapter 15). Christine had sporadic followers among Renaissance and Enlightenment humanists, the most notable of which was Mary Wollstonecraft, who published her provocative *Vindication of the Rights of Woman* in London in 1792 (see chapter 24). During the nineteenth century, Condorcet and Mill wrote reasoned pleas for female equality, as did the female novelist George Sand (see chapter 28). In America, the eloquence of Angelina Grimké (1805–1879) and other *suffragettes* (women advocating equality for women) was instrumental in winning women the right to vote in 1920.

Among the most impassioned advocates of the feminist movement was the novelist Virginia Woolf (1882–1941). Woolf argued that equal opportunity for education and economic advantage were even more important than the right to vote (British women gained the vote in 1918). In her novels and essays, Woolf proposed that women could become powerful only by achieving financial and psychological independence from men. Freedom, argued Woolf, is the prerequisite for creativity: for a woman to secure her own creative freedom, she must have money and the privacy provided by "a room of her own." The essay "A Room of One's Own" voices a response to a clergyman's remark that no female could have matched the genius of William Shakespeare. In the excerpt below, Woolf envisions Shakespeare's imaginary sister, Judith, in her sixteenth-century setting. She uses this fictional character to raise some challenging questions concerning the psychological aspects of female creativity.

READING 36.10 From Woolf's "A Room of One's Own" (1929)

. . . Let me imagine, since facts are so hard to come by, what 1
would have happened had Shakespeare had a wonderfully
gifted sister, called Judith, let us say. Shakespeare himself
went, very probably—his mother was an heiress—to the
grammar school, where he may have learnt Latin—Ovid, Virgil

and Horace—and the elements of grammar and logic. He was,
it is well known, a wild boy who poached rabbits, perhaps
shot a deer, and had, rather sooner than he should have done,
to marry a woman in the neighbourhood, who bore him a child
rather quicker than was right. That escapade sent him to seek 10
his fortune in London. He had, it seemed, a taste for the
theatre; he began by holding horses at the stage door. Very
soon he got work in the theatre, became a successful actor,
and lived at the hub of the universe, meeting everybody,
knowing everybody, practising his art on the boards, exercising
his wits in the streets, and even getting access to the palace of
the queen. Meanwhile his extraordinarily gifted sister, let
us suppose, remained at home. She was as adventurous, as
imaginative, as agog to see the world as he was. But she was
not sent to school. She had no chance of learning grammar 20
and logic, let alone of reading Horace and Virgil. She picked
up a book now and then, one of her brother's perhaps, and
read a few pages. But then her parents came in and told her
to mend the stockings or mind the stew and not moon about
with books and papers. They would have spoken sharply
but kindly, for they were substantial people who knew the
conditions of life for a woman and loved their daughter—
indeed, more likely than not she was the apple of her father's
eye. Perhaps she scribbled some pages up in an apple loft on
the sly, but was careful to hide them or set fire to them. Soon, 30
however, before she was out of her teens, she was to be
betrothed to the son of a neighbouring wool-stapler. She cried
out that marriage was hateful to her, and for that she was
severely beaten by her father. Then he ceased to scold her.
He begged her instead not to hurt him, not to shame him in
this matter of her marriage. He would give her a chain of beads
or a fine petticoat, he said; and there were tears in his eyes.
How could she disobey him? How could she break his heart?
The force of her own gift alone drove her to it. She made up a
small parcel of her belongings, let herself down by a rope one 40
summer's night and took the road to London. She was not
seventeen. The birds that sang in the hedge were not more
musical than she was. She had the quickest fancy, a gift like
her brother's, for the tune of words. Like him, she had a taste
for the theatre. She stood at the stage door; she wanted to
act, she said. Men laughed in her face. The manager—a fat,
loose-lipped man—guffawed. He bellowed something about
poodles dancing and women acting—no woman, he said,
could possibly be an actress. He hinted—you can imagine
what. She could get no training in her craft. Could she even 50
seek her dinner in a tavern or roam the streets at midnight?
Yet her genius was for fiction and lusted to feed abundantly
upon the lives of men and women and the study of their ways.
At last—for she was very young, oddly like Shakespeare the
poet in her face, with the same grey eyes and rounded
brows—at last Nick Greene the actor-manager took pity on
her; she found herself with child by that gentleman and so—
who shall measure the heat and violence of the poet's heart
when caught and tangled in a woman's body?—killed herself
one winter's night and lies buried at some cross-roads where 60
the omnibuses now stop outside the Elephant and Castle.

. . . any woman born with a great gift in the sixteenth
century would certainly have gone crazed, shot herself, or
ended her days in some lonely cottage outside the village, half

witch, half wizard, feared and mocked at. For it needs little skill in psychology to be sure that a highly gifted girl who had tried to use her gift for poetry would have been so thwarted and hindered by other people, so tortured and pulled asunder by her own contrary instincts, that she must have lost her health and sanity to a certainty. No girl could have walked to London and stood at a stage door and forced her way into the presence of actor-managers without doing herself a violence and suffering an anguish which may have been irrational—for chastity may be a fetish invented by certain societies for unknown reasons—but were none the less inevitable. Chastity had then, it has even now, a religious importance in a woman's life, and has so wrapped itself round with nerves and instincts that to cut it free and bring it to the light of day demands courage of the rarest. To have lived a free life in London in the sixteenth century would have meant for a woman who was poet and playwright a nervous stress and dilemma which might well have killed her. Had she survived, whatever she had written would have been twisted and deformed, issuing from a strained and morbid imagination. And undoubtedly, I thought, looking at the shelf where there are no plays by women, her work would have gone unsigned. That refuge she would have sought certainly. It was the relic of the sense of chastity that dictated anonymity to women even so late as the nineteenth century. Currer Bell,[1] George Eliot, George Sand, all the victims of inner strife as their writings prove, sought ineffectively to veil themselves by using the name of a man. Thus they did homage to the convention, which if not implanted by the other sex was liberally encouraged by them (the chief glory of a woman is not to be talked of, said Pericles, himself a much-talked-of man), that publicity in women is detestable. Anonymity runs in their blood. . . .

70

80

90

Q How does the figure of Shakespeare's fictional sister work to make Woolf's point?

Q How fragile, according to Woolf, is female creativity?

Postwar Feminism: de Beauvoir

The two world wars had a positive effect on the position of women. In the absence of men during wartime, women assumed many male jobs in agriculture and in industry. As Woolf predicted, the newly found financial independence of women gave them a sense of freedom and stimulated their demands for legal and social equality. In the Soviet Union, the communist regime put women to work in industry and on the battlefields. Women's roles in other regions beyond the West were also changing. In China, where women had been bought and sold for centuries, the People's Republic in 1949 closed all brothels, forbade arranged marriages, and enforced policies of equal pay for equal work.

Leaders of the feminist movement in the West demanded psychological independence as well as job equality;

their goals involved raising the consciousness of *both* sexes. The new woman must shed her passivity and achieve independence through responsible action, insisted the French novelist, social critic, and existentialist Simone de Beauvoir (1908–1986). In the classic feminist text *The Second Sex*, de Beauvoir dethroned the "myth of femininity"—the false and disempowering idea that women possess a unique and preordained "feminine" essence, which condemns them to a role of social and intellectual subordination to men. Reassessing the biological, psychological, and political reasons for women's dependency, she concluded that while Man defines Woman as "the Other" (or *second* sex), it is women themselves who complacently accept their subordinate position. De Beauvoir called on women everywhere "to renounce all advantages conferred upon them by their alliance" with men. She pursued this goal (unsuccessfully, according to some critics) in her own life: her fifty-year liaison with Jean-Paul Sartre constitutes one of the most intriguing partnerships of the century. Although both enjoyed love affairs with other people, they shared a lifelong marriage of minds.

In the following brief excerpt from *The Second Sex*, de Beauvoir explores the nature of female dependency upon men and the "metaphysical risk" of liberty.

READING 36.11 From de Beauvoir's
The Second Sex (1949)

If a woman discovers herself as the inessential, and never turns into the essential, it is because she does not bring about this transformation herself. Proletarians say "we." So do blacks. Positing themselves as subjects, they thus transform the bourgeois or whites into "others." Women —except in certain abstract gatherings such as conferences —do not use "we"; men say "women" and women adopt this word to refer to themselves; but they do not posit themselves authentically as Subjects. The proletarians made the revolution in Russia, the blacks in Haiti, the Indo-Chinese are fighting in Indochina. Women's actions have never been more than symbolic agitation; they have won only what men have been willing to concede to them; they have taken nothing; they have received. It is that they lack the concrete means to organize themselves into a unit that could posit itself in opposition. They have no past, no history, no religion of their own; and unlike the proletariat, they have no solidarity of labour or interests; they even lack their own space that makes communities of American blacks, or the Jews in ghettos, or the workers in Saint-Denis or Renault factories. They live dispersed among men, tied by homes, work, economic interests and social conditions to certain men —fathers or husbands—more closely than to other women. As bourgeois women, they are in solidarity with bourgeois men and not with women proletarians; as white women, they are in solidarity with white men and not with black women. The proletariat could plan to massacre the whole ruling class; a fanatic Jew or black could dream of seizing the secret of the atomic bomb and turning all of humanity entirely Jewish or entirely black: but a woman could not

1

10

20

30

[1] Currer Bell was the pseudonym for the British novelist Charlotte Brontë (1816–1855); for Eliot and Sand, see chapter 28.

even dream of exterminating males. The tie that binds her to her oppressors is unlike any other. The division of the sexes is a biological given, not a moment in human history. Their opposition took shape within an original *Mitsein*[1] and she has not broken it. The couple is a fundamental unit with the two halves riveted to each other: cleavage of society by sex is not possible. This is the fundamental characteristic of woman: she is the Other at the heart of a whole whose two components are necessary to each other. . . .

Now woman has always been, if not man's slave, at least his vassal; the two sexes have never divided the world up equally; and still today, even though her condition is changing, woman is heavily handicapped. In no country is her legal status identical to man's, and often it puts her at a considerable disadvantage. Even when her rights are recognized abstractly, long-standing habit keeps them from being concretely manifested in customs. Economically, men and women almost form two castes; all things being equal, the former have better jobs, higher wages and greater chances to succeed than their new female competitors; they occupy many more places in industry, in politics, and so on, and they hold the most important positions. In addition to their concrete power they are invested with a prestige whose tradition is reinforced by the child's whole education: the present incorporates the past, and in the past all history was made by males. At the moment that women are beginning to share in the making of the world, this world still belongs to men: men have no doubt about this, and women barely doubt it. Refusing to be the Other, refusing complicity with man, would mean renouncing all the advantages an alliance with the superior caste confers on them. Lord-man will materially protect liege-woman and will be in charge of justifying her existence: along with the economic risk, she eludes the metaphysical risk of a freedom that must invent its goals without help. Indeed, beside every individual's claim to assert himself as subject—an ethical claim—lies the temptation to flee freedom and to make himself into a thing: it is a pernicious path because the individual, passive, alienated and lost, is prey to a foreign will, cut off from his transcendence, robbed of all worth. But it is an easy path: the anguish and stress of authentically assumed existence are thus avoided. The man who sets the woman up as an *Other* will thus find in her a deep complicity. Hence woman makes no claim for herself as subject because she lacks the concrete means, because she senses the necessary link connecting her to man without positing its reciprocity, and because she often derives satisfaction from her role as *Other*. . . .

40

50

60

70

80

Q What circumstances, according to de Beauvoir, work to make the female "the Other"?

Q Is it still "a world that belongs to men"? (line 58).

---

[1] German for "co-existence."

America's Feminist Writers

During the 1960s, and especially in the United States, the struggle for equality between the sexes assumed a strident tone. Gender discrimination in both education and employment triggered demands for federal legislation on behalf of women. In 1960, the Pill, an oral contraceptive, was federally approved in the United States. Even as new methods of contraception gave women control over their reproductive function and therefore greater sexual freedom, the campaign to secure legal and political rights continued, generating protest marches and a spate of consciousness-raising literature. In 1963, Betty Friedan (1921–2006) published *The Feminine Mystique*, which claimed that American society—and commercial advertising in particular—had brainwashed women to prefer the roles of wives and mothers to other positions in life. Friedan was one of the first feminists to attack the theories of Sigmund Freud (see chapter 33), especially Freud's patriarchal view of women as failed men. She challenged women to question the existing order and to seek careers outside the home. With the founding of the National Organization for Women (NOW) in 1966, radical feminists called for a restructuring of all Western institutions.

Since the 1960s, there has been a virtual renaissance of poetry and fiction focused on the twin themes of gender equality and the search for female self-identity. As with the literature of black liberation, feminist writing often seethes with repressed rage and anger. Clearly, not all modern literature written by women addresses exclusively female issues—contemporary female writers have dealt with subjects as varied as boxing and the plight of the environment. Yet, in much of the postwar literature produced by women, three motifs recur: the victimization of the female, her effort to define her role in a society traditionally dominated by men, and her displacement from her ancient role as goddess and matriarch.

Plath and Sexton The first generation of feminist poets includes Sylvia Plath (1932–1963) and Anne Sexton (1928–1975). Plath's searing verse reflects her sense of dislocation in male-dominated society. In her most famous poem, "Lady Lazarus" (1962), she mingles Holocaust imagery with a litany of her failed efforts at suicide that culminates with a wrathful threat to "eat men" when, like the biblical Lazarus, she rises again.

Much like Plath, Sexton probes problems related to the socialization of women and the search for female identity. Deeply confessional, her verse often reflects upon her own troubled life, which (like Plath's) ended in suicide—an ironic fulfillment of Woolf's prophecy concerning the fate of Shakespeare's imaginary sister. In the autobiographical poem "Self in 1958," Sexton explores the images that traditionally have defined women: dolls, apparel, kitchens, and, finally, herself as an extension of her mother. Sexton's poem, which contemplates the female struggle for self-identity in modern society, recalls both Nora's plight in

Ibsen's *A Doll's House* (see chapter 30) and Woolf's observation that women "think through their mothers."

Sanchez, Rich, and Dove The African-American poet Sonia Sanchez (b. 1935) deals with the interrelated questions of racism and identity. Sanchez's poetry is more colloquial than Sexton's, and (like Baraka's) it is often fiercely confrontational. In the poem "Woman," Sanchez draws on the literary tradition in which eminent (and usually male) writers call upon the Classical gods for inspiration: she invokes the spiritual powers of Mother Earth to infuse her with courage and creative energy.

The poems of Adrienne Rich (1929–2012) are among the most challenging in the feminist canon. They were, to a large extent, impassioned responses to her shifting and often conflicting roles as American, Southerner, Jew, wife, mother, teacher, civil rights activist, feminist, and lesbian. Many of Rich's poems explore the complexities of personal and political relationships, especially as they are affected by gender. In the poem "Translations," she drew attention to the ways in which traditional gender roles polarize the sexes and potentially disempower women.

The youngest of the feminist poets in this group, Rita Dove (b. 1952), is the first African-American woman to have served as poet laureate in the United States (1993–1995). Dove's eight collections of poetry, one of which was awarded the Pulitzer Prize (1987), reach into the domains of the black feminist experience. In the short poem "Rosa," from the sequence of poems entitled "On the Bus with Rosa Parks," Dove pays homage to the heroism of the black woman who, riding a bus in Montgomery, Alabama, refused to give up her seat to a white man. (The incident triggered one of the earliest civil rights protests, a citywide boycott led by Martin Luther King.)

READING 36.12 Feminist Poems

Sexton's "Self in 1958" (1966)

What is reality?   1
I am a plaster doll; I pose
with eyes that cut open without landfall or nightfall
upon some shellacked and grinning person,
eyes that open, blue, steel, and close.   5
Am I approximately an I. Magnin[1] transplant?
I have hair, black angel,
black-angel-stuffing to comb,
nylon legs, luminous arms
and some advertised clothes.   10

I live in a doll's house
with four chairs,
a counterfeit table, a flat roof
and a big front door.
Many have come to such a small crossroad.   15

There is an iron bed,
(Life enlarges, life takes aim)
a cardboard floor,
windows that flash open on someone's city,
and little more.   20
Someone plays with me,
plants me in the all-electric kitchen,
Is this what Mrs. Rombauer[2] said?
Someone pretends with me—
I am walled in solid by their noise—   25
or puts me upon their straight bed.
They think I am me!
Their warmth? Their warmth is not a friend!
They pry my mouth for their cups of gin
and their stale bread.   30

What is reality
to this synthetic doll
who should smile, who should shift gears,
should spring the doors open in a wholesome disorder,
and have no evidence of ruin or fears?   35
But I would cry,
rooted into the wall that
was once my mother,
if I could remember how
and if I had the tears.   40

Sanchez's "Woman" (1978)

Come ride my birth, earth mother   1
tell me how i have become, became
this woman with razor blades between
her teeth.
      sing me my history O earth mother
about tongues multiplying memories   5
about breaths contained in straw.
pull me from the throat of mankind
where worms eat, O earth mother.
come to this Black woman. you.
rider of earth pilgrimages.   10
tell me how i have held five bodies
in one large cocktail of love
and still have the thirst of the beginning sip.
tell me. tellLLLLLL me. earth mother
for i want to rediscover me. the secret of me   15
the river of me. the morning ease of me.
i want my body to carry my words like aqueducts.
i want to make the world my diary
and speak rivers.

rise up earth mother   20
out of rope-strung-trees
dancing a windless dance
come phantom mother
dance me a breakfast of births
let your mouth spill me forth   25
so i creak with your mornings.

---

[1] A fashionable department store.

[2] Irma S. Rombauer, author of the popular cookbook *The Joy of Cooking*.

come old mother, light up my mind
with a story bright as the sun.

Rich's "Translations" (1972)

You show me the poems of some woman   1
my age, or younger
translated from your language

Certain words occur: *enemy, oven, sorrow*
enough to let me know   5
she's a woman of my time

obsessed
with Love, our subject:
we've trained it like ivy to our walls
baked it like bread in our ovens   10
worn it like lead on our ankles
watched it through binoculars as if
it were a helicopter
bringing food to our famine
or the satellite   15
of a hostile power

I begin to see that woman
doing things: stirring rice
ironing a skirt
typing a manuscript till dawn   20

trying to make a call
from a phonebooth

The phone rings unanswered
in a man's bedroom
she hears him telling someone else   25
Never mind. She'll get tired.
hears him telling her story to her sister
who becomes her enemy
and will in her own time
light her own way to sorrow   30

ignorant of the fact this way of grief
is shared, unnecessary
and political

Dove's "Rosa" (1998)

How she sat there,   1
the time right inside a place
so wrong it was ready.

That trim name with
its dream of a bench
to rest on. Her sensible coat.   5

Doing nothing was the doing:
the clean flame of her gaze
carved by a camera flash.

How she stood up   10

when they bent down to retrieve
her purse. That courtesy.

Q **What aspects of the female experience do each of these poems address?**

Q **How might these poems "empower" women?**

Feminist Art

The history of world art includes only a small number of female artists. Addressing this fact, the Australian-born feminist Germaine Greer (b. 1939) explained,

> There is . . . no female Leonardo, no female Titian, no female Poussin, but the reason does not lie in the fact that women have wombs, that they can have babies, that their brains are smaller, that they lack vigor, that they are not sensual. The reason is simply that you cannot make great artists out of egos that have been damaged, with wills that are defective, with libidos that have been driven out of reach and energy diverted into neurotic channels.

A sure indication of change, however, is the fact that, since the middle of the twentieth century, the number of women in the visual arts (and in music as well) has been greater than ever before in history. And, as with feminist poetry, much of the painting and sculpture produced by women artists since the 1960s has been driven by feminist concerns. A few examples will suffice to make this point.

Saint Phalle Bringing a feminist attention to the female body, the internationally acclaimed French sculptor Niki de Saint Phalle (1930–2003) fabricated gigantic sculptures that she called "Nanas." In 1963, Saint Phalle exhibited a monumental 80-foot-long, 20-foot-high, and 30-foot-wide Nana that viewers might enter through a doorway between the figure's legs. Inside was a cinema showing Greta Garbo movies, a telephone, a refreshment bar, and taped voices of romantic conversations between a man and a woman.

Mendieta In searching for a feminist aesthetic, women artists have brought attention to the female body as representative of nature's procreative forces. The Cuban-born Ana Mendieta (1948–1985) used photography and film to document performances inspired by Afro-Caribbean fertility rituals. For the series known as "Silhouettes," Mendieta immersed herself in pools of water, sand, and mud, and recorded 200 images of her body or its physical impressions on various earth surfaces. In the photograph *Tree of Life* from this series, the artist, encrusted with grass and mud, appears in the dual guises of dryad (a Classical tree nymph) and ancient priestess (Figure **36.13**). She stated: "My art is the way I establish the bonds that unite me to the universe."

Chicago The militant American feminist Judy Gerowitz (b. 1939), who in 1969 assumed the surname of her native city (hence, Judy Chicago), has been a lifelong

Niki de Saint Phalle's *Black Venus*, a hugely proportioned polyester "earth mother," wears a large red heart on her belly and flowers on her hips (Figure **36.11**). This exuberant creature is Saint Phalle's answer to the Western stereotypes of female beauty. She is more closely related to the ponderous fertility figures of prehistory, such as the Venus of Willendorf (Figure **36.12**), than to the refined Classical goddesses of the ancient Greeks and Romans. Indeed, she is the feminist reproof to the idealized female figure that dominated mainstream art through the nineteenth century.

Figure 36.11 NIKI DE SAINT PHALLE, *Black Venus*, 1965–1967. Painted polyester, 9 ft. 2 in. × 2 ft. 11 in. × 2 ft.

Figure 36.12 "Venus" of Willendorf, from Lower Austria, ca. 25,000–20,000 B.C.E. Limestone, height 4⅜ in.

advocate of women's art. Chicago pioneered some of the first art communities in which women worked together to produce, exhibit, and sell art. Her efforts ignited the visual arts with the consciousness-raising politics of the feminist movement. Between 1974 and 1979, Chicago directed a monumental project called *The Dinner Party*. This room-size installation consists of a triangular table (48 feet on each side) with thirty-nine place settings, each symbolizing a famous woman in myth or history (see LOOKING INTO, Figure **36.14**). To carry out this ambitious project, Chicago studied the traditionally female arts of embroidery and china painting, inventing at the same time new techniques for combining such dissimilar materials as ceramics and lace. Over 300 men and women contributed to this cooperative enterprise, which brought international attention to the cultural contributions of women in world history.

Sherman and Kruger The career of the American photographer Cindy Sherman (b. 1954) addresses one of the more recent concerns of feminist artists: the fact that the traditional Western *image* of the female—sweet, sexy, and servile—has been shaped by male needs and values.

Figure 36.13 ANA MENDIETA, *Tree of Life*, from the "Silhouettes" series, 1977. Original documentation of the earth/body performance, Iowa, 35 mm slide. Mendieta integrated the performance traditions of Afro-Caribbean religions into her feminist pieces. After 1980, she distanced herself from the feminist art movement, which she felt was too closely tied to white, middle-class values.

Chicago's *Dinner Party*

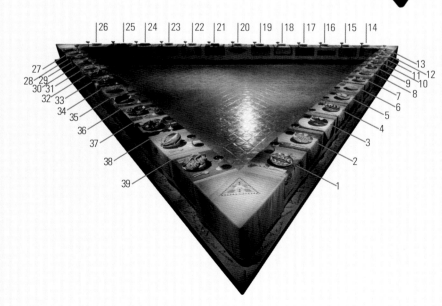

The feminist counterpart of the Last Supper, *The Dinner Party* pays homage to such immortals as Nefertiti, Sappho, Queen Elizabeth I, and Virginia Woolf. Each place setting includes a table runner embroidered with the notable woman's name, a napkin, utensils, a goblet, and a colorful high-relief ceramic plate, many of which bear a vulvalike butterfly image inspired by the personality or the accomplishments of the honoree. Chicago chose the triangle (a symbol of equality) for the shape of the table, as well as for each of the 999 porcelain tiles (inscribed with the names of additional famous females) that form the so-called Heritage Floor. The artist aimed, as she explained, "to end the ongoing cycle of omission in which women were written out of the historical record."

Figure 36.14
JUDY CHICAGO,
The Dinner Party,
1974–1979. Multimedia,
48 × 48 × 48 ft. With the ambitious combination of ceramics and textiles, Chicago introduced craft techniques into the arts of the 1970s. Each plate here is an independent artwork; each runner bears embroidery that includes the name of the honoree and her identifying symbol.

Wing I
From Prehistory to the
Roman Empire
1. Primordial Goddess
2. Fertile Goddess
3. Ishtar
4. Kali
5. Snake Goddess
6. Sophia
7. Amazon
8. Hatshepsut
9. Judith
10. Sappho
11. Aspasia
12. Boadaceia
13. Hypatia

Wing II
From the Beginnings of
Christianity to the Reformation
14. Marcella
15. Saint Bridget
16. Thodora
17. Hrosvitha
18. Trotula
19. Eleanor of Acquitaine
20. Hildegarde of Bingen
21. Petronilla de Meath
22. Christine de Pisan
23. Isabella d'Este
24. Elizabeth R.
25. Artemisia Gentilleschi
26. Anna van Schumann

Wing III
From the American to the
Women's Revolution
27. Anne Hutchinson
28. Sacajawea
29. Caroline Herschel
30. Mary Wollstonecraft
31. Sojourner Truth
32. Susan B. Anthony
33. Elizabeth Blackwell
34. Emily Dickinson
35. Ethel Smyth
36. Margaret Sanger
37. Natalie Barney
38. Virginia Woolf
39. Georgia O'Keeffe

Figure 36.15 CINDY SHERMAN, *Untitled #276*, 1993. Color photograph, edition of six, 6 ft. 8½ in. × 5 ft. 1 in., framed. Sitting in a curtained space, on a low throne, this flaxen-haired "Cinderella" assumes a vulgar pose. She holds, however, three stems of lilies, a symbol of purity traditionally associated with the Virgin Mary. Sherman underscores the ambiguity of her photographs' contents by deliberately leaving them untitled.

Chronology

1918   British women granted the right to vote

1920   American women granted the right to vote

1966   Founding of National Organization for Women (NOW)

1969   Police raid Stonewall Inn, a gay bar in New York City

2001   the Netherlands legalizes same-sex marriage

2013   the United States Supreme Court strikes down the Defense of Marriage Act

2014   legislation advanced to protect the rights of transgender people in India, Sweden, New Zealand and elsewhere

Well aware of the extent to which commercialism shapes identity, Barbara Kruger (b. 1945) creates photographs that deftly unite word and image to resemble commercial billboards. "Your Body is a Battleground," insists Kruger; by superimposing the message over the divided (positive and negative) image of a female face, the artist calls attention to the controversial issue of abortion in contemporary society (Figure **36.16**).

Gender Identity

The dual quest for racial and gender equality has also worked to raise public consciousness concerning the ways sex is used as a structuring principle in human culture and society. As distinct from *sex*, a biologically determined construct that designates the individual as either male or

Such images, say contemporary feminists, reflect the controlling power of the (male) "gaze." The theory of the "male gaze," which emerged among feminist critics of the 1960s, holds that the female image, usually conceived by male artists and rendered exclusively from the male perspective, reduces women to the status of objects. Just as Colescott and Saar use art to attack racial stereotypes, so Sherman makes visual assaults on gender stereotypes—those projected by the collective body of "great art" and by the modern-day phenomena of television, "girlie" magazines, and other mass media. Sherman's large, glossy studio photographs from the 1970s feature the artist herself in poses and attire that call attention to the body as a political or sexual object. In personalized narratives that resemble black-and-white movie stills, she recreates commercial stereotypes that mock the subservient roles that women play: the "little woman," the *femme fatale*, the baby doll, the "pin-up," and the lovesick teenager. Since the 1980s, Sherman has used the newest techniques in color photography to assault—often in visceral terms—sexual and historical stereotypes of women. She may replace the male image in a world-famous painting with a female image (often Sherman herself), use artificial body parts to "remake" the traditional nude, or flagrantly recast famous females from Western myth, history, and religion (Figure **36.15**).

Figure 36.16 BARBARA KRUGER, *Untitled ("Your Body is a Battleground")*, 1989. Photographic silkscreen on vinyl, 9 ft. 4 in. × 9 ft. 4 in.

female, *gender* is culturally determined. Assumptions concerning the sexual and social roles of males and females are rooted in traditions as old as Paleolithic culture and as venerated as the Bible. For many, sexual roles are fixed and unchanging. However, these assumptions, like so many others in the cultural history of the twentieth century, have come to be challenged and reassessed.

Gender issues accompanied a demand for equality on the part of those of untraditional sexual orientation—bisexuals, homosexuals (gays and lesbians), and transgendered individuals (those who identify with a gender other than that which they were biologically assigned at birth). In America, homosexuals date their "liberation" to June 1969, when they openly and violently protested a police raid on the Stonewall Inn, a gay bar in New York's Greenwich Village. Thereafter, the call for protection against harassment shifted to litigated demands for gender equality. While all societies have included a transgendered subculture, it was not until the last decades of the twentieth century that sexual and public issues intersected to produce some highly controversial questions. Should homosexuals serve in the armed forces? Should homosexual marriage be legalized? How does homosexuality affect the future of the traditional family? Should sexually explicit art receive public funding? Many of these questions have been answered by twenty-first century legislation. For instance, in 2001, the Netherlands became the first nation to legalize same-sex marriage. In 2013, the United States Supreme Court struck down the 1996 Defense of Marriage Act that blocked Federal recognition of gay marriage. To date, same-sex marriage has been recognized in seventeen American states. The most recent expression of the so-called gender revolution is the social movement to protect the rights of transgender individuals. Legislation to protect the rights of transgender individuals has been advanced in a number of countries, including India, Argentina, New Zealand, Sweden, and the Netherlands.

Science and Technology

1953	biophysicists determine the molecular structure of DNA
1953	Jonas Salk (American) tests an effective polio vaccine
1955	an American endocrinologist produces a successful birth-control pill
1967	Christian Bernard (South African) performs the first human heart transplant
1973	American biochemists isolate genes to make genetic engineering possible
1978	the world's first test-tube baby is born
1982	the fatal immune system disorder AIDS (Acquired Immune Deficiency Syndrome) is diagnosed

Figure 36.17 THE NAMES PROJECT, *AIDS Memorial Quilt*, as displayed on the National Mall facing the Capitol, Washington, D.C., October 1996.

There are a number of reasons why issues of human sexuality and gender identity became so visible in the culture of the late twentieth century: increasing sexual permissiveness (the consequence of improved pharmaceutical methods of contraception); the activity of the media (especially television and film) in broadcasting sexually explicit entertainment; and the appearance of the devastating pandemic called AIDS (Acquired Immune Deficiency Syndrome), a life-threatening disease resulting from a retrovirus named HIV that attacks the blood cells of the body, thus causing a failure of the autoimmune system. Collectively, these phenomena have represented an overwhelming challenge to traditional concepts of sexuality, sexual behavior, and (more generally) to conventional morality. They have also generated a provocative blurring of sex roles (which has been increasingly exploited in commercial advertising, video-sharing websites, and the popular media). And they continue to complicate the task of distinguishing between forms of expression that have mere shock value and those that represent a substantial creative achievement.

Gender Identity and the Arts

The AIDS pandemic left its mark on the late twentieth century in the form of a public arts project: the *Aids Memorial Quilt*, begun in 1985, which engaged 20,000 ordinary individuals, each of whom created a single 3- by 6-foot fabric panel in memory of someone who had died of an HIV-related disease. In 1992, AIDS activists assembled the panels in 16-foot squares and took them from San Francisco to Washington, D.C., to protest governmental inaction over the AIDS crisis. Commemorating the deaths of some 150,000 Americans, the *Aids Memorial Quilt* covered

15 acres of ground between the Washington Monument and the Lincoln Memorial (Figure **36.17**). The Names Project continues: in 2013, the quilt panels numbered 48,000, that is, more than double the figure of the original.

The photographs of Robert Mapplethorpe (1946–1989) are significant expressions of an artist who was himself a victim of AIDS. Mapplethorpe's fine-grained silver gelatin prints display exquisitely composed images ranging from still-life subjects to classically posed nudes. Although lacking explicit narrative, they reflect the artist's preoccupation with physical and sexual themes: male virility, sadomasochism, androgyny, and sexual identity. Mapplethorpe's stark black-and-white photographs depict contemporary sexuality in a manner that is at once detached and impassioned, but they often gain added power as gender-bending parodies of sexual stereotypes—witness the startling blurring of masculine and feminine cues in his *Self-Portrait* of 1980 (Figure **36.18**).

Themes of human sexuality have increasingly preoccupied contemporary writers. In her science-fiction fantasy *The Left Hand of Darkness* (1969), the American writer Ursula Le Guin (b. 1929) describes a distant planet, home to creatures with the sexual potential of both males and females. The ambisexuality of the characters in this fictional utopia calls into question human preconceptions about the defined roles of behavior for men and women. Through the device of science fiction, Le Guin suggests a shift in focus from the narrow view of male–female dualities (or opposites) to larger and more urgent matters of interdependence.

While Le Guin examines bisexuality in imaginary settings, other writers have dealt with the experience of homosexuality in day-to-day life. Among the eminent twentieth-century novelists who have dealt with explicitly gay themes and characters are E. M. Forster, James Baldwin, Gore Vidal, and André Gide. Set during the AIDS crisis, Bill Sherwood's *Parting Glances* (1986) is widely considered a landmark of gay cinema. And in the past quarter-century, a great number of gay and lesbian

television shows, videos, and films (of varying quality) have been produced throughout the world. Mass media have been particularly successful at bringing issues of gender identity, sexual "otherness," and the gay sensibility to a mass population.

By drawing attention to the ways in which matters of sexuality affect society and its institutions, contemporary art asserts that sexuality and power are as closely related

Figure 36.18 ROBERT MAPPLETHORPE, *Self-Portrait*, 1980. Silver gelatin print, 20 × 16 in. Questioning the conventional "markers" of male and female identity, Mapplethorpe appears here in drag, with fur stole and face make-up. In the late 1980s, American museum and gallery exhibitions of Mapplethorpe's photographs, which gave frank treatment to alternative lifestyles and sexual practices, raised intense public controversy and fired a debate over the funding of artists by the National Endowment for the Arts.

EXPLORING ISSUES

Issue-Driven Art

One of the most moving responses to the AIDS crisis is *Still/Here* (1994), a two-act dance-theater work produced by the African-American dancer/choreographer Bill T. Jones (b. 1952). Jones conceived the piece in part as a memorial to his partner, Arnie Zane, who died of AIDS in 1988. For the work, Jones combined dance and a vocal score with video imagery derived in part from workshops he conducted with AIDS victims. When it was first performed in 1994, *Still/Here* provoked heated criticism and debate. Critics questioned the value of art that showcased sickness and

death. Others defended the right as well as the responsibility of the artist to put art at the service of social action and reform.

More than twenty-five years later, many regard *Still/Here* as a tribute to the resilience of the human spirit in the face of life-threatening illness. But the work raises important questions. What role should issue-driven art play in contemporary life? If such art takes meaning and authority exclusively from its immediate historical context, can it be evaluated objectively for its broader aesthetic value? Are all issue-driven artworks activist in intention (see chapter 38)?

as race and power or gender and power. Tony Kushner's Pulitzer Prize-winning play *Angels in America: A Gay Fantasia on National Themes* (written in two parts: *Millennium Approaches*, 1990, and *Perestroika*, 1993) presents a radical vision of American society set against the AIDS epidemic and the politics of conservatism. Kushner (b. 1957) urges the old America—"straight," Protestant, and white—to look with greater objectivity at "the fringe" (the variety of ethnic, racial, and sexual minorities), which demands acceptance and its share of power. Kushner's landmark drama represents the movement for body-conscious politics and socially responsible art that animated the last decade of the twentieth century and continues to resonate in our own time.

LOOKING BACK

Anticolonialism and Liberation

- The quest for liberation from poverty, oppression, and inequality was a prevailing theme in twentieth-century history. In dozens of countries, movements for decolonization followed World War II.
- At the same time, racial and ethnic minorities fought valiantly to oppose discrimination as practiced by the majority culture. These crusades are yet ongoing among the populations of Eastern Europe, Latin America, the Middle East, Africa, and elsewhere.
- Western intrusion in Muslim lands has provoked protest, as evidenced in the poetry of Muhammad Iqbal.
- Liberation movements in Latin America were supported by the Catholic Church and by such writers as Pablo Neruda, whose poems condemn colonialism and commercial exploitation.

The Quest for Racial Equality

- The struggle of African-Americans to achieve freedom from the evils of racism has a long and dramatic history. From the Harlem Renaissance in the early twentieth century through the civil rights movement of the 1960s, the arts have mirrored that history.
- In the poems of Langston Hughes and Gwendolyn Brooks, and in the novels of Richard Wright, James Baldwin, Ralph Ellison, and Alice Walker, the plight and identity of African-Americans in white America have been central themes.
- The visual artist Romare Bearden engaged the world of jazz in collage; Betye Saar, Robert Colescott, and Kara Walker have tested the stereotypes of American racism by way of parody and satire.
- The impact of black culture in music and dance has been formidable. Blues and jazz giants from Louis Armstrong to Wynton Marsalis have produced a living body of popular music, while choreographers from Katherine Dunham to Alvin Ailey have inspired generations of dancers to draw on their African heritage.

The Quest for Gender Equality

- During the postwar era, women throughout the world worked to gain political, economic, and social equality.
- The writings of feminists Virginia Woolf and Simone de Beauvoir influenced women to examine the psychological conditions of their oppression.
- In America, the feminist movement elicited a virtual golden age in literature. The self-conscious poetry of Anne Sexton, Sonia Sanchez, Rita Dove, and Adrienne Rich is representative of this phenomenon.
- In the visual arts, at least two generations of women have redefined traditional concepts of female identity: first, by celebrating womanhood itself, and, more recently, by attacking outworn stereotypes.
- One of the most controversial of the twentieth century's liberation movements centered on issues of gender identity. Amidst the AIDS pandemic, Robert Mapplethorpe and Tony Kushner brought candor and perceptivity to matters of sexuality and sexual behavior.

Music Listening Selections

- Handy, "St. Louis Blues," 1914.
- Hardin/Armstrong, "Hotter Than That," 1927.
- Parker/Gillespie, "Koko," 1945.

Glossary

apartheid a policy of strict racial segregation and political and economic discrimination against the black population in South Africa

feminism the doctrine advocating equal social, political, and economic rights for women

scat singing a jazz performance style in which nonsense syllables replace the lyrics of a song

swing the jazz performer's practice of varying from the standard rhythms by playing just ahead of, or just behind, the beat; also, a big-band jazz style developed in the 1920s and flourishing in the age of large dance bands (1932–1942)

The Information Age
ca. 1960–present

*"In America, advertising enjoys universal popular adherence and
the American way of life is fashioned by it."*
Ellul

Figure 37.1 ROY LICHTENSTEIN, *Torpedo . . . Los!*, 1963. Oil on canvas, 5 ft. 8 in. × 6 ft. 8 in. Lichtenstein's large canvases, with their slickly finished surfaces and
flat, bold shapes, are burlesque versions of comic book heroes and mass-media advertisements. Ironically, the commercial world has now "reclaimed" Pop Art by quoting
Lichtenstein's imagery in advertising and fashion design.

Some historians date the end of Modernism to the decade of the Holocaust and the devastation of World War II, a period that saw the obliteration of utopian ideals and the rise of cynicism and doubt. But these sobering realities also formed the background for the Postmodern shift from an Industrial Age (dominated by farming and manufacturing) to an Information Age (dominated by radical changes in the technology of communication and the way we receive and process information). The agents of high technology, the mass media, and electronic modes of communication have facilitated this shift. In the fifteenth century, movable type brought about the print revolution, which transformed an essentially oral culture into one that depended on the book. In our own time, digital forms of communication have had an equally revolutionary effect: they have made more information available to a greater number of people at greater speed than ever before. And they have delivered much of that information in a visual form.

The information explosion had massive effects on the culture of the late twentieth century. It inspired literary styles that challenged traditional narrative genres and questioned the ways in which language serves meaning. Along with digitized forms of delivery, it contributed to a wealth of new styles and types of visual art, much of which is conceptual and interactive. In music and film, digital technology has affected everything from the production of sound to its storage and distribution. The culture of the last sixty years is challenging not only because of its diversity of styles and opinions, but also because it confronts the historical past with objectivity and skepticism.

The Information Explosion

Television and computers—the primary vehicles of the information explosion—have altered almost every aspect of life in our time. The wonderchild of electronics and the quintessential example of modern mass media, television originally transmitted sound and light by way of electromagnetic waves that sent information instantaneously into homes across the face of the earth. The very name "television" comes from the Greek word *tele*, meaning "far," and the Latin *videre*, meaning "to see"; hence "to see far." Television did not become common to middle-class life in the West until the 1950s, although it had been invented decades before then. By the 1960s, the events of a war in the jungles of Vietnam were being relayed via electronic communications satellite into American living rooms. In 1969, in a live telecast, the world saw the first astronauts walk on the surface of the moon. And in the early 1990s, during the Middle Eastern conflict triggered by the Iraqi invasion of Kuwait, those with access to television witnessed the first "prime-time war"—a war that was "processed" by censorship and television newscasting. Since the transition from analog to digital television in 2009, the news of the world has come into our homes with ever greater immediacy.

The second major technological phenomenon of the Information Age is the computer. Digital computers—machines that process information via numeric code—were first used widely in the 1950s. By the 1960s, computers utilizing electronic circuits were able to perform millions of calculations per second. Smaller and more reliable than ever before, computers have now come to facilitate a vast range of functions, from cellphone communication to rapid prototyping, a digital process that "prints" objects in three dimensions.

Computer technology accelerated the process of information production, storage, and retrieval. A single computer chip is capable of storing entire encyclopedias. Virtually unlimited amounts of information are available in various data banks, united by the World Wide Web, a system of electronically linked texts (or hypertexts) accessed by way of a series of interconnected computer networks known as the Internet.

Since the 1990s, information technology has rapidly proliferated. In 1998, the search engine known as Google became a website portal to other websites based on keyword searches. The world's first free, online, nonprofit English-language encyclopedia, Wikipedia, was launched in 2001. Publicly edited and continuously updated, it contains well over four million articles in 287 languages. Google currently vies with other companies to create a universal literary archive by putting all existing printed matter into an electronic library. The video-sharing website YouTube (2005) invites a polyglot audience to post

Science and Technology

1950	commercial color television becomes available
1953	first commercially successful computer introduced
1959	American engineers produce the first microchip (made from a silicon wafer)
1970	fiber optics technology is perfected to carry information thousands of times faster than copper cables
1972	first commercial videogame introduced
1975	first personal computer available
1979	first portable music device (the Walkman) produced
1983	first commercial cellular (wireless) phones produced

video "clips," while the image-hosting website Flickr (2004) provides a community resource for millions of photos and videos. Online postings—web-logs ("blogs")—exchange information and ideas on everything from current fashion fads to political policy. Fueling these activities are two prominent online social networking sites: Facebook, founded in 2004, and Twitter (2006), a site that enables users to send and read microblogs (text messages limited to 140 characters). Actively posting photos, opinions, and information, registered users of Facebook now exceed one billion worldwide, while the popularity of "tweeting" is reflected in the fact that, in 2013, users exchanged some 400 million "tweets" per day.

Big Data

Big data is the term for the phenomenon of mining and analyzing vast amounts of information available as a result of digital communication and storage. Such technology, which makes it possible to measure and analyze huge stores of data ("metadata"), may be viewed as the digital equivalent of the telescope or the microscope. In all fields, from biological science to sports and politics, the increasing volume and variety of data combine with sophisticated software to provide the basis for decision-making. Big data tools and techniques may be used for good or ill: for creating genome profiles that aid in medical cures, and for analyzing patterns of neighborhood crime so as to provide greater safety; or to manipulate financial programs for illicit gain, to assist hackers in evading or raiding government and corporate security systems, or to engage in identity

theft. Governments currently use big data for various kinds of surveillance; business enterprises use big data to target and exploit our personal buying habits, and, by extension, to shape our values. Clearly, big data may help politicians get elected; but will it help them to lead?

From Book to Screen

Book culture and the written language depend on linearity, syntactical order, and precision. By contrast, the culture of the Information Age is increasingly image-oriented (see Figure 37.7). By way of screens—television, computer, tablet, cell/smartphone, and camera—we receive ideas configured as pictures and logos, symbols and signs. Visual information (like music or film) is manipulated by dozens of digital processes: clipping, combining, distorting, mixing, and remixing. In contrast with the linear medium of print, electronic images are generated in diffuse, discontinuous bundles and rapidly dispatched fragments. As product and message fall to process and medium, all images tend to become homogenized, that is, uniform and alike. (As the communications theorist Marshall McLuhan (1911–1980) famously observed in 1964: "The medium is the message.") Further, electronic processing and the rapid diffusion of images via television and the Internet have worked to reduce distinctions between different types of information: the stuff of "popular" culture is often indistinguishable from that of "high" culture. Too frequently, the world of the screen has turned information, from protest marches to breakfast cereals, into marketable commodities, transforming culture into what one critic

EXPLORING ISSUES

The Perils of the Information Age

The French sociologist Jacques Ellul (1912–1994) blamed television for creating what he called a society of "mass man." He singled out advertising as the most pernicious condition assaulting human dignity. In *The Technological Society* (1964), Ellul observed:

> Advertising [affects] all people; or at least an overwhelming majority. Its goal is to persuade the masses to buy. . . .
> The inevitable consequence is the creation of the mass man. As advertising of the most varied products is concentrated, a new type of human being, precise and generalized, emerges. We can get a general impression of this new human type by studying America, where human beings tend clearly to become identified with the ideal of advertising. In America, advertising enjoys universal popular adherence and the American way of life is fashioned by it.

Ellul's view of advertising as a form of "psychological collectivism" that robs human beings of freedom and self-esteem dates from a time in which commercial advertising was dominated by printed

media and television. However, today's computerized forms of communication and data collection offer even greater resources for manipulating personal taste and values. At the same time, digital technology provides free resources for individual expression and interactive global enterprise (see chapter 38).

The dystopian novel *The Circle* (2013) by David Eggers (b. 1970) presents a timely (and all too recognizable) parable for our digital age. The heroine of the novel joins a company called the Circle that (much like Google or Facebook) seeks to gather, quantify, and share everything there is to be recorded. Obedient to the company logo, "All that happens must be known," she is pressed to renounce her privacy by "going transparent," that is, sharing the totality of her existence. Well beyond the tyranny of transparency, the consequences of information-sharing come to challenge her individual personhood. The age of big data raises the question: "What might be the perils of living in a world where all things and people can be endlessly observed?"

calls "a vast garage sale." Information overload and the gradual domination of the Internet over the printing press will surely transform cognition and communication in ways we have yet to discover.

New Directions in Science and Philosophy

The major developments of the last half-century followed from scientific advances that have made possible investigations into outer space—the universe at large—and inner space, the province of our own bodies. Science and technology have propelled humankind beyond planet earth and into the cosmos. At the same time, they have provided an unprecedented understanding of the genetic patterns that govern life itself. These phenomena have worked to make the planet smaller, the universe larger, and methods of navigating the two ever more promising.

String Theory

Since the middle of the twentieth century, physicists have tried to reconcile the insights of the two great intellectual systems advanced early in the century: Einstein's theory of relativity, which applies to vast, cosmological space, and quantum physics, which describes the realms of the very small. They seek to establish "a theory of everything," one that might explain the "fundamental of fundamentals" that governs the organization and complexity of matter. A new (but yet unproven) theory proposes that all matter—from the page of this book to the skin of a peach—consists of tiny loops of vibrating strings. *String* (or *Superstring*) *Theory*, most eloquently explained by the American physicist Brian Greene (b. 1962), describes a multidimensional universe in which loops of strings and oscillating globules of matter unite all of creation into vibrational patterns.* While the workings of such a universe can be simulated on a computer, language—other than the language of mathematics—is too frail to serve as an explanatory medium. Yet it is in the arts, and possibly in aesthetic theory, that the design of this elegant universe may be approximated. As the Norwegian physicist Niels Bohr (1885–1962) observed, "When it comes to atoms, language can be used only as in poetry."

Chaos Theory

Equally fascinating are the speculations of those who explore the shape and structure of matter itself. The proponents of *Chaos Theory* find that universal patterns underlie the seemingly random operations of nature. The catalyst for the development of Chaos Theory was the electronic computer, by which the mathematics of random patterns (applied to such matters as air turbulence and weather predictions) was first calculated. Predictable patterns repeat themselves in physical phenomena ranging from the formation of a snowflake to the rhythms of the

human heart. Chaos theorists (not only physicists, but also astronomers, mathematicians, biologists, and computer scientists) observe that while these patterns appear random, unstable, and disorderly, they are actually self-similar in scale, like the zigs and zags of a lightning bolt, or the oscillating motions of electric currents. To Einstein's famous assertion, "God does not play dice with the universe," these theorists might respond: "Not only does God play dice; but they are loaded."

The Human Genome

One of the major projects of the late twentieth century was the successful mapping of the *human genome*. By the year 2000, molecular biologists had been able (with the help of computers) to ascertain the order of nearly three billion units of DNA, thereby locating genes and determining their functions in the human cellular system. Ultimately, this enterprise is expected to revolutionize the practice

* Brian Greene, *The Elegant Universe: Superstrings, Hidden Dimensions and the Quest for the Ultimate Theory.* New York: Norton, 1999.

Science and Technology

1990	the internationally linked computer network (the Internet) becomes accessible to personal computers
1992	IBM invents the smartphone
1995+	advances in nanotechnology and microprocessing make possible minicomputers, palm televisions, smart bombs, etc.
2000+	wireless networks, broadband, digital television, and satellite radio become mainstream
2001	Apple releases its first-generation iPod (portable digital music device)
2004–2006	social media sites Facebook and Twitter founded
2005	the video-sharing website YouTube is launched
2007	wireless electronic reading devices become available

Science and Technology

1983	the first commercial use of MRI (Magnetic Resonance Imaging)
1990	the Human Genome Project is initiated
1996	Dolly, a cloned sheep, is born in Scotland
2000	scientists complete the mapping of the human genome
2005	first publicly available personal genetic blueprints
2007	human skin cells are found to be reprogrammable as stem cells
2010	the first full face transplant is completed in Spain

of medicine, in the preventive treatment of gene-related diseases, the diagnosis and prediction of hereditary diseases, and the repair and regeneration of tissue. (Already, such research has diminished the number of AIDS deaths internationally.)

The tools of genetic engineering have also given scientists the ability to clone life forms. They also promise the mitigation of what Freud described as one of humankind's greatest threats: the suffering "from our own body, which is doomed to decay and dissolution." From sports medicine to psychoanalysis, society has come to perceive human beings as mechanisms that can be improved, if not perfected, by the right diet, drugs, exercise, and a healthy lifestyle.

The 1990s brought exciting breakthroughs in the area of *cognitive neuroscience*, as new imaging technology showed how brain waves can influence matter. In recent German experiments in neural consciousness, patients wearing electrodes on their scalps modulate electrical signals to choose letters from a video screen—thus communicating with nothing but their own brains. These biofeedback experiments are reinforced by neurochemical research: the American biochemist Candace Pert (b. 1946) writes in her groundbreaking book *Molecules of Emotion* (1997), "We know that the immune system, like the central nervous system, has memory and the capacity to learn. Thus, it could be said that intelligence is located not only in the brain but in cells that are distributed throughout the body, and that the traditional separation of mental processes, including emotions, from the body, is no longer valid." As the gap between mind and body grows narrower, Eastern notions of the symbiosis of matter and spirit have received increased attention in the West. By way of popular literature (such as *Quantum Healing: Exploring the Frontier of Mind/Body Medicine*, 1990), the Indian-born endocrinologist Deepak Chopra (b. 1946) introduced Western audiences to holistic models of meditation and body control that have flourished in India for 2000 years.

Language Theory

While science moves forward optimistically to reveal the underlying natural order, philosophy has entered a phase of radical skepticism that denies the existence of any true or uniform system of thought. Contemporary philosophers have fastened on the idea, first popularized by the Austrian Ludwig Wittgenstein (1889–1951), that all forms of expression, and, indeed, all truths, are dominated by the limits of language as a descriptive tool. Wittgenstein, whose life's work was an inquiry into the ways in which language represents the world, argued that sentences (or propositions) were "pictures of reality." His groundbreaking theories on the philosophy of language were published two years after his death, under the title *Philosophical Investigations*.

Following Wittgenstein, philosophers tried to unlock the meaning of the *text* (that is, any mode of cultural expression) by way of a close analysis of its linguistic structure. Language theorists suggested that one must "deconstruct" or "take apart" discourse in order to "unmask" its many meanings. The leaders of *Deconstruction*, the French philosophers Jacques Derrida (1930–2004) and Michel Foucault (1926–1984), were influential in arguing that all human beings are prisoners of the very language they use to think and to describe the world. In *Of Grammatology* (1967), Derrida examined the relationship between speech and writing, and their roles in the effectiveness of communication. In a similar direction, Foucault's *The Archeology of Knowledge* (1969) suggests that language is not the servant, but the master, of those who use it; we fail to realize that we are forever submitting to its demands. Philosophers, he asserted, should abandon the search for absolute truths and concentrate on the discovery of meaning(s). "Deconstruction" became the popular method of analysis in philosophy, linguistics, and literary criticism in the late twentieth century.

The American philosopher Richard Rorty (1931–2007) was deeply troubled by the limits of both linguistic inquiry and traditional philosophy. Rorty argued that the great thinkers of the postphilosophical age are not the metaphysicians or the linguists but, rather, those artists whose works provide others with insights into achieving self-transformation. What Rorty called the "linguistic turn" describes the move (among writers and philosophers) to rethink language as verbal coding.

Literature in the Information Age

Postmodernism

The term "Postmodernism" came into use shortly before World War II to describe the reaction to or against Modernism, but by the late 1960s it had come to designate the cultural condition of the late twentieth century. Whether defined as a reaction against Modernism or as an entirely new form of Modernism, Postmodernism is a phenomenon that occurred principally in the West. As a style, it is marked by a bemused awareness of a historical past whose "reality" has been processed by mass communication and information technology.

Postmodern artists appropriate (or borrow) pre-existing texts and images from history, advertising, and the media. They offer alternatives to the high seriousness and introversion of Modernist expression, and move instead in the direction of parody (burlesque imitation), whimsy, paradox, and irony. Their playful amalgam of disparate styles mingles the superficial and the profound. Their seemingly incongruous "layering" of images calls to mind the fundamentals of Chaos Theory, which advances a geometry of the universe that is "broken up, twisted, tangled, intertwined."

In contrast with elitist Modernism, Postmodernism is self-consciously populist, even to the point of inviting the active participation of the beholder. Whereas Modern artists (consider Eliot or Kandinsky) exalt the artist as visionary and rebel, Postmodern artists bring wry skepticism to the creative act. Less preoccupied than the Modernists with formal abstraction and its redeeming power, Postmodernists acknowledge art as an information system and a commodity shaped by the electronic media, its messages, and its modes of communication.

The Postmodern stance is more disengaged than authorial, its message often enigmatic. Finally, Postmodernism is pluralistic, that is, it suggests that meaning is many-faceted and fleeting, rather than absolute and fixed; and that the individual has numerous (and often contradictory) identities.

Postmodern Fiction

Postmodern writers share the contemporary philosopher's disdain for rational structure and the Deconstructionist's fascination with the function of language. They tend to bypass traditional narrative styles in favor of techniques that parody the writer's craft, mingle past, present, and future events, leave situations unresolved, and freely mix the ordinary and the bizarre. This genre has been called "Metafiction"—fiction about fiction. It takes fragments of information out of their original literary/historical context and juxtaposes them with little or no commentary on their meaning. In a single story, a line from a poem by T. S. Eliot or a Shakespeare play may appear alongside a catchy saying or banal slogan from a television commercial, a phrase from a national anthem, or a shopping list, as if the writer were claiming all information as equally valuable.

In Postmodern fiction, characters undergo little or no development, plots often lack logical direction, and events—whether ordinary, perverse, or fantastic—may be described in the detached tone of a newspaper article. Like the television newscast, the language of Postmodern fiction is often diffuse, discontinuous, and filled with innuendo and "commentary." The American novelist Kurt Vonnegut (1922–2007) favored clipped sentences framed in the present tense. He created a kind of "videofiction" that seemed aimed at readers whose attention spans have been dwarfed by commercial television programming. The Italian novelist Italo Calvino (1923–1985) engages the reader in a hunt for meanings that lie in the spaces between the act of writing and the events the words describe. Calvino interrupts the story line of his novel *If On a Winter's Night a Traveler* (1979) to confront the reader, thus:

> For a couple of pages now you have been reading
> on, and this would be the time to tell you clearly
> whether this station where I have got off is a
> station of the past or a station of today; instead
> the sentences continue to move in vagueness,
>   grayness,
> in a kind of no man's land of experience reduced
> to the lowest kind of denominator. Watch out:
> it is surely a method of involving you gradually,
> capturing you in the story before you realize it—a
> trap. Or perhaps the author still has not made up
> his mind, just as you, reader, for that matter,
> are not sure what you would most like to read.

While Vonnegut and Calvino are representative of twentieth-century Metafiction, they are by no means the only writers whose prose works have a Postmodern stamp. The Nobel Prize-winning author Doris Lessing (1919–2013) conceived *The Golden Notebook* (1962) as a series of interwoven narrative fragments, diary entries, and personal notes. Her voice is that of a middle-aged feminist who struggles with the political and personal traumas of a postwar, Postmodern society.

It is too soon to determine which of the internationally renowned writers of the last half-century will leave landmarks in the history of culture. The following are likely candidates: Joan Didion (b. 1934), Tom Wolfe (b. 1930), and Don DeLillo (b. 1936). All three of these American authors employ the events of their time to produce *docufiction*—a literary genre that gives an original (and fictionalized) narrative context to contemporary events and situations. DeLillo captures the cinematic rush of American life in the compelling novel *Underworld*, which connects major worldwide phenomena—the atomic bomb, the cold war—to such everyday events as baseball and waste management. His style, in which the narrative moves back and forth in time, parallels a Postmodern propensity for disordering time sequences, readily apparent in contemporary cinema. DeLillo's concerns over international terrorism (see chapter 38), the ecology of the planet, urban violence, and the loss of spiritual and moral values are shared by many contemporary novelists. Most, however, such as Philip Roth (b. 1933), John Updike (1932–2009), and Margaret Atwood (b. 1939), have maintained a traditional narrative style. Atwood retains this style in dystopian works she calls "social science fiction," or "speculative fiction."

Urban violence, poverty, corporate greed, and the search for spiritual renewal in a commodity-driven world have inspired much of the literature of the late twentieth and early twenty-first centuries. Such writing is usually realistic and straightforward. One of the leading voices of the narrative genre is the American writer Joyce Carol Oates (b. 1938). Oates deals with the violent underlayer of contemporary urban society. In the story "Ace," she makes use of a highly concentrated kind of prose fiction that she calls the "miniature narrative." Its tale of random violence—the familiar fare of the daily broadcast television news—unfolds with cinematic intensity, an effect embellished by powerful present-tense narrative and vivid characterization.

READING 37.1 Oates' "Ace" (1988)

A gang of overgrown boys, aged eighteen to twenty-five,　　1
has taken over the northeast corner of our park again this
summer. Early evenings they start arriving, hang out until the
park closes at midnight. Nothing to do but get high on beer
and dope, the police leave them alone as long as they mind their
own business, don't hassle people too much. Now and then
there's fighting but nothing serious—nobody shot or stabbed.

　　Of course no girl or woman in her right mind would go
anywhere near them, if she didn't have a boyfriend there.

　　Ace is the leader, a big boy in his twenties with a mean　　10
baby-face, pouty mouth, and cheeks so red they look fresh-
slapped, sly little steely eyes curling up at the corners like he's
laughing or getting ready to laugh. He's six foot two weighing
maybe two hundred twenty pounds—lifts weights at the gym—
but there's some loose flabby flesh around his middle, straining

against his belt. He goes bare-chested in the heat, likes to sweat in the open air, muscles bunched and gleaming, and he can show off his weird tattoos—ace of spades on his right bicep, inky-black octopus on his left. Long shaggy hair the color of dirty sand and he wears a red sweatband for looks.

Nobody notices anything special about a car circling the park, lots of traffic on summer nights and nobody's watching then there's this popping noise like a firecracker and right away Ace screams and claps his hand to his eye and it's streaming blood—what the hell? Did somebody shoot him? His buddies just freeze not knowing what to do. There's a long terrible minute when everybody stands there staring at Ace not knowing what to do—then the boys run and duck for cover, scattering like pigeons. And Ace is left alone standing there, crouched, his hand to his left eye screaming, Help, Jesus, hey, help, my eye—Standing there crouched at the knee like he's waiting for a second shot to finish him off.

The bullet must have come at an angle, skimmed the side of Ace's face, otherwise he'd be flat-out dead lying in the scrubby grass. He's panicked though, breathing loud through his mouth saying, O Jesus, O Jesus, and after a minute people start yelling, word's out there's been a shooting and somebody's hurt. Ace wheels around like he's been hit again but it's only to get away, suddenly he's walking fast stooped over dripping blood, could be he's embarrassed, doesn't want people to see him, red headband and tattoos, and now he's dripping blood down his big beefy forearm, in a hurry to get home.

Some young girls have started screaming. Nobody knows what has happened for sure and where Ace is headed people clear out of his way. There's blood running down his chest, soaking into his jeans, splashing onto the sidewalk. His friends are scared following along after him asking where he's going, is he going to the hospital, but Ace glares up out of his one good eye like a crazy man, saying, Get the fuck away! Don't touch me! and nobody wants to come near.

On the street the cops stop him and there's a call put in for an ambulance. Ace stands there dazed and shamed and the cops ask him questions as if he's to blame for what happened, was he in a fight, where's he coming from, is that a bullet wound?—all the while a crowd's gathering, excitement in the air you can feel. It's an August night, late, eighty-nine degrees and no breeze. The crowd is all strangers, Ace's friends have disappeared. He'd beg the cops to let him go but his heart is beating so hard he can't get his breath. Starts swaying like a drunk man, his knees so weak the cops have to steady him. They can smell the panic sweat on him, running in rivulets down his sides.

In the ambulance he's held in place and a black orderly tells him he's O.K., he's going to be O.K., goin' to be at the hospital in two minutes flat. He talks to Ace the way you'd talk to a small child, or an animal. They give him some quick first aid trying to stop the bleeding but Ace can't control himself can't hold still, he's crazy with fear, his heart gives a half-dozen kicks then it's off and going—like a drum tattoo right in his chest. The ambulance is tearing along the street, siren going, Ace says O God O God O God his terrible heartbeat carrying him away.

He's never been in a hospital in his life—knows he's going to die there.

Then he's being hauled out of the ambulance. Stumbling

through automatic-eye doors not knowing where he is. Jaws so tight he could grind his teeth away and he can't get his breath and he's ashamed how people are looking at him, right there in the lights in the hallway people staring at his face like they'd never seen anything so terrible. He can't keep up with the attendants, knees buckling and his heart beating so hard hard but they don't notice, trying to make him walk faster, Come on man they're saying, you ain't hurt that bad, Ace just can't keep up and he'd fall if they weren't gripping him under the arms then he's in the emergency room and lying on a table, filmy white curtains yanked closed around him and there's a doctor, two nurses, What seems to be the trouble here the doctor asks squinting at Ace through his glasses, takes away the bloody gauze and doesn't flinch at what he sees. He warns Ace to lie still, he sounds tired and annoyed as if Ace is to blame, how did this happen he asks but doesn't wait for any answer and Ace lies there stiff and shivering with fear clutching at the underside of the table so hard his nails are digging through the tissue-paper covering into the vinyl, he can't see out of his left eye, nothing there but pain, pain throbbing and pounding everywhere in his head and the nurses—are there two? three?—look down at him with sympathy he thinks, with pity he thinks, they're attending to him, touching him, nobody has ever touched him so tenderly in all his life Ace thinks and how shamed he is hauled in here like this flat on his back like this bleeding like a stuck pig and sweating bare-chested and his big gut exposed quivering there in the light for everybody to see—

The doctor puts eight stitches in Ace's forehead, tells him he's damned lucky he didn't lose his eye, the bullet missed it by about two inches and it's going to be swollen and blackened for a while, next time you might not be so lucky he says but Ace doesn't catch this, his heart's going so hard. They wrap gauze around his head tight then hook him up to a machine to monitor his heartbeat, the doctor's whistling under his breath like he's surprised, lays the flat of his hand against Ace's chest to feel the weird loud rocking beat. Ace is broken out in sweat but it's cold clammy sick sweat, he knows he's going to die. The machine is going bleep-bleep-bleep high-pitched and fast and how fast can it go before his heart bursts?—he sees the nurses looking down at him, one of the nurses just staring at him, Don't let me die Ace wants to beg but he'd be too ashamed. The doctor is listening to Ace's heartbeat with his stethoscope, asks does he have any pain in his chest, has he ever had an attack like this before, Ace whispers no but too soft to be heard, all the blood has drained from his face and his skin is dead-white, mouth gone slack like a fish's and toes like ice where Death is creeping up his feet: he can feel it.

The heart isn't Ace's heart but just something inside him gone angry and mean pounding like a hammer pounding pounding pounding against his ribs making his body rock so he's panicked suddenly and wants to get loose, tries to push his way off the table—he isn't thinking but if he could think he'd say he wanted to leave behind what's happening to him here as if it was only happening in the emergency room, there on that table. But they don't let him go. There's an outcry in the place and two orderlies hold him down and he gives up, all the strength drained out of him and he gives up, there's no need to strap him down the way they do, he's finished. They hook him up to the heart monitor again and the terrible high-pitched bleeping starts again and he lies there shamed knowing he's going to die he's forgotten about the gunshot, his eye, who did it and was it on purpose meant for him and how can he get revenge, he's forgotten all that covered in sick clammy sweat his nipples puckered and the kinky hairs on his chest wet, even his belly button showing exposed from the struggle and how silly and sad his tattoos must look under these lights where they were never meant to be seen. 140

One of the nurses sinks a long needle in his arm, and there's another needle in the soft thin flesh of the back of his hand, takes him by surprise, they've got a tube in there, and something coming in hot and stinging dripping into his vein the doctor's telling him something he can't follow, This is to bring the heartbeat down the doctor says, just a tachycardia attack and it isn't fatal try to relax but Ace knows he's going to die, he can feel Death creeping up his feet up his legs like stepping 150 out into cold water and suddenly he's so tired he can't lift his head, couldn't get up from the table if they unstrapped him. And he dies—it's that easy. Like slipping off into the water, pushing out, letting the water take you. It's that easy.

They're asking Ace if he saw who shot him and Ace says, Naw, didn't see nobody. They ask does he have any enemies and he says, Naw, no more than anybody else. They ask can he think of anybody who might have wanted to shoot him and he says, embarrassed, looking down at the floor with his one good eye, Naw, can't think of nobody right now. So they let him go. 160

Next night Ace is back in the park out of pride but there's a feeling to him he isn't real or isn't the same person he'd been. One eye bandaged shut and everything looks flat, people staring at him like he's a freak, wanting to know What about the eye and Ace shrugs and tells them he's O.K., the bullet just got his forehead. Everybody wants to speculate who fired the shot, whose car it was, but Ace stands sullen and quiet thinking his own thoughts. Say he'd been standing just a little to one side the bullet would have got him square in the forehead or plowed right into his eye, killed him dead, it's something to think about 170 and he tries to keep it in mind so he'll feel good. But he doesn't feel good. He doesn't feel like he'd ever felt before. His secret is something that happened to him in the hospital he can't remember except to know it happened and it happened to him. And he's in a mean mood his head half-bandaged like a mummy, weird-looking in the dark, picking up on how people look at him and say things behind his back calling him Ace which goes through him like a razor because it's a punk name and not really his.

Mostly it's O.K. He hides how he feels. He's got a sense of 180 humor. He doesn't mind them clowning around pretending they hear gunshots and got to duck for cover, nobody's going to remember it for long, except once Ace stops laughing and backhands this guy in the belly, low below the belt, says in his old jeering voice, What do you know?—you don't know shit.

Q How would you describe the character Ace?

Q What aspects of contemporary American culture does Oates treat?

Postmodern Poetry

As with Postmodern fiction, so too with poetry; parody and ambivalence dominate. Multiple meanings or the absence of meaning itself are related to language, its ambiguities, and its role in shaping the self. In the poem "To Talk," the Mexican poet and critic Octavio Paz (1914–1999) deals with the idea of language as both self-defining and sacred.

More opaque are the poems of the American writer John Ashbery (b. 1927). While his verses are often playful, they are also usually cryptic and inscrutable. In the poem "Paradoxes and Oxymorons," Ashbery suggests that both language and life are incongruous, contradictory, and intrinsically human.

READING 37.2 Paz's "To Talk" (1987)

I read in a poem:	1
to talk is divine.	
But gods don't speak:	
they create and destroy worlds	
while men do the talking,	5
Gods, without words,	
play terrifying games.	

The spirit descends,
untying tongues,
but it doesn't speak words: 10
it speaks flames.
Language, lit by a god
is a prophecy
of flames and a crash
of burnt syllables: 15
meaningless ash.

Man's word
is the daughter of death.
We talk because we are
mortal: words 20
are not signs, they are years.
Saying what they say,
the names we speak
say time: they say us,
we are the names of time. 25
To talk is human.

Q What insights concerning the powers and perils of language does Paz convey in this poem?

READING 37.3 Ashbery's "Paradoxes and Oxymorons"[1] (1981)

This poem is concerned with language on a very plain level.   1
Look at it talking to you. You look out a window

---

[1] A paradox is a statement that seems contradictory or absurd, but may actually be true. An oxymoron is a combination of contradictory terms, such as "wise fool" or "cruel kindness."

Or pretend to fidget. You have it but you don't have it.
You miss it, it misses you. You miss each other.

This poem is sad because it wants to be yours, and cannot.   5
What's a plain level? It is that and other things,
Bringing a system of them into play. Play?
Well, actually, yes, but I consider play to be

A deeper outside thing, a dreamed role-pattern,
As in the division of grace these long August days   10
Without proof. Open-ended. And before you know it
It gets lost in the steam and chatter of typewriters.

It has been played once more. I think you exist only
To tease me into doing it, on your level, and then you aren't there
Or have adopted a different attitude. And the poem   15
Has set me softly down beside you. The poem is you.

— **Q** To what does "it" refer at each use here? Can you find any paradoxes or oxymorons in this poem?

Magic Realism

The term "Magic Realism" originated in the context of the visual arts where it characterized the paintings of Giorgio de Chirico and René Magritte (see chapter 33). As a literary term, it describes a genre in which unreal or surreal elements appear in an otherwise realistic setting. Magic Realism dominated Latin American fiction from the early 1920s through the literary explosion, the so-called Boom, that began in the late 1960s. Two of the most notable of Latin America's Magic Realists are the Colombian novelist Gabriel Garcia Marquez (1928–2014) and the Chilean author Isabel Allende (b. 1943). Both are brilliant storytellers who interweave Latin America's legendary history with universal themes of language and love. Allende has credited the influence of film and television for her ability to "think in images."

One of the earliest of the Latin American Magic Realists was the Argentinian Jorge Luis Borges (1899–1986). In his short stories and essays, Borges combined elements of Magic Realism—its unexpected shifts in time and place and its dreamlike, mythic settings—with a plurality of meanings and points of view common to Postmodernism. He cited among the basic devices of fantastic literature: the contamination of reality by dream, the voyage in time, and the "double." The fractured, reflexive self is both subject and object in "Borges and I," one of a group of parables and prose fragments that made up his most personal book, *The Maker* (1960).

— **READING 37.4** Borges' "Borges and I" (1960)

It's Borges, the other one, that things happen to. I walk   1
through Buenos Aires and I pause—mechanically now,
perhaps—to gaze at the arch of an entryway and its inner
door; news of Borges reaches me by mail, or I see his name

on a list of academics or in some biographical dictionary.
My taste runs to hourglasses, maps, eighteenth-century
typefaces, etymologies, the taste of coffee, and the prose of
Robert Louis Stevenson; Borges shares those preferences,
but in a vain sort of way that turns them into the accoutrements
of an actor. It would be an exaggeration to say that our   10
relationship is hostile—I live, I allow myself to live, so that
Borges can spin out his literature, and that literature is my
justification. I willingly admit that he has written a number
of sound pages, but those pages will not save *me*, perhaps
because the good in them no longer belongs to any individual,
not even to that other men, but rather to language itself, or to
tradition. Beyond that, I am doomed—utterly and inevitably—
to oblivion, and fleeting moments will be all of me that
survives in that other man. Little by little, I have been turning
everything over to him, though I know the perverse way he   20
has of distorting and magnifying everything. Spinoza believed
that all things wish to go on being what they are—stone
wishes eternally to be stone, and tiger, to be tiger. I shall
endure in Borges, not in myself (if, indeed, I am anybody at
all), but I recognize myself less in his books than in many
others', or in the tedious strumming of a guitar. Years ago
I tried to free myself from him, and I moved on from the
mythologies of the slums and outskirts of the city to games
with time and infinity, but those games belong to Borges now,
and I shall have to think up other things. So my life is a point-   30
counterpoint, a kind of fugue, and a falling away—and
everything winds up being lost to me, and everything falls into
oblivion, or into the hands of the other man.
I am not sure which of us it is that's writing this page.

— **Q** Based only on the evidence of this sketch, describe the setting, the age of the speaker(s), and his (their) main concerns. Borges considered this piece a parable; what might be the lesson of this parable?

Science Fiction

Science fiction has come to be one of our most entertaining literary genres. At its best, it evokes a sense of awe and a spirit of intellectual curiosity in the face of the unknown. It also is a vehicle by which writers express their concern for the future of the planet. During the twentieth century—a virtual golden age of science fiction—futurists contemplated the possibility of life in outer space, the interface between computers and human beings, the consequences of a nuclear disaster, and the potential for a bioengineered new species.

The beginnings of modern science fiction may be traced to the French novelist Jules Verne (1828–1905) and the British writer H. G. Wells (1866–1946). But the more recent flowering of the genre dates from the birth of space exploration—specifically the Soviet Union's historic launching of an artificial earth satellite (*Sputnik 1*) in 1957 and the American moon landing of 1969. These events triggered an outpouring of fiction related to space exploration. In 1950, Arthur C. Clarke (1917–2008), one of Britain's most successful writers, had produced the intriguing science-fiction story "The Sentinel," which in

1957	the first artificial satellite (*Sputnik 1*) is put into orbit by the Soviet Union
1969	an American astronaut is the first person to walk on the moon
1981	lasers are utilized for the study of matter
1990	the Hubble space telescope confirms the existence of extrasolar planets and fifty billion galaxies
1995	the Global Positioning System (GPS) goes into operation
2004	NASA scientists land rover probe on Mars
2005	International Space Station completed
2006	drones (unmanned aerial vehicles) are authorized by the Federal Aviation Administration for domestic use
2007	Computer imaging (CI) used to test spacecraft before production

turn became the basis for an extraordinary cinematic conceptualization of the space age—*2001: A Space Odyssey*.

In the last decades of the twentieth century, science fiction spawned a unique subgenre known as *cyberpunk*. Influenced by *Gravity's Rainbow* (1974), the dense masterpiece of Thomas Pynchon (b. 1937), cyberpunk deals with futuristic societies, dominated by computers, artificial intelligence, illicit drugs, and punk rock music. Pynchon's novel, an archetypal Postmodernist text, is packed with an encyclopedic array of references to (and puns on) world history, chemistry, mathematics, religion, film, and popular music.

The Visual Arts in the Information Age

In the last half-century the visual arts have been overwhelmingly diverse in style and technique. Collectively, they are characterized by an indebtedness to mass media and electronic technology, by an emphasis on process and medium, and by Postmodern parody and irony. High-tech materials—fiberglass, Plexiglas, stainless steel, neon, and polyester resin—have become as commonplace in the contemporary art world as marble, clay, and oil paints were in previous centuries. Performance and environmental art projects reach out of the studio and into daily life. The mixed-media experiments of early Modernism have now expanded to include film, video, television, and the computer.

The electronic media have revolutionized the visual arts of our time: computer-manipulated photographs, virtual environments, video games, and mixed-media installations are among the unique projects of the Information Age. The electronic synthesis of music, video, dance, and performance opens up new kinds of theatrical experience,

Science-Fiction Film

Directed by one of America's most brilliant filmmakers, Stanley Kubrick (1928–1999), *2001: A Space Odyssey* (1968) builds on the intriguing hypothesis of most science fiction: that intelligent life exists in outer space. The plot, which loosely follows Arthur C. Clarke's short story "The Sentinel," involves the quest to locate a mysterious four-million-year-old crystal monolith that appears to be emitting powerful radio waves in the direction of the planet Jupiter. Outfitted with a state-of-the-art spaceship called *Discovery*, which is engineered by a supercomputer named HAL-9000, the fictional heroes of the space odyssey set out for Jupiter. Their adventures include a contest of wills between the astronauts and the ruthless and deviant HAL, breathtaking encounters with the perils of outer space, and a shattering revelation of regeneration and rebirth. Kubrick's *2001* is the modern counterpart of ancient myth and legend. Like Homer's *Odyssey*, the film celebrates the adventures of a hero who, as part of a quest, challenges the unknown by force of wit and imagination. The vast, mysterious realm of outer space is the twentieth-century equivalent of Gilgamesh's untamed wilderness, Odysseus' wine-dark sea, and Dante's Christian cosmos. Just as the ancients looked across the lands beyond the sea to the earth's outermost reaches, so for moderns extraterrestrial space constitutes the unprobed celestial fringe of the universe. "On the deepest psychological level," explained Kubrick, "the film's plot symbolizes the search for God, and it postulates what is little less than a scientific definition of God."

In 1999, the American movie industry produced the first in a compelling science-fiction trilogy: *The Matrix*, followed by *The Matrix Reloaded* (2003) and *The Matrix Revolutions* (2003). The films picture a world dominated by an artificial intelligence that uses human beings as a source of energy. The known world—the matrix—is actually a computer simulation, a virtual reality planted inside each human mind. Drawing elements from Classical mythology, the Bible, Lewis Carroll's *Alice in Wonderland*, Zen Buddhism, and the choreography of gravity-defying martial arts, the film introduced a unique photographic technique ("flow motion") that employs more than 100 meticulously coordinated still cameras to create extraordinary special effects. *The Matrix*, which explores ideas of time and space by way of both content and form, has become the single greatest influence on science-fiction film of the twenty-first century.

some of which invite the interactive participation of the audience. In the Information Age, the image, and especially the moving image, has assumed a position of power over the printed word. In fact, the visual image has come to compete—in value and in authority—with all other forms of cultural expression.

Artists of the Information Age have joined popular musicians and world-class athletes in becoming the superstars of contemporary society. The art of prominent living painters, sculptors, and performance artists may command fortunes comparable to those of former industrial barons. Critics, gallery owners, and auction houses make use of the Internet to influence the marketing and commercialization of art, so that (for better or for worse) artists have become celebrities and art has become "big business."

Pop Art

Pop Art, the quintessential style of the Information Age, embraced the imagery of consumerism and celebrity culture as mediated by television, film, and magazines. As a style, "pop" departed dramatically from postwar abstraction, giving new life to the Western representational tradition. Its subject matter, however, while rendered in an overtly realistic style, was filtered through the prism of commercial advertising.

The term "Pop Art" was coined in the 1950s by a group of British artists who began pasting advertisements clipped from American magazines into their artworks. The movement came to fruition in New York a decade later. In the 1960s, some 60 percent of America's population owned television sets. Commercial products, stage and screen personalities, along with the newsworthy events of the day, came to life via an image-driven medium that—more

Figure 37.3 ANDY WARHOL, *Mint Marilyn Monroe*, 1962. Oil and silkscreen enamel on canvas, 20½ × 16½ in. Marilyn Monroe, a glamorous blonde film star of the 1950s, died from what was thought to be a drug overdose in 1962. A talented comic actor, she became an iconic figure in American entertainment history.

Figure 37.2 ANDY WARHOL, *Green Coca-Cola Bottles*, 1962. Acrylic, screenprint, and graphite pencil on canvas, 6 ft. 10½ in. × 4 ft. 9 in. Master of the mass-produced commodities of contemporary American life, Warhol was quoted as saying "Buying is more American than thinking . . ."

compelling than any printed vehicle—took its viewers hostage in their own living rooms.

The pioneer American Pop Artist Andy Warhol (1931–1987) dryly explained the meaning of the new style: "Pop Art," he observed, "is about liking things." Trained as a commercial artist, Warhol took some of his earliest subject matter from the shelves of the supermarket. He worked to depersonalize the subject by enlarging it or reproducing it in monotonous, postage-stamp rows resembling supermarket displays. Warhol hand-painted his first Brillo boxes on plywood, and inscribed Campbell's soup can labels and Coca-Cola bottles on canvas; but he soon turned to the photo-silkscreen technique of commercial advertising, reproducing these images mechanically, and thereafter employing studio assistants to replicate them. Works depicting natural disasters and social violence, such as the Birmingham, Alabama, race riots of the 1960s, were lifted from magazine and newspaper photos and transferred (as screenprints) to **silkscreen**; newsworthy events and stock images (such as the electric chair) share the deadpan objectivity of Warhol's Coca-Cola bottles (see Figure **37.2**) Rendered by way of "industrial image-making," his portraits of iconic political figures and celebrities, such as Elvis Presley and Marilyn Monroe (Figure **37.3**), challenged traditional distinctions between fine and applied art, even as they endorsed art as a saleable commodity.

Jasper Johns (b. 1930), an artist whose career has spanned more than half a century, shared Warhol's interest in commonplace objects. When Willem de Kooning quipped that Johns' high-powered art dealer could sell anything—even two beer cans—Johns created *Painted Bronze* (1960), a set of bronze-cast, hand-painted cans of ale (Figure **37.4**). Johns' beer cans, like his early paintings of flags and targets, are Neodada tributes to Marcel Duchamp (see Figure 33.6), whom Johns knew personally. Some critics see them as Postmodern parodies of the cherished icons of contemporary culture. But they are also mock-heroic commentaries on the fact that art, like beer, is a marketable commodity.

Among the most witty vehicles of pop parody are the monumental soft vinyl sculptures of Claes Oldenburg (b. 1929)—gigantic versions of such everyday items as clothespins, hot dogs, table fans, typewriter erasers, and toilets. Often enlarged ten to twenty times their natural size, these objects assume a comic vulgarity that forces us to reconsider their presence in our daily lives (Figure **37.5**).

The oversized paintings of Roy Lichtenstein (1923–1997), modeled on comic-book cartoons, bring attention to familiar clichés and stereotypes of popular entertainment. Violence and romance are trivialized in the fictional lives of Lichtenstein's clinging women and superheroes (see Figure **37.1**). Like other Pop Artists, Lichtenstein employed commercial techniques, including stencil and airbrush; he imitated the Benday dots used in advertising design to achieve tonal gradation.

The "pop" genre continues to be celebrated in the cheerfully kitsch creations of the America artist–impresario, Jeff Koons (b. 1955). Koons appropriates the novelties

Figure 37.5 CLAES OLDENBURG, *Clothespin*, Central Square, Philadelphia, 1976. Cor-ten (steel) and stainless steel, 45 ft. × 12 ft. 3 in. × 4ft. 6 in.

Figure 37.4 JASPER JOHNS, *Painted Bronze (Beer Cans)*, 1960. Painted bronze, 5½ × 8 × 4¼ in.

of the commercial gift-shop, and (with a staff of 125 studio assistants) repurposes them as gleaming stainless steel effigies. *Balloon Dog*, a monumental equestrian version of a children's party toy (Figure **37.6**), cast in several editions and colors, stands as a slick expression of the art world's contemporary romance with mass taste and the popular culture.

Assemblage

Art that combines two- and three-dimensional elements has a history that reaches back to the early twentieth century—recall Picasso's collages (see Figure 32.6) and Duchamp's modified ready-mades (see chapter 33). Since the middle of that century, however, the American artist Robert Rauschenberg (1925–2008) monumentalized the art of *assemblage* in works that incorporate what he wryly referred to as "the excess of the world." Boldly assembling old car tires, street signs, broken furniture, and other debris, Rauschenberg fathered landmark artworks

Figure 37.6 JEFF KOONS, *Balloon Dog (Yellow)*, 1994–2000. High chromium stainless steel with transparent color coating, 121 × 143 × 45 in. Koons has used this style to create balloon rabbits, monkeys, swans, and flowers. At auction in 2013, one of Koons' balloon dogs sold for a record $58.4 million, the highest price ever paid for a work of art by a living artist.

Art Film

Traditional film usually obeys a narrative sequence or presents a story; art film, however, such as Léger's *Ballet mécanique* (see chapter 34), explores the artistic potential of the medium itself. Between 1963 and 1968 Andy Warhol produced sixty experimental films. He focused a fixed camera on a single object and let it "roll" until the film ran out—thus bringing to film the (uniquely cinematic) "dead time" between "events," as John Cage had brought to music the "silence" between moments of sound. In *Outer and Inner Space* (1965), Warhol used double-screen formats to present multiple versions of his female "star" watching images of herself on televised videotape. He also exploited the "long take": in the homoerotic film *My Hustler* (1967), a single thirty-minute shot documents the interaction between two gay men who groom themselves before the bathroom sink.

Some art films depend exclusively on the associational nuances evoked by sequences of imaginatively juxtaposed images. Like Rauschenberg's collages, the experimental films of Bruce Conner (1930–2008) consist of footage assembled from old newsreels, pornographic movies, and Hollywood films. They achieve additional effect by being "choreographed" to a specific musical score, as was Conner's first film, *The Movie* (1958). As with music, art films defy explicit meaning; the power to arouse emotion lies with an ingenious cinematic union of image and sound.

he called "combines." Blurring the boundary between painting and sculpture, these artworks operate, as did the artist himself, "in the gap between art and life."

Rauschenberg was an extraordinary printmaker. For more than fifty years, he experimented with a wide variety of transfer techniques, lithograph, and silkscreen, to produce large-scale prints whose images are drawn from his own photographs, as well as from contemporary magazines and newspapers (Figure **37.7**). Disparate bits and pieces of cultural debris appear thrown together, as if all were equally valuable (or equally useless). But this bewildering array of visual information is assembled with an impeccable sensitivity to color, shape, and form. Rauschenberg's sly juxtaposition of familiar "found" images—like the visual scramble of Postmodern channel-grazing—invites viewers to create their own narratives.

Numerous artists have used assemblage to bring attention to the random and violent aspects of contemporary society. John Chamberlain (1927–2011) created seductive sculptures out of junked automobiles, whose corroded sheet-metal bodies and twisted steel bumpers suggest

Figure 37.7 ROBERT RAUSCHENBERG, *Buffalo II*, 1964. Oil on canvas with silkscreen, 8 × 6 ft. Rauschenberg used solvent transfer and screenprinting techniques to reproduce images from magazines and newspapers. The central strategy of his work, that of collecting and combining, informed both his prints and his three-dimensional pieces.

the transience of high-tech products and the dangers inherent in their misuse (Figure **37.8**). Louise Nevelson (1900–1988) collected wooden boxes, filled them with discarded fragments of found and machine-made objects, and painted them a uniform black, white, or gold. Like decaying altarpieces, these huge structures enshrine the vaguely familiar and haunting refuse of modern materialist culture (Figure **37.9**).

Geometric Abstraction

Not all contemporary artists embraced the ironic stance of pop and assemblage art. Some remained loyal to the non-objective style of *geometric abstraction*, first initiated in painting by Malevich and Mondrian (see chapter 32). Obedient to the credo of the Bauhaus architect Ludwig Mies van der Rohe that "less is more," these artists have pursued the machinelike purity of elemental forms, occasionally enlarging such forms to colossal sizes.

Early in his career, the American artist Frank Stella (b. 1936) painted huge canvases consisting of brightly colored, hard-edged geometric patterns that look as though they are made with a giant protractor (Figure **37.10**). The canvases in the "Protractor" series, which are named individually after the ancient circular cities of Asia Minor, depart from the standard square and rectangular format. Shaped like chevrons, circles, or triangles, they are fastened together to create unique geometric configurations. Stella's more recent artworks are flamboyant steel and aluminum pieces that capture in three dimensions the intensity of a

Figure 37.8 JOHN CHAMBERLAIN, *Debonaire Apache*, 1991. Painted and chromium-plated steel, 7 ft. 10 in. × 4 ft. 6¾ in. × 4 ft. 2½ in.

Figure 37.9 LOUISE NEVELSON, *Royal Tide IV*, 1960. Wood, with gold spray technique, 86 × 40 × 8 in. Nevelson, who came to the United States from Kiev, Ukraine, at the age of six, did not receive significant critical attention until she was sixty-eight years old. She selected wood as her creative medium, to avoid, as she explained, the distraction of color.

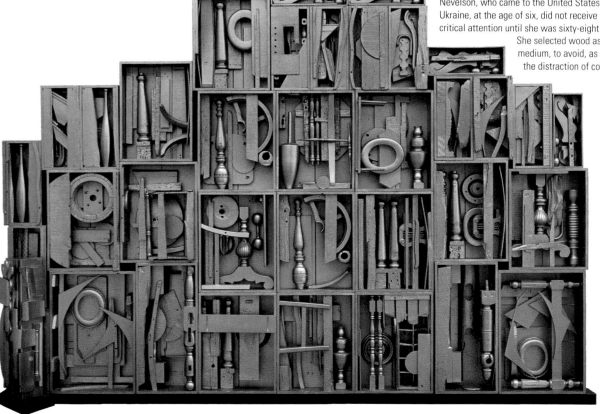

Figure 37.10 FRANK STELLA, *Tahkt-i-Sulayman I*, from the "Protractor" series, 1967. Polymer and fluorescent paint on canvas, 10 ft. ¼ in. × 20 ft. 2¼ in.

Jackson Pollock painting. Nevertheless, the artist continues to reject value-oriented art in favor of a style that is neutral and impersonal. "All I want anyone to get out of my paintings, and all I ever get out of them, is the fact that you can see the whole thing without confusion," explains Stella: "What you see is what you see."

Op Art

The idea that what one sees is determined by *how* one sees has been central to the work of Hungarian-born Victor Vasarely (1908–1997) and Britain's Bridget Riley (b. 1931). Both of these artists explore the operation of conflicting visual cues and the elemental effects of colors and shapes on the faculties of the human retina—a style known as *Optical Art*, or *Op Art*. In Riley's *Current* (Figure **37.11**), a series of curved black lines painted on a white surface creates the illusion of vibrating movement and elusive color—look for yellow by staring at the painting for a few minutes.

Minimalism

While Europeans pioneered optical abstraction, Americans led the way in the development of *Minimalism*. Minimalist sculptors developed a refined industrial aesthetic that featured elemental forms made of the high-tech materials. The geometric components of Minimalist artworks are usually factory-produced and assembled according to the artist's instructions.

Figure 37.11 BRIDGET RILEY, *Current*, 1964. Synthetic polymer paint on composition board, 4 ft. 10⅜ in. × 4 ft. 10⅞ in.

Figure 37.12 DONALD JUDD, *Untitled*, 1967. Green lacquer on galvanized iron, each unit 9 in. × 3 ft. 4 in. × 31 in. The space between the elements in this series takes on visual significance. As Judd explained, "Actual space is intrinsically more powerful and specific than paint on a flat surface."

Figure 37.13 ISAMU NOGUCHI, *Cube*, 1968. Steel subframe with aluminum panels, height 28 ft. Minimal sculptures play an important role as public artworks. This monumental piece playfully relieves the monotonous uniformity of high-rise office buildings in Manhattan's financial district.

The untitled stainless steel and Plexiglas boxes of Donald Judd (1928–1994) protrude from the wall with mathematical clarity and perfect regularity (Figure **37.12**). They resemble a stack of shelves, yet they neither contain nor support anything. The visual rhythms of Judd's serial forms create a dialogue between space and volume, between flat, bright enamel colors and dull or reflective metal grays, and between subtly textured and smooth surfaces.

More monumental in scale are the primal forms of the Japanese-American sculptor Isamu Noguchi (1904–1988). Poised on one corner of its steel and aluminum frame, Noguchi's gigantic *Cube* (Figure **37.13**) shares the purity of form and the mysterious resonance of the Egyptian pyramids and the crystal monolith in the film *2001*.

New Realism

During the 1970s, there emerged a new approach to figural realism that emphasized the stop-action stillness and sharp-focus immediacy of the photograph. *New Realism* (also called *Neorealism*, *Hyperrealism*, and *Photorealism*) differs from previous realist styles (including Social Realism and Pop Art) in its disavowal of narrative content and its indifference to moral, social, and political issues. Although decidedly representational, it is as impersonal as Minimal art.

Most New Realists do not seek to imitate natural phenomena; rather, they recreate an artificially processed view of reality captured by the photographic image. Richard Estes (b. 1936), for instance, paints urban still lifes based on fragments of the photographs that he himself makes (Figure **37.14**). A virtuoso painter, Estes tantalizes the eye with details refracted by polished aluminum surfaces and plate-glass windows.

Chuck Close (b. 1940) transfers a photographic image to canvas after both photograph and canvas have been ruled to resemble graph paper; each square of the photo is numbered to correspond to an equivalent square on the canvas. He then fills each square with tiny gradations of color that resemble the pixels of a television screen (Figure **37.15**). While his early monochromatic works resemble impersonal "mug shots," his more recent portraits have the familiar look of televised "talking heads." They make use of new techniques involving multiple dots of color within each square.

High-tech materials and techniques have made possible the fabrication of New Realist sculptures that are shockingly lifelike. Duane Hanson (1925–1996) used fiberglass-reinforced polyester resin to recreate the appearance of ordinary and often working-class individuals in their everyday occupations (Figure **37.16**). He cast his polyester figures from live models, then added wigs, clothing, and accessories. Hanson's "living dead" are pointedly symbolic of modern life at its most prosaic.

Figure 37.14 RICHARD ESTES, *Double Self-Portrait*, 1976. Oil on canvas, 24 × 36 ft. This is ostensibly a view of an urban restaurant, but the plate-glass façade takes in reflections of the buildings across the street, the sidewalk trees, and Estes himself (along with his photographic equipment).

Figure 37.15 CHUCK CLOSE, *Self-Portrait*, 1991. Oil on canvas, 100 × 84 in. After suffering a spinal blood clot in 1988, the partially paralyzed artist experimented with applying bits of colored paper and fingerprints to create the individual dots on the canvas.

Figure 37.16 DUANE HANSON, *Tourists*, 1970. Fiberglass and polyester polychromed, 5 ft. 4 in. × 5 ft. 5 in. × 3 ft. 11 in.

Total Art

The Information Age has generated new creative strategies that reach beyond the studio and the art gallery and into the public domain. With *total art*, process (and conception) is generally more important than product—the work of art itself. In the tradition of Duchamp's urinal (see Figure 33.6), the originality of the work lies with the artist's *idea*, its conception overriding any visual or formal concerns. Total art projects may take the form of communal rituals that involve planned (though usually not rehearsed) performance.

The seeds of total art are found in the aleatory enterprises of John Cage (see chapter 35) and in the daring experiments of the postwar Japanese Gutai Group (see chapter 35), whose artists/performers engaged their materials by pounding the canvas with paint-filled boxing gloves or hurling themselves against wet canvases. In one of the earliest European examples of *performance art*, a work entitled *Anthropometry*, the French artist Yves Klein (1928–1962) employed nude women as "human brushes" (Figure **37.17**). Klein's contemporary Jean Tinguely (1925–1991) made a distinctive comment on twentieth-century technology with a series of machines he programmed to self-destruct amid a public spectacle of noise, fire, and smoke.

A classic strain of total art, the *Happening*, was pioneered by the American artist Allan Kaprow (1927–2006). Kaprow, who coined the name for this conceptual genre, called the Happening "a performance that occurs in a given time and space." Played out on a city street, a beach, or in a private home, the Happening involved a structured series of actions and scripted gestures. While conceived and directed by the artist, it welcomed chance and random elements. During the 1960s, Kaprow wrote and orchestrated more than fifty Happenings, most of which engaged dozens of ordinary people in the dual roles of spectator and performer. *Fluids* (1967), a Happening staged in Pasadena, California, called for participants to construct a house of ice blocks and then witness the melting process that

Figure 37.17 YVES KLEIN, Performance of *Anthropometry ANT49*, 1960.

followed. Like a ritual or theater piece, the performance was *itself* the artwork. The only record of its occurrence might be a photograph or videotape.

Obviously, performance art has limited value as a saleable commodity; yet, it continues to attract artists and participants. A recent conceptual piece, *The Artist is Present* (2010), held at the Museum of Modern Art in New York City, invited an individual spectator to sit silently for an unspecified length of time across from the so-called grandmother of performance art, Marina Abramović (b. 1946). The work illustrates a unique conceptual movement known as "relational aesthetics." Here, the artist orchestrates a specific social exchange (such as a conversation or a communal meal), but generates no material object. Unlike the Happenings of the 1960s, such events are often neither photographed nor recorded. The "art" is interchangeable with the experience.

Performance art has also morphed into planned events that include political demonstrations, rock concerts, "raves" (high-energy festivals featuring electronic dance music), and Flashmobs (groups of people, usually organized via the Internet, who assemble briefly in public places to dance, sing, or otherwise perform)—all of which may be considered "staged" versions of total art.

Driven by ideas rather than by visual or formal concerns, the purest kind of conceptual art consists of written words or information in the form of directions or messages. Barbara Kruger's billboard-style posters, for instance (see Figure 36.16), combine photographic images and words that make cryptic comment on social and political issues. The American sculptor Jenny Holzer (b. 1950) carves paradoxical and often subversive messages in stone or broadcasts them electronically on public billboards. She often transmits her slogans by way of light-emitting diodes, a favorite medium of commercial advertising. In language that is at once banal and acerbic, Holzer informs us that "Lack of charisma can be fatal," "Myths make reality more intelligible," "Humanism is obsolete," "Decency is a relative thing," and "Ambivalence can ruin your life." Holzer's word-art tests the authority of public information, particularly as it is dispersed by contemporary media. Her most recent work expands on the project *Truth Before Power* (2004), which displays large silkscreened, declassified U.S. government documents, segments of which are obliterated by the censor's pen. By way of these cryptic pages—official memos, records of interrogation, and accounts by military personnel related to recent U.S. foreign policy in the Middle East—the artist addresses issues of secrecy, censorship, and the manipulation of information associated with the politics of war.

The most physically ambitious manifestation of total art is the *Earthwork*, which takes the natural landscape as both its medium and its subject. Independent of the gallery or museum, such environmental projects are usually colossal, heroic, and temporary. Some, like Smithson's *Spiral Jetty* (see Figure 38.9), have ecological implications; others, however, like the site-specific projects of the American husband-and-wife team Christo (b. 1935) and Jeanne-Claude (1935–2009), are aesthetic transformations

Figure 37.18 CHRISTO AND JEANNE-CLAUDE, *Running Fence*, Sonoma and Marin counties, California, 1972–1976. Nylon panels on cables and steel poles, height 18 ft., length 24½ miles. The installation of the "fence" mobilized the efforts of a large crew of workers and cost the artists over three million dollars. The fascinating history of this landmark piece is documented in films, photographs, and books.

of large physical spaces or landmarks. Using huge amounts of synthetic fabric, they have wrapped monumental public structures, such as the Pont Neuf in Paris and the Reichstag in Berlin; Christo and Jeanne-Claude have also reshaped nature, wrapping part of the coast of Australia and surrounding eleven islands in Miami's Biscayne Bay with over six million square feet of pink woven polypropylene fabric. In 2005, they lined the 23-mile footpath of Manhattan's Central Park with 7500 saffron-colored fabric flags—a 16-day-long spectacle called *The Gates*.

One of Christo and Jeanne-Claude's earliest projects, *Running Fence* (Figure **37.18**), involved the construction of a nylon "fence" 24½ miles long and 18 feet high. The nylon panels were hung on cables and steel poles and ran through Sonoma and Marin counties, California, to the Pacific Ocean. The fence itself, meandering along the California hills like a modern-day version of the Great Wall of China, remained on site for only two weeks.

Video Art

In the 1950s, the Korean artist and musician Nam June Paik (1932–2007) predicted that the television cathode-ray tube would replace the canvas as the medium of the future. The now-acclaimed "father of video art" was not far from the mark, for art that employs one or another form of electronic technology has come to dominate the art world. Video art had its beginnings in the 1960s.

Influenced by the visionary work of John Cage (see chapter 35), Paik introduced the first interactive experiments in sound and image. With the help of an electronic engineer, he launched video performance pieces and electronic installations, some of which included one of the earliest videosynthesizers—a device that made it possible to alter the shape and color of a video image.

In the 1990s, Paik assembled television sets, circuit boards, and other electronic apparatus to produce whimsical robots. More ambitious in size and conception, however, were the artist's multiscreen television installations. *Megatron* (1995), for instance, consists of 215 monitors programmed with a rapid-fire assortment of animated and live-video images drawn from East and West. The Seoul Olympic Games and Korean drummers, rock concert clips, girlie magazine nudes, and quick-cuts of Paik's favorite artists alternate with the national flags of various countries and other global logos (Figure **37.19**). The animated contours of a bird flying gracefully across a wall of screens brings magical unity to this ocular information blitz, while a two-channel audio track adds booming syncopated sound to the visual rhythms. Paik's wall of video monitors dazzles viewers with a kaleidoscopic barrage of images whose fast-paced editing imitates mainstream television and film.

In contrast with the frenzied dazzle of Paik's video projects, the art of Bill Viola (b. 1951) is profoundly subtle. Viola uses the video medium to deliver mesmerizing personal narratives. The artist's central themes are inspired

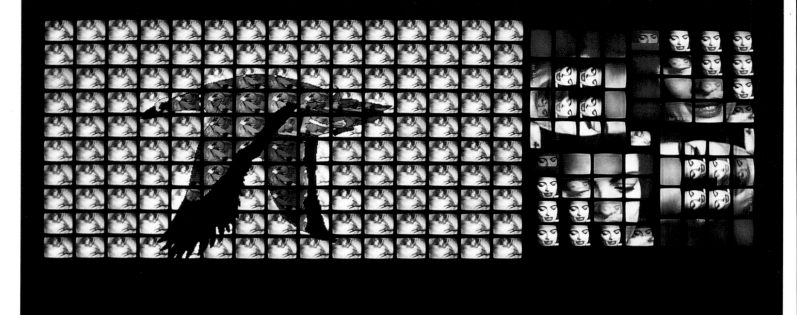

Figure 37.19 NAM JUNE PAIK, *Megatron*, 1995. 215 monitors, eight-channel color video and two-channel sound, left side 11 ft. 10½ in. × 22 ft. 6 in. × 23½ in.; right side 10 ft. 8 in. × 10 ft. 8 in. × 23½ in. Images flow by on these monitors as if seen from a rapidly passing car. Paik was the first to use the phrase "electronic superhighway" to describe the fast-paced media resources that link different parts of the planet.

by Zen Buddhism, Christian mysticism, and Sufi poetry. Viola's *Stations* (a reference to the Stations of the Cross, Christ's journey to Calvary), is a five-channel video and sound installation displaying moving images of the human body underwater. The nude bodies, projected upside down and reflected in polished black granite slabs below (Figure **37.20**) drift in and out of the frame, then suddenly plunge into the water in an explosion of light. This haunting cycle of muted order and disorder, which repeats itself in slow time, evokes a dreamlike mental image of the human journey from birth to death.

Viola's art is contemplative; it is deeply embedded in what the artist calls the "crisis of representation and identity," in which new media technology leaves viewers unsure as to whether an optical image is real or fabricated. According to Viola, "representing information" will be the main issue in the arts of the future. Video and sound installations, which became a major form of late twentieth-century expression, are closely related to the film experience. Both immerse the viewer in the moving image; but, as with Viola's work, video art concentrates experience in ways that envelop the viewer in three-dimensional space.

Figure 37.20 BILL VIOLA, *Stations* (view of the installation), 1994. Video/sound installation (continuously running): five channels of color video projections on five cloth screens suspended from the ceiling; five slabs of black granite on floor in front of each screen; five channels of amplified mono sound. 14 × 48 × 58 ft.

Since the 1970s, video installations have moved in the direction of theater. In 2004, Viola's specially created video sequences were used as a backdrop to the staging of Wagner's opera *Tristan and Isolde*. More elaborate in their staging, twenty-first century installations make use of holograms, laser beams, digital images, and computer-generated special effects (see chapter 38), all of which may be projected onto screens and walls to the accompaniment of live or electronic sound.

Architecture in the Information Age

Some contemporary critics link the birth of Postmodernism to the architecture of the 1960s and, specifically, to the demise of the International Style. The American Robert Venturi (b. 1925), who first introduced architectural Postmodernism in his book *Complexity and Contradiction in Architecture* (1966), countered Mies van der Rohe's dictum "less is more" with the claim "less is a bore." Venturi rejected the anonymity and austerity of the glass and steel skyscraper (see Figure 35.14) and the concrete high-rise (see Figure 32.24), along with the progressive utopianism of Modernists who hoped to transform society through functional form. Instead, he opted for an architecture that emphasized visual complexity, individuality, and outright fun.

In contrast to the machinelike purity of the International Style structure, the Postmodern building is a playful assortment of fragments "quoted" from architectural traditions as ill-mated as a fast-food stand and a Hellenistic temple. Postmodern architecture, like Postmodern fiction, engages a colorful mix of fragments in a whimsical and often witty manner. It shares with *Deconstructivist* literary theorists the will to dismantle and reassemble "the text" in a search for its multiple meanings. Just as there is (according to Deconstructivism) no single text for the whole of our experience, so there is no unifying pattern or defining style in the design of any single piece of architecture.

One example of this Postmodern aesthetic is the Piazza d'Italia in New Orleans, designed by Charles Moore (1925–1993). The plaza, which serves as an Italian cultural center, is a burlesque yet elegant combination of motifs borrowed from Pompeii, Palladio, and Italian Baroque architecture (Figure **37.21**). Its brightly colored colonnaded portico—looking every bit like a gaudy stage set—is adorned with fountains, neon lights, and polished aluminum balustrades. Moore's parodic grab-bag appropriation of the Italian heritage culminates in an apron shaped like a map of Italy that floats in the central pool of the piazza.

The Chinese-born American I. M. Pei (b. 1917) wedded Postmodern design to Minimalist principles in his inventive design for the courtyard of the Louvre Museum in Paris (Figure **37.22**). Three small steel and Plexiglas pyramids surround a central pyramid that covers the formal museum entrance. The large pyramid, which rises to a height of 70 feet, consists of 673 glass segments. Striking in its geometric simplicity, it looks back to Paxton's modular Crystal Palace (see Figure 30.27), to Buckminster Fuller's geodesic dome (see Figure 35.18), and to the steel-and-glass

Figure 37.21 PEREZ ASSOCIATES WITH CHARLES MOORE, RON FILSON, URBAN INNOVATIONS, INC., Piazza d'Italia, New Orleans, 1976–1979.

functionalism of the International Style (see Figure 32.22). The courtyard itself is a Postmodern triumph: it sets a twentieth-century version of the Great Pyramid at Giza amidst the wings of seventeenth-century Classical Baroque buildings. Futuristic in spirit, Pei's pyramid complex has become a kind of space station for the arts.

Since the beginning of the new millennium, many of the world's largest cities have been enjoying a "building boom." A great era of museum construction and expansion appears to be in progress. Museums have become sacred spaces, visited by millions not only to see great art, but also to enjoy an experience unlike that of other leisure activities. Some of the new art venues compete in their futuristic impact with Frank Lloyd Wright's Guggenheim Museum (see Figures 35.16 and 35.17). The expanded Milwaukee Museum of Art, designed by the Spanish-born Santiago Calatrava (b. 1951), is a case in point. Dominating the shore of Lake Michigan like the bleached skeleton of a large dinosaur, its signature element is a 90-foot-high glass-enclosed reception hall covered by a movable winglike sun screen (*brise-soleil*) made of 72 steel fins that control the temperature and light of the interior (Figure **37.23**). A 250-foot-long suspension bridge with angled cables links downtown Milwaukee to the lakefront and the museum. Calatrava, who has designed some extraordinary hotels and bridges throughout the world, brings a new bravura to steel-and-glass building construction.

Figure 37.22 I. M. PEI & ASSOCIATES, Louvre Pyramid, Paris, 1988. The angle of the slope of the pyramid that marks the Louvre entrance is almost identical to that of ancient Egypt's Great Pyramid of Khufu at Giza.

The architectural giant of our time, Frank Gehry (b. 1930), was born in Toronto, Canada, but lives and works in California. His early buildings reflect an interest in humble construction materials, such as plywood, corrugated zinc, stainless steel, and chainlink fencing, which he assembled in serial units. Gehry's structures, in which façades tilt, columns lean, and interior spaces are skewed, reflect his deliberate rejection of the Classical design principles of symmetry and stability. In later, more monumental projects that combine steel, titanium, glass, and limestone, he developed a vocabulary of undulating forms and irregular shapes inspired by everyday objects: a fish, a guitar, a bouquet of flowers.

One of Gehry's latest masterpieces is the Walt Disney Concert Hall in Los Angeles, California (Figure **37.24**). The 2265-seat hall engages glass curtain walls and a majestic multileveled lobby; but it is in the breathtaking design of the exterior, with its billowing, light-reflecting stainless steel plates, that the building achieves its singular magnificence. Gehry's creative process is intuitive: he designs "in his head," develops the contours on paper and in models, and then makes use of aerospace engineers and a sophisticated computer to direct the cutting of the actual building parts. His concert hall, like his highly acclaimed Guggenheim Museum in Bilbao, Spain (1997), combines the spontaneous vitality of action painting and the heroic stability of Minimal sculpture with the technology of the digital age.

Music in the Information Age

As with the visual arts and architecture, music since 1960 has been boldly experimental, stylistically diverse, and (with the exception of popular music) largely impersonal. Some late twentieth-century composers pursued the random style of John Cage, while others moved in the

Figure 37.23 SANTIAGO CALATRAVA, Milwaukee Art Museum, Minnesota, 2003. Calatrava stated that in designing the museum, he "worked to infuse the building with a certain sensitivity to the culture of the lake—the boats, the sails, and the always changing landscape."

Figure 37.24 FRANK GEHRY, Walt Disney Concert Hall, Los Angeles, California, 2003.

As architecture has become more sculptural, so sculpture has become more architectural. The Postminimalist works of the American sculptor Richard Serra (b. 1939) share Gehry's affection for organic design and geometric regularity. "There's an interconnection between the curvilinearity of Frank's building[s] and the obvious torquing of my pieces," says Serra. His monumental steel-rusted ellipses, which often measure more than 13 feet tall and 50 feet long (and can weigh well over 100 tons), reflect the direction in public art that invites the viewer to be a participant rather than simply an observer (Figure **37.25**). Serra expects the spectator to walk through and around the piece in time, that is, to become part of the piece itself.

Figure 37.25 RICHARD SERRA, *Band*, 2006. Weatherproof steel, 12 ft. 9 in. × 36 ft. 5 in. × 71 ft. 9½ in.

opposite direction, writing highly structured music that extends Schoenberg's serial techniques to pitch, counterpoint, and other aspects of composition.

Two further developments are notable: first, in a discipline dominated for centuries by men, women composers and conductors have become increasingly visible—witness the Pulitzer Prize-winning American composer Ellen Taaffe Zwilich (b. 1938), and Sarah Caldwell (1924–2006), the Metropolitan Opera's first female conductor. Caroline Shaw (b. 1982), the youngest recipient of the Pulitzer Prize for music, received this prestigious award for her *Partita for 8 voices* (2012), an *a cappella* piece with wordless melodies and novel voice effects (such as whispers, grunts, and sighs) produced in rhythmically precise patterns.

Second, electronic technology has affected all aspects of music, from composition and performance to distribution. Just as the electronic processes and media democratized the creation and distribution of images, so they have transformed the creation and reception of sound. The cheap and ready availability of digitally produced and reproduced music has worked virtually to eliminate the patronage system. It has also outmoded the avenues of commercial distribution that governed the music world of former decades.

Electronic Music

In addition to its practical and commercial functions, electronic technology was responsible for the birth of entirely new types of sound. The history of electronic music began in the late 1950s, when John Cage and other avant-garde composers first employed magnetic tape to record and manipulate sound. By splicing and reversing the taped sounds of various kinds of environmental noise—thunder, bird calls, train whistles, and ticking clocks— they introduced a musical genre known as *musique concrète*. This type of music made use of electronic equipment to record and/or modify pre-existing sounds, either natural, instrumental, or mechanically contrived.

The second kind of electronic music involves the use of special equipment to generate sound itself. "Pure" electronic music differs from *musique concrète* in its reliance on oscillators, wave generators, and other electronic devices. The pioneer in this type of music was the German composer Karlheinz Stockhausen (1928–2007). As musical director of the Studio for Electronic Music in Cologne, Germany, he employed electronic devices both by themselves and to manipulate and combine prerecorded sounds, including music generated by traditional instruments and voices. His compositions—atonal patterns of sounds and silence that lack any controlling frame of reference—renounce all conventional rules of rhythm and harmony. Editing taped sounds as a filmmaker edits footage, Stockhausen dispensed with a written score and composed directly on tape, thus assuming simultaneously the roles of composer and performer. Like a Kaprow Happening or a jazz improvisation, a Stockhausen composition is an artform in which process becomes identical with product.

The most revolutionary musical invention of the late 1960s was the computerized **synthesizer**, an electronic instrument capable of producing sounds by generating and combining signals of different frequencies. This artificial sound generator serves for both the production and manipulation of sound. Stockhausen's American contemporary Milton Babbitt (1916–2011) was the first composer to use the RCA Synthesizer to control the texture, timbre, and intensity of electronic sound. While traditional instruments produce only seventy to eighty pitches and a limited range of dynamic intensities, electronic devices like the synthesizer offer a range of frequencies from fifty to 15,000 cycles per second. This provides the potential for almost unlimited variability of pitch. Further, electronic instruments can execute rhythms at speeds and in complex patterns that are beyond the capability of live performers. Because such features defy traditional notation, electronic music is often graphed in acoustical diagrams that serve as "scores."

Since the 1970s, portable digital synthesizers have been attached to individual instruments. These allow musicians to manipulate the pitch, duration, and dynamics of sound even as the music is being performed. The synthesizer has facilitated the typically Postmodern technique known as *sampling*. A sample is a short, "borrowed" segment of recorded sound, which may be stored digitally, manipulated at will (stretched out, played backwards, and so on), then reintroduced into another musical phrase or composition. As one critic points out, what one does with sounds has become more important than what the sounds are. Electronic sampling, mixing, and remixing have generated sounds and strategies that, like the jump-cuts of Postmodern film, capture the fragmentation and tumultuousness of contemporary life.

Microtonality and Minimal Music

The Hungarian composer György Ligeti (1923–2006) took an interest in electronic music after meeting Stockhausen and other avant-garde composers in Cologne. While inspired by its unique sounds, he composed few electronic pieces. Nevertheless, in his instrumental works, he recreated some of its unique aural effects. To achieve the textures of electronic music, he made use of **microtonality** (the use of musical intervals smaller than the semitones of traditional European and American music). Almost completely lacking melody and harmony, Ligeti's technique, which he called "micropolyphony," produced dense clusters of sound: subtle, shimmering currents that murmur in a continuous, hypnotic flow. His instrumental *Atmospheres* (1961), and his choral work *Lux Eterna* (1966), both of which appear on the soundtrack of the film *2001*, achieved a new sonority that, as the composer explained, "is so dense that the individual interwoven instrumental voices are absorbed into the general texture and completely lose their individuality."

Ligeti's subtly shifting patterns of sound would become a hallmark of the musical style known as *Minimalism*. Minimal music, like Minimal art, reduces the vocabulary of expression to elemental or primary components that are repeated with only slight variations. In these "stripped-down" compositions, tonality and melody are usually simple, while rhythms and textures, built through minute repetition, are

See Music Listening Selections at end of chapter.

dense and complex. Minimalism has become widely popular among admirers of the Estonian composer Arvo Pärt (b. 1935), who embellishes austere and contemplative compositions with *tintinnabuli*, a weaving together of melodic lines that produces a bell-like prism of sound.

The most notable of Minimalist composers, Philip Glass (b. 1937), received his early training in the fundamentals of Western musical composition. In the 1970s, however, after touring Asia and studying with the sitar master Ravi Shankar (1920–2012), Glass began writing music that embraced the rhythmic structures of Indian *ragas*, progressive jazz, and rock and roll. The musical drama *Einstein on the Beach* (1976), which he produced in collaboration with the designer/director Robert Wilson (b. 1941), was the first opera performed at the Metropolitan Opera House in New York City to feature electronically amplified instruments.

Like traditional opera, *Einstein on the Beach* combines instrumental and vocal music, as well as recitation, mime, and dance. But it departs radically from operatic tradition in its lack of a narrative story line and character development, as well as in its instrumentation. The opera, which is performed with no intermissions over a period of four and a half hours, is not the story of Albert Einstein's life or work; rather, it is an extended poetic statement honoring the twentieth century's greatest scientist. The score consists of simple melodic lines that are layered and repeated in seemingly endless permutations. Mesmerizing and seductive, Glass' music recalls the texture of Gregorian chant, the sequenced repetitions of electronic tape loops, and the subtle rhythms of the Indian *raga*. Harmonic changes occur so slowly that one must, as Glass explains, learn to listen at "a different speed," a feat that closely resembles an act of meditation.

Historical themes and contemporary figures have continued to inspire much of the music of Glass. In 1980, he composed the opera *Satyagraha*, which celebrates the achievements of India's pacifist hero Mohandas Gandhi (see chapter 36). Sung in Sanskrit and English, the opera uses a text drawn from the *Bhagavad-Gita*, the sacred book of the Hindu religion. For the quincentennial commemoration of the Columbian voyage to the Americas, the composer wrote an imaginative modern-day analogue (*The Voyage*, 1992) that links the idea of great exploration to the theme of interplanetary travel. Glass' opera *Appomattox* (2007) deals with the role of racism in America, while *The Perfect American* (2013) takes as its subject the Hollywood icon Walt Disney.

Postmodern Opera

In the late twentieth century, opera found inspiration in newsworthy events such as international hijacking (John Adams' *Death of Klinghofer*), black nationalism (Anthony Davis' *X*), gay rights (Stewart Wallace's *Harvey Milk*), and the cult of celebrity—witness Ezra Laderman's *Marilyn* (Monroe), John Adams' *Nixon*, and Robert Xavier Rodriguez's *Frida* (Kahlo). Other composers turned to the classics of literature and art as subject matter for full-length

♪ See Music Listening Selections at end of chapter.

operas: Carlyle Floyd's *Of Mice and Men* (1970) is based on John Steinbeck's novel of the same name; William Bolcom's *A View from the Bridge* (1999) is an adaptation of the Arthur Miller play; John Harbison's *Gatsby* (1999) was inspired by F. Scott Fitzgerald's novel *The Great Gatsby*; and Tennessee Williams' classic play *A Streetcar Named Desire* (1998) received operatic treatment by the American composer André Previn. Few of these operas have attained the musical sophistication of the century's first typically Postmodern opera: *The Ghosts of Versailles* (1992) composed by John Corigliano (b. 1938). Scored for orchestra and synthesizer and cast in the style of a comic opera, *Ghosts of Versailles* takes place in three different (and interlayered) worlds: the eighteenth-century court of Versailles, the scenario of a Mozartean opera, and the realm of the afterlife—a place peopled by the ghosts of Marie Antoinette and her court. The score commingles traditional and contemporary musical styles, alternating pseudo-Mozartean lyricism with modern dissonance in a bold and inventive (although often astonishingly disjunctive) manner. In the spirit of Postmodernism, Corigliano made historical style itself the subject; his multivalent allegory tests the text against past texts by having one of his characters in the opera suddenly exclaim, "This is not opera; Wagner is opera."

Rock Music

The origins of the musical style called *rock* lay in the popular culture of the mid-1950s. The words "rocking" and "rolling," originally used to describe sexual activity, came to identify an uninhibited musical style that drew on a broad combination of popular American and African-American music, including country, swing, gospel, and rhythm and blues. Although no one musician is responsible for the birth of rock, the style gained popularity with such performers as Bill Haley, Little Richard, and Elvis Presley. In the hands of these flamboyant musicians, it came to be characterized by a high dynamic level of sound, fast and hard rhythms, a strong beat, and earthy, colloquial lyrics.

From its inception, rock music was an expression of a youth culture: the rock sound, associated with dancing, sexual freedom, and rebellion against restrictive parental and cultural norms, also mirrored the new consumerism of the postwar era. While 1950s rock and roll often featured superficial, "bubble gum" lyrics, 1960s rock became more sophisticated—the aural counterpart of Western-style Pop Art.

With the success of the Beatles—a British group of the 1960s—rock became an international phenomenon, uniting young people across the globe. The Beatles absorbed the music of Little Richard and also the rhythms and instrumentation of Indian classical music. They made imaginative use of electronic effects, such as feedback and splicing. Their compositions, which reflected the spirit of the Western counterculture, reached a creative peak in the album *Sergeant Pepper's Lonely Hearts Club Band* (1967). Although the electric guitar was in use well before the Beatles emerged, it was with this group that the instrument became the hallmark of rock music, and it remains the principal instrument of the rock musician.

During the 1960s, "establishment" America faced the protests of a youthful counterculture that was disenchanted with middle-class values, mindless consumerism, and bureaucratic authority. Counterculture "hippies"—the word derives from "hipster," an admirer of jazz and its subculture—exalted a neo-Romantic lifestyle that called for peaceful co-existence, a return to natural and communal habitation, more relaxed sexual standards, and experimentation with mind-altering drugs such as marijuana and lysergic acid diethylamide (LSD). The use of psychedelic drugs among members of the counterculture became associated with the emergence of a number of British and West Coast acid rock (or hard rock) groups, such as The Who and Jefferson Airplane. The music of these groups often featured earsplitting, electronically amplified sound and sexually provocative lyrics. The decade produced a few superb virtuoso performers, like the guitarist Jimi Hendrix (1942–1970). The 1960s also spawned the folk-rock hero Bob Dylan (b. 1941), whose songs gave voice to the anger and despair of the American counterculture. Dylan's lyrics, filled with scathing references to modern materialism, hypocrisy, greed, and warfare—specifically, the American involvement in Vietnam—attacked the moral detachment of contemporary authority figures.

Dance in the Information Age

Composed in conjunction with *Einstein on the Beach*, the choreography of Lucinda Childs (b. 1940)—who also danced in the original production—followed a Minimalist imperative. In line with the hypnotic rhythms of the piece, her choreography featured serial repetition of ritualized gestures and robotlike motions. Childs reduced the credo of pure dance to a set of patterned, geometric, recurrent body movements.

The most notable choreographer of our time, Seattle-born Mark Morris (b. 1956), allies dance to a closely studied musical score. Since the establishment of his own company in 1980, Morris has choreographed hundreds of original pieces inspired by specific works of music—from Mozart and Vivaldi to dance-hall tunes and rock. With comic wit and a reverence for technique, Morris often challenges ballet's gender conventions, assigning male dancers body movements traditionally consigned to females. Morris' landmark work *L'Allegro, il Penseroso ed il Moderato* (1988) is set to George Frideric Handel's oratorio of 1740, which takes its text from John Milton's famous poems of the same title. A brilliant union of poetry, music, and dance, the piece displays the structural clarity of Baroque style and the forthright simplicity of folk dance, a genre in which Morris had early training.

The role of improvisation in dance—the legacy of Merce Cunningham (see chapter 35)—has left a palpable mark: Companies such as the Sydney (Australia) Dance Company, Pilobolus, and Momix continue to produce exceptionally inventive repertories that embrace playful action and vigorous kinds of body movement, including acrobatics, aerobics, gymnastics, vaudeville, and street-dance. A highly original figure in contemporary choreography is the African-American Rennie Harris (b. 1964). Brought up in a crime-ridden section of North Philadelphia—without the luxury of formal dance training—Harris resolved to bring hip-hop dance to the concert stage. To achieve that goal, he founded his own dance company (Rennie Dance Puremovement) in 1992. His explosive choreography has transformed the violence of street gangs into a multimedia enterprise that features break-dancing (an acrobatic street-dance style) and electronically "souped up" sound.

LOOKING BACK

The Information Explosion

- The last decades of the twentieth century witnessed a transformation from an industrially based world culture to one shaped by mass media, electronic technology, and space travel.
- Digital technology has enhanced basic modes of communication, facilitated global homogeneity, and made possible the accumulation and transmission of huge amounts of information (so-called big data). The shift from book to screen has altered our way of perceiving reality and has had consequences for all the arts.
- The expansion of social media and the electronic mining and collection of

information raise complex cultural issues that have drawn the attention of those concerned with the right to privacy.

New Directions in Science and Philosophy

- Late twentieth-century advances in science have moved toward a greater understanding of both outer space and the inner workings of our bodies.
- Physicists continue to pursue a "theory of everything" that might reconcile Einstein's theory of relativity with the principles of quantum physics. String theorists have proposed a universal model consisting of tiny loops of vibrating strings. Chaos theorists identify common denominators

in nature: patterns that may seem random, but are actually self-similar.
- The mapping of the human genome by molecular biologists has led to major advances in medicine and experimentation in genetic engineering.
- Twentieth-century philosophers have generally abandoned the search for absolute truths, and instead, have given attention to the limits of language as a descriptive tool.

Literature in the Information Age

- The "Postmodern turn" accompanied the shift away from the anxious subjectivity and high seriousness of Modernism toward a skeptical and

- bemused attention to the history of culture and its myriad texts.
- Postmodern writers examine language as verbal coding and as a vehicle for both parody and social reform. They draw on the vast resources of history in works that often fictionalize history. The voice of the author may interrupt the narrative to produce the clipped rhythms of a video-fictional style.
- Some contemporary writers bring critical attention to the reality of urban violence and social inequity, while others explore the genres of Magic Realism and science fiction.

The Visual Arts in the Information Age

- The visual arts of the Information Age have not assumed any single, unifying style. Rather, they are diverse and eclectic, reflecting the Postmodern preoccupation with the media-shaped image, with parody and play, and with the contradictory nature of contemporary life. Distinctions between high and low art have become increasingly blurred.
- Andy Warhol was among the pioneers of American Pop Art, which glorified the mass-produced, commercial image. In the "combines" of Robert Rauschenberg, found objects became part of an inventive art of assemblage. Minimalism, championed by Donald Judd, utilized commercial and industrial materials in works that redefined the early twentieth-century credo of absolute abstraction.

At the other extreme, Hyperrealists provided a phenomenally detailed slice of life.
- The *process* of making art overtook the primacy of the *product*. Following the birth of the Happening, various kinds of total art emerged, including performance art, conceptual art, and site-specific earthworks that moved art out of the studio and into the environment.
- Nam June Paik and Bill Viola are two important figures in the birth and development of the widely popular genre of video art.

Architecture in the Information Age

- One of the earliest manifestations of Postmodernism was in architectural design, where architects united a playful assortment of historical styles within a single structure, such as the Piazza d'Italia in New Orleans.
- The new millennium has witnessed a trend toward sculptural architecture, most evident in the expansive (computer-aided) designs for museums and theaters conceived by Santiago Calatrava and Frank Gehry.

Music in the Information Age

- The music of the Information Age often deviated from traditional European modes of harmony and meter to incorporate microtonality, improvisation, and a variety of non-Western forms and instruments.

- The Minimalist compositions of Philip Glass feature hypnotic patterns of repetition inspired by traditional forms of Indian music. Contemporary subjects as well as historical themes dominate Postmodern operas, composed in a variety of musical idioms.
- Electronic technology has had a massive effect on all phases of musical culture, from composition to performance and distribution. Such technology facilitated the modification of pre-existing sound (as in "concrete music"), but also made possible the creation of a virtual golden age of electronic and electronically manipulated music.
- Rock music came to popularity as an expression of the youth culture of the 1960s. With the availability of portable digital synthesizers, and the increasingly complex techniques of mixing and sampling, rock has endured as a popular genre.

Dance in the Information Age

- The minimal choreography of Lucinda Childs and the radical innovations of Merce Cunningham have been complemented by new dance styles that feature acrobatics, gymnastics, vaudeville, and street-dance, including hip-hop.
- The inventive choreography of Mark Morris, unlike that of Cunningham, is directly inspired by and written for specific works of music.

Music Listening Selections

- Babbitt, *Ensembles for Synthesizer*, 1951, excerpt.
- Glass, *Einstein on the Beach*, "Knee Play 1," 1976.

Glossary

microtonality the use of musical intervals smaller than the semitones of traditional European and American music, but common to Indian and Arab Near Eastern music

musique concrète (French, "concrete music") a type of electroacoustic music that uses real or "concrete" sounds, such

as street noises, human voices, bird calls, and thunder, that are recorded, altered, and assembled on magnetic tape

silkscreen a printmaking technique employing a stenciled image cut and attached to finely meshed silk, through which printing ink is forced so as to transfer

the image to paper or cloth; also called "seriography"

synthesizer an integrated system of electronic components designed for the production and control of sound; it may be used in combination with a computer and with most musical instruments

Globalism:
The Contemporary World
ca. 1970–present

"To choose what is best for both the near and distant futures is a hard task, often seemingly contradictory and requiring knowledge and ethical codes which for the most part are still unwritten."
E. O. Wilson

Figure 38.1 ANDREAS GURSKY, *Pyongyang I*, 2007, C print, 13 ft. 10 in. × 6 ft. 10 in. × 2½ in. Gursky's photos, printed at colossal size, are digitally manipulated "records" of public events. The Arirang Festival was held in North Korea in 2007 to honor the late communist ruler Kim il Sung. More than 50,000 performers and 30,000 schoolchildren (holding colored flip cards) took part in a tightly choreographed visual display. Some critics see in these images the loss of individuality in a totalitarian society.

In 1962, the Canadian communications theorist Marshall McLuhan predicted the electronic transformation of planet earth into a "global village."* In the global village, communication between geographically remote parts of the world would be almost instantaneous, and every important new development— technological, ecological, political, economic, and intellectual— would affect every villager to some degree. Social and geographic mobility, receptivity to change, and a sense of collectivity would be the hallmarks of this new world community. Over the past five decades, McLuhan's futuristic vision has become a reality.

The roots of *globalism*—the interdependence of cultures and peoples in all parts of the world—are found in the industrial and commercial technology of the late nineteenth century. But the single factor that has been most significant in bringing together all parts of the world in the immediate exchange of information and ideas is electronic (and more recently digital) technology. The global community of the twenty-first century is challenged by some distinct problems: the effects of globalism on established religious, national, and ethnic traditions; the continuing threat of terrorism; and the future health of the world ecosystem. Globalism, its challenges, and its effects are the main themes of this chapter. In the arts, the focus is on the transformative influence of digital technology on traditional and untraditional genres. The multiple and often contradictory messages and styles in the arts of the global community make our own time one of the most exciting in the history of the humanistic tradition.

* The term was coined by the British Modernist Wyndham Lewis (1882–1957) in *America and Cosmic Man* (1948).

The Global Paradigm

Globalism has become the new model or paradigm for the contemporary world. While accelerated by digital technology, it owes much to a broad array of late twentieth-century developments: the success of anticolonial movements (see chapter 36), the fall of the Berlin Wall (1989) and subsequent collapse of the Soviet Union, and the end of the cold war (see chapter 35). With the elimination of these obstacles to freedom of communication among the populations of the earth, global cultural integration became a possibility, then a reality.

Television, the Internet, and video-sharing websites have been essential in dispersing visual images of international events, and effective in promoting Western values and consumer goods to other parts of the world. As Western consumer culture took hold across Asia and the Near East, it met a mixed reception (with some critics objecting to the "McDonaldization" of the planet). In India and China, its effects were transformative, while in some parts of the Muslim-occupied Near and Middle East, it was to produce virulent anti-Western antipathy (with enormous consequences for world peace), as well as popular movements for radical political change.

Globalism itself, however, remains an inevitable contemporary paradigm. In the international best-selling book *The World is Flat: A Brief History of the Twenty-First Century* (2005), the Pulitzer Prize-winning journalist Thomas L. Friedman describes a world that has become metaphorically "flat." With the collapse of most of the age-old barriers—physical, historical, and nationalistic—the global landscape offers a new, level playing field to all who choose to compete in the international marketplace. Interlinked digital networks, communication satellites, fiber-optic cables, and work-flow software provide an untrammeled exchange of data and the free flow of goods and ideas. These tools continue to transform the planet into a single world community.

Globalism and Tradition

Many parts of continental Africa have had a difficult time meeting the challenge of globalism. Following the end of colonialism and the withdrawal of Western powers from Africa, a void developed between African traditions and the modern ways of life that had been introduced by the European presence. Some African states, especially those crippled by poverty and epidemic disease, have faced serious problems arising from this void. Pleas for African unity, such as those made in the 1960s by Kwame Nkrumah (1909–1972), leader of Ghana, have gone unheeded; power struggles in some African countries have resulted in the emergence of totalitarian dictatorships, and age-old ethnic conflict has been reignited, all too often resulting in bloody civil wars and involving the recruitment of child soldiers (Figure **38.2**). Vast parts of Africa are thus caught in the sometimes devastating struggle between the old ways and the new.

Africa's leading English-language writer, Chinua Achebe (1930–2013), dealt sensitively with such problems. He is best known for his novel *Things Fall Apart* (1958), which remains the most widely read novel in African literature. In the short story "Dead Men's Path," Achebe examines the warp between premodern and modern traditions and the ongoing bicultural conflicts that plague many parts of Africa. At the same time, he probes the elusive, more universal tension between tradition and innovation, between spiritual and secular allegiance, and between faith and reason—polarities that continue to test human values in our time.

Figure 38.2 CHERI SAMBA, *Little Kadogo*, 2004. Acrylic on canvas, 78¾ × 106 in. Cheri Samba (b. 1956), a native of the Democratic Republic of Congo, depicts a *kadogo* (Swahili slang for "child soldier"), who raises his hands in surrender. The hand of an armed adult behind him warns, however, that the killing might very well continue.

READING 38.1 Achebe's "Dead Men's Path" (1972)

Michael Obi's hopes were fulfilled much earlier than he had   1
expected. He was appointed headmaster of Ndume Central
School in January 1949. It had always been an unprogressive
school, so the Mission authorities decided to send a young and
energetic man to run it. Obi accepted this responsibility with
enthusiasm. He had many wonderful ideas and this was an
opportunity to put them into practice. He had had a sound
secondary school education which designated him a "pivotal
teacher" in the official records and set him apart from the
other headmasters in the mission field. He was outspoken in   10
his condemnation of the narrow views of these older and
often less-educated ones.

    "We shall make a good job of it, shan't we?" he asked
his young wife when they first heard the joyful news of
his promotion.

    "We shall do our best," she replied. "We shall have such
beautiful gardens and everything will be just *modern* and
delightful. . . ." In their two years of married life she had
become completely infected by his passion for "modern
methods" and his denigration of "these old and superannuated   20
people in the teaching field who would be better employed as
traders in the Onitsha market." She began to see herself
already as the admired wife of the young headmaster, the
queen of the school.

    The wives of the other teachers would envy her position.
She would set the fashion in everything. . . . Then, suddenly,
it occurred to her that there might not be other wives.
Wavering between hope and fear, she asked her husband,
looking anxiously at him.

    "All our colleagues are young and unmarried," he said   30
with enthusiasm which for once she did not share.
"Which is a good thing," he continued.

    "Why?"

    "Why? They will give all their time and energy to the school."

    Nancy was downcast. For a few minutes she became
sceptical about the new school; but it was only for a few
minutes. Her little personal misfortune could not blind her to

her husband's happy prospects. She looked at him as he sat
folded up in a chair. He was stoop-shouldered and looked frail.   40
But he sometimes surprised people with sudden bursts of
physical energy. In his present posture, however, all his bodily
strength seemed to have retired behind his deep-set eyes,
giving them an extraordinary power of penetration. He was
only twenty-six, but looked thirty or more. On the whole, he
was not unhandsome.

    "A penny for your thoughts, Mike," said Nancy after a
while, imitating the woman's magazine she read.

    "I was thinking what a grand opportunity we've got at last
to show these people how a school should be run."   50

Ndume School was backward in every sense of the word.
Mr. Obi put his whole life into the work, and his wife hers too.
He had two aims. A high standard of teaching was insisted
upon, and the school compound was to be turned into a place
of beauty. Nancy's dream-gardens came to life with the coming
of the rains, and blossomed. Beautiful hibiscus and allamanda
hedges in brilliant red and yellow marked out the carefully
tended school compound from the rank neighbourhood bushes.

    One evening as Obi was admiring his work he was
scandalized to see an old woman from the village hobble right   60
across the compound, through a marigold flowerbed and the
hedges. On going up there he found faint signs of an almost
disused path from the village across the school compound to
the bush on the other side.

    "It amazes me," said Obi to one of his teachers who had
been three years in the school, "that you people allowed the
villagers to make use of this footpath. It is simply incredible."
He shook his head.

    "The path," said the teacher apologetically, "appears to be
very important to them. Although it is hardly used, it connects   70
the village shrine with their place of burial."

    "And what has that got to do with the school?" asked
the headmaster.

    "Well, I don't know," replied the other with a shrug of the
shoulders. "But I remember there was a big row some time ago
when we attempted to close it."

"That was some time ago. But it will not be used now," said Obi as he walked away. "What will the Government Education Officer think of this when he comes to inspect the school next week? The villagers might, for all I know, decide to use the schoolroom for a pagan ritual during the inspection."

Heavy sticks were planted closely across the path at the two places where it entered and left the school premises. These were further strengthened with barbed wire.

Three days later the village priest of Ani called on the headmaster. He was an old man and walked with a slight stoop. He carried a stout walking-stick which he usually tapped on the floor, by way of emphasis, each time he made a new point in his argument.

"I have heard," he said after the usual exchange of cordialities, "that our ancestral footpath has recently been closed. . . ."

"Yes," replied Mr. Obi. "We cannot allow people to make a highway of our school compound."

"Look here, my son," said the priest bringing down his walking-stick, "this path was here before you were born and before your father was born. The whole life of this village depends on it. Our dead relatives depart by it and our ancestors visit us by it. But most important, it is the path of children coming in to be born. . . ."

Mr. Obi listened with a satisfied smile on his face.

"The whole purpose of our school," he said finally, "is to eradicate just such beliefs as that. Dead men do not require footpaths. The whole idea is just fantastic. Our duty is to teach your children to laugh at such ideas."

"What you say may be true," replied the priest, "but we follow the practices of our fathers. If you re-open the path we shall have nothing to quarrel about. What I always say is: let the hawk perch and let the eagle perch." He rose to go.

"I am sorry," said the young headmaster. "But the school compound cannot be a thoroughfare. It is against our regulations. I would suggest your constructing another path, skirting our premises. We can even get our boys to help in building it. I don't suppose the ancestors will find the little detour too burdensome."

"I have no more words to say," said the old priest, already outside.

Two days later a young woman in the village died in childbed. A diviner was immediately consulted and he prescribed heavy sacrifices to propitiate ancestors insulted by the fence.

Obi woke up next morning among the ruins of his work. The beautiful hedges were torn up not just near the path but right round the school, the flowers trampled to death and one of the school buildings pulled down.

. . . That day, the white Supervisor came to inspect the school and wrote a nasty report on the state of the premises but more seriously about the "tribal-war situation developing between the school and the village, arising in part from the misguided zeal of the new headmaster."

Q **How does this story illustrate the conflict between tradition and innovation?**

Q **What might the path in this story symbolize?**

The Challenge of Globalism

Terrorism

Probably the greatest single threat to the contemporary global community is *terrorism*, the deliberate and systematic use of violence against civilians in order to destabilize political systems or advance political, religious, or ideological goals. As a combat tactic, terrorism is not new; however, rapid forms of communication and transportation, and the availability of more virulent weaponry, make contemporary terrorism both imminent and potentially devastating. Terrorist attacks have taken place all over the world, from Madrid to Mumbai. One of the most ruthless took the form of a coordinated air assault on New York's World Trade Center and the Pentagon in Washington, D.C. On September 11, 2001, Islamic militants representing the radical Muslim group known as al-Qaeda ("the base") hijacked four American airliners, flying two of them into the Twin Towers in Manhattan, and a third into the headquarters of the U. S. Department of Defense near the nation's capital. A fourth crashed before it could reach its target: the White House.

Masterminded by al-Qaeda's leader, Osama bin Laden (1957–2011), the attack, now called "9-11," killed more than 3000 civilians. Bin Laden justified the operation as retaliation for America's military presence and eco-political interference in the predominantly Muslim regions of the Middle East. The recurrence of radical Islamist assaults on other primarily Western targets throughout the world underline the troubling rift between two principal ideologies: the modern and dominantly Western separation of Church and state, and strict Qur'anic theocracy, by which religion and religious leaders dictate the governing order.

Eighteen months after 9-11, on suspicions of an Iraqi stockpile of chemical and biological weapons, a multinational coalition force invaded Iraq; that military intervention, which led to armed conflict between Shiite and Sunni factions, complicated the already tense situation in the Middle East. The war on terror has since spread to other regions, such as Afghanistan, where militant Sunni insurgents known as the Taliban seek to establish the rigid enforcement of Islamic law. And, since 2003, movements to end autocratic rule in various parts of the Middle East (including Egypt, Libya, Tunisia, Yemen, and Syria) have resulted in regional destabilization, and, in many cases, bloody civil wars.

The Arts and Terrorism

Initially, artists responded to the events of 9-11 by commemorating the destruction of the World Trade Center and those who died in the assault. One year after the attack, the composer John Adams (whom we met in chapter 37) premiered his choral eulogy *On the Transmigration of Souls*, which was awarded the 2003 Pulitzer Prize in music. Numerous photographs and films have revisited the tragic circumstances of the event, especially the experience of victims who escaped the burning buildings by jumping to their death. The American visual artist Carolee Schneemann (b. 1939), best known for her body-oriented

Figure 38.3 EL ANATSUI, *Between Earth and Heaven*, 2006. Aluminum, copper wire, 91 × 126 in. Widely regarded as Africa's most significant sculptor, El Anatsui teaches at the University of Nigeria.

The sculptures of the Ghanaian artist El Anatsui (b. 1944) reveal the intersection of traditional and contemporary African themes. *Between Earth and Heaven* (2006) consists of thousands of aluminum seals and screw caps from bottles of wine and liquor (Figure **38.3**). The caps are flattened and woven with copper wire to create large, shimmering metal tapestries. El Anatsui recycles discarded objects into compelling artworks whose designs and colors (gold, red, and black) have much in common with the decorative cotton-cloth textiles known as *kente* (Figure **38.4**). The handwoven *kente*— the name derives from the designs of baskets traditionally woven in the kingdom of Asante (modern Ghana)—belong to a royal textile tradition that reaches back to the eleventh century. Vibrant in color and complex in their patterns, these textiles have come to be associated with a pan-African identity.

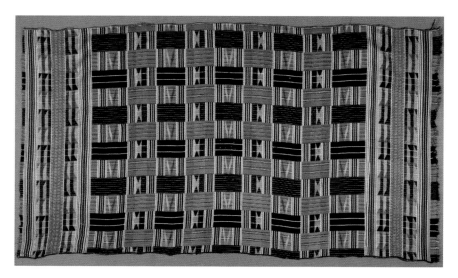

Figure 38.4 Asante *kente* textile, mid-twentieth century. Cotton, 3 ft. 11 in. × 6 ft. 7¼ in. The individual designs on the cloth are associated with seventeenth-century Asante kings who are said to have laid claim to specific signs and patterns.

performance pieces, treated the "jumper" image in stunning mixed-media artworks. One of these, *Terminal Velocity*, is a vertical grid of scanned newspaper photographs showing nine of the 200 or so individuals (some still unidentified) who leapt from the upper floors of the Twin Towers before the building collapsed (Figure **38.5**).

Literary reflection on 9-11 and its aftermath inspired (among other works) the novel *Falling Man* (2006) by Don DeLillo (see chapter 37), and Laurence Wright's carefully researched nonfiction study, *The Looming Tower: Al-Qaeda and the Road to 9-11* (2007). In 2013, the Canadian writer Margaret Atwood (see chapter 37) completed a fictional postapocalyptic trilogy, involving a lethal man-made plague unleashed by an ecoterrorist hacking collective called MaddAddam.

The global sense of insecurity in the face of international terrorism was powerfully voiced by two recently deceased Nobel Prize-winning poets: Wislawa Szymborska (1923–2012) and Seamus Heaney (1939–2013). Szymborska lived most of her life in communist-controlled Poland, a country that lost nearly one-fifth of its population during World War II. Her poems, while straightforward and conversational in tone, address personal and universal subjects and matters of moral urgency. "The Terrorist, He Watches," written in 1976, is a prescient anticipation of our current unease and apprehension.

The Irish Seamus Heaney shared with his countryman W. B. Yeats (see chapter 34) the gift of lyric brilliance. Heaney's ability to translate the small details of everyday experience into transcendent ideas was unsurpassed. While much of his poetry reflects his deep affection for the "bogs and barnyards" of rural life, one recent volume of poetry, *District and Circle*, responded to the violence of our time, specifically the 2005 terrorist attacks on London's subway system of which the District and Circle lines are a part. Prompted by the Roman poet Horace, Heaney grapples with the sobering fact that "anything can happen."

Figure 38.5 CAROLEE SCHNEEMANN, *Terminal Velocity*, 2001–2005. Black-and-white computer scans of falling bodies from 9-11, inkjet on paper, 8 × 7 ft. Collection of the artist. Schneemann enlarged scanned newspaper photographs (some by the American photojournalist Richard Drew). Collaging the photos onto a huge grid, she created a haunting image of corporeal vulnerability.

READING 38.2 Szymborska's "The Terrorist, He Watches" (1976)

The bomb will explode in the bar at twenty past one.   1
Now it's only sixteen minutes past.
Some will still have time to enter,
some to leave.

The terrorist's already on the other side.   5
That distance protects him from all harm
and, well, it's like the pictures:

A woman in a yellow jacket, she enters.
A man in dark glasses, he leaves.
Boys in jeans, they're talking.   10
Sixteen minutes past and four seconds.
The smaller one, he's lucky, mounts his scooter,
but that taller chap, he walks in.

Seventeen minutes and forty seconds.
A girl, she walks by, a green ribbon in her hair.   15
But that bus suddenly hides her.
Eighteen minutes past.
The girl's disappeared.
Was she stupid enough to go in, or wasn't she.
We shall see when they bring out the bodies.   20

Nineteen minutes past.
No one else appears to be going in.
On the other hand, a fat bald man leaves.
But seems to search his pockets and
at ten seconds to twenty past one   25
he returns to look for his wretched gloves.

It's twenty past one.
Time, how it drags.
Surely, it's now.
No, not quite.   30
Yes, now.
The bomb, it explodes.

Q **What does this poem suggest about the life of the individual in the global village?**

After Horace, Odes, I, 34

Anything can happen. You know how Jupiter[1]   1
Will mostly wait for clouds to gather head
Before he hurls the lightning? Well just now
He galloped his thunder cart and his horses

Across a clear blue sky. It shook the earth   5
and the clogged underearth, the River Styx,[2]
the winding streams, the Atlantic shore itself.
Anything can happen, the tallest towers

Be overturned, those in high places daunted,
Those overlooked regarded. Stropped-beak Fortune   10
Swoops, making the air gasp, tearing the crest off one,
Setting it down bleeding on the next.

Ground gives. The heaven's weight
Lifts up off Atlas like a kettle lid.[3]
Capstones shift. Nothing resettles right.   15
Telluric[4] ash and fire-spores boil away.

Q How does the poet's use of ancient mythology
contribute to the poem?

China: Global Ascendance

It is widely believed that the People's Republic of China
will be the next great global power. In the last three decades, China has experienced a cultural transformation of
enormous proportions. Once a country of rural villages,
this vast nation now claims more than 160 cities with a population of one million or more people in each. Currently,
China is the largest exporter on the planet. Still governed
by a communist regime, its rapid advances in industry,
technology, and the arts have made it a formidable presence on the global stage.

China's ascendance has not been unmarred by internal strife. Following the death of Mao Zedong in 1976
(see chapter 34), communist officials tightened control
over all forms of artistic expression. Nevertheless, young
Chinese artists and writers continued to work, either in
exile or at their own peril. In June 1989, at Tiananmen
Square in Beijing, thousands of student activists demonstrated in support of democratic reform. With Beethoven's
Ninth Symphony blaring from loudspeakers, demonstrators raised a plaster figure of the goddess of democracy
modeled on the Statue of Liberty. The official response to
this overt display of freedom resulted in the massacre of
some protesters and the imprisonment of others.

Since Tiananmen Square, literary publication has
remained under the watchful eye of the state, but efforts to

---

[1] Roman sky god.
[2] River in the underworld crossed by the souls of the dead.
[3] Mythic Titan condemned to support the heavens on his shoulders.
[4] Terrestrial.

control music and the visual arts have been relaxed. A large
body of Chinese literature, much of it written by women, has
examined the traumatic years of Mao's Cultural Revolution
(1966–1976). The enormous popularity of Western classical
music in China has created a talent pool of highly trained
performers. Outstanding filmmakers, such as Zhang Yimou
(see Film and Activism) have received worldwide attention. Even more dramatic is the upsurge in painting and
sculpture, where the Chinese have broken into the world
art market with works that depart radically from Chinese
tradition (and command huge prices in the West).

In the past four decades, artists—most of them rigorously trained in China's Central Academy—have had the
opportunity to explore the major styles and techniques of
their Western contemporaries, through international travel and mass electronic communication. In the early 1990s,
there emerged two overlapping (and still flourishing)
styles. The first, *political pop*, seized on Western icons and
images to glamorize or discredit various aspects of Chinese
life. The second, *cynical realism*, engaged commercial painting techniques to satirize social and political issues. Both
of these styles are evident in the "Great Criticism" series by
Wang Guangyi (b. 1956).

In one painting from the series (Figure **38.6**), bright
colors and broad, simplified shapes, reminiscent of the
Soviet-approved posters of the 1920s (see Figure 34.5),
send a sly and subversive message: three Maoist workers,
armed with the red flag of China, its mast an oversized
pen, advance boldly into the arena of commercial combat,
their mission approved by the official government stamps
stenciled on the surface of the canvas. Here, collectivist

Figure 38.6 WANG GUANGYI, *Coca-Cola*, from the series "Great Criticism,"
1993. Enamel paint on canvas, 4 ft. 11 in. × 3 ft. 11 in.

Figure 38.7 CAI GUO-QIANG, *Inopportune: Stage One*, 2005. Mixed media. Cai's installations are two- and three-dimensional "narratives" that regularly consume a series of rooms.

socialism engages capitalist consumerism, represented by such populist commodities as Coca-Cola, McDonald's hamburgers, and Marlboro cigarettes.

More recently, the Chinese art scene has exploded with an outpouring of photographic and video projects (see Figure 14.16), and elaborately choreographed mixed-media installations. The Chinese-born Cai Guo-Qiang (b. 1957) moved to Manhattan in 1995, bringing with him the age-old literary and artistic traditions of his homeland. Trained in stage design at the Shanghai Drama Institute, Cai captures in his public works the disquieting nature of contemporary life. Many of his installations explore the properties of gunpowder—an explosive invented by the Chinese for firework displays.

Cai's most ambitious project was an installation in 2004 of four works. The first piece, *Inopportune: Stage One*, featured a brilliant array of colored lights pulsing from long transparent rods that burst from nine identical Ford sedans (Figure **38.7**). The cars, suspended in midair along a 300-foot gallery, called to mind a sequence of images unfurling in a Chinese scroll, or a series of frozen film frames. *Inopportune: Stage Two*, installed in an adjacent gallery, consisted of nine prefabricated life-sized tigers pierced by hundreds of bamboo arrows—a reference to a popular thirteenth-century Chinese tale glorifying a hero who saves his village from a man-eating tiger. *Illusion* is a startling three-channel, ninety-second film projected on a huge screen of a phantom car bursting silently into flames, then

floating in a dreamlike manner through Manhattan's bustling, nocturnal Times Square. In front of the screen is an actual car filled with used fireworks. The fourth work is *Nine Cars*, a huge two-dimensional wall-hanging on which one sees nine exploding cars as "painted" by ignited gunpowder on paper. In this project Cai has mixed an assortment of traditions, symbols, and images to capture the violence of contemporary urban life. He claims that he uses the tools and materials of destruction and terror for healing purposes—the Chinese character for "gunpowder" translates literally as "fire medicine," which was once thought to cure the ailing body.

One of China's foremost (and most politically controversial) contemporary artists, Ai Weiwei (b. 1957), produces multimedia sculpture, photography, films, and performance art; but he is best known in the West as an outspoken critic of China's authoritarian regime. Ai's large installations, such as *Forever Bicycle* (Figure **38.8**), reference Chinese tradition by repurposing the most common

Figure 38.8 AI WEIWEI, *Forever Bicycle*, 2011. Deeply concerned with freedom of expression, Ai Weiwei attempts to transform China's "social landscape" both through his colossal installations and by way of critical commentary posted online.

mode of transportation in China. ("*Yong jiu*," the name of China's best-selling brand of bicycle, means "forever.") For this huge installation, Ai assembled 1,200 steel bicycles, which, while totally stationary, are layered so that they seem to be in motion. At once "social sculpture" and an expression of the artist's wit, the work is both visually provocative and obliquely personal—especially since the Chinese government has immobilized the activist artist by withholding his passport.

The building boom that China has enjoyed in the early twenty-first century was markedly accelerated by Beijing's role as the site of the 2008 Olympic Games. Representative of the global perspective, the architectural projects for the Olympics involved multinational participation and cooperation: the extraordinary Beijing airport—now the largest in the world—was the brainchild of the British architect Norman Foster (discussed later in this chapter); the National Stadium (nicknamed the "Bird's Nest" to describe its interwoven steel latticework) was designed by the Swiss architects Jacques Herzog and Pierre de Meuron in collaboration with Ai Weiwei; and the Aquatic Center (known as the "Water Cube") was designed and built by a consortium of Australian architects and Chinese engineers.

The Global Ecosystem

The future of the environment has become a major global concern. While modern industry brings vast benefits to humankind, it also threatens the global **ecosystem** (the ecological community and its physical environment). Sulphur dioxide emissions in one part of the world affect other parts of the world, causing acid rain that damages forests, lakes, and soil. Industrial pollution poisons the entire planet's oceans. Leaks from nuclear reactors (as occurred in 2011 at Japan's Fukushima Daiichi nuclear facility following a devastating tsunami) endanger populations thousands of miles away, and greenhouse gases (produced in part from the burning of the coal, oil, and natural gas that power the world's industries) contribute to global warming and increasingly dangerous changes in the earth's climate. Although such realities have inspired increasing concern for the viability of the ecosystem, they have only recently attracted the serious attention of world leaders.

A landmark figure in the study of ecological systems is the American sociobiologist Edward Osborne Wilson (b. 1929). A leading defender of the natural environment, Wilson's early work in evolutionary biology examined parallels between ants and other animal societies, including those of human beings. More recently, he proposed a new type of interdisciplinary research (which he calls "scientific humanism") that works to improve the human condition. In *The Diversity of Life*, Wilson makes a plea for the preservation of **biodiversity**, the variation of life forms within a given ecosystem. He seeks the development of a sound environmental ethic, shared by both "those who believe that life was put on earth in one divine stroke" and "those who perceive biodiversity to be the product of blind evolution." Wilson pleads for a practical ethic that will ensure the healthy future of the planet.

READING 38.4 From Wilson's *The Diversity of Life* (1992)

Every country has three forms of wealth: material, cultural, and biological. The first two we understand well because they are the substance of our everyday lives. The essence of the biodiversity problem is that biological wealth is taken much less seriously. This is a major strategic error, one that will be increasingly regretted as time passes. Diversity is a potential source for immense untapped material wealth in the form of food, medicine, and amenities. The fauna and flora are also part of a country's heritage, the product of millions of years of evolution centered on that time and place and hence as 10 much a reason for national concern as the particularities of language and culture.

The biological wealth of the world is passing through a bottleneck destined to last another fifty years or more. The human population has moved past 5.4 billion, is projected to reach 8.5 billion by 2025, and may level off at 10 to 15 billion by midcentury. With such a phenomenal increase in human biomass, with material and energy demands of the developing countries accelerating at an even faster pace, far less room will be left for most of the species of plants and animals in 20 a short period of time.

The human juggernaut creates a problem of epic dimensions: how to pass through the bottleneck and reach midcentury with the least possible loss of biodiversity and the least possible cost to humanity. In theory at least, the minimalization of extinction rates and the minimization of economic costs are compatible: the more that other forms of life are used and saved, the more productive and secure will our own species be. Future generations will reap the benefit of wise decisions taken on behalf of biological diversity by our generation. 30

What is urgently needed is knowledge and a practical ethic based on a time scale longer than we are accustomed to apply. An ideal ethic is a set of rules invented to address problems so complex or stretching so far into the future as to place their solution beyond ordinary discourse. Environmental problems are innately ethical. They require vision reaching simultaneously into the short and long reaches of time. What is good for individuals and societies at this moment might easily sour ten years hence, and what seems ideal over the next several decades could ruin future generations. To choose 40 what is best for both the near and distant futures is a hard task, often seemingly contradictory and requiring knowledge and ethical codes which for the most part are still unwritten.

If it is granted that biodiversity is at high risk, what is to be done? Even now, with the problem only beginning to come into focus, there is little doubt about what needs to be done. The solution will require cooperation among professions long separated by academic and practical tradition. Biology, anthropology, economics, agriculture, government, and law will have to find a common voice. Their conjunction has 50 already given rise to a new discipline, biodiversity studies, defined as the systematic study of the full array of organic diversity and the origin of that diversity, together with the

Figure 38.9 ROBERT SMITHSON, *Spiral Jetty*, Great Salt Lake, Utah, 1970. Rock, salt crystals, earth algae; coil 1500 ft. The lake itself had been degraded by abandoned oil derricks. Documentary drawings, photographs, and films of *Spiral Jetty*, along with the recent rehabilitation of the earthwork itself, have heightened public awareness of the fragile balance between nature and culture.

methods by which it can be maintained and used for the benefit of humanity. The enterprise of biodiversity studies is thus both scientific, a branch of pure biology, and applied, a branch of biotechnology and the social sciences. It draws from biology at the level of whole organisms and populations in the same way that biomedical studies draw from biology at the level of the cell and molecule. . . . 60

The evidence of swift environmental change calls for an ethic uncoupled from other systems of belief. Those committed by religion to believe that life was put on earth in one divine stroke will recognize that we are destroying the Creation, and those who perceive biodiversity to be the product of blind evolution will agree. Across the other great philosophical divide, it does not matter whether species have independent rights or, conversely, that moral reasoning is uniquely a human 70 concern. Defenders of both premises seem destined to gravitate toward the same position on conservation.

The stewardship of the environment is a domain on the near side of metaphysics where all reflective persons can surely find common ground. For what, in the final analysis, is morality but the command of conscience seasoned by a rational examination of consequences? And what is a fundamental precept but one that serves all generations? An enduring environmental ethic will aim to preserve not only the health and freedom of our species, but access to the world in which 80 the human spirit was born.

Q Why does Wilson contend that environmental problems are "innately ethical"?

Q Why does he regard "the stewardship of environment" as a global responsibility?

Environmental Art

What Wilson calls "the stewardship of environment" has captured the imagination of many visual artists. The Chinese-American conceptualist Mel Chin (b. 1951), for instance, has launched a novel project to leach toxic metals from highly contaminated soil. Chin shares the passions of the seminal eco-artist Robert Smithson (1938–1973), who pioneered one of the most important ecological landmarks of the late twentieth century: the piece known as *Spiral Jetty* (Figure **38.9**). Constructed on the edge of the Great Salt Lake in Utah, in waters polluted by abandoned oil mines, *Spiral Jetty* is a giant (1500-foot-long) coil consisting of 6650 tons of local black basalt, limestone, and earth. This snail-like symbol of eternity makes reference to ancient earthworks, such as those found in Neolithic cultures (see Figure 3.13), and to the origins of life in the salty waters of the primordial ocean; but it also calls attention to the way in which nature is constantly transforming the environment and its ecological balance.

When Smithson created *Spiral Jetty* in 1970, the lake was unusually shallow because of drought. Submerged for decades by rising waters, this iconic piece can now be seen again from ground level, its galactic coil partially encrusted with glittering white salt crystals that float in the algae-filled, rose-colored shallows. Earthworks like *Spiral Jetty* are often best appreciated from the air. Tragically, it was in the crash of a small airplane surveying a potential site that Smithson was killed.

Green Architecture

Architects have always given practical consideration to the environment in which they build. Now, however, in the face of rising fuel prices, global warming, and the degradation of the ecosystem because of industrial growth,

Figure 38.10 NORMAN FOSTER, Swiss Re building (30 St. Mary Axe), London, 2003.

Science and Technology

1962	Rachel Carson's *Silent Spring* argues that man-made chemicals are damaging the earth's ecosystem
1974	American scientists demonstrate that chlorofluorocarbons (CFCs) are eroding the earth's ozone layer
2006	Al Gore publishes *An Inconvenient Truth: The Planetary Emergency of Global Warming and What We Can Do About It*

the job of designing structures that do the least possible damage to the environment (a practice known as "green" or "sustainable" design), has become even more imperative. Green buildings—structures that are both friendly to the ecosystem and energy efficient—have been found to save money and preserve the environment. Although the United States launched the Green Building Council in 2000, fewer than 800 certified green buildings were constructed during the following seven years; however, the greening of architecture has become a global movement. It embraces architectural design that makes use of energy-efficient (and renewable) building materials, recycling systems that capture rainwater (for everyday use), solar panels that use sunlight to generate electricity, insulating glass, and other energy-saving devices and techniques.

Of the green buildings that have been constructed in the last ten years, one has already become a landmark: the Swiss Re office building (30 St. Mary Axe), designed in 2003 by the British architect Norman Foster (b. 1935), is London's first environmentally sustainable skyscraper (Figure **38.10**). Natural ventilation, provided by windows that open automatically, passive solar heating, and a double-glazed insulating glass skin (some 260,000 square feet of glass) are some of the features that work to reduce this forty-story building's energy costs by one-half of normal costs. While Foster's tower resembles a spaceship, its tall, rounded, picklelike shape has inspired Londoners to call it "the Gherkin."

Globalism and Ethnic Identity

Ethnic identity—that is, one's bond with a group that shares the same traditions, culture, and values—is a major theme in the global community. A "cluster" of traits (race, language, physical appearance, and religious values) that form one's self-image, ethnicity differentiates the self from mass culture and manifests itself in language, music, food, and ritual. The self-affirming significance of ethnic identity is apparent in the ancient Yoruba proverb: "I am because we are; what I am is what we are."

As the global village becomes more homogeneous, efforts to maintain ethnic identity have generated self-conscious reflection. In her poems, novels, and short stories, Leslie Marmon Silko (b. 1948) celebrates the Pueblo folklore of her Native American ancestors, while the Chinese-American writer Maxine Hong Kingston (b. 1940) blends fiction and nonfiction in novels that deal with family legends and native Chinese customs. The oral tradition—stories handed down from generation to generation, often by and through women—plays an important part in the works of these authors, even as it does in the preservation of ethnic identity.

Ethnicity has also become a dominant theme in the visual arts. While El Anatsui pays homage to his African identify in the fabrication of elaborate installations (see Figure 38.3), others treat ethnicity in photography and film. The contemporary Chinese artist Huang Yan has photographed his body tattooed with traditional Chinese landscape imagery (see Figure 14.16). The Iranian-born

Figure 38.11 SHIRIN NESHAT, *Rebellious Silence*, from the series "Women of Allah," 1994. Gelatin-silver print and ink.

Shirin Neshat (b. 1957), who now lives in New York City, employs film and photography to deal with conflicting ethnic values and lifestyles: Islamic and Western, ancient and modern, male and female. Her photographic series "Women of Allah" (1993–1997) explores the role of militant women who fought in the 1979 revolution that overthrew Iran's ruling dynasty. Neshat makes dramatic use of the *chador* (the large veil of black cloth that has become an ethnic symbol of Muslim women) to frame her face, which, intersected by a rifle, becomes the site of a poem (by the feminist writer Forough Farrokhzad, 1935–1967) transcribed in Farsi calligraphy (Figure **38.11**).

Latino Culture

The process of globalization and the rise of ethnicity have accelerated yet another major phenomenon: immigration—the age-old process of people moving from *mother* country to *other* country—which has increased dramatically in recent years. Every year, some 100 million people leave (or try to leave) their places of birth in search of political or economic advantage. This mass migration of peoples has resulted in the establishment of large ethnic communities throughout the world. The vast number of immigrants who have made the United States their home have had a dramatic impact: demographic changes, in the form of rising numbers of Asians and Latinos—persons

from the various Latin American countries—have changed the face of the economy, the urban environment, and the culture. If current trends continue, by the year 2050 Latinos will constitute 30 percent of the total population of the United States.

In all aspects of life, from literature and art to food and dance styles, there has been a flowering of Latino culture. With *The Mambo Kings Play Songs of Love* (1989), the first novel by a Hispanic to win the Pulitzer Prize, the Cuban-American Oscar Hijuelos (1951–2013) brought attention to the impact of Latin American music on American culture, and, more generally, to the role of memory in reclaiming one's ethnic roots. Contemporary writers, such as the Dominican-American Junot Diaz (b. 1968), author of the best-selling novel *The Brief Wondrous Life of Oscar Wao* (2008), have given voice to personal problems of adjustment in America's ethnic mosaic, and to the ways in which language and customs provide a vital sense of ethnic identity. These are the themes pursued by one of today's leading *Chicana* (Mexican-American female) authors, Sandra Cisneros (b. 1954). Cisneros, who describes the struggle of Chicana women in an alien society, writes in the familiar voice of everyday speech. Of her writing style, she says:

> It's very much of an anti-academic voice—a child's voice, a girl's voice, a poor girl's voice, a spoken voice, the voice of an American Mexican. It's in this rebellious realm of antipoetics that I tried to create a poetic text with the most unofficial language I could find.

Cisneros dates the birth of her own political consciousness from the moment (in a graduate seminar on Western literature) she recognized her "otherness," that is, her separateness from the dominant culture. A vignette from *The House on Mango Street*, her classic novel, describes the experience of a young girl growing up in the Latino section of Chicago. It illustrates the shaping role of language and memory in matters of identity.

┌─ **READING 38.5** Cisneros' "No Speak English" from
    The House on Mango Street (1984)

Mamacita[1] is the big mama of the man across the street,-   **1**
third-floor front. Rachel says her name ought to be *Mamasota*,[2]
but I think that's mean.

    The man saved his money to bring her here. He saved and
saved because she was alone with the baby boy in that
country. He worked two jobs. He came home late and he left
early. Every day.

    Then one day *Mamacita* and the baby boy arrived in a yellow
taxi. The taxi door opened like a waiter's arm. Out stepped a
tiny pink shoe, a foot soft as a rabbit's ear, then the thick   **10**
ankle, a flutter of hips, fuchsia roses and green perfume.
The man had to pull her, the taxicab driver had to push. Push,
pull. Push, pull. Poof!

[1] "Little Mama," also a term of endearment.
[2] "Big Mama."

All at once she bloomed. Huge, enormous, beautiful to look at, from the salmon-pink feather on the tip of her hat down to the little rosebuds of her toes. I couldn't take my eyes off her tiny shoes.

Up, up, up the stairs she went with the baby boy in a blue blanket, the man carrying her suitcases, her lavender hatboxes, a dozen boxes of satin high heels. Then we didn't see her. 20

Somebody said because she's too fat, somebody because of the three flights of stairs, but I believe she doesn't come out because she is afraid to speak English, and maybe this is so since she only knows eight words. She knows to say: *He not here* for when the landlord comes, *No speak English* if anybody else comes, and Holy smokes. I don't know where she learned this, but I heard her say it one time and it surprised me.

My father says when he came to this country he ate 30 hamandeggs for three months. Breakfast, lunch and dinner. Hamandeggs. That was the only word he knew. He doesn't eat hamandeggs anymore.

Whatever her reasons, whether she is fat, or can't climb the stairs, or is afraid of English, she won't come down. She sits all day by the window and plays the Spanish radio show and sings all the homesick songs about her country in a voice that sounds like a seagull.

Home. Home. Home is a house in a photograph, a pink house, pink as hollyhocks with lots of startled light. The man 40 paints the walls of the apartment pink, but it's not the same, you know. She still sighs for her pink house, and then I think she cries. I would.

Sometimes the man gets disgusted. He starts screaming and you can hear it all the way down the street.

Ay, she says, she is sad.

Oh, he says. Not again.

¿Cuándo, cuándo, cuándo?[3] she asks.

¡Ay, caray![4] We are home. This is home. Here I am and here I stay. Speak English. Speak English. Christ! 50

¡Ay, Mamacita, who does not belong, every once in a while lets out a cry, hysterical, high, as if he had torn the only skinny thread that kept her alive, the only road out to that country. And then to break her heart forever, the baby boy, who has begun to talk, starts to sing the Pepsi commercial he heard on T.V.

No speak English, she says to the child who is singing in the language that sounds like tin. No speak English, no speak English, and bubbles into tears. No, no, no, as if she can't believe her ears. 60

— **Q** **How does Cisneros bring Mamacita to life? What makes her a sympathetic figure?**

No less than in literature, the visual arts document the Latino effort to preserve or exalt ethnic identity: Yolanda López (b. 1942) appropriates a popular Latin American icon of political resistance—the Virgin of Guadalupe (see Figure 20.2). She transforms the Mother of God into the autobiographical image of an exuberant marathon

---

[3] "When?"
[4] An exclamation, loosely: "Good grief."

Figure 38.12 **YOLANDA LÓPEZ**, *Portrait of the Artist as the Virgin of Guadalupe*, part 3 from the *Guadalupe Triptych*, 1978. Oil pastel on paper, 30 × 24 in.

athlete outfitted in track shoes and star-studded cape (redolent of both Our Lady of Guadalupe and Wonder Woman, Figure **38.12**).

Ethnic Conflict

The exercise of ethnic identity has become a powerful social and political force in the global perspective. Having cast off the rule of foreign powers and totalitarian ideologies, ethnic peoples have sought to reaffirm their primary affiliations—to return to their spiritual roots. "Identity politics," the exercise of power by means of group solidarity, has—in its more malignant guise—pitted ethnic groups against each other in militant opposition. In Africa, the Middle East, the Balkans, the Indian subcontinent, and the former Soviet Union, efforts to revive or maintain ethnic identity have coincided with the bitter and often militant quest for solidarity and political autonomy. Nowhere is this more evident than in the ongoing conflict between Palestinians and Israelis who lay claim to the same ancient territories of the Middle East. Hostilities between the Arab (and essentially Muslim) population of Palestine and the Jewish inhabitants of Israel preceded the establishment of an independent Jewish state in 1947. However, these have become more virulent in the past few decades, and the move toward peaceful compromise seems to be remote.

The life of the Palestinian poet Mahmoud Darwish (1942–2008) was one of displacement and exile. Born to Sunni Muslim parents in a Palestinian village that was destroyed by Israel in 1948, Darwish lived in dozens of cities across the globe. Holding the bizarre status of a "present-absent alien," however, he remained a refugee from his homeland. Regarded by Palestinians as their poet laureate, this "poet in exile" published some twenty volumes of verse. His passion to redeem his lost homeland is expressed in a simple, yet eloquent, style illustrated in the poem "Earth Presses Against Us."

Darwish's Israeli counterpart, Yehuda Amichai (1924–2000), was born in Germany but moved to Palestine in 1936. Raised as an Orthodox Jew amidst Israel's turbulent struggle to become a state, Amichai began writing poetry in 1948. Israel's renowned poet takes as his themes the roles of memory, homeland, and religious faith. His poem "The Resurrection of the Dead" looks beyond the immediacy of ethnic turmoil to consider both the weight of past history and the promise of the future.

READING 38.6 The Poems of Darwish and Amichai

Darwish's "Earth Presses Against Us" (2003)

Earth is pressing against us, trapping us in the final passage. 1
To pass through, we pull off our limbs.
Earth is squeezing us. If only we were its wheat, we might die
and yet live.
If only it were our mother so that she might temper us with mercy.
If only we were pictures of rocks held in our dreams like mirrors.
We glimpse faces in their final battle for the soul, of those who
will be killed
by the last living among us. We mourn their children's feast.
We saw the faces of those who would throw our children out 10
of the windows
of this last space. A star to burnish our mirrors.
Where should we go after the last border? Where should birds fly
after the last sky?
Where should plants sleep after the last breath of air?
We write our names with crimson mist!
We end the hymn with our flesh.
Here we will die. Here, in the final passage.
Here or there, our blood will plant olive trees.

Amichai's "The Resurrection of the Dead" (2004)

We are buried below with everything we did, 1
with our tears and our laughs.
We have made storerooms of history out of it all,
galleries of the past, and treasure houses,
buildings and walls and endless stairs of iron and marble
in the cellars of time.
We will not take anything with us.
Even plundering kings, they all left something here.
Lovers and conquerors, happy and sad,
they all left something here, a sign, a house, 10
like a man who seeks to return to a beloved place
and purposely forgets a book, a basket, a pair of glasses,
so that he will have an excuse to come back to the beloved place.
In the same way we leave things here.

In the same way the dead leave us.

(Translated, from the Hebrew, by Leon Wieseltier.)

Q How does each of these poets deal with history, memory, and hope?

Q Why do you think there is no mention of religion in either poem?

The Visual Arts in the Global Village

The contemporary migration of artists from one part of the world to another, the media of television and film, and a rapidly expanding availability of digital technology link studio to gallery and artist to patron. Megasurveys and art fairs held regularly in Venice, Shanghai, Miami, and elsewhere invite the exchange of ideas and stimulate a vigorous multimillion-dollar commercial art market. The arts have become vehicles for global activism and for the expression of universally shared experience.

Art and Activism

Artists have always provided perspective on the social scene; however, since the late twentieth century, many artists have self-consciously assumed an activist stance. Overtly political and critical of the status quo, activist artists (such as Ai Weiwei, discussed above) seek to transform society by awakening its visionary potential or by demanding outright change. Such artists draw attention to ecological ruin and widespread drug use, to the threat of terrorism and the plight of marginalized populations, to decay in the quality of urban life and the erosion of moral values.

One of America's most outspoken social critics, Leon Golub (1922–2004), used figurative imagery to bring attention to state-sponsored aggression and political repression. Opposing both the Postmodern technology of war and America's military presence in Vietnam and Iraq, he painted large canvases showing mercenary soldiers carrying out acts of physical torture and gang violence (Figure **38.13**). Some of the assailants in these paintings stare blatantly at the viewer as they intimidate and mutilate their victims. Golub's oversized figures, whose national affiliations are deliberately left unidentified, appear against the indeterminate (usually red) background of his canvases, which he scraped and abraded to resemble ancient frescoes. Regarded during his lifetime as an "existential activist," Golub left visual statements that seem as relevant to our own time as to former centuries.

The Polish sculptor Magdalena Abakanowicz (b. 1930) practices a more subtle form of activism. Drawing on nontraditional methods of modeling, she casts hulking, life-sized figures that stage the global drama of the human condition (Figure **38.14**). Sisal, jute, and resin-stiffened burlap make up the substance of these one-of-a-kind humanoids, whose scarred and patched surfaces call to mind earth, mud, and the dusty origins of primordial creatures. Abakanowicz installs her headless, sexless forms (more recently cast in bronze) in groups that evoke a

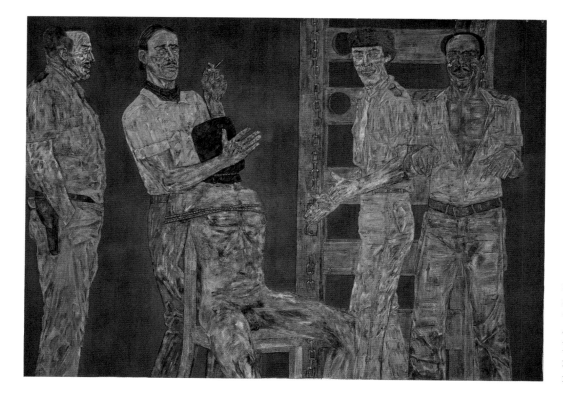

Figure 38.13 LEON GOLUB, *Interrogation II*, 1981. Acrylic on canvas, 10 × 14 ft. Some of the imagery in Golub's two series, "Mercenaries" and "Interrogation," was based on newspaper photographs documenting specific incidents of political suppression, intimidation, and torture.

sense of collective anonymity and vulnerability. She brings to these works her experience as a survivor of World War II (and Poland's repressive communist regime).

In today's big cities, from Belfast to Buenos Aires and from Manhattan to Moscow, street artists comment on urban problems, such as crime, domestic violence, and homelessness, in the form of public murals. At the same time, a rebel subculture consisting of

Film and Activism

The last fifty years has witnessed a golden age of cinematic creativity, one in which the film medium (in alliance with television) reached a new level of social influence. Its impact has been so great as to shape public opinion in the manner achieved by Eisenstein's seminal protest film, *Battleship Potemkin* (see chapter 34). The films of some directors/artists who emerged in the 1970s and 1980s reestablished the Hollywood film industry, which had faltered financially prior to the mid-1960s. The new directors, products of film schools rather than the Hollywood studio system, contributed to a critical reassessment of America's "master narratives" and dominant fictions: Arthur Penn's *Little Big Man* (1970), for example, exposed the myth of the Native American as "savage."

Robert Altman, one of America's finest director/artists, launched a biting satire on the Korean War (and war in general) with the film *M*A*S*H* (1970). The image of the passive, male-dependent female was transformed in the film *Thelma and Louise* (1991), directed by Ridley Scott, and the plight of transgendered individuals was explored in Kimberly Peirce's *Boys Don't Cry* (1999). Altman favored the telephoto zoom lens to probe the faces of his (usually) socially troubled characters; fractured sounds and bits of dialogue overlap or intrude from off-camera. To achieve lifelike spontaneity, Altman often invited his actors to improvise as he filmed. In *Nashville* (1974), he traded the single cinematic protagonist for some two dozen characters involved in a presidential election.

Issue-driven subjects were common fare in the history of late modern American film. But they have rarely been treated as powerfully as in Steven Spielberg's *Schindler's List* (1993), a story of the Holocaust (see chapter 34) adapted from Thomas

Keneally's prize-winning novel of 1982. A virtuoso filmmaker, Spielberg made brilliant use of the techniques of documentary newscasting to create visually shattering effects.

Activist cinema is by no means confined to the United States. In *Salaam Bombay!* (1988), filmed in the brothel district of Bombay, one of India's leading filmmakers, Mira Nair, exposed the sordid lives of that country's illiterate street urchins. China's internationally celebrated filmmaker and cinematographer Zhang Yimou (b. 1951) lived among the peasants of Shaanxi province prior to making films about China's disenfranchised rural population (*The Story of Qiu Ju*, 1992) and in particular its courageous women, many of whom remain hostage to feudal and patriarchal traditions (*Raise the Red Lantern*, 1991). An admirer of Ingmar Bergman and Akira Kurosawa (see chapter 35), Zhang rejected the socialist realism of the communist era in favor of purity of vision and fierce honesty. His films, at least three of which have been banned in China, are noted for their sensuous use of color and their troubling insights into moral and cultural issues.

Documentary films have played a major role in contemporary activism. Notable examples include *Everyday Rebellion: The Art of Change* (2013), which offers a global picture of contemporary nonviolent resistance movements; Jehane Noujaim's *The Square* (2013), which captures the violent political upheaval that took place between 2011 and 2013 in Cairo's Tahrir Square; and *KONY 2012*, a thirty-minute documentary film promoting a campaign to unseat the Ugandan leader Joseph Kony, responsible for the forced recruitment of child soldiers in Central Africa (see Figure 38.2). The film initially drew 97 million "views" on the video-sharing network YouTube.

Figure 38.14 MAGDALENA ABAKANOWICZ,
Crowd 1 (detail), 1986–1987. Burlap and resin, fifty standing life-sized figures, each 5 ft. 6⅞ in. × 23⅝ in. × 11¾ in. In their denial of individuality and human difference, these headless and sexless figures have been interpreted as a subtle criticism of Soviet ideology, that is, of communist collectivity; at the same time, they call to mind Ellul's "mass man."

Figure 38.15 BANKSY, *No Trespassing*, Mission Street, San Francisco, ca. 2010. (Now painted over.)

political and social activists post public protests as urban graffiti. Satiric, subversive, and often humorous, these sprayed, stenciled, drawn, or painted images, often accompanied by written messages, are either executed with the approval of civic authorities (thus "street art") or posted illegally (thus "graffiti"). The most notorious of contemporary graffiti personalities is the anonymous British figure known only as "Banksy." A painter, filmmaker, and political activist, Banksy has gained both a following and an unimpeachable reputation for some of the most incisive examples of antiwar, anticonsumerist, and antiauthoritarian imagery. In one instance, he makes use of an existing urban No Trespassing sign by adding the seated figure of a Native American—a sly comment linking America's displacement of its Native American population with the contemporary plight of the urban homeless (Figure **38.15**).

Immersive Environments

Room-sized installations, a version of total art (see chapter 37) that invites the participation of the spectator, have been popular for almost half a century. As early as 1968, a "Walk-in Infinity Chamber" by Stanley Landsman (b. 1930) dazzled viewers with mirrors and some 6000 miniature light bulbs. Contemporary installations, however, are much larger and more technically elaborate, often embracing recorded sound, digitally programmed lighting, and even specially orchestrated odors. The Brazilian artist Ernesto Neto (b. 1964) animates vast exhibition halls with temporary installations consisting of colored nylon fabric. From these soft, tentlike structures hang podlike sacs filled with herbs and aromatic substances. Designed to be "completed" by the physical presence of the viewer, Neto's

Figure 38.16 ERNESTO NETO, *Anthropodino*, 2009. Installation in Park Avenue Armory, New York. Neto claims his ideal space would be a cave in which gravity, balance, and the interaction between elements might produce a unique environment.

biomorphic, site-specific environments immerse spectators in an enveloping, multisensory space (Figure **38.16**).

The Weather Project, launched in 2003 by the Danish artist Olafur Eliasson (b. 1967) for the Turbine Hall of Tate Modern in London, used 200 computer-controlled yellow lamps to form a circular "sun" that glowed through vapor generated by humidifiers. Spectators, two million of whom experienced this unique immersive environment, saw themselves as tiny black shadows, reflected in a huge ceiling mirror (Figure **38.17**). While *The Weather Project* struck some as dismally postapocalyptic, others looked upon it as the futuristic counterpart of ritual sites like Stonehenge, the Neolithic project that served humankind's spiritual and communal needs.

The Digital Arts

All forms of expression, from art and architecture to music and dance, reflect the abundance and exchange of digitally transmitted information, that is, information expressed in discrete numerical codes used by computers or other electronic devices. Digital computers have put at our disposal the entire history of art. The Internet gives access to the contents of more than 5000 museums; and millions of photographic images are available on a variety of websites. In addition to their function in storing and distributing images, digital computers have transformed the manner

Figure 38.17 OLAFUR ELIASSON, *The Weather Project*, installation view at Tate Modern, London, 2003. Monofrequency lights, projection foil, haze machine, mirror oil, aluminum, and scaffolding. The giant yellow "sun" hangs 90 feet above the floor, while the mirrored ceiling reflects the movements of the spectators, many of whom are stretched out on the floor enjoying the misty golden ambiance.

in which art is made, sold, and experienced. Webcams, ink-jet printers, and painting software applications ("apps") empower every individual to create, advertise, and sell art. The World Wide Web provides a virtual theater in which one may assume an online identity—or more than one identity—in cyberspace.

"Digital art" describes a wide range of genres that employ the language of computers as a primary tool, medium, or creative partner. Digitization itself has revolutionized the art world by blurring the boundaries between the traditional genres of painting, sculpture, film, and photography, and by generating entirely new kinds of visual experience, such as **virtual reality**, animation, videogame art, Internet art, and two- and three-dimensional imaging. In the world of image-making, the laptop has become the studio.

Digital Photography

Digital technology has had a revolutionary impact on photography. In contrast with traditional (or **analog**) photography, which uses photographic film or plate to record real or contrived physical settings (see, for example, Figures 32.13, 34.1, 36.3 and 36.15), digital photography is of two main types: One involves the computerized manipulation of existing photographic resources (either digital or analog) to alter, rework, or assemble images (see Figures 38.1, 38.5 and 38.19). The other engages purely digital means (a geometric model or mathematical formula) to create an entirely new image. In the latter method, the artist may give the computer a set of instructions through which the image is digitally generated (see Figure 38.18).

The vast panoramas of the German artist Andreas Gursky (b. 1957) are representative of the first type of computer imaging. Gursky's photographs (often more than 15 feet in width) are the products of his world travels. His tours through Europe, Brazil, Mexico, Japan, Vietnam, and the United States document contemporary life: its concerts and public performances (see Figure **38.1**), its garbage dumps, stock exchanges, supermarkets, factories, prisons, and luxury hotels. Gursky's photographs are not, however, documentary: they are stitched together from transparencies of his own photographs, which undergo many rounds of editing, scanning, and proofing. By way of digitization, Gursky creates realistically detailed images in which (ironically) all individuality is lost. His works convey

the anonymity of "mass man," or what the artist himself calls the "aggregate state" of a globalized world.

An example of the second type of digital imaging is found in the works of Karl Sims (b. 1962). Sims, a graduate of the MIT Media Lab in Cambridge, Massachusetts, and a student of biotechnology, devised special computer-graphics techniques that generate abstract, three-dimensional simulations of genetic organisms (Figure **38.18**), and natural phenomena such as fog, smoke, and rain. According to Sims, his graphics of virtual creatures "unite several concepts: chaos, complexity, evolution, self-propagating entities, and the nature of life itself."

Digital Projects

Digital technology has inspired a wide range of new media projects, only a few of which can be mentioned in this chapter. In general, such technology has contributed to the monumental size and complexity of *site-specific installations*. One example, *The Bay Lights* (2014) launched by Leo Villareal (b. 1967), involved mounting 25,000 digitally programmed LEDs to the 300 vertical cables of the San Francisco–Oakland Bay Bridge. *The Bay Lights* will continue to glitter nightly for two years.

Reimagining global communication, the Japanese artist Noriko Yamaguchi (b. 1983) dons headphones and a body suit made of cellphone (*keitai*) keypads to "become" a human mobile phone—the telecommunications device that also functions as a television, credit card, video player,

Figure 38.18 KARL SIMS, *Galapagos*, 1997. Interactive media. This interactive artwork is part of a twelve-screen media installation that invites viewers to participate in the evolution of animated forms. Inspired by the theory of natural selection advanced by Darwin after he visited the Galapagos Islands in 1835, Sims invented a program whereby virtual "genetic" organisms appear to mutate and reproduce within the environment of the computer.

Contemporary Japanese artists have been particularly successful in using computer technology in various photographic and video projects. Yasumasa Morimura transforms Western masterpieces into camp spoofs in which he impersonates one or more of the central characters. In *Portrait (Futago)* (the Japanese word for "twins"; Figure **38.19**), Morimura turns Manet's *Olympia* (Figure **38.20**) into a drag queen decked out in a blond wig and rhinestone-trimmed slippers. Using himself as the model for both the nude courtesan and the maid, he revisualizes a landmark in the history of art and suggests, at the same time, the intersecting ("twin") roles of prostitute and slave. By "updating" Manet's *Olympia* (itself an "update" of a painting by Titian), Morimura also questions the authority of these historical icons, even as he makes sly reference to the postwar Japanese practice of copying Western culture. *Portrait* is a computer-manipulated color photograph produced from a studio setup—a combination of Postmodern techniques borrowed from fashion advertising. Here, and in his more recent photographs in which he impersonates contemporary icons and film divas (Madonna, Marilyn Monroe, and Liza Minnelli), Morimura pointedly tests classic stereotypes of identity and gender.

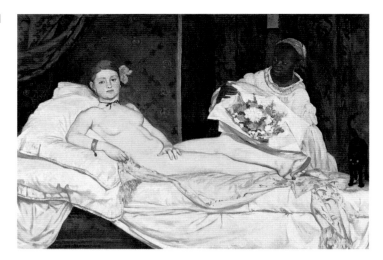

Figure 38.20 EDOUARD MANET, *Olympia*, 1863. Oil on canvas, 4 ft. 3¼ in. × 6 ft. 2¾ in.

Figure 38.19 YASUMASA MORIMURA, *Portrait (Futago)*, 1988. Color photograph, clear medium, 82½ × 118 in.

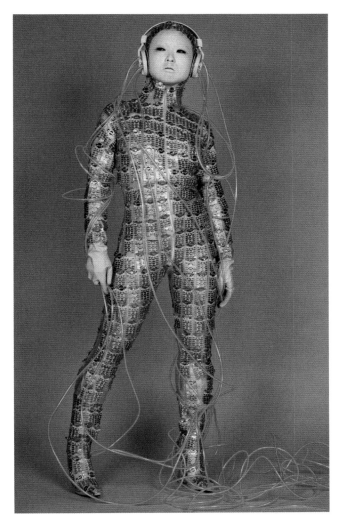

Figure 38.21 NORIKO YAMAGUCHI, *Keitai Girl*, 2003. The artist's use of white face make-up is a reference to *butoh*, a traditional Japanese dance form.

Digital Film

Digital technology has transformed the world of filmmaking. New technology, such as high-definition (HD) video, which gives visual images greater clarity, has begun to replace film stock altogether. The ease with which digital video can be produced, reproduced from film, and downloaded via computers has raised major issues concerning copyrights, but it has also made the archive of motion pictures readily available to a worldwide audience. The website YouTube, which welcomes video postings, has become a global forum for young and independent filmmakers, especially in the production of short and documentary films.

Computers have also revolutionized the way films are made: Computer-Generated Imaging (CGI) of realistic settings makes it unnecessary for filmmakers to use large-scale sets and locations. Special effects, achieved by way of computers, are used to juxtapose images in ways that distort reality. Like docufiction, films render believable what in actuality may be untrue. The film *Forrest Gump* (1994), for instance, shows its antihero shaking hands with the long-dead president John F. Kennedy.

Digital technology makes possible such hyperreal images as Steven Spielberg's dinosaurs (*Jurassic Park*, 1993), James Cameron's liquid-metal cyborgs (*Terminator 2*, 1991), and Larry and Andy Wachowski's extrordinary special effects in the science-fiction trilogy *The Matrix* (see Science-Fiction Film, chapter 37). *Terminator* was the first film to feature the computer-generated shape-shifting technique called "morphing." Just as CGI can create realistic settings, so it can replace human actors with computer-generated characters. The use of digital actors (as in the fantasy epic trilogy *The Lord of the Rings*, 2001–2003) blurs the border between the traditional live-action film and CGI animation. While digital artistry may not put live-action filmmaking in jeopardy, it provokes questions concerning differences between the original and the replica, the real and the virtual, truth and illusion.

Finally, film *animation* has undergone major changes since the early twentieth century, when still drawings and stop-motion techniques prevailed. The first feature-length, entirely computer-animated film, *Toy Story*, appeared in 1995. Since the turn of the twenty-first century, more sophisticated software for digital imaging, including three-dimensional graphics, has facilitated a greater range of color, movement, and special effects. In 2001, Hayao Miyazaki's award-winning *Spirited Away* brought Japanese *animé* to world attention, and in 2008 the Disney/Pixar science-fiction film *WALL-E* brought to life the story of a whimsical little robot who cleans up the garbage-ridden planet earth. The Pixar-produced adventure fantasy *Up* became, in 2009, the first computer-animated film to be presented in Disney Digital 3D.

portable music device, digital camera, and more (Figure **38.21**). Those who have the artist's telephone number may "dial up" Keitai Girl from their own cellular phones. Noriko's futuristic armor is part of a performance involving interactive lasers, fast, upbeat music, and a popular Japanese dance style known as *Para-Para*—a type of line dancing.

The latest advances in virtual reality immerse individuals in an interactive computer-simulated environment. By means of sophisticated digital software, virtual environments—both real and imagined—appear in three dimensions on a head-mounted display or glasses worn by viewers, or on a 360-degree screen. High-tech sensors detect the viewer's movements and commands. Like a giant video-game, virtual reality combines illusion, sound, and spoken texts. A synthesis of all kinds of retrievable information, such interactive hypermedia offer an image-saturated playground for the mind. However, the applications of VR go well beyond today's gaming systems, for use in education, city planning, advanced medicine, and elsewhere.

Probably the most exciting development in contemporary art is the opportunity it affords the individual to become part of the creative act. *Interactive art* projects, available in galleries, museums, and on computers or smartphones, make the viewer a partner in art-making. Such projects are distinctive in that they provoke a dialogue between the artwork and the spectator, offering the latter a means of altering the artwork itself. For instance, with *Electronic Eve* (1997), an interactive project conceived by the Greek video artist Jenny Marketou (b. 1944), "image consumers" create their own multimedia environment by selecting (through direct touch on the computer screen) from a database of video sequences, still images, computer graphics, texts, and sounds. In *Text Rain* (2005), an interactive installation by the American new-media artist Camille Utterback (b. 1970) and the Israeli Romy Achitov (b. 1958), viewers mirrored on a video projection screen interact with virtual falling letters to form words and phrases (Figure **38.22**). The letters belong to Evan Zimroth's poem "Talk You" (1993), which

Figure 38.22 CAMILLE UTTERBACK and **ROMY ACHITOV**, *Text Rain for Phaeno*, 2005. Computerized interactive media, 4 ft. 6 in. × 6 ft. Originally exhibited in 1999, this version of the piece was commissioned by Ansel Associates for the Phaeno Science Center in Wolfsburg, Germany.

deals with bodies and language. Utterback favors the digital medium because, she claims, "it is a perfect site to explore the interface between physical bodies and various representational systems."

The use of the computer in making art either alone or with others is no longer exclusive to professional artists. Digital art and design collectives such as Universal Everything (founded in 2004 by Matt Pyke) invite contributions from the public (through a smartphone app) to create digital artworks using **3D printing**, motion capture, and other new technology. Such projects might be considered a kind of crowdsourcing comparable to the collective enterprises of contemporary scientists and engineers.

Architecture in the Global Village

Since the 1960s, architects have made use of advanced three-dimensional modeling tools and sophisticated animation software. Now 3D printing promises to fabricate and construct houses in a twenty-four hour period. Contemporary technology has generated a futuristic vocabulary of folded, splintered, tilted, and boldly curved shapes that contrast with the well-defined axes, sharp edges, and clearly bounded space of older building styles. The architecture of our time embraces the experimental thrust of Russian Constructivism (see chapter 32), the Postmodern mix of whimsy and appropriation (see Figure 37.21), and the seductive morphing of Frank Gehry's breathtaking designs (see Figure 37.24). But, among contemporary architects, bulding-design reaches a higher level of structural complexity, tectonic fluidity, and plastic articulation.

The most dynamic figure in the development of the new "digital architecture" is the prize-winning visionary Zaha Hadid (b. 1950). Born in Baghdad and trained in London, Hadid has produced some of the most inventive structures of the past two decades. The Heydar Aliyev Center (2012) in Baku, Azerbaijan, reflects Hadid's gradual move away from the fractured, angular designs of her earlier buildings to a series of fluid forms (or "flow fields") with sinuous parabolic curves, that is, dynamic "curvilinearity" (Figure **38.23**). The 619,000-square-foot Center features a single continuous surface made of reinforced concrete coated with fiberglass, a medium that Hadid has also explored in her space-age furniture designs.

Music in the Global Village

Cultural interdependence and the willful fusion of disparate musical traditions have transformed contemporary music. Inspired by ancient and non-Western oral and instrumental forms of improvisation, much of today's music relies less on the formal score and more on the ear. The influence of Arabic chant, Indian *ragas*, and Latino beat is evident in both jazz and classical music. Cuban brass punctuates contemporary rock, shimmering Asian drones propel New Age music. The street music of black South Africa and traditional Zulu wedding songs inspired the rhythms of the rock album *Graceland* (1986), produced by the American songwriter Paul Simon (b. 1941).

The Intercultural Tapestry

Some contemporary composers create musical tapestries that utilize conventional Western instruments along with ancient musical ones (such as the Chinese flute or the *balafon*, an African version of the xylophone), producing textures that may be manipulated by electronic means. These innovations are evident in the compositions of Tan Dun (b. 1957), a Chinese-born composer who has lived in the United States since 1986. Tan's works, ranging from string quartets and operas to multimedia pieces and film scores, represent a spirit of cultural pluralism that blends Chinese opera, folk songs, and instruments with traditional Western techniques and traditions ranging from medieval chant and romantic harmonies to audacious aural experiments (in the style of John Cage) using the sounds of water, torn paper, and bird calls.

Tan's opera *The First Emperor* (2006) marries the singing style of Beijing opera and the use of Chinese instruments with Western performance style and a standard Western orchestra. Directed by the noted filmmaker Zhang Yimou, the opera tells the story of the visionary and brutal Qin Shi Huang Di, China's first imperial Son of Heaven (see chapter 7). Haunting and lyrical, the work is a bridge between East and West; it also anticipates a new musical possibility. As Tan Dun predicts: "Opera will no longer be a Western form, as it is no longer an Italian form."

One of the most notable experiments in contemporary intercultural music is the Silk Road Project, which involves

♪ See Music Listening Selections at end of chapter.

Figure 38.23 ZAHA HADID, Heydar Aliyev Center, Baku, Azerbaijan, 2012. The Center, with its swooping, undulating walls, encloses a conference hall, theater, and museum. Three-dimensional modeling, X-ray layering, and multiperspective projection are three of the digital tools used in Hadid's designs.

the exchange of Western musical traditions with those of the ancient Silk Road, the vast skein of trade routes that linked East Asia to Europe (see chapter 7). Begun in 1998, this extended effort to connect East and West was the brainchild of the renowned Japanese-American cellist Yo-Yo Ma (b. 1955). Ma aimed to revitalize the spirit of cultural exchange once facilitated by the Silk Road, which he calls "the Internet of Antiquity." In the current age of cultural pluralism, musicians from across Central Asia have joined with American virtuosos (selected by Ma) to produce works that integrate radically different compositional forms, instruments, and performance styles.

The global character of contemporary music is also evident in popular genres that engage issue-driven lyrics. The Jamaican musician Bob Marley (1945–1981) brought to the international scene the socially conscious music known as *reggae*—an eclectic style that draws on a wide variety of black Jamaican musical forms, including African religious music and Christian revival songs. Hip-hop (see chapter 36) and break-dancing (see chapter 37) have moved from their inner-city origins to assume an international scope. This "mutating hybrid" makes use of various musical traditions: modern (disco, salsa, reggae, rock) and ancient (African call-and-response). *Rap*—the vocal dimension of hip-hop—launches a fusillade of raw and socially provocative words chanted in rhymed couplets over an intense rhythmic beat.

The American avant-garde composer John Zorn (b. 1953) borrows harmonic and rhythmic devices from the domains of bluegrass, klezmer (Jewish folk music), and punk rock. The new-music collective known as Bang on a Can offers an eclectic mix of sounds that blur the boundary between classical and popular music. Part rock band and part amplified chamber group, its classically trained performers work in close collaboration with leading composers, jazz musicians, and pop artists. A recent work (*Timber*, 2013) by Bang on a Can's resident experimentalist Michael Gordon (b. 1956) calls for intense polyrhythmic percussion (involving neither pitches nor melody) performed on a series of thin wooden slabs of varying lengths and timbres. Such fusions of East and West, urban and folk, popular and classical styles, constitute the musical mosaic of the new millennium. While some critics lament that Western music has bifurcated into two cultures—art (or classical) music and popular music—the fact is that these two traditions are becoming more alike, or, more precisely, they share various features of a global musical menu.

Cybersounds

Digital technology has contributed enormously to global musical composition and performance. John Adams' opera *Doctor Atomic* (2005), which examines the role of Robert Oppenheimer in the genesis of the atom bomb, made use of electronically amplified instruments and computerized visual effects. Computerized images, infrared cameras, and digital projectors constitute some of the "spectacle-producing technology" now employed in staging operas such as Nico Muhly's *Two Boys* (2011), inspired by a real-life, Internet-related violent crime.

While musical instruments can be manipulated by computers, computers themselves have become "musical instruments." Equipped with a miniature keyboard, faders, and foot pedals, the computer is capable not only of producing a full range of sounds but also of producing and reproducing sounds more subtle and complex than any emitted by human voices or traditional musical instruments. Sound generators have come to replace live musicians in the studio and in some staged musical performances. The hyperinstrument projects of Tod Machover (b. 1953), who heads the MIT Media Lab in Cambridge, Massachusetts, engage electronically enhanced instruments, as well as "homemade" interactive instruments. Machover's "robotic opera," *Death and the Powers* (2010), employs forty computers, custom graphics, and software mapping to choreograph a chorus of "operabots" that join live singers in this century's first futuristic opera.

Using the computer itself to generate music, the American composer Barton McLean (b. 1938) draws (with a light pen) the contours of sound waves on the video screen of a sophisticated computer that "emits" the composition. Today, one can "compose" and produce music using a single laptop computer and a variety of sophisticated software tools, a phenomenon that abandons traditional performance practice and promotes the democratization of music, both classical and popular. The ultimate development in the global landscape may just follow from the availability of new kinds of visual programming language (such as Pure Data), which encourage musicians in different parts of the world to engage in live collaboration—that is, to create music together in real time.

Dance in the Global Village

Contemporary choreographers have been drawn increasingly to social issues and historical events: witness Charles Atlas' *Delusional* (1994), a meditation on death and decay in Bosnia, and Paul Taylor's 1999 spoof of the Ku Klux Klan (*Oh, You Kid*). The company known as Urban Bush Women, founded in 1984, uses dance to bring to light the histories of disenfranchised people. In their fiercely energetic performances, this Brooklyn-based ensemble of African, Caribbean, and black American women call on the spiritual traditions of the African diaspora. The Bangladeshi choreographer Akram Khan (b. 1974) blends classical Indian Kathak dance with contemporary improvisation in solo works such as *Desh* (Bengali for "homeland").

Returning to Vietnam fifteen years after fleeing her war-torn homeland, the choreographer Ea Sola (b. 1970)

Chronology

1947	Israel becomes an independent state
1954–1975	Vietnam War
1966–1976	Mao's Cultural Revolution
1989	Berlin Wall falls
1989	Massacre in Tiananmen Square
2001	al-Qaeda terrorists attack the United States
2003	United States and coalition forces invade Iraq
2005	terrorists attack London's subway system
2006	sectarian violence increases in Iraq
2008	global financial crisis and recession
2010–2012	revolutionary wave of demonstrations and protests (the "Arab Spring") begins in the Arab world, forcing rulers from power in Egypt, Tunisia, Libya, and Yemen
2013	civil war erupts in Syria
2014	militant group ISIS (Islamic State of Iraq and Syria) attempts to create a unified Islamic state in the Middle East
2014	renewed militant conflict between Palestinian Gaza and Israel

studied its traditional dance and music, both of which are present in her choreographed recollection of war, *Sécheresse et Pluie* (*Drought and Rain*, 1995). This work, as well as others by contemporary choreographers, reflects the influence of *butoh*, a Japanese dance form that features simple, symbolic movements performed in a mesmerizingly slow and hypnotic manner. *Ankoko butoh*, meaning "dance of utter darkness," grew out of ancient forms of Asian theater. Two other notable traditions have influenced contemporary choreography: Indian classical dance and German *Tanztheater* ("dance theater"), an expressionistic style that features everyday actions, speech, and theatrical props (including, occasionally, live animals).

LOOKING BACK

The Global Paradigm

- Globalism—the interdependence of cultures and peoples in all parts of the world—is the new model for contemporary society.
- Digital technology links all parts of the world, and electronic networks facilitate

the dissemination of values and goods. The sense of collectivity in the integrated landscape of the global village has become a hallmark of a new world community.

- In this post-colonial era, efforts to reconcile Modernist modes of life with waning ancient traditions have challenged

many regions, none more dramatically than Africa.

- The novels and short stories of Chinua Achebe deal with the warp between premodern and modern conditions in parts of Africa. Similarly, Africa's visual artists draw on past traditions in creative projects that often involve modern media.

The Challenge of Globalism

- Challenging the future of the global village, terrorism reflects an extremist response to ideological and political differences. The devastating attack of the radical Muslim group al-Qaeda on the United States on September 11, 2001, provoked a variety of creative and commemorative responses in literature, the visual arts, and music.
- The poets Wislawa Szymborska and Seamus Heaney both addressed the threat of terrorism in the global community.
- In the last three decades, China has emerged as a major world power. As state officials have somewhat loosened controls over artistic expression, China's academically trained painters and sculptors, along with a new generation of artists, have taken the world by storm with a variety of original projects.

The Global Ecosystem

- While environmental issues are not new, it is only recently that world leaders have begun to come together to address the ailing health of the global ecosystem.
- Edward Osborne Wilson, an early advocate for the preservation of the environment, has advanced "scientific humanism," an interdisciplinary discipline that values biodiversity and a sound environmental ethic.
- In the visual arts, earthworks and "green" architectural designs bring attention to the importance of a healthy ecosystem. The energy-efficient buildings of Norman Foster are models of environmentally sustainable projects that are both beautiful and practical.

Globalism and Ethnic Identity

- Ethnic identity has become a dominant theme in the global community.
- While immigration contributes to the blending of different ethnic populations, it has inspired efforts to maintain distinctive ethnic values and traditions. In the United States, large numbers of Latin Americans have introduced into American culture a unique array of culinary, musical, and dance styles. The growing number of female writers and artists who deal with ethnic identity is represented by the Mexican-American novelist Sandra Cisneros.
- Matters related to one's homeland and ethnic roots have provoked strife in many parts of the world, as illustrated by the ongoing conflict between Palestine and Israel. The role of memory in the painful progress toward peaceful co-existence is voiced in the poems of Yehuda Amichai and Mahmoud Darwish.

The Visual Arts in the Global Village

- The visual arts have become increasingly significant vehicles for global activism. Critical of the status quo, artists work to transform society by way of traditional media, as well as through photography, video, and digital resources.
- Film has become a dominant medium in the creative effort to bring attention to the plight of marginalized populations, criminal violence, and political unrest.
- Immersive environments and public art projects reflect the contemporary affection for greater size and spectacle.

The Digital Arts

- Computers and digital technology facilitate access to the arts of the entire world.
- Digital processes have become essential to making and sharing creative projects, to the blurring of traditional disciplines, and to the development of new techniques, such as animation, 3D imaging, and virtual reality.

Architecture in the Global Village

- Advanced digital tools have aided architects, such as Zaha Hadid, in creating a futuristic building style that features dynamic curvilinearity.

Music in the Global Village

- Western music and dance have responded to the influence of the cultures of Asia, Africa, and the Caribbean.
- Distinctions between popular and art (classical) music are becoming less pronounced.
- The compositions of Tan Dun and the efforts of the Silk Road Project and Bang on a Can are representative of the successful integration of widely diverse musical traditions.
- Digital technology has broadened the spectacular dimension of staged music and has facilitated the globalization of musical traditions and styles.

Dance in the Global Village

- Contemporary dance assumes a global dimension in choreography that reflects world events and the integration of ethnic dance styles.

Music Listening Selection

- Kalhor, *Gallop of a Thousand Horses*, the Silk Road Project, 2005.

Glossary

3D printing a technology of digital fabrication in which layers of material are built up to create a 3D form

analog (photography) traditional (camera and film) photography

biodiversity the preservation of all life forms in the ecosystem

ecosystem the ecological community and its physical environment

virtual reality the digital simulation of artificial environments

Picture Credits

The author and publishers wish to thank the following for permission to use copyright material. Every effort has been made to trace or contact copyright holders, but if notified of any omissions, Laurence King Publishing would be pleased to insert the appropriate acknowledgement in any subsequent edition of this publication.

Bold indicates Figure number or page/position of the image.

Cover

Top left: Photo © RMN-Grand Palais (Château de Versailles). Photo: Gérard Blot; **Top right:** The Art Institute of Chicago, Clarence Buckingham Collection (1928.1056). Photography © The Art Institute of Chicago; **Bottom left:** Courtesy National Gallery of Art, Washington, D.C., Gift of Mr. and Mrs. Robert Wood Bliss (1949.6.1); **Bottom right:** © Chuck Close, courtesy Pace Gallery. Photo: Ellen Page Wilson

Frontispiece and page xiv: © Wallace Collection, London/Bridgeman Images

Chapter 19

19.1 Yale University Art Gallery, Gift of Paul Mellon, B.A. 1929, L.H.D.H. 1967 (1956.16.3e); **19.2** © Victoria and Albert Museum, London; **19.3** Courtesy National Gallery of Art, Washington, D.C., Rosenwald Collection (1943.3.3554); **19.4** © Bristol Museum and Art Gallery/Bridgeman Images; **19.5** Photo © RMN-Grand Palais (Bibliothèque Nationale de France). Photo: BnF; **19.6** © The National Gallery, London/Scala, Florence; **19.7** Photo Scala, Florence; **19.8** Courtesy National Gallery of Art, Washington, D.C., Samuel H. Kress Collection (1952.5.33); **19.11** Courtesy National Gallery of Art, Washington, D.C., Rosenwald Collection (1943.3.3519); **19.12** SMB Kupferstichkabinett, Berlin/akg-images; **19.13** Unterlinden Museum, Colmar/The Art Archive; **19.14** Photo Fine Art Images/Heritage Images/Scala, Florence; **19.15** Detroit Institute of Arts; City of Detroit Purchase/Bridgeman Images; **19.16** © The Frick Collection, New York; **19.17** © The British Library Board, C.39.k.15, dedication and frontispiece; **19.18** Woburn Abbey, Bedfordshire/Bridgeman Images; **19.19** By permission of the Folger Shakespeare Library, Washington, D.C.

page 33: Cleveland Museum of Art, Ohio; Gift of the Hanna Fund/Bridgeman Images

Chapter 20

20.1 Fondo Edifici di Culto - Min. dell'Interno/Photo Scala, Florence; **20.2** National Palace, Mexico City/Gianni Dagli Orti/The Art Archive; **20.3** Fondo Edifici di Culto - Min. dell'Interno/Photo Scala, Florence; **20.4** Photo © Vatican Museums. All rights reserved; **20.5** Courtesy of the Ministero Beni e Att. Culturali/Photo Scala, Florence; **20.6** Photo Scala, Florence; **20.7** akg-images; **20.8** Courtesy of the Toledo Museum of Art (Toledo, Ohio), Purchased with funds from the Libbey Endowment, Gift of Edward Drummond Libbey, 1946.5; **20.9** © The National Gallery, London/Scala, Florence; **20.10** © Studio Fotografico Quattrone, Florence; **20.11** Mimmo Jodice/Corbis; **20.12** Courtesy of the Ministero Beni e Att. Culturali/Photo Scala, Florence; **20.13** © Vincenzo Pirozzi, Rome; **20.14** Yale University Art Gallery, Gift of Mrs. Charles B. Doolittle in memory of her sister Miss Helen Wells Seymour (1953.48.5); **20.15** Photo Scala, Florence; **20.16** James Anderson/akg-images; **20.17** © Vincenzo Pirozzi, Rome; **20.18** © Studio Fotografico Quattrone, Florence, **20.19** © Araldo de Luca; **20.20** Photo Scala, Florence; **20.21** Fondo Edifici di Culto - Min. dell'Interno/Photo Scala, Florence; **20.22** De Agostini Picture Library/SuperStock

Chapter 21

21.1 Château de Versailles/Giraudon/Bridgeman Images; **21.2** Photo © RMN-Grand Palais (Musée du Louvre). Photo: Stéphane Maréchalle; **21.3** Photo © RMN-Grand Palais (Musée du Louvre). Photo: Gérard Blot; **21.4** Photo © RMN-Grand Palais (Château de Versailles). Photo: Gérard Blot; **21.5** Photo © RMN-Grand Palais (Château de Versailles); **21.6** Erich Lessing/akg-images; **21.7** © Paul M.R. Maeyaert; **21.8** G. Dagli Orti/De Agostini Picture Library/Getty Images; **21.9** Château de Versailles/Giraudon/Bridgeman Images; **21.10** © Paul M.R. Maeyaert; **21.11** Photo © RMN-Grand Palais (Château de Versailles); **21.12** Photo © RMN-Grand Palais (Musée du Louvre). Photo: Stéphane Maréchalle; **21.13** © The National Gallery, London/Scala, Florence; **21.14** Photo Scala, Florence; **21.15** BPK, Bildagentur für Kunst, Kultur und Geschichte, Berlin/Photo Scala, Florence; **21.16** Bibliothèque Nationale, Paris/Collection Magnard/akg-images; **21.17** G. Dagli Orti/De Agostini Picture Library/akg-images; **21.18** Photo The Philadelphia Museum of Art/Art Resource, NY/Scala, Florence; **21.19** Paule Seux/hemis.fr/Getty Images; **21.20** © The Trustees of the Chester Beatty Library, Dublin (CBL In 03, f.143b); **21.21** Freer Gallery, Smithsonian Institution, Washington, D.C./Bridgeman Images; **21.22** © The British Library Board, Add.Or.948; **21.23** Jennie Lewis/Alamy; **21.24** Jean-Louis Nou/akg-images; **21.25** © The Palace Museum, Beijing. Photo: Chui Hu; **21.27** Gavin Hellier/Robert Harding World Imagery; **21.28** Freer Gallery, Smithsonian Institution, Washington, D.C./Bridgeman Images; **21.29** Photo © RMN-Grand Palais (Limoges, Cité de la Céramique). Photo: Jean-Gilles Berizzi; **21.30** Freer Gallery, Smithsonian Institution, Washington, D.C./Bridgeman Images; **21.31** The Art Institute of Chicago, Gift of Mrs. William M. Allison (1951.230). Photography © The Art Institute of Chicago; **21.32** © The Palace Museum, Beijing. Photo: Chui Hu; **21.33** National Treasure. Nezu Museum, Tokyo; **21.34** Tokyo National Museum/Granger Collection/The Art Archive; **21.35** The Art Institute of Chicago, Clarence Buckingham Collection (1928.1056). Photography © The Art Institute of Chicago; **21.36** Gitter-Yelen Collection

Chapter 22

22.1 Hermitage, St. Petersburg/Bridgeman Images; **22.2** © The National Gallery, London/Scala, Florence; **22.3** © The Chapter of St Paul's Cathedral; **22.5** McGraw-Hill Education; **22.6** Yale University Art Gallery, Gift of Mrs. Howard M. Morse (1957.45.17); **22.8** William H. Scheide Library, Princeton University, New Jersey; **22.9** akg-images

Chapter 23

23.1 Digital Image courtesy of the Getty's Open Content Program. The J. Paul Getty Trust (83.PB.388); **23.2** Sheila Terry/Science Photo Library; **23.3** © The National Gallery, London/Scala, Florence; **23.4** Photo © RMN-Grand Palais (Château de Versailles). Photo: Hervé Lewandowski; **23.5** De Agostini Picture Library/SuperStock; **23.6** Rijksmuseum, Amsterdam, (RP-T-1950-266-39); **23.7** Kunsthistorisches Museum, Vienna; **23.8** Courtesy National Gallery of Art, Washington, D.C., Andrew W. Mellon Collection (1937.1.56); **23.9** Cleveland Museum of Art, Ohio; Gift of the Hanna Fund/Bridgeman Images; **23.10** Courtesy National Gallery of Art, Washington, D.C., Andrew W. Mellon Collection (1937.1.58); **23.11** Mauritshuis, The Hague; **23.13** Courtesy National Gallery of Art, Washington, D.C., Widener Collection (1942.9.97); **23.14** © Wallace Collection, London/Bridgeman Images; **23.15** Courtesy National Gallery of Art, Washington, D.C., Gift of Mr. and Mrs. Robert Wood Bliss (1949.6.1); **23.16** Rijksmuseum, Amsterdam, De Bruijn-van der Leeuw Bequest, Muri, Switzerland (SK-A-4050); **23.17** Mauritshuis, The Hague; **23.18** Image © The Metropolitan Museum of Art, New York/Art Resource, NY/Scala, Florence

Chapter 24

24.1 Image © The Metropolitan Museum of Art, New York/Art Resource, NY/Scala, Florence; **24.2** Universal Images Group/Getty Images; **24.3** Bridgeman Images/Getty Images; **24.4** Musée National du Château de Malmaison, Rueil-Malmaison/Giraudon/Bridgeman Images; **24.5** De Agostini Picture Library/Getty Images; **24.6** Private Collection/Photo © Christie's Images/Bridgeman Images; **24.7** De Agostini Picture Library/Getty Images

Chapter 25

25.1 Courtesy National Gallery of Art, Washington, D.C., Rosenwald Collection (1944.5.87); **25.2** Library of Congress, Washington, D.C.; **25.3** Library of Congress, Washington, D.C.; **25.4** Bettmann/Corbis; **25.5** Courtesy National Gallery of Art, Washington, D.C., Rosenwald Collection (1944.5.11); **25.6** Photo Pierpont Morgan Library/Art Resource, NY/Scala, Florence; **25.7** Musée de la Ville de Paris, Musée Carnavalet, Paris/Giraudon/Bridgeman Images; **25.8** Photo © RMN-Grand Palais (Château de Versailles). Photo: Gérard Blot; **25.9** Musées Royaux des Beaux-Arts, Brussels/André Held/akg-images

Chapter 26

26.1 Courtesy National Gallery of Art, Washington, D.C., Chester Dale Collection (1943.7.2); **26.2** Photo Scala, Florence; **26.3** Image © The Metropolitan Museum of Art, New York/Art Resource, NY/Scala, Florence; **26.4** Bildarchiv Monheim/akg-images; **26.5** Photo © RMN-Grand Palais (Musée du Louvre). Photo: Stéphane Maréchalle; **26.6** Image © The Metropolitan Museum of Art, New York/Art Resource, NY/Scala, Florence; **26.7** Photo © RMN-Grand Palais (Château de Versailles). Photo: Gérard Blot; **26.8** © Wallace Collection, London/Bridgeman Images; **26.9** Image © The Metropolitan Museum of Art, New York/Art Resource, NY/Scala, Florence; **26.10** Photo © RMN-Grand Palais (Musée du Louvre). Photo: Franck Raux; **26.11** Courtesy National Gallery of Art, Washington, D.C., Samuel H. Kress Collection (1952.5.38); **26.12** North Carolina Museum of Art, Raleigh. Gift of Mr. and Mrs. Benjamin Cone (G.69.20.1); **26.13** Erich Lessing/akg-images; **26.14** Yale University Art Gallery (1966.106.3); **26.15** Photo Scala, Florence; **26.16** The National Trust Photolibrary/Alamy; **26.17** Courtesy of the Ministero Beni e Att. Culturali/Photo Scala, Florence; **26.18** © Victoria and Albert Museum, London; **26.19** © Angelo Hornak; **26.20** © Vincenzo Pirozzi, Rome; **26.21** Courtesy of The Library of Virginia; **26.22** Courtesy of the Bureau of Printing and Engraving, U.S. Department of the Treasury, Washington, D.C.; **26.23** Courtesy of The Library of Virginia; **26.24** Photo © RMN-Grand Palais (Musée du Louvre). Photo: Gérard Blot/Christian Jean; **26.25** Image © The Metropolitan Museum of Art, New York/Art Resource, NY/Scala, Florence; **26.26** Photo © RMN-Grand Palais (Musée du Louvre). Photo: Thierry Le Mage; **26.27** Photo Scala, Florence; **26.28** John Hay Library, Brown University Library, Rhode Island; **26.29** © Paul M.R. Maeyaert; **26.30** Bjanka Kadic/age fotostock/SuperStock; **26.31** © Paul M.R. Maeyaert; **26.32** Yoko Design, Thumbelina, T. Shooter and Anali/shutterstock.com; **26.34** Fine Art Images/SuperStock

page 207: © Crown Copyright: UK Government Art Collection

Chapter 27

27.1 Photograph © 2015 Museum of Fine Arts, Boston. Henry Lillie Pierce Fund 99.22; **27.2** akg-images; **27.3** © Victoria and Albert Museum, London; **27.4** Staatliche Antikensammlungen und Glyptothek, München. Photo: Renate Kühling; **27.5** Courtesy National Gallery of Art, Washington, D.C., Rosenwald Collection (1943.3.8997); **27.6** The Nelson-Atkins Museum of Art, Kansas City, Missouri. Purchase: William Rockhill Nelson Trust, 46-51/2. Photo: John Lamberton; **27.7** Erich Lessing/akg-images; **27.8** © The National Gallery, London/Scala, Florence; **27.9** Courtesy National Gallery of Art, Washington, D.C., Widener Collection (1942.9.10); **27.10** Erich Lessing/akg-images; **27.11** Image © The Metropolitan Museum of Art, New York/Art Resource, NY/Scala, Florence; **27.12** Courtesy of the Pennsylvania Academy of the Fine Arts, Philadelphia. General Fund (1917.1); **27.13** Image © The Metropolitan Museum of Art, New York/Art Resource, NY/Scala, Florence; **27.14** Image © The Metropolitan Museum of Art, New York/Art Resource, NY/Scala, Florence; **27.15** Corcoran Gallery of Art, Washington, D.C., USA Museum Purchase, Gallery Fund/Bridgeman Images; **27.16** Courtesy National Gallery of Art, Washington, D.C., Paul Mellon Collection (1965.16.347); **27.17** Smithsonian Institution, Washington, D.C. Photo: Peter T. Furst, Albany, New York; **27.18** Private collection. Photo: Peter T. Furst, Albany, New York; **27.19** Abby Aldrich Rockefeller Folk Art Museum. The Colonial Williamsburg Foundation. Gift of Marsha C. Scott (1976.609.14); **27.20** Brooklyn Museum, New York. Dick S. Ramsay Fund (40.340)

Chapter 28

28.1 Photo © RMN-Grand Palais (Château de Versailles). Photo: Franck Raux; **28.2** Wellcome Library, London; **28.3** © Crown Copyright: UK Government Art Collection; **28.4** Private Collection/Archives Charmet/Bridgeman Images; **28.5** Smithsonian Institution/Corbis; **28.6** Yale University Art Gallery, Anonymous gift (1947.188f); **28.7** Luigi Calamatta/Bridgeman Images/Getty Images

Chapter 29

29.1 Photo © RMN-Grand Palais (Musée du Louvre). Photo: Thierry Le Mage; **29.2** Photo © RMN-Grand Palais (Musée du Louvre). Photo: Thierry Le Mage; **29.3** White Images/Scala, Florence; **29.5** Musée du Louvre, Paris/Bridgeman Images; **29.6** Photo © RMN-Grand Palais (Musée du Louvre). Photo: Hervé Lewandowski; **29.7** Photo © RMN-Grand Palais (Musée du Louvre). Photo: Gérard Blot/Christian Jean; **29.8** imagebroker.net/SuperStock; **29.9** Hervé Champollion/akg-images; **29.10** Photo © RMN-Grand Palais (Musée d'Orsay). Photo: Franck Raux/René-Gabriel Ojéda; **29.11** Howard University Gallery of Art, Washington, D.C.; **29.12** © Peter Ashworth, London; **29.13** World Wide Photos, Inc. © Museum of the City of New York; **29.14** © Angelo Hornak, London; **29.15** Beethoven-Haus, Bonn/akg-images; **29.16** Musee de l'Opera, Paris/Bridgeman Images; **29.17** Photo © RMN-Grand Palais (Musée du Louvre)/Michel Urtado; **29.18** Erich Lessing/akg-images; **29.20** Photo © RMN-Grand Palais (Musée d'Orsay). Photo: Hervé Lewandowski; **29.21** © Victoria and Albert Museum, London; **29.22** © Ken Howard/Metropolitan Opera

Chapter 30

30.1 Photo © RMN-Grand Palais (Musée d'Orsay). Photo: Jean Schormans; **30.2** Kharbine-Tapabor/The Art Archive; **30.3** BPK, Bildagentur für Kunst, Kultur und Geschichte, Berlin/Photo Scala, Florence; **30.4** The University of Michigan Museum of Art (1956/1.21). © 2015 Artists Rights Society (ARS), New York/

VG Bild-Kunst, Bonn; **30.5** The Granger Collection/Topfoto; **30.6** RIA Novosti/Topfoto; **30.7** Photo © RMN-Grand Palais (Musée d'Orsay). Photo: Hervé Lewandowski; **30.8** Royal Photographic Society/National Media Museum/Science & Society Picture Library; **30.9** Library of Congress, Washington, D.C.; **30.10** Galerie Neue Meister, Dresden/© Staatliche Kunstsammlungen, Dresden/ Bridgeman Images; **30.11** Photo © RMN-Grand Palais (Musée d'Orsay). Photo: Gérard Blot/Hervé Lewandowski; **30.13** Courtesy National Gallery of Art, Washington, D.C., Rosenwald Collection (1954.12.22); **30.14** © The Research Library. The Getty Research Institute, Los Angeles (920048); **30.15** Image © The Metropolitan Museum of Art, New York/Art Resource, NY/Scala, Florence; **30.16** Photo © RMN-Grand Palais (Musée d'Orsay). Photo: Benoît Touchard/Mathieu Rabeau; **30.17** Photo © RMN-Grand Palais (Musée du Louvre). Photo: Hervé Lewandowski; **30.18** Bibliothèque Nationale, Paris/Giraudon/Bridgeman Images; **30.19** Photo © RMN-Grand Palais (Musée d'Orsay). Photo: Hervé Lewandowski; **30.20** Image © The Metropolitan Museum of Art, New York/Art Resource, NY/Scala, Florence; **30.21** Photo The Philadelphia Museum of Art/Art Resource, NY/Scala, Florence; **30.22** University of Pennsylvania School of Medicine/ akg-images; **30.23** Mauritshuis, The Hague; **30.24** Collection of the Hampton University Museum, Hampton, VA; **30.25** Courtesy National Gallery of Art, Washington, D.C., Rosenwald Collection (1958.3.29); **30.26** Image © The Metropolitan Museum of Art, New York/Art Resource, NY/Scala, Florence; **30.27** Library of Congress, Washington, D.C.; **30.28** © Paul M.R. Maeyaert; **30.29** Jack E .Boucher/Library of Congress, Washington, D.C.; **30.30** © Collection of the New-York Historical Society/ Bridgeman Images

Chapter 31

31.1 Photo © RMN-Grand Palais (Musée d'Orsay). Photo: Patrice Schmidt; **31.2** Fine Art Images/SuperStock; **31.3** © Kunstmuseum Bern; **31.4** Musée Marmottan, Paris/akg-images; **31.5** Photo © RMN-Grand Palais (Musée d'Orsay). Photo: Hervé Lewandowski; **31.6** Private Collection/Photo © Christie's Images/ Bridgeman Images; **31.7** © The Samuel Courtauld Trust, The Courtauld Gallery, London/Bridgeman Images; **31.8** Yale University Art Gallery, John Hay Whitney, B.A. 1926, Hon. 1956, Collection (1982.111.6); **31.9** Eadweard Muybridge/Photogravure Company of New York/Library of Congress, Washington, D.C.; **31.10** © Victoria and Albert Museum, London; **31.11** © Victoria and Albert Museum, London; **31.12** Image © The Metropolitan Museum of Art, New York/Art Resource, NY/Scala, Florence; **31.13** Digital Image, The Museum of Modern Art, New York/ Scala, Florence; **31.14** The Art Institute of Chicago, Robert A. Waller Fund (1910.2). Photography © The Art Institute of Chicago; **31.15** The Art Institute of Chicago, Helen Birch Bartlett Memorial Collection (1928.610). Photography © The Art Institute of Chicago; **31.16** © Bastin & Evrard Photodesigners. © 2015 Artists Rights Society (ARS), New York/SOFAM, Brussels; **31.17** Photo © RMN-Grand Palais (Musée des Beaux-Arts de la Ville de Paris). Photo: Agence Bulloz; **31.18** Image © The Metropolitan Museum of Art, New York/Art Resource, NY/Scala, Florence; **31.19** Photo © RMN-Grand Palais (Musée d'Orsay). Photo: René-Gabriel Ojéda; **31.20** Courtesy National Gallery of Art, Washington, D.C., Gift of Mrs. John W. Simpson (1942.5.36); **31.21** Detroit Institute of Arts/Bridgeman Images; **31.22** Arnold Genthe Collection/Library of Congress, Washington, D.C.; **31.23** Kunsthaus Zürich; **31.24** Photo © RMN-Grand Palais (Musée Rodin, Paris); **31.25** François Guénet/akg-images; **31.26** © Archives Musée Dapper, Paris. Photo: Hughes Dubois; **31.27** Ian Dagnall/Alamy; **31.28** Interfoto/ SuperStock; **31.29** Digital Image, The Museum of Modern Art, New York/Scala, Florence; **31.30** Photo © RMN-Grand Palais (Musée d'Orsay). Photo: Gérard Blot; **31.31** The Art Institute of Chicago, Helen Birch Bartlett Memorial Collection (1926.198). Photography © The Art Institute of Chicago; **31.32** The Art Institute of Chicago, Helen Birch Bartlett Memorial Collection (1926.224). Photography © The Art Institute of Chicago; **31.33** The Art Institute of Chicago, Helen Birch Bartlett Memorial Collection (1926.252). Photography © The Art Institute of Chicago; **31.34** Photo The Philadelphia Museum of Art/Art Resource, NY/ Scala, Florence

page 351: Digital Image, The Museum of Modern Art, New York/ Scala, Florence. © 2015 Estate of Pablo Picasso/Artists Rights Society (ARS), New York

Chapter 32

32.1 Photo The Philadelphia Museum of Art/Art Resource, NY/ Scala, Florence. © 2015 Estate of Pablo Picasso/Artists Rights Society (ARS), New York; **32.2** Digital Image, The Museum of Modern Art, New York/Scala, Florence. © 2015 Estate of Pablo Picasso/Artists Rights Society (ARS), New York; **32.3** Photo The Philadelphia Museum of Art/Art Resource, NY/Scala, Florence; **32.4** Musée Barbier Mueller, Geneva; **32.5** Photo © RMN-Grand Palais (Musée d'Orsay). Photo: Gérard Blot. © 2015 Artists Rights Society (ARS), New York/ADAGP, Paris; **32.6** Digital Image, The Museum of Modern Art, New York/Scala, Florence. © 2015 Estate of Pablo Picasso/Artists Rights Society (ARS), New York; **32.7** Digital Image, The Museum of Modern Art, New York/Scala, Florence. © 2015 Estate of Alexander Archipenko/ Artists Rights Society (ARS), New York; **32.8** Digital Image, The Museum of Modern Art, New York/Scala, Florence; **32.9** Photo The Philadelphia Museum of Art/Art Resource, NY/Scala, Florence. © Succession Marcel Duchamp/ADAGP, Paris/Artists Rights Society (ARS), New York 2015; **32.10** National Gallery of Denmark, Copenhagen. Photo © SMK. © 2015 Succession H. Matisse/ Artists Rights Society (ARS), New York; **32.11** © 2015 Succession H. Matisse/Artists Rights Society (ARS), New York; **32.12** Digital Image, The Museum of Modern Art, New York/Scala, Florence. © 2015 Artists Rights Society (ARS), New York/ADAGP, Paris; **32.13** Private Collection/Photo © Christie's Images/Bridgeman Images. © 2015 Center for Creative Photography, Arizona Board of Regents/Artists Rights Society (ARS), New York; **32.14** Digital Image, The Museum of Modern Art, New York/Scala, Florence. © 2015 Artists Rights Society (ARS), New York/ADAGP, Paris; **32.15** Digital Image, The Museum of Modern Art, New York/ Scala, Florence; **32.16** Munson Williams Proctor Arts Institute/Art Resource, NY/Scala, Florence. © 2014 Mondrian/Holtzman Trust c/o HCR International USA; **32.17** Collection Gemeentemuseum Den Haag; **32.18** Digital Image, The Museum of Modern Art, New York/Scala, Florence. © 2015 Artists Rights Society (ARS), New York/c/o Pictoright Amsterdam; **32.19** Photo Scala, Florence; **32.20** Andrea Jomolo/Scala, Florence. © 2015 Frank Lloyd Wright Foundation, Scottsdale, AZ/Artists Rights Society (ARS), NY; **32.21** H. Mark Weidman Photography/Alamy. © 2015 Frank Lloyd Wright Foundation, Scottsdale, AZ/Artists Rights Society (ARS), NY; **32.22** Digital Image, The Museum of Modern Art, New York/ Scala, Florence. © 2015 Artists Rights Society (ARS), New York/ VG Bild-Kunst, Bonn; **32.23** Bildarchiv Monheim/akg-images. © F.L.C./ADAGP, Paris/Artists Rights Society (ARS), New York 2015; **32.24** View Pictures Ltd/SuperStock. © F.L.C./ADAGP, Paris/ Artists Rights Society (ARS), New York 2015; **32.25** © 2015 Estate of Pablo Picasso/Artists Rights Society (ARS), New York

Chapter 33

33.1 Albright-Knox Art Gallery, Buffalo/SuperStock/The Art Archive. © Successió Miró/Artists Rights Society (ARS), New York/ADAGP, Paris 2015; **33.2** The National Museum of Art, Architecture and Design, Oslo. Photo: Børre Høstland; **33.3** Digital Image, The Museum of Modern Art, New York/Scala, Florence; **33.4** Digital Image, The Museum of Modern Art, New York/ Scala, Florence. © 2015 Artists Rights Society (ARS), New York/ SIAE, Rome; **33.5** Digital Image, The Museum of Modern Art, New York/Scala, Florence. © 2015 Artists Rights Society (ARS), New York/ADAGP, Paris; **33.6** Photo The Philadelphia Museum of Art/Art Resource, NY/Scala, Florence. © Succession Marcel Duchamp/ADAGP, Paris/Artists Rights Society (ARS), New York 2015; **33.7** Private Collection/Bridgeman Images. © Succession Marcel Duchamp/ADAGP, Paris/Artists Rights Society (ARS), New York 2015; **33.8** Digital Image, The Museum of Modern Art, New York/Scala, Florence. © 2015 Estate of Pablo Picasso/Artists Rights Society (ARS), New York; **33.9** Photo The Philadelphia Museum of Art/Art Resource, NY/Scala, Florence. © 2015 Artists Rights Society (ARS), New York; **33.10** Digital Image Museum Associates/LACMA/Art Resource, NY/Scala, Florence. © 2015 C. Herscovici/Artists Rights Society (ARS), New York; **33.11** Digital Image, The Museum of Modern Art, New York/Scala, Florence. © Salvador Dalí, Fundació Gala-Salvador Dalí, Artists Rights Society (ARS), New York 2015; **33.12** Bunuel-Dalí/SuperStock. © Salvador Dalí, Fundació Gala-Salvador Dalí, Artists Rights Society (ARS), New York 2015; **33.13** Dolores Olmedo, Mexico/ Nicolas Sapieha/The Art Archive. © 2015 Banco de México Diego Rivera Frida Kahlo Museums Trust, Mexico, D.F./Artists Rights Society (ARS), New York; **33.14** The Art Institute of Chicago, Alfred Stieglitz Collection, Gift of Georgia O'Keeffe (1947-712). Photography © The Art Institute of Chicago. © 2015 Georgia O'Keeffe Museum/Artists Rights Society (ARS), New York; **33.15** Digital Image, The Museum of Modern Art, New York/ Scala, Florence. © 2015 Artists Rights Society (ARS), New York/ ProLitteris, Zurich; **33.16** Erich Lessing/akg-images. © 2015 Artists Rights Society (ARS), New York/VG Bild-Kunst, Bonn

Chapter 34

34.1 © Lee Miller Archives, England 2015. All rights reserved; **34.2** © 2015 Artists Rights Society (ARS), New York/ADAGP, Paris; **34.3** Digital Image, The Museum of Modern Art, New York/ Scala, Florence. Art © Estate of George Grosz/Licensed by VAGA, New York, NY; **34.4** Digital Image, The Museum of Modern Art, New York/Scala, Florence. © 2015 Artists Rights Society (ARS), New York/ADAGP, Paris; **34.5** Fine Art Images/SuperStock; **34.6** Geoffrey Clements/Corbis. Art © T.H. Benton and R.P. Benton Testamentary Trusts/UMB Bank Trustee/Licensed by VAGA, New York, NY; **34.7** Photo The Philadelphia Museum of Art/Art Resource, NY/Scala, Florence. © 2015 Banco de México Diego Rivera Frida Kahlo Museums Trust, Mexico, D.F./Artists Rights Society (ARS), New York; **34.8** Dorothea Lange/Farm Security Administration, Office of War Information/Library of Congress, Washington, D.C.; **34.9** Museo Nacional de Arte Reina Sofia, Madrid. © 2015 Estate of Pablo Picasso/Artists Rights Society (ARS), New York; **34.10** White Images/Scala, Florence; **34.11** The Battleship Potemkin, 1925 directed by Sergei Eisenstein and Goskino/The Kobal Collection; **34.12** NSDAP/The Kobal Collection; **31.13** National Museum, Beijing/akg-images

Chapter 35

35.1 San Francisco Museum of Modern Art. Acquired through a gift of Peggy Guggenheim. © 1998 Kate Rothko Prizel & Christopher Rothko/Artists Rights Society (ARS), New York; **35.2** Arts Council Collection, Southbank Centre/Bridgeman Images. © The Estate of Francis Bacon. All rights reserved./ DACS, London/ARS, NY 2015; **35.3** Whitney Museum of American Art, New York. Purchase 55.35. © 2015 The Willem de Kooning Foundation/Artists Rights Society (ARS), New York; **35.4** Whitney Museum of American Art, New York. Purchase, with funds from the Friends of the Whitney Museum of American Art 57.10. © 2015 The Franz Kline Estate/Artists Rights Society (ARS), New York; **35.5** Gitter-Yelen Collection; **35.6** Rudolph Burckhardt/ Sygma/Corbis. © 2015 The Pollock-Krasner Foundation/Artists Rights Society (ARS), New York; **35.7** Image © The Metropolitan Museum of Art, New York/Art Resource, NY/Scala, Florence. © 2015 The Pollock-Krasner Foundation/Artists Rights Society (ARS), New York; **35.8** University of California, Berkeley Art Museum & Pacific Film Archive. Anonymous Gift (1966.63). © 2015 Helen Frankenthaler Foundation, Inc./Artists Rights Society (ARS), New York; **35.9** The Art Institute of Chicago, Friends of American Art Collection (1942.51). Photography © The Art Institute of Chicago; **35.10** Digital Image, The Museum of Modern Art, New York/Scala, Florence. Art © 2015 Alberto Giacometti Estate/Licensed by VAGA and ARS, New York; **35.11** Hirshhorn Museum and Sculpture Garden, Smithsonian Institution, Washington, D.C. Gift of Joseph H. Hirshhorn, 1966. Photography by Lee Stalsworth. Art © The George and Helen Segal Foundation/Licensed by VAGA, New York, NY; **35.12** Hirshhorn Museum and Sculpture Garden, Smithsonian Institution, Washington, D.C. Gift of the Joseph H. Hirshhorn Foundation, 1972. Photography by Lee Stalsworth. Art © The Estate of David Smith/Licensed by VAGA, New York, NY; **35.13** Courtesy National Gallery of Art, Washington, D.C., Gift of Mr. and Mrs. Klaus G. Peris (1996.120.3). © 2015 Calder Foundation, New York/Artists Rights Society (ARS), New York; **35.14** Angelo Hornak/Corbis. © 2015 Artists Rights Society (ARS), New York/VG Bild-Kunst, Bonn; **35.15** © Balthazar Korab, Korab Image, Minnesota; **35.16** Photo: Robert E. Mates © SRGF, NY; **35.17** Photo: David Heald © SRGF, NY; **35.18** Arcaid Images/Alamy; **35.19** Courtesy of The Merce Cunningham Trust. Robert Kovich and Chris Komar in Summerspace (1958). Photo by Jack Mitchell. Décor by Robert Rauschenberg. Art © Robert Rauschenberg Foundation/Licensed by VAGA, New York, NY

Chapter 36

36.1 © Kehinde Wiley. Courtesy of the artist.; **36.2** Digital Image, The Museum of Modern Art, New York/Scala, Florence. © 2015 The Jacob and Gwendolyn Lawrence Foundation, Seattle/Artists Rights Society (ARS), New York; **36.3** Courtesy the artist © Jeff Wall; **36.4** Collection of University of California, Berkeley Art Museum; purchased with the aid of funds from the National Endowment for the Arts (selected by the Committee for the Acquisition of Afro-American Art). Courtesy of Michael Rosenfeld Gallery, LLC, New York, NY; **36.5** © Robert Colescott Estate, Tucson, AZ, USA; **36.6** Artwork © 1998 Kara Walker. Courtesy of Sikkema Jenkins & Co. Photo by Dave Sweeney; **36.7** Photo Smithsonian American Art Museum/Art Resource, NY/Scala, Florence. Art © Romare Bearden Foundation/Licensed by VAGA, New York, NY; **36.8** Courtesy Hogan Jazz Archive, Tulane University; **36.9** The Broad Art Foundation, Santa Monica. Photograph © Douglas M. Parker Studio, Los Angeles. © The Estate of Jean-Michel Basquiat/ADAGP, Paris/ARS, New York 2015; **36.10** The New York Public Library/Art Resource, NY; **36.11** Whitney Museum of American Art, New York. Gift of the Howard and Jean Lipman Foundation, Inc. 68.73. © 2015 Niki Charitable Art Foundation. All rights reserved/ARS, NY/ADAGP, Paris; **36.12** Naturhistorisches Museum, Wien; **36.13** © The Estate of Ana Mendieta Collection, L.L.C. Courtesy Galerie Lelong, New York; **36.14** Collection of the Brooklyn Museum of Art. Photo: Donald Woodman. © 2015 Judy Chicago/ Artists Rights Society (ARS), New York; **36.15** Courtesy of the artist and Metro Pictures, New York; **36.16** Copyright: Barbara Kruger. Courtesy: Mary Boone Gallery, New York; **36.17** Peter Gridley/The Image Bank/Getty Images; **36.18** Self Portrait, 1980 © Copyright The Robert Mapplethorpe Foundation. Courtesy Art + Commerce

Chapter 37
37.1 Christie's Images, London/Scala, Florence. © Estate of Roy Lichtenstein; **37.2** Whitney Museum of American Art, New York. Purchase, with funds from the Friends of the Whitney Museum of American Art 68.25. © 2015 The Andy Warhol Foundation for the Visual Arts, Inc./Artists Rights Society (ARS), New York; **37.3** © 2015 The Andy Warhol Foundation for the Visual Arts, Inc./Artists Rights Society (ARS), New York; **37.4** Art © Jasper Johns/Licensed by VAGA, New York, NY; **37.5** Collection Centre Square Plaza, Fifteenth and Market streets, Philadelphia. Copyright 1976 Claes Oldenburg; **37.6** © Jeff Koons. The Metropolitan Museum of Art, The Iris and B. Gerald Cantor Roof Garden: "Jeff Koons on the Roof" (April 22–October 26, 2008). Photographed in April 2008. Image © The Metropolitan Museum of Art; **37.7** Art © Robert Rauschenberg Foundation/Licensed by VAGA, New York, NY; **37.8** Photograph courtesy of the Pace Gallery, New York. © 2015 Fairweather & Fairweather LTD/Artists Rights Society (ARS), New York; **37.9** © Rheinisches Bildarchiv Köln/Marion Mennicken (rba_c022558). © 2015 Estate of Louise Nevelson/Artists Rights Society (ARS), New York; **37.10** The Menil Collection Houston, Texas (83-131 DJ). © 2015 Frank Stella/Artists Rights Society (ARS), New York; **37.11** Digital Image, The Museum of Modern Art, New York/Scala, Florence. © Bridget Riley 2014. All rights reserved, courtesy Karsten Schubert, London; **37.12** Digital Image, The Museum of Modern Art, New York/Scala, Florence. Art © Judd Foundation. Licensed by VAGA, New York, NY; **37.13** Gloria K. Fiero. © 2015 The Isamu Noguchi Foundation and Garden Museum, New York/Artists Rights Society (ARS), New York; **37.14** Digital image, The Museum of Modern Art, New York/Scala, Florence. Courtesy Marlborough Gallery, New York. © Richard Estes; **37.15** © Chuck Close, courtesy Pace Gallery. Photo: Ellen Page Wilson; **37.16** Scottish National Gallery of Modern Art, Edinburgh. Purchased 1979 (GMA 2132). Art © Estate of Duane Hanson/Licensed by VAGA, New York, NY; **37.17** © 2015 Artists Rights Society (ARS), New York/ADAGP, Paris; **37.18** © Christo 1976. Photo: Jeanne-Claude, New York. Used with permission.; **37.19** Photo: Ellen Labenski © SRGF, NY. © Estate of Nam June Paik; **37.20** Photo: Charles Duprat. Used with permission of the Bill Viola Studio LLC, California; **37.21** © Norman McGrath, New York; **37.22** Photo © RMN-Grand Palais (Musée du Louvre). Photo: Gérard Blot; **37.23** Joseph Sohm/Visions of America/Corbis. © 2015 Santiago Calatrava/Artists Rights Society (ARS), New York/VEGAP, Madrid; **37.24** Kurt Krieger/Corbis; **37.25** Digital Image, Lorenze Kienzle/The Museum of Modern Art, New York/Scala, Florence. © 2015 Richard Serra/Artists Rights Society (ARS), New York

Chapter 38
38.1 Courtesy Sprüth Magers Berlin London. © 2015 Andreas Gursky/Artists Rights Society (ARS), New York/VG Bild-Kunst, Bonn; **38.2** © Chéri Samba. Courtesy C.A.A.C. - The Pigozzi Collection, Geneva. Photo: Christian Poite; **38.3** Image © The Metropolitan Museum of Art, New York/Art Resource, NY/Scala, Florence. Used with permission of the artist. Courtesy October Gallery, London; **38.4** Photo The Newark Museum/Art Resource, NY/Scala, Florence; **38.5** Photo: Susan Alzner. Image courtesy of the Artist. © 2015 Carolee Schneemann/Artists Rights Society (ARS), New York; **38.6** Image courtesy of the Artist and Hanart TZ Gallery; **38.7** Photo: Hiro Ihara. Courtesy Cai Studio; **38.8** Photo: Ai Weiwei. Reproduced by permission of the artist.; **38.9** Art © Estate of Robert Smithson/Licensed by VAGA, New York, NY; **38.10** VIEW Pictures Ltd./Alamy; **38.11** Courtesy of the Gladstone Gallery, New York; **38.12** All rights reserved. Used by permission of the artist. Image courtesy of The Chicano Studies Research Center, UCLA; **38.13** The Art Institute of Chicago, Gift of Society for Contemporary Art (1983.264). Photography © The Art Institute of Chicago. Art © Estate of Leon Golub/Licensed by VAGA, New York, NY; **38.14** Courtesy Marlborough Gallery, New York. © Magdalena Abakanowicz; **38.15** Radoslaw Lecyk/shutterstock.com; **38.16** Courtesy the artist; Tanya Bonakdar Gallery, New York; and Galeria Fortes Vilaça, São Paulo; **38.17** Photo: Eva-Lotta Jansson/Corbis. Courtesy the artist, neugerriemschneider, Berlin, and Tanya Bonakdar Gallery, New York. © Olafur Eliasson 2003; **38.18** Courtesy Karl Sims, **38.19** © 1988, Yasumasa Morimura; Courtesy of the artist and Luhring Augustine, New York; **38.20** Photo © RMN-Grand Palais (Musée d'Orsay). Photo: Hervé Lewandowski; **38.21** © Noriko Yamaguchi, courtesy MEM, Inc; **38.22** Photo courtesy of Virginia Museum of Contemporary Art. Used with permission of the artist.; **38.23** © Iwan Baan

Literary Credits

The author and publishers wish to thank the following for permission to use copyright material. Every effort has been made to trace or contact copyright holders, but if notified of any omissions or errors, Laurence King Publishing would be pleased to insert the appropriate acknowledgement in any subsequent edition of this publication.

Chapter 19
READING:
19.2 (pp. 489–490)**:** Desiderius Erasmus, from *The Praise of Folly,* translated by Hoyt H. Hudson, (Princeton University Press, 1941),copyright © 1941, 1969 Princeton University Press. Reprinted by permission of Princeton University Press.

19.4 (pp. 492–494): Miguel de Cervantes, from *Don Quixote: A Norton Critical Edition*, edited by Diana de Armas Wilson, translated by Burton Raffel (W. W. Norton), copyright © 1999 by W. W. Norton & Company, Inc. Used by permission of W. W. Norton & Company, Inc.

19.5 (pp. 494–496)**:** Michel de Montaigne, from "On Cannibals" from *The Complete Essays on Montaigne: Essays, Travel Journal. Letters*, translated by Donald M Frame, (Stanford University Press), copyright © 1943 by Donald M. Frame, copyright © 1948, 1957 by the Board of Trustees of the Leland Stanford Junior University. Renewed © 1971, 1976. All rights reserved. With the permission of Stanford University Press, www.sup.org.

Chapter 20
20.1 (p.39): from *The Spiritual Exercises of St. Ignatius of Loyola*, translated by Louis J. Puhl, S.J. (Newman Press, 1951). Reprinted by permission of Loyala Press. To order copies of this book call 1-800-621-1008 or visit www.loyolabooks.org.

Chapter 21
(p. 94)**:** Matsuo Basho, five haikus from *Introduction to Haiku* by Harold Gould Henderson (Doubleday, 1958), copyright © 1958 by Harold G. Henderson. Used by permission of Doubleday, an imprint of the Knopf Doubleday Publishing Group, a division of Random House, LLC. All rights reserved.

Chapter 24
24.5 (p. 143): Denis Diderot, from "Encyclopédie" from *Diderot's Selected Writings*, edited by Lester G. Crocker and translated by Derek Coltman (Macmillan, 1966), copyright © 1966 by The Macmillan Publishing Company. Reprinted with the permission of Scribner Publishing Group, a division of Simon & Schuster, Inc.

24.6 (pp. 146–147): Antoine Nicolas de Condorcet, from *Sketch for a Historical Picture of the Progress of the Human Mind*, translated by June Barraclough (Weidenfeld& Nicolson, 1955), copyright © 1955 George Weidenfeld & Nicolson Ltd. Reprinted by permission of The Orion Publishing Group.

Chapter 25
25.5 (pp. 165–167): Li Ju-chin, from *Flowers in the Mirror*, translated by Lin Tai-yi (University of California Press, 1965). Reproduced by permission of Peter Owen Ltd, London.

25.6 (pp. 168–169): Jean-Jacques Rousseau, from *Discourse on Inequality*, translated by Maurice Cranston (Viking Penguin, 1984), copyright © Maurice Cranston. Reprinted by permission of SLL/Sterling Lord Literistic, Inc.

Chapter 27
27.5 (pp. 220–221.): Shen Fu, from *Chapters from A Floating Life*, translated by Shirley M. Black, pp.63–65 (Oxford University Press, 1960). By permission of Oxford University Press.

(p.221): Shen Zhou, "Written on A Landscape Painting in an Album" from *The Columbia Anthology of Traditional Chinese Literature*, edited by Victor H. Mairr, translated by Daniel Bryant (Columbia University Press, 1994), copyright © 1994, University Press. Reprinted by permission of the publisher.

Chapter 28
28.4 (p. 245): Alexander Pushkin, "Napoleon" from *Collected Narrative and Lyrical Poetry*, translated by Walter Arndt (Ardis/Overlook, 1984). Reprinted by permission of the publisher.

28.7 (pp. 250–254): Johann Wolfgang von Goethe, "Prologue in Heaven" from *Faust: Parts 1 and 2*, translated by Louis McNeice (Oxford University Press, 1951). Reprinted by permission of David Higham Associates Ltd.

28.8 (p. 254): Heinrich Heine, "You Are Just Like a Flower" from *Heinrich Heine: Lyric Poems and Ballads*, translated by Ernst Feise (University of Pittsburgh Press), copyright © 1961, Ernst Feise. Reprinted by permission of the University of Pittsburgh Press.

Chapter 30
30.2 (pp. 281–283): Lin Tse-hsü, "Lin Tse-hsü's Moral Advice to Queen Victoria" from *China's Response to the West: A documentary Survey, 1839–1923* by Ssu-yu Têng and John King Fairbank, pp.24, 25–26, 27, (Cambridge, Mass.: Harvard University Press, 1954), copyright © 1954, 1979 by the President and Fellows of Harvard College. Renewed © 1982 by Sse-yu Têng and John King Fairbank.

30.7 (pp. 294–295): Fyodor Dostoevsky, from *Crime and Punishment*, translated by Jessie Coulson, pp.249–253, (Oxford University Press, 1987). By permission of Oxford University Press.

30.8 (p. 296): Gustave Flaubert, from *Madame Bovary: Provincial Manners*, translated by Margaret Mauldon, pp.257–259, (Oxford University Press, 2008). By permission of Oxford University Press.

30.10 (p. 298): Emile Zola, from *Germinal*, translated by Stanley and Eleanor Hochman (New American Library, 1970), translation copyright © 1970 by Stanley and Eleanor Hochman. Used by permission of Dutton Signet, a division of Penguin Group (USA) LLC and the translators.

30.11 (p. 299–300): Henrik Ibsen, "A Doll's House" from *Six Plays by Henrik Ibsen*, translated by Eva Le Gallienne (Random House, 1957), translation copyright © 1957 by Eva Le Gallienne. Used by permission of Modern Library, an imprint of Random House, a division of Random House LLC. All rights reserved, and Rebecca A. Lyman.

Chapter 31
31.1 (p. 321): Friedrich Nietzsche, *Twilight of the Idols, with The Antichrist and Ecce Homo*, translated by Anthony M Ludovicic, pp.61–62, 81, (Classics of World Literature, 2001).

Chapter 32
32.1 (p. 355)**:** Ezra Pound, "In a Station of the Metro" and "The Bathtub" from *Personae*, copyright © 1926 by Ezra Pound. Reprinted by permission of New Directions Publishing Corp.

32.2 (pp. 356–357): T.S. Eliot, "The Love Song of J. Alfred Prufrock" from *Collected Poems 1909–1962* (Faber & Faber, 1963), copyright © 1936 by Houghton Mifflin Harcourt Publishing Company, renewed © 1964 by Thomas Stearns Elliot. Reprinted by permission of Faber & Faber Ltd and Houghton Mifflin Harcourt Publishing Company. All rights reserved.

32.3 (p.358): Robert Frost, "The Road Not Taken" from *The Poetry of Robert Frost*, edited by Edward Connery Lathem (Jonathan Cape, 1969), copyright © 1944 by Robert Frost, copyright © 1916, 1969 by Henry Holt & Company, LLC. Used by permission of Henry Holt & Company, LLC. All rights reserved.

Chapter 33
33.1 (pp. 380–382): Sigmund Freud, from *Civilization and Its Discontents*, translated by David McLintock (Penguin Books, 2004), Sigmund Freud's German texts collected as Gesammelte Werke copyright © 1941, 1948 by Imago Publishing Co, Ltd. Translation copyright © David McLintock, 2002. Reproduced by permission of Penguin Books Ltd.

33.2 (pp. 383–384): Marcel Proust, from *Swann's Way: Within a Budding Grove (Remembrance of Things Past, Vol I)*, translated by C. K. Scott Moncrieff and Terence Kilmartin (Vintage, Chatto & Windus, 1981), translation copyright © 1981 by Random House and Chatto & Windus. Used by permission of Random House Group, an imprint and division of Random House LLC. All rights reserved, and The Random House Group Limited.

33.3 (pp. 385–386): Franz Kafka, from *The Metamorphosis and Other Stories*, translated by Stanley Appelbaum, (Dover Thrift Editions, 1996). Reproduced by permission of Dover Publications, Inc.

33.4 (p.387): E. E. Cummings, "she being Brand" from *Complete Poems: 1904–1962*, edited by George J. Firmage (Liveright Publishing, 1994), copyright 1926, 1954, copyright © 1991 by the Trustees for the E. E. Cummings Trust, copyright © 1985 by George James Firmage. Used by permission of Liveright Publishing Corporation.

Chapter 34

34.2 (p. 402): T. S. Eliot, "The Waste Land" from *Collected Poems 1909–1962* (Faber & Faber, 1974), copyright © T.S. Eliot 1963. Reprinted by permission of Faber and Faber Ltd.

34.5 (p. 414): Randall Jarrell, "The Death of the Ball Turret Gunner" from *The Complete Poems* (Faber & Faber, 1971), copyright © 1969, renewed © 1977 by Mary von S. Jarrell. Reprinted by permission of Farrar, Straus and Giroux, LLC. CAUTION: On-screen users are warned that this work is protected under copyright laws and downloading is strictly prohibited. The right to reproduce or transfer the work via any medium must be secured with Farrar, Straus and Giroux, LLC.

34.6 (p. 414): Kato Shuson, three haiku from *Modern Japanese Literature*, edited by Donald Keene, p.382 (Grove Press, 1956), copyright © 1956 by Grove Press. Used by permission of Grove/Atlantic, Inc. Any third party use of this material, outside of this publication, is prohibited.

34.7 (p. 415): Elie Wiesel, from *Night*, translated by Marion Wiesel (Hill and Wang, 2006), copyright © 2006 by Marion Wiesel. Reprinted by permission of Hill and Wang, a division of Farrar, Straus and Giroux, LLC.

Chapter 35

35.1 (pp. 425–427): Jean Paul Sartre, from *Existentialism and Human Emotions*, (Philosophical Library, 1947), copyright © 1957, 1985, Philosophical Library Inc. All rights reserved Reprinted by arrangement with Kensington Publishing Corp, www.kensingtonbooks.com.

35.2 (pp. 429–430): Samuel Beckett, from *Waiting for Godot*, pp.107–109, (Grove Press, 1954), copyright © 1954 by Grove Press, Inc.; renewed © 1982 by Samuel Beckett. Used by permission of Grove/Atlantic, Inc. Any third party use of this material, outside of this publication, is prohibited.

35.3 (p. 430): Dylan Thomas, "Do Not Go Gentle Into That Good Night" from *The Poems of Dylan Thomas,* copyright © 1952 by Dylan Thomas. Reprinted by permission of New Directions Publishing Corp.

Chapter 36

36.1 (p. 446): Mohammad Iqbal, "Revolution" and "Europe and Syria" from *Poems from Iqbal*, translated by V. Kiernan (John Murray, 1955).

36.2 (pp. 447–448): Pablo Neruda, "The United Fruit Co." from *Five Decades: Poems 1925–1970*, translated by Ben Belitt

(Grove Press, 1974), copyright © 1974 by Grove Press, Inc. And from Canto General, copyright © Fundación Pablo Neruda, 2014. Used by permission of Carmen Balcells Agency and Grove/Atlantic, Inc. Any third party use of this material, outside of this publication, is prohibited.

36.3 (p. 448): Langston Hughes, "Theme for English B" and "Harlem" from *The Collected Poems of Langston Hughes*, edited by Arnold Rampersad with David Roessel, Associate Editor, (Alfred A. Knopf, 1994), copyright © 1994 by the Estate of Langston Hughes. Used by permission of Alfred A. Knopf, an imprint of the Knopf Doubleday Publishing Group, a division of Random House LLC and Harold Ober Associates. All rights reserved.

36.4 (pp. 448–449): Gwendolyn Brooks, "The Mother" and "We Real Cool" from *Blacks* (Third World Press, 1991). Reprinted by consent of Brooks Permissions.

36.5 (pp. 449–451): Richard Wright, "The Ethics of Living Jim Crow" from *Uncle Tom's Children* (Harper and Row, 1937), copyright © 1937 by Richard Wright, renewed © 1965 by Ellen Wright. Reprinted by permission of HarperCollins Publishers.

36.6 (pp. 451–453): Dr. Martin Luther King Jr., 'Letter from Birmingham Jail' from *Why We Can't Wait* (1963), copyright © 1963 Dr. Martin Luther King, Jr., renewed © 1991 Coretta Scott King. Reprinted by arrangement with The Heirs to the Estate of Martin Luther King Jr., c/o Writers House as agent for the proprietor New York, NY.

36.7 (pp. 453–454): Malcolm X, "Message to the Grass Roots", from *Malcolm X Speaks*, 1965, pp.16–17, 19–20, copyright © 1965, 1989 by Betty Shabazz and Pathfinder Press. Reprinted by permission of Pathfinder Press.

36.8 (pp. 455–456): Ralph Ellison, from *Invisible Man* (Random House, 1952), copyright © 1947, 1948, 1952 by Ralph Ellison, renewed © 1975, 1976, 1980 by Ralph Ellison. Used by permission of Random House, an imprint and division of Random House LLC. All rights reserved.

36.9 (pp. 456–457): Alice Walker, "Elethia" from *You Can't Keep a Good Woman Down* (Harcourt Brace Jovanovich, 1981), copyright © 1979 by Alice Walker. Reprinted by permission of Houghton Mifflin Harcourt Publishing Company. All rights reserved.

36.11 (pp. 465–466): Simone de Beauvoir, from *The Second Sex*, translated by Constance Borde and Sheila Malovany-Chevallier, pp.8–10, translation copyright © 2009 by Constance Borde and Sheila Malovany-Chevallier. Used by permission of Alfred A. Knopf, an imprint of the Knopf Doubleday Publishing Group, a division of Random House LLC. All rights reserved.

36.12 (p. 467): Anne Sexton, "Self in 1958" from *Live or Die* (Houghton Mifflin, 1966), copyright © 1966 by Anne Sexton, renewed © 1994 by Linda G Sexton. Reprinted by permission of Houghton Mifflin Harcourt Publishing Company, and SLL/Sterling Lord Literistic, Inc. All rights reserved. (p.467–468): Sister Sonia Sanchez, "Woman" from *I've Been a Woman: New and Selected Poems* (Third World Press, 1985), copyright © 1985 by Sonia Sanchez. Reproduced by permission of the author. (p.468): Adrienne Rich, "Translations" from *Diving into The Wreck: Poems*

1971–1972 (W. W. Norton & Company, 1973), copyright © 1973 by W. W. Norton & Company, Inc. Used by permission of W. W. Norton & Company, Inc. (p.468): Rita Dove, "Rosa" from *On The Bus With Rosa Parks* (W.W. Norton & Company, 1999), copyright © 1999 by Rita Dove. Used by permission of W. W. Norton & Company, Inc.

Chapter 37

37.1 (pp. 480–482): Joyce Carol Oates, "Ace" from *The Assignation: Stories* (W. W. Norton & Co, 1989), copyright © 1988 by Joyce Carol Oates. Reprinted by permission of HarperCollins Publishers.

37.2 (p. 482): Octavio Paz, "To Talk" from *Collected Poems 1957–1987*, translated by Eliot Weinberger (1986), copyright © 1986 by Octavio Paz and Eliot Weinberger. Reprinted by permission of New Directions Publishing Corp.

37.3 (pp. 482–483): John Ashbery, "Paradoxes and Oxymorons" from *Shadow Train*, copyright © 1980, 1981 by John Ashbery. Reprinted by permission of Georges Borchardt, Inc., for the author.

37.4 (p. 483): Jorge Luis Borges, "Borges and I", translated by Antonios Sarhanis. Reprinted by permission of the translator.

Chapter 38

38.1 (pp. 504–505): Chinua Achebe, "Dead Men's Path" from *Girls at War and Other Stories* (Doubleday, 1973), copyright © 1972, 1973 by Chinua Achebe. Used by permission of Doubleday, an imprint of the Knopf Doubleday Publishing Group, a division of Random House LLC, and The Wylie Agency LLC. All rights reserved.

38.2 (p.507): Wislawa Szymborska, "The terrorist, he watches", from *People on a Bridge, Forest Books*, translated by Adam Czerniawski, 1990. Reproduced with permission of the translator.

38.3 (p.508) and in text (p. 508): Seamus Heaney , "Anything Can Happen" from *District and Circle*, copyright © 2006 by Seamus Heaney. Reprinted by permission of Farrar, Straus and Giroux, LLC and Faber and Faber Ltd. CAUTION: On-screen users are warned that this work is protected under copyright laws and downloading is strictly prohibited. The right to reproduce or transfer the work via any medium must be secured with Farrar, Straus and Giroux, LLC.

38.4 (pp. 510–511): Edward O. Wilson, from *The Diversity of Life*, pp.311–312, 351, (Cambridge, Mass.: The Belknap Press of Harvard University Press, 1992), copyright © 1992 by Edward O. Wilson. Reprinted by permission of the publisher.

38.5 (pp. 513–514): Sandra Cisneros, "No Speak English" from *The House on Mango Street* (Vintage Books), copyright © 1984 by Sandra Cisneros. Used by permission of Susan Bergholz Literary Services, New York, NY and Lamy, NM. All rights reserved.

38.6 (p. 515): Mahmoud Darwish, "Earth Presses Against US" from *Unfortunately, It Was Paradise: Selected Poems*, (University of California Press Books, 2013), copyright © 2013, The Regents of the University of California. Reprinted by permission of Copyright Clearance Center. And Yehuda Amichai, "The Resurrection of the Dead" translated by Leon Wieseltier, 2004. Reproduced with permission of the translator.

Index

Numbers in **bold** refer to figure numbers. Text excerpts are indicated by (quoted).